1861 Paul Broca, a French physician, discovers an area in the left frontal lobe of the brain that is critical for the production of spoken language (now called Broca's area).

Louis Pasteur advocates germ theory.

1869 Francis Galton, Charles Darwin's cousin, publishes *Hereditary Genius*, in which he claims that intelligence is inherited. In 1876 he coined the expression "nature and nurture" to correspond with "heredity and environment."

1874 Carl Wernicke, a German neurologist and psychiatrist, shows that damage to a specific area in the left temporal lobe disrupts ability to comprehend or produce spoken or written language (now called Wernicke's area).

1878 G. Stanley Hall receives from Harvard University the first Ph.D. degree in psychology awarded in the United States.

1879 Wilhelm Wundt establishes at the University of Leipzig, Germany, the first psychology laboratory, which becomes a Mecca for psychology students from all over the world.

1883 G. Stanley Hall, student of Wilhelm Wundt, establishes the first formal U.S. psychology laboratory at Johns Hopkins University.

1885 Hermann Ebbinghaus publishes *On Memory*, summarizing his extensive research on learning and memory, including the "forgetting curve."

1889 The first psychology laboratory in France is established at the Sorbonne, and the first International Congress of Psychology meets in Paris.

1890 William James, a Harvard University philosopher and psychologist, publishes *The Principles of Psychology*, describing psychology as "the science of mental life."

1891 James Mark Baldwin establishes the first psychology laboratory in the British Commonwealth at the University of Toronto.

1892 G. Stanley Hall spearheads the founding of the American Psychological Association (APA) and becomes its first president. (The first annual budget is $63.)

1893 Mary Whiton Calkins and Christine Ladd-Franklin are the first women elected to membership in the APA.

1894 Margaret Floy Washburn is the first woman to receive a Ph.D. degree in psychology (Cornell University).

Mary Whiton Calkins is refused admission to doctoral candidacy by Harvard because of her gender, despite Hugo Münsterberg's claim that she was the best student he had ever had there.

1896 John Dewey publishes "The Reflex Arc Concept in Psychology," which helps to formalize the school of psychology called functionalism.

1898 Edward L. Thorndike, Columbia University, publishes an article titled "Animal Intelligence," in which he describes his learning experiments with cats in "puzzle boxes." In 1905, he proposed the "law of effect."

1931 Margaret Floy Washburn is elected to the U.S. National Academy of Sciences, becoming the first female psychologist and only the second female scientist in any discipline to be so honored.

1932 Walter B. Cannon publishes *The Wisdom of the Body*, in which he coins the term *homeostasis*, discusses the fight-or-flight response, and identifies hormonal changes associated with stress.

1933 Inez Beverly Prosser is the first African-American woman to receive a doctoral degree in psychology from a U.S. institution (Ed.D., University of Cincinnati).

1935 Christiana Morgan and Henry Murray introduce the Thematic Apperception Test to elicit fantasies from people undergoing psychoanalysis.

1936 Egas Moniz, Portugese physician, publishes work on the first frontal lobotomy with humans.

1938 B. F. Skinner publishes *The Behavior of Organisms*, which describes operant conditioning of animals.

Louis L. Thurstone publishes *Primary Mental Abilities*, in which he proposes seven such abilities.

Ugo Cerletti and Lucino Bini use electroshock treatment with a human patient.

1939 David Wechsler publishes the Wechsler-Bellevue intelligence test, forerunner of the Wechsler Intelligence Scale for Children (WISC) and the Wechsler Adult Intelligence Scale (WAIS).

Mamie Phipps Clark receives a master's degree from Howard University. Research for her thesis, "The Development of Consciousness of Self in Negro Preschool Children," was extended in collaboration with Kenneth B. Clark, and their work was cited in the U.S. Supreme Court's 1954 decision to end racial segregation in public schools.

The Canadian Psychological Association is established. Edward Alexander Bott is a founder and becomes the first president in **1940.**

World War II provides many opportunities for psychologists to enhance the popularity and influence of psychology, especially in applied areas.

1943 Psychologist Starke Hathaway and physician J. Charnley McKinley publish the Minnesota Multiphasic Personality Inventory (MMPI).

1945 Karen Horney, who criticized Freud's theory of female sexual development, publishes *Our Inner Conflicts*.

1946 Benjamin Spock publishes *The Commonsense Book of Baby and Child Care*, which influences child rearing in North America for several decades.

Continued on inside back cover

Laura James, *People Waiting in the Sun*, acrylic, 1997

Laura James is a self-taught painter living and working in Brooklyn, New York. *People Waiting in the Sun* is typical of her style—incorporating bright colors, intricate patterns, and sometimes surreal objects to display her unique vision. Ms. James is a member of the Jamaica Artist Alliance, the Bridgeman Art Library in London, and the National Conference of Black Artists. Her paintings are widely exhibited and have reached as far as Japan, Africa, Canada, and the Caribbean.

Exploring PSYCHOLOGY

SIXTH EDITION

DAVID G. MYERS

Hope College
Holland, Michigan

WORTH PUBLISHERS

Grateful acknowledgment is given for permission to reprint the following photos: p. 1: Tom and Dee Ann McCarthy/Corbis; p. 36: Stephen Simpson/Taxi/Getty Images; p. 68: Johner/Photonica; p. 98: Paul Barton/Corbis; p. 140: Jason Dewey/Stone/Getty Images; p. 186: José Luis Pelaez, Inc./Corbis; p. 224: Larry Stanley/Index Stock Imagery/PictureQuest; p. 256: Ariel Skelley/Corbis; p. 292: Marc Romanelli/The Image Bank/Getty Images; p. 340: Kaz Mori/The Image Bank/Getty Images; p. 378: Sean Murphy/Stone/Getty Images; p. 428: Herve Collart/Corbis; p. 468: Image Source/SuperStock; p. 506: Zigy Kaluzny/Stone/Getty Images; p. 538: Owen Franken/Corbis

Credits for timeline photos, inside front and back covers (by date): 1637, Corbis-Bettmann; 1859, Granger Collection; 1878, 1879, 1890, Brown Brothers; 1893, 1894, Wellesley College Archives; 1898, Yale University Library; 1905, Sovfoto; 1913, 1920, 1933, 1939, Archives of the History of American Psychology, University of Akron; 1924, Larsen/Watson Papers, Archives of the History of American Psychology, University of Akron; 1938, Bettmann/Corbis; 1945, Corbis; 1951, Courtesy of Carl Rogers Memorial Library; 1954, Ted Polumbaum/*Life* magazine, © 1968 TimeWarner, Inc.; 1959, Chris Felver/Archive Images; 1963, Courtesy of CUNY Graduate School and University Center; 1966, Courtesy of John Garcia; 1971, Courtesy of Albert Bandura, Stanford University; 1974, Russell Fernald, Courtesy of the Stanford University News Service; 1979, Courtesy of Elizabeth Loftus, University of California, Irvine; 1981, Courtesy of the Archives, California Institute of Technology; 1993, Chet Snedden/American Airlines Corporate Communications.

Publisher: Catherine Woods

Development Editors: Nancy Fleming, Christine Brune

Marketing Manager: Katherine Nurre

Associate Managing Editor: Tracey Kuehn

Art Director, Cover Designer: Babs Reingold

Interior Designer: Lissi Sigillo

Layout Designer: Lee Ann Mahler

Illustration Coordinator: Bill Page

Illustrations: TSI Graphics, Alan Reingold, Shawn Kenney, Bonnie Hofkin, and Demetrios Zangos

Photo Editors: Meg Kuhta, Bianca Moscatelli

Photo Researcher: Julie Tesser

Production Manager: Sarah Segal

Composition: TSI Graphics

Printing and Binding: R. R. Donnelley and Sons

Cover Painting: Laura James, *People Waiting in the Sun*, acrylic, 1997

ISBN: 0-7167-1544-9 (paper); EAN: 9780716715443
        0-7167-8622-2 (case); EAN: 9780716786221
        0-7167-8645-1 (complimentary); EAN: 9780716786450

First printing 2004

All royalties from the sale of this book are assigned to the David and Carol Myers Foundation, which exists to receive and distribute funds to other charitable organizations.

Worth Publishers
41 Madison Avenue
New York, NY 10010
www.worthpublishers.com

For Tracey

David Myers received his psychology Ph.D. from the University of Iowa. He has spent his career at Hope College, Michigan, where he is the John Dirk Werkman Professor of Psychology and has taught dozens of introductory psychology sections. Hope College students have invited him to be their commencement speaker and voted him "outstanding professor."

Myers' scientific articles have appeared in more than two dozen scientific periodicals, including *Science, American Scientist, Psychological Science,* and the *American Psychologist.* His writings have also appeared in three dozen magazines, from *Today's Education* to *Scientific American* and in general audience books, including *The Pursuit of Happiness* and *Intuition: Its Powers and Perils.*

David Myers has chaired his city's Human Relations Commission, helped found a thriving assistance center for families in poverty, and spoken to hundreds of college and community groups. On behalf of fellow hard of hearing people, he is actively advocating the spread of assistive listening technology that can enable hearing aids to serve as wireless loudspeakers (see hearingloop.org). He bikes to work year-round and plays daily pick-up basketball. David and Carol Myers have raised two sons and a daughter.

contents in brief

contents

chapter 5
Sensation and Perception 141

chapter 6
States of Consciousness 187

chapter 7
Learning 225

chapter 8
Memory 257

Although a revised edition of this text appears every three years, it is a rare day between those editions when I do not harvest new information about the field I love and its applications to everyday life. Week by week, new information surprises us with discoveries about, for example, the ins and outs of brain activity, the powers and perils of intuition, and the roots and fruits of optimism. No wonder this book has changed dramatically since the first edition 15 years ago! Today's psychological science is more attuned to nature and nurture (see **TABLE 1**), to gender and cultural diversity (see **TABLES 2** and **3, p. xvi**), to an understanding of the power of our thought processes, and to the neuroscience revolution (see **TABLE 4, p. xvii**). We can also harness new ways to present information, both in books and via electronic media. These changes are exhilarating! Keeping up with new discoveries and technologies fills each day and connects me with many colleagues and friends.

The thousands of instructors and millions of students across the globe who have studied this book have contributed immensely to its development. Much of this has occurred spontaneously, through correspondence and conversations. Dozens of formal reviews from teaching psychologists and researchers around the world have also aided each revision. I look forward to continuing feedback as we strive, over future editions, to create an ever better book.

Table 1 Coverage of Evolution and Behavior Genetics

In addition to the coverage found in Chapter 3, ***the evolutionary perspective*** *is covered on the following pages:*

Anxiety disorders, pp. 480–481	Fear, p. 298	Puberty, onset of, p. 116
Attraction, pp. 73–74, 569	Hearing, pp. 156–157	Risk taking, p. 73
Biological predispositions in learning, pp. 233–234, 245	Hunger and taste preference, p. 348	Sensation, pp. 142, 159
Charles Darwin, p. 4	Instincts, pp. 341–342	Sensory adaptation, pp. 145, 176–177
Electromagnetic spectrum, sensitivity to, pp. 146–147	Intelligence, pp. 331–332	Sexual attraction, p. 73
	Language, pp. 302, 304–305	Sexuality, p. 357
Emotion, pp. 298, 385, 391, 392, 394	Love, p. 115	Sleep, p. 197
Emotion-detecting ability, p. 334	Need to belong, p. 371	Smell, pp. 163–164
Evolutionary perspective, defined, p. 8	Obesity, p. 349	Stress and the immune system, pp. 410, 416
	Overconfidence, pp. 299–300	

In addition to the coverage found in Chapter 3, ***behavior genetics*** *is covered on the following pages:*

Abuse, intergenerational transmission of, p. 249	Intelligence, pp. 317, 325–334	personality disorders, pp. 482–484, 485–486
Aggression, pp. 560–561	Learning, pp. 233–234, 245	schizophrenia, pp. 496–501
Biomedical therapies, pp. 529–534	Motor development, p. 104	Puberty, onset of, p. 115
Depth perception, pp. 167–168	Obesity and weight control, pp. 349, 353–355	Romantic love, pp. 130–131
Drives and incentives, p. 342	Perception, pp. 175–182	Sexuality, p. 357
Drug use, pp. 218–220	Personality traits, pp. 449–450	Sexual orientation, p. 367
Emotion and cognition, pp. 381–383	Psychological disorders:	Smell, p. 163
Fear, p. 365	anxiety disorders, pp. 480–482	Stress, personality, and illness, pp. 407–409, 411–413, 416
Happiness, pp. 399–401	bio-psycho-social perspective, pp. 471–472	
Hunger, taste preference, p. 348	depression, pp. 486–496	

Table 2 Coverage of the Psychology of Men and Women

Coverage of the **psychology of women and men** *can be found on the following pages:*

Alcoholism, p. 221
Behavioral effects of gender, p. 28
Biological sex/gender, p. 90
Body image, pp. 350–351
Depression, pp. 488, 494
Dieting, pp. 349, 355
Dream content, p. 200
Eating disorders, pp. 350–351
Emotion-detecting ability, pp. 334, 388–389
Emotional expression, pp. 133, 388–389
Empty nest, p. 131
Freud's views, pp. 432, 436–437
Gender and child-rearing, pp. 92–93
Gender roles, pp. 90–91
Generic pronoun "he," p. 309
Happiness, p. 400
Heart disease, pp. 408–409
Help-receiving, p. 574
Hormones and
    aggression, p. 561

sexual behavior, pp. 359–360
    sexual development, pp. 90, 115–117
Immune system, p. 410
Intelligence, pp. 332–350
    testing bias, p. 334
Life expectancy, p. 126
Marriage, pp. 417–418
Maturation, pp. 115–117
Menarche, p. 117
Menopause, pp. 124–125
Midlife crisis, pp. 129–130
Prejudice, pp. 294, 556–557
Obesity, pp. 349, 350
Pornography, pp. 360, 563
Psychological disorders, rates of, p. 502
Rape, pp. 563–564
REM sleep, arousal in, pp. 193–194
Risk taking, p. 73
Savant syndrome, p. 317

Schizophrenia, pp. 496, 498
Sense of smell, p. 163
Sexual abuse, pp. 72, 113–114, 211, 418
Sexual attraction, p. 73
Sexual disorders, p. 359
Sexuality, pp. 73–75, 357–361
Sexual orientation, pp. 364–369
Smoking, p. 100
Social connectedness, pp. 121, 417–418
Social Psychology, (Chapter 15), pp. 539–581
Stereotyping, p. 182
Stress:
    marital, pp. 417–418
    response, p. 403
    and sexual abuse, p. 418
Suicide, p. 490
Weight discrimination, p. 352
Women and work, p. 132
Women in psychology, pp. 4–5

Table 3 Coverage of Culture and Multicultural Experience

Coverage of **culture and multicultural experience** *permeates the chapters in the following discussions:*

Aging population, pp. 125–126
Aggression, pp. 559–560, 562, 563
AIDS, pp. 299, 410–411
Alcoholism, p. 211
Anger, pp. 394, 395
Attractiveness, pp. 570–571
Behavioral effects of culture, p. 28
Conformity, pp. 545, 547
Corporal punishment practices, p. 243
Culture and the self, pp. 460–463
Cultural norms, p. 87
Culture context effects, p. 182
Culture shock, pp. 87, 404–405
Deaf culture, pp. 62, 302, 305,
    307–310
Depression, pp. 488–489
Development:
    adolescence, p. 115
    attachment, pp. 112–114
    child-rearing, pp. 88–89
    cognitive development, p. 109
    developmental similarities, p. 89
    moral development, pp. 118–119
    motor development, p. 104
    social development, p. 110
Dieting, p. 349
Drugs, psychological effects of, p. 211
Dyslexia, p. 28
Emotion:
    emotion-detecting ability, p. 389

expressing, pp. 390–393
    experiencing, pp. 394–395
Enemy perceptions, p. 567
Gender:
    roles, pp. 90–91
    social connectedness, p. 119
Grief, expressing, p. 133
History of psychology, p. 2
Human diversity/kinship, p. 28
Hunger, p. 348
Individualism/collectivism, pp. 461–463
Intelligence, pp. 331–332
    testing bias, pp. 335–336
Language, pp. 85, 305, 308–309
Leaving the nest, p. 123
Life-expectancy, p. 125
Life satisfaction, pp. 397, 398, 399
Management styles, p. B-11
Marriage, p. 131
Meditation, p. 416
Memory, encoding, p. 264
Naturalistic observation, pace of life,
    p. 19
Need to belong, p. 372
Obesity, p. 354
Observational learning:
    television viewing, p. 122
    television and aggression, p. 250
Participative management, p. B-11
People with disabilities, p. 397

Personal space, p. 87
Prejudice, pp. 555, 556–557
Prejudice prototypes, p. 294
Psychological disorders:
    antisocial personality disorder, p. 486
    dissociative personality disorder, pp. 483–484
    eating disorders, pp. 350–351, 471
    rates of, p. 502
    schizophrenia, p. 502
    susto, p. 502
    taijin-kyofusho, p. 502
Psychotherapy:
    EMDR training, p. 525
    psychotherapists and values, pp. 528–529
Puberty and adult independence, p. 115
Self-esteem, pp. 400, 458
Self-serving bias, p. 459
Sexual attraction, p. 73
Sexual orientation, pp. 364–365
Smoking, pp. 212–213
Social-cultural perspective, p. 8
Social clock, pp. 129–130
Stress:
    adjusting to a new culture, p. 405
    poverty and inequality/life-expectancy, p. 406
Suicide, p. 490
Teen sexuality, pp. 361–362, 363–364
Testing bias, p. 335
See also Chapter 15, Social Psychology,
    pp. 539–581

Table 4 Neuroscience

In addition to the coverage found in Chapter 2, **neuroscience** *is covered on the following pages:*

Antisocial personality disorder, pp. 485–486

Autism, p. 108

Biofeedback, pp. 414–417, 420–421

Brain activity and
    aging, pp. 126, 128, 276
    aggression, p. 560–561
    dreams, p. 202
    emotion, pp. 163–164, 269, 384–385, 386
    sleep, pp. 191–193

Brain development:
    infancy and childhood, pp. 103–104
    adolescence, p. 117
    sexual differentiation *in utero*, p. 90

Brain development, experience and, pp. 83–84

Emotion and cognition, pp. 382–383

Fear-learning, p. 480

Fetal alcohol syndrome and brain abnormalities, pp. 100–101

Hallucinations and
    sleep, p. 203
    hallucinogens, pp. 215–216

Hormones and
    abuse, pp. 113–114
    development, pp. 90, 115–116

emotion, pp. 269, 384–385
    memory, p. 269
    sex, pp. 90, 115–116, 124–125, 269, 333–334, 383–384
    stress, pp. 403–404, 407, 410, 418
    weight control, pp. 346–347

Hunger, pp. 346–347

Intelligence, pp. 326–327

Language, statistical learning, pp. 306–308

Memory,
    physical storage of, p. 272
    and sleep, p. 202

Mirror neurons, pp. 248–249

Neuroscience perspective, defined, p. 8

Neurotransmitters and
    biomedical therapy:
        depression, pp. 491–492, 531–532
        ECT, pp. 533–534
        obsessive-compulsive disorder, p. 482
        psychosurgery, p. 534
        schizophrenia, pp. 530–531
    child abuse, pp. 113–114
    depression, pp. 471, 491–492
    drugs, pp. 210, 212, 215–216

exercise, p. 415
    narcolepsy, p. 199
    obsessive-compulsive disorder, p. 482
    schizophrenia, pp. 498–499
    smoking, p. 213

Pain, pp. 159–161
    phantom limb pain, p. 160

Parallel vs. serial processing, p. 150

Perception:
    brain damage and, pp. 141, 151–152
    color vision, pp. 153–155
    feature detection, pp. 150–151
    transduction, p. 84
    visual information processing, p. 150

Schizophrenia and brain abnormalities, pp. 498–499

Sensation:
    body position and movement, p. 164
    deafness, p. 158
    hearing, pp. 156–159
    sensory adaptation, p. 145
    smell, pp. 162–164
    taste, p. 162

Sexual orientation, pp. 366–368

Sleep, recuperation during, p. 197

Throughout its six editions, however, my vision for *Exploring Psychology* has not wavered: *to merge rigorous science with a broad human perspective in a book that engages both mind and heart.* My aim has been to create a state-of-the-art introduction to psychology, written with sensitivity to students' needs and interests. I aspire to help students understand and appreciate the wonder of important phenomena in their lives. I also want to convey the inquisitive spirit in which psychologists *do* psychology. The study of psychology, I believe, enhances our abilities to restrain intuition with critical thinking, judgmentalism with compassion, and illusion with understanding.

Believing with Thoreau that "anything living is easily and naturally expressed in popular language," I seek to communicate psychology's scholarship with crisp narrative and vivid storytelling. Writing as a solo author, I hope to tell psychology's story in a way that is warmly personal as well as rigorously scientific. I love to reflect on connections between psychology and other realms, such as literature, philosophy, history, sports, religion, politics, and popular culture. And I love to provoke thought, to play with words, and to laugh.

What's New?

This new edition retains its predecessor's voice and much of its content and organization. Yet it also reflects change on every page. In addition to the several hundred new references in this edition and updates on every page, I have introduced the following major changes to *Exploring Psychology*, sixth edition.

Expanded History of Psychology Coverage in Chapter 1

Psychology's history is taught in context throughout the book. But now, in response to many instructors' requests, students can also get an overview of psychology's story in Chapter 1. I had fun preparing this new section. My aim was to tell just enough of the story—aided by anecdotes and appealing artwork—to catch students' interest and to give them a perspective on the content of later chapters.

New Timeline by Charles Brewer

Charles Brewer (Furman University), noted psychology historian and longtime *Teaching of Psychology* editor, created an illustrated timeline of psychology's most significant events, from Ancient Greece to the present. This new feature fills the front and back inside covers, and a more detailed version can be found at www.worthpublishers.com/myers.

Revised Chapter 12, Personality

In response to feedback from many of you, I've modernized Chapter 12, Personality. The chapter's opening pages still cover the history of the psychoanalytic and humanistic perspectives, but this coverage is now followed by a more extensive discussion of contemporary research on traits, the social-cognitive perspective, the self, and the modern unconscious. Students will get a better sense of the contemporary nature of personality research, as well as an understanding of its historical roots.

New! Appendix B: Psychology at Work

Mindful of work's centrality to our lives, and also of the growing industrial/organizational (I/O) psychology subfield, I have written a new Psychology at Work appendix. Included in this new section are discussions of personnel psychology (interviewer intuition and skills, harnessing employee strengths), job satisfaction and engagement, management theories, leadership styles, and human factors psychology. My aim here was to identify some big and useful ideas emerging from contemporary I/O psychology.

Enhanced Coverage of Cognitive Psychology

Thanks partly to the burgeoning research on unconscious ("automatic") cognition, and to my own learning while writing a new book on the subject (*Intuition: Its Powers and Perils*), Chapter 9, Thinking, Language, and Intelligence, has been improved, and explanations in most chapters include enhanced coverage of the cognitive perspective.

Broader Coverage of Multicultural and Gender Issues, Including an Increasingly Global Perspective on Psychology

This edition presents an even more thoroughly cross-cultural perspective on psychology—reflected in research findings, text examples, and photos (see **TABLE 3,** page xvi). Coverage of the psychology of women and men is integrated throughout (see **TABLE 2,** page xvi). In addition, for this and succeeding editions I am working to offer a world-based psychology for our worldwide student readership. Thus, I continually search widely for research findings and text and photo examples, conscious that readers may be in Melbourne, Sheffield, Vancouver, or Nairobi. North American and European examples come easily, given that I reside in the United States, maintain contact with friends and colleagues in Canada, subscribe to several European periodicals, and live periodically in the United Kingdom. In addition to dozens of Canadian, British, Australian, and New Zealand examples, this edition offers significant coverage of Asian cultures and many mentions of other places worldwide. We are all citizens of a shrinking world, thanks to increased migration and the growing global economy. Thus, American students, too, benefit from information and examples that internationalize their world-consciousness. And if psychology seeks to explain *human* behavior (not just American or Canadian or Australian behavior), the broader the scope of studies presented, the more accurate is our picture of this world's people. My aim is to expose all students to the world beyond their own country. Thus, I continue to welcome input and suggestions from all readers.

Enhanced Critical Thinking Coverage

I introduce students to critical thinking in a very natural way throughout the book, with even more in this edition to encourage active learning of critical thinking principles.

- *Chapter 1 takes a unique, critical thinking approach to introducing students to psychology's research methods*, emphasizing the fallacies of our everyday intuition and common sense and, thus, the need for psychological science. *Critical thinking* is introduced as a key term in this chapter (p. 14).
- *Thinking Critically About . . . boxes* appear throughout the book, modeling for students a critical approach to some key issues in psychology. For example, see Thinking Critically About: Risks—Do We Fear the Right Things? (p. 298) (new to this edition). **TABLE 5** gives a complete list of these boxes.
- *Detective-style stories* throughout the narrative draw students into thinking critically about psychology's key research questions.
- *"Apply this" questions and activities* and *"Think about it" discussions* keep students active in their study of each chapter.

Table 5 Critical Thinking Topics

Critical thinking coverage and coverage of psychology's **scientific research** process can be found on the following pages:

Thinking Critically About . . . boxes:
Hot and Cold Streaks in Basketball and the Stock Market, p. 23
Extrasensory Perception, pp. 178–181
Risks—Do We Fear the Right Things? pp. 298–299
Lie Detection, pp. 386–387
Alternative Medicine—New Ways to Health or Old Snake Oil? pp. 420–421
How to Be a "Successful" Astrologer or Palm Reader, pp. 446–447
Insanity and Responsibility, p. 474
Do Video Games Teach or Release Violence?, p. 565

Critical Examinations of Pop Psychology:
Perceiving order in random events, pp. 21–23
Can subliminal tapes improve your life? pp. 26–27
Do we use only 10 percent of our brains? p. 55
Critiquing the evolutionary explanation, pp. 74–75
How great is the power of parenting? p. 82
Is there extrasensory perception? pp. 178–179
Can hypnosis enhance recall? Coerce action? Be therapeutic? Alleviate pain? pp. 204–206
Has the concept of "addiction" been stretched too far? pp. 208–210

Do animals exhibit language? pp. 312–315
Spirituality and faith communities, pp. 419, 422–424
Is repression a myth? pp. 437–438
How valid is the Rorschach test? pp. 434–435
Is Freud credible? pp. 435–438
Post-traumatic stress disorder, pp. 480–481
Is psychotherapy effective? pp. 520–523
Evaluating alternative therapies, pp. 523–526

Thinking Critically With Psychological Science:
The limits of intuition and common sense, pp. 11–13
Critical thinking introduced as a key term, p. 14
The scientific attitude, p. 14
The scientific method, pp. 15–16
Correlation and causation, p. 20
Illusory correlation, p. 21
Evaluating therapies, pp. 24–26
Statistical reasoning, p. A-1
Making inferences, pp. A-5–A-6

Scientific Detective Stories:
Is breast milk better than formula? p. 24
Language in the brain, p. 56
Our divided brains, pp. 59–60
Twin and adoption studies, pp. 76–79
How a child's mind develops, pp. 104–109

Aging and intelligence, pp. 128–129
Parallel processing, pp. 151–152
How do we see in color? pp. 153–155
Why do we sleep? pp. 194–197
Why do we dream? pp. 200–203
Is hypnosis an altered state of consciousness? pp. 207–208
How do we store memories in our brains? pp. 267–272
Memory construction, pp. 281–287
Risk assessment, pp. 298–299
Do animals exhibit language? pp. 312–315
Why do we feel hunger? pp. 345–347
What determines sexual orientation? pp. 365–369
The pursuit of happiness: Who is happy, and why? pp. 395–401
Why—and in whom—does stress contribute to heart disease? pp. 408–409
How and why is social support linked with health? pp. 417–419
Self-esteem versus self-serving bias, pp. 458–460
What causes mood disorders? pp. 488–495
Do prenatal viral infections increase risk of schizophrenia? p. 499
Is psychotherapy effective? pp. 520–523
Why do people fail to help in emergencies? pp. 574–576

- *Critical examinations of pop psychology* spark interest and provide important lessons in thinking critically about everyday topics.
- **NEW!** Each chapter now ends with a six-question Critical Thinker's Review. These new self-tests invite students to hone their critical reasoning skills while considering some application of a key concept covered in the chapter. Six categories of critical thinking (pattern recognition, practical problem solving, creative problem solving, scientific problem solving, psychological reasoning, and perspective taking) are included within each self-test.
- Appendix A: Statistical Reasoning in Everyday Life encourages students to focus on thinking smarter by applying simple statistical principles to everyday reasoning (pp. A-1 to A-9).

  See **TABLE 5** for a complete list of this text's coverage of critical thinking topics.

Enhanced Teaching and Learning Resources

Our supplements and media package have long been lauded for their quality, connectedness, accuracy, and abundance. This sixth edition features an even greater smorgasbord from which to choose. New items include the ultimate Web-based resource feast—the exciting **Instructor's Resource eLibrary** (see **FIGURE 1**); the new twenty-first–century *PsychSim* with all-new graphics; our *Digital Media Archive CD-ROM/DVD*; our *PsychInquiry Student CD-ROM*; a new positive psychology workbook, a new Special Edition of *Scientific American* on "The Brain"; and new video resources.

Successful SQ3R Study Aids

1. Exploring Psychology's *complete system of learning aids includes numbered "preview questions," which appear in this format throughout the book.*

Exploring Psychology has retained its popular system of study aids, integrated into an SQ3R structure that augments the narrative without disrupting it. Each chapter opens with a chapter outline that enables students to quickly *survey* its major topics. Numbered preview *questions* at the start of each new major topic define the learning objectives that will guide students as they *read*. *Rehearse It* quizzes at the end of each major section will stimulate students to rehearse what they have learned. (Students can check their answers against the key in Appendix C.) These test items offer a novel combination of crisp review of key ideas, and practice with

figure 1
Home page from the Instructor's Resource eLibrary

INSTRUCTOR'S RESOURCE eLIBRARY | for David G. Myers, *Exploring Psychology* 6th Edition

Search [ ] [All sources ▲] [All types ▲] [go]
[Search tips]

→ New Collection
→ Open Collection: [Default Collec.. ▲]
→ Update my profile
→ Log off

Browse by: Book table of contents | **Source** | Resource type

Myers, *Exploring Psychology* 6e

+ Book Companion Site
+ Faculty Guide: Scientific American Frontiers
+ Faculty Guide: The Human Experience
+ Faculty Guide: The Mind
+ Instructor's Resources
+ PsychInquiry
+ PsychOnline
+ PsychSim 5
+ Special Scientific American Issue on the Human Brain
+ Textbook

Help

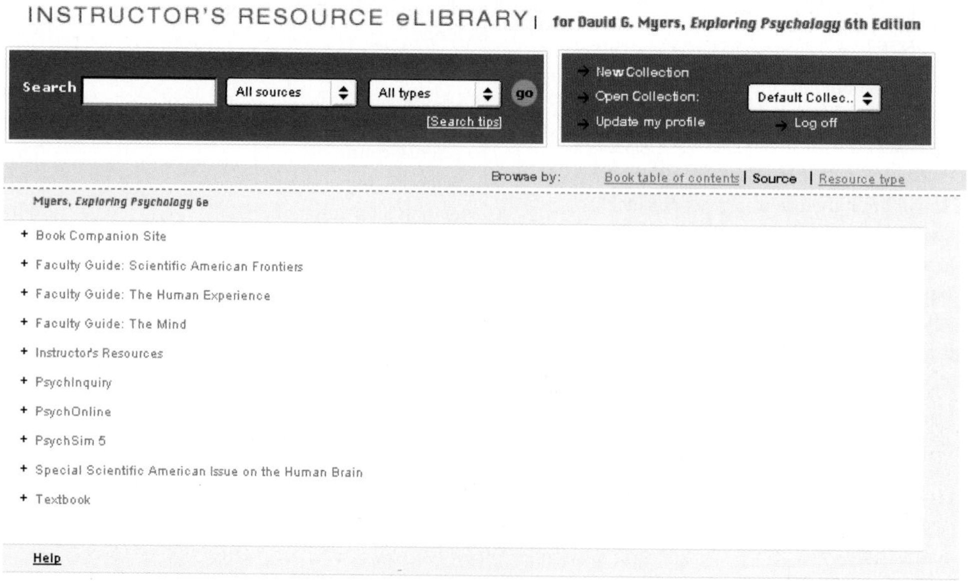

the multiple-choice test format. The chapter-ending *Review* is structured as a set of answers to the numbered preview questions. A **NEW** self-test, A Critical Thinker's Review, at the end of each chapter offers students an opportunity to review and apply key concepts for even better retention. All **key terms** are defined in the margins for ready reference while students are being introduced to the new term in the narrative (see sample at right). Periodic Thinking Critically About and Close-Up boxes encourage development of critical thinking skills as well as application of the new concepts. The Tips for Studying Psychology section at the end of Chapter 1 explains the SQ3R-based system of study aids, suggesting how students can *survey*, *question*, *read*, *rehearse*, and *review* the material for maximum retention.

▶ **key terms** Look for complete definitions of each important term in the margin near its introduction in the narrative.

In the margins of this book, students will find interesting and informative review notes, and quotes from researchers and others that will encourage them to be active learners and apply what they are learning.

Goals for the Sixth Edition

Throughout this revision, I have steadfastly followed eight principles:

1. ***To exemplify the process of inquiry*** I strive to show students not just the outcome of research, but how the research process works. Throughout, the book tries to excite the reader's curiosity. It invites readers to imagine themselves as participants in classic experiments. Several chapters introduce research stories as mysteries that progressively unravel as one clue after another falls into place. (See, for example, the history of research on the brain's processing of language—page 56.)

2. ***To teach critical thinking*** By presenting research as intellectual detective work, I exemplify an inquiring, analytical mind-set. Whether students are studying development, cognition, or statistics, they will become involved in, and see the rewards of, critical reasoning. Moreover, they will discover how an empirical approach can help them evaluate competing ideas and claims for highly publicized phenomena—ranging from subliminal persuasion, ESP, and alternative therapies, to astrology, basketball streak-shooting, and repressed and recovered memories.

3. ***To put facts in the service of concepts*** My intention is not to fill students' intellectual file drawers with facts, but to reveal psychology's major concepts—to teach students how to think, and to offer psychological ideas worth thinking about. In each chapter I emphasize those concepts I hope students will carry with them long after they complete the course. Always, I try to follow Albert Einstein's dictum that "everything should be made as simple as possible, but not simpler."

4. ***To be as up to date as possible*** Few things dampen students' interests as quickly as the sense that they are reading stale news. While retaining psychology's classic studies and concepts, I also present the discipline's most important recent developments. Nearly 700 references in this edition are dated 2000 to 2004.

5. ***To integrate principles and applications*** Throughout—by means of anecdotes, case histories, and the posing of hypothetical situations—I relate the findings of basic research to their applications and implications. Where psychology can illuminate pressing human issues—be they racism and sexism, health and happiness, or violence and war—I have not hesitated to shine its light.

6. ***To enhance comprehension by providing continuity*** Many chapters have a significant issue or theme that links subtopics, forming a thread that ties the chapter together. Chapter 7, Learning, conveys the idea that bold thinkers can serve as intellectual pioneers. Chapter 9, Thinking, Language, and Intelligence, raises the issue of human rationality and irrationality. Chapter 13, Psychological Disorders, conveys empathy for, and understanding of, troubled lives. "The uniformity of a work," observed Edward Gibbon, "denotes the hand of a single artist." Because this book has a single author, other threads, such as behavior genetics and cultural diversity, weave throughout the whole book, and students hear a consistent voice.

7. ***To reinforce learning at every step*** Everyday examples and rhetorical questions encourage students to process the material actively. Concepts presented earlier are frequently applied, and thereby reinforced, in later chapters. For instance, in Chapter 5, Sensation and Perception, students learn that much of our information processing occurs *outside* of our conscious awareness. Ensuing chapters reinforce this concept. The SQ3R system of pedagogical aids augments learning without interrupting the text narrative. A marginal glossary helps students master important terminology. Major sections begin with numbered preview questions and end with Rehearse It sections for self-testing on key concepts. End-of-chapter reviews repeat the preview questions and answer them. And the new end-of-chapter Critical Thinker's Reviews invite students to review and apply key concepts in memorable ways.

8. ***To convey respect for human unity and diversity*** Time and again, readers will see evidence of our human kinship—our shared biological heritage, our common mechanisms of seeing and learning, hungering and feeling, loving and hating. They will also better understand the dimensions of our diversity—our *individual* diversity in development and aptitudes, temperament and personality, and disorder and health; and our *cultural* diversity in attitudes and expressive styles, child-rearing and care for the elderly, and life priorities.

The Multimedia Supplements Package

Exploring Psychology, sixth edition, offers a host of new electronic and print supplements titles.

NEW! Instructor's Resource eLibrary (IReL) The *IReL* is the ultimate integrator, bringing together all the existing text and supplementary resources in a single, easy-to-use Web interface with a Google™-like search engine. The *IReL* includes materials from the textbook, *Instructor's Resources,* and electronic supplements, including PowerPoint slides and modules from *PsychSim* and *PsychOnline.* Through simple browse and search tools, adopting instructors can quickly access virtually any piece of content in the package and either download it to their computer's hard drive or create a Web page to share with students.

NEW! Worth Digital Media Archive CD-ROM This dual-platform *Instructor's Presentation CD-ROM* contains a rich collection of more than 40 digitized video clips of classic experiments and research. Footage includes Albert Bandura's Bobo doll experiment, Harold Takooshian's bystander studies, Jean Piaget's conservation experiment, Harry Harlow's monkey experiments, Stanley Milgram's obedience study, and Ulric Neisser's selective attention studies. The *Digital Media Archive* clips are compressed in MPEG format and are compatible with Microsoft PowerPoint software. The clips are also available in DVD and VHS formats.

NEW! PsychSim 5 is a major update and expansion of Thomas Ludwig's (Hope College) award-winning package of multimedia activities for introductory psychology. The content coverage has doubled, with more than 40 simulated experiments, demonstrations, and other activities covering important psychology topics in a brief, focused, yet whimsical manner. The new graphics are, methinks, pretty spectacular.

NEW! Instructor's Resource CD-ROM, containing an electronic version of the *Instructor's Resources,* including line art and JPEG from the text, lecture guides, and prebuilt PowerPoint presentations.

NEW! PsychInquiry: Student Activities in Research and Critical Thinking Developed by Thomas Ludwig and a team of contributors, this new CD-ROM—customized for *Exploring Psychology,* sixth edition—contains dozens of highly interactive activities designed to help students learn about psychological research and to improve their critical thinking. These activities enable students to work hands-on with descriptive, correlational, and experimental research to help them hone the critical thinking mind-set required for psychological research.

PsychInquiry activities are complete with animations, video, fresh illustrations, and self-assessment instruments that draw students into the discipline. *PsychInquiry* also offers a handful of more extensive research activities for use as classroom projects or lab assignments.

NEW! Special *Scientific American* Issue "Improving the Mind and Brain" This September 2003 single-topic issue from *Scientific American* magazine features the latest findings from the most distinguished researchers in the field. This issue covers a range of fascinating subjects, including helping the brain repair itself, learning and brain plasticity, new ways to treat mood disorders, alternatives to shock therapy, cognitive enhancement, and the changing landscape of neurobioethics.

NEW! Expanded Myers Psychology Web Companion (www.worthpublishers.com/myers) provides an even wider variety of activities and study aids organized by *Exploring Psychology*, sixth edition, chapters. Features include new self-tests for every chapter written by *Test Bank* author John Brink (Calvin College); Chapter Overviews; Thinking Critically Exercises; Web links; Tom Ludwig's (Hope College) award-winning programs *PsychQuest* and *PsychSim*; other simulations and demonstrations; and key-term flashcards.

PsychOnline is a wonderful set of online resources authored by Thomas Ludwig and a team of contributors. With *PsychOnline*, you pick and choose from a buffet of resources that can be used as a complete online course or a component of a more traditional lecture-based course.

NEW! Pursuing Human Strengths: A Positive Psychology Guide supplement by Martin Bolt (Calvin College) aims to help students build up their own strengths. Closely following the research, this workbook provides a brief overview of nine positive traits, including hope, self-respect, commitment, and joy. It also offers self-assessment activities that help students gauge how much of the trait they have developed, and how they might work further toward fostering these traits.

NEW! *Making Sense of Psychology on the Web* with CD-ROM by Connie K. Varnhagen (University of Alberta) is a brief booklet that helps students locate reliable information on the Web, evaluate sites, and organize research. The guide includes a CD-ROM containing *Research HyperFolio*, software that enables students to collect snippets of text, illustrations, video clips, and audio clips from the Web or other electronic sources and compile them into worksheets and an easily accessible filing cabinet.

NEW! *Psychology: The Human Experience* Teaching Modules, available in VHS or DVD formats. This new Emmy-award-winning series includes more than three hours of footage from the new Introductory Psychology telecourse, *Psychology: The Human Experience,* produced by Coast Learning Systems in collaboration with Worth Publishers. These brief clips are ideal for lecture, and a faculty guide is available to help integrate each clip. Footage contains noted scholars, the latest research, and beautiful animations.

NEW! *The Many Faces of Psychology* Video, edited by Frank Vattano (Colorado State University) and Martin Bolt (Calvin College) is now available in VHS and DVD. This video is a terrific way to begin your psychology course. It introduces psychology as a science and a profession, illustrating basic and applied methods. This new 22-minute video presents some of the major areas in which psychologists work and teach, including biological, cognitive, neuroscience, clinical/counseling, human factors, industrial/organizational, school psychology, sports psychology, health psychology, forensics, social, developmental, and rehabilitation.

***Scientific American* Frontiers Video Collection, second edition,** is a renowned series hosted by Alan Alda. These 10- to 12-minute modules provide an excellent way to show how psychological research is actually conducted, focusing on the work of Steve Sumi, Renee Baillargeon, Carl Rosengren, Laura Pettito, Steven Pinker, Barbara Rothbaum, Bob Stickgold, Irene Pepperberg, Marc Hauser, Linda Bartoshuk, and Michael Gazzaniga.

The Mind Video Teaching Modules, **second edition,** offers 35 brief, engaging video clips to enhance and illustrate lecture topics.

The Brain Video Teaching Modules, **second edition,** offers more engaging video clips to help you teach.

Image and Lecture Gallery (www.worthpublishers.com/ILG) is a convenient way to access electronic versions of lecture materials. Registered users can browse, search, and download illustrations from Worth titles and prebuilt PowerPoint presentation files for specific chapters. Instructors can also create personal folders on a personalized home page for easy organization of the materials.

PowerPoint Slides are available and can be used as is, or customized to fit your needs. There are four prebuilt versions available for each chapter: 1) chapter text only, 2) chapter art and illustrations, 3) lecture presentations by James McCubbin (Clemson University), and 4) topic-based lectures by Harvey Shulman (Ohio State University).

Presentation Manager Pro 2.0 is an easy-to-operate CD-ROM that includes materials compatible with most commercially available presentation software programs. Included on the CD are our pre-built PowerPoint lectures and all the art from the textbook. With Presentation Manager Pro, instructors can build classroom presentations using graphic materials from the book, and your own digital material (including video) imported from the Internet or other sources. **WebCT** and **Blackboard** are available free to all adopters. With these course organizational software systems, instructors can create a course Web site and/or online course with content, threaded discussions, quizzing, an online grade book, a course calendar, and more! This book's graphic and media content is available in the WebCT and Blackboard formats.

Online Testing is now available with Diploma from the Brownstone Research Group. Instructors can now create and administer secure exams over a network and over the Internet with questions that incorporate multimedia and interactive exercises. The program includes impressive security features and grade book and result-analysis features.

In addition to all these fabulous resources, *Exploring Psychology*, sixth edition, is accompanied by smartly updated versions of the widely acclaimed print supplements package.

The updated and better-than-ever ***Instructor's Resources*** by Martin Bolt (Calvin College) has been hailed as the finest set of psychology teaching resources ever assembled, including ready-to-use demonstration handouts, detailed lecture/discussion ideas, student projects, classroom exercises, and video and film suggestions.

The ***Student Study Guide*** by Richard O. Straub (University of Michigan, Dearborn) follows the text's content and offers the following for every major section in the text: a new "Thinking Critically" feature, Stepping Through the Section, Self-Tests, Web Sightings Internet activities, and Cross-Check crossword puzzles. The Guide also includes Cornelius Rea's (Douglas College, British Columbia) helpful "Focus on Vocabulary and Language" feature, designed to help clarify idioms and other phrases potentially unfamiliar to students for whom English is a second language.

The ***Test Bank*** by John Brink (Calvin College) is broken into two banks, providing over 4000 multiple-choice factual/definitional and conceptual questions plus essay questions. Each question is page-referenced to the textbook, tied into the *Instructor's Resources'* list of learning objectives, and rated for level of difficulty. The second Test Bank includes optional questions on *PsychQuest* and *PsychSim* computer simulations and *The Brain* and *The Mind* videos.

The Critical Thinking Companion by Jane Halonen (James Madison University) and Cynthia Gray (Alverno College) is now available in a second edition. This collection of engaging, challenging, and fun critical thinking exercises is tied to the main topics in *Exploring Psychology*, sixth edition. The *Critical Thinking Companion* would work particularly well with this edition of *Exploring Psychology*, given the new Critical Thinker's Review sections at the end of each chapter, which address each of Halonen's six categories of critical thinking.

In Appreciation

If it is true that "whoever walks with the wise becomes wise," then I am wiser for all the wisdom and advice received from expert colleagues. Aided by several hundred consultants and reviewers over the last two decades, *Exploring Psychology* has become a better, more accurate book than one author alone (this author, at least) could write. My indebtedness continues to each of the teacher-scholars whose influence I acknowledged in the five previous editions.

My gratitude now extends to the colleagues who contributed criticism, corrections, and creative ideas related to the content of this new edition. For their expertise and encouragement, I thank the following reviewers:

Susan Becker, *Mesa State College*

Stephanie Berk, *University of Pittsburgh*

Jay Brown, *Southwest Missouri State University*

Shelley Coley, *Jefferson State Community College*

Carl Granrud, *University of Northern Colorado*

Mary M. Boggiano, *University of Alabama at Birmingham*

Paul Mallery, *La Sierra University*

Gary McCullough, *University of Texas of the Permian Basin*

Kathleen Mentink, *Chippewa Valley Technical College*

Donna Nelson, *Winthrop University*

Michelle Pilati, *Rio Hondo College*

Colleen Pilgrim, *Schoolcraft College*

Paul K. Presson, *Westminster College*

Christopher Randall, *Troy State University*

Tammy Ruff, *Nashville Community College*

Adeny Schmidt, *La Sierra University*

Jeff Sinn, *Winthrop University*

Mary Ellen Dello Stritto, *Ball State University*

Cynthia Terres, *Coastal Carolina University*

Fernelle Warren, *Troy State University*

ShawnaLee K. Washam, *Aims Community College*

At Worth Publishers a host of people played key roles in creating this sixth edition. Christine Brune, chief editor of the parent book and associate editor of this briefer version, is a wonder worker. She offers just the right mix of encouragement, gentle admonition, attention to detail, and passion for excellence. An author could not ask for more.

Nancy Fleming served in a dual capacity—as chief editor of this new edition and as copyeditor. It is a rare and gifted editor who can both "think big" and "think small" in working with a manuscript. Nancy does both with unusual sensitivity and grace.

Laura Pople and Reid Sherline worked long hours to create the fabulous new *Instructor's Resource eLibrary*. It is a pioneering contribution to the teaching of psychology.

Publisher Catherine Woods helped construct and execute the plan for this new edition and was a trusted sounding board as we faced decisions along the way. Media and Supplements Editor Andrea Musick coordinated production of the huge supplements package for this edition. Betty Probert efficiently edited and produced the core print supplements. Editorial Assistant Matthew Driskill provided invaluable support in commissioning reviews, mailing information to professors, and performing numerous other daily tasks related to the book's development and production. Lee Mahler did a splendid job of laying out each page. Debbie Goodsite and Meg Kuhta located the myriad photographic illustrations.

Associate Managing Editor Tracey Kuehn displayed tenacity, commitment, and impressive organization in leading Worth's gifted artistic production team and coordinating editorial input throughout the production process. Senior Production Manager Sarah Segal masterfully kept the book to its tight schedule, and Babs Reingold and Lissi Sigillo created the distinctive design and art program. Production Manager Stacey Alexander did her usual excellent work of producing the many core print supplements.

To achieve our goal of supporting the teaching of psychology, this teaching package must not only be authored, reviewed, edited, and produced, but also made available to teachers of psychology. For their exceptional success in doing that, our author team is grateful to Worth Publishers' professional sales and marketing team. We are especially thankful for Marketing Manager Kate Nurre and Executive Marketing Manager Renée Altier, both for their tireless efforts to inform our teaching colleagues of our efforts to assist their teaching, and for the joy of working with them.

At Hope College, the supporting team members for this edition included Kathryn Brownson, who researched countless bits of information, proofed hundreds of pages, and, with the assistance of Rachel Brownson, prepared the Name Index and Reference section. She also crafted the new beginning to the Personality chapter. Typesetters Phyllis and Richard Vandervelde worked faithfully and joyfully to enter or revise every one of the more than 300,000 words and finally to code them for electronic delivery.

Again, I gratefully acknowledge the influence and editing assistance of my writing coach, poet Jack Ridl, whose influence resides in the voice you will be hearing in the pages that follow. He more than anyone cultivated my delight in dancing with the language and taught me to approach writing as a craft that shades into art.

After hearing countless dozens of people say that this book's supplements have taken their teaching to a new level, I reflect on how fortunate I am to be a part of a team on which everyone has produced on-time work marked by the highest professional standards. For their remarkable talents, their long-term dedication, and their friendship, I thank Martin Bolt, John Brink, Thomas Ludwig, and Richard Straub.

Finally, my gratitude extends to the many students and instructors who have written to offer suggestions or just an encouraging word. It is for them, and for those about to begin their study of psychology, that I have done my best to introduce the field I love.

When those who paint the Golden Gate Bridge finish, it is time to start over again. So with this book. The ink is barely dry before one begins envisioning the next edition. By the time you read this, I will be gathering information for the seventh edition. Your input will again influence how this book continues to evolve. So, please, do share your thoughts.

David Myers

Hope College
Holland, Michigan 49422-9000
USA
www.davidmyers.org

Exploring PSYCHOLOGY

chapter 1

Thinking Critically With Psychological Science

Hoping to satisfy their curiosity about people and to remedy their own woes, millions turn to "psychology." They listen to talk-radio counseling, read articles on psychic powers, attend stop-smoking hypnosis seminars, and absorb self-help books on the meaning of dreams, the path to ecstatic love, the roots of personal happiness.

Others, intrigued by claims of psychological truth, wonder: Do mothers and infants bond in the first hours after birth? Should we trust childhood sexual abuse memories that get "recovered" in adulthood—and prosecute the alleged predators? Are first-born children more driven to achieve? Does handwriting offer clues to personality? Does psychotherapy heal?

For these questioners, as for most people whose exposure to psychology comes from popular books, magazines, and TV, psychologists analyze personality, offer counseling, and dispense child-rearing advice.

Do they? Yes, and much more. Consider some of psychology's questions that from time to time you may wonder about:

- Have you ever found yourself reacting to something just as one of your biological parents would—perhaps in a way you vowed you never would—and then wondered how much of your personality you inherited? *To what extent are personality differences predisposed by one's genes? To what extent by the home and neighborhood environments?*
- Have you ever played peekaboo with a 6-month-old infant and wondered why the baby finds the game so delightful? The baby reacts as though, when you momentarily move behind a door, you actually disappear—only to reappear later out of thin air. What do babies actually perceive and think?
- Have you ever awakened from a nightmare and, with a wave of relief, wondered why you had such a crazy dream? How often, and why, do we dream?
- Have you ever wondered what leads to school and work success? Are some people just born smarter? *Does sheer intelligence explain why some people get richer, think more creatively, or relate more sensitively?*
- Have you ever gotten depressed or anxious and wondered whether you'll ever feel "normal"? *What triggers our bad moods—and our good ones?*
- Have you ever worried about how to act among people of a different culture, race, or gender? *In what ways are we alike as members of the human family? How do we differ?*

Such questions provide grist for psychology's mill because psychology is a science that seeks to answer all sorts of questions about us all: how we think, feel, and act.

A smile is a smile the world around Throughout this book, you will see examples not only of our cultural and gender diversity but also of the similarities that define our shared human nature. People in different cultures vary in when and how often they smile, but a smile *means* the same thing anywhere in the world.

WHAT IS PSYCHOLOGY?

Psychology's Roots

Once upon a time, on a planet in your neighborhood of the universe, there came to be people. Soon thereafter, these creatures became intensely interested in themselves and in one another. They wondered, *"Who are we? From where come our*

"I have made a ceaseless effort not to ridicule, not to bewail, not to scorn human actions, but to understand them."

Benedict Spinoza, A Political Treatise, 1677

1

thoughts? Our feelings? Our actions? And how are we to understand—and to master or manage—those around us?" Psychology's answers to these wonderings have developed from international roots in philosophy and biology into a science that aims to describe and explain how we think, feel, and act. Understanding the roots of today's psychology helps us appreciate psychologists' varied perspectives.

Prescientific Psychology

1. How long have people been thinking and writing about the questions that fascinate psychologists today?[1]

We can trace many of psychology's current questions back through human history. These early thinkers wondered: How do our minds work? How do our bodies relate to our minds? How much of what we know comes built in? How much is acquired through experience? In India, for example, Buddha pondered how sensations and perceptions combine to form ideas. In China, Confucius stressed the powers of ideas and of an educated mind. In ancient Israel, Hebrew scholars anticipated today's psychology by linking mind and emotion to the body; people we said to think with their hearts and feel with their bowels.

In ancient Greece, the philosopher-teacher Socrates (469–399 B.C.) and his student Plato concluded that mind is separable from body and continues after the body dies, and that knowledge is innate—built within us. As Socrates lay dying, Plato's future student, Aristotle, was entering the world in another part of Greece. Aristotle's love of data distinguished him from Socrates and Plato, who derived principles by logic. An intellectual ancestor of today's scientists, Aristotle derived principles from careful observations. His observations told him that "the soul is not separable from the body, and the same holds good of particular parts of the soul" (*De Anima*). Moreover, he said knowledge is *not* preexisting (sorry, Socrates and Plato); instead, it grows from the experiences stored in our memories.

The next 2000 years brought few enduring new insights into human nature, but that changed in the 1600s, when modern science began to flourish. With it came new theories of human behavior, and new versions of the ancient debates. A frail but brilliant Frenchman named René Descartes (1595–1650) agreed with Socrates and Plato about the existence of innate ideas and the mind's being "entirely distinct from the body" and able to survive its death. Descartes' concept of mind forced him to conjecture, as people have ever since, how the immaterial mind and physical body communicate. A scientist as well as a philosopher, Descartes dissected animals and concluded that the fluid in the brain's cavities contained "animal spirits." These spirits, he surmised, flowed from the brain through what we call the nerves (which he thought were hollow) to the muscles, provoking movement. Memories formed as experiences opened pores in the brain, into which the animal spirits also flowed. Descartes was right that nerve paths are important and that they enable reflexes. Yet, genius though he was, and standing upon the accumulated knowledge from 99+ percent of our human history, he hardly had a clue of what today's average 12-year-old knows. Indeed, most of the scientific story of our self-exploration—the story told in this book's chapters—has been written in but the last historical eye blink of human time.

Meanwhile, across the English channel in Britain, science was taking a more down-to-earth form, centered on experiment, experience, and common-sense judgment. Francis Bacon (1561–1626) became one of the founders of modern science, and his influence lingers in the experiments of today's psychological science. Bacon also was fascinated by the human mind and its failings. Anticipating what we have

A seventeenth-century view of nerves
In his *Treatise of Man*, Descartes proposed the hydraulics of a simple reflex.

Bettmann/Corbis

---

[1]A Preview Question will appear at the beginning of each major section of a chapter. Search actively for the answer to the question as you read through the section. Answers are available in the form of a numbered chapter review at the end of the chapter.

come to appreciate about our mind's hunger to perceive patterns even in random events, he wrote that "the human understanding, from its peculiar nature, easily supposes a greater degree of order and equality in things than it really finds" (*Novum Organuum*). He also foresaw research on our eagerness to selectively notice and remember events that confirm our beliefs: "All superstition is much the same whether it be that of astrology, dreams, omens, retributive judgments, or the like, in all of which the deluded believers observe events which are fulfilled, but neglect and pass over their failure, though it be much more common."

Some 50 years after Bacon's death, John Locke (1632–1704), a British political philosopher, sat down to write a one-page essay on "our own abilities" for an upcoming discussion with friends. After 20 years and hundreds of pages, Locke had completed one of history's latest and greatest late papers (*Essay Concerning Human Understanding*), in which he famously argued that the mind at birth is a blank slate—a "white paper"—on which experience writes. This idea, adding to Bacon's legacy, helped form modern **empiricism**, the view that knowledge originates in experience and that science should, therefore, rely on observation and experimentation.

Psychological Science Is Born

2. What event defines the birth of psychology as we know it today? What were structuralism and functionalism, and how did they differ?

Philosophers' thinking about thinking continued until the birth of psychology as we know it, on a December day in 1879, in a small room on the third floor of a shabby building at Germany's University of Leipzig. There, two young men were helping a long-faced, austere, middle-aged professor, Wilhelm Wundt, create an experimental apparatus. Their machine measured the time lag between people's hearing a ball hit a platform and their pressing a telegraph key (Hunt, 1993). Later, the researchers compared this lag to the time required for slightly more complex tasks. Curiously, people responded in about one-tenth of a second when asked to press the key as soon as the sound occurred—and in about two-tenths of a second when asked to press the key as soon as they were aware of perceiving the sound. Wundt was seeking to measure "atoms of the mind"—the fastest and simplest mental processes. Thus began what many consider psychology's first experiment, launching the first psychology laboratory, staffed by Wundt and psychology's first graduate students.

Before long, this new science of psychology became organized into different branches, or schools of thought, each promoted by pioneering thinkers. These early schools included *structuralism* and *functionalism*, described here, and Gestalt psychology, behaviorism, and psychoanalysis, described in later chapters.

THINKING ABOUT THE MIND'S STRUCTURE Soon after receiving his Ph.D. in 1892, Wundt's student Edward Bradford Titchener joined the Cornell University faculty and introduced **structuralism**. As physicists and chemists discerned the structure of matter, so Titchener aimed to discover the elements of mind. His method was to engage people in self-reflective *introspection* (looking inward), training them to report elements of their experience as they looked at a rose, listened to a metronome, smelled a scent, or tasted a substance. What were their immediate sensations, their images, their feelings? And how did these relate to one another? Titchener shared with the English essayist C. S. Lewis (1960, pp. 18–19) the view that "there is one thing, and only one in the whole universe which we know more about than we could learn from external observation." That one thing, Lewis said, is ourselves. "We have, so to speak, inside information."

▶ **empiricism** the view that (a) knowledge comes from experience via the senses, and (b) science flourishes through observation and experiment.

▶ **structuralism** an early school of psychology that used introspection to explore the elemental structure of the human mind.

*Throughout this book, important concepts are **bold faced**. As you study, you can find these terms with their definitions in a nearby margin and in the Glossary at the end of the book.*

Information sources are cited in parentheses, with name and date, then provided fully in the References section at the book's end.

Wilhelm Wundt Established the first psychology laboratory at the University of Leipzig, Germany.

Edward Bradford Titchener
Used introspection to search for the mind's structural elements.

"The rose is smooth-petaled, sweetly aromatic,..."

Monika Suteski

"You don't know your own mind."

Jonathan Swift, Polite Conversation, *1738*

▶ **functionalism** a school of psychology that focused on how mental and behavioral processes function—how they enable the organism to adapt, survive, and flourish.

Alas, structuralism waned as introspection waned. Introspection required smart, verbal people. It also proved somewhat unreliable, its results varying from person to person and experience to experience. And just as the very act of measuring an atomic particle can alter what is measured, so the act of reflecting on an experience can alter the memory of it. Recent studies indicate that people's recollections frequently err, as do their self-reports about what has caused them to help or hurt another (Myers, 2002). Often we just don't know why we feel what we feel and do what we do.

THINKING ABOUT THE MIND'S FUNCTIONS Unlike those hoping to assemble the structure of mind from simple elements—which was rather like trying to understand a car by examining its disconnected parts—philosopher-psychologist William James thought it more fruitful to consider the evolved *functions* of our thoughts and feelings. Smelling is what the nose does; thinking is what the brain does. But *why* do the nose and brain do these things? Under the influence of evolutionary theorist Charles Darwin, James assumed that thinking, like smelling, developed because it was adaptive—it contributed to our ancestors' survival. Consciousness serves a function. It enables us to consider our past, adjust to our present circumstances, and plan our future.

As a **functionalist**, James encouraged explorations of down-to-earth emotions, memories, will power, habits, and moment-to-moment streams of consciousness. His psychology was "full-bodied" and "warm-hearted," wrote another famed psychologist, Ernest Hilgard (1987, p. 50).

James' greatest legacy, however, came less from his laboratory than from his Harvard teaching and his writing. When not plagued by ill health and depression, James was an impish, outgoing, and joyous man, who once recalled that "the first lecture on psychology I ever heard was the first I ever gave." During one of his wise-cracking lectures, a student interrupted and asked him to get serious (Hunt, 1993). He was reportedly one of the first American professors to solicit end-of-course student evaluations of his teaching.

James displayed great spunk in 1890, when—over the objections of Harvard's president—he admitted Mary Calkins into his graduate seminar (Scarborough & Furumoto, 1987). When Calkins joined, all the other students dropped. (In those years women lacked even the right to vote.) So James tutored her alone. Later she finished all the requirements for a Harvard Ph.D., outscoring all the male students on the qualifying exams. Alas, Harvard denied her the degree she had earned, offering her instead a degree from Radcliffe College, its undergraduate sister school for women. Calkins resisted the unequal treatment and refused the degree.

More than a century later, psychologists and psychology students were lobbying Harvard to posthumously award the Ph.D. she earned (*Feminist Psychologist*, 2002).

William James and Mary Whiton Calkins James, legendary teacher-writer, mentored Calkins, who became a pioneering memory researcher and American Psychological Association president.

Margaret Floy Washburn The first woman to receive a psychology Ph.D.; synthesized animal behavior research in *The Animal Mind.*

Calkins nevertheless became a distinguished memory researcher and the American Psychological Association's (APA's) first female president in 1905. What a different world from the recent past—1996 to 2002—when women claimed two-thirds or more of new psychology Ph.D.s and were five of the seven elected presidents of the science-oriented American Psychological Society. In Canada and Europe, too, most recent psychology doctorates have been earned by women.

When Harvard denied Calkins psychology's first female psychology Ph.D., that left the honor to Margaret Floy Washburn, who later wrote an influential book, *The Animal Mind,* and became the second female APA president in 1921. Although Washburn's thesis was the first foreign study Wundt published in his journal, her gender meant she was barred from joining the organization of experimental psychologists founded by Titchener, her own graduate adviser (Johnson, 1997).

James' influence reached even further through his dozens of well-received articles, which moved the publisher Henry Holt to offer a contract for a textbook of the new science of psychology. James agreed and began work in 1878, with an apology for requesting two years to finish his writing. The work proved an unexpected chore and actually took him 12 years. (Why am I not surprised?) But more than a century later, people still read *Principles of Psychology* and marvel at the brilliance and elegance with which James introduced psychology to the educated public.

Psychological Science Develops

3. How has the science of psychology's focus changed since its birth in the late nineteenth century? What is the modern definition of psychology?

This young science of psychology developed from the more established fields of philosophy and biology. Wundt was a German philosopher and physiologist. James was an American philosopher. Ivan Pavlov, who pioneered the study of learning, was a Russian physiologist. Sigmund Freud, controversial personality theorist, was an Austrian physician. Jean Piaget, the last century's most influential observer of children, was a Swiss biologist. This list of pioneering psychologists—"Magellans of the mind," as Morton Hunt (1993) called them—illustrates psychology's origins in many disciplines and countries.

▶ **psychology** the science of behavior and mental processes.

▶ **nature-nurture issue** the longstanding controversy over the relative contributions that genes and experience make to the development of psychological traits and behaviors.

It is no wonder, then, that psychology has developed along many lines, or that its practitioners have sometimes disagreed about the very definition of *psychology*. Early psychologists Wundt and Titchener focused on *inner* sensations, images, and feelings. James, too, engaged in introspective examination of the stream of consciousness and of emotion. Thus, until the 1920s, *psychology* was defined as "the science of mental life."

From the 1920s into the 1960s, American psychologists, initially led by flamboyant and provocative John B. Watson and later by the equally provocative B. F. Skinner, dismissed introspection and redefined *psychology* as "the science of observable behavior." After all, said these "behaviorists," science is rooted in observation. You cannot observe a sensation, a feeling, or a thought, but you *can* observe and record people's *behavior* as they respond to different situations.

In the 1960s, psychology began to recapture its initial interest in mental processes through studies of how our minds process and retain information. To encompass psychology's concern with observable behavior *and* with inner thoughts and feelings, today we define **psychology** as *the science of behavior and mental processes*.

Let's unpack this definition. *Behavior* is anything an organism *does*—any action we can observe and record. Yelling, smiling, blinking, sweating, talking, and questionnaire marking are all observable behaviors. *Mental processes* are the internal subjective experiences we infer from behavior—sensations, perceptions, dreams, thoughts, beliefs, and feelings.

For many psychologists, the key word in psychology's definition is *science*. Psychology, as I will emphasize throughout this book, is less a set of findings than a way of asking and answering questions. As a science, psychology attempts to sift opinions and evaluate ideas with careful observation and rigorous analysis. In its attempt to describe and explain human nature, psychological science welcomes hunches and plausible-sounding theories. And it puts them to the test. If a theory works—if the data support its predictions—so much the better for that theory. If the predictions fail, the theory will be revised or rejected.

My aim in this text, then, is not merely to report results but also to show you how psychologists play their game. You will see how researchers evaluate conflicting opinions and ideas. And you will learn how all of us, whether scientists or simply curious people, can think smarter when describing and explaining the events of our lives.

John B. Watson and Rosalie Rayner Working with Rayner, Watson championed psychology as the science of behavior and demonstrated conditioned responses on "Little Albert."

B. F. Skinner A leading "behaviorist," who rejected introspection and studied how consequences shape behavior.

Contemporary Psychology

Like its pioneers, today's psychologists are citizens of many lands. The International Union of Psychological Science has 69 member nations, from Albania to Zimbabwe. Nearly everywhere, membership in psychological societies is mushrooming—from 4183 American Psychological Association members and affiliates in 1945 to more than 160,000 today, with similarly rapid growth in Britain (**FIGURE 1.1**). In China, five universities had psychology departments in 1985; by the century's end, there were 50 (Jing, 1999). Worldwide, some 500,000 people have been trained as psychologists, and 130,000 of them belong to European psychological organizations (Tikkanen, 2001). Moreover, thanks to international publications, joint meetings, and the Internet, collaboration and communication cross borders now more than ever: "We are moving rapidly towards a single world of psychological science," reports Robert Bjork (2000). Psychology is *growing* and it is *globalizing*.

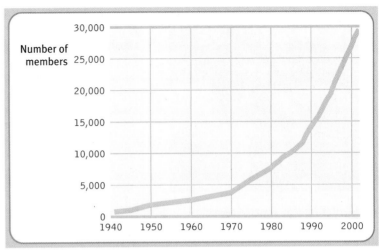

figure 1.1
British Psychological Society membership

Today's psychologists debate some enduring issues and view behavior from differing perspectives. They also teach, work, and do research in many different subfields.

Psychology's Perspectives

4. What theoretical perspectives do psychologists take?

During its short history, psychology has wrestled with some issues that will reappear throughout this book. The biggest and most persistent issue (and the focus of Chapter 3) concerns *the relative contributions of biology and experience.* Do our human traits develop through experience, or do we come equipped with them? As we have seen, the ancient Greeks debated this, and Locke and Descartes rekindled the debate in the 1600s. Today's psychologists explore this **nature-nurture** debate by asking, for example:

- How are differences in intelligence, personality, and psychological disorders influenced by heredity and by environment?
- Is children's grammar innate or formed by experience?
- Are sexual behaviors more "pushed" by inner biology or "pulled" by external incentives?
- Should we treat depression as a disorder of the brain or a disorder of thought—or both?
- How are humans alike (because of their common biology and evolutionary history) and different (because of their differing environments)?
- Are gender differences biologically predisposed or socially constructed?

The debate continues. Yet over and over again we will see that in contemporary science the nature-nurture tension dissolves: *Nurture works on what nature endows.* Our species is biologically endowed with an enormous capacity to learn and adapt. Moreover, every psychological event (every thought, every emotion) is simultaneously a biological event. Thus depression can be *both* a thought disorder and a brain disorder.

This book looks at behavior, thought, and emotion from differing perspectives. Consider, for example, how the complementary perspectives described in **TABLE 1.1,** page 8, can shed light on anger.

Like peas in a pod Because identical twins have the same genes, they are ideal participants in studies designed to shed light on hereditary and environmental influences on temperament, intelligence, and other traits. Studies of identical and fraternal twins provide a rich array of findings—described in later chapters—that underscore the importance of both nature and nurture.

Dennis Degnan/Corbis

Tim Wright/Corbis

Views of anger How would each of psychology's perspectives explain what's going on here?

table 1.1 Psychology's Current Perspectives

Perspective	Focus	Sample Questions
Neuroscience	How the body and brain enable emotions, memories, and sensory experiences	How are messages transmitted within the body? How is blood chemistry linked with moods and motives?
Evolutionary	How the natural selection of traits promotes the perpetuation of one's genes	How does evolution influence behavior tendencies?
Behavior genetics	How much our genes and our environment influence our individual differences	To what extent are psychological traits such as intelligence, personality, sexual orientation, and vulnerability to depression attributable to our genes? To our environment?
Psychodynamic	How behavior springs from unconscious drives and conflicts	How can someone's personality traits and disorders be explained in terms of sexual and aggressive drives or as the disguised effects of unfulfilled wishes and childhood traumas?
Behavioral	How we learn observable responses	How do we learn to fear particular objects or situations? What is the most effective way to alter our behavior, say, to lose weight or stop smoking?
Cognitive	How we encode, process, store, and retrieve information	How do we use information in remembering? Reasoning? Solving problems?
Social-cultural	How behavior and thinking vary across situations and cultures	How are we—as Africans, Asians, Australians, or North Americans —alike as members of one human family? As products of different environmental contexts, how do we differ?

- Someone working from a *neuroscience perspective* might study the brain circuits that produce the physical state of being "red in the face" and "hot under the collar."
- Someone working from an *evolutionary perspective* might analyze how anger facilitated the survival of our ancestors' genes.
- Someone working from a *behavior genetics perspective* might study how heredity and experience influence our individual differences in temperament.
- Someone working from a *psychodynamic perspective* might view an outburst as an outlet for unconscious hostility.
- Someone working from a *behavioral perspective* might study the facial expressions and body gestures that accompany anger, or might attempt to determine which external stimuli result in angry responses or aggressive acts.
- Someone working from a *cognitive perspective* might study how our interpretation of a situation affects our anger and how our anger affects our thinking.
- Someone working from a *social-cultural perspective* might explore which situations produce the most anger, and how expressions of anger vary across cultural contexts.

Such perspectives needn't contradict one another. Rather, they are complementary outlooks on the same biological state. It's like explaining why grizzly bears hibernate. Is it because hibernation enhanced their ancestors' survival and reproduction? Because their inner physiology drives them to do so? Because cold environments hinder food gathering during winter? Such perspectives are complementary, because "everything is related to everything else" (Brewer, 1996).

So bear in mind psychology's limits. Don't expect it to answer the ultimate questions posed by Russian novelist Leo Tolstoy (1904): "Why should I live? Why should

I do anything? Is there in life any purpose which the inevitable death that awaits me does not undo and destroy?" Instead, expect that psychology will help you understand why people think, feel, and act as they do. Then you should find the study of psychology fascinating and useful.

Psychology's Subfields

5. What are psychology's specialized subfields?

Picturing a chemist at work, you probably envision a white-coated scientist surrounded by glassware and high-tech equipment. Picture a psychologist at work and you would be right to envision

- a white-coated scientist probing a rat's brain.
- an intelligence researcher measuring how quickly an infant becomes bored with (looks away from) a familiar picture.
- an executive evaluating a new "healthy life-styles" training program for employees.
- someone at a computer keyboard analyzing data on whether adopted teens' temperaments more closely resemble those of their adoptive parents or those of their biological parents.
- a therapist listening carefully to a client's depressed thoughts.
- a traveler en route to another culture to collect data on variations in human values and behaviors.
- a teacher or writer sharing the joy of psychology with others.

The cluster of subfields that we call psychology has less unity than most other sciences. But there is a payoff: Psychology is a meeting ground for different disciplines and is thus a perfect home for those with wide-ranging interests. In their diverse activities, from biological experimentation to cultural comparisons, a common quest unites the tribe of psychology: to describe and explain behavior and the mind underlying it.

Some psychologists conduct **basic research** that builds psychology's knowledge base. In the pages that follow we will meet a wide variety of such researchers:

- *Biological psychologists* exploring the links between brain and mind
- *Developmental psychologists* studying our changing abilities from womb to tomb
- *Cognitive psychologists* experimenting with how we perceive, think, and solve problems
- *Personality psychologists* investigating our persistent traits
- *Social psychologists* exploring how we view and affect one another

These psychologists also may conduct **applied research** that tackles practical problems. So do other psychologists, such as *industrial/organizational psychologists* as they study and advise on behavior in the workplace. They use psychology's concepts and methods to help organizations and companies select and train employees more effectively, to boost morale and productivity, to design products, and to implement systems.

Although most psychology textbooks focus on psychological science, psychology is also a helping profession devoted to such practical issues as how to have a happy

▶ **basic research** pure science that aims to increase the scientific knowledge base.

▶ **applied research** scientific study that aims to solve practical problems.

"I'm a social scientist, Michael. That means I can't explain electricity or anything like that, but if you ever want to know about people I'm your man."

Psychology: A science and a profession Psychologists experiment with, observe, test, and treat behavior. Here we see psychologists recording children's behavior, testing a child, and doing face-to-face therapy.

I see you! A biological psychologist might view this child's delighted response as evidence for brain maturation. A cognitive psychologist might see it as a demonstration of the baby's growing knowledge of his surroundings. For a cross-cultural psychologist, the role of grandparents in different societies might be the issue of interest.

"Once expanded to the dimensions of a larger idea, [the mind] never returns to its original size."

Oliver Wendell Holmes, 1809–1894

You can use these Rehearse It questions to gauge whether you are ready for the next section. The answers are in Appendix C in the back of this book.

marriage, how to overcome anxiety or depression, and how to raise thriving children. **Clinical psychologists** study, assess, and treat troubled people. After graduate school training, they administer and interpret tests, provide psychotherapy, manage mental health programs, and conduct basic and applied research. By contrast, **psychiatrists**, who also often provide psychotherapy, are medical doctors licensed to prescribe drugs and otherwise treat physical causes of psychological disorders. (Some clinical psychologists are lobbying for a similar right to prescribe mental health–related drugs, and in 2002 the state of New Mexico granted that right to specially trained and licensed psychologists.)

With perspectives ranging from the biological to the social, and with settings from the laboratory to the clinic, psychology relates to many disciplines. More and more, psychology connects with fields ranging from mathematics to biology to sociology to philosophy. And more and more, psychology's methods and findings aid other disciplines. Psychologists teach in medical schools, law schools, and theological seminaries, and they work in hospitals, factories, and corporate offices. They engage in interdisciplinary studies, such as psychohistory (the psychological analysis of historical characters), psycholinguistics (the study of language and thinking), and psychoceramics (the study of crackpots).[2]

Psychology also influences modern culture. Knowledge transforms us. Learning about the solar system and the germ theory of disease alters the way people think and act. Learning psychology's findings also changes people: They less often judge psychological disorders as a moral failing, treatable by punishment and ostracism. They less often regard and treat women as men's mental inferiors. They less often view and rear children as ignorant willful beasts in need of taming. "In each case," notes Morton Hunt (1990, p. 206), "knowledge has modified attitudes, and, through them, behavior." Once aware of psychology's well-researched ideas—about how body and mind connect, how a child's mind grows, how we construct our perceptions, how we remember (and misremember) our experiences, how people across the world differ (and are alike)—your mind may never again be quite the same.

[2]Confession time: I wrote the last part of this sentence on April Fools' Day.

rehearse it!

1. The science of psychology was born in December 1879, when a psychologist and his students measured the time lag between people's hearing a ball hit a platform and their pressing a key. The psychologist who ran this experiment and established the first psychology lab was
   a. Charles Darwin.
   b. William James.
   c. Edward Bradford Titchener.
   d. Wilhelm Wundt.

2. A popular psychology textbook was written in 1890. Its famous author was
   a. Wilhelm Wundt.
   b. Mary Whiton Calkins.
   c. Charles Darwin.
   d. William James.

3. The definition of *psychology* has changed several times since the late 1800s. In the early twentieth century, _____ redefined *psychology* as "the science of observable behavior."
   a. James Watson
   b. René Descartes
   c. William James
   d. Edward Bradford Titchener

4. Psychology is now defined as the science of behavior and mental processes. The perspective in psychology that focuses on how behavior and thought differ from situation to situation and from culture to culture is the
   a. cognitive perspective.
   b. behavioral perspective.
   c. social-cultural perspective.
   d. neuroscience perspective.

5. In the history of psychology, one of the main debates has been over the nature-nurture issue. Nature is to nurture as
   a. personality is to intelligence.
   b. biology is to experience.
   c. intelligence is to biology.
   d. psychological traits are to behaviors.

6. The behavioral perspective in psychology emphasizes observable responses and how they are acquired and modified. A behavioral psychologist would be most likely to study
   a. the effect of school uniforms on classroom behaviors.
   b. the hidden meaning in children's themes and drawings.
   c. the age at which children can learn algebra.

   d. whether certain mathematical abilities appear to be inherited.

7. A psychologist who treats emotionally troubled adolescents at the local mental health agency is most likely to be a/an
   a. research psychologist.
   b. psychiatrist.
   c. industrial/organizational psychologist.
   d. clinical psychologist.

8. A psychologist who conducts basic research to expand psychology's knowledge base would be most likely to
   a. design a computer screen with limited glare and assess the effect on computer operators' eyes after a day's work.
   b. treat older people who are overcome by depression.
   c. observe 3- and 6-year-old children solving puzzles and analyze differences in their abilities.
   d. interview children with behavioral problems and suggest treatments.

Answers can be found in Appendix C.

WHY DO PSYCHOLOGY?

Although in some ways we outsmart the smartest computers, our intuition often goes awry. To err is human. Enter psychological science. With its procedures for gathering and sifting evidence, science restrains error. As we familiarize ourselves with its strategies and incorporate its underlying principles into our daily thinking, we can think smarter. *Psychologists use the science of behavior and mental processes to better understand why people think, feel, and act as they do.*

What About Intuition and Common Sense?

6. Why are the answers that flow from the scientific approach more reliable than those based on intuition and common sense?

In sifting reality from illusion, won't intuition and plain common sense suffice for everyday life? Some say psychology merely documents what people already know and dresses it in jargon: "So what else is new—you get paid for using fancy methods to prove what my grandmother knew?"

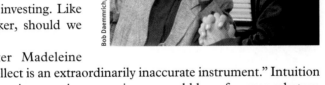

Others scorn a scientific approach because of their faith in human intuition. Advocates of "intuitive management" urge us to distrust statistical predictors and tune into our hunches when hiring, firing, and investing. Like *Star Wars'* Luke Skywalker, should we trust the force within?

Actually, notes writer Madeleine L'Engle, "The naked intellect is an extraordinarily inaccurate instrument." Intuition can lead us astray. We sometimes err in presuming we could have foreseen what we know happened.

The limits of intuition Personnel interviewers tend to be overconfident of their gut feelings about job applicants. Their confidence stems partly from their recalling cases where their favorable impression proved right, and from their ignorance about rejected applicants who succeeded elsewhere.

Did We Know It All Along? The Hindsight Bias

How easy it is to seem astute when drawing the bull's eye after the arrow has struck. *After* each stock market downswing—after the bursting of the dot-com bubble, for example—investment gurus say "the market was obviously overdue for a correction." After the first World Trade Center tower was hit on 9/11, some said people in the second tower *should* have immediately evacuated (it became obvious only later that it was not an accident). But *before* the arrow strikes, the stock market drops, and the terrorists attack, these results are anything but obvious. Finding out that something has happened makes it seem inevitable. Psychologists call this 20/20 hindsight vision the **hindsight bias**, also known as the *I-knew-it-all-along phenomenon* (Slovic & Fischhoff, 1977; Wood, 1979).

This phenomenon is easy to demonstrate: Give half the members of a group some purported psychological finding, and the other half an opposite result. Tell the first group, "Psychologists have found that separation weakens romantic attraction. As the saying goes, 'Out of sight, out of mind.'" Ask them to imagine why this might be true. Most people can, and nearly all will then regard this true finding as unsurprising.

Tell the second group just the opposite—that "psychologists have found that separation strengthens romantic attraction. As the saying goes, 'Absence makes the heart grow fonder.'" People given this result can also easily explain it, and they overwhelmingly see it as unsurprising common sense. Obviously, when both a supposed finding and its opposite seem like common sense, there is a problem.

Such errors in our recollections and explanations show why we need psychological research. Just asking people how and why they felt or acted as they did can

"Life is lived forwards, but understood backwards."

Philosopher Søren Kierkegaard, 1813–1855

▶ **clinical psychology** a branch of psychology that studies, assesses, and treats people with psychological disorders.

▶ **psychiatry** a branch of medicine dealing with psychological disorders; practiced by physicians who sometimes provide medical (for example, drug) treatments as well as psychological therapy.

▶ **hindsight bias** the tendency to believe, after learning an outcome, that one would have foreseen it. (Also known as the *I-knew-it-all-along phenomenon*.)

Hindsight bias *After* the horror of 9/11 it seemed obvious that the American intelligence service should have taken advance warnings more seriously, that airport security should have anticipated box-cutter–wielding terrorists, that occupants of the second World Trade Center tower should have known to play it safe and leave. With 20/20 hindsight, everything seems obvious.

"Anything seems commonplace, once explained."

Dr. Watson to Sherlock Holmes

NON SEQUITUR

sometimes be misleading—*not* because common sense is usually wrong, but because it is after the fact. Common sense describes what has happened more easily than it predicts what will happen.

Nevertheless, Grandmother is often right. As Yogi Berra once said, "You can observe a lot by watching." (We have Berra to thank for other gems, such as "Nobody ever comes here—it's too crowded," and "If the people don't want to come out to the ballpark, nobody's gonna stop 'em.") Because we're all behavior watchers, it would be surprising if many of psychology's findings had *not* been foreseen. Many people believe that love breeds happiness, and they are right (we have what Chapter 10 calls a deep "need to belong").

But sometimes Grandmother's intuition has it wrong. Informed by countless casual observations, our intuition may tell us that familiarity breeds contempt, that dreams predict the future, and that emotional reactions coincide with menstrual phase. As we will see in later chapters, the available evidence suggests that these commonsense ideas are wrong, wrong, and wrong. Throughout this book we will see how research has both inspired and overturned popular ideas—about aging, about sleep and dreams, about personality. And we will also see how it has surprised us with discoveries about how the brain's chemical messengers control our moods and memories, about animal abilities, and about the effects of stress on our capacity to fight disease.

Overconfidence

Our everyday thinking is limited not only by our after-the-fact common sense but also by our human tendency to be overly confident. As Chapter 9 explains, we tend to think we know more than we do. Asked how sure we are of our answers to factual questions (Is Boston north or south of Paris?), we tend to be more confident than correct.[3] Or consider these three anagrams, which Richard Goranson (1978) asked people to unscramble:

WREAT → WATER

ETRYN → ENTRY

GRABE → BARGE

Fun anagram solutions from Wordsmith.org:

Elvis = lives

Dormitory = dirty room

Slot machines = cash lost in 'em

[3]Boston is south of Paris.

Reflect for a moment: About how many seconds do you think it would have taken you to unscramble each of those?

Once people know the target word, hindsight makes it seem obvious—so much so that they become overconfident. They think they would have seen the solution in only 10 seconds or so, when in reality the average problem solver spent 3 minutes, as you also might, given a similar anagram without the solution: OCHSA (see page 14 to check your answer).

Are we any better at predicting our social behavior? To find out, Robert Vallone and his associates (1990) had students predict at the beginning of the school year whether they would drop a course, vote in an upcoming election, call their parents more than twice a month, and so forth. On average, the students felt 84 percent confident in making these self-predictions. Later quizzes about their actual behavior showed their predictions were correct only 71 percent of the time. Even when they were 100 percent sure of themselves, their self-predictions erred 15 percent of the time.

The point to remember: Hindsight and overconfidence bias lead us to overestimate our intuition. But scientific inquiry, fed by skepticism and humility, helps us sift reality from illusion.

The Scientific Attitude

7. What attitudes characterize scientific inquiry?

Underlying all science is, first, a hard-headed *curiosity,* a passion to explore and understand without misleading or being misled. Some questions (Is there life after death?) are beyond science. To answer them in any way requires a leap of faith. With many other ideas (Can some people demonstrate ESP?), the proof is in the pudding. No matter how sensible or crazy-sounding an idea, the hard-headed question is, Does it work? When put to the test, can its predictions be confirmed?

This scientific approach has a long history. As ancient a figure as Moses used such an approach. How do you evaluate a self-proclaimed prophet? His answer: Put the prophet to the test. If the predicted event "does not take place or prove true," then so much the worse for the prophet (*Deuteronomy* 18:22). Magician James Randi uses Moses' approach when testing those claiming to see auras around people's bodies:

> **Randi:** *Do you see an aura around my head?*
> **Aura-seer:** *Yes, indeed.*
> **Randi:** *Can you still see the aura if I put this magazine in front of my face?*
> **Aura-seer:** *Of course.*
> **Randi:** *Then if I were to step behind a wall barely taller than I am, you could determine my location from the aura visible above my head, right?*

Randi tells me that no aura-seer has yet agreed to take this simple test.

When subjected to such scrutiny, crazy-sounding ideas sometimes find support. More often, science relegates crazy-sounding ideas to the mountain of forgotten claims of perpetual motion machines, miracle cancer cures, and out-of-body travels into centuries past. To sift reality from fantasy, sense from nonsense, therefore requires a scientific attitude: being skeptical but not cynical, open but not gullible.

As scientists, psychologists also approach the world of behavior with a *curious skepticism.* They persistently ask two questions: What do you mean? How do you know? In business, the motto is "Show me the money." In science, it is "Show me the evidence."

Consider some familiar claims: that parental behaviors determine their children's sexual orientation; that lie detectors tell the truth; that astrologers can analyze your character and predict your future based on the position of the planets at your birth. As you will see in the chapters that follow, putting such claims to the test has led most psychologists to doubt them. In the arena of competing ideas, skeptical testing can reveal which ones best match the facts. "To believe with certainty," says a Polish proverb, "we must begin by doubting."

"We don't like their sound. Groups of guitars are on their way out."

Decca Records, in turning down a recording contract with the Beatles in 1962

"Computers in the future may weigh no more than 1.5 tons."

Popular Mechanics, 1949

"The telephone may be appropriate for our American cousins, but not here, because we have an adequate supply of messenger boys."

British expert group evaluating the invention of the telephone

"They couldn't hit an elephant at this dist–."

General John Sedgwick's last words, uttered during a U.S. Civil War battle, 1864

"The scientist . . . must be free to ask any question, to doubt any assertion, to seek for any evidence, to correct any errors."

Physicist J. Robert Oppenheimer, Life, October 10, 1949

"A skeptic is one who is willing to question any truth claim, asking for clarity in definition, consistency in logic, and adequacy of evidence."

Philosopher Paul Kurtz, The Skeptical Inquirer, 1994

The amazing Randi The magician James Randi exemplifies skepticism. He has tested and debunked a variety of psychic phenomena.

Rob Kinmonth

"My deeply held belief is that if a god anything like the traditional sort exists, our curiosity and intelligence are provided by such a god. We would be unappreciative of those gifts . . . if we suppressed our passion to explore the universe and ourselves."

Carl Sagan, Broca's Brain, *1979*

Throughout this book, you will encounter Thinking Critically boxes. Each highlights careful thinking about some interesting or important issue. In addition, at the end of each chapter, you will find A Critical Thinker's Review of the key concepts. This feature uses six categories of critical thinking to help you become a smarter thinker and to provide a memorable way for you to review the chapter.

"The real purpose of the scientific method is to make sure Nature hasn't misled you into thinking you know something you don't actually know."

Robert M. Pirsig, Zen and the Art of Motorcycle Maintenance, *1974*

Solution to anagram on page 13: CHAOS.

Putting a scientific attitude into practice requires not only skepticism but also *humility*, because we may have to reject our own ideas. In the last analysis, what matters is not my opinion or yours, but the truths nature reveals in response to our questioning. If people don't behave as our ideas predict, then so much the worse for our ideas. This is the humble attitude expressed in one of psychology's early mottos: "The rat is always right."

Historians of science tell us that these attitudes of curiosity, skepticism, and humility helped make modern science possible. Many of its founders were people whose religious convictions made them humble before nature and skeptical of mere human authority (Hooykaas, 1972; Merton, 1938). Of course, scientists, like anyone else, can have big egos and may cling to their preconceptions. We all view nature through the spectacles of our preconceived ideas. Yet the ideal that unifies psychologists with all scientists is the curious, skeptical, humble scrutiny of competing ideas. As a community, scientists check and recheck one another's findings and conclusions.

Critical Thinking

This scientific attitude prepares us to think smarter. Smart thinking, called **critical thinking**, examines assumptions, discerns hidden values, evaluates evidence, and assesses conclusions. Whether reading a news report or listening to a conversation, critical thinkers ask questions. Like scientists, they wonder, How do they know that? What's this person's agenda? Is the conclusion based on anecdote and gut feelings, or on evidence? Does the evidence justify a cause-effect conclusion? What alternative explanations are possible? Carried to an extreme, healthy skepticism can degenerate into a negative cynicism that scorns any unproven idea. Better to have a critical attitude that produces humility—an awareness of our own vulnerability to error and an openness to surprises and new perspectives.

Has psychology's critical inquiry been open to surprising findings? The answer, as ensuing chapters illustrate, is plainly yes. Believe it or not . . .

- massive losses of brain tissue early in life may have minimal long-term effects (see page 59).
- within days, newborns can recognize their mother's odor and voice (see pages 101–102).
- brain damage can leave a person able to learn new skills, yet be unaware of such (see pages 60–61).
- diverse groups—men and women, old and young, rich and working class, those with disabilities and without—report roughly comparable levels of personal happiness (see pages 396–398).
- electroconvulsive ("shock") therapy is often a very effective treatment for severe depression (see page 533).

And has critical inquiry convincingly debunked popular presumptions? The answer, as ensuing chapters also illustrate, is again yes. The evidence indicates that . . .

- sleepwalkers are *not* acting out their dreams and sleeptalkers are *not* verbalizing their dreams (see Chapter 6).
- our past experiences are *not* all recorded verbatim in our brains; with brain stimulation or hypnosis, one *cannot* simply "play the tape" and relive long-buried or repressed memories (see Chapter 8).
- most people do *not* suffer from unrealistically low self-esteem (see page 458).
- opposites do *not* generally attract (see page 571).

HOW DO PSYCHOLOGISTS ASK AND ANSWER QUESTIONS?

Psychologists arm their scientific attitude with the *scientific method*: They make observations, form theories, and then refine their theories in the light of new observations.

The Scientific Method

8. How do psychologists use the scientific method to construct theories?

In everyday conversation, we tend to use *theory* to mean "mere hunch." In science, *theory* is linked with observation. A scientific **theory** *explains* through an integrated set of principles that *organizes* and *predicts* behaviors or events. By organizing isolated facts, a theory simplifies things. There are too many facts about behavior to remember them all. By linking facts and bridging them to deeper principles, a theory offers a useful summary. When we connect the observed dots, we may discover a coherent picture.

A good theory of depression, for example, helps us organize countless observations concerning depression into a much shorter list of principles. Say we observe over and over that people with depression describe their past, present, and future in gloomy terms. We might therefore theorize that low self-esteem contributes to depression. So far so good: Our self-esteem principle neatly summarizes a long list of facts about people with depression.

Yet no matter how reasonable a theory may sound—and low self-esteem seems a reasonable explanation of depression—we must put it to the test. A good theory doesn't just sound appealing. It must imply testable predictions, called **hypotheses**. By enabling us to test and reject or revise the theory, such predictions give direction to research. They specify what results would support the theory and what results would disconfirm it. To test our self-esteem theory of depression, we might give people a test of self-esteem on which they respond to statements such as "I have good ideas." Then we could see whether, as we hypothesized, people who report poorer self-images also score higher on a depression scale (**FIGURE 1.2**, on page 16).

In testing our theory, we should be aware that it can bias subjective observations. Having theorized that depression springs from low self-esteem, we may see what we expect. We may perceive depressed people's neutral comments as self-disparaging.

As a check on their biases, psychologists report their research precisely enough—with clear **operational definitions** of concepts—to allow others to **replicate** (repeat) their observations. If other researchers re-create a study with different

▶ **critical thinking** thinking that does not blindly accept arguments and conclusions. Rather, it examines assumptions, discerns hidden values, evaluates evidence, and assesses conclusions.

▶ **theory** an explanation using an integrated set of principles that organizes and predicts observations.

▶ **hypothesis** a testable prediction, often implied by a theory.

▶ **operational definition** a statement of the procedures (operations) used to define research variables. For example, *intelligence* may be operationally defined as what an intelligence test measures.

▶ **replication** repeating the essence of a research study, usually with different participants in different situations, to see whether the basic finding extends to other participants and circumstances.

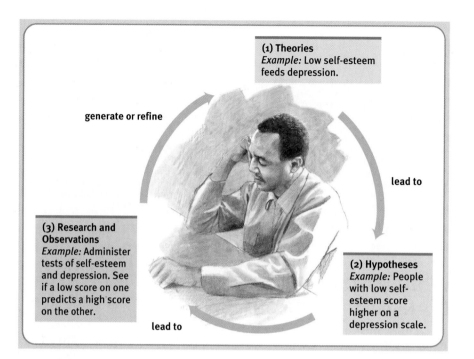

(1) Theories
Example: Low self-esteem feeds depression.

generate or refine

lead to

(3) Research and Observations
Example: Administer tests of self-esteem and depression. See if a low score on one predicts a high score on the other.

lead to

(2) Hypotheses
Example: People with low self-esteem score higher on a depression scale.

participants and materials and get similar results, then our confidence in the finding's reliability grows. The first study of hindsight bias aroused psychologists' curiosity. Now, after many successful replications with differing people and questions, we feel sure of the phenomenon's power.

In the end, our theory will be useful if it (1) effectively *organizes* a range of self-reports and observations and (2) implies clear *predictions* that anyone can use to check the theory or to derive practical applications. (If we boost people's self-esteem, will their depression lift?) Eventually, our research will probably lead to a revised theory (such as the one on pages 492–495) that better organizes and predicts what we know about depression.

Our research strategies include descriptive, correlational, and experimental methods. We test hypotheses and refine our theories by making *observations* that *describe* behavior, detecting *correlations* that help *predict* behavior, and doing *experiments* that help *explain* behavior. To think critically about popular psychology claims, we need to recognize these designs and to know what conclusions they allow.

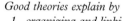

Good theories explain by
1. organizing and linking observed facts.
2. implying hypotheses that offer testable predictions and, sometimes, practical applications.

Description

9. How do psychologists observe and describe behavior?

The starting point of any science is description. In everyday life, all of us observe and describe people, often drawing conclusions about why they behave as they do. Professional psychologists do much the same, only more objectively and systematically.

The Case Study

Among the oldest research methods is the **case study**, in which psychologists study one individual in great depth in the hope of revealing things true of us all. Some examples: Much of our early knowledge about the brain came from case studies of individuals who suffered a particular impairment after damage to a certain brain region. Sigmund Freud constructed his theory of personality from a handful of case studies. Developmental psychologist Jean Piaget taught us about children's thinking after carefully observing and questioning but a few children. Studies of only a few chimpanzees have revealed their capacity for understanding and language. Intensive case studies are sometimes very revealing.

"'Well my dear,' said Miss Marple, 'human nature is very much the same everywhere, and of course, one has opportunities of observing it at closer quarters in a village.'"

Agatha Christie, The Tuesday Club Murders, 1933

Although case studies can also suggest hypotheses for further study, they sometimes mislead us: An individual may be atypical. Unrepresentative information can lead to mistaken judgments and false conclusions. Indeed, anytime a researcher mentions a finding ("Smokers die younger: 95 percent of men over 85 are nonsmokers") someone is sure to offer a contradictory case ("Well, I have an uncle who smoked two packs a day and lived to be 89"). Anecdotal cases—dramatic stories, personal experiences, even psychological case examples—have a way of overwhelming general truths. Highly publicized school shootings can raise alarm about school violence even while school violence rates are subsiding. Numbers can be numbing (in one study of 1300 dream reports concerning a kidnapped child, only 5 percent correctly envisioned the child as dead—see page 179). Anecdotes are often more startling. ("But I know a man who dreamed his sister was in a car accident, and two days later she was badly injured.")

The point to remember: Individual cases can suggest fruitful ideas. What's true of all of us can be glimpsed in any one of us. But to discern the general truths that cover individual cases, we must answer questions with other methods.

The Survey

The **survey** method, commonly used in both descriptive and correlational studies, looks at many cases in less depth. A survey asks people to report their behavior or opinions. Questions about everything from sexual practices to political opinions get put to the public. Harris and Gallup polls have revealed that 72 percent of Americans think there is too much TV violence, 84 percent favor equal job opportunities for homosexual people, 89 percent say they face high stress, 95 percent believe in God, and 96 percent would like to change something about their appearance. But asking questions is tricky, and the answers may well depend on your wording and your choice of respondents.

WORDING EFFECTS Even subtle changes in the order or wording of questions can have major effects. Should cigarette ads or pornography be allowed on television? People are much more likely to approve "not allowing" such things than "forbidding" or "censoring" them. In one national survey, only 27 percent of Americans approved of "government censorship" of media sex and violence, though 66 percent approved of "more restrictions on what is shown on television" (Lacayo, 1995). People are similarly much more approving of "aid to the needy" than of "welfare," of "affirmative action" than of "preferential treatment," and of "revenue enhancers" than of "taxes." Because wording questions is such a delicate matter, critical thinkers will reflect on how the phrasing of a question might have affected the opinions respondents expressed.

SAMPLING You can describe human experience using common sense, dramatic anecdotes, personal experience, and arbitrary samples. But for an accurate picture of the experiences and attitudes of a whole population, there's only one game in town—the representative sample.

We can extend this point to everyday thinking, as we generalize from samples we observe. We meet a few students and attend a few classes during a visit to a college and infer from those instances how friendly the campus is and how good the teaching is. We observe the weather during a three-day visit to Copenhagen and then tell our friends about the climate there.

Overgeneralizing from such select samples is tempting, especially when they are vivid cases. Given (a) a statistical summary of a professor's student evaluations and (b) the vivid comments of two irate students, an administrator's impression of the professor may be influenced as much by the two unhappy students as by the many favorable evaluations in the statistical summary. Standing in the checkout line at the supermarket, George sees the woman in front of him pay with government-provided food stamps and then watches with dismay as she drives away in a fancy car. In both situations, the temptation to generalize from a few vivid but unrepresentative cases is nearly irresistible.

▶ **case study** an observation technique in which one person is studied in depth in the hope of revealing universal principles.

▶ **survey** a technique for ascertaining the self-reported attitudes or behaviors of people, usually by questioning a representative, random sample of them.

The case of the conversational chimpanzee In intensive case studies of chimpanzees, psychologists have explored the intriguing question of whether language is uniquely human. Here Nim Chimpsky signs *hug* as his trainer, psychologist Herbert Terrace, shows him the puppet Ernie. But is Nim really capable of using language? We'll explore that issue in Chapter 9.

The point to remember: The best basis for generalizing is from a representative sample of cases.

If you wished to survey the students at your college or university, how could you survey a representative sample of the total student **population**—the whole group you wanted to study and describe? Typically, by choosing a **random sample**, one in which every person in the entire group has an equal chance of participating.

To sample the students at your institution randomly, you would *not* send each of them a questionnaire. (The conscientious people who return it would not be a random sample.) Rather, you would aim for a representative sample by, say, using a table of random numbers to pick participants from a student listing and then making sure you involve as many as possible. Large representative samples are better than small ones, but a small representative sample of 100 is better than an unrepresentative sample of 500.

The point to remember: Before believing survey findings, think critically: Consider the sample. You cannot compensate for an unrepresentative sample by simply adding more people.

The random-sampling principle also works in national surveys. Imagine that you had a giant barrel containing 60 million white beans mixed with 40 million red beans. A scoop that randomly sampled 1500 of them would contain about 60 percent white and 40 percent red beans, give or take 2 or 3 percent. Sampling voters in a national election survey is like sampling the beans; 1500 randomly sampled people, drawn from all areas of a country, provide a remarkably accurate snapshot of the opinions of a nation.

Because gathering a random sample can be a huge task, some don't make the effort. Shere Hite's book *Women and Love* reported survey findings based on only a 4.5 percent response rate from mailings to an unrepresentative sample of 100,000 women. The response was doubly unrepresentative because not only did she have a modest, self-selected return, but the women initially contacted were members of women's organizations. Nonetheless, "It's 4500 people. That's enough for me," reported Hite. And it was apparently enough for *Time* magazine, which made a cover story of her findings—that 70 percent of women married five or more years were having affairs, and that 95 percent of women felt emotionally harassed by the men they love (Wallis, 1987). Evidently it didn't matter that on less publicized surveys, *randomly* sampled American women expressed much higher levels of satisfaction. And only 1 in 7 reported having had an affair during their current marriage—a level of faithfulness replicated in British, French, and Danish surveys (Greeley, 1991, 1994). Without random sampling, large samples like Hite's—including call-in phone samples and TV Web site polls—often merely give misleading results.

Naturalistic Observation

A third descriptive research method involves watching and recording the behavior of organisms in their natural environment. These **naturalistic observations** range from watching chimpanzee societies in the jungle, to using unobtrusive measures of parent-child interactions in different cultures, to recording students' self-seating patterns in the lunchrooms of multiracial schools.

Like the case study and survey methods, naturalistic observation does not *explain* behavior. It *describes* it. Nevertheless, descriptions can be revealing. We once thought, for example, that only humans use tools. Then naturalistic observation revealed that chimpanzees sometimes insert a stick in a termite mound and withdraw it, eating the stick's load of termites. Such naturalistic observations, recalls chimpanzee observer Jane Goodall (1998), paved the way for later studies of animal thinking, language, and emotion. "Observations, made in the natural habitat, helped to show that the societies and behavior of animals are far more complex than previously supposed," thus expanding our understanding of our fellow animals. We

---

With very large samples, estimates become quite reliable. E is estimated to represent 12.7 percent of the letters in written English. E, in fact, is 12.3 percent of the 925,141 letters in Melville's Moby Dick; *12.4 percent of the 586,747 letters in Dickens'* A Tale of Two Cities; *and 12.1 percent of the 3,901,021 letters in 12 of Mark Twain's works (*Chance News, *1997).*

"How would you like me to answer that question? As a member of my ethnic group, educational class, income group, or religious category?"

▶ **population** all the cases in a group, from which samples may be drawn for a study. (Note: Except for national studies, this does *not* refer to a country's whole population.)

▶ **random sample** a sample that fairly represents a population because each member has an equal chance of inclusion.

▶ **naturalistic observation** observing and recording behavior in naturally occurring situations without trying to manipulate and control the situation.

▶ **correlation coefficient** a statistical measure of the extent to which two factors vary together, and thus of how well either factor predicts the other.

later learned that chimps and baboons also use deception to achieve their aims. Psychologists Andrew Whiten and Richard Byrne (1988) repeatedly saw one young baboon pretending to have been attacked by another as a tactic to get its mother to drive the other baboon away from its food.

Naturalistic observations are also done with humans. Here's one funny finding: We humans laugh 30 times more often in social situations than in solitary situations. (Have you noticed how seldom you laugh when alone?) And when we do laugh, 17 muscles contort our mouth and squeeze our eyes, and we emit a series of 75-millisecond vowel-like sounds that are spaced about one-fifth of a second apart (Provine, 2001).

Naturalistic observation also enabled Robert Levine and Ara Norenzayan (1999) to compare the pace of life in 31 countries. By operationally defining *pace of life* as walking speed, the speed with which postal clerks completed a simple request, and the accuracy of public clocks, they concluded that life is fastest paced in Japan and Western Europe, and slower paced in economically less developed countries. People in colder climates also tend to live at a faster pace (and are more prone to die from heart disease). Naturalistic observation is often used to describe behavior. But this study, showing how pace of life is associated with culture and climate, illustrates how naturalistic observation can also be used with correlational research, our next topic.

Naturalistic observation Some psychologists study human and animal behavior in natural environments. As University of St. Andrews psychologist Richard Byrne observes an adult gorilla, recording its behavior on a hand-held computer, a curious infant approaches and investigates his camera lens cap.

Correlation

Describing behavior is a first step toward predicting it. When surveys and naturalistic observations reveal that one trait or behavior accompanies another, we say the two *correlate*. The **correlation coefficient** is a statistical measure of relationship: It reveals how closely two things vary together and thus how well either one *predicts* the other. Knowing how much aptitude test scores *correlate* with school success tells us how well the scores *predict* school success.

A *positive* correlation (between 0 and +1.00) indicates a *direct* relationship, meaning that two things increase together or decrease together. Some examples:

- According to some studies, the amount of violence viewed on television correlates about +.3 with aggressive social behavior; people's TV-viewing habits therefore modestly predict their aggressiveness (or vice versa).
- Genetically identical twins correlate about +.6 on tests of extraversion, which means that the outgoingness of either twin gives a reasonable clue to that of the other (Bouchard & others, 1990).
- University of Michigan surveys of 71,000 representatively sampled high school seniors revealed that the more hours students worked on a job, the less they slept and exercised and the more they used cigarettes, alcohol, and other drugs (ISR, 1994).

A *negative* correlation—equally predictive—indicates an *inverse* relationship: As one thing increases, the other decreases. Our earlier findings on self-esteem and depression illustrate a negative correlation: People who score *low* on self-esteem tend to score *high* on depression. Negative correlations could go as low as –1.00, which means that, like people on the opposite ends of a teeter-totter, one set of scores goes down precisely as the other goes up.

Though informative, psychology's correlations usually leave most of the variation among individuals unpredicted. As we will see, there is a correlation between parents' abusiveness and their children's later abusiveness when they become parents. But this does not mean that most abused children become abusive. The correlation simply indicates a statistical relationship: Although most abused children do not grow into abusers, nonabused children are even less likely to become abusive. Correlations point us toward predictions, but usually imperfect ones.

▶ **illusory correlation** the perception of a relationship where none exists.

Correlation and Causation

10. Why do correlations permit prediction but not explanation?

We have seen that correlations, however imperfect, do help us predict and restrain the illusions of our flawed intuition. Watching violence correlates with (and therefore predicts) aggression. But does that mean it causes aggression? Does low self-esteem cause depression? If, based on the correlational evidence, you assume that they do, you have much company. Among the most irresistible thinking errors made both by laypeople and by professional psychologists is assuming that correlation proves causation. But no matter how strong the relationship, it does not!

Correlation need not mean causation
Length of marriage correlates with hair loss in men. Does this mean that marriage causes men to lose their hair (or that balding men make better husbands)? In this case, as in many others, a third factor obviously explains the correlation: Golden anniversaries and baldness both accompany aging.

For example, what about the negative correlation between self-esteem and depression? Perhaps low self-esteem does cause depression. But as **FIGURE 1.3** suggests, we'd get the same correlation of low self-esteem and depression if depression caused people to be down on themselves, or if something else—a third factor such as heredity or brain chemistry—caused both low self-esteem and depression. Among men, length of marriage correlates positively with hair loss—because both are associated with a third factor, age.

This point is so important—so basic to thinking smarter with psychology—that it merits one more example, from a survey of 12,118 adolescents: The more teens feel loved by their parents, the less likely they are to behave in unhealthy ways—having early sex, smoking, abusing alcohol and drugs, exhibiting violence (Resnick & others, 1997). "Adults have a powerful effect on their children's behavior right through the high school years," gushed an Associated Press story on the study. But the correlation comes with no built-in cause-effect arrow. Thus, the AP could as well have said, "Well-behaved teens feel their parents' love and approval; out-of-bounds teens more often think their parents are disapproving jerks."

A New York Times *writer reported a massive survey showing that "adolescents whose parents smoked were 50 percent more likely than children of nonsmokers to report having had sex." He concluded (would you agree?) that the survey indicated a causal effect—that "to reduce the chances that their children will become sexually active at an early age" parents might "quit smoking" (O'Neil, 2002).*

The point to remember: Correlation indicates the *possibility* of a cause-effect relationship, *but it does not prove causation.* Knowing that two events are correlated need not tell us anything about causation. Remember this principle and you will be wiser as you see reports of scientific studies in the news and in this book.

figure 1.3
Three possible cause-effect relationships People low in self-esteem are more likely to report depression than are those high in self-esteem. One possible explanation of this negative correlation is that a bad self-image causes depressed feelings. But, as the diagram indicates, other cause-effect relationships are possible.

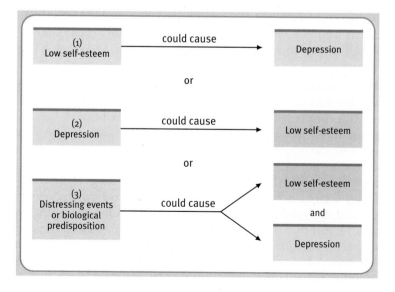

Illusory Correlations

11. How accurately does the naked eye detect correlations?

Correlations make visible the relationships that we might otherwise miss. They also restrain our "seeing" relationships that actually do not exist. A perceived nonexistent correlation is an **illusory correlation**. When we *believe* there is a relationship between two things, we are likely to *notice* and *recall* instances that confirm our belief (Trolier & Hamilton, 1986).

Illusory correlations help explain many a superstitious belief, such as the presumption that more babies are born when the moon is full or that infertile couples who adopt become more likely to conceive (Gilovich, 1991) (**FIGURE 1.4**). Such illusory thinking helps explain why for so many years people believed (and many still do) that sugar made children hyperactive, that getting cold and wet caused one to catch a cold, and that weather changes trigger arthritis pain. We are, it seems, very willing to perceive patterns, whether they're there or not, but not so willing to test our hypotheses.

Because we are sensitive to dramatic or unusual events, we are especially likely to notice and remember the occurrence of two such events in sequence—say, a premonition of an unlikely phone call followed by the call. When the call does not follow the premonition, we are less likely to note and remember the nonevent.

	Conceive	Do not conceive
Adopt	confirming evidence	disconfirming evidence
Do not adopt	disconfirming evidence	confirming evidence

The point to remember: When we notice random coincidences, we may forget that they are random and instead see them as correlated. Thus, we can easily deceive ourselves by seeing what is not there.

Perceiving Order in Random Events

Illusory correlations arise from our natural eagerness to make sense of our world—what poet Wallace Stevens called our "rage for order." Given even random data, we look for order, for meaningful patterns. And we usually find such, because *random sequences often don't look random.* Consider a random coin flip: If someone flipped a coin six times, which of the following sequences of heads (H) and tails (T) would be most likely: HHHTTT or HTTHTH or HHHHHH?

Daniel Kahneman and Amos Tversky (1972) found that most people believe HTTHTH would be the most likely random sequence. Actually, all are equally likely (or, you might say, equally unlikely) to occur. A bridge or poker hand of 10 through Ace, all of hearts, would seem extraordinary; actually, it would be no more or less likely than any other specific hand of cards (**FIGURE 1.5**).

In random sequences, seeming patterns and streaks (such as repeating digits) occur more often than people expect. To demonstrate this phenomenon for myself (as you can do), I flipped a coin 51 times, with these results:

1. H	10. T	19. H	28. T	37. T	46. H
2. T	11. T	20. H	29. H	38. T	47. H
3. T	12. H	21. T	30. T	39. H	48. T
4. T	13. H	22. T	31. T	40. T	49. T
5. H	14. T	23. H	32. T	41. H	50. T
6. H	15. T	24. T	33. T	42. H	51. T
7. H	16. H	25. T	34. T	43. H	
8. T	17. T	26. T	35. T	44. H	
9. T	18. T	27. H	36. H	45. T	

Michael Newman Jr./PhotoEdit

figure 1.4
Illusory correlation in everyday life
Many people believe infertile couples become more likely to conceive a child after adopting a baby. This belief arises from their attention being drawn to such cases. The many couples who adopt without conceiving or conceive without adopting grab less attention. To determine whether there actually is a correlation between adoption and conception, we need data from all four cells in this figure. (From Gilovich, 1991.)

figure 1.5
Two random sequences Your chances of being dealt either of these hands are precisely the same: 1 in 2,598,960.

Bizarre-looking, perhaps. But actually no more unlikely than any other number sequence.

BIZARRE SEQUENCE OF COMPUTER-GENERATED RANDOM NUMBERS

© 1990 by Sidney Harris/*American Scientist Magazine.*

On the 2002 anniversary of 9/11, New York State's three-pick lottery numbers came up 9–1–1.

On March 11, 1998, Utah's Ernie and Lynn Carey gained three new grandchildren when three of their daughters gave birth—on the same day (Los Angeles Times, 1998).

Given enough random events, something weird will happen
Evelyn Marie Adams was the beneficiary of one of those extraordinary, chance events when she won the New Jersey lottery a second time.

UPI/Corbis-Bettmann

Looking over the sequence, patterns jump out: Tosses 10 to 22 provided an almost perfect pattern of pairs of tails followed by pairs of heads. On tosses 30 to 38 I had a "cold hand," with only one head in eight tosses. But my fortunes immediately reversed with a "hot hand"—seven heads out of the next nine tosses.

What explains these patterns? Was I exercising some sort of paranormal control over my coin? Did I snap out of my tails funk and get in a heads groove? No such explanations are needed, for these are the sorts of streaks found in any random data. Comparing each toss to the next, 24 of the 50 comparisons yielded a changed result—just the sort of near 50-50 result we expect from coin tossing. Despite the seeming patterns in these data, the outcome of one toss gives no clue to the outcome of the next toss.

However, some happenings seem so extraordinary that we struggle to conceive an ordinary, chance-related explanation (as applies to our coin-tosses). In such cases, statisticians often are less mystified. When Evelyn Marie Adams won the New Jersey lottery *twice*, newspapers reported the odds of her feat as 1 in 17 trillion. Bizarre? Actually, 1 in 17 trillion are the odds that a given person who buys a single ticket for two New Jersey lotteries will win both times. But statisticians Stephen Samuels and George McCabe (1989) report that, given the millions of people who buy U.S. state lottery tickets, it was "practically a sure thing" that someday, somewhere, someone would hit a state jackpot twice. Indeed, say fellow statisticians Persi Diaconis and Frederick Mosteller (1989), "with a large enough sample, any outrageous thing is likely to happen." "The really unusual day would be one where nothing unusual happens," adds Diaconis (2002). An event that happens to but one in 1 billion people every day occurs about six times a day, 2000 times a year. (For two provocative instances of random sequences that don't look random, see Thinking Critically About Hot and Cold Streaks in Basketball and the Stock Market on page 23.)

Streaks in Basketball and the Stock Market on page 23.)

rehearse it!

12. In psychology, a good theory implies hypotheses, or predictions that can be tested. When hypotheses are tested, the result is typically
    a. increased skepticism.
    b. rejection of the merely theoretical.
    c. confirmation or revision of the theory.
    d. personal bias on the part of the investigator.

13. Psychology's basic *research strategies* are description, correlation, and experimentation. Which of the following would you use in an attempt to predict college grades from high school grades?
    a. A case study
    b. Naturalistic observation
    c. Correlational research
    d. Experimental research

14. You wish to take an accurate poll in a certain country by questioning people

who truly represent the country's adult population. Therefore, you need to make sure the people are
    a. at least 30 percent urban dwellers.
    b. registered voters.
    c. a very large sample of the population.
    d. a random sample of the population.

15. Suppose a psychologist finds that the *more* natural childbirth training classes a woman attends, the *less* pain medication she requires during childbirth. The relationship between the number of training sessions and the amount of pain medication required is a
    a. positive correlation (direct relationship).
    b. negative correlation (inverse relationship).
    c. cause-effect relationship.
    d. controlled experiment.

16. Knowing that two events are correlated does not tell us what is the cause and what is the effect. However, it does provide
    a. a basis for prediction.
    b. an explanation of events.
    c. proof that as one increases, the other also increases.
    d. an indication that an underlying third factor is at work.

17. Some people wrongly perceive that their dreams predict future events. This is an example of a/an
    a. negative correlation.
    b. positive correlation.
    c. illusory correlation.
    d. naturalistic correlation.

Answers can be found in Appendix C.

Hot and Cold Streaks in Basketball and the Stock Market

Misinterpreted random sequences are common in sports and investing. In both arenas, the statistical facts collide with commonsense intuition.

Basketball Players' "Hot Hands"

Every basketball player and every fan intuitively "knows" that players have hot and cold streaks. Players who have "hot hands" can't seem to miss. Those who have "cold" ones can't find the center of the hoop. When Thomas Gilovich, Robert Vallone, and Amos Tversky (1985) interviewed Philadelphia 76ers, the players estimated they were about 25 percent more likely to make a shot after they had just made one than after a miss. In one survey, 9 in 10 basketball fans agreed that a player "has a better chance of making a shot after having just *made* his last two or three shots than he does after having just *missed* his last two or three shots." Believing in shooting streaks, players will feed the ball to a teammate who has just made two or three shots in a row. Many coaches will bench the player who has just missed three in a row.

The only trouble is (believe it or not), it isn't true! When Gilovich and his collaborators studied detailed individual shooting records, they found that the 76ers—and the Boston Celtics, the New Jersey Nets, the New York Knicks, and Cornell University's men's and women's basketball players—were equally likely to score after a miss and after

a basket. A typical 50 percent shooter averages 50 percent after just missing three shots, and 50 percent after just making three shots. It works with free throws, too. Celtics star Larry Bird made 88 percent of his free throws after making a free throw and 91 percent after missing. (Did this reduce Larry Bird to a mere puppet, manipulated by statistical laws? No, his skill was reflected in his 90 percent average.)

Why, then, do players and fans alike believe that players are more likely to score after scoring and to miss after missing? (The same phenomenon turns up in baseball, where the individual and team streaks and slumps that fascinate sportswriters are to be expected, given mere random variation [Myers, 2002].) It's because streaks do occur, more than people expect in random sequences. In any series of 20 shots by a 50 percent shooter (or any 20 flips of a coin), there is a 50-50 chance of 4 baskets (or heads) in a row, and it is quite possible that one person out of five will have a streak of 5 or 6. Players and fans notice these random streaks and so form the errant conclusion that "when you're hot, you're hot" (**FIGURE 1.6**).

Mutual Funds: Does Past Performance Predict Future Returns?

The same misinterpretation of random sequences occurs when investors believe that a mutual fund that has had a string of good years will

likely outperform one that has had a string of bad years. Based on that assumption, investment magazines report mutual funds' performance. But, as economist Burton Malkiel (1989, 1995) documents, past performances of mutual funds do *not* predict their future performance. If on January 1 of each year since 1980 we had bought the previous year's top-performing funds, our hot funds would not have beaten the next year's market average. If we had put our money instead on the *Forbes* "Honor Roll" of funds each year for the two decades following 1975, we would have pulled in 13.5 percent (compared with the market's overall 14.9 percent annual return). Of the top 81 Canadian funds during 1994, 40 performed above average and 41 below average during 1995 (Chalmers, 1995).

When funds have streaks of several good or bad years, we may nevertheless think that past success predicts future success. "Randomness is a difficult notion for people to accept," notes Malkiel. "When events come in clusters and streaks, people look for explanations and patterns. They refuse to believe that such patterns—which frequently occur in random data—could equally well be derived from tossing a coin. So it is in the stock market as well."

The point to remember: When watching basketball, choosing stocks, or flipping coins, remember that our intuition often misleads us. Random sequences frequently don't look random. Expect streaks.

figure 1.6
Who is the chance shooter? Here are 21 consecutive shots, each scoring either a basket or a miss, by two players who each make 11. Within this sample of shots, which player's sequence looks more like what we would expect in a random sequence? (See page 24; adapted from Barry Ross, *Discover*, 1987.)

Player A

Player B

Answer to question in Figure 1.6 (page 23): For these players, chance shooting, like chance coin tossing, should produce a change in outcome about 50 percent of the time. Player B, whose outcomes may look more random, actually has fewer streaks than would be expected by chance. Seventy percent of the time (14 times out of 20), Player B's outcome changes on successive shots. Player A's next outcome differs from the last 10 times out of 20.

▶ **experiment** a research method in which an investigator manipulates one or more factors (independent variables) to observe the effect on some behavior or mental process (the dependent variable). By random assignment of participants, the experiment controls other relevant factors.

▶ **placebo** [pluh-SEE-bo; Latin for "I shall please"] an inert substance or condition that may be administered instead of a presumed active agent, such as a drug, to see if it triggers the effects believed to characterize the active agent.

▶ **double-blind procedure** an experimental procedure in which both the research participants and the research staff are ignorant (blind) about whether the research participants have received the treatment or a placebo. Commonly used in drug-evaluation studies.

▶ **placebo effect** any effect on behavior caused by a placebo.

▶ **experimental condition** the condition of an experiment that exposes participants to the treatment, that is, to one version of the independent variable.

▶ **control condition** the condition of an experiment that contrasts with the experimental condition and serves as a comparison for evaluating the effect of the treatment.

▶ **random assignment** assigning participants to experimental and control conditions by chance, thus minimizing preexisting differences between those assigned to the different groups.

▶ **independent variable** the experimental factor that is manipulated; the variable whose effect is being studied.

▶ **dependent variable** the experimental factor—in psychology, the behavior or mental process—that is being measured; the variable that may change in response to manipulations of the independent variable.

Experimentation

12. How do experiments clarify or reveal cause-effect relationships?

Happy are they "who have been able to perceive the causes of things," remarked the Roman poet Virgil. We endlessly wonder and debate *why* we act as we do. Why do some people smoke? Have babies while they are still children? Do stupid things when drunk? Become troubled teens and open fire on their classmates? Though psychology cannot answer these questions directly, it has helped us to understand what influences drug use, sexual behaviors, thinking when drinking, and aggression.

Many factors influence our everyday behavior. To isolate cause and effect—say, in looking for possible causes of depression—psychologists sometimes try to statistically control for other factors. For example, many studies have found that breast-fed infants grow up with somewhat higher intelligence scores than those of infants bottle-fed with cows milk (Angelsen & others, 2001; Gale & Martyn, 1996; Johnson & others, 1996; Lucas & others, 1992; Mortensen & others, 2002; Quinn & others, 2001). Mother's milk correlates modestly but positively with later intelligence. But does this mean that smarter mothers (who more often breast-feed) have smarter children? Or, as some researchers believe, do the nutrients of mother's milk contribute to brain development? To help answer this question, researchers have "controlled for" (statistically removed differences in) maternal age, education, and intelligence. Still, breast-fed infants exhibit slightly higher intelligence as young children.

The clearest and cleanest way to isolate cause and effect is, however, to **experiment**. Experiments enable a researcher to focus on the possible effects of one or more factors by (1) *manipulating the factors of interest* and (2) *holding constant ("controlling") other factors*. Knowing that correlations of infant nutrition and later intelligence can't possibly control for all other possible factors, a British research team led by Alan Lucas (1998) decided to experiment, using 424 hospital preterm infants. With parental permission, the researchers randomly assigned some infants to standard infant formula feedings and others to donated breast milk feedings. When given intelligence tests at age 8, the children nourished with breast milk had significantly higher intelligence scores than their formula-fed counterparts. No single experiment is conclusive, of course, but by randomly assigning infants to a feeding condition, these researchers were able to hold constant all factors except nutrition. This rigorous design helps eliminate alternative explanations and supports the conclusion that, so far as the developing intelligence of preterm infants is concerned, breast is best.

If behavior changes when we vary an experimental factor, such as infant nutrition, then we know the factor is having an effect. *The important point to remember:* Unlike correlational studies, which uncover naturally occurring relationships, an experiment manipulates a factor to determine its effect. Let's consider some more experiments.

Evaluating Therapies

Our tendency to seek new remedies when we are ill or emotionally down can produce misleading testimonies. When our health or emotions return to normal, we attribute the return to something we have done. If three days into a cold we start taking vitamin C tablets and find our cold symptoms lessening, the pills may seem more potent than they are (an illusion of control). If, after nearly failing the first exam, we listen to a "peak learning" subliminal tape and then improve on the next exam, we may credit the tape rather than conclude that our performance has returned to our average. In the 1700s, blood-letting *seemed* effective. Sometimes people improved after the treatment; when they didn't, the practitioner inferred the disease was too far advanced to be reversed. So, whether or not a remedy is truly effective, enthusiastic users will probably endorse it. To find out whether it actually is effective, we must experiment.

And that is precisely how new drug treatments and new methods of psychological therapy are evaluated (Chapter 14). In many of these studies, the participants are *blind* (uninformed) about what treatment, if any, they are receiving. One group receives the treatment. Others receive a pseudotreatment—an inert **placebo** (perhaps a pill with no drug in it). Often neither the participant nor the research assistant collecting the data knows whether the participant's group is receiving the treatment. This **double-blind procedure** enables researchers to check a treatment's actual effects apart from the research participants' (and their own) enthusiasm for it and from the healing power of belief. The **placebo effect** is well documented with pain, depression, and anxiety (Kirsch & Sapirstein, 1998). Just *thinking* one is getting a treatment can boost one's spirits, relax one's body, and lead to symptom relief.

The double-blind procedure creates an **experimental condition** in which people receive the treatment, and a contrasting **control condition** without the treatment. By **randomly assigning** people to these conditions, we can be fairly certain that the two groups are otherwise identical in age, attitudes, and every other characteristic. With random assignment, as occurred with the infants in the breast milk experiment, we can also know that any later differences between people in the experimental and control conditions must be the result of the treatment.

Another example: On the advice of their physicians, millions of postmenopausal women turned to hormone replacement therapy after correlational studies found that women on replacement hormones had lower rates of heart disease, stroke, and colon cancer. But women who got the therapy were perhaps more likely to be receiving medical care, exercising, and eating well. So, did the hormones make women healthy or did healthy women take the hormones? In 2002, the National Institutes of Health announced the surprising results of a massive experiment that randomly assigned 16,608 healthy women to either replacement hormones or a placebo: Compared with women in the control condition, women receiving the hormones had *more* health problems (Love, 2002).

And an even more potent example: The drug Viagra was approved for use after 21 clinical trials, including an experiment in which researchers randomly assigned 329 men with impotence to either an experimental condition (Viagra) or a control condition (a placebo). It was a double-blind procedure—neither the men nor the person who gave them the pills knew which drug they were receiving. The result: At peak doses, 69 percent of Viagra-assisted attempts at intercourse were successful, compared with 22 percent for men receiving the placebo (Goldstein & others, 1998). Viagra worked.

This simple experiment manipulated just one drug factor. We call this experimental factor the **independent variable** because we can vary it independently of other factors, such as the men's age, weight, and personality (which random assignment controls). Experiments examine the effect of one or more independent variables on some measurable behavior, called the **dependent variable** because it can vary *depending* on what takes place during the experiment. Both variables are given precise operational definitions, which specify the procedures that manipulate the independent variable (the precise drug dosage and timing in this study) or measure the dependent variable (the questions that assessed the men's responses). These definitions answer the "What do you mean?" question with a level of precision that enables others to repeat the study.

Let's recap. A variable is anything (infant nutrition, intelligence, hair color—whatever) that can vary. Experiments aim to *manipulate* an *independent* variable, *measure* the *dependent* variable, and *control* all other variables. An experiment has at least two different conditions: a comparison or control condition and an experimental condition. Random assignment equates the conditions before any treatment effects. In this way, an experiment tests the effect of at least one independent variable (what we measure) on at least one dependent variable (what we manipulate). **TABLE 1.2,** on page 26, compares the features of psychology's research methods.

Note the distinction between random sampling *in surveys and random* assignment *in experiments. Random sampling helps us generalize to a larger population. Random assignment controls extraneous influences, which helps us infer cause and effect.*

table 1.2 Comparing Research Methods

Research Method	Basic Purpose	How Conducted	What Is Manipulated	Possible Problems
Descriptive	To observe and record behavior	Do case studies, surveys, or naturalistic observations	Nothing	Atypical sample; biased observations
Correlational	To detect naturally occurring relationships; to assess how well one variable predicts another	Compute statistical association, sometimes among survey responses	Nothing	Does not specify cause and effect
Experimental	To explore cause and effect	Manipulate one or more factors; use random assignment	The independent variable(s)	Sometimes not feasible; results may not generalize to other contexts

These concepts—experimental and control conditions, independent and dependent variables, random assignment—are important, yet easily confused. So let's put them to work with another intriguing set of experiments.

Can Subliminal Tapes Improve Your Life?

A new generation of entrepreneurs would have you believe so. We are bombarded by mail-order catalogs, cable television ads, and bookstores offering tapes whose imperceptibly faint messages supposedly "reprogram your unconscious mind for success and happiness." While struggling students listen to soothing music, subliminal messages (those below one's hearing threshold) are said to persuade the unconscious that "I am a good student. I love learning." Procrastinators can be similarly reprogrammed: "I set my priorities. I get things done ahead of time!"

Is there anything to these claims? Could positive subliminal messages help us, even a little? Chapter 5 will show that subliminal sensation is for real. We, in fact, do process much information without conscious awareness. And under certain conditions, a stimulus too weak to recognize can affect us, *briefly*.

But does this subtle, fleeting effect extend to the powerful, enduring influence claimed by the subliminal tape merchants? Anthony Greenwald and his colleagues (1991) wanted to find out, so they randomly assigned university students to listen daily for five weeks to commercial subliminal tapes claiming to improve either self-esteem or memory. But the researchers had manipulated an experimental factor. On half the tapes they switched the labels. Some students *thought* they were receiving affirmations of self-esteem when they actually were hearing the memory enhancement tape. Others got the self-esteem tape but *thought* their memory was being recharged (**FIGURE 1.7**).

Were the tapes effective? Their scores on tests for both self-esteem and memory, taken before and after the five weeks, revealed zilch. No effects. None. And yet, those who *thought* they had heard a memory tape *believed* their memories had improved. A similar result occurred for those who thought they had heard a self-esteem tape. The tapes had no effects, yet the students *perceived* themselves receiving the benefits they *expected*. When reading this research, you can hear echoes of the testimonies that ooze from the mail-order tape catalogs. Many customers, having bought what is not supposed to be heard, and having indeed not heard it, actually write things like, "I really know that your tapes were invaluable in reprogramming my mind." Greenwald conducted 16 double-blind experiments evaluating subliminal self-help tapes over one 10-year period. His results were uniform: Not one had any therapeutic effect (Greenwald, 1992).

Experiments can also help us evaluate social programs. Do early childhood education programs boost impoverished children's chances for success? What are the effects of different anti-smoking campaigns? Does school sex education

In this experiment, what was the independent variable? The dependent variable? (See page 28.)

figure 1.7
Design of the subliminal tapes experiment Students' self-esteem and memory abilities were assessed before and after listening to subliminal tapes purporting to increase either self-esteem or memory. Half the students, however, received deliberately mislabeled tapes.

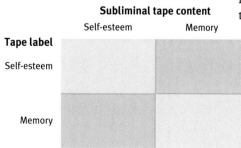

Subliminal tape content

	Self-esteem	Memory
Tape label		
Self-esteem		
Memory		

reduce teen pregnancies? To answer these questions, we can experiment: If an intervention is welcomed but resources are scarce, we could use a lottery to randomly assign some people (or regions) to experience the new program and others to a control condition. If later the two groups differ, there will be less to argue about (Passell, 1993).

rehearse it!

18. A researcher wants to determine whether noise level affects the blood pressure of elderly people. In one group she varies the level of noise in the environment and records blood pressures. In this experiment, the level of noise is the
    a. control condition.
    b. dependent variable (the factor being measured).
    c. independent variable (the factor being manipulated).
    d. cause of any blood pressure variations.

19. To test the effect of a new drug on depression, we randomly assign people to control and experimental conditions. Those in the experimental condition take a pink pill containing the new medication; those in the control group take a pink pill that contains no medication. Which statement is true?
    a. The medication is the dependent variable.
    b. Depression is the independent variable.
    c. Participants in the control group take a placebo.
    d. Neither the experimental nor the control group is told the purpose of the experiment.

20. To eliminate the biasing effect of a researcher's positive expectations on the outcome of a health clinic's research experiment,
    a. patients are randomly assigned to the control and experimental groups (random assignment).
    b. members of the experimental group are carefully matched for age, sex, income, and level of education with members of the control group (controlled selection).
    c. neither the patients nor the researcher will know whether a given person has been assigned to the experimental or control condition (double-blind procedure).
    d. people in the experimental group are chosen by selecting every tenth person in an alphabetical listing of all the clinic's patients (random selection).

21. Description is to explanation as case study is to
    a. correlation.
    b. naturalistic observation.
    c. experiment.
    d. survey.

Answers can be found in Appendix C.

FREQUENTLY ASKED QUESTIONS ABOUT PSYCHOLOGY

We have seen how case studies, surveys, and naturalistic observations help us describe behavior. We have also noted that correlational studies assess the relationship between two factors, which indicates how well knowing one thing lets us predict another. We have examined the logic that underlies experiments, which use control conditions and random assignment of participants to isolate the effects of an independent variable on a dependent variable. We have reflected on how a scientific approach can restrain biases.

You are now prepared to understand what lies ahead and to think critically about psychological matters. Yet, even knowing this much, you may still be approaching psychology with a mixture of curiosity and apprehension. So before we plunge in, let's consider some frequently asked questions.

13. Can laboratory experiments illuminate everyday life?

When you see or hear about psychological research, do you ever wonder whether people's behavior in the lab will predict their behavior in real life? For example, does detecting the blink of a faint red light in a dark room have anything useful to say about flying a plane at night? Does our tendency to remember best the first and last items in a list of unrelated words tell us anything about why we remember the names of certain people we meet at a party? After viewing a violent, sexually explicit film, does an aroused man's increased willingness to push buttons that he thinks will electrically shock a woman really say anything about whether violent pornography makes a man more likely to abuse a woman?

Before you answer, consider: The experimenter *intends* the laboratory environment to be a simplified reality—one in which important features of everyday life can be simulated and controlled. Just as an aeronautical wind tunnel enables an engineer to re-create atmospheric forces under controlled conditions, a laboratory experiment enables a psychologist to re-create psychological forces under controlled conditions.

The experiment's purpose, notes Douglas Mook (1983), is not to re-create the exact behaviors of everyday life but to test theoretical principles. *It is the resulting principles—not the specific findings—that help explain everyday behaviors.*

A cultured greeting Because culture shapes people's understanding of social behavior, actions that seem ordinary to us may seem quite odd to visitors from far away. Yet underlying these differences are powerful similarities. Schoolchildren everywhere greet their teachers with respect, although not necessarily with the formality of this young Japanese schoolchild.

Answer to question on page 26: In the subliminal tapes experiment, the primary independent variable was the type of subliminal message, self-esteem versus memory. (This experiment actually had a second independent variable as well: people's beliefs about which tape they received.) The primary dependent variable was improvement on the self-esteem and memory measures.

"All people are the same; only their habits differ."

Confucius, 551–479 B.C.

▶ **culture** the enduring behaviors, ideas, attitudes, and traditions shared by a large group of people and transmitted from one generation to the next.

When psychologists apply laboratory research on aggression to actual violence, they are applying theoretical *principles* of aggressive behavior, principles they have refined through many experiments. Similarly, it is the principles of the visual system, developed from experiments in artificial settings (such as looking at red lights in the dark), that we apply to more complex behaviors, such as night flying. And many investigations show that principles derived in the laboratory *do* typically generalize to the everyday world (Anderson & others, 1999).

The point to remember: As psychologists, our concerns lie less with particular behaviors than with the general principles that help explain many behaviors.

14. Does behavior depend on one's culture and gender?

If culture shapes behavior, what can psychological studies done in one culture, often with white North Americans, really tell us about people in general? As we will see time and again, **culture**—shared ideas and behaviors that one generation passes on to the next—matters. Our culture influences our standards of promptness and frankness, our attitudes toward premarital sex and varying body shapes, our tendency to be casual or formal, and much, much more. Being aware of such differences, we can restrain our assumptions that others will think and act as we do. Given the growing mixing and clashing of cultures, our need for such awareness is urgent.

You will see throughout this book that gender matters too. Researchers report gender differences in what we dream, in how we express and detect emotions, and in our risk for alcoholism, depression, and eating disorders. Not only is studying such differences interesting, it also is potentially beneficial. For example, many researchers believe that women carry on conversations more readily to build relationships; men usually talk to give information and advice (Tannen, 1990). Knowing this difference can help us prevent conflicts and misunderstandings in everyday relationships.

Likewise, it's important to remember that psychologically as well as biologically, women and men are overwhelmingly similar. Whether female or male, we learn to walk at about the same age. We experience the same sensations of light and sound. We feel the same pangs of hunger, desire, and fear. We exhibit similar overall intelligence and well-being. We also tend to exhibit and perceive the very behaviors our culture expects of males and females.

Our shared biological heritage does, however, unite us as a universal human family. The same underlying processes guide people everywhere:

- People diagnosed with dyslexia, a reading disorder, exhibit the same brain malfunction whether they are Italian, French, or British (Paulesu & others, 2001).
- Variation in languages—spoken and gestured—may impede communication across cultures, yet all languages share deep principles of grammar, and people from opposite hemispheres can communicate with a smile or a frown.
- People in different cultures do vary in feelings of loneliness, but across cultures shyness, low self-esteem, and being unmarried magnify loneliness (Jones & others, 1985; Rokach & others, 2002).
- Most Japanese prefer their fish raw and most North Americans prefer theirs cooked, but the same principles of hunger and taste influence all of us when we sit down to a meal. We are each in certain respects like all others, like some others, and like no other. Studying people of all races and cultures helps us discern our similarities and our differences, our human kinship and our diversity.

The point to remember: Even when specific attitudes and behaviors vary across cultures, as they often do, the underlying processes are much the same. A children's song says it well: "We're all the same and different."

15. Why do psychologists study animals?

Many psychologists study animals because they find them fascinating. They want to understand how different species learn, think, and behave. Psychologists also study animals to learn about people, by doing experiments that are permissible only with animals. Rats, critics say, are not long-tailed people. Yet human physiology resembles that of many other animals. Animal experiments have therefore led to treatments for human diseases—insulin for diabetes, vaccines to prevent polio and rabies, transplants to replace defective organs. We humans are not like animals. We *are* animals.

Likewise, the same processes by which humans see, exhibit emotion, and become obese are present in rats and monkeys. To discover more about the basics of human learning, researchers even study sea slugs. To understand how a combustion engine works, you would do better to study the engine of a lawn mower than that of a Mercedes. Like Mercedes engines, humans are complex. But it is precisely the simplicity of the sea slug's nervous system that makes it so revealing of the neural mechanisms of learning.

16. Is it ethical to experiment on animals?

If we share important similarities with other animals, then should we not respect them? "We cannot defend our scientific work with animals on the basis of the similarities between them and ourselves and then defend it morally on the basis of differences," noted Roger Ulrich (1991). The animal protection movement protests the use of animals in psychological, biological, and medical research. Researchers remind us that the world's 30 million mammals used each year in research are but a fraction of 1 percent of the billions of animals killed annually for food (which means the average person eats 20 animals a year). While researchers each year conduct experiments on some 200,000 dogs and cats cared for under humane regulations, humane animal shelters are forced to kill 50 times that many (Goodwin & Morrison, 1999).

Only 7 percent of psychology's studies have involved animals, 95 percent of which were rats, mice, rabbits, or birds. Electric shock was used in about 10 percent of these studies (Coile & Miller, 1984; Gallup & Suarez, 1985). In British psychology departments, where animal use dropped by two-thirds in the dozen years after 1977, only 4 percent of animal studies involved electric shock, all with rats (Thomas & Blackman, 1991).

Animal protection organizations, such as Psychologists for the Ethical Treatment of Animals, advocate naturalistic observation of animals rather than laboratory manipulation. However, many researchers say this is not the morality of good versus evil but of compassion for animals versus compassion for people. How many of us would have attacked Pasteur's experiments with rabies, which caused some dogs to suffer but led to a vaccine that spared millions of people, and dogs, from agonizing death? And would we really wish to have deprived ourselves of the animal research that led to effective methods of training children with mental disorders; of understanding aging; of relieving fears and depression; of controlling obesity, alcoholism, and stress-related pain and disease?

Out of this heated debate, two issues emerge. The basic one is whether it is right to place the well-being of humans above that of animals. In experiments on stress and cancer, is it right that mice get tumors in hopes that people might not? Is our use of other animals as natural as the behavior of carnivorous hawks, cats, and whales? (No other animals assign rights to those who are lower on the food chain.)

If we give human life first priority, the second issue is the priority given the well-being of the animals in research. What safeguards should protect animals? Most researchers today feel ethically obligated to enhance the well-being of captive animals and protect them from needless suffering. In one survey of animal researchers, 98 percent or more supported government regulations protecting primates, dogs, and cats, and 74 percent supported regulations providing for the humane care of rats and mice (Plous & Herzog, 2000). Many professional associations and funding agencies now have guidelines for the humane use of animals. For example, British Psychological Society guidelines now call for housing animals under reasonably natural living conditions, with companions for social animals (Lea, 2000). Humane care also leads to more effective science, because pain and stress would distort the animals' behavior during experiments.

"Rats are very similar to humans except that they are not stupid enough to purchase lottery tickets."

Dave Barry, July 2, 2002

"I believe that to prevent, cripple, or needlessly complicate the research that can relieve animal and human suffering is profoundly inhuman, cruel, and immoral."

Psychologist Neal Miller, 1983

"The righteous know the needs of their animals."

Proverbs 12:10

Animal research benefiting animals
Thanks partly to research on the benefits of novelty, control, and stimulation, these Bronx Zoo gorillas are enjoying improved quality of life.

"The greatness of a nation can be judged by the way its animals are treated."

Mahatma Gandhi, 1869–1948

"It is doubtless impossible to approach any human problem with a mind free from bias."

Simone De Beauvoir, The Second Sex, 1953

figure 1.8
What do you see? People interpret ambiguous information to fit their preconceptions. Did you see a duck or a rabbit? Before showing some friends this image, ask them if they can see the duck lying on its back (or the bunny in the grass). (From Shepard, 1990.)

Animals have themselves benefited from animal research. One Ohio team of research psychologists measured stress hormone levels in samples of millions of dogs brought each year to animal shelters, and they devised methods of handling and stroking them that reduced stress and eased their transition to adoptive homes (Tuber & others, 1999). Thanks to animal behavior studies, formerly idle Bronx Zoo animals are now staving off listless boredom by working for their supper, as would their counterparts in the wild (Stewart, 2002). Other studies have helped improve care and management in animals' natural habitats. By revealing our behavioral kinship with animals and the remarkable intelligence of some animals, experiments have also led to an increase in our empathy for them. At its best, a psychology concerned for humans and sensitive to animals serves the welfare of both.

17. Is it ethical to experiment on people?

If the image of animals or people receiving supposed electric shocks troubles you, you may find it a relief that most psychological research involves no such stress. With people, blinking lights, flashing words, and pleasant social interactions are more common.

Occasionally, though, researchers do temporarily stress or deceive people, but only when they believe it is essential to a justifiable end, such as understanding and controlling violent behavior or studying mood swings. Such experiments wouldn't work if the participants knew all there was to know about the experiment beforehand. Either the procedures would be ineffective or the participants, wanting to be helpful, might try to confirm the researchers' predictions.

Ethical principles developed by the American Psychological Association (1992) and the British Psychological Society (1993) urge investigators to (1) obtain the informed consent of potential participants, (2) protect them from harm and discomfort, (3) treat information about individual participants confidentially, and (4) fully explain the research afterward. Moreover, most universities today screen research proposals through an ethics committee that safeguards the well-being of every participant.

18. Is psychology free of value judgments?

Psychology is definitely not value-free. Values affect what we study, how we study it, and how we interpret results. Consider: Researchers' values influence their choice of research topics—whether to study worker productivity or worker morale, sex discrimination or gender differences, conformity or independence. Values can even color "the facts." Our preconceptions can bias our observations and interpretations; sometimes we see what we want or expect to see (**FIGURE 1.8**). Even the words we use to describe a phenomenon can reflect our values. Labeling the sex acts we do not practice as "perversions" or as "sexual variations" conveys a value judgment. The same holds true in everyday speech, when one person's "rigidity" is another's "consistency," or one person's "faith" is another's "fanaticism." Our labeling someone as "firm" or "stubborn," "careful" or "picky," "discreet" or "secretive" reveals our feelings. Both in and out of psychology, labels describe and labels evaluate.

Popular *applications* of psychology also contain hidden values. If you defer to "professional" guidance about how to live—how to raise children, how to achieve self-fulfillment, what to do with sexual feelings, how to get ahead at work—you are accepting value-laden advice. A science of behavior and mental processes can certainly help us reach our goals, but it cannot decide what those goals should be.

19. Is psychology potentially dangerous?

If some people see psychology as merely common sense, others have a different concern—that it is becoming dangerously powerful. Is it an accident that astronomy is the oldest science and psychology the youngest? Exploring the external universe is one thing, but exploring our own inner universe seems even more dangerous and threatening. Might psychology be used to manipulate people?

Knowledge, like all power, can be used for good or evil. Nuclear power has been used to light up cities—and to demolish them. Persuasive power has been used to educate people—and to deceive them. The power of mind-altering drugs has been used to restore sanity—and to destroy it.

Although psychology does indeed have the power to deceive, its purpose is to enlighten. Every day, psychologists are exploring ways to enhance learning, creativity, and compassion. Psychology also speaks to many of our world's great problems—war, overpopulation, prejudice, family dysfunction, crime—all of which involve attitudes and behaviors. And psychology speaks to our deepest longings—for nourishment, for love, for happiness. True, psychology cannot address all of life's great questions, but it speaks to some mighty important ones.

rehearse it!

22. In a laboratory experiment, features of everyday life can be simulated, manipulated, and controlled. The laboratory environment is designed to help us
    a. exactly re-create the events of everyday life.
    b. re-create psychological forces under controlled conditions.
    c. create opportunities for naturalistic observation.
    d. minimize the use of animals and humans in psychological research.

23. Which of the following is true regarding gender differences and similarities?
    a. Differences between the genders outweigh any similarities.
    b. Despite some gender differences, the underlying processes of human behavior are the same.
    c. Both similarities and differences between the genders depend more on biology than on environment.
    d. Gender differences are so numerous, it is difficult to make meaningful comparisons.

24. The animal protection movement has protested the use of animals in all fields of scientific research. In defending their experimental research with animals, psychologists have noted that
    a. animals' physiology and behavior can tell us much about our own.
    b. they do not torture or needlessly exploit animals.
    c. advancing the well-being of humans justifies animal experimentation.
    d. All of the above

Answers can be found in Appendix C.

TIPS FOR STUDYING PSYCHOLOGY

20. How can psychological principles help you as a student?

The investment you are making in studying psychology should enrich your life and enlarge your vision. Although many of life's significant questions are beyond psychology, some very important ones are illuminated by even a first psychology course. Through painstaking research, psychologists have gained insights into brain and mind, depression and joy, dreams and memories. Even the unanswered questions can enrich us, by renewing our sense of mystery about "things too wonderful" for us yet to understand. What is more, your study of psychology can help teach you *how to ask and answer important questions*—how to think critically as you evaluate competing ideas and claims.

Having your life enriched and your vision enlarged (and getting a decent grade) requires effective study. As you will see in Chapter 8, to master information you must *actively process* it. Your mind is not like your stomach, something to be filled passively; it is more like a muscle that grows stronger with exercise. Countless experiments reveal that people learn and remember material best when they put it in their own words, rehearse it, and then review and rehearse it again.

The **SQ3R** study method incorporates these principles (Robinson, 1970). SQ3R is an acronym for its five steps: *S*urvey, *Q*uestion, *R*ead, *R*ehearse, *R*eview.

To study a chapter, first *survey*, taking a bird's-eye view as you note its headings. Notice how the chapter is organized.

As you prepare to read each section, use its heading or the preview question to form a *question* that you should answer. For this section, you might have asked, "How can I most effectively and efficiently master the information in this book?"

Then *read*, actively searching for the answer. At each sitting, read only as much of the chapter as you can absorb without tiring. Usually, a single main chapter section will do—the Frequently Asked Questions section you just finished, for example. Relating what you are reading to your own life will improve understanding and retention. Reading the occasional Close-Up and Thinking Critically boxes will also help.

▶ **SQ3R** a study method incorporating five steps: *Survey, Question, Read, Rehearse, Review.*

Having read a section, *rehearse* in your own words what you read. Test yourself by trying to answer your question, rehearsing what you can recall, then glancing back over what you can't recall.

Finally, *review:* Read over any notes you have taken, again with an eye on the chapter's organization, and quickly review the whole chapter.

Survey, question, read, rehearse, review. I have organized this book's chapters to facilitate your use of the SQ3R study system. Each chapter begins with a chapter outline that aids your *survey.* Headings and preview *questions* suggest issues and concepts you should consider as you *read.* The material is organized into sections of readable length, and at the end of each section there are *Rehearse* It questions that help you test yourself before moving on. The chapter *Reviewing* sections, as well as the Critical Thinker's *Review* and the key terms help you check your mastery of important concepts. Survey, question, read. . . .

Five additional study tips may further boost your learning:

1. *Distribute your study time.* One of psychology's oldest findings is that "spaced practice" promotes better retention than "massed practice." You'll remember material better if you space your time over several study periods rather than cram it into one long study blitz. Better to give your study of this text one hour a day, with one day off a week, than six hours at a time. Doing this requires a disciplined approach to managing your time. (Richard Straub explains time management in the *Student Study Guide* that accompanies this text.) For example, rather than trying to read an entire chapter in a single sitting, read just one section and then turn to something else.

2. *Learn to think critically.* Whether reading or in class, note people's *assumptions and values.* What perspective or bias underlies an argument? *Evaluate evidence.* Is it anecdotal? Correlational? Experimental? *Assess conclusions.* Are there alternative explanations?

3. *In class, listen actively.* As psychologist William James urged a century ago, "No reception without reaction, no impression without . . . expression." Listen for the main ideas and subideas of a lecture. Write them down. Ask questions during and after class. In class, as in your private study, process the information actively and you will understand and retain it better.

4. *Overlearn.* Psychology tells us that overlearning improves retention. Most of us are prone to overestimating how much we know. You may understand a chapter as you read it, but by devoting extra study time to testing yourself and reviewing what you think you know, you will retain your new knowledge long into the future.

5. *Be a smart test-taker.* If a test contains both multiple-choice questions and an essay question, turn first to the essay. Read the question carefully, noting exactly what the instructor is asking. On the back of a page, pencil in a list of points you'd like to make and then organize them. Before writing, put aside the essay and work through the multiple-choice questions. (As you do so, your mind may continue to mull over the essay question. Sometimes the objective questions will bring pertinent thoughts to mind.) Then reread the essay question, rethink your answer, and start writing. When finished, proofread to eliminate spelling and grammatical errors that make you look less competent than you are. When reading multiple-choice questions, don't confuse yourself by trying to imagine how each alternative might be right. Try instead to recall the answer *before* reading the alternatives given. Answer the question as if it were a fill-in-the-blank; first cover the answers and complete the sentence in your mind, and then find the alternative that best matches your own answer.

While exploring psychology, you will learn much more than effective study techniques. Psychology deepens our appreciation for how we humans perceive, think, feel, and act. By so doing it can indeed enrich our lives and enlarge our vision. Through this book I hope to help guide you toward that end. As educator Charles Eliot said a century ago: "Books are the quietest and most constant of friends, and the most patient of teachers."

chapter review

REVIEWING

Thinking Critically With Psychological Science

WHAT IS PSYCHOLOGY?

1. How long have people been thinking and writing about the questions that fascinate psychologists today?

Psychology traces its roots back through recorded history to the writings of many scholars who spent their lives wondering about people—in India, China, the Middle East, and Europe. In their attempt to understand human nature, they looked carefully at how our minds work and how our bodies relate to our minds.

More than 2000 years ago, Buddha and Confucius focused on the powers and origins of ideas. In other parts of the world, ancient Hebrew scholars, Socrates, his student Plato, and Plato's student Aristotle pondered whether mind and body are connected or distinct, and whether human ideas are innate or result from experience. In the 1600s, René Descartes and John Locke reengaged aspects of those ancient debates, and Locke coined his famous description of the mind as a "white paper."

2. What event defines the birth of psychology as we know it today? What were structuralism and functionalism, and how did they differ?

Psychology as we know it today was born in a laboratory in Germany in the late 1800s, when Wilhelm Wundt ran the first true experiments in psychology's first lab. Soon, the new discipline formed branches: structuralism, which searched for the basic elements of the mind, and functionalism, which tried to explain why we do what we do. William James, a functionalist, wrote the first text for the new discipline.

3. How has the science of psychology's focus changed since its birth in the late nineteenth century? What is the modern definition of psychology?

After beginning as a "science of mental life," psychology evolved in the 1920s into a "science of observable behavior." After rediscovering the mind in the 1960s, psychology now views itself as a "science of behavior and mental processes."

4. What theoretical perspectives do psychologists take?

Psychologists view behavior and mental processes from various perspectives. These currently include the neuroscience, evolutionary, behavior genetics, psychodynamic, behavioral, cognitive, and social-cultural perspectives.

5. What are psychology's specialized subfields?

Psychology's subfields encompass basic research (often done by biological, developmental, cognitive, personality, and social psychologists), applied research (sometimes conducted by organizational/industrial psychologists), and clinical applications.

WHY DO PSYCHOLOGY?

6. Why are the answers that flow from the scientific approach more reliable than those based on intuition and common sense?

If intuition and common sense were trustworthy, we would have less need for scientific inquiry and critical thinking. But without such thinking we readily succumb to *hindsight bias*, or the I-knew-it-all-along phenomenon. Learning the outcome of a study (or of an everyday happening) can make it seem like obvious common sense. But things seldom seem so obvious before the fact. We also are routinely *overconfident* of our judgments, thanks partly to our bias to seek information that confirms them. Such biases lead us to overestimate our unaided intuition. Although limited by the testable questions it can address, a scientific approach can help us sift reality from illusion.

7. What attitudes characterize scientific inquiry?

Scientific inquiry begins with an eagerness to *skeptically* scrutinize competing ideas and an open-minded *humility* before nature. Putting ideas, even crazy-sounding ideas, to the test helps us winnow sense from nonsense. The *curiosity* that drives us to test ideas and to expose their underlying assumptions carries into everyday life as critical thinking.

HOW DO PSYCHOLOGISTS ASK AND ANSWER QUESTIONS?

8. How do psychologists use the scientific method to construct theories?

Research stimulates the construction of *theories*, which organize the *observations* and imply predictive *hypotheses*. These hypotheses (predictions) are then tested to validate and refine the theory and to suggest practical applications. Precise operational definitions enable other researchers to *replicate* (repeat) observations.

9. How do psychologists observe and describe behavior?

Through individual case studies, surveys among random samples of a population, and naturalistic observations, psychologists observe and describe behavior and mental processes. In generalizing from observations, remember: Representative samples are a better guide than vivid examples.

10. Why do correlations permit prediction but not explanation?

The strength of the relationship between one factor and another is expressed in their *correlation coefficient*. Knowing how closely two things are positively or negatively correlated tells us how much one predicts the other. But correlation is only a measure of relationship; it does not reveal cause and effect.

11. *How accurately does the naked eye detect correlations?*

Correlations help us to see relationships that the naked eye might miss and to discount illusory correlations and random events that might otherwise look significant.

12. *How do experiments clarify or reveal cause–effect relationships?*

By constructing a controlled reality in an *experiment*, psychologists can manipulate one or more factors and discover how these independent variables affect a particular behavior, the dependent variable.

FREQUENTLY ASKED QUESTIONS ABOUT PSYCHOLOGY

13. *Can laboratory experiments illuminate everyday life?*

By intentionally creating a controlled, artificial environment in the lab, researchers aim to test theoretical principles. These principles help us to understand, describe, explain, and predict everyday behaviors.

14. *Does behavior depend on one's culture and gender?*

Although attitudes and behaviors vary across cultures, the principles that underlie them vary much less. Cross-cultural psychology explores both our cultural differences and the universal similarities that define our human kinship.

Gender is also a fact of life. Although gender differences tend to capture attention, it is important to remember the much greater similarities between men and women.

15. *Why do psychologists study animals?*

Some psychologists study animals out of an interest in animal behavior. Others do so because knowledge of the physiologi-

cal and psychological processes of animals permits a better understanding of the similar processes operating in humans.

16. *Is it ethical to experiment on animals?*

Only about 7 percent of all psychological experiments involve animals, and under ethical and legal guidelines these animals rarely experience pain. Nevertheless, animal rights groups raise an important issue: Is an animal's temporary suffering justified if it leads to the relief of human suffering?

17. *Is it ethical to experiment on people?*

Occasionally researchers temporarily stress or deceive people in order to learn something important. Professional ethical standards provide guidelines for the treatment of human as well as animal participants.

18. *Is psychology free of value judgments?*

Psychology is not value-free. Psychologists' own values influence their choice of research topics, their theories and observations, their labels for behavior, and their professional advice.

19. *Is psychology potentially dangerous?*

Knowledge is power that can be used for good or evil. Applications of psychology's principles have so far been mostly for the good, and psychology addresses some of humanity's greatest problems and deepest longings.

TIPS FOR STUDYING PSYCHOLOGY

20. *How can psychological principles help you as a student?*

Experiments have shown that learning and memory are enhanced by active study. The SQ3R study method—survey, question, read, rehearse, and review—applies the principles derived from these experiments.

A CRITICAL THINKER'S REVIEW OF CHAPTER 1

At the end of each chapter, you will find A Critical Thinker's Review. This feature is intended to help you test your knowledge of the chapter content while building your reasoning and problem-solving skills. In each of these end-of-chapter self-tests, I use expert Jane Halonen's six categories of critical thinking (from *The Critical Thinking Companion for Introductory Psychology*, 2001), described below. There will be one question for each of the six categories at the end of each chapter. The thinking skills you learn to use in this review may help your studies in other classes as well.

1. Pattern recognition: Acknowledge significant differences and recognize meaningful patterns in those differences. Finding patterns helps us to think more effectively, and quickly, about a situation.

2. Practical problem solving: Determine that a behavior represents a significant discrepancy from an orderly, workable world, and then develop a functional strategy for dealing with the concern.

3. Creative problem solving: We again need to notice a troublesome discrepancy in behavior, but this time developing a strategy for dealing with the issue involves making novel connections between previously unrelated or disconnected ideas.

4. Scientific problem solving: Resolving a difficulty with this type of critical thinking requires using experimentation to establish systematic explanations for the relationships among various factors.

5. Psychological reasoning: Use psychological principles to create, defend, or challenge an argument about behavior. Use what you're learning in this course to discuss important issues with family and friends!

6. Perspective taking: Identifying the values and experiences that influence our own and others' behaviors will help us think more clearly and comprehensively about an issue. Taking another's point of view on an issue can be very enlightening.

You'll see, in parentheses below, which of the categories is addressed by each question. You should be able to answer each question in a short paragraph.

1. Why do many psychologists try to consider questions or issues from more than one perspective? (psychological reasoning)

2. Matthew's friend asks, "Are you ready for the history test?" Matthew scans his notes and everything looks familiar, so he says, confidently, "Yes." However, Matthew's performance on the test is not impressive. What human tendency is Matthew displaying, and why is it important to study more than we think is needed? (practical problem solving)

3. Outside the community library, you are approached by a woman with what she claims is a survey on whether the city should hire an additional librarian. She says, "Do you agree that our city dollars should not be wasted on extraneous municipal staff positions?" What does the wording of this question tell you about what this woman hopes to accomplish? (perspective taking)

4. Here are three recently reported correlations, with interpretations drawn by journalists. Knowing just these correlations, can you come up with other possible explanations? (creative problem solving)

   a. Alcohol use is associated with violence.
   Journalists' interpretation: Drinking lowers inhibitions, unleashing aggressive behavior.

   b. Educated people live longer, on average, than less-educated people.
   Journalists' interpretation: Education lengthens life and enhances health.

   c. Teens engaged in team sports use drugs, smoke, have sex, carry weapons, and eat junk food less often than teens who do not engage in team sports.
   Journalists' interpretation: Team sports encourage healthy living.

5. Why, when testing a new drug for blood pressure, would we learn more about its effectiveness from giving it to half of the participants in a group of 1000 than to all 1000 participants? (scientific problem solving)

6. In what ways does the field of psychology *fit* your preconceptions (what you expected when you signed up for the class) and in what ways has it surprised you so far? (pattern recognition)

Answers can be found in Appendix C.

TERMS AND CONCEPTS TO REMEMBER

empiricism, p. 3
structuralism, p. 3
functionalism, p. 4
psychology, p. 6
nature-nurture issue, p. 7
basic research, p. 9
applied research, p. 9
clinical psychology, p. 10
psychiatry, p. 10
hindsight bias, p. 11
critical thinking, p. 14

theory, p. 15
hypothesis, p. 15
operational definition, p. 15
replication, p. 15
case study, p. 16
survey, p. 17
population, p. 18
random sample, p. 18
naturalistic observation, p. 18
correlation coefficient, p. 19
illusory correlation, p. 21

experiment, p. 24
placebo, p. 25
double-blind procedure, p. 25
placebo effect, p. 25
experimental condition, p. 25
control condition, p. 25
random assignment, p. 25
independent variable, p. 25
dependent variable, p. 25
culture, p. 28
SQ3R, p. 31

To continue your study and review of Thinking Critically With Psychological Science, visit this book's Web site at www.worthpublishers.com/myers. You will find practice tests, review activities, and Web links for more information on topics related to Thinking Critically With Psychological Science.

chapter2

Neuroscience and Behavior

No principle is more central to today's psychology, or to this book, than this: *Everything psychological is simultaneously biological.* Your every idea, every mood, every urge is a biological happening. You think, feel, and act with your body. (Try laughing, crying, or loving without it.) Without your body—your genes, your brain, your body chemistry, your appearance—you are, indeed, nobody. Although we find it convenient to talk separately of biological and psychological influences on behavior, we need to remember: To think, feel, or act without a body would be like running without legs.

Today's science is riveted on the most amazing parts of our body—our brain, its component neural systems, and their genetic blueprints. The brain's ultimate challenge? To understand itself. How does our brain organize and communicate with itself? How does our heredity prewire the brain, and our experience modify it? How does the brain process the information we need to shoot a basketball? To delight in a guitarist's notes? To remember our first kiss?

On the timescale of human existence, the last 150 years are but a few ticks of the clock. Yet that's how recently a scientific understanding of the brain-mind connection began to emerge. We have come far since the early 1800s, when the German physician Franz Gall invented *phrenology*, a popular but ill-fated theory that claimed bumps on the skull could reveal our mental abilities and our character traits. Phrenology did, however, correctly focus attention on the idea that various brain regions have particular functions. Within little more than the last century, we have also realized that the body is composed of cells; that among these are nerve cells that conduct electricity and "talk" to one another by sending chemical messages across a tiny gap that separates them; that specific brain systems serve specific functions (though not the functions Gall supposed); and that from the information processed in these different brain systems, we construct our experience of sights and sounds, meanings and memories, pain and passion. You and I are privileged to live in a time when discoveries about the interplay of our biology and behavior are occurring at an exhilarating pace.

Throughout this book you will find examples of how our biology underlies our behavior and mental processes. By studying the links between biological activity and psychological events, **biological psychologists** are gaining a better understanding of sleep and dreams, depression and schizophrenia, hunger and sex, stress and disease. We therefore begin our study of psychology with a look at its biological roots.

▶ **biological psychology** a branch of psychology concerned with the links between biology and behavior. (Some biological psychologists call themselves *behavioral neuroscientists, neuropsychologists, behavior geneticists, physiological psychologists,* or *biopsychologists.*)

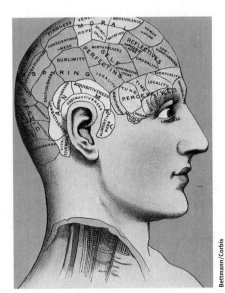

A wrongheaded theory
Despite initial acceptance of Gall's speculations, bumps on the skull tell us nothing about the brain's underlying functions. Nevertheless, some of his assumptions have held true: Different parts of the brain do control different aspects of behavior.

Bettmann/Corbis

NEURAL COMMUNICATION

In this book we start small and build from the bottom up—from neurons up to the brain in this chapter, and to the environmental and cultural influences that interact with our biology in later chapters. We will also work from the top down, as we consider how our thinking and emotions influence our brain and our health. At all levels, psychologists examine how we process information—how we take in information; how we organize, interpret, and store it; and how we use it.

For scientists, it is a happy fact of nature that the information systems of humans and other animals operate similarly—so similarly, in fact, that you could not distinguish between small samples of brain tissue from a human and a monkey. This similarity allows researchers to study simple animals, such as squids and sea slugs, to discover how our neural systems operate. And it allows them to study other mammals' brains to understand the organization of our own. Though the human brain is more complex, it follows the same principles that govern all of the animal world.

Neurons

2. What are neurons, and how do they transmit information?

Our body's neural information system is complexity built from simplicity. Its building blocks are **neurons**, or nerve cells. There are many different types of neurons, but all are variations on the same theme (**FIGURE 2.1**). Each consists of a cell body and its branching fibers. The bushy **dendrite** fibers receive information and conduct it toward the cell body. From there, **axon** fibers pass the message along to other neurons or to muscles or glands. Unlike the short dendrites, axons are sometimes very long, projecting several feet through the body. Motor neurons, which control muscles, are the neural system's giant redwoods. A neuron carrying orders to a leg muscle has a cell body and axon roughly on the scale of a basketball attached to a rope 4 miles long.

A neuron fires an impulse when it receives signals from sense receptors stimulated by pressure, heat, or light, or when it is stimulated by chemical messages from neighboring neurons. The impulse, called the **action potential**, is a brief electrical charge that travels down the axon. A layer of fatty tissue, called the **myelin sheath**, insulates the axons of some neurons and helps speed their impulses. The myelin sheath's importance is evident in multiple sclerosis, a disease in which the myelin sheath degenerates. The result is a slowing of all communication to muscles and the eventual loss of muscle control.

figure 2.1
A motor neuron

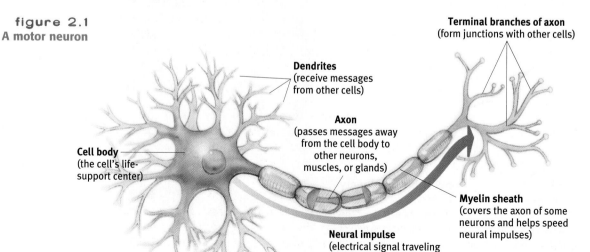

Dendrites
(receive messages from other cells)

Terminal branches of axon
(form junctions with other cells)

Axon
(passes messages away from the cell body to other neurons, muscles, or glands)

Cell body
(the cell's life-support center)

Myelin sheath
(covers the axon of some neurons and helps speed neural impulses)

Neural impulse
(electrical signal traveling down the axon)

Depending on the type of fiber, the neural impulse travels at speeds ranging from a sluggish 2 miles per hour to, in some myelinated fibers, a breakneck 200 or more miles per hour. But even this top speed is 3 million times slower than that of electricity through a wire. We measure brain activity in milliseconds (thousandths of a second) and computer activity in nanoseconds (billionths of a second). That helps to explain why, unlike the nearly instantaneous reactions of a high-speed computer, your reaction to a sudden event, such as a child darting in front of your car, may take a quarter-second or more. Your brain is vastly more complex than a computer, but not faster at executing simple responses.

Each neuron in your brain is itself a miniature decision-making device that performs complex calculations. From hundreds, even thousands of other neurons, it receives signals on its dendrites and cell body. Some of these signals are *excitatory*, somewhat like pushing a neuron's accelerator. Other signals are *inhibitory*, more like pushing its brake. If excitatory signals minus inhibitory signals exceed a minimum intensity, called the **threshold,** the combined signals trigger an action potential. (Think of it this way: If the excitatory party animals outvote the inhibitory party poopers, the party's on.) The action potential transmits down the axon, which branches into junctions with hundreds or thousands of other neurons and with the body's muscles and glands.

Increasing the stimulus above the threshold, however, will not increase the action potential's intensity. How then do we detect the intensity of a stimulus? How do we distinguish a gentle touch from a big hug? The neuron's reaction is an *all-or-none response*: Like guns, neurons either fire or they don't. But a strong stimulus—a slap on the back rather than a tap—can trigger *more* neurons to fire and to fire more often. But it does not affect the action potential's speed.

How Neurons Communicate

3. How do nerve cells communicate?

Neurons interweave so intricately that even with a microscope it is hard to see where one neuron ends and another begins. Scientists once believed that the branching axon of one cell fused with the dendrites of another in an uninterrupted fabric. Then a Spanish anatomist, Santiago Ramon y Cajal (1852–1934), described gaps between individual nerve cells and concluded that the individual neurons must function as independent agents within the nervous system. At the same time, the British physiologist Sir Charles Sherrington (1857–1952) noticed that neural impulses were taking an unexpectedly long time to travel a neural pathway. Sherrington inferred there must be a brief interruption in the transmission.

We now know that the axon terminal of one neuron is in fact separated from the receiving neuron by a gap less than a millionth of an inch wide. Sherrington called this junction the **synapse**, and the gap is called the *synaptic gap* or *cleft*. To Cajal, these near-unions of neurons—"protoplasmic kisses," he called them—were another of nature's marvels. How do the neurons execute the protoplasmic kiss? How does it cross the tiny synaptic gap? The answer is one of the important scientific discoveries of our age.

When the action potential reaches the knoblike terminals at an axon's end, it triggers the release of chemical messengers, called **neurotransmitters** (**FIGURE 2.2**, page 40). Within 1/10,000th of a second, the neurotransmitter molecules cross the synaptic gap and bind to receptor sites on the receiving neuron—as precisely as a key fits a lock. For an instant, the neurotransmitter unlocks tiny channels at the receiving site. This allows electrically charged atoms to enter the receiving neuron, thereby either exciting or inhibiting its readiness to fire. Excess neurotransmitters are reabsorbed by the sending neuron in a process called *reuptake*. Many drugs increase the availability of selected neurotransmitters by blocking their reuptake.

▶ **neuron** a nerve cell; the basic building block of the nervous system.

▶ **dendrite** the bushy, branching extensions of a neuron that receive messages and conduct impulses toward the cell body.

▶ **axon** the extension of a neuron, ending in branching terminal fibers, through which messages pass to other neurons or to muscles or glands.

▶ **action potential** a neural impulse; a brief electrical charge that travels down an axon. The action potential is generated by the movement of positively charged atoms in and out of channels in the axon's membrane.

▶ **myelin [MY-uh-lin] sheath** a layer of fatty tissue segmentally encasing the fibers of many neurons; enables vastly greater transmission speed of neural impulses as the impulse hops from one node to the next.

▶ **threshold** the level of stimulation required to trigger a neural impulse.

▶ **synapse [SIN-aps]** the junction between the axon tip of the sending neuron and the dendrite or cell body of the receiving neuron. The tiny gap at this junction is called the *synaptic gap* or *cleft*.

▶ **neurotransmitters** chemical messengers that traverse the synaptic gaps between neurons. When released by the sending neuron, neurotransmitters travel across the synapse and bind to receptor sites on the receiving neuron, thereby influencing whether that neuron will generate a neural impulse.

"All information processing in the brain involves neurons 'talking to' each other at synapses."

Neuroscientist Solomon H. Snyder (1984)

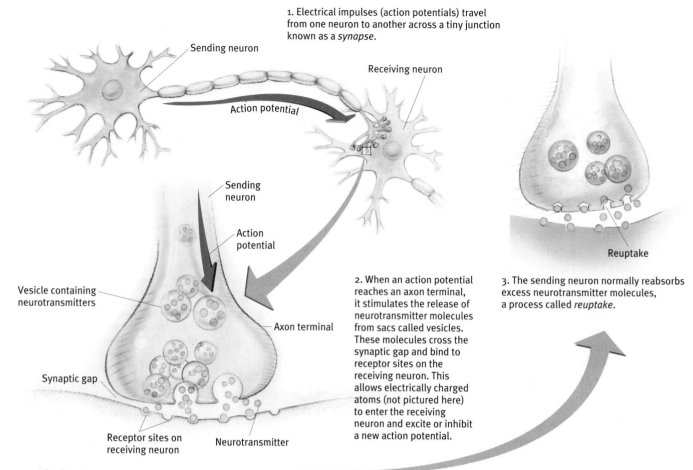

1. Electrical impulses (action potentials) travel from one neuron to another across a tiny junction known as a *synapse.*

Sending neuron

Receiving neuron

Action potential

Sending neuron

Action potential

Vesicle containing neurotransmitters

Axon terminal

Synaptic gap

Receptor sites on receiving neuron

Neurotransmitter

2. When an action potential reaches an axon terminal, it stimulates the release of neurotransmitter molecules from sacs called vesicles. These molecules cross the synaptic gap and bind to receptor sites on the receiving neuron. This allows electrically charged atoms (not pictured here) to enter the receiving neuron and excite or inhibit a new action potential.

Reuptake

3. The sending neuron normally reabsorbs excess neurotransmitter molecules, a process called *reuptake.*

figure 2.2
How neurons communicate

How Neurotransmitters Influence Us

4. How do neurotransmitters influence human behavior?

"When it comes to the brain, if you want to see the action, follow the neurotransmitters."

Neuroscientist Floyd Bloom (1993)

As researchers discovered dozens of different neurotransmitters, they also encountered new questions: Are certain neurotransmitters found only in specific places? What are their effects? Can we boost or diminish these effects through drugs or diet? Could such changes affect our moods, memories, or mental abilities?

Later in this text, we examine the role of neurotransmitters in depression and euphoria, hunger and thinking, addictions and therapy. For now, let's glimpse how neurotransmitters influence our motions and our emotions. We now know that a particular neural pathway in the brain may use only one or two neurotransmitters (**FIGURE 2.3**), and that particular neurotransmitters may have particular effects on behavior and emotions (**TABLE 2.1** offers examples).

figure 2.3
Neurotransmitter pathways
Each of the brain's differing chemical messengers has designated pathways where it operates, as shown here for dopamine and serotonin (Carter, 1998).

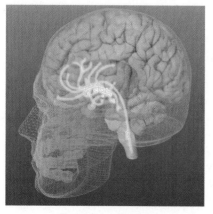

Dopamine pathways

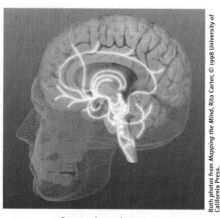

Serotonin pathways

Both photos from *Mapping the Mind,* Rita Carter, © 1998 University of California Press.

table 2.1 Some Neurotransmitters and Their Functions

Neurotransmitter	Function	Examples of Malfunctions
Acetylcholine (ACh)	Enables muscle action, learning, and memory.	Undersupply, as ACh-producing neurons deteriorate, marks Alzheimer's disease.
Dopamine	Influences movement, learning, attention, and emotion.	Excess dopamine receptor activity linked to schizophrenia. Starved of dopamine, the brain produces the tremors and decreased mobility of Parkinson's disease.
Serotonin	Affects mood, hunger, sleep, and arousal.	Undersupply linked to depression. Prozac and some other antidepressant drugs raise serotonin levels.
Norepinephrine	Helps control alertness and arousal.	Undersupply can depress mood.
GABA (gamma-aminobutyric acid)	A major inhibitory neurotransmitter.	Undersupply linked to seizures, tremors, and insomnia.
Glutamate	A major excitatory neurotransmitter; involved in memory.	Oversupply can overstimulate brain, producing migraines or seizures (which is why some people avoid MSG, monosodium glutamate, in food).

Duomo/Corbis

Molecules and muscles When your body moves, a flood of acetylcholine molecules triggers the muscle action.

Acetylcholine (ACh) is one of the best-understood neurotransmitters. In addition to its vital role in learning and memory, ACh is the messenger at every junction between a motor neuron and skeletal muscle. When ACh is released to our muscle cells, the muscle contracts.

If the transmission of ACh is blocked, the muscles cannot contract. Curare, a poison that certain South American Indians apply to the tips of their hunting darts, occupies and blocks ACh receptor sites, leaving the neurotransmitter unable to affect the muscles. Struck by one of these darts, an animal becomes paralyzed. Botulin, a poison that can form in improperly canned food, causes paralysis by blocking ACh release from the sending neuron. (Injections of botulin—Botox— smooth wrinkles by paralyzing the underlying facial muscles.) By contrast, the venom of the black widow spider causes a synaptic flood of ACh. The result? Violent muscle contractions, convulsions, and possible death.

The Endorphins

An exciting discovery about neurotransmitters occurred when Candace Pert and Solomon Snyder (1973) attached a radioactive tracer to morphine, showing them where it was taken up in an animal's brain. Their discovery: The morphine, an opiate drug that elevates mood and eases pain, bound to receptors in areas linked with mood and pain sensations.

It was hard to imagine why the brain would contain these "opiate receptors" unless it had its own naturally occurring opiates. Why would the brain have a chemical lock, unless it also had a corresponding key? Researchers soon confirmed that the brain does indeed contain several types of neurotransmitter molecules similar to morphine. Named **endorphins** (short for *end*ogenous [produced within] m*orphin*e), these natural opiates are released in response to pain and vigorous exercise. They may therefore help explain all sorts of good feelings, such as the "runner's high," the painkilling effects of acupuncture, and the indifference to pain in some severely injured people, such as David Livingstone reported in his 1857 *Missionary Travels*:

> I heard a shout. Starting, and looking half round, I saw the lion just in the act of springing upon me. I was upon a little height, he caught my shoulder as he sprang, and we both came to the ground below together. Growling horribly close to my ear, he shook me as a

▶ **endorphins [en-DOR-fins]** "morphine within"—natural, opiatelike neurotransmitters linked to pain control and to pleasure.

Physician Lewis Thomas, on the endorphins: "There it is, a biologically universal act of mercy. I cannot explain it, except to say that I would have put it in had I been around at the very beginning, sitting as a member of a planning committee."

The Youngest Science, *1983*

▶ **nervous system** the body's speedy, electrochemical communication system, consisting of all the nerve cells of the peripheral and central nervous systems.

▶ **central nervous system (CNS)** the brain and spinal cord.

▶ **peripheral nervous system (PNS)** the sensory and motor neurons that connect the central nervous system (CNS) to the rest of the body.

▶ **nerves** neural "cables" containing many axons. These bundled axons, which are part of the peripheral nervous system, connect the central nervous system with muscles, glands, and sense organs.

terrier does a rat. The shock produced a stupor similar to that which seems to be felt by a mouse after the first shake of the cat. It caused a sort of dreaminess in which there was no sense of pain nor feeling of terror, though [I was] quite conscious of all that was happening. . . . This peculiar state is probably produced in all animals killed by the carnivora; and if so, is a merciful provision by our benevolent Creator for lessening the pain of death.

How Drugs and Other Chemicals Alter Neurotransmission

If indeed the endorphins lessen pain and boost mood, why not flood the brain with artificial opiates, thereby intensifying the brain's own "feel-good" chemistry? One problem is that when flooded with opiate drugs such as heroin and morphine, the brain may stop producing its own natural opiates. When the drug is withdrawn, the brain may then be deprived of any form of opiate. For a drug addict, the result is discomfort that persists until the brain resumes production of its natural opiates or receives more artificial opiates. As we will see in later chapters, mood-altering drugs, from alcohol to nicotine to heroin, share a common effect: They trigger unpleasant, lingering aftereffects. For suppressing the body's own neurotransmitter production, nature charges a price.

Various drugs affect communication at the synapse, often by either exciting or inhibiting neurons' firing. *Agonists* excite. An agonist molecule may be similar enough to the neurotransmitter to mimic its effects, or it may block the neurotransmitter's reuptake (**FIGURE 2.4**). Some opiate drugs, for example, produce a temporary "high" by amplifying normal sensations of arousal or pleasure. *Antagonists* inhibit. An antagonist can be a drug molecule that inhibits a neurotransmitter's release. Or it may be enough like the natural neurotransmitter to occupy its receptor site and block its effect but not similar enough to stimulate the receptor (rather like foreign coins that fit into, but won't operate, a soda or candy machine). Curare

figure 2.4
Agonists and antagonists

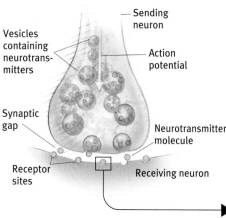

Neurotransmitters carry a message from a sending neuron across a synapse to receptor sites on a receiving neuron.

This neurotransmitter molecule has a molecular structure that precisely fits the receptor site on the receiving neuron, much as a key fits a lock.

This agonist molecule excites. It is similar enough in structure to the neurotransmitter molecule that it mimics its effects on the receiving neuron. Morphine, for instance, mimics the action of endorphins by stimulating receptors in brain areas involved in mood and pain sensations.

This antagonist molecule inhibits. It has a structure similar enough to the neurotransmitter to occupy its receptor site and block its action, but not similar enough to stimulate the receptor. Curare poisoning paralyzes its victims by blocking ACh receptors involved in muscle movement.

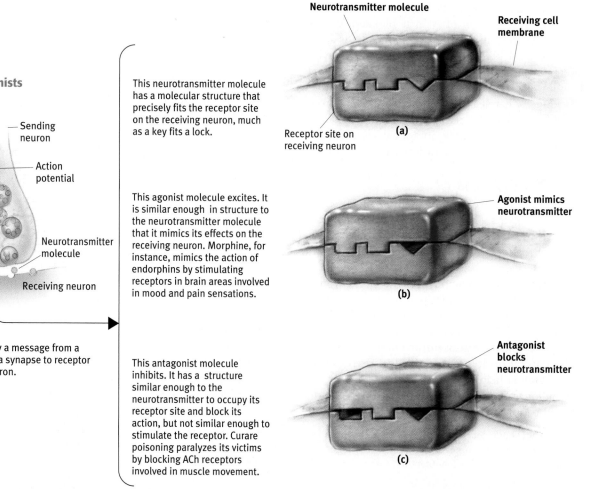

poison causes paralysis by blocking receptors for acetylcholine, a neurotransmitter that produces muscle movement.

Neurotransmitter research is leading to new drug therapies, but designing such drugs can be harder than it sounds. A *blood-brain barrier* enables the brain to fence out unwanted chemicals circulating in the blood, and some chemicals don't have the right shape to slither through this barrier. Scientists know, for example, that the tremors of Parkinson's disease result from the death of nerve cells that produce dopamine. Giving the patient dopamine doesn't help, because dopamine cannot cross the blood-brain barrier. But L-dopa, a raw material the brain can convert to dopamine, can sneak through, enabling many patients to regain better muscular control.

rehearse it!

1. The neuron fiber that carries messages to other neurons is the
   a. dendrite.   c. cell body.
   b. axon.   d. myelin.

2. The neuron's response to stimulation is an *all-or-none* response, meaning that the intensity of the stimulus determines
   a. whether or not an impulse is generated.
   b. how fast an impulse is transmitted.
   c. how intense an impulse will be.
   d. whether the stimulus is excitatory or inhibitory.

3. There is a minuscule space between the axon of a sending neuron and the dendrite or cell body of a receiving neuron. This small space is called the
   a. axon terminal.
   b. sac or vesicle.
   c. synaptic gap.
   d. threshold.

4. When the action potential reaches the axon terminal of a neuron, it triggers the release of chemical messengers called
   a. dendrites.
   b. synapses.

   c. neural impulses.
   d. neurotransmitters.

5. Endorphins are released in the brain in response to
   a. morphine or heroin.
   b. pain or vigorous exercise.
   c. antagonists.
   d. all of the above.

Answers can be found in Appendix C.

THE NERVOUS SYSTEM

5. *What are the major divisions of the nervous system, and what are their basic functions?*

Neurons communicating with other neurons form our body's primary information system, the **nervous system** (**FIGURE 2.5**). The brain and spinal cord form the **central nervous system (CNS)**. The **peripheral nervous system (PNS)** links the central nervous system with the body's sense receptors, muscles, and glands. The sensory and motor axons carrying this PNS information are bundled into the electrical cables that we know as **nerves**. The optic nerve, for example, bundles a million axon fibers into a single cable carrying the information that each eye sends to the brain (Mason & Kandel, 1991).

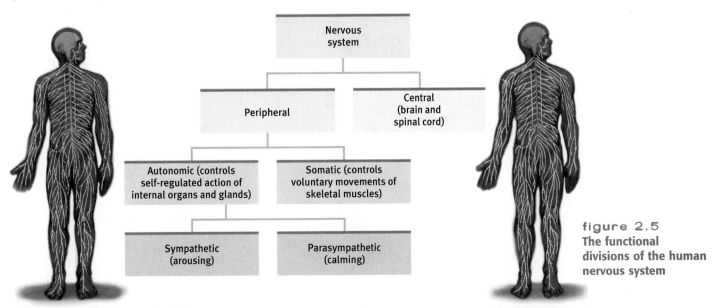

figure 2.5
The functional divisions of the human nervous system

Information travels in the nervous system through three types of neurons. The **sensory neurons** send information from the body's tissues and sensory organs inward to the brain and spinal cord, which process the information. This processing involves a second class of neurons, the central nervous system's own **interneurons**, which enable its internal communication. The central nervous system then sends instructions out to the body's tissues via the **motor neurons**. Our complexity, though, resides mostly in our interneuron systems. Our nervous system has a few million sensory neurons, a few million motor neurons, but billions and billions of interneurons. Supporting these billions of nerve cells are nine times as many *glial cells*—"glue cells" that guide neural connections, provide nutrients and insulating myelin, and mop up debris.

The Peripheral Nervous System

Our peripheral nervous system has two components—somatic and autonomic. The **somatic nervous system** controls the movements of our skeletal muscles. As you reach the bottom of the next page, the somatic nervous system will report to your brain the current state of your skeletal muscles and carry instructions back, triggering your hand to turn the page.

Our **autonomic nervous system** controls the glands and the muscles of your internal organs. (*Autonomic* means self-regulating.) Like an automatic pilot, this system may be consciously overridden. But usually it operates on its own to influence internal functioning, including heartbeat, digestion, and glandular activity.

The autonomic nervous system is a dual system (**FIGURE 2.6**). The **sympathetic nervous system** arouses you for defensive action. If something alarms or enrages

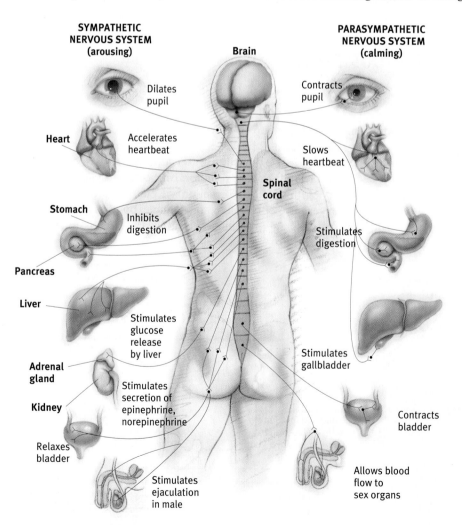

figure 2.6
The dual functions of the autonomic nervous system The autonomic nervous system controls the more autonomous (or self-regulating) internal functions. Its sympathetic division arouses and expends energy. Its parasympathetic division calms and conserves energy, allowing routine maintenance activity. For example, sympathetic stimulation accelerates heartbeat, whereas parasympathetic stimulation slows it.

SYMPATHETIC NERVOUS SYSTEM (arousing)

Dilates pupil
Accelerates heartbeat
Inhibits digestion
Stimulates glucose release by liver
Stimulates secretion of epinephrine, norepinephrine
Relaxes bladder
Stimulates ejaculation in male

Brain

Spinal cord

Heart
Stomach
Pancreas
Liver
Adrenal gland
Kidney

PARASYMPATHETIC NERVOUS SYSTEM (calming)

Contracts pupil
Slows heartbeat
Stimulates digestion
Stimulates gallbladder
Contracts bladder
Allows blood flow to sex organs

you, the sympathetic system will accelerate your heartbeat, slow your digestion, raise your blood sugar, dilate your arteries, and cool you with perspiration, making you alert and ready for action. (Lie-detection machines measure such stress responses, which may or may not accompany lies.) When the stress subsides, the **parasympathetic nervous system** produces opposite effects. It conserves energy as it calms you by decreasing your heartbeat, lowering your blood sugar, and so forth. In everyday situations, the sympathetic and parasympathetic nervous systems work together to keep you in a steady internal state.

The Central Nervous System

From the simplicity of neurons "talking" to other neurons arises the complexity of the central nervous system that enables our humanity—our thinking, feeling, and acting. Tens of billions of neurons, each communicating with thousands of other neurons, yield an ever-changing wiring diagram that dwarfs a powerful computer. Your brain alone has some 30 billion neurons, each having roughly 10,000 contacts with other neurons. A grain-of-sand–sized speck of your brain contains some 100,000 neurons and one billion "talking" synapses (Ramachandran & Blakeslee, 1998).

Neurons cluster into work groups called *neural networks*. To understand why neurons tend to connect with nearby neurons, Stephen Kosslyn and Oliver Koenig (1992, p. 12) invite us to "think about why cities exist; why don't people distribute themselves more evenly across the countryside?" Like people networking with people, neurons network with nearby neurons with which they can have short, fast connections. One of the great remaining scientific mysteries is how this neural machinery organizes itself into these complex circuits capable of learning, feeling, and thinking.

The spinal cord is an information highway connecting the peripheral nervous system to the brain. Ascending neural fibers send up sensory information, and descending fibers send back motor-control information.

The neural pathways governing our **reflexes**, our automatic responses to stimuli, illustrate the spinal cord's work. A simple spinal reflex pathway is composed of a single sensory neuron and a single motor neuron. These often communicate through an interneuron. The knee-jerk response, for example, involves one such simple pathway; a headless warm body could do it.

Another such pathway enables the pain reflex (**FIGURE 2.7**). When your fingers touch a flame, neural activity excited by the heat travels via sensory neurons to

▶ **sensory neurons** neurons that carry incoming information from the sense receptors to the central nervous system.

▶ **interneurons** central nervous system neurons that internally communicate and intervene between the sensory inputs and motor outputs.

▶ **motor neurons** neurons that carry outgoing information from the central nervous system to the muscles and glands.

▶ **somatic nervous system** the division of the peripheral nervous system that controls the body's skeletal muscles. Also called the *skeletal nervous system.*

▶ **autonomic [aw-tuh-NAHM-ik] nervous system** the part of the peripheral nervous system that controls the glands and the muscles of the internal organs (such as the heart). Its sympathetic division arouses; its parasympathetic division calms.

▶ **sympathetic nervous system** the division of the autonomic nervous system that arouses the body, mobilizing its energy in stressful situations.

▶ **parasympathetic nervous system** the division of the autonomic nervous system that calms the body, conserving its energy.

▶ **reflex** a simple, automatic, inborn response to a sensory stimulus, such as the knee-jerk response.

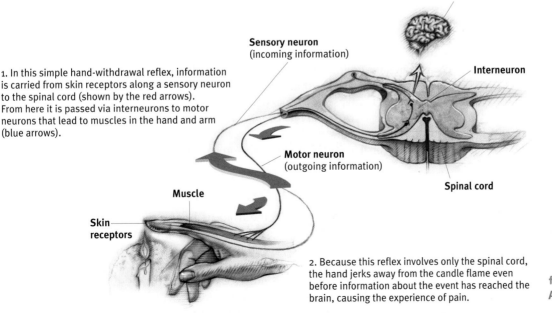

1. In this simple hand-withdrawal reflex, information is carried from skin receptors along a sensory neuron to the spinal cord (shown by the red arrows). From here it is passed via interneurons to motor neurons that lead to muscles in the hand and arm (blue arrows).

Brain

Sensory neuron (incoming information)

Interneuron

Motor neuron (outgoing information)

Spinal cord

Muscle

Skin receptors

2. Because this reflex involves only the spinal cord, the hand jerks away from the candle flame even before information about the event has reached the brain, causing the experience of pain.

figure 2.7
A simple reflex

"The body is made up of millions and millions of crumbs."

interneurons in your spinal cord. These interneurons respond by activating motor neurons to the muscles in your arm. That's why it feels as if your hand jerks away not by your choice, but on its own.

Because the simple pain reflex pathway runs through the spinal cord and out, your hand jerks from the candle's flame *before* your brain receives and responds to the information that causes you to feel pain. Information travels to and from the brain by way of the spinal cord. Were the top of your spinal cord severed, you would not feel pain. Nor would you feel pleasure. Your brain would literally be out of touch with your body. You would lose all sensation and voluntary movement in body regions whose sensory and motor neurons connect with the spinal cord below its point of injury.

With the severing of the brain center that keeps the brakes on erections, men paralyzed below the waist are easily capable of an erection (a simple reflex) if their genitals are stimulated (Goldstein, 2000). Females similarly paralyzed respond with vaginal lubrication. But, depending on where and how completely the spinal cord is severed, they may be genitally unresponsive to erotic images and have no genital feeling (Kennedy & Over, 1990; Sipski & Alexander, 1999). To produce bodily pain or pleasure, the sensory information must reach the brain.

rehearse it!

6. The autonomic nervous system controls internal functions, such as heart rate and glandular activity. The word *autonomic* means
   a. peripheral.
   b. voluntary.
   c. self-regulating.
   d. arousing.

7. Usually, the sympathetic nervous system arouses us for action and the parasympathetic nervous system calms us down. Together, the two systems make up the
   a. autonomic nervous system.
   b. somatic nervous system.
   c. central nervous system.
   d. peripheral nervous system.

8. The neurons of the spinal cord are part of the
   a. somatic nervous system.
   b. central nervous system.
   c. autonomic nervous system.
   d. peripheral nervous system.

Answers can be found in Appendix C.

THE BRAIN

Imagine that just moments before your death, someone removed your brain from your body and kept it alive by pumping enriched blood through it as it floated in a tank of cerebral fluid. Would you now still be in there? Further imagine, to carry our fantasy to its limit, that someone transplanted your still-living brain into the body of a person with severe brain damage. To whose home should the recovered patient return?

That we can imagine such questions illustrates how convinced we are that we live in our heads. And for good reason: The brain enables the mind—seeing, hearing, remembering, thinking, feeling, speaking, dreaming. It is the brain that self-reflectively analyzes the brain. When we're thinking about our brain, we're thinking *with* our brain—by firing millions of synapses and releasing billions of neurotransmitter molecules. Indeed, say neuroscientists, the *mind is what the brain does*. But precisely where and how are the mind's functions tied to the brain? (To see how scientists explore such questions, see the Close-Up on The Tools of Discovery on page 48.)

"I am a brain, Watson. The rest of me is a mere appendix."

Sherlock Holmes, in Arthur Conan Doyle's *"The Adventure of the Mazarin Stone"*

Lower-Level Brain Structures

Clues to an animal's capacities come from its brain structures. In primitive vertebrate (backboned) animals, such as sharks, the brain primarily regulates basic survival functions: breathing, resting, and feeding. In lower mammals, such as rodents, a more complex brain enables emotion and greater memory. In advanced mammals, such as humans, the brain processes more information, letting us act with foresight. To enable this increasing complexity, species have elaborated new brain systems on top of the old, much as the Earth's landscape covers the old with the

"You're certainly a lot less fun since the operation."

new. Digging down, one discovers the fossil remnants of the past—brainstem components still performing much as they did for our distant ancestors. Starting with the brainstem and working up, let's now explore the brain.

The Brainstem

6. What are the functions of the brainstem and its associated structures?

The brain's basement—its oldest and innermost region—is the **brainstem**. It begins where the spinal cord enters the skull and swells slightly, forming the **medulla**. Here lie the controls for your heartbeat and breathing. If the top of a cat's brainstem is severed from the rest of the brain above it, the animal will still breathe and live—and even run, climb, and groom (Klemm, 1990). But cut off from the brain's higher region, it won't purposefully run or climb to get food.

The brainstem is also the crossover point, where most nerves to and from each side of the brain connect with the body's opposite side. This peculiar cross-wiring is but one of many surprises the brain has to offer.

Inside the brainstem, between your ears, lies the **reticular** ("netlike") **formation**, a finger-shaped network of neurons that extends from the spinal cord right up to the thalamus (see Figure 2.8). As the spinal cord's sensory input travels up to the thalamus, some of it travels through the reticular formation, which filters incoming stimuli and relays important information to other areas of the brain. Among its other functions, the reticular formation helps control arousal.

In 1949, Giuseppe Moruzzi and Horace Magoun discovered that electrically stimulating the reticular formation of a sleeping cat almost instantly produced an awake, alert animal. But when Magoun *severed* a cat's reticular formation from higher brain regions, without damaging the nearby sensory pathways, the cat lapsed into a coma from which it never awakened.

The Thalamus

Atop the brainstem sits the brain's sensory switchboard, a joined pair of egg-shaped structures called the **thalamus** (**FIGURE 2.8**). It receives information from all the senses except smell and routes it to the higher brain regions that deal with seeing, hearing, tasting, and touching. Think of the thalamus as being to sensory input what London is to England's trains: a hub through which traffic passes en route to various destinations. The thalamus also receives some of the higher brain's replies, which it then directs to the medulla and to the cerebellum.

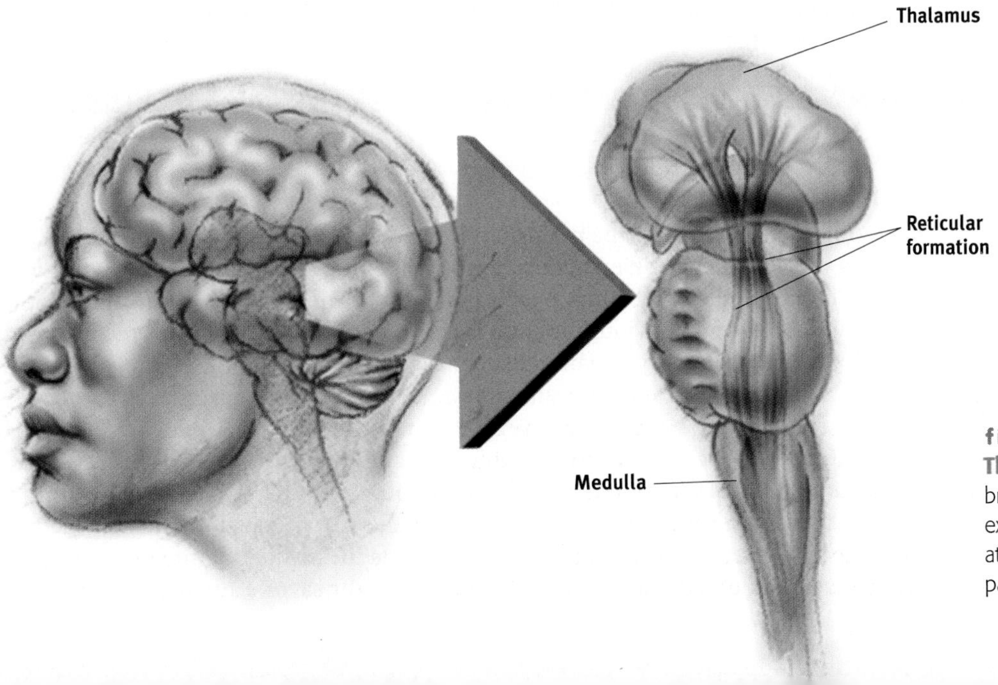

▶ **brainstem** the oldest part and central core of the brain, beginning where the spinal cord swells as it enters the skull; the brainstem is responsible for automatic survival functions.

▶ **medulla** [muh-DUL-uh] the base of the brainstem; controls heartbeat and breathing.

▶ **reticular formation** a nerve network in the brainstem that plays an important role in controlling arousal.

▶ **thalamus** [THAL-uh-muss] the brain's sensory switchboard, located on top of the brainstem; it directs messages to the sensory receiving areas in the cortex and transmits replies to the cerebellum and medulla.

Thalamus

Reticular formation

Medulla

figure 2.8
The brainstem and thalamus The brainstem, including the medulla, is an extension of the spinal cord. The thalamus is attached to its top. The reticular formation passes through both structures.

CLOSE-UP

The Tools of Discovery

It is exciting to consider how fast and how far the neurosciences have progressed within a lifetime. For centuries, we had no tools high-powered yet gentle enough to explore the living human brain. Now, however, techniques for peering into the thinking, feeling brain are doing for psychology what the microscope did for biology and the telescope did for astronomy.

Clinical Observation

The oldest method of studying brain-mind connections is to observe the effects of specific brain diseases and injuries. Physicians noted that damage to one side of the brain often caused numbness or paralysis on the body's opposite side, suggesting that the right side of the body is wired to the brain's left side, and vice versa. Others noticed that damage to the back of the brain disrupted vision, and that damage to the left-front part of the brain produced speech difficulties. Gradually, these early explorers were mapping the brain.

Manipulating the Brain

Today's scientists do not need to await brain injuries. They can elec-trically, chemically, or magnetically *stimulate* various parts of the brain and note the effects. They can also surgically **lesion** tiny clusters of normal or defective cells in specific brain areas, leaving their surroundings unharmed. For example, a lesion in one area of the hypothalamus in a rat's brain reduces eating, causing the rat to starve unless force-fed. A lesion in another area produces *over*eating.

Recording the Brain's Electrical Activity

Right now, your mental activity is giving off telltale electrical, metabolic, and magnetic signals that would enable neuroscientists to eavesdrop on your brain. The tips of modern microelectrodes are so small they can detect the electrical pulse in a single neuron. For example, we can now detect exactly where the information goes in a cat's brain when someone strokes its whisker.

We can also snoop on the mass action of billions of neurons as their electrical activity sweeps in regular waves across the brain's surface. The **electroencephalogram (EEG)** is an amplified tracing of such waves (**FIGURE 2.9**).

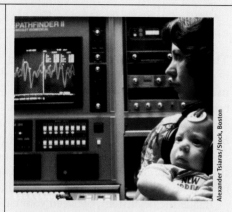

figure 2.9
An electroencephalograph providing amplified tracings of waves of electrical activity in the brain Here it is detecting brain response to sound, making possible an early evaluation of what may be a hearing impairment.

Neuroimaging Techniques

Other new windows into the brain give us a Supermanlike ability to see inside the brain without lesioning it. One such tool, the **PET (positron emission tomography) scan** (**FIGURE 2.10**), depicts brain activity by showing each brain area's consumption of its chemical fuel, the sugar glucose (see Figure 2.21, page 57). Active neurons are glucose hogs. A person is given a temporarily radioactive form of glucose, and

The Cerebellum

Extending from the rear of the brainstem is the **cerebellum**, meaning "little brain," which is what its two wrinkled hemispheres rather look like (**FIGURE 2.12**). As you will see in Chapter 8, the cerebellum enables one type of nonverbal learning and memory. However, its most obvious function is coordinating voluntary movement. If you injured your cerebellum, you would likely have difficulty walking, keeping your balance, or shaking hands. Your movements would be jerky and exaggerated.

Note: These lower brain functions all occur without any conscious effort. This illustrates another of our recurring themes: *Our brain processes most information outside of our awareness.* We are aware of the *results* of our brain's labor (say, our current visual experience) but not of *how* we construct the visual image. Likewise, whether we are asleep or awake, our brainstem manages its life-sustaining functions, freeing our higher brain regions to dream or to think, talk, or savor a memory.

▶ **cerebellum [sehr-uh-BELL-um]** the "little brain" attached to the rear of the brainstem; it helps coordinate voluntary movement and balance.

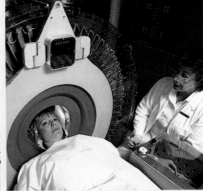

figure 2.10
The PET scan To obtain a PET scan, researchers inject volunteers with a low and harmless dose of a short-lived radioactive sugar. Detectors around the subject's head pick up the release of gamma rays from the sugar, which has concentrated in active brain areas. A computer then processes and translates these signals into a map of the brain at work.

the PET scan locates and measures the radioactivity, thereby detecting where this "food for thought" goes. By noting these "hot spots," researchers can see which brain areas are most active as the person performs mathematical calculations, listens to music, or daydreams.

In **MRI (magnetic resonance imaging)** scans, the head is put in a strong magnetic field, which aligns the spinning atoms of brain molecules. Then a brief pulse of radio waves disorients the atoms momentarily. When the atoms return to their normal spin, they release signals that provide a detailed picture of the brain's soft tissues. MRI scans can, for example, reveal enlarged fluid-filled brain areas in some patients who have schizophrenia, a disabling psychological disorder (**FIGURE 2.11**).

A special application of MRI can reveal the brain's functioning as well as its structure. Where the brain is especially active, blood goes. MRI scans, taken less than a second apart, show the brain lighting up (with increased oxygen-laden blood-flow) as a research participant performs different mental functions. As the person looks at a face, a *functional MRI* (fMRI) machine detects blood rushing to the back of the brain, which processes visual information (see Figure 2.17, page 54). Such snapshots of the brain's activity provide new insights into how the brain divides its labor.

Clearly, this is the golden age of brain science. To be learning about the neurosciences now is like studying world geography while Magellan was exploring the seas.

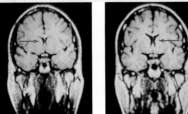

figure 2.11
MRI scan of a healthy individual (left) and a person with schizophrenia (right) Note the enlarged fluid-filled brain region in the image on the right.

▶ **lesion [LEE-zhuhn]** tissue destruction. A brain lesion is a naturally or experimentally caused destruction of brain tissue.

▶ **electroencephalogram (EEG)** an amplified recording of the waves of electrical activity that sweep across the brain's surface. These waves are measured by electrodes placed on the scalp.

▶ **PET (positron emission tomography) scan** a visual display of brain activity that detects where a radioactive form of glucose goes while the brain performs a given task.

▶ **MRI (magnetic resonance imaging)** a technique that uses magnetic fields and radio waves to produce computer-generated images that distinguish among different types of soft tissue; allows us to see structures within the brain.

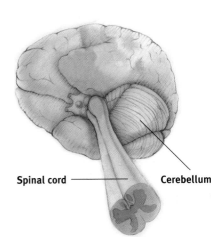

Spinal cord ——— Cerebellum

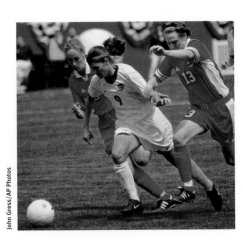

figure 2.12
The brain's organ of agility Hanging at the back of the brain, the cerebellum coordinates our movements, as when Mia Hamm directs the ball precisely.

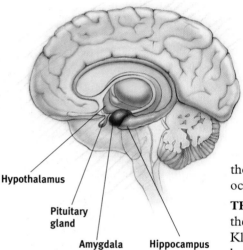

figure 2.13
The limbic system Limbic structures form a doughnut-shaped neural system between the brain's older parts and its cerebral hemispheres. Although part of the hormonal (endocrine) system, not the brain, the pituitary gland is controlled by the limbic system's hypothalamus, just above it.

Labels: Hypothalamus · Pituitary gland · Amygdala · Hippocampus

The Limbic System

7. What are the functions of limbic system structures?

At the border ("limbus") of the brain's older parts and the cerebral hemi-spheres—the two halves of the brain—is a doughnut-shaped neural system, the **limbic system** (**FIGURE 2.13**). We will see in Chapter 8 how one limbic system component, the *hippocampus*, processes memory. (If animals or humans lose their hippocampus to surgery or injury, they become unable to lay down new memories of facts and episodes.) For now, let's look at the limbic system's links to emotions such as fear and anger, and to basic motives such as those for food and sex. The limbic system's influence on emotions and motives occurs partly through its control of the body's hormones.

THE AMYGDALA In the limbic system, two almond-shaped neural clusters, called the **amygdala**, influence aggression and fear. In 1939, psychologist Heinrich Klüver and neurosurgeon Paul Bucy surgically lesioned the part of a rhesus monkey's brain that included the amygdala. The result? The normally ill-tempered monkey turned into the most mellow of creatures. Poke it, pinch it, do virtually anything that normally would trigger a ferocious response, and still the animal remained placid. What then might happen if we electrically stimulated the amygdala in a normally placid domestic animal such as a cat? Do so in one spot and the cat prepares to attack, hissing with its back arched, its pupils dilated, its hair on end. Move the electrode only slightly within the amygdala, cage the cat with a small mouse, and now it cowers in terror.

These experiments confirm the amygdala's role in rage and fear, not to mention the perception of such emotions and the processing of emotional memories (Anderson & Phelps, 2000; Poremba & Gabriel, 2001). Still, we must be careful not

The amygdala

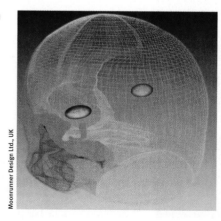

Moonrunner Design Ltd., UK

Frank Siteman/Stock, Boston

Aggression as a brain state Back arched and fur fluffed, this fierce cat is ready to attack. Electrical stimulation of a cat's amygdala provokes reactions such as the one shown here, suggesting its role in emotions like rage. Which division of the autonomic nervous system is activated by such stimulation? (See page 52.)

to think of the amygdala as *the* control center for aggression and fear. The brain is *not* neatly organized into structures that correspond to our categories of behavior. Actually, both aggressive and fearful behavior involve neural activity in all levels of the brain. Even within the limbic system, stimulating neural structures other than the amygdala can evoke such behavior. If you put a charge to your car's dead battery, you can activate the engine. Yet the battery is merely one link in an integrated system.

THE HYPOTHALAMUS Another of the limbic system's fascinating structures lies just below (*hypo*) the thalamus, and so is called the **hypothalamus**. Neuroscientists, by lesioning or stimulating different areas in the hypothalamus, have isolated within it neural networks that perform specific maintenance duties for the body. Some neural clusters influence hunger; still others regulate thirst, body temperature, and sexual behavior.

The hypothalamus both monitors blood chemistry and takes orders from other parts of the brain. For example, thinking about sex (in your brain's cerebral cortex) can stimulate your hypothalamus to secrete hormones. Through these hormones, the hypothalamus controls the adjacent "master gland," the pituitary (see Figure 2.13), which in turn influences hormone release by other glands, which the hypothalamus monitors. (Note the interplay between the nervous and hormone systems: The brain influences the hormone system, which in turn influences the brain.)

The story of a remarkable discovery about the hypothalamus illustrates how progress in scientific research often occurs—when curious, open-minded investigators make an unexpected observation. Two young McGill University neuropsychologists, James Olds and Peter Milner (1954), were trying to implant electrodes in the reticular formations of white rats when they made a magnificent mistake. In one rat, they incorrectly placed an electrode in what was later discovered to be a region of the hypothalamus (Olds, 1975). Curiously, the rat kept returning to the place on its tabletop enclosure where it had been stimulated by this misplaced electrode, as if seeking more stimulation. Upon discovering their mistake, they alertly recognized that they had stumbled upon a brain center that provides a pleasurable reward.

In a meticulous series of experiments, Olds (1958) went on to locate other "pleasure centers," as he called them. (What the rats actually experience only they know. And they aren't telling. Today's scientists do not want to attribute human feelings to rats, so they refer to *reward centers*, not "pleasure centers.") When Olds allowed rats to trigger their own stimulation in these areas by pressing a pedal, he noticed that they would sometimes do so at a feverish pace—up to 7000 times per hour—until they dropped from exhaustion. Moreover, they would do anything to get this stimulation, even cross an electrified floor that a starving rat would not cross to reach food (**FIGURE 2.14**).

Similar reward centers in or near the hypothalamus were later discovered in many other species, including goldfish, dolphins, and monkeys. In fact, animal research has revealed both a general reward system that triggers the release of the neurotransmitter dopamine and specific centers associated with the pleasures of eating, drinking, and sex. Animals, it seems, come equipped with built-in systems that reward activities essential to survival.

By using brain stimulation to reward rats for turning left or right (when electrodes stimulate a brain region that makes them feel as if their left or right whiskers have been touched), Sanjiv Talwar and his colleagues (2002) trained rats that had never been outdoors to navigate natural environments. By pressing buttons on a laptop, the researchers can direct a rat—which carries a receiver, power source, and video camera on a backpack—to turn

▶ **limbic system** a doughnut-shaped system of neural structures at the border of the brainstem and cerebral hemispheres; associated with emotions such as fear and aggression and drives such as those for food and sex. Includes the hippocampus, amygdala, and hypothalamus.

▶ **amygdala** [uh-MIG-duh-la] two almond-shaped neural clusters that are components of the limbic system and are linked to emotion.

▶ **hypothalamus** [hi-po-THAL-uh-muss] a neural structure lying below (*hypo*) the thalamus; it directs several maintenance activities (eating, drinking, body temperature), helps govern the endocrine system via the pituitary gland, and is linked to emotion.

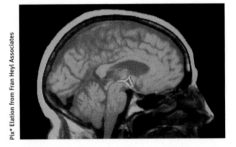

Pix* Elation from Fran Heyl Associates

The hypothalamus This small but important structure, colored in red in this MRI brain scan photograph, helps keep the body's internal environment in a steady state by regulating thirst, hunger, and body temperature. Its activity also influences experiences of pleasurable reward.

"If you were designing a robot vehicle to walk into the future and survive, . . . you'd wire it up so that behavior that ensured the survival of the self or the species—like sex and eating—would be naturally reinforcing."

Candace Pert (1986)

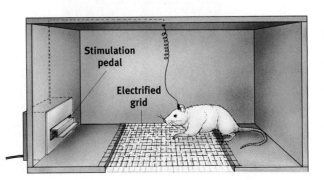

Stimulation pedal

Electrified grid

figure 2.14 Rat with an implanted electrode With an electrode implanted in a reward center of its hypothalamus, the rat readily crosses an electrified grid, accepting the painful shocks, to press a lever that sends electrical impulses to its "pleasure centers."

Ratbot on a pleasure cruise When stimulated by remote control, this rat could be guided to navigate across a field and even up a tree.

Sanjiv Talwar, SUNY Downstate

The cat on page 50 is aroused via its sympathetic nervous system.

on cue, climb trees, scurry along branches, and turn around and come back down. Their work suggests future applications in search-and-rescue operations.

Dramatic findings like these have led people to wonder whether humans, too, might have limbic centers for pleasure. Indeed we do. One neurosurgeon used electrodes to calm violent patients. Stimulated patients reported mild pleasure; however, unlike Olds' rats, they were not driven to a frenzy by it (Deutsch, 1972; Hooper & Teresi, 1986). Some researchers believe that addictive disorders, such as alcoholism, drug abuse, and binge eating, may stem from a *reward deficiency syndrome*—a genetically disposed deficiency in the natural brain systems for pleasure and well-being that leads people to crave whatever provides that missing pleasure or relieves negative feelings (Blum & others, 1996).

rehearse it!

13. The limbic system, a doughnut-shaped structure at the border of the brain's older parts and the cerebral hemispheres, is associated with basic motives, emotions, and memory functions. Two parts of the limbic system are the amygdala and the
    a. reticular formation.
    b. hippocampus.
    c. thalamus.
    d. medulla.

14. A ferocious response to electrical brain stimulation would lead you to suppose that the electrode had been touching the
    a. medulla.   c. hypothalamus.
    b. pituitary.   d. amygdala.

15. The neural structure that most directly regulates eating, drinking, and body temperature is the
    a. cerebellum.   c. thalamus.
    b. hypothalamus.   d. amygdala.

16. The reward centers discovered by Olds and Milner were located in regions of the
    a. cerebral cortex.
    b. brainstem.
    c. hypothalamus.
    d. spinal cord.

Answers can be found in Appendix C.

The Cerebral Cortex

Your **cerebral cortex** is an intricate covering of interconnected neural cells that, like bark on a tree, forms a thin surface layer on your cerebral hemispheres. It is your body's ultimate control and information-processing center.

With the elaboration of the cerebral cortex, tight genetic controls relax and the organism's adaptability increases. Frogs and other amphibians have a small cortex and operate extensively on preprogrammed genetic instructions. The larger cortex of mammals offers increased capacities for learning and thinking, enabling them to be more adaptable.

The people who first dissected and labeled the brain used the language of scholars—Latin and Greek. Their words are actually attempts at graphic description: For example, cortex means "bark," cerebellum is "little brain," and thalamus is "inner chamber."

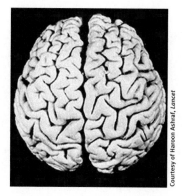

Courtesy of Haroon Ashraf, *Lancet*

Einstein's brain
For you and me, as well as for Albert Einstein (whose brain is shown here), this small wrinkled organ is far more complex than the most sophisticated computer. What you see here is only a portion of the brain's outer layer. Most of its surface lies hidden within its convoluted folds.

Structure of the Cortex

8. How is the cerebral cortex organized?

If you opened a human skull, exposing the brain, you would see a wrinkled organ, shaped somewhat like the meat of an oversized walnut. Without those wrinkles, a flattened cortex would require triple the area—roughly that of a very large pizza—to fit inside the skull.

Eighty percent of the brain's weight lies in the ballooning left and right cerebral hemispheres, which are mostly filled with axon connections between the brain's surface and its other regions. The cortex—the thin surface layer of the cerebral hemispheres—contains some 20 to 23 billion nerve cells and 300 trillion synaptic connections (de Courten-Myers, 2002). Being human takes a lot of nerve.

Each brain hemisphere is divided into four regions, or *lobes*. Starting at the front of your brain and going around over the top, there are the **frontal lobes** (behind your forehead), the **parietal lobes** (at the top and to the rear), the **occipital lobes** (at the back of your head), and the **temporal lobes** (just above your ears). These lobes are convenient geographic subdivisions separated by prominent folds ("fissures") (**FIGURE 2.15**). Each lobe carries out many functions, and many functions require the interplay of several lobes.

If flattened, a human cortex would cover about four pages of this book. A chimpanzee's would cover one page, a monkey's a postcard, and a rat's a postage stamp. (Calvin, 1996.)

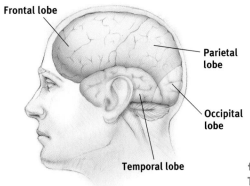

Frontal lobe

Parietal lobe

Occipital lobe

Temporal lobe

figure 2.15
The basic subdivisions of the cortex

Functions of the Cortex

9. What are the functions of the cerebral cortex?

More than a century ago, autopsies of people partially paralyzed or speechless revealed damaged cortical areas. But this rather crude evidence did not convince researchers that specific parts of the cortex perform specific functions. After all, if control of speech and movement were diffused across the cortex, damage to almost any area might produce the same effect. A television would go dead with its power cord cut, but we would be deluding ourselves if we thought we had "localized" the picture in the cord.

MOTOR FUNCTIONS Scientists have, however, localized simpler brain functions. For example, in 1870, when German physicians Gustav Fritsch and Eduard Hitzig applied mild electrical stimulation to the cortexes of dogs, they made an important discovery: They could make different body parts move. The effects were selective: Stimulation caused movement only when applied to an arch-shaped region at the back of the frontal lobe, running roughly from ear to ear across the top of the brain. This arch we now call the **motor cortex** (**FIGURE 2.16**, page 54). Moreover, when the researchers stimulated specific parts of this region in the left or right hemisphere, specific body parts moved on the *opposite* side of the body.

A half-century ago, neurosurgeons Otfrid Foerster in Germany and Wilder Penfield in Montreal mapped the motor cortex in hundreds of wide-awake patients. Before putting the knife to the brain, the surgeons needed to know the possible side effects of removing different parts of the cortex. They painlessly (the brain has no sensory receptors) stimulated different cortical areas and noted the body responses. Like Fritsch and Hitzig, they found that when they stimulated different areas of the motor cortex at the back of the frontal lobe, different body parts moved. (Kids, don't try this without parental supervision.) They were now able to map the motor cortex according to the body parts it controlled (see Figure 2.16, page 54). Interestingly, those areas of the body requiring precise control, such as the fingers and mouth, occupied the greatest amount of cortical space.

Neuroscientist José Delgado demonstrated the mechanics of motor behavior. In a human patient, he stimulated a spot on the left motor cortex that triggered the right hand to make a fist. Asked to keep the fingers open during the next stimulation, the patient, whose fingers closed despite his best efforts, remarked, "I guess, Doctor, that your electricity is stronger than my will" (Delgado, 1969, p. 114). More recently, scientists have been able to predict a monkey's arm motion a tenth of a second before it moves—by repeatedly measuring motor cortex activity

▶ **cerebral [seh-REE-bruhl] cortex** the intricate fabric of interconnected neural cells that covers the cerebral hemispheres; the body's ultimate control and information-processing center.

▶ **frontal lobes** the portion of the cerebral cortex lying just behind the forehead; involved in speaking and muscle movements and in making plans and judgments.

▶ **parietal [puh-RYE-uh-tuhl] lobes** the portion of the cerebral cortex lying at the top of the head and toward the rear; includes the sensory cortex.

▶ **occipital [ahk-SIP-uh-tuhl] lobes** the portion of the cerebral cortex lying at the back of the head; includes the visual areas, which receive visual information from the opposite visual field.

▶ **temporal lobes** the portion of the cerebral cortex lying roughly above the ears; includes the auditory areas, each of which receives auditory information primarily from the opposite ear.

▶ **motor cortex** an area at the rear of the frontal lobes that controls voluntary movements.

Demonstration: *Try moving your right hand in a circular motion, as if polishing a table. Now start your right foot doing the same motion synchronized with the hand. Now reverse the foot motion (but not the hand). Tough, huh? But easier if you try moving the* left *foot opposite to the right hand. The left and right limbs are controlled by opposite sides of the brain. So their opposed activities interfere less with one another.*

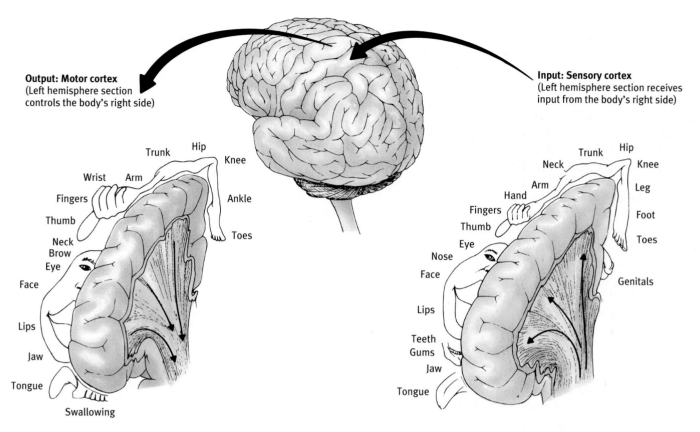

Output: Motor cortex
(Left hemisphere section controls the body's right side)

Input: Sensory cortex
(Left hemisphere section receives input from the body's right side)

figure 2.16
Left hemisphere tissue devoted to each body part in the motor cortex and the sensory cortex As you can see from this classic though inexact representation, the amount of cortex devoted to a body part is not proportional to that part's size. Rather, the brain devotes more tissue to sensitive areas and to areas requiring precise control. Thus, the fingers have a greater representation in the cortex than does the upper arm. However, the neural wiring is complex. Individual muscles are linked with multiple neural clusters, which in turn may also link with other muscles.

preceding specific arm movements (Gibbs, 1996). By similarly eavesdropping on the brain, could we enable someone—perhaps a paralyzed person—to control machines, hands free, to move a robotic limb or command a cursor to write e-mail or surf the Web? Stay tuned. Research toward this goal is currently under way.

SENSORY FUNCTIONS If the motor cortex sends messages out to the body, where does the cortex receive *incoming* messages? Penfield identified a cortical area that specializes in receiving information from the skin senses and from the movement of body parts. This area, parallel to the motor cortex and just behind it at the front of the parietal lobes, we now call the **sensory cortex** (see Figure 2.16). Stimulate a point on the top of this band of tissue, and a person may report being touched on the shoulder; stimulate some point on the side, and the person may feel something on the face.

The more sensitive a body region, the greater the area of the sensory cortex devoted to it; your supersensitive lips project to a larger brain area than do your toes (see Figure 2.16). (That's one reason we kiss with our lips rather than touch toes.) Similarly, rats have a large area of the brain devoted to their whisker sensations, owls to their hearing sensations, and so forth.

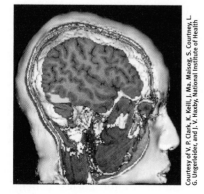

figure 2.17
New technology shows the brain in action This functional MRI (fMRI) scan shows the visual cortex—the occipital lobes—activated (color representation of increased bloodflow) as the subject looks at faces. When the person stops looking at faces, the region instantly calms down.

Courtesy of V. P. Clark, K. Keill, J. Ma. Maisog, S. Courtney, L. G. Ungerleider, and J. V. Haxby, National Institute of Health

Scientists have also identified where the cortex receives input from senses other than touch. At this moment, you are receiving visual information in the occipital lobes at the very back of your brain (**FIGURE 2.17**). A bad enough bash there and you would go blind. Stimulated there, you might see flashes of light or dashes of color. (In a sense, we *do* have eyes in the back of our head!) From these occipital lobes, the visual information you are now processing goes to other areas that specialize in tasks such as identifying words, detecting emotions, and recognizing faces.

Any sound you are now hearing you processed with the auditory areas in your temporal lobes (**Figure 2.18**). Most of this auditory information travels a circuitous route from one ear to the auditory receiving area above your opposite ear. If you were stimulated there, you might hear a sound. The sound needn't be real. MRI scans of people with schizophrenia reveal that auditory areas of the temporal lobe are active during auditory hallucinations (Lennox & others, 1999). Even the phantom ringing sound experienced by people with hearing loss is—if heard in one ear—associated with activity in the temporal lobe on the brain's opposite side (Muhlnickel & others, 1998).

ASSOCIATION AREAS So far, we have pointed out small areas of the cortex that either receive sensory information or direct muscular responses. In humans, that leaves a full three-fourths of the thin wrinkled layer, the cerebral cortex, uncommitted to sensory or muscular activity. What then goes on in this vast region of the brain? Neurons in these **association areas** (the peach-colored areas in **Figure 2.19**) integrate information. They associate various sensory inputs with stored memories—a very important part of thinking.

Electrically probing the association areas doesn't trigger any observable response. So, unlike the sensory and motor areas, we can't so neatly specify the functions of the association areas. Their silence seems to have led to one of pop psychology's most widespread falsehoods: that we ordinarily use only 10 percent of our brains. This fabrication—"one of the hardiest weeds in the garden of psychology," writes Donald McBurney (1996, p. 44)—implies that if we could activate our whole brain, we would be far smarter than those who drudge along on 10 percent brain power. But surgically lesioned animals and brain-damaged humans bear witness that the association areas are not dormant. (The brain has no appendix—no apparently purposeless tissue.) Rather, these areas interpret, integrate, and act on information processed by the sensory areas.

The frontal lobes' association areas enable us to judge, plan, and process new memories. People with damaged frontal lobes may have intact memories, score high on intelligence tests, and be able to bake a cake—yet be unable to plan ahead to *begin* baking the cake for the birthday party.

Frontal lobe damage also can alter personality, removing a person's inhibitions. Consider the classic case of railroad worker Phineas Gage. One afternoon in 1848, Gage, then 25 years old, was packing gunpowder into a rock with a tamping iron. A

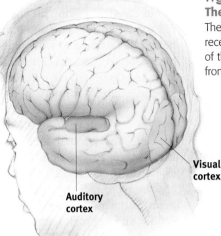

figure 2.18
The visual cortex and auditory cortex The occipital lobes at the rear of the brain receive input from the eyes. An auditory area of the temporal lobes receives information from the ears.

Visual cortex

Auditory cortex

▶ **sensory cortex** the area at the front of the parietal lobes that registers and processes body sensations.

▶ **association areas** areas of the cerebral cortex that are not involved in primary motor or sensory functions; rather, they are involved in higher mental functions such as learning, remembering, thinking, and speaking.

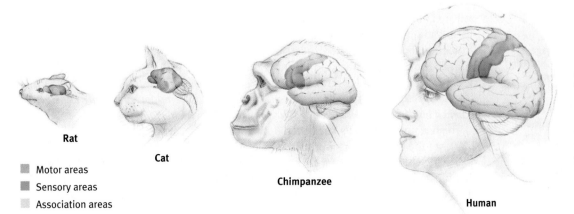

Rat

Cat

Chimpanzee

Human

■ Motor areas
■ Sensory areas
■ Association areas

figure 2.19
Areas of the cortex in four mammals More intelligent animals have increased "uncommitted" or association areas of the cortex. These vast areas of the brain are responsible for integrating and acting on information received and processed by sensory areas.

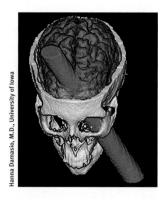

Phineas Gage reconsidered Using measurements of his skull (which was kept as a medical record) and modern neuroimaging techniques, researcher Hanna Damasio and her colleagues (1994) have reconstructed the probable path of the rod through Gage's brain.

▶ **aphasia** impairment of language, usually caused by left hemisphere damage either to Broca's area (impairing speaking) or to Wernicke's area (impairing understanding).

▶ **Broca's area** controls language expression—an area of the frontal lobe, usually in the left hemisphere, that directs the muscle movements involved in speech.

▶ **Wernicke's area** controls language reception—a brain area involved in language comprehension and expression; usually in the left temporal lobe.

spark ignited the gunpowder, shooting the rod up through his left cheek and out the top of his skull, leaving his shish-kebabed frontal lobes massively damaged. To everyone's amazement, Gage was immediately able to sit up and speak, and after the wound healed he returned to work. Although his mental abilities and memories were intact, his personality was not. The affable, soft-spoken Phineas Gage was now irritable, profane, and dishonest. He eventually lost his job and ended up earning his living as a fairground exhibit. This person, said his friends, was "no longer Gage." With his frontal lobes ruptured, Gage's moral compass became disconnected from his behavior.

The association areas of the other lobes also perform mental functions. For example, the parietal lobes, parts of which were large and unusually shaped in Einstein's normal-weight brain, are involved in mathematical and spatial reasoning (Witelson & others, 1999). An area on the underside of the right temporal lobe enables us to recognize faces. If a stroke or head injury destroyed this area of your brain, you would still be able to describe facial features and to recognize someone's gender and approximate age, yet be strangely unable to identify the person as, say, Nelson Mandela or even your mother.

LANGUAGE Complex human abilities, such as language, result from the intricate coordination of many brain areas. For example, consider this curious finding: Damage to any one of several cortical areas can cause **aphasia**, an impaired use of language. It is even more curious that some people with aphasia can speak fluently but cannot read (despite good vision), while others can comprehend what they read but cannot speak. Still others can write but not read, read but not write, read numbers but not letters, or sing but not speak. This all is very puzzling. After all, we think of speaking and reading, or writing and reading, or singing and speaking as merely different examples of the same general ability.

Researchers began to sort out how the brain processes language after a discovery by French physician Paul Broca in 1865. Broca discovered that after damage to a specific area of the left frontal lobe, later called **Broca's area**, a person would struggle to form words, yet often would be able to sing familiar songs with ease. A decade later, German investigator Karl Wernicke discovered that after damage to a specific area of the left temporal lobe (**Wernicke's area**) people could speak only meaningless words and were unable to comprehend others' words.

Norman Geschwind assembled these clues into an explanation of how we use language. When you read aloud, the words (1) register in the visual area, (2) are relayed to a third brain area, the *angular gyrus*, which transforms the words into an auditory code, which is (3) received and understood in the nearby Wernicke's area, and (4) sent to Broca's area, which (5) controls the motor cortex as it creates the pronounced word (**FIGURES 2.20** and **2.21**). Depending on which link in this chain is damaged, a different form of aphasia occurs. Damage to the angular gyrus leaves the person able to speak and understand but unable to read. Damage to Wernicke's area disrupts understanding. Damage to Broca's area disrupts speaking. The general principle bears repeating: *Complex abilities result from the intricate coordination of many brain areas.*

The same is true of reading a word: The brain computes the words' forms, sounds, and meanings using different neural networks (Posner & Carr, 1992). Thus fMRI scans show that jokes playing on meaning ("Why don't sharks bite lawyers? . . . Professional courtesy") are processed in a different brain area than jokes playing on language sounds ("What kind of lights did Noah use on the ark? . . . Flood lights") (Goel & Dolan, 2001). Think about it: *What you experience as a continuous, indivisible stream of perception is actually but the visible tip of the information-processing iceberg, most of which lies beneath the surface of your conscious awareness.*

To sum up, the mind's subsystems are localized in particular brain regions (**FIGURE 2.22**), yet the brain acts as a unified whole. Moving your hand; recognizing faces; even perceiving color, motion, and depth—all depend on specific neural networks. Yet complex functions such as language, learning, and loving involve the coordination of many brain areas. Both principles—specialization and integration—appear in research on the brain's two hemispheres.

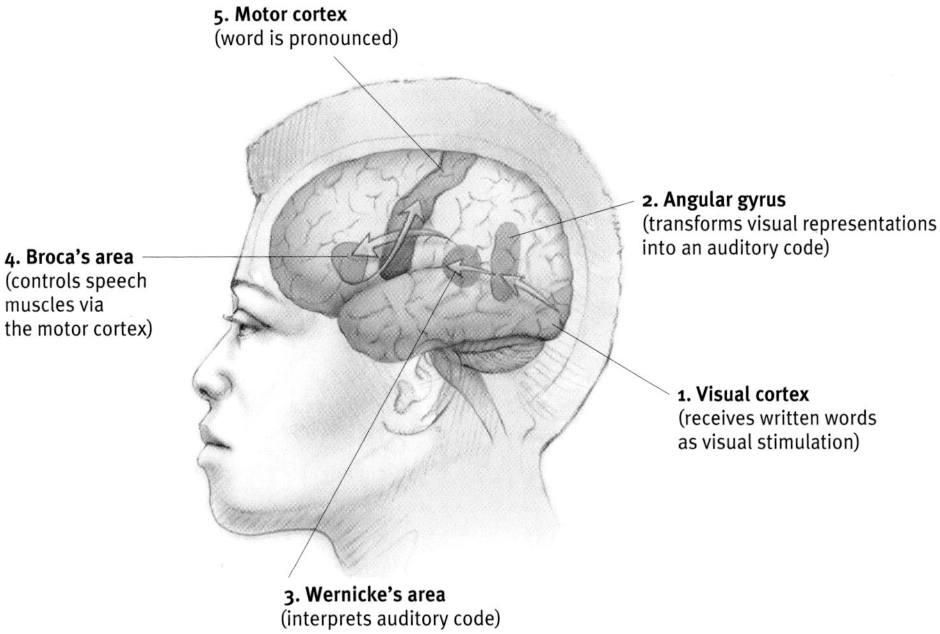

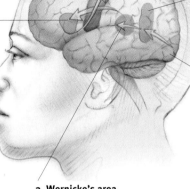

5. Motor cortex
(word is pronounced)

2. Angular gyrus
(transforms visual representations
into an auditory code)

4. Broca's area
(controls speech
muscles via
the motor cortex)

1. Visual cortex
(receives written words
as visual stimulation)

3. Wernicke's area
(interprets auditory code)

figure 2.20
**Specialization and integration in
language**

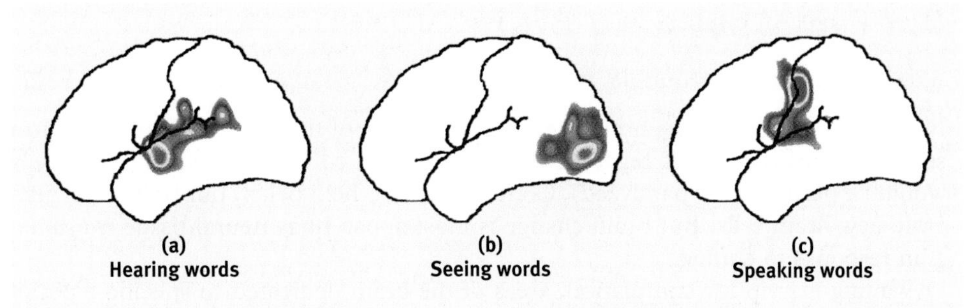

(a)
Hearing words

(b)
Seeing words

(c)
Speaking words

figure 2.21
**Brain activity when hearing, seeing,
and reading words** PET scans such as
these detect the activity of different areas of
the brain. The red blotches show where the
brain is rapidly consuming the brain's normal
fuel, glucose.

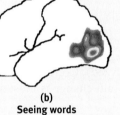

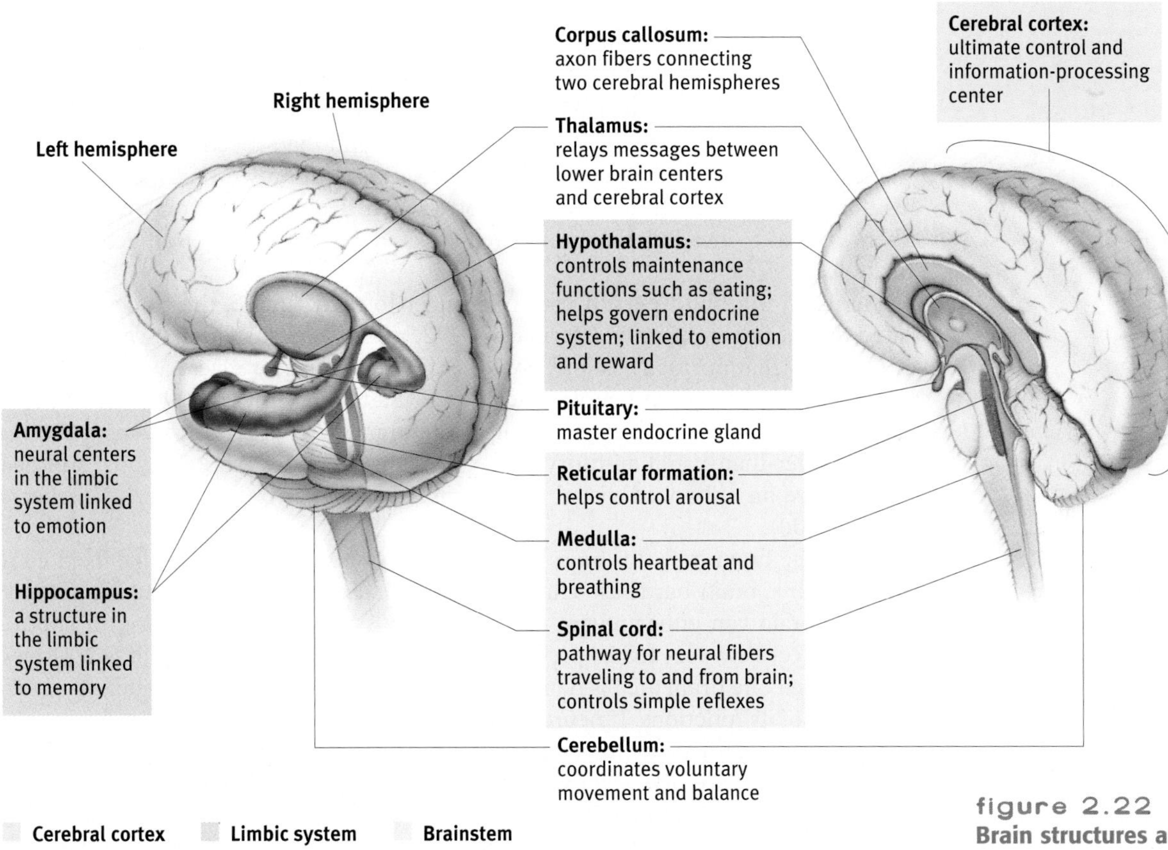

Right hemisphere

Left hemisphere

Corpus callosum:
axon fibers connecting
two cerebral hemispheres

Cerebral cortex:
ultimate control and
information-processing
center

Thalamus:
relays messages between
lower brain centers
and cerebral cortex

Hypothalamus:
controls maintenance
functions such as eating;
helps govern endocrine
system; linked to emotion
and reward

Amygdala:
neural centers
in the limbic
system linked
to emotion

Pituitary:
master endocrine gland

Reticular formation:
helps control arousal

Medulla:
controls heartbeat and
breathing

Hippocampus:
a structure in
the limbic
system linked
to memory

Spinal cord:
pathway for neural fibers
traveling to and from brain;
controls simple reflexes

Cerebellum:
coordinates voluntary
movement and balance

Cerebral cortex Limbic system Brainstem

figure 2.22
Brain structures and their functions

17. The motor cortex is the brain region that controls voluntary muscle movement. If a neurosurgeon stimulated your right motor cortex, you would most likely
    a. see light.
    b. hear a sound.
    c. feel a touch on the right arm.
    d. move your left leg.

18. The sensory cortex registers and processes body sensations, with the more sensitive body regions having the greatest representation. Which of

the following has the greatest representation?
    a. Knee
    b. Toes
    c. Forehead
    d. Thumb

19. About three-fourths of the cerebral cortex is not committed to any specific sensory or muscular function. The "uncommitted" areas are called
    a. occipital lobes.
    b. fissures.
    c. association areas.
    d. Wernicke's area.

20. Judging and planning are enabled by the
    a. occipital lobes.
    b. parietal lobes.
    c. frontal lobes.
    d. temporal lobes.

21. The area in the brain that, if damaged, might impair your ability to form words is
    a. Wernicke's area.
    b. Broca's area.
    c. the left occipital lobe.
    d. the angular gyrus.

Answers can be found in Appendix C.

BRAIN REORGANIZATION

Our Ever-Changing Brain

10. Is the brain capable of reorganizing itself if damaged?

Nurture's sculpting of the brain is evident in studies of the brain's **plasticity**. Most severed neurons will not regenerate (if your spinal cord were severed, you likely would be permanently paralyzed). Contrary to long-held belief, our brains can generate new brain cells. But brain change is most apparent as neural tissue *reorganizes* in response to damage.

Waiting in vain for stimulation, areas of the brain dedicated to specific types of information seem to look for other signals to process. If a body part is amputated, for example, sensory fibers that terminate on adjacent areas of the sensory cortex may invade the brain tissue that's no longer receiving sensory input. Lose a finger and the sensory cortex that received its input will begin to receive input from the adjacent fingers. As Figure 2.16 on page 54 shows, the hand is between the face and the arm regions on the sensory cortex. This explains a mysterious phenomenon: When stroking the face of someone whose hand had been amputated, V. S. Ramachandran found the person felt the sensations not only on his face but also on his nonexistent ("phantom") fingers. Ditto when stroking the arm, whose sensory fibers had also invaded the brain area vacated by the hand (Ramachandran & Blakeslee, 1998).

Similarly, if a blind person uses one finger to read Braille, the brain area dedicated to that finger expands (Barinaga, 1992a). The sense of touch invades the part of the brain that normally helps people see. PET scans also reveal activation of the *visual* cortex when blind people read Braille (Sadato & others, 1996). In addition, MRI scans show how experience sculpts the brain. Well-practiced pianists likewise have a larger-than-usual auditory cortex area that encodes piano sounds, and deaf people have an enhanced visual cortex with greater peripheral vision (Bavelier & others, 2000).

Thus, the brain may not be as "hard-wired" as once thought. Unlike fixed computer circuits, brain hardware changes with time. In response to changing stimulation, the brain can either rewire itself with new synapses or (according to another theory) select new uses for its prewired circuits (Gazzaniga, 1992; Kolb & Whishaw, 1998). When one brain area is damaged, other areas may in time reorganize and take over some of its functions. If neurons are destroyed, nearby neurons may partly compensate for the damage by making new connections that replace the lost ones. These new connections are one way the brain struggles to recover from a minor stroke.

Our brains are most plastic, though, when we are young children (Kolb, 1989). Children are born with a surplus of neurons. If an injury destroys one part of a

▶ **plasticity** the brain's capacity for modification, as evident in brain reorganization following damage (especially in children) and in experiments on the effects of experience on brain development.

▶ **corpus callosum** [KOR-pus kah-LOW-sum] the large band of neural fibers connecting the two brain hemispheres and carrying messages between them.

child's brain, the brain will compensate by putting other surplus areas to work. Thus, if the speech areas of an infant's left hemisphere are damaged, the right hemisphere will take over much of its language function.

As an extreme example of plasticity, consider children whose medical condition required removing an *entire* hemisphere. One Johns Hopkins medical team, reflecting on the 58 child hemispherectomies they have performed, reports being "awed" by how well children retain their memory, personality, and humor after removal of either brain hemisphere (Vining & others, 1997).

Brain plasticity Believe it or not, this 4-year-old is functioning with only half a brain. Her right hemisphere was surgically removed to eliminate seizures. Now neurons in her left hemisphere have made countless new connections to take over the tasks once performed by her right hemisphere.

Our Divided Brain

For more than a century, clinical evidence has shown that the brain's two sides serve differing functions. Accidents, strokes, and tumors in the left hemisphere generally impair reading, writing, speaking, arithmetic reasoning, and understanding. Similar lesions in the right hemisphere seldom have such dramatic effects.

By 1960 the left hemisphere was, therefore, well accepted as the "dominant" or "major" hemisphere, and its silent companion to the right as the "subordinate" or "minor" hemisphere. The left, verbal hemisphere is rather like the moon's facing side—the one easiest to observe and study. (For about 1 in 10 people, including one-fourth of all left-handers, speech is processed in the right hemisphere.) The other side is there, of course, but backstage. Then researchers found that the "minor" right hemisphere was not so limited after all. The story of this discovery is a fascinating chapter in psychology's history.

"You wouldn't want to have a date with the right hemisphere."

Michael Gazzaniga, 2000

Splitting the Brain

> **11.** *What is a split brain, and what does it reveal about brain functioning?*

In 1961, two Los Angeles neurosurgeons, Philip Vogel and Joseph Bogen, speculated that major epileptic seizures were caused by an amplification of abnormal brain activity that reverberated between the two hemispheres. They therefore wondered whether they could reduce seizures in their patients with uncontrollable epilepsy by cutting communication between the two sides of the brain. To do this, Vogel and Bogen knew they would have to sever the **corpus callosum**, the wide band of axon fibers connecting the brain's two hemispheres (**FIGURE 2.23**).

Corpus callosum

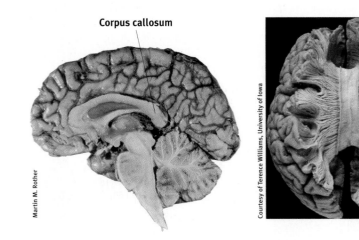

figure 2.23
The corpus callosum This large band of neural fibers connects the two brain hemispheres. To photograph the half brain shown at left, the hemispheres were separated by cutting through the corpus callosum and lower brain regions. In the view on the right, a surgeon has cut back brain tissue to expose the corpus callosum and bundles of fibers coming out from it.

figure 2.24
The information highway from eye to brain Information from the left half of your field of vision goes to your right hemisphere, and information from the right half of your visual field goes to your left hemisphere, which usually controls speech. (Note, however, that each eye receives sensory information from both the right and left visual fields.) The data received by either hemisphere are quickly transmitted to the other across the corpus callosum. In a person with a severed corpus callosum, this information sharing does not take place.

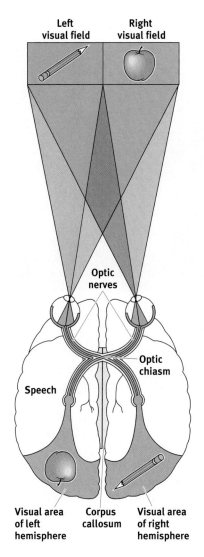

Left visual field · Right visual field

Optic nerves

Optic chiasm

Speech

Visual area of left hemisphere · Corpus callosum · Visual area of right hemisphere

The surgeons had reason to believe such an operation would not be incapacitating. Psychologists Roger Sperry, Ronald Myers, and Michael Gazzaniga had divided the brains of cats and monkeys in this manner with no serious ill effects. So Vogel and Bogen operated. The result? The seizures were all but eliminated and the patients with these **split brains** were surprisingly normal, their personalities and intellect hardly affected. Waking from the surgery, one patient even managed to quip that he had a "splitting headache" (Gazzaniga, 1967).

Sperry and Gazzaniga's ingenious experiments on such patients have provided a key to understanding the hemispheres' functions. As **FIGURE 2.24** illustrates, the peculiar nature of our visual wiring enabled Sperry and Gazzaniga to send information to the patient's left or right brain—by having the patient stare at a spot and then flashing a stimulus to its right or left. (They could do this with you, too, but in your intact brain the telltale hemisphere that received the information would instantly call the news to its partner across the valley. The split-brain surgery severs the phone cables—the corpus callosum—across the valley.) Finally, the researchers quizzed each hemisphere separately.

In an early experiment, Gazzaniga (1967) asked split-brain people to stare at a dot as he flashed HE•ART on a screen (**FIGURE 2.25**). Thus, HE appeared in the patients' left visual field (which transmits to the right brain) and ART in their right field (which transmits to the left brain). When he then asked them what they had seen, the patients *said* they had seen ART. But when asked to *point* to the word, they were startled when their left hand (controlled by the right brain) pointed to HE. Given an opportunity to express itself, each hemisphere reported only what it had seen. The left hand intuitively knew what it could not verbally report.

figure 2.25
Testing the divided brain When an experimenter flashes the word HEART across the visual field, the split-brain person reports seeing the portion of the word transmitted to her left hemisphere. However, if asked to indicate with her left hand what she saw, she points to the portion of the word transmitted to her right hemisphere. (From Gazzaniga, 1983.)

"Look at the dot."

Two words separated by a dot are momentarily projected.

"What word did you see?"

Art

or

"Point with your left hand to the word you saw."

HE ART

Similarly, when a picture of a spoon was flashed to their right hemisphere, the patients could not say what they had seen. But when asked to identify what they had viewed by feeling an assortment of hidden objects with their left hand, they readily selected the spoon. If the experimenter said, "Right!" the patient might reply, "What? Right? How could I possibly pick out the right object when I don't know what I saw?" It is, of course, the left hemisphere doing the talking here, bewildered by what the nonverbal right hemisphere knows.

A few people who have had split-brain surgery have been for a time bothered by the unruly independence of their left hand, which might unbutton a shirt while the right hand buttoned it or put grocery store items back on the shelf after the right hand put them in the cart. It was as if each hemisphere was thinking "I've half a mind to wear my green (blue) shirt today." One woman, after a massive stroke in her corpus callosum, complained that occasionally her left hand would fly up to her throat and try to strangle her, requiring her right hand to push it away (Ramachandran & Blakeslee, 1998). Indeed, said Sperry (1964), split-brain surgery leaves people "with two separate minds." (Reading these reports, I fantasize a split-brain person enjoying a solitary game of "rocks, paper, scissors"—left versus right hand.)

When the "two minds" are at odds, the left hemisphere seems to act as the brain's press agent, doing mental gymnastics to rationalize reactions it does not understand. If a patient follows an order sent to the right hemisphere ("Walk"), the interpretive left hemisphere will offer a ready explanation ("I'm going into the house to get a Coke"). Thus, Michael Gazzaniga (1988), who considers split-brain patients "the most fascinating people on earth," concludes that the conscious left hemisphere is an "interpreter" that instantly constructs theories to explain our behavior.

These experiments demonstrate that the right hemisphere understands simple requests and easily perceives objects. With a split brain, both hemispheres can comprehend and follow an instruction to copy—*simultaneously*—different figures with the left and right hand (Franz & others, 2000). But the right hemisphere surpasses the left at copying drawings, and also at recognizing faces, perceiving differences, perceiving emotion, and expressing emotion through the more expressive left side of the face. Most of the body's paired organs—kidneys, lungs, breasts—perform identical functions, providing a backup system should one side fail. Not so the brain's two halves. They are a biological odd couple, serving differing functions, each seemingly with a mind of its own.

Studying Hemispheric Differences in the Intact Brain

What about the 99.99+ percent of us with undivided brains? Have scientists found our hemispheres to be similarly specialized? Yes they have, in several different types of studies. For example, when a person performs a *perceptual* task, brain waves, bloodflow, and glucose consumption reveal increased activity in the *right* hemisphere; when a person speaks or calculates, activity increases in the *left* hemisphere.

Which one is happier? Look at the center of one face, then the other. Does one appear happier? Most people say the right face does. Some researchers think this is because the right hemisphere, which is skilled in emotion processing, receives information from the left half of each face (when looking at its center).

"Do not let your left hand know what your right hand is doing."

Matthew 6:3

Try this Joe, a split-brain patient, can simultaneously draw two different shapes.

Question: *If we flashed a red light to the right hemisphere of a split-brain patient and flashed a green light to the left hemisphere, would each observe its own color? Would the person be aware that the colors differ? What would the person verbally report seeing? (Answers on page 62.)*

▶ **split brain** a condition in which the two hemispheres of the brain are isolated by cutting the connecting fibers (mainly those of the corpus callosum) between them.

On occasion, hemispheric specialization has been even more dramatically shown by briefly sedating an entire hemisphere. To check for the locus of language before surgery, a physician may inject a sedative into the neck artery that feeds blood to the hemisphere on its side of the body. Before the drug is injected, the patient is lying down, arms in the air, conversing easily. You can likely predict what happens when the drug flows into the artery going to the left hemisphere: Within seconds, the person's right arm falls limp and, if the left hemisphere controls language, the subject becomes speechless until the drug wears off. When the drug goes into the artery to the right hemisphere, the *left* arm falls limp, but the person can still speak.

Which hemisphere would you suppose enables sign language among Deaf people? The right, because of its visual-spatial superiority? Or the left, because of its preparedness to process language? Studies reveal that, just as hearing people use the left hemisphere to process speech, Deaf people use the left hemisphere to read signs (Corina & others, 1992; Hickok & others, 2001). A stroke in the left hemisphere will disrupt a Deaf person's signing, much as it would disrupt a hearing person's speaking. Broca's area is similarly involved in both spoken and signed speech production (Corina, 1998). To the brain, language is language, whether spoken or signed.

About 90 percent of the human population is right-handed. The remaining 10 percent (somewhat more among males, somewhat less among females) is left-handed. Tests reveal that about 95 percent of right-handers process speech primarily in their left hemispheres, which tend to be slightly larger (Springer & Deutsch, 1985). Left-handers are more diverse. More than half process speech in the left hemisphere, as right-handers do. About a quarter process language in the right hemisphere; the other quarter use both hemispheres more or less equally.

Although the left hemisphere is adept at making quick, literal interpretations of language, the right hemisphere excels in making subtle inferences (Beeman & Chiarello, 1998; Beeman & others, 1994; Bowden & Beeman, 1998). If "primed" with the flashed word *foot*, the left hemisphere will be especially quick to then recognize the closely associated word *heel*. But if primed with *foot*, *cry*, and *glass*, the right hemisphere will more quickly recognize another word that is distantly related to all three (*cut*). And if given an insightlike problem—what word goes with *high*, *district*, and *house*?—the right hemisphere has better access to the solution. (The right hemisphere more quickly than the left recognizes that the solution is *school*.) As one patient explained after suffering right-hemisphere stroke damage, "I understand words, but I'm missing the subtleties." Thus, the right hemisphere helps us modulate our speech to make meaning clear—as when we ask "What's that in the road ahead?" instead of "What's that in the road, a head?" (Heller, 1990).

Answers to questions on page 61: Yes. No. Green.

Even babies exhibit asymmetry, by favoring the left side of their mouth when beginning a smile, and the right side when using baby language—babbling. From simply looking at the two hemispheres, which appear alike to the naked eye, who would suppose that they contribute so uniquely to the harmony of the whole? Yet a variety of observations—of people with split brains and people with normal brains—converge beautifully, leaving little doubt that we have unified brains with specialized parts.

rehearse it!

22. Plasticity refers to the brain's ability to reorganize itself after damage. Especially plastic are the brains of
    a. split-brain patients.
    b. young adults.
    c. young children.
    d. right-handed people.

23. The brain structure that enables the right and left hemispheres to communicate is
    a. the medulla.
    b. Broca's area.
    c. Wernicke's area.
    d. the corpus callosum.

24. An experimenter flashes the word HERON across the visual field of a split-brain patient. HER is transmitted to his right hemisphere and ON to his left hemisphere. When asked to indicate what he saw, the patient
    a. *says* he saw HER but *points* to ON.
    b. *says* he saw ON but *points* to HER.
    c. *says* he saw HERON but *points* to HER.
    d. *says* he saw HERON but *points* to ON.

25. The study of split-brain patients has allowed us to observe the special functions of each hemisphere of the brain. The left hemisphere excels in
    a. processing language.
    b. visual perceptions.
    c. recognition of emotion.
    d. recognition of faces.

26. Damage to the brain's right hemisphere is most likely to reduce a person's ability to
    a. recite the alphabet rapidly.
    b. recognize the emotional content of facial expressions.
    c. understand verbal instructions.
    d. solve arithmetic problems.

Answers can be found in Appendix C.

THE ENDOCRINE SYSTEM

12. How does the endocrine system—the body's slower information system—transmit its messages?

Interconnected with the nervous system is the second of the body's communication systems, the **endocrine system** (FIGURE **2.26**). The endocrine system's glands secrete another form of chemical messengers, **hormones**. Hormones originate in one tissue, travel through the bloodstream, and affect other tissues, including the brain. When they act on the brain, they influence our interest in sex, food, and aggression.

Some hormones are chemically identical to neurotransmitters (those chemical messengers that diffuse across a synapse and excite or inhibit an adjacent neuron). The endocrine system and nervous system are therefore kindred systems: They both secrete molecules that activate receptors elsewhere. But unlike the speedy nervous system, zipping messages from eyes to brain to hand in a fraction of a second, endocrine messages trudge along. If the nervous system's communication delivers messages rather like e-mail, the endocrine system is the body's snail mail. Several seconds or more may elapse before the bloodstream carries a hormone from an endocrine gland to its target tissue. But these endocrine messages are often worth the wait because their effects usually outlast the effects of a neural message.

The endocrine system's hormones influence many aspects of our lives—growth, reproduction, metabolism, mood—working to keep everything in balance while we respond to stress, exertion, and our own thoughts. In a moment of danger, for example, the autonomic nervous system orders the **adrenal glands** on top of the kidneys to release *epinephrine* and *norepinephrine* (also called *adrenaline* and *noradrenaline*). These hormones increase heart rate, blood pressure, and blood sugar, providing us with a surge of energy. When the emergency passes, the hormones—and the feelings of excitement—linger a while.

▶ **endocrine [EN-duh-krin] system** the body's "slow" chemical communication system; a set of glands that secrete hormones into the bloodstream.

▶ **hormones** chemical messengers, mostly those manufactured by the endocrine glands, that are produced in one tissue and affect another.

▶ **adrenal [ah-DREEN-el] glands** a pair of endocrine glands just above the kidneys. The adrenals secrete the hormones epinephrine (adrenaline) and norepinephrine (noradrenaline), which help to arouse the body in times of stress.

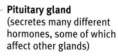

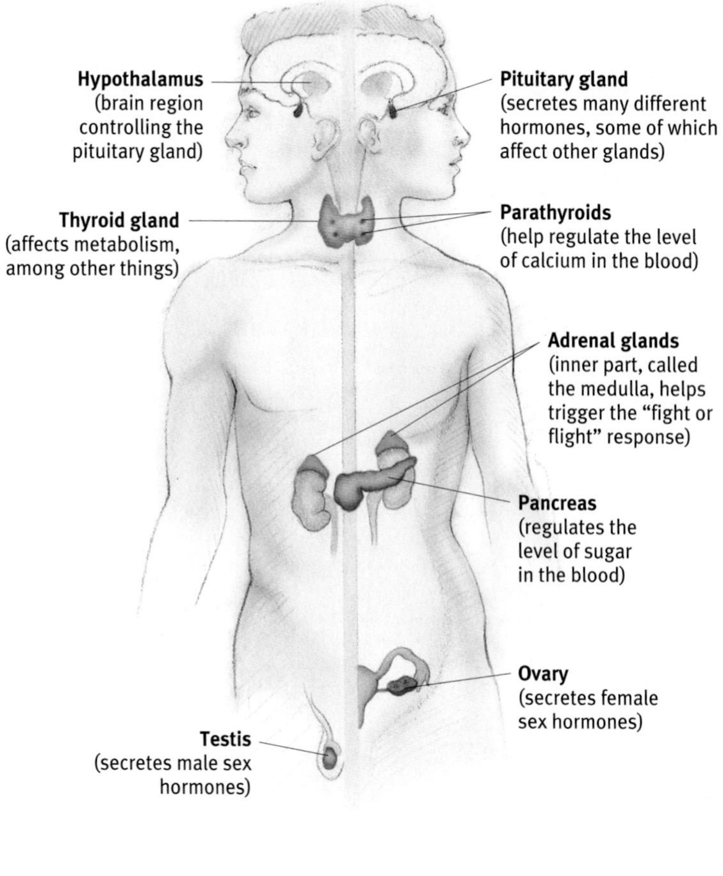

Hypothalamus
(brain region controlling the pituitary gland)

Pituitary gland
(secretes many different hormones, some of which affect other glands)

Thyroid gland
(affects metabolism, among other things)

Parathyroids
(help regulate the level of calcium in the blood)

Adrenal glands
(inner part, called the medulla, helps trigger the "fight or flight" response)

Pancreas
(regulates the level of sugar in the blood)

Ovary
(secretes female sex hormones)

Testis
(secretes male sex hormones)

figure 2.26
The body's major endocrine glands

▶ **pituitary gland** the endocrine system's most influential gland. Under the influence of the hypothalamus, the pituitary regulates growth and controls other endocrine glands.

The most influential endocrine gland is the **pituitary gland**, a pea-sized structure located in the base of the brain, where it is controlled by an adjacent brain area, the hypothalamus. The pituitary releases hormones that influence growth, and its secretions also influence the release of hormones by other endocrine glands. The pituitary, then, is really a sort of master gland (whose own master is the hypothalamus). For example, under the brain's influence, the pituitary triggers your sex glands to release sex hormones. These in turn influence your brain and behavior.

This feedback system (brain → pituitary → other glands → hormones → brain) reveals the intimate connection of the nervous and endocrine systems: the nervous system directing endocrine secretions, which then affect the nervous system. Conducting and coordinating this whole electrochemical orchestra is that maestro we call the brain.

● ● ●

"You are your synapses."

Joseph Le Doux, The Synaptic Self, *2002*

We have glimpsed the truth of our overriding principle: Everything psychological is simultaneously biological. This chapter has focused on how our thoughts, feelings, and actions arise from our specialized yet integrated brain. In chapters to come, we will further explore the significance of the biological revolution in psychology.

From nineteenth-century phrenology to today's neuroscience, we have come a long way. Yet what is unknown still dwarfs what is known. We can describe the brain. We can learn the functions of its parts. We can study how the parts communicate. But how do we get mind out of meat? How does the electrochemical whir in a hunk of tissue the size of a head of lettuce give rise to elation, a creative idea, or that memory of Grandmother?

"If the human brain were so simple that we could understand it, we would be so simple that we couldn't."

Emerson M. Pugh, quoted by George E. Pugh, The Biological Origin of Human Values, *1977*

The mind boggles both at what is known and what is not. Interviews with leading brain scientists reveal their own awe and wonder. Others ponder philosophical mysteries: How does the material brain give rise to consciousness? To what extent can a thing understand itself? The mind seeking to understand the brain—that is indeed among the ultimate scientific challenges.

rehearse it!

27. The endocrine system, the second and slower bodily communication system, produces chemical messengers that travel through the bloodstream and affect other tissues. These chemical substances are
    a. hormones.
    b. neurotransmitters.
    c. endorphins.
    d. glands.

28. The pituitary gland releases hormones that influence growth and the activity of other glands. The pituitary gland is part of the
    a. endocrine system.
    b. peripheral nervous system.
    c. sympathetic nervous system.
    d. central nervous system.

Answers can be found in Appendix C.

chapter review

Neuroscience and Behavior

1. Why do psychologists study biology?

As a first step in understanding our behavior and mental processes, biological psychologists examine the biological roots of how we think, feel, and act.

NEURAL COMMUNICATION

2. What are neurons, and how do they transmit information?

The body's neural circuitry consists of billions of nerve cells, called neurons, which are the elementary components of the nervous system, the body's speedy electrochemical information system. A neuron receives signals from external stimuli and from other neurons through its branching dendrites and cell bodies, combines these signals in the cell body, and, if the signals exceed a certain threshold, transmits an electrical impulse (the action potential) down its axon.

3. How do nerve cells communicate?

When electrical signals reach the end of the axon, they stimulate the release of chemical messengers called neurotransmitters. These molecules pass on their excitatory or inhibitory messages as they traverse the tiny gap (synapse) between neurons and bind to receptor sites on neighboring neurons.

4. How do neurotransmitters influence human behavior?

Dozens of different neurotransmitters have been discovered, and the functions of some are now well understood. Learning about endorphins, the feel-good neurotransmitters, has helped us understand how drugs affect our brain chemistry. Some drugs (agonists) mimic particular neurotransmitters; others (antagonists) block them.

THE NERVOUS SYSTEM

5. What are the major divisions of the nervous system, and what are their basic functions?

The nervous system consists of the central nervous system (CNS) and the peripheral nervous system (PNS). The interneurons in the brain and spinal cord (the CNS) communicate with the sensory and motor neurons that form nerves in the PNS. The peripheral nervous system also has two main divisions, the somatic and the autonomic. The somatic nervous system directs voluntary movements and reflexes. The autonomic nervous system, through its sympathetic and parasympathetic divisions, controls our involuntary muscles and the glands of the internal organs.

THE BRAIN

Scientists have studied the brain through lesioning, electroencephalograms, and PET and MRI scans.

6. What are the functions of the brainstem and its associated structures?

Within the brainstem, the medulla controls heartbeat and breathing, and the reticular formation controls arousal and attention. The cerebellum, attached to the rear of the brainstem, coordinates muscle movement. On top of the brainstem is the thalamus, the brain's sensory switchboard.

7. What are the functions of limbic system structures?

The limbic system has been linked primarily to memory, emotions, and drives. For example, one of its neural centers, the amygdala, is involved in aggressive and fearful responses. Another, the hypothalamus, has been linked to various bodily maintenance functions and to pleasurable rewards. The hypothalamus also controls the endocrine system.

8. How is the cerebral cortex organized?

The cerebral cortex is a thin, wrinkled sheet of neurons with trillions of interconnections. Prominent folds divide each hemisphere into four lobes—the frontal, parietal, occipital, and temporal.

9. What are the functions of the cerebral cortex?

Small, well-defined regions within the cerebral lobes control muscle movement (the motor cortex) and receive information from the body senses (the sensory cortex). However, most of the cortex—its association areas—is uncommitted to such functions and is therefore free to process other information.

Some brain regions serve specific functions. In general, however, human emotions, thoughts, and behaviors result from the intricate coordination of many brain areas. Language, for example, depends on a chain of events in several brain regions, particularly Broca's area, Wernicke's area, and the angular gyrus. Damage to an area of the brain involved in language may cause one of several types of aphasia.

BRAIN REORGANIZATION

10. Is the brain capable of reorganizing itself if damaged?

If one hemisphere is damaged early in life (in the first five years), the other will pick up many of its functions, thus demonstrating the brain's plasticity. Although the brain is less plastic later in life, nearby neurons may partially compensate for damaged ones, as when a patient recovers from a minor stroke.

11. What is a split brain, and what does it reveal about brain functioning?

A split brain is one whose corpus callosum, the large band of nerve fibers connecting the two brain hemispheres, has been severed. Experiments on split-brain patients have refined our knowledge of each hemisphere's special functions. By testing the two hemispheres separately, researchers have confirmed that for most people the left hemisphere is the more verbal and that the right hemisphere excels in visual perception and the recognition of emotion. Studies of normal people with intact brains confirm that each hemisphere makes unique contributions to the integrated functioning of the brain.

THE ENDOCRINE SYSTEM

12. How does the endocrine system—the body's slower information system—transmit its messages?

Hormones released by the glands of the endocrine system travel through the bloodstream and affect other tissues, including the brain. The endocrine system's master gland, the pituitary, influences hormone release by other glands. The adrenal glands are activated in stressful times by the autonomic nervous system.

A CRITICAL THINKER'S REVIEW OF CHAPTER 2

You've now studied and reviewed **Neuroscience and Behavior**. For even better retention, reflect on these concepts at a deeper level. If you need to refresh your memory of the six categories of critical thinking shown in parentheses below, see page 34. See if you can answer each of these questions in a short paragraph.

1. Knowing what you now know about the endorphin response, explain why the immediate pain you experience from a paper cut could possibly be greater than the pain from a terrible accident that severed your arm. (pattern recognition)

2. One way researchers have learned about normal neurotransmitter functioning is by introducing a non-natural substance, such as the drug morphine, and watching where it goes in our body. What could researchers learn about normal neurotransmitter functioning by watching this process? (scientific problem solving)

3. Imagine that you are a neuroscientist, and you are trying to help a right-handed man whose neural deficiency seems to be preventing him from successfully using a fork. Describe for your patient and his family how the information would normally flow through the various parts of his nervous system. (practical problem solving)

4. What information could a neuroscientist working with the patient in Question 3 acquire from a single MRI scan of the patient's brain? Why might a functional MRI be a more useful technique in this case? (psychological reasoning)

5. Imagine that you lost a thumb. What would happen in your sensory cortex in response to this change? How would you experience the sensory cortex change? (perspective taking)

6. Geniene is having trouble speaking. We know her problem is not an inability to speak, because when someone tells her what to say, she can repeat it with reasonable accuracy. However, she is unable to read aloud. Besides this inability, Geniene appears to have normal vision. What two areas in Geniene's brain may be causing her problem? (creative problem solving)

Answers can be found in Appendix C.

TERMS AND CONCEPTS TO REMEMBER

biological psychology, p. 37

neuron, p. 38

dendrite, p. 38

axon, p. 38

action potential, p. 38

myelin sheath, p. 38

threshold, p. 39

synapse [SIN-aps], p. 39

neurotransmitters, p. 39

endorphins [en-DOR-fins], p. 41

nervous system, p. 43

central nervous system (CNS), p. 43

peripheral nervous system (PNS), p. 43

nerves, p. 43

sensory neurons, p. 44

interneurons, p. 44

motor neurons, p. 44

somatic nervous system, p. 44

autonomic [aw-tuh-NAHM-ik] nervous system, p. 44

sympathetic nervous system, p. 44

parasympathetic nervous system, p. 45

reflex, p. 45

brainstem, p. 47

medulla [muh-DUL-uh], p. 47

reticular formation, p. 47

thalamus [THAL-uh-muss], p. 47

lesion [LEE-zhuhn], p. 48

electroencephalogram (EEG), p. 48

PET (positron emission tomography) scan, p. 48

cerebellum [sehr-uh-BELL-um], p. 48

MRI (magnetic resonance imaging), p. 49

limbic system, p. 50

amygdala [uh-MIG-duh-la], p. 50

hypothalamus [hi-po-THAL-uh-muss], p. 51

cerebral [seh-REE-bruhl] cortex, p. 52

frontal lobes, p. 53

parietal [puh-RYE-uh-tuhl] lobes, p. 53

occipital [ahk-SIP-uh-tuhl] lobes, p. 53

temporal lobes, p. 53

motor cortex, p. 53

sensory cortex, p. 54

association areas, p. 55

aphasia, p. 56

Broca's area, p. 56

Wernicke's area, p. 56

plasticity, p. 58

corpus callosum [KOR-pus kah-LOW-sum], p. 59

split brain, p. 60

endocrine [EN-duh-krin] system, p. 63

hormones, p. 63

adrenal [ah-DREEN-el] glands, p. 63

pituitary gland, p. 64

To continue your study and review of Neuroscience and Behavior, visit this book's Web site at www.worthpublishers.com/myers. You will find Practice Tests, Review Activities, and Web links for more information on topics related to Neuroscience and Behavior.

chapter3

The Nature and Nurture of Behavior

What makes you you? To answer, we must first understand how you come to be so much like everyone else. Whatever our differences, we are the leaves of one tree. Our human family shares not only a common biological heritage—cut us and we bleed— but also common behavioral tendencies. Our shared brain architecture predisposes us to sense the world, develop language, and feel hunger through identical mechanisms.

Our kinship appears in our social behaviors as well. Whether we live in the Arctic or the tropics, we prefer sweet tastes to sour. We divide the color spectrum into similar colors. And we feel drawn to behaviors that produce and protect offspring. Regardless of our culture or our gender, we regard female features that signify youth and health— and reproductive potential—as attractive. Whether our last name is Wong, Nkomo, Smith, or Gonzales, at about eight months we start fearing strangers, and as adults we prefer the company of those whose attitudes and attributes are similar to our own. Coming from different parts of the globe, we know how to read one another's smiles and frowns. As members of one species, we affiliate, conform, reciprocate favors, punish offenses, organize hierarchies of status, and grieve a child's death. A visitor from outer space could drop in anywhere and find humans dancing and feasting, singing and worshiping, playing sports and games, laughing and crying, living in families, and forming groups. Taken together, such universal behaviors reveal our human nature.

Telling the story of you also requires explaining your individuality. Why are you more or less intelligent? Happy? Aggressive? Why is one person gay or lesbian while another is straight? Why is one person unable to keep pounds off while another can't put them on? Also, what's the source of our *group* differences in whether we think plump is beautiful or unattractive, whether we conceal or express anger, whether we tend to do our own thing or honor others' expectations?

Psychology's answer to these questions begins with a look back at how our species developed the body-mind system that enabled our distant ancestors to navigate their physical worlds, hunt, gather food, engage others, and reproduce. The story continues as we look at the genetic inheritance that designs each unique new body-mind system. Psychologists are exploring how—and how much—our individual heredity predisposes our differing personalities, preferences, and abilities. To what extent are we shaped by our heredity (our *nature*) and by our life history (including the *nurture* we have received since our conception)?

The conclusions—that *nature* is crucially important, and that *nurture* is crucially important—are central to today's psychology. Genes—and the rest of our bodies— matter. Culture—and everything we experience from womb to tomb—matters. Consider, then, how nature and nurture work together to shape us.

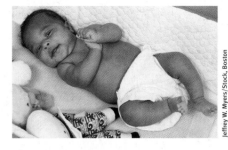

The nurture of nature Parents everywhere wonder: Will my baby grow up to be peaceful or aggressive? Homely or attractive? Successful or struggling at every step? What comes built-in, and what is nurtured—and how?

GENES: OUR BIOLOGICAL BLUEPRINT

1. Our genes predispose our biology; does this mean they determine our behaviors?

Behind the story of our body and our brain—surely the most awesome thing on our little planet—is the heredity that interacts with our experience to create both our universal human attributes and our individual traits. Barely more than a century ago, who would have guessed that every cell nucleus in your body contains the genetic master code for your entire body? It's as if every room in the Tower of London had a bookcase containing the architect's plans for the entire building. These plans run to 46 books—23 donated by your mother (from her egg) and 23 by your father (from his sperm). These books, called **chromosomes,** are each composed of a coiled chain of the molecule **DNA** (deoxyribonucleic acid). Small segments, called **genes,** of the giant DNA molecules form the words of these chromosome books (**FIGURE 3.1**, page 70). All told, each of us has 30,000 or so of these gene words. Each gene is a self-replicating unit capable of synthesizing proteins—the building blocks of our physical development.

▶ **chromosomes** threadlike structures made of DNA molecules that contain the genes.

▶ **DNA (deoxyribonucleic acid)** a complex molecule containing the genetic information that makes up the chromosomes.

▶ **genes** the biochemical units of heredity that make up the chromosomes; a segment of DNA capable of synthesizing a protein.

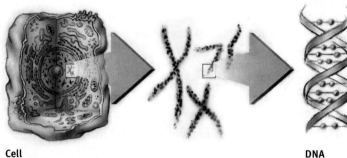

figure 3.1
The genes: Their location and composition
Contained in the nucleus of each of the trillions of cells in your body are chromosomes. Each chromosome contains a coiled chain of the molecule DNA. Genes are DNA segments that form templates for the production of proteins. By directing the manufacture of proteins, the genes determine our individual biological development.

Nucleus
(the inner area of a cell that houses chromosomes and genes)

Chromosome
(threadlike structure made largely of DNA molecules)

Gene
(segment of DNA containing the code for a particular protein; determines our individual biological development)

Cell
(the basic structural unit of a living thing)

DNA
(a spiraling, complex molecule containing genes)

"We share half our genes with the banana."

Evolutionary biologist Robert May, president of Britain's Royal Society, 2001

Genetically speaking, every other human is close to being your identical twin. Even the person you like least is your near-clone, sharing about 99.9 percent of your DNA (Plomin & Crabbe, 2000). But geneticists and psychologists are interested in the occasional variations found at particular gene sites in the DNA—variations that in their many combinations define each person's uniqueness. The differences are few. But vive la différence! Slight person-to-person variations from the common pattern give clues to why one person has a disease that another does not, why one person is short and another tall, why one is happy and another depressed.

Human traits are influenced by *gene complexes*—many genes acting in concert. How tall you are, for example, reflects the height of your face, the size of your vertebrae, the length of your leg bones, and so forth—each of which may be influenced by different genes. Complex human traits such as intelligence, happiness, and aggressiveness are similarly influenced by groups of genes. Still, researchers have discovered that variations in a single gene are part of the recipe for certain forms of Alzheimer's disease, for alcoholism, for schizophrenia, for reading disabilities—and the list grows.

Our genetic predispositions help explain both our shared human nature and our individual differences. Evolutionary psychology and behavior genetics together shed light on both human nature and human diversity.

EVOLUTIONARY PSYCHOLOGY: MAXIMIZING FITNESS

2. How do evolutionary psychologists use natural selection to explain behavior tendencies?

A fox is a wild and wary animal. If you capture a fox and try to befriend it, be careful. Stick your hand in the cage and, if the timid fox can't flee, it probably will make a snack of your fingers. Working at the Russian Academy of Science's Institute of Cytology and Genetics, Dmitry Belyaev was wondering how our human ancestors had domesticated dogs from their wolf forebears. Might he, within a comparatively short stretch of time, accomplish a similar feat by transforming the fearful fox into a friendly fox?

To find out, Belyaev set to work with 30 male and 100 female foxes. From their offspring he selected and mated the tamest 5 percent of males and 20 percent of females, measuring tameness by the foxes' responses to attempts to feed, handle, and stroke them. Over more than 30 generations of foxes, Belyaev and his successor, Lyudmila Trut, repeated that simple procedure. Today, 40 years and 45,000 foxes later, they have a new breed of foxes that, in Trut's (1999) words, are "docile, eager to please and unmistakably domesticated. . . . Before our eyes, 'the Beast' has turned into 'beauty,' as the aggressive behavior of our herd's wild [ancestors] entirely disap-

"Thanks for almost everything, Dad."

peared." So friendly and eager for human contact are they, so inclined to whimper to attract attention and to lick people like affectionate cats, that the cash-strapped institute has seized on a way to raise funds—by marketing its foxes to people as house pets.

As Belyaev and Trut demonstrated, when certain traits are *selected*—by conferring a reproductive advantage upon them—those traits, over time, come to prevail. Dog breeders, as Robert Plomin and his colleagues (1997) remind us, have given us sheepdogs that herd, retrievers that retrieve, trackers that track, and pointers that point. Psychologists, too, have bred dogs, mice, and rats whose genes predispose them to be serene or reactive, quick learners or slow learners.

Natural Selection

In life outside the laboratory, the same selection process confers an advantage to other organisms. Bacteria that resist a hospital's antibiotics will multiply rapidly as other bacteria die off. Over time, the natural result has been many hospitals plagued by antibiotic-resistant bacteria. Deep in the sea, many years ago, a mutant shark with keener-than-normal smell was able to find more prey, enabling it to live longer and leave more offspring. As nature continued over countless generations to give an edge to sharks best suited to their ecological niche, an exquisitely effective predator came into being.

Does **natural selection** also explain our human tendencies? Do we fear snakes and heights, for example, because our ancestors who feared them were more likely to survive and spread their genes? Nature has indeed selected advantageous variations from among the **mutations** (random errors in gene replication) and the new gene combinations produced at each human conception.

But the tight genetic leash that predisposes an ant's nest building, a dog's retrieving, or a cat's pouncing is looser on humans. The genes selected during our ancestral history provide more than a long leash; they endow us with a great capacity to learn and therefore to adapt to life in varied environments—from the tundra to the jungle. Genes and experience together wire the brain. Our adaptive flexibility in responding to different environments contributes to our fitness—our ability to survive and reproduce.

Yet in the big picture our lives are remarkably alike. Visit the international arrivals area at London's Heathrow Airport, a world hub where arriving passengers meet their excited loved ones. There you will see the same delighted joy in the faces of Kenyan grandmothers, Chinese children, and homecoming Britons. Although human differences grab our attention, our deep similarities also demand explanation.

These behavioral similarities arise from our biological similarity. Of our few genetic differences, only 6 percent are differences among races. Only 8 percent are differences among groups within a race. The rest—over 85 percent—are individual variations within local groups. The typical genetic difference between two Icelandic villagers or between two Kenyans is much greater than the *average* difference between the two groups. Thus, notes geneticist Richard Lewontin (1982), if after a worldwide catastrophe only Icelanders or Kenyans survived, the human species would suffer only "a trivial reduction" in its genetic diversity.

Why are we all so much alike? At the dawn of human history, our ancestors faced certain questions: Who is my ally, who my foe? What food should I eat? With whom should I mate? Some individuals answered those questions more successfully than others. Those disposed to eat nourishing rather than poisonous food survived to contribute their genes to later generations; those who deemed leopards "nice to pet" did not.

Similarly successful were those who mated with someone with whom they could produce and nurture offspring. Over generations, the genes of individuals not so disposed tended to be lost from the human gene pool. As further mutations occurred, genes providing an adaptive edge continued to be selected. The result, say **evolutionary psychologists**, is behavioral tendencies and thinking and learning capacities that prepared our Stone Age ancestors to survive, reproduce, and send

L.N. Trut, *American Scientist* (1999) 87: 160–169

From beast to beauty Forty years into the fox-breeding experiment, most of the offspring are devoted, affectionate, and capable of forming strong bonds with people.

▶ **natural selection** the principle that, among the range of inherited trait variations, those that lead to increased reproduction and survival will most likely be passed on to succeeding generations.

▶ **mutation** a random error in gene replication that leads to a genetic change.

▶ **evolutionary psychology** the study of the evolution of behavior and the mind, using principles of natural selection.

their genes into the future. Nature selected the fittest adaptations, which also include the human diversity that allows Arctic and equatorial dwellers to thrive in their distinct environments.

As inheritors of this prehistoric genetic legacy, we are predisposed to behave in ways that promoted our ancestors' surviving and reproducing. We love the taste of sweets and fats, which once were hard to come by but which prepared our ancestors to survive famines. Ironically, with famine rare in Western cultures, and sweets and fats beckoning us from store shelves, fast-food outlets, and vending machines, obesity has become a growing problem. We are, in some ways, biologically prepared for a world that no longer exists.

Evolution has been an organizing principle for biology for a long time. But only recently, in "the second Darwinian revolution," have psychologists attempted to harness evolutionary principles. Charles Darwin (1859) anticipated this application of evolutionary principles to psychology. In concluding *The Origin of Species*, he foresaw "open fields for far more important researches. Psychology will be based on a new foundation" (p. 346).

Those who are troubled by an apparent conflict between scientific and religious accounts of human origins may find it helpful to recall that different perspectives of life can be complementary (Chapter 1). For example, the scientific account attempts to tell us when and how; religious creation stories usually aim to tell about an ultimate who and why. As Galileo explained to the Grand Duchess Christina, "The Bible teaches how to go to heaven, not how the heavens go."

Only 35 percent of the American public finds Darwin's evolutionary theory "supported by evidence" (Brooks, 2001). Yet, notes Jared Diamond (2001), "virtually no contemporary scientists believe that Darwin was basically wrong." In today's world, Karl Marx is dead, Sigmund Freud is dying, and Darwin lives. Marxism didn't work. Freud, as we will see, was wrong about much. But Darwin's big idea lives on as an organizing principle for biology and, increasingly, for psychology.

Regardless of how the vigorous debate over evolutionary psychology ends, evolutionary psychologists have been on a roll. Psychologists, as we will see, are now using evolutionary principles to explore questions such as these:

- Why do infants start to fear strangers about the time they become mobile?
- Why are biological fathers so much less likely than unrelated boyfriends to abuse and murder the children with whom they share a home?
- Why are most parents so passionately devoted to their children?
- Why do so many more people have phobias about spiders and snakes than about more dangerous guns and electricity?
- How and why do men and women differ? For example, why are men quicker than women to perceive friendliness as sexual interest, to initiate sexual relations, and to feel jealous rage over a mate's having sex with someone else?

To see how evolutionary psychologists think and reason, let's pause to explore this last question: How—and why, according to evolutionary psychology—do women's sexuality and men's sexuality differ?

Sexuality

Psychologists Roy Baumeister, Kathleen Catanese, and Kathleen Vohs (2001) invite us to consider which **gender** has the stronger sex drive. More specifically, which desires more frequent sex, thinks more about sex, masturbates more often, initiates more sex, and makes more sacrifices to gain sex? The answers are men, men, men, men, and men. Indeed, "with few exceptions anywhere in the world," agree cross-cultural psychologist Marshall Segall and his colleagues (1990, p. 244), "males are more likely than females to initiate sexual activity." This difference is among the largest of gender differences in sexuality. There are others:

- In a 2001 survey of 281,064 entering American college students, 55 percent of men but only 32 percent of women agreed that "if two people really like each other, it's all right for them to have sex even if they've known each other for a very short time" (Sax & others, 2001). "I can imagine myself being comfortable and enjoying 'casual' sex with different partners," agreed 48 percent of men and 12 percent of women in one survey of 4901 Australians (Bailey & others, 2000).

▶ **gender** in psychology, the characteristics, whether biologically or socially influenced, by which people define *male* and *female*.

● In a careful survey of 3432 U.S. 18- to 59-year-olds, 48 percent of the women but only 25 percent of the men cited affection as a reason for first intercourse. And how often do they think about sex? "Every day" or "several times a day," acknowledged 19 percent of the women and 54 percent of the men (Laumann & others, 1994).

● Such gender differences characterize both heterosexual and homosexual people. Gay men report more interest in uncommitted sex, more responsiveness to visual sexual stimuli, and more concern with their partner's physical attractiveness than do lesbians (Bailey & others, 1994). (Aware of HIV risks, gay men are, however, having fewer partners than in 1985 [Altman, 1999].)

An Evolutionary Explanation

As biologists use natural selection to explain the mating behaviors of many species, so evolutionary psychologists use natural selection to explain women's more relational and men's more recreational approaches to sex. Their explanation goes like this: While a woman incubates and nurses one infant, a male can spread his genes through other females. Our natural yearnings are our genes' way of reproducing themselves. In our ancestral history, women most often sent their genes into the future by pairing wisely, men by pairing widely. "Humans are living fossils—collections of mechanisms produced by prior selection pressures," says evolutionary psychologist David Buss (1995).

And what do men and women find attractive in the other sex? Some aspects of attractiveness cross place and time. Men in 37 cultures, from Australia to Zambia, judge women as more attractive if they have a youthful appearance (**FIGURE 3.2**, page 74). Evolutionary psychologists say that men drawn to healthy, fertile-appearing women—women with smooth skin and a youthful shape suggesting many childbearing years to come—have stood a better chance of sending their genes into the future. From yesterday's Stone Age figurines to today's *Playboy* centerfolds and beauty pageant winners—and regardless of cultural variations in ideal weight—men feel most attracted to women whose waists are roughly a third narrower than their hips—a sign of future fertility (Singh, 1993).

Women also feel attracted to healthy-looking men, but especially to those who seem mature, dominant, bold, and affluent (Singh, 1995). Such attributes, say the evolutionary psychologists, connote a capacity to support and protect (Buss, 1996, 2000; Geary, 1998).

Evolutionary psychologists are also not surprised that each sex tends to advertise the qualities that maximize its odds of attracting desirable partners: women by spending time and money on appearance, men by trying to establish their status and dominance. In singles ads, for example, women tend to offer looks and seek status; men do the reverse (Rajecki & others, 1991). Why do even successful men lust after ever more money and power? Some psychologists speculate that such attributes are to men what antlers are to a

"It's not that gay men are oversexed; they are simply men whose male desires bounce off other male desires rather than off female desires."

Steven Pinker, How the Mind Works, *1997*

Canada's famed Starbuck Holstein bull sired more than 200,000 offspring.

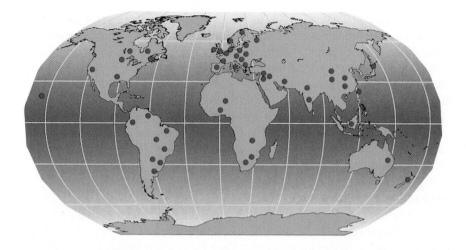

figure 3.2
Worldwide mating preferences David Buss and an international team of collaborators surveyed the mating preferences of 10,047 people in 37 cultures depicted by the dots (from Buss, 1994b). Everywhere, men more than women preferred attractive physical features suggesting youth and health—and reproductive potential. Everywhere, women more than men preferred mates with resources and social status. This gender difference, evolutionary psychologists believe, is the result of natural selection favoring those whose choices help perpetuate their genes.

stag or tail feathers to a male peacock. Men needn't consciously think, "I'm trying to outdo my male rivals in the competition for female attention." They're just designed to want to outdo their rivals (and to provide for their offspring), because those who did so in the past put more of their genes into our human gene pool.

Women also prefer mates with the potential for long-term mating and investment in their joint offspring (Gangestad & Simpson, 2000). They prefer stick-around dads over likely cads. The offspring of men who stayed around probably had greater survival prospects. Long-term mates contribute protection and support. Thus, for men there are genetic tradeoffs between seeking to distribute one's genes widely and being willing to co-parent.

There is a principle at work here, say evolutionary psychologists: Nature selects behaviors that increase the likelihood of sending one's genes into the future. As mobile gene machines, we are designed to prefer whatever worked for our ancestors in their environments. They were predisposed to act in ways that would leave grand-children—had they not been, we wouldn't be here. And as carriers of their genetic legacy, we are similarly predisposed.

Critiquing the Evolutionary Explanation

Without disputing nature's selection of traits that enhance gene survival, critics see problems with evolutionary psychology. It often, they say, starts with an effect (such as the gender sexuality difference) and works backward to propose an explanation. If men were uniformly loyal to their mates, might we not reason that the children of committed, supportive fathers more often survived to perpetuate their genes? Might not men also be better off bonded to one woman—both to increase the otherwise slim odds of impregnation and to keep her from the advances of competing men? Might not a ritualized bond—a marriage—also spare women from chronic male harrassment? Such suggestions are, in fact, evolutionary explanations for why humans tend to pair off monogamously. Although more men than women desire multiple sexual partners, the things men and women seek in a mate "are remark-ably similar," argue Lynn Carol Miller and her colleagues (2002). Most men and women wish for a single, long-term partner (Pedersen & others, 2002).

And what about those species, such as chimpanzees and bonobos, in which ardent females mate with numerous males? Does this ensure that the males, not knowing the true paternity of a female's offspring, will join in tolerating or protecting them? One can hardly lose at hindsight explanation, which is, said paleontologist Stephen Jay Gould (1997), mere "speculation [and] guesswork in the cocktail party mode."

Critics also emphasize that much of who we are is *not* hard-wired (which evolu-tionary psychologists don't dispute). Cultural expectations bend the genders, and what's attractive varies somewhat with time and place. The voluptuous Marilyn

"I had a nice time, Steve. Would you like to come in, settle down, and raise a family?"

Monroe ideal of the 1950s has been replaced by the turn-of-the-century leaner, athletic female image. Moreover, if socialized to value lifelong commitment, men may sexually bond with one partner; if socialized to accept casual sex, women may willingly have sex with many partners.

To some extent, gender differences in mate preferences are universal across cultures. But gender differences also vary with a culture's social and family structures. Show Alice Eagly and Wendy Wood (1999; Wood & Eagly, 2002) a culture with gender inequality—where men are providers and women are homemakers—and they will show you a culture where men strongly desire youth and domestic skill in their potential mates, and where women seek status and earning potential in their mates. Show Eagly and Wood a culture with gender equality, and they will show you a culture with smaller gender differences in mate preferences. They draw their conclusions from an analysis of the same 37 cultures studied earlier by David Buss.

Some critics worry about the social consequences of evolutionary psychology. Does it suggest a genetic determinism that strikes at the heart of progressive efforts to remake society (Rose, 1999)? Does it undercut ethical theory and moral responsibility? Could it be used to rationalize "high-status men marrying a series of young, fertile women" (Looy, 2001)?

Evolutionary psychologists calm concerns about genetic determinism by reminding us that humans have a great capacity for learning and social progress. (We come equipped to adapt and survive, whether living in igloos or tree houses.) They point to the coherence and explanatory power of evolutionary principles. They offer testable predictions (for example, that we will favor others to the extent they share our genes or can later reciprocate our favors). And they remind us that the study of how we came to be who we are need not dictate how we ought to act. Sometimes understanding our propensities helps us overcome them.

---

rehearse it!

1. Every cell nucleus in your body contains the genetic master code for your entire body. _____ are threadlike structures made largely of DNA molecules.
   a. Gene complexes   c. Chromosomes
   b. Nuclei   d. Cells

2. Each person's genetic blueprint combines contributions from the mother's egg and the father's sperm. When the egg and sperm unite, each contributes
   a. one chromosome pair.
   b. 23 chromosomes.
   c. 23 chromosome pairs.
   d. 30,000 chromosomes.

3. Evolutionary psychologists study how we came to be who we are. They are most likely to focus on
   a. how we differ from one another.
   b. the links between biology and behavior.
   c. natural selection of the fittest adaptations.
   d. random assignment of genes over several generations.

Answers can be found in Appendix C.

BEHAVIOR GENETICS: PREDICTING INDIVIDUAL DIFFERENCES

3. How do behavior geneticists explain individual differences?

Evolutionary psychologists apply Darwin's big idea to explain our universal human tendencies and our diversity and adaptability. **Behavior geneticists** more intensively assess our differences from one another. How much are our differences shaped by our differing genetic blueprints? And how much by our **environment**—every external influence, from maternal nutrition while in the womb to social support while nearing the tomb—reacting to our genetic traits? More specifically, to what extent are we formed by our upbringing? By our culture? And by our current circumstance?

To disentangle the threads of heredity and environment, behavior geneticists often use two sets of tweezers: twin studies and adoption studies.

▶ **behavior genetics** the study of the relative power and limits of genetic and environmental influences on behavior.

▶ **environment** every nongenetic influence, from prenatal nutrition to the people and things around us.

Womb mates In hopes of assessing genetic and environmental influences, behavioral geneticists have studied tens of thousands of twin pairs.

Michael Newman/PhotoEdit, Inc.

Twin Studies

To tease apart environment and heredity, it would be nice if we could control the home environment while varying heredity. Happily for our purposes, nature has given us ready-made subjects for this experiment: identical versus fraternal twins. **Identical twins**, who develop from a single fertilized egg that splits in two, are *genetically* identical (**FIGURE 3.3**). They are nature's own human clones—indeed, clones who share not only the same genes but the same conception, uterus, birth date, and cultural history.

Fraternal twins, who develop from separate eggs, are genetically no more similar than ordinary brothers and sisters. A person whose identical twin has Alzheimer's disease has a 60 percent risk of sharing the disease; if the affected twin is fraternal, the risk is only 30 percent (Plomin & others, 1997). Such a difference suggests a genetic influence.

figure 3.3
Same egg, same genes; different eggs, different genes Identical twins develop from a single fertilized egg, fraternal twins from two.

Identical
twins

Fraternal
twins

Same
sex only

Same or
opposite sex

Behavior geneticists ask: Are identical twins, being genetic clones of one another, behaviorally more similar than fraternal twins? Studies of nearly 13,000 pairs of Swedish twins, of 7000 Finnish twin pairs, and of 3810 Australian twin pairs provide a consistent answer: On both extraversion (outgoingness) and neuroticism (emotional instability), identical twins are much more similar than fraternal twins. In explaining individual differences, genes matter.

Other dimensions of personality and ability also reflect genetic influences. When John Loehlin and Robert Nichols (1976) gave a battery of questionnaires to 850 U.S. twin pairs, identical twins were much more similar than fraternals in many ways—in abilities, personality traits, and interests. However, the identical twins, more than fraternal twins, also reported being treated alike. So, did their experience rather than their genes account for their similarity? No, said Loehlin and Nichols; identical twins whose parents treated them alike were *not* psychologically more alike than identical twins who were treated less similarly.

If a young woman cloned herself, her daughter would also be her identical twin. If 25 years later the woman died, her husband would be left with a daughter who resembled the woman he loved and married. Would it be wrong for them to marry? (Adapted from Talbot, 2001.)

Separated Twins

Imagine the following science fiction experiment: A mad scientist decides to separate identical twins at birth, then rear them in differing environments. Better yet, consider a true story:

On a chilly Ohio Saturday morning in February 1979, some time after divorcing his first wife, Linda, Jim Lewis awoke in his modest, middle-class home next to his second wife, Betty. Jim—a romantic, affectionate type—was determined that this marriage would work and made a habit of leaving love notes to Betty around the house. As Jim lay in bed he thought about others he had loved, including his son, James Alan, and his faithful dog, Toy.

Having outfitted a workshop in a corner of his basement, Jim looked forward to spending some of the day's free time on his woodworking hobby. He had derived

▶ **identical twins** twins who develop from a single fertilized egg that splits in two, creating two genetically identical organisms.

▶ **fraternal twins** twins who develop from separate eggs. They are genetically no closer than brothers and sisters, but they share a fetal environment.

many hours of satisfaction from building furniture, picture frames, and an assortment of other items, including a circular white bench around a tree in his front yard. Jim also liked to spend free time driving his Chevy, watching stock-car racing, and drinking Miller Lite beer.

Jim was basically healthy. Having undergone a vasectomy, he was done having children. His blood pressure was a little high, perhaps related to his chain-smoking habit. He chewed his fingernails to the nub. And he suffered occasional half-day migraine headaches— "like somebody's hitting you with a two-by-four in the back of the neck." He had become overweight a while back but had shed some of the pounds.

What was extraordinary about Jim Lewis, however, was that at that same moment (I am not making this up) there existed another man—also named Jim—for whom all these things (right down to the dog's name) were also true.[1] This other Jim—Jim Springer—just happened, 38 years earlier, to have been his womb mate. Thirty-seven days after their birth, these two genetically identical twins were separated, adopted by blue-collar families, and reared with no contact or knowledge of the other's whereabouts until one February day when Jim Lewis' phone rang. The caller was his genetic clone (who, having been told he had a twin, set out to find him).

One month after that fateful encounter, the brothers became the first twin pair tested by University of Minnesota psychologist Thomas Bouchard and his colleagues, thus beginning a study of separated twins that extends to the present (Holden, 1980a,b; Wright, 1998). When given tests measuring their intelligence, personality, heart rate, and brain waves, the Jim twins—despite 38 years of separation— were virtually as alike as the same person tested twice. Their voice intonations and inflections were so similar that, hearing a playback of an earlier interview, Jim Springer guessed "That's me." Wrong—it was his brother.

Identical twins Oskar Stohr and Jack Yufe presented equally striking similarities. One was raised by his grandmother in Germany as a Catholic and a Nazi, while the other was raised by his father in the Caribbean as a Jew. Nevertheless, they share traits and habits galore. They like spicy foods and sweet liqueurs, have a habit of falling asleep in front of the television, flush the toilet before using it, store rubber bands on their wrists, and dip buttered toast in their coffee. Stohr is domineering toward women and yells at his wife, as did Yufe before he and his wife separated.

Aided by publicity in magazine and newspaper stories, Bouchard and his colleagues (1990; DiLalla & others, 1996; Segal, 1999) have located and studied more than 70 pairs of identical twins reared apart. They continue to find similarities not only of tastes and physical attributes but also of personality, abilities, attitudes, interests, and even fears.

In Sweden, which has a national registry of 70,000 twin pairs, Nancy Pedersen and her co-workers (1988) identified 99 separated identical twin pairs and more than 200 separated fraternal twin pairs. Compared with equivalent samples of identical twins reared together, the separated identical twins had more dissimilar personalities. Still, separated twins were more alike if genetically identical than if fraternal. Separation shortly after birth (rather than, say, at age 8) didn't amplify their personality differences.

The startling twin similarity stories do not impress Bouchard's critics. They contend that if any two strangers were to spend hours comparing their behaviors and

Identical twins are people two
Identical twins Gerald Levey and Mark Newman were separated at birth and raised in different homes. When reunited at age 31, they discovered that they both volunteered as firefighters. Research has shown remarkable similarities in the life choices of separated identical twins, lending support to the idea that genes influence personality.

Twins Lorraine and Levinia Christmas, driving to deliver Christmas presents to each other near Flitcham, England, collided (Shepherd, 1997).

"In some domains it looks as though our identical twins reared apart are . . . just as similar as identical twins reared together. Now that's an amazing finding and I can assure you none of us would have expected that degree of similarity."

Thomas Bouchard (1981)

---

[1]Actually, this description of the two Jims errs in one respect: Jim Lewis named his son James Alan. Jim Springer named his James Allan.

Coincidences are not unique to twins. Patricia Kern of Colorado was born March 13, 1941, and named Patricia Ann Campbell. Patricia DiBiasi of Oregon also was born March 13, 1941, and named Patricia Ann Campbell. Both had fathers named Robert, worked as bookkeepers, and at the time of this comparison had children ages 21 and 19. Both studied cosmetology, enjoyed oil painting as a hobby, and married military men, within 11 days of each other. They are not genetically related (from an AP report, May 2, 1983).

life histories, they would probably discover many coincidental similarities. If researchers created a control group of biologically unrelated pairs of the same age, sex, and ethnicity, who did not grow up together but who were as similar to one another in economic and cultural background as are separated twin pairs, wouldn't these pairs also exhibit striking similarities (Joseph, 2001)? (Bouchard replies that separated fraternal twins do not exhibit similarities comparable to those of separated identical twins.) Even the more impressive data from the personality assessments are clouded by the reunion of many of the separated twins some years before they were tested. Moreover, separated twins share an appearance and the responses it evokes. And adoption agencies tend to place separated twins in similar homes.

Nevertheless, the twin studies illustrate why scientific thinking has shifted toward a greater appreciation of genetic influences. Genes-R-Us.

Adoption Studies

Another real-life experiment, adoption, creates two groups of relatives: the adoptees' genetic relatives (biological parents and siblings) and environmental relatives (adoptive parents and siblings). For any given trait we can therefore ask whether adopted children are more like their adoptive parents, who contribute a home environment, or their biological parents, who contributed their genes. While sharing the same home environment, do adopted siblings come to share traits?

The stunning finding from studies of hundreds of adoptive families—toppling many of our cherished notions about parental influence—is that people who grow up together, whether biologically related or not, do not much resemble one another in personality (McGue & Bouchard, 1998; Plomin & others, 1998; Rowe, 1990). Adoptees' traits bear more similarities to their biological parents than to their caregiving adoptive parents.

If parental nurture mattered as much as most people suppose, then shouldn't people's personalities be more alike if they were reared in the same home? Shouldn't it matter whether the parents work or don't, fight or don't, drink or don't? Whether the house is a crowded apartment or a spacious estate? Whether the kitchen is stocked with green veggies or Twinkies, the family room with books or toy guns, the neighborhood school with computers or metal detectors? The finding is stunning enough to bear repeating: So far as personality development is concerned, environmental factors shared by a family's children have virtually no impact on their personalities. Two adopted children reared in the same home are no more likely to share personality traits with one another than with the child down the block. For chimpanzees too, heredity shapes personalities; being raised in the same zoo hardly matters (Weiss & others, 2000). Add this to the finding that identical twins, whether they grow up together or apart, are about as similar as we would expect from their shared genes, and the effect of shared rearing environment seems shockingly modest.

"Mom may be holding a full house while Dad has a straight flush, yet when Junior gets a random half of each of their cards his poker-hand may be a loser."

David Lykken (2001)

What we have here is perhaps "the most important puzzle in the history of psychology," contends Steven Pinker (2002): Why are children in the same family so different? (Even biological siblings tend to be strikingly different.) Why do the shared genes and the shared family environment (the family's social class, the parents' personalities and marital status, day care versus home care, the neighborhood) have so little discernible effect on children's personalities? Is it because each sibling nevertheless has differing experiences—differing peer influences and life events? Is it because siblings—despite sharing half their genes—have very different combinations of genes? Does parental influence therefore affect an easygoing child one way, an emotionally reactive child another? "Child-rearing is not something a parent does to a child," notes Judith Rich Harris (1998). "It is something the parent and the child do together. . . . I would have been pegged as a permissive parent with my first child, a bossy one with my second."

So is adoptive parenting a fruitless venture? Even if the personalities of adopted children do not much resemble those of their adoptive parents, adoption matters (Brodzinsky & Schechter, 1990). Although the genetic leash limits the family environment's influence on personality, parents do influence their children's attitudes, values, manners, faith, and politics. A pair of adopted children or identical twins *will* have more similar religious beliefs if reared in the same home (Kelley & De Graaf, 1997; Rohan & Zanna, 1996). Parenting matters!

David Young-Wolff/PhotoEdit, Inc.

Family ties Studies of adoptive families have provided new clues to hereditary and environmental influences. How similar would you expect adopted children to be to their adoptive parents? To their biological parents?

Moreover, in adoptive homes, child neglect and abuse and even parental divorce are rare. (Adoptive parents are carefully screened; natural parents are not.) So it is not surprising that, despite a somewhat greater risk of psychological disorder, most adopted children thrive, especially when adopted as infants (Benson & others, 1994; Wierzbicki, 1993). They score higher than their biological parents on intelligence tests. Seven in eight report feeling strongly attached to one or both adoptive parents. As children of self-giving parents, they grow up to be more self-giving and altruistic than average (Sharma & others, 1998). And they generally become happier and more stable people than they would have been in a stressed or neglectful environment. In one Swedish study, infant adoptees grew up with fewer problems than were experienced by children whose biological mothers had initially registered them for adoption but then decided to raise the children themselves (Bohman & Sigvardsson, 1990). Clearly, to benefit from adoption, children need not have personalities that resemble those of their adoptive parents.

The greater uniformity of adoptive homes—mostly healthy, nurturing homes—helps explain the lack of striking differences when comparing child outcomes of different adoptive homes (Stoolmiller, 1999).

Temperament Studies

As most parents will tell you after having their second child, babies differ even before gulping their first breath. Consider one quickly apparent aspect of personality. An infant's **temperament** includes inborn emotional excitability—whether reactive, intense, and fidgety, or easygoing, quiet, and placid. From the first weeks of life, "difficult" babies are more irritable, intense, and unpredictable. "Easy" babies are cheerful, relaxed, and predictable in feeding and sleeping (Chess & Thomas, 1987).

Temperament endures. Consider these findings:

- The most emotionally reactive newborns tend also to be the most reactive 9-month-olds (Wilson & Matheny, 1986; Worobey & Blajda, 1989).
- Four-month-olds who react to changing scenes with arched back, pumping legs, and crying are usually fearful and inhibited in their second year. Those who react with relaxed smiles are usually fearless and sociable in their second year (Kagan, 1990).
- Exceptionally inhibited and fearful 2-year-olds often are still relatively shy as 8-year-olds; about half will become introverted adolescents (Kagan & others, 1992, 1994).
- The most emotionally intense preschoolers tend to be relatively intense as young adults (Larsen & Diener, 1987). In one study that is following more than 900 New Zealanders through time, emotionally reactive and impulsive 3-year-olds developed into somewhat more impulsive, aggressive, and conflict-prone 21-year-olds (Caspi, 2000).

"Oh, he's cute, all right, but he's got the temperament of a car alarm."

▶ **temperament** a person's characteristic emotional reactivity and intensity.

▶ **interaction** the effect of one factor (such as environment) depends on another factor (such as heredity).

Heredity seems to predispose temperament differences. Physiological tests reveal that anxious, high-strung infants have high and variable heart rates and a reactive nervous system (Kagan & others, 1992). They become more physiologically aroused when facing new or strange situations. Compared with fraternal twins, identical twins have more similar temperaments (Emde & others, 1992; Gabbay, 1992; Robinson & others, 1992). Such evidence adds to the emerging conclusion that our biologically rooted temperament helps form our enduring personality (McCrae & others, 2000; Rothbart & others, 2000).

Group Differences

If genetic influences help explain individual differences in traits such as aggressiveness, can the same be said of group differences between men and women, or between people of different races? Not necessarily. Individual differences in height and weight are highly heritable. Yet nutritional rather than genetic influences explain why, as a group, today's adults are taller and heavier than those of a century ago. The two groups differ, but not because human genes have changed in a mere century's eyeblink of time. As with height and weight, so with personality and intelligence scores: Heritable individual differences need not imply heritable group differences. If some individuals are genetically disposed to be more aggressive than others, that needn't explain why some groups are more aggressive than others. Putting people in a new social context can change their aggressiveness.

Nature Enables Nurture

Among our similarities, the most important—the behavioral hallmark of our species—is an enormous adaptive capacity. Some human traits, such as having two eyes, develop the same in virtually every environment. But most psychologically interesting traits are expressed in particular environments. We all are driven to eat, but depending on our culturally learned tastes, we may have a yen for fish eyes, black bean salad, or chicken legs. Go barefoot for a summer and you will develop toughened, callused feet—a biological adaptation to friction. Meanwhile, your shod neighbor will remain a tenderfoot. The difference between the two of you is, of course, an effect of environment. But it is also the product of a biological mechanism. Our shared biology enables our developed diversity (Buss, 1991).

An analogy may help: Genes and environment—nature and nurture—work together like two hands clapping, with the environment reacting to and shaping what nature predisposes. Thus, asking whether your personality is more a product of your genes or environment is like asking whether water's wetness is due more to its hydrogen or its oxygen, or whether the area of a field is more the result of its length or width. We could, however, ask whether the *differing* areas of various fields are more the result of differences in their length or width. For psychological traits, human differences are nearly always the result of both genetic and environmental variations. Thus (to give a preview of coming attractions), eating disorders are genetically influenced: Some individuals are more at risk than others. But culture also bends the twig, for eating disorders are primarily a contemporary Western cultural phenomenon.

Gene-Environment Interaction

To say that genes and experience are *both* important is true, but it is an oversimplification. More precisely, their effects intertwine. Imagine two babies, one genetically predisposed to be attractive, sociable, and easygoing, the other less so. Assume further that the first baby attracts more affectionate and stimulating care than the second and so develops into a warmer and more outgoing person. As the two children grow older, the more naturally outgoing one more often seeks activities and friends that encourage further social confidence.

"Men's natures are alike; it is their habits that carry them far apart."

Confucius, Analects, ~500 B.C

"Heredity deals the cards; environment plays the hand."

Psychologist Charles L. Brewer (1990)

Genetic-environmental influence
People respond differently to a Rowan Atkinson (here playing Mr. Bean) than to a David Beckham.

What has caused their resulting personality differences? We cannot say simply that individual personalities are due *x* percent to genes and *y* percent to experience, because neither heredity nor experience dances alone. Our genetically influenced traits *evoke* significant responses in others. Thus, an aggressive child may be yelled at by a teacher who talks warmly to the child's model classmates.

This helps explain why identical twins reared in different families recall their parents' warmth as remarkably similar—almost as similar as if they had had the same parents (Plomin & others, 1988, 1991, 1994). Fraternal twins recall their early family life more differently—even if reared in the same family! "Children experience us as different parents, depending on their own qualities," notes Sandra Scarr (1990). Moreover, as we grow older we also *select* environments well suited to our natures.

So, from conception onward, we are the product of a cascade of **interactions** between our genetic predispositions and our surrounding environments. Our genes affect how people react to and influence us. Biological appearances have social consequences. Asking whether genes or experiences are more important is therefore like asking whether an engine or a steering wheel is more important for driving a car. So, forget nature *versus* nurture; think nurture *via* nature.

"I thought that sperm-bank donors remained anonymous."

rehearse it!

4. Studies of identical and fraternal twins offer an opportunity to assess genetic and environmental influences on behavior. Fraternal twins result when
a. a single egg is fertilized by a single sperm and then splits.
b. a single egg is fertilized by two sperm and then splits.
c. two eggs are fertilized by two sperm.
d. two eggs are fertilized by a single sperm.

5. Adoption studies seek to reveal genetic influences on personality. They do this mainly by
a. comparing adopted children with nonadopted children.
b. evaluating whether adopted children more closely resemble their adoptive parents or their biological parents.
c. studying the effect of prior neglect on adopted children.
d. studying the effect of one's age at adoption.

6. Although development is lifelong, there is stability of personality over time. For example,
a. temperament is a product of learning and can therefore be unlearned.
b. temperament seems to be biologically based and tends to remain stable throughout life.
c. temperament changes significantly during adolescence.
d. fraternal twins tend to have more similar temperaments than do identical twins.

Answers can be found in Appendix C.

"So I blame you for everything—whose fault is that?"

ENVIRONMENTAL INFLUENCE

4. To what extent are our lives shaped by parental nurture, prenatal nutrition, early stimulation, and peer influences?

Genetic influences predict roughly 40 to 50 percent of our individual variations in many personality traits. When asked what accounts for the rest, many people presume it is parental nurture.

But Peter Neubauer and Alexander Neubauer (1990, pp. 20–21) illustrate how, with hindsight, we may inappropriately credit or blame our parents:

> Identical twin men, now age thirty, were separated at birth and raised in different countries by their respective adoptive parents. Both kept their lives neat—neat to the point of pathology. Their clothes were preened, appointments met precisely on time, hands scrubbed regularly to a raw, red color. When the first was asked why he felt the need to be so clean, his answer was plain.
>
> "My mother. When I was growing up she always kept the house perfectly ordered. She insisted on every little thing returned to its proper place, the clocks—we had dozens of clocks—each set to the same noonday chime. She insisted on this, you see. I learned from her. What else could I do?"
>
> The man's identical twin, just as much a perfectionist with soap and water, explained his own behavior this way: "The reason is quite simple. I'm reacting to my mother, who was an absolute slob."

How Much Credit (or Blame) Do Parents Deserve?

Parents typically feel enormous pride in their children's successes, and guilt or shame over their failures. They beam when folks offer congratulations for the child who wins an award. They wonder where they went wrong with the child repeatedly called into the principal's office. Freudian psychiatry and psychology have been among the sources of such ideas, by blaming problems from asthma to schizophrenia on "bad mothering." And society reinforces such parent-blaming: Believing that parents shape their children as a potter molds clay, people readily praise parents for their children's virtues and blame them for their children's vices. Popular culture of the 1990s endlessly proclaimed the psychological harm toxic parents inflict on their fragile children. "The major source of human misery" is the "neglected, wounded child" within each of us, claimed author-lecturer John Bradshaw (1990, p. 7).

But do parents really produce future adults with an inner wounded child by being (take your pick from the toxic parent lists) overbearing—or uninvolved? Pushy—or ineffectual? Overprotective—or distant? Are children really so easily wounded by well-meaning but occasionally exhausted parents? If so, should we then blame our parents for our failings, and ourselves for our children's failings? Should we shame the parents of troubled children or pass city ordinances that punish them for their children's misdeeds? Or does all the talk of wounding fragile children through normal parental mistakes trivialize the brutality of real abuse?

If parental handling shapes children's personalities, then children who share the same parents should be somewhat similar, yes? But as we have seen, behavior geneticists have repeatedly found this to be untrue. Shared environmental influences—including the home influences that siblings share—typically account for less than 10 percent of children's personality differences (though they account for more of their beliefs and values). In the words of behavior geneticists Robert Plomin and Denise Daniels (1987), "Two children in the same family [are on average] as different from one another as are pairs of children selected randomly from the population." To developmental psychologist Sandra Scarr (1993), this implies that "parents should be given less credit for kids who turn out great and blamed less for kids who don't."

If parental influence on personality is more limited than popular psychology supposes, what aspects of the environment do matter? Here, for starters, are four: prenatal environment, early experience, peer influence, and culture.

Even among chimpanzees, when one infant is hurt by another, the victim's mother will often attack the offender's mother (Goodall, 1968).

"If you want to blame your parents for your own adult problems, you are entitled to blame the genes they gave you, but you are not entitled—by any facts I know—to blame the way they treated you. . . . We are not prisoners of our past."

Martin Seligman, **What You Can Change and What You Can't,** *1994*

Prenatal Environment

"Nurture" begins in the womb, as embryos receive differing nutrition and varying levels of exposure to toxic agents. Even identical twins may receive not-so-identical prenatal nurture. Two-thirds of identical twins share the same placenta, and thus a more similar prenatal environment (though one might get a richer blood supply and weigh more at birth). Other identical twins have separate placentas (**Figure 3.4**). In this arrangement, one placenta sometimes has a more advantageous placement that provides better nourishment and therefore a better placental barrier against viruses. Early indications are that, compared with same-placenta identical twins, those who develop with separate placentas are somewhat less similar in their psychological traits (Phelps & others, 1997).

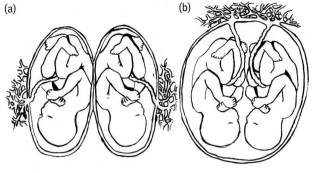

figure 3.4
Two placental arrangements in identical twins Identical twins may (a) have separate placentas and blood sources, as do fraternal twins. Or they may (b) share the same placental blood. Researchers are now studying how this variation predicts later differences between identical twins. (From Davis & others, 1995.)

Experience and Brain Development

Experience helps develop the brain's neural connections. Even if forgotten, early learning helps prepare our brains for thought and language, and also for later experiences. But how do early experiences leave their "marks" in the brain? Mark Rosenzweig and David Krech reared some young rats in solitary confinement and others in a communal playground (**Figure 3.5**). When their brains were then analyzed, the rats who died with the most toys had won. Those living in the enriched environment, which simulated a natural environment, usually developed a heavier and thicker brain cortex.

Rosenzweig (1984; Renner & Rosenzweig, 1987) was so surprised by this discovery that he repeated the experiment several times before publishing his findings. The effects are great enough that, shown brief video clips of rats, you could tell from their activity and curiosity whether their rearing was impoverished or enriched (Renner & Renner, 1993). After 60 days of being housed in enriched environments, report Bryan Kolb and Ian Whishaw (1998), rats' brain weight increases 7 to 10 percent and the number of synapses mushrooms about 20 percent—"an extraordinary change!" Such results have motivated improvements in the environments we provide for laboratory, farm, and zoo animals—and for children in institutions.

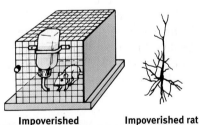

Impoverished environment

Impoverished rat brain cell

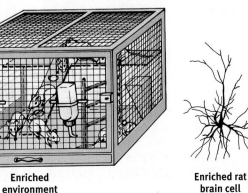

Enriched environment

Enriched rat brain cell

figure 3.5
Experience affects brain development Mark Rosenzweig and David Krech reared rats either alone in an environment without playthings, or with others in an environment enriched with playthings that were changed daily. In 14 of 16 repetitions of this basic experiment, the rats placed in the enriched environment developed significantly more cerebral cortex (relative to the rest of the brain's tissue) than did those in the impoverished environment.

Stringing the circuits young String musicians who started playing before age 12 have larger and more complex neuron circuits controlling the note-making left-hand fingers than do string musicians whose training started later (Elbert & others, 1995).

Courtesy of C. Brune

Several research teams have found that the stimulation of touch or massage benefits infant rats and premature babies (Field, 2001; Meaney & others, 1988). "Handled" infants of both species gain weight more rapidly and develop faster neurologically. William Greenough and his University of Illinois colleagues (1987) further discovered that repeated experiences modify a rat's neural tissue—at the very spot in the brain that processes the experience. After brain maturation provides us with an abundance of neural connections, experience preserves our activated connections while allowing our unused ones to degenerate. The result by puberty is a massive loss of unemployed neural pathways.

Here, then, at the juncture of nurture and nature, is where a child's enriched environment activates and preserves connections that, given impoverished experiences, might have died off from disuse. There is a biological reality to early childhood education. During early childhood—while the excess connections are still on call—youngsters can most easily master the grammar and accent of another language. Lacking any exposure to written or signed language before adolescence, the person will never master any language (see pages 307–308).

Likewise, lacking visual experience during the early years, people whose vision is restored by cataract removal never achieve normal perceptions (see pages 175–176). The brain cells normally assigned to vision have died or been diverted to other uses. For us to have optimum brain development, normal stimulation during the early years is critical. The maturing brain seems governed by a rule: Use it or lose it.

The brain's development does not, however, end with childhood. Throughout life our neural tissue is changing. Both nature and nurture sculpt our synapses. Sights and smells, touches and tugs activate and strengthen some neural pathways while others weaken from disuse. Similar to pathways through a forest, less traveled paths gradually disappear, popular paths are broadened. Our genes dictate our overall brain architecture, but experience directs the details. If a monkey is trained to push a lever with a finger several thousand times a day, the brain tissue that controls the finger changes to reflect the experience. Human brains work similarly. The wiring of Eric Clapton's brain reflects the thousands of hours he has spent playing the guitar. Likewise, while learning to keyboard or in-line skate or perform a laboratory task, we perform with increasing skill as our brain incorporates the learning (**FIGURE 3.6**).

"Nature and nurture . . . are simply two different ways of making deposits in the brain's synaptic ledgers."

Joseph Le Doux, The Synaptic Self, 2002

figure 3.6
A trained brain A well-learned finger-tapping task activates more motor cortex neurons (orange area, right) than were active in the same brain before training (left). (From Karni & others, 1998.)

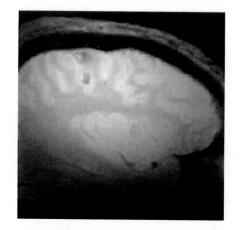
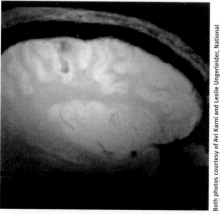

Both photos courtesy of Avi Karni and Leslie Ungerleider, National Institute of Mental Health

Peer Influence

As children mature, what sorts of experiences do the work of nurturing? Peer influences on development may exceed parental influences, argues Judith Harris (1998, 2000a). Consider:

● Preschoolers who disdain a certain food despite parents' urgings often will eat the food if put at a table with a group of children who like it.

● A child who hears English spoken with one accent at home and another in the neighborhood and at school will invariably adopt the accent of the peers, not the parents. Moreover, immigrant children who are placed in peer groups of nonimmigrants quickly lose their parents' culture. "When in Rome, they become Romans," notes Harris. "Even if their parents happen to be British or Chinese or Mesquakie."

● Direct parental influences on smoking are less important than many people suppose. Rather, teens who start smoking typically have *friends* who model smoking, who suggest its pleasures, and who offer cigarettes (Rose & others, 1999).

Part of the similarity to peers may result from a "selection effect," as kids seek out peers with similar attitudes and interests. Those who smoke (or don't) may select as friends those who also smoke (or don't). But our sensitivity to peers makes biological sense, suggests Harris (1998). Parental nurture is essential to our early survival, and parental influence is especially discernible while children are in the home. But in the long run, we are destined to play with, work with, and mate with peers. Small wonder that nature predisposes us to be acutely sensitive to their styles and opinions (another example of how our evolved nature *enables* our cultural nurture).

Other psychologists remind us that individual parents matter (Collins & others, 2000; Eisenberg & others, 1998a,b; Vandell, 2000). The power of parenting to shape our differences is clearest at the extremes. Chapter 4 will provide the sharpest examples—the abused who become abusive, the neglected who become neglectful, the loved but firmly handled children who become self-confident and socially competent. The power of the family environment also shows up in the remarkable academic and vocational successes of children of the refugee Asian boat people—successes attributed to close-knit, supportive, even demanding families (Caplan & others, 1992).

Howard Gardner (1998) concludes that parents and peers are complementary:

> Parents are more important when it comes to education, discipline, responsibility, orderliness, charitableness, and ways of interacting with authority figures. Peers are more important for learning cooperation, for finding the road to popularity, for inventing styles of interaction among people of the same age. Youngsters may find their peers more interesting, but they will look to their parents when contemplating their own futures. Moreover, parents choose the neighborhoods and schools that supply the peers.

It may be scary to realize how risky it is to have and raise children. In procreation, a woman and a man shuffle their gene decks and deal a life-forming hand to their child-to-be, who is then subjected to countless influences beyond their control. Knowing that lives are formed by influences beyond parents' control is another reason for caution in crediting parents for their children's achievements and blaming them for their children's troubling traits. And if our children are not formless blobs to be sculpted by parental nurture, then perhaps we parents can relax a bit more and love our children for who they are.

"Men resemble the times more than they resemble their fathers."

Ancient Arab proverb

Sybil Shackman

Peer power As we develop we must play, work, mate, and partner with peers. No wonder children and youth are so sensitive and responsive to peer influences.

Culture

5. How do cultural norms affect our behavior?

Compared with the narrow path taken by flies, fish, and foxes, nature has built for us a longer, wider road along which environment drives us. The mark of our species—nature's great gift to us—is our ability to learn and adapt. We come equipped with a huge cerebral hard drive ready to receive many gigabytes of cultural software.

Culture is the behaviors, ideas, attitudes, and traditions shared by a large group of people and transmitted from one generation to the next (Brislin, 1988). If we all lived in homogeneous ethnic groups in separate regions of the world, as some people still do, cultural diversity would be less relevant. In Japan, 99 percent of the country's 126 million people are of Japanese descent. Internal cultural differences are therefore minimal compared with those found in Los Angeles, where the public schools recently taught 82 different languages, or in Toronto or Vancouver, where minorities are one-third of the population and many are immigrants (as are 17 percent of all Canadians and 24 percent of Australians) (Iyer, 1993; Statistics Canada, 2002; Trewin, 2001). I am ever mindful that the readers of this book are culturally diverse. You reach from Australia to Africa and from Singapore to Sweden.

Variation Across Cultures

We see our adaptability in cultural variations among our beliefs and our values, in how we raise our children and bury our dead, in what we wear (or whether we wear anything at all). Riding along with a unified culture is like biking with the wind: As it carries us along, we hardly notice it is there. When we try riding *against* the wind we feel its force. Face to face with a different culture, we become aware of the cultural winds. Visiting Europe, most North Americans notice the smaller cars, the left-handed use of the fork, the uninhibited attire on the beaches. Stationed in the

Uniform requirements People in individualist Western cultures sometimes see traditional Japanese culture as confining. But from the Japanese perspective the same tradition expresses a "serenity that comes to people who know exactly what to expect from each other" (Weisz & others, 1984).

Kevin R. Morris/Corbis

Middle East, European and American soldiers alike realized how liberal their home cultures were. A decade of working with refugee immigrants sensitized psychologist Mary Pipher (2002) to her own culture:

> Like most Americans I only speak English fluently. I value freedom and personal space. I am time-conscious. I am comfortable with only certain forms of touch. A certain amount of eye contact and distance between bodies seems right to me. Some things seem much more edible than others. Certain clothes—jeans and T-shirts—feel best to me. I do not cover my head when I go out and I wear shoes inside my house. I like to talk.

Arriving in North America, visitors from some cultures struggle to understand why many people wear their dirty *street* shoes in the house, or why people find it fun to eat a picnic lunch out in the woods amid flies and ants.

Each cultural group evolves its own **norms**—the rules for accepted and expected behavior. Many South Asians, for example, use only the right hand's fingers for eating. The Japanese have norms for taking off street shoes, and the British have a norm for orderly waiting in line. Sometimes social expectations seem oppressive: "Why should it matter how I dress?" Yet, norms grease the social machinery. Prescribed, well-learned behaviors free us from self-preoccupation. When we know when to clap or bow, which fork to pick up first at the dinner party, and what sorts of gestures and compliments are appropriate, we can relax and enjoy one another without fear of embarrassment or insult. Likewise, having a well-understood norm for greeting people in one's culture—by shaking hands or kissing each cheek—precludes awkward moments of indecision about whether to lead with one's hand or cheek.

When cultures collide, their differing norms often befuddle. For example, if someone invades our **personal space**—the portable buffer zone we like to maintain around our bodies—we feel uncomfortable. Scandinavians, North Americans, and the British prefer more personal space than do Latin Americans, Arabs, and the French (Sommer, 1969). At a social gathering, a Mexican seeking a comfortable conversation distance may end up walking around a room with a backpedaling American. (You can experience this at a party by playing Space Invader as you talk with someone.) To the American, the Mexican may seem intrusive; to the Mexican, the American may seem cold and standoffish.

Cultures also vary in their expressiveness. Those with roots in northern European culture often perceive people from Mediterranean cultures as warm and charming but inefficient. The Mediterraneans, in turn, see northern Europeans as efficient but cold and preoccupied with punctuality (Triandis, 1981).

Cultures vary in their pace of life, too. A British businessperson may feel frustrated by a Latin American client who arrives 30 minutes after the time set for lunch. People from time-conscious Japan—where bank clocks keep exact time, pedestrians walk briskly, and postal clerks fill requests speedily—may find themselves growing impatient when visiting Indonesia, where clocks keep less accurate time and the pace of life is more leisurely (Levine & Norenzayan, 1999). In adjusting to their host countries, the first wave of U.S. Peace Corps volunteers reported that two of their greatest culture shocks, after the language difference, were the differing pace of life and the people's differing sense of punctuality (Spradley & Phillips, 1972).

Variation Over Time

Consider, too, how rapidly cultures may change over time. English poet Geoffrey Chaucer (1342–1400) is separated from a modern Briton by only 20 generations, but the two would converse with great difficulty. In the thinner slice of history since 1960, most Western cultures have changed with remarkable speed. Middle-class people fly to places they once only read about, e-mail those they once snail-mailed, and work in air-conditioned comfort where they once sweltered. They enjoy the convenience of on-line holiday shopping, cell phone calling, and—enriched by doubled per-person

Robert Azzi/Woodfin Camp & Associates

Culture influences personal space
Behavior that is seen as appropriate in one culture may violate the norms of another group. In Arab countries, such as Saudi Arabia, people typically require less personal space than do members of some European and North American groups.

Cross-cultural communication can also suffer in translation, as in these signs for English-speaking tourists (Lederer, 1987; Triandis, 1994):

- *In a Greek tailor shop: "Because of a big rush, we will execute customers in strict rotation."*
- *An Italian laundry: "Ladies, leave your clothes here and spend the afternoon having a good time."*
- *A Danish airline: "We take your bags and send them in all directions."*
- *A Moscow hotel room: "If this is your first visit to the USSR, you are welcome to it."*
- *A detour sign in Japan: "Stop: Drive Sideways."*

▶ **culture** the enduring behaviors, ideas, attitudes, and traditions shared by a large group of people and transmitted from one generation to the next.

▶ **norm** an understood rule for accepted and expected behavior. Norms prescribe "proper" behavior.

▶ **personal space** the buffer zone we like to maintain around our bodies.

real income—eating out two and a half times as often as did their parents back in the culture of 1960. With greater economic independence, today's women are more likely to marry for love and less likely to endure abusive relationships out of economic need. Various minorities enjoy expanded human rights.

But some changes seem not so wonderfully positive. Had you fallen asleep in the United States in 1960 and awakened near the end of the millennium, you would have opened your eyes to a culture with a doubled rate of divorce, a nearly tripled rate of teen suicide, a quadrupled rate of reported juvenile violent crime, a quintupled prison population, and an escalating incidence of depression (Myers, 2000). You would also find Americans spending more hours at work, fewer hours sleeping, and fewer hours with friends and family (Frank, 1999; Putnam, 2000). Similar cultural transformations have occurred in Canada, Britain, Australia, and New Zealand.

Whether we love or loathe these changes, we cannot fail to be impressed by their breathtaking speed. And we cannot explain them by changes in the human gene pool, which evolves far too slowly to account for high-speed cultural transformations. Cultures vary. Cultures change. And cultures shape our lives.

Culture and Child Rearing

Child-rearing practices are not immune to the variations in cultural values from one time and place to another. Do you prefer children who are independent or children who comply with what others think?

If you live in a Westernized culture, the odds are you prefer the former. Westernized countries derived from northern Europe are noted for their *individualism* (giving priority to personal goals and identity). Most parents in these societies want their children to think for themselves. "You are responsible for yourself," Western families and schools tell their children. "Follow your conscience. Be true to yourself. Discover your gifts. Think through your personal needs." But these cultural values represent change over time. A half-century ago, Western parents placed greater priority on obedience, respect, and sensitivity to others (Alwin, 1990; Remley, 1988). "Be true to your traditions," they taught their children. "Be loyal to your heritage and country. Show respect toward your parents and other superiors."

Unlike most Westerners, who now raise their children to be independent, many Asians, Africans, and Central and South Americans favor *collectivism* (giving priority to group goals and identity). They tend to live in communal cultures, cultures that focus on cultivating emotional closeness. Rather than being given their own bedrooms and entrusted to day care, infants and toddlers typically sleep with their mothers and spend their days close to a family member (Morelli & others, 1992; Whiting & Edwards, 1988). Children of communal cultures grow up with a stronger sense of "family self"—a feeling that what shames the child shames the family, and what brings honor to the family, brings honor to the self. Compared with Westerners, people in Japanese and Chinese cultures, for example, exhibit greater shyness toward strangers and greater concern for social harmony and loyalty (Bond, 1988; Cheek & Melchior, 1990; Triandis, 1994). "My parents will be disappointed in me" is a concern expressed by 7 percent of American and Italian teenagers and 14 percent of Australian teens, but by nearly 25 percent of teens in Taiwan and Japan (Atkinson, 1988).

Parental involvement promotes development Parents in every culture facilitate their children's discovery of their world, but cultures differ in what they deem important. Asian cultures place more emphasis on school and hard work than does North American culture. This may help explain why Japanese and Taiwanese children get higher scores on mathematics achievement tests.

José Luis Pelaez, Inc./Corbis

Children across place and time have thrived under various child-rearing systems. Upper-class British parents traditionally handed off routine caregiving to nannies, then sent their children off to boarding school at about age 10. These children generally grew up to be pillars of British society, just like their parents and their boarding-school peers. In the African Gusii society, babies nurse freely but spend most of the day on their mother's back—with lots of body contact but little face-to-face and language interaction. When the mother becomes pregnant, the toddler is weaned and handed over to someone else, often an older sibling. Westerners may wonder about the negative effects of this lack of verbal interaction, but then the African Gusii would in turn wonder about Western mothers pushing their babies around in strollers and leaving them in playpens and car seats (Small, 1997). Such diversity in child rearing cautions us against presuming that our culture's way is the only way to rear children successfully.

Developmental Similarities Across Groups

Because we are so mindful of how others differ from us, we often fail to notice the similarities predisposed by our shared biology. Cross-cultural research can help us by leading us to appreciate both our cultural diversity *and* our human kinship. Compared with the person-to-person differences within groups, the differences between groups are small. Regardless of our culture, we humans share the same life cycle. We all speak to our infants in similar ways and respond similarly to their coos and cries (Bornstein & others, 1992a,b). All over the world, the children of parents who are warm and supportive feel better about themselves and are less hostile than are the children of parents who are punitive and rejecting (Rohner, 1986; Scott & others, 1991).

Within a culture, ethnic subgroups may behave differently and yet be influenced similarly. Differences sometimes attributed to race may therefore actually result from other factors. David Rowe and his colleagues (1994, 1995) illustrate this with an analogy: Black men tend to have higher blood pressure than white men. Suppose that (1) in both groups salt consumption correlates with blood pressure, and (2) salt consumption is higher among black men than among white men. What then might we expect? A blood pressure "race difference" that may actually be, at least partly, a *diet* difference.

And that, say Rowe and his colleagues, parallels psychological findings: Behavior differences, like blood pressure differences, can result from differing inputs to the same process. Although American Hispanic, Asian, black, and white ethnic groups differ in school achievement and delinquency, the differences are "no more than skin deep." To the extent that family structure, peer influences, and parental education predict behavior in one ethnic group, they do so for other groups as well.

So in surface ways we may differ, but as members of one species we seem subject to the same psychological forces. As members of different ethnic and cultural groups, our languages vary, yet they reflect universal principles of grammar. Our tastes vary, yet they reflect common principles of hunger. Our social behaviors vary, but they reflect pervasive principles of human influence (Chapter 15).

"We recognize that we are the products of many cultures, traditions, and memories; that mutual respect allows us to study and learn from other cultures; and that we gain strength by combining the foreign with the familiar."

U.N. Secretary-General Kofi Annan, Nobel Peace Prize lecture, 2001

"When someone has discovered why men in Bond Street wear black hats he will at the same moment have discovered why men in Timbuctoo wear red feathers."

G. K. Chesterton, Heretics, 1908

rehearse it!

9. In psychology, *personal space* refers to the portable buffer zone we like to maintain around our bodies. This space varies according to cultural norms. Which of the following prefer *less* personal space than the others?
   a. Americans   c. Arabs
   b. British   d. Scandinavians

10. Cultural values vary over time and place. Western cultures are to _____ as Asian and African cultures are to _____.
   a. obedience; emotional closeness
   b. independence; social harmony
   c. loyalty; interdependence
   d. respect; morality

11. Human developmental processes tend to _____ from one group to another because we are members of _____.
   a. be the same; the same ethnic group
   b. be the same; the same species
   c. differ; different species
   d. differ; different ethnic groups

Answers can be found in Appendix C.

THE NATURE AND NURTURE OF GENDER

6. How do nature and nurture interact to define us as male or female?

Earlier we considered one significant gender difference—in sexual interests and behaviors. Let's recap this chapter's theme—that nature and nurture together predispose our behavior—by considering other gender variations.

The Nature of Gender

In domains where men and women have faced similar challenges—regulating heat with sweat, developing tastes that nourish, growing calluses where the skin meets friction—the sexes are similar. Even when describing the ideal mate, both men and women put traits such as "kind," "honest," and "intelligent" at the top of their lists. But in some domains pertinent to mating, evolutionary psychologists contend, guys act like guys whether they are elephants or elephant seals, rural peasants or corporate presidents. Such differences between the sexes arise, genetically, from their differing sex chromosomes and, physiologically, from their differing concentrations of sex hormones.

Males and females are variations on a single form. Seven weeks after conception, you were anatomically indistinguishable from someone of the other sex. Then your genes activated your biological sex. Your sex was determined by your twenty-third pair of chromosomes, the sex chromosomes. The member of the pair that came from your mother was an **X chromosome**. From your father, you received the one chromosome out of 46 that is not unisex. This was either an X chromosome, making you a girl, or a **Y chromosome**, making you a boy. The Y chromosome includes a single gene that throws a master switch triggering the testes to develop and produce the principal male hormone, **testosterone**, which at about the seventh week starts the development of external male sex organs. (Females also have testosterone, but less of it.) Another key period for sexual differentiation falls during the fourth and fifth prenatal months, when different brain-wiring patterns for males and females develop under the influence of the male's greater testosterone and the female's ovarian hormones (Fitch & Dennenberg, 1998; Udry, 2000).

The Nurture of Gender

Although biologically influenced, gender is also socially constructed. What biology initiates, culture accentuates.

"Sex brought us together, but gender drove us apart."

Gender Roles

In psychology, as in the theater, a **role** refers to a cluster of prescribed actions—the behaviors we expect of those who occupy a particular social position. One set of norms defines our culture's **gender roles**—our expectations about the way men and women behave. Traditionally, men have initiated dates, driven the car, and picked up the check; women have decorated the home, bought and cared for the children's clothes, and selected the wedding gifts. And consider work roles: In Australia, women devote 54 percent more time to unpaid household work and 71 percent more time to child care than do men (Trewin, 2001). In the United States, married mothers do 90 percent of the laundry and 13 percent of the car maintenance (Acock & Demo, 1994). And, I do not have to tell you

Gender roles have changed, but not every male has changed with them.

which parent, about 90 percent of the time in two-parent families, stays home with a sick child, arranges for the baby-sitter, or calls the doctor (Maccoby, 1995).

Gender roles can smooth social relations, saving awkward decisions about who does what. But they often do so at a cost: If we deviate from such conventions, we may feel anxious.

Evolution seemingly predisposes men everywhere to be aggressive and dominant in order to serve their reproductive goals, and predisposes women to the interpersonal skills that serve their reproductive goals (Archer, 1996). But we know that some gender roles are not rigidly fixed by evolution, because they vary across cultures. In nomadic societies of food-gathering people, there is minimal division of labor by sex. Boys and girls receive much the same upbringing. However, in agricultural societies, women remain close to home, working in the fields and staying with the children; men often roam more freely, herding cattle or sheep. Such societies typically socialize their children into distinct gender roles (Segall & others, 1990; Van Leeuwen, 1978).

Gender roles everywhere have tended to limit women's rights and power. "There are no human societies in which women dominate men," notes Felicia Pratto (1996). In 2002, women were 14.3 percent of the world's national legislators, 5 percent of the presidents and prime ministers of the world's countries, and 0 percent of the Nobel awardees in economics since the prize was first awarded in 1901 (CIA, 2002; IPU, 2002).

Gender roles vary over time as well as across cultures:

- As we began the last century, only one country—New Zealand—granted women the right to vote. As we ended it, only one democracy—Kuwait—did not (Briscoe, 1997).
- With the flick of an apron, the number of U.S. college women hoping to be full-time homemakers plunged during the late 1960s and early 1970s (**FIGURE 3.7**). In 1970, one in 10 entering U.S. law students were women; in 2001, half were (Glater, 2001). Over the decades since 1930, women's assertiveness has increased and decreased with their social status—up until the end of World War II, then down until the mid-1960s, then up again (Twenge, 2001).
- Gender ideas also vary across generations. When families emigrate from Asia to Canada and the United States, the immigrant children often grow up with peers who assume gender roles different from those of the immigrant parents. Daughters, especially, may feel torn between competing sets of norms (Dion & Dion, 2001).

► **X chromosome** the sex chromosome found in both men and women. Females have two X chromosomes; males have one. An X chromosome from each parent produces a female child.

► **Y chromosome** the sex chromosome found only in males. When paired with an X sex chromosome from the mother, it produces a male child.

► **testosterone** the most important of the male sex hormones. Both males and females have it, but the additional testosterone in males stimulates the growth of the male sex organs in the fetus and the development of the male sex characteristics during puberty.

► **role** a set of expectations (norms) about a social position, defining how those in the position ought to behave.

► **gender role** a set of expected behaviors for males and for females.

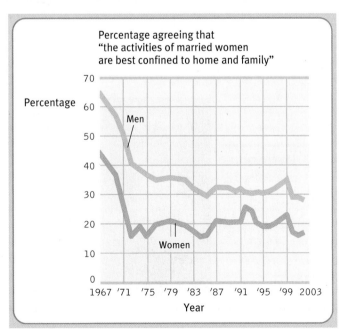

Percentage agreeing that "the activities of married women are best confined to home and family"

figure 3.7
Changing attitudes about gender roles U.S. college students' endorsement of the traditional view of women's role has declined dramatically. Men's and women's attitudes have also converged. (From Dey & others, 1991; Sax & others, 2002.)

Hulton Archive/Getty Images

▶ **gender identity** one's sense of being male or female.

▶ **gender-typing** the acquisition of a traditional masculine or feminine role.

▶ **social learning theory** the theory that we learn social behavior by observing and imitating and by being rewarded or punished.

▶ **gender schema theory** the theory that children learn from their cultures a concept of what it means to be male and female and that they adjust their behavior accordingly.

"How is it gendered?"

Gender and Child Rearing

Society assigns each of us to a *gender*, the social category of male or female. The inevitable result is our strong **gender identity**, our sense of being male or female. To varying extents, we also become **gender-typed**. That is, some boys more than others exhibit traditionally masculine traits and interests, and some girls more than others become distinctly feminine.

Social learning theory assumes that children learn gender-linked behaviors by observing and imitating and by being rewarded or punished. "Nicole, you're such a good mommy to your dolls"; "Big boys don't cry, Alex." But modeling and rewarding is not done by parents alone, because the differences in the way parents rear boys and girls aren't enough to explain gender-typing (Lytton & Romney, 1991). In fact, even when their families discourage traditional gender-typing, children organize themselves into "boy worlds" and "girl worlds," each guided by rules for what boys and girls do.

A later version of social learning theory, called *social-cognitive theory*, also recognizes the importance of children's emerging gender conceptions (Bussey & Bandura, 1999). So, too, does **gender schema theory**, which also combines social learning theory with cognition: Out of your struggles to comprehend the world came concepts, or *schemas*, including a schema for your own gender (Bem, 1987, 1993). Gender became a lens (a schema) through which you view your experiences (**Figure 3.8**). Before age 1, children begin to discriminate male and female voices and faces (Martin & others, 2002). After age 2, language forces children to begin organizing their worlds on the basis of gender. English, for example, uses the pronouns *he* and *she*; other languages classify objects as masculine ("*le* train") or feminine ("*la* table"). Through language, dress, toys, and

figure 3.8
Two theories of gender-typing
Social learning theory proposes that gender-typing evolves through imitation and reinforcement. Gender schema theory proposes that one's concept of maleness and femaleness influences one's perceptions and behavior.

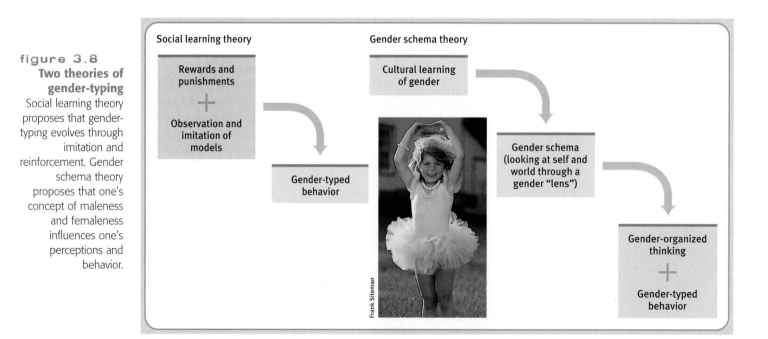

Mitchel Gerber/Corbis

Gender-typing Popular culture, from children's movies to professional wrestling, often appeals to boys' and girls' eagerness to categorize the world by gender, with images of macho men and coy, helpless women.

songs, social learning shapes gender schemas. Children then compare themselves with their concept of gender ("I am male—thus, masculine, strong, aggressive," or "I am female—therefore, feminine, sweet, and helpful") and adjust their behavior accordingly.

rehearse it!

12. The fertilized egg will develop into a boy if it receives
    a. an X chromosome from its mother.
    b. an X chromosome from its father.
    c. a Y chromosome from its mother.
    d. a Y chromosome from its father.

13. Gender roles vary across cultures and over time. "Gender role" refers to our

    a. sense of being male or female.
    b. expectations about the way males and females behave.
    c. biological sex.
    d. beliefs about how men and women should earn a living.

14. Psychologists differentiate between our biological sex and our gender. As a

consequence of the gender assigned to us by society, we develop a gender identity, which means that we
a. exhibit traditional masculine or feminine roles.
b. are socially categorized as male or female.
c. have a sense of being male or female.
d. have an ambiguous biological sex.

Answers can be found in Appendix C.

POSTSCRIPT: REFLECTIONS ON NATURE AND NURTURE

"There are trivial truths and great truths," reflected the physicist Niels Bohr on some of the paradoxes of modern science. "The opposite of a trivial truth is plainly false. The opposite of a great truth is also true." It appears true that our ancestral history helped form us as a species. Where there is variation, natural selection, and heredity, there will be, on some scale, evolution. The unique gene combination created when our mother's egg engulfed our father's sperm also helped form us, as individuals. Genes predispose both our shared humanity and our individual differences. This is a great truth about human nature. Genes form us.

But it also is true that our experiences help form us. In the womb, in our families, and in our peer social relationships, we learn ways of thinking and acting. Even differences initiated by our nature may be amplified by our nurture. If our genes and hormones mix predisposes males to be more aggressive than females, culture may magnify this gender difference through norms that encourage males to be macho and females to be the kinder, gentler sex. If men are inclined to roles that demand physical power, and women to more nurturing roles, each may then exhibit the actions expected of those who fill such roles and find themselves shaped accordingly. Roles remake their players. Presidents in time become more presidential, servants more servile. In such ways, our life experiences in local environments and surrounding cultures help form us. This, too, is a great truth about human nurture. Our experiences form us.

● ● ●

If nature and nurture—genes and scenes—jointly form us, are we "nothing but" the product of nature and nurture?

We *are* the product of nature and nurture, but we are also an open system. Genes are all-pervasive but not all-powerful. Constrained by the dictates of their DNA, organisms construct themselves in particular places and times. Sometimes people defy their genetic bent to reproduce, by electing celibacy. Culture, too, is all-pervasive but not all-powerful. Sometimes people defy peer pressures, by asserting their freedom and doing the opposite of the expected. To excuse our failings by blaming our nature and nurture is what philosopher-novelist Jean-Paul Sartre called "bad faith"—attributing responsibility for one's fate to bad genes or bad influences.

In reality, we are both the creatures and the creators of our worlds. We are—it is a great truth—the products of our genes and environments. Nevertheless—another great truth—the stream of causation that shapes the future runs through our present choices. Our decisions today design our environments tomorrow. Mind matters. The human environment is not like the weather—something that just happens. We are its architects. Our hopes, goals, and expectations influence our future. And that is what enables cultures to vary and to change so quickly.

● ● ●

I know from my mail and from public opinion surveys that some readers feel troubled by the naturalism and evolutionism of contemporary science. They worry that a science of behavior (and evolutionary science in particular) will destroy our sense of the beauty, mystery, and spiritual significance of the human creature. For those concerned, I offer some reassuring thoughts.

When Isaac Newton explained the rainbow in terms of light of differing wavelengths, the poet Keats feared that Newton had destroyed the rainbow's mysterious beauty. Yet, notes Richard Dawkins (1998) in *Unweaving the Rainbow,* Newton's analysis led to Maxwell's theory of electromagnetism and onward to an even deeper mystery—Einstein's theory of special relativity. Moreover, nothing about Newton's optics need diminish our appreciation for the dramatic elegance of a rainbow arching across a rain-darkened sky.

When Galileo assembled evidence that the Earth revolved around the Sun, not vice versa, he did not offer irrefutable proof for his theory. Rather he offered a coherent explanation for a variety of observations, such as the changing shadows cast by the Moon's mountains. His explanation eventually won the day because it described and explained things in a way that made sense, that hung together. Darwin's big idea likewise is a coherent view of natural history. It offers an organizing principle that unifies various observations.

Although some people of faith may find the scientific idea of human origins troubling, many others find it congenial with their spirituality. In the fifth century, St.

Augustine (quoted by Wilford, 1999) wrote, "The universe was brought into being in a less than fully formed state, but was gifted with the capacity to transform itself from unformed matter into a truly marvelous array of structures and life forms." Some 1600 years later, Pope John Paul II in 1996 welcomed science-religion dialogue, finding it noteworthy that evolutionary theory "has been progressively accepted by researchers, following a series of discoveries in various fields of knowledge." Evolution, he concluded, is "more than just a theory."

Meanwhile, many people of science are awestruck at the emerging understanding of the universe and the human creature. It boggles the mind—the entire universe popping out of a point some 14 billion years ago, and instantly inflating to cosmological size. Had the energy of this Big Bang been the tiniest bit less, the universe would have collapsed back on itself. Had it been the tiniest bit more, the result would have been a soup too thin to support life. Had gravity been a teeny bit stronger or weaker, or had the weight of a carbon proton been a wee bit different, our universe just wouldn't have worked.

What caused this almost-too-good-to-be-true fine-tuned universe? Why is there something rather than nothing? What made it—like Baby Bear's porridge—"just right"? How did it come to be, in the words of Harvard-Smithsonian astrophysicist Owen Gingerich (1999), "so extraordinarily right, that it seemed the universe had been expressly designed to produce intelligent, sentient beings"? Is there a benevolent superintelligence behind it all? Have there instead been an infinite number of universes born and we just happen to be the lucky inhabitants of one that, by chance, was exquisitely fine-tuned to give birth to us? Or does that idea violate Occam's razor, the principle that we should prefer the simplest of competing explanations? On most of these matters, science is silent. Faced with such mind-boggling questions, a humble, awed, scientific silence is appropriate, suggested philosopher Ludwig Wittgenstein: "Whereof one cannot speak, thereof one must be silent."

Rather than fearing or restraining science, we can welcome its enlarging our understanding and awakening our sense of awe. In *The Fragile Species*, Lewis Thomas (1992) described his utter amazement that the Earth in time gave rise to bacteria and eventually to Bach's *Mass in B-Minor*. In a short 4 billion years, life has come from nothing to structures as complex as a 6-billion-unit strand of DNA and the incomprehensible intricacy of the human brain. Nature, says cosmologist Paul Davies (1992, 1999), seems cunningly devised to produce extraordinary, self-replicating, information-processing systems—us. Although we appear to have been created from dust, over eons of time, the end result is a priceless creature, one rich with potentials beyond our imagining.

"The causes of life's history [cannot] resolve the riddle of life's meaning."

Stephen Jay Gould, Rocks of Ages: Science and Religion in the Fullness of Life, *1999*

"The larger the island of knowledge, the longer the shoreline of wonder."

Ralph W. Sockman

chapter review

REVIEWING

The Nature and Nurture of Behavior

GENES: OUR BIOLOGICAL BLUEPRINT

1. Our genes predispose our biology; does this mean they determine our behaviors?

Genes (DNA segments that form the chromosomes) are the biochemical units of heredity. They provide the blueprint for protein molecules, the building blocks of our physical and behavioral development. Our genetic predispositions help explain our behaviors, but they do not determine them.

EVOLUTIONARY PSYCHOLOGY: MAXIMIZING FITNESS

2. How do evolutionary psychologists use natural selection to explain behavior tendencies?

Evolutionary psychologists study how natural selection has shaped our universal behavior tendencies. They reason that if organisms vary, if only some mature to produce surviving offspring, and if certain inherited behavior tendencies assist that survival, then nature must select those tendencies. They believe this helps explain gender differences in sexuality. Critics maintain that evolutionary psychologists make too many hindsight explanations.

BEHAVIOR GENETICS: PREDICTING INDIVIDUAL DIFFERENCES

3. How do behavior geneticists explain individual differences?

Behavior geneticists use methods such as twin, adoption, and temperament studies to identify the extent to which various traits and disorders are inherited.

Studies of the inheritance of temperament, and of twins and adopted children, provide scientific support for the idea that nature *and* nurture influence one's developing personality. Genes and environment, biological and social factors, direct our life courses as their effects intertwine.

ENVIRONMENTAL INFLUENCE

4. To what extent are our lives shaped by parental nurture, prenatal nutrition, early stimulation, and peer influences?

Parental nurture matters, but it is not the sole determinant of who we are or become. Genetic influences are pervasive, but so are prenatal environments, early experiences, cultures, and peer influences. Sculpted by experience, neural interconnections multiply rapidly after birth.

5. How do cultural norms affect our behavior?

Human variations across cultures and over time show how differing norms, or expectations, guide behavior. Cultures differ in their norms for personal space, expressiveness, and pace of life. They also differ in their emphasis on the individual versus the group.

THE NATURE AND NURTURE OF GENDER

6. How do nature and nurture interact to define us as male or female?

Gender is a social category, and it illustrates the interaction between nature and nurture. Although males and females share similarly adaptive bodily procedures, differing sex chromosomes and differing concentrations of sex hormones lead to significant physiological sex difference. Yet gender differences vary widely depending upon cultural socialization through social learning and gender schemas.

A CRITICAL THINKER'S REVIEW OF CHAPTER 3

You've now studied and reviewed **The Nature and Nurture of Behavior**. For even better retention, reflect on these concepts at a deeper level. If you need to refresh your memory of the six categories of critical thinking shown in parentheses below, see page 34. See if you can answer each of these questions in a short paragraph.

1. Whose explanation of gender differences in sexuality do you find most persuasive—that of evolutionary psychologists or their critics? Now switch gears completely and write a few persuasive lines about the explanation with which you are least likely to align yourself. Do you still feel as strongly opposed to that perspective? (perspective taking)

2. How might behavior geneticists investigate the heritability of intelligence with sets of identical twins raised together and sets of fraternal twins raised together? (scientific problem solving)

3. Steven is a third-grader who for his age is very large, strong, and "tough" looking. However, Steven has a sweet, sensitive personality. Use the concept of genetic and environmental interaction to explain how Steven could be drawn into a group of bullies in his school. (psychological reasoning)

4. Many researchers have recently concluded that the shared home environment has less effect on children's development than is often supposed, and that peer influences matter more than we realized. What evidence supports that conclusion? (practical problem solving)

5. Why are so few women worldwide in top leadership positions? Use what you have learned about the nature and nurture of gender to try to explain this phenomenon. (creative problem solving)

6. James states that our evolutionary heritage has fixed our gender-specific behaviors. He claims "guys can't help being jerks who run around in search of one-night stands." His friend Charlie retorts that humans have exhibited dramatic behavior variations across cultures and over time. Explain why Charlie's argument counters James's statement. (pattern recognition)

Answers can be found in Appendix C.

TERMS AND CONCEPTS TO REMEMBER

chromosomes, p. 69

DNA (deoxyribonucleic acid), p. 69

genes, p. 69

natural selection, p. 71

mutation, p. 71

evolutionary psychology, p. 71

gender, p. 72

behavior genetics, p. 75

environment, p. 75

identical twins, p. 76

fraternal twins, p. 76

temperament, p. 79

interaction, p. 81

culture, p. 86

norm, p. 87

personal space, p. 87

X chromosome, p. 90

Y chromosome, p. 90

testosterone, p. 90

role, p. 90

gender role, p. 90

gender identity, p. 92

gender-typing, p. 92

social learning theory, p. 92

gender schema theory, p. 92

To continue your study and review of The Nature and Nurture of Behavior, visit this book's Web site at www.worthpublishers.com/myers. You will find practice tests, review activities, and Web links for more information on topics related to The Nature and Nurture of Behavior.

chapter4

The Developing Person

In mid-1978, the newest astonishment in medicine . . . was the birth of an English baby nine months after conception in a dish. The older surprise, which should still be fazing us all, is that a solitary sperm and a single egg can fuse and become a human being. . . . This has been going on under our eyes for so long a time that we've gotten used to it; hence the outcries of amazement at this really minor technical modification of the general procedure—nothing much, really, beyond relocating the beginning of the process from the fallopian tube to a plastic container.

Lewis Thomas, *The Medusa and the Snail*, 1979

The developing person is no less a wonder after birth than in the womb. As we journey through life—from womb to tomb—when, how, and why do we develop? We can't help but notice how people differ. However, to **developmental psychologists**, who study physical, mental, and social changes throughout the human life cycle, discerning our commonalities is just as important. Virtually all of us began walking around age 1 and talking by age 2. As children, we each engaged in social play in preparation for life's work. As adults, we all smile and cry, love and loathe, and occasionally ponder the fact that someday we will die. Psychology's developmental perspective examines how people are continually developing, from infancy through old age. Much of its research centers on three major issues:

1. *Nature/nurture:* How do genetic inheritance (*our nature*) and experience (*the nurture we receive*) influence our development?
2. *Continuity/stages:* Is development a gradual, continuous process like riding an escalator, or does it proceed through a sequence of separate stages, like climbing rungs on a ladder?
3. *Stability/change:* Do our early personality traits persist through life, or do we become different persons as we age?

In Chapter 3, we engaged the nature/nurture issue. At this chapter's end, we will reflect on the continuity and stability issues.

"Nature is all that a man brings with him into the world; nurture is every influence that affects him after his birth."

Francis Galton, English Men of Science, 1874

PRENATAL DEVELOPMENT AND THE NEWBORN

1. How does life develop before birth?

Conception

Nothing is more natural than a species reproducing itself. Yet nothing is more wondrous. Consider human reproduction. The process starts when a woman's ovary releases a mature egg, a cell roughly the size of the period at the end of this sentence, and when the 200 million or more sperm deposited during intercourse begin their race upstream toward it.

Like space voyagers approaching a huge planet, the sperm approach a cell 85,000 times their own size. The relatively few that make it to the egg release digestive enzymes that eat away the egg's protective coating, allowing a sperm to penetrate (**FIGURE 4.1**, page 100). But the egg is hardly passive. As soon as one sperm begins to penetrate, the egg's surface blocks out the others. Meanwhile, fingerlike projections sprout around the successful sperm and pull it in. Before half a day elapses, the egg nucleus and the sperm nucleus fuse. The two have become one. Consider it your most fortunate of moments. Among 200 million sperm, the one needed to make you, in combination with that one particular egg, won the race.

Study Tip: *Treat each main section of a chapter as if it were a short chapter—an amount suitable for reading in one sitting. To assist your doing so, each section begins with a preview question and ends with a Rehearse It! quiz.*

▶ **developmental psychology** a branch of psychology that studies physical, cognitive, and social change throughout the life span.

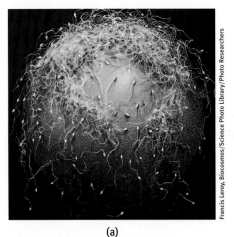

(a)

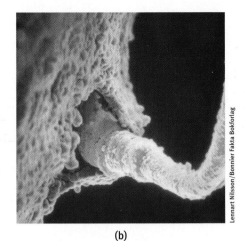

(b)

figure 4.1
Life is sexually transmitted
(a) Sperm cells surround an ovum (egg). (b) As one sperm penetrates the egg's jellylike outer coating, a series of chemical events begins that will cause sperm and egg to fuse into a single cell. If all goes well, that cell will subdivide again and again to emerge 9 months later as a 100-trillion-cell human being.

"From the very moment that the sperm hits the egg, a precarious trip on the thin edge of biological extinction has begun."

Ralph Blair, Nevertheless Joy! *1989*

Prenatal development	
zygote:	conception to 2 weeks
embryo:	2 weeks through 8 weeks
fetus:	9 weeks to birth

"You shall conceive and bear a son. So then drink no wine or strong drink."

Judges 13:7

figure 4.2
Prenatal development (a) The embryo grows and develops rapidly. At 40 days, the spine is visible and the arms and legs are beginning to grow. (b) Five days later, the inch-long embryo's proportions have begun to change. The rest of the body is now bigger than the head, and the arms and legs have grown noticeably. (c) By the end of the second month, when the fetal period begins, facial features, hands, and feet have formed. (d) As the fetus enters the fourth month, its 3 ounces could fit in the palm of your hand.

Prenatal Development

Fewer than half of all fertilized eggs, called **zygotes**, survive beyond the first 2 weeks (Grobstein, 1979). But for you and me, good fortune prevailed. Beginning as one cell, each of us became 2 cells, then 4—each cell just like the first. Then, within the first week, when this cell division had produced a zygote of some 100 cells, the cells began to *differentiate*—to specialize in structure and function. How identical cells do this—as if one decides "I'll become a brain, you become intestines!"—is a scientific puzzle that developmental biologists are just beginning to solve.

About 10 days after conception, the increasingly diverse cells attach to the mother's uterine wall, beginning approximately 37 weeks of the closest human relationship. The zygote's outer part attaches to the uterine wall, forming the placenta, through which nourishment passes. The inner cells become the **embryo** (**FIGURE 4.2**). Over the next 6 weeks, organs begin to form and function. The heart begins to beat, and the liver begins to make red blood cells.

By 9 weeks after conception, the organism looks unmistakably human. It is now a **fetus**. By the end of the sixth month, organs such as the stomach are sufficiently formed and functional to allow a prematurely born fetus a chance of survival.

At each prenatal stage, genetic *and* environmental factors affect our development. The placenta transfers nutrients and oxygen from mother to fetus, while screening out many potentially harmful substances. But some substances slip by. The placental screen can admit **teratogens**—harmful agents such as particular viruses and drugs. If the mother is a heroin addict, her baby will be born a heroin addict. If she carries the AIDS virus, her baby may also. A pregnant woman never smokes alone; she and her fetus both experience reduced blood oxygen and a shot of nicotine. If she is a heavy smoker, her fetus may receive fewer nutrients and be born underweight and at risk for various problems.

There is no known safe amount of alcohol for a pregnant woman. Even light drinking can affect the fetal brain (Braun, 1996; Day, 2002). Alcohol enters the

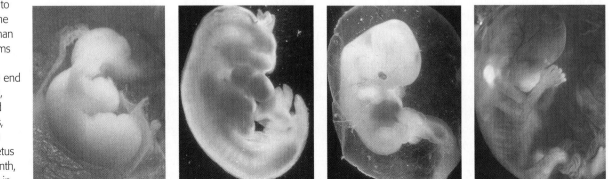

(a)　　(b)　　(c)　　(d)

woman's bloodstream—and her fetus'—and depresses activity in both their central nervous systems. If she drinks heavily, her baby will be at risk for birth defects and mental retardation. For 1 in 750 infants, the effects are visible as **fetal alcohol syndrome (FAS)**, marked by a small, misproportioned head and lifelong brain abnormalities that lead to learning disabilities and behavior problems. Research with rats indicates that even a single drinking binge during the brain growth spurt period (comparable in humans to 6 months' gestation) can kill many millions of brain cells (Ikonomidou & others, 2000).

The Competent Newborn

2. What are some of the newborn's abilities?

Having survived prenatal hazards, we as newborns came equipped with reflexes ideally suited for our survival. We withdrew our limbs to escape pain. If a cloth over our face interfered with our breathing, we turned our head from side to side and swiped at it.

New parents are often in awe of the coordinated sequence of reflexes by which their baby gets food. The **rooting reflex** illustrates this: When something touches their cheek, babies open their mouth and vigorously "root" for a nipple. Finding one, they automatically close on it and begin sucking—which itself requires a coordinated sequence of tonguing, swallowing, and breathing. Failing to find satisfaction, the hungry baby may cry—a behavior parents are predisposed to find highly unpleasant and very rewarding to relieve.

Moreover, psychologists have discovered that we are born preferring sights and sounds that facilitate social responsiveness. As newborns, we turn our heads in the direction of human voices. We gaze longer at a drawing of a facelike image (**FIGURE 4.3**) than at a bull's-eye pattern; yet we gaze more at a bull's-eye pattern—which has contrasts much like those of the human eye—than at a solid disk (Fantz, 1961). We prefer to look at objects 8 to 12 inches away, which, wonder of wonders, just happens to be the approximate distance between a nursing infant's eyes and its mother's (Maurer & Maurer, 1988).

Our perceptual abilities develop continuously during the first months of life. Within days after birth, our brain's neural networks were stamped with the smell of our mother's body. Thus, a week-old nursing baby, placed between a gauze pad from its mother's bra and one from another nursing mother, will usually turn toward the

Margin glossary

▶ **zygote** the fertilized egg; it enters a 2-week period of rapid cell division and develops into an embryo.

▶ **embryo** the developing human organism from about 2 weeks after fertilization through the second month.

▶ **fetus** the developing human organism from 9 weeks after conception to birth.

▶ **teratogens** agents, such as chemicals and viruses, that can reach the embryo or fetus during prenatal development and cause harm.

▶ **fetal alcohol syndrome (FAS)** physical and cognitive abnormalities in children caused by a pregnant woman's heavy drinking. In severe cases, symptoms include noticeable facial misproportions.

▶ **rooting reflex** a baby's tendency, when touched on the cheek, to open the mouth and search for the nipple.

Prepared to feed and eat Animals are predisposed to respond to their offsprings' cries for nourishment.

figure 4.3
Newborns' preference for faces When shown these two stimuli with the same elements, Italian newborns spent nearly twice as many seconds looking at the facelike image (Johnson & Morton, 1991). Canadian newborns—average age 53 minutes in one study—display the same apparently inborn preference to look toward faces (Mondloch & others, 1999).

CLOSE-UP

How Do We Know What Infants See and Remember?

Can a newborn see well enough to distinguish shapes? Can a 3-month-old recognize faces? Does a 5-month-old have a concept of number? If babies could talk, we would ask them. But they can't, so psychologists let behavior do the talking. Developmental researchers, for example, exploit a simple form of learning called **habituation**—a decrease in responding with repeated stimulation. A novel stimulus gets attention when first presented. But the more often the stimulus is presented, the weaker the response becomes. This seeming boredom with familiar stimuli gives us a way to ask infants—some as young as 7 hours old—what they see and remember.

Janine Spencer, Paul Quinn, and their colleagues (1997; Quinn, 2002), used a novelty preference procedure to ask 4-month olds how they recognize cats and dogs. The researchers first showed the infants a series of images of cats or dogs. Which of the two animals in **FIGURE 4.4** do you think the infants would find more novel (measured in looking time) after seeing a series of cats? It was the hybrid animal with the dog's head (or with a cat's head, if they had previously viewed a series of dogs). This suggests that infants, like adults, focus first on the face, not the body.

Other researchers using the habituation phenomenon report

figure 4.4
Quick—which is the cat? Researchers used cat-dog hybrid images such as these to test how infants categorize animals.

Courtesy Paul Quinn, © John Wiley & Sons.

▶ **habituation** decreasing responsiveness with repeated stimulation. As infants gain familiarity with repeated exposure to a visual stimulus, their interest wanes and they look away sooner.

that infants can also discriminate colors, shapes, and sounds and can understand some basic concepts of numbers and physics (for example, that two solid objects cannot occupy the same space).

Why have such elegantly simple studies been done only recently? Researcher Alan Slater (1994) explains: To recognize a new stimulus as different, an infant must remember the initial stimulus. Until the early 1980s, researchers assumed a newborn's brain was too immature to enable such memory. Then, as their appreciation for a newborn's abilities grew, they devised new ways to test the scope of infant cognition.

---

smell of its own mother's pad (MacFarlane, 1978). At 3 weeks, if given a pacifier that sometimes turns on recordings of its mother's voice and sometimes that of a female stranger's, an infant will suck more vigorously when it hears its now-familiar mother's voice (Mills & Melhuish, 1974). So not only can we as young infants see what we need to see, and smell and hear well, but we are already using our sensory equipment to learn.

---

rehearse it!

1. Developmental psychologists tend to focus on three major issues. Which of the following is not one of those issues?
   a. Nature/nurture
   b. Uniqueness/commonality
   c. Stability/change
   d. Continuity/stages

2. The 9 months of prenatal development prepare the individual for survival outside the womb. The body organs first begin to form and function during the period of the _____; within 6 months, during the period of the _____, the organs are sufficiently functional to allow a chance of survival.
   a. zygote; embryo   c. embryo; fetus
   b. zygote; fetus   d. placenta; fetus

3. Teratogens are chemicals that pass through the placenta's screen and may harm an embryo or fetus. Which of the following is *not* a teratogen?
   a. Oxygen   c. Alcohol
   b. Heroin   d. Nicotine

4. Stroke a newborn's cheek and he or she will root for a nipple. This illustrates
   a. a reflex.
   b. sensorimotor learning.
   c. differentiation.
   d. a gender difference.

Answers can be found in Appendix C.

INFANCY AND CHILDHOOD

During infancy, a baby grows from newborn to toddler, and during childhood from toddler to teenager. We all traveled this path, developing physically, cognitively, and socially. From infancy on, brain and mind, neural hardware and cognitive software, develop together. The association areas of the cortex—those linked with thinking, memory, and language—are the last brain areas to develop. As they do, the child's mental abilities surge ahead (Chugani & Phelps, 1986; Thatcher & others, 1987).

▶ **maturation** biological growth processes that enable orderly changes in behavior, relatively uninfluenced by experience.

"It is a rare privilege to watch the birth, growth, and first feeble struggles of a living human mind."

Annie Sullivan, in Helen Keller's
The Story of My Life, *1903*

Physical Development

3. How do the brain and motor skills develop during infancy and childhood?

Brain Development

While you resided in your mother's womb, your body was forming nerve cells at an exploding rate of nearly one-quarter million per *minute*. On the day you were born, you had most of the brain cells you would ever have. However, at birth your nervous system was immature: After birth, the neural networks that eventually enabled you to walk, talk, and remember had a wild growth spurt (**Figure 4.5**). From ages 3 to 6, the brain's neural network is sprouting most rapidly in the frontal lobes, which enable rational planning (and which continue developing into adolescence and beyond). Fiber pathways supporting language and agility proliferate into puberty, after which a pruning process shuts down excess connections, which wither away, while strengthening others (Paus & others, 1999; Thompson & others, 2000).

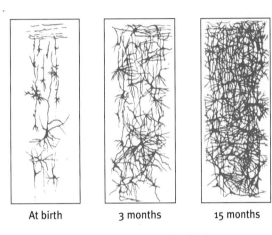

At birth   3 months   15 months

figure 4.5
Drawings of human cerebral cortex sections In humans, the brain is immature at birth. As the child matures, the neural networks grow increasingly more complex.

figure 4.6
Infant at work Babies only 3 months old can learn that kicking moves a mobile—and can retain that learning for a month. (From Rovee-Collier, 1989, 1997.)

A flower unfolds in accord with its genetic blueprint. So do we, experiencing an orderly sequence of genetically designed biological growth processes called **maturation**. Maturation decrees many of our commonalities—from standing before walking, to using nouns before adjectives. Severe deprivation or abuse will retard development, and ample experiences with parents who talk and read to the child will help sculpt neural connections. Yet the genetic growth tendencies are inborn. Maturation sets the basic course of development; experience adjusts it.

MATURATION AND INFANT MEMORY The lack of neural connections helps explain why our earliest memories seldom predate our third birthdays (Howe & Courage, 1993; Nelson, 1993). We see this in the memories of a group of preschoolers who experienced an emergency fire evacuation caused by a burning popcorn maker. Seven years later they were able to recall the alarm and what caused it—*if* they were 4 to 5 years old at the time. Those who experienced the event as 3-year-olds could not remember the cause and usually misrecalled being already outside when the alarm sounded (Pillemer, 1995). Other studies confirm that the average age of earliest conscious memory is 3.5 years (Bauer, 2002). By 4 to 5 years, childhood amnesia is giving way to remembered experiences (Bruce & others, 2000).

Although we consciously recall little from before age 4, some memories exist during and beyond those early years. Given occasional reminders, 3-month-old infants who learn that moving their leg propels a mobile will remember the association for at least a month (**Figure 4.6**).

Courtesy of Carolyn Rovee-Collier, Rutgers University

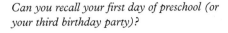

Can you recall your first day of preschool (or your third birthday party)?

Motor Development

The developing brain also enables physical coordination. As an infant's muscles and nervous system mature, more complicated skills emerge. With minor exceptions, the sequence of physical (motor) development is universal. Babies roll over before they sit unsupported, and they usually creep on all fours before they walk. These behaviors reflect not imitation but a maturing nervous system; blind children, too, crawl and walk.

Triumphant toddlers
Roll, crawl, walk, run—the sequence of these motor development milestones is the same the world around, though babies reach them at varying ages.

There are, however, individual differences in the timing of this sequence. In the United States, for example, 25 percent of all babies walk by age 11 months, and 90 percent by age 15 months (Frankenburg & others, 1992).

Genes play a major role. Identical twins typically begin sitting up and walking on nearly the same day (Wilson, 1979). Biological maturation—including the rapid development of the cerebellum at the back of the brain—creates our readiness to learn walking at about age 1. Experience before that time has a limited effect. This is true for other physical skills, including bowel and bladder control. Before necessary muscular and neural maturation, no pleading, harassment, or punishment will produce successful toilet training.

"This is the path to adulthood. You're here."

Cognitive Development

4. How did Piaget view the development of a child's mind, and what are current researchers' views?

"Who knows the thoughts of a child?" wondered poet Nora Perry. As much as anyone of his generation, developmental psychologist Jean Piaget (pronounced Pee-ah-ZHAY) knew. His interest began in 1920, when he was working in Paris to develop questions for children's intelligence tests. While administering tests to find out at what age children could answer certain questions correctly, Piaget became intrigued by children's *wrong* answers. Where others saw childish mistakes, Piaget saw intelligence at work. The errors made by children of a given age, he noted, were often strikingly similar.

A half-century spent with children convinced Piaget that a child's mind is not a miniature model of an adult's. Piaget revolutionized our understanding of children's minds, much as Copernicus revolutionized our understanding of the solar system, suggests William Damon (1995). Until Piaget, most people—forgetting their own preschool days—assumed children "simply knew less, not *differently*, than adults" (p. 100). Thanks partly to his work, we now understand that "children reason in wildly illogical ways about problems whose solutions are self-evident to adults" (Brainerd, 1996).

Piaget further believed that a child's mind develops through a series of stages, in an upward march from the newborn's simple reflexes to the adult's abstract reasoning power. An 8-year-old child therefore comprehends things that a 3-year-old can-

▶ **schema** a concept or framework that organizes and interprets information.

▶ **assimilation** interpreting one's new experience in terms of one's existing schemas.

▶ **accommodation** adapting one's current understandings (schemas) to incorporate new information.

▶ **cognition** all the mental activities associated with thinking, knowing, remembering, and communicating.

▶ **sensorimotor stage** in Piaget's theory, the stage (from birth to about 2 years of age) during which infants know the world mostly in terms of their sensory impressions and motor activities.

▶ **object permanence** the awareness that things continue to exist even when not perceived.

Two-year-old Gabriella has learned the schema for "cow" from her picture books.

Gabriella sees a moose and calls it a "cow." She is trying to assimilate this new animal into an existing schema. Her mother tells her, "No, it's a moose."

Gabriella accommodates her schema for large, shaggy animals and continues to modify that schema to include "mommy moose," "baby moose," and so forth.

not. An 8-year-old might grasp the analogy "getting an idea is like having a light turn on in your head." Trying to teach the same analogy to a 3-year-old would be fruitless. Our adult minds likewise engage in reasoning uncomprehended by 8-year-olds.

Piaget felt that the driving force behind this intellectual progression is our unceasing struggle to make sense of our experience. His core idea is that "children are active thinkers, constantly trying to construct more advanced understandings of the world" (Siegler & Ellis, 1996). To this end, the maturing brain builds concepts, which Piaget called **schemas**. Schemas (or schemes) are mental molds into which we pour our experience. By adulthood we have built countless schemas, ranging from cats and dogs to our concept of love.

To explain how we use and adjust our schemas, Piaget proposed two concepts. First, we **assimilate** new experiences—we interpret them in terms of our current understandings (schemas). Having a simple schema for *dog*, for example, a toddler may call all four-legged animals *doggies*. But we also adjust, or **accommodate**, our schemas to fit the particulars of new experiences. The child soon learns that the original *doggie* schema is too broad and accommodates by refining the category. As children interact with the world, they construct and modify their schemas.

Pouring experience into mental molds
We use our existing schemas to *assimilate* new experiences. But sometimes we need to *accommodate* (adjust) our schemas to include new experiences.

"Childhood has its own way of seeing, thinking, and feeling, and there is nothing more foolish than the attempt to put ours in its place."

Philosopher Jean-Jacques Rousseau, 1798

An impossible object Look carefully at the "devil's tuning fork" at left. Now look away—no, better first study it some more—and then look away and draw it. . . . Not so easy, is it? Because this tuning fork is an impossible object, you have no schema for such an image.

Piaget's Theory and Current Thinking

Cognition refers to all the mental activities associated with thinking, knowing, remembering, and communicating. Piaget believed that children experience spurts of change followed by greater stability as they move from one cognitive developmental plateau to the next. These plateaus form four stages (**TABLE 4.1**, page 106), each with distinctive characteristics that permit specific kinds of thinking. To appreciate how a child's mind grows, let's look at Piaget's stages in the light of our current thinking about cognitive development.

SENSORIMOTOR STAGE During Piaget's **sensorimotor stage**, from birth to nearly age 2, babies take in the world through their sensory and motor interactions with objects—through looking, hearing, touching, mouthing, and grasping.

Very young babies seem to live in the present: What is out of sight is out of mind. In one of his tests, Piaget would show an infant an appealing toy and then flop his beret over it to see whether the infant searched for the toy. Before the age of 6 months, the infant did not. Young infants lack **object permanence**—the awareness that objects continue to exist when not perceived. By 8 months, infants begin exhibiting memory for things no longer seen. If you hide a toy, the infant will momentarily look for it. Within another month or two, the infant will look for it even after being restrained for several seconds.

Jean Piaget "If we examine the intellectual development of the individual or of the whole of humanity, we shall find that the human spirit goes through a certain number of stages, each different from the other" (1930).

table 4.1 Piaget's Stages of Cognitive Development		
Typical Age Range	**Description of Stage**	**Developmental Phenomena**
Birth to nearly 2 years	*Sensorimotor* Experiencing the world through senses and actions (looking, touching, mouthing, and grasping)	• Object permanence • Stranger anxiety
About 2 to 6 years	*Preoperational* Representing things with words and images but lacking logical reasoning	• Pretend play • Egocentrism • Language development
About 7 to 11 years	*Concrete operational* Thinking logically about concrete events; grasping concrete analogies and performing arithmetical operations	• Conservation • Mathematical transformations
About 12 through adulthood	*Formal operational* Abstract reasoning	• Abstract logic • Potential for mature moral reasoning

But does object permanence in fact blossom at 8 months, much as tulips blossom in spring? Today's researchers see development as more continuous than Piaget did, and they now view object permanence as unfolding gradually. Even young infants will look for a toy where they saw it hidden a second before.

Consider, too, some simple experiments that demonstrate baby logic:

- Like adults staring in disbelief at a magic trick, infants look longer at an unexpected scene of a car seeming to pass through a solid object, a ball stopping in midair, or an object violating object permanence by magically disappearing (Baillargeon, 1995, 1998; Wellman & Gelman, 1992). Babies seem to have a more intuitive grasp of simple laws of physics than Piaget realized.
- Babies also have a head for numbers. Karen Wynn (1992, 2000) showed 5-month-old infants one or two objects. Then she hid the objects behind a screen, and then visibly removed or added one (**FIGURE 4.7**). When she lifted the screen, the infants sometimes did a double take, staring longer when shown a wrong number of objects. Later experiments showed that babies' number sense extends to such things as drumbeats and motions (Spelke, 2000; Wynn & others, 2002). If accustomed to a Daffy Duck puppet jumping three times on stage, they show surprise if it jumps only twice. Clearly, infants are smarter than Piaget appreciated.

The educated public's new appreciation for infant competence enabled a spoof headline in a 2002 Onion: "STUDY REVEALS: BABIES ARE STUPID" (based on "research" showing that infants cannot learn to read a map or scuba dive).

Object permanence Infants younger than 6 months seldom understand that things continue to exist when they are out of sight. But for this infant, out of sight is definitely not out of mind.

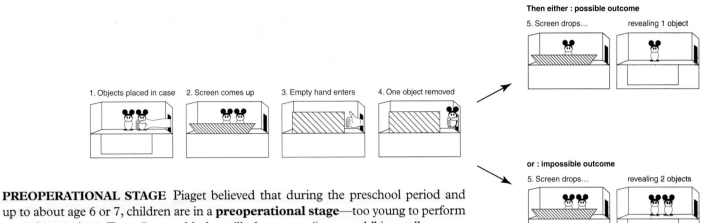

Then either : possible outcome

1. Objects placed in case   2. Screen comes up   3. Empty hand enters   4. One object removed

5. Screen drops...   revealing 1 object

or : impossible outcome

5. Screen drops...   revealing 2 objects

figure 4.7
Baby math Shown a numerically impossible outcome, infants stare longer. (From Wynn, 1992.)

PREOPERATIONAL STAGE Piaget believed that during the preschool period and up to about age 6 or 7, children are in a **preoperational stage**—too young to perform mental operations. For a 5-year-old, the milk that seems "too much" in a tall, narrow glass may become an acceptable amount if poured into a short, wide glass. This is because the child focuses only on the height dimension and is incapable of performing the *operation* of mentally pouring it back. A child lacks the concept of **conservation**—the principle that quantity remains the same despite changes in shape.

Piaget did not view the stage transitions as abrupt. Even so, symbolic thinking appears at an earlier age than he supposed. Judy DeLoache (1987) discovered this when she showed children a model of a room and hid a model toy in it (a miniature stuffed dog behind a miniature couch). The 2½-year-olds easily remembered where to find the miniature toy, but they could not use the model to locate an actual stuffed dog behind a couch in a real room. Three-year-olds—only 6 months older—usually went right to the actual stuffed animal in the real room, showing that they *could* think of the model as a symbol for the room. Piaget probably would have been surprised.

Egocentrism Piaget contended that preschool children are **egocentric**: They cannot perceive things from another's point of view. They may think the Sun and Moon follow them around. Asked to "show Mommy your picture," 2-year-old Gabriella holds the picture up facing her own eyes. Three-year-old Gray makes himself "invisible" by putting his hands over his eyes, assuming that if he can't see someone, they can't see him. Children's conversations also reveal their egocentrism, as one young boy demonstrated (Phillips, 1969, p. 61):

"Do you have a brother?"
"Yes."
"What's his name?"
"Jim."
"Does Jim have a brother?"
"No."

TV-watching preschoolers who block your view of the television assume that you see what they see. When preschoolers are on the phone, they may respond to questions by nodding their head, as if the listener could see them. When relating to a young child, remember that such behaviors reflect a cognitive limitation: The egocentric preschoolers are not intentionally "selfish" or "inconsiderate." They simply have not developed the ability to take another's viewpoint. Parents who abuse their children generally have no understanding of these limits.

Theory of Mind Although still egocentric, preschoolers begin forming a **theory of mind**. Rather than thinking of people as breathing wind-up dolls, they come to realize that people have minds. When Little Red Riding Hood realizes her "grandmother" is really a wolf, she swiftly revises her ideas about the creature's intentions and races away.

As their ability to infer others' mental states develops, children will seek to understand what made a playmate angry, when a sibling will share, and what might make a parent buy a toy. The preschooler's growing ability to tease, empathize, and persuade stems from a growing ability to take another's perspective. Between about

Question: *If most 2½-year-olds do not understand how miniature dolls and toys can symbolize real objects, should anatomically correct dolls be used when questioning such children about alleged physical or sexual abuse? Judy DeLoache (1995) reports that "very young children do not find it natural or easy to use a doll as a representation of themselves."*

▶ **preoperational stage** in Piaget's theory, the stage (from about 2 to 6 or 7 years of age) during which a child learns to use language but does not yet comprehend the mental operations of concrete logic.

▶ **conservation** the principle (which Piaget believed to be a part of concrete operational reasoning) that properties such as mass, volume, and number remain the same despite changes in the forms of objects.

▶ **egocentrism** in Piaget's theory, the preoperational child's inability to take another's point of view.

▶ **theory of mind** people's ideas about their own and others' mental states—about their feelings, perceptions, and thoughts and the behaviors these might predict.

Piaget's test of conservation
This preoperational child does not yet understand the principle of conservation of substance. Closed beakers with identical volumes seem suddenly to hold different amounts after one is merely inverted.

FAMILY CIRCUS ® BIL KEANE

"Don't you remember, Grandma? You were in it with me."

DENNIS THE MENACE

"Cut it up into a LOT of slices, Mom. I'm really hungry!"

3½ and 4, for example, children come to realize that others may hold false beliefs (Wellman & others, 2001). Jennifer Jenkins and Janet Astington (1996) showed Toronto children a Band Aids box and asked them what was inside. The children naturally expected Band Aids, and so were surprised to discover that the box actually contained pencils. Asked what a child who had never seen the box would think was inside, 3-year-olds typically answered "pencils." By age 4 to 5, the children's "theory of mind" had leapt forward, and they delighted in anticipating their friends' false belief that the box would hold Band Aids.

Children with *autism*, a disorder characterized by deficient communication and social interaction, have difficulty inferring others' thoughts and feelings (Klein & Kihlstrom, 1998; Yirmiya & others, 1998). They do not appreciate that playmates and parents might view things differently. Most children learn that another child's pouting mouth signals sadness, and that twinkling eyes mean happiness or mischief. A child with autism (which is related to malfunctions of brain areas that enable attending to others) fails to understand these signals (Frith & Frith, 2001).

CONCRETE OPERATIONAL STAGE By the time children are about 6 or 7 years of age, said Piaget, they enter the **concrete operational stage**. Given concrete materials, they begin to grasp conservation—that change in shape does not mean change in quantity. They can mentally pour milk back and forth between glasses of different shapes. They also enjoy jokes that allow them to use their new understanding of conservation:

> Mr. Jones went into a restaurant and ordered a whole pizza for his dinner. When the waiter asked if he wanted it cut into 6 or 8 pieces, Mr. Jones said, "Oh, you'd better make it 6, I could never eat 8 pieces!" (McGhee, 1976)

During the concrete operational stage, said Piaget, children fully gain the mental ability to comprehend mathematical transformations and conservation. When my daughter Laura was 6, I was astonished at her inability to reverse arithmetic operations. Asked, "What is 8 plus 4?" she required 5 seconds to compute "12," and another 5 seconds to then compute 12 minus 4. By age 8, she could answer the second question instantly.

FORMAL OPERATIONAL STAGE By age 12, our reasoning expands from the purely concrete (involving actual experience) to encompass abstract thinking (involving imagined realities and symbols). As children approach adolescence, said Piaget, many become capable of solving hypothetical propositions and deducing consequences: *If this, then that.* Systematic reasoning, what Piaget called **formal operational** thinking, is now within their grasp.

But once again, critics say, the rudiments of Piaget's cognitive stages begin earlier than he realized. Consider this simple but abstract problem:

If John is in school, then Mary is in school. John is in school. What can you say about Mary?

Formal operational thinkers have no trouble answering correctly. But neither do most 7-year-olds (Suppes, 1982).

Reflecting on Piaget's Theory

Piaget's stage theory is controversial. For some things, it gets high marks. Studies around the globe, from aboriginal Australia to Algeria to North America, reveal that human cognition everywhere unfolds basically in the sequence he proposed (Segall & others, 1990). However, today's researchers see development as more continuous than did Piaget. By detecting the beginnings of each type of thinking at earlier ages, they have revealed conceptual abilities Piaget missed. Moreover, they see formal logic as a smaller part of cognition than he did.

What remains of Piaget's ideas about the child's mind? Plenty—enough to merit his being singled out in 1999 by *Time* magazine as one of the twentieth century's 20 most influential scientists and thinkers and, more recently, to be named in a survey of British psychologists as the greatest twentieth-century psychologist (*Psychologist*, 2003). Piaget identified significant cognitive milestones and stimulated worldwide interest in how the mind develops. His emphasis was less on the ages at which children typically reach specific milestones than on their sequence—a sequence that later research has shown is pretty much as he described (Lourenco & Machado, 1996). Piaget would not be surprised that today, as part of our own cognitive development, we are adapting his ideas to accommodate new findings.

What are the implications of all this for parents and teachers? Piaget contended that children construct their understandings from their *interactions* with the world. This implies that children are not passive receptacles waiting to be filled with a teacher's knowledge. Teachers would do better to build on what children already know, engaging them in concrete demonstrations and stimulating them to think for themselves. Future parents and teachers, remember: Young children are incapable of adult logic. Realize that what is simple and obvious to you—that getting off a teeter-totter will cause a friend on the other end to crash—may be incomprehensible to a 3-year-old. And accept children's cognitive immaturity as adaptive. It is nature's strategy for keeping children close to protective adults and providing time for learning and socialization (Bjorklund & Green, 1992).

▶ **concrete operational stage** in Piaget's theory, the stage of cognitive development (from about 6 or 7 to 11 years of age) during which children gain the mental operations that enable them to think logically about concrete events.

▶ **formal operational stage** in Piaget's theory, the stage of cognitive development (normally beginning about age 12) during which people begin to think logically about abstract concepts.

"Assessing the impact of Piaget on developmental psychology is like assessing the impact of Shakespeare in English literature."

Developmental psychologist Harry Beilin (1992)

---

rehearse it!

5. The orderly sequence of biological growth is called maturation. Maturation explains why
   a. children with autism have difficulty inferring others' thoughts and feelings.
   b. most children have begun walking by about 12 months.
   c. enriching experiences may affect brain tissue.
   d. differences between the sexes are minimal.

6. Most of us have no conscious memories of events that occurred before our third birthday because
   a. we are not born with enough brain cells to form memories.
   b. we were not given the extra "handling" and environmental stimulation we needed.
   c. the connections between our brain cells had not yet become complex enough to form permanent memories.

   d. we do not enter the memory stage of cognition until our third year.

7. As the infant's muscles and nervous system mature, more complicated skills emerge. Which of the following is true of motor-skill development?
   a. It is determined solely by genetic factors.
   b. The sequence, but not the timing, is universal.
   c. The timing, but not the sequence, is universal.
   d. Environment creates a readiness to learn.

8. According to Piaget, the preoperational stage extends from about age 2 to 6. During this period, the young child's thinking is
   a. abstract.   c. conservative.
   b. negative.   d. egocentric.

9. The principle of conservation explains why a pint of milk remains a pint, whether poured into a tall thin glass or

   a round goblet. Children acquire the mental operations necessary to understand conservation during
   a. infancy.
   b. the sensorimotor stage.
   c. the preoperational stage.
   d. the concrete operational stage.

10. Piaget's stage theory continues to inform our understanding of cognitive development in childhood. However, many researchers believe that
    a. Piaget's "stages" begin earlier and development is more continuous than Piaget realized.
    b. children do not progress as rapidly as Piaget predicted.
    c. few children really progress to the concrete operational stage.
    d. there is no way of testing much of Piaget's theoretical work.

Answers can be found in Appendix C.

▶ **stranger anxiety** the fear of strangers that infants commonly display, beginning by about 8 months of age.

▶ **attachment** an emotional tie with another person; shown in young children by their seeking closeness to the caregiver and showing distress on separation.

Social Development

5. How do the bonds of attachment form between parents and infants?

From birth, babies are social creatures. In all cultures, infants develop an intense bond with their caregivers. Beginning with a newborn's attraction to humans in general, infants soon come to prefer familiar faces and voices, then to coo and gurgle when given their mother's or father's attention. Soon after object permanence emerges and children become mobile, a curious thing happens: They develop a fear of strangers, called **stranger anxiety**. Beginning at about 8 months, they may greet strangers by crying and reaching for their familiar caregivers. "No! Don't leave me!" their distress seems to say. At about this age, children have schemas for familiar faces; when they cannot assimilate the new face into these remembered schemas, they become distressed (Kagan, 1984). This illustrates an important principle: The brain, mind, and social-emotional behavior develop together.

At 12 months, many infants cling tightly to a parent when they are frightened or expect separation. Reunited after being separated, they shower the parent with smiles and hugs. No social behavior is more striking than this intense and mutual infant-parent bond. Called **attachment**, it is a powerful survival impulse that keeps infants close to their caregivers.

Stranger anxiety
A newly emerging ability to evaluate people as unfamiliar and possibly threatening helps protect babies 8 months and older.

Origins of Attachment

A number of elements work to create the parent-infant bond. Infants become attached to those—typically their parents—who are comfortable, familiar, and responsive to their needs.

BODY CONTACT For many years, developmental psychologists reasoned that infants became attached to those who satisfied their need for nourishment. It made sense. But an accidental finding overturned this explanation. During the 1950s, University of Wisconsin psychologist Harry Harlow bred monkeys for his learning studies. To equalize the infant monkeys' experiences and to isolate any disease, he separated the monkeys from their mothers shortly after birth and raised them in sanitary individual cages, which included a cheesecloth baby blanket (Harlow & others, 1971).

figure 4.8
Monkey with two "mothers"
Psychologist Harry Harlow reared monkeys with two artificial mothers—one a bare wire cylinder with a wooden head and an attached feeding bottle, the other a cylinder with no bottle but covered with foam rubber and wrapped with terry cloth. Harlow's discovery surprised many psychologists: The monkeys much preferred contact with the comfortable cloth mother, even while feeding from the nourishing mother.

Surprisingly, the infants became intensely attached to their blankets: When the blankets were taken to be laundered, the monkeys became distressed.

Harlow recognized that this attachment to the blanket contradicted the idea that attachment derives from an association with nourishment. But how could he show this more convincingly? To pit the drawing power of a food source against the contact comfort of the blanket, Harlow created two artificial mothers. One was a bare wire cylinder with a wooden head, the other a cylinder wrapped with terry cloth. By attaching a bottle he could associate either with nourishment.

When reared with both a nourishing wire mother and a nonnourishing cloth mother, the monkeys overwhelmingly preferred the comfy cloth mother (**FIGURE 4.8**). Like human infants clinging to their mothers, the monkeys would cling to their cloth mother when anxious. They also used her as a secure base from which to venture into the environment, as if attached to the mother by an invisible elastic band that stretched so far and then pulled the infant back. Further studies revealed other qualities—rocking, warmth, and feeding—that made the cloth mother even more appealing.

Human infants, too, become attached to parents who are soft and warm and who rock, feed, and pat. And human attachment also consists of one person providing another with a *safe haven* when distressed and a *secure base* from which to explore. As we mature, our secure base and safe haven shift—from parents to peers and partners (Cassidy & Shaver, 1999). But at all ages we are social creatures. We gain strength when someone offers, by words and actions, a safe haven: "I will be here. I am interested in you. Come what may, I will actively support you" (Crowell & Waters, 1994).

FAMILIARITY Contact is one key to attachment. Another is familiarity. In many animals, attachments based on familiarity form during a sensitive **critical period**—an optimal period shortly after birth when certain events must take place to facilitate proper development (Bornstein, 1989). The first moving object a gosling, duckling, or chick sees during the hours shortly after hatching is normally its mother. From then on, the young fowl follows her, and her alone.

This rigid attachment process, called **imprinting**, was explored by Konrad Lorenz (1937). He wondered: What would ducklings do if *he* was the first moving creature they observed? What they did was follow him around: Everywhere that Konrad went, the ducks were sure to go.

Children—unlike ducklings—do not imprint. However, they do become attached to what they've known. "Mere exposure" to people and things fosters fondness (see pages 568–569). Children like to reread the same books, rewatch the same movies, reenact family traditions. They prefer to eat familiar foods, live in the same familiar neighborhood, attend school with the same old friends. Familiarity is a safety signal. Familiarity breeds content.

Lee Kirkpatrick (1999) reports that for some people a perceived relationship with God functions as do other attachments—by providing a secure base for exploration and a safe haven when threatened.

Attachment When French pilot Christian Moullec takes off in his microlight plane, his imprinted geese, which he reared since their hatching, follow closely.

RESPONSIVE PARENTING What accounts for attachment differences? Placed in a strange situation (usually a laboratory playroom), about 60 percent of infants display *secure attachment*. In their mother's presence they play comfortably, happily exploring their new environment. When she leaves, they are distressed; when she returns, they seek contact with her. Other infants show *insecure attachment*. They are less likely to explore their surroundings; they may even cling to their mother. When she leaves, they either cry loudly and remain upset or seem indifferent to their mother's going and returning (Ainsworth, 1973, 1989; Kagan, 1995; van IJzendoorn & Kroonenberg, 1988).

Mary Ainsworth (1979) studied attachment differences by observing mother-infant pairs at home during their first six months. Later she observed the 1-year-old infants in a "strange situation" without their mothers. Sensitive, responsive mothers—those who noticed what their babies were doing and responded appropriately—

▶ **critical period** an optimal period shortly after birth when an organism's exposure to certain stimuli or experiences produces proper development.

▶ **imprinting** the process by which certain animals form attachments during a critical period very early in life.

Harlow Primate Laboratory, University of Wisconsin

figure 4.9
Social deprivation and fear Monkeys raised by artificial mothers were terror-stricken when placed in strange situations without their surrogate mothers. (Today's climate of greater respect for animal welfare prevents such primate studies.)

"Out of the conflict between trust and mistrust, the infant develops hope, which is the earliest form of what gradually becomes faith in adults."

Erik Erikson, 1983

Does father love matter? An ill-fated Cuba-to-America immigration attempt left young Elián González's mother dead and his father still in Cuba. U.S. officials debated for months before taking Elián from relatives in Miami and returning him to his father. Critics said that if it had been Elián's mother in Cuba, there would have been no hesitation in returning him to her.

had infants who exhibited secure attachment. Insensitive, unresponsive mothers—mothers who attended to their babies when they felt like doing so but ignored them at other times—had infants who often became insecurely attached. Harlow's monkey studies, in which the artificial structures were certainly the ultimate unresponsive mothers, produced even more striking effects. When put in strange situations without their artificial mothers, the deprived infants were terrified (**FIGURE 4.9**).

But is attachment style the result of parenting or of genetically influenced *temperament*—one's characteristic emotional reactivity and intensity? Shortly after birth, some babies are noticeably "difficult"—irritable, intense, and unpredictable. Others are "easy"—cheerful, relaxed, and feeding and sleeping on predictable schedules (Chess & Thomas, 1987). By neglecting such inborn differences, chides Judith Harris (1998), the parenting studies are like "comparing foxhounds reared in kennels with poodles reared in apartments." So, to separate nature and nurture, Dutch researcher Dymphna van den Boom (1990) varied parenting while controlling temperament. (Pause and think: If you were the researcher, how might you have done this?)

Van den Boom's solution was to randomly assign one hundred 6- to 9-month-old temperamentally difficult infants to either an experimental condition, in which mothers received personal training in sensitive responding, or to an untreated control condition in which they did not. When 12 months old, 68 percent of the experimental-condition infants were rated securely attached; of the control-condition infants, only 28 percent were.

As these examples indicate, researchers have more often studied mother care than father care. Infants who lack a caring mother are said to suffer "maternal deprivation"; those lacking the care of a father are said merely to experience "father absence." But evidence increasingly indicates that fathers are more than just mobile sperm banks. Across nearly 100 studies worldwide, a father's love and acceptance has been comparable to a mother's love in predicting offsprings' health and well-being (Rohner & Veneziano, 2001).

Developmental theorist Erik Erikson (1902–1994) would not have been surprised by the effects of early caregiving. Erikson, in collaboration with his wife, Joan Erikson, said that securely attached children approach life with a sense of **basic trust**—a sense that the world is predictable and reliable. He attributed basic trust not to one's continuing positive environment or inborn temperament, but to early parenting. He theorized that infants blessed with sensitive, loving caregivers form a lifelong attitude of trust rather than fear. Nor would Erikson have been surprised that our adult styles of romantic love exhibit either secure, trusting attachment; insecure, anxious attachment; or the avoidance of attachment (Feeney & Noller, 1990; Shaver & Hazan, 1993; Simpson & others, 1992). Although debate continues, many researchers now believe that our early attachments form the foundation for our adult relationships (Fraley, 2002).

Whether children stay home or attend a day-care center, whether they live in North America, Guatemala, or the Kalahari Desert, anxiety over separation from parents peaks at around 13 months, then gradually declines (**FIGURE 4.10**). Does this mean our need for and love of others also fades away? Hardly. In fact, in other ways our capacity for love grows, and our pleasure in touching and holding

AP/Wide World Photos

those we love never ceases. The power of early attachment does nonetheless gradually relax, allowing us to move out into a wider range of situations and communicate with strangers more freely. Indeed, much of the life cycle story boils down to a poignant rhythm of attachment and separation—from the attachment of fetal life to the separation of birth, from infant attachment to adolescent separation, from the attachments of marriage and parenthood to the separation of death.

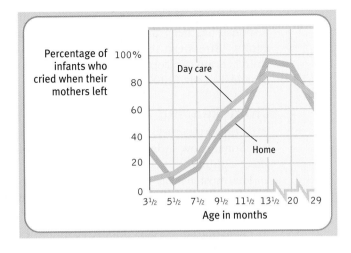

figure 4.10
Infants' distress over separation from parents In one experiment, groups of infants were left by their mothers in an unfamiliar room. In both groups, the percentage who cried when the mother left peaked at about 13 months. (From Kagan, 1976.) Whether the infant had experienced day care made little difference.

Deprivation of Attachment

If secure attachment nurtures social competence, what happens when circumstances prevent a child from forming attachments? In all of psychology, there's no sadder research literature. Babies reared in institutions without the stimulation and attention of a regular caregiver, or locked away at home under conditions of abuse or extreme neglect, are often withdrawn, frightened, even speechless. Those abandoned in Romanian orphanages during the 1980s looked "frighteningly like Harlow's monkeys" (Carlson, 1995). If institutionalized more than 8 months, they often bore lasting emotional scars (Chisholm, 1998; Malinosky-Rummell & Hansen, 1993; Rutter & others, 1998).

Harlow's monkeys similarly bore scars if reared in total isolation, without even an artificial mother. As adults, when placed with other monkeys their age, they either cowered in fright or lashed out in aggression. When they reached sexual maturity, most were incapable of mating. If artificially impregnated, females often were neglectful, abusive, even murderous toward their first-born.

In humans, too, the unloved often become the unloving. Most abusive parents report having been neglected or battered as children (Kempe & Kempe, 1978). Many condemned murderers report the same. One study of 14 young men awaiting execution for juvenile crimes found that all but two had histories of brutal physical abuse (Lewis & others, 1988).

But does this mean that today's victim is predictably tomorrow's victimizer? The answer is no. Though most abusers were indeed abused, most abused children do *not* later become violent criminals or abusive parents. Most children growing up under adversity, as did the surviving children of the Holocaust, are resilient; they become normal adults (Helmreich, 1992; Masten, 2001).

But other children, especially those who experience no sharp break from their abusive past, are not so dramatically resilient. Some 30 percent of those abused do abuse their children—a rate four times higher than the national rate of child abuse (Kaufman & Zigler, 1987; Widom, 1989a,b). Moreover, young children terrorized through sexual abuse, physical abuse, or wartime atrocities (being beaten, witnessing torture, and living in constant fear) may suffer other lasting wounds—often nightmares, depression, and a troubled adolescence involving substance abuse, binge eating, or aggression (Kendall-Tackett & others, 1993; Polusny & Follette, 1995; Trickett & McBride-Chang, 1995).

Although children are resilient, extreme childhood trauma can leave footprints on the brain. When normally placid golden hamsters are repeatedly threatened and attacked while young, the effects linger into their adult lives. They grow up to be cowards when caged with same-sized hamsters, or bullies when caged with weaker ones (Ferris, 1996). Such animals show changes in the brain chem-

"What is learned in the cradle, lasts to the grave."

French proverb

▶ **basic trust** according to Erik Erikson, a sense that the world is predictable and trustworthy; said to be formed during infancy by appropriate experiences with responsive caregivers.

ical serotonin, which calms aggressive impulses. A similarly sluggish serotonin response has been found in abused children who become aggressive teens and adults. "Stress can set off a ripple of hormonal changes that permanently wire a child's brain to cope with a malevolent world," concludes abuse researcher Martin Teicher (2002).

Child-Rearing Practices

Parenting styles vary. Some parents spank, some reason. Some are strict, some are lax. Some show little affection, some liberally hug and kiss. Do such differences affect children?

The most heavily researched aspect of parenting has been how, and to what extent, parents seek to control their children. Several investigators have identified three parenting styles:

1. *Authoritarian* parents impose rules and expect obedience: "Don't interrupt." "Do keep your room clean." "Don't stay out late or you'll be grounded." "Why? Because I said so."
2. *Permissive* parents submit to their children's desires, make few demands, and use little punishment.
3. *Authoritative* parents are both demanding and responsive. They exert control not only by setting rules and enforcing them but also by explaining the reasons and, especially with older children, encouraging open discussion and allowing exceptions when making the rules.

Too hard, too soft, and just right, these styles have been called. For studies by Stanley Coopersmith (1967), Diana Baumrind (1996), and John Buri and others (1988) reveal that children with the highest self-esteem, self-reliance, and social competence usually have warm, concerned, *authoritative* parents. Although the participants in most studies have been middle-class white families, studies with families of other races and in more than 200 cultures worldwide confirm the social and academic corrrelates of loving and authoritative parenting (Rohner & Veneziano, 2001; Steinberg & Morris, 2001).

But wait. Before jumping to conclusions about the results of different parenting styles, heed this caution: *Correlation is not causation.* The association between certain parenting styles (being firm but open) and certain childhood outcomes (social competence) is correlational. There are other possible explanations for this parenting-competence link (**FIGURE 4.11**).

● Perhaps children's traits influence parenting more than vice versa. Parental warmth and control vary somewhat from child to child even in the same family (Holden & Miller, 1999). So perhaps socially mature, agreeable, easygoing children *elicit* greater trust and warmth from their parents, and less competent and less cooperative children elicit less. Twin studies support this possibility (Kendler, 1996).

● Perhaps there may be some underlying third factor. Maybe, for example, competent parents and their competent children share genes that predispose social competence.

Parents struggling with conflicting advice and with the stresses of child-rearing should remember that *all advice reflects*

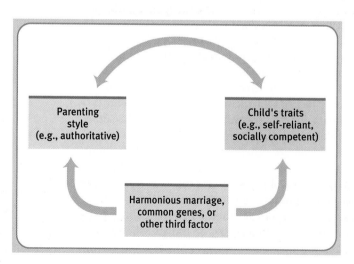

figure 4.11
The correlation between authoritative parenting and social competence in children Three possible explanations are (1) parenting may influence children's competence; (2) children's social competence may influence parenting; or (3) both may be influenced by an underlying third factor.

Parenting style (e.g., authoritative)

Child's traits (e.g., self-reliant, socially competent)

Harmonious marriage, common genes, or other third factor

the advice-giver's values. For those who prize unquestioning obedience from a child, an authoritarian style may have the desired effect. For those who value children's sociability and self-reliance, authoritative firm-but-open parenting is advisable.

The investment in raising a child buys many years not only of joy and love but of worry and irritation. Yet for most parents, a child is one's biological and social legacy—one's personal investment in the human future. To paraphrase psychiatrist Carl Jung, we reach backward into our parents and forward into our children, and through their children into a future we will never see, but about which we must therefore care.

"You are the bows from which your children as living arrows are sent forth."

Kahlil Gibran, The Prophet, *1923*

rehearse it!

11. After about 8 months of age, infants develop schemas for familiar objects. Faced with a new babysitter, they will show distress, a behavior referred to as
    a. conservation.
    b. stranger anxiety.
    c. imprinting.
    d. maturation.

12. Body contact facilitates attachment between infant and parent. In a series

of experiments, Harry Harlow found that monkeys raised with artificial mothers tended, when afraid, to cling to
    a. the wire mother.
    b. the cloth mother.
    c. whichever mother held the feeding bottle.
    d. other infant monkeys.

13. From the very first weeks of life, infants differ in their characteristic emotional

reactions, with some infants being intense and anxious, while others are easygoing and relaxed. These differences are usually explained as differences in
    a. attachment.
    b. imprinting.
    c. temperament.
    d. parental responsiveness.

Answers can be found in Appendix C.

ADOLESCENCE

Many psychologists once believed that childhood sets our traits. Today's developmental psychologists see development as lifelong. At a five-year high school reunion, former soul mates may be surprised at the divergence of their paths; a decade later, they may have trouble sustaining a conversation.

As this life-span perspective emerged, psychologists began to look at how maturation and experience shape us not only in infancy and childhood, but also in adolescence and beyond. **Adolescence** is life between childhood and adulthood. It starts with the physical beginnings of sexual maturity and ends with the social achievement of independent adult status.

To G. Stanley Hall (1904), one of the first psychologists to describe adolescence, the tension between biological maturity and social dependence created a period of "storm and stress." Indeed, after age 30, many who grow up in independence-fostering Western cultures look back on their teenage years as a time they would not want to relive, a time when their peers' social approval was imperative, their sense of direction in life was in flux, and their feeling of alienation from their parents was deepest (Arnett, 1999; Macfarlane, 1964). Despite the mood swings, adolescence can also be a time of vitality without the cares of adulthood, a time of rewarding friendships, of heightened idealism and a growing sense of life's exciting possibilities (Coleman, 1980).

How will you look back on your life 10 years from now? Are you making choices that someday you will recollect with satisfaction?

Physical Development

6. What major physical changes occur during adolescence?

Adolescence begins with **puberty,** the time when one is maturing sexually. Puberty follows a surge of hormones, which may intensify moods and which trigger a two-year period of rapid physical development, usually beginning at about age 11 in girls and at about age 13 in boys. About the time of puberty, boys' growth propels them to greater height than their female counterparts (**FIGURE 4.12**, page 116). During this growth spurt, the **primary sex characteristics**—the reproductive organs and

▶ **adolescence** the transition period from childhood to adulthood, extending from puberty to independence.

▶ **puberty** the period of sexual maturation, during which a person becomes capable of reproducing.

▶ **primary sex characteristics** the body structures (ovaries, testes, and external genitalia) that make sexual reproduction possible.

figure 4.12
Height differences Throughout childhood, boys and girls are similar in height. At puberty, girls surge ahead briefly, but then boys overtake them at about age 14. (Data from Tanner, 1978.) Recent studies suggest that sexual development and growth spurts are beginning somewhat earlier than was the case a half-century ago (Herman-Giddens & others, 2001).

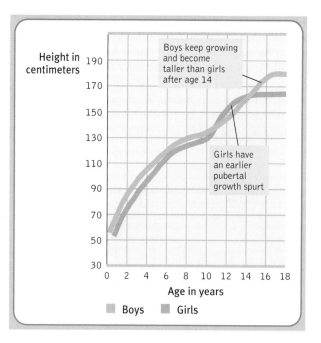

external genitalia—develop dramatically. So do **secondary sex characteristics**, the nonreproductive traits such as breasts and hips in girls, facial hair and deepened voice in boys, pubic and underarm hair in both sexes (**FIGURE 4.13**). A year or two before puberty, however, boys and girls often feel the first stirrings of attraction toward those of the other (or their own) sex (McClintock & Herdt, 1996).

Both physically and socially, kids have been getting older younger. Earlier puberty has coincided with increasing child obesity and father absence, and heavier girls and those without biological fathers at home are indeed prone to earlier puberty (Ellis & others, 1999, 2000; Kaplowitz, 2001). It makes sense, say some evolutionary psychologists, that when body fat can support pregnancy and nursing and when parent-child bonds are weak and survival seems iffy, a female would be disposed to reproduce early.

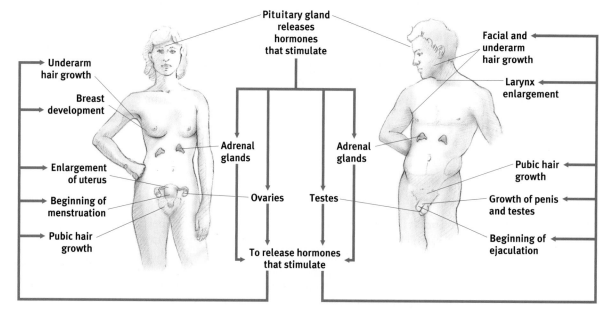

figure 4.13
Body changes at puberty At about age 11 in girls and age 13 in boys, a surge of hormones triggers a variety of physical changes.

In girls, puberty starts with breast development, which now often begins by age 10 (Brody, 1999). But puberty's landmarks are the first ejaculation in boys, usually by about age 14, and the first menstrual period in girls, usually within a year of age 12. The first menstrual period, called **menarche** (meh-NAR-key), is a memorable event. Nearly all adult women recall it and remember experiencing a mixture of feelings—pride, excitement, embarrassment, and apprehension (Greif & Ulman, 1982; Woods & others, 1983). Girls who have been prepared for menarche usually experience it as a positive life transition. Most men similarly recall their first ejaculation ("spermarche"), which usually occurs as a nocturnal emission (Fuller & Downs, 1990).

Just as in the earlier life stages, the *sequence* of physical changes in puberty (for example, breast buds and visible pubic hair before menarche) is far more predictable than their *timing*. Some girls start their growth spurt at 9, some boys as late as age 16. Though such variations have little effect on height at maturity, they may have psychological consequences. Early maturation pays dividends for boys. Early developing boys, being stronger and more athletic during their early teen years, tend to be more popular, self-assured, and independent, though also more at risk for alcohol use and premature sexual activity (Steinberg & Morris, 2001). But for girls, early maturation can be stressful. If a young girl's body is out of sync with her own emotional maturity and her friends' physical development and experiences, she may begin associating with older adolescents or may suffer teasing or sexual harrassment. It's not only when we mature that counts, but how people react to our genetically influenced physical development. Remember: *Heredity and environment interact.*

Adolescents' brains are also a work in progress. Until puberty, brain cells increase their connections, like trees growing more roots and branches. Then, during adolescence, comes a selective pruning of unused connections (Durston & others, 2001). What we don't use, we lose. It's rather like traffic engineers reducing congestion by eliminating certain streets and constructing new beltways that move traffic more efficiently.

Frontal lobe development appears to lag behind that of the emotional limbic system. This helps explain teens' occasional impulsiveness, emotional storms, and risky behaviors (Casey & others, 2000). With frontal lobe maturation during the teens and early twenties comes improved judgment, impulse control, and the ability to plan for the long term. The brain with which we begin our teens differs from the brain with which we end our teens.

Tweens: Eleven going on fifteen
Sexual maturity and interests emerge at younger ages than a half-century ago, as reflected in preteens' toys, music, and clothes.

Owen Franken/Stock, Boston

▶ **secondary sex characteristics** nonreproductive sexual characteristics, such as female breasts and hips, male voice quality, and body hair.

▶ **menarche** [meh-NAR-key] the first menstrual period.

"If a gun is put in the control of the prefrontal cortex of a hurt and vengeful 15-year-old, and it is pointed at a human target, it will very likely go off."

National Institutes of Health brain scientist Daniel R. Weinberger, "A Brain Too Young for Good Judgment," 2001

Cognitive Development

7. How did Piaget and Kohlberg describe cognitive and moral development during adolescence?

Adolescents' developing ability to reason gives them a new level of social awareness and moral judgment. As young teenagers become capable of thinking about their thinking, and of thinking about other people's thinking, they begin imagining what other people are thinking about *them.* (Adolescents might worry less about what others think of them if they knew how similarly self-preoccupied their peers are.) As their cognitive abilities mature, many adolescents think about what is ideally possible and criticize their society, their parents, and even their own shortcomings.

"When the pilot told us to brace and grab our ankles, the first thing that went through my mind was that we must all look pretty stupid."

Jeremiah Rawlings, age 12, after a 1989 DC-10 crash in Sioux City, Iowa

"Ben is in his first year of high school, and he's questioning all the right things."

"It is a delightful harmony when doing and saying go together."

Michel Eyquem de Montaigne (1533–1592)

Developing Reasoning Power

During the early teen years, reasoning is often self-focused. Adolescents may think their private experiences are unique. They may assume their parents just can't understand what it feels like to be dating or to hate school: "But, Mother, *you* don't really know how it feels to be in love" (Elkind, 1978).

Gradually, though, most achieve the intellectual summit that Piaget called *formal operations.* Preadolescents reason concretely, but adolescents become more capable of abstract logic: *If* this, *then* that. We can see this new abstract reasoning power as adolescents ponder and debate human nature, good and evil, truth and justice. Having perhaps envisioned God as an old man in the clouds when they were first capable of symbolic thinking in early childhood, they may now seek a deeper conception of God and existence (Elkind, 1970; Worthington, 1989). Adolescents' ability to reason hypothetically and deduce consequences also enables them to detect inconsistencies in others' reasoning and to spot hypocrisy. This can lead to heated debates with parents and silent vows never to lose sight of their own ideals (Peterson & others, 1986).

Developing Morality

A crucial task of childhood and adolescence is discerning right from wrong and developing character—the psychological muscles for controlling impulses. To be a moral person is to *think* morally and *act* accordingly.

Piaget (1932) believed that children's moral judgments build on their cognitive development. Agreeing with Piaget, Lawrence Kohlberg (1981, 1984) sought to describe the development of *moral reasoning,* the thinking that occurs as we consider right and wrong. Kohlberg posed moral dilemmas (for example, whether a person without money to buy medicine should steal the drugs to save a loved one's life), and he asked children, adolescents, and adults if the action was right or wrong. He then analyzed their answers for evidence of stages of moral thinking.

His findings led him to believe that as we develop intellectually, we pass through three basic levels of moral thinking:

- *Preconventional morality* Before age 9, most children have a preconventional morality of self-interest: They obey either to avoid punishment or to gain concrete rewards.
- *Conventional morality* By early adolescence, morality usually evolves to a more conventional level that cares for others and upholds laws and social rules simply because they are the laws and rules.
- *Postconventional morality* Some of those who develop the abstract reasoning of formal operational thought may come to a third level. Postconventional morality affirms people's agreed-upon rights or follows what one personally perceives as basic ethical principles.

Demonstrating their reasoning ability Although on opposite sides of the debate over the U.S. invasion of Iraq, these teens demonstrate their newfound ability to think logically about abstract topics. According to Piaget, they are in the final cognitive stage, formal operations.

Kohlberg's claim was that these levels form a moral ladder from the bottom rung of a young child's immature, preconventional morality, to the top rung of an adult's self-defined ethical principles, which only some attain. As with all stage theories, the sequence is unvarying. We begin on the bottom rung and ascend to varying heights.

Research confirms that children in various cultures progress from the level Kohlberg called preconventional into the stages of his conventional level (Edwards, 1981, 1982; Snarey, 1985, 1987). And as our *thinking* matures, our *behavior* also becomes less selfish and more caring (Krebs & Van Hesteren, 1994; Miller & others, 1996). However, the postconventional level is more controversial. It appears mostly in the European and North American educated middle class, which prizes *individualism*—giving priority to one's own goals rather than to group goals (Eckensberger, 1994; Miller & Bersoff, 1995). Critics therefore contend that the theory is biased against the moral reasoning of those in communal societies such as China and India—and also against Western women, whose morality may be based slightly less on abstract, impersonal principles and more on caring relationships (Jaffee & Hyde, 2000).

Today's character education programs tend to focus both on discussing moral issues and their implications, and on *doing* the right thing. Thus, they teach children *empathy* for others' feelings, and also the self-discipline needed to restrain one's own impulses—to delay small gratifications now to enable bigger rewards later. (Those who do learn to *delay gratification* become more socially responsible, academically successful, and productive [Funder & Block, 1989; Mischel & others, 1988, 1989].) They often engage students in responsible action through "service learning." When teens tutor, clean up their neighborhoods, and assist the elderly, their sense of competence and desire to serve increases and their school absenteeism and drop-out rates diminish (Andersen, 1998; Piliavin, 2003).

"This might not be ethical. Is that a problem for anybody?"

"I am a bit suspicious of any theory that says that the highest moral stage is one in which people talk like college professors."

James Q. Wilson, The Moral Sense, *1993*

Social Development

> *8. What tasks and challenges do adolescents face en route to mature adulthood, and are they the same for males and females?*

Theorist Erik Erikson (1963) contended that each stage of life has its own "psychosocial" task, a crisis that needs resolution. Young children wrestle with issues of *trust* (page 112), then *autonomy* (independence), then *initiative* (**TABLE 4.2**, page 120). School-age children strive for *competence*, feeling able and productive. The adolescent's task, said Erikson, is to synthesize past, present, and future possibilities into a clearer sense of self. Adolescents wonder "Who am I as an individual? What do I want to do with my life? What values should I live by? What do I believe in?" Erikson called this quest the adolescent's "search for identity."

Forming an Identity

To refine their sense of identity, adolescents in Western cultures usually try out different "selves" in different situations—perhaps acting out one self at home, another with friends, and still another at school and work. If two of these situations overlap—as when a teenager brings home friends—the discomfort can be considerable. The teen asks, "Which self should I be? Which is the real me?" This role confusion usually gets resolved by forming a self-definition that unifies the various selves into a consistent and comfortable sense of who one is—an **identity**.

▶ **identity** one's sense of self; according to Erikson, the adolescent's task is to solidify a sense of self by testing and integrating various roles.

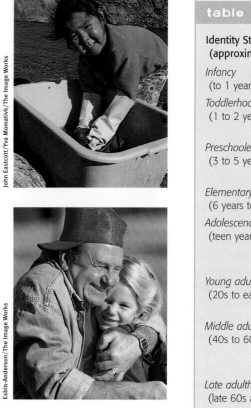

John Eastcott/Yva Momatiuk/The Image Works

Esbin-Anderson/The Image Works

table 4.2 Erikson's Stages of Psychosocial Development

Identity Stage (approximate age)	Issues	Description of Task
Infancy (to 1 year)	*Trust vs. mistrust*	If needs are dependably met, infants develop a sense of basic trust.
Toddlerhood (1 to 2 years)	*Autonomy vs. shame and doubt*	Toddlers learn to exercise will and do things for themselves, or they doubt their abilities.
Preschooler (3 to 5 years)	*Initiative vs. guilt*	Preschoolers learn to initiate tasks and carry out plans, or they feel guilty about efforts to be independent.
Elementary school (6 years to puberty)	*Competence vs. inferiority*	Children learn the pleasure of applying themselves to tasks, or they feel inferior.
Adolescence (teen years into 20s)	*Identity vs. role confusion*	Teenagers work at refining a sense of self by testing roles and then integrating them to form a single identity, or they become confused about who they are.
Young adulthood (20s to early 40s)	*Intimacy vs. isolation*	Young adults struggle to form close relationships and to gain the capacity for intimate love, or they feel socially isolated.
Middle adulthood (40s to 60s)	*Generativity vs. stagnation*	The middle-aged discover a sense of contributing to the world, usually through family and work, or they may feel a lack of purpose.
Late adulthood (late 60s and up)	*Integrity vs. despair*	When reflecting on his or her life, the older adult may feel a sense of satisfaction or failure.

But not always. Erikson noticed that some adolescents forge their identity early, simply by taking on their parents' values and expectations. (Traditional, less individualistic cultures inform adolescents who they are, rather than leaving them to decide on their own.) Other adolescents may adopt a negative identity that defines itself in opposition to parents and society but in conformity with a particular peer group—the jocks, the preppies, the geeks, the goths. Still others never quite seem to find themselves or to develop strong commitments. For most people, the identity question—Who am I?—is lifelong.

The late teen years, when many people begin attending college or working full time, provide new opportunities for trying out possible roles. As seniors, many college students have achieved a clearer identity than they had as first-year students (Waterman, 1988). Their identity typically incorporates an increasingly positive self-concept. In several nationwide studies, researchers have given young Americans

"I am becoming still more independent of my parents; young as I am, I face life with more courage than Mummy; my feeling for justice is immovable, and truer than hers. I know what I want, I have a goal, an opinion, I have a religion, and love. Let me be myself and then I am satisfied. I know that I'm a woman, a woman with inward strength and plenty of courage."

Anne Frank, Diary of a Young Girl, *1947*

Who shall I be today?
By varying the way they look, adolescents try out different "selves." Although we eventually form a consistent and stable sense of identity, the "self" we present may change with the situation.

David Vance/The Image Bank

David Delossy/The Image Bank

tests of self-esteem. (Sample item: "I am able to do things as well as most other people.") During the early to mid-teen years, self-esteem falls, but it then rebounds during the late teens and twenties (Robins & others, 2002; Twenge & Campbell, 2001).

Developing Intimacy

Erikson contended that the adolescent identity stage is followed in young adulthood by a developing capacity for **intimacy**, the ability to form emotionally close relationships. Once you have a clear and comfortable sense of who you are, said Erikson, you are ready for close relationships.

GENDER AND SOCIAL CONNECTEDNESS To Carol Gilligan and her colleagues (1982, 1990), the "normal" struggle to create one's separate identity describes individualist males more than relationship-oriented females. Gilligan believes females are less concerned than males with viewing themselves as separate individuals and more concerned with "making connections."

These gender differences surface early, in children's play. Boys typically play in large groups with an activity focus and little intimate discussion. Girls usually play in smaller groups, often with one friend. Their play is less competitive than boys' and more imitative of social relationships. Both in play and other settings, females are more open and responsive to feedback than are males (Maccoby, 1990; Roberts, 1991).

As teens, girls spend more time with friends and less time alone (Wong & Csikszentmihalyi, 1991). The gender difference in connectedness continues through adulthood. When coping with stress, women more often turn to others for support (Tamres & others, 2002). Being more *interdependent*, women also use conversation more to explore relationships; men use it to communicate solutions (Tannen, 1990). As friends, women talk more often and more openly (Berndt, 1992; Dindia & Allen, 1992). And while men enjoy doing activities "side-by-side," women take more pleasure in talking "face-to-face" (Wright, 1989). New studies from several countries also reveal gender differences in communication:

- *New Zealand:* Given a sample of students' e-mail notes, people correctly guessed the writer's gender 66 percent of the time (Thomson & Murachver, 2001). (Males less often offered apologies, disclosed emotion and personal information, and used such hedges as "it was *sort of* interesting.")
- *United States:* When using computers, girls spend less time playing games and more time e-mailing friends (Crabtree, 2002).
- *France:* Women make 63 percent of telephone calls, and when talking to a woman stay connected longer (7.2 minutes) than men do when talking to other men (4.6 minutes) (Smoreda & Licoppe, 2000).

Both men and women report their friendships with women to be more intimate, enjoyable, and nurturing (Rubin, 1985; Sapadin, 1988). When wanting understanding and someone with whom to share worries and hurts, both men and women usually turn to women. And, although 69 percent of people say they have a close relationship with their father, 90 percent feel close to their mother (Hugick, 1989). Women provide most of the care to the very young and the very old.

Gender differences in connectedness and other traits peak in late adolescence and early adulthood—the very years most commonly studied. As teenagers, girls become progressively less assertive and more flirtatious; boys become more domineering and unexpressive. But by age 50, these differences have diminished. Women become more assertive and self-confident, and men more empathic and less domineering (Maccoby, 1998).

Some see biological wisdom in these changing gender roles. They speculate that, during dating, mating, and early parenthood, social expectations lead both sexes to downplay traits that interfere with their roles. As long as men are expected to provide and protect, they forgo their more dependent and tender sides (Gutmann, 1977). As long as women are expected to nurture, they forgo their impulses to be assertive and independent. When they graduate from these early adult roles, men and women are freer to develop and express their previously inhibited tendencies.

▶ **intimacy** in Erikson's theory, the ability to form close, loving relationships; a primary developmental task in late adolescence and early adulthood.

Question: *Why does it take 200 million sperm to fertilize one egg?*
Answer: *Because they won't stop for directions.*

"What's the difference between a man and E.T.? E.T. phoned home."

Anonymous

"In the long years liker must they grow; The man be more of woman, she of man."

Alfred Lord Tennyson, The Princess, *1847*

"How was my day? How was my day? Must you micromanage my life?"

Separating From Parents

As adolescents in Western cultures seek to form their own identities, they begin to separate themselves from their parents (Paikoff & Brooks-Gunn, 1991). The preschooler who can't be close enough to mother, who loves to touch and cling to her, becomes the 14-year-old who wouldn't be caught dead holding hands with Mom. The transition occurs gradually (**FIGURE 4.14**). By adolescence, arguments occur more often, usually over mundane things—household chores, bedtime, homework (Tesser & others, 1989).

For a minority of parents and their adolescents, differences lead to estrangement and to great stress (Steinberg & Morris, 2001). But for most, disagreement at the level of bickering is not destructive. One study of 6000 adolescents in 10 countries, from Australia to Bangladesh to Turkey, found that most liked their parents (Offer & others, 1988). "We usually get along, but . . ." adolescents often report (Galambos, 1992; Steinberg, 1987). Positive relations with parents support positive peer relations. High school girls who have the most affectionate relationships with their mothers tend also to enjoy the most intimate friendships with girlfriends (Gold & Yanof, 1985). And teens who feel close to their parents tend to be healthy and happy and to do well in school (Resnick & others, 1997). Of course, we can state this correlation the other way: Misbehaving teens are more likely to have tense parental relationships.

Adolescence is typically a time of diminishing parental influence and growing peer influence. Asked in a survey if they had "ever had a serious talk" with their child about illegal drugs, 85 percent of American *parents* answered yes. But the teens sometimes tuned out this earnest advice, for only 45 percent could recall such a serious talk (Morin & Brossard, 1997). Instead, what their friends are—what "everybody's doing"— they often become.

As we noted in Chapter 3, heredity does much of the heavy lifting in forming individual differences in character and personality, and peer influences do much of the rest. Teens are herd animals. They talk, dress, and act more like their peers than their parents. In teen calls to hotline counseling services, peer relationships are the most discussed topic (Boehm & others, 1999). For those who feel excluded, the pain is acute. "The social atmosphere in most high schools is poisonously clique-driven and exclusionary," observes social psychologist Elliot Aronson (2001). Most excluded "students suffer in silence. . . . A small number act out in violent ways against their classmates." When rejected adolescents withdraw, they are vulnerable to loneliness, low self-esteem, and depression (Steinberg & Morris, 2001). Peer approval matters. But teens see their parents as having more influence in other

Nine times out of ten, it's all about peer pressure.

Compared with teens elsewhere, teens in the United States spend more time watching TV and hanging out with friends (both predictors of negative outcomes) and less time on schoolwork (Larson, 2001).

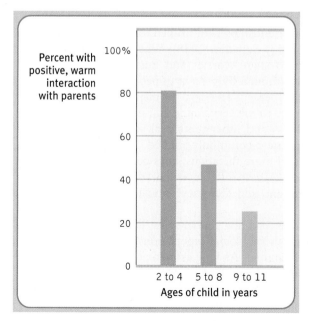

Percent with positive, warm interaction with parents

figure 4.14
The changing parent-child relationship Interviews from a large, national study of Canadian families reveal that the typically close, warm relationships between parents and preschoolers loosen among children of older ages. (Data from Statistics Canada, 1999.)

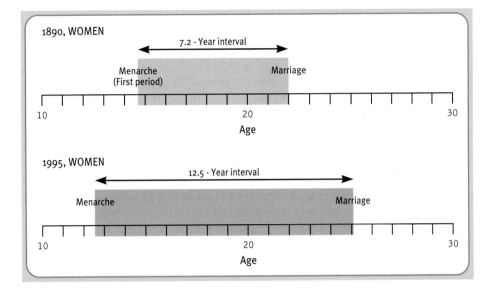

figure 4.15
Adolescence is being stretched from both ends In the 1890s the average interval between a woman's first menstrual period and marriage, which typically marked a transition to adulthood, was about 7 years; today in industrialized countries it is nearly 12 years (Guttmacher, 2000). Although many adults are unmarried, later marriage combines with prolonged education and earlier menarche to help stretch out adolescence.

areas—in shaping their religious faith and practices, and in thinking about college and career choices, for example (*Emerging Trends*, 1997).

As people mature in young adulthood, the emotional ties between parents and children continue to loosen. During their early twenties, many still lean heavily on their parents. By their late twenties, most feel more comfortably independent of their parents and better able to empathize with them as fellow adults (Frank, 1988; White, 1983). This graduation from adolescence to adulthood is now taking longer.

In the Western world, adolescence now roughly corresponds to the teen years, but at earlier times—and in some developing countries today—adolescence was a brief interlude between the dependence of childhood and the responsibilities of adulthood. Shortly after sexual maturity, society bestowed adult responsibilities and status on the young person, often marking the event with an elaborate initiation. The new adult then worked, married, and had children.

With compulsory schooling, adult independence began occurring later. In industrialized cultures from Europe to Australia, adolescents are taking more time to finish college, to leave the nest, and to establish careers. In the United States, for example, the average age at first marriage has increased more than 4 years since 1960 (to 27 for men, 25 for women). Earlier sexual maturity, related to improved nutrition, and later independence have widened the once-brief interlude between biological maturity and social independence (**FIGURE 4.15**). That gap—the years spent morphing from child to adult—is adolescence.

rehearse it!

14. Adolescence is marked by the onset of
a. an identity crisis.
b. puberty.
c. separation anxiety.
d. parent-child conflict.

15. Dramatic developments in the sex characteristics take place during the adolescent growth spurt. Primary sex characteristics relate to _____; secondary sex characteristics refer to _____.
a. ejaculation; menarche
b. breasts and facial hair; ovaries and testes
c. emotional maturity; hormone surges
d. reproductive organs; nonreproductive traits

16. According to Piaget, the ability to think logically about abstractions indicates
a. concrete operational thought.
b. egocentrism.
c. formal operational thought.
d. conservation.

17. According to Kohlberg, preconventional morality focuses on _____; conventional morality is more concerned with _____
a. upholding laws and social rules; self-interest
b. self-interest; basic ethical principles
c. upholding laws and social rules; basic ethical principles
d. self-interest; upholding laws and social rules

18. Erikson contended that each stage of life has its own special psychosocial task or challenge. The *primary* task during adolescence is to
a. attain formal operations.
b. forge an identity.
c. develop a sense of intimacy with another person.
d. live independent of parents.

19. The differences among individuals within each gender are much greater than the differences between men and women. Nevertheless, women more than men exhibit a concern for
a. independence and self-reliance.
b. social connections.
c. competitive achievement.
d. social stereotyping.

Answers can be found in Appendix C.

ADULTHOOD

At one time, psychologists viewed center-of-life years between adolescence and old age as one long plateau. No longer. Those who follow the unfolding of people's adult lives now believe our development continues. Physically, cognitively, and especially socially, people at age 50 differ from their 25-year-old selves.

It is more difficult to generalize about adulthood stages than about life's early years. If you know that James is a 1-year-old and Jamal is a 10-year-old, you could say a great deal about each child. Not so with adults who differ by a similar number of years. The boss may be 30 or 60; the marathon runner may be 20 or 50; a 19-year-old can be a parent who supports a child or a child who gets an allowance. Yet our life courses are in some ways similar. Our bodies, our minds, and our relationships undergo some changes in common with those of our childhood friends, who in other ways now seem so very different.

Physical Development

9. How do our bodies change in middle and late adulthood?

Our physical abilities—muscular strength, reaction time, sensory keenness, and cardiac output—all crest by the mid-twenties. Like the declining daylight after the summer solstice, declining physical prowess begins imperceptibly. Athletes are often the first to notice. World-class sprinters and swimmers peak in their teens or early twenties. Women, because they mature earlier than men, also peak earlier. But most of us—especially those of us whose daily lives do not require top physical performance—hardly perceive the early signs of decline.

Physical Changes in Middle Adulthood

Middle-age (post-40) athletes know all too well that physical decline gradually accelerates (**FIGURE 4.16**). As a 61-year-old who regularly plays basketball, I now find myself occasionally wondering whether my team really needs me down court. But even diminished vigor is sufficient for normal activities. Moreover, during early and middle adulthood, physical vigor has less to do with age than with a person's health and exercise habits. Many of today's physically fit 50-year-olds run 4 miles with ease, while sedentary 25-year-olds find themselves huffing and puffing up two flights of stairs. Even many 70-year-olds don't yet feel old.

For women, aging means a gradual decline in fertility. Among women 35 to 39, a single act of intercourse is half as likely to produce a pregnancy as it would be for a woman 19 to 26 (Dunson & others, 2002). But women's foremost biologi-

---

"I am still learning."

Michelangelo, 1560, at age 85

"Happy fortieth. I'll take the muscle tone in your upper arms, the girlish timbre of your voice, your amazing tolerance for caffeine, and your ability to digest french fries. The rest of you can stay."

How old does a person have to be before you think of him or her as old? The average 18- to 29-year-old says 67. The average person 60 and over says 76 (Yankelovich, 1995).

figure 4.16
Gradually accelerating decline An analysis of aging and batting averages of all twentieth-century major league baseball players revealed a gradual but accelerating decline in players' later years (Schall & Smith, 2000). The career performance record of the great Willie Mays is illustrative.

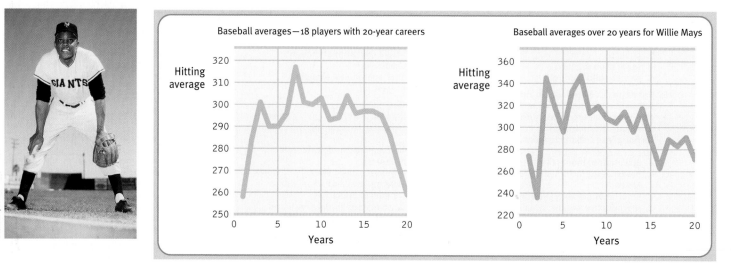

cal sign of aging is **menopause**, the ending of the menstrual cycle, usually beginning within a few years of age 50. The image of menopausal emotionality and depression clashes with reality: Menopause usually does *not* create psychological problems for women. Studies following thousands of American and Australian middle-aged women for up to 10 years have all found them no more or less depressed if experiencing menopause (Busch & others, 1994; Dennerstein & others, 2000; Matthews, 1992; McKinlay & others, 1987a,b). A woman's expectations and attitudes influence the emotional impact of menopause. Does she see it as a sign that she is losing her femininity and sexual attractiveness and growing old? Or does she view it as liberation from menstrual periods, fears of pregnancy, and children's demands?

Men experience no equivalent to menopause—no cessation of fertility, no sharp drop in sex hormones. They do experience a more gradual decline in sperm count, testosterone level, and speed of erection and ejaculation. Some may also experience psychological distress related to their perception of decreased virility and declining physical capacities. But most men age without such problems.

After middle age, most men and women remain capable of satisfying sexual activity. When people over 60 were surveyed by the National Council on Aging, 39 percent expressed satisfaction with the amount of sex they were having and 39 percent said they wished for sex more frequently (Leary, 1998).

Physical Changes in Later Life

Is old age "more to be feared than death" (Juvenal, *Satires*)? Or is life "most delightful when it is on the downward slope" (Seneca, *Epistulae ad Lucilium*)? What is it like to grow old?

SENSORY ABILITIES As we have seen, physical decline begins in early adulthood, but we are not usually acutely aware of it until later life. Visual sharpness diminishes, and adaptation to changes in light level slows. Muscle strength, reaction time, and stamina also diminish noticeably, as do hearing, distance perception, and the sense of smell (**FIGURE 4.17**). In later life, the stairs get steeper, the print gets smaller, and people seem to mumble more.

With age, the eye's pupil shrinks and its lens becomes less transparent, reducing the amount of light reaching the retina. In fact, a 65-year-old retina receives only about one-third as much light as its 20-year-old counterpart (Kline & Schieber, 1985). Thus, to see as well as a 20-year-old when reading or driving, a 65-year-old needs three times as much light—a reason for buying cars with untinted windshields. This also explains why older people sometimes ask younger people, "Don't you need better light for reading?"

▶ **menopause** the time of natural cessation of menstruation; also refers to the biological changes a woman experiences as her ability to reproduce declines.

"There are no lifestyle changes, surgical procedures, vitamins, antioxidants, hormones or techniques of genetic engineering available today that have been demonstrated to influence the processes of aging."

Position Statement on Human Aging signed by 51 scientists who study aging, 2002

"For some reason, possibly to save ink, the restaurants had started printing their menus in letters the height of bacteria."

Dave Barry, Dave Barry Turns Fifty, 1998

figure 4.17
The aging senses
Sight, smell, and hearing all are less acute among those over age 70. (From Doty & others, 1984.)

Proportion of normal (20/20) vision when identifying letters on an eye chart

Percent correct when identifying smells

Percent correct when identifying spoken words

Age in years

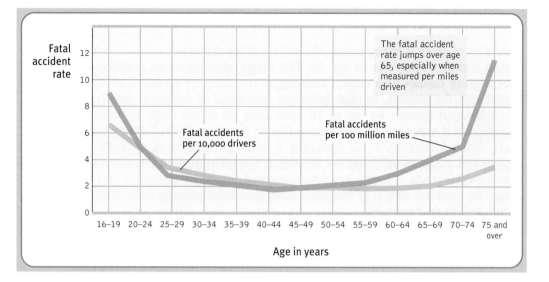

figure 4.18
Age and fatal accidents Slowing reactions contribute to increased accident risks among those 75 and older (Stock, 1995). Would you favor driver exams based on performance, not age, to screen out those whose slow reactions or sensory impairments indicate accident risk?

HEALTH For those growing older, there is both bad and good news about health. The bad news: The body's disease-fighting immune system weakens, making the elderly more susceptible to life-threatening ailments such as cancer and pneumonia. The good news: Thanks partly to a lifetime's accumulation of antibodies, older people *less* often suffer short-term ailments, such as common flu and cold viruses. For example, those over 65 are half as likely as 20-year-olds and one-fifth as likely as preschoolers to suffer upper respiratory flu each year (National Center for Health Statistics, 1990). This is one reason older workers have lower absenteeism rates (Rhodes, 1983).

Aging levies a tax on the brain by slowing our neural processing. Up to the teen years, we process information with greater and greater speed (Fry & Hale, 1996; Kail, 1991). But compared with teens and young adults, older people take a bit more time to react, to solve perceptual puzzles, even to remember names (Bashore & others, 1997; Verhaeghen & Salthouse, 1997). Speed slows especially when the task becomes complex (Cerella, 1985; Poon, 1987). At video games, most 70-year-olds are no match for a 20-year-old. And, as **FIGURE 4.18** indicates, fatal car accident rates per mile sharply increase after age 75. By age 75, they reach the relatively high teenage level (National Research Council, 1990).

During aging, brain regions important to memory begin to atrophy (Schacter, 1996). In young adulthood, a small, gradual net loss of brain cells begins, contributing by age 80 to a brain weight reduction of 5 percent or so. Aging may proceed more slowly in women. Not only do women worldwide live four years longer than men, their brains shrink more slowly than men's (Coffey & others, 1998).

The birth of new cells and the proliferation of neural connections, especially in those who remain active, helps compensate for the cell loss (Coleman & Flood, 1986). This helps explain the common finding that adults who remain active—physically, sexually, and mentally—retain more of their capacity for such activities in later years. Physical exercise enhances muscles, bones, and energy and helps prevent obesity and heart disease. It also, it now seems, stimulates brain cell development, thanks perhaps to increased oxygen and nutrient flow (Kempermann & others, 1998). And that may explain why sedentary older adults randomly assigned to a walking program exhibited enhanced memory and sharpened judgment (Kramer & others, 1999). We are more likely to rust from disuse than to wear out from overuse. "Use it or lose it" is sound advice.

Cognitive Development

10. In what ways do memory and intelligence change as we age?

Among the most controversial questions in the study of the human life span is whether adult cognitive abilities, such as memory, creativity, and intelligence, parallel the gradually accelerating decline of physical abilities.

Keeping the biological clock running smoothly How quickly people age depends in part on their health habits. As this cheerful group makes clear, the more active people remain, the more vigor they retain.

Aging and Memory

As we age, we remember some things well. Looking back in later life, people most vividly recall not only recent happenings but also their experiences in life's second two decades (Holmes & Conway, 1999; Rubin & others, 1998). Asked to recall the one or two most important events over the last half-century, they tend to name events from their teens or twenties. Whatever one experienced around this stage of life—the Great Depression, World War II, the civil rights movement, the Vietnam war (or, for current twenty-somethings, perhaps the events of 9/11)—becomes pivotal (Pillemer, 1998; Schuman & Scott, 1989). Our teens and twenties are also the time when we experience so many of life's memorable "firsts"—first date, first job, first going to college, first meeting your parents-in-law.

For some types of learning and remembering, early adulthood is indeed a peak time. In one experiment, Thomas Crook and Robin West (1990) invited 1205 people to learn some names. Fourteen videotaped people said their names, using a common format: "Hi, I'm Larry." Then the same individuals reappeared and said, for example, "I'm from Philadelphia"—thus providing a visual and voice cue for remembering the person's name. As **FIGURE 4.19** shows, everyone remembered more names after a second and third replay of the introductions, but younger adults consistently surpassed older adults in their name recall. Similar results appear in other studies. Within hours after Prime Minister Margaret Thatcher announced her resignation, young and old British people recalled how they heard the news. When asked again 11 months later, 90 percent of the younger group, but only 42 percent of the older group, told the same story (Cohen & others, 1994). Perhaps it's not surprising, then, that nearly two-thirds of people over age 40 say their memory is worse than it was 10 years ago (KRC, 2001).

But consider another experiment. David Schonfield and Betty-Anne Robertson (1966) asked adults of various ages to learn a list of 24 words. Without giving any clues, the researchers asked some to *recall* as many words as they could from the list, and others simply to *recognize* words, using multiple-choice questions. Again, younger adults had better recall (**FIGURE 4.20**). But the researchers found no similar memory decline with age on the recognition tests. Tests also reveal that, unless given a jolt of caffeine, recognition memory is better for older adults early in the day

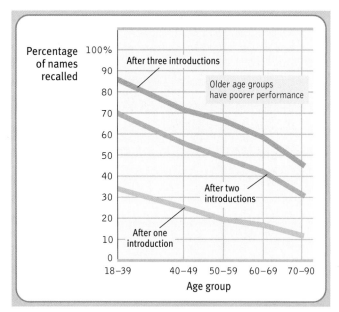

figure 4.19
Tests of recall Recalling new names introduced once, twice, or three times is easier for younger adults than for older ones. (Data from Crook & West, 1990.)

If you are within five years of 20, what experiences from your last year will you likely never forget? If you are older, what do you remember most vividly from that era of your life?

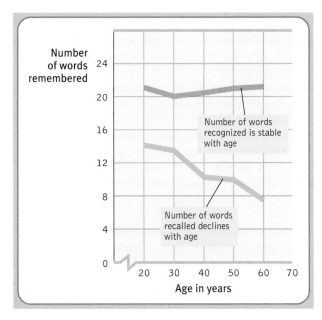

figure 4.20
Recall and recognition in adulthood In this experiment, the ability to *recall* new information declined during early and middle adulthood, but the ability to *recognize* new information did not. (From Schonfield & Robertson, 1966.)

rather than late (May & others, 1993; Ryan & others, 2002). So, how well older people remember depends: Are they being asked simply to *recognize* what they have tried to memorize (minimal decline) or to *recall* it without clues (greater decline)?

Forgetting seems also to depend on the type of information. If the information is meaningful, older people's rich web of existing knowledge will help them to catch it. Their capacity to learn and remember skills also shows less decline (Graf, 1990; Labouvie-Vief & Schell, 1982; Perlmutter, 1983).

Aging and Intelligence

What happens to our broader intellectual powers as we age? Do they gradually decline, as does our ability to recall new material? Or do they remain constant, as does our ability to recognize meaningful material?

PHASE I: CROSS-SECTIONAL EVIDENCE FOR INTELLECTUAL DECLINE In **cross-sectional studies**, researchers test and compare people of various ages. When giving intelligence tests to representative samples of people, researchers consistently find that older adults give fewer correct answers than do younger adults. David Wechsler (1972), creator of the most widely used adult intelligence test, therefore concluded that "the decline of mental ability with age is part of the general [aging] process of the organism as a whole." As everyone "knew," you couldn't teach an old dog new tricks.

PHASE II: LONGITUDINAL EVIDENCE FOR INTELLECTUAL STABILITY After colleges began giving intelligence tests to entering students about 1920, several psychologists saw their chance to study intelligence **longitudinally**—retesting the same people over a period of years. What they expected to find was a decrease in intelligence after about age 30 (Schaie & Geiwitz, 1982). What they actually found was a surprise: Until late in life, intelligence remained stable. On some tests, it even increased.

How then are we to account for the findings from the cross-sectional studies? In retrospect, researchers saw the problem. When a cross-sectional study compares 70-year-olds and 30-year-olds, it compares people not only of two different ages but of two different eras. It compares generally less-educated people (born, say, in the early 1900s) with better-educated people (born after 1950), people raised in large families with people raised in smaller families, people growing up in less affluent families with people raised in more affluent families. According to this more optimistic view, the myth that intelligence sharply declines with age is laid to rest. As everyone "knows," given good health you're never too old to learn.

PHASE III: IT ALL DEPENDS But the controversy continues. For one thing, longitudinal studies have their own pitfalls. Those who survive to the end of longitudinal studies may be bright, healthy people whose intelligence is least likely to decline. (Perhaps people who died younger and were removed from the study had declining intelligence.) Adjusting for the loss of subjects, as did a recent study following more than 2000 people over age 75 in Cambridge, England, reveals a steeper intelligence decline. This is especially so as people age after 85 (Brayne & others, 1999). Current research indicates that whether intelligence increases or decreases with age depends on the type of intellectual performance we measure. **Crystallized intelligence**—one's accumulated knowledge as reflected in vocabulary and analogies tests—*increases* up to old age. **Fluid intelligence**—one's ability to reason speedily and abstractly, as when solving novel logic problems—*decreases* slowly up to age 75 or so, then more rapidly, especially after age 85 (Cattell, 1963; Horn, 1982). We can see this pattern in the intelligence scores of a national sample of adults. After adjustments for education, verbal scores (reflecting crystallized intelligence) held relatively steady from ages 20 to 74. Nonverbal, puzzle-solving intelligence declined (**FIGURE 4.21**).

These cognitive differences help explain why mathematicians and scientists produce much of their most creative work during their late twenties or early thirties,

▶ **cross-sectional study** a study in which people of different ages are compared with one another.

▶ **longitudinal study** research in which the same people are restudied and retested over a long period.

▶ **crystallized intelligence** one's accumulated knowledge and verbal skills; tends to increase with age.

▶ **fluid intelligence** one's ability to reason speedily and abstractly; tends to decrease during late adulthood.

▶ **social clock** the culturally preferred timing of social events such as marriage, parenthood, and retirement.

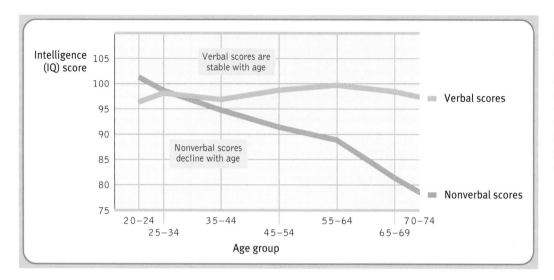

figure 4.21
Intelligence and age After adjustments for education, verbal intelligence scores hold steady with age, while nonverbal intelligence scores decline. (Intelligence scores from standardization sample of the Wechsler Adult Intelligence Scale, based on norms for 25- to 34-year-olds.) (Adapted from Kaufman & others, 1989.)

whereas those in literature, history, and philosophy tend to produce their best work in their forties, fifties, and beyond, after accumulating more knowledge (Simonton, 1988, 1990). For example, poets (who depend on fluid intelligence) reach their peak output earlier than prose authors (who need a deeper knowledge reservoir)— a finding observed in every major literary tradition, for both living and dead languages. So, intellectual performance can either increase or decrease with age, depending on what we assess and how we assess it.

"In youth we learn, in age we understand."

Marie Von Ebner-Eschenbach, Aphorisms, *1883*

Social Development

Many of the differences between younger and older adults are created not by the physical and cognitive changes that accompany aging but by life events associated with family relationships and work. A new job means new relationships, new expectations, and new demands. Marriage brings the joy of intimacy and the stress of merging your life with another's. The birth of a child introduces responsibilities and significantly alters your life focus. The death of a loved one creates an irreplaceable loss and a need to reaffirm your own life. Do these normal events of adult life shape a predictable sequence of life changes?

Adulthood's Ages and Stages

11. Is the journey from adolescence to death marked by stages that serve as developmental milestones?

As people enter their forties, they undergo a transition to middle adulthood, a time when they realize that life will soon be mostly behind them instead of ahead of them. Some psychologists have argued that for many the "midlife transition" is a crisis, a time of great struggle, of regret, or even of feeling struck down by life. The popular image of the midlife crisis is a man who forsakes his family for a younger girlfriend and a hot sports car. But the fact—reported by large samples of people— is that unhappiness, job dissatisfaction, marital dissatisfaction, divorce, anxiety, and suicide do *not* surge during the early forties (Hunter & Sundel, 1989; Mroczek & Kolarz, 1998). Divorce, for example, is most common among those in their twenties, suicide among those in their seventies and eighties. One study of emotional instability in nearly 10,000 men and women found "not the slightest evidence" that distress peaks anywhere in the midlife age range (**FIGURE 4.22**, page 130).

   There is another reason skeptics question age-linked stages such as the "midlife crisis." The **social clock**—the cultural prescription of "the right time" to leave home, get a job, marry, have children, and retire—varies from culture to culture and

"Midway in the journey of our life I found myself in a dark wood, for the straight way was lost."

Dante, The Divine Comedy, *1314*

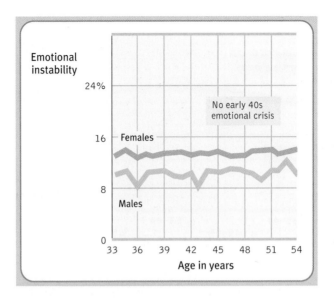

figure 4.22
Early-forties midlife crises? Among 10,000 people responding to a national health survey, there was no early forties increase in emotional instability ("neuroticism") scores. (From McCrae & Costa, 1990.)

Resetting the social clock
The social clock once prescribed that university graduation should occur around age 22. Today, more students are earning degrees at other ages.

era to era. In Jordan, 40 percent of brides are in their teens; in Hong Kong, only 3 percent are (United Nations, 1992). In Western Europe, fewer than 10 percent of men over 65 remain in the work force, as do 16 percent in the United States, 36 percent in Japan, and 69 percent in Mexico (Davies & others, 1991). And the once rigid sequence for Western women—of student to worker to wife to at-home mom to worker again—has loosened. Contemporary women occupy these roles in any order or all at once. For women and men, life events—marriage, parenthood, vocational changes, divorce, nest emptying, relocation, and retirement—mark transitions to new life stages whenever they occur, and they are occurring at increasingly unpredictable ages. The social clock still ticks, but people feel freer about being out of sync with it.

Adulthood's Commitments

12. What do psychologists view as adulthood's two primary commitments?

Two basic aspects of our lives do, however, dominate adulthood. Erik Erikson called them *intimacy* (forming close relationships) and *generativity* (being productive and supporting future generations). Researchers have chosen various terms—*affiliation* and *achievement*, *attachment* and *productivity*, *commitment* and *competence*. Sigmund Freud (1935) put it most simply: The healthy adult, he said, is one who can *love* and *work*.

LOVE Across time and place, human societies have nearly always included a relatively monogamous bond between men and women and a bond between parents and their children. We flirt, fall in love, and marry—one person at a time. "Pair-bonding is a trademark of the human animal," observed anthropologist Helen Fisher (1993). From an evolutionary perspective, the arrangement makes sense: Parents who cooperated to nurture their children to maturity were more likely to have their genes passed along to posterity than parents who didn't.

"One can live magnificently in this world if one knows how to work and how to love."

Leo Tolstoy, 1856

The bond of love is most satisfying and enduring when marked by a similarity of interests and values, a sharing of emotional and material support, and intimate self-disclosure (see Chapter 15). Marriage bonds are also likely to last when couples marry after age 20 and are well educated. Compared with their counterparts of 40 years ago, people in Western countries *are* better educated and marrying later. Yet, ironically, they are twice as likely to divorce. This partly reflects women's lessened economic dependence and men and women's rising expectations. We now hope not only for an enduring bond, but also for a mate who is a wage earner, caregiver, intimate friend, and warm and responsive lover. To judge from the divorce rate—both Canada and the United States now have about one divorce for every two marriages—marriage has become a union that often defies management (Bureau of the Census, 2002). In Europe, divorce is only slightly less common.

Love Intimacy, attachment, commitment—love by whatever name—is central to healthy and happy adulthood.

Might test-driving life together in a "trial marriage" minimize divorce risk? In a 2001 Gallup survey of American twenty-somethings, 62 percent thought it would (Whitehead & Popenoe, 2001). In reality, 10 studies in Europe, Canada, and the United States have found those who cohabited before marriage actually had *higher* divorce rates than those who did not (Myers, 2000). Those who cohabit tend to be initially less committed to the ideal of enduring marriage, and they become even less marriage-supporting while cohabiting.

Nonetheless, the institution of marriage endures. Worldwide, reports the United Nations, 9 in 10 heterosexual adults marry (Lowy, 2000). In Western countries, 3 in 4 who divorce will remarry—and their second marriages are virtually as happy as the average first marriage (Vemer & others, 1989). They are not alone. Surveys of more than 40,000 Americans since 1972 reveal that 40 percent of married adults and 23 percent of unmarried adults report being "very happy." Lesbian couples, too, report greater well-being than those who are alone (Wayment & Peplau, 1995). Marriage is a predictor not only of happiness but also of health, sexual satisfaction, and income. Moreover, neighborhoods with high marriage rates typically have low rates of social pathologies such as crime, delinquency, and emotional disorders among children (Myers, 2000).

Often, love bears children. For most people, the most enduring of life changes, having a child, is a happy event. However, when children begin to absorb time, money, and emotional energy, satisfaction with the marriage itself may decline. This is especially likely among employed women who, more than they expected, carry the traditional burden of doing the chores at home (Belsky & others, 1986; Hackel & Ruble, 1992). The effort to create an equitable relationship can pay double dividends, making for a more satisfying marriage, which also breeds better parent-child relations (Erel & Burman, 1995).

Although love bears children, children eventually leave home. This departure is a significant event, and a sometimes difficult separation. But seven national surveys reveal that the empty nest is for most people a happy place (Adelmann & others, 1989; Glenn, 1975). Compared with middle-aged women who still have children at home, those whose nest has emptied report greater happiness and greater enjoyment of their marriage. Many parents experience what sociologists Lynn White and John Edwards (1990) call a "postlaunch honeymoon," especially if they maintain close relationships with their children.

What do you think? Does marriage correlate with happiness because marital support and intimacy breed happiness, because happy people more often marry and stay married, or both?

If you have left home, did your parents suffer the "empty nest syndrome"—a feeling of distress focusing on a loss of purpose and relationship? Did they mourn the lost joy of listening for you in the wee hours of Saturday morning? Or did they seem to discover a new freedom, relaxation, and (if still married) renewed satisfaction with their own relationship?

Job satisfaction and life satisfaction Work can provide us with a sense of identity and competence and opportunities for accomplishment. Perhaps this is why challenging and interesting occupations enhance people's happiness.

For more on work, see Appendix B.

WORK For many adults, the answer to "Who are you?" depends a great deal on the answer to "What do you do?" Was Freud right? Does work, including a career, indeed contribute to self-fulfillment and life satisfaction? One approach to answering this question has been to compare the roughly equal numbers of North American women who are or are not employed. From their studies at the Wellesley College Center for Research on Women, Grace Baruch and Rosaline Barnett (1986) conclude that what matters is not which roles a woman occupies—paid worker, wife, and/or mother—but the quality of her experience in those roles.

For women and men, choosing a career path is difficult, especially in today's changing work environment. During the first two years of college or university, few students can predict their later careers. Most shift from their initially intended majors, many find their postcollege employment in fields not directly related to their majors, and most will change careers (Rothstein, 1980). In the end, happiness is about having work that fits your interests and provides you with a sense of competence and accomplishment. And for those who choose to marry, it is having a partner who is a close, supportive companion and who sees you as special, and/or having loving children whom you like and feel proud of.

Well-Being Across the Life Span

We're all aging. This moment marks the oldest you have ever been. To live is to grow older. That means we all can look back with satisfaction or regret, and forward with hope or dread. When people are asked what they would have done differently if they could relive their lives, their most common answer is "taken my education more seriously and worked harder at it" (Kinnier & Metha, 1989). Other regrets—"I should have told my father I loved him," "I regret that I never went to Europe"—also focus less on mistakes made than on the things one *failed* to do (Gilovich & Medvec, 1995).

In later life, income shrinks, work is often taken away, the body deteriorates, recall fades, energy wanes, family members and friends die or move away, and the great enemy, death, looms ever closer. Small wonder that many presume the over-65 years to be the worst of times (Freedman, 1978). But they are not, as Ronald Inglehart (1990) discovered when he amassed interviews conducted during the 1980s with representative samples of nearly 170,000 people in 16 nations. Older people report as much happiness and satisfaction with life as younger people do (**FIGURE 4.23**). If anything, positive feelings grow after midlife and negative feelings subside (Mroczek, 2001; Charles & others, 2001). Given that growing older is an outcome of living, an outcome nearly all of us prefer to early dying, this finding is comforting.

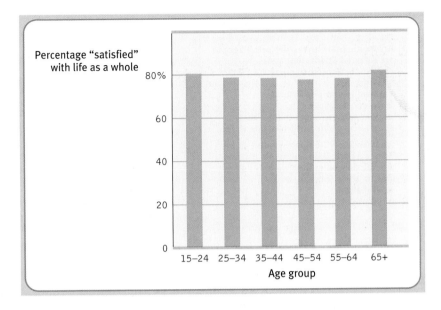

figure 4.23
Age and life satisfaction With the tasks of early adulthood behind them, many older adults have more time to pursue personal interests. No wonder their satisfaction with life remains high, and may even rise if they are healthy and active. As this graph based on multinational surveys shows, age differences in life satisfaction are trivial. (Data from Inglehart, 1990.)

Death and Dying

Most of us will suffer and cope with the deaths of relatives and friends. Usually, the most difficult separation is from one's spouse—a loss suffered by five times more women than men. Grief is especially severe when the death of a loved one comes suddenly and before its expected time on the social clock. The accidental death of a child or the sudden illness that claims a 45-year-old life partner may trigger a year or more of mourning flooded with memories, eventually subsiding to a mild depression that sometimes continues for several years (Lehman & others, 1987). When, as usually happens, death comes at a more expected late-life time, the grieving may be shorter lived.

The normal range of reactions to a loved one's death is wider than most suppose. Some cultures encourage public weeping and wailing; others hide grief. Within any culture, some individuals grieve more intensely and openly. Contrary to popular misconceptions, however,

- those who express the strongest grief immediately do not purge their grief more quickly (Bonanno & Kaltman, 1999; Wortman & Silver, 1989).
- "grief work" is not reliably healing. During the acute grieving period after losing a spouse, men are more at risk for ill health than women are, but this apparently is not because of women's greater ability to express emotions and work through grief. Grieving spouses who talk often with others adjust no better than those who grieve more privately (Bonanno, 2001; Stroebe & others, 2001, 2002).
- terminally ill and bereaved people do not go through predictable stages, such as denial, anger, and so forth (Nolen-Hoeksema & Larson, 1999). Given similar losses, some people grieve hard and long, others more lightly and briefly.

We can be grateful for the waning of death-denying attitudes. Facing death with dignity and openness helps people complete the life cycle with a sense of life's meaningfulness and unity—the sense that their existence has been good and that life and death are parts of an ongoing cycle. Although death may be unwelcome, life itself can be affirmed even at death. This is especially so for people who review their lives not with despair but with what Erik Erikson called a sense of *integrity*—a feeling that one's life has been meaningful and worthwhile.

"Do not go gentle into that good night, Old age should burn and rave at close of day; Rage, rage against the dying of the light."

Dylan Thomas, "Do not go gentle into that good night," 1952, poem written to his father as the father lay dying peacefully

"Consider, friend, as you pass by, as you are now, so once was I. As I am now, you too shall be. Prepare, therefore, to follow me."

Scottish tombstone epitaph

20. Some types of learning and remembering peak in early adulthood. By age 65, a person would be most likely to experience a decline in the ability to
    a. recall and list all the items in a chapter glossary.
    b. select the correct definition in a multiple-choice question.
    c. evaluate whether a statement is true or false.
    d. exercise sound judgment in answering an essay question.

21. In longitudinal studies the same people are retested at different ages. Longitudinal research suggests that intelligence
    a. steadily declines with age.
    b. peaks at age 25.
    c. generally increases in later life.
    d. remains stable until very late in life.

22. Freud defined the healthy adult as one who is able to love and work. Erikson agreed, observing that the adult struggles to attain intimacy and
    a. affiliation.
    b. identity.
    c. competence.
    d. generativity.

23. Contrary to what many people assume,
    a. older people are much happier than adolescents.
    b. men in their forties express much greater dissatisfaction with life than do women of the same age.
    c. people of all ages report similar levels of happiness.
    d. those whose children have recently left home—the empty nesters—have the lowest level of happiness of all groups.

Answers can be found in Appendix C.

REFLECTIONS ON TWO MAJOR DEVELOPMENTAL ISSUES

13. What conclusions can we draw from research on the issues of continuity versus stages and of stability versus change in lifelong development?

We began our survey of developmental psychology by identifying three pervasive issues: (1) how development is steered by genes and by experience, (2) whether development is a gradual, continuous process or a series of discrete stages, and (3) whether development is characterized more by stability over time or by change. We considered the first issue in Chapter 3. It is time to reflect on the second and third.

Continuity and Stages

Adults are vastly different from infants. But do they differ as a giant redwood differs from its seedling—a difference created by gradual, cumulative growth? Or do they differ as a butterfly differs from a caterpillar—a difference of distinct stages?

TOO MUCH COFFEE MAN BY SHANNON WHEELER

Stages of the life cycle

Generally speaking, researchers who emphasize experience and learning see development as a slow, continuous shaping process. Those who emphasize biological maturation tend to see development as a sequence of genetically predetermined stages or steps; although progress through the various stages may be quick or slow, everyone passes through the stages in the same order.

Are there clear-cut stages of psychological development, as there are physical stages such as walking before running? We have considered the stage theories of Jean Piaget on cognitive development, Lawrence Kohlberg on moral development, and Erik Erikson on psychosocial development. And we have seen their stage theories criticized: Young children have some abilities that Piaget attributed to later stages. Kohlberg's work appears biased by a worldview characteristic of educated males in individualistic cultures and, possibly, by too much emphasis on thinking over acting. Erikson's ideas are contradicted by research showing that adult life does not progress through a fixed, predictable series of steps.

Although research casts doubt on the idea that life proceeds through neatly defined, age-linked stages, the concept of stage remains useful. There are spurts of brain growth during childhood and puberty that correspond roughly to Piaget's stages (Thatcher & others, 1987). And stage theories contribute a developmental perspective on the whole life span, by suggesting how people of one age think and act differently when they arrive at a later age.

Stability and Change

This leads us to the final question: Over time, are people's personalities consistent, or do they change? If reunited with a long-lost grade school friend, would you instantly recognize that "it's the same old Andy"? Or does a person during one period of life seem like a different person at a later period?

Researchers who have followed lives through time have found evidence for both stability and change. There is continuity to personality and yet, happily for troubled children and adolescents, life is a process of becoming: The struggles of the present may be laying a foundation for a happier tomorrow. More specifically, researchers generally agree on the following points:

As adults grow older, there is continuity of self.

1. The first two years of life provide a poor basis for predicting a person's eventual traits (Kagan & others, 1978, 1998). Older children and adolescents also change. Although delinquent children have elevated rates of work problems, substance abuse, and crime, many confused and troubled children have blossomed into mature, successful adults (Moffitt & others, 2002; Roberts & others, 2001; Thomas & Chess, 1986). As people grow older, however, personality does gradually stabilize (Costa & McCrae, 1989; Klohnen & Bera, 1998; Stein & others, 1986).

2. Some characteristics, such as temperament, are more stable than others, such as social attitudes (Moss & Susman, 1980). But attitudes, too, become more stable with age (Krosnick & Alwin, 1989).

3. In some ways, we all change with age. Most shy, fearful toddlers begin opening up by age 4, and in the years after adolescence, most people become calmer and more self-disciplined, agreeable, and self-confident (McCrae & Costa, 1994; Roberts & others, 2003). Many a 20-year-old goof-off has matured into

"At 70, I would say the advantage is that you take life more calmly. You know that 'this, too, shall pass'!"

Eleanor Roosevelt, 1954

a 40-year-old business or cultural leader. Such changes can occur without changing a person's position *relative* to others of the same age. The hard-driving young adult may mellow by later life yet still be a relatively hard-driving senior citizen.

Finally, we should remember that life requires *both* stability and change. Stability enables us to depend on others, motivates our concern for the healthy development of children, and provides our identity. Change motivates our concerns about present influences, sustains our hope for a brighter future, and lets us adapt and grow with experience.

rehearse it!

24. Developmental researchers who emphasize learning and experience tend to believe in _____; those who emphasize biological maturation tend to believe in _____.
    a. nature; nurture
    b. continuity; stages

    c. stability; change
    d. randomness; predictability

25. Although development is lifelong, there is stability of personality over time. For example,
    a. most personality traits emerge in infancy and persist throughout life.

    b. temperament tends to remain stable throughout life.
    c. few people change significantly after adolescence.
    d. people tend to undergo greater personality changes as they age.

Answers can be found in Appendix C.

chapter review

The Developing Person

PRENATAL DEVELOPMENT AND THE NEWBORN

1. How does life develop before birth?

Developmental psychologists examine how we develop physically, cognitively, and socially from conception to death. The life cycle begins when one sperm cell, out of the some 200 million ejaculated, unites with an egg. The nuclei of the egg and sperm fuse to form a zygote. Attached to the uterine wall, the developing embryo begins to form body organs. By 9 weeks, the fetus is recognizably human. The mother eats, drinks, and breathes for two, so that any teratogens she ingests can reach the developing child and place it at risk.

2. What are some of the newborn's abilities?

Researchers have discovered that newborns are born with sensory equipment and reflexes that facilitate their interacting with adults and securing nourishment. For example, they quickly learn to discriminate the smell and sound of their mothers.

INFANCY AND CHILDHOOD

3. How do the brain and motor skills develop during infancy and childhood?

Within the brain, nerve cells form before birth. Sculpted by maturation and experience, their interconnections multiply rapidly after birth. We lose conscious memories of experiences from those earliest years. Infants' more complex physical skills—sitting, standing, walking—develop in a predictable sequence whose actual timing is a function of individual maturation rate and culture.

4. How did Piaget view the development of a child's mind, and what are current researchers' views?

Jean Piaget's observations of children convinced him—and almost everyone else—that the mind of a child is not that of a miniature adult. Piaget theorized that our mind develops by forming schemas that help us *assimilate* our experiences and that must occasionally be altered to *accommodate* new information. In this way, children progress from the simplicity of the *sensorimotor* stage of the first two years to more complex stages of thinking, which include a developing "theory of mind."

Piaget believed that preschool children, in the *preoperational stage*, are egocentric and unable to perform simple logical operations. At about age 6 or 7 they enter the *concrete operational stage* and can perform concrete operations, such as those required to comprehend the principle of conservation.

And by about age 12, children enter the *formal operational stage*, in which systematic reasoning is within their grasp.

Recent research supports the sequence Piaget proposed for the unfolding of human cognition, but it also shows that young children are more capable, and their development more continuous, than he believed. The cognitive abilities that emerge at each stage apparently begin developing in a rudimentary form in the previous stage.

5. How do the bonds of attachment form between parents and infants?

Infants become attached to their mothers and fathers not simply because mothers and fathers gratify biological needs but, more important, because they are comfortable, familiar, and responsive. In many animals, this attachment process, called imprinting, occurs during a critical period.

If denied responsive care, or if abused, both monkey and human infants may become pathetically withdrawn, anxious, and eventually abusive. Once an attachment forms, infants who are separated from their caregivers will, for a time, display stranger anxiety. Infants' differing attachment styles reflect both their individual temperament and the responsiveness of their parents and child-care providers. Parenting styles—permissive, authoritative, and authoritarian—reflect varying degrees of control. Children with the highest self-esteem, self-reliance, and social competence tend to have been reared by authoritative parents.

ADOLESCENCE

Due to earlier maturation and prolonged education, adolescence—the transition years between biological maturity and social independence—has lengthened in many countries.

6. What major physical changes occur during adolescence?

During adolescence, both primary and secondary sex characteristics develop dramatically. Boys seem to benefit from "early" maturation, girls from "late" maturation. The brain's frontal lobes mature during adolescence and the early twenties, enabling improved judgment, impulse control, and long-term planning.

7. How did Piaget and Kohlberg describe cognitive and moral development during adolescence?

Piaget theorized that adolescents develop the capacity for formal operations, which enables them to reason abstractly. Today's developmentalists find the rudiments of formal logic appearing earlier than Piaget believed.

Kohlberg contended that moral thinking likewise proceeds through a sequence of stages, from a preconventional morality of self-interest, to a conventional morality concerned with gaining others' approval or doing one's duty, to (in some people) a postconventional morality of agreed-upon rights or universal ethical principles. But morality also lies in actions. Moreover, say Kohlberg's critics, the postconventional level represents morality from the perspective of individualist, middle-class males.

8. *What tasks and challenges do adolescents face en route to mature adulthood, and are they the same for males and females?*

Erik Erikson theorized that a chief task of adolescence is solidifying one's sense of self—one's identity. This often means "trying on" a number of different roles. For many people the struggle for identity continues in the adult years as new relationships emerge and new roles are assumed. Gender differences in connectedness and other traits tend to peak during late adolescence. During adolescence, parental influence diminishes and peer influence increases. The transition from adolescence to adulthood is now taking longer—for some, into the mid-twenties.

ADULTHOOD

9. *How do our bodies change in middle and late adulthood?*

The barely perceptible physical declines of early adulthood begin to accelerate during middle adulthood. For women, a significant physical change is menopause, which generally seems to be a smooth rather than rough transition. For both men and women, perceptual acuity, strength, and stamina decline after 65, but short-term ailments are fewer.

10. *In what ways do memory and intelligence change as we age?*

As the years pass, recall begins to decline, especially for meaningless information, but recognition memory remains strong. Fluid intelligence declines in later life but crystallized intelligence does not.

11. *Is the journey from adolescence to death marked by stages that serve as developmental milestones?*

Although some theorists have maintained that adults progress through an orderly sequence of age-related stages, current research indicates that people are not so predictable. More important are life events, and the loosening of strict dictates of the social clock—the culturally preferred timing of social events.

12. *What do psychologists view as adulthood's two primary commitments?*

Adulthood's two major commitments are love (Erikson's *intimacy*—forming close relationships, especially with family) and work (productive activity, or what Erikson called *generativity*). Life events involving love and work influence adult development in unanticipated ways and vary with culture. Marriage seems more likely to last when people marry after age 20 and are well-educated, but Western couples who marry today are more than twice as likely to divorce as were those who married in 1960. Few people grow old gratefully, but most age gracefully, retaining a sense of well-being throughout life. Those who live to old age must, however, cope with the deaths of friends and family members and with the prospect of their own deaths. Erikson's view of the crisis of late adulthood pits integrity against despair.

REFLECTIONS ON TWO MAJOR DEVELOPMENTAL ISSUES

13. *What conclusions can we draw from research on the issues of continuity versus stages and of stability versus change in lifelong development?*

Although the stage theories of Piaget, Kohlberg, and Erikson have been modified in the light of later research, each theory usefully alerts us to differences among people of different ages. The discovery that people's traits continue to change in later life has helped create a new emphasis on lifelong development. Nevertheless, there is also an underlying consistency to most people's temperament and personality traits.

A CRITICAL THINKER'S REVIEW OF CHAPTER 4

You've now studied and reviewed **The Developing Person.** For even better retention, reflect on these concepts at a deeper level. If you need to refresh your memory of the six categories of critical thinking shown in parentheses below, see page 34. See if you can answer each of these questions in a short paragraph.

1. Your friend—a heavy smoker—hopes to become pregnant soon. She says she will stop smoking as soon as she learns she is pregnant. What can you tell her to convince her that the time to stop smoking is before she is pregnant? (psychological reasoning)

2. Ugandan babies tend to begin walking at an earlier age than babies of European descent. Researchers have presumed that this difference is a product of the infants' nurture. Others might wonder if credit should instead go to their genetically predisposed nature. How might we test these alternatives? (scientific problem solving)

3. How do Piaget's first three stages of cognitive development explain why young children are not just miniature adults in the way they think? (creative problem solving)

4. To predict whether a teenager smokes marijuana, you can ask how many of the teen's friends smoke it. One explanation for this correlation is peer influence. What's another? (perspective taking)

5. Jacintha would like to study adult memory in university professors. She is considering a longitudinal study, in which the same people are restudied and retested over a long period of time. She would need to test the professors repeatedly over the next 30 years. However, she is not sure she wants to spend 30 years completing this study! What approach could Jacintha use instead that would allow her to complete this study much more quickly? (pattern recognition)

6. Mr. Johnson, a counselor at a nearby high school, is trying hard to help students deal with the recent, tragic death of a classmate. Mr. Johnson is convinced that the students must all express their grief openly, and go through several specific stages of grieving, before they will be "healed." Some of the students he's trying to help seem to be feeling worse than ever. What can you tell Mr. Johnson that might help him deal with the students more effectively? (practical problem solving)

Answers can be found in Appendix C.

TERMS AND CONCEPTS TO REMEMBER

developmental psychology, p. 99
zygote, p. 100
embryo, p. 100
fetus, p. 100
teratogens, p. 100
fetal alcohol syndrome (FAS), p. 101
rooting reflex, p. 101
habituation, p. 102
maturation, p. 103
schema, p. 105
assimilation, p. 105
accommodation, p. 105
cognition, p. 105

sensorimotor stage, p. 105
object permanence, p. 105
preoperational stage, p. 107
conservation, p. 107
egocentrism, p. 107
theory of mind, p. 107
concrete operational stage, p. 108
formal operational stage, p. 108
stranger anxiety, p. 110
attachment, p. 110
critical period, p. 111
imprinting, p. 111
basic trust, p. 112

adolescence, p. 115
puberty, p. 115
primary sex characteristics, p. 115
secondary sex characteristics, p. 116
menarche [meh-NAR-key], p. 117
identity, p. 119
intimacy, p. 121
menopause, p. 125
cross-sectional study, p. 128
longitudinal study, p. 128
crystallized intelligence, p. 128
fluid intelligence, p. 128
social clock, p. 129

To continue your study and review of The Developing Person, visit this book's Web site at www.worthpublishers.com/myers. You will find practice tests, review activities, and Web links for more information on topics related to The Developing Person.

chapter5

Sensation and Perception

Twenty-four hours a day, stimuli from the outside world bombard your body. Meanwhile, in a silent, cushioned, inner world, your brain floats in utter darkness. This raises a question, one that predates psychology by thousands of years and helped inspire its beginnings a little more than a century ago: *How does the world out there get in?*

To modernize the question: How do we construct our representations of the external world? How do we represent a campfire's flicker, crackle, and smoky scent as patterns of active neural connections? And how, from this living neurochemistry, do we create our conscious experience of the fire's motion and temperature, its aroma and beauty?

To represent the world in our head, we must detect physical energy from the environment and encode it as neural signals, a process traditionally called **sensation**. And we must select, organize, and interpret our sensations, a process traditionally called **perception**. In our everyday experiences, sensation and perception blend into one continuous process. In this chapter, we slow down that process to study its parts.

We start with the sensory receptors and work up to higher levels of processing. Psychologists refer to sensory analysis that starts at the entry level as **bottom-up processing**. Our minds also interpret what our senses detect. We construct perceptions drawing both on sensations coming bottom-up to the brain and on our experience and expectations, which psychologists call **top-down processing**.

Failures of perception may occur anywhere between sensory detection and perceptual interpretation. For example, the eyes of a person born with cataracts may be unable to detect light, rendering the brain's higher-level visual processing equipment useless. People with brain damage reveal the importance of other links in the sensation-perception chain. After losing a temporal lobe area essential to recognizing faces, patient "E.H." suffers from a condition called *prosopagnosia*. She has complete sensation but incomplete perception. She can sense visual information—indeed may accurately report the features of a face—yet she is unable to recognize it. Shown an unfamiliar face, she does not react. Shown a familiar face, her autonomic nervous system responds with measurable perspiration. Still, she hasn't a clue who the person is. Shown her own face in a mirror, she is again stumped. Because of her brain damage, she cannot process top-down—she cannot relate her stored knowledge to the sensory input.

> ▶ **sensation** the process by which our sensory receptors and nervous system receive and represent stimulus energies from our environment.
>
> ▶ **perception** the process of organizing and interpreting sensory information, enabling us to recognize meaningful objects and events.
>
> ▶ **bottom-up processing** analysis that begins with the sense receptors and works up to the brain's integration of sensory information.
>
> ▶ **top-down processing** information processing guided by higher-level mental processes, as when we construct perceptions drawing on our experience and expectations.

Detail, *The Forest Has Eyes* by Bev Doolittle © The Greenwich Workshop, Inc., Trumbull, CT.

What's going on here? Our sensory and perceptual processes work together to help us sort out the complex images in this Bev Doolittle painting, *The Forest Has Eyes*. Bottom-up processing enables our sensory systems to detect the lines, angles, and colors that form the horses, rider, and surroundings. Using top-down processing, we consider the painting's title, notice the apprehensive expressions, and then direct our attention to aspects of the painting that will give those observations meaning.

Animals' sensory abilities suit their historical ecological niches
Manatees hear what their ancestors needed to hear, which was not the low-frequency sounds of boat noise. The manatee's meager sensitivity to low-pitch sounds explains the failure of two decades of manatee protection. Slowing boats did not halt the collisions that have decimated Florida's population of these gentle giants (Gerstein, 2002).

Branden D. Cole/Corbis

SENSING THE WORLD: SOME BASIC PRINCIPLES

Sensory systems enable organisms to obtain needed information. Consider:

- A frog, which feeds on flying insects, has eyes with receptor cells that fire only in response to small, dark, moving objects. A frog could starve to death knee-deep in motionless flies. But let one zoom by and the frog's "bug detector" cells snap awake.
- A male silkworm moth has receptors so sensitive to the odor of the female sex-attractant that a single female silkworm moth need release only a billionth of an ounce per second to attract every male silkworm moth within a mile. That is why there continue to be silkworms.
- We are similarly designed to detect what are, for us, the important features of our environments. Our ears are most sensitive to sound frequencies that include human voice consonants and a baby's cry.

Nature's sensory gifts suit each recipient's needs.

Sensory limits
A mosquito's buzz can sound like a dive-bomber, thanks to our low threshold for sounds at its pitch. But a shrieking, dive-bombing bat will seem silent, its cries too high-pitched for us to hear. Our ears are most sensitive to the pitch range of human speech.

Thresholds

We exist in a sea of energy. At this moment, you and I are being struck by x-rays and radio waves, ultraviolet and infrared light, and sound waves of very high and very low frequencies. To all of these we are blind and deaf. But human senses hardly exhaust the sensory possibilities (Hughes, 1999). Other animals detect the world that lies beyond human experience. Birds use their magnetic compass. Bats and dolphins locate prey with sonar (bouncing echoing sound off objects). On a cloudy day, bees navigate by detecting polarized light from an invisible (to us) sun.

The shades on our own senses are open just a crack, allowing us only a restricted awareness of this vast sea of energy. **Psychophysics** is the study of how this physical energy relates to our psychological experience. What stimuli can we detect? At what intensity? How sensitive are we to changing stimulation?

Absolute Thresholds

1. What is an absolute threshold, and are we influenced by stimuli below it?

To some kinds of stimuli we are exquisitely sensitive. Standing atop a mountain on an utterly dark, clear night, we can, given normal senses, see a candle flame atop another mountain 30 miles away. We can feel the wing of a bee falling on our cheek. We can even smell a single drop of perfume in a three-room apartment (Galanter, 1962).

Our awareness of these faint stimuli illustrates our **absolute thresholds**—the minimum stimulation necessary to detect a particular stimulus (light, sound, pressure, taste, odor) 50 percent of the time. To test your absolute threshold for sounds, a psychologist—or a hearing specialist—would expose each of your ears to varying sound levels. For each pitch, the test would define where half the time you correctly detect the sound and half the time you do not. For each of the senses, that 50-50 point defines your absolute threshold.

▶ **psychophysics** the study of relationships between the physical characteristics of stimuli, such as their intensity, and our psychological experience of them.

▶ **absolute threshold** the minimum stimulation needed to detect a particular stimulus 50 percent of the time.

▶ **subliminal** below one's absolute threshold for conscious awareness.

Subliminal Stimulation

In 1956, controversy erupted over a false report that New Jersey movie audiences were unwittingly being influenced by imperceptible flashed messages to DRINK COCA-COLA and EAT POPCORN (Pratkanis, 1992). Many years later, the controversy erupted anew. Advertisers were said to manipulate consumers by imperceptibly printing the word *sex* on crackers and by embedding erotic images in liquor ads. Rock recordings were said to contain "satanic messages" that could be heard if the recordings were played backward and that, even when played forward, could unconsciously persuade the unwitting listener. Hoping to penetrate our unconscious, entrepreneurs offer audiotapes to help us lose weight, stop smoking, or improve our memories. These tapes contain soothing ocean sounds that mask unheard messages such as, "I am thin," "Smoke tastes bad," or "I do well on tests. I have total recall of information." Claims like these make two assumptions: that unconsciously we can sense **subliminal** (literally, "below threshold") stimuli (**FIGURE 5.1**), and that, without our awareness, these stimuli have extraordinary suggestive powers. Can we? Do they?

Can we be affected by stimuli so weak as to be unnoticed? Recent experiments hint that, under certain conditions, the answer may be yes. One experiment subliminally flashed either emotionally positive scenes (kittens, a romantic couple) or negative scenes (a werewolf, a dead body) an instant before participants viewed slides of people (Krosnick & others, 1992). Although the participants consciously perceived only a flash of light, they gave more positive ratings to people whose photos had been associated with positive scenes. People somehow looked nicer if their photo immediately followed unperceived kittens rather than an unperceived werewolf. Unfamiliar Chinese characters seemed nicer if preceded by a flashed but unperceived smiling face rather than a scowling face (Murphy & Zajonc, 1993). Sometimes we *feel* what we do not know and cannot describe.

An imperceptibly brief stimulus evidently triggers a weak response that evokes a feeling, though not a conscious awareness of the stimulus. But does the fact of subliminal *sensation* verify entrepreneurial claims of subliminal *persuasion*? Can advertisers really manipulate us with "hidden persuasion"? The near-consensus among research psychologists is no. The laboratory research reveals a *subtle, fleeting* effect on *thinking*. Priming thirsty people with the subliminal word *thirst* might therefore, for a brief interval, make a thirst-quenching beverage ad more persuasive (Strahan & others, 2002). But the subliminal tape hucksters claim something different: a *powerful, enduring* effect on *behavior*.

How to think uncritically without psychology: James Vicary, an unemployed marketing researcher, masterminded the EAT POPCORN subliminal advertising hoax with the help of uncritical reporters and broadcasters. Vicary reportedly collected big fees from advertising firms for his promised services—and then disappeared (Rogers, 1993, 1994).

"The heart has its reasons which reason does not know."

Pascal, Pensées, 1670

figure 5.1

Absolute threshold Do I smell it or not? When stimuli are detectable less than 50 percent of the time, they are "subliminal." Absolute threshold is the intensity at which we can detect a stimulus half the time.

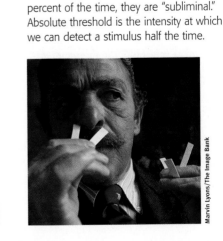

Marvin Lyons/The Image Bank

Subliminal persuasion?
Although subliminally presented stimuli *can* subtly influence people, experiments discount attempts at subliminal advertising and self-improvement. (The playful message here is not, however, subliminal—because you can easily perceive it.)

Experiments, such as the one described in Chapter 1, show that commercial subliminal tapes have no effect beyond that of a placebo—an effect of one's belief in them (Moore, 1988; Pratkanis & others, 1994; Smith & Rogers, 1994). The Canadian Broadcasting Corporation used a popular Sunday night TV show to flash a subliminal message 352 times (*Advertising Age*, 1958). Asked to guess the message, not one of the almost 500 letter writers did. Nearly half, however, reported feeling strangely hungry or thirsty during the show. But this was merely an effect of expectations. The actual message was TELEPHONE NOW. The effect of these 352 subliminal messages on Canadian telephone usage? Zilch.

Difference Thresholds

2. How does the magnitude of a stimulus influence our threshold for detecting differences?

To function effectively, we need absolute thresholds low enough to allow us to detect important sights, sounds, textures, tastes, and smells. We also need to detect small differences among stimuli. A musician must detect minute discrepancies in an instrument's tuning. A wine taster must detect the slight flavor difference between two vintage wines. Parents must detect the sound of their own child's voice amid other children's voices.

The difference threshold
In this computer-generated copy of the Twenty-third Psalm, each line of the typeface changes imperceptibly. How many lines are required for you to experience a just noticeable difference?

The LORD is my shepherd;
    I shall not want.
He maketh me to lie down
        in green pastures:
    he leadeth me
        beside the still waters.
He restoreth my soul:
    he leadeth me
        in the paths of righteousness
        for his name's sake.
Yea, though I walk through the valley
        of the shadow of death,
        I will fear no evil:
    for thou art with me;
        thy rod and thy staff
        they comfort me.
Thou preparest a table before me
        in the presence of mine enemies:
    thou anointest my head with oil,
        my cup runneth over.
Surely goodness and mercy
        shall follow me
        all the days of my life:
    and I will dwell
        in the house of the LORD
        for ever.

The **difference threshold** (also called the *just noticeable difference*, or *jnd*) is the minimum difference a person can detect between any two stimuli half the time. The difference threshold increases with the magnitude of the stimulus. Thus, if you add 10 grams to a 100-gram weight, you will detect the difference; add 10 grams to a 1-*kilogram* weight and you will not, because the difference threshold has increased. More than a century ago, Ernst Weber noted that regardless of their magnitude, two stimuli must differ by a constant proportion for their difference to be perceptible. This principle—that the difference threshold is not a constant amount but some constant *percentage* of the stimulus—is so simple and so widely applicable that we still refer to it as **Weber's law**. The exact proportion varies, depending on the stimulus. For the average person to perceive their differences, two lights must differ in intensity by 8 percent. Two objects must differ in weight by 2 percent. And two tones must differ in frequency by only 0.3 percent (Teghtsoonian, 1971).

▶ **difference threshold** the minimum difference between two stimuli required for detection 50 percent of the time. We experience the difference threshold as a just noticeable difference. (Also called *just noticeable difference* or *jnd*.)

▶ **Weber's law** the principle that, to be perceived as different, two stimuli must differ by a constant minimum percentage (rather than a constant amount).

▶ **sensory adaptation** diminished sensitivity as a consequence of constant stimulation.

Weber's law is a rough approximation. It works well for nonextreme sensory stimuli, and it parallels some of our life experiences. If the price of a 50-cent chocolate bar goes up by 5 cents, shoppers might notice the change; similarly, it might take a $5000 price hike in a $50,000 Mercedes to raise the eyebrows of its potential buyers. In both cases, the price went up by 10 percent. Weber's principle: Our thresholds for detecting differences are a roughly constant proportion of the size of the original stimulus.

Sensory Adaptation

3. What function does sensory adaptation serve?

Entering your neighbors' living room, you smell an unpleasant odor. You wonder how they can stand the stench, but within minutes you no longer notice it. Jumping into a swimming pool, you shiver and complain about how cold it is. A short while later a friend arrives and you exclaim, "C'mon in. Water's fine!" These examples illustrate **sensory adaptation**—our diminishing sensitivity to an unchanging stimulus. (To experience this phenomenon, move your watch up your wrist an inch: You will feel it—but only for a few moments.) After constant exposure to a stimulus, our nerve cells fire less frequently.

Why, then, if we stare at an object without flinching, does it not vanish from sight? Because, unnoticed by us, our eyes are always moving, quivering just enough to guarantee that stimulation on the inner surface of the eye continually changes.

But what if we actually could stop our eyes from moving? Would sights seem to vanish, as odors do? To find out, psychologists have devised ingenious instruments for maintaining a constant image on the eye's inner surface. Imagine that we have fitted a volunteer, Mary, with one of these instruments—a miniature projector mounted on a contact lens (**FIGURE 5.2a**). When Mary's eye moves, the image from the projector moves as well. Thus, everywhere that Mary looks, the scene is sure to go.

If we project the profile of a face through such an instrument, what will Mary see? At first, she will see the complete profile. But within a few seconds, as her sensory receptors begin to fatigue, things get weird. Bit by bit, the image vanishes, only later to reappear and then disappear—in recognizable fragments or as a whole (Figure 5.2b).

Although sensory adaptation reduces our sensitivity, it offers an important benefit: It enables us to focus on *informative* changes in our environment without being distracted by the uninformative constant stimulation of garments, odors, and street noise. Our sensory receptors are alert to novelty; bore them with repetition and they free our attention for more important things. *This reinforces a fundamental lesson:* We perceive the world not exactly as it is, but as it is useful for us to perceive it.

Our sensitivity to changing stimulation helps explain television's attention-getting power. Cuts, edits, zooms, pans, and sudden noises demand attention. Television researchers marvel at TV's hold on themselves. Even during interesting conversations, notes media researcher Percy Tannenbaum (2002), "I cannot for the life of me stop from periodically glancing over to the screen."

Sensory thresholds and adaptation are not the only commonalities among the senses. All the senses receive sensory stimulation, transform it into neural information, and deliver that information to the brain. How do the senses work? How do we see? Hear? Smell? Taste? Feel pain? Let's start with vision, the sense people prize the most.

"We need above all to know about changes; no one wants or needs to be reminded 16 hours a day that his shoes are on."

Neuroscientist David Hubel (1979)

For 9 in 10 people—but, curiously, for only 1 in 3 of those with schizophrenia—this eye flutter turns off when the eye is following a moving target (Holzman & Matthysse, 1990).

"My suspicion is that the universe is not only queerer than we suppose, but queerer than we can suppose."

J. B. S. Haldane, Possible Worlds, 1927

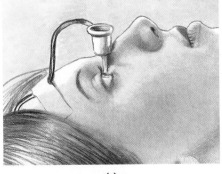

(a)

BEER   PEER   PEEP   BEE   BE

(b)

figure 5.2

Now you see it, now you don't!
(a) A projector mounted on a contact lens makes the projected image move with the eye. (b) Initially the person sees the stabilized image, but soon she sees fragments fading and reappearing. (From "Stabilized images on the retina" by R. M. Pritchard. Copyright © 1961 Scientific American, Inc. All Rights Reserved.)

rehearse it!

1. To construct meaning out of our external environment, we select, organize, and interpret sensory information. This is the process of
   a. sensation.
   b. sensory adaptation.
   c. encoding.
   d. perception.

2. Sensation is to _____ as perception is to _____.
   a. absolute threshold; difference threshold
   b. bottom-up processing; top-down processing
   c. interpretation; detection
   d. conscious awareness; persuasion

3. The absolute threshold is the minimum stimulation a person can detect 50 percent of the time. Knowing your absolute threshold for sound tells you

   a. the smallest difference you can detect between two sounds.
   b. how likely you are to hear a particular faint sound.
   c. why you become used to background noise.
   d. whether you are being affected by subliminal stimulation.

4. People wonder whether subliminal stimuli, such as undetectably faint sights or sounds, influence us. Subliminal stimuli are
   a. too weak to be processed by the brain in any way.
   b. consciously perceived more than 50 percent of the time.
   c. strong enough to affect our behavior.
   d. below the absolute threshold for conscious awareness.

5. To be perceived as different, two lights must differ in intensity by at least 8 percent. This illustrates a general principle called Weber's law, which states that for a difference to be perceived, two stimuli must differ by
   a. a fixed or constant amount.
   b. a constant minimum percentage.
   c. a constantly changing amount.
   d. more than 7 percent.

6. Sensory adaptation reduces our sensitivity to some stimuli in the environment, such as unpleasant smells. Sensory adaptation also has survival benefits. It helps us focus on
   a. the world as it really is.
   b. underlying phenomena and stimuli.
   c. constant features of the environment.
   d. important changes in the environment.

Answers can be found in Appendix C.

▶ **wavelength** the distance from the peak of one light or sound wave to the peak of the next. Electromagnetic wavelengths vary from the short blips of cosmic rays to the long pulses of radio transmission.

▶ **hue** the dimension of color that is determined by the wavelength of light; what we know as the color names *blue, green,* and so forth.

▶ **intensity** the amount of energy in a light or sound wave, which we perceive as brightness or loudness, as determined by the wave's amplitude.

VISION

Part of our genius is our body's ability to convert one sort of energy to another. Our sensory systems convert stimulus energy into neural messages. Your eyes, for example, receive light energy and manage an amazing feat: They *transduce* (transform) the energy into neural messages that the brain then processes into what you consciously see. How does such a remarkable thing happen?

The Stimulus Input: Light Energy

4. What are the characteristics of the wavelengths we see as visible light?

Scientifically speaking, what strikes our eyes is not color but pulses of electromagnetic energy that our visual system experiences as color. What we see as visible light is but a thin slice of the whole spectrum of electromagnetic radiation. As **FIGURE 5.3** illustrates, this *electromagnetic spectrum* ranges from imperceptibly short waves of gamma rays, to the narrow band that we see as visible light, to the long waves of radio transmission.

Two physical characteristics of light and sound help determine our sensory experience of them. Light's **wavelength**—the distance from one wave peak to the next (**FIGURE 5.4a**)—determines its **hue** (the color we experience, such as blue or green).

Differing eyes
When it comes to vision, humans and bees are on different wavelengths. Compare the way a human eye and a bee's eye register a flower. The bee detects reflected ultraviolet wavelengths, enabling it to see the pollen where it will find nutrients. The differing ecological niches occupied by different species demand sensitivity to different stimuli.

Human eye

Bee's eye

Both photos: Thomas Eisner

figure 5.3
The spectrum of electromagnetic energy This spectrum ranges from gamma rays as short as the diameter of an atom to radio waves over a mile long. The narrow band of wavelengths visible to the human eye (shown enlarged) extends from the shorter waves of blue-violet light to the longer waves of red light. Other organisms are sensitive to differing portions of the spectrum. For instance, bees cannot see red but can see ultraviolet light (see photos on page 146).

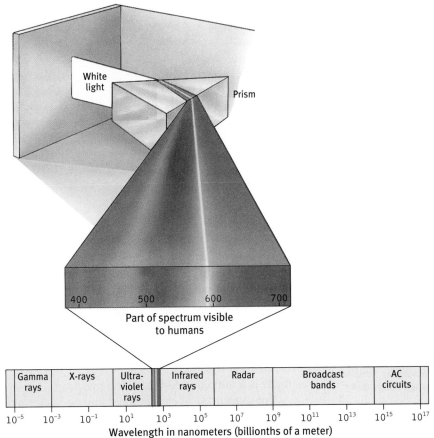

Intensity, the amount of energy in light waves (determined by a wave's *amplitude*, or height), influences brightness (Figure 5.4b). To understand *how* we transform physical energy into a sensation of color, we first need to understand our mind's window, the eye.

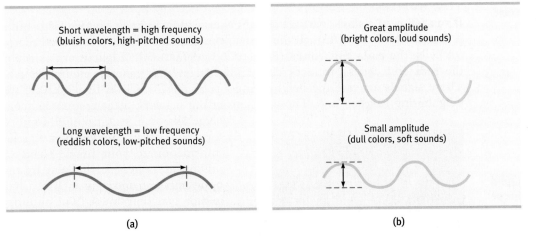

(a)   (b)

figure 5.4
The physical properties of waves (a) Waves vary in wavelength, the distance between successive peaks. Frequency, the number of complete wavelengths that can pass a point in a given time, depends on the wavelength. The shorter the wavelength, the higher the frequency. (b) Waves also vary in amplitude, the height from peak to trough. Wave amplitude determines the intensity of colors and sounds.

The Eye

5. How does the eye transform light energy into neural messages?

Light enters the eye through the *cornea*, which protects the eye and bends light to provide focus. The light then passes through the *pupil*, a small adjustable opening (**FIGURE 5.5**, page 148). The pupil's size, and therefore the amount of light entering

figure 5.5

The eye Light rays reflected from the candle pass through the cornea, pupil, and lens. The curvature and thickness of the lens change to bring either nearby or distant objects into focus on the retina. Light rays travel in straight lines. So rays from the top of the candle strike the bottom of the retina and those from the left side of the candle strike the right side of the retina. The candle's retinal image is thus upside-down and reversed.

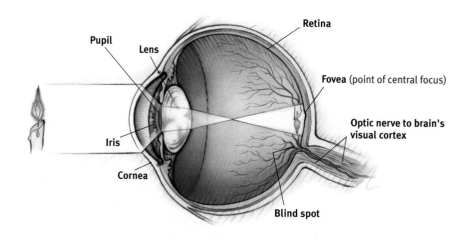

▶ **accommodation** the process by which the eye's lens changes shape to focus near or far objects on the retina.

▶ **retina** the light-sensitive inner surface of the eye, containing the receptor rods and cones plus layers of neurons that begin the processing of visual information.

▶ **rods** retinal receptors that detect black, white, and gray; necessary for peripheral and twilight vision, when cones don't respond.

▶ **cones** receptor cells that are concentrated near the center of the retina and that function in daylight or in well-lit conditions. The cones detect fine detail and give rise to color sensations.

▶ **optic nerve** the nerve that carries neural impulses from the eye to the brain.

▶ **blind spot** the point at which the optic nerve leaves the eye, creating a "blind" spot because no receptor cells are located there.

the eye, is regulated by the *iris*, a colored muscle surrounding the pupil. The iris adjusts light intake by dilating and constricting in response to light intensity and even to inner emotions. (When we're feeling amorous, our telltale dilated pupils subtly signal our interest.) The uniqueness of each iris enables iris-scanning machines to confirm someone's identity.

Behind the pupil is a *lens* that focuses the incoming rays into an image on the eye's light-sensitive back surface. It does so by changing its curvature in a process called **accommodation**. The eyeball's light-sensitive surface on which the rays focus is a multilayered tissue, the **retina**.

For centuries, scientists have known that when the image of a candle passes through a small opening, its mirror image appears inverted on a dark wall behind (as in Figure 5.5). This was baffling. If the retina receives an upside-down image, how can we see the world right side up?

Eventually, scientists discovered that the retina doesn't read the image as a whole. Rather, its millions of receptor cells convert light energy into neural impulses. These impulses are sent to the brain and constructed *there* into a perceived, upright-seeming image.

The Retina

If you followed a single particle of light energy into your eye, you would see that it first makes its way through the retina's outer layer of cells to its buried receptor cells, the **rods** and **cones** (**FIGURE 5.6** and **TABLE 5.1**). Light energy striking the rods and cones produces chemical changes that generate neural signals. These signals activate the neighboring *bipolar cells*, which in turn activate the neighboring *ganglion cells*. The axons from the network of ganglion cells converge like the strands of a rope to form an **optic nerve** that carries information to your brain. Nearly a million messages can be sent by the optic nerve at once, through nearly a million ganglion fibers. (The auditory nerve, which enables hearing, carries much less information through its mere 30,000 fibers.) Where the optic nerve leaves the eye there are no receptor cells—creating a **blind spot** (Figures 5.6 and **5.7**).

Rods enable black-and-white vision; cones enable you to see color. If illumi-

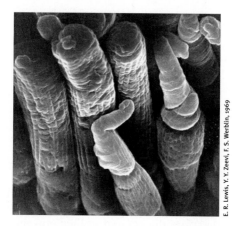

Rod-shaped rods and cone-shaped cones As the scanning electron microscope shows, rods and cones are well named. The rods are more sensitive to light than are the color-sensitive cones, which is why the world looks colorless at night. Some nocturnal animals, such as toads, mice, rats, and bats, have retinas made up almost entirely of rods, allowing them to function well in dim light. These creatures probably have very poor color vision.

E. R. Lewis, Y. Y. Zeevi, F. S. Werblin, 1969

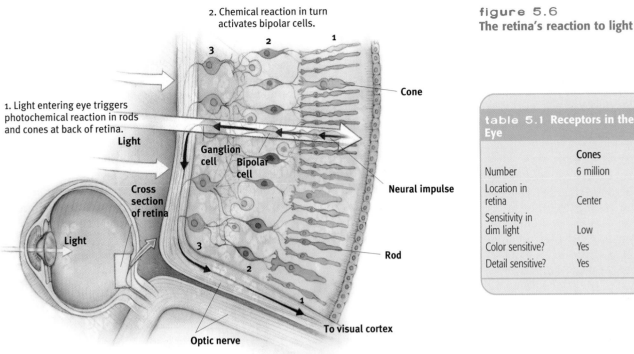

2. Chemical reaction in turn activates bipolar cells.

1. Light entering eye triggers photochemical reaction in rods and cones at back of retina.

Light

Ganglion cell

Bipolar cell

Cross section of retina

Light

Cone

Neural impulse

Rod

To visual cortex

Optic nerve

3. Bipolar cells then activate the ganglion cells, the axons of which converge to form the optic nerve. This nerve transmits information to the visual cortex in the brain's occipital lobe.

figure 5.6
The retina's reaction to light

table 5.1 Receptors in the Human Eye		
	Cones	Rods
Number	6 million	120 million
Location in retina	Center	Periphery
Sensitivity in dim light	Low	High
Color sensitive?	Yes	No
Detail sensitive?	Yes	No

nation diminishes, the cones become ineffectual, which is why you do not see colors in dim light. The rods, however, remain sensitive in dim light, and several rods will funnel their faint energy output onto a single bipolar cell. Thus, cones and rods each provide a special sensitivity—cones to detail and rods to faint light.

When you enter a darkened theater or turn off the light at night, your pupils dilate to allow more light to reach the rods in the retina's periphery. It typically takes 20 minutes or more before your eyes fully adapt. You can demonstrate dark adaptation by closing or covering one eye for up to 20 minutes. Then make the light in the room not quite bright enough to read this book with your open eye. Now open the dark-adapted eye and read (easily). This period of dark adaptation is yet another instance of the remarkable adaptiveness of our sensory systems, for it parallels the average natural twilight transition between the sun's setting and darkness.

Knowing just this much about the eye, can you imagine why a cat sees so much better at night than you do? (See page 152 for answer.)

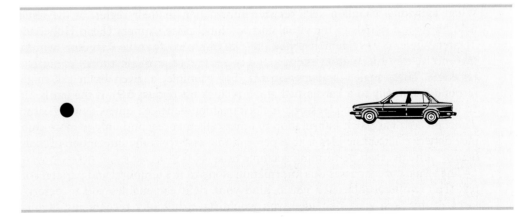

figure 5.7
The blind spot Where the optic nerve leaves the eye (Figure 5.6), there are no receptor cells. This creates a blind spot in our vision. To demonstrate, close your left eye, look at the spot, and move the page to a distance from your face (about a foot) at which the car disappears. In everyday vision, the blind spot doesn't impair your vision because your eyes are moving and because one eye catches what the other misses.

Visual Information Processing

6. How is visual information processed in the brain?

Turn your eyes to the left, close them, and then gently rub the right side of your right eyelid with your fingertip. Note the patch of light to the left, moving as your finger moves. Why do you see light? Why at the left? (See page 152 for answer.)

Visual information percolates through progressively more abstract levels. At the entry level, the retina—which is actually a piece of the brain that migrates to the eye during early fetal development—processes information before routing it to the brain's cortex. The retina's neural layers are not just passing along electrical impulses; they also help to encode and analyze the sensory information. The third neural layer in a frog's eye, for example, contains the "bug detector" cells that fire only in response to moving flylike stimuli. The information from the retina's nearly 130 million receptor rods and cones is received and transmitted by the million or so ganglion cells, whose fibers make up the optic nerve. But most information processing occurs in the brain. Any given area of the retina relays its information to a corresponding location in the visual cortex at the back of the brain (**FIGURE 5.8**).

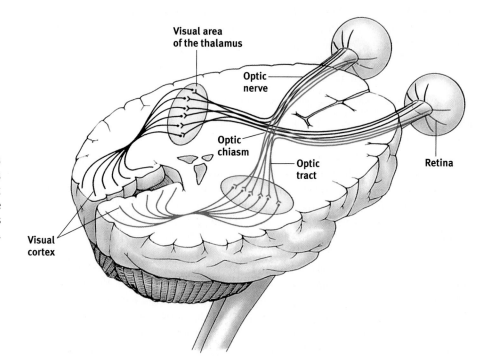

figure 5.8
Pathway from the eyes to the visual cortex
Neurons in the optic nerves run to the thalamus, where they synapse with neurons that run to the visual cortex.

Feature Detection

When individual ganglion cells register information in their region of the visual field, they send signals to the visual cortex. Nobel prize winners David Hubel and Torsten Wiesel (1979) demonstrated that the brain has **feature detector** neurons that receive this information and respond to a scene's specific features—to particular edges, lines, angles, and movements. For example, a given brain cell might respond maximally to a bar flashed at a 2 o'clock tilt (**FIGURE 5.9**). If the bar is tilted further—say, to a 3 o'clock or 1 o'clock position—the cell quiets down. Feature detection cells pass such information to other cells that respond only to more complex patterns. The basic idea is that perceptions arise from the interaction of many neuron systems, each performing a simple task.

The visual cortex passes this information along to the temporal and parietal cortex. One temporal lobe area just behind your right ear enables you to perceive faces. If this area were damaged, you would have difficulty recognizing familiar

▶ **feature detectors** nerve cells in the brain that respond to specific features of the stimulus, such as shape, angle, or movement.

▶ **parallel processing** the processing of several aspects of a problem simultaneously; the brain's natural mode of information processing for many functions, including vision. Contrasts with the step-by-step (serial) processing of most computers and of conscious problem solving.

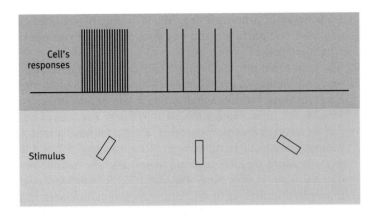

figure 5.9
Electrodes record how individual cells in this monkey's visual cortex respond to different visual stimuli Hubel and Wiesel won a Nobel prize for their discovery that most cells in the visual cortex respond only to particular features—for example, to the edge of a surface or to a bar at a 30-degree angle in the upper right part of the field of vision. Other cells integrate information from these simpler ones.

faces but could recognize other objects. Other brain areas light up fMRI scans when a person views images of the human body or of inanimate objects (Downing & others, 2001). Damage in these areas blocks other perceptions while sparing face recognition. Some researchers believe that amazingly specific combinations of temporal lobe activity occur as people look at faces, shoes, cats, houses, and other object categories (**FIGURE 5.10**).

"We can tell if a person is looking at a shoe, a chair, or a face, based on the pattern of their brain activity," notes researcher James Haxby (2001).

Other high-level brain cells respond to specific visual scenes, such as a face or an arm movement in a particular direction. Psychologist David Perrett and his colleagues (1988, 1992, 1994)

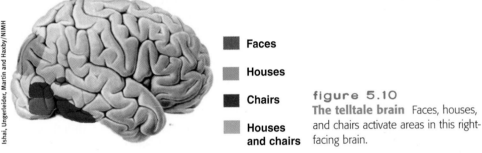

Faces

Houses

Chairs

Houses and chairs

figure 5.10
The telltale brain Faces, houses, and chairs activate areas in this right-facing brain.

report that for biologically important objects and events, monkey brains (and surely ours as well) have a "vast visual encyclopedia" distributed as cells that respond to one stimulus but not to others. Perrett identified nerve cells that specialize in responding to a specific gaze, head angle, posture, or body movement. Other supercell clusters integrate this information and fire only when the cues collectively indicate the direction of someone's attention and approach. This instant analysis, which aided our ancestors' survival, also helps a soccer goalie anticipate the direction of an impending kick and helps a pedestrian anticipate another pedestrian's next movement.

Well-developed supercells Brazil's Ronaldo instantly processed visual information about the positions and movements of the German defenders and goalie and somehow managed to get the ball around them all to put Brazil ahead 2–0 in this World Cup 2002 final game.

Parallel Processing

Unlike most computers, which do step-by-step serial processing, our brains engage in **parallel processing**. That means we can do several things at once. We construct our perceptions by integrating the work of different visual teams, working in parallel. Destroy or disable the neural workstation for a visual subtask and something peculiar results, as happened in these actual cases of visual disabilities produced by brain damage (from Hoffman, 1998):

Answer to question on page 149: Cats can see better than you can at night for at least two reasons: A cat's pupils can open much wider than yours, letting in more light; and a cat has a higher proportion of light-sensitive rods (Moser, 1987). But there is a trade-off: With fewer cones, a cat sees neither details nor color as well as you do.

Answer to question on page 150: You have this sensation because your retinal cells are so responsive that even pressure triggers them. But your brain interprets their firing as light. Moreover, it interprets the light as coming from the left—the direction light normally comes from when it activates the right side of the retina.

"I am fearfully and wonderfully made."

King David, Psalms 139:14

- Looking at an American flag, Ms. W is able to see lines and stars. But "it's like you have one part here and one part there, and you put them together to see what they make."
- Mr. I, an artist until suffering a concussion at age 65, no longer perceives colors, only shades of gray. Tomatoes look black, flowers an assortment of grays. Even his once vivid imagination of colors is now gone.
- Ms. M, having suffered stroke damage near the rear of both sides of her brain, can no longer perceive movement. People moving about a room seem "suddenly here or there but I have not seen them moving." It's a challenge to pour tea into a cup because the fluid appears frozen and she cannot perceive the rising in the cup. (You could experience this same loss of motion detection if given disruptive magnetic stimulation to the corresponding neural area in your brain.)

These and other cases suggest that the brain divides a visual scene into subdimensions such as color, depth, movement, and form and works on each aspect simultaneously (Livingstone & Hubel, 1988). The distribution of visual tasks to different neural work teams explains the peculiar cases of visual disability. Having lost a portion of their brain's visual cortex to surgery or stroke, people may experience blindness in part of their field of vision, a phenomenon called *blindsight*. Shown a series of sticks in the blind field, they report seeing nothing. Yet when asked to guess whether the sticks are vertical or horizontal, they unerringly offer the correct response. When told, "You got them all right," they are astounded. There are, it seems, little minds—"parallel processing" systems—operating unseen.

Indeed, "sight unseen" is how University of Durham psychologist David Milner (2003) describes the brain's two visual systems—"one that gives us our conscious perceptions, and one that guides our actions." The second he calls "the zombie within." Milner describes a woman with brain damage who can see fine details—the hairs on the back of a hand—without being able to recognize the hand. Asked to use her thumb and forefinger to estimate an object's size, she can't do it. Yet when reaching for the object, her thumb and forefinger are appropriately placed. She knows more than she is aware of.

Other senses process information with similar speed and intricacy. Opening the back door, you recognize the aroma wafting from the kitchen even before you step inside. Answering the phone, you recognize the friend calling from the moment she says "Hi." A fraction of a second after such events stimulate the senses, millions of neurons have simultaneously coordinated in extracting the essential features, comparing them with past experience, and identifying the stimulus (Freeman, 1991).

This scientific understanding of sensory information processing is illustrated by neuropsychologist Roger Sperry's (1985) reflection: The "insights of science give added, not lessened, reasons for awe, respect, and reverence." Think about it: As you look at someone, the visual information is sent to your brain as millions of neural impulses, then constructed into its component features, and finally, in some as yet mysterious way, composed into a meaningful perceived image, which is then compared with previously stored images and recognized as, for example, your grandmother. The whole process (**FIGURE 5.11**) is more complex than taking a car apart, piece by piece, transporting it to a different location, then having specialized workers reconstruct it. That all of this happens instantly, effortlessly, and continuously is indeed awesome.

Parallel processing Studies of brain-damaged patients suggest that the brain delegates the work of processing color, motion, form, and depth to different areas. After taking a scene apart, how does the brain integrate these subdimensions into the perceived image? The answer to this question is the Holy Grail of vision research.

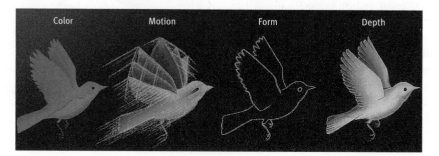

Tim Bieber/The Image Bank

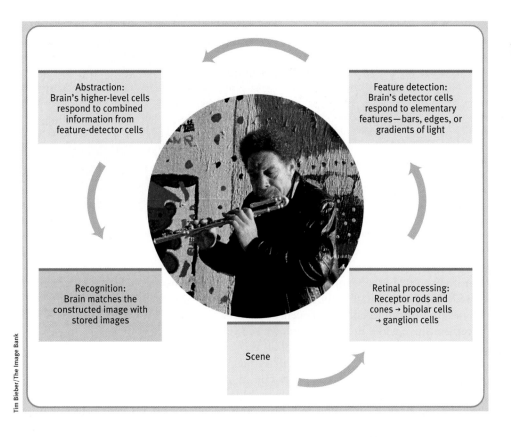

figure 5.11
A simplified summary of visual information processing

Abstraction:
Brain's higher-level cells respond to combined information from feature-detector cells

Feature detection:
Brain's detector cells respond to elementary features—bars, edges, or gradients of light

Recognition:
Brain matches the constructed image with stored images

Retinal processing:
Receptor rods and cones → bipolar cells → ganglion cells

Scene

Color Vision

7. What theories contribute to our understanding of color vision, and how does color constancy affect our perception of color?

We talk as though objects possess color. We say, "A tomato is red." Perhaps you have pondered the old question, "If a tree falls in the forest and no one hears it, does it make a sound?" We can ask the same of color: If no one sees the tomato, is it red?

The answer is no. First, the tomato is everything *but* red, because it *rejects* (reflects) the long wavelengths of red. Second, the tomato's color is our mental construction. As Isaac Newton (1704) noted, "The [light] rays are not coloured." Color, like all aspects of vision, resides not in the object but in the theater of our brains. Even while dreaming, we may perceive things in color.

In the study of vision, one of the most basic and intriguing mysteries is how we see the world in color. How, from the light energy striking the retina, does the brain manufacture our experience of color—and of such a multitude of colors? Our difference threshold for colors is so low that we can discriminate some 7 million different color variations (Geldard, 1972).

At least most of us can. For about 1 person in 50, vision is color-deficient—and that person is usually male, because the defect is genetically sex-linked. To understand why some people's vision is color-deficient, it will help to first understand how normal color vision works.

Modern detective work on the mystery of color vision began in the nineteenth century when Hermann von Helmholtz built on the insights of an English physicist, Thomas Young. Young and von Helmholtz knew that any color can be created by combining the light waves of three primary colors—red, green, and blue. So they inferred that the eye must have three types of receptors, one for each primary color of light.

Years later, researchers measured the response of various cones to different color stimuli and confirmed the **Young-Helmholtz trichromatic (three-color) theory**, which simply states that the retina has three types of color receptors, each especially

"Only mind has sight and hearing; all things else are deaf and blind."

Epicharmus, Fragments, 550 B.C.

▶ **Young-Helmholtz trichromatic (three-color) theory** the theory that the retina contains three different color receptors— one most sensitive to red, one to green, one to blue—which when stimulated in combination can produce the perception of any color.

Fritz Goro, *LIFE* Magazine, © 1971 Time Warner, Inc.

figure 5.12
Subtractive and additive color mixing
Mixing paint colors subtracts wavelengths. Mixing all three primary colors leaves you with black. Mixing lights is additive, because wavelengths from each light in the mix reach the eye, and mixing all three primary light colors creates white.

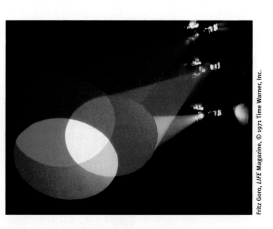

Subtractive color mixing   Additive color mixing

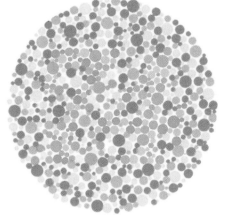

figure 5.13
Color-deficient vision People who suffer red-green deficiency have trouble perceiving the number within the design.

sensitive to one of three colors. And surprise! Those colors are, indeed, red, green, or blue. When we stimulate combinations of these cones, we see other colors. For example, there are no receptors especially sensitive to yellow. Yet when both red- and green-sensitive cones are stimulated, we see yellow.

If you are trying to make sense of all this by thinking back to mixing paints, you had better think again. Mixing paints is *subtractive color mixing* because it *subtracts* wavelengths from the reflected light. The more colors you mix in, the fewer wavelengths can be reflected back. So, mixing blue and yellow paint leaves only green to be reflected back. Combining red, blue, and yellow means no light waves will be reflected and you will see brown or black. But mixing *lights*, as Young and von Helmholtz did, is *additive color mixing*, because the process adds wavelengths and thus *increases* light—combining red, blue, and green lights makes white light (**Figure 5.12**).

Most color-deficient people are not actually "colorblind." They simply lack functioning red- or green-sensitive cones. Their vision is dichromatic (two-color) instead of trichromatic, making it difficult to distinguish red and green, as in **Figure 5.13** (Boynton, 1979). Dogs, too, lack receptors for the wavelengths of red, giving them only limited, dichromatic color vision (Neitz & others, 1989).

Soon after Young and von Helmholtz proposed the trichromatic theory, physiologist Ewald Hering pointed out that other parts of the color vision mystery remained unsolved. For example, we see yellow when mixing red and green light. But how is it that those blind to red and green can often still see yellow? And why does yellow appear to be a pure color and not a mixture of red and green, the way purple is of red and blue?

Hering found a clue in the well-known occurrence of *afterimages*. When you stare at a green square for a while and then look at a white sheet of paper, you see red, green's *opponent color*. Stare at a yellow square and you will later see its opponent color, blue, on the white paper (as in the flag demonstration in **Figure 5.14**). Hering surmised that there were two additional color processes, one responsible for red-versus-green perception, and one for blue-versus-yellow.

figure 5.14
Afterimage effect Stare at the center of the flag for a minute and then shift your eyes to the dot in the white space beside it. What do you see? (After tiring your neural response to black, green, and yellow, you should see their opponent colors.) Stare at a white wall and note how the size of the flag grows with the projection distance!

A century later, researchers confirmed Hering's **opponent-process theory**. *After* leaving the receptor cells, visual information is analyzed in terms of the opponent colors red and green, blue and yellow, and also black and white. In the retina and in the thalamus (where impulses from the retina are relayed en route to the visual cortex), some neurons are turned "on" by red but turned "off" by green. Others are turned on by green but off by red (DeValois & DeValois, 1975). Opponent processes explain afterimages, such as in the flag demonstration, in which we tire our green response by staring at green. When we then stare at white (which contains all colors, including red), only the red part of the green/red pairing will fire normally.

The present solution to the mystery of color vision is therefore roughly this: Color processing occurs in two stages. The retina's red, green, and blue cones respond in varying degrees to different color stimuli, as the Young-Helmholtz trichromatic theory suggested. Their signals are then processed by the nervous system's opponent-process cells, en route to the visual cortex.

Color Constancy

Our experience of color depends on something more than the wavelength information received by our trichromatic cones and transmitted through the opponent-process cells.

That something more is the surrounding *context*. If you view only part of a tomato, its color will seem to change as the light changes. But if you see the whole tomato as one item in a bowl of fresh vegetables, its color will remain roughly constant as the lighting and wavelengths shift—a phenomenon known as **color constancy**. Dorothea Jameson (1985) notes that a chip colored blue under indoor lighting matches the wavelengths reflected by a gold chip in the sunlight. Yet bring a bluebird indoors and it won't look like a goldfinch. Likewise, a green leaf hanging from a brown branch may, when the illumination changes, reflect the same light energy that formerly came from the brown branch. Yet to us the leaf stays greenish and the branch stays brownish. Put on yellow-tinted ski goggles and the snow, after a second, looks as white as before.

Though we take this color constancy for granted, the phenomenon is truly remarkable. It demonstrates that our experience of color comes not just from the object—the color is not in the isolated leaf—but from everything around it as well. You and I see color thanks to our brains' computations of the light reflected by any object *relative to its surrounding objects*.

In a context that does not vary, we maintain color constancy. But what if we change the context? Because the brain computes the color of an object relative to its context, the perceived color changes (as is dramatically apparent in **Figure 5.15**). This principle—that we perceive objects not in isolation but in their environmental context—is especially significant for artists, interior decorators, and clothing designers. Our perception of the color of a wall or of a swatch of paint on a canvas is determined not just by the paint in the can but by the surrounding colors. The take-home lesson: Comparisons govern our perceptions.

▶ **opponent-process theory** the theory that opposing retinal processes (red-green, yellow-blue, white-black) enable color vision. For example, some cells are stimulated by green and inhibited by red; others are stimulated by red and inhibited by green.

▶ **color constancy** perceiving familiar objects as having consistent color, even if changing illumination alters the wavelengths reflected by the object.

R. Beau Lotto at University College, London

figure 5.15
Color depends on context
Believe it or not, these three blue disks are identical in color.

7. Two physical characteristics of light help determine our sensory experience of it. The characteristic that determines the color we experience, such as blue, or green, is
a. intensity.
b. wavelength.
c. amplitude.
d. hue.

8. The blind spot is located in the area of the retina in which
a. there are rods but no cones.
b. there are cones but no rods.
c. the optic nerve leaves the eye.
d. the bipolar cells meet the ganglion cells.

9. Rods and cones are the eye's receptor cells. Cones are especially sensitive to _____ light and are responsible for our _____ vision.
a. bright; black-and-white
b. dim; color

c. bright; color
d. dim; black-and-white

10. According to Hubel and Wiesel, the brain includes cells that respond maximally to certain bars, edges, and angles. These cells are called
a. rods and cones.
b. feature detector cells.
c. bug detectors.
d. ganglion cells.

11. Unlike most computers, the brain is capable of simultaneously processing separate aspects of an object or problem. We call this ability
a. parallel processing.
b. feature detection.
c. recognition.
d. accommodation.

12. Researchers today believe that the Young-Helmholtz and Hering theories together account for color vision. The

Young-Helmholtz theory shows that the eye contains _____ and the Hering theory accounts for the nervous system's having _____.
a. opposing retinal processes; three pairs of color receptors
b. opponent-process cells; three types of color receptors
c. three pairs of color receptors; opposing retinal processes
d. three types of color receptors; opponent-process cells

13. We perceive tomatoes and stringbeans as consistently red and green, respectively, even though shifting illumination may alter their reflective wavelengths. This demonstrates the phenomenon of
a. afterimages.
b. color constancy.
c. trichromatic vision.
d. color processing.

Answers can be found in Appendix C.

▶ **visual capture** the tendency for vision to dominate the other senses, as when we perceive voices in films as coming from the screen we see rather than from the projector behind us.

▶ **audition** the sense of hearing.

▶ **frequency** the number of complete wavelengths that pass a point in a given time (for example, per second).

▶ **pitch** a tone's highness or lowness; depends on frequency.

THE OTHER SENSES

For humans, vision is the major sense. More of our brain cortex is devoted to vision than to any other sense. Moreover, when there is a conflict between visual and other sensory information, vision tends to dominate or "capture" the other senses. This phenomenon of **visual capture** is an everyday experience. When viewing a movie for which the projector provides the sound, we nevertheless perceive the sound as coming from the screen, where we *see* the actors talking. While viewing a roller coaster ride on a giant wraparound movie screen, we may brace ourselves, even though our other senses tell us we're not moving. In both cases, vision has captured the other senses.

Yet without our senses of hearing, touch, taste, smell, and body motion and position, our capacities for experiencing the world would be vastly diminished.

Hearing

Like our other senses, our hearing, or **audition**, is highly adaptive. We hear a wide range of sounds, but we hear best those sounds with frequencies in a range corresponding to that of the human voice. We also are remarkably sensitive to faint sounds, an obvious boon to our ancestors' survival when hunting or being hunted or to our need to detect a child's whimper. (If our ears were much more sensitive, we would hear a constant hiss from the movement of air molecules.) We are also acutely sensitive to differences in sounds. We easily detect differences among thousands of human voices, helping us to recognize immediately the voice of almost anyone we know.

For hearing as for seeing, one fundamental question remains—How do we do it? How do we translate sound energy into neural messages that the brain interprets as a particular sound coming from a particular place?

The Stimulus Input: Sound Waves

8. What are the characteristics of the air pressure waves that we hear as meaningful sounds?

Hit a piano key and the resulting stimulus energy is sound waves—jostling molecules of air, each bumping into the next. The resulting waves of compressed and expanded air are like the ripples on a pond circling out from where a stone has been tossed. As

The sounds of music A violin's short, fast waves create a high pitch, an accordion's longer, slower waves a low pitch. Differences in the waves' height, or amplitude, also create differing degrees of loudness.

McCarthy/Peter Arnold

we swim in our ocean of moving air molecules, our ears detect these brief air pressure changes. The ears then transform them into nerve impulses, which our brain decodes as sounds. The strength, or amplitude, of sound waves determines their *loudness*. Waves also vary in length, and therefore in **frequency** (recall Figure 5.4, page 147). Their frequency determines their **pitch**: Long waves have low frequency—and low pitch. Short waves have high frequency—and high pitch. A piccolo produces much shorter, faster sound waves than does a tuba.

Decibels are the measuring unit for sound energy. The absolute threshold for hearing is arbitrarily defined as zero decibels. Every 10 decibels correspond to a tenfold increase in sound. Thus, normal conversation (60 decibels) is 10,000 times louder than a 20-decibel whisper. And a tolerable 100-decibel passing subway train is 10 billion times louder than the faintest detectable sound. When prolonged, however, exposure to sounds above 85 decibels can produce hearing loss (**FIGURE 5.16**).

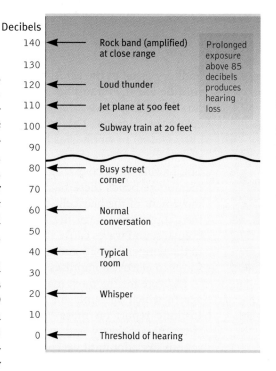

Decibels
140	Rock band (amplified) at close range
130	
120	Loud thunder
110	Jet plane at 500 feet
100	Subway train at 20 feet
90	
80	Busy street corner
70	
60	Normal conversation
50	
40	Typical room
30	
20	Whisper
10	
0	Threshold of hearing

Prolonged exposure above 85 decibels produces hearing loss

figure 5.16
The intensity of some common sounds At close range, the thunder that follows lightning has 120-decibel intensity.

The Ear

9. How does the ear transform sound energy into neural messages?

To hear, we must somehow convert sound waves into neural activity. But how? The human ear accomplishes this feat through an intricate mechanical chain reaction (**FIGURE 5.17**). First, the visible outer ear channels the sound waves through the

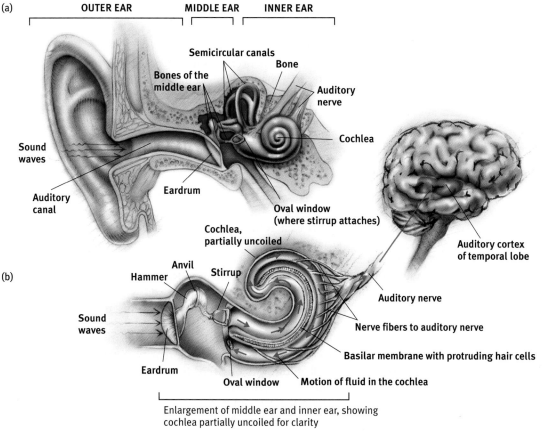

figure 5.17
How we transform sound waves into nerve impulses that our brain interprets
(a) The outer ear funnels sound waves to the eardrum. The bones of the middle ear amplify and relay the eardrum's vibrations through the oval window into the fluid-filled cochlea. (b) As shown in this detail of the middle and inner ear, the resulting pressure changes in the cochlear fluid cause the basilar membrane to ripple, bending the hair cells on the surface. Hair cell movements trigger impulses at the bases of the nerve cells, whose fibers converge to form the auditory nerve.

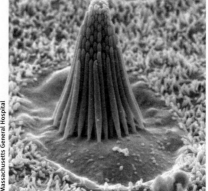

Be kind to your inner ear's hair cells
When vibrating in response to sound, the 50 to 60 cilia shown here atop a hair cell produce an electrical signal.

Ironically, even health clubs and fitness spas—which commonly blast 100+ decibel music—may be damaging their patrons' hearing health. They might take a cue from Pete Townshend of the Who, who sent Hearing Education and Awareness for Rockers a check for $10,000, acknowledging his own hearing loss.

figure 5.18
How we locate sounds Sound waves strike one ear sooner and more intensely than the other. From this information, our nimble brains compute the sound's location. As you might therefore expect, people who lose all hearing in one ear often have difficulty locating sounds.

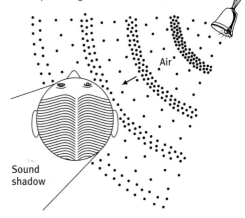

Air

Sound
shadow

auditory canal to the *eardrum*, a tight membrane that vibrates with the waves. The **middle ear** then transmits the eardrum's vibrations through a piston made of three tiny bones (the *hammer, anvil,* and *stirrup*) to a snail-shaped tube in the **inner ear** called the **cochlea**. The incoming vibrations cause the cochlea's membrane (the *oval window*) to vibrate, jostling the fluid that fills the tube. This motion causes ripples in the *basilar membrane*, which is lined with *hair cells*, so named because of their tiny hairlike projections. At the end of this sequence, the rippling of the basilar membrane bends these hair cells, not unlike the wind bending a wheat field. The movement of the hair cells triggers impulses in the adjacent nerve fibers, which in turn converge to form the auditory nerve. By means of this mechanical chain of events, sound waves cause the hair cells of the inner ear to send neural messages up to the temporal lobe's auditory cortex. From vibrating air to moving piston to fluid waves to electrical impulses to the brain: Voilà! We hear.

My vote for the most magical part of the hearing process is the hair cells, damage to which accounts for most hearing loss. A 1997 Howard Hughes Medical Institute report on these "quivering bundles that let us hear" marvels at their "extreme sensitivity and extreme speed." A cochlea has 16,000 of them, which sounds like a lot until we compare that with an eye's 120 million or so photoreceptors. But consider their responsiveness. Deflect the tiny bundles of cilia on the tip of a hair cell by the width of an atom—the equivalent of displacing the top of the Eiffel Tower by half an inch—and the alert hair cell triggers a neural response. Moreover, at the highest perceived frequency they can turn neural current on and off a thousand times per second!

As you might expect of something so sensitive, they are, however, delicate and fragile. Blast them with incessant jackhammer or headset sounds and the hair cells' cilia will begin to wither or fuse. Hair cells have been likened to shag carpet fibers. Walk around on them and they will spring back with a quick vacuuming. But leave a heavy piece of furniture on them for a long time and they may never rebound. Small wonder that with industrialization, power tools, and loud recreations, the proportion of 45- to 64-year-old Americans who "cannot hear and understand normal speech" shot up 87 percent in the two decades following 1971 (National Health Interview Survey, 1994). Although rock and roll may be here to stay, the sad truth for some rock musicians is that their hearing may not be.

As a general rule, if you cannot talk over a noise, it is potentially harmful, especially if prolonged (Roesser, 1998). (People who spend their day behind a power mower or above a jackhammer should be wearing earplugs.) And if we experience ringing of the ears after exposure to loud machinery or music we have been bad to our unhappy hair cells. As pain alerts us to possible bodily harm, so ringing of the ears alerts us to possible hearing damage. It is hearing's equivalent of bleeding. "Condoms or, safer yet, abstinence," say sex educators. "Earplugs or walk away," say hearing educators.

How Do We Locate Sounds?

Why don't we have one big ear—perhaps above our one nose? The better to hear you, as the wolf said to Red Riding Hood. Just as the placement of our eyes allows us to sense visual depth (page 168), the placement of our two ears allows us to enjoy stereophonic ("three-dimensional") hearing. The slightly different messages sensed by the two microphones used in creating a stereophonic recording mimic the slightly different sound messages received by our two ears.

Two ears are better than one for at least two reasons: If a car to the right honks, your right ear receives a more *intense* sound, and it receives sound slightly *sooner* than your left ear (**FIGURE 5.18**). Because sound travels 750 miles per hour and our ears are but 6 inches apart, the intensity difference and the time lag are extremely small. However, our sensitive auditory system can actually detect such minute differences (Brown & Deffenbacher, 1979; Middlebrooks & Green, 1991). A just noticeable difference in the direction from which two sounds come corresponds to a time difference of just 0.000027 second!

So how well do you suppose we do at locating a sound that is equidistant from our two ears, such as those that come from directly ahead, behind, overhead, or beneath us? Not very well. Why? Because such sounds strike the two ears simultaneously. Sit with closed eyes while a friend snaps fingers around your head. You will easily point to the sound when it comes from either side, but you will likely make some mistakes when it comes from directly ahead, behind, above, or below. That is why, when trying to pinpoint a sound, you cock your head, so that your two ears will receive slightly different messages.

Touch

10. How do we sense touch and feel pain?

If you had to lose one sense, which would you prefer it to be? If you could have only one, which would you want?

Although not the first sense to come to mind, touch could be our priority sense. Right from the start, touch is essential to our development. Infant rats deprived of their mothers' grooming touch produce less growth hormone and have a lower metabolic rate—a good way to keep alive until the mother returns, but a reaction that stunts growth if she's delayed. Infant monkeys allowed to see, hear, and smell—but not touch—their mothers become desperately unhappy; those separated by a screen with holes that allow touching are much less miserable. As we noted in Chapter 3, premature babies gain weight faster and go home sooner if they are stimulated by hand massage. As lovers, we yearn to touch—to kiss, to stroke, to snuggle.

Humorist Dave Barry may be right to say that the skin "keeps people from seeing the inside of your body, which is repulsive, and it prevents your organs from falling onto the ground." But skin does much more. Our "sense of touch" is actually a mix of at least four distinct skin senses—pressure, warmth, cold, and pain. Within the skin are different types of specialized nerve endings. Touching various spots on the skin with a soft hair, a warm or cool wire, and the point of a pin reveals that some spots are especially sensitive to pressure, others to warmth, others to cold, still others to pain.

Surprisingly, there is no simple relationship between what we feel at a given spot and the type of specialized nerve ending found there. Only pressure has identifiable receptors. The relationship between warmth, cold, and pain and the receptors that respond to them remains a mystery. Other skin sensations are variations of the basic four (pressure, warmth, cold, and pain):

- Stroking adjacent pressure spots creates a tickle.
- Repeated gentle stroking of a pain spot creates an itching sensation.
- Touching adjacent cold and pressure spots triggers a sense of wetness, which you can experience by touching dry, cold metal.

Touch sensations involve more than tactile stimulation, however. A self-produced tickle produces less somatosensory cortex activation than the same tickle from something or someone else (Blakemore & others, 1998). The brain is wise enough to be most sensitive to unexpected stimulation.

Pain

Be thankful for occasional pain. Pain is your body's way of telling you something has gone wrong. Drawing your attention to a burn, a break, or a rupture, it tells you to change your behavior immediately. The rare people born without the ability to feel pain may experience severe injury without ever being alerted by pain's danger signals. Usually, they die by early adulthood. Without the discomfort that makes us occasionally shift position, their joints fail from excess strain, and without the warnings of pain, the effects of unchecked infections and injuries accumulate (Neese, 1991). More

▶ **middle ear** the chamber between the eardrum and cochlea containing three tiny bones (hammer, anvil, and stirrup) that concentrate the vibrations of the eardrum on the cochlea's oval window.

▶ **inner ear** the innermost part of the ear, containing the cochlea, semicircular canals, and vestibular sacs.

▶ **cochlea [KOHK-lee-uh]** a coiled, bony, fluid-filled tube in the inner ear through which sound waves trigger nerve impulses.

Bruce Ayres/Stone/Getty Images

The precious sense of touch As William James wrote in his *Principles of Psychology* (1890), "Touch is both the alpha and omega of affection."

"When belly with bad pains doth swell, It matters naught what else goes well."

Sadi, *The Gulistan, 1258*

Putting pain out of mind Vigorously rubbing sore feet helps reduce pain sensations, perhaps by stimulating the spinal cord's large fibers and closing the pain "gate" described in gate-control theory.

numerous are those who endure chronic pain, which is rather like an alarm that won't shut off. The suffering of people with persistent or recurring backaches, arthritis, headaches, and cancer-related pain prompts us to try to understand pain.

What Is Pain?

Pain is a property not only of the senses—of the region where we feel it—but of the brain as well. As the dreamer may see with eyes closed and the listener may hear a ringing during utter silence, so some 7 in 10 amputees may feel pain or movement in their nonexistent limbs (Melzack, 1992, 1993). (An amputee may also try to step off a bed onto a phantom limb or to lift a cup with a phantom hand.) Even those born without a limb sometimes perceive sensations from the absent limb. The brain, Melzack (1998) surmises, comes prepared to anticipate "that it will be getting information from a body that has limbs."

These *phantom limb sensations* indicate that with pain, as with sights and sounds, the brain can misinterpret the spontaneous central nervous system activity that occurs in the absence of normal sensory input. A similar phenomenon occurs with other senses. People with hearing loss often experience the sound of silence: phantom sounds—a ringing-in-the-ears sensation known as *tinnitus*. People who lose vision to glaucoma, cataracts, diabetes, or macular degeneration sometimes experience phantom sights—nonthreatening hallucinations (Ramachandran & Blakeslee, 1998). (As she became legally blind, my clear-thinking mother-in-law would occasionally see silent visitors to her room doing strange things like walking on the back of her couch.) Nerve damage in the taste system can similarly produce taste phantoms, such as ice water seeming sickeningly sweet (Goode, 1999). Others have experienced phantom smells, such as nonexistent rotten food. The moral: To see, hear, taste, smell, and feel, we require not only a body but also a brain. No brain, no pain.

Unlike vision, however, the pain system is not located in a simple neural cord running from a sensing device to a definable area in the brain. Moreover, there is no one type of stimulus that triggers pain (as light triggers vision), and there are no special receptors (like the retina's rods and cones) for pain. In fact, at low intensities, the stimuli that produce pain also cause other sensations, including warmth or coolness, smoothness or roughness.

Although no theory of pain explains all the available findings, psychologist Ronald Melzack and biologist Patrick Wall's (1965, 1983) classic **gate-control theory** still provides a useful model. Melzack and Wall believe that the spinal cord contains a neurological "gate" that either blocks pain signals or allows them to pass on to the brain. The spinal cord contains small nerve fibers that conduct most pain signals, and larger fibers that conduct most other sensory signals. When tissue is injured, the small fibers activate and open the neural gate, and you feel pain. Large-fiber activity closes the pain gate, turning pain off.

Thus, one way to treat chronic pain is to stimulate (electrically, by massage, or by acupuncture) "gate-closing" activity in the large neural fibers (Wall, 2000). Rubbing the area around your stubbed toe will create competing stimulation that will block some of the pain messages. If you place ice on a bruise,

The pain in sprain is mainly in the brain Kerri Strug had just sprained her left ankle so severely that she would be unable to do gymnastics for months afterward. Yet with this near-perfect vault, she helped carry her team to a 1996 Olympic gold medal.
Because pain is a phenomenon of the conscious brain, athletes sometimes endure serious injuries while focusing their attention outside their bodies.

you not only will control the swelling but will also trigger gate-closing cold messages. Some people with arthritis wear a small, portable electrical stimulation unit next to a painful area. When the unit stimulates nerves in the area, the person feels a vibrating sensation rather than pain (T. Murphy, 1982).

Melzack and Wall believe the pain gate can also be closed by information from the brain. These brain-to-spinal-cord messages help explain some striking psychological influences on pain. When we are distracted from pain and soothed by the release of endorphins, our experience of pain may be greatly diminished. Sports injuries may go unnoticed, until the after-game shower. During a 1989 basketball game, Ohio State University player Jay Burson broke his neck—and kept playing. Clearly, there is more to pain than what stimulates the sense receptors.

There is also more to our *memories* of pain than the pain we experienced. In experiments, and after medical procedures, people overlook a pain's duration. Their memory snapshots instead record its peak moment and how much pain they felt at the end. Daniel Kahneman and his co-researchers (1993) discovered this when they asked people to immerse one hand in painfully cold water for 60 seconds, and then the other hand in the same painfully cold water for 60 seconds followed by a slightly less painful 30 seconds more. Curiously, when asked which trial they would prefer to repeat, most preferred the longer trial, with more net pain—but less pain at the end.

For medical personnel, the implication is clear: It's better to taper down a painful procedure than to switch it off abruptly. In one experiment, a physician did this for some patients undergoing colon exams—lengthening the discomfort by a minute, but lessening its intensity (Kahneman, 1999). Although this milder discomfort added to the net pain experience, patients given this "taper down" treatment later recalled the exam as less painful than those whose pain ended abruptly. In a parallel phenomenon, people rate an imagined terrible life with a moderately bad year added on as better than a terrible life that ends abruptly without the moderately bad year. And they rate an imagined wonderful life that ends abruptly as better than one with added mildly pleasant years (Diener & others, 2001).

Pain Control

If pain is where body meets mind—if it is indeed a physical and a psychological phenomenon—then it should be treatable both physically and psychologically. Depending on the type of symptoms, pain control clinics select one or more therapies from a list that includes drugs, surgery, acupuncture, electrical stimulation, massage, exercise, hypnosis, relaxation training, and thought distraction.

The Lamaze method of childbirth combines relaxation (through deep breathing and muscle relaxation), counterstimulation (through gentle massage), and distraction (through focusing attention on, say, a pleasant photograph).

Distracting people with pleasant images ("Think of a warm, comfortable environment") or drawing their attention away from the painful stimulation ("Count backward by 3's") is an especially effective way to increase pain tolerance (Fernandez & Turk, 1989; McCaul & Malott, 1984). The principle works in health care situations. A well-trained nurse may distract needle-shy patients by chatting with them and asking them to look away when inserting the needle. Because pain is in the brain, diverting the brain's attention may gain relief.

> ▶ **gate-control theory** the theory that the spinal cord contains a neurological "gate" that blocks pain signals or allows them to pass on to the brain. The "gate" is opened by the activity of pain signals traveling up small nerve fibers and is closed by activity in larger fibers or by information coming from the brain.

"Pain is increased by attending to it."
Charles Darwin, Expression of Emotions in Man and Animals, *1872*

"From there to here, from here to there, funny things are everywhere."
Dr. Seuss, One Fish, Two Fish, Red Fish, Blue Fish, *1960*

Although Lamaze training reduces labor pain, most Lamaze patients request a local anesthetic during labor. Some—having expected a "natural, painless birth"—feel needless guilt and failure. Pain researcher Ronald Melzack therefore advocates—as does the Lamaze program itself—childbirth training that prepares a woman "to cope with an event which is often extremely painful and, at the same time, one of the most fulfilling peak experiences in her life" (Melzack, 1984).

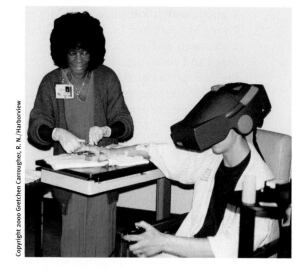

Copyright 2000 Gretchen Carrougher, R. N./Harborview

Virtual-reality pain control
For burn victims undergoing painful skin repair, an illusory virtual reality can reduce pain by powerfully distracting attention (Hoffman & others, 2001).

► **sensory interaction** the principle that one sense may influence another, as when the smell of food influences its taste.

Taste

11. How do we experience taste?

Like touch, our sense of taste mostly involves four basic sensations. Taste's sensations are sweet, sour, salty, and bitter (McBurney & Gent, 1979). Other tastes are mixtures of these. Until recently, investigators were frustrated in their search for specialized nerve fibers for each of these four basic taste sensations. New research indicates we have bitter-sensing and sweet-sensing receptors, as well as a receptor for a seeming fifth taste sensation—the meaty taste of *umami*, best experienced as the flavor enhancer monosodium glutamate (Chaudhari & others, 2000; Nelson & others, 2001; Smith & Margolskee, 2001).

Taste is a chemical sense. Inside each little bump on the top and sides of your tongue are 200 or more taste buds, each containing a pore that catches food chemicals. These molecules are sensed by 50 to 100 taste receptor cells that project antennalike hairs into the pore. Some of these receptors respond mostly to sweet-tasting molecules, others to salty-, sour-, or bitter-tasting ones. It doesn't take much to trigger a response. If a stream of water is pumped across your tongue, the addition of a concentrated salty or sweet taste for but one-tenth of a second will get your attention (Kelling & Halpern, 1983). When a friend asks for "just a taste" of your soft drink, you can squeeze off the straw after a mere fraction of a second.

Taste receptors reproduce themselves every week or two, so if you burn your tongue with hot food it hardly matters. However, as you grow older, the number of taste buds decreases, as does taste sensitivity (Cowart, 1981). (No wonder adults enjoy strong-tasting foods that children resist.) Smoking and alcohol use accelerate the decline in taste buds and sensitivities.

Taste buds are certainly essential for taste, but there's more to taste than meets the tongue. Hold your nose, close your eyes, and have someone feed you various foods. A slice of apple may be indistinguishable from a chunk of raw potato; a piece of steak may taste like cardboard; without their smells, a cold cup of coffee may be hard to distinguish from a glass of red wine. To savor a taste, we normally breathe the aroma through our nose—which is why eating is not much fun when you have a bad cold, and why people who lose their sense of smell may think they have also lost their sense of taste. Smell not only adds to our perception of taste, it also changes it: A drink's strawberry odor enhances our perception of its sweetness. This is **sensory interaction** at work—the principle that one sense may influence another. Smell plus texture plus taste equals flavor.

Sensory interaction can also influence what we hear. If we *see* a speaker saying one syllable while *hearing* another, we may perceive a third syllable that blends both inputs. Seeing the mouth movements for *ga* while hearing *ba* we may perceive *da*—a phenomenon known as the McGurk effect, after its discoverers, psychologist Harry McGurk and his assistant John MacDonald (1976). Much the same is true with touch and vision. In detecting events, the brain can combine simultaneous touch and visual signals, thanks to neurons projecting from the somatosensory cortex back to the visual cortex (Macaluso & others, 2000). So, the senses interact: seeing, hearing, touching, tasting, and smelling are not totally separate channels. In interpreting the world, the brain blends their inputs.

Smell

12. How does our sense of smell work?

Inhale, exhale. Inhale, exhale. Breaths come in pairs—except at two moments: birth and death. Each day, you inhale and exhale nearly 20,000 breaths of life-sustaining air, bathing your nostrils in a stream of scent-laden molecules. The resulting experiences of smell *(olfaction)* are strikingly intimate: You inhale something of whatever or whoever it is you smell.

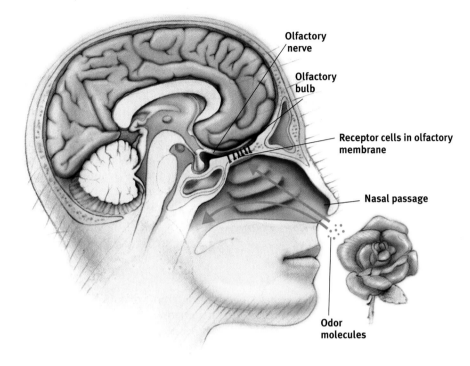

Olfactory
nerve

Olfactory
bulb

Receptor cells in olfactory
membrane

Nasal passage

Odor
molecules

figure 5.19
The sense of smell If you are to smell a rose, airborne molecules of its fragrance must reach receptors at the top of your nose. Sniffing swirls air up to the receptors, enhancing the aroma. The receptor cells send messages to the brain's olfactory bulb, and then onward to the temporal lobe's primary smell cortex and to the parts of the limbic system involved in memory and emotion (not illustrated here).

Like taste, smell is a chemical sense. We smell something when molecules of a substance carried in the air reach a tiny cluster of 5 million receptor cells at the top of each nasal cavity (**FIGURE 5.19**). These olfactory receptor cells, waving like sea anemones on a reef, respond selectively—to the aroma of a cake baking, to a wisp of smoke, to a friend's fragrance. Instantly they alert the brain through their axon fibers. Even nursing infants and their mothers have a literal chemistry to their relationship. They quickly learn to recognize each other's scents (McCarthy, 1986). Aided by smell, a mother fur seal returning to a beach crowded with pups will find her own. Our own sense of smell is less impressive than the acuteness of our seeing and hearing. Looking out across a garden we see its forms and colors in exquisite detail and hear a variety of birds singing, yet we smell little of it without settling our nose into the blooms.

Precisely how olfactory receptors work remains a mystery. Unlike light, which can be separated into its spectral colors, an odor cannot be separated into more elemental odors. The olfaction system has no parallel to the retina, which detects myriad colors with sensory cells dedicated to red, green, or blue. Olfactory receptors recognize odors individually.

Humans have 10 to 20 million olfactory receptors. A bloodhound has some 200 million (Herz, 2001).

Odor molecules come in many shapes and sizes, so many in fact that it takes many different receptors to detect them. A large family of some 1000 genes design the 1000 or so receptor proteins that recognize particular odor molecules (Axel, 1995). As a key slips into a lock, so odor molecules slip into these receptors. Yet we seem not to have a distinct receptor for each detectable odor. This suggests that some odors trigger a combination of receptors, whose activity the olfactory cortex interprets. As the alphabet's 26 letters can combine to form many words, so odor molecules bind to different receptor arrays, producing the 10,000 odors we can detect (Malnic & others, 1999).

Odors also have the power to evoke memories and feelings. A hotline runs between the brain area that gets information from the nose and the brain's ancient limbic centers associated with memory and emotion. Smell is primitive. Eons before the elaborate analytical areas of our cerebral cortex had fully evolved, our mammalian ancestors sniffed for food—and for predators.

In *Remembrance of Things Past*, the French novelist Marcel Proust described how the aroma and flavor of a bit of cake soaked in tea resurrected long-forgotten

The olfactory brain Information from the taste buds (orange arrow) travels to an area of the temporal lobe not far from that where olfactory information is received. The brain's circuitry for smell (red arrow) also connects with areas involved in memory storage, which helps explain why a smell can trigger a memory explosion.

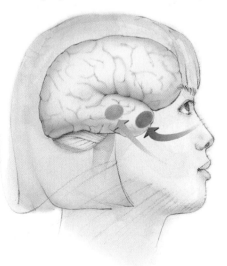

▶ **kinesthesis [kin-ehs-THEE-sehs]** the system for sensing the position and movement of individual body parts.

▶ **vestibular sense** the sense of body movement and position, including the sense of balance.

Impress your friends with your new word for the day: People unable to see are said to experience blindness. People unable to hear experience deafness. People unable to smell experience anosmia.

memories of his aunt's bedroom in the old family house. "The smell and taste of things," he noted, "bears unfaltering, in the tiny and almost impalpable drop of their essence, the vast structure of recollection."

Laboratory studies confirm that, though it's difficult to recall odors by name, we do indeed have a remarkable capacity to recognize long-forgotten odors and their associated personal episodes (Engen, 1987; Schab, 1991). Pleasant odors can evoke pleasant memories (Ehrlichman & Halpern, 1988). The smell of the sea, the scent of a perfume, or an aroma of a favorite relative's kitchen can bring to mind a happy time. Such is the power of an odor to switch on memories and to retrieve associated emotions. It's a phenomenon understood by the British travel agent chain Lunn Poly. To evoke memories of lounging on sunny, warm beaches, the company has piped the aroma of coconut suntan oil into its shops (Fracassini, 2000).

Body Position and Movement

13. How do our senses monitor our body's position and movement?

With only the five familiar senses we have so far considered, we could not put food in our mouths, stand up, or reach out and touch someone. We would be helpless. To know just how to move your arms to grasp someone's hand, you need a sixth sense. You need to know the current position of your arms and hands and then be aware of their changing positions as you move them. For you to take just one step requires feedback from, and instructions to, some 200 muscles.

We come equipped with millions of position and motion sensors. They are all over our bodies—in the muscles, tendons, and joints—and they are continually providing information to our brains. If we twist our wrists one degree, the sensors immediately report it. This sense of our body parts' position and movement is **kinesthesis**.

One can momentarily imagine being blind or deaf. Close your eyes, plug your ears, and experience the dark stillness. But what would it be like to live without touch or kinesthesis—without, therefore, being able to sense the positions of your limbs when awakening during the night? Ian Waterman of Hampshire, England, knows. In 1972, at age 19, Waterman contracted a rare viral infection that destroyed the nerves that enabled his sense of light touch and of body position and movement. People with this condition report feeling disembodied, as though their body is dead, not real, not theirs (Sacks, 1985). With prolonged practice, Waterman has learned to walk and eat—by visually focusing on his limbs and directing them accordingly. But if the lights go out, he crumples to the floor, unable to move until they come back on (Azar, 1998). Even for the rest of us, vision interacts with kinesthesis. Stand with your right heel in front of your left toes. Easy. Now close your eyes and you will probably wobble.

A companion **vestibular sense** monitors the head's (and thus the body's) position and movement. The biological gyroscopes for this sense of equilibrium are in the inner ear. In the *semicircular canals*, which look like a three-dimensional pretzel (Figure 5.17a, page 157), and the *vestibular sacs*, which connect the canals with the cochlea, are substances that move when the head rotates or tilts. This movement stimulates hairlike receptors which send the messages to the cerebellum at the back of the brain, thus enabling us to sense our body position and to maintain our balance.

If you twirl around and then come to an abrupt halt, neither the fluid in your semicircular canals nor your kinesthetic receptors immediately will return to their neutral state. The aftereffect fools your dizzy brain with the sensation that you're still spinning. This illustrates a principle that underlies our upcoming discussion of perceptual illusions: Mechanisms that normally give us an accurate experience of the world can, under special conditions, fool us. Understanding how we get fooled provides clues to how our perceptual system works.

The intricate vestibular sense
Thank your inner ears for the information that enables your brain to monitor your body's position.

Bob Daemmrich/The Image Works

PERCEPTUAL ORGANIZATION

14. What did the Gestalt psychologists contribute to our understanding of how the brain organizes sensations into perceptions?

▶ **gestalt** an organized whole. Gestalt psychologists emphasized our tendency to integrate pieces of information into meaningful wholes.

We have examined the processes by which we sense sights and sounds, tastes and smells, touch and movement. Now our central question is, how do we see not just shapes and colors, but a rose in bloom, a familiar face, a sunset? How do we hear not just a mix of pitches and rhythms, but a child's cry of pain, the hum of distant traffic, a symphony? In short, how do we *organize* and *interpret* our sensations so that they become meaningful perceptions?

Early in the twentieth century, a group of German psychologists became intrigued with how the mind organizes sensations into perceptions. Given a cluster of sensations, the human perceiver organizes them into a **gestalt**, a German word meaning a "form" or a "whole." The Gestalt psychologists provided compelling demonstrations of gestalt perception and described principles by which we organize our sensations into perceptions. They also were fond of saying that in perception the whole may exceed the sum of its parts. Combine sodium, a corrosive metal, with chlorine, a poison gas, and something very different emerges—table salt. Likewise, a unique perceived form emerges from an object's components (Rock & Palmer, 1990), as it does in **FIGURE 5.20**. Note that the individual elements of the figure are really nothing but eight blue circles, each containing three converging white lines. When we view them all together, however, we see a *whole*, a form, a Necker cube.

As you read further about the Gestalt psychologists' organizational principles, keep in mind the fundamental truth they illustrate: Our brains do more than merely register information about the world. Perception is not just opening a shutter and letting a picture print itself on the brain. We constantly filter sensory information and infer perceptions in ways that make sense to us. Mind matters.

figure 5.20
A Necker cube What do you see: circles containing white lines, or a cube? If you stare at the cube, you may notice that it reverses location, moving the tiny X in the center from the front edge to the back. At times the cube may seem to float in front of the page, with circles behind it; other times the circles may become holes in the page through which the cube appears, as though it were floating behind the page. There is far more to perception than meets the senses.

Form Perception

15. How do the principles of figure-ground and grouping contribute to our perception of form?

Imagine designing the new video/computer systems that, like your eye/brain system, can recognize faces at a glance. What abilities will they need?

figure 5.21
Reversible figure and ground

Figure and Ground

To start with, the systems need to recognize the faces as distinct from their backgrounds. Likewise, our first perceptual task is to perceive any object, called the *figure*, as distinct from its surroundings, called the *ground*. Among the voices you hear at a party, the one you attend to becomes the figure; all others, part of the ground. As you read, the words are the figure; the white paper, the ground. In **FIGURE 5.21**, the **figure-ground** relationship continually reverses—but always we organize the stimulus into a figure seen against a ground. Such reversible figure-and-ground illustrations demonstrate again that the same stimulus can trigger more than one perception.

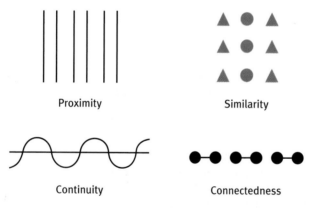

figure 5.22
Organizing stimuli into groups We could perceive the stimuli shown here in many ways, yet people everywhere see them similarly. The Gestalt psychologists believed this shows that the brain uses "rules" to order sensory information into wholes.

Proximity

Similarity

Continuity

Connectedness

Grouping

Having discriminated figure from ground, we (and our video/computer system) now have to organize the figure into a meaningful form. Some basic features of a scene—such as color, movement, and light/dark contrast—we process instantly and automatically (Treisman, 1987). To bring order and form to these basic sensations, our minds follow certain rules for **grouping** stimuli together (**FIGURE 5.22**). These rules, identified by the Gestalt psychologists and applied even by 6-month-old infants, illustrate the idea that the perceived whole differs from the sum of its parts (Quinn & others, 2002; Rock & Palmer, 1990):

> ***Proximity*** We group nearby figures together. We see not six separate lines (above left), but three sets of two lines.
> ***Similarity*** Figures similar to each other we group together. We see the triangles and circles above as vertical columns of similar shapes, not as horizontal rows of dissimilar shapes.
> ***Continuity*** We perceive smooth, continuous patterns rather than discontinuous ones. The pattern above could be a series of alternating semicircles, but we perceive it as two continuous lines—one wavy, one straight.
> ***Connectedness*** Because they are uniform and linked, we perceive each of the spots and lines above as a single unit.
> ***Closure*** We fill in gaps to create a complete, whole object. Thus we assume that the circles (far left) are complete but partially blocked by the (illusory) triangle. Add nothing more than little line segments that close off the circles and now your brain may stop constructing a triangle (near left).

Photo by Walter Wick. Reprinted from GAMES Magazine. Copyright 1983 PCS Games Limited Partnership.

figure 5.23
Grouping principles You probably perceive this doghouse as a gestalt—a whole (though impossible) structure. Actually, your brain imposes this sense of wholeness on the picture. As the photo on page 175 shows, Gestalt grouping principles such as closure and continuity are at work here.

Usually, these grouping principles help us construct reality. Sometimes, however, they lead us astray, as when we look at the doghouse in **Figure 5.23**.

Depth Perception

16. How do we see the world in three dimensions?

Two-dimensional images fall on our retinas, yet we somehow organize three-dimensional perceptions. Seeing objects in three dimensions, called **depth perception**, enables us to estimate their distance from us. At a glance, we estimate the distance of an oncoming car or the height of a house. This ability is partly innate. Eleanor Gibson and Richard Walk (1960) discovered this using a miniature cliff with a drop-off covered by sturdy glass. Gibson's inspiration for these experiments occurred while she was picnicking on the rim of the Grand Canyon. She wondered: Would a toddler peering over the rim perceive the dangerous drop-off and draw back?

Back in their Cornell University laboratory, Gibson and Walk placed 6- to 14-month-old infants on the edge of a safe canyon—a **visual cliff** (**Figure 5.24**). Their mothers then coaxed them to crawl out onto the glass. Most refused to do so, indicating that they could perceive depth. Perhaps by crawling age the infants had *learned* to perceive depth. Yet newborn animals with virtually no visual experience—

▶ **figure-ground** the organization of the visual field into objects (the *figures*) that stand out from their surroundings (the *ground*).

▶ **grouping** the perceptual tendency to organize stimuli into coherent groups.

▶ **depth perception** the ability to see objects in three dimensions although the images that strike the retina are two-dimensional; allows us to judge distance.

▶ **visual cliff** a laboratory device for testing depth perception in infants and young animals.

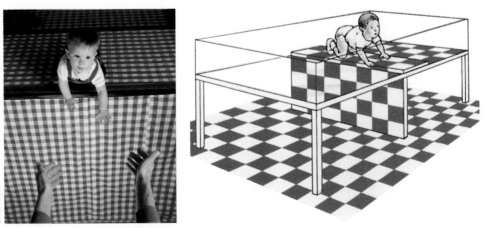

Enrico Feroelt

figure 5.24
Visual cliff Eleanor Gibson and Richard Walk devised this miniature cliff with a glass-covered drop-off to determine whether crawling infants and newborn animals can perceive depth. Even when coaxed, infants are reluctant to venture onto the glass over the cliff.

▶ **binocular cues** depth cues, such as retinal disparity and convergence, that depend on the use of two eyes.

▶ **monocular cues** distance cues, such as linear perspective and overlap, available to either eye alone.

▶ **retinal disparity** a binocular cue for perceiving depth: By comparing images from the two eyeballs, the brain computes distance—the greater the disparity (difference) between the two images, the closer the object.

▶ **convergence** a binocular cue for perceiving depth; the extent to which the eyes converge inward when looking at an object.

including young kittens, a day-old goat, and newly hatched chicks—respond similarly. Under normal circumstances, each species, by the time it is mobile, has the perceptual abilities it needs. What is more, by 3 months of age, infants are using Gestalt perception principles, by looking more at novel groupings of objects (Quinn & others, 2002).

Biological maturation predisposes our wariness of heights. Experience amplifies it. Infants' wariness increases with their experiences of crawling, no matter when they begin to crawl. When infants' movement is enhanced by a walker, they become even more wary of heights (Campos & others, 1992).

How do we do it? How do we transform two differing two-dimensional retinal images into a single three-dimensional perception? Some depth cues—**binocular cues**—require both eyes. Others—**monocular cues**—are available to each eye separately.

Binocular Cues

Try this: With both eyes open, hold two pens or pencils in front of you and touch their tips together. Now do so with one eye closed. The task should become noticeably more difficult, demonstrating the importance of binocular cues in judging the distance of nearby objects. Two eyes are better than one.

Because our eyes are about 2½ inches apart, our retinas receive slightly different images of the world. When the brain compares these two images, the difference between them—their **retinal disparity**—provides an important cue to the relative distance of different objects. When you hold your finger directly in front of your nose, your retinas receive quite different views. (You can see this if you close one eye and then the other, or create a finger sausage as in **FIGURE 5.25**.) At a greater distance—say, when you hold your finger at arm's length—the disparity is smaller.

The creators of three-dimensional (3-D) movies simulate or exaggerate retinal disparity by photographing a scene with two cameras placed a few inches apart (a feature we might want to build into our seeing computer). When we view the movie through spectacles that allow the left eye to see only the image from the left camera and the right eye only the image from the right camera, the 3-D effect mimics normal retinal disparity. Similarly, twin cameras in airplanes can take photos of terrain for integration into 3-D maps.

Can you find the three-dimensional Greek letter psi (Ψ) in the computer-generated "stereogram" in **FIGURE 5.26**? Cross your eyes slightly (or look at a pencil tip 3 inches or so above the page), and see if you can perceive the psi

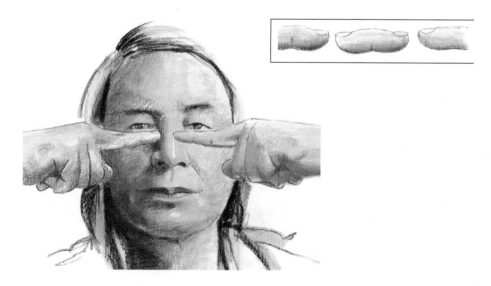

figure 5.25
The floating finger sausage
Hold your two index fingers about 5 inches in front of your eyes, with their tips half an inch apart. Now look beyond them and note the weird result. Move your fingers out farther and the retinal disparity—and the finger sausage—will shrink.

figure 5.26
Two eyes + brain = depth If you are having trouble seeing the 3-D image, try holding the picture close to your face, so that the center of it touches your nose, then slowly move it backward without changing the focus of your eyes. About a foot from your face, the 3-D image should emerge. The image appears because the picture contains two views of the psi, from slightly different angles. When the brain fuses these two into one, you see the image in three dimensions. (Some people are able to reverse the depth by relaxing and looking through the image, as if to a point behind it.)

image (at which point you will no longer feel that your eyes are crossed). The image looks so real you may be able to measure its distance from the page with a ruler.

But notice that you cannot trace the outline of the 3-D image on the page—because it isn't on the page. Notice also that if you close one eye, the image immediately disappears, confirming that the image exists only in your brain. The perceived depth, from two slightly different images lying on top of one another, occurs as each eye focuses on one image and the brain integrates the two versions into a single 3-D image. This illustrates dramatically one of this chapter's fundamental lessons: Perception is not merely projecting the world onto our brains. Rather, sensations are disassembled into information bits that the brain then reassembles into its own functional model of the external world. *Our brains construct our perceptions.*

Another binocular cue to distance is **convergence**, a neuromuscular cue caused by the eyes' greater inward turn when they view a near object. The brain notes the angle of convergence, then computes whether you are focusing on this printed page or on something else across the room. The greater the inward strain, the closer the object.

Monocular Cues

How do we judge whether a person is 10 or 100 meters away? In both cases, the retinal disparity while looking straight ahead is slight. At such distances we depend on monocular cues such as the following:

Relative size

Relative size If we assume that two objects are similar in size, we perceive the one that casts the smaller retinal image as farther away. To a driver, distant pedestrians appear smaller, which also means that small-looking pedestrians (children) may sometimes be misperceived as more distant than they are (Stewart, 2000).

Otto Greule, Jr./Allsport/Getty Images

Interposition If one object partially blocks our view of another, we perceive it as closer. The painting below purposely confuses figure and ground by interposition.

Interposition
The depth cues provided by interposition make this an impossible scene.

Relative height We perceive objects higher in our field of vision as farther away. Because we perceive the lower part of a figure-ground illustration as closer, we perceive it as figure (Vecera & others, 2002). Invert the illustration below and the black becomes ground, like a night sky.

Figure this
Thanks to relative height, lower objects seem closer—and thus are usually perceived as figure.

Relative height may contribute to the illusion that vertical dimensions are longer than identical horizontal dimensions. Is the vertical line in the diagram at right longer, shorter, or equal in length to the horizontal line? Measure and see.

Relative height

Relative motion (motion parallax) As we move, objects that are actually stable may appear to move. If while riding in a train you fix your gaze on some object—say, a house—the objects closer than the house (the fixation point) appear to move backward. The nearer an object is, the faster it seems to move.

Objects beyond the fixation point appear to move with you: The farther away the object, the lower its apparent speed. Your brain uses these speed and direction clues to compute the objects' relative distances.

Relative motion   Direction of passenger's motion ➡   **Relative motion**

Linear perspective Parallel lines, such as railroad tracks, appear to converge with distance. The more the lines converge, the greater their perceived distance. Linear perspective can contribute to rail-crossing accidents, by leading people to overestimate a train's distance (Leibowitz, 1985). (A train's massive size also makes it appear to be moving more slowly than it is.)

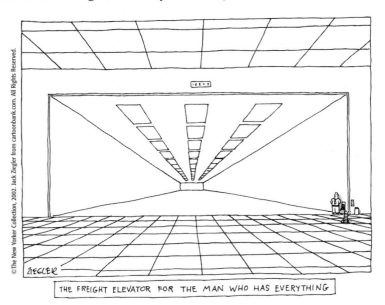

THE FREIGHT ELEVATOR FOR THE MAN WHO HAS EVERYTHING

Linear perspective

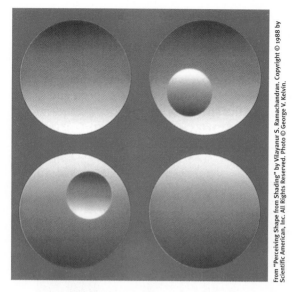

Light and shadow

Light and shadow Nearby objects reflect more light to our eyes. Thus, given two identical objects, the dimmer one seems farther away. This illusion can also contribute to accidents, as when a fog-shrouded vehicle, or one with only its parking lights on, seems farther away than it is. Shading, too, produces a sense of depth consistent with the assumed light source. Invert the illustration at left and the hollow becomes a hill, because our brains follow a simple rule: *Assume that light comes from above.*

Artists use such monocular cues to convey depth on a flat canvas (**FIGURE 5.27**). So do people who must gauge depth with but one eye. In 1960, the University of Washington football team won the year's biggest game, thanks partly to the superb passing of Bob Schloredt. Schloredt, who was obviously skilled at judging his receiver's distance, used monocular cues for distance. He was blind in his left eye.

figure 5.27
Perspective techniques
By the time that "Bristol, Broad Quay" was painted (c. 1730, Anonymous), techniques for depicting three dimensions on a flat surface were well established. Note the effective use of distance cues such as interposition, linear perspective, and relative size and height.

Perceptual Constancy

17. How do perceptual constancies help us to organize our sensations into meaningful perceptions?

So far we have noted that our video/computer system must first perceive objects as we do—as having a distinct form, location, and perhaps motion. Its next task is even more challenging: to recognize the object without being deceived by changes in its size, shape, brightness, or color. **Perceptual constancy** enables us to perceive an object as unchanging even though the stimuli we receive from it change. You glance at someone ahead of you on the sidewalk and instantly recognize a classmate. In less time than it takes to draw a breath, information reaching your eyes has been sent to

▶ **perceptual constancy** perceiving objects as unchanging (having consistent lightness, color, shape, and size) even as illumination and retinal images change.

your brain, where work teams comprising millions of neurons have extracted the essential features, compared them with stored images, and identified the person. Replicating this human perceptual feat, which has intrigued perception researchers for decades, provides a monumental challenge for our seeing computer.

Shape and Size Constancies

Sometimes an object whose actual shape cannot change *seems* to change shape with the angle of our view (**FIGURE 5.28**). More often, thanks to *shape constancy*, we perceive the form of familiar objects as constant even while our retinal images of them change. When a door opens, it casts a changing shape on our retinas, yet we still manage to perceive the door as having a constant doorlike shape (**FIGURE 5.29**).

figure 5.28
Perceiving shape Do the tops of these tables have different dimensions? They appear to. But—believe it or not—they are identical. (Measure and see.) With both tables we adjust our perceptions relative to our viewing angle.

Thanks to *size constancy* we perceive objects as having a constant size, even while our distance from them varies. Size constancy leads us to perceive a car as large enough to carry people, even when we see its tiny image from two blocks away. This illustrates the close connection between an object's perceived *distance* and perceived *size*. Perceiving an object's distance gives us cues to its size. Likewise, knowing its general size—that the object is, say, a car—provides us with cues to its distance.

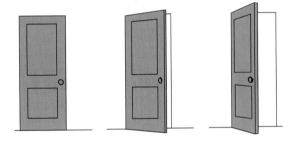

figure 5.29
Shape constancy A door casts an increasingly trapezoidal image on our retinas as it opens, yet we still perceive it as rectangular.

SIZE-DISTANCE RELATIONSHIP It is a marvel how effortlessly size perception occurs. Given an object's perceived distance and the size of its image on our retinas, we instantly and unconsciously infer the object's size. Although the monsters in **FIGURE 5.30a** cast the same retinal images, the linear perspective tells our brain that the monster in pursuit is farther away. We therefore perceive it as larger.

This interplay between perceived size and perceived distance helps explain several well-known illusions. For example, can you imagine why the moon looks up to 50 percent larger near the horizon than when high in the sky? For at least 22 centuries, scholars have wondered and have argued about reasons for the *moon illusion* (Hershenson, 1989). One reason is that cues to objects' distances at the horizon

(a)

(b)

figure 5.30
The interplay between perceived size and distance (a) The monocular cues for distance make the pursuing monster look larger than the pursued. It isn't.
(b) This visual trick, called the Ponzo illusion, is based on the same principle as the fleeing monsters. The two red bars cast identical-sized images on our retinas. But experience tells us that a more distant object can create the same-sized image as a nearer one only if it is actually larger. As a result, we perceive the bar that seems farther away as larger. (From Shepard, 1990.)

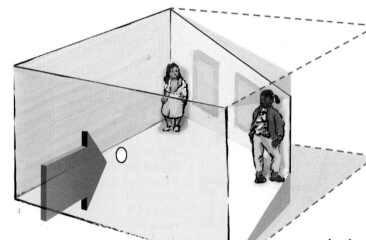

figure 5.31
The illusion of the shrinking and growing girls This distorted room, designed by Adelbert Ames, appears to have a normal rectangular shape when viewed through a peephole with one eye. The girl in the near corner appears disproportionately large because we judge her size based on the false assumption that she is the same distance away as the girl in the far corner.

figure 5.32
Brightness contrast Squares A and B are identical in color, believe it or not. (If you don't believe me, photocopy the illustration, cut out the squares, and compare.) But we perceive B as lighter.

Courtesy Edward Adelson

make the moon behind them seem farther away than the moon high in the night sky (Kaufman & Kaufman, 2000). Thus, the horizon moon—like the distant monster in Figure 5.30a and the distant bar in the *Ponzo illusion* in Figure 5.30b—seems larger. Take away these distance cues—by looking at the horizon moon (or each monster or each bar) through a paper tube—and the object immediately shrinks.

Size-distance relationships also explain why in **FIGURE 5.31** the two same-age girls seem so different in size. As the diagram reveals, the girls are actually about the same size, but the room is distorted. Viewed with one eye through a peephole, its trapezoidal walls produce the same images as those of a normal rectangular room viewed with both eyes. Presented with the camera's one-eyed view, the brain makes the reasonable assumption that the room *is* normal and that each of the girls is therefore the same distance from us. And given the different sizes of the images on the retina, our brain ends up calculating that the girls are very different in size.

Our occasional misperceptions reveal the workings of our normally effective perceptual processes. The perceived relationship between distance and size is generally valid, but under special circumstances it can lead us astray—as when helping to create the moon illusion, and the Ames Room illusion.

Lightness Constancy

White paper reflects 90 percent of the light falling on it; black paper, only 10 percent. In sunlight the black paper may reflect 100 times more light than does the white paper indoors, but it still looks black (McBurney & Collings, 1984). This illustrates *lightness constancy* (also called *brightness constancy*); we perceive an object as having a constant lightness even while its illumination varies. Perceived lightness depends on *relative luminance*—the amount of light an object reflects relative to its surroundings. If you view sunlit black paper through a narrow tube so nothing else is visible, it may look gray, because in bright sunshine it reflects a fair amount of light. View it without the tube and it is again black, because it reflects much less light than the objects around it. The phenomenon is similar to that of color constancy (page 155). As light changes, a red apple in a fruit bowl retains its redness, because our brain computes the light reflected by any object relative to its surrounding objects.

Perceived lightness stays roughly constant, given an unchanging context. But what happens when the surrounding context changes? As **FIGURE 5.32** shows, the visual system computes brightness and color relative to surrounding objects. Thus, perceived lightness changes with context.

Form perception, depth perception, motion perception, and perceptual constancy illuminate how we organize our visual experiences. Perceptual organization applies to other senses, too. It explains why we perceive a clock's steady ticking not as a tick-tick-tick but as grouped sounds, say, TICK-tick, TICK-tick. Listening to an unfamiliar language, we have trouble hearing where one word stops and the next one begins. Listening to our own language, we automatically hear distinct words. This, too, is a form of perceptual organization. But it is more, for we even organize a string of letters—THEDOGATEMEAT—into words that make an intelligible phrase, more likely "The dog ate meat" than "The do gate me at" (McBurney & Collings, 1984). This process involves not only organization but interpretation—discerning meaning in what we perceive.

Photo by Walter Wick. Reprinted from GAMES Magazine. Copyright © 1983 PSC Games Limited Partnership.

The solution Another view of the impossible doghouse in Figure 5.23 (page 167) reveals the secrets of this illusion. From the photo angle in Figure 5.23, the grouping principle of closure leads us to perceive the boards as continuous.

rehearse it!

21. Gestalt psychologists identified the principles by which we organize our perceptions. Our tendencies to fill in the gaps and to perceive a pattern as continuous are two different examples of the organizing principle called
    a. figure-ground.
    b. depth perception.
    c. shape constancy.
    d. grouping.

22. In their experiments, Gibson and Walk used a visual cliff to test depth perception in infants and young animals. Their results suggest that
    a. infants have not yet developed depth perception.
    b. crawling infants perceive depth.
    c. we have no way of knowing whether infants can perceive depth.
    d. humans differ significantly from animals in being able to perceive depth in infancy.

23. The images that fall on our retinas are two-dimensional, or flat. Yet we perceive the world as having three-dimensional depth. Depth perception underlies our ability to
    a. discriminate figure from ground.
    b. perceive objects as having a constant shape or form.
    c. judge distances.
    d. fill in the gaps in a figure.

24. In estimating distances, we use both binocular cues, which depend on both eyes, and monocular cues, which are available to either eye alone. Examples of monocular cues are interposition and
    a. closure.
    b. retinal disparity.
    c. linear perspective.
    d. convergence.

25. Form perception and perceptual constancy are organizing principles that apply to hearing as well as vision. For example, in listening to a concerto, you follow the solo instrument and perceive the orchestra as accompaniment; this illustrates the organizing principle of
    a. figure-ground.
    b. shape constancy.
    c. grouping.
    d. depth or distance perception.

Answers can be found in Appendix C.

PERCEPTUAL INTERPRETATION

Philosophers have debated the origin of our perceptual abilities: Is it nature or nurture? German philosopher Immanuel Kant (1724–1804) maintained that knowledge comes from our *inborn* ways of organizing sensory experiences. Indeed, we come equipped to process sensory information. But British philosopher John Locke (1632–1704) argued that through our experiences we also *learn* to perceive the world. Indeed, we learn to link an object's distance with its size. So, just how important is experience? How radically does it shape our perceptual interpretations?

Sensory Deprivation and Restored Vision

18. What does research on sensory restriction and restored vision reveal about the effects of experience on perception?

Writing to John Locke, William Molyneux wondered whether "a man *born* blind, and now adult, taught by his *touch* to distinguish between a cube and a sphere" could, if made to see, visually distinguish the two. Locke's answer was no, because the man would never have *learned* to see the difference.

Molyneux's hypothetical case has since been put to the test with dozens of adults who, though blind from birth, have gained sight (Gregory, 1978; von Senden, 1932). Most had been born with cataracts—clouded lenses that allowed them to see only diffused light, rather as you or I might see a diffuse fog through a Ping-Pong ball sliced in half. When their cataracts were surgically removed, the patients could distinguish figure from ground and could sense colors—suggesting that these aspects of perception are innate. But much as Locke supposed, the formerly blind patients often could not recognize by sight objects that were familiar by touch.

Seeking to gain more control than is provided by clinical cases, researchers have conducted Molyneux's imaginary experiment with infant kittens and monkeys. In one experiment, they outfitted them with goggles through which the animals could see only diffuse, unpatterned light (Wiesel, 1982). After infancy, when their goggles were removed, these animals exhibited perceptual limitations much like those of humans born with cataracts. Their eyes had not degenerated; their retinas still relayed signals to their visual cortex. But lacking stimulation, the cortical cells had not developed normal connections. Thus, the animals remained functionally blind to shape.

In both humans and animals, a similar period of sensory restriction does no permanent harm if it occurs later in life. Cover the eye of an animal for several months during adulthood, and its vision will be unaffected after the eye patch is removed. Remove cataracts that develop after early childhood, and a human, too, will enjoy normal vision. The effects of visual experiences during infancy in cats, monkeys, and humans suggest there is a *critical period* (page 111) for normal sensory and perceptual development. Experience guides, sustains, and maintains the brain's neural organization.

Learning to see At age 3, Mike May lost his vision in an explosion. On March 7, 2000, after a new cornea restored vision to his right eye, he got his first look at his wife and children. Alas, although signals were reaching his long dormant visual cortex, it lacked the experience to interpret them. Faces, apart from features such as hair, were not recognizable. Expressions eluded him. Yet he can see an object in motion and is gradually learning to navigate his world and to marvel at such things as dust floating in sunlight (Abrams, 2002).

Mike May, Allison Allano Photography

Human infants born with an opaque lens (cataract) will typically have corrective surgery within a few months. The brain network responsible for the corrected eye then rapidly develops, enabling improved visual acuity with as little as one hour's visual experience (Maurer & others, 1999). Congenitally deaf kittens and human infants given cochlear implants exhibit a similar "awakening" of the pertinent brain area (Klinke & others, 1999; Sirenteanu, 1999). Nurture sculpts what nature has endowed.

Perceptual Adaptation

19. How adaptable is our ability to perceive the world around us?

Given a new pair of glasses, we may feel slightly disoriented, even dizzy. Within a day or two, we adjust. Our **perceptual adaptation** to changed visual input makes the world seem normal again. But imagine a far more dramatic new pair of glasses—one that shifts the apparent location of objects 40 degrees to the left. When you first put them on and toss a ball to a friend, it sails off to the left. Walking forward to shake hands with the person, you veer to the left.

Could you adapt to this distorted world? Chicks cannot. When fitted with such lenses, they continue to peck where food grains *seem* to be (Hess, 1956; Rossi, 1968). But we humans adapt to distorting lenses quickly. Within a few minutes your throws would again be accurate, your stride on target. Remove the lenses and you would experience an aftereffect: At first your throws would err in the *opposite* direction, sailing off to the right; but again, within minutes you would readapt.

▶ **perceptual adaptation** in vision, the ability to adjust to an artificially displaced or even inverted visual field.

▶ **perceptual set** a mental predisposition to perceive one thing and not another.

Indeed, given an even more radical pair of glasses—one that literally turns the world upside down—you could still adapt. Psychologist George Stratton (1896) experienced this when he invented, and for eight days wore, optical headgear that flipped left to right *and* up to down, making him the first person to experience a right-side-up retinal image while standing upright.

At first, Stratton felt disoriented. When he wanted to walk, he found himself searching for his feet, which were now "up." Eating was nearly impossible. He became nauseated and depressed. But Stratton persisted, and by the eighth day he could comfortably reach for something in the right direction and walk without bumping into things. When Stratton finally removed the headgear, he readapted quickly. Later experiments replicated Stratton's experience (Dolezal, 1982; Kohler, 1962). After a period of adjustment, people wearing the optical gear have even been able to ride a motorcycle, ski the Alps, and fly an airplane.

Psychologists have recently demonstrated adaptation to other sorts of reversed worlds. Kaoru Sekiyama (2000) invited four Japanese students to live for over a month with reversed left-right vision. Like Stratton, they initially were disoriented and nauseated. Within a few weeks, however, they were able to ride bicycles. When the experiment ended, they, too, readapted quickly. They had become "biperceptual," explained Sekiyama, likening his participants to bilingual immigrants who, upon returning to their native country, can quickly transition from a new language back to their old language. After living for a year in Britain, where, after some months, driving on the left became automatic, I worried whether it would take awhile to readjust to right-sided driving. It did not. Drivers who switch between left- and right-sided worlds are like bilingual and biperceptual persons; when their worlds switch, they quickly reawaken their dormant schemas for driving on the other side.

Like Stratton, Stuart Anstis (2000) experimented on himself, by viewing the world through a video camera that inverted light—meaning he saw the world as a photographic negative. White became black, and dark shadows were now light. On one occasion he swatted at a black bug crawling across a colleague's forehead. The bug was actually a patch of sunlight dancing on his annoyed colleague's bald head. Anstis was quickly able to read people's expressions, but during his three days in the inverted light he was often at a loss in recognizing people.

Did all these people adjust by perceptually converting their strange worlds to "normal" views? Actually no. The world around them still seemed above their heads or on the wrong side of them. But by actively moving about in these topsy-turvy worlds, they adapted to the context and learned to coordinate their movements.

Perceptual adaptation "Oops, missed," thinks Dr. Hubert Dolezal as he views the world through inverting goggles. Yet, believe it or not, kittens, monkeys, and humans can adapt to an inverted world.

Courtesy of Hubert Dolezal

Perceptual Set

20. How do our assumptions, expectations, and contexts affect our perceptions?

As everyone knows, to see is to believe. As many people also know, but do not fully appreciate, to believe is to see. Our experiences, assumptions, and expectations may give us a **perceptual set**, or mental predisposition, that greatly influences what we perceive. People perceive an adult-child pair as looking more alike when told they are parent and child (Bressan & Dal Martello, 2002). And consider: Is the image in the center picture of **FIGURE 5.33** a man playing the saxophone or a woman's face? What we see in such a drawing can be influenced by first looking at either of the two unambiguous versions (Boring, 1930). **Continued on page 180**

figure 5.33
Perceptual set What do you see in the center picture: a male saxophonist or a woman's face? Glancing first at one of the two unambiguous versions of the picture is likely to influence your interpretation.

From Shepard (1990)

Continued on page 180

Thinking Critically About:

Extrasensory Perception

Can we perceive only what we sense? Or, without sensory input, are we capable of **extrasensory perception (ESP)**? Are there indeed people—any people—who can read minds, see through walls, or foretell the future? In laboratory experiments, **parapsychologists**—those who study paranormal (literally, beyond the normal) occurrences—have at times been astonished at psychics who seem capable of discerning the contents of sealed envelopes, influencing the roll of a die, or drawing a picture of what someone else is viewing at an unknown remote location. Five British universities now have parapsychology units staffed by Ph.D. graduates of Edinburgh University's parapsychology program (Morris, 2000). But other research psychologists and scientists—including 96 percent of the scientists in the National Academy of Sciences—have been skeptical (McConnell, 1991). If ESP is real, we would need to overturn the scientific understanding that we are creatures whose minds are tied to our physical brains and whose perceptual experiences of the world are built of sensations. However, sometimes new

evidence does overturn our scientific preconceptions. Before we evaluate claims of ESP, let's review them.

Claims of ESP

Claims of paranormal phenomena include astrological predictions, psychic healing, communication with the dead, and out-of-body experiences. Of these, the most testable and (for a sensation/perception chapter) most relevant claims are for three varieties of ESP:

Telepathy, or mind-to-mind communication—one person sending thoughts to another or perceiving another's thoughts.

Clairvoyance, or perceiving remote events, such as sensing that a friend's house is on fire.

Precognition, or perceiving future events, such as a political leader's death or a sporting event's outcome.

Premonitions or Pretensions?

Can psychics see into the future? Although one might wish for a psychic stock forecaster, the tallied forecasts of "leading psychics" reveal meager accuracy. No greedy—or charitable—psychic was able to predict the outcome of the $331 million Big Game jackpot in 2002. Moreover, between 1978 and 1985, the New Year's predictions of the *National Enquirer*'s favorite psychics yielded 2 accurate predictions out of 486 (Strentz, 1986). During the 1990s, tabloid psychics were all wrong in predicting surprising events (Madonna did not become a gospel singer, the Statue of Liberty did not lose both arms in a terrorist blast, Queen Elizabeth did not abdicate her throne to enter a convent.) And the new-century psychics missed the big-news events such as the Florida presidential

Which supposed ability does Psychic Pizza claim?

ballot controversy and the horror of 9/11. Where were the precogs on 9/10 when we needed them?

Analyses of psychic visions offered to police departments reveal that these, too, are no more accurate than guesses made by others (Reiser, 1982). Psychics working with the police do, however, generate dozens or even hundreds of predictions. This increases the odds of an occasional correct guess, which psychics can then report to the media. Moreover, vague predictions can later be interpreted ("retrofitted") to match events that provide a perceptual set for interpreting them. Nostradamus, a sixteenth-century French psychic, explained in an unguarded moment that his ambiguous prophecies "could not possibly be understood till they were interpreted after the event and by it." Police departments are wise to all this. When Jane Ayers Sweat and Mark Durm

SNAPSHOTS

"A person who talks a lot is sometimes right."

Spanish proverb

(1993) asked the police department's of America's 50 largest cities whether they ever used psychics, 65 percent said they never had. Of those that had, not one had found it helpful. Thousands of psychics reportedly overwhelmed police with mispredictions of the whereabouts of Washington, D.C., intern Chandra Levy, whose body was discovered by a jogger on a wooded hill a year after her disappearance (Radford, 2002).

Are the spontaneous "visions" of everyday people any more accurate? Consider our dreams. Do they foretell the future, as about half of university students believe (Messer & Griggs, 1989)? Or do they only seem to do so because we are more likely to recall or reconstruct dreams that seem to have come true? More than 60 years ago, two Harvard psychologists (Murray & Wheeler, 1937) tested the prophetic power of dreams. After aviator Charles Lindbergh's baby son was kidnapped and murdered but before the body was discovered, the researchers invited the public to report their dreams about the child. Of the 1300 dream reports submitted, how many accurately envisioned the child dead? Five percent. And how many also correctly anticipated the body's location—buried among trees? Only 4 of the 1300. Although this number was surely no better than chance, to those 4 dreamers the accuracy of their *apparent* precognitions must have seemed uncanny.

Throughout the day, each of us imagines many events. Occasionally an unlikely imagining is bound to occur and to astonish us when it does. If you tell everyone in a group of 100 to think "heads" before each tosses six coins, someone is likely to get heads every time (whether thinking heads or not) and to feel

eerie afterward. Given the billions of events in the world each day, and given enough days, the improbable becomes inevitable.

One skeptic, magician James Randi, long offered $10,000 to anyone who could demonstrate "*any paranormal ability*" before a group of competent experts. With pledges from others, his offer—"to anyone who proves a genuine psychic power under proper observing conditions"—several years ago was upped to $1 million, on deposit with Goldman-Sachs (Randi, 1999). Still, after three decades, no winner.

Large as Randi's offer is, the scientific seal of approval would be worth far more to anyone whose claims could be authenticated. To refute those who say there is no ESP, one need only produce a single person who can demonstrate a single, reproducible ESP phenomenon. (To refute those who say pigs can't talk would take but one talking pig.) So let's stop here and see if the claims made for ESP can withstand the demands of critical inquiry.

Putting ESP to Experimental Test

In the past, there have been all kinds of strange ideas—that bumps on the head reveal character traits, that bloodletting is a cure-all, that each sperm cell contains a miniature person. When faced with such claims—or with claims of mind reading or out-of-body travel or communication with the dead—how can we separate bizarre ideas from those that sound bizarre but are true? At the heart of science is a simple answer: *Test them to see if they*

Testing psychic powers in the British population Hertfordshire University psychologist Richard Wiseman created a "mind machine" to see if people can influence or predict a coin toss. Using a touch-sensitive screen, visitors to festivals around the country were given four attempts to call heads or tails. Using a random-number generator, a computer then decided the outcome. When the experiment concluded in January 2000, nearly 28,000 people had predicted 110,972 tosses—with 49.8 percent correct.

work. If they do, so much the better for the ideas. If they don't, so much the better for our skepticism.

▶ **extrasensory perception (ESP)** the controversial claim that perception can occur apart from sensory input. Said to include *telepathy, clairvoyance,* and *precognition.*

▶ **parapsychology** the study of paranormal phenomena, including ESP and psychokinesis.

Continued on next page

This scientific attitude has led both believers and skeptics to agree that what parapsychology needs to give it credibility is a reproducible phenomenon and a theory to explain it. Seeking a phenomenon, how might we test ESP claims in a controlled experiment? An experiment differs from a staged demonstration. On stage, the "psychic," like a magician, controls what the audience sees and hears. The "effects" are typically mind blowing. In the laboratory, the experimenter controls what the psychic sees and hears. Time and again, skeptics note, so-called psychics have exploited unquestioning audiences with amazing performances in which they *appeared* to communicate with the spirits of the dead, read minds, or levitate objects—only to have it revealed that their acts were a hoax, or nothing more than the illusions of stage magicians.

> *"A psychic is an actor playing the role of a psychic."*
>
> Psychologist-magician Daryl Bem (1984)

Knowing how easily we can be deceived, and lacking reproducible results, most research psychologists remain skeptical. But some have become newly intrigued by findings published by social psychologist Daryl Bem and parapsychologist Charles Honorton (1994) using the *ganzfeld procedure*. The procedure would place you in a reclining chair, play hissing white noise through headphones, and shine diffuse red light through halved Ping-Pong balls strapped over your eyes. Ostensibly, this reduction of external distractions would put you in an ideal state to receive thoughts from someone else, which you might hear as small voices from within.

Building on earlier studies using this procedure, Bem and Honorton isolated a "sender" and "receiver" in separate, shielded chambers and had the sender concentrate for half an hour on one of four randomly selected visual images. The receivers were then asked which of four images best matched the images they experienced during the session. Over 11 studies, the receivers beat chance (25 percent accurately matched) by a small but statistically significant margin (32 percent accurately matched).

Recall that psychology-based critical inquiry always asks two questions: *What do you mean? And how do you know (what's your evidence)?* Parapsychologists say the ganzfeld tests of ESP offer clear answers to both questions. Skeptic Ray Hyman (1994, 1996) granted that their methodology surpasses that of previous ESP experiments,

---

Continued from page 177

> *"The temptation to form premature theories upon insufficient data is the bane of our profession."*
>
> Sherlock Holmes, in Arthur Conan Doyle's The Valley of Fear, 1914

Everyday examples of perceptual set abound. In 1972, a British newspaper published genuine, unretouched photographs of a "monster" in Scotland's Loch Ness—"the most amazing pictures ever taken," stated the paper. If this information creates in you the same perceptual set it did in most of the paper's readers, you, too, will see the monster in the photo reproduced in **FIGURE 5.34a**. But when Steuart Campbell (1986) approached the photos with a different perceptual set, he saw a curved tree trunk—very likely the same tree trunk others had seen in the water the day the photo was shot. Moreover, with this different perceptual set, you may now notice that the object is floating motionless, without any rippling water or wake around it—hardly what we would expect of a lively monster. Apparently aided by perceptual set, thousands of others have marveled at a face on the moon, Mother Teresa on a cinnamon bun, Jesus on a pancake, and the word *Allah* on a sliced potato.

Our perceptual set can influence what we hear as well as what we see. Consider the kindly airline pilot who, on a takeoff run, looked over at his depressed co-pilot

figure 5.34
Believing is seeing
What do you perceive in these photos? (a) Is this Nessie, the Loch Ness monster, or a log? (b) Are these flying saucers or clouds? We often perceive what we expect to see.

(a)

(b)

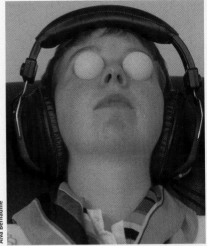

Alva Bernadine

The ganzfeld procedure Hoping to detect faint telepathy signals, some parapsychologists subject volunteers to sensory deprivation to minimize distractions.

these experiments. Would this be the first reliable ESP phenomenon? Or one more dashed hope?

Alas, Julie Milton and Richard Wiseman's (1999, 2001) statistical digest of 30 follow-up ganzfeld experiments found no effect. "We conclude that the ganzfeld technique does not at present offer a replicable method for producing ESP in the laboratory." But—hold the phone—the studies and the debate continue (Bem & others, 2001; Storm & Ertel, 2001, 2002).

Until new evidence emerges, we are left with this observation: After thousands of experiments, *a reproducible ESP phenomenon has never been discovered, nor has anyone produced any individual who can convincingly demonstrate psychic ability.* A National Research Council investigation of ESP similarly concluded that "the best available evidence does not support the contention that

these phenomena exist" (Druckman & Swets, 1988). And in 1995, a CIA-commissioned report evaluated 10 years of military testing of psychic spies. Twenty million dollars had been invested. The result? The program produced nothing. Given so many disappointing laboratory results and vague or erroneous psychic visions, the psychic spy program was finally scrapped (Hyman, 1996; Waller, 1995).

Recall from Chapter 1 that the scientific attitude involves skeptical but open-minded scrutiny of competing ideas. As critical thinkers, we can be open to new ideas without being gullible, discerning without being cynical. We can be critical thinkers, yet—knowing that our understanding of nature is incomplete—we can agree with Shakespeare's Hamlet that "there are more things in heaven and earth, Horatio, than are dreamt of in your philosophy."

but he questioned certain procedural details that may have introduced bias. Intrigued, other researchers set to work replicating

and said, "Cheer up." The co-pilot heard the usual "Gear up" and promptly raised the wheels—before they left the ground (Reason & Mycielska, 1982). Clearly, much of what we perceive comes not just from the world "out there" but also from what's behind our eyes and between our ears. What determines our perceptual set? Our preexisting schemas for male saxophonists and women's faces, for monsters and tree trunks, for airplane lights and UFOs all influence how we interpret ambiguous sensations with top-down processing.

When shown the phrase:
Mary had a
a little lamb
many people perceive what they expect, and miss the repeated word. Did you?

Context Effects

A given stimulus may trigger radically different perceptions, partly because of our differing schemas, but also because of the immediate context. Some examples:

- Imagine hearing a noise interrupted by the words "eel is on the wagon." Likely, you would actually perceive the first word as *wheel*. Given "eel is on the orange," you would hear *peel*. This curious phenomenon, discovered by Richard Warren, suggests that the brain can work backward in time to allow a later stimulus to determine how we perceive an earlier one. The context creates an expectation that, top-down, influences our perception as we match our bottom-up signal against it (Grossberg, 1995).
- Did the pursuing monster in Figure 5.30a on page 173 look aggressive? Did the identical pursued one seem frightened? If so, you experienced a context effect.
- Is the "magician's cabinet" in **FIGURE 5.35** (page 182) sitting on the floor or hanging from the ceiling? How we perceive it depends on the context defined by the rabbits.
- Did the speaker say "cults and sects" or "cults and sex"? Did the critic advocate "attacks" or "a tax" on our politicians? In both instances, we must discern the meaning from the surrounding words.

IT'S AMAZING HOW PEOPLE SLOW DOWN WHEN YOU POINT A HAIR DRYER AT THEM.

figure 5.35
Context effects: The magician's cabinet Is the box in the far left frame lying on the floor or hanging from the ceiling? What about the one on the far right? In each case, the context defined by the inquisitive rabbits guides our perceptions. (From Shepard, 1990.)

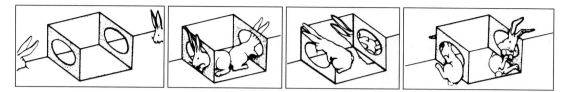

Culture and context effects What is above the woman's head? In one study, nearly all the East Africans who were questioned said the woman was balancing a metal box or can on her head and that the family was sitting under a tree. Westerners, for whom corners and boxlike architecture are more common, were more likely to perceive the family as being indoors, with the woman sitting under a window. (Adapted from Gregory & Gombrich, 1973.)

Even hearing sad rather than happy music can predispose people to perceive a sad meaning in spoken homophonic words—*mourning* rather than *morning, die* rather than *dye, pain* rather than *pane* (Halberstadt & others, 1995).

In Seattle's county hospital where I was once an orderly, we occasionally faced the task of transporting a dead body through crowded hallways without alarming the patients or their visitors. Our solution was to exploit the "Kulechov effect" by creating a context that matched people's schemas for sleeping and sedated patients: With the body's face uncovered and the sheet turned down in normal fashion, we could wheel an apparently "sleeping" body past those unsuspecting.

In everyday life, perceptual sets—for example, stereotypes about gender or culture—can color the context. Without the obvious cues of pink or blue, people will struggle over whether to call the new baby "he" or "she." But told an infant is "David," people (especially children) may perceive "him" as bigger and stronger than if the same infant is called "Diana" (Stern & Karraker, 1989). Some gender differences, it seems, exist merely in the eyes of their beholders.

The effects of perceptual set and context show how experience helps us construct perception. "We hear and apprehend only what we already half know," said Thoreau. The river of perception is fed by two streams, sensation and cognition. To return to the question—is perception innate or learned?—we can answer: It's both. "Simple" perceptions are the brain's creative products.

rehearse it!

26. Locke believed that our perception of the world is learned through experience. Support for his view can be found in
    a. the writings of Immanuel Kant.
    b. research on critical periods and sensory restriction.
    c. research on perceptual set and context.
    d. theories of color vision.

27. In some cases, surgeons have restored vision to patients who have been blind from birth. The newly sighted individu-

als were able to sense colors but had difficulty
    a. recognizing objects by touch.
    b. recognizing the shapes of objects.
    c. distinguishing figure from ground.
    d. distinguishing between bright and dim light.

28. Experiments in which volunteers wear glasses that displace or invert their visual fields show that, after a period of disorientation, they learn to function quite well. This ability is called

    a. visual capture.
    b. perceptual set.
    c. sensory interaction.
    d. perceptual adaptation.

29. Our perceptual set influences what we perceive. This mental predisposition reflects our
    a. experiences, assumptions, and expectations.
    b. perceptual adaptation.
    c. objectivity, realism, and intelligence.
    d. perceptual constancy.

Answers can be found in Appendix C.

To feel awe and to gain a deep reverence for life, we do not need to look any further than our own perceptual system and its capacity for organizing formless nerve impulses into colorful sights, vivid sounds, and evocative smells. Within our ordinary perceptual experiences lies much that is truly extraordinary—surely much more than has so far been dreamt of in our psychology. A century of research has revealed many of the secrets of sensation and perception, yet for future generations of researchers there remain profound and genuine mysteries to solve.

chapter review

REVIEWING

Sensation and Perception

SENSING THE WORLD: SOME BASIC PRINCIPLES

Sensation—receiving and representing stimulus energies from our environment—involves bottom-up processing. Perception—the process of selecting, organizing, and interpreting sensory information—involves top-down processing. Psychophysics is the study of how sensations are perceived.

1. What is an absolute threshold, and are we influenced by stimuli below it?

We—like other species—sense only a portion of the sea of energy that surrounds us, but to this portion, which enables us to survive and thrive, we are exquisitely sensitive. Our absolute threshold for any stimulus is the minimum stimulation necessary for us to detect it 50 percent of the time. Experiments reveal that we *can* process some information from stimuli too weak to recognize. But the restricted conditions under which this occurs would not enable unscrupulous opportunists to exploit us with subliminal messages.

2. How does the magnitude of a stimulus influence our threshold for detecting differences?

To survive and thrive, an organism must have difference thresholds low enough to detect minute changes in important stimuli. In humans, a difference threshold (also called a just noticeable difference, or *jnd*) increases in proportion to the stimulus—a principle known as Weber's law.

3. What function does sensory adaptation serve?

The phenomenon of sensory adaptation helps to focus our attention on informative changes in stimulation by diminishing our sensitivity to constant or routine odors, sounds, and so forth.

VISION

4. What are the characteristics of the wavelengths that we see as visible light?

Each sense receives stimulation, transforms it into neural signals, and sends these neural messages to the brain. The energies we experience as visible light are a thin slice from the broad spectrum of electromagnetic radiation. The perceived hue (blue, green, and so on) of light depends on its wavelength. The brightness of light depends on its intensity.

5. How does the eye transform light energy into neural messages?

After entering the eye and being focused by a cameralike lens (through the process of accommodation), light waves strike the retina. The retina's light-sensitive rods and color-sensitive cones convert the light energy into neural impulses, which travel along the optic nerve to the brain. The point at which the optic nerve leaves the eye is the blind spot.

6. How is visual information processed in the brain?

In the cortex, individual neurons, called feature detectors, respond to specific features of a visual stimulus, and their information is pooled for interpretation by higher-level brain cells. Subdimensions of vision (color, movement, depth, and form) are processed separately and simultaneously, illustrating the brain's capacity for parallel processing. The visual pathway faithfully represents retinal stimulation, but the brain's representation incorporates our assumptions, interests, and expectations.

7. What theories contribute to our understanding of color vision, and does color constancy affect our perception of color?

Research on how we see color supports two nineteenth-century theories. First, as the Young-Helmholtz trichromatic (three-color) theory suggests, the retina contains three types of cones. Each is most sensitive to the wavelengths of one of the three primary colors of light (red, green, or blue). Second, as opponent-process theory maintains, the nervous system codes the color-related information from the cones into pairs of opponent colors, as demonstrated by the phenomenon of afterimages and as confirmed by measuring opponent processes within visual neurons of the thalamus. The phenomenon of color constancy under varying illumination shows that our brains construct our experience of color.

THE OTHER SENSES

Although vision tends to dominate our other senses (visual capture), our other senses, including hearing (audition), are highly adaptive.

8. What are the characteristics of the air pressure waves that we hear as meaningful sounds?

The pressure waves we experience as sound vary in frequency, which determines a tone's pitch (its highness or lowness). These waves also vary in amplitude, which determines their loudness. Sound energy is measured in decibels. Prolonged exposure to sounds above 85 decibels can produce hearing loss.

9. *How does the ear transform sound energy into neural messages?*

Through a mechanical chain of events, the sound waves traveling down the auditory canal cause minuscule vibrations in the eardrum. Transmitted via the bones of the middle ear to the fluid-filled cochlea in the inner ear, these vibrations create movement in tiny hair cells, triggering neural messages to the brain. We localize sound by detecting minute differences in the loudness and timing of the sounds received by each ear.

10. *How do we sense touch and feel pain?*

Our sense of touch is actually four senses—pressure, warmth, cold, and pain—that combine to produce other sensations, such as a tickle. One theory of pain is that a "gate" in the spinal cord either opens to permit pain signals traveling up small nerve fibers to reach the brain, or closes to prevent their passage. Because pain is both a physiological and a psychological phenomenon, it often can be controlled through a combination of physical and psychological treatments.

11. *How do we experience taste?*

Taste, a chemical sense, is likewise a composite of five basic sensations—sweet, sour, salty, bitter, and umami. Other tastes are mixtures of these five. Taste receptors are located in the taste buds. Aromas that interact with information from the taste receptors also affect our perception of taste. This is an example of sensory interaction.

12. *How does our sense of smell work?*

Like taste, smell is a chemical sense, but there are no basic sensations for smell, as there are for touch and taste. Airborne molecules activate receptor cells located at the top of each nasal cavity. These receptors and their associated proteins recognize individual odor molecules. Some odors trigger a combination of receptors. Odors can spontaneously evoke memories and their associated emotions.

13. *How do our senses monitor our body's position and movement?*

Our effective functioning requires a *kinesthetic sense*, which notifies the brain of the position and movement of body parts, and a *vestibular sense*, which monitors the position and movement of the whole body. Millions of position and motion sensors in the muscles, tendons, and joints are receptors for our kinesthetic sense. Receptors for the vestibular sense are located in the inner ear.

PERCEPTUAL ORGANIZATION

14. *What did the Gestalt psychologists contribute to our understanding of how the brain organizes sensations into perceptions?*

The early Gestalt psychologists were impressed with the seemingly innate way in which we organize fragmentary sensory data into whole perceptions (gestalts). They studied how our minds structure the information that comes to us.

15. *How do the principles of figure-ground and grouping contribute to our perception of form?*

To recognize an object, we must first perceive it (see it as a figure) as distinct from its surroundings (the ground). We must also organize the figure into a meaningful form. Several Gestalt principles of grouping—proximity, similarity, continuity, connectedness, and closure—describe this process.

16. *How do we see the world in three dimensions?*

Research on the visual cliff reveals that many species perceive the world in three dimensions at, or very soon after, birth. We transform two-dimensional retinal images into three-dimensional depth perceptions by use of binocular cues (such as retinal disparity and convergence) and monocular cues (such as interposition, relative size, relative height, relative motion, linear perspective, and light and shadow).

17. *How do perceptual constancies help us to organize our sensations into meaningful perceptions?*

Because of size, shape, and lightness constancy, objects appear to have unchanging characteristics regardless of their true distance from us or their actual shape or illumination. These perceptual constancies explain several well-known visual illusions, such as the moon and the Ames Room illusions.

PERCEPTUAL INTERPRETATION

18. *What does research on sensory restriction and restored vision reveal about the effects of experience on perception?*

For many species, infancy is a critical period during which experience must activate the brain's innate visual mechanisms. If cataract removal restores eyesight to adults who were blind from birth, they remain unable to perceive the world normally. Generally, they can distinguish figure from ground and can perceive colors, but they are unable to recognize shapes and forms. In controlled experiments, infant animals have been reared with severely restricted visual input. When their visual exposure is returned to normal, they, too, suffer enduring visual handicaps.

19. *How adaptable is our ability to perceive the world around us?*

Human vision is remarkably adaptable. Given glasses that shift the world slightly to the left or right, turn it upside down, or reverse it, people manage to adapt their movements and, with practice, to move about with ease.

20. *How do our assumptions, expectations, and contexts affect our perceptions?*

Clear evidence that perception is influenced by our experience—our learned assumptions and beliefs—as well as by sensory input comes from the many demonstrations of perceptual set and context effects. The ideas we have stored in memory help us to interpret otherwise ambiguous stimuli, which helps explain why some of us "see" monsters, faces, and UFOs that others do not.

Our expectations also influence our views on ESP. For several reasons, especially the lack of a reproducible ESP effect, most research psychologists remain skeptical.

A CRITICAL THINKER'S REVIEW OF CHAPTER 5

You've now studied and reviewed **Sensation and Perception.** For even better retention, reflect on these concepts at a deeper level. If you need to refresh your memory of the six categories of critical thinking shown in parentheses below, see page 34. See if you can answer each of these questions in a short paragraph.

1. For the purposes of this book, we discuss sensation and perception separately, but in reality the distinction is hazy. What is the rough distinction between sensation and perception, and why is it considered hazy? (psychological reasoning)

2. Olivia is the director of a children's choir that is barely scraping by financially. She really needs to raise the yearly tuition from $500 to $750, but she doesn't want to lose families in the process. Keeping in mind Weber's law, how would you suggest she accomplish her goals? (creative problem solving)

3. Deirdre is intensely interested in the sense of smell. She often talks about how many of her memories are connected to smells, and she claims that smell is more complex than our senses of vision, touch, or taste. How might she support this claim—how is smell different from these other senses? (scientific problem solving)

4. John has completely color-deficient vision. What sorts of dangers and challenges does this present in his daily life? (perspective taking)

5. How does the study of illusions inform our understanding of normal perceptions? (pattern recognition)

6. Tatiana and Ariana watch a television show with lions hunting zebras. Tatiana is upset at the carnage, while Ariana is matter-of-fact about the life-feeds-on-life principle. How could context and perceptual set have affected their very different points of view? (practical problem solving)

Answers can be found in Appendix C.

TERMS AND CONCEPTS TO REMEMBER

sensation, p. 141
perception, p. 141
bottom-up processing, p. 141
top-down processing, p. 141
psychophysics, p. 142
absolute threshold, p. 142
subliminal, p. 143
difference threshold, p. 144
Weber's law, p. 144
sensory adaptation, p. 145
wavelength, p. 146
hue, p. 146
intensity, p. 147
accommodation, p. 148
retina, p. 148
rods, p. 148
cones, p. 148

optic nerve, p. 148
blind spot, p. 148
feature detectors, p. 150
parallel processing, p. 151
Young-Helmholtz trichromatic (three-color) theory, p. 153
opponent-process theory, p. 155
color constancy, p. 155
visual capture, p. 156
audition, p. 156
frequency, p. 157
pitch, p. 157
middle ear, p. 158
inner ear, p. 158
cochlea [KOHK-lee-uh], p. 158
gate-control theory, p. 160
sensory interaction, p. 162

kinesthesis [kin-ehs-THEE-sehs], p. 164
vestibular sense, p. 164
gestalt, p. 165
figure-ground, p. 166
grouping, p. 166
depth perception, p. 167
visual cliff, p. 167
binocular cues, p. 168
monocular cues, p. 168
retinal disparity, p. 168
convergence, p. 169
perceptual constancy, p. 172
perceptual adaptation, p. 176
perceptual set, p. 177
extrasensory perception (ESP), p. 178
parapsychology, p. 178

To continue your study and review of Sensation and Perception, visit this book's Web site at www.worthpublishers.com/myers. You will find practice tests, review activities, and Web links for more information on topics related to Sensation and Perception.

chapter6

States of Consciousness

Now playing at an inner theater near you: the premiere showing of a sleeping person's vivid dream. This never-before-seen mental movie features captivating characters wrapped in a plot so original and unlikely, yet so intricate and so seemingly real, that the viewer later marvels at its creation.

Waking from a troubling dream, wrenched by its emotions, who among us has not wondered about this weird state of consciousness? How does our brain so creatively, colorfully, and completely construct this alternative, conscious world? In the shadowland between our dreaming and waking consciousness, we may even wonder for a moment which is real. And what shall we make of other altered states of consciousness—hypnosis, drug-altered hallucinations, and near-death visions?

But first questions first: What is consciousness? In every science there are concepts so fundamental they are nearly impossible to define. Biologists agree on what is alive but not on precisely what life is. In physics, matter and energy elude simple definition. To psychologists, consciousness is similarly a fundamental yet slippery concept.

"Neither [psychologist] Steve Pinker nor I can explain human subjective consciousness. . . . We don't understand it."

Evolutionary biologist Richard Dawkins (1999)

WAKING CONSCIOUSNESS

1. What is consciousness, and how does it function?

At its beginning, psychology was "the description and explanation of states of consciousness" (Ladd, 1887). But the difficulty of scientifically studying consciousness led many psychologists during the first half of the last century to turn to direct observations of behavior—an approach favored by an emerging school of psychology called *behaviorism* (page 228). By the 1950s, psychology no longer defined itself as the study of consciousness or "mental life" but rather as the science of behavior. Psychology had nearly lost consciousness. Consciousness was viewed as resembling a car's speedometer: "It doesn't make the car go, it just reflects what's happening" (Seligman, 1991, p. 24).

By 1960, mental concepts began to reenter psychology. Advances in neuroscience made it possible to relate brain activity to various mental states—waking, sleeping, dreaming. Researchers began studying consciousness altered by hypnosis and drugs. Psychologists of all persuasions were affirming the importance of mental processes (cognition). Psychology was regaining consciousness.

For most psychologists today, **consciousness** is our awareness of ourselves and our environment. Consciousness brings varied information to the surface, enabling us to reflect and plan. When we learn a complex concept or behavior—say, driving a car—consciousness focuses our concentration on the car and the traffic. This awareness varies with our attentional spotlight. With practice, driving becomes automatic and no longer requires our undivided attention—freeing our consciousness to focus on other things. Consciousness assembles information from various sources, enabling us to reflect on our past and plan for our future.

"Psychology must discard all reference to consciousness."

Behaviorist John B. Watson (1913)

Jeff Greenberg/PhotoEdit

Consciousness Our awareness is but the visible surface of our brain's information processing.

▶ **selective attention** the focusing of conscious awareness on a particular stimulus, as in the cocktail party effect.

Selective Attention

Perceptions come to us moment by moment, one perception vanishing as the next appears. This illustrates an important principle: Our conscious attention is *selective*.

Selective attention means that at any moment we focus our awareness on only a limited aspect of all that we experience. Indeed, a *very* limited aspect: By one estimate, our five senses take in 11,000,000 bits of information per second, of which we consciously process about 40 (Wilson, 2002). Yet we intuitively make great use of the other 10,999,960 bits. Until reading this sentence, you have been unaware that your shoes are pressing against your feet or that your nose is in your line of vision. Now, suddenly, your attentional spotlight shifts. Your feet feel encased, your nose stubbornly intrudes on the page before you. While attending to these words, you've also been blocking from awareness information coming from your peripheral vision. But you can change that. While staring at the X below, notice what surrounds the book (the edges of the page, your desk top, and so forth).

X

Another example of selective attention, the *cocktail party effect*, is the ability to attend selectively to only one voice among many. Imagine hearing two conversations over a headset, one in each ear, and being asked to repeat the message in your left ear while it is spoken. When paying attention to what is being said in your left ear, you won't perceive what is said in your right. If you are asked later what language your right ear heard, you may draw a blank (though you could report the speaker's gender and loudness). At the level of conscious awareness, whatever has your attention pretty much has your undivided attention. That explains why, in a University of Utah experiment, students conversing on a cell phone were slower to detect and respond to traffic signals during a driving simulation (Strayer & Johnston, 2001).

In other experiments, people also exhibit a remarkable lack of awareness of happenings in their visual environment. After a brief visual interruption, a big Coke bottle may disappear from the scene, a railing may rise, clothing color may change, and, more often than not, viewers don't notice (Resnick & others, 1997; Simons, 1996; Simons & Levin, 1998). This *change blindness* even occurs among people giving directions to a construction worker who, unnoticed by two-thirds of them, is replaced by another construction worker (**FIGURE 6.1**). Out of sight, out of mind.

Can stimuli that we do not notice affect us? Indeed yes. In one experiment, women students listened through headphones as a prose passage played in one ear. Their task was to repeat its words out loud and to check them against a written transcript (Wilson, 1979). Meanwhile, some simple, novel tunes played in the other ear. The tunes were not subliminal—the women could hear them easily. But with their attention selectively focused on the prose passage, the women were no more aware of the tunes than you normally are of your shoes. Thus, when they later heard these tunes interspersed among new ones, they could not recognize them (just as we cannot recall a conversation to which we paid no attention). Nevertheless, when asked to rate how much they liked each tune, they *preferred* the ones previously played. Their preferences revealed what their conscious memories could not.

Driven to distraction In one simulated driving experiment, students whose attention was diverted by cell-phone conversation (rather than merely listening to the radio) missed twice as many traffic signals as those not talking on the phone.

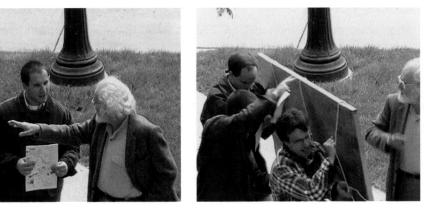

figure 6.1
Change blindness While a man (wearing glasses) provides directions to a construction worker, two experimenters rudely pass between them carrying a door. During this interruption, the original construction worker is replaced by a different person wearing different colored clothing. In this experiment by Daniel Simons and Daniel Levin, most people, focused on their direction giving, do not notice the switch.

Levels of Information Processing

Conscious awareness enables us to exert voluntary control and to communicate our mental states to others. Yet consciousness is but the tip of the information-processing iceberg. Research reported throughout this book reveals that we process much information outside our awareness. We register and react to stimuli we do not consciously perceive. We perform well-learned tasks automatically, as when keyboarding without attending to where the letters are. When we meet someone, we instantly and unconsciously react to their gender, age, and appearance, and then become aware of our response. We change our attitudes and reconstruct our memories with no awareness of doing so.

Unlike the processing of subconscious information, which occurs simultaneously on many parallel tracks, conscious processing takes place in sequence (serially). Consciousness is relatively slow and has limited capacity, but is skilled at solving novel problems. It is like a chief executive, whose many assistants automatically take care of routine business. Traveling a familiar route, your hands and feet do the driving while your mind engages in conversation. Running on automatic pilot allows consciousness—the mind's CEO—to monitor the whole system and deal with new challenges.

Novel tasks require our conscious attention. Try this: If you are right-handed, you can move your right foot in a smooth counterclockwise circle, and you can write the number 3 repeatedly with your right hand—but probably not at the same time. (If you are musically inclined, try something equally difficult: Tap a steady three times with your left hand while tapping four times with your right hand.) Both tasks require conscious attention, which can be in only one place at a time. If time is nature's way of keeping everything from happening at once, then consciousness is nature's way of keeping us from thinking and doing everything at once.

SLEEP AND DREAMS

Sleep—the irresistible tempter to whom we inevitably succumb. Sleep—the equalizer of presidents and peasants. Sleep—sweet, renewing, mysterious sleep. Sleep's age-old mysteries have intrigued us for centuries.

"I love to sleep. Do you? Isn't it great? It really is the best of both worlds. You get to be alive and unconscious."

Comedian Rita Rudner, 1993

Dolphins can sleep while moving.

Now, some of these mysteries are being solved. In laboratories throughout the world, thousands have slept attached to recording devices while others observe. By recording sleepers' brain waves and muscle movements, by observing and waking them from time to time, the sleep watchers glimpse things that a thousand years of common sense never told us. Perhaps you can anticipate some of their discoveries. Are the following statements true or false?

1. When people dream of performing some activity, their limbs often move in concert with the dream (page 194).
2. Sleepwalkers are acting out their dreams (pages 199–200).
3. Sleep experts recommend treating insomnia with an occasional sleeping pill (page 198).
4. Some people dream every night; others seldom dream (page 194).

All these statements (adapted from Palladino & Carducci, 1983) are false. Let's see why.

Biological Rhythms and Sleep

2. How do our age-old biological rhythms influence our daily functioning and our sleep and dreams?

Like the ocean, life has its rhythmic tides. Over varying time periods, our bodies fluctuate, and with them, our minds. Let's look more closely at two of those biological rhythms—our 24-hour biological clock and our 90-minute sleep cycle.

Circadian Rhythm

The rhythm of the day parallels the rhythm of life—from our waking to a new day's birth to our nightly return to what Shakespeare called "death's counterfeit." Our bodies roughly synchronize with the 24-hour cycle of day and night through a biological clock called the **circadian rhythm** (from the Latin *circa*, "about," and *dies*, "day"). Our body temperature rises as morning approaches, peaks during the day, dips for a time in early afternoon (when many people take siestas), and then begins to drop again before we go to sleep. Awake at 4:00 A.M., with a depressed body, we may fret over concerns: Does a lovers' spat signal a split? Does a child's moodiness mean more trouble ahead? By midday, our body energized, we fret less. Pulling an all-nighter, we feel groggiest about 4:00 A.M., and then a second wind after our normal wake-up time arrives.

Recent evidence suggests that thinking is sharpest and memory most accurate when people are at their daily peak in circadian arousal. Some of us are morning-loving "larks," others evening-energized "owls." With age, we tend to shift from being owls to larks. Most university students are "evening persons," report Cynthia May and Lynn Hasher (1998). Their performance typically improves across the day. Most older adults are "morning persons," with their performance declining as the day wears on. In retirement homes, all is quiet by mid-evening; in university dorms, the day is far from over.

A transcontinental flight disrupts our circadian rhythm and we experience jet lag, mainly because we are awake when our circadian rhythm cries "Sleep!" Studies in the laboratory and with shift workers reveal that bright light helps reset our biological clocks (Czeisler & others, 1986, 1989; Eastman & others, 1995). Thus, to speed the resetting of your biological clock after a long flight, spend the first day outdoors. Bright light in the morning facilitates awakening (and protects against depression). Bright light at night helps delay sleep (Oren & Terman, 1998).

Light tweaks the circadian clock by activating light-sensitive retinal proteins, which trigger signals to a brain region that controls the circadian clock (Lavie, 2001; Young, 2000). It does so partly by causing the brain's pineal gland to decrease (in the morning) or increase (in the evening) its production of sleep-inducing melatonin (**FIGURE 6.2**).

▶ **circadian [ser-KAY-dee-an] rhythm** the biological clock; regular bodily rhythms (for example, of temperature and wakefulness) that occur on a 24-hour cycle.

▶ **REM sleep** rapid eye movement sleep, a recurring sleep stage during which vivid dreams commonly occur. Also known as *paradoxical sleep*, because the muscles are relaxed (except for minor twitches) but other body systems are active.

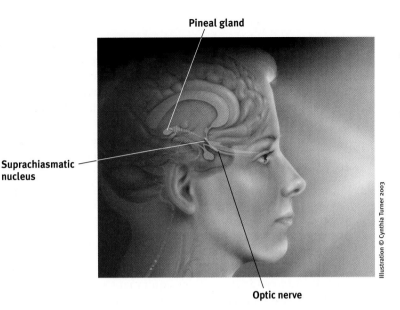

Pineal gland

Suprachiasmatic nucleus

Optic nerve

Illustration © Cynthia Turner 2003

figure 6.2
The biological clock Light striking the retina causes a neural center in the hypothalamus (the "suprachiasmatic nucleus") to alter the production of biologically active substances, such as melatonin production by the pineal gland.

We can reset our biological clocks by adjusting our sleep schedules. If we stay up late and sleep in on weekends, we may end up with "Sunday night insomnia" and "Monday morning blues." Those who sleep till noon on Sunday and then go to bed just 11 hours later in preparation for the new workweek often find sleep elusive. They are like New Yorkers whose biology is on California time, or like someone who has just flown east from Perth to Sydney.

Curiously—given that our ancestors' body clocks were attuned to the rising and setting sun of the 24-hour day—many of today's young adults adopt something closer to a 25-hour day, by staying up too late to get 8 hours of sleep. For this, we can thank (or blame) Thomas Edison, inventor of the light bulb. Being bathed in light, even in a cave, is like traveling one time zone west—it nudges our 24-hour biological clock back (Czeisler & others, 1999; Dement, 1999). This helps explain why rotating shift workers and store clerks servicing a 24/7 culture adapt better to progressively later shifts than to earlier ones, and why until our later years we must discipline ourselves to go to bed on time and force ourselves to get up. Most animals, too, when placed under unnatural constant illumination, exceed a 24-hour day. Artificial light delays sleep.

If our natural circadian rhythm were attuned to a 23-hour cycle, would we instead need to discipline ourselves to stay up later at night and sleep in longer in the morning? Do older adults, who typically prefer an earlier waking and bedtime than university students, have a shorter circadian rhythm?

Sleep Stages

3. What is the biological rhythm of our sleep?

There is also a biological rhythm during our sleep. About every 90 or 100 minutes we pass through a cycle of five distinct sleep stages. This elementary fact apparently was unknown until 8-year-old Armond Aserinsky went to bed one night in 1952. His father, Eugene, a University of Chicago graduate student, needed to test an electroencephalograph he had been repairing during the day (Aserinsky, 1988; Seligman & Yellen, 1987). He placed electrodes near Armond's eyes to record the rolling eye movements believed to occur during sleep. Before long, the machine went wild, tracing deep zigzags on the graph paper. Aserinsky thought the machine was still broken. But as the night proceeded, the activity periodically recurred. This indicated, Aserinsky finally realized, fast, jerky eye movements accompanied by energetic brain activity. When he awakened Armond during one such episode, the boy reported he was having a dream. Aserinsky had discovered what we now know as **REM sleep** (rapid eye movement sleep).

To find out if similar cycles occur during adult sleep, Nathaniel Kleitman (1960) and Aserinsky pioneered procedures that have now been used with thousands of volunteers. To appreciate both their methods and findings, imagine yourself as a

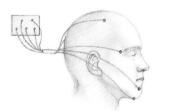

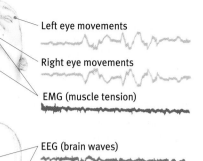

Left eye movements

Right eye movements

EMG (muscle tension)

EEG (brain waves)

figure 6.3
Measuring sleep activity
Sleep researchers measure brain-wave activity, eye movements, and muscle tension by electrodes that pick up weak electrical signals from the brain, eye, and facial muscles. (From Dement, 1978.)

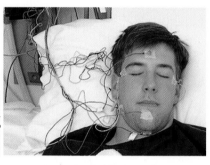

Can you recall the moment you fell asleep last night? Or, at best, your last moments of waking?

participant. As the hour grows late, you begin to fight sleepiness and yawn in response to reduced brain metabolism. Yawning stretches your neck muscles and increases your heart rate, which increases your alertness (Moorcroft, 2003). When you are ready for bed, the researcher glues electrodes to your scalp (to detect your brain waves), just outside the corners of your eyes (to detect eye movements), and on your chin (to detect muscle tension) (**FIGURE 6.3**). Other devices allow the researcher to record your heart rate, your respiration rate, and the degree of your genital arousal.

When you are in bed with your eyes closed, the researcher in the next room sees on the EEG the relatively slow **alpha waves** of your awake but relaxed state (**FIGURE 6.4**). As you adapt to all this equipment and grow tired, you slip into **sleep**. Sleep is a state that we do not know we are in until we leave it. Our dive into sleep—marked by the slowed breathing and the irregular brain waves of Stage 1—happens in an unrecognized moment (**FIGURE 6.5**).

Sleep researcher William Dement (1999) observed the moment the perceptual door between the brain and outside world slammed shut in one of his 15,000 subjects. Dement asked this sleep-deprived young man, lying on his back with eyelids taped open, to press a button every time a strobe light flashed in his eyes (averaging about every 6 seconds). After a few minutes the subject missed one. Asked why, he said, "Because there was no flash." But there was a flash—which he missed because (as his brain activity revealed) he had fallen asleep for two seconds. Unaware that he had done so, he had missed not only the flash 6 inches from his nose but also the abrupt moment of his entry into sleep.

During this brief Stage 1 sleep you may experience fantastic images, resembling **hallucinations**—sensory experiences that occur without a sensory stimulus. You may have a sensation of falling (at which moment your body may suddenly jerk) or of floating weightlessly. Such "hypnogogic" sensations may later become incorporated into memories. People who claim to have been abducted by aliens—often shortly after getting in bed—commonly recall being floated off their beds.

Soon, you relax more deeply and begin about 20 minutes of Stage 2 sleep, characterized by the periodic appearance of *sleep spindles*—bursts of rapid, rhythmic brain-wave activity. Although you can still be awakened without too much difficulty during this phase, you are now clearly asleep. Sleeptalking—usually garbled or nonsensical—can occur during this or any other sleep stage (Mahowald & Ettinger, 1990).

Then for the next few minutes you go through the transitional Stage 3 to the deep sleep of Stage 4. First in Stage 3, and increasingly in Stage 4, your brain emits large, slow **delta waves**. These stages together are called *slow-wave sleep*. They last for about 30 minutes, during which you are hard to awaken. Curiously, it is at

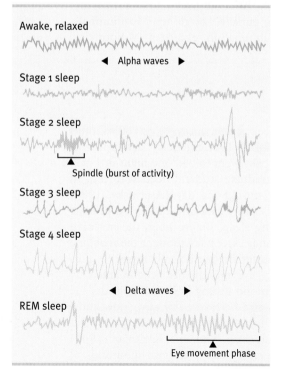

Awake, relaxed

◀ Alpha waves ▶

Stage 1 sleep

Stage 2 sleep

Spindle (burst of activity)

Stage 3 sleep

Stage 4 sleep

◀ Delta waves ▶

REM sleep

Eye movement phase

figure 6.4
Brain waves and sleep stages The regular alpha waves of an awake, relaxed state are quite different from the slower, larger delta waves of deep Stage 4 sleep. Although the rapid REM sleep waves resemble the near-waking Stage 1 sleep waves, the body is more aroused during REM sleep than during Stage 1 sleep. (From Dement, 1978.)

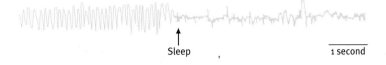

figure 6.5
The moment of sleep We seem unaware of the moment we fall into sleep, but someone eavesdropping on our brain waves could tell. (From Dement, 1999.)

the end of the deep sleep of Stage 4 that children may wet the bed or begin walking in their sleep. About 20 percent of 3- to 12-year-olds have at least one episode of sleepwalking, usually lasting 2 to 10 minutes; some 5 percent have repeated episodes (Giles & others, 1994).

Even when you are deeply asleep, your brain somehow processes the meaning of certain stimuli. You move around on your bed, but you manage not to fall out of it. If you sleep with your babies, you will not roll over and suffocate them (assuming you are not intoxicated). The occasional roar of passing vehicles may leave deep sleep undisturbed, but the cry from a baby's nursery quickly interrupts it. So does the sound of your name—a stimulus our selective attention is ever alert for. EEG recordings confirm that the brain's auditory cortex responds to sound stimuli even during sleep (Kutas, 1990). All this reminds us of one of this book's basic lessons: *We process most information outside our conscious awareness.*

REM Sleep

About an hour after you first fall asleep, a strange thing happens. Rather than continuing in deep slumber, you ascend from your initial sleep dive. Returning through Stage 3 and Stage 2 (where you spend about half your night), you enter the most intriguing sleep phase of all—REM sleep (**Figure 6.6**). For about 10 minutes, your brain waves become rapid and saw-toothed, more like those of the nearly awake Stage 1 sleep. But unlike Stage 1 sleep, during REM sleep your heart rate rises, your breathing becomes rapid and irregular, and every half-minute or so your eyes dart around in a momentary burst of activity behind closed lids. Because anyone watching a sleeper's eyes can notice these REM bursts, it is amazing that science was ignorant of REM sleep until 1952.

Except during very scary dreams, your genitals become aroused during REM sleep, and you have an erection or increased vaginal lubrication and clitoral engorgement, regardless of whether the dream's content is sexual (Karacan &

▶ **alpha waves** the relatively slow brain waves of a relaxed, awake state.

▶ **sleep** periodic, natural, reversible loss of consciousness—as distinct from unconsciousness resulting from a coma, general anesthesia, or hibernation. (Adapted from Dement, 1999.)

▶ **hallucinations** false sensory experiences, such as seeing something in the absence of an external visual stimulus.

▶ **delta waves** the large, slow brain waves associated with deep sleep.

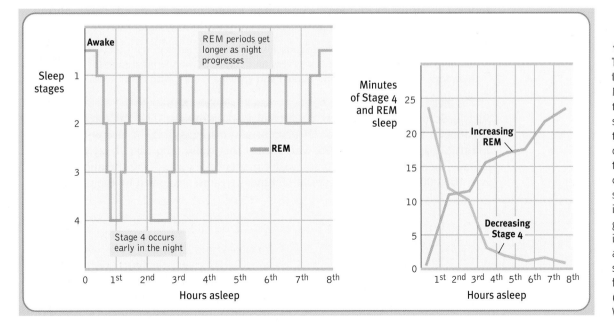

figure 6.6
The stages in a typical night's sleep Most people pass through the five-stage sleep cycle several times, with the periods of Stage 4 sleep and then Stage 3 sleep diminishing and REM sleep periods increasing in duration. The second graph plots this increasing REM sleep and decreasing deep sleep based on data from 30 young adults. (From Cartwright, 1978; Webb, 1992.)

Some sleep deeply, some not
The fluctuating sleep cycle enables safe sleep for these soldiers on the battlefield. One benefit of communal sleeping is that someone will probably be awake or easily roused in the event of a threat during the night.

"Boy are my eyes tired! I had REM sleep all night long."

Question: *Does eating spicy foods cause one to dream more?*
Answer: *Any food that causes you to awaken more increases your chance of recalling a dream (Moorcroft, 2003).*

People rarely snore during dreams. When REM starts, snoring stops.

others, 1966). The phenomenon has been studied mostly in men, from whom measurements are more easily recorded. In young men, sleep-related erections outlast REM periods, lasting 30 to 45 minutes on average (Karacan & others, 1983; Schiavi & Schreiner-Engel, 1988). A typical 25-year-old man therefore has an erection during nearly half his night's sleep, a 65-year-old man for one-quarter. Many men troubled by "erectile disorder" (impotence) have morning erections, suggesting that the problem is not between their legs.

Although your brain's motor cortex is active during REM sleep, your brainstem blocks its messages, leaving your muscles relaxed—so relaxed that, except for an occasional finger, toe, or facial twitch, you are essentially paralyzed. Moreover, you cannot easily be awakened. Thus, REM sleep is sometimes called *paradoxical* sleep; the body is internally aroused and externally calm.

Even more intriguing than the paradoxical nature of REM sleep is what the rapid eye movements announce: the beginning of a dream. Even those who claim they never dream will, more than 80 percent of the time, recall a dream after being awakened during REM sleep. Unlike the fleeting images of Stage 1 sleep, REM sleep dreams are often emotional and usually storylike—but never acted out, thanks to REM's protective paralysis. People occasionally recall dreams when awakened from stages other than REM sleep, but these dreams usually contain a thought ("I was thinking about my exam today") or a single vague image ("I was trying to borrow something from someone"). REM dreams are more richly hallucinatory.

My husband and I were at some friends' house, but our friends weren't there. Their TV had been left on, but otherwise it was very quiet. After we wandered around for a while, their dogs finally noticed us and barked and growled loudly, with bared teeth.

The sleep cycle repeats itself about every 90 minutes. As the night wears on, deep Stage 4 sleep gets progressively briefer and then disappears. The REM sleep period gets longer. By morning, 20 to 25 percent of our average night's sleep—some 100 minutes—has been REM sleep. This means that those who say, "I rarely dream" actually spend about 600 hours a year experiencing some 1500 dreams, or more than 100,000 dreams over a typical lifetime—dreams swallowed by the night.

Why Do We Sleep?

4. How does sleep loss affect us? What is sleep's function?

The idea that "everyone needs 8 hours of sleep" is not true. Newborns spend nearly two-thirds of their day asleep, most adults no more than one-third. Age-related differences in average time spent sleeping are rivaled by differences in the normal amount of sleep among individuals at any age. Some people thrive with fewer than 6 hours of sleep per night; others regularly sleep 9 hours or more. Sleep patterns may be genetically influenced. When Wilse Webb and Scott Campbell (1983) checked the pattern and duration of sleep among fraternal and identical twins, only the identical twins were strikingly similar.

Sleep patterns are also culturally influenced. Because of modern light bulbs, shift work, and social diversions, people in industrialized nations are able to sleep less than they did a century ago. People who would have gone to bed at 9:00 P.M. are now up until 11:00 P.M. Thomas Edison (1948, pp. 52, 178) was pleased to accept credit for this. For him, lost sleep meant more time and opportunity:

> When I went through Switzerland in a motor-car, so that I could visit little towns and villages, I noted the effect of artificial light on the inhabitants. Where water power and electric light had been developed, everyone seemed normally intelligent. When these appliances did not exist, and the natives went to bed with the chickens, staying there till daylight, they were far less intelligent.

Allowed to sleep unhindered, most humans will sleep at least 9 hours a night, reports Stanley Coren (1996). With that much sleep, we do not become groggy. We awake refreshed, sustain better moods, and perform more efficient and accurate work than do those who get less sleep. With a succession of 5-hour nights, however, we accumulate sleep debt that is not paid off by one 10-hour sleep—which explains why we can feel sleepy even after a long sleep. "The brain keeps an accurate count of sleep debt for at least two weeks," says William Dement (1999, p. 64). Deprived of sleep, we also begin to feel terrible, as our bodies yearn for sleep. Try to stay awake and eventually we will lose. In the tiredness battle, sleep always wins.

Obviously, then, we need sleep. Sleep commands roughly one-third of our lives—some 25 years, on average. But why? It seems an easy question to answer: Just keep people awake for several days and note how they deteriorate. If you were a volunteer in such an experiment, how do you think it would affect your body and mind?

Of course, you would become terribly drowsy at times—especially during the hours when your biological clock programs you to sleep. But could a lack of sleep physically damage you? Would it noticeably alter your biochemistry or body organs? Would you become emotionally disturbed? Mentally disoriented?

The Effects of Sleep Loss

A major effect of lessened sleep is not only sleepiness but a general malaise (Mikulincer & others, 1989). People today more than ever suffer from sleep patterns that thwart their having an energized feeling of well-being. Four in 10 young adults say they are sleepy at work two or more days a week (National Sleep Foundation, 2000). Teenagers typically need 8 or 9 hours sleep, but they now average nearly 2 hours less sleep a night than their counterparts of 80 years ago (Holden, 1993; Maas, 1999). Many fill this need by using their first class for an early siesta and after-lunch study hall for a slumber party. Even when awake, they often function below their peak.

At Stanford University, William Dement (1997) reports, 80 percent of students are "dangerously sleep deprived." Such individuals "are at high risk for some sort of accident. . . . Sleep deprivation [entails] difficulty studying, diminished productivity, tendency to make mistakes, irritability, fatigue." A large sleep debt "makes you stupid," says Dement (1999, p. 231). But let's put this positively: To manage your life with enough sleep to awaken naturally and well rested is to be more alert, productive, healthy, and happy. For teens, that's easier said than done. The one who staggers glumly out of bed in response to an unwelcome alarm, yawns through morning classes, and feels half-depressed much of the day may be energized at 11 P.M. and mindless of the next day's looming sleep deficit (Carskadon, 2002).

In experiments, the U.S. Navy and the National Institutes of Health have paid volunteers to spend 14 hours daily in bed for at least a week. For the first few days, the volunteers in both experiments averaged 12 hours sleep a day or more, apparently paying off a sleep debt that averaged 25 to 30 hours. That accomplished, they then settled back to 7.5 to 9 hours sleep a night and, with no sleep

Gallup 2001 poll:
"Usually, how many hours sleep do you get at night?"

5 or less	*16%*
6	*27*
7	*28*
8	*28*

2001 average = 6.7 hours
1942 average = 7.6 hours

"Tiger Woods said that one of the best things about his choice to leave Stanford for the professional golf circuit was that he could now get enough sleep."

Stanford sleep researcher William Dement, 1997

In a 2001 Gallup poll, 61 percent of men, but only 47 percent of women, said they got enough sleep.

*To test whether you are one of the many sleep-deprived students, see **Table 6.1**.*

In 1989, Michael Doucette was named America's Safest Driving Teen. In 1990, while driving home from college, he fell asleep at the wheel and collided with an oncoming car, killing both himself and the other driver. Michael's driving instructor later acknowledged never having mentioned sleep deprivation and drowsy driving (Dement, 1999).

"Drowsiness is red alert!"

William Dement, The Promise of Sleep, 1999

debt, felt energized and happier. "What this means to me," reflected Dement (1999, p. 72) "is that millions of us are living a less than optimal life and performing at a less than optimal level, impaired by an amount of sleep debt that we're not even aware we carry."

As a demonstration of the costs of sleep deprivation, Stanley Coren capitalized on a naturally occurring experiment that manipulates sleep length—the "spring forward" to daylight time and "fall backward" to standard time. Searching millions of records, he found that in both Canada and the United States, accidents increase immediately after the shortened sleep associated with the spring time change. In Canada, for example, traffic accidents during 1991 and 1992 were 7 percent higher on the Monday after the spring time change than on the Monday before, and they were 7 percent *lower* on the Monday following the extra sleep bestowed by the fall time change (**Figure 6.7**).

Sleep deprivation can also be devastating for driving and piloting. Some 30 percent of Australian highway deaths occur when drivers fall asleep on long, monotonous roads (Maas, 1999). Driver fatigue also contributes to an estimated 20 percent of American traffic accidents (Brody, 2002). "Rest. That's what I need is rest," said Eastern Airlines Captain James Reeves to the control tower on a September 1974 morning—30 minutes before crashing his airliner at low altitude, killing the crew and all 68 passengers (Moorcroft, 1993). Consider also the *Exxon Valdez* oil spill; Union Carbide's Bhopal, India, disaster; and the Three Mile Island and Chernobyl nuclear accidents—they all occurred after midnight, when operators in charge were likely to be drowsiest. Severely sleep-deprived, the *Exxon Valdez* mate at the helm was unresponsive to clear signals to turn his vessel back into the shipping lanes.

Other effects of sleep loss are subtle. One such effect is suppression of the disease-fighting immune system (Beardsley, 1996; Irwin & others, 1994). Sleep deprivation suppresses immune cells that fight off viral infections and cancer, which helps explain why people who sleep 7 to 8 hours a night tend to outlive those who are chronically sleep deprived (Dement, 1999). When infections do set in, we typically sleep more, boosting our immune cells. Chronic sleep debt also alters metabolic and hormonal functioning in ways that mimic aging and are conducive to obesity, hypertension, and memory impairment (Spiegel & others, 1999). Other effects include irritability, slowed performance, and impaired creativity, concentration, and communication (Harrison & Horne, 2000). When sleepy frontal lobes confront an unexpected situation, misfortune often results.

figure 6.7
Traffic accidents and time changes
On the Monday after the spring time change, when people lose sleep, accidents increased as compared with the Monday before. In the fall, accidents are increased because of greater snow, ice, and darkness, but they diminish after the time change. (Adapted from Coren, 1996.)

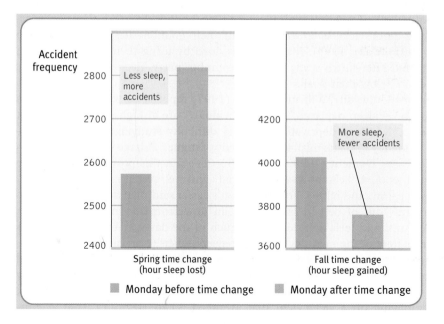

table 6.1 Are You Sleep Deprived?

Cornell University psychologist James Maas reports that most college students suffer the consequences of sleeping less than they should. To see if you are in that group, answer the following true-false questions:

True False

☐ ☐ 1. I need an alarm clock in order to wake up at the appropriate time.
☐ ☐ 2. It's a struggle for me to get out of bed in the morning.
☐ ☐ 3. Weekday mornings I hit the snooze bar several times to get more sleep.
☐ ☐ 4. I feel tired, irritable, and stressed out during the week.
☐ ☐ 5. I have trouble concentrating and remembering.
☐ ☐ 6. I feel slow with critical thinking, problem solving, and being creative.
☐ ☐ 7. I often fall asleep watching TV.
☐ ☐ 8. I often fall asleep in boring meetings or lectures or in warm rooms.
☐ ☐ 9. I often fall asleep after heavy meals or after a low dose of alcohol.
☐ ☐ 10. I often fall asleep while relaxing after dinner.
☐ ☐ 11. I often fall asleep within five minutes of getting into bed.
☐ ☐ 12. I often feel drowsy while driving.
☐ ☐ 13. I often sleep extra hours on weekend mornings.
☐ ☐ 14. I often need a nap to get through the day.
☐ ☐ 15. I have dark circles around my eyes.

If you answered "true" to three or more items, you probably are not getting enough sleep. To determine your sleep needs, Maas recommends that you "go to bed 15 minutes earlier than usual every night for the next week—and continue this practice by adding 15 more minutes each week—until you wake without an alarm clock and feel alert all day."

(Quiz reprinted with permission from James B. Maas, Power sleep: The revolutionary program that prepares your mind and body for peak performance *[New York: HarperCollins, 1999].)*

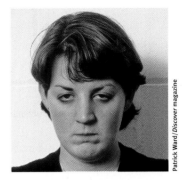

Sleepless and suffering This fatigued, sleep-deprived person may also experience a depressed immune system, impaired concentration, and greater vulnerability to accidents.

Sleep Theories

So nature charges us for our sleep debt. But why do we have this need for sleep? We have very few answers, but sleep may have evolved for three reasons: First, sleep *protects.* When darkness precluded our ancestors' hunting and food gathering and made travel treacherous, they were better off asleep in a cave, out of harm's way. Walk around a strange room in the dark and you will crash into things. Imagine your distant ancestors trying to navigate around rocks and cliffs at night. Surely those who didn't attempt to do so were more likely to leave descendants. We sleep as suits our ecological niche. Animals with the most need to graze and the least ability to hide tend to sleep less. Elephants and horses sleep 3 to 4 hours a day, gorillas 12 hours, and cats 14 hours. For bats and eastern chipmunks, both of which sleep 20 hours, to live is hardly more than to eat and to sleep (Moorcroft, 2003).

Second, sleep helps us recuperate. It helps *restore* body tissues, especially those of the brain. During the time we are awake, our active brain produces the chemical adenosine, which inhibits certain neurons, making us sleepy. (Caffeine blocks adenosine's activity.) During sleep, adenosine concentration declines (Porkka-Heiskanen & others, 1997). As we sleep, our brain is nevertheless active, repairing and reorganizing itself and consolidating memories. Sleep is food for the brain.

Sleep may also play a role in the *growth* process. During deep sleep, the pituitary gland releases a growth hormone. As adults grow older, they release less of this hormone, and they spend less time in deep sleep (Pekkanen, 1982). These physiological discoveries are beginning to solve the ongoing riddle of sleep.

"Sleep faster, we need the pillows."
Yiddish proverb

"Corduroy pillows make headlines."
Anonymous

Sleep Disorders

5. What are the major sleep disorders?

No matter what their normal need for sleep, some 10 to 15 percent of adults complain of **insomnia**—persistent problems in falling or staying asleep. True insomnia is not the occasional inability to sleep that we experience when anxious or excited. For any stressed organism, being vigilant is natural and adaptive. Americans who report frequently experiencing stress average nearly an hour less sleep a night than do those rarely stressed (Moore, 2002). A personal conflict during the day often means a fitful sleep that night (Brisette & Cohen, 2002). Moreover, from middle age on, sleep is seldom uninterrupted. Being occasionally awakened becomes the norm, not something to fret over or treat with medication.

Some people fret unnecessarily about their sleep (Coren, 1996). In laboratory studies, insomnia complainers do get less sleep than others, but they typically overestimate—by about double—how long it took them to fall asleep. They also underestimate by nearly half how long they actually slept. Even if we have been awake only an hour or two, we may *think* we have had very little sleep, because it's the waking part we remember. When researchers awaken people repeatedly during the night, some recall having slept soundly.

The most common quick fixes for true insomnia, sleeping pills and alcohol, can aggravate the problem. Both reduce REM sleep and can leave a person with next-day blahs. Relying on such, one comes to need bigger doses to get an effect. Then when the drug is discontinued, the insomnia can worsen. Scientists are searching for natural chemicals that are abundant during sleep, hoping they might be synthesized as a sleep aid without side effects. In the meantime, sleep experts offer other natural alternatives:

- Relax before bedtime, using dimmer light.
- Avoid caffeine (this includes chocolate) after late afternoon and avoid rich foods before bedtime. A glass of milk may help. (Milk provides raw materials for the manufacture of serotonin, a neurotransmitter that facilitates sleep.)
- Sleep on a regular schedule (rise at the same time even after a restless night) and avoid naps. A regular sleep schedule boosts daytime alertness, too, as shown in an experiment in which University of Arizona students slept 7.5 hours a night on either a varying or consistent schedule (Manber & others, 1996).
- Exercise regularly but not in the late evening (late afternoon is best).
- Reassure yourself that a temporary loss of sleep causes no great harm, certainly nothing worth losing sleep over. "Sleep is like love or happiness," notes Wilse Webb (1992, p. 170). "If you pursue it too ardently it will elude you."
- If nothing else works, aim for less sleep; go to bed later or get up earlier.

Rarer but also more troublesome than insomnia are the sleep disorders narcolepsy and sleep apnea. People who suffer **narcolepsy** (from *narco*, "numbness,"

"The lion and the lamb shall lie down together, but the lamb will not be very sleepy."

Woody Allen, in the movie Love and Death, 1975

"In 1757 Benjamin Franklin gave us the axiom, 'Early to bed, early to rise, makes a man healthy, wealthy, and wise.' It would be more accurate to say 'consistently to bed and consistently to rise . . .'"

James B. Maas, Power Sleep, 1999

Stress robs sleep Urban police officers, especially those under stress, report poorer sleep quality and less sleep than average (Neylan & others, 2002).

and *lepsy*, "seizure") experience periodic, overwhelming sleepiness. This usually lasts less than 5 minutes, but sometimes occurs at the most inopportune times, perhaps just after taking a terrific swing at a softball or when laughing loudly, shouting angrily, or having sex (Dement, 1978, 1999). In severe cases, the person may collapse directly into a brief period of REM sleep, with its accompanying loss of muscular tension.

Those who suffer from narcolepsy—1 in 2000 people, estimates the Stanford University Center for Narcolepsy (2002)—must live with extra caution. As a traffic menace, "snoozing is second only to boozing," says the American Sleep Disorders Association, and those with narcolepsy are especially at risk (Aldrich, 1989). At the century's end, one team of researchers discovered a gene causing narcolepsy in dogs (Lin & others, 1999). Then researchers discovered the more immediate cause of narcolepsy—a relative absence of a hypothalamic neural center that produces a neurotransmitter called hypocretin (Taheri & others, 2002; Thannickal & others, 2000). Narcolepsy, it is now clear, is a brain disease; it is not just "in your mind." And this gives hope that narcolepsy might be effectively relieved in humans, as it already has been in dogs, by a drug that mimics the missing hypocretin (Siegel, 2000).

The National Institutes of Health reports that 1 in 20 people (mostly overweight men) suffer from **sleep apnea**—a disorder that was unknown before modern sleep research. They intermittently stop breathing during sleep. (*Apnea* means "with no breath.") After an airless minute or so, decreased blood oxygen arouses the sleeper to awaken and snort in air for a few seconds. The process can repeat more than 400 times a night, depriving the person of slow-wave sleep. Apart from complaints of

Archivo Iconografico, S.A./Corbis

sleepiness and irritability during the day—and their mates' complaints about their loud "snoring"—apnea sufferers are often unaware of their disorder. Sleep apnea leaves millions of people tired and sometimes irritable during the day and therefore, like those who suffer narcolepsy, at increased risk of traffic accidents (Teran-Santos & others, 1999). As the number of obese people increases, so does sleep apnea. Anyone who snores at night, who feels tired during the day, and who possibly has high blood pressure as well, should be checked for apnea (Dement, 1999).

A third sleep disorder—**night terrors**—targets mostly children. The person might sit up or walk around, talk incoherently, experience a doubling of heart and breathing rates, and appear terrified (Hartmann, 1981). The night-terror sufferer seldom wakes up fully during the episode and recalls little or nothing the next morning—at most, a fleeting, frightening image. Night terrors are not nightmares (which, like other dreams, typically occur during early morning REM sleep). As with sleepwalking, night terrors usually occur during the first few hours of Stage 4. Family members often try to awaken and reassure the person with night terrors.

Children also are most prone to sleepwalking and sleeptalking, disorders that run in families. Finnish twin studies reveal that occasional childhood sleepwalking occurs for about one-third of those with a sleepwalking fraternal twin and half of those with a sleepwalking identical twin. The same is true for sleeptalking (Hublin & others, 1997, 1998). Sleepwalking is usually harmless and

Dan McCoy/Rainbow

▶ **insomnia** recurring problems in falling or staying asleep.

▶ **narcolepsy** a sleep disorder characterized by uncontrollable sleep attacks. The sufferer may lapse directly into REM sleep, often at inopportune times.

▶ **sleep apnea** a sleep disorder characterized by temporary cessations of breathing during sleep and consequent momentary reawakenings.

▶ **night terrors** a sleep disorder characterized by high arousal and an appearance of being terrified; unlike nightmares, night terrors occur during Stage 4 sleep, within 2 or 3 hours of falling asleep, and are seldom remembered.

Imagine observing a person with narcolepsy in medieval times. Might such symptoms and their associated hallucinations have seemed like demon possession?

Did Brahms need his own lullabies?
Cranky, overweight, and nap prone, Johannes Brahms exhibited common symptoms of sleep apnea (Margolis, 2000).

Night terrors and nightmares Night terrors occur within 2 or 3 hours of falling asleep, during Stage 4 sleep. Nightmares occur toward morning, during REM sleep. (From Hartmann, 1984.)

unrecalled the next morning. Sleepwalkers typically return to bed on their own or are guided there by a family member. Young children, who have the deepest and lengthiest Stage 4 sleep, are the most likely to experience both night terrors and sleepwalking. As we grow older and deep Stage 4 sleep diminishes, so do night terrors and sleepwalking. After age 40, sleepwalking is rare.

rehearse it!

3. Our body temperature tends to rise and fall in sync with a biological clock, which is referred to as
   a. the circadian rhythm.
   b. narcolepsy.
   c. REM sleep.
   d. hypnogogic sensations.

4. Stage 1 sleep is a twilight zone of light sleep. During Stage 1 sleep, a person is most likely to experience
   a. sleep spindles.
   b. hallucinations.
   c. night terrors or nightmares.
   d. rapid eye movements.

5. In the deepest stage of sleep—surprisingly, the stage when people sleepwalk—the brain emits large, slow delta waves. This deep stage of sleep is called

   a. Stage 2.
   b. Stage 4.
   c. REM sleep.
   d. paradoxical sleep.

6. An electroencephalograph shows that during sleep we pass through a cycle of five stages, each with characteristic brain waves. As the night progresses, the REM stage
   a. gradually disappears.
   b. becomes briefer and briefer.
   c. remains about the same.
   d. becomes progressively longer.

7. Various theories have been proposed to explain why we need sleep. They include all but which of the following?
   a. Sleep has survival value.
   b. Sleep helps us recuperate.
   c. Sleep rests the eyes.

   d. Sleep plays a role in the growth process.

8. Two relatively rare sleep disorders are narcolepsy and sleep apnea. With narcolepsy, the person _____; with sleep apnea, the person _____.
   a. has persistent problems falling asleep; experiences a doubling of heart and breathing rates
   b. experiences a doubling of heart and breathing rates; has persistent problems falling asleep
   c. intermittently stops breathing; suffers periodic, overwhelming sleepiness
   d. suffers periodic, overwhelming sleepiness; intermittently stops breathing

Answers can be found in Appendix C.

Dreams

Discovering the link between REM sleep and dreaming opened a new era in dream research. Instead of relying on someone's hazy recall hours or days after having a dream, researchers could catch dreams as they happened. They could awaken people during or within 3 minutes after a REM sleep period and hear a vivid account.

What We Dream

6. What do we dream?

"I do not believe that I am now dreaming, but I cannot prove that I am not."

Philosopher Bertrand Russell (1872–1970)

Would you suppose that people dream if blind from birth? Studies of blind people in France, Hungary, Egypt, and the United States all found them dreaming of using their nonvisual senses—hearing, touching, smelling, tasting (Buquet, 1988; Taha, 1972; Vekassy, 1977).

A popular sleep myth: If you dream you are falling and hit the ground (or if you dream of dying), you die. Unfortunately, those who could confirm these ideas are not around to do so. Some people, however, have had such dreams and are alive to report them.

REM dreams—"hallucinations of the sleeping mind"—are vivid, emotional, and bizarre. Several times a night, you are the creator and producer of a surrealistic mental movie in which events frequently occur in a jumbled sequence, scenes change suddenly, people appear and disappear, and physical laws, such as gravity, may be violated. Yet, **dreams** are so vivid we may confuse them with reality. Awakening from a nightmare, a 4-year-old may complain of a bear in the house.

Occasionally, we may be sufficiently aware during a dream to wonder whether we are, in fact, dreaming. When experiencing such *lucid dreams*, some people are able to test their state of consciousness. If they can perform some absurd act, such as floating in the air, then they know they are dreaming.

We spend six years of our life in dreams, many of which are anything but sweet. For both women and men, 8 in 10 dreams are marked by negative emotions (Domhoff, 1999). People commonly dream of repeatedly failing in an attempt to do something; of being attacked, pursued, or rejected; or of experiencing misfortune (Hall & others, 1982). When awakened during REM sleep, people report dreams with sexual imagery less often than you might think. In one study, only 1 in 10 dreams among young men and 1 in 30 among young women had sexual overtones (Domhoff, 1996.) More commonly, we dream of events in our daily lives, a meeting at work, taking an exam, relating to a family member or friend.

MAXINE

The story line of our dreams—what Sigmund Freud called their **manifest content**—sometimes incorporates traces of previous days' experiences and pre-occupations (De Koninck, 2000):

- Robert Stickgold and his colleagues (2000) had people play the computer game "Tetris" for seven hours and then repeatedly awakened them during their first hour of sleep; three-fourths reported experiencing images of the game's falling blocks.
- After suffering a trauma, people commonly report nightmares.
- People in hunter-gatherer societies often dream of animals; urban Japanese rarely do (Mestel, 1997).

The sensory stimuli of our sleeping environment may also intrude. A particular odor or the telephone's ringing may be instantly and ingeniously woven into the dream story. In one experiment, William Dement and Edward Wolpert (1958) lightly sprayed cold water on dreamers' faces. Compared with sleepers who did not get the cold-water treatment, these sleepers were more likely to dream about water—about a waterfall, a leaky roof, or even about being sprayed by someone. Even while in REM sleep, focused on internal stimuli, we maintain some awareness of changes in our external environment.

So, could we learn a foreign language by listening to tapes while we sleep? If only it were so easy. While sleeping we can learn to associate a sound with a mild electric shock (and to react to the sound accordingly). But we do not remember taped information played while we are soundly asleep (Eich, 1990; Wyatt & Bootzin, 1994). In fact, anything that happens during the 5 minutes just before we fall asleep is typically lost from memory (Roth & others, 1988). This explains why sleep apnea patients, who repeatedly awaken with a gasp and then immediately fall back to sleep, do not recall the episodes. It also explains why dreams that momentarily awaken us are mostly forgotten by morning. To remember a dream, get up and stay awake for a few minutes.

Why We Dream

7. What is the function of dreams?

In his landmark book *The Interpretation of Dreams*, published in 1900, Freud offered "the most valuable of all the discoveries it has been my good fortune to make." He argued that by fulfilling wishes, a dream provides a psychic safety valve that discharges otherwise unacceptable feelings. According to Freud, a dream's manifest content is a censored, symbolic version of its **latent content**, which consists of unconscious drives and wishes that would be threatening if expressed directly. Although most dreams have no overt sexual imagery, Freud nevertheless believed that most adult dreams can be "traced back by analysis to *erotic wishes*." In Freud's view, a gun, for example, might be a disguised representation of a penis.

"For what one has dwelt on by day, these things are seen in visions of the night."

Menander of Athens (342–292 B.C.), Fragments

▶ **dream** a sequence of images, emotions, and thoughts passing through a sleeping person's mind. Dreams are notable for their hallucinatory imagery, discontinuities, and incongruities, and for the dreamer's delusional acceptance of the content and later difficulties remembering it.

▶ **manifest content** according to Freud, the remembered story line of a dream (as distinct from its latent content).

▶ **latent content** according to Freud, the underlying meaning of a dream (as distinct from its manifest content). Freud believed that a dream's latent content functions as a safety valve.

Freud considered dreams the key to understanding our inner conflicts. However, his critics say it is time to wake up from Freud's dream theory, which actually is a scientific nightmare. Some contend that even if dreams are symbolic, they could be interpreted any way one wished. Others maintain that dreams hide nothing. A dream about a gun is a dream about a gun. Legend has it that even Freud, who loved to smoke cigars, remarked that "sometimes, a cigar is just a cigar."

Freud's wish-fulfillment theory of dreams has in large part given way to other theories. Researchers who see dreams as *information processing* believe that dreams may help sift, sort, and fix the day's experiences in our memory. We have known for some time that REM sleep facilitates memory (McGrath & Cohen, 1978). In experiments, people have heard unusual phrases or learned to find hidden visual images before bedtime. If awakened every time they began REM sleep, they remembered less the next morning than if awakened during other sleep stages (Empson & Clarke, 1970; Karni & Sagi, 1994). Moreover, while people generally improved on a learned task the next day after a night of memory consolidation, those deprived of both slow-wave and REM sleep didn't do as well (even after two nights of recovery sleep) as those who slept on their new learning (Stickgold & others, 2000, 2001).

Other studies confirm that we sleep, in part, to remember. The brain regions that buzz as rats learn to navigate a maze, or as people learn to perform a visual-discrimination task, buzz again later during REM sleep (Louie & Wilson, 2001; Maquet, 2001). So precise were the activity patterns that the scientists could tell where in the maze the rat would be if awake. A night of solid sleep (and dreaming) does, it seems, have an important place in our lives.

The benefits to be gained from sleeping on learning is important news for teens and college students, researcher Robert Stickgold (2000) believes. Many students suffer from a kind of sleep bulimia, with binge sleeping on the weekend. "But if you don't get good sleep and enough sleep after you learn new stuff, you won't integrate it effectively into your memories," Stickgold notes. That may help explain why high school students with high grades (A and B averages) average 25 minutes more sleep a night and go to bed 40 minutes earlier than their C, D, and F classmates (Wolfson & Carskadon, 1998).

Another explanation of why we dream proposes that dreams may also serve a *physiological function.* Perhaps dreams—or the associated brain activity of REM sleep—provide the sleeping brain with periodic stimulation. As you may recall from Chapter 3, stimulating experiences develop and preserve the brain's neural pathways. This theory makes sense from a developmental point of view. Infants, whose neural networks are fast developing, spend a great deal of time in REM sleep (**FIGURE 6.8**).

"When people interpret [a dream] as if it were meaningful and then sell those interpretations, it's quackery."

Sleep researcher J. Allan Hobson (1995)

Question: *Given (1) how sleep consolidates memory and (2) the results of a 2001 Gallup Poll in which 79 percent of teens wished for more sleep, would you favor American secondary schools starting around 9 A.M. as do many secondary schools in other countries, such as Great Britain?*

Rapid eye movements also stir the liquid behind the cornea; this delivers fresh oxygen to corneal cells, preventing their suffocation.

figure 6.8
Sleep across the life span As we age, our sleep patterns change. During our first two weeks, we spend about two-thirds of our day asleep, half of that time in REM sleep. During our first few months, we spend progressively less time in REM sleep. During our first 20 years, we spend progressively less time asleep (Snyder & Scott, 1972).

Tom Prettyman/PhotoEdit

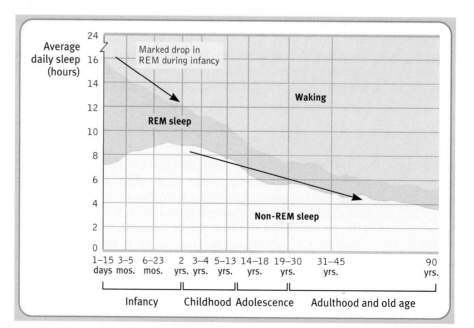

Other physiological theories propose that dreams erupt from neural activity that spreads upward from the brainstem (Antrobus, 1991; Hobson, 1988). According to one version—the *activation-synthesis* theory—this neural activity is random, and dreams are the brain's attempt to make sense of it. Much as a neurosurgeon can produce hallucinations by stimulating different parts of a patient's cortex, so can stimulation originating within the brain. These internal stimuli activate brain areas that process visual images, but not the visual cortex area, which receives raw input from the eyes. As Freud might have expected, the emotion-related limbic system also becomes active during REM sleep, while frontal lobe regions responsible for inhibition and rational thought are idling (which explains why our dreams are less inhibited than we are). PET scans of sleeping people reveal increased activity in several brain areas, especially the amygdala (Maquet & others, 1996). Add the limbic system's emotional tone to the brain's visual bursts and—voilà!—we dream. Damage either the limbic system or the visual centers active during dreaming and dreaming itself may be impaired (Domhoff, 2003).

The activation-synthesis theory, then, is that dreams spring from the mind's relentless effort to make sense of unrelated visual bursts, which are given their emotional tone by the limbic system. Dreams are the brain's interpretation of its own activity.

There is one thing dream theorists agree on: We *need* REM sleep. Deprived of it by repeatedly being awakened, people return more and more quickly to the REM stage after falling back to sleep. When finally allowed to sleep undisturbed, they literally sleep like babies—with increased REM sleep, a phenomenon called **REM rebound**. Withdrawing REM-suppressing sleeping medications also increases REM sleep, but with accompanying nightmares.

Most other mammals also experience REM sleep and REM rebound. Animals' need for REM sleep suggests that its causes and functions are deeply biological. That REM sleep occurs in mammals—and not in animals such as fish, whose behavior is less influenced by learning—also fits the information-processing theory of dreams. All of this reminds us once again of a basic lesson: *Biological and psychological explanations of behavior are partners, not competitors.*

But if dreams lack the disguised meanings that Freud supposed, and instead serve physiological functions, are they therefore psychologically meaningless? Not necessarily. Every psychologically meaningful experience involves an active brain. Moreover, say advocates of dream reflection, dreams may be akin to abstract art—amenable to more than one meaningful interpretation, and illuminating to ponder.

▶ **REM rebound** the tendency for REM sleep to increase following REM sleep deprivation (created by repeated awakenings during REM sleep).

"Those dreams that on the silent night intrude, and with false flitting shapes our minds delude . . . are mere productions of the brain. And fools consult interpreters in vain."

Jonathan Swift, "On Dreams," 1727

---

rehearse it!

9. According to Sigmund Freud, dreams are the key to understanding our inner conflicts. In interpreting dreams, Freud was most interested in their
   a. information-processing function.
   b. physiological function.
   c. manifest content, or story line.
   d. latent content, or symbolic meaning.

10. Some theories of dreaming propose that dreams serve a physiological pur-

pose. One such theory suggests that dreams
   a. are the brain's attempt to make sense of random neural activity.
   b. provide a rest period for overworked brains.
   c. are manifestations of the sensory stimuli that intrude on our sleep.
   d. prevent the brain from being disturbed by periodic stimulations.

11. The tendency for REM sleep to increase following REM sleep deprivation is referred to as
   a. paradoxical sleep.
   b. deep sleep.
   c. REM rebound.
   d. slow-wave sleep.

Answers can be found in Appendix C.

HYPNOSIS

8. What is hypnosis, and what powers does a hypnotist have over a hypnotized subject?

Imagine you are about to be hypnotized. The hypnotist invites you to sit back, fix your gaze on a spot high on the wall, and relax. In a quiet, low voice the hypnotist suggests, "Your eyes are growing tired. . . . Your eyelids are becoming heavy . . . now

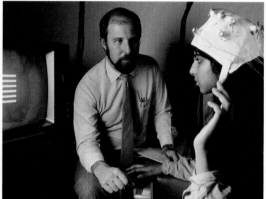

Subject to influence As a deeply hypnotized woman sits before a TV screen, researcher David Spiegel asks her to imagine that a cardboard box is blocking the screen. When a stimulus appears on the screen, her brain waves do not display the normal response. Such findings, Spiegel argues, suggest that hypnosis can alter brain functioning.

heavier and heavier. . . . They are beginning to close. . . . You are becoming more deeply relaxed. . . . Your breathing is now deep and regular. . . . Your muscles are becoming more and more relaxed. Your whole body is beginning to feel like lead."

After a few minutes of this hypnotic induction you may undergo **hypnosis**. When the hypnotist suggests, "Your eyelids are shutting so tight that you cannot open them even if you try," it may indeed seem beyond your control to open your eyelids. Told to forget the number 6, you may be puzzled when you count 11 fingers on your hands. Invited to smell a sensuous perfume that is actually ammonia, you may linger delightedly over its pungent odor. Told that you cannot see a certain object, such as a chair, you may indeed report that it is not there, although you manage to avoid the chair when walking around.

And if instructed to forget all these happenings once out of the hypnotic state, you may later report **posthypnotic amnesia**, a temporary memory loss rather like being unable to recall a familiar name. Although people *say* they don't remember "forgotten" material, the material must be "in there," for it can affect later behavior and be recalled at a prearranged signal (Kihlstrom, 1985; Spanos & others, 1985).

Before considering whether the hypnotic state is actually an *altered* state of consciousness, let's first consider some areas of general agreement.

Facts and Falsehoods

Can Hypnosis Work for Anyone?

Those who study hypnosis agree that its power resides not in the hypnotist but in the subject's openness to suggestion (Bowers, 1984). Hypnotists have no magical mind-control power; they merely engage people's ability to focus on certain images or behaviors. But what powers does hypnosis have?

Can Anyone Experience Hypnosis?

To some extent, nearly everyone is suggestible. When people standing upright with their eyes closed are told repeatedly that they are swaying back and forth, most will indeed sway a little. In fact, postural sway is one of the items on the Stanford Hypnotic Susceptibility Scale that assesses a person's hypnotizability. The people who respond to such suggestions without hypnosis are the people who respond with hypnosis (Kirsch & Braffman, 2001). During hypnosis, a hypnotist gives a brief hypnotic induction and then presents a series of suggested experiences that range from easy (one's outstretched arms will move together) to difficult (with eyes open one will see a nonexistent person).

Those who are highly hypnotizable—say, the 20 percent who can carry out a suggestion not to smell or react to a bottle of ammonia held under the nose—frequently become deeply absorbed in imaginative activities (Lynn & Rhue, 1986; Silva & Kirsch, 1992). Typically, they have rich fantasy lives and easily become absorbed in the imaginary events of a novel or movie. Many researchers refer to hypnotic "susceptibility" as hypnotic *ability*, a label with more positive connotations—the "ability" to focus attention totally on a task, to become imaginatively absorbed in it, to entertain fanciful possibilities.

"Excellent hypnotic subjects choose to become absorbed in suggestions in the same way that many people become absorbed in movies and novels."

Nicholas P. Spanos, Multiple Identities and False Memories, 1996

Can Hypnosis Enhance Recall of Forgotten Events?

Can hypnotic procedures enable people to relive earlier experiences? To recall kindergarten classmates? To retrieve forgotten or suppressed details of a crime? Should testimony obtained under hypnosis be admissible in court?

Most people believe—wrongly, as Chapter 8 will explain—that our experiences are all "in there," that everything that happens to us gets recorded in our brains and can be recalled if only we are able to break through our own defenses (Loftus, 1980). In one community survey, three in four people agreed with the inaccurate statement that hypnosis enables people to "recover accurate memories as far back as birth" (Johnson & Hauck, 1999). But 60 years of research dispute the claims of *age regression*—the supposed ability to relive childhood experiences. Age-regressed people act as they *believe* children would, but they typically miss the mark by out-performing real children of the specified age (Silverman & Retzlaff, 1986). They may, for example, *feel* childlike and print much as they know a 6-year-old would, but they sometimes do so with perfect spelling and typically without any change in their adult brain waves, reflexes, and perceptions.

Researchers have also found that "hypnotically refreshed" memories combine fact with fiction. Thus, American, Australian, and British courts increasingly ban testimony from witnesses who have been hypnotized (Druckman & Bjork, 1994; Gibson, 1995; McConkey, 1995).

Striking examples of memories created under hypnosis come from the tens of thousands of people who since 1980 have reported being abducted by UFOs, abused in satanic cults, or adored during a past life. Studies reveal that most reports of UFOs have come from people who are predisposed to believe in aliens, are highly hypnotizable, and have undergone hypnosis (Newman & Baumeister, 1996; Nickell, 1996).

Can Hypnosis Force People to Act Against Their Will?

Researchers Martin Orne and Frederick Evans (1965) demonstrated that hypnotized people *could* be induced to perform an apparently dangerous act. The participants followed a request to dip one hand briefly into fuming "acid," then throw the "acid" in a research assistant's face. When interviewed a day later, they exhibited no memory of their acts and emphatically denied they would ever follow orders to commit such an act.

Had hypnosis given the hypnotist a special power to control these people against their will? To find out, Orne and Evans unleashed that enemy of so many illusory beliefs—the control group: Orne asked some other people to *pretend* they were hypnotized. The laboratory experimenter, unaware that the control subjects had not been hypnotized, treated all participants the same. The result? All the *un*hypnotized participants (perhaps believing that the laboratory context assured safety) performed the same acts as those who were hypnotized.

Such studies illustrate a principle that Chapter 15 emphasizes: An authoritative person in a legitimate context can induce people—hypnotized or not—to perform some unlikely acts. Hypnosis researcher Spanos (1982) put it directly: "The overt behaviors of hypnotic subjects are well within normal limits."

Can Hypnosis Be Therapeutic?

Hypnotherapists do nothing magical. They simply try to help patients harness their own healing powers (Baker, 1987). **Posthypnotic suggestions** have helped alleviate headaches, asthma, warts, and stress-related skin disorders. One woman, who for more than 20 years suffered from open sores all over her body, was asked to imagine herself swimming in shimmering, sunlit liquids that would cleanse her skin and to experience her skin as smooth and unblemished. Within three months, her sores had disappeared (Bowers, 1984).

In one statistical digest of 18 studies, the average client whose therapy was supplemented with hypnosis showed greater improvement than 70 percent of other therapy patients (Kirsch & others, 1995, 1996). Hypnosis seemed especially helpful for treatment of obesity. However, drug, alcohol, and smoking addictions do not respond well to hypnosis (Nash, 2001). In controlled studies, hypnosis speeds the disappearance of warts, but so do the same positive suggestions given without hypnosis (Spanos, 1991, 1996). Hypnosis and positive suggestions both can alter people's expectations.

"Hypnosis is not a psychological truth serum and to regard it as such has been a source of considerable mischief."

Researcher Kenneth Bowers (1987)

See Chapter 8 for a more detailed discussion of how people may construct false memories.

"It wasn't what I expected. But facts are facts, and if one is proved to be wrong, one must just be humble about it and start again."

Agatha Christie's Miss Marple

▶ **hypnosis** a social interaction in which one person (the hypnotist) suggests to another (the subject) that certain perceptions, feelings, thoughts, or behaviors will spontaneously occur.

▶ **posthypnotic amnesia** supposed inability to recall what one experienced during hypnosis; induced by the hypnotist's suggestion.

▶ **posthypnotic suggestion** a suggestion, made during a hypnosis session, to be carried out after the subject is no longer hypnotized; used by some clinicians to help control undesired symptoms and behaviors.

Joel Gordon

The Lamaze method of childbirth
Like hypnosis, the Lamaze method uses breathing and concentration techniques that draw attention away from pain. Women for whom the method works tend to have high hypnotic ability (Venn, 1986).

Can Hypnosis Alleviate Pain?

Yes, hypnosis *can* relieve pain (Druckman & Bjork, 1994; Montgomery & others, 2000). When unhypnotized subjects put their arms in an ice bath, they feel intense pain within 25 seconds. When hypnotizable subjects do the same after being given suggestions to feel no pain, they indeed report feeling little pain. As some dentists know, even light hypnosis can reduce fear, and thus hypersensitivity to pain. Nearly 10 percent of us can become so deeply hypnotized that even major surgery can be performed without anesthesia. Half of us can gain at least some pain relief from hypnosis.

How can this be? One theory of hypnotic pain relief finds the answer in **dissociation**, a split between different levels of consciousness. Hypnosis, it suggests, dissociates the sensation of the pain stimulus (of which the subject is still aware) from the emotional suffering that defines our experience of pain. The ice water therefore feels cold—very cold—but not painful.

Another theory proposes that hypnotic pain relief results from selective attention, as when an injured athlete, caught up in the competition, feels little or no pain until the game ends. Support for this view comes from several studies showing that hypnosis relieves pain—for example, the pain women experience during childbirth—no better than does merely relaxing and distracting people (Chaves, 1989; D'Eon, 1989). PET scans reveal that hypnosis reduces brain activity in a region involved in attending to painful stimuli, but not in the somatosensory cortex that receives the raw sensory input (Rainville & others, 1997).

The unanswered question of how hypnosis relieves pain—by *dissociating* the pain sensation from conscious awareness, or merely by focusing *attention* on other things—brings us to the basic issue: Is hypnosis a unique psychological state?

Explaining the Hypnotized State

9. Is hypnosis an extension of normal consciousness or an altered state of consciousness?

We have seen that hypnosis involves heightened suggestibility. We have also seen that hypnotic procedures do not endow a person with special powers. But they can sometimes enhance a person's recall of real (and unreal) past events, aid in overcoming psychologically influenced ailments, and help alleviate pain. So, just what is hypnosis?

Hypnosis as a Social Phenomenon

Some skeptics believe that hypnotic phenomena may simply reflect the workings of normal consciousness and the power of social influence (Lynn & others, 1990; Spanos & Coe, 1992). In Chapter 5 we saw how powerfully our interpretations influence ordinary perceptions. Especially in the case of pain, for which the effects of hypnosis seem most dramatic, our perceptions follow our attention. Moreover, imaginative people can manufacture vivid perceptions with or without hypnosis (Barber, 2000). In an experiment with London university students, those who were most suggestible to feeling warm, tingly, and relaxed while holding New Age crystals (whether real or fake) also scored high on hypnotic suggestibility (French & others, 2001).

No one is proposing that people are consciously faking hypnosis. Rather, they seem to be acting the role of "good hypnotic subjects" and allowing the hypnotist to direct their fantasies. Like actors who get caught up in their roles, they begin to feel and behave in ways appropriate to the hypnotic role. The more they like and trust the hypnotist and feel motivated to demonstrate hypnotic behavior, the more they do so (Gfeller & others, 1987). "The hypnotist's ideas become the subject's thoughts," explains Theodore Barber (2000), "and the subject's thoughts produce the hypnotic experiences and behaviors." If told later to scratch their ear when they

▶ **dissociation** a split in consciousness, which allows some thoughts and behaviors to occur simultaneously with others.

▶ **hidden observer** Hilgard's term describing a hypnotized subject's awareness of experiences, such as pain, that go unreported during hypnosis.

hear the word *psychology*, subjects will likely do so—but—only if they think the experiment is still under way (and scratching is therefore expected). If an experimenter eliminates the motivation for their acting hypnotized—by stating that hypnosis reveals their "gullibility"—subjects become unresponsive.

Based on such findings, advocates of the *social influence theory* contend that hypnotic phenomena are *not* unique to hypnosis. They argue that hypnotic phenomena—like behavior associated with other supposed altered states, such as dissociative identity disorder (pages 482–484) and spirit or demon possession—are an extension of everyday social behavior (Spanos, 1994, 1996). Hypnotic subjects are imaginative role players.

Hypnosis as Divided Consciousness

Most hypnosis researchers grant that normal social and cognitive processes play a part in hypnosis, but they nevertheless believe hypnosis is more than trying to be a "good subject." For one thing, hypnotized subjects will *sometimes* carry out suggested behaviors on cue, even when they believe no one is watching (Perugini & others, 1998). Moreover, many practitioners remain convinced that certain phenomena *are* unique to hypnosis, which is accompanied by distinctive brain activity (Kosslyn & others, 2000).

To famed researcher Ernest Hilgard (1986, 1992), hypnosis involved not only social influence but also a special state of dissociated (divided) consciousness (**FIGURE 6.9**). Hilgard viewed hypnotic dissociation as a vivid form of everyday mind splits.

Consider: Putting a child to bed, we might read *Goodnight Moon* for the fourteenth time while mentally organizing a busy schedule for the next day. With practice, you could even read and comprehend a short story while copying dictated words, much as you can doodle while listening to a lecture or finish typing a sentence while starting a conversation, or as a skilled pianist can talk to an audience while playing a familiar piece (Hirst & others, 1978).

Hilgard was especially intrigued by people's subjective experience of hypnosis. This phenomenon spurred further inquiry. Hypnotized subjects, as we noted earlier, report far less pain than others when they place their arms in ice water. But when asked to press a key if "some part" of them does feel the pain, they invariably press the key. To Hilgard, this suggested that a dissociated consciousness, a **hidden observer**, is passively aware of what is happening.

The divided-consciousness theory of hypnosis provoked controversy, because what the "hidden observer" reports varies with what the experimenter seems to want. But this much seems clear: You and I process much information without conscious awareness. In hypnosis as in life, *much of our behavior occurs on autopilot.* Thus, when hypnotized people write answers to questions about one topic while talking or reading about

"The total possible consciousness may be split into parts which co-exist but mutually ignore each other."

William James, Principles of Psychology, *1890*

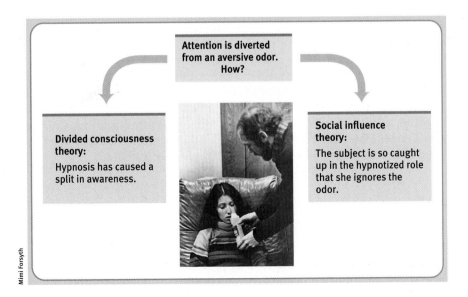

figure 6.9
Explaining hypnosis How can she do it? How can this hypnotized young woman show no reaction to the terrible smell of ammonia? Divided-consciousness theory and social influence theory offer possible explanations.

Mimi Forsyth

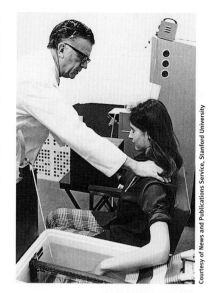

Demonstrating the "hidden observer" A hypnotized subject being tested by Ernest Hilgard exhibits no pain when her arm is placed in an ice bath. But asked to press a key if some part of her feels the pain, she does so. To Hilgard, this suggested that hypnosis divides consciousness into one part that is unaware of pain and another part—a "hidden observer"—that is aware of it.

Courtesy of News and Publications Service, Stanford University

a different topic, they display an accentuated form of normal dissociation of cognition from behavior. So, when today's researchers refer to a "hypnotic state," note Irving Kirsch and Steven Jay Lynn (1995, 1998a,b), they merely refer to the subjective experience of hypnosis, not to a unique trance state.

We have seen other examples of unconscious information processing in the chapters on sensation and perception, and we will see more in later chapters on learning, memory, and thinking. Without doubt, there is much more to thinking and acting than we are conscious of. Our information processing, which starts with selective attention, *is* divided into simultaneous conscious and subconscious realms.

But still, there is also little doubt that social influences do play an important role in hypnosis. So, might the two views—social influence and divided consciousness—be bridged? Researchers John Kihlstrom and Kevin McConkey (1990) believe there is no contradiction between the two approaches, which are converging toward a "unified account of hypnosis." Hypnosis, they suggest, is an extension *both* of normal principles of social influence *and* of everyday dissociations between our conscious awareness and our automatic behaviors.

DRUGS AND CONSCIOUSNESS

There is controversy about whether hypnosis uniquely alters consciousness, but there is little dispute that drugs do. **Psychoactive drugs** are chemicals that change perceptions and moods. Let's imagine a day in the life of a legal-drug user. It begins with a wake-up latté. By midday, several cigarettes have calmed frazzled nerves. Leaving work early makes time for a happy-hour drink, providing a relaxing and sociable prelude to a dental appointment, where nitrous oxide makes an otherwise painful experience mildly pleasurable. A diet pill before dinner helps stem the appetite, and its stimulating effects can later be partially offset with a nightcap and two Tylenol PMs. Before drifting off into REM-depressed sleep, our hypothetical drug user is dismayed by a news report of "rising drug abuse."

© 1992 by Sidney Harris.

"Just tell me where you kids got the idea to take so many drugs."

Dependence and Addiction

10. What are dependence and addiction? Can substance abusers overcome their addictions?

Continued use of a psychoactive drug produces **tolerance**: The user experiences *neuroadaptation* (the brain's counteracting the disruption to its normal functioning). Thus, the user requires larger and larger doses to experience the drug's effect. A person who rarely drinks alcohol might get tipsy on one can of beer, but an experienced drinker may not get tipsy until the second six-pack (**Figure 6.10**). Ironically, despite the connotations of "tolerance," alcoholics' brains, hearts, and livers suffer damage from the excessive alcohol they are "tolerating."

Users who stop taking psychoactive drugs may experience the undesirable side effects of **withdrawal**. As the body responds to the drug's absence, the user may feel physical pain and intense cravings, indicating a **physical dependence** on the drug. People can also develop **psychological dependence**, particularly for stress-relieving drugs. Although such drugs may not be physically addictive, they nevertheless become an important part of the user's life, often as a way of relieving negative emotions. With either physical or psychological dependence, the user's primary focus becomes obtaining and using the drug.

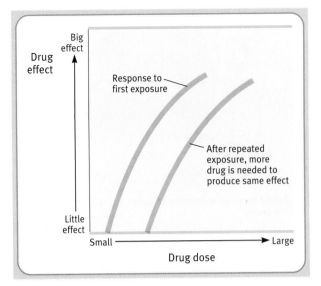

Misconceptions About Addiction

An *addiction* has traditionally meant a craving for a substance, with physical symptoms such as aches, nausea, and distress following sudden withdrawal. In recent pop psychology, the supposedly irresistible seduction of addiction has been extended to cover many behaviors formerly considered bad habits or even sins. Has the concept been stretched too far? Are addictions as irresistible as commonly believed? Many drug researchers believe the following three myths about addiction are *false*:

1. ***Addictive drugs quickly corrupt; for example, morphine taken to control pain is powerfully addictive and often leads to heroin abuse.*** After taking a psychoactive drug, some people—perhaps 10 percent—do indeed have a hard time using it in moderation or stopping altogether. However, there are many more controlled, occasional users than addicts of drugs such as alcohol and marijuana (Gazzaniga, 1988; Siegel, 1990). "Even for a very addictive drug like cocaine, only 15 to 16 percent of people become addicted within 10 years of first use," report Terry Robinson and Kent Berridge (2003). Moreover, people typically don't become addicted when using drugs medically. Those given morphine to control pain rarely develop the cravings of the addict who uses morphine as a mood-altering drug (Melzack, 1990).

2. ***Addictions can't be overcome voluntarily; therapy is a must.*** Some addicts do benefit from treatment programs. Alcoholics Anonymous, for example, has supported many people in overcoming their alcohol dependence. But critics say that the recovery rates of treated and untreated groups differ less than one might suppose. Therapy or group support may be helpful, but people often recover on their own.

    Moreover, viewing addiction as a disease, as diabetes is a disease, can undermine self-confidence and the will to change cravings that, without treatment, "one can't fight." And that, critics say, would be unfortunate, for many people do voluntarily stop using addictive drugs, without treatment. Some 70 percent of smokers who seek treatment for their addiction later return to smoking, whereas most of America's 41 million ex-smokers kicked the habit on their own.

3. ***We can extend the concept of addiction to cover not just drug dependencies, but a whole spectrum of repetitive, pleasure-seeking behaviors.*** We can, and we have, but should we? The addiction-as-disease-needing-treatment idea has been suggested for a host of driven behaviors, including overeating, shopping, exercise, sex, gambling, and work. Initially, we may use the term metaphorically ("I'm a science fiction addict"), but if we begin taking the metaphor as reality, addiction can become an all-purpose excuse. Those who embezzle to feed their "gambling addiction," who surf the Web half the night to satisfy their "Internet addiction," or who abuse or betray to indulge their "sex addiction" can then explain away their behavior as an illness.

figure 6.10
Drug tolerance With repeated exposure to a psychoactive drug, the drug's effect lessens. Thus, it takes bigger doses to get the desired effect.

"About 70 percent of Americans have tried illicit drugs, but . . . only a few percent have done so in the last month. . . . Past age 35, the casual use of illegal drugs virtually ceases." Having sampled the pleasures and their aftereffects, "most people eventually walk away."

Neuropsychologist Michael Gazzaniga (1997)

▶ **psychoactive drug** a chemical substance that alters perceptions and mood.

▶ **tolerance** the diminishing effect with regular use of the same dose of a drug, requiring the user to take larger and larger doses before experiencing the drug's effect.

▶ **withdrawal** the discomfort and distress that follow discontinuing the use of an addictive drug.

▶ **physical dependence** a physiological need for a drug, marked by unpleasant withdrawal symptoms when the drug is discontinued.

▶ **psychological dependence** a psychological need to use a drug, such as to relieve negative emotions.

"That is not one of the seven habits of highly effective people."

A University of Illinois campus survey showed that before sexual assaults, 80 percent of the male assailants and 70 percent of the female victims had been drinking (Camper, 1990). Another survey of 89,874 American collegians found alcohol or drugs involved in 79 percent of unwanted sexual intercourse experiences (Presley & others, 1997).

figure 6.11
Alcoholism shrinks the brain MRI scans show brain shrinkage in women with alcoholism (left) compared with women in a control group (right).

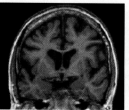

Scan of woman
with alcoholism

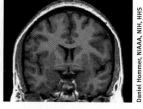

Scan of woman
without alcoholism

Daniel Hommer, NIAAA, NIH, HHS

Sometimes, though, behaviors such as gambling or cybersex do become compulsive and dysfunctional, much like abusive drug taking (Griffiths, 2001). Is there justification for stretching the addiction concept to cover social behaviors? Debates over the addiction-as-disease model continue.

Psychoactive Drugs

There are at least three categories of psychoactive drugs: *depressants*, *stimulants*, and *hallucinogens*. Drugs in all three categories do their work at the brain's synapses, by stimulating, inhibiting, or mimicking the activity of neurotransmitters, the brain's chemical messengers. But our expectations also play a role in the way these drugs affect us.

Depressants

> *11. What are depressants, and what are their effects?*

Depressants, or "downers"—drugs such as alcohol, barbiturates (tranquilizers), and opiates—calm neural activity and slow body functions.

ALCOHOL True or false? In large amounts, alcohol is a depressant; in small amounts, it is a stimulant.

False. Small doses of "spirits" may, indeed, enliven a drinker, but they do so by slowing brain activity that controls judgment and inhibitions. When provoked, people under alcohol's influence respond more aggressively than usual. If asked to help, people under alcohol's influence respond more willingly than usual. Alcohol is an equal-opportunity drug: It *increases* harmful tendencies—as when sexually coercive college men lower their dates' sexual inhibitions by getting them to drink (Abbey, 1991; Mosher & Anderson, 1986)—and it *increases* helpful tendencies—as when tipsy restaurant patrons leave extravagant tips (M. Lynn, 1988). Thus, alcohol makes us more aggressive or helpful or self-disclosing or sexually daring—when such tendencies are already present. *The urges you feel when sober are the ones you will more likely act upon if intoxicated.*

Low doses of alcohol relax the drinker by slowing sympathetic nervous system activity. With larger doses, alcohol can become a staggering problem: Reactions slow, speech slurs, skilled performance deteriorates. Paired with sleep deprivation, alcohol becomes a potent sedative. (Although either sleep deprivation or booze can put a driver at risk, their combination is deadlier yet.) These physical effects, combined with lowered inhibitions, contribute to alcohol's worst consequences—the several hundred thousand lives claimed worldwide each year in alcohol-related accidents and violent crime. Accidents occur despite most drinkers' belief (when sober) that driving while under the influence of alcohol is wrong and despite their insisting that they wouldn't do so. Yet as their blood-alcohol level rises, people's moral judgments become less mature, their qualms about drinking and driving lessen—and virtually all will drive home from a bar, even if given a breathalyzer test and told they are intoxicated (Denton & Krebs, 1990; MacDonald & others, 1995).

Alcohol affects not only judgment but also memory. It does not impair short-term recall for what just happened, nor does it affect existing long-term memories. Rather, it disrupts the *processing* of recent experiences into long-term memories. Thus, the day after being intoxicated, heavy drinkers may not recall whom they met or what they said or did the night before. This memory blackout stems partly from an inability to transfer memories from the intoxicated to the sober state (Eich, 1980). Blackouts after drinking may also result from the way alcohol suppresses REM sleep. (Recall that people deprived of REM sleep have difficulty fixing their day's experiences into permanent memories.) Prolonged and excessive drinking can also affect cognition by shrinking the brain, which MRI scans show is especially striking in women, who have less of a stomach enzyme that digests alcohol (Wuethrich, 2001) (**FIGURE 6.11**).

Don't drink and drive With billboards like this one that shows the appalling consequences of driving under the influence of alcohol, Mothers Against Drunk Driving (MADD) has vigorously promoted awareness of the dangers of alcohol abuse. The group has also lobbied for stiffer penalties for drunk drivers.

Alcohol has another intriguing effect on consciousness: It reduces self-awareness (Hull & others, 1986). Compared with people who feel good about themselves, those who want to suppress their awareness of failures or shortcomings are more likely to drink. Losing a business deal, a game, or a romance will sometimes elicit a drinking binge.

Alcohol also focuses one's attention on the immediate situation and away from any future consequences. This facilitates urges that a person might otherwise resist (Steele & Josephs, 1990). In surveys, over half of rapists acknowledge drinking before committing their offense (Seto & Barbaree, 1995). The effect reaches onto college campuses. Sexually active university students are less likely to use condoms when intoxicated (MacDonald & others, 1996, 2000). University women under alcohol's influence find an attractive but sexually promiscuous man a more appealing potential date than they do when sober. It seems, surmise Sheila Murphy and her colleagues (1998), "that when people have been drinking, the restraining forces of reason may weaken and yield under the pressure of their desires."

As with other psychoactive drugs, alcohol's behavioral effects stem not only from its alteration of brain chemistry but also from the user's expectations. Many studies have found that when people *believe* that alcohol affects social behavior in certain ways, and *believe*, rightly or wrongly, that they have been drinking alcohol, they will behave accordingly (Leigh, 1989).

Consider one such experiment by David Abrams and Terence Wilson (1983). They gave Rutgers University men who volunteered for a study on "alcohol and sexual stimulation" either an alcoholic or a nonalcoholic drink. (Both drinks had a strong taste that masked any alcohol.) In each group, half the participants thought they were drinking alcohol and half thought they were not. After being shown an erotic movie clip, the men who *thought* they had consumed alcohol were more likely to report having strong sexual fantasies and feeling guilt-free. Being able to *attribute* their sexual responses to alcohol released their inhibitions—whether they actually had drunk alcohol or not. If, as commonly believed, liquor is the quicker pick-her-upper, the effect lies partly in that powerful sex organ, the mind.

This research illustrates an important principle: A drug's psychological effects are powerfully influenced by the user's expectations. And that explains why drug experiences vary with cultures (Ward, 1994). If one culture assumes that a particular drug produces euphoria (or aggression or sexual arousal) and another does not, each culture may find its expectations fulfilled.

BARBITURATES The **barbiturate** drugs, or *tranquilizers*, mimic the effects of alcohol. Because they depress sympathetic nervous system activity, barbiturates such as Nembutal and Seconal are sometimes prescribed to induce sleep or reduce anxiety. In larger doses, they can lead to impaired memory and judgment. In combination with alcohol—as when people take a sleeping pill after an evening of heavy drinking—the total depressive effect on body functions can be lethal. With sufficient doses,

Facts: College and university students drink more alcohol than their nonstudent peers, and they spend more on alcohol than on books and other beverages combined. Fraternity and sorority members drink three times as much as other students (Atwell, 1986; Malloy & others, 1994). Although few university students believe they have an alcohol problem, many meet the criteria for alcohol abuse (Marlatt, 1991). As students mature with age, they drink less.

Fact: In a Harvard School of Public Health survey of 18,000 students at 140 colleges and universities, almost 9 in 10 students reported abuse by intoxicated peers, including sleep and study interruption, insults, sexual advances, and property damage (Wechsler & others, 1994). In a follow-up survey, 44 percent of students admitted binge drinking within the previous two weeks (Wechsler & others, 2002).

Fact: Drinking contributes to 1400 American college student deaths, 70,000 sexual assaults, and 500,000 injuries annually (Hingson & others, 2002).

Fact: Alcohol kills more people than all illegal drugs combined. So does tobacco (Siegel, 1990).

▶ **depressants** drugs (such as alcohol, barbiturates, and opiates) that reduce neural activity and slow body functions.

▶ **barbiturates** drugs that depress the activity of the central nervous system, reducing anxiety but impairing memory and judgment.

▶ **opiates** opium and its derivatives, such as morphine and heroin; they depress neural activity, temporarily lessening pain and anxiety.

▶ **stimulants** drugs (such as caffeine, nicotine, and the more powerful amphetamines and cocaine) that excite neural activity and speed up body functions.

▶ **amphetamines** drugs that stimulate neural activity, causing speeded-up body functions and associated energy and mood changes.

barbiturates by themselves can also cause death, which makes them the drugs often chosen by those attempting suicide.

OPIATES The **opiates**—opium and its derivatives, morphine and heroin—also depress neural functioning. The pupils constrict, the breathing slows, and the user becomes lethargic. For a few hours, blissful pleasure replaces pain and anxiety. But for short-term pleasure one pays a long-term price, which for the heroin user is the gnawing craving for another fix, the need for progressively larger doses, the week-long physical anguish of withdrawal—and for some, the ultimate price: death by overdose.

The pathway to addiction is treacherous. When repeatedly flooded with an artificial opiate, the brain eventually stops producing its own opiates, the endorphins. If the drug is then withdrawn, the brain lacks the normal level of these painkilling neurotransmitters. The result is the discomfort of withdrawal.

Stimulants

12. What are stimulants, and what are their effects?

Stimulants, or "uppers," temporarily excite neural activity and arouse body functions. The most widely used stimulants are caffeine, nicotine, the powerful **amphetamines**, the even more powerful cocaine, and Ecstasy. Stimulants speed up body functions, hence the nickname "speed" for amphetamines. Strong stimulants increase heart and breathing rates. Pupils dilate, appetite diminishes (because blood sugar increases), and energy and self-confidence rise. For these reasons, people use stimulants to stay awake, lose weight, or boost mood or athletic performance. As with other drugs, the benefits come with a price. When drug stimulation ends, the user experiences a compensating slowdown and may crash into fatigue, headaches, irritability, and depression. Like the depressants, stimulants—including coffee and caffeinated sodas—can be addictive (Silverman & others, 1992).

NICOTINE Imagine that cigarettes were harmless—except, once in every 25,000 packs, an occasional innocent-looking one is filled with dynamite instead of tobacco. Not such a bad risk of having your head blown off. But with 250 million packs a day consumed worldwide, we could expect more than 10,000 gruesome daily deaths (more than three times the 9/11 fatalities each and every day)—surely enough to have cigarettes banned everywhere.[1]

The lost lives from these dynamite-loaded cigarettes approximate those from today's actual cigarettes. Each year throughout the world, tobacco kills some 4 million of its 1.2 billion customers, reports the World Health Organization (2002). (Imagine the outrage if terrorists took down an equivalent of 25 loaded jumbo jets today, let alone tomorrow and every day thereafter.) And the worst is yet to come. Given present trends, according to the WHO, the death rate will soon grow to 10 million annually, meaning that *half a billion* (say that number slowly) people alive today will be killed by tobacco (Lopez, 1999). A teen-to-the-grave smoker has a 50 percent chance of dying from the habit, and the death is often agonizing and premature, as the Philip Morris company acknowledged in 2001. Responding to Czech Republic complaints about the health care costs of tobacco, Philip Morris reassured the Czechs that there was actually a net "health care cost savings due to early mortality" and the resulting savings on pensions and elderly housing (Herbert, 2001). Smoke a cigarette and nature will charge you 12 minutes—ironically, just about the length of time you spend smoking it (*Discover*, 1996). Eliminating smoking would increase life expectancy more than any other preventive measure.

Nonsmokers not only live healthier, they live happier. Smoking correlates with higher rates of depression, chronic disabilities, and divorce (Doherty & Doherty, 1998; Vita & others, 1998). Nondepressed teens who smoke suffer a quadrupled risk of developing depression (Goodman, 2000). Healthy living seems to add both years to life and life to years.

"There is an overwhelming medical and scientific consensus that cigarette smoking causes lung cancer, heart disease, emphysema, and other serious diseases in smokers. Smokers are far more likely to develop serious diseases, like lung cancer, than nonsmokers."

Philip Morris Companies, Inc., 1999

SNAPSHOTS

Once upon a time, peer pressure caused Bob to start smoking.

Twenty years later, it forces him to quit.

© Jason Love

[1] This analogy, adapted here with world-based numbers, was suggested by mathematician Sam Saunders, as reported by K. C. Cole (1998).

When and why do people start smoking? Smoking is a "pediatric disease." It usually begins during early adolescence and is especially common among those who get low grades, who drop out of school, who feel less competent and in control of their future, and whose friends, parents, and siblings smoke (Chassin & others, 1987; Schulenberg & others, 1994). If you are in college or university, and if by now the cigarette manufacturers haven't attracted your business, they almost surely never will.

Why do people not stop smoking? Three in four have tried (Niemi & others, 1989). However, once addicted to nicotine we find it very hard to quit. Tobacco products are as addictive as heroin and cocaine. Indeed, some who have kicked the heroin habit have been unable to also stop smoking. Surveys in Britain and the United States show that at least one in three of those who try cigarettes become hooked—a higher addiction rate than for heroin and cocaine (Heishman & others, 1997).

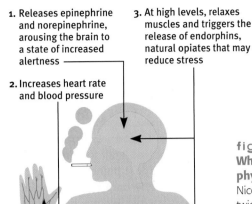

1. Releases epinephrine and norepinephrine, arousing the brain to a state of increased alertness

2. Increases heart rate and blood pressure

3. At high levels, relaxes muscles and triggers the release of endorphins, natural opiates that may reduce stress

4. Reduces circulation to extremities

5. Suppresses appetite for carbohydrates

figure 6.12
Where there's smoke . . . : The physiological effects of nicotine
Nicotine reaches the brain within 7 seconds, twice as fast as intravenous heroin. Within minutes, the amount in the blood soars.

As with other addictions, a smoker becomes *dependent*; each year fewer than one of every seven smokers who want to quit will do so. A smoker also develops *tolerance*, eventually needing larger and larger doses to get the same effect. Quitting causes nicotine-*withdrawal* symptoms, including craving, insomnia, anxiety, and irritability. And all it takes to relieve these aversive states is a cigarette—a portable nicotine dispenser.

As with all addictive drugs, nicotine use is not only compulsive and mood-altering, it is also reinforcing. Smoking both terminates aversive cravings and offers a pleasurable lift. Nicotine triggers the release of epinephrine and norepinephrine, which in turn diminish appetite and boost alertness and mental efficiency (**FIGURE 6.12**). More importantly, nicotine also stimulates the central nervous system to release neurotransmitters that calm anxiety and reduce sensitivity to pain. For example, nicotine increases dopamine by stimulating its release (Nowak, 1994). These rewards keep people smoking even when they wish they could stop—indeed, even when they know they are committing slow-motion suicide. And it also helps explain why, even if given low-nicotine cigarettes, the smoker will end up smoking more of them to maintain a roughly constant level of nicotine in the blood. Although quitting is seldom easy, the Centers for Disease Control report that half of Americans who have ever smoked have quit. More than 90 percent did so on their own, often after repeated attempts. For those who endure, the acute craving and withdrawal symptoms gradually dissipate over the ensuing six months (Ward & others, 1997).

COCAINE In national surveys, 5 percent of high school seniors reported having tried cocaine during the past year (Johnston & others, 2004). Nearly half said they had smoked *crack*, a potent form of cocaine. Cocaine addiction is a fast track from euphoria to crash. When animals and people chew coca leaves, only small amounts of cocaine enter the bloodstream, and they do so gradually, without seeming ill effects (Siegel, 1990). But when extracted cocaine is sniffed ("snorted"), and especially when injected or smoked ("free-based"), it enters the bloodstream quickly. The result: a "rush" of euphoria that lasts 15 to 30 minutes. Because the rush depletes the brain's supply of the neurotransmitters dopamine, serotonin, and norepinephrine, a crash of agitated depression occurs as the drug's effect wears off

"To cease smoking is the easiest thing I ever did; I ought to know because I've done it a thousand times."

Mark Twain, 1835–1910

Asked "If you had to do it all over again, would you start smoking?" more than 85 percent of adult smokers answer "No" (Slovic & others, 2002).

The recipe for Coca-Cola originally included an extract of the coca plant, creating a cocaine tonic for tired elderly people. Between 1896 and 1905, Coke was indeed "the real thing."

▶ **Ecstasy (MDMA)** a synthetic stimulant and mild hallucinogen. Produces euphoria and social intimacy, but with short-term health risks and longer-term harm to serotonin-producing neurons and to mood and cognition.

▶ **hallucinogens** psychedelic ("mind-manifesting") drugs, such as LSD, that distort perceptions and evoke sensory images in the absence of sensory input.

▶ **LSD** a powerful hallucinogenic drug; also known as *acid* (*lysergic acid diethylamide*).

▶ **near-death experience** an altered state of consciousness reported after a close brush with death (such as through cardiac arrest); often similar to drug-induced hallucinations.

(**FIGURE 6.13**). Crack works even faster and produces a briefer but more intense high, a more intense crash, and a craving for more crack, which wanes after several hours but then returns several days later (Gawin, 1991).

Regular cocaine users become addicted. Monkeys have become so strongly addicted that they will press a lever more than 12,000 times to gain each cocaine injection (Siegel, 1990). Human and animal cocaine users may experience emotional disturbance, suspiciousness, convulsions, cardiac arrest, or respiratory failure. In situations that trigger aggression, ingesting cocaine may increase aggressive reactions. Caged rats fight when given foot shocks, and they fight even more when given cocaine and foot shocks. Likewise, humans who have ingested high-dose cocaine impose higher shock levels on an opponent in a laboratory experiment than do those who have received a placebo (Licata & others, 1993).

As with all psychoactive drugs, cocaine's psychological effects depend not only on the dosage and form in which one takes the drug but also on one's expectations, one's personality, and the situation—a mix of factors. Given a placebo, cocaine users who *think* they are taking cocaine often have a cocainelike experience (Van Dyke & Byck, 1982).

ECSTASY Ecstasy, a street name for MDMA (methylenedioxymethamphetamine), is both a stimulant and a mild hallucinogen. As an amphetamine derivative, it triggers the release of the neurotransmitter dopamine. But its major effect is to release stored serotonin and to block its reabsorption, thus prolonging serotonin's feel-good flood (Braun, 2001). (As we will see in Chapter 14, some antidepressant drugs more moderately elevate serotonin, by blocking its reabsorption.) During the late 1990s, Ecstasy became a fast-growing "club drug" commonly taken at night clubs and all-night raves (Landry, 2002). Beginning about a half-hour after taking an Ecstasy pill, and for the next 3 to 4 hours, users commonly experience emotional elevation and, given a social context, feelings of connectedness with those around them ("I love everyone.").

There are, however, reasons not to be ecstatic about Ecstasy. One immediate effect is dehydration and, when combined with prolonged dancing, the risk of severe overheating, increased blood pressure, and death. One long-term effect of

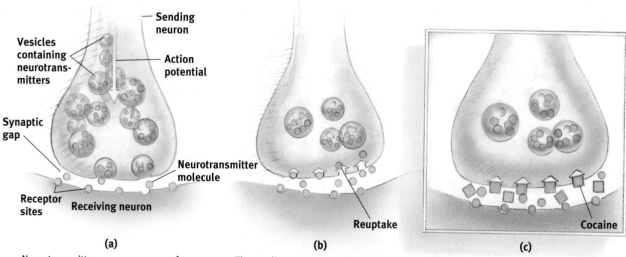

(a)
Neurotransmitters carry a message from a sending neuron across a synapse to receptor sites on a receiving neuron.

(b)
The sending neuron normally reabsorbs excess neurotransmitter molecules, a process called reuptake.

(c)
By binding to the sites that normally reabsorb neurotransmitter molecules, cocaine blocks reuptake of dopamine, norepinephrine, and serotonin (Ray & Ksir, 1990). The extra neurotransmitter molecules therefore remain in the synapse, intensifying their normal mood-altering effects and producing a euphoric rush. When the cocaine level drops, the absence of these neurotransmitters produces a crash.

figure 6.13
Cocaine euphoria and crash

repeated leaching of brain serotonin is damage to serotonin-producing neurons, leading to reduced serotonin levels and increased risk of depressed mood (Croft & others, 2001; McCann & others, 2001). Other research reveals that Ecstasy interferes with serotonin's control of the circadian clock (explaining the drug's disruption of sleep), suppresses the disease-fighting immune system, and impairs memory and other cognitive functions (Biello & Dafters, 2001; Pacifici & others, 2001; Reneman & others, 2001). Ecstasy delights for the night but dispirits the morrow.

Hallucinogens

13. What are hallucinogens, and what are their effects?

Hallucinogens distort perceptions and evoke sensory images in the absence of sensory input (which is why these drugs are also called *psychedelics*, meaning "mind-manifesting"). Some are natural substances, such as the mild hallucinogen marijuana. Others are synthetic, the best known of which are LSD and MDMA (Ecstasy).

LSD In 1943, chemist Albert Hofmann, the creator of **LSD** (lysergic acid diethylamide) took the first "acid trip." After accidentally ingesting some of the chemical, Hofmann reported that he "perceived an uninterrupted stream of fantastic pictures, extraordinary shapes with intense, kaleidoscopic play of colors" (Siegel, 1984). LSD and other powerful hallucinogens are chemically similar to (and therefore block the actions of) a subtype of the neurotransmitter serotonin (Jacobs, 1987).

The emotions of an LSD trip vary from euphoria to detachment to panic. As with all drug use, a person's current mood and expectations color the LSD experience. Despite emotional variations, the resulting perceptual distortions and hallucinations have commonalities. Psychologist Ronald Siegel (1982) reports that no matter whether you provoke your brain to hallucinate by loss of oxygen, extreme sensory deprivation, or drugs, "it will hallucinate in basically the same way." The experience typically begins with simple geometric forms, such as a lattice, a cobweb, or a spiral. The next phase consists of more meaningful images; some may be superimposed on a tunnel or funnel, others may be replays of past emotional experiences. When the hallucinogenic experience peaks, people frequently feel separated from their bodies and experience dreamlike scenes as though they were real—so real that users may become panic-stricken or harm themselves.

These hallucinatory sensations are strikingly similar to the **near-death experience** reported by about one-third of those who survive a brush with death, as when revived from cardiac arrest (Moody, 1976; Ring, 1980; Schnaper, 1980). Psychologist Ronald Siegel (1980) reports that one may experience visions of tunnels and bright lights or beings of light (**Figure 6.14**), a replay of old memories, and out-of-body sensations.

Given that oxygen deprivation and other insults to the brain are known to produce hallucinations, it is difficult to resist wondering whether near-death experiences are manufactured by the brain under stress. Patients who have experienced temporal lobe seizures have reported similarly profound mystical experiences, as have solitary sailors and polar explorers while enduring monotony, isolation, and cold (Suedfeld & Mocellin, 1987).

The hug drug MDMA, known as Ecstasy, produces a euphoric high and feelings of intimacy. But repeated use destroys serotonin-producing neurons and may permanently deflate mood and impair memory.

figure 6.14
Near-death vision or hallucination? Psychologist Ronald Siegel (1977) reports that people under the influence of hallucinogenic drugs often see "a bright light in the center of the field of vision. . . . The location of this point of light create[s] a tunnel-like perspective."

▶ **THC** the major active ingredient in marijuana; triggers a variety of effects, including mild hallucinations.

MARIJUANA Marijuana consists of the leaves and flowers of the hemp plant, which for 5000 years has been cultivated for its fiber. Marijuana's major active ingredient is **THC** (delta-9-tetrahydrocannabinol). Whether smoked or eaten, THC produces a mix of effects that makes the drug difficult to classify. (Smoking gets the drug into the brain in about 7 seconds, producing a greater effect than does eating the drug, which causes its peak concentration to be reached at a slower, unpredictable rate.) Like alcohol, marijuana relaxes, disinhibits, and may produce a euphoric high. But marijuana also acts as a mild hallucinogen by amplifying sensitivity to colors, sounds, tastes, and smells.

As with other drugs, the marijuana user's experience varies, depending on the situation. If the person feels anxious or depressed, taking the drug may intensify these feelings. In other situations, using marijuana can be not only pleasurable but therapeutic. For those who suffer the pain, nausea, and severe weight loss associated with AIDS, marijuana may spell relief (Watson & others, 2000). (For a time, marijuana was also used to control nausea from chemotherapy and pain from glaucoma, but more effective medications are now available.) Marijuana's therapeutic uses have motivated legislation legalizing the drug for such patients. The medical uses are, however, compromised by the toxicity of marijuana smoke—which, like cigarette smoke, can cause cancer, lung damage, and pregnancy complications. For medical uses, the Institute of Medicine recommends delivering the THC with a medical inhaler.

The National Academy of Sciences (1982, 1999) research reviews have identified other not-so-pleasant marijuana consequences. Like alcohol, marijuana impairs the motor coordination, perceptual skills, and reaction time necessary for safely operating an automobile or other machine. "THC causes animals to misjudge events," reports Ronald Siegel (1990, p. 163). "Pigeons wait too long to respond to buzzers or lights that tell them food is available for brief periods; and rats turn the wrong way in mazes." Marijuana also disrupts memory formation and interferes with immediate recall of information learned only a few minutes before. Such cognitive effects outlast the period of smoking (Pope & Yurgelun-Todd, 1996; Smith, 1995). Clearly, getting high is not conducive to learning.

Scientists have shed light on marijuana's cognitive, mood, and motor effects with the discovery of concentrations of THC-sensitive receptors in the brain's frontal lobes, limbic system, and motor cortex (Iversen, 2000). Recall from Chapter 2 that the 1970s discovery of the receptors for morphine led to the discovery of morphine-like neurotransmitters (the endorphins). Similarly, the discovery of "cannabinoid receptors" has led to the follow-up discovery of naturally occurring THC-like molecules that bind with cannabinoid receptors, perhaps helping to control pain.

Unlike alcohol, which the body eliminates within hours, THC and its byproducts linger in the body for a month or more. Thus, contrary to the usual tolerance phenomenon, regular users may achieve a high with smaller amounts of the drug than occasional users would need to get the same effect.

Although marijuana is not as addictive as cocaine or nicotine, it changes brain chemistry, much as cocaine and heroin do, and it may make the brain more susceptible to cocaine and heroin addiction (Tanda & others, 1997). One study that followed 654 junior high students into their early twenties found that adolescents who heavily used marijuana developed more health and family problems than did nonusers (Newcomb & Bentler, 1988).

Despite their differences, the psychoactive drugs summarized in **TABLE 6.2** share a common feature: They trigger negative aftereffects that offset their immediate positive effects. The aftereffects illustrate a more general principle: Emotions tend to produce opposing emotions, which linger after the original emotions disappear. With repetition, the opposing emotions grow stronger. This emotions-trigger-opposing-emotions principle parallels that of drug-induced pleasures; the pleasures wane as the drug exacts its compensatory price. That helps explain both tolerance and withdrawal. As the opposing, negative aftereffects get stronger, it takes larger

"How strange would appear to be this thing that men call pleasure! And how curiously it is related to what is thought to be its opposite, pain! . . . Wherever the one is found, the other follows up behind."

Plato, *Phaedo, fourth century* B.C

table 6.2 A Guide to Selected Psychoactive Drugs

Drug	Type	Pleasurable Effects	Adverse Effects
Alcohol	Depressant	Initial high followed by relaxation and disinhibition	Depression, memory loss, organ damage, impaired reactions
Heroin	Depressant	Rush of euphoria, relief from pain	Depressed physiology, agonizing withdrawal
Caffeine	Stimulant	Increased alertness and wakefulness	Anxiety, restlessness, and insomnia in high doses; uncomfortable withdrawal
Methamphetamine ("speed," "ice")	Stimulant	Euphoria, alertness, energy	Irritability, insomnia, hypertension, seizures
Cocaine	Stimulant	Rush of euphoria, confidence, energy	Cardiovascular stress, suspiciousness, depressive crash
Nicotine	Stimulant	Arousal and relaxation, sense of well-being	Heart disease, cancer (from tars)
Ecstasy (MDMA)	Stimulant; mild hallucinogen	Emotional elevation, disinhibition	Dehydration and overheating, depressed mood and cognitive functioning
Marijuana	Mild hallucinogen	Enhanced sensation, relief of pain, distortion of time, relaxation	Disrupted memory, lung damage from smoke

and larger doses to produce the desired high (tolerance), causing the aftereffects to worsen in the drug's absence (withdrawal). This in turn creates a need to switch off the withdrawal symptoms by taking yet more of the drug.

Influences on Drug Use

14. *Why do some people become regular users of consciousness-altering drugs?*

Drug use by North American youth increased during the 1970s. Then, with increased drug education and a more realistic and deglamorized media depiction of taking drugs, drug use declined sharply. Since the early 1990s, the cultural antidrug voice has softened and drugs are once again being glamorized in some music and films. And drug use has rebounded, renewing public concern. Consider the trends:

- In the University of Michigan's annual survey of 15,000 high school seniors, the proportion who believe there is "great risk" in regular marijuana use rose from 35 percent in 1978 to 79 percent in 1991, then retreated to 55 percent in 2003 (Johnston & others, 2004).
- After peaking in 1978, marijuana use by high school seniors declined through 1992, but then rose through the mid-1990s (**FIGURE 6.15**, page 218).
- In the UCLA/American Council on Education annual survey of new college and university students, support for the legalization of marijuana dropped from 53 percent in 1977 to 17 percent in 1989; support rebounded to 40 percent in 2002 (Astin & others, 1997; Sax & others, 2002).

Similar ups and downs in attitude and usage since the late 1970s appear in Canadian and British surveys (Conner & McMillan, 1999; Smart & others, 1991). By the mid-1990s, 57 percent of students surveyed at 10 British universities said they had tried marijuana.

In the real world, alcohol accounts for one-sixth or less of beverage use. In television's world, drinking alcohol occurs more often than the combined drinking of coffee, tea, soft drinks, and water (Gerbner, 1990).

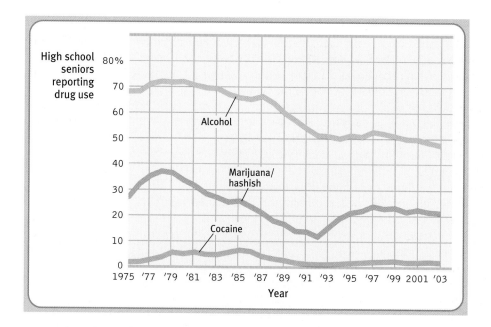

figure 6.15
Trends in drug use The percentage of high school seniors who report having used alcohol, marijuana, or cocaine during the past 30 days declined from the late 1970s to 1992. (From Johnston & others, 2004.)

Other studies reveal a changing national attitude toward alcohol in the United States. More than at any time since Prohibition, health- and safety-conscious people see alcohol less as a beverage to be enjoyed than as a drug to be shunned. The number of new U.S. collegians who reported abstaining from drinking beer during the preceding year has doubled, from 25 percent in 1981 to 54 percent in 2002. Four in 10 Americans declare themselves "total abstainer[s]" (Gallup, 2002). Hard liquor consumption per person dropped 60 percent from 1977 to 1997 (Nephew & others, 1999). When the alcohol industry started substituting wine coolers for wine and nonalcoholic beer for alcoholic, it was clear that attitudes were changing.

The apparent lesson: Effectively inform people about the health hazards of using cocaine, marijuana, alcohol, or tobacco and—without therapy, support groups, or medicines—many will simply stop.

Biological Influences

Some people may be biologically vulnerable to alcohol. For example, evidence accumulates that heredity influences some aspects of alcohol use and abuse (Crabbe, 2002):

- Adopted individuals are more susceptible to alcoholism if one or both biological parents has a history of alcoholism.
- Having an identical twin with alcoholism puts one at increased risk for alcohol problems.
- Boys who at age 6 are excitable, impulsive, and fearless (genetically influenced traits) are more likely as teens to smoke, drink, and use other drugs (Masse & Tremblay, 1997).
- Compared with other children, children whose parents abuse alcohol have a higher tolerance for multiple alcoholic drinks taken over an hour or two.
- Researchers have bred rats and mice that prefer alcoholic drinks to water. One such strain has reduced levels of a brain chemical called NPY; mice engineered to overproduce NPY are very sensitive to alcohol's sedating effect and drink little.
- Molecular geneticists have identified genes that are more common among people and animals predisposed to alcoholism. These genes may, for example, produce deficiencies in the brain's natural dopamine reward system.

Psychological and Cultural Influences

Psychological and social factors may also exert an important influence. In their studies of youth and young adults, Michael Newcomb and L. L. Harlow (1986) found that one psychological factor is the feeling that one's life is meaningless and directionless, a common feeling among school dropouts who subsist without job skills, without privilege, with little hope. When young unmarried adults leave home, alcohol and other drug use increases; when they marry and have children, it decreases (Bachman & others, 1997). Yet the ups and downs of marijuana usage over time seem not due to youth becoming more rebellious (which they have not). What predicts usage is instead the ups and downs in how risky the young people perceive marijuana use to be (**FIGURE 6.16**).

Other studies reveal that heavy users of alcohol, marijuana, and cocaine often have experienced significant stress or failure and are depressed. Monkeys, too, end up with a taste for booze when stressed by permanent separation from their mothers at birth (Small, 2002). By temporarily dulling the pain of self-awareness, alcohol may offer a way to avoid having to cope with depression, anger, anxiety, or insomnia. The relief may be temporary, but as Chapter 7 explains, behavior is often controlled more by its immediate than by its later consequences.

Especially for teenagers, drug use can also have social roots, evident in differing rates of drug use across cultural groups. In the United States, alcohol and other drug addiction rates are extremely low among the Amish, Mennonites, Mormons, and Orthodox Jews (Trimble, 1994). What do you suppose is the rate of drug usage among African-American students—low or high? Independent government studies of drug use in households nationwide and among 12,272 high schoolers in all 50 states reveal that African-American teens have sharply lower rates of drinking, smoking, and cocaine use (Bass & Kane-Williams, 1993; Kann & others, 1993).

Peer culture is a major social influence. By their words and examples, peers influence attitudes about drugs. They also throw the parties and provide the drugs. If an adolescent's friends use drugs, the odds are that he or she will, too. If the friends do not, the opportunity may not even arise.

Peer influence is not just a matter of what friends do and say but also of what adolescents *believe* their friends are doing and favoring. Young adolescents consume more alcohol when, as often happens, they overestimate their friends' use (Aas & Klepp, 1992; Graham & others, 1991). In one survey of sixth graders in 22 states,

Warning signs of alcoholism
- *Drinking binges*
- *Regretting things done or said when drunk*
- *Feeling low or guilty after drinking*
- *Failing to honor a resolve to drink less*
- *Drinking to alleviate depression or anxiety*
- *Avoiding family or friends when drinking*

Annual Beer and Wine Consumption, Liters per Person

	Beer	Wine
France	41	67
Germany	143	25
Italy	23	57
New Zealand	110	15
Australia	102	19
United Kingdom	106	12
United States	87	7
Sweden	59	12

Source: Australian Social Trends, *1995.*

Humorist Dave Barry (1995) recalling why he smoked his first cigarette the summer he turned 15: "Arguments against smoking: 'It's a repulsive addiction that slowly but surely turns you into a gasping, gray-skinned, tumor-ridden invalid, hacking up brownish gobs of toxic waste from your one remaining lung.' Arguments for smoking: 'Other teenagers are doing it.' Case closed! Let's light up!"

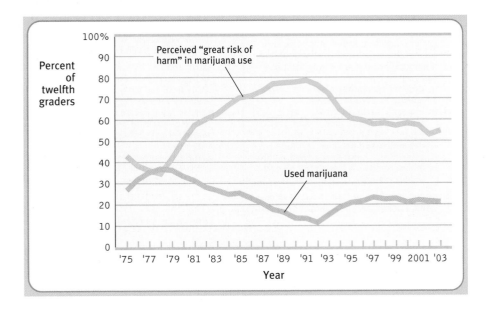

figure 6.16
Perceived marijuana risk and actual use As the percentage of twelfth graders perceiving a "great risk" in regular marijuana use increases, the percentage having used it in the previous 30 days decreases. (Data from Johnston & others, 2004.)

14 percent believed their friends had smoked marijuana, though only 4 percent acknowledged doing so (Wren, 1999). At the university level, drinking dominates social occasions partly because students overestimate their fellow students' enthusiasm for alcohol (Prentice & Miller, 1993; Self, 1994). Thinking that few students share their concerns about the risks associated with alcohol, most students surrender to the perceived norm.

People are more likely to stop using drugs if their beginning use was influenced by their peers (Kandel & Raveis, 1989). When friends stop or the social network changes, they typically stop. For example, more than 9 in 10 soldiers who became drug-addicted while in Vietnam ceased their drug use after returning home. Teenagers who come from happy families and do well in school tend not to use drugs, largely because they rarely associate with those who do (Oetting & Beauvais, 1987, 1990). As always with correlations, the traffic between friends' and one's own drug use may be two-way: Our friends influence us, but we also select as friends those who share our likes and dislikes.

The findings suggest three possible channels of influence for drug prevention and treatment programs: (1) education about the long-term costs of a drug's temporary pleasures, (2) efforts to boost people's self-esteem and purpose in life, and (3) attempts to modify peer associations or to "inoculate" youth against peer pressures by training them in "refusal skills." Said more directly, people rarely abuse drugs if they understand the physical and psychological costs, feel good about themselves and the directions their lives are taking, and are in a peer group that disapproves of using drugs. These educational, psychological, and social factors help explain why 42 percent of American high school dropouts, but only 15 percent of college graduates, smoke (Ladd, 1998).

rehearse it!

15. Continued use of a psychoactive drug produces tolerance. This means that the user will
    a. feel physical pain and intense craving.
    b. be irreversibly addicted to the substance.
    c. need to take bigger doses to get the desired effect.
    d. be able to take smaller doses to get the desired effect.

16. Depressants are drugs that reduce neural activity and slow down body functions. The depressants include alcohol, barbiturates,
    a. and opiates.
    b. cocaine, and morphine.
    c. caffeine, nicotine, and marijuana.
    d. and amphetamines.

17. Alcohol is a depressant that, in significant doses, powerfully affects behavior. For example, drinking alcohol may make a person more helpful or more self-disclosing; conversely, it may make a person more aggressive or more sexually daring. These alcohol effects result from

    a. alcoholic blackouts or memory losses.
    b. deprivation of REM sleep.
    c. sensory arousal and hallucinations.
    d. the lowering of inhibitions.

18. Nicotine and cocaine stimulate neural activity, speed up body functions, and
    a. induce sensory hallucinations.
    b. interfere with memory.
    c. induce a temporary sense of well-being.
    d. lead to heroin use.

19. Ecstasy, which produces euphoria and social intimacy, is both a stimulant and a mild hallucinogen. Its long-term use can
    a. depress sympathetic nervous system activity and lead to death.
    b. increase the brain's supply of dopamine and reduce inhibitions.
    c. deplete the brain's supply of dopamine and produce agitation.
    d. destroy serotonin-producing neurons and permanently deflate mood and impair memory.

20. About one-third of those who have survived a brush with death have reported

near-death experiences, which are strikingly similar to the hallucinations evoked by
    a. amphetamines.
    b. barbiturates.
    c. LSD.
    d. marijuana.

21. Smoking marijuana can relieve certain kinds of pain and nausea. It also
    a. impairs motor coordination, perception, reaction time, and memory.
    b. inhibits people's emotions.
    c. increases male sex hormone levels.
    d. stimulates brain cell development.

22. Marijuana use by young North Americans generally declined from the late 1970s until the early 1990s and then began to increase again. *Social* explanations for drug use today focus on the powerful effect of peer influence. An important *psychological* contributor to drug use is
    a. inflated self-esteem.
    b. the feeling that life is meaningless and directionless.
    c. academic and job pressures.
    d. overprotective parents.

Answers can be found in Appendix C.

chapter review

REVIEWING

States of Consciousness

WAKING CONSCIOUSNESS

1. What is consciousness, and how does it function?

Psychology has returned to the study of consciousness—our awareness of ourselves and our environment. At any moment our selective attention makes us conscious of a very limited amount of all that we are capable of experiencing, as when we attend to one voice among many at a party (the cocktail party effect). Speedy, parallel processing handles subconscious information. Conscious processing of novel tasks is serial and much slower.

SLEEP AND DREAMS

2. How do our age-old biological rhythms influence our daily functioning and our sleep and dreams?

Our daily schedule of waking and sleeping is timed with a body clock known as the circadian rhythm. Each night's sleep also has a rhythm of its own.

3. What is the biological rhythm of our sleep?

Beginning with the alpha waves of the awake but relaxed state, it cycles from transitional Stage 1 sleep, in which hallucinations may occur, to deep Stage 4 sleep, characterized by delta waves, and back up to the more internally active REM sleep stage. Periods of Stage 4 sleep progressively shorten, and periods of dream-laden REM sleep lengthen through the night.

4. How does sleep loss affect us? What is sleep's function?

Depriving people of sleep has not conclusively revealed why, physiologically, we need sleep. Several theories have been proposed. One is that sleep has evolutionary value. Others are that it helps restore brain tissues and consolidate memories. Sleep is linked with the release of pituitary growth hormone.

5. What are the major sleep disorders?

The disorders of sleep include insomnia (recurring wakefulness), narcolepsy (uncontrollable lapsing into REM sleep), sleep apnea (the temporary cessation of breathing while sleeping), and night terrors (high arousal and terrified appearance occurring during Stage 4 sleep).

6. What do we dream?

Although conscious thoughts can occur during any sleep stage, waking people during REM sleep yields predictable "dreamlike" reports; waking them during other sleep stages yields only an occasional fleeting image. Our dreams are mostly of ordinary events; they often relate to everyday experiences and more frequently involve anxiety or misfortune than triumphant achievements.

7. What is the function of dreams?

Freud believed that a dream's manifest content, or story line, is a censored version of its latent or hidden content, which gratifies our unconscious wishes. Newer explanations of why we dream suggest that dreams (1) help process information from the day and fix it in memory, (2) serve a physiological function, and/or (3) are the brain's efforts to string periodic hallucinations (from activity bursts in brain areas that process visual images) into a story line. Despite their differences, most theorists agree that REM sleep and its associated dreams serve an important function, as shown by the REM rebound that occurs following REM deprivation.

HYPNOSIS

8. What is hypnosis, and what powers does a hypnotist have over a hypnotized subject?

Psychologists agree that hypnosis is a social interaction in which the hypnotist suggests to a subject that certain perceptions, feelings, thoughts, or behaviors will occur spontaneously. They also agree that people are suggestible in varying degrees, and that hypnotized people can no more be made to act against their will than can nonhypnotized people. Hypnosis can be at least temporarily therapeutic (through posthypnotic suggestion), and hypnotizable people can enjoy significant pain relief (perhaps through dissociation).

9. Is hypnosis an extension of normal consciousness or an altered state of consciousness?

There is debate whether hypnosis is a by-product of normal social and cognitive processes or an altered state of consciousness, perhaps involving a dissociation between levels of consciousness (the hidden observer).

DRUGS AND CONSCIOUSNESS

Psychoactive drugs are perception- and mood-altering substances. A surprising number of these drugs, such as caffeine, nicotine, and alcohol, are legal and a part of everyday life.

10. What are dependence and addiction? Can substance abusers overcome their addictions?

The use of psychoactive drugs often leads to tolerance and physical and/or psychological dependence. Users who are physically dependent will experience withdrawal when they try to stop taking the drug. The three types of psychoactive drugs are depressants, stimulants, and hallucinogens.

11. *What are depressants, and what are their effects?*

Alcohol, barbiturates, and the opiates are examples of depressants, which dampen neural activity and slow down body functions. Alcohol decreases inhibitions, both harmful and helpful, and impairs judgment. Alcohol also disrupts the processing of recent experiences into long-term memory and reduces self-awareness. User expectation strongly influences alcohol's behavioral effects. Barbiturates can be especially dangerous in combination with alcohol. The harmful aftereffects of opiates oppose and offset the temporary pleasure they induce.

12. *What are stimulants, and what are their effects?*

Caffeine, nicotine, the amphetamines, cocaine, and Ecstasy are examples of stimulants, which stimulate neural activity and arouse body functions. The reinforcing effects of nicotine make smoking a difficult habit to kick, but increased knowledge of its devastating health effects has led to a decreasing percentage of Americans who smoke. All stimulants, but especially cocaine and crack, produce a crash of agitated depression as the drug wears off. This reinforces the use of increased amounts of the drug to get out of the depression, leading regular cocaine and crack users to become addicted. As with nearly all psychoactive drugs, stimulants act at the synapses by influencing the brain's neurotransmitters, and their effects depend on dosage and the user's personality and expecta-

tions. Ecstasy, which is also a mild hallucinogen, can destroy serotonin-producing neurons and permanently deflate mood and impair memory.

13. *What are hallucinogens, and what are their effects?*

LSD and marijuana are examples of hallucinogens, which distort perception and evoke sensory images without sensory input. Both LSD and marijuana can distort the user's judgments of time and, depending on the setting in which they are taken, can alter sensation and perception. Similar hallucinations are reported in near-death experiences, perhaps as a result of oxygen deprivation in the brain. Although THC, the major active ingredient in marijuana, can be therapeutic for those enduring glaucoma, AIDS, or chemotherapy, it corrodes health, judgment, and memory.

14. *Why do some people become regular users of consciousness-altering drugs?*

Drug use among teenagers and young adults declined during the 1980s and into the early 1990s. Nevertheless, psychological factors (such as stress, depression, and feelings of hopelessness) and social factors (such as peer pressure) combine to lead many people to experiment with—and become dependent on—drugs. Some people also appear to have a greater biological susceptibility to dependence on drugs such as alcohol.

A CRITICAL THINKER'S REVIEW OF CHAPTER 6

You've now studied and reviewed **States of Consciousness.** For even better retention, reflect on these concepts at a deeper level. If you need to refresh your memory of the six categories of critical thinking shown in parentheses below, see page 34. See if you can answer each of these questions in a short paragraph.

1. Your friend Jake is intently watching TV in the next room. You call out "Mind if I eat the last cookie?" There is no response, so you eat it. Jake is later angry, because he insists that you never asked. How can you show Jake that "selective attention" really exists? (scientific problem solving)

2. Eliza shows classic signs of sleep deprivation. She has a hard time concentrating, and she often falls asleep during even the most interesting lectures. She claims she gets plenty of sleep, yet she always has to set her alarm and often hits the "snooze" button several times before getting out of bed in the morning. She drinks a lot of cola at night while studying, because she says it quenches her thirst. She also regularly works out at night before going to bed. And her bedtimes and wake-up times fluctuate wildly throughout the week. Based on what you've learned from reading about sleep research, what changes would you recommend to Eliza so that she can feel more alert during the day? (practical problem solving)

3. Karena is convinced she is suffering from narcolepsy. She has a tendency to fall asleep at what she considers inopportune times, such as late at night while watching TV with friends, or when she's in the library trying to study. When she falls asleep—leaning back on the couch or with her head on her desk—she is hard to awaken. She says she often begins dreaming during these "naps." What questions do we need to ask of Karena to help her determine whether she is truly suffering from narcolepsy? What else could be causing her to nod off? (pattern recognition)

4. Byron was not doing well in his university courses, and he had a hard time mustering the energy to get out of bed each day. A friend suggested he see a hypnotist to help uncover and resolve the inner conflicts she is sure are disrupting his functioning. After several sessions, Byron became convinced he had been abducted by aliens, who landed on his rooftop in their spaceship and performed painful medical procedures on him. He is understandably upset and, because he worries the aliens will come back, he cannot sleep at night. What can you tell Byron about hypnosis and recall of forgotten events that will help dispel his fears? (perspective taking)

5. A U.S. government survey of 27,616 current or former alcohol drinkers found that 40 percent of those who began drinking before age 15 grew dependent on alcohol. The same was true of only 10 percent of those who first imbibed at ages 21 or 22 (Grant & Dawson, 1998). What possible explanations can you think of for this correlation between early use and later abuse? (creative problem solving)

6. Your parents lecture you about not drinking and driving, but then they often drive themselves home after having several drinks with friends. When you point out this inconsistency, they tell you that they are older and can "handle it" better than a young adult. Using what you now know about the physiological effects of alcohol, explain why this is not true. (psychological reasoning)

Answers can be found in Appendix C.

TERMS AND CONCEPTS TO REMEMBER

consciousness, p. 187

selective attention, p. 188

circadian [ser-KAY-dee-an] rhythm, p. 190

REM sleep, p. 191

alpha waves, p. 192

sleep, p. 192

hallucinations, p. 192

delta waves, p. 192

insomnia, p. 198

narcolepsy, p. 198

sleep apnea, p. 199

night terrors, p. 199

dream, p. 200

manifest content, p. 201

latent content, p. 201

REM rebound, p. 203

hypnosis, p. 204

posthypnotic amnesia, p. 204

posthypnotic suggestion, p. 205

dissociation, p. 206

hidden observer, p. 207

psychoactive drug, p. 208

tolerance, p. 208

withdrawal, p. 209

physical dependence, p. 209

psychological dependence, p. 209

depressants, p. 210

barbiturates, p. 211

opiates, p. 212

stimulants, p. 212

amphetamines, p. 212

Ecstasy (MDMA), p. 214

hallucinogens, p. 215

LSD, p. 215

near-death experience, p. 215

THC, p. 216

To continue your study and review of States of Consciousness, visit this book's Web site at www.worthpublishers.com/myers. You will find practice tests, review activities, and Web links for more information on topics related to States of Consciousness.

chapter7

Learning

When a chinook salmon first emerges from its egg in a stream's gravel bed, its genes provide most of the behavioral instructions it needs for life. It knows instinctively how and where to swim, what to eat, and how to protect itself from predators. Following a built-in plan, the young salmon soon begins its trek to the sea. After some four years in the ocean, the mature salmon returns to its birthplace. It navigates hundreds of miles to the mouth of its home river and then, guided by the scent of its home stream, begins an upstream odyssey to its ancestral spawning ground. Once there, the salmon seeks out the exact conditions of temperature, gravel, and water flow that will facilitate its breeding. It then mates and, its life mission accomplished, dies.

Unlike the salmon, we are not born with a genetic blueprint for life. Much of what we do we learn from experience. Although we struggle to find the life direction a salmon is born with, our learning gives us more flexibility. We can learn how to build grass huts or snow shelters, submarines or space stations, and thereby adapt to almost any environment. Indeed, nature's most important gift to us may be our *adaptability*—our capacity to learn new behaviors that enable us to cope with changing circumstances.

"Actually, sex just isn't that important to me."

1. What is learning?

No topic is closer to the heart of psychology than **learning**, *a relatively permanent change in an organism's behavior due to experience.* In earlier chapters we considered the learning of visual perceptions, of moral ideas, of a drug's expected effect. In later chapters we will consider how learning shapes our thought and language, our motivations and emotions, our personalities and attitudes.

Learning in all such realms breeds hope. What is learnable, we can potentially teach—a fact that encourages parents, educators, coaches, and animal trainers. What has been learned we can potentially change by new learning—an assumption that underlies counseling, psychotherapy, and rehabilitation programs. No matter how unhappy, unsuccessful, or unloving we are, that need not be the end of our story.

By definition, experience is key to learning. More than 200 years ago, philosophers such as John Locke and David Hume echoed Aristotle's conclusion from 2000 years earlier: We learn by association. Our minds naturally connect events that occur in sequence: We *associate* them. If, after seeing and smelling freshly baked bread, you eat some and find it satisfying, then the next time you see and smell fresh bread, your experience will lead you to expect that eating it will be satisfying again. And if you associate a sound with a frightening consequence, then your fear may be aroused by the sound itself. As one 4-year-old exclaimed after watching a TV character get mugged, "If I had heard that music, I wouldn't have gone around the corner!" (Wells, 1981).

Simpler animals can learn simple associations. When disturbed by a squirt of water, the sea snail *Aplysia* will protectively withdraw its gill. If the squirts continue, as happens naturally in choppy water, the withdrawal response diminishes. (The snail's response "habituates.") But if the sea snail repeatedly receives an electric shock just after being squirted, its withdrawal response to the squirt instead becomes stronger. The animal associates the squirt with the impending shock. More complex animals can learn more complex associations, especially those that bring favorable consequences. Seals in an aquarium will repeat behaviors, such as slapping and barking, that prompt people to toss them a herring.

By linking two events that occur close together, both the sea snail and the seals exhibit **associative learning**. The sea snail associates the squirt with impending shock; the seals associate slapping and barking with receiving a herring (**FIGURE 7.1**, page 226). In both cases, the animals learned something important to their survival: to associate the past with the immediate future.

"Learning is the eye of the mind."

Thomas Drake, Bibliotheca Scholastica
Instructissima, *1633*

▶ **learning** a relatively permanent change in an organism's behavior due to experience.

▶ **associative learning** learning that certain events occur together. The events may be two stimuli (as in classical conditioning) or a response and its consequences (as in operant conditioning).

figure 7.1
Associative learning: Learning to associate two events

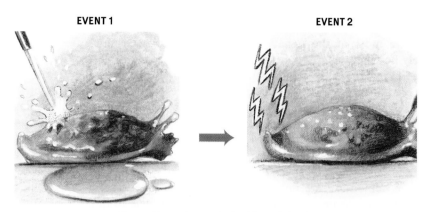

Sea snail associates splash with a tail shock

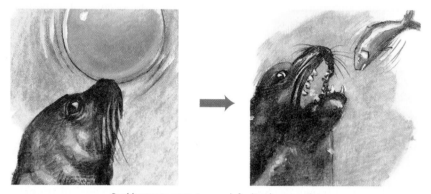

Seal learns to expect a snack for its showy antics

Elise Amendola/AP Photo

Nature without appropriate nurture
When captive-bred Mexican gray wolves were first freed, their life experience left them unprepared for self-protection and survival.

Which type of conditioning does the sea snail illustrate? What about the seal? (See page 228.)

Most of us would be unable to name the order of the songs on our favorite CD. Yet hearing the end of one piece cues (by association) an anticipation of the next. Likewise, when singing your national anthem, you associate the end of each line with the beginning of the next. (Pick a line out of the middle and notice how much harder it is to recall the previous *line.)*

The significance of an animal's learning is illustrated by the challenges that captive-bred animals face when reintroduced to the wild. After being bred and raised in captivity, 11 Mexican gray wolves—extinct in the United States since 1977—were released in Arizona's Apache National Forest in 1998. Eight months later, the lone survivor of this initial effort was recaptured. The pen-reared wolves had learned how to hunt—and to move 100 feet away from people—but had not learned to run from a human with a gun. The gray wolves' experience is not unusual. Of 145 documented reintroductions of 115 species in the twentieth century, only 11 percent produced self-sustaining populations in the wild. Keiko—the killer whale of Free Willy fame—had all the right genes for being dropped right back into his Icelandic home waters, but not the life experience. Successful adaptation requires both nature (the needed genetic predispositions) and nurture (a history of appropriate learning).

Conditioning is the process of learning associations. In *classical conditioning*, we learn to associate two stimuli and thus to anticipate events. We learn that a flash of lightning signals an impending crack of thunder, and so we start to brace ourselves when lightning flashes nearby (**FIGURE 7.2**).

In *operant conditioning*, we learn to associate a response and its consequence and thus to repeat acts followed by rewards and avoid acts followed by punishment. We learn that pushing a vending machine button relates to the delivery of a candy bar (**FIGURE 7.3**).

To simplify, we will consider these two types of associative learning separately. Often, though, they occur together in the same situation. A clever Japanese rancher reportedly herds cattle by outfitting them with electronic pagers, which he calls from his cell phone. After a week of training, the cattle learn to associate two stimuli—the beep on their pager and the arrival of food (classical conditioning). But they also learn to associate their hustling to the food trough with the pleasure of eating (operant conditioning).

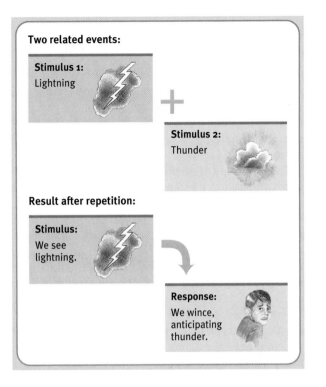

figure 7.2
Classical conditioning

The concept of conditioning by association, however, leaves many questions: What principles influence the learning and the loss of associations? How can we apply these principles? And what really are the associations: Does the beep on a steer's pager evoke a mental representation of food, to which the steer responds by coming to the trough? Or does it make little sense to explain conditioned associations in terms of cognitive processes?

Conditioning is not the only form of learning. Through *observational learning*, we learn from others' experiences and examples. Complex animals, such as chimpanzees, sometimes learn behaviors merely by observing others perform them. If one animal watches another learn to solve a puzzle that gains a food reward, the observing animal may perform the trick more quickly.

In all these ways—by classical and operant conditioning and by observation—we humans learn and adapt to our environments. We learn to expect and prepare for significant events such as food or pain (classical conditioning). We also learn to repeat acts that bring good results and to avoid acts that bring bad results (operant conditioning). By watching others, we learn new behaviors (observational learning). And, through language, we also learn things we have neither experienced nor observed. Of all the world's creatures, we humans are the most capable of changing through learning.

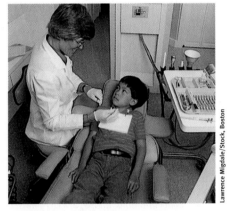

Conditioned fear Because of pain experienced during previous visits to the dentist chair, this young patient has learned to expect discomfort.

Response: Pushing vending machine button

Consequence: Receiving a candy bar

Behavior strengthened

figure 7.3
Operant conditioning

► **classical conditioning** a type of learning in which an organism comes to associate stimuli. A neutral stimulus that signals an unconditioned stimulus (UCS) begins to produce a response that anticipates and prepares for the unconditioned stimulus. Also called *Pavlovian conditioning*.

► **behaviorism** the view that psychology (1) should be an objective science that (2) studies behavior without reference to mental processes. Most research psychologists today agree with (1) but not with (2).

► **unconditioned response (UCR)** in classical conditioning, the unlearned, naturally occurring response to the unconditioned stimulus (UCS), such as salivation when food is in the mouth.

► **unconditioned stimulus (UCS)** in classical conditioning, a stimulus that unconditionally— naturally and automatically— triggers a response.

► **conditioned response (CR)** in classical conditioning, the learned response to a previously neutral conditioned stimulus (CS).

► **conditioned stimulus (CS)** in classical conditioning, an originally irrelevant stimulus that, after association with an unconditioned stimulus (UCS), comes to trigger a conditioned response.

Answers to questions on page 226: The sea snail illustrates classical conditioning. The seal illustrates operant conditioning.

CLASSICAL CONDITIONING

2. How does classical conditioning demonstrate learning by association?

Although the idea of learning associations had long generated philosophical discussion, only in the early twentieth century did psychology's most famous research verify it. For many people, the name Ivan Pavlov (1849–1936) rings a bell. His experiments are classics, and the phenomenon he explored we justly call **classical conditioning** (or *Pavlovian conditioning*).

Pavlov's work also laid the foundation for psychologist John B. Watson's idea that human behavior, though biologically influenced, is mainly a bundle of conditioned responses. In searching for laws underlying learning, Watson (1913) urged his colleagues to discard reference to inner thoughts, feelings, and motives. The science of psychology should instead study how organisms respond to stimuli in their environments, said Watson. "Its theoretical goal is the prediction and control of behavior. Introspection forms no essential part of its methods." Simply said, psychology should be an objective science based on *observable behavior*. This view, which influenced North American psychology during the first half of the twentieth century, Watson called **behaviorism**. Watson and Pavlov shared both a disdain for "mentalistic" concepts such as consciousness and a belief that the basic laws of learning were the same for all animals—whether dogs or humans. Although few researchers today would agree that psychology should avoid the study of mental processes, nearly all would agree that classical conditioning is a basic form of learning by which all organisms adapt to their environment.

Pavlov's Experiments

Pavlov was driven by a lifelong passion for research. After setting aside his initial plan to follow his father into the Russian Orthodox priesthood, Pavlov received a medical degree at age 33 and spent the next two decades studying the digestive system. This work earned him Russia's first Nobel prize in 1904. But it was his novel experiments on learning, to which he devoted the last three decades of his life, that earned this feisty scientist his place in history.

Pavlov's new direction came when his creative mind seized on an incidental finding. After studying salivary secretion in dogs, he knew that when he put food in a dog's mouth the animal would invariably salivate. He also noticed that when he worked with the same dog repeatedly, the dog began salivating to stimuli associated with food—to the mere sight of the food, to the food dish, to the presence of the person who regularly brought the food, or even to the sound of that person's approaching footsteps. Because these "psychic secretions" interfered with his experiments on digestion, Pavlov considered them an annoyance—until he realized they pointed to a simple but important form of learning. From that time on, Pavlov studied learning, which he hoped might enable him to better understand the brain's workings.

Sovfoto

At first, Pavlov and his assistants tried to imagine what the dog was thinking and feeling as it drooled in anticipation of the food. This only led them into fruitless debates. So to explore the phenomenon more objectively, they experimented. They paired various neutral stimuli, such as a tone, with food in the mouth to see if the dog would begin salivating to the neutral stimuli alone. To eliminate the possible influence of extraneous stimuli, they isolated the dog in a small room, secured it in a harness, and attached a device that diverted its saliva to a measuring instrument

Ivan Pavlov "Experimental investigation . . . should lay a solid foundation for a future true science of psychology" (1927).

(**FIGURE 7.4**). From an adjacent room they could present food—at first by sliding in a food bowl, later by blowing meat powder into the dog's mouth at a precise moment. If a neutral stimulus—something the dog could see or hear—now regularly signaled the arrival of food, would the dog associate the two stimuli? If so, would it begin salivating to the neutral stimulus in anticipation of the food?

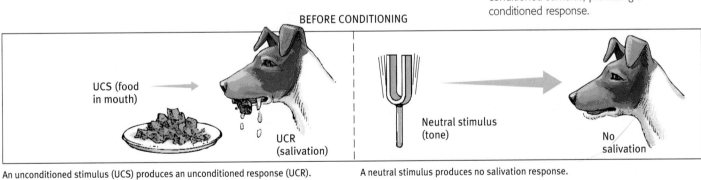

figure 7.4
Pavlov's device for recording salivation The dog's saliva was collected drop by drop in a tube. (Adapted from Goodwin, 1991.)

The answers proved to be yes and yes. Just before placing food in the dog's mouth to produce salivation, Pavlov sounded a tone. After several pairings of tone and food, the dog began salivating to the tone alone, in anticipation of the meat powder. Using this procedure, Pavlov conditioned dogs to salivate to other stimuli—a buzzer, a light, a touch on the leg, even the sight of a circle.

Because salivation in response to food in the mouth was unlearned, Pavlov called it an **unconditioned response (UCR)**. Food in the mouth automatically, *unconditionally*, triggers a dog's salivary reflex (**FIGURE 7.5**). Thus, Pavlov called the food stimulus an **unconditioned stimulus (UCS)**.

Salivation in response to the tone was *conditional* upon the dog's learning the association between the tone and the food. One translation of Pavlov therefore calls the salivation the "conditional reflex" (Todes, 1997). Today we call this learned response the **conditioned response (CR)**. The previously irrelevant tone stimulus that now triggered the conditional salivation we call the **conditioned stimulus (CS)**. It's easy to distinguish these two kinds of stimuli and responses. Just remember: conditioned = learned; *un*conditioned = *un*learned.

A second example, drawn from more recent experiments, may help. An experimenter sounds a tone just before delivering an air puff to your eye. After several repetitions, you blink to the tone alone. What is the UCS? The UCR? The CS? The CR?[1]

[1]UCS=air puff; UCR=blink to air puff; CS=tone; CR=blink to tone

figure 7.5
Pavlov's classic experiment Pavlov presented a neutral stimulus (a tone) just before an unconditioned stimulus (food in mouth). The neutral stimulus then became a conditioned stimulus, producing a conditioned response.

BEFORE CONDITIONING

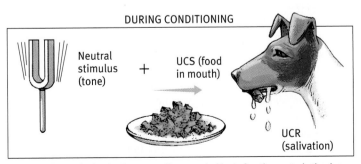

UCS (food in mouth)

UCR (salivation)

An unconditioned stimulus (UCS) produces an unconditioned response (UCR).

Neutral stimulus (tone)

No salivation

A neutral stimulus produces no salivation response.

DURING CONDITIONING

Neutral stimulus (tone) + UCS (food in mouth)

UCR (salivation)

The unconditioned stimulus is repeatedly presented just after the neutral stimulus. The unconditioned stimulus continues to produce an unconditioned response.

AFTER CONDITIONING

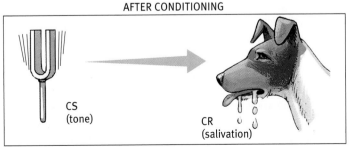

CS (tone)

CR (salivation)

The neutral stimulus alone now produces a conditioned response (CR), thereby becoming a conditioned stimulus (CS).

PEANUTS

If Pavlov's demonstration of associative learning was so simple, what did he do for the next three decades? How did his research factory generate 532 papers on salivary conditioning (Windholz, 1997)? He and his associates explored the causes and effects of classical conditioning. Their experiments identified five major conditioning processes: acquisition, extinction, spontaneous recovery, generalization, and discrimination.

Acquisition

3. How do the processes of acquisition, extinction, spontaneous recovery, generalization, and discrimination affect a CR?

To understand the **acquisition**, or initial learning, of the stimulus-response relationship, Pavlov and his associates first had to confront the question of timing: How much time should elapse between presenting the neutral stimulus (the tone, the light, the touch, or whatever) and the unconditioned stimulus? They found that, in most cases, the answer was not much. With many species and procedures, half a second works well. What do you suppose would happen if the food (UCS) appeared *before* the tone (CS) rather than after? Would conditioning occur?

Not likely. Although there are exceptions, conditioning seldom occurs when the CS comes after the UCS. This finding fits the presumption that classical conditioning is biologically adaptive. It helps organisms *prepare* for good or bad events. Pavlov's tone (CS) signals an important biological event—the arrival of food (UCS). To a deer in the forest, the sound of a snapping twig (CS) may come to signal a predator (UCS). If the good or bad event had already occurred, the CS would not likely signal anything significant.

Michael Domjan (1992, 1994, 1997) showed how the CS signals an important biological event by conditioning the sexual arousal of male Japanese quail. Just before presenting an approachable female, the researchers turned on a red light. Over time, with the red light continuing to herald a female's impending arrival, it caused the male quail to become excited (and to copulate with her more quickly when she arrived). Moreover, the male quail developed a preference for their cage's red-light district. Exposure to sexually conditioned stimuli also caused them to release more semen and sperm (Domjan & others, 1998). All in all, the quail's capacity for classical conditioning gives it a reproductive edge. This illustrates the larger lesson that conditioning serves a function: It helps an animal survive and reproduce—by responding to cues that help it gain food, avoid dangers, defeat rivals, locate mates, and produce offspring (Hollis, 1997).

In humans, too, objects, smells, and sights associated with sexual pleasure become conditioned stimuli for sexual arousal. Psychologist Michael Tirrell (1990) recalls: "My first girlfriend loved onions, so I came to associate onion breath with kissing. Before long, onion breath sent tingles up and down my spine. Oh what a feeling!" (Questions: What is the unconditioned stimulus here? What is the conditioned response? See **FIGURE 7.6**.)

Check yourself: If the aroma of cake baking sets your mouth to watering, what is the UCS? The CS? The CR? (See page 233.)

Remember:

UCS = **Un**Conditioned **S**timulus
UCR = **Un**Conditioned **R**esponse
CS = **C**onditioned **S**timulus
CR = **C**onditioned **R**esponse

▶ **acquisition** the initial stage in classical conditioning; the phase associating a neutral stimulus with an unconditioned stimulus so that the neutral stimulus comes to elicit a conditioned response. In operant conditioning, the strengthening of a reinforced response.

▶ **extinction** the diminishing of a conditioned response; occurs in classical conditioning when an unconditioned stimulus (UCS) does not follow a conditioned stimulus (CS); occurs in operant conditioning when a response is no longer reinforced.

▶ **spontaneous recovery** the reappearance, after a rest period, of an extinguished conditioned response.

Updating Pavlov's Understanding

4. Do cognitive processes and biological constraints affect classical conditioning?

Pavlov's and Watson's disdain for "mentalistic" concepts such as consciousness has given way to a growing realization that they underestimated the importance of *cognitive processes* (thoughts, perceptions, expectations) and *biological constraints* on an organism's learning capacity.

Cognitive Processes

The early behaviorists believed that the learned behaviors of various organisms could be reduced to mindless mechanisms. The idea that rats and dogs exhibit cognition therefore struck many psychologists as unnecessary. No longer. Robert Rescorla and Allan Wagner (1972) argued that when two significant events occur close together in time, an animal learns the *predictability* of the second event. If a shock always is preceded by a tone, and then sometimes also by a light that accompanies the tone, a rat will react with fear to the tone but not to the light. Although the light is always followed by the shock, the tone better predicts impending shock. The more predictable the association, the stronger the conditioned response. It's as if the animal learns an *expectancy*, an awareness of how likely it is that the UCS will occur.

This principle helps explain why classical conditioning treatments that ignore cognition often have limited success. For example, people receiving therapy for alcoholism sometimes are given alcohol spiked with a nauseating drug. Will they then associate alcohol with sickness? If classical conditioning were merely a matter of "stamping in" stimulus associations, we might hope so, and—to some extent—this does occur (as we will see on pages 514–515). However, those receiving the drink are aware that they can blame their nausea on the drug, not on the alcohol. This cognition often weakens the association between alcohol and feeling sick. So, even in classical conditioning, it is not only the simple CS–UCS association but also the thought that counts.

Biological Predispositions

Ever since Darwin, scientists have assumed that all animals share a common evolutionary history and resulting commonalities in their makeup and functioning. Pavlov and Watson, for example, believed the basic laws of learning were essentially similar in all animals. So it should make little difference whether one studied pigeons or people. Moreover, it seemed that any natural response could be conditioned to any neutral stimulus. As learning researcher Gregory Kimble proclaimed in 1956, "Just about any activity of which the organism is capable can be conditioned and . . . these responses can be conditioned to any stimulus that the organism can perceive" (p. 195).

Twenty-five years later Kimble (1981) humbly acknowledged that "half a thousand" scientific reports had proven him wrong. More than the early behaviorists realized, an animal's capacity for conditioning is constrained by its biology. Each species' biological predispositions prepare it to learn the associations that enhance its survival. Environments are not the whole story.

Among those who challenged the prevailing behaviorist environmentalism was John Garcia. While researching the effects of radiation on laboratory animals, Garcia and Robert Koelling (1966) noticed that rats began to avoid drinking the water from the plastic bottles in radiation chambers. They wondered whether classical conditioning might be the culprit. Might the rats have linked the plastic-tasting water (a CS) to the sickness (UCR) triggered by the radiation (UCS)?

To test their hunch, Garcia and Koelling gave the rats a particular taste, sight, or sound (CS) and later also gave them radiation or drugs that led to nausea and vomiting (UCR). Two startling findings emerged: First, even if sickened as late as

▶ **generalization** the tendency, once a response has been conditioned, for stimuli similar to the conditioned stimulus to elicit similar responses.

▶ **discrimination** in classical conditioning, the learned ability to distinguish between a conditioned stimulus and stimuli that do not signal an unconditioned stimulus.

"All brains are, in essence, anticipation machines."

Daniel C. Dennett, Consciousness Explained, *1991*

Answer to questions on page 230: The cake (and its taste) are the UCS. The associated aroma is the CS. Salivation to the aroma is the CR.

John Garcia As the laboring son of California farmworkers, Garcia attended school only in the off-season during his early childhood years. After entering junior college in his late twenties, and earning his Ph.D. in his late forties, he received the American Psychological Association's Distinguished Scientific Contribution Award "for his highly original, pioneering research in conditioning and learning." He was also elected to the National Academy of Sciences.

Courtesy of John Garcia

Taste aversion If you became violently ill after eating mussels, you probably would have a hard time eating them again. Their smell and taste would have become a CS for nausea. This learning occurs readily because our biology prepares us to learn taste aversions to toxic foods.

"Once bitten, twice shy."

G. F. Northall, *Folk-Phrases, 1894*

figure 7.9
Nausea conditioning in cancer patients

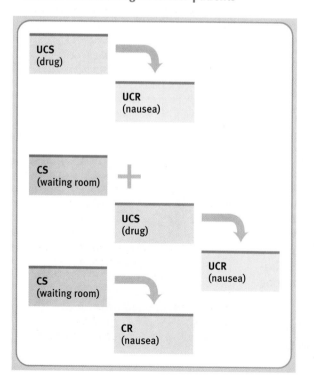

several hours after tasting a particular novel flavor, the rats thereafter avoided that flavor. This appeared to violate the notion that for conditioning to occur, the UCS must follow the CS immediately.

Second, the sickened rats developed aversions to tastes but not to sights or sounds. This contradicted the behaviorists' idea that any perceivable stimulus could serve as a CS. But it made adaptive sense, because for rats the easiest way to identify tainted food is to taste it. (If sickened after sampling a new food, they thereafter avoid the food—which makes it difficult to eradicate a population of "bait-shy" rats by poisoning.) Birds, which hunt by sight, appear biologically primed to develop aversions to the *sight* of tainted food (Nicolaus & others, 1983).

Humans, too, seem biologically prepared to learn some things rather than others. If you get violently ill four hours after eating contaminated mussels, you will probably develop an aversion to the taste of mussels but not to the sight of the associated restaurant, its plates, the people you were with, or the music you heard there. Similarly, we more easily learn to fear snakes and spiders than to fear flowers (Cook & others, 1986). Again, it makes sense: Such animals harm us more frequently than do flowers.

All these cases support Charles Darwin's principle that natural selection favors traits that aid survival. Nature prepares the members of each species to learn those things crucial to their survival. Someone who readily learns a taste aversion is unlikely to eat the same toxic food again and is more likely to survive and leave descendants. Indeed, all sorts of bad feelings, from nausea to anxiety to pain, serve good purposes. Like the low-oil light on a car dashboard, each alerts the body to a threat (Neese, 1991).

Garcia and Koelling's provocative findings extended to other species. In one well-known study, coyotes and wolves that were tempted into eating sheep carcasses laced with a sickening poison developed an aversion to sheep meat (Gustavson & others, 1974, 1976). Two wolves that were later penned with a live sheep seemed actually to fear it.

Such research suggests possible humane ways for controlling predators and agricultural pests. This is but one instance in which psychological research that began with the discomfort of some laboratory animals enhanced the welfare of many more animals. In this case, the research saved the sheep from the coyotes. The coyotes in turn were saved from angry ranchers and farmers who, with their livestock no longer endangered, were less adamant about destroying the coyotes. Later experiments revealed that conditioned taste aversion could successfully prevent baboons from raiding African gardens, racoons from attacking chickens, and ravens and crows from feeding on crane eggs—all while preserving predators who occupy an important ecological niche (Garcia & Gustavson, 1997).

The discovery of biological constraints on learning affirms a deep principle: *Learning enables animals to adapt to their environments.* Adaptation shows us why animals would be responsive to stimuli that announce significant events, such as food or pain. Animals are generally predisposed to associate a CS with a UCS that follows predictably and immediately—for causes often immediately precede effects.

Adaptation also helps explain exceptions, such as the taste-aversion finding. In this case, effect need not follow cause immediately—poisoned food usually causes sickness quite a while after the food has been eaten. Similarly, cancer patients who suffer nausea and vomiting beginning more than an hour following chemotherapy often develop classically conditioned nausea to stimuli associated with taking the drug (**FIGURE 7.9**). After four or five clinic visits, they may react to its sight, sound, and smell with anxiety and anticipatory nausea (Hall, 1997). (Under normal circumstances, such revulsion to sickening stimuli is adaptive.) The conditioned stimuli elicit the associated nausea. Thus, merely returning to the clinic's waiting room or seeing the nurses can provoke sick feelings (Burish & Carey, 1986; Davey, 1992).

Pavlov's Legacy

5. Why is Pavlov's work important?

What, then, remains of Pavlov's ideas about conditioning? A great deal. All the researchers we have met so far in this chapter agree that classical conditioning is a basic form of learning. Judged by today's knowledge of cognitive processes and biological predispositions, Pavlov's ideas were incomplete. But if we see further than Pavlov did, it is because we stand on his shoulders.

Why does Pavlov's work remain so important? If he had taught us only that old dogs can learn new tricks, his experiments would long ago have been forgotten. Why should anyone care that a dog can be conditioned to salivate at the sound of a tone? The importance lies first in this fact: Many other responses to many other stimuli can be classically conditioned in many other organisms—in fact, in every species tested, from earthworms to fish to dogs to monkeys to people (Schwartz, 1984). Thus, classical conditioning is one way that virtually all organisms learn to adapt to their environment.

Second, Pavlov showed us how a process such as learning can be studied objectively. Pavlov was proud that his methods involved virtually no subjective judgments or guesses about what went on in the dogs' minds. The salivary response is an overt behavior measurable as so many drops or cubic centimeters of saliva. Pavlov's success therefore suggested a scientific model for how the young discipline of psychology might proceed—by isolating the elementary building blocks of complex behaviors and studying them with objective laboratory procedures.

Applications of Classical Conditioning

In later chapters on motivation, emotions and health, psychological disorders, and therapy, we will see how Pavlov's principles of classical conditioning apply to human health and well-being. Some examples:

- Former crack cocaine users often feel a craving when they again encounter cues (people, places) associated with previous highs. Thus, drug counselors advise addicts to steer clear of settings associated with the euphoria of previous drug use.
- Counselors sometimes provide people who abuse alcohol with aversive experiences that may reverse their positive associations with alcohol (pages 514–515).
- Classical conditioning even works on the body's disease-fighting immune system. When a particular taste accompanies a drug that influences immune responses, the taste by itself may come to produce an immune response (page 412).

Pavlov's work also provided a basis for John Watson's (1913) idea that human emotions and behavior, though biologically influenced, are mainly a bundle of conditioned responses. In one famous study, Watson and Rosalie Rayner (1920; Harris, 1979) showed how specific fears might be conditioned (**FIGURE 7.10**, page 236). Their subject was an 11-month-old infant named Albert. Like most infants, "Little Albert" feared loud noises but not white rats. Watson and Rayner presented him with a white rat and, as he reached to touch it, struck a hammer against a steel bar just behind his head. After seven repetitions of seeing the rat and then hearing the frightening noise, Albert burst into tears at the mere sight of the rat (an ethically troublesome study by today's standards). What is more, five days later Albert showed generalization of his conditioned response by reacting with fear to a rabbit, a dog, and a sealskin coat, but not to dissimilar objects such as toys.

Although Little Albert's fate is unknown, Watson's is not. After losing his professorship at Johns Hopkins University over an affair with Rayner (whom he later married), he became the

"[Psychology's] factual and theoretical developments in this century—which have changed the study of mind and behavior as radically as genetics changed the study of heredity—have all been the product of objective analysis—that is to say, behavioristic analysis."

Psychologist Donald Hebb (1980)

In Watson and Rayner's experiment, what was the UCS? The UCR? The CS? The CR? (See page 237.)

Brown Brothers

John B. Watson Watson (1924) admitted to "going beyond my facts" when offering his famous boast: "Give me a dozen healthy infants, well-formed, and my own specified world to bring them up in and I'll guarantee to take any one at random and train him to become any type of specialist I might select—doctor, lawyer, artist, merchant-chief, and, yes, even beggar-man and thief, regardless of his talents, penchants, tendencies, abilities, vocations, and race of his ancestors."

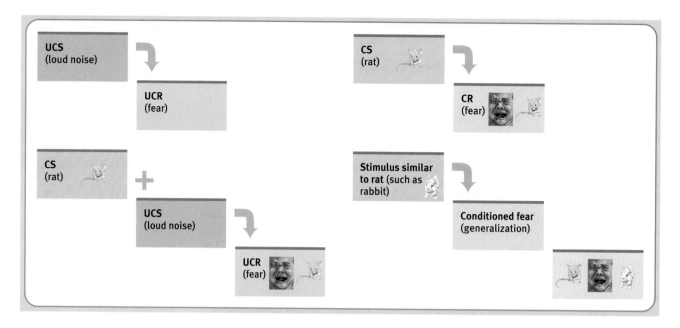

figure 7.10
Little Albert's conditioning
The pairing of a laboratory rat with a terribly loud noise gave Little Albert a conditioned fear (the CR) of both rats (the CS) and similar furry things (generalization).

J. Walter Thompson advertising agency's resident psychologist. There he used his knowledge of associative learning to conceive many successful campaigns, including one for Maxwell House that helped make the "coffee break" an American custom (Hunt, 1993).

Some psychologists had difficulty repeating Watson and Rayner's findings with other children, but the work with Little Albert has had legendary significance for many psychologists. Some have wondered if each of us might not be a walking repository of conditioned emotions. Might our worst emotions be controlled by the application of extinction procedures or by conditioning new responses to emotion-arousing stimuli? One therapist told a patient, who for 30 years had feared going into an elevator alone, to force himself to enter 20 elevators a day. Within 10 days, his fear nearly vanished (Ellis & Becker, 1982). In Chapter 14 we will see more examples of how psychologists use behavioral techniques to treat emotional disorders.

OPERANT CONDITIONING

6. What is operant conditioning, and how does it differ from classical conditioning?

Classical conditioning associates neutral stimuli with important stimuli that produce responses, which often are automatic. It's one thing to teach an animal to salivate at the sound of a tone or a child to fear cars in the street; it's something else to teach an elephant to walk on its hind legs or a child to say *please*. Another type of associative learning explains—and trains—such behaviors. Through **operant conditioning** subjects associate behaviors with their consequences. Thus, they become more likely to repeat rewarded (reinforced) behaviors and less likely to repeat punished behaviors.

Both classical and operant conditioning involve acquisition, extinction, spontaneous recovery, generalization, and discrimination. Yet their difference is straightforward: Classical conditioning forms associations between stimuli (a CS and the UCS it signals). It also involves **respondent behavior**—behavior that occurs as an *automatic* response to some stimulus (such as salivating in response to meat powder and later in response to a tone). Operant conditioning involves **operant behavior**, so-called because the act *operates* on the environment to *produce* rewarding or punishing stimuli. We can therefore distinguish classical from operant conditioning by asking: *Is the organism learning associations between events that it doesn't control (classical conditioning)? Or is it learning associations between its behavior and resulting events (operant conditioning)?*

Skinner's Experiments

B. F. Skinner (1904–1990) was a college English major and an aspiring writer who, seeking a new direction, entered graduate school in psychology. He went on to become modern behaviorism's most influential and controversial figure. Skinner's work elaborated a simple fact of life that psychologist Edward L. Thorndike (1874–1949) called the **law of effect**: *Rewarded behavior is likely to recur.* Using Thorndike's law of effect as a starting point, Skinner developed a "behavioral technology" that revealed principles of behavior control. These principles also enabled him to teach pigeons such unpigeonlike behaviors as walking in a figure 8, playing Ping-Pong, and keeping a missile on course by pecking at a target on a screen.

For his pioneering studies with rats (and later with pigeons), Skinner designed an **operant chamber**, popularly known as the *Skinner box* (**FIGURE 7.11**, page 238). The box is typically soundproof, with a bar or key that an animal presses or pecks to release a reward of food or water, and a device that records these responses.

▶ **operant conditioning** a type of learning in which behavior is strengthened if followed by a reinforcer or diminished if followed by a punisher.

▶ **respondent behavior** behavior that occurs as an automatic response to some stimulus.

▶ **operant behavior** behavior that operates on the environment, producing consequences.

▶ **law of effect** Thorndike's principle that behaviors followed by favorable consequences become more likely.

▶ **operant chamber** a chamber, also known as a *Skinner box*, containing a bar or key that an animal can manipulate to obtain a food or water reinforcer, with attached devices to record the animal's rate of bar pressing or key pecking. Used in operant conditioning research.

Answer to question on page 235: The UCS was the loud noise; the UCR was the startled fear response; the CS was the rat; the CR was fear.

Charlotte van Oyen Witvliet

The law of effect at Stingray City For 35 years, Cayman Islands fishing crews have gathered conch and cleaned them over this barrier reef. Stingrays in the surrounding bay gradually became accustomed to these yummy treats. Noticing the rays congregating, scuba divers then began feeding the increasingly friendly rays by hand. Today, tourists can do the same and can even pet the rays as they graze past them.

figure 7.11
A Skinner box Inside the box, the rat presses a bar for a food reward. Outside, a measuring device records the animal's accumulated responses.

Experiments by Skinner and other operant researchers did far more than teach us how to pull habits out of a rat. They explored the precise conditions that foster efficient and enduring learning. In his experiments, Skinner used **shaping**, a procedure in which *reinforcers*, such as food, gradually guide an animal's actions toward a desired behavior.

Shaping Behavior

Imagine that you wanted to condition a hungry rat to press a bar. After observing how the animal naturally behaves before training, you would build on its existing behaviors. You might give the rat a food reward each time it approaches the bar. Once the rat is approaching regularly, you would require it to move closer before rewarding it, then closer still; finally, you would require it to touch the bar before you gave it the food. With this method of *successive approximations*, you reward responses that are ever-closer to the final desired behavior, and you ignore all other responses. By making rewards contingent on desired behaviors, researchers and animal trainers gradually *shape* complex behaviors.

By shaping nonverbal organisms to discriminate between stimuli, a psychologist can also determine what they perceive. Can a dog distinguish colors? Can a baby discriminate sounds? If we can shape them to respond to one stimulus and not to another, then obviously they can perceive the difference. Experiments show that some animals are remarkably capable of forming concepts; they demonstrate this by discriminating between classes of events or objects. If an experimenter reinforces a pigeon for pecking after seeing a human face, but not after seeing other images, the pigeon will learn to recognize human faces (Herrnstein & Loveland, 1964). After being trained to discriminate among flowers, people, cars, and chairs, pigeons can usually identify in which of these categories a new pictured object belongs (Bhatt & others, 1988; Wasserman, 1993). With training, pigeons have even been taught to discriminate between Bach's music and Stravinsky's (Porter & Neuringer, 1984).

In the shaping procedure, the trainer builds on the organism's existing behaviors by expecting and immediately rewarding successively closer approximations of a desired behavior. In everyday life, too, we continually reward and shape the

A discriminating creature
University of Windsor psychologist Dale Woodyard uses a food reward to train this manatee to discriminate between objects of different shapes, colors, and sizes. A manatee can remember such responses for a year or more.

HI AND LOIS

Reprinted with special permission of King Features Syndicate.

> **shaping** an operant conditioning procedure in which reinforcers guide behavior toward closer and closer approximations of a desired goal.

> **reinforcer** in operant conditioning, any event that *strengthens* the behavior it follows.

behavior of others, said Skinner, but we often do so unintentionally. Sometimes we unthinkingly reward behaviors we find annoying. Billy's whining, for example, annoys his mystified parents, but look how they typically deal with Billy.

Billy: *Could you tie my shoes?*
Father: *(Continues reading paper.)*
Billy: *Dad, I need my shoes tied.*
Father: *Uh, yeah, just a minute.*
Billy: *DAAAAD! TIE MY SHOES!*
Father: *How many times have I told you not to whine? Now, which shoe do we do first?*

Billy's whining is positively reinforced, because he gets something desirable—his dad's attention. Dad's response is negatively reinforced because it gets rid of something aversive—Billy's whining.

Or consider the way some teachers use reinforcers. On a wall chart, the teacher pastes gold stars after the names of children scoring 100 percent on spelling tests. All children take the same tests. As everyone can then see, some children, the academic all-stars, easily get 100 percent. The others get no reward. The teacher would be better advised to apply the principles of operant conditioning—to reinforce all spellers for gradual improvements (successive approximations toward perfect spelling of words they find challenging).

Principles of Reinforcement

7. What are the basic types of reinforcers?

People often refer rather loosely to the power of "rewards." This idea gains a more precise meaning in Skinner's concept of **reinforcement**, any event that strengthens, or increases the frequency of, a preceding response. A *positive* reinforcer may be a tangible reward. It may be praise or attention. Or it may be an activity—being able to borrow the car when the dishes are done, or to have a break after an hour of study.

Most people think of reinforcers as rewards. Actually, anything that serves to increase behavior is a reinforcer—even students being yelled at, if yelling *increases* the offending behavior. Reinforcers vary with circumstance. What's reinforcing to one person (rock concert tickets) may not be to another. What's reinforcing in one situation (food when hungry) may not be in another.

There are two basic kinds of reinforcement (**TABLE 7.1**). One type (positive reinforcement) strengthens a response by *presenting* a typically pleasurable stimulus after a response. Food is a positive reinforcer for hungry animals; attention, approval, and money are positive reinforcers for most people. The other type (negative reinforcement) strengthens a response by reducing or *removing* an aversive stimulus. Taking aspirin may relieve a headache. Dragging on a

table 7.1
Ways to Increase Behavior

Operant Conditioning Term	Description	Possible Examples
Positive reinforcement	*Add* a desirable stimulus	Getting a hug; watching TV
Negative reinforcement	*Remove* an aversive stimulus	Fastening seatbelt to turn off beeping

Positive reinforcement An A grade positively reinforces this boy's effort, as do his classmates' smiles and his teacher's praise.

cigarette will reduce a nicotine addict's pangs. Pushing the snooze button silences the annoying alarm. All these consequences, assuming they do affect behavior, provide negative reinforcement. When someone stops nagging or whining, that, too, is a reinforcer. (Note that contrary to popular usage, negative reinforcement *removes* an aversive event.)

So imagine a worried student who, after goofing off and getting a bad exam grade, studies harder for the next exam. The student's studying may be reinforced by reduced anxiety (negative reinforcement) and by a better grade (positive reinforcement). Whether it works by giving something desirable or by reducing something aversive, *reinforcement is any consequence that strengthens behavior.*

PRIMARY AND CONDITIONED REINFORCERS Primary **reinforcers**—getting food when hungry or being relieved of electric shock—are innately satisfying. **Conditioned reinforcers**, also called *secondary reinforcers*, are learned. They get their power through association with primary reinforcers. If a rat in a Skinner box learns that a light reliably signals that food is coming, the rat will work to turn on the light. The light has become a secondary reinforcer associated with food. Our lives are filled with potential secondary reinforcers—money, good grades, a pleasant tone of voice, a word of praise—each of which may have been linked with more basic rewards. Secondary reinforcers greatly enhance our ability to influence one another.

IMMEDIATE AND DELAYED REINFORCERS Let's return to the imaginary shaping experiment in which you were conditioning a rat to press a bar. Before performing this "wanted" behavior, the hungry rat will engage in a sequence of "unwanted" behaviors—scratching, sniffing, and moving around. Whichever of these behaviors immediately precedes the food reinforcer becomes more likely to recur. If you delay the reinforcement of bar pressing for longer than 30 seconds, allowing other incidental behaviors to intervene and be reinforced, virtually no learning to press the bar will occur.

Unlike rats, humans do respond to reinforcers that are greatly delayed: the paycheck at the end of the week, the good grade at the end of the semester, the trophy at the end of the season. Indeed, to function effectively we must learn to postpone immediate rewards for greater long-term rewards. In laboratory testing, some 4-year-old children show an ability to delay gratification; in choosing a candy, they would rather have a big reward tomorrow than a small one right now. As they mature, these children tend to become socially competent and high achieving (Mischel & others, 1989). A big step toward maturity—and toward gaining the most satisfying life—is learning to delay gratification, to control one's impulses in order to achieve more valued rewards (Logue, 1998a,b).

But to our detriment, small but immediate consequences are sometimes more alluring than big but delayed consequences. Smokers, alcoholics, and other drug users may know that their immediate pleasure—the kick that often comes within seconds—is more than offset by future ill effects. Still, immediate reinforcement prevails. Hangovers do not prevent further drinking, and drugs such as nicotine and cocaine that provide the most immediate reinforcement are the most strongly addictive (Marlatt, 1991). Likewise, for many teens the immediate gratification of risky, unprotected sex in passionate moments prevails over the delayed gratifications of safe sex or saved sex (Loewenstein & Furstenberg, 1991). And the immediate enjoyment of staying up to watch another TV show may outweigh the prospect of tomorrow's day-long sluggishness.

▶ **primary reinforcer** an innately reinforcing stimulus, such as one that satisfies a biological need.

▶ **conditioned reinforcer** a stimulus that gains its reinforcing power through its association with a primary reinforcer; also known as *secondary reinforcer*.

▶ **continuous reinforcement** reinforcing the desired response every time it occurs.

▶ **partial (intermittent) reinforcement** reinforcing a response only part of the time; results in slower acquisition of a response but much greater resistance to extinction than does continuous reinforcement.

▶ **fixed-ratio schedule** in operant conditioning, a schedule of reinforcement that reinforces a response only after a specified number of responses.

"Oh, not bad. The light comes on, I press the bar, they write me a check. How about you?"

Reinforcement Schedules

8. How do different reinforcement schedules affect behavior?

So far, most of our examples assume **continuous reinforcement**: The desired response is reinforced every time it occurs. Under such conditions, learning occurs rapidly. But when the reinforcement stops—when we disconnect the food delivery chute—extinction also occurs rapidly. If the experimenter withholds food pellets, the rat soon stops pressing the bar. If a normally dependable candy machine fails to deliver a chocolate bar twice in a row, we stop putting money into it (although a week later we may exhibit spontaneous recovery by trying again).

Real life often does not provide continuous reinforcement. A salesperson does not make a sale with every pitch, nor does an angler get a bite with every cast. But they persist because their efforts have occasionally been rewarded. Researchers have explored several **partial (intermittent) reinforcement** schedules, in which responses are sometimes reinforced, sometimes not (Nevin, 1988). Initial learning is typically slower with intermittent reinforcement, which makes continuous reinforcement preferable until a behavior is mastered. But intermittent reinforcement produces greater persistence—greater *resistance to extinction*—than is found with continuous reinforcement. Imagine a pigeon that has learned to peck a key to obtain food. When the experimenter gradually phases out the delivery of food until it occurs only rarely and unpredictably, pigeons may peck 150,000 times without a reward (Skinner, 1953). With intermittent reinforcement, hope springs eternal.

Corresponding human examples come readily to mind. Slot machines reward gamblers occasionally and unpredictably. This intermittent reinforcement affects them much as it affects pigeons: They keep trying, sometimes interminably. There is also a valuable lesson here for parents. *Occasionally* giving in to children's demanding tantrums for the sake of peace and quiet intermittently reinforces the tantrums. That is the very best procedure for making a behavior persist.

Skinner (1961) and his collaborators compared four schedules of partial reinforcement. Some are rigidly fixed, some unpredictably variable.

Fixed-ratio schedules reinforce behavior after a set number of responses. Like people paid on a piecework basis—say, for every 30 pieces—laboratory animals may be reinforced on a fixed ratio of, say, one reinforcer for every 30 responses. Once conditioned, the animal will pause only briefly after a reinforcer and will then return to a high rate of responding (**FIGURE 7.12**). Because resting while on a fixed-ratio schedule

> *"The charm of fishing is that it is the pursuit of what is elusive but attainable, a perpetual series of occasions for hope."*
>
> Scottish author John Buchan (1875–1940)

In operant conditioning, acquisition is the strengthening of a reinforced response. Extinction occurs when a response is no longer reinforced. Generalization and discrimination occur as organisms respond to various stimuli and experience consequences.

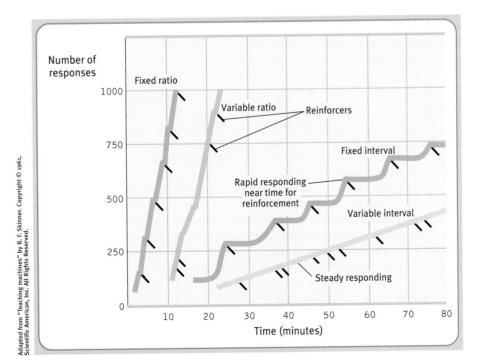

figure 7.12
Intermittent reinforcement schedules
Skinner's laboratory pigeons produced these response patterns to each of four reinforcement schedules. (Reinforcers are indicated by diagonal marks.) For people, as for pigeons, reinforcement linked to number of responses (a ratio schedule) produces a higher response rate than reinforcement linked to amount of time elapsed (interval schedule). But the predictability of the reward also matters. An unpredictable (variable) schedule produces more consistent responding than a predictable (fixed) schedule.

reduces rewards, employees often find such arrangements tiring. Unions have therefore pressured employers to replace piecework pay with hourly wage schedules.

Variable-ratio schedules provide reinforcers after an unpredictable number of responses. This is what gamblers and anglers experience—unpredictable reinforcement—and what makes gambling and fishing so hard to extinguish. Like the fixed-ratio schedule, the variable-ratio schedule produces high rates of responding, because reinforcers increase as the number of responses increases.

Fixed-interval schedules reinforce the first response after a fixed time period. Like people checking more frequently for the mail as the delivery time approaches, or checking to see if the cookies are done or the Jell-O is set, pigeons on a fixed-interval schedule peck a key more frequently as the anticipated time for reward draws near, producing a choppy stop-start pattern rather than a steady rate of response (see Figure 7.12).

Variable-interval schedules reinforce the first response after *varying* time intervals. Like the "You've got mail" that finally rewards persistence in rechecking for e-mail, variable-interval schedules tend to produce slow, steady responding. This makes sense, because there is no knowing when the waiting will be over.

Animal behaviors differ, yet Skinner (1956) contended that these reinforcement principles of operant conditioning are universal. It matters little, he said, what response, what reinforcer, or what species you use. The effect of a given reinforcement schedule is pretty much the same: "Pigeon, rat, monkey, which is which? It doesn't matter. . . . Behavior shows astonishingly similar properties."

Door-to-door salespeople are reinforced by which schedule? People checking the oven to see if the cookies are done are on which schedule? Airline frequent-flyer programs that offer a free flight after every 25,000 miles of travel use which reinforcement schedule? (See page 246.)

Punishment

9. How does punishment affect behavior?

The effect of **punishment** is opposite to that of reinforcement. Reinforcement increases a behavior; punishment decreases it. Thus, a punisher is any consequence that *decreases* the frequency of a preceding behavior, usually by administering an undesirable consequence or withdrawing a desirable one (see **TABLE 7.2**). Swift and sure punishers can powerfully restrain unwanted behavior. The dog that learns to come running at the sound of the electric can opener will stop coming if its master starts running the can opener to attract and catch it for banishment to the basement. The rat that is shocked after touching the forbidden object and the child who loses a treat after running into the street will learn not to repeat the behavior.

Boys Town psychologist Robert Larzelere (1996, 1999, 2000) notes a problem with human punishment studies, which often find that spanked children are at increased risk for aggression, depression, and low self-esteem. Well, yes, says Larzelere, just as people who have received radiation treatments are more likely to die of cancer, and people who have undergone psychotherapy are more likely to suffer depression—because they had preexisting problems that triggered the treatments. If one adjusts for preexisting cancer or depression—or antisocial behavior—then radiation, psychotherapy, or an occasional single swat or two to misbehaving 2- to 6-year-olds looks more effective. That is especially so if the swat is combined with a generous dose of reasoning and positive parenting, and if it is used only as a backup to enhance the effectiveness of milder disciplinary tactics such as reasoning and time-out.

Nevertheless, say advocates of nonviolent parenting, physical punishment has drawbacks (Marshall, 2002). Punished behavior is not forgotten; it is suppressed. This temporary suppression may (negatively) reinforce the parents' punishing behavior. The child swears, the parent swats, the parent hears no more swearing from the child, and the parent feels the punishment was successful in stopping the behavior. But was it? If the punishment is avoidable, the punished behavior may reappear in safe settings. The child may simply learn discrimination and thus not to swear around the house but to swear elsewhere. The driver who is hit with a couple of speeding tickets may buy a radar detector and speed freely when no radar patrol is around.

table 7.2 Types of Punishers		
Type	Description	Possible Examples
Positive punishment	Administer an aversive stimulus	Spanking; a parking ticket
Negative punishment	Withdraw a desirable stimulus	Time-out from privileges such as TV; revoked driver's license

Physical punishment may increase aggressiveness by demonstrating that aggression is a way to cope with problems. This helps explain why so many aggressive delinquents and abusive parents come from abusive families (Straus & Gelles, 1980; Straus & others, 1997). Moreover, punishment can create fear; the person receiving the punishment may associate the fear not only with the undesirable behavior but also with the person who administers it or with the situation in which it occurs. Thus, a child may come to fear the punitive teacher and want to avoid school. For such reasons, most European countries have banned hitting children in schools and child-care institutions (Leach, 1993, 1994). Eleven countries, including those in Scandinavia, have further outlawed hitting by parents, thereby extending to children the same legal protection given to spouses (EPOCH, 2000).

Even though punishment suppresses unwanted behavior, it often does not guide one toward more desirable behavior. Punishment tells you what *not* to do; reinforcement tells you what *to* do. Thus, punishment combined with reinforcement is usually more effective than punishment alone. This approach has been used with children who bite themselves or bang their heads. They may be mildly punished (say, with a squirt of water in the face) whenever they bite themselves, but also be rewarded with positive attention and food when they behave well. The approach also works in the classroom. The teacher whose feedback on a paper says "No, but try this . . ." and "Yes, that's it!" reduces unwanted behavior by reinforcing alternative behaviors.

Parents of delinquent youth often lack this awareness of how to reinforce desirable behavior without screaming or hitting (Patterson & others, 1982). Training programs for such parents help them reframe contingencies from dire threats to positive incentives—from "You clean up your room this minute or no dinner!" to "You're welcome at the dinner table after you get your room cleaned up." When you stop to think about it, many threats of punishment are just as forceful, and perhaps more effective, if rephrased positively. Thus, "If you don't get your homework done, there'll be no TV" would better be phrased as . . .

To sum up, most psychologists therefore favor an emphasis on reinforcement rather than on punishment. Notice people doing something right and affirm them for it.

Updating Skinner's Understanding

Skinner granted the existence of private processes and the biological underpinnings of behavior. Nevertheless, many psychologists criticized him for discounting the importance of these processes and predispositions.

Cognition and Operant Conditioning

10. Do cognitive processes and biological constraints affect operant conditioning?

A mere eight days before dying of leukemia, Skinner (1990) stood before the American Psychological Association convention for one final critique of "cognitive science," which he viewed as a throwback to early twentieth-century introspectionism. Skinner died resisting the growing belief that cognitive processes—thoughts, perceptions, expectations—have a necessary place in the science of psychology and even in our understanding of conditioning. (He regarded thoughts and emotions as behaviors that follow the same laws as other behaviors.) Yet we have seen several hints that cognitive processes might be at work in operant learning. For example, animals on a fixed-interval reinforcement schedule respond more and more frequently as the time approaches when a response will produce a reinforcer. The animals behave as if they expected that repeating the response would soon produce the reward.

To a strict behaviorist, however, talk of "expectations" is unnecessary; it is enough to say that responses reinforced under certain conditions recur when those conditions recur. Moreover, talk of expectations and other cognitions begs the question of what

▶ **variable-ratio schedule** in operant conditioning, a schedule of reinforcement that reinforces a response after an unpredictable number of responses.

▶ **fixed-interval schedule** in operant conditioning, a schedule of reinforcement that reinforces a response only after a specified time has elapsed.

▶ **variable-interval schedule** in operant conditioning, a schedule of reinforcement that reinforces a response at unpredictable time intervals.

▶ **punishment** an event that *decreases* the behavior that it follows.

For more information on animal behavior, see books by (I am not making this up) Robin Fox and Lionel Tiger.

▶ **cognitive map** a mental representation of the layout of one's environment. For example, after exploring a maze, rats act as if they have learned a cognitive map of it.

▶ **latent learning** Animals, like people, can learn from experience, with or without reinforcement. After exploring a maze for 10 days, rats received a food reward at the end of the maze. They quickly demonstrated their prior learning of the maze—by immediately doing as well as (and even better than) rats that had been reinforced for running the maze.

▶ **intrinsic motivation** a desire to perform a behavior for its own sake and to be effective.

▶ **extrinsic motivation** a desire to perform a behavior due to promised rewards or threats of punishment.

"Bathroom? Sure, it's just down the hall to the left, jog right, left, another left, straight past two more lefts, then right, and it's at the end of the third corridor on your right."

Tiger Woods' intrinsic motivation
"I remember a daily ritual that we had: I would call Pop at work to ask if I could practice with him. He would always pause a second or two, keeping me in suspense, but he'd always say yes. . . . In his own way, he was teaching me initiative. You see, he never pushed me to play" (quoted in *USA Weekend*, 1997).

causes them. It is not enough to say that evil thoughts predisposed Mohamed Atta and fellow terrorists to hijack and fly planes into the World Trade Center towers and the Pentagon. We want to know what would cause such thoughts and behavior.

Evidence of cognitive processes has come from studying rats in mazes. Rats exploring a maze, with no obvious reward, are like people driving around a new town. The rats seem to develop a **cognitive map**, a mental representation of the maze. This occurs even if they are carried passively through the maze in a wire basket. When an experimenter then places a reward in the maze's goal box, the rats immediately perform as well as rats that have been reinforced with food for running the maze.

During their explorations, the rats seemingly experience **latent learning**—learning that becomes apparent only when there is some incentive to demonstrate it. The conclusion: Learning can occur without reinforcement or punishment. As the cognitive-mapping experiments suggest, there is more to learning than associating a response with a consequence. There is also cognition. In Chapter 9 we will encounter striking evidence of animals' cognitive abilities in solving problems and in using aspects of language.

INTRINSIC MOTIVATION   The cognitive perspective has also led to an important qualification concerning the power of rewards: Unnecessary rewards sometimes carry hidden costs. Most people think that offering tangible rewards will boost anyone's interest in an activity (Boggiano & others, 1987). Actually, promising children a reward for a task they already enjoy can backfire. In experiments, children promised a payoff for playing with an interesting puzzle or toy later play with the toy less than do children who are not paid to play (Deci & others, 1999; Tang & Hall, 1995). It is as if the children think, "If I have to be bribed into doing this, then it must not be worth doing for its own sake."

Excessive rewards can undermine **intrinsic motivation**—the desire to perform a behavior effectively and for its own sake. Intrinsically motivated people work and play seeking enjoyment, interest, self-expression, or challenge. **Extrinsic motivation** is seeking external rewards and avoiding threatened punishment. If youth sports coaches aim to promote enduring interest and activity, and not just to pressure players into winning, they should focus on the intrinsic joy of play and reaching one's potential, note motivation researchers Edward Deci and Richard Ryan (1985, 1992, 2000).

To sense the difference between extrinsic and intrinsic motivation, you might reflect on your own current experience. Are you feeling pressured to get this reading finished before a deadline? Worried about your course grade? Eager for rewards that depend on your doing well? If yes, then you are extrinsically motivated (as, to some extent, almost all students are). Are you also finding the course material interesting? Does learning it lead you to feel more competent? If there were no grade at stake, might you be curious enough to want to learn the material for its own sake? If yes, intrinsic motivation also fuels your efforts.

A person's interest often survives when a reward is used neither to bribe nor to control but to signal a job well done, as in a "most improved player" award (Boggiano & others, 1985). If a reward boosts your feeling of competence after doing good work, your enjoyment of the task may increase. Rewards, rightly administered, can motivate high performance and creativity (Eisenberger & Rhoades, 2001; Henderlong & Lepper, 2002).

Biological Predispositions

As with classical conditioning, an animal's natural predispositions constrain its capacity for operant conditioning. When you reinforce a hamster's behavior with food, you can easily condition it to dig or to rear up, because these are among the animal's natural behaviors when searching for food. But it is difficult to use food as a reinforcer to shape hamster behaviors—such as face washing—that aren't normally associated with food or hunger (Shettleworth, 1973). Similarly, pigeons easily learn to flap their wings to avoid being shocked and to peck to obtain food, because it is natural for them to flee with their wings and eat with their beaks. However, they have a hard time learning to peck in order to avoid a shock or to flap their wings to obtain food (Foree & LoLordo, 1973). Biological constraints predispose organisms to learn associations that are naturally adaptive.

Skinner's former associates Keller Breland and Marian Breland (1961) came to appreciate biological predispositions while using operant procedures to train animals for circuses, TV shows, and movies. The Brelands had originally assumed that operant principles would work on almost any response that any animal could make. But after training 6000 animals of 38 different species, from chickens to whales, they concluded that biological predispositions were more important than they had supposed. In one act, they trained pigs to pick up large wooden "dollars" and deposit them in a piggy bank. After learning this behavior, however, the animals began to drift back to their natural ways. They would drop the coin, push it with their snouts as pigs are prone to do, pick it up again, and then repeat the sequence—delaying their food reinforcer. As this "instinctive drift" illustrates, "misbehaviors" occurred when the animals reverted to their biologically predisposed patterns.

Natural athletes Animals can most easily learn and retain behaviors that draw on their biological predispositions, such as cats' inborn tendency to leap high and land on their feet.

"Never try to teach a pig to sing. It wastes your time and annoys the pig."

Mark Twain (1835–1910)

Skinner's Legacy

B. F. Skinner was one of the most controversial intellectual figures of the late twentieth century. He stirred a hornet's nest by repeatedly insisting that external influences (not internal thoughts and feelings) shape behavior and by urging the use of operant principles to influence people's behavior at school, work, and home. Recognizing that behavior is shaped by its consequences, we should administer rewards in ways that promote more desirable behavior.

Skinner's critics objected, saying that he dehumanized people by neglecting their personal freedom and by seeking to control their actions. Skinner's reply: People's behavior is already haphazardly controlled by external consequences, so why not administer those consequences for human betterment? In place of the punishments used in homes, schools, and prisons, would not reinforcers be more humanitarian? And if it is humbling to think that we are shaped by our histories, this very idea also gives us hope that we can shape our future.

B. F. Skinner "I am sometimes asked, 'Do you think of yourself as you think of the organisms you study?' The answer is yes. So far as I know, my behavior at any given moment has been nothing more than the product of my genetic endowment, my personal history, and the current setting" (1983).

Applications of Operant Conditioning

11. How might educators, business managers, and other individuals apply operant conditioning?

We have seen applications of operant conditioning principles, and in later chapters we will see how psychologists apply these principles to problems ranging from high blood pressure to social withdrawal. Behavioral economists are applying operant principles to their studies of consumer behavior and of drug use and abuse. Reinforcement technologies are also at work in schools, businesses, and homes.

AT SCHOOL A generation ago, Skinner and others advocated the use of teaching machines and textbooks that would shape learning in small steps and provide immediate reinforcement for correct responses. Such machines and texts, they said,

Computer-assisted learning
Computers have helped realize Skinner's goal of individually paced instruction with immediate feedback.

Answer to question on page 242: Door-to-door salespeople are reinforced on a variable-ratio schedule (after varying numbers of rings). Cookie checkers are reinforced on a fixed-interval schedule. Frequent-flyer programs use a fixed-ratio schedule.

would revolutionize education and free teachers to concentrate on their students' special needs.

To envision Skinner's idea, imagine two math teachers, each with a class of academically diverse students. Teacher A gives the whole class the same math lesson, knowing that some students will readily understand the concepts and that others will be frustrated. With so many different children, how can one teacher guide them individually? The whiz kids breeze through unchallenged; the slower learners experience failure. Faced with a similar class, Teacher B paces the material according to each student's rate of learning and provides prompt feedback with positive reinforcement to both slow and fast learners. Does the individualized instruction of Teacher B seem unrealistic?

Although the predicted revolution has not occurred, to the end of his life Skinner (1986, 1988, 1989) believed the ideal was achievable. "Good instruction demands two things," he said. "Students must be told immediately whether what they do is right or wrong and, when right, they must be directed to the step to be taken next." Computers were his final hope. For reading and math drills, the computer could be Teacher B—engaging the student actively, pacing material according to the student's rate of learning, quizzing the student to find gaps in understanding, providing immediate feedback, and keeping flawless records for the supervising teacher. With on-line testing systems improving and more and more interactive student software and Web-based learning becoming available, we are closer than ever before to achieving Skinner's ideal.

AT WORK Believing reinforcers influence productivity, business managers have capitalized on psychological research. Many companies now enable their employees to share profits and to participate in company ownership. When workers' productivity boosts rewards for everyone, their motivation, morale, and cooperative spirit often increase (Deutsch, 1991). Reinforcement for jobs well done is especially effective in boosting productivity when the desired performance is *well-defined and achievable*. The message for managers? Reward specific behaviors, not vaguely defined merit. Even criticism triggers the least resentment and the greatest performance boost when specific and considerate (Baron, 1988).

It is also wise to make the reinforcement *immediate*. When IBM legend Thomas Watson observed an achievement, he would write the employee a check on the spot (Peters & Waterman, 1982). But rewards need not be material, nor should they be so substantial that they become political and a source of discouragement to those who don't receive them. An effective manager may simply walk the floor and sincerely affirm people for good work, or write notes of appreciation for a completed project. As Skinner said, "How much richer would the whole world be if the reinforcers in daily life were more effectively contingent on productive work?"

AT HOME Parents can take helpful advantage of operant conditioning. Parent-training researchers Michelle Wierson and Rex Forehand (1994) remind us that when parents say "get ready for bed" and then cave in to protests or defiance, they reinforce such behaviors. Eventually, exasperated, they may yell at their child or gesture menacingly, at which point the child's fearful compliance in turn reinforces the parents' angry

behavior. Over time, a destructive parent-child relationship develops. To disrupt this cycle, Wierson and Forehand offer these recommendations for parents:

● Give children attention and other reinforcers when they are behaving *well.* Target a specific behavior, reward it, and watch it increase.

● Ignore whining. If whining has triggered attention in the past, it may temporarily increase when ignored. Over time, if not reinforced, it will diminish.

● When children misbehave or are defiant, do not yell at or hit them. Simply explain the misbehavior and give them *time-out*—remove them from any reinforcing surroundings for a specified time.

Finally, we can use operant conditioning on ourselves, by reinforcing our most desired behaviors and extinguishing those undesired. To take charge of your own behavior, psychologists suggest these step-by-step procedures:

1. *State your goal*—say, to stop smoking, eat less, or study or exercise more—in measurable terms, and make your intention public. You might, for example, aim to boost your study time by an hour a day and announce that goal to some supportive friends.
2. *Monitor* how often you engage in the behavior you wish to promote. You might log your current study time, noting under what conditions you do and don't study. (When I began writing textbooks, I logged my time and was astonished to discover how much time I was wasting.)
3. *Reinforce* the desired behavior. To increase your study time, allow yourself a snack (or some other reinforcing activity) only after specified periods of study. Agree with your friends that you will join them for weekend activities only if you have met your weekly studying goal.
4. *Reduce the incentives* gradually while giving yourself a mental pat on the back as your new behaviors become more habitual.

"I wrote another five hundred words. Can I have another cookie?"

Contrasting Conditioning Techniques

The last four decades of research have changed psychologists' views of both classical and operant conditioning (summarized in **TABLE 7.3**). Learning, like so much else, depends on both nature and nurture. As we have seen, biological predispositions make learning some associations easier than learning others. Yet animals exhibit more sophisticated cognitive processes than once seemed likely. And rewarding people to do what they already enjoy may undermine their interest.

"O! This learning, what a thing it is."

*William Shakespeare, **The Taming of the Shrew,**
1597*

table 7.3 Comparison of Classical and Operant Conditioning		
	Classical Conditioning	**Operant Conditioning**
Response	Involuntary, automatic	"Voluntary," operates on environment
Acquisition	Associating events; CS announces UCS.	Associating response with a consequence (reinforcer or punisher).
Extinction	CR decreases when CS is repeatedly presented alone.	Responding decreases when reinforcement stops.
Cognitive processes	Subjects develop expectation that CS signals the arrival of UCS.	Subjects develop expectation that a response will be reinforced or punished; they also exhibit latent learning, without reinforcement.
Biological predispositions	Natural predispositions constrain what stimuli and responses can easily be associated.	Organisms best learn behaviors similar to their natural behaviors; unnatural behaviors instinctively drift back toward natural ones.

rehearse it!

8. Salivating in response to a tone paired with food is a (an) _____; pressing a bar to obtain food is a (an) _____.
   a. primary reinforcer; secondary reinforcer
   b. secondary reinforcer; primary reinforcer
   c. operant behavior; respondent behavior
   d. respondent behavior; operant behavior

9. Thorndike's law of effect states that "rewarded behavior is likely to recur." This law became the basis for operant conditioning and the "behavioral technology" developed by
   a. Ivan Pavlov.
   b. John Garcia.
   c. B. F. Skinner.
   d. John B. Watson.

10. B. F. Skinner taught rats to press a bar to obtain a food pellet. To guide the rat's natural behavior toward the desired behavior, he used
   a. shaping.
   b. punishment.
   c. taste aversion.
   d. discrimination.

11. A reinforcer is anything presented after a response that increases the frequency of that response. Imagine that your dog barks at every noise it hears. The barking disturbs you, so you put the dog outside when it starts to bark. The stopping of the barking is for you the termination of an aversive stimulus, or a
   a. positive reinforcer.
   b. negative reinforcer.
   c. punishment.
   d. primary reinforcer.

12. Continuous reinforcement—reinforcement of the desired response every time it occurs—makes for rapid learning and, when reinforcement stops, for rapid extinction. A partial reinforcement schedule that reinforces a response at unpredictable times is a
   a. fixed-interval schedule.
   b. variable-interval schedule.
   c. fixed-ratio schedule.
   d. variable-ratio schedule.

13. A medieval proverb notes that "a burnt child dreads the fire." In behavioral terms, the burning is an example of a

   a. primary reinforcer.
   b. negative reinforcer.
   c. punisher.
   d. positive reinforcer.

14. Most researchers today believe that cognitive processes can play an important role in learning. Evidence for the effect of cognition (thoughts, perceptions, and expectations) comes from studies in which rats
   a. spontaneously recover previously learned behavior.
   b. develop cognitive maps.
   c. exhibit respondent behavior.
   d. generalize responses.

15. Rats were carried passively through a maze and given no reward. In later trials involving food rewards, they immediately did as well as rats that had been reinforced for running the maze. The rats that had learned without reinforcement demonstrate
   a. modeling.
   b. biological predisposition.
   c. shaping.
   d. latent learning.

Answers can be found in Appendix C.

LEARNING BY OBSERVATION

12. What is observational learning?

From drooling dogs, running rats, and pecking pigeons we have learned much about the basic processes of learning. But conditioning principles alone do not tell us the whole story. Among higher animals, especially humans, learning need not occur through direct experience. **Observational learning**, in which we observe and imitate others, also plays a big part. A child who sees his big sister burn her fingers on the stove has thereby learned not to touch it. The process of observing and imitating a specific behavior is often called **modeling**. We learn all kinds of social behaviors by observing and imitating models.

We can glimpse the roots of observational learning in other species. Shortly after a fight, stumptail macaque monkeys often reconcile with one another by approaching their opponent and making friendly contact. Rhesus macaque monkeys rarely make up quickly. If, however, rhesus monkeys grow up with forgiving older stumptails, then more often than not, their fights, too, are followed by reconciliation within three minutes (de Waal & Johanowicz, 1993). Monkey see, monkey do. By observing others, gorillas learn and generalize complex actions, such as how to use both hands to prepare plants for eating (Byrne & Russon, 1998). Even rats, pigeons, and crows observe others and learn (Dugatkin, 2002).

Imitation is all the more striking in humans. So many of our ideas, fashions, and habits travel by imitation that these transmitted cultural elements now have a name: *memes*. We humans are the supreme meme machines, notes Susan Blackmore (1999, 2000). Our catch-phrases, hem lengths, ceremonies, foods, traditions, vices, and fads (think Harry Potter) all spread by one person copying another.

Recently, neuroscientists have discovered **mirror neurons** (in a frontal lobe area adjacent to the brain's motor cortex) that provide a neural basis for observa-

"Children need models more than they need critics."

Joseph Joubert, Pensées, 1842

▶ **observational learning** learning by observing others.

▶ **modeling** the process of observing and imitating a specific behavior.

▶ **mirror neurons** frontal lobe neurons that fire when performing certain actions or when observing another doing so. The brain's mirroring of another's action may enable imitation, language learning, and empathy.

tional learning. When a monkey performs a task such as grasping, holding, or tearing, these neurons fire (Rizzolatti & others, 2002). But they also fire when the monkey observes another monkey performing the same task. When one monkey sees, these neurons will mirror what another monkey does. And it's not just monkey business. PET scans reveal that humans, too, have mirror neurons in this brain area. Mirror neurons help give rise to children's empathy and to their theory of mind (their inferring another's mental state). As adults, we often feel what another feels, and we find it harder to frown when viewing a smile than when viewing a frown (Dimberg & others, 2000, 2002).

The imitation of models thus shapes children's development. Shortly after birth, an infant may imitate an adult who sticks out his tongue. By 9 months, infants will imitate novel play behaviors. And by age 14 months they will imitate acts modeled on television (Meltzoff, 1988; Meltzoff & Moore, 1989, 1997). To persuade children to smoke, simply expose them to parents, older youth, and attractive media models who smoke. To encourage children to read, read to them and surround them with books and people who read. To increase the odds of your children practicing your religion, worship and attend other religious activities with them.

Bandura's Experiments

Albert Bandura "Learning would be exceedingly laborious, not to mention hazardous, if people had to rely solely on the effects of their own actions to inform them what to do" (1977).

Picture this scene from a famous experiment devised by Albert Bandura, the pioneering researcher of observational learning (Bandura & others, 1961). A preschool child is at work on a drawing. An adult in another part of the room is working with some Tinkertoys. The adult then gets up and for nearly 10 minutes pounds, kicks, and throws a large inflated Bobo doll around the room, while yelling such remarks as, "Sock him in the nose. . . . Hit him down. . . . Kick him."

After observing this outburst, the child is taken to another room where there are many appealing toys. Soon the experimenter interrupts the child's play and explains that she has decided to save these good toys "for the other children." She now takes the frustrated child to an adjacent room containing a few toys, including a Bobo doll. Left alone, what does the child do?

Compared with children not exposed to the adult model, those who observed the model's aggressive outburst were much more likely to lash out at the doll. Apparently, observing the adult model beating up the doll lowered their inhibitions. But something more than lowered inhibitions was at work, for the children also imitated the very acts they had observed and used the very words they had heard.

What determines whether we will imitate a model? Bandura believes part of the answer is reinforcements and punishments—those received by the model as well as by the imitator. We look and we learn. By looking, we learn to anticipate a behavior's consequences in situations like those we are observing. We are especially likely to imitate those we perceive as similar to ourselves, as successful, or as admirable.

Applications of Observational Learning

The bad news from Bandura's studies is that antisocial models—in one's family or neighborhood, or on TV—may have antisocial effects (pages 562–564). In the first eight days after the 1999 Columbine High School massacre, every U.S. state except Vermont had to deal with copycat threats or incidents. Pennsylvania alone had 60 threats of school violence (Cooper, 1999). By watching TV programs, children may "learn" that physical intimidation is an effective way to control others, that free and easy sex brings pleasure without later misery or disease, or that men are supposed to be tough and women gentle.

Observational learning also helps us understand how abusive parents might have aggressive children and why many men who beat their wives had wife-battering fathers (Stith & others, 2000). The lessons we learn as children are not easily

Meltzoff, A. N. (1988). Imitation of televised models by infants. *Child Development, 59,* 1221–1229. Photos courtesy of A. N. Meltzoff and M. Hanuk.

Learning from observation
This 14-month-old boy in Andrew Meltzoff's laboratory is imitating behavior he has seen on TV. In the top photo the infant leans forward and carefully watches the adult pull apart a toy. In the middle photo he has been given the toy. In the bottom photo he pulls the toy apart, imitating what he has seen the adult do.

"The problem with television is that the people must sit and keep their eyes glued to a screen: The average American family hasn't time for it. Therefore the showmen are convinced that . . . television will never be a serious competitor of [radio] broadcasting."

New York Times, *1939*

▶ **prosocial behavior** positive, constructive, helpful behavior. The opposite of antisocial behavior.

unlearned as adults, and they are sometimes visited on future generations. Critics note that the intergenerational transmission of abuse could be genetic. But with monkeys, at least, we know it can be environmental. In study after study, young monkeys that received high levels of aggression when reared apart from their mothers grew up to be perpetrators of aggression (Chamove, 1980).

Positive Observational Learning

The good news is that **prosocial** (positive, helpful) models can have prosocial effects. People who exemplify nonviolent, helpful behavior can prompt similar behavior in others. Mahatma Gandhi and Martin Luther King, Jr., both drew on the power of modeling, making nonviolent action a powerful force for social change. Parents are powerful models. Research indicates that European Christians who risked their lives to rescue Jews from the Nazis usually had a close relationship with at least one parent who modeled a strong moral or humanitarian concern; this was also true for U.S. civil rights activists in the 1960s (London, 1970; Oliner & Oliner, 1988).

Models are most effective when their actions and words are consistent. Sometimes, however, models say one thing and do another. Many parents seem to operate according to the principle "Do as I *say*, not as I do." Experiments suggest that children learn to do both (Rice & Grusec, 1975; Rushton, 1975). Exposed to a hypocrite, they tend to imitate the hypocrisy by doing what the model did and saying what the model said.

Television and Observational Learning

Some not-so-good examples of observational learning come from research on media models of aggression. Wherever television exists, it becomes the source of much observational learning. During their first 18 years, most children in developed countries spend more time watching TV than they spend in school. In Australia, 99.2 percent of households have television and 56 percent have multiple sets (Trewin, 2001). In the United States, where 9 in 10 teens watch TV daily, someone who lives to 75 will have spent 9 years staring at the tube (Gallup, 2002; Kubey & Csikszentmihalyi, 2002). Two-thirds of U.S. homes have three or more sets, which helps explain why parents' reports of what their children watch hardly correlate with children's reports of what they watch (Donnerstein, 1998).

In urban homes across the world, including those of South America and Asia, television is now commonplace. With more than a billion TV sets now in homes worldwide, CNN reaching 150 countries, and MTV broadcasting in 17 languages, television has created a global pop culture (Gunderson, 2001; Lippman, 1992). One can watch American programs in Perth or Prague and catch the latest rock videos from Newfoundland to the tiny Himalayan kingdom of Bhutan, where television was introduced in 1999 and soon began influencing speech and children's behavior (Keys, 2001).

Does the reel world reflect the real world? On evening dramas broadcast in the United States during the 1980s and early 1990s and often exported to the rest of the world, only one-third of the characters were women. Fewer than 3 percent were visibly old. One percent were Hispanic. Only 1 in 10 was married (Gerbner, 1993).

U.S. network programs have offered about 3 violent acts per hour during prime time, and 18 per hour during children's Saturday morning programs (Gerbner & others, 1994). Unlike the real world, where 87 percent of crimes are nonviolent, in TV world 13 percent of crimes are nonviolent (Bushman & Anderson, 2001). During the late twentieth century, the average child viewed some 8000 TV murders and 100,000 other acts of violence before finishing elementary school (Huston & others, 1992). If one includes cable programming and video rentals, the violence numbers escalate. (Popular rental films like *Die Hard 2*, with its 264 deaths, are much more violent than major network programs.) An analysis of more than 3000 network and cable programs aired during 1996/1997 revealed that nearly 6 in 10 featured violence, that 74 percent of the violence went unpunished, that 58 percent did not show the victims' pain, and that nearly half the incidents involved justified violence and nearly half involved an attractive perpetrator. These conditions define the recipe for the violence-viewing effect described below (Donnerstein, 1998).

Does viewing televised aggression influence some people to commit aggression? Was the judge who in 1993 tried two British 10-year-olds for their murder of a 2-year-old right to suspect that one possible influence was the aggressors' exposure to "violent video films"? Were the American media right to think that the teen assassins who killed 13 of their Columbine High School classmates had been influenced by repeated viewings of *Natural Born Killers* and by frequently playing splatter games such as *Doom*? To answer similar questions, researchers have conducted both correlational and experimental studies (Hearold, 1986; Wood & others, 1991).

Correlational studies do link violence viewing with violent behavior.

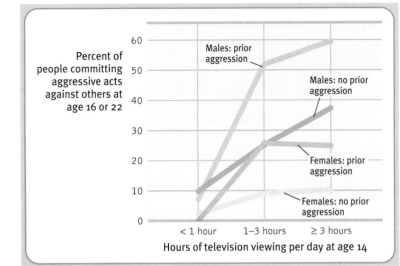

- The more hours children spend watching violent programs, the more at risk they are for aggression and crime as teens and adults (Eron, 1987; Turner & others, 1986).
- Compared with those who watch less than an hour of TV daily at age 14, those who watch more than three hours at this age commit five times as many aggressive acts at age 16 or 22 (**Figure 7.13**).
- In the United States and Canada, homicide rates doubled between 1957 and 1974, coinciding with the introduction and spread of television. Moreover, census regions that were late in acquiring television had their homicide rate jump correspondingly later.
- White South Africans were first introduced to television in 1975. A similar near-doubling of the homicide rate began after 1975 (Centerwall, 1989).

figure 7.13
TV viewing time at age 14 predicts later aggressive acts Data from 707 individuals, reported by Jeffrey Johnson & others (2002).

"There is absolutely no doubt," concluded the 1993 American Psychological Association Commission on Violence and Youth, "that higher levels of viewing violence on television are correlated with increased acceptance of aggressive attitudes and increased aggressive behavior."

But as we know from Chapter 1, correlation does not imply causation. So these correlational studies do not prove that viewing violence *causes* aggression (Freedman, 1988; McGuire, 1986). Maybe aggressive children prefer violent programs. Maybe children of neglectful or abusive parents are both more aggressive and more often left in front of the TV. Maybe television simply reflects, rather than affects, violent trends.

To pin down causation, experimenters have randomly assigned some viewers to view violence and others to view entertaining nonviolence. Does viewing cruelty

TV's greatest effect may stem from what it displaces. Children and adults who spend four hours a day watching television spend four fewer hours in active pursuits—talking, studying, playing, reading, or socializing with friends. What would you have done with your extra time if you had never watched television, and how might you therefore be different?

Violence viewing leads to violent play Research has shown that viewing media violence does lead to increased expression of aggression in the viewers, as with these boys imitating pro wrestlers.

"Thirty seconds worth of glorification of a soap bar sells soap. Twenty-five minutes worth of glorification of violence sells violence."

U.S. Senator Paul Simon, Remarks to the Communitarian Network, 1993

Gallup surveys asked American teens (Mazzuca, 2002): "Do you feel there is too much violence in the movies, or not?"

1977: 42 percent said yes.

1999: 23 percent said yes.

A model grandma This boy is learning to cook by observing his grandmother. As the sixteenth-century proverb states, "Example is better than precept."

prepare people to react more cruelly when irritated? To some extent, it does. "The consensus among most of the research community," reported the National Institute of Mental Health (1982), "is that violence on television does lead to aggressive behavior by children and teenagers who watch the programs." This is especially so when an attractive person commits seemingly justified, realistic violence that goes unpunished and causes no visible pain or harm (Donnerstein, 1998).

"Don't you understand? This is life, *this is what is happening. We can't* switch to another channel."

The violence effect seems to stem from a combination of factors including *imitation* (Geen & Thomas, 1986). One research team observed a sevenfold increase in violent play immediately after children viewed the "Power Rangers" (Boyatzis & others, 1995). Boys often precisely imitated the characters' flying karate kicks and other violent acts.

Prolonged exposure to violence also desensitizes viewers; they become more indifferent to it when later viewing a brawl, whether on TV or in real life (Rule & Ferguson, 1986). While spending three evenings watching sexually violent movies, male viewers in one experiment became progressively less bothered by the rapes and slashings. Three days later, they also expressed less sympathy for domestic violence victims than did research participants who had not been exposed to the films, and they rated the victims' injuries as less severe (Mullin & Linz, 1995). Indeed, as Edward Donnerstein and his co-researchers (1987) suggested, an evil psychologist could hardly imagine a better way to make people indifferent to brutality than to expose them to a graded series of scenes, from fights to killings to the mutilations in slasher movies. Watching cruelty fosters indifference. What a change from the showing of the first story film, *The Great Train Robbery*, in 1903. In a scene where a cowboy fires his pistol at the camera, report Brad Bushman and Craig Anderson (2001), "The first audiences who saw the film reacted by running out of the theatre screaming."

Our knowledge of learning principles comes from the work of thousands of investigators. This chapter has focused on the ideas of a few pioneers—Pavlov, Watson, Skinner, and Bandura. They illustrate the impact that can result from single-minded devotion to a few well-defined problems and ideas. These researchers defined the issues and impressed on us the importance of learning. As their legacy demonstrates, intellectual history is often made by people who risk going to extremes in pushing ideas to their limits (Simonton, 2000).

---

rehearse it!

16. Children learn many social behaviors by imitating parents and other models. This type of learning is called
   a. observational learning.
   b. reinforced learning.
   c. operant conditioning.
   d. classical conditioning.

17. Parents are powerful models of behavior. They are *most* effective in getting their children to imitate them if
   a. their words and actions are consistent.
   b. they have outgoing personalities.
   c. the father works and the mother stays home to care for the children.

   d. they carefully explain why a behavior is acceptable in adults but not in children.

18. Bandura believes that modeling is not automatic. Whether a child will imitate a model depends in part on the
   a. child's family connections to the model.
   b. child's ability to distinguish right from wrong.
   c. rewards and punishments received by the model and by the imitator.
   d. child's age in relation to that of the model.

19. There is considerable controversy about the effects of heavy exposure to television programs showing violence. However, most experts agree that repeated viewing of television violence
   a. makes all viewers significantly more aggressive.
   b. has little effect on viewers.
   c. dulls the viewer's sensitivity to violence.
   d. makes viewers angry and frustrated.

Answers can be found in Appendix C.

chapter review

REVIEWING

Learning

1. *What is learning?*

   All animals, especially humans, adapt to their environments aided by learning. Through associative learning, we come to link certain events. The process of learning associations between events is called conditioning. Through classical conditioning, we learn to anticipate important events, such as impending food or pain. Through operant conditioning, we learn to repeat acts that bring desired results and to avoid acts that bring punishment. Through observational learning, we learn from the experience and example of others.

CLASSICAL CONDITIONING

2. *How does classical conditioning demonstrate learning by association?*

   Although associative learning had been discussed for centuries, it remained for Ivan Pavlov to capture the phenomenon of classical conditioning. Pavlov repeatedly presented a neutral stimulus (such as a tone) just before an unconditioned stimulus (UCS, such as food) triggered an unconditioned response (UCR, such as salivation). After several repetitions, the tone alone (now the conditioned stimulus—CS) began triggering a conditioned response (CR, such as salivation). Further experiments on acquisition revealed that classical conditioning was usually greatest when the CS was presented just before the UCS, thus preparing the organism for what was coming.

   Pavlov's work laid a foundation for John B. Watson's belief that psychology should study only overt behavior, without considering unobservable mental activity. He called this position behaviorism.

3. *How do the processes of acquisition, extinction, spontaneous recovery, generalization, and discrimination affect a CR?*

   The first stage in response learning involves the association of a CS with the UCS (acquisition). Responses are subsequently weakened if they are not reinforced (extinction), but they may reappear after a rest pause (spontaneous recovery). Responses may be triggered by stimuli similar to the conditioned stimulus (generalization) but not by dissimilar stimuli (discrimination).

4. *Do cognitive processes and biological constraints affect classical conditioning?*

   The behaviorists' optimism that learning principles would generalize from one response to another and from one species to another has been tempered. Conditioning principles, we now know, are cognitively and biologically constrained. In classical conditioning, animals learn when to expect an unconditioned stimulus. Moreover, biological predispositions make learning some associations easier than learning others. For example, rats are biologically disposed to learn associations between, say, a peculiar taste and a sickness-producing drink, which they will then avoid. But they don't learn to avoid a sickening drink announced by a noise.

5. *Why is Pavlov's work important?*

   Pavlov's conditioning principles generalize to many species and are applicable to humans, especially to the learning of emotions such as fear. His objective methods illustrated how psychology could proceed as a science.

   Pavlov's work provided a basis for John B. Watson's early work on conditioned emotions and behavior. One outgrowth of this work is the behavioral therapy used to treat some emotional disorders.

OPERANT CONDITIONING

6. *What is operant conditioning, and how does it differ from classical conditioning?*

   Through classical (Pavlovian) conditioning, an organism associates different stimuli that it does not control and responds to them automatically (respondent behavior). Through operant conditioning, the organism associates its operant behaviors with their consequences. Expanding on Edward Thorndike's law of effect, B. F. Skinner and other researchers found that the behavior of rats or pigeons placed in a Skinner box can be shaped by rewarding closer and closer approximations of the desired behavior.

7. *What are the basic types of reinforcers?*

   Reinforcers can be positive (when presented after a response) or negative (when they cause an aversive stimulus to be withdrawn); primary (unlearned) or secondary (learned through association with primary reinforcers); and immediate or delayed. Regardless of type, all reinforcers strengthen the behaviors that they follow.

8. *How do different reinforcement schedules affect behavior?*

   Partial reinforcement schedules (fixed-interval, fixed-ratio, variable-interval, and variable-ratio) produce slower acquisition of the target behavior than does continuous reinforcement. They also produce greater resistance to extinction.

9. *How does punishment affect behavior?*

Like reinforcement, punishment is most effective when immediate and consistent. Although punishment decreases the frequency of the behavior it follows, it is not simply the logical opposite of reinforcement, for punishment can result in several undesirable side effects, such as increased aggression and fear of the punisher.

10. *Do cognitive processes and biological constraints affect operant conditioning?*

Many psychologists criticized Skinner (as they did Pavlov) for underestimating the importance of cognitive and biological constraints. For example, research on cognitive mapping and latent learning points to the importance of cognitive processes in learning. Excess rewards can undermine intrinsic motivation by leading people to attribute their behavior to the rewards.

11. *How might educators, business managers, and other individuals apply operant conditioning?*

Skinner stimulated vigorous intellectual debate on the nature of human freedom and the strategies and ethics of managing people. Nevertheless, his operant principles are being applied in schools, the workplace, and homes. For example, computer-assisted instruction both shapes and reinforces learning. Immediate reinforcement boosts worker productivity. And individuals can strengthen their own desired behavior and extinguish unwanted behavior.

LEARNING BY OBSERVATION

12. *What is observational learning?*

The type of learning Albert Bandura called observational learning results from watching others' behavior and imitating it. Recent research indicates that neurons in the frontal lobe of the brain may be involved in this type of learning. In experiments, children tend to imitate what a model both does and says, whether the behavior is prosocial or antisocial. Such experiments have stimulated research on social modeling in the home, on television, and within peer groups. Children are especially likely to imitate those they perceive to be like them, successful, or admirable.

A CRITICAL THINKER'S REVIEW OF CHAPTER 7

You've now studied and reviewed **Learning**. For even better retention, reflect on these concepts at a deeper level. If you need to refresh your memory of the six categories of critical thinking shown in parentheses below, see page 34. See if you can answer each of these questions in a short paragraph.

1. Holden is feeling somewhat lonely during his first week away at college. While unpacking his things, he finds his dog's old toy at the bottom of his duffle bag. The smell of the toy brings to mind many happy times playing with his dog at home and makes him feel better. Why does Holden feel better? Would Holden's roommate also feel better if he smelled the toy? Use the terminology you've learned in this chapter to explain. (pattern recognition)

2. Two-year-old Antonia received a painful hornet sting in the ear. Now she is terribly afraid of all flying bugs, including flies and mosquitoes. Use principles of conditioning to explain Antonia's fears and to suggest what her parents might do to help her overcome them. (practical problem solving)

3. Ian has learned about positive reinforcement in his psychology course, and he would like to use this technique to help his two school-aged sons develop good study habits. Ian decides that after each son finishes his homework, he will be allowed to watch television. This seems to be working for his older son, who works hard for this privilege, but not for his younger son, who doesn't seem to care about the television but does seem to enjoy his father's frequent visits to his room to check on his homework progress. Why aren't the younger son's study habits being improved by Ian's efforts? Use principles of operant conditioning to explain. (perspective taking)

4. Five-year-old Thomas has already gotten into trouble several times at his new school for hitting his classmates. Whenever things don't go his way, he lashes out physically. When the teacher discusses the problem with Thomas' parents, she learns that the parents often use physical punishment at home but feel it's "not working." They are eager to help change Thomas' disruptive behaviors. What research results might the teacher offer to help Thomas' parents modify his behavior? (creative problem solving)

5. Lily has an idea for her thesis paper in psychology. She has noticed wildly varying scores on the vocabulary portion of her city's schools' standardized testing of 12-year-olds. She wonders whether teaching styles—specifically views on *latent learning* of vocabulary, the idea that children expand their vocabulary naturally while reading many different types of literature and seeing new words in context—may be related in any way to those scores. She knows that some city schools believe in latent learning of vocabulary. Other schools believe children will broaden their vocabulary only by doing specific exercises that drill them on the meaning of lists of vocabulary words. How might Lily test whether these two different ways of learning are related to the standardized test scores? (scientific problem solving)

6. Jason's parents and older friends all smoke, but they advise him not to. Juan's parents and friends don't smoke, but they say nothing to deter him from doing so. Who will be more likely to start smoking, Jason or Juan? (psychological reasoning)

Answers can be found in Appendix C.

TERMS AND CONCEPTS TO REMEMBER

learning, p. 225

associative learning, p. 225

classical conditioning, p. 228

behaviorism, p. 228

unconditioned response (UCR), p. 229

unconditioned stimulus (UCS), p. 229

conditioned response (CR), p. 229

conditioned stimulus (CS), p. 229

acquisition, p. 230

extinction, p. 231

spontaneous recovery, p. 231

generalization, p. 232

discrimination, p. 232

operant conditioning, p. 237

respondent behavior, p. 237

operant behavior, p. 237

law of effect, p. 237

operant chamber, p. 237

shaping, p. 238

reinforcement, p. 239

primary reinforcer, p. 240

conditioned reinforcer, p. 240

continuous reinforcement, p. 241

partial (intermittent) reinforcement, p. 241

fixed-ratio schedule, p. 241

variable-ratio schedule, p. 242

fixed-interval schedule, p. 242

variable-interval schedule, p. 242

punishment, p. 242

cognitive map, p. 244

latent learning, p. 244

intrinsic motivation, p. 244

extrinsic motivation, p. 244

observational learning, p. 248

modeling, p. 248

mirror neurons, p. 248

prosocial behavior, p. 250

To continue your study and review of Learning, visit this book's Web site at www.worthpublishers.com/myers. You will find practice tests, review activities, and Web links for more information on topics related to Learning.

chapter8

Memory

Be thankful for memory. We take it for granted, except when it malfunctions. But it is our memory, notes Rebecca Rupp (1998, p. xvii), that "allows us to recognize friends, neighbors, and acquaintances and call them by their names; to knit, type, drive, and play the piano; to speak English, Spanish, or Mandarin Chinese." It is our memory that accounts for time and defines our life. It is our memory that enables us to sing our national anthem, find our way home, and locate the food and water we need for survival. It is our shared memories that bind us together as Irish or Aussies, as Serbs or Scots. And it is our memories that occasionally pit us against those whose offenses we cannot forget.

In large part, you are what you remember. Without memory, there would be no savoring joyful moments past, no guilt or anger over painful recollections. You would instead live in an enduring present. Each moment would be fresh. But each person would be a stranger, every language foreign, every task—dressing, cooking, biking—a novel challenge. You would even be a stranger to yourself, lacking that continuous sense of self that extends from your distant past to your momentary present.

"It isn't so astonishing, the number of things I can remember, as the number of things I can remember that aren't so."

Mark Twain (1835–1910)

"Waiter, I'd like to order, unless I've eaten, in which case bring me the check."

THE PHENOMENON OF MEMORY

Your memory is your mind's storehouse, the reservoir of your accumulated learning. To the Roman statesman Cicero, memory was "the treasury and guardian of all things." To a psychologist, **memory** is any indication that learning has persisted over time. It is our ability to store and retrieve information.

Studying memory's extremes has helped researchers understand how memory works. Some studies have explored the roots and fruits of memory loss. At age 92, my father suffered a small stroke that had but one peculiar effect. His genial personality was intact. He was as mobile as before. He knew us and while poring over family photo albums could reminisce in detail about his past. But he lost most of his facility for laying down new memories of conversations and everyday episodes. He could not tell me what day of the week it was. Told repeatedly of his brother-in-law's death, he still expressed surprise on hearing the news.

Memory lost and found Larry Treadgold, an engineer, invented a paging system that serves as a kind of artificial memory for his son Adrian. Brain-injured in an auto accident, the young man can retain information for as long as he pays attention. But as soon as he is distracted, the information fades. The paging system allows a central computer to take over memory functions, reminding him, for example, to "take your 8:00 A.M. medications; call 123–4567 to confirm." If Adrian fails to confirm, the computer continues to page him and eventually contacts an emergency number.

▶ **memory** the persistence of learning over time through the storage and retrieval of information.

257

MR. TOTAL RECALL

Which is more important—your experiences or your memories of them?

Hours after the space shuttle Challenger *explosion in 1986, people recalled where they had heard the news. Yet they were sometimes wildly inaccurate when again recalling their whereabouts 1 to 3 years later (McCloskey & others, 1988; Neisser, 1997). One woman recalled hearing it from someone running through her dorm screaming, "The space shuttle blew up." Actually, she had learned about it from friends over lunch.*

At the other extreme are some people who would be medal winners in a memory Olympics, such as Russian journalist Shereshevskii, or S, as psychologist Alexander Luria (1968) called him. S' memory not only allowed him merely to listen while other reporters were scribbling notes, it also earned him a place in virtually every modern book on memory. You and I can repeat back a string of about 7 digits—almost surely no more than 9. S could repeat up to 70 digits or words, provided they were read about 3 seconds apart in an otherwise silent room. Moreover, he could recall them backward as easily as forward. His accuracy was unerring, even when he was asked to recall a list as much as 15 years later, after having memorized hundreds of other lists. "Yes, yes," he might recall. "This was a series you gave me once when we were in your apartment. . . . You were sitting at the table and I in the rocking chair. . . . You were wearing a gray suit and you looked at me like this. . . ."

Do these memory feats make your own memory seem feeble? If so, consider: Your capacity for remembering countless voices, sounds, and songs; tastes, smells, and textures; faces, places, and happenings is pretty staggering. Imagine viewing more than 2500 slides of faces and places, for only 10 seconds each. Later you see 280 of these slides one at a time, paired with a previously unseen slide. If you are like the subjects in this experiment by Ralph Haber (1970), you would recognize 90 percent of those you saw before.

Your memory capacity is perhaps most apparent in your recall of unique and highly emotional moments in your past. One of my vivid memories is of my only hit in an entire season of Little League baseball. Perhaps yours is of a car accident, your first romantic kiss, your first day as an immigrant in a new country, or your surroundings when you heard some tragic news. Most Americans over 50 feel sure of exactly what they were doing when they heard the news of President Kennedy's assassination (Brown & Kulik, 1982). Seven months after Princess Diana's death, most Britishers could still recall what they had also reported the day after her death—their whereabouts on hearing the news (Wynn & Gilhooly, 1999). And you likely recall where you first heard the news on 9/11—"one of those moments in which history splits and we define the world as 'before' and 'after,'" said the next morning's *New York Times*. This clarity for our memories of surprising, significant events leads some psychologists to call them **flashbulb memories**. It's as if the brain commands, "Capture this!"

How do we accomplish such memory feats? How can we remember things we have not thought about for years, yet forget the name of someone we met a minute ago? How can two people's memories of the same event be so different? How are memories stored in our brains? Why can even our flashbulb memories sometimes prove dead wrong (as researchers will likely again show when they recontact people whom they queried immediately after 9/11)? Why will you be likely later in this chapter to misrecall this sentence: *"The angry rioter threw the rock at the window"*? How can we improve our memories? These will be our questions as we review a century of research on memory.

Information Processing

1. How do psychologists describe the human memory system?

To think about memory, we first need a model of how it works. Building a memory is in some ways like my information processing in creating this book. For each edition, I first glimpse countless items of information, including some 100,000 journal article titles. Most of it I ignore, but some things merit temporary storage in my briefcase for more detailed processing later. Most of these items I eventually discard. The rest—typically about 3000 articles and news items—gets organized and filed for long-term storage. Later, I retrieve this information and draw from it as I spin the story of today's psychology. In forming memories, you, too, must select, process, store, and retrieve information. You follow this process not only in the "cramming" you do to study in your college courses, but also in your processing of countless daily events.

Our memory is in some ways like a computer's information-processing system. To remember any event, we must *get information into our brain* (**encoding**), *retain that information* (**storage**), and later *get it back out* (**retrieval**). Consider how a computer *encodes*, *stores*, and *retrieves* information. First, it translates input (keystrokes) into an electronic language, much as the brain encodes sensory information into a neural language. The computer permanently stores vast amounts of information on a disk, from which it can later be retrieved.

Like all analogies, the computer model has its limits, however. Our memories are less literal and more fragile than a computer's. Moreover, most computers process information speedily but sequentially, even while alternating between tasks. The brain is slower but does many things at once—in parallel.

This chapter uses Richard Atkinson and Richard Shiffrin's classic and influential *three-stage processing* model of memory (1968), which suggests that we give birth to memories through three stages. We first record to-be-remembered information as a fleeting **sensory memory**, from which it is processed into a **short-term memory** bin, where we encode it for **long-term memory** and later retrieval (**FIGURE 8.1**).

As we will see, this three-step process is limited and fallible. Bombarded with information, we cannot possibly focus on everything at once. Instead we shine the flashlight beam of our attention on certain incoming stimuli—often novel or important stimuli. These incoming stimuli, along with images we retrieve from our long-term memory, get displayed on our mental screen as conscious short-term memories. These rapidly decay unless used or rehearsed.

THE FAR SIDE BY GARY LARSON

More facts of nature: All forest animals, to this very day, remember exactly where they were and what they were doing when they heard that Bambi's mother had been shot.

▶ **flashbulb memory** a clear memory of an emotionally significant moment or event.

▶ **encoding** the processing of information into the memory system—for example, by extracting meaning.

▶ **storage** the retention of encoded information over time.

▶ **retrieval** the process of getting information out of memory storage.

▶ **sensory memory** the immediate, initial recording of sensory information in the memory system.

▶ **short-term memory** activated memory that holds a few items briefly, such as the seven digits of a phone number while dialing, before the information is stored or forgotten. *Working memory* is a similar concept that focuses more on the processing of briefly stored information.

▶ **long-term memory** the relatively permanent and limitless storehouse of the memory system.

figure 8.1
Atkinson-Shiffrin's three-stage processing model of memory

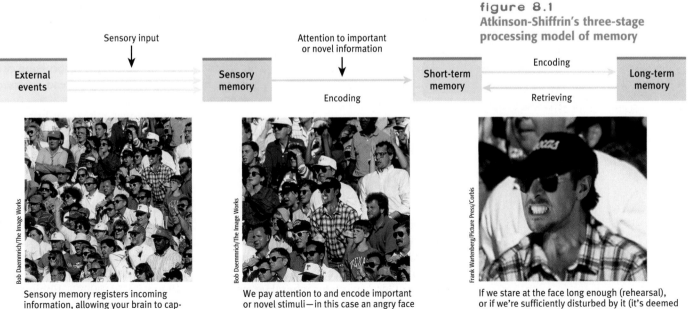

Sensory memory registers incoming information, allowing your brain to capture for a fleeting moment a sea of faces.

We pay attention to and encode important or novel stimuli—in this case an angry face in the crowd.

If we stare at the face long enough (rehearsal), or if we're sufficiently disturbed by it (it's deemed "important"), we will encode it for long-term storage, and we may, an hour later, be able to call up an image of the face.

▶ **automatic processing** unconscious encoding of incidental information, such as space, time, and frequency, and of well-learned information, such as word meanings.

▶ **effortful processing** encoding that requires attention and conscious effort.

▶ **rehearsal** the conscious repetition of information, either to maintain it in consciousness or to encode it for storage.

▶ **spacing effect** the tendency for distributed study or practice to yield better long-term retention than is achieved through massed study or practice.

▶ **serial position effect** our tendency to recall best the last and first items in a list.

The newer concept of *working memory* clarifies the short-term memory concept by focusing more on how we attend to, rehearse, and manipulate information in temporary storage (Engle, 2002). We do not just display information on-screen; we actively associate new and old information and solve problems. Working memory is roughly like a computer's random-access memory (RAM), which integrates information coming in from our keyboard with that retrieved from long-term storage on the hard drive. Part of this working memory is visible on our short-term screen.

ENCODING: GETTING INFORMATION IN

2. How do the sights, sounds, and other sensations we experience get selectively encoded and transferred into the memory system?

How We Encode

Some encoding occurs automatically, freeing your attention to simultaneously process information that requires effort. Thus, your memory for the route you walked to your last class is handled by **automatic processing**. Your learning of this chapter's concepts requires **effortful processing** (**FIGURE 8.2**).

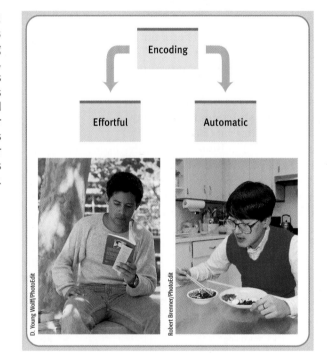

figure 8.2
Automatic versus effortful processing
Some information, such as this chapter's concepts, requires effort to encode and remember. Other information, such as where you ate dinner yesterday, you process automatically.

Automatic Processing

Often with little or no effort, you encode an enormous amount of information about *space*, *time*, and *frequency*: During an exam, you may recall the place on a textbook page where forgotten material appears. To guess where you left your coat, you can re-create a sequence of a day's events. Passing a classmate, you may realize that "this is the third time I've run into you this afternoon." Effort may help us retain such memories, yet they form almost automatically. Not only does *automatic processing* occur effortlessly, it is difficult to shut off. When you hear or read a familiar word in your native language, whether an insult or a compliment, it is virtually impossible not to register its meaning automatically.

Some types of automatic processing we learn. For example, learning to read reversed sentences at first requires effort:

.citamotua emoceb nac gnissecorp luftroffE

After practice, some *effortful processing* becomes more automatic, much as reading from right to left becomes easy for students of Hebrew (Kolers, 1975).

Effortful Processing

3. How much does rehearsal aid in forming memories?

We encode and retain vast amounts of information automatically, but we remember other types of information only with effort and attention. When learning novel information such as names, we can boost our memory through **rehearsal**, or conscious repetition. This was shown long ago by the pioneering researcher of verbal memory, German philosopher Hermann Ebbinghaus (1850–1909). Ebbinghaus was to the study of memory what Ivan Pavlov was to the study of conditioning. Ebbinghaus became impatient with philosophical speculations about memory and decided to study it scientifically. To do so, he chose to study his own learning and forgetting of novel verbal materials.

Ebbinghaus needed to find verbal material that was not familiar. His solution was to form a list of all possible nonsense syllables created by sandwiching a vowel between two consonants. Then, for a particular experiment, he would randomly select a sample of the syllables. To get a feel for how Ebbinghaus tested himself, rapidly read aloud, eight times over, the following list (from Baddeley, 1982). Then try to recall the items:

JIH, BAZ, FUB, YOX, SUJ, XIR, DAX, LEQ, VUM, PID, KEL, WAV, TUV, ZOF, GEK, HIW.

The day after learning such a list, Ebbinghaus could recall few of the syllables. But were they entirely forgotten? As **FIGURE 8.3** portrays, the more frequently he repeated the list aloud on day 1, the fewer repetitions he required to relearn the list on day 2. Here, then, was a simple beginning principle: *The amount remembered depends on the time spent learning.* Even after we learn material, additional rehearsal (*overlearning*) increases retention.

The point to remember is that for novel verbal information, practice—effortful processing—does indeed make perfect. And that helps us understand some other interesting phenomena:

- The *next-in-line effect*: When people go around a circle reading words or saying their names, their poorest memories are for what was said by the person just before them (Bond & others, 1991; Brenner, 1973). When next in line, we focus on our own performance and often fail to process the last person's words.
- Information presented in the seconds just before sleep seldom is remembered (Wyatt & Bootzin, 1994). When our consciousness fades before we've processed the information, all is lost. Information presented in the *hour* before sleep, as we will see, is well remembered.
- Taped information played during sleep is registered by the ears but is not remembered (Wood & others, 1992). Without opportunity for rehearsal, "sleep learning" doesn't occur.

We also retain information better when our rehearsal is distributed over time (as when learning classmates' names), a phenomenon called the **spacing effect** (Bjork, 1999; Dempster, 1988).

In a 9-year experiment, Harry Bahrick and three of his family members (1993) practiced foreign language word translations for a given number of times, at intervals ranging from 14 to 56 days. Their consistent finding: The longer the space between practice sessions, the better their retention up to 5 years later. Reflecting on the spacing effect, Bahrick saw a practical implication: Restudying material for comprehensive final exams, capstone review courses, and senior examinations will enhance lifelong retention. Spreading out learning—say, over a semester or a year, rather than over shorter terms—should also help. *Spaced study beats cramming.* To paraphrase Ebbinghaus (1885), those who learn quickly also forget quickly.

To memorize such things as a phone number, "expanding" spaced rehearsal works well. Thomas Landauer (2001) explains: "Rehearse the name or number you are trying to memorize, wait a few seconds, rehearse again, wait a little longer, rehearse again, then wait longer still and rehearse yet again. The waits should be as long as possible without losing the information."

A phenomenon you have surely experienced further illustrates the benefits of rehearsal. Experimenters have shown people a list of items (words, names, dates, even odors) and then immediately asked them to recall the items in any order (Reed, 2000). As people struggle to recall the list, they often demonstrate the **serial position effect**: They remember the last and first items better than they

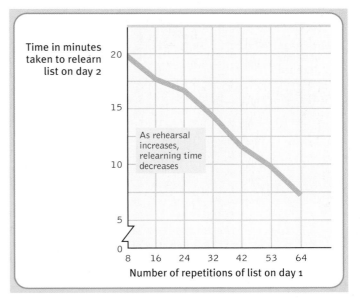

As rehearsal increases, relearning time decreases

figure 8.3
Ebbinghaus' retention curve
Ebbinghaus found that the more times he practiced a list of nonsense syllables on day 1, the fewer repetitions he required to relearn it on day 2. Said simply, the more time we spend learning novel information, the more we retain. (From Baddeley, 1982.)

"The mind is slow in unlearning what it has been long in learning."
    Roman philosopher Seneca (4 B.C.–A.D. 65)

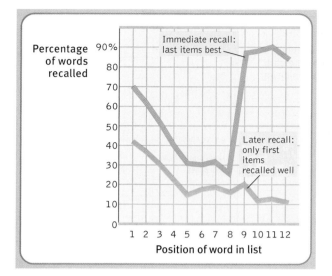

figure 8.4
The serial position effect After being presented with a list of words or names, people immediately recall the last items well (perhaps because they are still "on-screen"), and quite often the first few items nearly as well. But later they recall the first items best. (From Craik & Watkins, 1973.)

Here is another sentence I will ask you about later: The fish attacked the swimmer.

How many Fs *are in the following sentence? FINISHED FILES ARE THE RESULTS OF YEARS OF SCIENTIFIC STUDY COMBINED WITH THE EXPERIENCE OF YEARS. (See page 266.)*

▶ **imagery** mental pictures; a powerful aid to effortful processing, especially when combined with semantic encoding.

▶ **mnemonics** [nih-MON-iks] memory aids, especially those techniques that use vivid imagery and organizational devices.

do those in the middle (**Figure 8.4**). Perhaps because the last items are still in short-term memory, people briefly recall them especially quickly and well. But after a delay—after they shift their attention from the last items—their recall is best for the first items. As an everyday parallel, imagine being introduced to several people. As you meet each person, you repeat (rehearse) all their names starting from the beginning. By the time you meet the last person, you will have spent more time rehearsing the earlier names than the later ones; thus, the next day you will probably more easily recall the earlier names. Also, learning the first few names may interfere with your learning the later ones.

But, sometimes merely repeating information, such as the new phone number we are about to dial, is not enough to store it for later recall (Craik & Watkins, 1973; Greene, 1987). Our memory system also processes information by encoding its significant features.

What We Encode

4. What methods of effortful processing aid in forming memories?

We process information in three key ways—by encoding its meaning, by encoding its image, and by mentally organizing it. To some extent, we do these things automatically. But in each case, there are effortful strategies for enhancing memory.

Encoding Meaning

When processing verbal information for storage, we usually encode its meaning, associating what we read or hear with what we already know or imagine. Thus, whether we hear "eye-screem" as "ice cream" or "I scream" depends on how the context and our experience guide us to interpret the sounds.

Try it yourself: Can you repeat the sentence about the rioter from page 258? ("The angry rioter threw . . .") Perhaps, like the subjects in an experiment by William Brewer (1977), you recalled the rioter sentence as you encoded it when you read it (for example, "The angry rioter threw the rock *through* the window") and not as it was written ("The angry rioter threw the rock *at* the window"). As such recall indicates, we tend not to remember things exactly as they were. Rather, *we remember what we encoded.* Studying for an exam, you may remember your lecture notes rather than the lecture itself. Gordon Bower and Daniel Morrow (1990) liken our minds to theater directors who, given a raw script, imagine a finished stage production. Asked later to recall what we heard or read, we recall not the literal text but the mental model we constructed from it.

But given too raw a script, we have trouble creating a mental model. Put yourself in the place of the students whom John Bransford and Marcia Johnson (1972) asked to remember the following recorded passage:

> The procedure is actually quite simple. First you arrange things into different groups. Of course, one pile may be sufficient depending on how much there is to do. . . . After the procedure is completed one arranges the materials into different groups again. Then they can be put into their appropriate places. Eventually they will be used once more and the whole cycle will then have to be repeated. However, that is part of life.

When the students heard the paragraph you have just read, without a meaningful context, they remembered little of it. When told that the paragraph was about washing clothes (something additionally meaningful to them), they remembered much more of it—as you probably could now after rereading it.

Such research suggests the benefits of rephrasing what we read and hear into meaningful terms. From his experiments on himself, Ebbinghaus estimated that, compared with learning nonsense material, learning meaningful material required only one-tenth the effort. As memory researcher Wayne Wickelgren (1977, p. 346) noted, "The time you spend thinking about material you are reading and relating it to previously stored material is about the most useful thing you can do in learning any new subject matter."

Encoding Imagery

We struggle to memorize formulas, definitions, and dates, yet we can easily picture where we were yesterday, who was with us, where we sat, and what we wore. Our earliest memories—probably of something that happened at age 3 or 4—almost surely involve visual **imagery**, or mental pictures.

In a variety of experiments, researchers have documented the benefits of mental images. For example, we remember words that lend themselves to picture images better than we remember abstract, low-imagery words. (When I quiz you later, which three of these words—*typewriter, void, cigarette, inherent, fire, process*—will you most likely recall?) Similarly, you probably still recall the sentence about the rock-throwing rioter, not only because of the meaning you encoded but also because the sentence lent itself to a visual image. As the example suggests, and as certain memory experts believe, memory for concrete nouns is aided by encoding them *both* semantically and visually (Marschark & others, 1987; Paivio, 1986). Two codes are better than one.

Thanks to the durability of our most vivid images, we recall our experiences with mental snapshots of their best or worst moments. Thus, the best moment of a pleasure or joy, and the worst moment of a pain or frustration, often colors our memories more than does its duration (Fredrickson & Kahneman, 1993). Recalling the high points while forgetting the mundane moments may explain a phenomenon Terrence Mitchell, Leigh Thompson, Erika Peterson, and Randy Cronk (1997) call *rosy retrospection*: People tend to recall events such as a camping holiday more positively than they evaluated them at the time. They remember their visit to Disney World less for the muggy heat and long lines than for the surroundings, food, and rides.

Imagery is at the heart of many memory aids. **Mnemonic** (nih-MON-ik) devices (so named after the Greek word for memory) were developed by ancient Greek scholars and orators as aids to remembering lengthy passages and speeches. Using the "method of loci," they imagined themselves moving through a familiar series of locations, associating each place with a visual representation of the to-be-remembered topic. Then, when speaking, the orator would mentally revisit each location and retrieve the associated image.

Other mnemonic devices involve both acoustic and visual codes. For example, the "peg-word" system requires that you first memorize a jingle: *"One is a bun; two is a shoe; three is a tree; four is a door; five is a hive; six is sticks; seven is heaven; eight is a gate; nine is swine; ten is a hen."* Without much effort, you will soon be able to count by peg-words instead of numbers: bun, shoe, tree . . . and then to visually associate the peg-words with to-be-remembered items. Now you are ready to challenge anyone to give you a grocery list to remember. Carrots? Imagine them stuck into a bun. Milk? Fill the shoe with it. Paper towels? Drape them over the tree branch. Think "bun, shoe, tree" and you see their associated images: carrots, milk, paper towels. With few errors (Bugelski & others, 1968), you will be able to recall the items in any order and to name any given item.

Organizing Information for Encoding

Meaning and imagery enhance our memory partly by helping us organize information. When Bransford and Johnson's laundry paragraph (page 262) became meaningful, we could mentally organize its sentences into a sequence. Mnemonic devices help organize material for our later retrieval.

"A thing when heard, remember, strikes less keen on the spectator's mind than when 'tis seen."

Horace, Ars Poetica, 8 B.C.

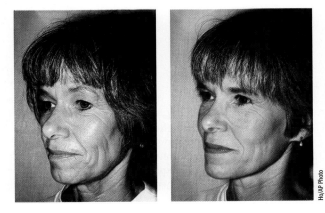

The imagery principle Plastic surgery researcher Darrick Antell observes that "you can talk until you're blue in the face about all the health hazards" of tanning and smoking. But show people photos of identical twins, only one of whom has aged under the influence of tanning and smoking, and they will learn and remember. Sixty-year-old Gay Black, left, was an avid tanner and onetime smoker, unlike her younger-looking identical twin, Gwen Sirota, right.

Ho/AP Photo

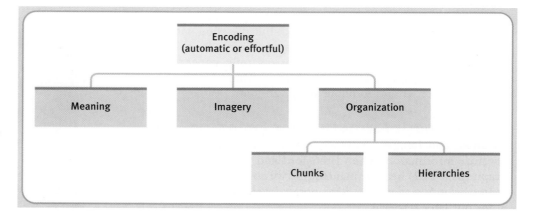

1. ◁⊃Ọ◅⊓◁⊓ (LANGUAGE reversed/upside down)
2. K L C I S N E

3. KLCISNE NVESE YNA NI CSTTIH TNDO
4. NICKELS SEVEN ANY IN STITCH DONT

5. NICKELS SEVEN ANY IN STITCH DONT
   SAVES AGO A SCORE TIME AND
   NINE WOODEN FOUR YEARS TAKE

6. DONT TAKE ANY WOODEN NICKELS
   FOUR SCORE AND SEVEN YEARS AGO
   A STITCH IN TIME SAVES NINE

figure 8.5
Effects of chunking on memory
When we organize information into meaningful units, such as letters, words, and phrases, we recall it more easily. (From Hintzman, 1978.)

Memory researchers agree that Canada's postal codes, with alternating numbers and letters, are especially hard to memorize (Hebert, 2001). A1C 5S7 would be more easily remembered if chunked by letters and numbers, as ACS 157.

春夏秋冬

figure 8.6
An example of chunking—for those who read Chinese After looking at these characters, can you reproduce them exactly? If so, you are literate in Chinese.

CHUNKING To experience the importance of organization, glance for a few seconds at row 1 of **FIGURE 8.5**, then look away and try to reproduce what you saw. Impossible, yes? But you can easily reproduce the second row, which is no less complex. Similarly, I bet you found row 4 much easier to remember than row 3, although both contain the same letters. And you could remember the sixth cluster more easily than the fifth, although both contain the same words.

As this demonstrates, we more easily recall information when we can organize it into meaningful units, or chunks. **Chunking** occurs so naturally that we take it for granted. If you are a native English speaker, you can reproduce perfectly the 150 or so line segments that make up the words in the three phrases of item 6 in Figure 8.5. It would astonish someone unfamiliar with the language.

I am similarly awed at the ability of someone literate in Chinese to glance at **FIGURE 8.6** and then to reproduce all of the strokes; or of a chess master who, after a 5-second look at the board during a game, can recall the exact positions of most of the pieces (Chase & Simon, 1973); or of a varsity basketball player who, given a 4-second glance at a basketball play, can recall the positions of the players (Allard & Burnett, 1985). We all remember information best when we can organize it into personally meaningful arrangements.

Chunking also aids our recall of unfamiliar material. One mnemonic technique chunks it into a more familiar form by creating words (called *acronyms*) or sentences from the first letters of words to be remembered. Should you ever need to recall the names of North America's five Great Lakes, just remember HOMES (*H*uron, *O*ntario, *M*ichigan, *E*rie, *S*uperior). Want to remember the colors of the rainbow in order of wavelength? Think of the mnemonic ROY G. BIV (*r*ed, *o*range, *y*ellow, *g*reen, *b*lue, *i*ndigo, *v*iolet).

HIERARCHIES When people develop expertise in an area, they process information not only in chunks but also in hierarchies composed of a few broad concepts divided and subdivided into narrower concepts and facts. By organizing knowledge in hierarchies, we, too, can retrieve information efficiently. This chapter therefore aims not only to teach you the elementary facts of memory but also to help you organize these facts around broad principles, such as encoding; subprinciples, such as automatic and effortful processing; and still more specific concepts, such as meaning, imagery, and organization (**FIGURE 8.7**).

Gordon Bower and his colleagues (1969) demonstrated the benefits of hierarchical organization. They presented words either randomly or grouped into categories. When the words were organized into groups, recall was two to three times better. Such results show the benefits of organizing what you study—of giving special attention to chapter outlines, headings, previews, and review para-

figure 8.7
Organization benefits memory
When we organize words or concepts into hierarchical groups, as illustrated here with concepts in this chapter, we remember them better than when we see them presented randomly.

graphs and questions. If you can master a chapter's concepts with their overall organization, your recall should be effective at test time. Taking lecture and text notes in outline format—a type of hierarchical organization—may also prove helpful.

How many of the six quiz words on page 263 can you now recall? Of these, how many are high-imagery words? How many are low-imagery?

rehearse it!

1. Human memory involves information processing. We take information in, retain it, and later get it back out. In psychological terms, these steps are
   a. retrieval, encoding, and storage.
   b. encoding, storage, and retrieval.
   c. storage, encoding, and retrieval.
   d. retrieval, storage, and encoding.

2. Short-term memory is an intermediate stage of memory where information is held before it is stored or forgotten. The newer concept of working memory
   a. clarifies the idea of short-term memory by focusing on behind-the-scenes information processing.
   b. splits short-term memory into two substages—sensory memory and working memory.
   c. splits short-term memory into two areas—working (retrievable) memory and inaccessible memory.
   d. clarifies the idea of short-term memory by introducing the element of rehearsal.

3. Rehearsal is the conscious repetition of information a person wants to remember, either in the short or long term. Rehearsal is part of
   a. automatic processing.
   b. effortful processing.
   c. forgetting.
   d. retrieval.

4. Psychologists have found that when people are shown a list of words and are immediately tested, they tend to recall the first and last items on the list more readily than those in the middle (called the serial position effect). When people are *retested* after a delay, they are most likely to recall
   a. the first items on the list.
   b. the first and last items on the list.
   c. a few items at random.
   d. the last items on the list.

5. Many people use visual imagery to help them remember material that would otherwise be difficult to master.

Memory aids that use visual imagery, peg-words, or other organizational devices are called
   a. acronyms.
   b. nonsense material.
   c. mental pictures.
   d. mnemonics.

6. Chunking is a way of organizing information into familiar and manageable units. A related technique involves organizing material into broad categories, which are then divided into sub-categories. This technique, used in chapter outlines and organizational charts, is called
   a. serial position.
   b. peg-words.
   c. hierarchial organization.
   d. mental pictures.

Answers can be found in Appendix C.

STORAGE: RETAINING INFORMATION

If you later recall something you experienced, you must, somehow, have stored and retrieved it. Anything stored in long-term memory lies dormant, waiting to be reawakened by a cue. What is our temporary and our long-term memory storage capacity? Let's start with the first memory store noted in the three-stage processing model (Figure 8.1 on page 259)—our fleeting sensory memory.

Sensory Memory

5. How does sensory memory work?

Consider what one intriguing memory experiment revealed about our sensory memory—the initial recording of sensory information in the memory system. As part of his doctoral research, George Sperling (1960) showed people three rows of three letters each for only 1/20th of a second (**FIGURE 8.8**). It was harder than reading by flashes of lightning. After the nine letters disappeared from the screen, people could recall only about half of them.

Was it because they had insufficient time to glimpse them? No, Sperling cleverly demonstrated that even at faster than lightning-flash speed, people actually *can* see and recall all the letters, but only momentarily. Rather than ask them to recall all nine letters at once, Sperling would sound a high, medium, or low tone immediately *after* flashing the nine letters. This cue directed participants to report only the letters of the top, middle, or bottom row, respectively. Now they rarely missed a letter, showing that all nine letters were momentarily available for recall.

figure 8.8
Momentary photographic memory
When George Sperling flashed a group of letters similar to this for 1/20th of a second, people could recall only about half of the letters. But when signaled to recall a particular row *immediately* after the letters had disappeared, they could do so with near-perfect accuracy.

▶ **chunking** organizing items into familiar, manageable units; often occurs automatically.

▶ **iconic memory** a momentary sensory memory of visual stimuli; a photographic or picture-image memory lasting no more than a few tenths of a second.

▶ **echoic memory** a momentary sensory memory of auditory stimuli; if attention is elsewhere, sounds and words can still be recalled within 3 or 4 seconds.

Sperling's experiment revealed that we have a fleeting photographic memory called **iconic memory**. For an instant, our eyes register an exact representation of a scene and we can recall any part of it in amazing detail—but only for a few tenths of a second. If Sperling delayed the tone signal by more than half a second, the iconic memory was gone and the subjects once again recalled only about half the letters. Our visual screen clears quickly, as it must, so that new images can be superimposed over old ones.

We also have an impeccable, though fleeting, memory for auditory sensory images, called **echoic memory** (Cowan, 1988; Lu & others, 1992). However, if partially interpreted, the auditory echo disappears more slowly. The last few words spoken seem to linger for 3 or 4 seconds. Picture yourself in conversation, as your attention veers to the TV. If your mildly irked conversational partner asks, "What did I just say?" you will recover the last few words from your mind's echo chamber.

Answer to question on page 262: Partly because your initial processing of the letters was primarily acoustic rather than visual, you probably missed some of the six Fs, especially those that sound like a V rather than an F.

Short-Term Memory

6. What are the limits of short-term memory?

Among the vast amounts of information registered by our sensory memory, we illuminate some with our attentional flashlight. We also retrieve information from long-term storage for "on-screen" display. But unless we meaningfully encode or rehearse that information, it quickly disappears. During your finger's trip from phone book to phone, your memory of a telephone number may evaporate.

To find out how quickly a short-term memory will disappear, Lloyd Peterson and Margaret Peterson (1959) asked people to remember three-consonant groups, such as *CHJ*. To prevent rehearsal of the letters, the researchers asked participants, for example, to start at 100 and count aloud backwards by threes. After 3 seconds, people recalled the letters only about half the time; after 12 seconds, they seldom recalled them at all (**Figure 8.9**). Without active processing, short-term memories have a limited life.

Short-term memory is limited not only in duration but also in capacity. As noted earlier, our short-term memory typically stores just seven or so bits of information (give or take two). George Miller (1956) enshrined this recall capacity as the *Magical Number Seven, plus or minus two*. Not surprisingly, when some phone companies began requiring all callers to dial an area code in addition to a seven-digit number, many people reported trouble retaining the just-looked-up number.

The Magical Number Seven has become psychology's contribution to an intriguing list of magic sevens—the seven wonders of the world, the seven seas, the seven deadly sins, the seven primary colors, the seven musical scale notes, the seven days of the week—seven magical sevens.

Our short-term recall is slightly better for random digits (such as those of a phone number) than for random letters, which sometimes have similar sounds. It is slightly better for information we hear than for images we see. Both children and adults have short-term recall for roughly as many words as they can speak in 2 seconds (Cowan, 1994; Hulme & Tordoff, 1989). With information chunks (for example, letters meaningfully grouped as ABC, FBI, KGB, BBC, CIA) and without rehearsal, the average person retains only about four chunks in short-term memory (Cowan, 2001). Suppressing rehearsal by saying "the the the" while hearing random digits also reduces memory to about four items. The basic principle: At any given moment, we can consciously process only a very limited amount of information.

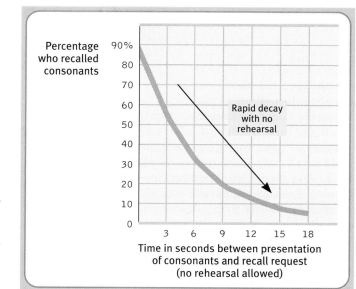

**figure 8.9
Short-term
memory decay**
Unless rehearsed,
verbal information
may be quickly
forgotten. (From
Peterson & Peterson,
1959.)

Percentage who recalled consonants

Rapid decay with no rehearsal

Time in seconds between presentation of consonants and recall request (no rehearsal allowed)

Long-Term Memory

7. How large and durable is our long-term memory?

In Arthur Conan Doyle's *A Study in Scarlet*, Sherlock Holmes offers a popular theory of memory capacity:

> I consider that a man's brain originally is like a little empty attic, and you have to stock it with such furniture as you choose. . . . It is a mistake to think that that little room has elastic walls and can distend to any extent. Depend upon it, there comes a time when for every addition of knowledge you forget something that you knew before.

Contrary to Holmes' belief, our capacity for storing long-term memories is essentially limitless. By one careful estimate, the average adult has about a billion bits of information in memory and a storage capacity that is probably a thousand to a million times greater (Landauer, 1986). So, our brains are *not* like attics, which once filled can store more items only if we discard old ones.

The point is vividly illustrated by those who have performed phenomenal memory feats. Consider Rajan Mahadevan, a University of Tennessee psychologist. Give him a block of 10 digits from the first 30,000 or so digits of pi and, after a few moments of mental searching for the string, he'll pick up the series from there, firing numbers like a machine gun (Delaney & others, 1999; Thompson & others, 1993). He also can repeat 50 random digits—backwards. It is not a genetic gift, he says; anyone could learn to do it. But given the genetic influence on so many human traits, and knowing that Rajan's father memorized Shakespeare's complete works, one wonders.

Storing Memories in the Brain

8. How are memories recorded in the brain?

I marveled at my aging mother-in-law, a retired pianist and organist. At age 88 her blind eyes could no longer read music. But let her sit at a keyboard and she would flawlessly play any of hundreds of hymns, including ones she had not thought of for 20 years. Where did her brain store those thousands of sequenced notes? For a time, some memory researchers believed that brain stimulation during surgery provided evidence that our whole past, not just well-practiced music, is "in there," in complete detail, just waiting to be relived. Even today, 6 in 10 university students agree that "everything we learn is permanently stored" although sometimes inaccessible (Brown & others, 1996). Perhaps some of them have heard of memories apparently awakened during brain surgery. To predict possible side effects of brain surgery, Wilder Penfield (1969) helped map the brain's motor cortex by electrically stimulating wide-awake patients. Occasionally, Penfield's patients would report hearing things, such as "a mother calling her little boy." Penfield assumed he was activating long-lost experiences etched permanently on the brain.

Scrutinizing these famous reports, memory researchers Elizabeth Loftus and Geoffrey Loftus (1980) discovered these flashbacks were extremely rare, occurring in only a handful of Penfield's 1100 stimulated patients. Moreover, the content of these few recollections suggested the experiences were being invented, not relived. As if they had been dreaming, people would recall being in locations they had never visited. Despite the brain's vast storage capacity, we do not store most information with the exactness of a tape recorder. Rather, say memory researchers, forgetting occurs as new experiences interfere with our retrieval (page 278) and as the physical memory trace gradually decays.

But what exactly is the "memory trace"? Recent research provides new clues to memory's physical basis. While cognitive psychologists study our memory "software," neuroscientists explore our memory "hardware"—how and where we physically store information in our brains.

R. J. Erwin/Photo Researchers

Clark's Nutcracker Among animals, one contender for champion memorist would be a mere birdbrain—the Clark's Nutcracker—which during winter and early spring can locate up to 6000 caches of buried pine seeds (Shettleworth, 1993).

"Our memories are flexible and superimposable, a panoramic blackboard with an endless supply of chalk and erasers."

Elizabeth Loftus and Katherine Ketcham,
The Myth of Repressed Memory, 1994

The search for physical evidence of memory has at times been exasperating. One psychologist, Karl Lashley (1950), trained rats to solve a maze, then cut out pieces of the rats' cortexes and retested their memory of the maze. No matter what small cortex section he removed, the rats retained at least a partial memory of how to solve the maze. Lashley's conclusion: Memories do not reside in single, specific spots.

Are memories instead rooted in the brain's ongoing electrical activity? If so, then temporarily shutting down that activity should eliminate them, much as a power failure eliminates the settings on a digital clock radio. Testing that idea, Ralph Gerard (1953) first trained hamsters to turn right or left to get food, and then lowered their body temperature until the brain's electrical activity ceased. When the hamsters were revived and their brains were active again, would they remember which way to turn? Yes. Their long-term memories survived the electrical blackout. In commenting on the elusiveness of the memory trace, one memory researcher, with tongue only partly in cheek, said, "I must admit that memories are more of a spiritual than a physical reality. When you try to touch them, they turn to mist and disappear" (Loftus & Ketcham, 1994, p. 4). To know how our brain stores and effortlessly retrieves a flood of details "defies comprehension," said one awestruck neuroscientist (Doty, 1998).

Recently, the search for the physical basis of memory—for information incarnated in matter—has focused on the synapses.

Synaptic Changes

Neuroscientists are expanding the search for the location of memories by exploring changes within and between single neurons. Memories begin as impulses whizzing through brain circuits, somehow leaving permanent neural traces. Where does the neural change occur? The available clues point to the synapses—the sites where nerve cells communicate with one another through their neurotransmitter messengers. Recall from Chapter 2 how experience modifies the brain's neural networks. Given increased activity in a particular pathway, neural interconnections form or strengthen.

Eric Kandel and James Schwartz (1982) observed changes in the sending neurons of a simple animal, the California sea snail, *Aplysia*. Its mere 20,000 or so nerve cells are unusually large and accessible, enabling the researchers to observe synaptic changes during learning. Chapter 7 noted how the sea snail can be classically conditioned (with electric shock) to reflexively withdraw its gills when squirted with water, much as a shell-shocked soldier jumps at the sound of a snapping twig. By observing sea snails' neural connections before and after conditioning, Kandel and Schwartz pinpointed changes. When learning occurs, the snail releases more of the neurotransmitter serotonin at certain synapses. These synapses then become more efficient at transmitting signals.

Increased synaptic efficiency makes for more efficient neural circuits. In experiments, rapidly stimulating certain memory-circuit connections has increased their sensitivity for hours or even weeks to come. The sending neuron now needs less prompting to release its neurotransmitter, and receptor sites may increase (**FIGURE 8.10**). This prolonged strengthening of potential neural firing, called

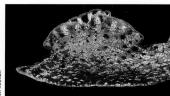

Aplysia This much-studied California sea snail has increased our understanding of the neural basis of learning.

"The biology of the mind will be as scientifically important to this [new] century as the biology of the gene [was] to the twentieth century."

Eric Kandel, acceptance remarks for a
2000 Nobel prize

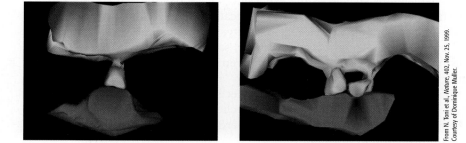

figure 8.10
Doubled receptor sites Electron microscope images show just one receptor site (gray) reaching toward a sending neuron before long-term potentiation (left) and two afterward (right). (From Toni & others, 1999.)

long-term potentiation (LTP), provides a neural basis for learning and remembering associations. We know now that drugs that block LTP interfere with learning (Lynch & Staubli, 1991). Mutant mice engineered to lack an enzyme needed for LTP can't learn their way out of a maze (Silva & others, 1992). And rats given a drug that enhances LTP will learn a maze with half the usual number of mistakes (Service, 1994). At the turn of the century, neuroscientists were discovering protein molecules that serve to build synaptic connections and enhance long-term memory (McGaugh, 2000). These findings raise hopes that researchers may someday discover drugs or "brain-specific" nutrients to synthesize these proteins and enhance human memory, especially for those whose memory is fading (McDaniel & others, 2002).

After long-term potentiation has occurred, passing an electric current through the brain won't disrupt old memories. But the current will wipe out very recent experiences. Such is the experience both of laboratory animals and of depressed people given electroconvulsive therapy. A blow to the head can do the same. Like sleepers who can't remember what they heard just before losing consciousness, football players and boxers momentarily knocked unconscious typically have no memory of events just before the knock-out (Yarnell & Lynch, 1970). The information in short-term memory before the blow did not have time to consolidate into long-term memory.

Stress Hormones and Memory

The stress hormones that humans and animals produce when excited or stressed make more glucose energy available to fuel brain activity. This hormone surge signals the brain that something important has happened. Moreover, the amygdala, which processes emotion, boosts activity in the brain's memory-forming areas (Hamann & others, 2002). The result: Arousal sears events onto the brain. Conversely, people given a drug that blocks stress hormones will later have more trouble remembering the details of an upsetting story (Cahill & others, 1994). Weaker emotion means weaker memories.

Emotion-triggered hormonal changes help explain why we long remember exciting or shocking events, such as our first kiss, an earthquake, or 9/11. People who experienced the 1989 San Francisco earthquake had perfect recall a year and a half later of where they were and what they were doing (as they had recorded within a day or two of the quake). Others' memories for the circumstances under which they merely *heard* about the quake were more prone to errors (Neisser & others, 1991; Palmer & others, 1991). (A second important reason for the durability of dramatic experiences is our reliving and rehearsing them—as did most people who experienced the earthquake and told their stories to countless others.)

The point to remember, according to James McGaugh (1994), is that "stronger emotional experiences make for stronger, more reliable memories." After traumatic experiences—a wartime ambush, a house fire, a rape—vivid recollections of the horrific event may intrude again and again. It is as if they were burned in.

Storing Implicit and Explicit Memories

A memory-to-be enters the cortex through the senses, then winds its way into the brain's depths. Precisely where it goes depends on the type of information, as dramatically illustrated by those who, as in the case of my father mentioned earlier, suffer from a type of **amnesia** in which they are unable to form new memories.

Neurologist Oliver Sacks (1985, pp. 26–27) describes one such patient, Jimmie, who had brain damage. Jimmie had no memories—thus, no sense of elapsed time—beyond his injury in 1945. Asked in 1975 to name the U.S. President, he replied, "FDR's dead. Truman's at the helm."

► **long-term potentiation (LTP)** an increase in a synapse's firing potential after brief, rapid stimulation. Believed to be a neural basis for learning and memory.

► **amnesia** the loss of memory.

Stress hormones and memory When we are greatly aroused, as are these firefighters putting out a blaze, our stress hormones help make memories indelible.

Tom Carter/PhotoEdit

▶ **implicit memory** retention independent of conscious recollection. Also called *procedural memory*.

▶ **explicit memory** memory of facts and experiences that one can consciously know and "declare." (Also called *declarative memory*.)

▶ **hippocampus** a neural center located in the limbic system that helps process explicit memories for storage.

When Jimmie gave his age as 19, Sacks set a mirror before him: "Look in the mirror and tell me what you see. Is that a 19-year-old looking out from the mirror?"

Jimmie turned ashen, gripped the chair, cursed, then became frantic: "What's going on? What's happened to me? Is this a nightmare? Am I crazy? Is this a joke?" When his attention was diverted to some children playing baseball, his panic ended, the dreadful mirror forgotten.

Sacks showed Jimmie a photo from *National Geographic*. "What is this?" he asked. "It's the moon," Jimmie replied.

"No, it's not," Sacks answered. "It's a picture of the Earth taken from the moon."

"Doc, you're kidding? Someone would've had to get a camera up there!"

"Naturally."

"Hell! You're joking—how the hell would you do that?" Jimmie's wonder was that of a bright young man from 55 years ago reacting with amazement to his travel back to the future.

Careful testing of these unique people reveals something even stranger: Although incapable of recalling new facts or anything they have recently done, Jimmie and others with similar conditions can learn. Shown hard-to-find figures in pictures (in the *Where's Waldo?* series), they can quickly spot them again later. They can learn to read reversed mirror-image writing or do a jigsaw puzzle, and they have even been taught complicated job skills (Schacter, 1992, 1996; Xu & Corkin, 2001). They can be classically conditioned. However, *they do all these things with absolutely no awareness of having learned them.*

These amnesia victims are in some ways like people with brain damage who cannot consciously recognize faces but whose physiological responses to familiar faces reveal an implicit (unconscious) recognition. Their behaviors challenge the idea that memory is a single, unified system. Instead, we seem to have two memory systems operating in tandem (**FIGURE 8.11**). Whatever has destroyed conscious recall in these individuals with amnesia has not destroyed their unconscious capacity for learning. They can learn *how* to do something—called **implicit memory** (*procedural memory*). But they may not know and declare *that* they know—called **explicit memory** (*declarative memory*). Having read a story once, they will read it faster a second time, showing implicit memory. But there will be no explicit memory, for they cannot recall having seen the story before. Having played golf on a new course, they will forget it completely, yet the more they play the course, the more their game will improve. If repeatedly shown the word *perfume*, they will not recall having seen it. But if asked the first word that comes to mind in response to the letters *per*, they surprise themselves by saying *perfume*, readily displaying their learning. They retain their past but do not explicitly recall it. Perhaps you recall the experiment in which Tetris game players, while afterward falling asleep, dreamt of Tetrislike pieces floating down (page 201). Three of the participants suffered amnesia and therefore had no recollection of the game, no idea why they were awakened, and no clue why they dreamt of falling blocks (Stickgold & others, 2000).

The two-track memory system reinforces an important principle introduced in Chapter 5's description of parallel processing: Mental feats such as vision, thinking, and memory may seem to be single abilities, but they are not. Rather, we split information into different components for separate and simultaneous processing.

figure 8.11
Memory subsystems
We process and store our explicit and implicit memories separately. Thus, one may lose explicit memory (becoming amnesic), yet display implicit memory for material one cannot consciously recall.

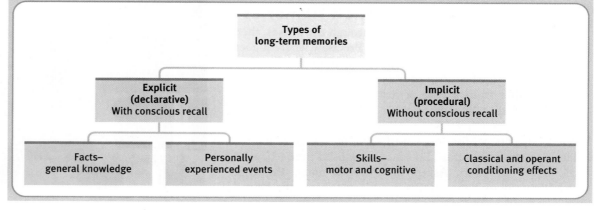

THE HIPPOCAMPUS One way to discover how memory works is to study its malfunctions. For example, these remarkable patients provoke us to wonder: Do our explicit and implicit memory systems involve separate brain regions? Scans of the brain in action, and autopsies of people who had amnesia, reveal that new explicit memories of names, images, and events are laid down via a limbic system structure called the **hippocampus** (**Figure 8.12**). The hippocampus again lights up on a PET scan when people recall words (using explicit memory) (Squire, 1992).

Damage to the hippocampus disrupts some types of memory. Chickadees and other birds can store food in hundreds of places and return to these unmarked caches months later, but not if their hippocampus has been removed (Sherry & Vaccarino, 1989). Like the cortex, the hippocampus is lateralized. (You've got two of them, one just above each ear and about an inch and a half straight in.) Damage to the left or right hippocampus seems to produce different results. Patients with left hippocampus damage have trouble remembering verbal information, but they have no trouble recalling visual designs and locations. For those with right hippocampus damage, the problem is reversed (Schacter, 1996).

Monkeys who lose their hippocampus to surgery also lose most of their recall for things learned during the preceding month, though their older memories remain intact (Squire & Zola-Morgan, 1991; McGaugh, 2000). The hippocampus seems to act as a loading dock where the brain registers and temporarily stores the elements of a remembered episode—its smell, feel, sound, and location. But then, much as I shift older files to a basement store room, memories migrate for storage elsewhere.

Our brain's librarian assigns different information to different regions. Brain scans reveal that, once stored, our mental encores of past experience activate various parts of the frontal and temporal lobes (Fink & others, 1996; Gabrieli & others, 1996; Markowitsch, 1995). Calling up a telephone number and holding it in working memory activates a region of the left frontal cortex; recalling a party scene would more likely activate a region of the right hemisphere.

There is no longer any doubt: Our memories are not in one place. Many brain regions are active as we encode, store, and retrieve different kinds of information. Savoring that memory of your first kiss requires a mental symphony conductor that retrieves snippets from various cortical storage sites and integrates them with the emotional associations provided by your amygdala.

THE CEREBELLUM Although your hippocampus is a temporary processing site for your explicit memories, you could lose it and still lay down memories for skills and conditioned associations. Joseph Le Doux (1996) recounts a brain-damaged French patient whose amnesia left her unable to recognize her physician as, each day, he shook her hand and introduced himself. One day, after reaching for his hand, she yanked hers back, for the physician had pricked her with a tack in his palm. The next time he returned to introduce himself she refused to shake his hand but couldn't explain why. Having been classically conditioned, she just wouldn't do it.

Hoping to locate such implicit memories, psychologist Richard Thompson and his fellow explorers David Krupa and Judith Thompson studied how a rabbit's brain learns to associate a tone with an impending air puff in the eye (and thus to blink in anticipation of the puff). First, they traced the pathway connecting the brain's reception of the tone with the blink response. They discovered that it runs to the brainstem through a part of the cerebellum (at the back of the head) and that if they cut this pathway, the learned response would be lost. It was like cutting the cords to your stereo speakers, which would confirm the cord's part in the electronic path but might still leave you wondering where the music is stored. Their next step was to administer a drug during the rabbits' eye-blink training, temporarily deadening different parts of the neural pathway. This pinpointed the implicit memory—in the cerebellum. The rejuvenated rabbits failed to display the learned response only when the cerebellum was deactivated during training (Krupa & others, 1993; Steinmetz, 1999). Human patients with a damaged cerebellum are likewise incapable of simple eye-blink conditioning (Daum & Schugens, 1996; Green & Woodruff-Pak, 2000).

"[Brain-scanning] technologies are revolutionizing the study of the brain and mind in the same way that the telescope revolutionized the study of the heavens."

Endel Tulving (1996)

figure 8.12
The hippocampus Explicit memories for facts and episodes are processed in the hippocampus and fed to other brain regions for storage.

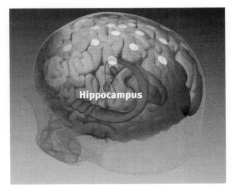

Weidenfeld & Nicolson archives

Emotional memories involve the amygdala. Those with amygdala damage don't learn the sort of fear conditioning displayed by the woman who feared the physician's hand; with an intact amygdala but a damaged hippocampus, they learn but don't explicitly remember (Dolan, 2002).

Our dual explicit-implicit memory system helps explain infantile amnesia: The reactions and skills we learned during infancy reach far into our future, yet as adults we recall nothing (explicitly) of our first three years. Our conscious minds are blank, not only because we index so much of our explicit memory by words that nonspeaking children have not learned, but also because the hippocampus is one of the last brain structures to mature.

---

rehearse it!

7. Sensory information is initially recorded in our sensory memory. This memory may be visual (_____ memory) or auditory (_____ memory).
   a. implicit; explicit
   b. iconic; echoic
   c. declarative; procedural
   d. long-term; short-term

8. Our capacity for storing long-term memories is essentially limitless. However, our short-term memory for new information is limited. When confronted with a list of novel items, most people can immediately recall
   a. only the first items on the list.
   b. a series of about 20 items.
   c. a series of about 7 items.
   d. only meaningful items.

9. Researchers have found that long-term potentiation (LTP) provides a neural basis for learning and memory. LTP refers to
   a. emotion-triggered hormonal changes.
   b. the role of the hippocampus in processing explicit memories.
   c. an increase in a synapse's firing potential after brief, rapid stimulation.
   d. aging people's potential for learning.

10. A person who has amnesia following damage to the hippocampus typically has difficulties in learning new facts and recalling recent events. However, the person may well be able to recall the more distant past and certain well-learned skills, such as how to ride a bicycle or hem a dress. Memories of skills are
   a. explicit memories.
   b. implicit memories.
   c. iconic memories.
   d. echoic memories.

11. The physical basis of memory—how and where memories are physically stored in the brain—is not yet well understood. However, research suggests that the hippocampus, a neural center in the limbic system of the brain, plays an important role. The hippocampus may function as a
   a. temporary processing site for explicit memories.
   b. temporary processing site for implicit memories.
   c. permanent storage area for emotion-based memories.
   d. permanent storage for iconic and echoic memories.

Answers can be found in Appendix C.

Remembering things past Even if Madonna and Paul Newman had not become famous, their high school classmates would most likely still recognize their yearbook photos.

RETRIEVAL: GETTING INFORMATION OUT

9. How do we get information out of memory?

To most people, memory is **recall**, the ability to retrieve information not in conscious awareness. To a psychologist, memory is any sign that something learned has been retained. So *recognizing* or more quickly *relearning* information also indicates memory.

Long after you cannot recall most of the people in your high school graduating class, you may still be able to **recognize** their yearbook pictures from a photographic lineup and pick their names from a list of names. Harry Bahrick and his colleagues (1975) reported that people who had graduated 25 years earlier could not *recall* many of their old classmates, but they could *recognize* 90 percent of their pictures and names.

Our speed at **relearning** can reveal memory. If you once learned something and then forgot it, you probably will relearn it more quickly than you originally learned it. When you study for a final exam or resurrect a language used in early childhood, the relearning is easier. Tests of recognition and of time spent relearning reveal that we remember more than we can recall.

Our recognition memory is impressively quick and vast. "Is your friend wearing a new or old outfit?" "Old." "Is this seconds-long movie clip from a film you've ever seen?" "Yes." "Have you ever before seen this person—this minor variation on the same old human features (two eyes, one nose, and so on)?" "No." Before the mouth can form our answer to any of millions of such questions, the mind knows, and knows that it knows.

Retrieval Cues

When retrieving information on the Internet, one needs the correct keywords. Like Web information, memories can't be accessed unless we have the right cues for retrieving them—reminders, or clues telling us where to look. Do you recall the gist of the second sentence I asked you to remember (on page 262)? If not, does the word *shark* help? Experiments show that *shark* (likely what you visualized) more readily retrieves the image you stored than does the sentence's actual word, *fish* (Anderson & others, 1976).

You can think of a memory as held in storage by a web of associations. To retrieve a specific memory, you first need to identify one of the strands that leads to it, a process called **priming**. Philosopher-psychologist William James referred to priming as the "wakening of associations." Often our associations are activated, or primed, without our awareness. As **Figure 8.13** indicates, seeing or hearing the word *rabbit* primes associations with *hare* even though we may not recall having seen or heard *rabbit*.

Priming has been called "memoryless memory"—memory without remembering, invisible memory. If, walking down a hallway, you see a poster of a missing child, you will then be "primed" to interpret an ambiguous adult-child interaction as a possible kidnapping (James, 1986). Although you don't consciously remember the poster, it predisposes your interpretation. (As we saw in Chapter 5, even subliminal stimuli can briefly prime responses to later stimuli.)

Retrieval cues often prime our memories of earlier experiences. Mnemonic devices provide us with handy retrieval cues: ROY G. BIV; HOMES; bun, shoe, tree. But, the best retrieval cues come from the associations formed at the time we encode a memory. Those cues can be experiences as well as words. Tastes, smells, and sights often evoke our recall of associated episodes. To call up visual cues when trying to recall something, we may mentally place ourselves in the original context. For British theologian John Hull (1990, p. 174) this became difficult after losing his sight. On one occasion when his wife asked him what he had done that day he had difficulty recalling. "I knew I had been somewhere, and had done particular things with certain people, but where? I could not put the conversations I had had into a context. There was no background, no features against which to identify the place. Normally, the memories of people you have spoken to during the day are stored in frames which include the background."

Multiple-choice questions test our
a. recall.
b. recognition.
c. relearning.

Fill-in-the-blank questions test our _____. (See page 275 for answers to these questions.)

> **"Memory is not like a container that gradually fills up; it is more like a tree growing hooks onto which memories are hung."**
>
> Psychologist Peter Russell, *The Brain Book,* 1979

Ask a friend two rapid-fire questions: (a) How do you pronounce the word spelled by the letters s-h-o-p? (b) What do you do when you come to a green light? If your friend answers "stop" to the second question, you have demonstrated priming.

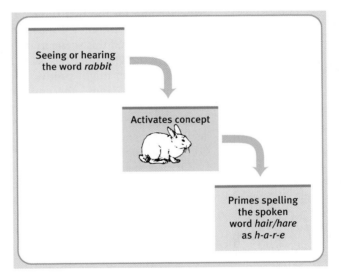

figure 8.13
Priming—awakening associations After seeing or hearing *rabbit*, we are later more likely to spell the spoken word as *h-a-r-e*. The spreading of associations unconsciously activates related associations. This phenomenon is called priming. (Adapted from Bower, 1986.)

Figure content:
Seeing or hearing the word *rabbit* → Activates concept → Primes spelling the spoken word *hair/hare* as *h-a-r-e*

Context Effects

It does help to put yourself back in the context where you experienced something. Duncan Godden and Alan Baddeley (1975) discovered this when they had scuba divers listen to a list of words in two different settings, either 10 feet underwater or sitting on the beach. As **Figure 8.14** (page 274) illustrates, the divers recalled more words when they were retested in the same place.

You have probably experienced similar context effects. You return to where you once lived or to the school you once attended and are flooded with retrieval cues and memories. Even taking an exam in the same room where you are taught may help a little. In several experiments, Carolyn Rovee-Collier (1993) found that a familiar context activates memories even in 3-month-olds. After infants learned that kicking a crib mobile would make it move (via a connecting ribbon from the ankle), the infants kicked more when tested again in the same crib with the same bumper than when in a different context.

▶ **recall** a measure of memory in which the person must retrieve information learned earlier, as on a fill-in-the-blank test.

▶ **recognition** a measure of memory in which the person need only identify items previously learned, as on a multiple-choice test.

▶ **relearning** a memory measure that assesses the amount of time saved when learning material for a second time.

▶ **priming** the activation, often unconsciously, of particular associations in memory.

figure 8.14
The effects of context on memory
Words heard underwater are best recalled underwater; words heard on land are best recalled on land. (Adapted from Godden & Baddeley, 1975.)

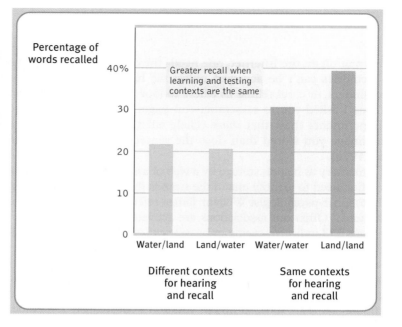

"Do you ever get that strange feeling of vujà dé? Not déjà vu; vujà dé. It's the distinct sense that, somehow, something just happened that has never happened before. Nothing seems familiar. And then suddenly the feeling is gone. Vujà dé."

George Carlin, Funny Times, December 2001

CALLAHAN

"I wonder if you'd mind giving me directions. I've never been sober in this part of town before."

▶ **déjà vu** that eerie sense that "I've experienced this before." Cues from the current situation may subconsciously trigger retrieval of an earlier experience.

▶ **mood-congruent memory** the tendency to recall experiences that are consistent with one's current good or bad mood.

Sometimes, being in a context similar to one we've been in before may trigger the experience of **déjà vu** (French for "already seen")—that eerie sense that "I've been in this exact situation before." The 60 percent of people who report having had this experience (McAneny, 1996) often wonder, "How could I recognize a situation I'm experiencing for the first time?" Those who suppose a paranormal explanation may think of reincarnation ("I must have experienced this in a previous life") or precognition ("I viewed this scene in my mind before experiencing it"). Posing the question differently ("Why do I feel as if I recognize this situation?"), we can see how our memory system might produce déjà vu (Alcock, 1981). If we have previously been in a similar situation, the current situation may be loaded with cues that unconsciously retrieve the earlier experience. Thus, if in such a context you see a stranger who looks and walks like one of your friends, the similarity may give rise to an eerie feeling of recognition. Because the feeling conflicts with your knowing that the person is a stranger, you may think, "I've seen that person in this situation before."

Or perhaps, suggests James Lampinen (2002), a situation seems familiar when moderately similar to several events. Imagine you briefly encounter my dad, my brothers, my sister, my children, and a few weeks later meet me. Perhaps you might think, "I've been with this guy before." Although no one in my family looks just like me (lucky them), they all look somewhat like me and you might form a "global match" to the similarity.

Moods and Memories

Associated words, events, and contexts are not the only retrieval cues. Events in the past may have aroused a specific *emotion* that later can prime us to recall its associated events. Cognitive psychologist Gordon Bower (1983) explained it this way: "An emotion is like a library room into which we place memory records. We best retrieve those records by returning to that emotional room." What we learn in one state—be it joyful or sad, drunk or sober—is sometimes more easily recalled when we are again in that state, a subtle phenomenon called *state-dependent memory*. What people learn when depressed or drunk they don't recall well in *any* state (depression disrupts encoding and alcohol disrupts storage). But they recall it slightly better when again depressed or drunk. Someone who hides money when drunk may forget the location until drunk again.

For example, consider how our moods bias our memories (Fiedler & others, 2001). We seem to associate good or bad events with their accompanying emotions, which become retrieval cues. Thus, our memories are somewhat **mood-congruent**.

Being depressed sours memories by priming negative associations, which we then use to explain our current mood. If put in a buoyant mood—whether under hypnosis or just by the day's events (a World Cup soccer victory for the German subjects of one study)—people recall the world through rose-colored glasses (DeSteno & others, 2000; Forgas & others, 1984; Schwarz & others, 1987). They judge themselves competent and effective, other people benevolent, happy events more likely.

Knowing this connection, we should not be surprised that in some studies *currently* depressed people recall their parents as rejecting, punitive, and guilt-promoting, whereas *formerly* depressed people describe their parents much as do those who have never suffered depression (Lewinsohn & Rosenbaum, 1987; Lewis, 1992). No wonder Robert Bornstein and others (1991) report that adolescents' ratings of parental warmth give little clue to how the same adolescents will rate their parents six weeks later. When teenagers are down, their parents seem inhuman; as their mood brightens, their parents morph from devils into angels. You and I may nod our heads knowingly. Yet, in a good or bad mood, we persist in attributing to reality our own changing judgments and memories.

Moods also influence how we *interpret* other people's behavior. In a bad mood we read someone's look as a glare; in a good mood we encode the same look as interest. How we perceive the world depends on our mood. Passions exaggerate.

Your mood's effect on retrieval helps explain why moods persist. When happy, you recall happy events and therefore see the world as a happy place, which helps prolong the good mood. When depressed, you recall sad events, which darkens your interpretations of current events. As we will see in Chapter 13, this process maintains depression's vicious cycle.

Mood and memory
Elated, we remember other happy times and expect more such times. Mood serves as a retrieval cue, activating other memories associated with the same emotion. These memories help sustain the current mood.

Dan McCoy/Rainbow

"When a feeling was there, they felt as if it would never go; when it was gone, they felt as if it had never been; when it returned, they felt as if it had never gone."

George MacDonald, *What's Mine's Mine, 1886*

Answers to questions on page 273: Multiple-choice questions test recognition. Fill-in-the-blank questions test recall.

---

rehearse it!

12. To measure long-term memory, psychologists test a person's ability to *recall* information. They also test ability to *recognize* what has been learned, and they measure *relearning* time. A psychologist who asks you to write down as many objects as you can remember having seen a few minutes earlier is testing your
a. recall.
b. recognition.
c. recall and recognition.
d. relearning.

13. To gain access to a memory, a person activates an association that leads to that memory. The association may be activated by a specific odor, visual image, or mnemonic; all of these are examples of
a. relearning.
b. déjà vu.
c. declarative memories.
d. retrieval cues.

14. In some cases, retrieval may be enhanced by being in a context similar to one you have already experienced. The resulting feeling that "you've been there before" is known as
a. déjà vu.
b. mood-congruent memory.

c. relearning.
d. an explicit memory.

15. When happy, we tend to recall happy times. When depressed, we more often recall depressing events. This tendency to recall experiences that are consistent with our current emotions is called
a. mnemonics.
b. chunking.
c. repression.
d. mood-congruent memory.

Answers can be found in Appendix C.

FORGETTING

10. *Why do we forget? At what points in the memory system can our memory fail us?*

Amid all the applause for memory—all the efforts to understand it, all the books on how to improve it—have any voices been heard in praise of forgetting? William James (1890, p. 680) was such a voice: "If we remembered everything, we should on most occasions be as ill off as if we remembered nothing." To discard the clutter of useless or out-of-date information—where we parked the car yesterday, a friend's old phone number, restaurant orders already cooked and served—is surely a blessing (Bjork, 1978). The Russian memory whiz S, whom we met at the beginning of

"Happiness is nothing more than health and a poor memory."

Physician Albert Schweitzer (1875–1965)

this chapter, was haunted by his junk heap of memories. They dominated his consciousness. He had difficulty thinking abstractly—generalizing, organizing, evaluating. A good memory is helpful, but so is the ability to forget.

More often, however, our memory dismays and frustrates us. Memories are quirky. My own memory can easily call up such episodes as that wonderful first kiss with the woman I love or trivial facts like the number of sheep in Scotland. Then it abandons me when I'm trying to recall that new colleague's name or where I left my sunglasses. Memory researcher Daniel Schacter (1999) enumerates seven ways our memories fail us—the seven sins of memory, he calls them. These include
Three sins of forgetting:

- *Absent-mindedness*—inattention to details produces encoding failure (our mind is elsewhere as we lay down the car keys).
- *Transience*—storage decay over time (unused information fades).
- *Blocking*—inaccessibility of stored information (it may be on the tip of our tongue, but we experience retrieval failure—we cannot get it out).

Three sins of distortion:

- *Misattribution*—confusing the source of words in someone else's mouth or remembering a movie scene as an actual happening.
- *Suggestibility*—the lingering effects of misinformation (a leading question—"Did Mr. Jones touch your private parts?"—later becomes a young child's false memory).
- *Bias*—belief-colored recollections (someone's current feelings toward their fiancé may color their recalled initial feelings).

One sin of intrusion:

- *Persistence*—unwanted memories (being haunted by images of a sexual assault).

Let's first consider the sins of forgetting, then those of distortion and intrusion.

Encoding Failure

What causes us to forget? One answer is that we failed to encode the information (**Figure 8.15**). Thus, it never entered long-term memory. Age can affect encoding efficiency. The same brain areas that jump into action when young adults are encoding new information are less responsive among older adults. This slower encoding helps explain age-related memory decline (Grady & others, 1995). (As Chapter 4 noted, older people tend to recall less than younger adults do, but they usually remember as well as younger people when given reminders or a recognition test.)

But no matter how young we are, we selectively attend to few of the myriad sights and sounds continually bombarding us. As our "change blindness" (page 188) demonstrates, much of what we sense we never notice. Consider something you have looked at countless times: What letters accompany the number 5 on your telephone? Or where is the number 0 on your calculator? For most of us, these questions are surprisingly difficult.

As we noted earlier, we encode some information—where we had dinner yesterday—automatically; other types of information—like the concepts in this chapter—require effortful processing. Without effort, many memories never form.

Cellist Yo-Yo Ma forgot his 266-year-old, $2.5 million cello in a New York taxi. (He later recovered it.)

"Amnesia seeps into the crevices of our brains, and amnesia heals."

Joyce Carol Oates, "Words Fail, Memory Blurs, Life Wins," 2001

"Each of us finds that in [our] own life every moment of time is completely filled. [We are] bombarded every second by sensations, emotions, thoughts . . . nine-tenths of which [we] must simply ignore. The past [is] a roaring cataract of billions upon billions of such moments: Any one of them too complex to grasp in its entirety, and the aggregate beyond all imagination. . . . At every tick of the clock, in every inhabited part of the world, an unimaginable richness and variety of 'history' falls off the world into total oblivion."

English novelist-critic C. S. Lewis (1967)

figure 8.15
Forgetting as encoding failure We cannot remember what we have not encoded.

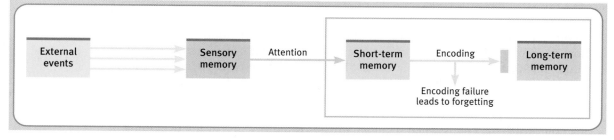

External events → Sensory memory → Attention → Short-term memory → Encoding → Long-term memory

Encoding failure leads to forgetting

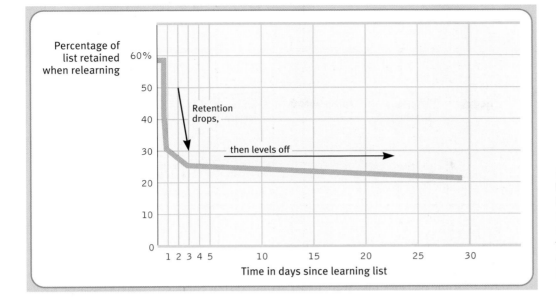

figure 8.16
Ebbinghaus' forgetting curve After learning lists of nonsense syllables, Ebbinghaus studied how much he retained up to 30 days later. He found that memory for novel information fades quickly, then levels out. (Adapted from Ebbinghaus, 1885.)

Storage Decay

Even after encoding something well, we sometimes later forget it. To study the durability of our stored memories, Ebbinghaus (1885) learned more lists of nonsense syllables and measured how much he retained when relearning each list, from 20 minutes to 30 days later. His famous "forgetting curve" (**FIGURE 8.16**) indicates that much of what we learn we may indeed quickly forget. Later experiments made the forgetting curve into one of psychology's laws: The course of forgetting is initially rapid, then levels off with time (Wixted & Ebbesen, 1991).

Harry Bahrick (1984) extended Ebbinghaus' finding. He examined the forgetting curve for Spanish vocabulary learned in school. Compared with those just completing a high school or college Spanish course, those who had been out of school for 3 years had forgotten much of what they had learned (**FIGURE 8.17**). However, after roughly 3 years, their forgetting leveled off; what people remembered then, they still remembered 25 and more years later, even if they had not used their Spanish at all.

One explanation for these forgetting curves is a gradual fading of the physical memory trace. As we learn more about the physical storage of memory, we may come to understand better how memory storage can decay. But memories also fade because of the accumulation of other learning that disrupts our retrieval.

figure 8.17
The forgetting curve for Spanish learned in school Compared with people just completing a Spanish course, those 3 years out of the course remembered much less. Compared with the 3-year group, however, those who studied Spanish even longer ago did not forget much more. (Adapted from Bahrick, 1984.)

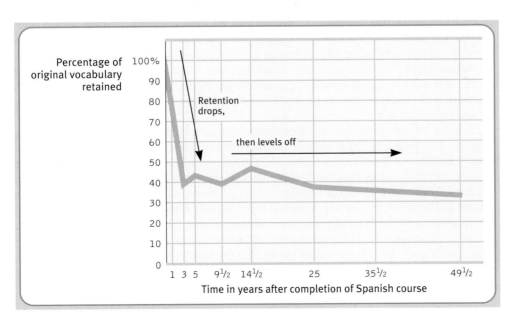

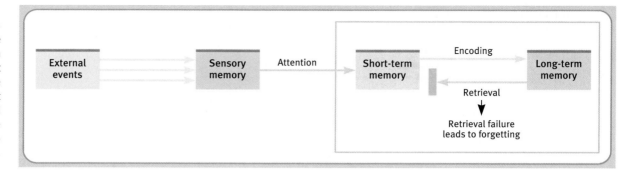

figure 8.18
Retrieval failure We store in long-term memory what's important to us or what we've rehearsed. But sometimes even stored information cannot be accessed, which leads to forgetting.

Retrieval Failure

We have seen that forgotten events are like books you can't find in your campus library—some because they were never acquired (not encoded), others because they were discarded (stored memories decayed).

But there is a third possibility: Even if the book is stored and available, it may be inaccessible. Perhaps you don't have the information needed to look it up and retrieve it. Information sometimes gets into our brain and, though we know it is there, we cannot get it out (**FIGURE 8.18**). A name may lie poised on the tip of the tongue, waiting to be retrieved. But given retrieval cues ("It begins with an *M*"), we may easily retrieve an elusive memory. Retrieval problems contribute to older adults' occasional memory failures. Forgetting is often not memories discarded but memories unretrieved.

Interference

Learning some items may interfere with retrieving others, especially when the items are similar. If someone gives you a phone number, you may be able to recall it later. But if two more people give you their numbers, each successive number will be more difficult to recall. Likewise, if you buy a new combination lock or get a new phone number, the old one may interfere. Such **proactive** (*forward-acting*) **interference** occurs when something you learned earlier disrupts your recall of something you experience later. As you collect more and more information, your mental attic never fills, but it certainly gets cluttered.

Benton Underwood (1957) found that those who learn different lists of words on successive days have more and more difficulty remembering each new list the next day. This proactive interference explains why Ebbinghaus, after memorizing countless lists of nonsense syllables during his career, could remember only about one-fourth of a new list of syllables on the day after he learned it—far fewer than you as a novice could remember after learning a single list.

Retroactive (*backward-acting*) **interference** occurs when new information makes it harder to recall something you learned earlier (**FIGURE 8.19**). For example, learning new students' names typically interferes with a teacher's recall of the names of previous students.

You can minimize retroactive interference by reducing the number of interfering events—say, by going for a walk or to sleep shortly after learning new information. John Jenkins and Karl Dallenbach (1924) discovered the sleep benefit in a classic experiment. Day after day, two people each learned some nonsense syllables, then tried to recall them after up to eight hours of being awake or asleep at night. As **FIGURE 8.20** shows, forgetting occurred more rapidly after being awake and involved with other activities. The investigators surmised that "forgetting is not so much a matter of the decay of old impressions and associations as it is a matter of interference, inhibition, or obliteration of the old by the new" (1924, p. 612). Later experiments have confirmed that the hour before a night's sleep (but not the minute before sleep) is a good time to commit information to memory (Fowler & others, 1973).

▶ **proactive interference** the disruptive effect of prior learning on the recall of new information.

▶ **retroactive interference** the disruptive effect of new learning on the recall of old information.

figure 8.19
Proactive and retroactive interference

Interference is an important cause of forgetting, and may explain why ads viewed during violent or sexual TV programs are so forgettable (Bushman & Bonacci, 2002). But we should not overstate the point. Sometimes old information can facilitate our learning of new information. Knowing Latin may help us to learn French—a phenomenon called *positive transfer*. It is when old and new information compete with each other that interference occurs.

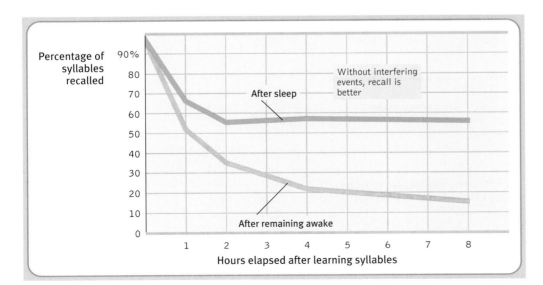

figure 8.20
Retroactive interference More forgetting occurred when a person stayed awake and experienced other new material. (From Jenkins & Dallenbach, 1924.)

Motivated Forgetting

The huge cookie jar in our kitchen was jammed with freshly baked chocolate chip cookies. Still more were cooling across racks on the counter. Twenty-four hours later, not a crumb was left. Who had taken them? During that time, my wife, three children, and I were the only people in the house. So while memories were still fresh, I conducted a little memory test. Andy acknowledged wolfing down as many as 20. Peter admitted eating 15. Laura guessed she had stuffed her then-6-year-old body with 15 cookies. My wife, Carol, recalled eating 6, and I remembered consuming 15 and taking 18 more to the office. We sheepishly accepted responsibility for 89 cookies. Still, we had not come close; there had been 160.

In experiments that parallel the cookie-memory phenomenon, Michael Ross and his colleagues (1981) found that people unknowingly revise their own histories. After Ross persuaded a group of people that brushing their teeth frequently is desirable, they (more than other people) recalled having frequently brushed their teeth in the last two weeks. Having taken a highly touted study skills course, students later inflated their estimates of self-improvement. By *de*flating their evaluations of their previous study habits, they convinced themselves that they had really benefited (Conway & Ross, 1984). To remember our past is often to revise it.

Why do our memories fail us? Why did my family and I not encode, store, and retrieve the actual number of cookies each of us ate? As **FIGURE 8.21** reminds us, we automatically encode sensory information in amazing detail. So was it a storage problem? Might our memories of cookies, like Ebbinghaus' memory of nonsense syllables, have vanished almost as fast as the cookies themselves? Or might the information still be intact but irretrievable because it would be embarrassing to remember?[1]

[1]One of my cookie-scarfing sons, on reading this in his father's textbook years later, confessed that he had fibbed "a little."

"[It is] necessary to remember that events happened in the desired manner. And if it is necessary to rearrange one's memories . . . then it is necessary to forget that one has done so. The trick of doing this can be learned like any other mental technique. . . . It is called doublethink."

George Orwell, Nineteen Eighty-Four, 1948

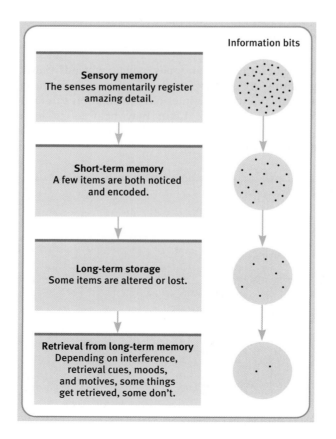

figure 8.21
When do we forget? Forgetting can occur at any memory stage. As we process information, we filter, alter, or lose much of it.

Information bits

Sensory memory
The senses momentarily register amazing detail.

Short-term memory
A few items are both noticed and encoded.

Long-term storage
Some items are altered or lost.

Retrieval from long-term memory
Depending on interference, retrieval cues, moods, and motives, some things get retrieved, some don't.

With his concept of **repression**, Sigmund Freud proposed that our memory systems do indeed self-censor painful information. To protect our self-concept and to minimize anxiety, we supposedly repress painful memories. But the submerged memory lingers, said Freud, and with patience and effort may be retrieved by some later cue or during therapy. One reported case involved a woman with an intense, unexplained fear of running water. One day an aunt solved the mystery. She whispered, "I have never told." The words relit a blown-out candle in the mind; they cued the woman's memory of an incident when, as a disobedient young child, she wandered away from a family picnic and became trapped under a waterfall—until being rescued by her aunt, who promised not to tell her parents (Kihlstrom, 1990). Such stories have fed the now-common belief, shared by 9 in 10 university students, that "memories for painful experiences are sometimes pushed into unconsciousness" (Brown & others, 1996). Repression was central to Freud's psychology and became part of psychology's lore. Most everyone believes it. Therapists assume it often. Yet increasing numbers of memory researchers think repression rarely, if ever, occurs. Earlier we noted that emotions and associated stress hormones *strengthen* memories. But what about horrible happenings? Do people typically have trouble remembering traumatic experiences, or trouble forgetting them? Stay tuned.

> ▶ **repression** in psychoanalytic theory, the basic defense mechanism that banishes from consciousness anxiety-arousing thoughts, feelings, and memories.

MEMORY CONSTRUCTION

11. How accurate are our memories?

Picture yourself having this experience:

> You go to a fancy restaurant for dinner. You are seated at a table with a white tablecloth. You study the menu. You tell the server you want prime rib, medium rare, a baked potato with sour cream, and a salad with blue cheese dressing. You also order some red wine from the wine list. A few minutes later the server returns with your salad. Later the rest of the meal arrives. You enjoy it all, except the prime rib is a bit overdone.

Were I immediately to quiz you on this paragraph (adapted from Hyde, 1983), you could surely retrieve considerable detail. For example, without looking back, answer the following questions:

1. What kind of salad dressing did you order?
2. Was the tablecloth red checked?
3. What did you order to drink?
4. Did the server give you a menu?

You were probably able to recall exactly what you ordered, and maybe even the color of the tablecloth. Does retrieval therefore consist merely of "reading" the information stored in our brain's library? We do have an enormous capacity for storing and reproducing the incidental details of our daily experience. But we often construct our memories as we encode them, and we may also alter our memories as we withdraw them from the memory bank. Like a scientist who infers a dinosaur's appearance from its remains, we infer our past from stored information plus what we now assume. Did the server give you a menu? Not in the paragraph given. Nevertheless, many answer yes. By filtering information and filling in missing pieces, your schema for restaurants directed your memory construction.

Misinformation and Imagination Effects

In more than 200 experiments, involving more than 20,000 people, Elizabeth Loftus has shown how eyewitnesses similarly reconstruct their memories when questioned. In one classic experiment with John Palmer, Loftus showed people a film of a traffic accident and then quizzed them about what they saw (Loftus &

Depiction of actual accident

figure 8.22
Memory construction
When people who saw the film of a car accident were asked a leading question, they recalled a more serious accident than they had witnessed. (From Loftus, 1979.)

Leading question:
"About how fast were the cars going when they smashed into each other?"

Memory construction

"Memory is insubstantial. Things keep replacing it. Your batch of snapshots will both fix and ruin your memory. . . . You can't remember anything from your trip except the wretched collection of snapshots."

Annie Dillard, "To Fashion a Text," 1988

Palmer, 1974). Those asked, "How fast were the cars going when they *smashed* into each other?" gave higher speed estimates than those asked, "How fast were the cars going when they *hit* each other?" A week later, the researchers asked the viewers if they recalled seeing any broken glass. Compared with those who had been asked the question with *hit*, those asked the question with *smashed* were more than twice as likely to say yes, they had seen broken glass (**FIGURE 8.22**). In fact, the film showed no broken glass.

In many follow-up experiments around the world, people have witnessed an event, received or not received misleading information about it, and then taken a memory test. The repeated result is a **misinformation effect**: After exposure to subtle misinformation, many people misremember. They have misrecalled a yield (give way) sign as a stop sign, hammers as screwdrivers, Coke cans as peanut cans, *Vogue* magazine as *Mademoiselle*, "Dr. Henderson" as "Dr. Davidson," breakfast cereal as eggs, and a clean-shaven man as a man with a mustache (Loftus & others, 1992). As a memory fades with time following an event, the injection of misinformation becomes easier (Loftus, 1992).

So unwitting is the misinformation effect that people later find it nearly impossible to discriminate between their memories of real and suggested events (Schooler & others, 1986). This difficulty was strikingly true among those who three years later misrecalled where they were when they heard of the space shuttle *Challenger*'s explosion (Neisser & Harsch, 1992). When shown their own accounts, handwritten the day after the explosion, many were surprised. Some felt so sure of their false memories that they insisted their original version must have been flawed.

As we recount an experience, we fill in memory gaps with plausible guesses and assumptions. After more retellings, we often recall the guessed details, which have now been absorbed into our memories, as if we had actually observed them (Roediger & others, 1993). Others' vivid retelling of an event may also implant false memories.

Even repeatedly *imagining* nonexistent actions and events can create false memories. In one laboratory experiment, students who repeatedly imagined simple acts such as breaking a toothpick or picking up a stapler later experienced "imagination inflation"; they were more likely to think they had actually done such things during the experiment's first phase (Goff & Roediger, 1998). In another experiment, by Maryanne Garry and others (1996), university students noted whether they had experienced certain childhood events, such as breaking a window with their hand. Two weeks later, half were asked to imagine themselves experiencing four of these events—for example, running, tripping, falling, and cutting a hand as it crashed through a window. After vividly imagining the fictional event, one-fourth of them became more likely to believe that such events may actually have happened during their childhood.

Imagined events later seem more familiar, and familiar things seem more real. Thus the more vividly people can imagine things, the more likely they are to inflate their imaginations into memories (Loftus, 2001; Porter & others, 2000). People who believe they have been abducted by aliens for medical exams on spaceships tend to have powerful imaginations and, in memory tests, to be more susceptible to false memories (Clancy & others, 2002). Those who believe they have recovered memories of childhood sexual abuse likewise tend to have vivid imaginations and to score high on false memory tests (Clancy & others, 2000; McNally & others, 2000, 2001).

DOONESBURY

To see how far the mind's search for a fact will go in creating a fiction, Richard Wiseman and his University of Hertfordshire colleagues (1999) staged eight seances, each attended by 25 curious people. During the supposed seance, the medium—actually a professional actor and magician—asked everyone to concentrate on the moving table. Although it never moved, he suggested that it had: "That's good. Lift the table up. That's good. Keep concentrating. Keep the table in the air." When questioned two weeks later, 34 percent of the participants recalled having actually seen the table levitate.

Memory construction helps explain why "hypnotically refreshed" memories of crimes so easily incorporate errors, some of which originate with the hypnotist's leading questions. ("Did you hear loud noises?") It explains why dating partners who fall in love *over*estimate their first impressions of one another ("It was love at first sight"), while those who break up *under*estimate their earlier liking ("We never really clicked") (McFarland & Ross, 1987). And it explains why people who are asked how they felt 10 years ago about marijuana or gender issues recall attitudes closer to their current views than to the views they actually reported a decade earlier (Markus, 1986).

Source Amnesia

When we encode memories, we distribute different aspects of them to different parts of the brain. Among the frailest parts of a memory is its source. Thus, we may recognize someone but have no idea where we have seen the person. Or we imagine or dream an event and later be unsure whether it really happened. Or we may hear something and later recall seeing it (Henkel & others, 2000). In all these cases, we retain the image, but not the context in which we acquired it.

Australian psychologist Donald Thompson found his own work on memory distortion ironically haunting him when authorities brought him in for questioning about a rape. Although he was a near-perfect match to the victim's memory of the rapist, he had an airtight alibi. Just before the rape occurred, Thompson was being interviewed on live television. He could not possibly have made it to the crime scene. Then it came to light that the victim had been watching the interview—ironically about face recognition—and had experienced source amnesia, confusing her memories of Thompson with those of the rapist (Schacter, 1996).

"Memory isn't like reading a book; it's more like writing a book from fragmentary notes."

Psychologist John F. Kihlstrom (1994)

▶ **misinformation effect** incorporating misleading information into one's memory of an event.

Authors and songwriters sometimes suffer source amnesia. They think an idea came from their own creative imagination, when in fact they are unintentionally plagiarizing something they earlier read or heard.

Debra Poole and Stephen Lindsay (1995, 2001, 2002) experimented with Piaget's **source amnesia** (also called *source misattribution*). They had preschoolers interact with "Mr. Science," who engaged them in demonstrations such as blowing up a balloon with baking soda and vinegar. Three months later, their parents on three successive days read them a story about themselves and Mr. Science. The stories described some things they had experienced and some they had not. When asked by a new interviewer what Mr. Science had done with them—"Did Mr. Science have a machine with ropes to pull?"—4 in 10 children spontaneously recalled Mr. Science doing things that were only in the story.

Children's Eyewitness Recall

Because memory is reconstruction as well as reproduction, we can't be sure whether a memory is real by how real it feels. Much as perceptual illusions may seem like real perceptions, unreal memories feel like real memories. If memories can be sincere, yet sincerely wrong, might children's recollections of sexual abuse be prone to err? Who is most often victimized—abused children whose recollections are disbelieved or falsely accused adults whose reputations are ruined?

At issue is the credibility of children's reports. As we have seen, interviewers who ask leading questions can plant false memories of a story they expect to hear. We also know that children sometimes are credible eyewitnesses in criminal cases, but that they tend to be suggestible. In 90 percent of studies making age comparisons, preschoolers were more suggestible than were older children or adults (Bruck & Ceci, 1999). In these studies, many young children have falsely reported that a nurse licked their knee, a man had put "something yucky" in their mouth, their doctor had put a stick in their genitals, and someone had touched their private parts. When suggestive interview techniques are added, most preschoolers can be induced to report false events, such as seeing a thief steal food in their day-care center (Bruck & others, 1998). Nevertheless, if questioned about their experiences in words they understand, children often accurately recall what happened and who did it (Goodman & others, 1990; Howe, 1997; Pipe, 1996). Children are especially credible when involved adults have not talked with them prior to the interview and when their disclosure is made in a first interview with a neutral person who asks nonleading questions.

Stephen Ceci (1993) thinks "it would be truly awful to ever lose sight of the enormity of child abuse." Yet Ceci and Maggie Bruck's (1993a, 1995) studies of children's memories have sensitized them to children's suggestibility. In one study, they asked 3-year-olds to show on anatomically correct dolls where a pediatrician had touched them. Fifty-five percent of the children who had not received genital examinations pointed to either genital or anal areas.

In another study, Ceci and Bruck had a child choose a card from a deck of possible happenings, then an adult read from the card. For example, "Think real hard, and tell me if this ever happened to you. Can you remember going to the hospital with a mousetrap on your finger?" After 10 weekly interviews, with the same adult repeatedly asking children to think about several real and fictitious events, a new adult asked the same question. The stunning result: 58 percent of preschoolers produced false (often vivid) stories regarding one or more events they had never experienced. Here is one from a boy who initially had denied the mousetrap incident (Ceci & others, 1994):

> My brother Colin was trying to get Blowtorch [an action figure] from me, and I wouldn't let him take it from me, so he pushed me into the wood pile where the mousetrap was. And then my finger got caught in it. And then we went to the hospital, and my mommy, daddy, and Colin drove me there, to the hospital in our van, because it was far away. And the doctor put a bandage on this finger.

▶ **source amnesia** attributing to the wrong source an event that we have experienced, heard about, read about, or imagined. (Also called *source misattribution*.) Source amnesia, along with the misinformation effect, is at the heart of many false memories.

Given such detailed stories, professional psychologists who specialize in interviewing children were often fooled. They could not reliably separate real memories from false ones. Nor could the children themselves. The above child, reminded that his parents had told him several times that the mousetrap incident never happened—that he had imagined it—protested, "But it really did happen. I remember it!"

"[The] research leads me to worry about the possibility of false allegations. It is not a tribute to one's scientific integrity to walk down the middle of the road if the data are more to one side."

Stephen Ceci (1993)

Repressed or Constructed Memories of Abuse?

During the 1990s, psychology's most intense controversy—the "memory wars"—concerned claims of repressed and recovered memories of childhood sexual abuse. During 2002, such claims surfaced again amid seemingly more credible accusations of sexual abuse by some priests. Are clinicians who have guided people in "recovering" memories of childhood abuse triggering false memories that damage innocent adults, or are they uncovering the truth?

Some therapists have reasoned with patients that "people who've been abused often have your symptoms, so you probably were abused. Let's see if, aided by hypnosis or drugs, or helped to dig back and visualize your trauma, you can recover it." In one American survey, the average therapist estimated that 11 percent of the population—some 34 million people—have repressed memories of childhood sexual abuse (Kamena, 1998). In another survey, of British and American doctoral-level therapists, 7 in 10 said they had used techniques such as hypnosis or drugs to help clients recover suspected repressed memories of childhood sexual abuse (Poole & others, 1995).

As we might expect from the research on source amnesia and the misinformation effect, many patients exposed to such techniques do form an image of a threatening person. With further visualization, the image grows more vivid, leaving the patient stunned, angry, and ready to confront or sue the equally stunned and devastated parent or other relative, who, as the therapist has predicted, vigorously denies the accusation. One woman in her thirty-second therapy session recalled that her father had abused her at age 15 months. After such aided recall, actress Roseanne Barr (1991) claimed to recall sexual abuse beginning in infancy.

Without questioning the professionalism of most therapists, skeptics compare the uncorroborated accusations suggested by some therapists with a 1990s reenactment of the Salem witch trials. Clinicians who use "memory work" techniques such as "guided imagery," hypnosis, and dream analysis to recover memories "are nothing more than merchants of mental chaos, and, in fact, constitute a blight on the entire field of psychotherapy," charged some scientific critics (Loftus & others, 1995). Irate clinicians countered that those who dispute recovered memories of abuse add to abused women's trauma and play into the hands of child molesters.

In an effort to find a sensible common ground that might resolve this ideological battle, study panels have been convened and public statements made by the American Medical, American Psychological, and American Psychiatric Associations; the Australian Psychological Society; the British Psychological Society; and the Canadian Psychiatric Association. Those committed to protecting abused children and those committed to protecting wrongly accused adults agree on the following:

- *Injustice happens*. Some innocent people have been falsely convicted. Some guilty people have evaded responsibility by casting doubt on their truth-telling accusers.
- *Incest and other sexual abuse happens*. And it happens more often than we once supposed. There is no characteristic "survivor syndrome" (Kendall-Tackett & others, 1993). However, sexual abuse can leave its victims predisposed to problems ranging from sexual dysfunction to depression.

- *Forgetting happens*. Many abused people either were very young when abused or may not have understood the meaning of their experience—circumstances under which forgetting is "utterly common." Forgetting isolated past events, both negative and positive, is an ordinary part of everyday life.
- *Recovered memories are commonplace.* Cued by a remark or an experience, we recover memories of long-forgotten events, both pleasant and unpleasant. What is debated is whether the unconscious mind sometimes forcibly represses painful experiences and, if so, whether these can be retrieved by certain therapist-aided techniques.
- *Memories "recovered" under hypnosis or the influence of drugs are especially unreliable.* (Recall from Chapter 6 the ease with which "age-regressed" hypnotized subjects incorporate suggestions into their memories, even memories of "past lives.")
- *Memories of things happening before age 3 are also unreliable*. People do not reliably recall happenings of any sort from their first 3 years—a phenomenon called *infantile amnesia*. Most psychologists—including most clinical and counseling psychologists—therefore are skeptical of "recovered" memories of abuse during infancy (Gore-Felton & others, 2000; Knapp & Vande Creek, 2000).
- *Memories, whether real or false, can be emotionally upsetting.* If a false memory of abuse becomes a real part of one's history, the accuser as well as the accused may suffer. Like real traumas, such experiences can then cause lasting suffering.

To more closely approximate therapist-aided recall, Elizabeth Loftus and her colleagues (1996) have experimentally implanted false memories of childhood traumas. In one study, she had a trusted family member recall for a teenager three real childhood experiences and a false one—a vivid account of the child's being lost for an extended time in a shopping mall at age 5 until being rescued by an elderly person. Two days later, one participant, Chris, said, "That day I was so scared that I would never see my family again." Two days after that he began to visualize the flannel shirt, bald head, and glasses of the old man who supposedly had found him. Told the story was made up, Chris was incredulous: "I thought I remembered being lost . . . and looking around for the guys. I do remember that, and then crying, and Mom coming up and saying, 'Where were you? Don't you . . . ever do that again.' "

Such is the memory construction process by which people can recall being abducted by UFOs, victimized by a satanic cult, molested in a crib, or living a past life. Thousands of reasonable, normally functioning human beings, notes Loftus, "speak in terror-stricken voices about their experience aboard flying saucers. They *remember*, clearly and vividly, being abducted by aliens" (Loftus & Ketcham, 1994, p. 66).

Loftus knows firsthand the phenomenon she studies. At a family reunion, an uncle told her that at age 14, she had found her mother's drowned body. Shocked, she denied it. But the uncle was adamant, and over the next three days she began to wonder if *she* had a repressed memory. "Maybe that's why I'm so obsessed with this topic." As the now-upset Loftus pondered her uncle's suggestion, she "recovered" an image of her mother lying in the pool, face down, and of herself finding the body. "I started putting everything into place. Maybe that's why I'm such a workaholic. Maybe that's why I'm so emotional when I think about her even though she died in 1959."

Then her brother called and said there had been a mistake. Her uncle now remembered what other relatives also confirmed: Aunt Pearl, not Loftus, had found the body (Loftus & Ketcham, 1994; Monaghan, 1992).

"When memories are 'recovered' after long periods of amnesia, particularly when extraordinary means were used to secure the recovery of memory, there is a high probability that the memories are false."

Royal College of Psychiatrists Working Group on Reported Recovered Memories of Child Sexual Abuse (Brandon & others, 1998).

TODAY'S SPECIAL GUEST

BRUNDAGE MORNALD, OF BATTLE CREEK, MONTANA
UNDER HYPNOSIS, MR. MORNALD RECOVERED LONG-BURIED MEMORIES OF A PERFECTLY NORMAL, HAPPY CHILDHOOD.

But then again, Loftus also knows firsthand the reality of sexual abuse. A male baby-sitter molested her when she was 6 years old. She has not forgotten. And that makes her wary of those whom she sees as trivializing real abuse by suggesting and seeking out uncorroborated traumatic experiences, then accepting them uncritically as fact. The enemies of the truly victimized are not only those who prey and those who deny, she says, but those whose writings and allegations "are bound to lead to an increased likelihood that society in general will disbelieve the genuine cases of childhood sexual abuse that truly deserve our sustained attention" (Loftus, 1993).

Courtesy of Elizabeth Loftus, University of California, Irvine

Elizabeth Loftus "The research findings for which I am being honored now generated a level of hostility and opposition I could never have foreseen. People wrote threatening letters, warning me that my reputation and even my safety were in jeopardy if I continued along these lines. At some universities, armed guards were provided to accompany me during speeches."
Elizabeth Loftus, on receiving the American Psychological Society's William James Fellow Award, 2001

So, does repression ever occur? Or is this concept—the cornerstone of Freud's theory and of so much popular psychology—misleading? In Chapter 12, we will return to this hotly debated issue. As we will see, this much now appears certain: The most common response to a traumatic experience (witnessing a parent's murder, experiencing the horrors of a Nazi death camp, being terrorized by a hijacker or a rapist, escaping the collapsing World Trade Center towers) is not banishment of the experience into an active but inaccessible unconscious. Rather, such experiences are typically etched on the mind as vivid, persistent, haunting memories.

"Horror sears memory, leaving . . . the consuming memories of atrocity."

Robert Kraft, **Memory Perceived: Recalling the Holocaust, 2001**

rehearse it!

16. In some cases, forgetting may be due to encoding failure. That is, meaningless information may not be transferred from
    a. the environment into sensory memory.
    b. sensory memory into long-term memory.
    c. long-term memory into short-term memory.
    d. short-term memory into long-term memory.

17. Forgetting may result from storage decay. Ebbinghaus found that about three days after a session of learning nonsense syllables, people have forgotten much of what they learned. Ebbinghaus' "forgetting curve" shows that as time goes on, our retention of the nonsense syllables tends to
    a. increase slightly.
    b. decrease noticeably.
    c. decrease greatly.
    d. level out.

18. Experiments show that the hour before sleep is a good time to memorize information. For example, studying a vocabulary list before going to sleep minimizes the disrupting effects of all the other new words and terms that might, in the course of a school day, claim our attention. Going to sleep after learning new material minimizes
    a. the misinformation effect.
    b. amnesia.
    c. retroactive interference.
    d. proactive interference.

19. People unknowingly revise or rearrange their memories of events. According to Sigmund Freud, painful or unacceptable memories are self-censored, or blocked from consciousness, through a mechanism called
    a. repression.
    b. proactive interference.
    c. the misinformation effect.
    d. physical decay of the memory trace.

20. Because we often alter information as we encode it and because we tend to fill in memory gaps with our assumptions about events, our memories are generally not exact reproductions of events. One reason for this memory reconstruction is
    a. proactive interference.
    b. the misinformation effect.
    c. retroactive interference.
    d. the eyewitness recall effect.

21. Aspects of our memories are distributed to different parts of the brain. Thus, while we may recognize a face in the crowd, we may not be able to recall where we know the person from. This is called
    a. the misinformation effect.
    b. amnesia.
    c. source amnesia.
    d. repression.

Answers can be found in Appendix C.

IMPROVING MEMORY

12. How might we apply memory principles to everyday situations, such as remembering a person's name or even the material of this chapter?

Now and then we are dismayed at our forgetfulness—at our embarrassing inability to recall someone's name, at forgetting to bring up a point in conversation, at forgetting to bring along something important, at finding ourselves standing in a room

SQ3R: **S**urvey, **Q**uestion, **R**ead, **R**ehearse, **R**eview

"I have discovered that it is of some use when you lie in bed at night and gaze into the darkness to repeat in your mind the things you have been studying. Not only does it help the understanding, but also the memory."

Leonardo da Vinci (1452–1519)

"Knit each new thing on to some acquisition already there."

William James, Principles of Psychology, 1890

Thinking and memory Most of what we know is not the result of efforts to memorize. We learn because we're curious and because we spend time thinking about our experiences. Actively thinking as we read, by rehearsing and relating ideas, yields the best retention.

unable to recall why we are there (Herrmann, 1982). Is there anything we can do to minimize such misdeeds of our memory system? Much as biology benefits medicine and botany benefits agriculture, so can the psychology of memory benefit education. Sprinkled throughout this chapter and summarized here for easy reference are concrete suggestions for improving memory. The SQ3R study technique introduced in Chapter 1 incorporates several of these strategies.

Study repeatedly to boost long-term recall. Overlearn. To learn a name, say it to yourself after being introduced; wait a few seconds and say it again; wait longer and say it again. Provide yourself with many separate study sessions by taking advantage of life's little intervals—riding on the bus, walking across campus, waiting for class to start.

Spend more time rehearsing or actively thinking about the material. Speed-reading (skimming) complex material—with minimal rehearsal—yields little retention. Rehearsal and critical reflection help more. It pays to study actively!

Make the material personally meaningful. To build a network of retrieval cues, take thorough text and class notes in your own words. Mindlessly repeating information is relatively ineffective. It is better to form images, understand and organize information, relate the material to what you already know or have experienced, and put it in your own words. Without such cues, you may find yourself stuck when a question uses phrasing different from the rote forms you memorized. To increase retrieval cues, form as many associations as possible.

To remember a list of unfamiliar items, use mnemonic devices. Associate items with peg-words. Make up a story that incorporates vivid images of the items. Chunk information into acronyms.

Refresh your memory by activating retrieval cues. Mentally re-create the situation and the mood in which the original learning occurred. Return to the same location. Jog your memory by allowing one thought to cue the next.

Flip Chalfant/The Image Bank

Minimize interference. Study before sleeping. Do not study in close proximity topics that are likely to interfere with each other, such as Spanish and French.

Test your own knowledge, both to rehearse it and to help determine what you do not yet know. If you must *recall* information later, do not be lulled into overconfidence by your ability to *recognize* it. Test your recall. Outline sections on a blank page. Define concepts listed at each chapter's end *before* turning back to their definitions. Take practice tests; the study guides that accompany many texts, including this one, can help.

chapter review

R E V I E W I N G
Memory

THE PHENOMENON OF MEMORY

1. How do psychologists describe the human memory system?

Memory is the persistence of learning over time. Psychologists have proposed several information-processing models of memory. We will use the influential three-stage processing model which suggests that we (1) register fleeting *sensory memories*, some of which are (2) processed into on-screen *short-term* or *working memories*, a tiny fraction of which are (3) encoded for *long-term memory* and, possibly, later retrieval. We are particularly likely to remember vivid events that form flashbulb memories. The computer is one convenient model for thinking about human memory.

ENCODING: GETTING INFORMATION IN

2. How do the sights, sounds, and other sensations we experience get selectively encoded and transferred into the memory system?

Some types of information, notably concerning space, time, and frequency, we encode mostly automatically (automatic processing). Other types of information, including much of our processing of meaning, imagery, and organization, require effortful processing.

3. How much does rehearsal aid in forming memories?

Without rehearsal, much information (such as a new phone number) is lost within three seconds. The more we rehearse information, the better we retain it—especially if our rehearsal is spaced out over time (spacing effect) rather than massed. When learning a list of words or names, our later recall is often best for those learned first, which we may have rehearsed more (the serial position effect).

4. What methods of effortful processing aid in forming memories?

Effortful encoding of meaning, imagery, and organization enhances long-term retention. Mnemonic devices exploit the memorability of visual images and of information that is organized into chunks (chunking). Organizing information into hierarchies also aids memory.

STORAGE: RETAINING INFORMATION

5. How does sensory memory work?

Information first enters the memory system through the senses. We register and briefly store visual images via iconic memory and sounds via echoic memory.

6. What are the limits of short-term memory?

Our short-term memory for information just presented is limited—a seconds-long retention up to about seven items, depending on the information and how it is presented.

7. How large and durable is our long-term memory?

Our capacity for storing information permanently in long-term memory is essentially unlimited.

8. How are memories recorded in the brain?

The search for the physical basis of memory has recently focused on the synapses and their neurotransmitters; on the long-term potentiation of brain circuits, such as those running through the hippocampus; and on the effects of stress hormones on memory. Studies of people with brain damage reveal that we have two types of memory—explicit (declarative) memories processed by the hippocampus, and implicit (nondeclarative) memories processed by the cerebellum and the amygdala.

RETRIEVAL: GETTING INFORMATION OUT

9. How do we get information out of memory?

Psychologists interested in memory study not only our ability to retrieve information we have learned earlier (recall), but also our ability to identify items previously learned (recognition) and to relearn information quickly. To be remembered, information that is "in there" must be retrieved, with the aid of associations (cues) that prime the memory. Cues sometimes come from returning to the original context. Mood affects memory, too. While in a good or bad mood, we tend to retrieve memories congruent with that mood. This tendency helps explain why moods persist.

FORGETTING

10. Why do we forget? At what points in the memory system can our memory fail us?

One explanation of forgetting is that we fail to encode information for entry into our memory system. Without effortful processing, we never notice or process much of what we sense. Memories may also fade after storage—often rapidly at first, and then leveling off. Forgetting also results from retrieval failure. Retrieval-related forgetting may be caused by a lack of retrieval cues, by proactive interference, or even, said Freud, by motivated forgetting.

MEMORY CONSTRUCTION

11. How accurate are our memories?

Memories are not stored as exact copies, and they certainly are not retrieved as such. Rather, we construct our memories, using both stored and new information. Thus, when eyewitnesses are subtly exposed to misinformation after an event, they often believe they saw the misleading details as part of the event. People also exhibit source amnesia, by attributing something heard, read, or imagined to a wrong source. Memory researchers are especially suspicious of claims of long-repressed memories of sexual abuse, UFO abduction, or other traumas "recovered" with the aid of a therapist or suggestive book. More than we once supposed, incest and abuse happen. But unless the victim was a child too young to remember any early experiences, such traumas are usually remembered vividly, not banished into an active but inaccessible unconscious.

IMPROVING MEMORY

12. How might we apply memory principles to everyday situations, such as remembering a person's name or even the material of this chapter?

The psychology of memory suggests concrete strategies for improving memory, which are incorporated into the SQ3R method. These include repeated, spaced study; active rehearsal; encoding of well-organized, vivid, meaningful associations; mnemonic techniques; returning to contexts and moods that are rich with associations; minimizing interference; and self-testing and rehearsal.

A CRITICAL THINKER'S REVIEW OF CHAPTER 8

You've now studied and reviewed **Memory**. For even better retention, reflect on these concepts at a deeper level. If you need to refresh your memory of the six categories of critical thinking shown in parentheses below, see page 34. See if you can answer each of these questions in a short paragraph.

1. In a week, you will be expected to participate in a graded discussion of key historical figures in your World History class. What strategy could you employ to learn and retain information about these people so that you are ready by next week? What might you do to make sure you retain this information beyond next week? (practical problem solving)

2. Your friend tells you that her brother, Brad, was in a car accident six months ago, and his neurologist told the family that Brad's hippocampus was severely damaged and he would no longer be able to form new memories of events, images, or names. Your friend has noticed that Brad has learned to do a new jigsaw puzzle, and that his skill at using an exercise bike in his physical therapy class is steadily improving. She wonders if this is evidence that the neurologist's diagnosis was wrong. What can you tell your friend? (pattern recognition)

3. Your biology instructor favors fill-in-the-blank tests; your psychology instructor uses nothing but multiple-choice questions. In which class might it be easier to do well on the tests? Explain. (psychological reasoning)

4. After Shonte's store is robbed at gunpoint, she is asked to go to the police department to identify possible suspects. When she sees the lineup of men who supposedly fit the description she gave after the robbery, she really isn't sure which one of them did it. She points to a man on the far left and says, "I think it might have been him." The attending officer responds, "He *does* look like a criminal, doesn't he?! That's great, you got him. Nice work." Later in court, Shonte *confidently* testifies that she's sure the man she identified in the lineup was the culprit. However, DNA evidence contradicts Shonte's eyewitness testimony. Using what you know about memory construction, explain how Shonte's confidence level about identifying the suspect could have changed so dramatically. (perspective taking)

5. What would happen if we had perfect memories? What might life be like if we remembered *all* our waking experiences and *all* our dreams? (creative problem solving)

6. Your friend Casey tells you she is sure she is ready for the big chemistry test. She says she doesn't need to take the self-test at the end of the chapter, because she has looked through her notes many times, and everything looks very familiar. Why might Casey not be ready for the test? Explain. (scientific problem solving)

TERMS AND CONCEPTS TO REMEMBER

memory, p. 257

flashbulb memory, p. 258

encoding, p. 259

storage, p. 259

retrieval, p. 259

sensory memory, p. 259

short-term memory, p. 259

long-term memory, p. 259

automatic processing, p. 260

effortful processing, p. 260

rehearsal, p. 260

spacing effect, p. 261

serial position effect, p. 261

imagery, p. 263

mnemonics [nih-MON-iks], p. 263

chunking, p. 264

iconic memory, p. 266

echoic memory, p. 266

long-term potentiation (LTP), p. 269

amnesia, p. 269

implicit memory, p. 270

explicit memory, p. 270

hippocampus, p. 271

recall, p. 272

recognition, p. 272

relearning, p. 272

priming, p. 273

déjà vu, p. 274

mood-congruent memory, p. 274

proactive interference, p. 278

retroactive interference, p. 278

repression, p. 281

misinformation effect, p. 282

source amnesia, p. 284

To continue your study and review of Memory, visit this book's Web site at www.worthpublishers.com/myers. You will find practice tests, review activities, and Web links for more information on topics related to Memory.

chapter 9

Thinking, Language, and Intelligence

Throughout history, we humans have deplored our own foolishness and celebrated our wisdom. The poet T. S. Eliot was struck by "the hollow men . . . Headpiece filled with straw." But Shakespeare's Hamlet extolled the human species as "noble in reason! . . . infinite in faculties! . . . in apprehension how like a god!" In the preceding chapters, we have likewise marveled both at our capabilities and at our propensity to err.

We have studied the human brain—3 pounds of wet tissue containing circuitry more complex than the planet's telephone networks. We have appreciated the competence of newborn infants. We have relished the human sensory system, which disassembles visual stimuli into millions of nerve impulses, distributes them for parallel processing, and then reassembles them into clear and colorful perceived images. We have pondered our memory's seemingly limitless capacity and the ease with which we process information, consciously and unconsciously. Little wonder, then, that our species, by refining ideas over time, has the collective genius to invent the camera, the car, and the computer; to unlock the atom and crack the genetic code; to travel out to space and into the oceans' depths.

Yet we have also seen that our species is kin to the other animals, influenced by the same principles that produce learning in rats and pigeons. We have noted that we assimilate reality into our preconceptions and succumb to perceptual illusions. We have seen how easily we deceive ourselves about pseudopsychic claims, hypnotic regression, and false memories. Little wonder, then, that we sometimes imagine we can read minds and travel outside our bodies; that we form distorted images of other ethnic, age, and gender groups; that we are bound by biological principles common to many creatures.

In this chapter, we encounter further instances of these two images of the human condition—the rational and the irrational. We will see how we form concepts, solve problems, and make judgments. We will look at our flair for language and ask whether our species alone has this capability. We will consider the role of our intelligence. And we will reflect on how deserving we are of our name, *Homo sapiens*—wise human.

> ► **cognition** the mental activities associated with thinking, knowing, remembering, and communicating.

> ► **concept** a mental grouping of similar objects, events, ideas, or people.

THINKING

Previous chapters explained how we receive, perceive, store, and retrieve information. Now we consider how our cognitive system uses this information. Thinking, or **cognition**, refers to all the mental activities associated with processing, understanding, remembering, and communicating. *Cognitive psychologists* study these mental activities, including the logical and sometimes illogical ways in which we create concepts, solve problems, make decisions, and form judgments. By thinking about thinking, and by alerting us to common errors in our thinking, cognitive psychologists help us think *smart*. Their research helps us to appreciate both the powers and the limits of our intuition, and to reason more effectively.

Concepts

1. What are the functions of concepts?

To think about the countless events, objects, and people in our world, we simplify things. We form **concepts**—mental groupings of similar objects, events, and people. The concept *chair* sums up a variety of items—a baby's high chair, a reclining chair, the chairs around a dining room table, a dentist's chair.

Imagine life without concepts. We would need a different name for every object and idea. We could not ask a child to "throw the ball" because there would be no concept of *ball*. Instead of saying, "They were angry," we would have to describe facial expressions, vocal intensities, gestures, and words. Such concepts as *ball* and *angry* provide us with much information without much cognitive effort.

To simplify things further, we organize concepts into hierarchies. Cab

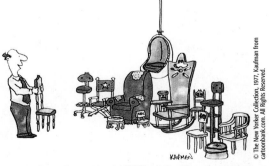

"Attention, everyone! I'd like to introduce the newest member of our family."

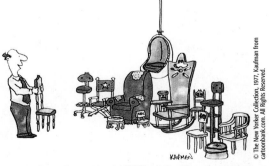

Daniel J. Cox/Liaison/Getty Images

J. Messerschmidt/The Picture Cube

A bird and a . . . ? If asked to imagine a bird, most people quickly come up with a mental picture that is something like this American robin. It takes them a bit longer to conceptualize a penguin as a bird because it doesn't match their prototype of a small, feathered, flying creature.

drivers organize their cities into geographical sectors, which subdivide into neighborhoods and again into blocks. The earliest naturalists simplified and ordered the overwhelming complexity of some 5 million living species by clustering them into two basic categories—the plant and animal kingdoms. Then they divided these basic categories into smaller and smaller subcategories—vertebrates, bony fish, and Atlantic salmon, for instance.

We form some concepts by definition. Told the rule that a triangle has three sides, we thereafter classify all three-sided geometric forms as triangles. More often, however, we form our concepts by developing **prototypes**—a mental image or best example that incorporates all the features we associate with a category (Rosch, 1978). The more closely something matches our prototype of a concept, the more readily we recognize it as an example of the concept. A robin and a goose both satisfy our definition of *bird*: a two-footed animal that has wings and feathers and hatches from an egg. Yet people agree more quickly that "A robin is a bird" than that "A goose is a bird." For most of us, the robin, with its beak, size, and easy flying, is the birdier bird; it more closely resembles our bird prototype.

If something fails to match our prototype, we may have trouble classifying it. Thus, we might be slow to recognize nonflying penguins and kiwis as birds. Similarly, we are slow to perceive an illness when our symptoms don't fit one of our disease prototypes (Bishop, 1991). People whose heart attack symptoms (shortness of breath, a dull weight in the chest) don't match their prototype of a heart attack (sharp chest pain) may not seek help.

Solving Problems

2. What strategies do we use to solve problems, and what obstacles hinder our problem solving?

One tribute to our rationality is our ability to form and use concepts. Another is our skill at solving problems as we cope with novel situations. What's the best route around this traffic jam? How shall we respond to a friend's criticism? How can we get into the house when we've lost our keys?

Some problems we solve through trial and error. Thomas Edison tried thousands of light bulb filaments before stumbling upon one that worked. For other problems, we may follow an **algorithm**, a step-by-step procedure that guarantees a solution. Told to find another word using all the letters in *SPLOYOCHYG*, we could try each letter in each position, but generating and examining the 907,200 resulting permutations would be exasperating. Because step-by-step algorithms can be laborious (well-suited to computers), we often solve problems with simple strategies, called **heuristics**. Thus, in rearranging the letters of *SPLOYOCHYG*, we might exclude letter combinations such as two *Y*'s together. By using heuristics and then applying trial and error, you may hit upon the answer (page 296).

Heuristic searching To search for chutney you could search every supermarket aisle (an algorithm) or check the mustard, spice, and gourmet sections (heuristics). The heuristic approach is often speedier, but an algorithmic search guarantees you will find it eventually.

Spencer Grant/Liaison/Getty Images

Sometimes we are unaware of using any problem-solving strategy; the answer just comes to us. We can all recall occasions when we puzzled over a problem for some time. Then, suddenly, the pieces fell together and we perceived the solution. Such sudden flashes of inspiration we call **insight**. Ten-year-old Johnny Appleton displayed insight in solving a problem that had stumped construction workers: how to rescue a young robin that had fallen into a narrow 30-inch-deep hole in a cement block wall. Johnny's solution: to slowly pour in sand, giving the bird enough time to keep its feet on top of the constantly rising sand (Ruchlis, 1990).

Insight provides a sense of satisfaction. After solving a difficult problem or discovering how to resolve a conflict, we feel happy. The joy of a joke may similarly lie in our capacity for insight—our sudden comprehension of an unexpected ending or a double meaning, as illustrated in the two jokes rated funniest (among 2 million ratings of 40,000 submitted jokes) in an Internet humor study co-sponsored by Richard Wiseman (2002) and the British Association for the Advancement of Science. First, the runner-up:

> Sherlock Holmes and Dr. Watson are going camping. They pitch their tent under the stars and go to sleep. Sometime in the middle of the night Holmes wakes Watson up.
>
> **Holmes:** *"Watson, look up at the stars, and tell me what you deduce."*
> **Watson:** *"I see millions of stars and even if a few of those have planets, it's quite likely there are some planets like Earth, and if there are a few planets like Earth out there, there might also be life. What does it tell you, Holmes?"*
> **Holmes:** *"Watson, you idiot, somebody has stolen our tent!"*

And roll the drums for the winner:

> A couple of New Jersey hunters are out in the woods when one of them falls to the ground. He doesn't seem to be breathing, his eyes are rolled back in his head. The other guy whips out his cell phone and calls the emergency services. He gasps to the operator: "My friend is dead! What can I do?" The operator, in a calm soothing voice says: "Just take it easy. I can help. First, let's make sure he's dead." There is a silence, then a shot is heard. The guy's voice comes back on the line: "OK, now what?"

Obstacles to Problem Solving

Inventive as we can be in solving problems, the correct answer may elude us. Two cognitive tendencies—*confirmation bias* and *fixation*—often mislead our search for a solution.

CONFIRMATION BIAS A major obstacle to problem solving, **confirmation bias**, is our eagerness to search for information that confirms our ideas. In an experiment with British university students, Peter Wason (1960) demonstrated this phenomenon. Wason gave students the three-number sequence 2-4-6 and asked them to guess the rule he had used to devise the series. (The rule was simple: any three ascending numbers.) Before submitting their answers, the students generated their own sets of three numbers, and each time Wason told them whether their sets conformed to his rule. Once they had done enough testing to feel *certain* they had the rule, they were to announce it.

The result? Seldom right but never in doubt. Most of Wason's students convinced themselves of a wrong rule. Typically, they formed a wrong idea ("Maybe it's counting by twos") and then searched only for confirming evidence (by testing 6-8-10, 100-102-104, and so forth). Reflecting on many experiments, Wason (1981) observed that "ordinary people evade facts, become inconsistent, or systematically defend themselves against the threat of new information relevant to the issue." Such experiments reveal that we seek evidence that will verify our ideas more eagerly than we seek evidence that might refute them (Klayman & Ha, 1987; Skov & Sherman, 1986).

In business, for example, managers are more likely to follow the successful careers of those they once hired than to track the achievements of those they rejected, leading them to confirm their own perceived hiring ability.

FIXATION Another major obstacle to problem solving is **fixation**—the inability to see a problem from a fresh perspective. Once we incorrectly represent the problem, it's hard to restructure how we approach it. Try to solve the matchstick problem in **FIGURE 9.1**. If your attempts to solve the problem were fixated on two-dimensional solutions, then the three-dimensional solution shown in **FIGURE 9.3** (page 297) will have eluded you.

Another type of fixation goes by the awkward but appropriate label **functional fixedness**. This is our tendency to perceive the functions of objects as fixed and

▶ **prototype** a mental image or best example of a category. Matching new items to the prototype provides a quick and easy method for including items in a category (as when comparing feathered creatures to a prototypical bird, such as a robin).

▶ **algorithm** a methodical, logical rule or procedure that guarantees solving a particular problem. Contrasts with the usually speedier—but also more error-prone—use of *heuristics*.

▶ **heuristic** a simple thinking strategy that often allows us to make judgments and solve problems efficiently; usually speedier but also more error-prone than *algorithms*.

▶ **insight** a sudden and often novel realization of the solution to a problem; it contrasts with strategy-based solutions.

▶ **confirmation bias** a tendency to search for information that confirms one's preconceptions.

▶ **fixation** the inability to see a problem from a new perspective; an impediment to problem solving.

▶ **functional fixedness** the tendency to think of things only in terms of their usual functions; an impediment to problem solving.

"The human understanding, when any proposition has been once laid down . . . forces everything else to add fresh support and confirmation."

Francis Bacon, Novum Organum, *1620*

figure 9.1
The matchstick problem How would you arrange six matches to form four equilateral triangles?

figure 9.2
The candle-mounting problem Using these materials, how would you mount the candle on a bulletin board? (From Duncker, 1945.)

unchanging. A person may ransack the house for a screwdriver when a dime would have turned the screw. As an example, try the candle-mounting problem in **FIGURE 9.2**. You perhaps experienced functional fixedness because most people think of the matchbox as having only the function of holding matches. Another use for it is shown in **FIGURE 9.4**, page 299. Perceiving and relating familiar things in new ways is part of creativity.

Answer to SPLOYOCHYG anagram on page 294: PSYCHOLOGY.

Making Decisions and Forming Judgments

3. How do heuristics, overconfidence, and framing influence our decisions and judgments?

When making each day's hundreds of judgments and decisions—Is it worth the bother to take an umbrella? Can I trust this person? Should I shoot the basketball or pass to the player who's hot?—we seldom take the time and effort to reason systematically. We just follow our intuition. After interviewing policymakers in government, business, and education, social psychologist Irving Janis (1986) concluded that they "often do not use a reflective problem-solving approach. How do they usually arrive at their decisions? If you ask, they are likely to tell you . . . they do it mostly by the *seat of their pants*."

Using and Misusing Heuristics

Those mental shortcuts we call heuristics often do help us make reasonable seat-of-the-pants decisions. Thanks to the mind's automatic information processing, intuitive judgments are instantaneous. But the price we sometimes pay for this efficiency—quick but bad judgments—can be costly. To gain an idea of how heuristics determine our intuitive judgments—and how they occasionally lead even the smartest people into dumb decisions—consider two heuristics identified by cognitive psychologists Amos Tversky and Daniel Kahneman (1974): *representativeness* and *availability*.

"In creating these problems, we didn't set out to fool people. All our problems fooled us, too."

Amos Tversky (1985)

"The information-processing shortcuts—called heuristics—which are normally both highly efficient and immensely time-saving in day-to-day situations, work systematically against us in the market-place. . . . The tendency to underestimate or altogether ignore past probabilities in making a decision is undoubtedly the most significant problem of intuitive predictions."

David Dreman, Contrarian Investment Strategy: The Psychology of Stock Market Success, 1979

▶ **representativeness heuristic** judging the likelihood of things in terms of how well they seem to represent, or match, particular prototypes; may lead one to ignore other relevant information.

▶ **availability heuristic** estimating the likelihood of events based on their availability in memory; if instances come readily to mind (perhaps because of their vividness), we presume such events are common.

THE REPRESENTATIVENESS HEURISTIC To judge the likelihood of things in terms of how well they represent particular prototypes is to use the **representativeness heuristic**. To illustrate, consider:

> A stranger tells you about a person who is short, slim, and likes to read poetry, and then asks you to guess whether this person is more likely to be a professor of classics at an Ivy League university or a truck driver (adapted from Nisbett & Ross, 1980). Which would be the better guess?

If you are like most people, you answered "professor" because the description seems more *representative* of Ivy League scholars than of truck drivers. The representativeness heuristic enabled you to make a snap judgment. But it also led you to ignore other relevant information. When I help people think through this question, the typical conversation goes something like this:

Question: First, let's figure out how many professors fit the description. How many
            Ivy League universities do you suppose there are?
Answer: Oh, about 10, I suppose.
Question: How many classics professors would you guess there are at each?
Answer: Maybe 4.
Question: Okay, that's 40 Ivy League classics professors. What fraction of these are
            short and slim?

Answer: Let's say half.

Question: And, of these 20, how many like to read poetry?

Answer: I'd say half—10 professors.

Question: Okay, now let's figure how many truck drivers fit the description. How many truck drivers do you suppose there are?

Answer: Maybe 400,000.

Question: What fraction are short and slim?

Answer: Not many—perhaps 1 in 8.

Question: Of these 50,000, what percentage like to read poetry?

Answer: Truck drivers who like poetry? Maybe 1 in 100—oh, oh, I can see where this is going—that leaves me with 500 short, slim, poetry-reading truck drivers.

Comment: Yup. So, although the person I've described may be much more representative of classics professors than of truck drivers, this person is still (even if we accept your stereotypes) 50 times more likely to be a truck driver than a classics professor.

The representativeness heuristic influences many of our daily decisions. To judge the likelihood of something, we intuitively compare it with our mental representation of that category—of, say, what truck drivers are like. If the two match, that fact usually overrides other considerations of statistics or logic.

THE AVAILABILITY HEURISTIC
The **availability heuristic** operates when we base our judgments on the availability of information in our memories. If instances of an event are easily available—if they come to mind readily—we presume such events are common. The faster people can remember an instance of some event ("a broken promise"), the more they expect it to recur (MacLeod & Campbell, 1992). Cognitively available events *are* more likely to recur—but not always. To see this, make a guess: Does the letter *k* appear more often as the first or third letter in English usage?

Because words beginning with *k* come to mind more easily than words having *k* as their third letter, most people guess that *k* occurs more frequently as the first letter. Actually, *k* is much more likely to appear as the third letter. So far in this chapter, words such as *know, kingdom,* and *kin* are outnumbered 51 to 10 by words such as *make, likely, asked,* and *acknowledged.*

The availability heuristic also affects our social judgments, as Ruth Hamill and her co-workers demonstrated (1980). They presented people with a single, vivid welfare case, in which a recipient had several unruly children receiving long-term welfare. Statistically, this case was exceptional: Most people who received welfare did so for four years or less (Duncan & others, 1988). Yet when the statistical reality was pitted against the single vivid case, the memorable case had greater influence on people's opinions about welfare recipients.

A memorable picture sometimes overwhelms a thousand statistics. When a little girl, Jessica McClure, fell into a Texas well, the attention of hundreds of millions of people worldwide was riveted on her three-day rescue. During those three days, more than 100,000 invisible children—"mere statistics" on some world health ledger—died of preventable starvation, diarrhea, and disease (Gore, 1992).

figure 9.3
Solution to the matchstick problem
To solve this problem, you must break the fixation of limiting your considerations to two-dimensional solutions.

"The problem is I can't tell the difference between a deeply wise, intuitive nudge from the Universe and one of my own bone-headed ideas!"

© B. Veley. Used by permission.

"The human understanding is most excited by that which strikes and enters the mind at once and suddenly, and by which the imagination is immediately filled and inflated. It then begins almost imperceptibly to conceive and suppose that everything is similar to the few objects which have taken possession of the mind."

Francis Bacon, Novum Organum, *1620*

When the D.C. area snipers killed 10 people during an October 2002 three-week shooting spree, the world was aghast. Although less noticed, 30 other Americans are murdered with firearms each day.

Thinking Critically About:

Risks—Do We Fear the Right Things?

"Most people reason dramatically, not quantitatively," said Oliver Wendell Holmes. Especially since 9/11, many people fear flying more than driving. Yet National Safety Council (2001) data reveal that in the last half of the 1990s Americans were, mile for mile, 37 times more likely to die in a vehicle crash than on a commercial flight.

Why do we fear the wrong things? Why do we fear terrorism more than accidents—which kill nearly as many per *week* in just the United States as did terrorism with its 2527 worldwide deaths in all of the 1990s (Johnson, 2001)? Even with the horror of 9/11, more Americans in 2001 died of food poisoning (which scares few) than of terrorism (which scares many). And why do so many smokers (whose habit shortens their lives, on average, by about five years) fret before flying (which, averaged across people, shortens life by one day)?

Psychological science has identified four influences on our intu-

AP/Wide World Photos

Vivid events are more available to memory Images of 9/11 etched a sharper image in our minds than did the millions of fatality-free flights on U.S. airlines during 2002. Such dramatic events, being readily available to memory, shape our perceptions of risk.

itions about risk. First, we fear *what our ancestral history has prepared us to fear.* Human emotions were road tested in the Stone Age. Yesterday's risks prepare us to fear snakes, lizards, and spiders, although all three combined now kill virtually no one in developed countries. Flying may be far safer than biking, but our biological past predisposes us to fear confinement and heights, and therefore flying.

Second, we fear *what we cannot control.* Downhill skiing, by one estimate, poses 1000 times the health and injury risk of food preservatives (Slovic, 1987). Yet many people gladly assume the risk of skiing, which they control, but avoid preservatives. Driving we control, flying we do not. "We are loathe to let others do unto us what we happily do to ourselves," noted risk analyst Chauncey Starr.

Third, we fear *what is immediate.* Teens are often indifferent to smoking's toxicity because they live more for the present than for the distant

---

▶ **overconfidence** the tendency to be more confident than correct—to overestimate the accuracy of one's beliefs and judgments.

"Don't believe everything you think."

Bumper sticker

Overconfidence

Our use of intuitive heuristics when forming judgments, our eagerness to confirm the beliefs we already hold, and our knack for explaining away failures combine to create **overconfidence**, a tendency to overestimate the accuracy of our knowledge and judgments. Across various tasks, people overestimate what their performance was, is, or will be (Metcalfe, 1998).

People are also more confident than correct when answering such questions as, "Is absinthe a liqueur or a precious stone?" (It's a licorice-flavored liqueur.) On questions where only 60 percent of people answer correctly, respondents typically feel 75 percent confident. Even when people feel 100 percent certain of their answers to such questions, they err about 15 percent of the time (Fischhoff & others, 1977).

Overconfidence plagues decisions outside the laboratory, too. It was an overconfident Hitler who invaded Russia, an overconfident Lyndon Johnson who waged war with North Vietnam, an overconfident Slobodan Milosovic who marched into Kosovo. Stockbrokers and investment managers market their services with confidence that they can outperform the market average in picking stocks, despite overwhelming evidence to the contrary (Malkiel, 1985, 1995). A purchase of stock X,

future. Much of a plane's threat is telescoped into the moments of takeoff and landing, while the dangers of driving are diffused across many moments to come, each trivially dangerous.

Fourth, we fear *what is most readily available in memory*. Horrific images of United Flight 175 slicing into the World Trade Center form indelible memories. And these indelible, available memories serve as our measuring rods as we intuitively judge risks. Thousands of safe car trips (for those who have survived to read this) have extinguished our anxieties about driving.

In less familiar realms, vivid, memorable images dominate our fears. A handful of massively publicized anthrax victims in 2001 riveted America's attention in a way that more than 20,000 annual influenza fatalities or 30,000 suicidal, homicidal, and accidental gun deaths never could.

Vivid events also cause us to overestimate the odds and distort our comprehension of risks and probable outcomes. We comprehend Andrew "Jack" Whittaker's winning $315 million in a 2002 Powerball lottery. We do not comprehend the more than 560 million losing tickets enabling his jackpot. We comprehend the 266 passengers and crew who died on those 9/11 flights. We do not comprehend the vast numbers of accident-free flights—16 *million* consecutive fatality-free takeoffs and landings during one stretch of the 1990s (Tolchin, 1994). Dramatic outcomes capture our attention; probabilities we hardly grasp. The result: We overvalue lottery tickets, overestimate flight risk, and underestimate the dangers of driving.

Because we fear too little those threats that will claim lives undramatically, one by one (rather than in bunches), and in the future rather than the immediate present, we will also spend hundreds of billions to save thousands of lives instead of spending a few billion to save millions.

Alternatively, $1.5 billion a year would be the U.S. share of a global effort to cut world hunger in half by 2015 (Bread for the World, 2002). And $10 billion a year would spare *29 million* world citizens from developing AIDS by 2010, according to a joint report by representatives of the United Nations, the World Health Organization, and others (Altman, 2002). A few tens of billions spent on alternative energy sources could help avert the anticipated enormous future toll of global warming. While agonizing over missed signals of the impending horror of 9/11, are we missing the clearer indications of greater horrors to come?

The point to remember: It is perfectly normal to fear purposeful violence from those who hate us. When terrorists strike again, we will all recoil in horror. But smart thinkers will also want to check their fears against facts. By so doing, we can take away the terrorists' omnipresent weapon: exaggerated fear.

---

recommended by a broker who judges this to be the time to buy, is usually balanced by a sale made by someone who judges this to be the time to sell. Despite their confidence, buyer and seller can't both be right.

Roger Buehler and his colleagues (1994) were struck by how routinely planners exhibit overconfidence in estimating how quickly and inexpensively they can do a project. In 1957, planners predicted the Sydney Opera House would be completed in 1963 for $7 million. A reduced version actually opened in 1973 at a cost of $102 million. (Even as I wrote this we were moving into a new kitchen that our architect estimated would take one month, our contractor estimated would take three months, and that actually took five months.) Students, too, are routinely overconfident about how quickly they can do assignments and write papers, Buehler reports; they typically expect to finish projects ahead of schedule. But in fact, the projects generally get finished after about twice the number of days they predicted. Although people know they have often underestimated completion times, they remain overly confident of their next prediction.

Overconfidence does have adaptive value. Failing to appreciate one's potential for error when making military, economic, or political judgments can have devastating

figure 9.4
Solution to the candle-mounting problem Solving this problem requires recognizing that a box need not always serve as a container. (From Duncker, 1945.)

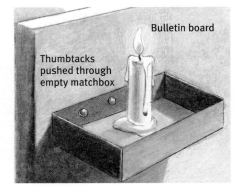

Bulletin board

Thumbtacks pushed through empty matchbox

Predict your own behavior
When will you finish reading this chapter?

"When you know a thing, to hold that you know it; and when you do not know a thing, to allow that you do not know it; this is knowledge."

Confucius (551–479 B.C.), Analects

consequences, but so can a lack of self-confidence. People who err on the side of overconfidence live more happily, find it easier to make tough decisions, and seem credible (Baumeister, 1989; Taylor, 1989). Moreover, when given prompt and clear feedback on the accuracy of their judgments—as weather forecasters are after each day's predictions—people soon learn to assess their accuracy more realistically (Fischhoff, 1982). The wisdom to know when we know a thing and when we do not is born of experience.

Framing Decisions

A further test of rationality is whether the same issue, presented in two different but logically equivalent ways, will elicit the same answer. For example, one surgeon tells someone that 10 percent of people die while undergoing a particular surgery. Another tells someone that 90 percent survive. The information is the same. The effect is not. To both patients and physicians, the risk seems greater to those who hear that 10 percent will die (McNeil & others, 1988; Marteau, 1989; Rothman & Salovey, 1997).

The way we present an issue is called **framing**, and its effects are sometimes striking. Consumers respond more positively to ground beef described as "75 percent lean" rather than "25 percent fat" (Levin & Gaeth, 1988; Sanford & others, 2002). Nine in 10 college students rate a condom as effective if it has a supposed "95 percent success rate" in stopping the AIDS virus; only 4 in 10 think it successful when given a "5 percent failure rate" (Linville & others, 1992). And people express more surprise when a "1 in 20" event happens than when an equivalent "10 in 200" event happens (Denes-Raj & others, 1995). People told that a chemical exposure is projected to kill 10 of every 10 million people (imagine 10 dead people!) feel more frightened than if told the fatality risk is an infinitesimal .000001 (Kraus & others, 1992).

Consider how the framing effect influences economic and business decisions:

● Merchants mark up their "regular prices" to appear to offer huge savings on "sale prices." A $100 coat marked down from $150 by Store X can seem like a better deal than the same coat priced regularly at $100 by Store Y (Urbany & others, 1988).

● Many find taking a 7 percent pay cut in a period of zero inflation much more objectionable than receiving a 5 percent pay raise when inflation is 12 percent (Kahneman & others, 1986).

● FedEx doesn't charge extra to pick up at your door; instead, they offer a "drop-off discount." Likewise, my dentist doesn't charge more if we pay later, though she does offer a 5 percent discount for immediate cash payment. FedEx and my dentist both understand that a fee framed as a forfeited discount irritates customers less than one framed as a surcharge, although they add up to the same thing.

That our judgments can flip-flop so dramatically is startling. It suggests that our judgments and decisions may not be well reasoned, and that those who understand the power of framing can use it to influence important decisions—for example, by framing survey questions to support or reject a particular viewpoint.

"This CD player costs less than players selling for twice as much."

The Belief Perseverance Phenomenon

4. How do our preexisting beliefs influence our decision making?

An additional source of irrationality is **belief perseverance**, our tendency to cling to our beliefs in the face of contrary evidence. Belief perseverance often fuels social conflict. Charles Lord and his colleagues (1979) revealed how this happens when they studied people with opposing views of capital punishment. Those on both sides studied two supposedly new research findings, one supporting and the other refuting the claim that the death penalty deters crime. Each side was more impressed by the study that supported its beliefs, and each readily disputed the other study. Thus, showing the pro– and anti–capital-punishment groups the *same* mixed evidence actually *increased* their disagreement.

If you want to rein in the belief perseverance phenomenon, a simple remedy exists: *Consider the opposite.* When Lord and his colleagues (1984) repeated the capital-punishment study, they asked some of their participants to be "as *objective* and *unbiased* as possible." The plea did nothing to reduce the biased evaluation of evidence. They asked another group to consider "whether you would have made the same high or low evaluations had exactly the same study produced results on the *other* side of the issue." Having imagined and pondered *opposite* findings, these people became much less biased in their evaluations of the evidence.

If people interpret ambiguous evidence as supporting their preexisting belief, would their belief be demolished by information that clearly discredits its basis? Not necessarily. Craig Anderson and Lee Ross discovered that a false belief can be surprisingly difficult to change once a person has ideas that support it. In one study with Mark Lepper (1980), they asked people to consider whether risk-takers or cautious people make better fire fighters. Then they told half the people about a risk taker who was an excellent fire fighter and about a cautious person who was a poor fire fighter. From these cases, the participants surmised that risk takers tend to be better fire fighters. "Risk takers are braver," was the typical explanation. The researchers gave the other participants two cases suggesting the opposite conclusion, leading people to infer, for example, that "cautious people think before they act. They're less likely to make foolish mistakes."

The researchers then discredited the basis for the beliefs; they truthfully informed both groups that the cases were simply made up for the experiment. Did discrediting the evidence undermine the newly formed beliefs? Not by much, because they held on to their *explanations* for why these new beliefs made sense. Although the evidence was gone, their theory survived.

The more we come to appreciate why our beliefs might be true, the more tightly we cling to them. Once people have explained to themselves why they believe a child is "gifted" or "learning disabled," or why candidate X or Y will be more likely to preserve peace, or why company Z is a stock worth owning, they tend to ignore the evidence that undermines that belief. Prejudice persists. Once beliefs form and get justified, it takes more compelling evidence to change them than it did to create them.

● ● ●

We have seen how our irrational thinking can plague our efforts to solve problems, make wise decisions, form valid judgments, and reason logically. Moreover, these perils of intuition appear even when people are offered extra pay for thinking smart, even when they are asked to justify their answers,

▶ **framing** the way an issue is posed; how an issue is framed can significantly affect decisions and judgments.

▶ **belief perseverance** clinging to one's initial conceptions after the basis on which they were formed has been discredited. (*Confirmation bias*—searching for belief-support information—contributes to belief perseverance.)

"Once you have a belief, it influences how you perceive all other relevant information. Once you see a country as hostile, you are likely to interpret ambiguous actions on their part as signifying their hostility."

Political scientist Robert Jervis (1985)

"I'm happy to say that my final judgment of a case is almost always consistent with my prejudgment of the case."

"To begin with, it was only tentatively that I put forward the views I have developed . . . but in the course of time they have gained such a hold upon me that I can no longer think in any other way."

Sigmund Freud, Civilization and Its Discontents, *1930*

Belief perseverance Do risk takers or cautious people make better fire fighters? Once we've formed opinions on a question like this and developed reasons for our views, we tend to cling to our beliefs—even if the basis for our opinion is undermined.

"Even though I am not religious, the amazement and wonder I have about the human mind is closer to religious awe than dispassionate analysis."

Bill Gates, 1997

and even when they are expert physicians or clinicians (Shafir & LeBoeuf, 2003). From this we might conclude that our heads are indeed filled with straw. All in all, these and many other findings suggest "bleak implications for human rationality" (Nisbett & Borgida, 1975). Still, we should not forget that our cognition can be effective and wonderfully efficient: It enables our survival and our inventive genius.

rehearse it!

1. We use the concept *bird* to think and talk about a variety of creatures, all of which have wings and feathers. A concept is
   a. a mental grouping of similar things.
   b. an example of insight.
   c. a fixation on certain characteristics.
   d. a hierarchy.

2. Sometimes we solve problems through trial and error, trying hundreds or even thousands of solutions before finding one that works. At other times we are more methodical or systematic. The most systematic procedure for solving a problem is
   a. a heuristic.
   b. an algorithm.
   c. insight.
   d. intuition.

3. A major obstacle to problem solving is the confirmation bias, the tendency to search for information that confirms our preconceptions while ignoring information that might prove us wrong.

Another obstacle to problem solving is fixation, which is
   a. an error we make when we base our judgments on certain vivid memories.
   b. the art of framing the same question in two different ways.
   c. the inability to view a problem from a new perspective.
   d. a rule of thumb for judging the likelihood of an event in terms of our mental image of it.

4. You move into a new neighborhood and notice that your next-door neighbor is very neatly dressed, wears glasses, and is reading a Greek play. Given a choice between her being a librarian and a store clerk, you incorrectly guess that she is a librarian. Your incorrect judgment is probably due to
   a. the availability heuristic.
   b. confirmation bias.
   c. overconfidence.
   d. the representativeness heuristic.

5. After the events of 9/11 by foreign-born terrorists, some observers initially assumed that the 2003 East Coast blackout was probably the work of foreign-born terrorists. This assumption illustrates
   a. belief perseverance.
   b. the availability heuristic.
   c. functional fixedness.
   d. confirmation bias.

6. The way an issue is posed can affect our decisions and judgments. For example, consumers respond more positively to ground beef described as "75 percent lean" rather than "25 percent fat." In this case people's reactions were influenced by
   a. belief perseverance.
   b. fixation.
   c. confirmation bias.
   d. framing.

Answers can be found in Appendix C.

LANGUAGE

The most tangible indication of our thinking power is **language**—our spoken, written, or signed words and the ways we combine them as we think and communicate. Humans have long and proudly proclaimed that language sets us above all other animals. "When we study human language," asserted linguist Noam Chomsky (1972), "we are approaching what some might call the 'human essence,' the qualities of mind that are, so far as we know, unique" to humans. To cognitive scientist Steven Pinker (1990), language is "the jewel in the crown of cognition." Consider language's "vast expressive powers," says Pinker (1998). You sometimes sit for hours "listening to other people make noise as they exhale, because those hisses and squeaks contain *information*."

When the human vocal tract evolved the capacity to utter vowels, our capacity for language exploded, catapulting our species forward (Diamond, 1989). Whether spoken, written, or signed, language enables us to communicate complex ideas from person to person and to transmit civilization's accumulated knowledge across generations. Monkeys mostly know what they see. Thanks to language we know much that we've never seen.

Language Development

5. When do children acquire language, and how do they master this complex task?

▶ **language** our spoken, written, or signed words and the ways we combine them to communicate meaning.

▶ **babbling stage** beginning by about 4 months, the stage of speech development in which the infant spontaneously utters various sounds at first unrelated to the household language.

Make a quick guess: How many words did you learn in one average day during the years between your first birthday and your high school graduation?

The average secondary school graduate knows some 80,000 words (Miller & Gildea, 1987). That averages (after age 1) to nearly 5000 words learned each year, or 13 each day! How you did it—how the 5000 words a year you learned could so far outnumber the roughly 200 words a year that your schoolteachers consciously taught you—is one of the great human wonders. Before children can add 2 + 2, they are creating their own original and grammatically appropriate sentences. College students also have an astonishing facility for language. With remarkable efficiency, you can selectively sample the tens of thousands of words in your memory, effortlessly combine them on the fly with near-perfect word order, and spew them out three words a second (Vigliocco & Hartsuiker, 2002).

It's an amazing feat, given how many ways there are to mess up. It's as if there were elves down in our head's basement busily hammering together sentences that get piped up and shoved out of our mouth or off our hands. How did your language ability unfold, and how can we explain it?

Acquiring Language

Children's language development moves from simplicity to complexity. Infants start without language (*in fantis* means "not speaking"). Yet by 4 months of age, babies can read lips and discriminate speech sounds. They prefer to look at a face that matches a sound, so we know they can recognize that *ah* comes from wide open lips and *ee* from a mouth with corners pulled back (Kuhl & Meltzoff, 1982). At about this age, babies enter a **babbling stage** in which they spontaneously utter a variety of sounds, such as *ah-goo*.

Babbling is not an imitation of adult speech, for it includes sounds from various languages, even sounds that do not occur in the household's language. From this early babbling, a listener could not identify an infant as being, say, French, Korean, or Ethiopian. Deaf infants acquiring sign language babble (repeat syllablelike gestures) (Petitto & Marentette, 1991). It seems, then, that before nurture molds our speech, nature enables a wide range of possible sounds. Many of these natural babbling sounds are consonant-vowel pairs formed by simply bunching the tongue in front of the mouth (da-da, na-na, ta-ta) or by the lips (ma-ma), both of which babies do naturally for feeding (MacNeilage & Davis, 2000).

Eventually our babbling comes to resemble the characteristic sounds and intonations of our household language. By the time infants are about 10 months old, their babbling has changed so that a trained ear can identify the language of the household (de Boysson-Bardies & others, 1989). Sounds outside the infant's native tongue begin to disappear, as does the ability to discriminate those sounds.

Clever though controversial experiments by Janet Werker (1989) reveal that at 6 months infants can perceive subtle sound differences in other languages, but by 12 months they cannot (**FIGURE 9.5**). Without exposure to other languages, we

Although you probably know about 80,000 words, you use only 150 words for about half of what you say.

figure 9.5
Testing for speech sound perception
We are all born with the ability to recognize speech sounds from all the world's languages. In Janet Werker's lab, an infant is reinforced with applause and by activating toy animals when he looks to the right after hearing a changed sound (as in *ba, ba, ba, ba, da, da*). Adult Hindi-speakers and young infants from English-speaking homes can easily discriminate two Hindi *t* sounds not spoken in English. By about age 1, however, English-speaking listeners rarely perceive the sound difference. (Adapted from Werker, 1989.)

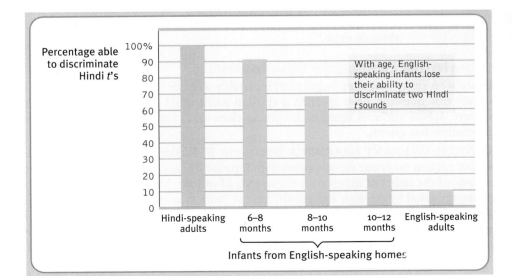

Percentage able to discriminate Hindi *t*'s

With age, English-speaking infants lose their ability to discriminate two Hindi *t* sounds

Hindi-speaking adults — 6–8 months — 8–10 months — 10–12 months — English-speaking adults

Infants from English-speaking homes

"Got idea. Talk better. Combine words. Make sentences."

became functionally deaf to speech sounds outside our native language (Pallier & others, 2001). So, by adulthood those who speak only English cannot discriminate certain Japanese language sounds. Nor can Japanese adults with no training in English distinguish between the English *r* and *l*. Thus (believe it or not), *la-la-ra-ra* may sound like the same repeated syllable to a Japanese adult. This makes life challenging for the Japanese tourist who is told the train station is "just after the next light." The next what? After the street veering right, or farther down, after the traffic light?

Around the first birthday (the exact age varies from child to child), most children enter the **one-word stage**. Having already learned that sounds carry meanings, they begin to use sounds to communicate meaning. Their first words usually contain only one syllable—*ma* or *da*, for instance—and may be barely recognizable. But family members quickly learn to understand the infant's language, and gradually it conforms more and more to the family's language. At this one-word stage, an inflected word may equal a sentence. "Doggy!" may mean "Look at the dog out there!"

Children typically use more and more single words during the second year. At about 18 months, their word learning steadily increases, from a word per week to a word per day. Before their second birthday, they usually enter the **two-word stage**, when they start uttering two-word sentences (**TABLE 9.1**). Language at this stage is characterized by **telegraphic speech**: Like telegrams (TERMS ACCEPTED SEND MONEY), this early form of speech contains mostly nouns and verbs (*Want juice*). Also like telegrams, it follows rules of syntax; the words are in a sensible order. The English-speaking child typically says adjectives before nouns—*big doggy* rather than *doggy big*.

There seems to be no "three-word stage." Once children move out of the two-word stage, they quickly begin uttering longer phrases (Fromkin & Rodman, 1983). Although the sentences may still resemble a telegraphed message, they continue to follow the rules of syntax (*Mommy get ball*). By early elementary school, the child understands complex sentences and begins to enjoy the humor conveyed by double meanings: "You never starve in the desert because of all the sand-which-is there."

table 9.1 Summary of Language Development	
Month (approximate)	Stage
4	Babbles many speech sounds
10	Babbling reveals household language
12	One-word stage
24	Two-word, telegraphic speech
24+	Language develops rapidly into complete sentences

Explaining Language Development

Those who study language acquisition inevitably wonder how we do it. Attempts to answer this question have sparked a spirited intellectual controversy. The nature-nurture debate surfaces again and, here as elsewhere, appreciation for innate predisposition has grown.

SKINNER: OPERANT LEARNING Behaviorist B. F. Skinner (1957) believed that we can explain language development with familiar learning principles, such as association (of the sights of things with the sounds of words); imitation (of the words and syntax modeled by others); and reinforcement (with success, smiles, and hugs when the child says something right). Thus, Skinner (1985) argued, babies learn to talk in many of the same ways that animals learn to peck keys and press bars: "Verbal behavior evidently came into existence when, through a critical step in the evolution of the human species, the vocal musculature became susceptible to operant conditioning." And what happens when there is minimal reinforcement for speaking? Hearing children of Deaf parents, whose exposure to spoken language is more passive, much of it via television, learn sign normally but spoken language more slowly (Messer, 2000). (Those who often overhear a second language during childhood do, however, later learn to speak it with a more nativelike accent [Au & others, 2002]).

CHOMSKY: INBORN UNIVERSAL GRAMMAR Linguist Noam Chomsky (1959, 1987) thinks Skinner's ideas were naive. Surely, Chomsky has said, a Martian scientist observing children in a single-language community would conclude that language is almost entirely inborn. But it isn't. Children do learn their environment's language. However, they acquire untaught words and grammar at too extraordinary a rate to be explained solely by learning principles. They generate all sorts of sentences they have never heard (sometimes with novel errors)—sentences they could not be imitating. (No parent teaches the sentence, "I hate you, Daddy.") There are 3,628,800 ways to arrange this sentence's 10 words. Only a handful of them make any sense. Yet any 4-year-old could pick them out from among the 3,628,700+ nonsensical orderings.

Moreover, many of the errors young children make result from *overgeneralizing* logical grammatical rules, such as adding *-ed* to make the past tense (from de Cuevas, 1990):

> **Child:** *My teacher holded the baby rabbits and we petted them.*
> **Mother:** *Did you say your teacher held the baby rabbits?*
> **Child:** *Yes.*
> **Mother:** *Did you say she held them tightly?*
> **Child:** *No, she holded them loosely.*

Chomsky (1987) likens the behaviorist view of how language develops to filling a bottle with water. He instead views language development as "helping a flower to grow in its own way." It is, he believes, akin to sexual maturation: Given adequate nurture, it just "happens to the child." All human languages have the same grammatical building blocks, such as nouns and verbs, subjects and objects, negations and questions.

Our 6000 human languages are therefore dialects of the "universal grammar" for which our brains are prewired (Baker, 2001). Thanks to our inborn universal grammar, we readily learn the specific grammar of whatever language we hear. It happens so naturally—as naturally as birds learning to fly—that training hardly helps. Expose children to language and they will soak it up. If raised in isolation, they develop without language. If not exposed to language, a *group* of children will, however, make up their own. Without exposure to language, deaf children, too, will over time create their own with gestures, complete with grammar.

Other worlds may have languages that, for us humans, are unlearnable, but our world does not. Chomsky maintains that our language acquisition capacity is like a box—a "language acquisition device"—in which grammar switches are thrown as children experience their language. Thus, English-speaking children learn to put the object of a sentence last ("She ate an apple"). Japanese-speaking children put the object before the verb ("She an apple ate"). We are born with the hardware and an operating system; experience writes the software (**FIGURE 9.6**, page 306).

Slightly more than half the world's 6000 languages are spoken by fewer than 10,000 people. And slightly more than half the world's population speaks one of the top 20 languages (Gibbs, 2002).

Susan Meiselas/Magnum Photos

Creating a language Brought together as if on a desert island (actually a school), Nicaragua's young deaf children over generations refined their own Nicaraguan Sign Language, complete with words and intricate grammar. Our biological predisposition for language does not create language in a vacuum. But activated by a social context, nature and nurture work creatively together (Osborne, 1999; Senghas & Coppola, 2001).

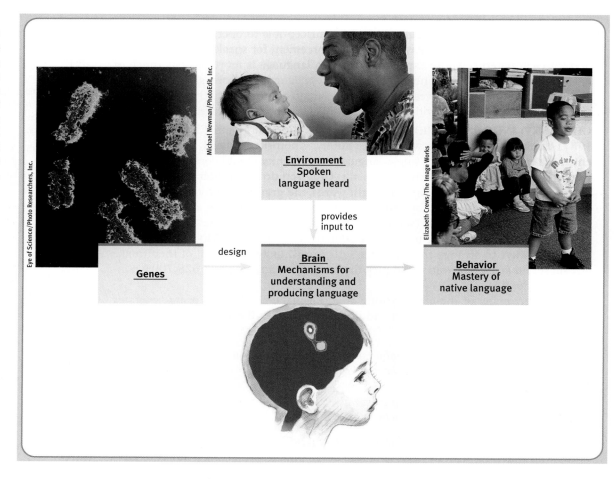

figure 9.6
Nature and nurture
Genes design the mechanisms for a language, and experience activates them as it modifies the brain. Grow up in Paris and you will speak French (environment matters), but not if you are a cat (genes matter).

Environment
Spoken language heard

provides input to

design

Genes

Brain
Mechanisms for understanding and producing language

Behavior
Mastery of native language

COGNITIVE SCIENTISTS: STATISTICAL LEARNING Human infants display a remarkable ability to learn statistical aspects of human speech. When you or I listen to an unfamiliar language, the syllables all run together. Someone unfamiliar with English might, for example, hear the "United Nations" as the Uneye Tednay Shuns. Before our first birthday, our brains were discerning word breaks by statistically analyzing which syllables most often go together. Jenny Saffran and her colleagues (1996) showed this by exposing 8-month-old infants to a computer voice speaking an unbroken, monotone string of nonsense syllables (*bidakupadotigolabubidaku . . .*). After just two minutes of exposure, the infants were able to recognize (as indicated by their attention) three-syllable sequences that appeared repeatedly.

Little statistician Human infants come with a remarkable capacity to statistically analyze language and discern words and grammatical rules. This is a tribute to both nature and nurture—to our biological machinery for learning language.

Follow-up research offers further testimony to infants' surprising knack for soaking up language. Seven-month-old infants can learn simple sentence structures. After repeatedly hearing syllable sequences that follow one rule, such as *ga-ti-ga* and *li-na-li* (an ABA pattern), they listen longer to syllables in a different sequence, such as *wo-fe-fe* (an ABB pattern) rather than *wo-fe-wo*. Their detecting the difference between the two patterns suggests that babies come with a built-in readiness to learn grammatical rules (Marcus & others, 1999).

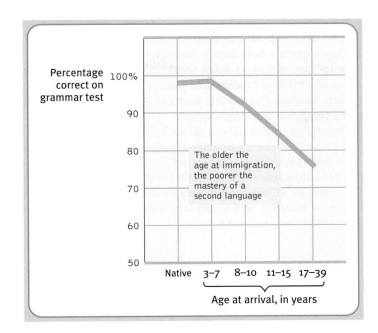

Percentage correct on grammar test

The older the age at immigration, the poorer the mastery of a second language

Native   3–7   8–10   11–15   17–39

Age at arrival, in years

figure 9.7
New language learning gets harder with age Young children have a readiness to learn language. Ten years after coming to the United States, Asian immigrants took a grammar test. Those who arrived before age 8 understood American English grammar as well as native speakers. Those who arrived later did not. (From Johnson & Newport, 1991.)

Childhood is a critical period for mastering grammar. Those who learn a second language as adults usually speak it with the accent of their first language. Do they master the foreign grammar better than the accent? To find out, Jacqueline Johnson and Elissa Newport (1991) gave Korean and Chinese immigrants to the United States a grammar test, requiring them to identify each of 276 sentences ("Yesterday the hunter shoots a deer") as grammatically correct or incorrect. Some of the test-takers had immigrated in early childhood, others as adults. Regardless of their age at immigration, each had been in the United States for approximately 10 years. Nevertheless, as **FIGURE 9.7** reveals, those who learned their second language early learned it best. Chomsky would say that once the grammar switches are thrown during a child's developing years, mastering another grammar becomes more difficult.

The impact of early experience is evident in comparisons of deaf and hearing children. Hearing children of hearing-speaking parents and deaf children of Deaf-signing parents have much in common. As noted earlier, both groups babble as infants—hearing children by repeating sounds, deaf children by repeating elementary sign gestures (Petitto & Marentette, 1991). Both groups develop vocabularies at comparable rates (Meier, 1991). For both groups, later-than-usual exposure to language (at age 2 or 3) unleashes their brain's idle language capacity, producing a rush of language. But consider the 90+ percent of deaf children born to hearing-nonsigning parents. These children typically do not experience language during their early years. Compared with deaf children exposed to sign language from birth, those who learn to sign as teens or adults are not like birds that, having missed exposure to their species' song during the weeks before maturity, never learn to sing. But they are like immigrants who learn English after childhood. They can master the basic words and learn to order them, but they never become as fluent as native signers in producing and comprehending subtle grammatical differences (Newport, 1990). Moreover, the late-learners show less brain activity in right hemisphere regions that are active as native signers read sign language (Newman & others, 2002).

Brain scans reveal a difference in how the brain records a second language learned early versus a second language learned later in life. Adults who learned a second language early in life use the same *patch of frontal lobe tissue when recounting an event in either the native or the second language. Those who learned their second tongue after childhood display activity in an* adjacent *brain area while using their second language (Kim & others, 1997).*

"Childhood is the time for language, no doubt about it. Young children, the younger the better, are good at it; it is child's play. It is a one-time gift to the species."

Lewis Thomas, The Fragile Species, *1992*

Not! Deaf children of Deaf-signing parents and hearing children of hearing parents have much in common. They develop language skills at about the same rate, and they are equally effective at opposing parental wishes and demanding their way.

▶ **linguistic determinism** Whorf's hypothesis that language determines the way we think.

To summarize, children's genes design complex brain wiring that prepares them to learn language as they interact with their caregivers. Skinner's emphasis on learning helps explain how infants acquire their language as they interact with others. (So does infants' ability to learn statistical probabilities in speech.) Chomsky's emphasis on our built-in readiness to learn grammar rules helps explain why preschoolers acquire language so readily and use grammar so well. Once again, we see biology and experience working together.

Returning to our debate about how deserving we are of our name *Homo sapiens*, let's pause to issue an interim report card. On decision making and judgment, our error-prone species might rate a C+. On problem solving, where humans are inventive yet vulnerable to fixation, we would probably receive better marks, perhaps a B. On cognitive efficiency, our fallible but quick heuristics earn us an A. And when it comes to learning and using language, the awestruck experts would surely award the human species an A+.

Thinking and Language

6. What is the relationship between thinking and language?

Thinking and language intricately intertwine. Asking which comes first is one of psychology's chicken-and-egg questions. Do our ideas come first and we wait for words to name them? Or are our thoughts conceived in words and therefore unthinkable without them?

Language Influences Thinking

Linguist Benjamin Lee Whorf contended that language determines the way we think. According to Whorf's (1956) **linguistic determinism** hypothesis, different languages impose different conceptions of reality: "Language itself shapes a man's basic ideas." The Hopi, Whorf noted, have no past tense for their verbs. Therefore, he contended, a Hopi could not so readily *think* about the past.

Whorf's hypothesis would probably not occur to people who speak only one language and view that language as simply a vehicle for thought. But to those who speak two dissimilar languages, such as English and Japanese, it seems obvious that a person thinks differently in different languages (Brown, 1986). Unlike English, which has a rich vocabulary for self-focused emotions such as anger, Japanese has many words for interpersonal emotions such as sympathy (Markus & Kitayama, 1991). Many bilinguals report that they have a different sense of self, depending on which language they are using (Matsumoto, 1994). After emigrating from Asia to North America, bilinguals may even reveal different personalities when taking the same personality test in their two languages (Dinges & Hull, 1992). Michael Ross, Elaine Xun, and Anne Wilson (2002) demonstrated this by inviting China-born, bilingual University of Waterloo students to describe themselves in English or Chinese. When describing themselves in English, their self-descriptions were typically Canadian: They expressed mostly positive self-statements and moods. When responding in Chinese, they were typically Chinese: They reported more agreement with Chinese values and roughly equal positive and negative self-statements and moods. Their language use seemed to shape how they thought of themselves.

"All words are pegs to hang ideas on."

Henry Ward Beecher,
Proverbs from Plymouth Pulpit, 1887

Learn a language and you learn about a culture. When a language becomes extinct—the likely fate of most of the world's 6000 remaining languages—the world loses the culture and thinking that hang on that language. "To destroy a people, destroy their language," observed poet Joy Harjo.

But to say that language *determines* the way we think is much too strong. A Papua New Guinean without our words for shapes and colors nevertheless perceives them much as we do (Rosch, 1974). Our words do *influence* what we think (Hardin & Banaji, 1993; Özgen & Davies, 2002). Whether living in Britain or New Guinea, people use their language when classifying and remembering colors (Davidoff & others,

"Language is not a straight jacket."

Psychologist Lila Gleitman, American Association
for the Advancement of Science Convention, 2002

1999). If English is your native language, imagine that while viewing three colors you called two of them "yellow" and one of them "blue." Later you would likely see and recall the yellows as being more similar. People in the Berinmo tribe, which has different words for two shades of yellow, would better recall the distinctions between the two yellows.

Consider, too, that people use generic pronouns selectively, as in "the doctor . . . he" and "the secretary . . . she" (MacKay, 1983). If *he* and *his* were truly gender-free, we shouldn't skip a beat when hearing that "a nurse must answer his calls" or that "man, like other mammals, nurses his young." That we are startled indicates that *his* carries a gender connotation that clashes with our idea of *nurse*.

To expand language is to expand the ability to think. In young children, thinking develops hand in hand with language (Gopnik & Meltzoff, 1986). And what is true for preschoolers is true for everyone: *It pays to increase your word power.* That's why most textbooks, including this one, introduce new words—to teach new ideas and new ways of thinking.

Increased word power helps explain what McGill University researcher Wallace Lambert (1992; Lambert & others, 1993) calls the "bilingual advantage." Bilingual children, who learn to inhibit their unspoken language, can better inhibit their attention to irrelevant information. If asked to say whether a sentence is grammatically correct ("Why is the cat barking so loudly?") they can more efficiently focus on the grammar alone (Bialystok, 2001).

Lambert helped devise a Canadian program that enables English-speaking children to be immersed in French. (From 1981 to 1999, the number of non-Quebec Canadian children immersed in French rose from 65,000 to 280,000 [Commissioner, 1999].) For most of their first three years in school, the English-speaking children are taught entirely in French, and thereafter gradually shift by the end of their schooling to classes mostly in English. Not surprisingly, the children attain a natural French fluency unrivaled by other methods of language teaching. Moreover, compared with similarly capable children in control conditions, they do so without detriment to their English fluency, and with increased aptitude scores, math scores, and appreciation for French-Canadian culture (Genesee & Gándara, 1999).

So, for English-speaking Canadians, immersion followed by bilingual education pays dividends. Does bilingual education for children in a linguistic minority also pay dividends? Advocates of "English-only" education doubt it. They argue that bilingual programs are expensive, ineffective, and detrimental to non–English-speaking children's assimilation into their English-based cultures (Porter, 1998). But some studies find that such children benefit from bilingual education, if in "two-way" schools where they, together with English-speaking children, experience half their classes in English and half in their native language. Compared with non–English-speaking children dropped into English-only schools, those in the two-way schools tend to develop higher self-esteem. They drop out less frequently. And they eventually attain higher levels of academic achievement and English proficiency (August & Hakuta, 1998; Padilla & Benavides, 1992; Thomas & Collier, 1998).

Increasing word power through sign language has also had great benefits for deaf people, who for thousands of years were viewed as incompetent to inherit property, marry, be educated, or have challenging work (Sacks, 1990). Since the spread of signed instruction, Deaf people, when exposed to signing as preschoolers and then schooled in their language, become literate. It is never easy to learn one native language and then have to read and write another, such as English. Nevertheless, deaf children with native sign fluency—learned, for example, as children of signing Deaf parents—outperform other signing deaf children on measures of intelligence and academic achievement (Isham & Kamin, 1993). Whether we are Deaf or hearing, language transforms experience. Language connects us to the past and the future. Language fuels our imagination. Language links us to one another.

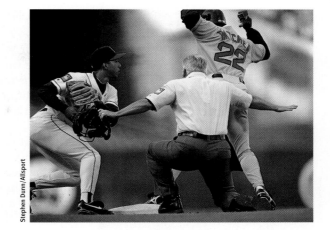

Stephen Dunn/Allsport

A safe sign We have outfielder William Hoy to thank for baseball sign language. The first deaf player to join the major leagues (1892), he invented hand signals for "Strike!" "Safe!" (shown here) and "Yerr Out!" (Pollard, 1992). Such gestures worked so well that referees in all sports now use invented signs, and fans are fluent in sports sign language.

Many native English speakers, including most Americans, are monolingual. Most humans are bilingual or multilingual. Does monolingualism limit people's ability to comprehend the thinking of other cultures?

Mental practice Before each turn at bat during his 70–home-run season, Mark McGwire would imagine the pitcher throwing the baseball, imagine how the ball would move, and "imagine smashing the ball with his Paul Bunyan swing" (Olney, 1998).

A thoughtful art Playing the piano engages thinking without language. In the absence of a piano, mental practice can sustain one's skill.

Thinking in Images

When you are alone, do you talk to yourself? Is "thinking" simply conversing with yourself? Without a doubt, words convey ideas. But aren't there times when ideas precede words? To turn on the cold water in your bathroom, in which direction do you turn the handle? To answer this question, you probably thought not in words but with procedural memory—a mental picture of how you do it. Indeed, we often think in images. Artists think in images. So do composers, poets, mathematicians, athletes, and scientists. Albert Einstein reported that he achieved some of his greatest insights through visual images and later put them into words.

Pianist Liu Chi Kung showed the value of thinking in images. One year after placing second in the 1958 Tchaikovsky piano competition, Liu was imprisoned during China's cultural revolution. Soon after his release, after seven years without touching a piano, he was back on tour, the critics judging his musicianship better than ever. How did he continue to develop without practice? "I did practice," said Liu, "every day. I rehearsed every piece I had ever played, note by note, in my mind" (Garfield, 1986).

Athletes in many fields now supplement physical with mental practice. For Olympic athletes, "mental practice has become a standard part of training," reports Richard Suinn (1997). Golf great Jack Nicklaus has said that he would "watch a movie" in his head before each shot. In a laboratory test, Georgia Nigro (1984) demonstrated the wisdom of mental practice. She had people actually throw darts 24 times at a target, then had half the people throw 24 darts mentally, and, finally, had everyone throw another 24 darts. Only those who had mentally practiced showed any improvement.

Young members of the U.S. Figure Skating Association have exhibited similar improvement in their performance ratings for jumps and spins following mental practice while listening to their skating music (Garza & Feltz, 1998). And several experiments on mental practice and basketball foul shooting have found comparable benefits. In one such experiment (Savoy & Beitel, 1996), conducted with the University of Tennessee women's team over 35 games, the team's free-throw shooting increased from approximately 52 percent in games following standard physical practice to some 65 percent after mental practice. During the mental practice, players repeatedly imagined making foul shots under various conditions, including being "trash-talked" by their opposition. The experiment's dramatic conclusion occurred when Tennessee won the national championship game in overtime, thanks in part to their foul shooting.

Mental rehearsal can also help you achieve an academic goal. In one study, Shelley Taylor and her UCLA colleagues (1998) engaged introductory psychology students who were a week away from facing a midterm exam. Some were told to visualize themselves scanning the posted grade list, seeing their A, beaming with joy, and feeling proud. Repeating this "outcome simulation" 5 minutes each day until the exam had little effect, adding only 2 points to their exam scores, compared with scores of student counterparts not engaging in any mental simulation. But the researchers had another group visualize themselves effectively studying—reading the chapters, going over notes, eliminating distractions, declining an offer to go out. Repeating this "process simulation" for 5 minutes each day had a beneficial effect. Compared with the control students, this second group of students began studying sooner, spent more time at it, and beat the control group average by 8 points. From such experiments, the researchers conclude that it is better to spend your fantasy time planning how to get somewhere than to dwell on the imagined destination.

More evidence of thinking without language comes from earlier chapters: Much of our information processing occurs outside of consciousness, beyond language. Inside the ever-active brain, many streams of activity flow in parallel, function automatically, are remembered implicitly, and only occasionally surface as conscious words. "Thinking lite," this unconscious processing has been called—"one-fourth the effort of regular thinking." So, yes, there certainly is cognition without language.

What, then, should we say about the relationship between thinking and language? As we have seen, language does influence our thinking. But if thinking did not also affect language, there would never be any new words. And new words and new combinations of old words express new ideas. The basketball term *slam dunk* was coined after the act itself had become fairly common. So, let us say that *thinking affects our language, which then affects our thought.*

Psychological research on thinking and language mirrors the mixed views of our species by those in fields such as literature and religion. The human mind is simultaneously capable of striking intellectual failures and of vast intellectual power. Some misjudgments have disastrous consequences, so we do well to appreciate our capacity for error. Yet our heuristics often serve us well, and they certainly are efficient. Moreover, our ingenuity at problem solving and our extraordinary power of language surely, among the animals, rank humankind as almost "infinite in faculties."

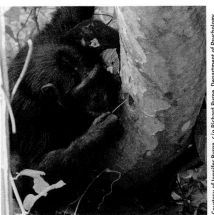

The interplay of thought and language The traffic runs both ways between thinking and language. Thinking affects our language, which affects our thought.

Elizabeth Crews/The Image Works

---

rehearse it!

7. Children progress from babbling to one-word communications and then to sentences of two words. The one-word stage of speech development is usually reached at about
   a. 4 months.   c. 1 year.
   b. 6 months.   d. 2 years.

8. B. F. Skinner believed that we learn language the same way we learn other behaviors—through association, imitation, and reinforcement. Skinner's behaviorist view is most helpful in explaining
   a. the onset of babbling.
   b. the speech behavior of deaf infants.
   c. the seemingly effortless mastery of grammatical rules by very young children.

   d. why children learn their household's language.

9. According to Noam Chomsky, we are biologically prepared to acquire language and are born with a readiness to learn the grammatical rules of the language we hear or see. He believes all we need to acquire language is
   a. instruction in grammar.
   b. exposure to language in early childhood.
   c. reinforcement for babbling and other early verbal behaviors.
   d. imitation and drill.

10. Benjamin Lee Whorf proposed that our language determines the way we perceive and think about the world.

Although we now know that language influences, rather than determines, our thinking, Whorf's hypothesis does help explain why
a. a person who learns a second language thinks differently in that language.
b. children have a built-in readiness to learn grammatical rules.
c. children's babbling contains sounds not found in the languages spoken in their homes.
d. artists, athletes, and others are able to think in visual images.

Answers can be found in Appendix C.

Animal Thinking and Language

7. Do animals—in some sense we can identify with—think? Do they even exhibit language?

If in our use of language we humans are, as the psalmist long ago rhapsodized, "little lower than God," where do other animals fit in the scheme of things? Are they "little lower than human"? In part, the answer lies in the extent to which animals share our capacity for thinking and language.

Do Animals Think?

Animals, especially the great apes, display remarkable capacities for thinking. They can, for example, form concepts. After monkeys learn to classify cats and dogs, certain frontal lobe neurons in their brains fire in response to new "catlike" images, others to new "doglike" images (Freedman & others, 2001). Pigeons—mere bird-brains—can sort objects according to their similarity. Shown pictures of cars, cats, chairs, and flowers, they readily learn to identify the categories. Shown a picture of a never-before-seen chair, the pigeon will reliably peck a key that represents "chairs" (Wasserman, 1995).

Chimpanzee inventiveness A wild chimpanzee shows ingenuity by using a stick to fish for ants living in the tree.

Courtesy of Jennifer Byrne, c/o Richard Byrne, Department of Psychology, University of St. Andrews, Scotland

Chimpanzee culture On the western bank of one Ivory Coast river, a mother uses a stone hammer to open a nut while a youngster watches. On the river's other side, a few miles away, chimps have not learned this trick.

We aren't the only creatures that display insight. German psychologist Wolfgang Köhler (1925) observed apparent insight while studying chimpanzees placed on an island off the coast of Africa. In one experiment with a caged chimp named Sultan, Köhler placed a piece of fruit and a long stick well beyond reach, and a short stick inside the cage. Spying the short stick, Sultan grabbed it and tried to reach the fruit. But the stick, by design, was too short. After several unsuccessful attempts, Sultan dropped the stick and paused to survey the situation. Then suddenly, as if thinking "Aha!" he jumped up, seized the short stick again, and used it to pull in the longer stick—which he then used to reach the fruit. Sultan's actions displayed animal cognition, claimed Köhler, and showed that there is more to learning than conditioning.

Thanks to problem solving shaped by reinforcement, forest-dwelling chimpanzees have become natural tool users (Boesch-Achermann & Boesch, 1993). They can select appropriate branches or stones to use as hammers in cracking nuts. They can also break off a reed or a stick, strip the twigs and leaves, carry it to a termite mound, fish for termites by twisting it just so, and then carefully remove it without scraping off many termites. One anthropologist, trying to mimic the chimpanzee's deft termite fishing, failed miserably.

Researchers have found at least 39 local customs related to chimp tool use, grooming, and courtship (Whiten & Boesch, 2001). One group may slurp ants directly from the stick, while another group plucks them off individually. One group may break nuts with a stone hammer, another with a wooden hammer. Such group differences, along with differing dialects and hunting styles, occur within subspecies and thus seem not to be genetic. Rather, they are the chimpanzee equivalent of cultural diversity. Like humans, chimpanzees—often younger ones—invent customs and pass them on to their peers and offspring. So do orangutans (van Schaik & others, 2003).

Do Animals Exhibit Language?

Without doubt, animals communicate. Vervet monkeys have different alarm cries for different predators: a barking call for a leopard, a cough for an eagle, and a chuttering for a snake. Hearing the leopard alarm, other vervets climb the nearest tree. Hearing the eagle alarm, they rush into the bushes. Hearing the snake chutter, they stand up and scan the ground (Byrne, 1991). Whales also communicate, with clicks and wails. And honeybees do a dance that informs other bees of the direction and distance of the food source. The question is, however, do animals' communications make up a language?

Smart bird brain Alex, an African gray parrot trained and tested by University of Arizona professor Irene Pepperberg (2002), displays numerical competence when shown novel assortments of objects. Asked, for example, "How many red blocks?" or "How many green balls?" Alex, with a brain the size of a walnut, answers correctly more than 80 percent of the time.

THE CASE OF THE APES The greatest challenge to humanity's claim to be the only language-using species has come from reports of apes that "talk" with people. Genetically speaking, our closest relatives are the chimpanzees, and the chimpanzees' closest relatives are not other apes, but us (Sagan & Druyan, 1992). Knowing that chimpanzees could not vocalize more than a few words, University of Nevada researchers Allen Gardner and Beatrix Gardner (1969) tried to teach sign language words to a chimpanzee named Washoe, as though she were a deaf human child. After four years, Washoe could use 132 signs. At age 32, Washoe had a vocabulary of 181 signs (Sanz & others, 1998). The Gardners' announcement of the success of their efforts aroused enormous scientific and public interest. One *New York Times* reporter, having learned American sign language from his Deaf parents, visited

Seeing a doll floating in her water, Washoe signed, "Baby in my drink."

Washoe and exclaimed, "Suddenly I realized I was conversing with a member of another species in my native tongue."

Human language may have evolved from gestured communications (Corballis, 1999, 2002). If so, it is no wonder that our ape relatives have produced many gestured words but few spoken words. It is no wonder that gestures survive as part of hearing people's speech (even when talking on the phone!). It is no wonder that signing so readily develops among deaf people as an alternative to speech. It is no wonder that congenitally blind people produce gestures similar to those of sighted people, even if they believe the listener is also blind (Iverson & Goldin-Meadow, 1998). It is no wonder that prohibiting gestures disrupts speech that has spatial content (for example, when describing an apartment layout). And it's therefore no wonder that gesturing lightens the cognitive load carried by speech. Gestures leave the speaker's mind less taxed and freer to remember recently learned information. People told not to gesture put more effort into communicating with words alone, and therefore have more trouble remembering lists of words or numbers (Goldin-Meadow & others, 2001). For both humans and apes, communication entails gestures.

Gesture researcher Robert Krauss (1998) recalls his grandfather telling of two men walking on a bitter winter day. One chattered away while the second nodded, saying nothing. "Schmuel, why aren't you saying anything?" the first friend finally wondered. "Because," replied Schmuel, "I forgot my gloves."

Further evidence of gestured "ape language" surfaced during the 1970s. Usually apes signed just single words, but sometimes they strung signs together to form intelligible sentences. Washoe signed, "You me go out, please." Apes even appeared to combine words creatively. Washoe designated a swan as a "water bird." Koko, a gorilla trained by Francine Patterson (1978), reportedly described a long-nosed Pinocchio doll as an "elephant baby." Lana is a chimpanzee that "talks" by punching buttons wired to a computer that then translates her punches into English. One day, she wanted her trainer's orange, but she had no word for *orange*. She did however know her colors and the word for *apple*, so she improvised: "?Tim give apple which-is orange" (Rumbaugh, 1977).

As reports of ape language accumulated, it seemed that they might indeed be "little lower than human." Granted, their vocabularies and sentences are simple, rather like those of a 2-year-old child, yet the apes do seem to share what we humans have considered our unique ability.

BUT CAN APES REALLY TALK? By the late 1970s, fascination with "talking apes" turned toward cynicism: Were the chimps language champs or were the researchers chumps? The ape language researchers were making monkeys out of themselves, said the skeptics, who raised the following arguments:

- Apes gain their limited vocabularies only with great difficulty. They are hardly like speaking or signing children, who effortlessly soak up dozens of new words a week. Saying that apes can learn language because they can sign words is like saying humans can fly because they can jump.
- Chimpanzees can make signs or push buttons in sequence to get a reward, just as Moscow circus bears can learn to ride unicycles. But pigeons, too, can peck a sequence of keys to get grain (Straub & others, 1979). No one says the pigeon is "talking."

But is this language? The ability of chimpanzees to express themselves in American Sign Language (ASL) raises questions about the very nature of language. Here, the trainer is asking, "What is this?" The sign in response is "Baby." Does the response constitute language?

Another "talking" chimpanzee Lana has learned to speak by punching word symbols on a computer keyboard. When she presses a key, the symbol lights up.

"[Our] view that [we are] unique from all other forms of animal life is being jarred to the core."

Duane Rumbaugh and
Sue Savage-Rumbaugh (1978)

- Apes can certainly use symbols meaningfully. But "Give orange me give eat orange me eat orange . . ." is a far cry from the exquisite syntax of a 3-year-old (Pinker, 1995). To the child, "you tickle" and "tickle you" communicate different ideas. A chimpanzee might sign the phrases interchangeably.
- After training a chimp he named Nim Chimsky, Herbert Terrace (1979) concluded that much of chimpanzees' signing is nothing more than apes aping their trainers' signs.
- Presented with ambiguous information, people, thanks to their "perceptual set," tend to see what they want or expect to see. Interpreting chimpanzee signs as language may be little more than the trainers' wishful thinking, claimed Terrace. (When Washoe signed *water bird*, she perhaps was separately naming *water* and *bird*.)

"Chimps do not develop language," concludes Steven Pinker (1995). "But that is no shame on them; humans would surely do no better if trained to hoot and shriek like chimps, to perform the waggle-dance of the bee, or any of the other wonderful feats in nature's talent show."

In science as in politics, controversy can stimulate progress. The provocative claim that "apes share our capacity for language" and the skeptical rejoinder that "apes no use language" (as Washoe might have put it) have moved psychologists toward a greater appreciation of both apes' remarkable capabilities and our own. Everyone agrees: Humans alone possess language, if by the term we mean verbal or signed expression of complex grammar. If we mean, more simply, the ability to communicate through a meaningful sequence of symbols, then apes are indeed capable of language.

Although chimpanzees do not have our facility for language, their abilities to think and communicate continue to impress their trainers. After her second infant died, a depressed Washoe repeatedly asked "Baby?" and became withdrawn when told "Baby dead, baby gone, baby finished." Two weeks later, caretaker-researcher Roger Fouts (1992, 1997) had better news for Washoe: "I have baby for you." Washoe reacted to the signed news with instant excitement, her hair on end, swaggering and panting while signing over and again, "Baby, my baby." When Fouts then introduced the foster infant, Loulis, it took several hours for them to warm to each other, whereupon Washoe broke the ice by signing, "Come baby" and cuddling Loulis. In the months that followed, Loulis picked up 68 signs simply by observing Washoe and three other language-trained chimps.

Moreover, Washoe, Loulis, and the others now sign spontaneously. They ask one another to *chase, tickle, hug, come,* or *groom*. People who sign can actually eavesdrop on these chimp-to-chimp conversations with near-perfect agreement about what the chimps are saying, 90 percent of which pertains to social interaction, reassurance, or play (Fouts & Bodamer, 1987). The chimps are even modestly bilingual; they can translate spoken English words into signs (Shaw, 1989–1990).

More stunning is the discovery by Sue Savage-Rumbaugh and her colleagues (1993) that pygmy chimpanzees can learn to comprehend the semantic nuances of spoken English. Kanzi, one such chimp with the grammatical abilities of a 2½-year-old, happened onto language while observing his adoptive mother being language trained. Kanzi has behaved intelligently whether asked, "Can you show me the light?" or "Can you bring me the [flash]light?" or "Can you turn the light on?" Kanzi also knows the spoken words *snake, bite,* and *dog*. Given stuffed animals and asked—for the first time—to "make the dog bite the snake," he put the snake to the dog's mouth. For chimps as for humans, early life is the critical time for learning language. If raised without early exposure to speech or word symbols, the chimps are unable as adults to gain language competence (Rumbaugh & Savage-Rumbaugh, 1994).

Yes, trained apes' language capabilities are modest by human standards. Yet their cognitive powers remain impressive. If Kanzi "had a vocal tract, he would be talking," exclaimed Duane Rumbaugh (1994). Realizing this, we see

"Although humans make sounds with their mouths and occasionally look at each other, there is no solid evidence that they actually communicate with each other."

once again how animal research can increase our respect for the creatures studied. Believing that animals could not think, Descartes and other philosophers argued that they were living robots without any moral rights. Animals, it has been said at one time or another, cannot plan, conceptualize, count, use tools, show compassion, or use language (Thorpe, 1974). Today, we know better. We have seen primates exhibit insight, show family loyalty, communicate with one another, display altruism, transmit cultural patterns across generations, and comprehend the syntax of human speech. Accepting and working out the moral implications of all this is an unfinished task for our own thinking species.

"He says he wants a lawyer."

rehearse it!

11. *Insight* is defined as a sudden and often novel realization of a problem's solution. Of the examples discussed in this section, the problem-solving behavior that most closely resembled insight was
    a. Alex the parrot's answer to questions about colors and numbers.
    b. Sultan the chimpanzee's use of a short stick to pull in a long stick.
    c. Kanzi the chimpanzee's ability to understand subtle grammatical differences in English sentences.
    d. Washoe the chimpanzee's use of sign language to request food.

12. There is much controversy over whether apes can be taught to use language in the way that humans do. However, most researchers of ape sign language agree that apes can
    a. communicate through symbols.
    b. reproduce most human speech sounds.
    c. create new sentences and meanings.
    d. surpass a human 3-year-old in language skills.

Answers can be found in Appendix C.

INTELLIGENCE

So far, we have considered how humans, in general, think and communicate. But do we humans not differ from one another in our intellectual capacities? No controversy in psychology has been more heated than the question of whether there exists in each person a general intellectual capacity that can be measured and quantified as a number. School boards, courts, and scientists debate the usefulness and fairness of intelligence and aptitude tests. Should such tests be used to rank individuals and to determine whether to admit them to a particular college or to hire them in a particular job? Do groups differ in native intelligence?

Let's therefore consider: What is intelligence? How is it assessed? And to what extent does it result from nature (heredity) rather than nurture (environment)? Is intelligence testing society's best means of identifying those who would benefit from special opportunities? Or is intelligence testing a potent discriminatory weapon camouflaged as science?

The Origins of Intelligence Testing

8. When and why were intelligence tests created?

Intelligence is a concept intended to explain why some people perform better than others on cognitive tasks. Robert Sternberg (1997) speaks for many experts in viewing **intelligence** as the mental abilities needed to select, adapt to, and shape environments. Intelligent behavior reflects a capacity to learn from experience, to solve problems, and to reason clearly. To understand the concept of intelligence, it helps first to know the history of intelligence testing.

Alfred Binet: Predicting School Achievement

The modern intelligence-testing movement began at the dawn of the twentieth century when the French government passed a law requiring that all children attend school. Teachers soon faced an overwhelming range of individual differences. Some children, including many newcomers to Paris, seemed incapable of benefiting from

▶ **intelligence** the mental abilities needed to select, adapt to, and shape environments. It involves the abilities to profit from experience, solve problems, reason, and successfully meet challenges and achieve goals.

Alfred Binet "The scale, properly speaking, does not permit the measure of intelligence, because intellectual qualities . . . cannot be measured as linear surfaces are measured" (Binet & Simon, 1905).

"The IQ test was invented to predict academic performance, nothing else. If we wanted something that would predict life success, we'd have to invent another test completely."

Social psychologist Robert Zajonc (1984b)

the regular school curriculum and in need of special classes. But how could the schools objectively identify children with special needs?

The government was reluctant to trust teachers' subjective judgments of children's learning potential. Academic slowness might merely reflect inadequate prior education. Also, teachers might prejudge children on the basis of their social backgrounds. To minimize bias, France's minister of public education in 1904 commissioned Alfred Binet (1857–1914) and others to study the problem.

Binet and his collaborator, Théodore Simon, began by assuming that all children follow the same course of intellectual development but that some develop more rapidly. On tests, therefore, a "dull" child should perform as does a typical younger child, and a "bright" child as does a typical older child.

Binet and Simon set out to measure what came to be called a child's **mental age**, the chronological age typical of a given level of performance. The average 9-year-old has a mental age of 9. Children with below average mental ages, such as 9-year-olds who perform at the level of a typical 7-year-old, would struggle with schoolwork considered normal for their age.

To measure mental age, Binet and Simon developed varied reasoning and problem-solving questions that might predict school achievement, and they tried many of them out on Binet's two daughters. By then testing "bright" and "backward" Parisian schoolchildren on these questions, Binet and Simon succeeded: They found items that did predict how well the children handled schoolwork. Note that Binet and Simon made no assumptions about *why* a particular child was slow, average, or precocious. Rather, their test had a single practical purpose: to identify French schoolchildren needing special attention. Binet hoped the test would be used to improve children's education, but he also feared it would be used to label children and limit their opportunities (Gould, 1981).

Lewis Terman: The Innate IQ

Binet might have been dismayed to discover that the test he designed as a practical guide for identifying slow learners in need of special help would soon be used as a numerical measure of inherited intelligence. After Binet's death in 1911, Stanford University professor Lewis Terman (1877–1956) attempted to use Binet's test but found that the Paris-developed age norms worked poorly with California schoolchildren. So Terman revised the test. He adapted some of Binet's original items, added others, established new age norms, and extended the upper end of the test's range from teenagers to "superior adults." Terman gave his revision the name it retains today—the **Stanford-Binet**.

For such tests, German psychologist William Stern derived the famous **intelligence quotient**, or **IQ**. The IQ was simply a person's mental age divided by chronological age and multiplied by 100 to get rid of the decimal point:

$$IQ = \frac{mental\ age}{chronological\ age} \times 100$$

Thus, an average child, whose mental and chronological ages are the same, has an IQ of 100. But an 8-year-old who answers questions as would a typical 10-year-old has an IQ of 125.

Most current intelligence tests, including the Stanford-Binet, no longer compute an IQ. The original IQ formula works fairly well for children but not for adults. (Should a 40-year-old who does as well on the test as an average 20-year-old be assigned an IQ of only 50?) Today's intelligence tests therefore produce a mental ability score based on the test-taker's performance *relative to the average performance of others the same age*. As on the original Stanford-Binet, current tests define this score so that 100 is average, with about two-thirds of all people scoring between 85 and 115. Although there is no longer any intelligence *quotient*, the term "IQ" still lingers in everyday vocabulary as a shorthand expression for "intelligence test score."

Mrs. Randolph takes mother's pride too far.

What Is Intelligence?

9. Is intelligence a single general ability or several distinct abilities?

Reading all the conflicting ideas about intelligence can leave you feeling as Alice in Wonderland felt after reading "Jabberwocky": "Somehow it seems to fill my head with ideas—only I don't exactly know what they are." So let's see if we can refine the concept.

One General Ability or Several Specific Abilities?

You probably know some people with talents in science, others who excel at the humanities, and still others gifted in athletics, art, music, or dance. You may also know a talented artist who is dumbfounded by the simplest mathematical problems, or a brilliant math student with little aptitude for literary discussion. Perhaps you have wondered whether people's mental abilities are too diverse to justify labeling them with the single word *intelligence* or quantifying them with a number from some single scale. How might you test this idea?

To find out whether there might be a general ability factor that runs throughout our specific mental abilities, psychologists study how various abilities relate to one another. A statistical method called **factor analysis** enables researchers to identify clusters of test items that measure a common ability. For example, people who do well on vocabulary items often do well on paragraph comprehension, a cluster that helps define a verbal intelligence factor. Other clusters include a spatial ability factor and a reasoning ability factor.

Charles Spearman (1863–1945), who helped develop factor analysis, believed there is also a **general intelligence**, or *g*, factor that underlies the specific factors. Spearman granted that people often have special abilities that stand out. But he also noted that those who score high on one factor, such as verbal intelligence, typically score higher than average on other factors, such as spatial or reasoning ability. So there is at least a tendency for different abilities to come in the same package. Spearman believed that this commonality, the *g* factor, underlies all of our intelligent behavior, from navigating the sea to excelling in school.

Not so, says Howard Gardner (1983, 1999), a modern representative of the view that intelligence comes in different packages. He notes that brain damage may diminish one type of ability but not others. He observes that different abilities enabled our ancestors to cope with different environmental challenges (finding their way home, reading others' emotions, solving problems). And he studies people with exceptional abilities, including those who excel in only one. People with **savant syndrome**, for example, often score low on intelligence tests but have an island of brilliance—some incredible ability, as in computation, drawing, or musical memory (Treffert & Wallace, 2002). Many are also diagnosed with autism, which mostly

► **mental age** a measure of intelligence test performance devised by Binet; the chronological age that most typically corresponds to a given level of performance. Thus, a child who does as well as the average 8-year-old is said to have a mental age of 8.

► **Stanford-Binet** the widely used American revision (by Terman at Stanford University) of Binet's original intelligence test.

► **intelligence quotient (IQ)** defined originally as the ratio of mental age (*ma*) to chronological age (*ca*) multiplied by 100 (thus, IQ = *ma/ca* × 100). On contemporary intelligence tests, the average performance for a given age is assigned a score of 100.

► **factor analysis** a statistical procedure that identifies clusters of related items (called *factors*) on a test; used to identify different dimensions of performance that underlie one's total score.

► **general intelligence (*g*)** a general intelligence factor that Spearman and others believed underlies specific mental abilities and is therefore measured by every task on an intelligence test.

► **savant syndrome** a condition in which a person otherwise limited in mental ability has an exceptional specific skill, such as in computation or drawing.

"g is one of the most reliable and valid measures in the behavioral domain . . . and it predicts important social outcomes such as educational and occupational levels far better than any other trait."

Behavior geneticist Robert Plomin (1999)

Ethan Hill

Islands of genius: Savant syndrome
Leslie Lemke (far left) is blind and has never had a piano lesson. Yet he can play thousands of pieces flawlessly, even after a single hearing. At 14, several hours after hearing Tchaikovsky's *Piano Concerto No. 1* for the first time, he played it without hesitation.

Kim Peek (center), the inspiration for the character Raymond Babbit in the movie *Rain Man*, depends on his father for many of his daily needs. Yet Peek knows more than 7600 books by heart, as well as all U.S. area codes, Zip codes, and TV stations.

Alonzo Clemons (near left), despite a developmental disability, can create perfect replicas of any animal he briefly sees. His bronze figures have earned him a national reputation.

afflicts males, and about 4 in 5 people with savant syndrome are males. These individuals may have virtually no language ability, yet be able to compute numbers as quickly and accurately as an electronic calculator or to identify almost instantly the day of the week that corresponds to any given date in history (Miller, 1999).

Gardner (1998) also speculates about a ninth possible intelligence—"existential intelligence"—the ability "to ponder large questions about life, death, existence."

Using such evidence, Gardner argues that we do not have *an* intelligence, but instead have *multiple* intelligences, each relatively independent of the others. In addition to the verbal and mathematical aptitudes assessed by standard tests, he identifies distinct aptitudes for musical accomplishment, for spatially analyzing the visual world, for mastering movement skills (as in dance), and for insightfully understanding ourselves, others, and our natural environment. In simple words, you can think of these eight intelligences as word smarts, number smarts, music smarts, space smarts, body smarts, self smarts, people smarts, and nature smarts. As exemplars of these alternative intellects, Gardner offers poet T. S. Eliot, scientist Albert Einstein, composer Igor Stravinsky, artist Pablo Picasso, dancer Martha Graham, psychiatrist Sigmund Freud, leader Mahatma Gandhi, and naturalist Charles Darwin.

According to Gardner (1998), the computer programmer, the poet, the street-smart adolescent who becomes a crafty executive, and the point guard on the basketball team exhibit different kinds of intelligence. He notes,

> If a person is strong (or weak) in telling stories, solving mathematical proofs, navigating around unfamiliar terrain, learning an unfamiliar song, mastering a new game that entails dexterity, understanding others, or understanding himself, one simply does not know whether comparable strengths (or weaknesses) will be found in other areas.

A general intelligence score is therefore like the overall rating of a city—which doesn't give you much specific information about its schools, streets, or nightlife.

Wouldn't it be wonderful if the world were so just, responds intelligence researcher Sandra Scarr (1989), that being weak in any area would often be compensated by genius in some other area? Alas, the world is not just, for there remains some tendency for different skills to correlate. For example, people with mental disadvantages often have lesser physical abilities as well; Special Olympics gives them and others a chance to enjoy fair competition. Moreover, general intelligence scores predict performance on various complex tasks and in various jobs; *g* matters (Gottfredson, 2002a,b; Reeve & Hakel, 2002).

While Robert Sternberg (1985, 1999) agrees with Gardner's idea of multiple intelligences, he distinguishes more simply among three aspects of intelligence:

- *Analytical (academic problem-solving) intelligence*—assessed by intelligence tests, which present well-defined problems having a single right answer.
- *Creative intelligence*—demonstrated in reacting adaptively to novel situations and generating novel ideas.
- *Practical intelligence*—often required for everyday tasks, which are frequently ill-defined, with multiple solutions.

Spatial intelligence genius In 1998, World Checkers Champion Ron "Suki" King of Barbados set a new record by simultaneously playing 385 players in 3 hours and 44 minutes. Thus, while his opponents often had hours to plot their game moves, King could devote only about 35 seconds to each game. Yet he still managed to win all 385 games!

Courtesy of Cameras on Wheels

Traditional intelligence tests assess academic intelligence. They predict school grades reasonably well but do less well in predicting vocational success. People who demonstrate keen practical intelligence may or may not have distinguished themselves in school. Managerial success, for example, depends less on the academic abilities assessed by an intelligence test score (assuming the score is average or above) than on a shrewd ability to manage oneself, one's tasks, and other people. Today's millionaires had average college grades—"a 2.92 undergraduate grade point average"—contends a book ad for *The Millionaire Mind*.

Sternberg and Richard Wagner's (1993, 1995) test of practical managerial intelligence measures whether test-takers know how to write effective memos, how to motivate people, when to delegate tasks and responsibilities, how to read people, and how to promote their own careers. Business executives who score high on this test tend to earn higher salaries and receive better performance ratings than do those who score low. In a similar finding, Stephen Ceci and Jeffrey Liker (1986) report that racetrack fans' expertise in handicapping horses—a practical but complex cognitive task—is unrelated to their intelligence test scores.

Although Sternberg (1998, 1999) and Gardner (1998) differ on specific points, they agree that multiple abilities can contribute to life success. (Neither candidate in the 2000 U.S. presidential election had scored exceptionally high on college entrance aptitude tests, notes Sternberg [2000], yet both have been very successful.) They also agree that the differing varieties of giftedness add spice to life and challenges for education. Under Gardner's or Sternberg's influence, many teachers have been trained to appreciate the varieties of ability and to apply multiple intelligence theory in their classrooms. Evaluations of these programs are under way.

Emotional Intelligence

10. Is our ability to manage our own emotions and to empathize with others a form of intelligence?

Also distinct from academic intelligence is what Nancy Cantor and John Kihlstrom (1987) first called *social intelligence*—the know-how involved in comprehending social situations and managing oneself successfully. A critical part of social intelligence is what Peter Salovey and John Mayer (1990; Salovey & others, 2002) call **emotional intelligence**—the ability to perceive, express, understand, and manage emotions. Emotionally intelligent people are self-aware. They manage their emotions without being hijacked by overwhelming depression, anxiety, or anger. They can delay gratification in pursuit of long-range rewards, rather than being overtaken by immediate impulses. Their empathy enables them to read others' emotions. They handle others' emotions skillfully, knowing what to say to a grieving friend, how to encourage colleagues, and how to manage conflicts well. Simply said, they are emotionally smart, and thus they often succeed in careers, marriages, and parenting where other academically smarter (but emotionally less intelligent) people fail. One study, led by emotion researcher Carroll Izard (2001), assessed 5-year-olds' ability to recognize and label facial emotions. Even after controlling for verbal aptitude and temperament, the 5-year-olds who could most accurately discern emotions became 9-year-olds who easily made friends, cooperated with the teacher, and effectively managed their emotions.

Emotional intelligence is not necessarily related to academic aptitude. In extreme cases, brain damage may diminish emotional intelligence while leaving academic intelligence intact. Antonio Damasio, a University of Iowa neuroscientist known for his registry of more than 2000 brain-damaged patients, tells of Elliot, a man with normal intelligence and memory. Since removal of a brain tumor, Elliot has lived without emotion. "I never saw a tinge of emotion in my many hours of conversation with him," Damasio (1994) reported, "no sadness, no impatience, no frustration." Shown disturbing pictures of injured people, destroyed communities, and natural disasters, Elliot shows—and realizes he feels—no emotion. Like Mr.

"You're wise, but you lack tree smarts."

▶ **emotional intelligence** the ability to perceive, express, understand, and regulate emotions.

Emotional intelligence Some people, even if they don't score high on standard intelligence tests, are gifted at perceiving, understanding, and expressing emotions.

Spock, or the human-appearing android Data of *Star Trek: The Next Generation*, he knows but he cannot feel. Lacking emotional signals, Elliot's social intelligence plummeted. Unable to intuitively adjust his behavior in response to others' feelings, he lost his job. He went bankrupt. His marriage collapsed. He remarried and divorced again. At last report, he was dependent on custodial care from a sibling and a disability check.

Some scholars—including even multiple-intelligence man Howard Gardner (1999)—are concerned that concepts such as "emotional intelligence" stretch *intelligence* too far. It is wise to stretch the concept to include not only our processing of words, numbers, and logic, but also space, music, and information about ourselves and others, says Gardner. But let us also, he says, respect emotional sensitivity, creativity, motivation, and morality as important but different. Stretch a word to mean everything we prize and it will lose its meaning.

In defense of academic smarts—the *g* factor—researchers point to studies in which traditional intelligence scores *do* to some extent predict both occupational status and job performance (Brody, 1997; Schmidt & Hunter, 1998). For example, intelligence matters most in mentally demanding jobs. Meteorology more than meter reading requires intelligence to excel. However, once admitted to a vocation, those who become highly successful have other traits as well—they are conscientious, well-connected, and doggedly energetic. Thus, high intelligence does more to get you into a profession (via the schools and training programs that take you there) than it does to make you successful once there.

So it seems that the academic aptitude tapped by intelligence tests is indeed important. Yet our competence in everyday living requires much that traditional intelligence tests do not measure. We might, then, liken mental abilities to physical abilities. Athleticism is not one thing but many. The ability to run fast is distinct from the strength needed for power lifting, which is distinct from the eye-hand coordination required to throw a ball on target. A champion weightlifter rarely has the potential to be a skilled ice skater. Yet there remains some tendency for good things to come packaged together—for running speed and throwing accuracy to correlate, thanks to general athletic ability. Similarly, intelligence involves several distinct abilities, which cluster together in the same individual often enough to define a small general intelligence factor.

"I worry about [intelligence] definitions that collapse assessments of our cognitive powers with statements about the kind of human beings we favor."

Howard Gardner, "Rethinking the Concept of Intelligence," 2000

Creativity and Intelligence

11. What is creativity, and what fosters this ability?

Pierre de Fermat, a seventeenth-century mischievous genius, challenged mathematicians of his day to match his solutions to various number theory problems. He jotted his most famous challenge—his so-called last theorem, after mathematicians solved all his others—in a book alongside Pythagoras' formula: $a^2 + b^2 = c^2$. The equation has infinite integer solutions, such as $a = 3$, $b = 4$, $c = 5$. But there are no solutions, said Fermat, for similar higher order problems. Thus, $x^3 + y^3 = z^3$ has no integer solutions, nor does the 4th or 5th power sum. "I have a truly marvelous demonstration of this proposition, which this margin is too narrow to contain" (Singh & Riber, 1997).

For more than three centuries, the puzzle baffled the greatest mathematical minds, even after a $2 million prize (in today's dollars) was offered in 1908 to who-

Everyone held up their crackers as David threw the cheese log into the ceiling fan.

FURIOUS GEORGE

Imaginative thinking Cartoonists often display creativity as they see things in new ways or make unusual connections.

ever first created a proof. Like countless others, Princeton mathematician Andrew Wiles had pondered the problem for more than 30 years and had come to the brink of a solution. Then, one morning, out of the blue, the "incredible revelation"—the fix to the one remaining difficulty—struck him. "It was so indescribably beautiful; it was so simple and so elegant. I couldn't understand how I'd missed it and I just stared at it in disbelief for 20 minutes. Then during the day I walked around the department, and I'd keep coming back to my desk looking to see if it was still there. It was still there. I couldn't contain myself, I was so excited. It was the most important moment of my working life" (Singh, 1997, p. 25).

Wiles' incredible moment illustrates **creativity**—the ability to produce ideas that are both novel and valuable.

Studies of intelligence and creativity suggest that a certain level of aptitude is necessary but not sufficient for creativity. In general, people who do well on intelligence tests also do well on creativity tests. ("How many uses can you think of for a brick?") But beyond a certain level—a score of about 120—the correlation between intelligence scores and creativity shrivels. Exceptionally creative architects, mathematicians, scientists, and engineers usually score no higher on intelligence tests than do their less creative peers (MacKinnon & Hall, 1972; Simonton, 2000). So clearly there is more to creativity than what intelligence tests reveal. Studies of creative people suggest five other components of creativity (Sternberg, 1988; Sternberg & Lubart, 1991, 1992):

After picking up a Nobel prize in Stockholm, physicist Richard Feynman stopped in Queens, New York, to look at his high school record. "My grades were not as good as I remembered," he reported, "and my IQ was [a good, though unexceptional] 124" (Faber, 1987).

1. ***Expertise*** is a well-developed base of knowledge. "Chance favors only the prepared mind," observed Louis Pasteur. The more ideas, images, and phrases we have to work with, through our accumulated learning, the more chances we have to combine these mental building blocks in novel ways. Wiles' well-developed base of knowledge put the needed theorems and methods at his disposal.

2. ***Imaginative thinking skills*** provide the ability to see things in new ways, to recognize patterns, to make connections. Having mastered the basic elements of a problem, we redefine or explore the problem in a new way. Copernicus first developed expertise regarding the solar system and its planets and then redefined the system as revolving around the Sun, not the Earth. Wiles' imaginative solution combined two important but incomplete solutions.

3. ***A venturesome personality*** tolerates ambiguity and risk, perseveres in overcoming obstacles, and seeks new experiences rather than following the pack. Inventors, for example, have a willingness to persist after failures. Thomas Edison tried countless substances for his light bulb filament. Andrew Wiles says he labored in isolation from the mathematics community partly to stay focused and avoid distraction.

4. ***Intrinsic motivation*** is creativity's fourth component. As psychologist Teresa Amabile points out, "People will be most creative when they feel

▶ **creativity** the ability to produce novel and valuable ideas.

▶ **Wechsler Adult Intelligence Scale (WAIS)** the WAIS is the most widely used intelligence test; contains verbal and performance (nonverbal) subtests.

▶ **aptitude test** a test designed to predict a persons future performance; *aptitude* is the capacity to learn.

▶ **achievement test** a test designed to assess what a person has learned.

▶ **standardization** defining meaningful scores by comparison with the performance of a pretested "standardization group."

▶ **normal curve** the symmetrical bell-shaped curve that describes the distribution of many physical and psychological attributes. Most scores fall near the average, and fewer and fewer scores lie near the extremes.

motivated primarily by the interest, enjoyment, satisfaction, and challenge of the work itself—rather than by external pressures" (Amabile & Hennessey, 1992). Creative people focus not so much on extrinsic motivators—meeting deadlines, impressing people, or making money—as on the intrinsic pleasure and challenge of their work. Asked how he solved such difficult scientific problems, Isaac Newton reportedly answered, "By thinking about them all the time." Wiles concurred: "I was so obsessed by this problem that for eight years I was thinking about it all the time—when I woke up in the morning to when I went to sleep at night" (Singh & Riber, 1997).

5. ***A creative environment*** sparks, supports, and refines creative ideas. After studying the careers of 2026 prominent scientists and inventors, Dean Keith Simonton (1992) noted that the most eminent among them were in fact not lone geniuses. Rather, they were mentored, challenged, and supported by their relationships with colleagues. Such people often have the emotional intelligence needed to network effectively with peers. Even Wiles, a relative loner, stood on the shoulders of others and wrestled his problem with the collaboration of a former student.

Assessing Intelligence

12. What do intelligence tests measure, and by what criteria can we judge these tests?

How do we assess intelligence? Movie hero Forrest Gump's answer, "Stupid is as stupid does," catches the spirit of psychology's simplest answer: Intelligent is as intelligent does on an IQ test. In other words, intelligence is whatever intelligence tests measure. So, what are these tests, and what makes a test credible?

Recall that Lewis Terman and his colleagues recognized that items developed for Parisians did not provide a satisfactory standard for evaluating Americans. They revised the test and standardized the new version by testing 2300 native-born, white Americans of differing socioeconomic levels. Ironically, they then used this standard to evaluate immigrant groups and nonwhite Americans (Van Leeuwen, 1982). As a 6-year-old Romanian, David Wechsler was among the Eastern European immigrants of the early 1900s who took this test and were mistakenly classified as feeble-minded because they did not know their new culture. Many years later, Wechsler, then a psychologist, created what is now the most widely used intelligence test, the **Wechsler Adult Intelligence Scale (WAIS)**. After creating the **WAIS**, Wechsler developed the *Wechsler Intelligence Scale for Children (WISC)* for school-age children and still later a test for preschool children. The WAIS consists of 11 subtests, as illustrated in **FIGURE 9.8**. It yields not only an overall intelligence score, as does the Stanford-Binet, but also separate "verbal" and "performance" (nonverbal) scores. Striking differences between the two scores alert the examiner to possible learning problems. For example, a verbal score much lower than the same person's performance score might indicate a reading or language disability. The tests also provide clues to cognitive strengths a teacher or an employer might build upon.

Matching patterns Block design puzzles test the ability to analyze patterns. Wechsler's individually administered intelligence test comes in forms suited for adults (WAIS) and children (WISC).

Lew Merrim/Photo Researchers, Inc.

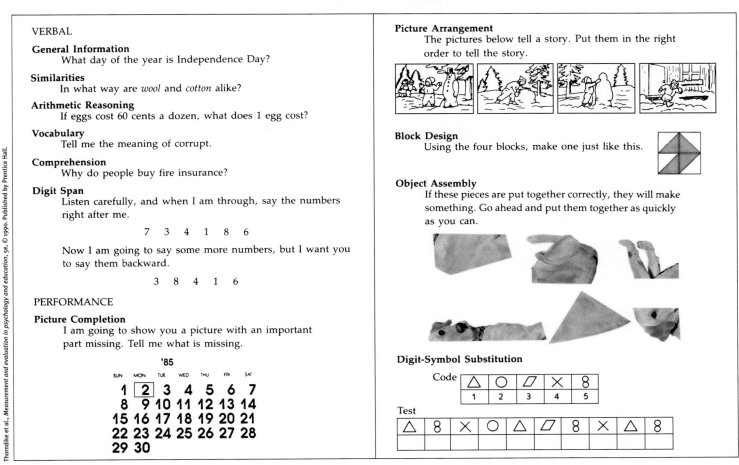

figure 9.8
Sample items from the Wechsler Adult Intelligence Scale (WAIS) subtests (From Thorndike & Hagen, 1977.)

Principles of Test Construction

To be widely accepted, psychological tests—whether tests of **aptitude** (the capacity to learn) or **achievement** (what has already been learned)—must meet three criteria: They must be *standardized*, *reliable*, and *valid*. The Stanford-Binet and Wechsler tests meet these requirements.

STANDARDIZATION The number of questions you answer correctly on an intelligence test would tell us almost nothing. To evaluate your performance, we need a basis for comparing it with others' performance. To enable meaningful comparisons, test-makers first give the test to a representative sample of people. When individuals later take the test following the same procedures, their scores can be compared with the standards defined by the sample. This process of defining meaningful scores relative to a pretested group is called **standardization**.

Standardized test results typically form a *normal distribution*, a bell-shaped pattern of scores that forms the **normal curve** (**FIGURE 9.9**). No matter what we measure—people's heights, weights, or mental aptitudes—scores often form a roughly symmetrical, bell-shaped distribution clustered around the average. On an intelligence test, we call this average score 100. As we move out from the average (toward either extreme), we find fewer and fewer people. Within each age group, the Stanford-Binet and the Wechsler tests assign any person a score according to how much that person's performance deviates above or below the average. As Figure 9.9 shows, a performance higher than all but 2 percent of all scores earns an intelligence score of 130. A raw score that is comparably *below* 98 percent of all the scores earns an intelligence score of 70.

figure 9.9
The normal curve Scores on aptitude tests tend to form a normal, or bell-shaped, curve. For example, the Wechsler scale calls the average score 100. To keep the average score near 100, such scales are periodically restandardized with current populations.

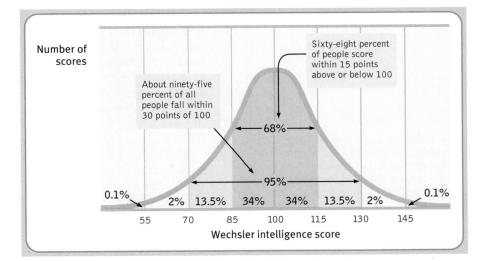

CLOSE-UP

Extremes of Intelligence

One way to glimpse the validity and significance of any test is to compare people who score at the two extremes of the normal curve. The two groups should differ noticeably, and they do.

In one famous project begun in 1921, Lewis Terman studied more than 1500 California schoolchildren with IQ scores over 135. Contrary to the popular notion that intellectually gifted children are frequently maladjusted because they are "in a different world" from their nongifted peers, Terman's high-scoring children, like those in later studies, were healthy, well adjusted, and unusually successful academically. When restudied over the next seven decades, most had attained high levels of education (Austin & others, 2002; Holahan & Sears, 1995). The group included many doctors, lawyers, professors, scientists, and writers, but no Nobel prize winners. (Terman did test one future Nobel laureate in physics, but excluded him from the gifted sample because his measured IQ wasn't high enough [Cassandro & Simonton, 2003].) Johns Hopkins University studies have similarly tracked math-

Michael O'Neill

A gifted child At age 10, Lenny Ng became the youngest child to score a perfect 800 on the SAT math test. At age 16, his math project won a $20,000 scholarship in the 1993 Westinghouse Science Talent Search. Contrary to the notion that such precocious children suffer socially, high-aptitude children are typically well adjusted. By his early twenties, Ng was a postdoctoral mathematics researcher at Stanford, after graduating with highest honors from Harvard, winning a national math competition, and then earning a Ph.D. from MIT.

ematically precocious youngsters into early scientific achievement (Lubinski & Benbow, 2000; Stanley, 1997). In another study following preteens who had aptitude scores among the top .01 percent (1 in

10,000), the rate of their later seeking doctoral degrees was more than 50 times greater than average (Lubinski & others, 2001).

These whiz kids remind one of Jean Piaget, who by age 7 was devoting his free time to studying birds, fossils, and machines; who by 15 began publishing scientific articles on mollusks; and who later went on to become the twentieth-century's most famous developmental psychologist (Hunt, 1993). Children with extraordinary academic gifts are sometimes more isolated, introverted, and in their own worlds (Winner, 2000). But most thrive.

At the other extreme of the normal curve are those whose intelligence test scores fall below 70. To be labeled as having **mental retardation**, a child must have both a low test score *and* difficulty adapting to the normal demands of independent living. Only about 1 percent

"Joining Mensa means that you are a genius. . . . I worried about the arbitrary 132 cutoff point, until I met someone with an IQ of 131 and, honestly, he was a bit slow on the uptake."

Steve Martin, 1997

RELIABILITY Comparing your test scores with those of the standardizing group still won't tell us much about you unless the test has **reliability**. A good test must yield dependably consistent scores. To check a test's reliability, researchers retest people using either the same test or another form of it. If the two scores generally agree, or *correlate*, the test is reliable. As an alternative, the researcher may split a test in half and see whether scores derived from odd and even questions agree. Assuming that one's basic ability has not changed between two adjacent testings, any score difference reflects "error" variation related to such things as luck, fatigue, and anxiety.

The higher the correlation between the *test-retest* or the *split-half* scores, the higher the test's reliability. The tests we have considered so far—the Stanford-Binet, the WAIS, and the WISC—all have reliabilities of about +.9, which is very high. When retested, people's scores generally match their first score closely.

VALIDITY High reliability does not ensure a test's **validity**—the extent to which the test actually measures what it is supposed to measure or predicts what it is supposed to predict. If you use an inaccurate tape measure to measure people's heights,

▶ **reliability** the extent to which a test yields consistent results, as assessed by the consistency of scores on two halves of the test, on alternate forms of the test, or on retesting.

▶ **validity** the extent to which a test measures or predicts what it is supposed to. (See also *content validity* and *predictive validity*.)

of the population meets both criteria, with males outnumbering females by 50 percent (American Psychiatric Association, 1994). As **TABLE 9.2** indicates, most individuals with mental retardation can, with support, live in mainstream society.

Mental retardation sometimes has a known physical cause. **Down syndrome**, for example, is a disorder of varying severity caused by an extra chromosome in the person's genetic makeup.

During the last two centuries, the pendulum of opinion about how best to care for people with mental retardation has made a complete swing. Until the mid-nineteenth century, they were cared for at home. Many of those with the most severe disabilities died, but people with milder forms of retardation often found a place in a farm-based society. Then, residential schools for slow learners were established. By the twentieth centu-ry, many of these institutions had become warehouses, providing residents with little attention, no privacy, and no hope. Parents often were told to separate themselves permanently from their impaired child before they became attached.

In the last half of the twentieth century, the pendulum swung back to normalization—encouraging people to live in their own communities as normally as their functioning permits. Children with mild retardation are educated in less restrictive environments, and many are integrated, or *mainstreamed,* into regular classrooms. Most grow up with their own families, then move into a protected living arrangement, such as a group home. The hope, and often the reality, is a happier and more dignified life.

table 9.2 Degrees of Mental Retardation

Level	Typical Intelligence Scores	Percentage of Persons With Retardation	Adaptation to Demands of Life
Mild	50–70	85%	May learn academic skills up to sixth-grade level. Adults may, with assistance, achieve self-supporting social and vocational skills.
Moderate	35–49	10%	May progress to second-grade level academically. Adults may contribute to their own support by laboring in sheltered workshops.
Severe	20–34	3–4%	May learn to talk and to perform simple work tasks under close supervision but are generally unable to profit from vocational training.
Profound	Below 20	1–2%	Require constant aid and supervision.

Source: Reprinted with permission from the Diagnostic and Statistical Manual of Mental Disorders, *Fourth Edition. Copyright 1994 American Psychiatric Association.*

▶ **mental retardation** a condition of limited mental ability, indicated by an intelligence score below 70 and difficulty in adapting to the demands of life; varies from mild to profound.

▶ **Down syndrome** a condition of retardation and associated physical disorders caused by an extra chromosome in one's genetic makeup.

your height report would have high reliability (consistency) but low validity. It is enough for some tests that they have **content validity**, meaning the test taps the pertinent behavior. The road test for a driver's license has content validity because it samples the tasks a driver routinely faces. Course exams have content validity if they assess one's mastery of a representative sample of course material.

Other tests are evaluated in terms of how well they agree with some **criterion**, an independent measure of what the test aims to assess. For some tests, the criterion is future performance. For example, aptitude tests must have **predictive validity** (also called *criterion-related validity*), which means they predict future achievement.

Are general aptitude tests as predictive as they are reliable? As critics are fond of noting, the answer is plainly no. The predictive power of aptitude tests is fairly strong in the early grades, but later it weakens. A better predictor of future grades is past grades, which reflect both aptitude and motivation. More generally, the best predictor of future behavior is a large sample of past behavior of the same sort.

▶ **content validity** the extent to which a test samples the behavior that is of interest (such as a driving test that samples driving tasks).

▶ **criterion** the behavior (such as future college grades) that a test (such as the SAT) is designed to assess; thus, the measure used in defining whether the test has predictive validity.

▶ **predictive validity** the success with which a test predicts the behavior it is designed to predict; it is assessed by computing the correlation between test scores and the criterion behavior. (Also called *criterion-related validity*.)

Genetic and Environmental Influences on Intelligence

13. Is intellect influenced more by heredity or environment?

Intelligence seems to run in families. But why? Are our intellectual abilities mostly inherited? Or primarily molded by our environment?

Few issues arouse such passion or have such serious political implications. Consider: If we mainly inherit our differing mental abilities, and if success reflects those abilities, then people's socioeconomic standing will correspond to their inborn differences. This could lead to those on top believing their intellectual birthright justifies their social positions.

If, on the other hand, mental abilities are primarily nurtured by the environ- ments that raise and inform us, then children from disadvantaged environments can expect to lead disadvantaged lives. In this case, people's standing will result from their unequal opportunities. For now, as best we can, let us set aside such political implications and examine the evidence.

Genetic Influences

Do people who share the same genes also share comparable mental abilities? As you can see from **FIGURE 9.10**, which summarizes many studies, the answer is clearly yes. In support of the genetic contribution to intelligence, researchers cite four sets of findings:

"There are more studies addressing the genet- ics of g than any other human characteristic."

Robert Plomin (1999)

- The intelligence test scores of identical twins are virtually as similar as those of the same person taking the same test twice (Lykken, 1999; Plomin, 2001). Fraternal twins, who typically share only half their genes, have much less simi- lar scores. Likewise, identical twins reared separately have similar scores— similar enough to lead twin researcher Thomas Bouchard (1996) to estimate that "about 70 percent" of intelligence score variation "can be attributed to genetic variation." Other researchers have offered estimates from 50 to 75 percent (Devlin & others, 1997; Neisser & others, 1996; Plomin, 2003).

- Brain scans reveal that identical twins have very similar gray matter volume. Moreover, unlike fraternal twins, their brains are virtually the same in areas associated with verbal and spatial intelligence (Thompson & others, 2001).

Smart scientist, smart mouse Working with Ya-Ping Tang and others, Princeton University biologist Joe Z. Tsien genetically engineered a strain of smart mice. Such work may shed new light on the biology of human intelligence.

- Are there genes for genius? Among the many genes that combine to influence intelligence, one, located on chromosome 6, has recently been identified. In two studies, the gene was carried by about one-third of children with very high intelligence scores but by only one-sixth of those with average scores (Chorney & others, 1998). Another project comparing the genes of people of high versus average intelligence has made slow progress in trying to identify the many genes that contribute to cognitive ability (Plomin, 2003).

- By inserting an extra gene into fertilized mouse eggs, researchers have produced smarter mice—mice that excel at learning and remembering the location of a hidden underwater platform or recognizing cues that signal impending shock (Tsien, 2000). The gene engineers a neural receptor involved in memory.

But there is also some evidence pointing to an effect of environment. Fraternal twins, who are genetically no more alike than any other siblings—but who are treated more alike because they are the same age—tend to score more alike than other siblings.

Seeking to disentangle genes and environment, researchers have also asked whether adopted children and their siblings, thanks to their shared environment, share similar aptitudes. During childhood, the intelligence test scores of adoptive siblings correlate modestly. Researchers have also compared the intelligence test scores of adopted children with those of (a) their biological parents, the providers of their genes, and (b) their adoptive parents, the providers of their home environment. Over time, adopted children accumulate experience in their differing adoptive families. So would you expect the family environment effect to grow with age and the genetic legacy effect to shrink?

If you would, behavior geneticists have a surprise for you. With age, mental similarities between adopted children and their adoptive families disappear as parental influence wanes; by adulthood, the correlation is roughly zero (McGue & others,

"I told my parents that if grades were so important they should have paid for a smarter egg donor."

figure 9.10
Intelligence: Nature and nurture The most genetically similar people have the most similar intelligence scores. Remember: 1.0 indicates a perfect correlation; zero indicates no correlation at all. (Data from McGue & others, 1993.)

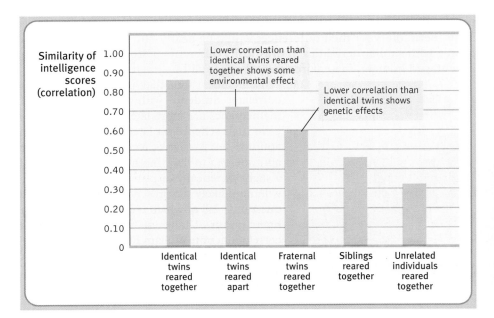

figure 9.11
Who do adopted children resemble? As the years went by in their adoptive families, Colorado Adoption Project children's verbal ability scores became modestly more like their *biological* parents' scores. (Adapted from Plomin & DeFries, 1998.)

Child-parent correlation in verbal ability scores

- Children and their birth parents
- Adopted children and their birth parents
- Adopted children and their adoptive parents

3 years   16 years

A check on your understanding of heritability: If environments become more equal, the heritability of intelligence would

a. increase.

b. decrease.

c. be unchanged.

(See page 330.)

1993). Such findings contradict the widely held belief that, as we accumulate life experience, the environmental influence on traits such as intelligence increases. In fact, the *opposite* seems true: With age, genetic influences become more apparent (Bouchard, 1995, 1996a). Adopted children's intelligence scores become more like those of their biological parents (**FIGURE 9.11**), and identical twins' similarities continue or increase into their eighties (McClearn & others, 1997; Plomin & others, 1997).

To say that the **heritability** of intelligence—the variation in intelligence test scores attributable to genetic factors—is 50 percent (or a tad more) does *not* mean that your genes are responsible for 50 percent of *your* intelligence and your environment for the rest. It means that we can attribute to heredity 50 percent *of the variation in intelligence* (among those studied). This point is so often misunderstood that I repeat: We can never say what percentage of an *individual's* intelligence is inherited. Heritability refers instead to the extent to which *differences among people* are attributable to genes. Heritability *never* pertains to an individual, only to why people differ.

Even this conclusion must be qualified, because heritability can vary from study to study. For example, environmental differences are more predictive of intelligence scores among children of less-educated parents—among whom family environments may vary widely (Rowe & others, 1999). To see why, consider humorist Mark Twain's proposal to raise boys in barrels to age 12, feeding them through a hole. Given the boys' equal environments, differences in their individual intelligence test scores at age 12 could be explained only by their heredity. Thus, heritability for their differences would be nearly 100 percent. But if we raise people with similar heredities in drastically different environments (barrels versus advantaged homes), the environmental effect will be greater.

"Selective breeding has given me an aptitude for the law, but I still love fetching a dead duck out of freezing water."

Remember, too, that genes and environment correlate. Students with a natural aptitude for mathematics are more likely to select math courses in high school and later to score well on math aptitude tests—thanks *both* to their natural math aptitude *and* to their math experience. If you have a slight genetically disposed intelligence edge, you will more likely stay in school, read books, and ask questions—all of which will amplify your cognitive brain power. Thanks to such gene-environment correlation, note William Dickens and James Flynn (2001), modest genetic advantages can be socially multiplied into big performance advantages. Our genes shape the experiences that shape us.

Environmental Influences

Genes make a difference. Even if we were all raised in the same intellectually stimulating environment, we would have differing aptitudes. But we have also seen that heredity doesn't tell the whole story. In ways sometimes predisposed by our genes, our life experiences matter.

Human environments are rarely as impoverished as the dark and barren cages inhabited by deprived rats that develop thinner-than-normal brain cortexes (see Chapter 3). Yet severe life experiences do leave marks on us. Biology and experience intertwine (**FIGURE 9.12**).

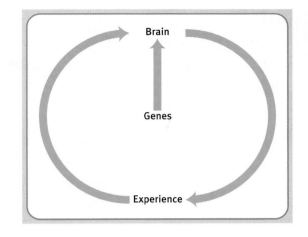

figure 9.12
figure 9.12
The plastic brain The brain is shaped by genes and experience, working together.

EARLY INTERVENTION EFFECTS In a destitute Iranian orphanage, Psychologist J. McVicker Hunt (1982) observed the dramatic effects of early experiences and demonstrated the impact of early intervention. The typical child Hunt observed there could not sit up unassisted at age 2 or walk at age 4. The little care the infants received was not in response to their crying, cooing, or other behaviors, so the children did not develop any sense of personal control over their environment. They were instead becoming passive "glum lumps." Extreme deprivation was bludgeoning native intelligence.

Aware of the benefits of responsive caregiving, Hunt began a program of "tutored human enrichment." For instance, he trained caregivers to play vocal games with infants. They first imitated the babies' babbling. Then they led the babies in vocal follow-the-leader by shifting from one familiar sound to another. Then they began to teach sounds from the Persian language.

The results were dramatic. By 22 months of age, all 11 infants who received these language-fostering experiences could name more than 50 objects and body parts. So charming had the infants become that most were adopted—an unprecedented success for the orphanage.

Hunt's findings testify to the importance of environment. There is no doubt that severe disadvantage takes a toll (Ramey & Ramey, 1992). And when the infant malnutrition associated with severe poverty is relieved with nutritional supplements, poverty's effect on physical and cognitive development lessens (Brown & Pollitt, 1996).

Do such findings indicate a way to "give your child a superior intellect"? Some popular books claim that with intensive preschool training such is possible, but most experts are doubtful (Bruer, 1999). Although malnutrition, sensory deprivation, and social isolation can retard normal brain development, the difference between normal and "enriched" environments matters less. There is no environmental recipe for superbabies, beyond normal exposure to sights, sounds, and speech. Sandra Scarr's (1984) verdict still is widely shared: "Parents who are very concerned about providing special educational lessons for their babies are wasting their time."

Hunt would probably have agreed with Scarr that extra instruction has little effect on the intellectual development of children from stimulating environments. But he was optimistic when it came to children from disadvantaged environments. Indeed, his 1961 book, *Intelligence and Experience*, helped launch Project Head Start in 1965. Head Start, a U.S. government-funded preschool program, serves 900,000 children, most of whom come from families below the poverty level. It aims to enhance children's chances for success in school and beyond by boosting their cognitive and social skills.

Does it succeed? Researchers study Head Start and other preschool programs by comparing children who experience the program with their counterparts who

"There is a large body of evidence indicating that there is little if anything to be gained by exposing middle-class children to early education."

*Developmental psychologist
Edward F. Zigler (1987)*

▶ **heritability** the proportion of variation among individuals that we can attribute to genes. The heritability of a trait may vary, depending on the range of populations and environments studied.

Getting a head start To increase readiness for schoolwork and expand children's notions of where school might lead them, Project Head Start offers educational activities. Here children in a classroom learn about colors and those on a field trip learn what firefighters do.

Answer to question on page 328: Heritability—variation explained by genetic influences—will increase as environmental variation decreases.

don't. Quality programs, offering individual attention, increase children's school readiness, which decreases their likelihood of repeating a grade or being placed in special education. Generally, the aptitude benefits dissipate over time (reminding us that life experience *after* Head Start matters, too). Psychologist Edward Zigler, the program's first director, nevertheless believes there are long-term benefits (Zigler & Styfco, 2001). High-quality preschool programs can provide at least a small boost to emotional intelligence—creating better attitudes toward learning and reducing school dropouts and criminality (Reynolds & others, 2001).

SCHOOLING EFFECTS Schooling itself is an intervention that pays dividends reflected in intelligence scores. Stephen Ceci and Wendy Williams (1997) have amassed evidence that schooling and intelligence contribute to each other (and that both enhance later income). High intelligence is conducive to prolonged schooling. But it is also true that intelligence scores tend to rise during the school year and drop over the summer months. They decline when students' schooling is discontinued. Completing high school elevates intelligence scores over those obtained by comparable children who leave school early. And consider this: Children whose birthdays just make the cutoff point for school entrance temporarily have higher intelligence scores than those born only slightly later, who are a year behind them in school (**FIGURE 9.13**).

figure 9.13
The schooling effect On a test of nonverbal intelligence administered by Sorel Cahan and Nora Cohen of Hebrew University, older children within a grade tended to score slightly higher than their younger classmates. The large gap between the end of one line and the beginning of the next reflects the extra year of schooling among children who are virtually the same age. (From Neisser, 1997.)

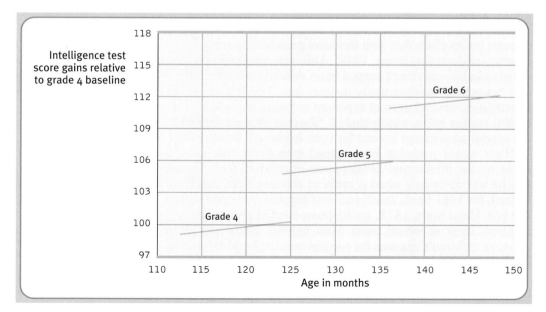

Group Differences in Intelligence Test Scores

14. How, and why, do ethnic and gender groups differ in aptitude test performance?

If there were no group differences in aptitude scores, psychologists could politely debate hereditary and environmental influences in their ivory towers. But there are group differences. What are they? And what shall we make of them?

Ethnic Similarities and Differences

Fueling this discussion are two disturbing but agreed-upon facts:

- Racial groups differ in their average scores on intelligence tests.
- High-scoring people (and groups) are more likely to attain high levels of education and income.

A statement by 52 intelligence researchers explains: "The bell curve for Whites is centered roughly around IQ 100; the bell curve for American Blacks roughly around 85; and those for different subgroups of Hispanics roughly midway between those for Whites and Blacks" (Avery & others, 1994). Comparable results come from other academic aptitude tests. In recent years, the Black-White difference has diminished somewhat, and among children has dropped to 10 points in some recent studies (Neisser & others, 1996). Yet the test score gap stubbornly persists.

There are differences among other groups as well. European New Zealanders outscore native Maori New Zealanders. Israeli Jews outscore Israeli Arabs. Most Japanese outscore the stigmatized Japanese minority, the Burakumin. And those who can hear outscore those born deaf (Braden, 1994; Steele, 1990; Zeidner, 1990).

Everyone further agrees that such *group* differences provide little basis for judging individuals. Women outlive men by six years, but knowing someone's sex doesn't tell us with any precision how long that person will live. Even Charles Murray and Richard Herrnstein (1994), whose writings drew attention to Black-White differences, reminded us that "millions of Blacks have higher IQs than the average White."

Swedes and Kenyans differ in complexion and language. The first is genetic, the second environmental. So what about intelligence scores?

As we have seen, heredity contributes to individual differences in intelligence. Does that mean it also contributes to group differences? Some psychologists believe it does (Herrnstein & Murray, 1994; Rowe, 1997). Some have speculated that different climates and survival challenges could have led to racial differences in aptitudes (Lynn, 1991, 2001; Rushton, 1990, 1998).

But we have also seen that group differences in a heritable trait may be entirely environmental, as in our earlier barrel-versus-home–reared boys example. Consider one of nature's experiments: Allow some children to grow up hearing their culture's dominant language, while others, born deaf, do not. Then give them an intelligence test rooted in that language, and (no surprise) those with expertise in the test's language will score highest. Although individual performance differences may be substantially genetic, the group difference is not.

Or consider this: If each identical twin were exactly as tall as his or her co-twin, heritability would be 100 percent. Imagine that we then separated some young twins and gave only half of them a nutritious diet, and that the well-nourished twins all grew to be exactly 3 inches taller than their counterparts—an environmental effect comparable with that actually observed in both Britain and America, where adolescents are several inches taller than their counterparts were a half-century ago (Angoff, 1987; Lynn, 1987). What would the heritability of height now be for our well-nourished twins? Still 100 percent, because the variation in height within the group would remain entirely predictable from the heights of their malnourished identical siblings. So even perfect heritability within groups would not eliminate the possibility of a strong environmental impact on the group differences.

Since 1850, the average Dutch man has grown from 5 feet 4 inches to today's 5 feet 10 inches (Bogin, 1998).

In prosperous country X everyone eats all they want. In country Y the rich are well fed, but the semistarved poor are often thin. In which country will the heritability of body weight be the greatest? (See page 333.)

The culture of scholarship The children of Indochinese refugee families studied by Nathan Caplan, Marcella Choy, and James Whitmore (1992) typically excel in school. On weekday nights after dinner, the family clears the table and begins homework. Family cooperation is valued, and older siblings help younger ones.

"Do not obtain your slaves from Britain, because they are so stupid and so utterly incapable of being taught."

Cicero, 106–43 B.C.

Despite the gender equivalence in intelligence test scores, males are more likely than females to overestimate their own test scores. Both males and females tend to rate their fathers' scores higher than their mothers', their brothers' scores higher than their sisters', and their sons' scores higher than their daughters' (Furnham 2001; Furnham & others, 2002a,b).

Might the racial gap be similarly environmental? Consider:

- Genetics research reveals that under the skin, the races are remarkably alike (Cavalli-Sforza & others, 1994; Lewontin, 1982). Individual differences within a race are much greater than differences between races. The average genetic difference between two Icelandic villagers or between two Kenyans greatly exceeds the group difference between Icelanders and Kenyans. Moreover, looks can deceive. Light-skinned Europeans and dark-skinned Africans are genetically closer than are dark-skinned Africans and dark-skinned Aboriginal Australians.
- Asian students outperform North American students on math achievement and aptitude tests. But this difference appears to be a recent phenomenon and may reflect conscientiousness more than competence. Asian students also attend school 30 percent more days per year and spend much more time in and out of school studying math (Geary & others, 1996; Larson & Verma, 1999; Stevenson, 1992).
- The intelligence test performance of today's better-fed, better-educated, and more test-prepared population exceeds that of the 1930s population—by the same margin that the intelligence test score of the average White today exceeds that of the average Black (Flynn, 1987, 1999). No one attributes the generational group difference to genetics.
- White and black infants have scored equally well on an infant intelligence measure (preference for looking at novel stimuli—a predictor of future intelligence scores [Fagan, 1992]).
- Race is hardly a neatly defined biological category. With increasingly mixed ancestries, more and more people are resisting racial categorization. (What race is Tiger Woods?)
- In different eras, different ethnic groups have experienced golden ages—periods of remarkable achievement. Twenty-five hundred years ago it was the Greeks and the Egyptians, then the Romans; in the eighth and ninth centuries, genius seemed to reside in the Arab world; 500 years ago it was the Aztec Indians and the peoples of Northern Europe. Today, people marvel at Asians' technological genius. Cultures rise and fall over centuries; genes do not. That fact makes it difficult to attribute a natural superiority to any race.

Gender Similarities and Differences

In science, as in everyday life, differences, not similarities, excite interest. Compared with the anatomical and physiological similarities between men and women, our sex differences are relatively minor. Yet it's the differences we find exciting. Similarly, in the psychological domain, gender similarities vastly outnumber gender differences, but most people find those differences more newsworthy. Girls are better spellers: At the end of high school, only 30 percent of males spell better than the average female (Lubinski & Benbow, 1992). Girls are more verbally fluent; more sensitive to touch, taste, and odor; and more capable of remembering words and the location of objects (Halpern, 2000). Boys outnumber girls at the low extremes and therefore in special education classes (Kleinfeld, 1998). Boys tend to talk later and to stutter more often. In remedial reading classes, boys outnumber girls three to one (Finucci & Childs, 1981). Among high school underachievers, boys outnumber girls by two to one (McCall & others, 1992).

MATH AND SPATIAL APTITUDES In math grades, the average girl typically equals or surpasses the average boy (ETS, 1992; Kimball, 1989). And on math tests given to more than 3 million representatively sampled people in 100 independent studies, males and females obtained nearly identical average scores (Hyde & others, 1990). But again—despite greater diversity within the genders than between them—group differences make the news. Although females have

World Math Olympics Champs After outscoring 350,000 of their U.S. peers, these boys all had perfect scores in competition with math whizzes from 68 other countries.

an edge in math computation, males in 20 of 21 countries scored higher in math problem solving (Bronner, 1998; Hedges & Nowell, 1995). For example, male high school seniors average 45 points higher on the 200- to 800-point SAT math test (literally meaning that they average 4 more correct answers on the 60-question test).

The score differences are sharpest at the extremes. Among 12- to 14-year-olds scoring extremely high on SAT math, boys have outnumbered girls 13 to 1, and within that precocious group the boys more often went on to earn a degree in the inorganic sciences and engineering (Benbow & others, 2000). In other Western countries, virtually all math prodigies participating in the International Mathematics Olympiad have been males. More female math prodigies have, however, reached the top levels in non-Western countries such as China (Halpern, 1991). And through 2002, of the 78 U.S. national spelling bee champions, 42 were girls.

The average male edge seems most reliable in tests like the one shown in **FIGURE 9.14**, which involve speedily rotating three-dimensional objects in one's mind (Collins & Kimura, 1997; Halpern, 2000). Such spatial ability helps when fitting suitcases into a car trunk, playing chess, or doing certain types of geometry problems.

Working from an evolutionary perspective, David Geary (1995, 1996) and Irwin Silverman and his colleagues (1992, 1998) speculate that skills in navigating within three-dimensional space helped our ancestral fathers in tracking their prey and making their way home. In contrast, the survival of our ancestral mothers was enhanced by keen memory for the location of edible plants—a legacy that lives today in women's superior memory for objects and their location.

In studies of more than 100,000 American adolescents, girls also modestly surpassed boys in memory for picture associations (Hedges & Nowell, 1995). And among nearly 200,000 students taking Germany's Test for Medical Studies, young women year after year have surpassed men in remembering facts from short medical cases (Stumpf & Jackson, 1994). (My wife, who remembers many of my experiences for me, tells me that if she died I'd be a man without a past.)

In the first 56 years of the Putnam Mathematical Competition—the Olympics of college math—all of the nearly 300 awardees were men (Arenson, 1997). In 1997, a woman broke the male grip by joining 5 men in the winner's circle. In 1998 Melanie Wood became the first female member of a U.S. math Olympics team (Shulman, 2000). Her training began at an early age: When mall-shopping with her then-4-year-old daughter, Melanie's mother would alleviate her child's boredom by giving her linear equations to solve.

Answer to question on page 331: Heritability—differences due to genes—will be greater in country X, where environmental differences in nutrition are minimal.

Which two circles contain a configuration of blocks identical to the one in the circle at the left?

Standard   **Responses**

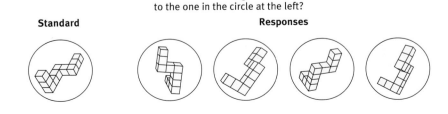

figure 9.14
The mental rotation test This is a test of spatial abilities. Which two responses show a different view of the standard? (From Vandenberg & Kuse, 1978.) (See page 334 for answers.)

Who wants to be a millionaire? In the first half-year of this once-popular American quiz show, only 1 in 10 contestants who made it to the hot seat were women. The qualifying questions—requiring a competitive, speed-based, sequential ordering of information—seemed to favor men. A different format, such as challenging contestants to detect facial emotions, might have favored women.

Answers to the mental rotation test on page 333: the first and fourth alternatives.

Do natural sex differences therefore explain why most mathematicians and more than 9 in 10 rated chess players and American architects, engineers, and mapmakers are men? Or why the world chess body has therefore found it necessary to hold separate competitions for men and women? Exposure to high levels of male sex hormones during the prenatal period does enhance spatial abilities (Berenbaum & others, 1995). But social expectations also shape boys' and girls' interests and abilities (Crawford & others, 1995; Eccles & others, 1990). Traditionally, math and science have been considered masculine subjects. Many parents send their sons to computer camps and give their daughters more encouragement in English. Thus, the male edge in math problem solving grows with age, becoming detectable only after elementary school.

EMOTION-DETECTING ABILITY Recall that part of emotional intelligence is empathic accuracy in reading others' emotions. Some of us are more sensitive to emotional cues. Robert Rosenthal, Judith Hall, and their colleagues (1979; McClure, 2000) demonstrated this by showing hundreds of people brief film clips of portions of a person's emotionally expressive face or body, sometimes with a garbled voice added. For example, after a two-second scene revealing only the face of an upset woman, the researchers asked whether the woman was criticizing someone for being late or was talking about her divorce. Rosenthal and Hall found that some people are much better emotion detectors than others are, and that women are better at it than men.

Some psychologists speculate that women's ability to detect emotions helped our ancestral mothers read emotions in their infants and would-be lovers, which may in turn have fueled cultural tendencies to encourage women's empathic skills. Such skills may, as noted in Chapter 4, explain women's somewhat greater responsiveness in both positive and negative emotional situations.

The Question of Bias

15. Are intelligence tests biased and discriminatory?

Knowing there are group differences in intelligence test scores leads us to wonder whether intelligence tests are biased. The answer depends on two very different definitions of *bias*. One meaning is that the tests detect not only innate differences in intelligence but also performance differences caused by cultural experiences (as when little David Wechsler scored low). In this sense, everyone agrees that intelligence tests are biased. An intelligence test measures your developed abilities, which reflect, in part, your education and experiences.

Another meaning of *bias* hinges on whether a test is less valid for some groups than for others—whether it predicts future behavior only for some groups of test-takers. For example, if the SAT accurately predicted the college achievement of women but not that of men, then the test would be biased. The near-consensus among psychologists, as summarized by the National Research Council's Committee on Ability Testing and the American Psychological Association's Task Force on Intelligence, is that the major aptitude tests are *not* biased in this statistical meaning of the term (Neisser & others, 1996; Wigdor & Garner, 1982). The predictive validity of the SAT or of a standard intelligence test is roughly the same for women and men, for Blacks and Whites, and for rich and poor. If an intelligence test score of 95 predicts C grades, the rough prediction usually applies equally to both genders and all ethnic and economic groups. If anything, the SAT overpredicts the college achievements of non-Asian minority students (Steele, 1997).

To predict school performance accurately, an aptitude test must mirror any gender or racial bias in school teaching and testing. Among students given a difficult math test by Steven Spencer and his colleagues (1997), men outperformed equally capable women—except when the women had been led to expect that women usually do as well as men on the test. Otherwise, the women apparently felt apprehensive, which affected their performance. Claude Steele, Steven Spencer, and Joshua Aronson (2002) have observed the same self-fulfilling effect of negative racial stereotypes. They found this **stereotype threat** phenomenon in black students' verbal aptitude scores, which were lower when they took tests under conditions designed to make black students feel threatened. Stereotype threat also explains why women have scored higher when given math tests without men being tested with them, and why Blacks have scored higher when tested by Blacks than when tested by Whites (Danso & Esses, 2001; Inzlicht & Ben-Zeev, 2000).

What then can we realistically conclude about aptitude tests and bias? The tests do seem biased in one sense—sensitivity to performance differences caused by cultural experience. But they are not biased in another—statistical prediction for different groups.

Does this mean the tests are discriminatory? Again, the answer can be yes or no. In one sense, yes, their purpose is to discriminate—to distinguish among individuals. In another sense, their purpose is to reduce discrimination by reducing reliance on subjective criteria for school and job placement—criteria such as whom you know, what you look like, or how much the interviewer happens to like "your kind of person." Many pioneers of mental testing saw themselves as social progressives who were sometimes uncovering abilities—diamonds in the rough—when few expected to find them. (The educational system is very good at finding those who score in the top 1 or 2 percent on intelligence-related tests and then offering a first-class education that may lead to a first-class job.) Banning aptitude tests would lead those who decide on admissions and jobs to rely more on other considerations, such as their personal opinions. Civil service tests, for example, were devised to discriminate more fairly and objectively, by reducing the political, racial, and ethnic discrimination that preceded their use.

Perhaps, then, our aim should be threefold. First, we should realize the benefits that Alfred Binet foresaw for

▶ **stereotype threat** a self-confirming concern that one will be evaluated based on a negative stereotype.

"Math class is tough!"

"Teen talk" talking Barbie doll (introduced February 1992, recalled October 1992)

J. Griffin/The Image Works

Untestable compassion Intelligence test scores are only one part of the picture of a whole person. They don't measure the abilities, talent, and commitment of, for example, people who devote their lives to helping others.

"Almost all the joyful things of life are outside the measure of IQ tests."

Madeleine L'Engle, A Circle of Quiet, 1972

What time is it now? On page 300, did you underestimate or overestimate how quickly you would finish the chapter?

tests of mental abilities—to enable schools to recognize who might best benefit from early intervention. Second, we must remain alert to Binet's fear that intelligence test scores may be misinterpreted as literal measures of a person's worth and fixed potential. And finally, we must remember that *intelligence test scores reflect only one aspect of personal competence.* Our practical intelligence and emotional intelligence matter, too, as do other forms of talent and character. The competence that general intelligence tests sample is important; it helps enable life success. But it is far from all-important. The carpenter's spatial ability differs from the programmer's logical ability, which differs from the poet's verbal ability. Because there are many ways of being successful, our personal and cultural differences—regardless of their origins—are variations on the human theme of adaptability.

rehearse it!

20. A current view is that about 50 percent of intelligence score variation among individuals can be attributed to heredity. The strongest support for heredity's influence on intelligence is the finding that
    a. identical twins, but not other siblings, have nearly identical intelligence test scores.
    b. the correlation between intelligence test scores of fraternal twins is higher than that for other siblings.
    c. unrelated people living in the same environment tend not to have similar intelligence test scores.
    d. children whose birthdays just make the cutoff point for school entrance temporarily have higher intelligence test scores than those born only slightly later.

21. The heritability of a trait may vary, depending on the range of populations and environments studied. To say that the heritability of intelligence is about 50 percent means that 50 percent of
    a. an individual's intelligence is due to genetic factors.
    b. the similarities between men and women are attributable to genes.
    c. the variation in intelligence within a group of people is attributable to genetic factors.
    d. intelligence is due to the mother's genes and the rest is due to the father's genes.

22. Within the limits set by heredity, experiences help shape intelligence. The experience that has the clearest, most profound effect on intellectual development is
    a. being enrolled in a Head Start program.
    b. growing up in an economically disadvantaged home or neighborhood.
    c. being raised in a very neglectful home or institution.
    d. being exposed to very stimulating toys and lessons in infancy.

Answers can be found in Appendix C.

chapter review

REVIEWING

Thinking, Language, and Intelligence

Our cognitive system receives, perceives, and retrieves information, which we then use to think and communicate, sometimes wisely, sometimes foolishly. In this chapter we have explored cognition—how we form concepts, solve problems, make decisions and judgments, use language, and exhibit intelligence.

THINKING

1. *What are the functions of concepts?*

Concepts simplify and order the world by organizing it into a hierarchy of categories. Concepts often form around prototypes, or best examples of a category. Matching objects and ideas with prototypes is an efficient way of making snap judgments about what belongs in a specific category.

2. *What strategies do we use to solve problems, and what obstacles hinder our problem solving?*

When faced with new situations for which no well-learned response will do, we may use such strategies as algorithms and heuristics. Sometimes the solution comes in a flash of insight. We do, however, face certain obstacles to successful problem solving. The confirmation bias predisposes us to verify rather than challenge our hypotheses. And fixations, such as mental set and functional fixedness, may prevent our taking a needed fresh perspective on a problem.

3. *How do heuristics, overconfidence, and framing influence our decisions and judgments?*

Our use of heuristics, such as the representativeness and availability heuristics, provides highly efficient but occasionally misleading guides for making quick decisions and forming intuitive judgments. Our tendencies to seek confirmation of our hypotheses and to use quick and easy heuristics can blind us to our vulnerability to error, a phenomenon known as overconfidence. And the way someone poses, or frames, a question affects our responses.

4. *How do our preexisting beliefs influence our decision making?*

We tend to show a belief bias in our reasoning, accepting as more logical those conclusions that agree with our beliefs. We also exhibit belief perseverance, clinging to our ideas because the explanation we accepted as valid lingers in the mind even after the basis for the ideas has been discredited. Yet despite our capacity for error and our susceptibility to bias, human cognition is remarkably efficient and adaptive. As we gain expertise in a field, we grow adept at making quick, shrewd judgments.

LANGUAGE

5. *When do children acquire language, and how do they master this complex task?*

Among the marvels of nature is a child's ability to acquire language. The ease with which children progress from the babbling stage through the one-word stage to the telegraphic speech of the two-word stage and beyond has sparked a lively debate concerning how they do it. Behaviorist B. F. Skinner proposed that we learn language by the familiar principles of association, imitation, and reinforcement. Challenging this claim, linguist Noam Chomsky argued that children are biologically prepared to learn words and use grammar. For mastery of grammar, the learning that occurs during life's first few years is critical.

6. *What is the relationship between thinking and language?*

Words convey ideas, and different languages embody different ways of thinking. Although the linguistic determinism hypothesis suggested that language *determines* thought, it is more accurate to say that language *influences* thought. Studies of the effects of using the generic pronoun *he*, for example, reveal the influence of words.

We sometimes think in images rather than in words, and we invent new words to describe new ideas. So we might say that our thinking affects our language, which then affects our thought.

7. *Do animals—in some sense that we can identify with—think? Do they even exhibit language?*

Evidence accumulates that primates at some level count, display insight, create tools, and transmit cultural innovations. Animals obviously communicate, but a vigorously debated issue is whether language is a uniquely human ability. Several teams of psychologists have taught various species of apes, including a number of chimpanzees, to communicate with humans by using sign language or by pushing buttons wired to a computer. Apes have developed considerable vocabularies. They string words together to express meaning and to make and follow requests. Skeptics point out significant differences between apes' and humans' facilities with language, especially in their respective abilities to order words grammatically. Nevertheless, these studies reveal that apes have considerable cognitive ability.

INTELLIGENCE

8. *When and why were intelligence tests created?*

Intelligence can be defined as the mental abilities needed to select, adapt to, and shape environments. In the early 1900s, French psychologist Alfred Binet and his colleague Théodore Simon developed questions in an attempt to measure mental age and thus to help predict children's future progress in the Paris school system. Lewis Terman of Stanford University adapted Binet's test and offered his Stanford-Binet as a way to direct people toward occupations for which they were deemed well suited. William Stern derived the intelligence quotient (IQ) to define performance on Terman's test.

9. *Is intelligence a single general ability or several distinct abilities?*

Psychologists agree that people have specific abilities, such as verbal and mathematical aptitudes. However, they debate whether a general intelligence (*g*) factor runs through them all. Factor analysis and studies of special conditions, such as the savant syndrome, have identified clusters of mental aptitudes. Howard Gardner has identified at least eight multiple intelligences, and Robert Sternberg specifies three components of intelligence: analytical, creative, and practical.

10. *Is our ability to manage our own emotions and to empathize with others a form of intelligence?*

Psychologists have recently described emotional intelligence as the ability to perceive, understand, and regulate emotions. Emotionally intelligent people are especially self-aware, and their empathy enables them to read others' emotions.

11. *What is creativity, and what fosters this ability?*

Intelligence correlates weakly with creativity. Increases in intelligence beyond a necessary threshold level are not linked with increased creativity. Creative people generally have a reasonable level of intelligence, but also a developed expertise, imaginative thinking skills, a venturesome personality, intrinsic motivation, and a creative environment.

12. *What do intelligence tests measure, and by what criteria can we judge these tests?*

The most widely used intelligence test is the Wechsler Adult Intelligence Scale (WAIS). All good tests—whether aptitude tests (designed to predict ability to learn a particular skill) or achievement tests (designed to assess current competence)—must be *standardized*, so that any person's performance can be meaningfully compared with others'. They must also be *reliable*, so they yield dependably consistent scores. And they must be *valid*, so they measure what they are supposed to measure *(content validity)* or predict, on the basis of a specified *criterion*, what they are supposed to predict *(predictive validity)*. Test scores usually fall into a bell-shaped distribution, the normal curve. The average score is assigned an arbitrary number (such as 100 on an intelligence test). Aptitude tests are highly reliable, but their validity is more modest (as judged by their predictions of academic success).

At the extremes of the bell curve are the gifted and those with mental retardation. One cause of mental retardation is Down syndrome.

13. *Is intellect influenced more by heredity or by environment?*

Studies of twins, family members, and adopted children point to a significant hereditary contribution to intelligence scores. Heritability, the variation in a trait that can be attributed to genes, pertains only to variation of a characteristic within a group, not to the origin of a characteristic in any individual. Heritability of intelligence increases as environmental differences decrease. These studies, plus others that compare children reared in extremely impoverished environments or in different cultures, indicate that life experiences also significantly influence intelligence test performance.

14. *How, and why, do ethnic and gender groups differ in aptitude test performance?*

Like individuals, groups vary in intelligence test scores. Hereditary variation *within* a group need not signify a hereditary explanation of *between*-group differences. In the case of the racial gaps in test scores, the evidence suggests that environmental differences are largely, perhaps entirely, responsible. Girls have tended to score higher on spelling tests and on reading others' emotions, boys on math and spatial relations tests. Psychologists debate evolutionary and cultural explanations of gender differences in specific abilities.

15. *Are intelligence tests biased and discriminatory?*

Aptitude tests aim to predict how well a test-taker will perform in a given situation. So they are necessarily "biased" in the sense that they are sensitive to performance differences caused by cultural experience. But *bias* can also mean what psychologists commonly mean by the term—that a biased test predicts less accurately for one group than for another. In this sense of the term, most experts do not consider the major aptitude tests to be significantly biased.

A CRITICAL THINKER'S REVIEW OF CHAPTER 9

You've now studied and reviewed **Thinking, Language, and Intelligence**. For even better retention, reflect on these concepts at a deeper level. If you need to refresh your memory of the six categories of critical thinking shown in parentheses below, see page 34. See if you can answer each of these questions in a short paragraph.

1. Your cousin Sam is a 22-year-old smoker who has refused to fly since the U.S. terrorist attacks of 9/11. Instead he drives himself on long road trips. What could you say to Sam to explain why his risk assessment doesn't make sense? (perspective taking)

2. If children are not yet even speaking, would they nevertheless benefit from having parents and other caregivers read to them? (creative problem solving)

3. If your dog barks at a stranger at the front door, does this qualify as *language*? What if the dog yips in a telltale way to let you know she needs to go out? (pattern recognition)

4. Joseph is a student at Harvard Law School. He carries a straight-A average, writes a small column for the *Harvard Law Review*, and will be working for a Supreme Court Justice the year after he graduates. Joseph's grandmother, Judith, is very proud of her grandson and says he is way more intelligent than she ever was. But Joseph is also very proud of Judith. As a young woman, Judith was imprisoned by the Nazis. When the war ended, she walked out of Germany, contacted an agency helping refugees travel to the United States, and began a new life as an assistant chef in her cousin's restaurant. According to the definition of intelligence in this chapter, why is Joseph not the only intelligent person in this story? (psychological reasoning)

5. Fiona wants to find out if leg strength predicts running speed. She correlates the muscular strength of the 10 fastest runners in her school with their 100-meter times—and finds only a weak correlation. But even if strong muscles do enable speed, we could have expected this result. Why? Is Fiona's study *valid*? (scientific problem solving)

6. The Romanos have enrolled their 2-year-old son, who they believe is gifted, in a special program that claims to "give your child a superior mind." Why is this endeavor of questionable value? (practical problem solving)

TERMS AND CONCEPTS TO REMEMBER

cognition, p. 293

concept, p. 293

prototype, p. 294

algorithm, p. 294

heuristic, p. 294

insight, p. 294

confirmation bias, p. 295

fixation, p. 295

functional fixedness, p. 295

representativeness heuristic, p. 296

availability heuristic, p. 297

overconfidence, p. 298

framing, p. 300

belief perseverance, p. 301

language, p. 302

babbling stage, p. 303

one-word stage, p. 304

two-word stage, p. 304

telegraphic speech, p. 304

linguistic determinism, p. 308

intelligence, p. 315

mental age, p. 316

Stanford-Binet, p. 316

intelligence quotient (IQ), p. 316

factor analysis, p. 317

general intelligence (*g*), p. 317

savant syndrome, p. 317

emotional intelligence, p. 319

creativity, p. 321

Wechsler Adult Intelligence Scale (WAIS), p. 322

aptitude test, p. 323

achievement test, p. 323

standardization, p. 323

normal curve, p. 323

mental retardation, p. 324

reliability, p. 324

validity, p. 324

Down syndrome, p. 325

content validity, p. 325

criterion, p. 325

predictive validity, p. 325

heritability, p. 328

stereotype threat, p. 335

To continue your study and review of Thinking, Language, and Intelligence, visit this book's Web site at www.worth-publishers.com/myers. You will find practice tests, review activities, and Web links for more information on topics related to Thinking, Language, and Intelligence.

chapter10

Motivation

"What's my motivation?" the actor asks the director. In our everyday conversation, "What motivated you to do *that*?" is a way of asking "What *caused* your behavior?" To psychologists, a **motivation** is a need or desire that *energizes* behavior and *directs* it toward a goal. Consider motivation in these situations:

▶ **motivation** a need or desire that energizes and directs behavior.

- *Hunger:* David Mandel (1983), a former Nazi concentration camp inmate, recalled how a starving "father and son would fight over a piece of bread. Like dogs." One father, whose 20-year-old son stole his bread from under his pillow while he slept, went into a deep depression, asking over and over again how his son could do such a thing. The next day the father died. "Hunger does something to you that's hard to describe," Mandel explained.
- *Sexuality:* In the Old Testament's *Song of Solomon* love poems, a woman and a man express their intense sexual passion for one another. "I am sick with love," she declares. "O that his left hand were under my head, and that his right hand embraced me!" He, in turn, pronounces her "delectable." "You are stately as a palm tree, and your breasts are like its clusters. I say I will climb the palm tree and lay hold of its branches."
- *Belonging:* At age 2½, "Baby Jessica" panicked as she was wrenched from her adoptive family—the only family she had ever known. A court ruling in this painful custody battle placed her with her biological parents hundreds of miles away. As social animals, we all have something of Jessica within us—a sense of who we belong to, of who is "us."
- *Achievement:* In Texas, a school truant officer discovers Alfredo Gonzales, age 14, picking fruit and sends him off to the first day of school in his life. Although placed at the lowest skill level and paddled for asking questions in Spanish—he knows no English—Alfredo decides "I could do better." Today he is a highly educated college administrator who works to motivate youth to wake up, as he did, to "their own potential, and to gain a desire to achieve it."

Although other identifiable motives exist (including thirst and curiosity), a close look at these four reveals the interplay between nature (the physiological "push") and nurture (the cognitive and cultural "pulls").

MOTIVATIONAL CONCEPTS

Before considering specific motives, let's step back and see how psychologists have understood motivation. Three perspectives have been influential: instinct theory (now replaced by the evolutionary perspective), drive-reduction theory (emphasizing the interaction between inner pushes and external pulls), and arousal theory (emphasizing the urge for an optimum level of stimulation). A fourth perspective, Abraham Maslow's hierarchy of needs, describes how some motives are, if unsatisfied, more basic and compelling than others.

Instincts and Evolutionary Psychology

1. What underlying assumption is shared by instinct theory and evolutionary psychology?

Early in the twentieth century, as the influence of Charles Darwin's evolutionary theory grew, it became fashionable to classify all sorts of behaviors as instincts. If people criticized themselves, it was because of their "self-abasement instinct." If they boasted, it reflected their "self-assertion instinct." After scanning 500 books, one sociologist compiled a list of 5759 supposed human instincts! Before long, this fad for naming instincts collapsed under its own weight. It was like "explaining" a bright child's low grades by labeling the child an "underachiever." To name a behavior is *not* to explain it.

"What do you think . . . should we get started on that motivation research or not?"

Same motive, different wiring
The more complex the nervous system, the more adaptable the organism. Both the woman and the weaverbird satisfy their need for shelter in ways that reflect their inherited capacities. The woman's behavior is flexible; she can learn whatever skills she needs to build a house. The bird's behavior pattern is fixed; it can build only this kind of nest.

To qualify as an **instinct**, a complex behavior must have a fixed pattern throughout a species and be unlearned (Tinbergen, 1951). Such behaviors are common in other species (recall imprinting in birds and the return of salmon to their birthplace). Human behavior, too, exhibits certain innate tendencies, including simple fixed patterns such as an infant's rooting and sucking. Most psychologists, though, view human behavior as directed by physiological needs *and* psychological wants.

Although instinct theory failed to explain human motives, the underlying assumption that genes predispose species-typical behavior remains as strong as ever. We saw this in Chapter 3's explanation of our human similarities. We also saw this in Chapter 7's discussion of our biological predisposition to learn certain aversions. And we will see this in later discussions of how evolution might influence our phobias, our helping behaviors, and our romantic attractions. Evolutionary psychology is now in its heyday.

Drives and Incentives

2. How does drive-reduction theory help us understand the forces that energize and direct some of our behavior?

When the original instinct theory of motivation collapsed, it was replaced by **drive-reduction theory**—the idea that a physiological need creates an aroused state that *drives* the organism to reduce the need by, say, eating or drinking. With few exceptions, when a physiological need increases, so does a psychological drive—an aroused, motivated state.

The physiological aim of drive reduction is **homeostasis**—the maintenance of a steady internal state. An example of homeostasis (literally "staying the same") is the body's temperature-regulation system, which works like a thermostat. Both systems operate through feedback loops. Sensors feed room temperature to a control device. If room temperature cools, the control device switches on the furnace. Likewise, if our body temperature cools, blood vessels constrict to conserve warmth, and we feel driven to put on more clothes or seek a warmer environment. Similarly, if the water level in our cells drops, sensors detect our need for water and we feel thirsty (**FIGURE 10.1**).

Not only are we *pushed* by our "need" to reduce drives, we also are *pulled* by **incentives**—positive or negative stimuli that lure or repel us. This is one way our individual learning histories influence our motives. Depending on our learning, the aroma of fresh roasted peanuts (or toasted ants), the sight of someone we find attractive, and the threat of disapproval can all motivate our behavior. Our internal needs energize and direct our behavior, but these external incentives do as well. The lure of money may energize us quite apart from any need-based drive.

figure 10.1
Drive-reduction theory

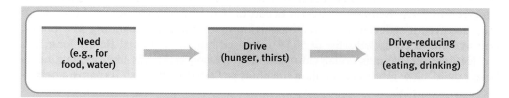

When there is both a need and an incentive, we feel strongly driven. The food-deprived person who smells baking bread feels a strong hunger drive. In the presence of that drive, the baking bread becomes a compelling incentive. For each motive, we can therefore ask, "How is it pushed by our inborn physiological needs and pulled by incentives in the environment?"

Optimum Arousal

3. What type of motivated behavior does arousal theory attempt to explain?

We are much more than homeostatic systems, however. Our biological rhythms cycle through times of arousal. Also, far from reducing a physiological need or minimizing tension, some motivated behaviors *increase* arousal. Well-fed animals will leave their shelter to explore, seemingly in the absence of any need-based drive. From taking such risks, animals may, however, gain information and resources (Renner, 1992).

Curiosity drives monkeys to monkey around trying to figure out how to unlock a latch that opens nothing or how to open a window that allows them to see outside their room (Butler, 1954). It drives the 9-month-old infant who investigates every accessible corner of the house. It drives the scientists whose work this text discusses. And it drives explorers and adventurers. Asked

Driven by curiosity Baby monkeys and small people are fascinated by things they've never handled before. Their drive to explore the relatively unfamiliar is one of several motives that do not fill any immediate physiological need.

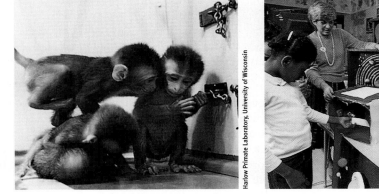
Harlow Primate Laboratory, University of Wisconsin

George Ancona//International Stock

why he wanted to climb Mount Everest, George Mallory answered, "Because it is there." Those who, like Mallory, enjoy high arousal are most likely to enjoy intense music, novel foods, and risky behaviors (Zuckerman, 1979).

Despite having all our biological needs satisfied, we feel driven to experience stimulation. Without it, we feel bored and look for a way to increase arousal to some optimum level. However, with too much stimulation comes stress, and we then look for a way to decrease arousal.

A Hierarchy of Motives

4. What is the basic idea behind Maslow's hierarchy of needs?

Some needs take priority over others. At this moment, with your needs for air and water satisfied, other motives—such as your desire to achieve—energize and direct your behavior. Let your need for water go unsatisfied and your thirst will preoccupy you. But if you were deprived of air, your thirst would disappear.

Abraham Maslow (1970) described these priorities as a **hierarchy of needs** (**FIGURE 10.2**, page 344). At the base of this pyramid are our physiological needs, such as those for food and water. Only if these needs are met are we prompted to meet our need for safety, and then to meet the uniquely human needs to give and receive love and to enjoy self-esteem. Beyond this, said Maslow (1971), lies the highest of human needs: to actualize one's full potential. (More on self-esteem and self-actualization in Chapter 12.)

Maslow's hierarchy is somewhat arbitrary; the order of such needs is not universally fixed. People have starved themselves to make a political statement.

▶ **instinct** a complex behavior that is rigidly patterned throughout a species and is unlearned.

▶ **drive-reduction theory** the idea that a physiological need creates an aroused tension state (a drive) that motivates an organism to satisfy the need.

▶ **homeostasis** a tendency to maintain a balanced or constant internal state; the regulation of any aspect of body chemistry, such as blood glucose, around a particular level.

▶ **incentive** a positive or negative environmental stimulus that motivates behavior.

▶ **hierarchy of needs** Maslow's pyramid of human needs, beginning at the base with physiological needs that must first be satisfied before higher-level safety needs and then psychological needs become active.

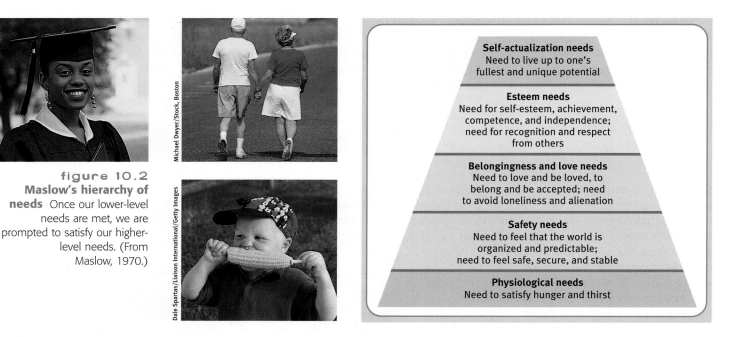

figure 10.2
Maslow's hierarchy of needs Once our lower-level needs are met, we are prompted to satisfy our higher-level needs. (From Maslow, 1970.)

Self-actualization needs
Need to live up to one's fullest and unique potential

Esteem needs
Need for self-esteem, achievement, competence, and independence; need for recognition and respect from others

Belongingness and love needs
Need to love and be loved, to belong and be accepted; need to avoid loneliness and alienation

Safety needs
Need to feel that the world is organized and predictable; need to feel safe, secure, and stable

Physiological needs
Need to satisfy hunger and thirst

"Hunger is the most urgent form of poverty."

Alliance to End Hunger, 2002

Nevertheless, the simple idea that some motives are more compelling than others provides a framework for thinking about motivation, and life-satisfaction surveys in 39 nations support this basic idea (Oishi & others, 1999). In poorer nations that lack easy access to money and the food and shelter it buys, financial satisfaction more strongly predicts subjective well-being. In wealthy nations, where most are able to meet basic needs, home-life satisfaction matters more. Self-esteem matters most in individualist nations, whose citizens tend to focus more on personal achievements than on family and community identity.

Let's now consider four representative motives, beginning at the basic, physiological level with hunger and working up through sexual motivation to the higher-level needs to belong and to achieve. At each level, we shall see how environmental factors interact with what is physiologically given.

rehearse it!

1. Although instinct theory fails to explain most human behavior, the existence of simple fixed patterns such as an infant's rooting and sucking suggests some innate tendencies in humans. Indeed, the underlying assumption of instinct theory—that _____—is as strong as ever.
   a. physiological needs arouse psychological states
   b. genes predispose species-typical behavior
   c. physiological needs increase arousal
   d. external needs energize and direct behavior

2. Drive-reduction theory proposes that a need, or deprivation (for example, a lack of water), leads to an aroused state or drive; this in turn motivates the organism to act to reduce this drive (drink a glass of water) and restore internal stability. The maintenance of a balanced internal state is called
   a. instinct.
   b. pursuit of stimulation.
   c. a hierarchy of needs.
   d. homeostasis.

3. Motivated behaviors satisfy a variety of needs. When feeling bored, we may look for ways to
   a. reduce physiological needs.
   b. search out respect from others.
   c. increase arousal.
   d. ensure stability.

4. Behavior is also influenced by incentives in the environment. For example, a pile of leaves in the driveway may motivate you to get out the rake; your neighbor's disapproval may motivate you to turn down your radio. To explain the effects of external incentives, we must refer to
   a. biological needs.
   b. instinct.
   c. individual learning histories.
   d. homeostasis.

5. According to Abraham Maslow, we are not prompted to satisfy psychological needs, such as the need to be accepted or loved, until we have satisfied more basic needs. The most basic needs are physiological needs, including the need for food, water, and oxygen; just above these are
   a. safety needs.
   b. self-esteem needs.
   c. belongingness needs.
   d. psychological needs.

Answers can be found in Appendix C.

GARFIELD

THE TV ADVERTISERS DIDN'T WASTE ANY TIME

I'VE BEEN ON A DIET ONE DAY AND THEY'RE ALREADY RUNNING MORE FOOD COMMERCIALS

HUNGER

A vivid demonstration of the supremacy of physiological needs came about following reports of starvation in World War II prison camps and occupied areas. To learn more about the results of semistarvation, scientist Ancel Keys and his colleagues (1950) solicited volunteers for an experiment. More than 100 conscientious objectors to the war volunteered, and from them the researchers selected 36 men. First, they fed them just enough to maintain their initial weight. Then, for six months, they cut this food level in half.

The effects soon became visible. Without thinking about it, the men began conserving energy; they appeared listless and apathetic. Their body weights dropped rapidly, eventually stabilizing at about 25 percent below their starting weights. But the psychological effects were especially dramatic. Consistent with Maslow's idea of a needs hierarchy, the men became obsessed with food. They talked food. They daydreamed food. They collected recipes, read cookbooks, and feasted their eyes on delectable forbidden foods. At the same time, they lost interest in sex and social activities. They became preoccupied with their unfulfilled basic needs. As one participant reported, "If we see a show, the most interesting part of it is contained in scenes where people are eating. I couldn't laugh at the funniest picture in the world, and love scenes are completely dull."

The Physiology of Hunger

5. What physiological factors cause us to feel hungry?

Keys' semistarved subjects felt their hunger in response to a homeostatic system designed to maintain normal body weight and an adequate nutrient supply. But what precisely triggers hunger? Is it the pangs of an empty stomach? That is how it feels. And so it seemed after A. L. Washburn, working with Walter Cannon (Cannon & Washburn, 1912), intentionally swallowed a balloon. When inflated in his stomach, the balloon transmitted his stomach contractions to a recording device (**FIGURE 10.3**, page 346). While his stomach was being monitored, Washburn pressed a key each time he felt hungry. The discovery: Washburn was indeed having stomach contractions whenever he felt hungry.

Would hunger persist without stomach pangs? Researchers answered that question early in the twentieth century, when they removed some rats' stomachs and attached their esophagi to their small intestines (Tsang, 1938). Did the rats continue to eat? Indeed they did. Some hunger persists similarly in humans whose ulcerated or cancerous stomachs have been removed. In fact, one can feel some hunger even on a full stomach. Animals that fill their stomachs by eating low-calorie food will eat more than animals that consume a less filling, high-calorie diet (McHugh & Moran, 1978). If the pangs of an empty stomach are not the only source of our hunger, what else matters?

"Never get a tattoo when you're drunk and hungry."

"Nobody wants to kiss when they are hungry."

Dorothea Dix, 1801–1887

"The full person does not understand the needs of the hungry."

Irish proverb

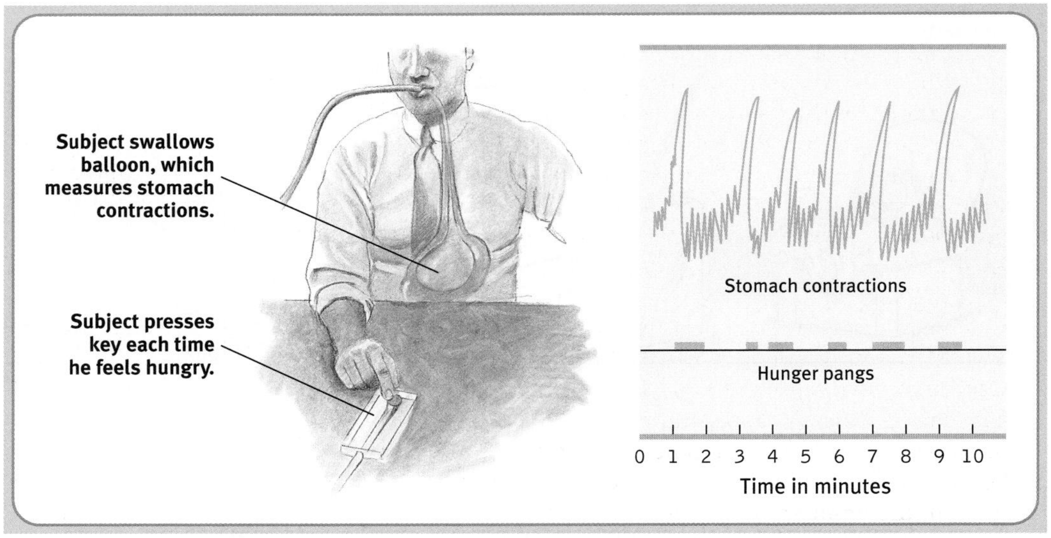

figure 10.3
Monitoring stomach contractions
Using this procedure, Washburn showed that stomach contractions (transmitted by the stomach balloon) accompany our feelings of hunger (indicated by a key press). (From Cannon, 1929.)

Subject swallows balloon, which measures stomach contractions.

Subject presses key each time he feels hungry.

Stomach contractions

Hunger pangs

0 1 2 3 4 5 6 7 8 9 10
Time in minutes

One interesting line of research is focusing on *ghrelin*, a hunger-arousing hormone secreted by an empty stomach. When people with severe obesity undergo bypass surgery that seals off part of the stomach, the remaining stomach then produces much less ghrelin, and their appetites lessen (Lemonick, 2002). But other chemicals also affect hunger.

Body Chemistry and the Brain

People and other animals automatically regulate their caloric intake to prevent energy deficits and maintain a stable body weight. This suggests that the body is somehow, somewhere, keeping tabs on its available resources. One such resource is the blood sugar **glucose**. Increases in the hormone *insulin* diminish blood glucose, partly by converting it to stored fat. The body is normally adept at maintaining its blood glucose level. But if that level drops, hunger increases. You do not consciously feel this change in your blood chemistry. Rather, your brain is automatically monitoring information on your body's internal state. Signals from your stomach, intestines, and liver (indicating whether glucose is being deposited or withdrawn) all signal your brain to motivate eating or not. But where in the brain are these messages integrated? During the 1940s and 1950s, researchers located hunger controls within the hypothalamus, a small but complex neural traffic intersection buried deep in the brain (**FIGURE 10.4**).

Actually, there are two distinct hypothalamic centers that help control eating. Experiments during the 1960s suggested that activity along the sides of the hypothalamus, known as the *lateral hypothalamus*, brings on hunger. When electrically stimulated there, a well-fed animal would begin to eat; when the area was destroyed, even a starving animal had no interest in food. We now know that if a rat is deprived of food and its blood sugar levels wane, the lateral hypothalamus will churn out another hunger-triggering hormone, *orexin*. When given orexin, rats become ravenously hungry (Sakurai & others, 1998).

Activity in the lower mid-hypothalamus, the *ventromedial hypothalamus*, depresses hunger. Stimulate this area and an animal will stop eating; destroy it and the animal's stomach and intestines will process food more rapidly, causing it to eat more often and to become extremely fat (Duggan & Booth, 1986; Hoebel & Teitelbaum, 1966). This discovery explained why some patients with tumors near the base of the brain (in what we now realize is the hypothalamus) eat excessively and become very overweight (Miller, 1995).

How do these complementary areas of the hypothalamus work? One theory is that they influence how much glucose is converted to fat and how much is left available to fuel immediate activity (and minimize hunger). After ventromedial lesions,

figure 10.4
The hypothalamus As we saw in Chapter 2, the hypothalamus (colored red) performs various body maintenance functions, including control of hunger. Blood vessels supply the hypothalamus, enabling it to respond to our current blood chemistry as well as to incoming neural information about the body's state.

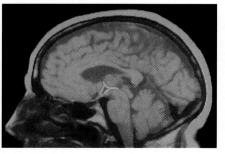

Pix•ELATION from Fran Heyl Associates

rats produce more fat and use less fat for energy, rather like a miser who runs every bit of extra money to the bank and resists taking any out (Pinel, 1993). Recent experiments also reveal a brain system that monitors the body's state and reports to the hypothalamus, which processes the information and sends it along to the frontal lobes, which decide behavior (Winn, 1995).

The hypothalamus monitors levels of the body's appetite hormones (see **TABLE 10.1**). Experimental manipulation of these hormones has raised hopes for an appetite-reducing medication. Such a pill might counteract the body's hunger-producing chemicals, such as ghrelin, the empty-stomach hormone that stimulates appetite. Or perhaps it might increase levels of *PYY*, a digestive hormone that *suppresses* appetite.

An older hunger theory proposes that manipulating the lateral and ventromedial hypothalamus alters the body's "weight thermostat," predisposing us to keep our body at a particular weight level, called its **set point** (Keesey & Corbett, 1983). When semi-starved rats fall below their normal weight, biological pressures act to restore the lost weight: Hunger increases and energy expenditure decreases. If body weight rises—as happens when rats are force-fed—hunger decreases and energy expenditure increases. This stable weight toward which semistarved and overstuffed rats return is their set point. In rats and humans, heredity influences body type and set point.

Human bodies regulate weight much as rats' bodies do—through the control of food intake and energy output. Despite day-to-day variations in your eating, your body regulates your weight much better than you could through conscious efforts to control food intake precisely. If your body weight rises above its set point, you will tend to feel less hungry; if your weight drops below, you will tend to eat more. Consider that over the next 40 years you will eat about 20 tons of food. If during those years you increase your daily intake by just .01 ounce more than required for your energy needs, you will gain 24 pounds (Martin & others, 1991). With astonishing precision, your body will automatically balance your energy intake and expenditure.

Evidence for the brain's control of eating A lesion near the ventromedial (middle) area of the hypothalamus caused this rat's weight to triple.

"To put it simply, PYY is the fullness hormone and ghrelin is the hunger hormone."

Hunger researcher Stephen R. Bloom (2002)

table 10.1 Some Appetite Hormones

Insulin	Hormone secreted by pancreas; controls blood glucose
Orexin	Hunger-triggering hormone secreted by hypothalamus
Ghrelin	Hormone secreted by empty stomach; sends "I'm hungry" signals to the brain
PYY	Digestive tract hormone; sends "I'm *not* hungry" signals to the brain

To maintain its set-point weight, your body adjusts not only food intake and energy output but also its **basal metabolic rate**—its rate of energy expenditure in maintaining basic body functions when the body is at rest. By the end of their 24 weeks of semistarvation, the conscientious objectors who participated in the World War II experiment had stabilized at three-quarters of their normal weight—while eating half of what they previously did. The stabilization resulted from reduced energy expenditure, achieved partly by physical lethargy and partly by a 29 percent drop in their basal metabolic rate. In a reverse experiment—in which volunteers were overfed 1000 calories a day for eight weeks—those who gained the least weight tended to spend the extra caloric energy by fidgeting more (Levine & others, 1999).

Some researchers, however, doubt that the body has a precise set point that drives hunger. They believe that slow, sustained changes in body weight can, for example, alter one's set point. Given unlimited access to tasty foods, people and other animals tend to overeat and gain weight. This casts doubt on the idea that our bodies have a preset tendency to maintain optimum weight (Assanand & others, 1998). And they also note that psychological factors sometimes drive our feelings of hunger.

▶ **glucose** the form of sugar that circulates in the blood and provides the major source of energy for body tissues. When its level is low, we feel hunger.

▶ **set point** the point at which an individual's "weight thermostat" is supposedly set. When the body falls below this weight, an increase in hunger and a lowered metabolic rate may act to restore the lost weight.

▶ **basal metabolic rate** the body's resting rate of energy expenditure.

The Psychology of Hunger

6. What psychological influences affect our eating behavior and feelings of hunger?

Our eagerness to eat is indeed pushed by our physiological state—our body chemistry and hypothalamic activity. Yet there is more to hunger than meets the stomach. This was strikingly apparent when Paul Rozin and his trickster colleagues (1998) tested two patients with amnesia who had no memory for events occurring more than a minute ago. If, 20 minutes after eating a normal lunch, the patients were offered another, both readily consumed it . . . and usually a third meal offered 20 minutes after the second was finished. This suggests that part of knowing when to eat is our memory of our last meal. As time accumulates since we last ate, we anticipate eating again and start feeling hungry.

An acquired taste For Alaskan natives, but not for most other North Americans, whale blubber is a tasty treat. People everywhere learn to enjoy the fatty, bitter, or irritating foods prescribed by their culture.

Richard Olsenius/Black Star

Taste Preference: Biology or Culture?

Psychologists have studied how we eat and how our eating is influenced by hunger and taste. As our hunger diminishes, our eating behavior changes. Eliot Stellar (1985) discovered this after outfitting people with a special dental retainer engineered to record each chew and swallow. The device answers questions about our eating that you may never have thought to ask. During a meal of sandwich snacks, how often does the average person swallow? Every 14 seconds. How many chews per swallow? On average, 19. How fast do people chew? Some 1.8 chews per second. As the meal progresses and both hunger and food tastiness decrease, people chew more. Ironically, the better a food tastes, the *less* time we leave it in our mouth.

Body chemistry and environmental factors together influence not only when we feel hunger, but what we feel hungry for—our taste preference. When feeling tense or depressed, do you crave starchy carbohydrate-laden foods? Carbohydrates help boost levels of the neurotransmitter serotonin, which has calming effects.

Our preferences for sweet and salty tastes are genetic and universal. Other taste preferences are conditioned, as when people given highly salted foods develop a liking for excess salt (Beauchamp, 1987), or when people develop an aversion to a food eaten before becoming violently ill. (The frequency of children's illnesses provides many chances for them to learn food aversions.)

Culture affects taste, too. Bedouins enjoy eating the eye of a camel, which most North Americans would find repulsive. Similarly, most North Americans and Europeans shun dog, rat, and horse meat, all of which are prized elsewhere, but they welcome beef, which Hindus would not think of eating. Such preferences vary with exposure (Pliner & Pelchat, 1991; Rozin, 1976).

We humans have a natural dislike of many things that are unfamiliar, including novel foods (especially novel animal-based rather than vegetarian foods). In experiments, people have tried novel fruit drinks or ethnic foods. With repeated exposure, their appreciation for the new taste typically increases; moreover, exposure to one set of novel foods increases our willingness to try another (Pliner, 1982; Pliner & others, 1993). This "neophobia" surely was adaptive for our ancestors, protecting them from potentially toxic substances. Other taste preferences are also adaptive. For example, the spices most commonly used in the recipes of hot climates, where food—expecially meat—spoils more quickly, inhibit the growth of bacteria (**FIGURE 10.5**). Pregnancy-related nausea is another example of adaptive taste preferences. This nausea causes food aversions that protect the developing embryo, and such taste aversions peak about the tenth week, when the embryo is most vulnerable.

figure 10.5
Some like it hot Countries with hot climates, in which food historically spoiled more quickly, feature recipes with more hot (bacteria-inhibiting) spices (Sherman & Flaxman, 2001). India averages nearly 10 spices per meat recipe, Finland 2 spices.

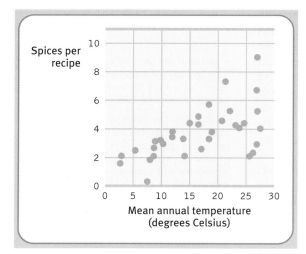

Obesity and Weight Control

7. What factors predispose some people to become and remain obese?

Why do some people gain weight while others eat the same amount and seldom add a pound? And why do so few overweight people win the battle of the bulge? What hope is there for the 65 percent of Americans who, according to the Centers for Disease Control, are overweight?

First, the good news about fat. It is an ideal form of stored energy that provides the body with a high-calorie fuel reserve to carry it through periods when food is scarce—a common occurrence in the feast-or-famine existence of our prehistoric ancestors. (Think of that spare tire around the middle as an energy storehouse—biology's counterpart to a hiker's waist-borne snack pack.) No wonder that in most developing societies today, as in Europe in earlier centuries—in fact, wherever people face famine—obesity signals affluence and social status (Furnham & Baguma, 1994).

Cultures without a thin-ideal for women are also cultures without eating disorders. For example, Ghanians idealize a larger body size than do Americans—and experience fewer eating disorders (Cogan & others, 1996). The same is true of African-American women compared with European-American women (Parker & others, 1995).

The bad news is that in those parts of the world where food and sweets are now abundantly available, the adaptive tendency to store fat has become maladaptive. Being slightly overweight poses only modest health risks (Ernsberger & Koletsky, 1999; Miller, 1999). Fitness matters more than being a little overweight. But the National Institutes of Health report that significant obesity (**FIGURE 10.6**) increases the risk of diabetes, high blood pressure, heart disease, gallstones, arthritis, sleep disorders, and certain types of cancer. The risks are greater for apple-shaped people who carry their weight in pot bellies than for pear-shaped people with ample hips and thighs (Greenwood, 1989).

Peter Paul Rubens, The Prado, Madrid/The Bridgeman Art Library, Superstock

Rubens' *The Garden of Love* In other times and places, plumper bodies have been idealized.

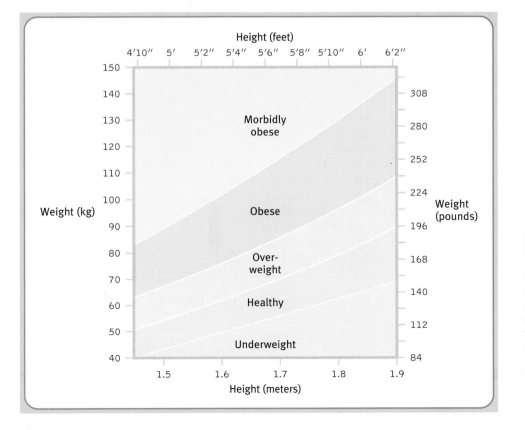

figure 10.6
Obesity measured as body mass index (BMI) Government guidelines encourage a body mass index (BMI) under 25. The World Health Organization and many countries define obesity as a BMI of 30 or more. The bands of shading are based on BMI measurements for those heights and weights. BMI is calculated by using the following formula:

$$BMI = \frac{\text{Weight in kg (pounds} \times .45)}{\text{Squared height in meters}}$$
(inches divided by 4)

CLOSE-UP

Eating Disorders

Psychological influences on eating behavior are strikingly evident when a motive for abnormal thinness overwhelms normal homeostatic pressures.

Persons with **anorexia nervosa** drop significantly below normal weight (typically, by 15 percent or more) yet feel fat and are obsessed with losing weight. Even when emaciated, the person continues to limit food intake. The disorder usually develops in adolescence, 9 times out of 10 in females.

Those with **bulimia nervosa** have repeated episodes of overeating followed by compensatory vomiting, laxative use, fasting, or excessive exercise. Bulimia patients eat the way some alcoholics drink—in spurts, sometimes under the influence of friends who are bingeing (Crandall, 1988). Most binge-purge eaters are women in their late teens or early twenties. Like those with anorexia, they are preoccupied with food (craving sweet and high-fat foods), are fearful of becoming overweight, and are depressed or anxious (Hinz & Williamson, 1987; Johnson & others, 2002). Their depression and shame are felt most keenly during and following binges. About half of those with anorexia also display the binge-purge-depression symptoms of bulimia. But unlike anorexia, bulimia is marked by weight fluctuations within or above normal ranges, making the condition easy to hide.

Researchers report that the families of bulimia patients have a higher-than-usual incidence of alcoholism, obesity, and depression. In contrast, anorexia patients often come from families that are competitive, high-achieving, and

Dying to be thin Anorexia was identified and named in the 1870s, when it appeared among affluent adolescent girls (Brumberg, 2000). This 1930s photo illustrates the physical condition.

Reprinted by permission of *The New England Journal of Medicine*, 207, (Oct. 5, 1932), 613–617.

protective (Pate & others, 1992; Yates, 1989, 1990). They set high standards, fret about falling short of expectations, and are intensely concerned with how others perceive them (Polivy & Herman, 2002; Striegel-Moore & others, 1993). Eating disorders are only slightly, if at all, related to a childhood history of sex abuse. Thus, they do *not* provide (as some have speculated) a telltale sign of such abuse (Smolak & Murnen, 2002; Stice, 2002).

Families may provide a fertile ground for the growth of eating disorders in another way, however. Mothers of girls with eating disorders are themselves often focused on their own weight and on their daughters' weight and appearance (Pike & Rodin, 1991). Anorexia always begins as a weight-loss diet, and the self-induced vomiting of bulimia nearly always begins after a dieter has broken diet restrictions and gorged.

Genetics, too, may influence susceptibility to eating disorders. If twins are identical rather than fraternal, the chances of the other twin's sharing the disorder are somewhat greater (Fairburn & others, 1999).

There is, however, a cultural explanation for the fact that anorexia and bulimia occur mostly in women and mostly in weight-conscious cultures. Body ideals vary across culture and time. In India, women students rate their ideals as close to their actual shape. In much of Africa—where poverty, AIDS, and hunger mean thinness, and prosperity means plumpness—bigger is better (Knickmeyer, 2001). In Western cultures, however, the rise in eating disorders has coincided with a dramatic increase over the last 50 years in women having a poor body image, according to a recent analysis of 222 studies of 141,000 people over 50 years (Feingold & Mazzella, 1998).

Other research confirms that those vulnerable to eating disorders are those who most idealize thinness and have the greatest body dissatisfaction (Stice, 2002; Thompson & Stice, 2001; Vohs & others, 2001). Not surprisingly, those people are most often women. In one national

© 1999 Shannon Burns www.shannonburns.com/cartoon4.htm

"Thanks, but we don't eat."

"Gee, I had no idea you were married to a supermodel."

> *"Why do women have such low self-esteem? There are many complex psychological and societal reasons, by which I mean Barbie."*
>
> *Dave Barry, 1998*

survey, nearly one-half of U.S. women reported feeling negative about their appearance and preoccupied with being or becoming overweight (Cash & Henry, 1995). And in a turn-of-the-century British survey of 3500 bank and university staff, men were more likely to *be* overweight and women were more likely to *perceive* themselves as overweight (Emslie & others, 2001). Similar gender differences appeared in an experiment led by Barbara Fredrickson (1998), who had University of Michigan men and women put on a sweater or a swim suit and complete a math test while alone in a changing room. For the women but not the men, wearing the swimsuit triggered self-consciousness and shame that disrupted their math performance.

Part of the cultural pressure is surely transmitted by the "thin-ideal" exemplified in fashion magazines, advertisements, and even in some toys. What do you suppose happens when young women

> *"Diana remained throughout a very insecure person at heart, almost childlike in her desire to do good for others, so she could release herself from deep feelings of unworthiness, of which her eating disorders were merely a symptom."*
>
> *Charles, Ninth Earl of Spencer, eulogizing his sister Princess Diana, 1997*

repeatedly encounter magazine images of fashion models, who tend to be unnaturally thin (Tovee & others, 1997)? Eric Stice and Heather Shaw (1994) and Heidi Posavac and colleagues (1998) report that women tend to feel more ashamed, depressed, and dissatisfied with their own bodies—the very attitudes that predispose eating disorders. When Stice and his colleagues (2001) gave some adolescent girls (but not others) a 15-month subscription to a teen fashion magazine (*Seventeen*), vulnerable girls (who were already dissatisfied, idealizing thinness, and lacking social support) exhibited

increased body dissatisfaction and eating disorder tendencies. But even ultra-thin models do not define the impossible standard of the classic Barbie fashion doll. Adjusted to a height of 5 feet 7 inches, her 32-16-29 figure (in centimeters: 82 bust, 41 waist, and 73 hips) defines a body shape approximated by fewer than 1 in 100,000 women (Norton & others, 1996).

It seems clear that the sickness of today's eating disorders lies not just within the victims but also within our weight-obsessed culture—a culture that says, in countless ways, "Fat is bad," that motivates millions of women to be "always dieting," and that encourages eating binges by pressuring women to live in a constant state of semistarvation. "You can't be too rich or too thin," declared the Duchess of Windsor. Eating disorder specialists disagree.

▶ **anorexia nervosa** an eating disorder in which a normal-weight person (usually an adolescent female) diets and becomes significantly (15 percent or more) underweight, yet, still feeling fat, continues to starve.

▶ **bulimia nervosa** an eating disorder characterized by episodes of overeating, usually of high-calorie foods, followed by vomiting, laxative use, fasting, or excessive exercise.

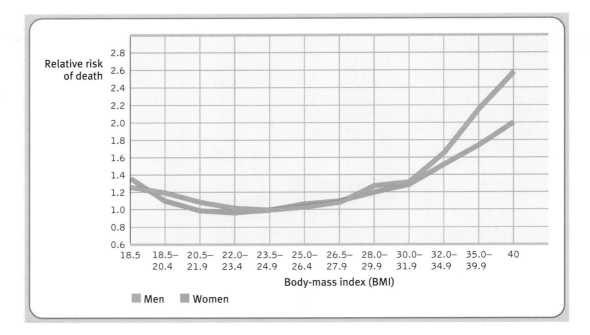

figure 10.7
Obesity and mortality Relative risk of death among healthy nonsmokers rises with extremely high or low body mass index. (Data from 14-year study of 1.05 million Americans, Calle & others, 1999.)

Not surprisingly, then, a massive recent study—following more than 1 million Americans over 14 years—revealed that being significantly overweight can cut life short (Calle & others, 1999). The death rate was especially high among very over-weight men (**FIGURE 10.7**).

The Social Effects of Obesity

The social and psychological effects of obesity can also be socially toxic, affecting both how you are treated and how you feel about yourself. Obese people know the stereotype: slow, lazy, and sloppy (Crandall, 1994, 1995; Ryckman & others, 1989). Many people see obesity as a matter of choice or as reflecting a lack of self-discipline or a personality problem—a maladjusted way of reducing anxiety, dealing with guilt, or gratifying an "oral fixation." Widen people's images on a video monitor (making them look fatter) and observers suddenly rate them as less sincere, less friendly, meaner, and more obnoxious (Gardner & Tockerman, 1994). In personal ads, women often advertise, and men often state their preference for, slimness (Miller & others, 2000; Smith & others, 1990).

The social effects of obesity were clear in a study that followed 370 obese 16- to 24-year-old women (Gortmaker & others, 1993). When restudied seven years later, two-thirds of the women were still obese. They also were less like-ly to be married, and they were making less money—$7000 a year less—than an equally intelligent comparison group of some 5000 other women.

In one clever experiment, Regina Pingitore and her colleagues (1994) demonstrated weight discrimination. They videotaped mock job interviews in which professional actors appeared as either normal-weight or overweight applicants. In one condition, the actors wore makeup and prostheses that made them look 30 pounds heavier. When appearing overweight, the same person, using the same lines, intonation, and gestures, was rated as less wor-thy of hiring. The weight bias was especially strong against women applicants (**FIGURE 10.8**). Other studies reveal that weight discrimi-nation, though hardly discussed, is greater than race and gender discrimination. It occurs at every stage of the employment cycle—hiring, placement, promotion, compensation, discipline, and dis-charge (Roehling, 2000).

figure 10.8
Gender and weight discrimination When women applicants were made to look overweight, university students were less willing to think they would hire them. Among men applicants, weight mattered less. (Data from Pingitore & others, 1994.)

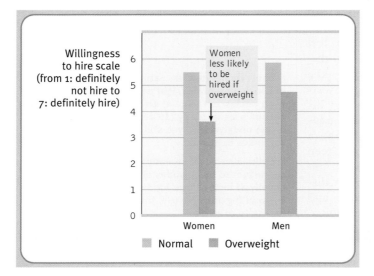

Weight discrimination takes its toll at home, too. In studies of patients who were especially unhappy with their weight—those who had lost an average of 100 pounds after short-cutting digestion with intestinal bypass surgery—4 in 5 said their children had asked them not to attend school functions. And 9 in 10 said they would rather have a leg amputated than be obese again (Rand & Macgregor, 1990, 1991).

Why don't obese people drop their excess baggage and free themselves of all this pain? The answer lies in the psychology of fat.

The Physiology of Obesity

Research on the physiology of obesity challenges the stereotype of severely overweight people being weak-willed gluttons. First, consider the arithmetic of weight gain: People get fat by consuming more calories than they expend. The energy equivalent of a pound of fat is 3500 calories; therefore, dieters have been told they will lose a pound for every 3500-calorie reduction in their diet. Surprise: This conclusion is false. Why? Read on.

FAT CELLS The immediate determinants of body fat are the size and number of fat cells. A typical adult has about 30 billion of these miniature fuel tanks, half of which lie near the skin's surface. A fat cell can vary from relatively empty, like a deflated balloon, to overly full. In an obese person, fat cells may swell to two or three times their normal size and then divide. Once the number of fat cells increases—due to genetic predisposition, early childhood eating patterns, or adult overeating—it never decreases. Fat cells may shrink on a diet, but they never disappear (Sjöstrum, 1980).

SET POINTS AND METABOLISM Another way our bodies maintain fat is that fat tissue has a low metabolic rate. Compared with other tissue, fat takes less food energy to maintain. Thus, once we become fat, we require less food to maintain our weight than we did to attain it. The "weight thermostat" of an obese person's body is set to maintain body weight within a higher-than-average range. When weight drops below the set-point (or "settling point") range, the person's hunger increases and metabolism decreases. In a classic experiment (Bray, 1969), obese patients whose daily food intake was reduced from 3500 to 450 calories lost only 6 percent of their weight—partly because their metabolic rates dropped about 15 percent (**FIGURE 10.9**). Thus, the body adapts to starvation by burning off fewer calories, and to extra calories by burning off more. That is why reducing your food intake by 3500 calories may not reduce your weight by 1 pound. That is why further weight loss comes slowly following the rapid weight losses that occur during the initial three weeks or so of a rigorous diet. And that is why when a diet ends, amounts of food that worked to maintain weight before the diet may increase it, because the body is still conserving energy.

figure 10.9
The effects of a severe diet on obese patients' body weight and metabolism After seven days on a 3500-calorie diet, six obese patients were given only 450 calories a day for the next 24 days. Body weight declined only 6 percent and then leveled off, because metabolism dropped about 15 percent. (From Bray, 1969.)

Phyllis Picardi/Stock, Boston

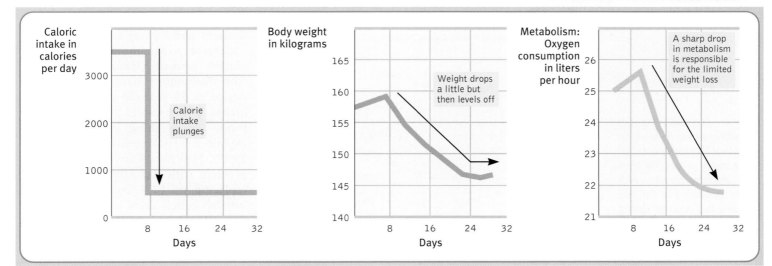

Caloric intake in calories per day — Calorie intake plunges

Body weight in kilograms — Weight drops a little but then levels off

Metabolism: Oxygen consumption in liters per hour — A sharp drop in metabolism is responsible for the limited weight loss

In Britain, as elsewhere, not all pounds are sterling We humans were not designed for a world filled with energy-saving cars and tools, and high-calorie foods. In hunting and gathering societies, obesity is almost unknown (Brown, 1993).

In Gallup surveys from 1990 to 2001, the average American's reported body weight rose 10 pounds—to 153 for women and 189 for men (Saad, 2002). That comes to a collective weight gain of well over a billion pounds.

"We have the Surgeon General coming out with yet another official report—entitled 'Americans: What a Bunch of Whales.'"

Dave Barry, 2002

Individual differences in resting metabolism also explain why two people of the same height, age, and activity level can maintain the same weight, even if one of them eats much less than the other does. Most overweight people are just normal people whose bodies predispose them to weigh more. This appears true despite findings that people—obese people, especially—tend to overestimate their physical activity and underestimate their caloric intake (Brownell & Wadden, 1992; Lichtman & others, 1992).

THE GENETIC FACTOR Studies of adoptees and twins reveal a genetic influence on body weight. Consider:

● Despite shared family meals, the body weights of adoptive siblings are uncorrelated with one another and with those of their adoptive parents. Rather, people's weights resemble those of their biological parents (Grilo & Pogue-Geile, 1991).

● Identical twins have closely similar weights, even when reared apart (Plomin & others, 1997; Stunkard & others, 1990). Across studies, their weight correlates .74. The much lower .32 correlation among fraternal twins suggests that genes explain two-thirds of our varying body mass (Maes & others, 1997).

The genetic influence is surely complex, with some genes influencing when our intestines signal "full," others dictating how efficiently we burn calories or convert extra calories to fat, and still others prompting us to fidget or sit still.

Genes aren't the whole story behind obesity, however. Genes cannot explain why obesity is six times more common among lower-class than among upper-class women, more common among Americans than among Europeans, and more common among Americans today than in 1900. Western cultures have become like animal feedlots—places where farmers fatten animals by restricting their exercise and offering abundant fattening food. Lack of exercise and high-calorie foods help create human feedlots, aided by larger serving sizes (Big Gulps, Double Whoppers) and a tripled percentage of meals eaten at fast-food restaurants since 1997 (Farley & Cohen, 2001). Compared with their counterparts in the early 1900s, people are eating a higher-fat, higher-sugar diet, expending fewer calories, and suffering higher rates of diabetes at younger ages (Thompson, 1998).

Across the developed world, weight increase has accelerated. Your parents and grandparents at age 30 likely weighed less than you did or will. In Britain, the average woman's dress size has increased from size 12 in 1951 to size 16 today; just since 1980, adult obesity rates have nearly tripled, to 21 percent (Hawkes, 2002; Merriman, 1999). And over the last 40 years, as health experts have cajoled Americans to lose weight, the adult obesity rate has more than doubled to 31 percent (**FIGURE 10.10**). And so it goes, pretty much everywhere this book is being read. Australia, similar to Britain and America, classifies some 55 percent of its population as overweight (Australian Bureau of Statistics, 1999; Halsey & Webb, 2000). In Canada, the proportion of people classified as overweight has increased by 60 percent since 1985 (Statistics Canada, 1999).

The bottom line: New stadiums, theaters, and subway cars are offering wider seats to accommodate this population growth (Hampson, 2000). The Washington State Ferries abandoned its 50-year-old standard of 18 inches per person. "Eighteen-inch butts are a thing of the past," explained a spokesperson (Shepherd, 1999). New York City, facing a large problem with Big Apple bottoms, is replacing its 17.5 inch bucket-style subway bench seats with bucketless seats (Hampson, 2000). In the end, today's people need more room.

figure 10.10 Trading risks As smoking, which kills some 400,000 Americans a year, has been dropping, obesity, which now contributes to 300,000 deaths, has been increasing. (Source: Centers for Disease Control and Prevention.)

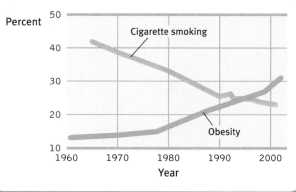

Note how these findings reinforce a familiar lesson from our earlier study of intelligence: There can be high levels of heritability (genetic influence on individual differences) without heredity explaining group differences. Genes mostly determine why one person today is heavier than another. Environment mostly determines why people today are heavier than their counterparts 50 years ago.

LOSING WEIGHT Perhaps you shake your head in sympathy with obese people: "Slim chance they (or we) have of becoming and staying thin. If they lose weight on a diet, their metabolism slows and their hungry fat cells cry out, 'Feed me!' They're fated for fat!" Indeed, the condition of an obese person's body reduced to average weight is much like that of a semistarved body. Held under normal set point, each body "thinks" it is starving. Having lost weight, formerly obese people look normal, but their fat cells may be abnormally small, their metabolism slowed, and, like the semistarved volunteers in Keys' study, their minds obsessed with food.

BOTTOM LINERS

"It works as well as most other diet plans. . . . I've lost over $200 in less than three weeks."

All this explains why, short of drastic surgery to tie off part of the stomach and small intestine, most people who succeed on a weight-loss program eventually regain most of the weight (Garner & Wooley, 1991; Jeffery & others, 2000). Programs that modify one's life-style and ongoing eating behavior have better carryover to postdiet weight management. Yet the participants in these programs, too, typically regain much of their lost weight (**Figure 10.11**).

But that's not for lack of trying, especially by people with two X chromosomes. In one survey of 108,000 adults, 29 percent of men and 44 percent of women were actively trying to lose weight (Serdula & others, 1999). Asked if they would rather "be five years younger or weigh 15 pounds less," 29 percent of men and 48 percent of women said they would prefer losing the weight (*Responsive Community*, 1996). The gender difference for teenagers is even larger: 15 percent of boys and 44 percent of girls have reported trying to lose weight (Centers for Disease Control, 1991).

With fat cells, set points, metabolism, and genetic factors all tirelessly conspiring to make losing weight a big problem, what advice can psychology offer if you wish to shed excess pounds? For some helpful hints, see the Close-Up feature on page 356.

For most people, the only long-term result of participating in a commercial weight-loss program is a thinner wallet.

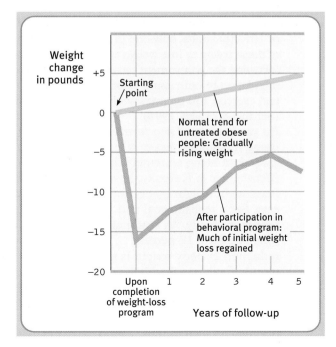

figure 10.11
Weight-loss programs and weight change Behavior management weight-loss programs promote weight loss, but most lost weight is regained. (From Brownell & Jeffery, 1987.)

Weight change in pounds

+5 — Starting point

0

Normal trend for untreated obese people: Gradually rising weight

−5

−10

After participation in behavioral program: Much of initial weight loss regained

−15

−20

Upon completion of weight-loss program | 1 | 2 | 3 | 4 | 5

Years of follow-up

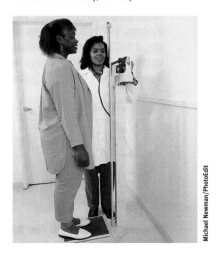

Helpful Hints for Losing Weight

People struggling with obesity are well advised to seek medical evaluation and guidance. For others who wish to take off a few pounds, researchers have offered these tips.

Begin only if you feel motivated and self-disciplined. For most people, permanent weight loss requires making a career of staying thin—a lifelong change in eating habits combined with gradually increased exercise.

Minimize exposure to tempting food cues. Keep tempting foods out of the house or out of sight. Stay out of the sweets and chips shops. Go to the supermarket only on a full stomach. Eat simple meals, with only a few different foods; given more variety, people consume more (Raynor & Epstein, 2001).

Take steps to boost your metabolism. Inactive people are often overweight (**FIGURE 10.12**). One of the few predictors of successful long-term weight loss is exercise both during and after changing your eating patterns (Jeffery & others, 2000; McGuire & others, 1999; Wadden & others, 1998). Exercise, such as brisk walking, running, and swimming, not only empties fat cells, builds muscle, and makes you feel better, it also temporarily speeds up metabolism and can help lower your set point (Bennett, 1995; Kolata, 1987; Thompson & others, 1982). Even brief bouts of exercise—four 10-minute walks a day—provide benefits (Jakicic &

"I looked at you and thought, I bet this man runs marathons."

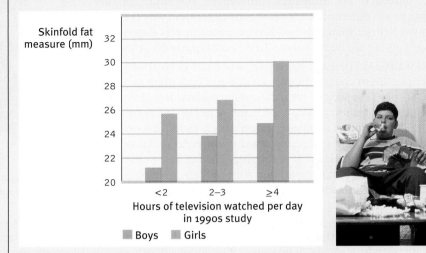

Skinfold fat measure (mm)

Hours of television watched per day in 1990s study

■ Boys ■ Girls

Tony Freeman/PhotoEdit

figure 10.12
Couch potatoes beware: A correlational study of TV watching and obesity In a 1980s study of 6671 young people 12 to 17 years old, and in a 1990s follow-up study of 4063 individuals 8 to 16 years old, obesity was more common among those who watched the most television (Andersen & others, 1998; Dietz & Gortmaker, 1985). Of course, overweight people may avoid activity, preferring to sit and watch TV. But the association between TV watching and obesity remained when many other factors were controlled, suggesting that inactivity and snacking while watching TV do contribute to obesity. Also, as life-styles have become more sedentary and TV watching has increased, so has the percentage of overweight people in Britain, North America, and elsewhere. When California children were placed in a TV-reduction educational program, they watched less—and lost weight (Robinson, 1999).

others, 1999). Lack of exercise helps explain why so few succeed in losing weight permanently. In a Centers for Disease Control study of 107,000 adults, only one in five of those trying to lose weight were following the government recommendation to both count calories and exercise 150 minutes weekly (Serdula & others, 1999).

Be realistic and moderate. Being moderately heavy is less risky than being extremely thin (Ernsberger & Koletsky, 1999). Permanent weight loss is not easy. Set a realistic goal and take it gradually. "A reasonable time line for a 10 percent reduction in body weight is six months," advises the National Institutes of Health (1998).

Eat healthy foods. Whole grains, fruits, vegetables, and healthy fats such as those found in olive oil and fish help regulate appetite and artery-clogging cholesterol (Taubes, 2001, 2002).

Don't starve all day and eat one big meal at night. This eating pattern, common among overweight people, slows metabolism.

Beware of the binge. Among people who consciously restrain their eating, drinking alcohol or feeling anxious or depressed can unleash the urge to eat (Herman & Polivy, 1980). So can being distracted from monitoring your eating (Ward & Mann, 2000). (Ever notice that you eat more when out with friends?) Once the diet is broken, the person often thinks "what the heck" and then binges (Polivy & Herman, 1985, 1987). A lapse need not become a full collapse: Remember, most people occasionally lapse.

rehearse it!

6. The hypothalamus, a structure deep within the brain, controls feelings of hunger and fullness, in part by evaluating changes in blood chemistry. Hunger occurs in response to high blood insulin and
   a. high blood glucose and low levels of ghrelin.
   b. low blood glucose and high levels of ghrelin.
   c. decreased energy expenditure and high levels of PYY.
   d. stimulation of any part of the hypothalamus.

7. One theory maintains that our bodies tend to stay at a particular weight level, or set point. Changes in the basal metabolic rate help keep us at this weight. For example, when our weight falls below the set point, we feel hungrier (and eat more) and lethargic (and reduce our energy expenditure). The operation of this "weight thermostat" is an example of

   a. homeostasis.
   b. an eating disorder.
   c. individual learning.
   d. binge-purge episodes.

8. Some of our responses to food and eating are learned; others are genetic and universal. Which of the following is a genetically disposed response to food?
   a. An aversion to eating cats and dogs
   b. An interest in novel foods
   c. A preference for sweet and salty foods
   d. An aversion to carbohydrates

9. Both anorexia nervosa and bulimia nervosa are eating disorders characterized by abnormal eating patterns. Which of the following is true regarding bulimia nervosa?
   a. People with bulimia continue to want to lose weight even when they are underweight.
   b. Bulimia is marked by weight fluctuations within or above normal ranges.

   c. Bulimia patients often come from middle-class families that are competitive, high-achieving, and protective.
   d. If one twin is diagnosed with bulimia, the chances of the other twin's sharing the disorder are greater if they are fraternal rather than identical twins.

10. Obese people find it very difficult to lose weight permanently. This is due to several factors, including the fact that
   a. with dieting, fat cells shrink and then disappear.
   b. the set point of obese people is lower than average.
   c. with dieting, basal metabolic rate increases.
   d. there is a genetic influence on body weight.

Answers can be found in Appendix C.

SEXUAL MOTIVATION

Sex is part of life. Had this not been so for all your ancestors, you would not be reading this book. Sexual motivation is nature's clever way of making people procreate, thus enabling our species' survival. When two people feel attracted, they hardly stop to think of themselves as guided by their genes. As the pleasure we take in eating is nature's inventive method of getting our body nourishment, so the pleasure of sex is our genes' way of preserving and spreading themselves.

"I love the idea of there being two sexes, don't you?"

Describing Sexual Behavior

8. What behavior patterns must a theory of sexual motivation explain?

Unable to answer his students' questions about people's sexual practices, Indiana University biologist Alfred Kinsey and his colleagues (1948, 1953) set out to find some answers. Kinsey's confidential interviews with 18,000 people—85 percent conducted by himself or his associate Wardell Pomeroy—asked more than 350 rapid-fire questions. Social scientists were quick to point out what Kinsey readily acknowledged—that his nonrandom sample contained an overrepresentation of well-educated white urbanites.

Because we do not know whether Kinsey's sample accurately represented the nation's sexual practices in the 1940s, let alone those of today, his precise findings can be misleading. Moreover, Kinsey and Pomeroy's questioning encouraged (some say, demanded) admission of sexual activity. They never asked subjects *whether* they had engaged in a particular activity; they asked them *when* they had first engaged in it (thus making it easier for people to divulge their behavior).

"Maybe . . . it starts with a kiss."

Prenatal photographer Lennart Nillson, answering the question "When does life begin?"

Dellenback, reprinted by permission of the Kinsey Institute for Research in Sex, Gender, and Reproduction, Inc.

Alfred Kinsey The controversial biologist, shown here conducting one of his interviews, did not begin with sexually explicit questions. Rather, he first helped people feel at ease by asking nonthreatening questions about family background, health, and education.

A nonsmoking 50-year-old male has about a 1 in a million chance of a heart attack during any hour. This increases to merely 2 in a million during the hour following sex (with no increase for those who exercise regularly). Compared with risks associated with heavy exertion or anger, this risk seems not worth losing sleep (or sex) over (Muller & others, 1996).

By today's standards of random sampling and nonleading questioning, Kinsey's tactics, and thus his results, are problematic. Yet his surveys were less misleading than some of the haphazard sexual surveys reported more recently in the popular press. Recall from Chapter 1 that when popular "sex reports" begin with a biased sample of people (such as subscribers to selected magazines) and receive replies from only 3 percent of this nonrandom sample, there is good reason to doubt the generality of their findings.

The Physiology of Sex

What happens in our bodies during sexual arousal? What causes sexual arousal?

The Sexual Response Cycle

9. What are the stages of the human sexual response cycle?

The headlines created by Kinsey's 1940s surveys reappeared after some 1960s studies in which scientists recorded the physiological responses of volunteers who masturbated or had intercourse. With the help of 382 female and 312 male volunteers—an atypical sample, consisting only of people able and willing to display arousal and orgasm while being observed in a laboratory—gynecologist-obstetrician William Masters and his collaborator Virginia Johnson (1966) monitored or filmed more than 10,000 sexual "cycles."

Their description of the **sexual response cycle** identified four stages, similar in men and women. During the initial *excitement phase*, the genital areas become engorged with blood, causing the man's penis to become partially erect and the woman's clitoris to swell and the inner lips covering her vagina to open up. Her vagina also expands and secretes lubricant, and her breasts and nipples may enlarge.

In the *plateau phase*, excitement peaks as breathing, pulse, and blood pressure rates continue to increase. The penis becomes fully engorged and some fluid—frequently containing enough live sperm to enable conception—may appear at its tip. Vaginal secretion continues to increase, the clitoris retracts, and orgasm feels imminent.

Masters and Johnson observed muscle contractions all over the body during *orgasm*; these were accompanied by further increases in breathing, pulse, and blood pressure rates. A woman's arousal and orgasm facilitate conception by helping propel semen from the penis, positioning the uterus to receive sperm, and drawing the sperm farther inward. A woman's orgasm therefore not only reinforces intercourse, which is essential to natural reproduction, it also increases retention of deposited sperm (Furlow & Thornhill, 1996). In the excitement of the moment, men and women are hardly aware of all this but are more aware of their rhythmic genital contractions creating a pleasurable feeling of sexual release. The feeling apparently is much the same for both sexes. In one study, a panel of experts could not reliably distinguish between descriptions of orgasm written by men and those written by women (Vance & Wagner, 1976).

After orgasm, the body gradually returns to its unaroused state as the engorged genital blood vessels release their accumulated blood—relatively quickly if orgasm has occurred, relatively slowly otherwise. (It's like the nasal tickle that goes away rapidly if you have sneezed, slowly otherwise.) During this *resolution phase*, the male enters a **refractory period**, lasting from a few minutes to a day or more, during which he is incapable of another orgasm. The female's refractory period is not very long, which may make it possible for her to have another orgasm if restimulated during or soon after resolution.

Masters and Johnson sought not only to describe the human sexual response cycle but also to understand and treat the inability to complete it. **Sexual disorders** are problems that consistently impair sexual functioning. Some involve sexual motivation, especially lack of sexual energy and arousability. Others include, for men, *premature ejaculation* and *erectile disorder* (inability to have or maintain an erection), and, for women, *orgasmic disorder* (infrequently or never experiencing orgasm).

What causes such problems? The idea that personality disorders are to blame has been largely discounted. Researchers have found that men or women with sexual disorders can often be helped by receiving behaviorally oriented therapy where, for example, men may learn ways to control their urge to ejaculate, and women are trained to bring themselves to orgasm.

Hormones and Sexual Behavior

10. How do sex hormones influence human sexual development and arousal?

Sex hormones have two effects: They direct the development of male and female sex characteristics, and (especially in nonhuman animals) they activate sexual behavior. In most mammals, nature neatly synchronizes sex with fertility. The female becomes sexually receptive ("in heat") when production of the female hormone **estrogen** peaks at ovulation. (In experiments, researchers stimulate receptivity by injecting female animals with estrogen.) Male hormone levels are more constant, and researchers cannot so easily manipulate the sexual behavior of male animals by hormone treatments (Feder, 1984). Nevertheless, castrated male rats—having lost their testes, which manufacture the male sex hormone **testosterone**—gradually lose much of their interest in receptive females. They gradually regain it if injected with testosterone.

Hormones more loosely influence human sexual behavior. At ovulation, women's sexual desire is only slightly higher than at other times (Harvey, 1987; Meuwissen & Over, 1992). Women's sexuality also differs from that of other mammalian females in being more responsive to testosterone level than to estrogen level (Meston & Frohlich, 2000; Reichman, 1998). If a woman's natural testosterone level is lowered, as happens with removal of the ovaries or adrenal glands, her sexual interest may wane. But it can often be restored by a testosterone-replacement drug.

In men, normal fluctuations in testosterone levels, from man to man and hour to hour, have little effect on sexual drive (Byrne, 1982). Indeed, fluctuations in male hormones are partly a *response* to sexual stimulation. When James Dabbs and his colleagues (1987, 2000) had male collegians converse separately with another male student and with a female student, the men's testosterone levels rose with the social arousal, but especially after talking with the female. Thus, sexual arousal can be a cause as well as a consequence of increased testosterone levels.

Although normal short-term hormonal changes have little effect on men's and women's desire, large hormone shifts over the life span have a greater effect. A person's interest in dating and sexual stimulation usually increases with the pubertal surge in sex hormones. Male testosterone levels surge during puberty, which helps explain adolescent boys' behavior.

If the hormonal surge is precluded—as happened during the 1600s and 1700s with prepubertal boys who were castrated to preserve their soprano voices for Italian opera—the normal development of sex characteristics and sexual desire does not occur (Peschel & Peschel, 1987). Among adult men who suffer castration, sex drive typically falls as testosterone levels decline (Hucker & Bain, 1990). Male sex offenders similarly lose much of their sexual urge when voluntarily taking Depo-Provera, a drug that

▶ **sexual response cycle** the four stages of sexual responding described by Masters and Johnson—excitement, plateau, orgasm, and resolution.

▶ **refractory period** a resting period after orgasm, during which a man cannot achieve another orgasm.

▶ **sexual disorder** a problem that consistently impairs sexual arousal or functioning.

▶ **estrogen** a sex hormone, secreted in greater amounts by females than by males. In nonhuman female mammals, estrogen levels peak during ovulation, promoting sexual receptivity.

▶ **testosterone** the most important of the male sex hormones. Both males and females have it, but the additional testosterone in males stimulates the growth of the male sex organs in the fetus and the development of the male sex characteristics during puberty.

"Fill'er up with testosterone."

reduces testosterone level to that of a prepubertal boy (Money & others, 1983). By contrast, men with high testosterone levels tend to be energetic, ambitious, and rambunctious (Dabbs, 2000). In later life, as sex hormone levels decline, the frequency of sexual fantasies and intercourse declines as well (Leitenberg & Henning, 1995). For men with abnormally low testosterone levels, testosterone-replacement therapy often increases sexual desire and also energy and vitality (Yates, 2000).

To summarize: We might compare human sex hormones, especially testosterone, to the fuel in a car. Without fuel, a car will not run. But if the fuel level is minimally adequate, adding more fuel to the gas tank won't change how the car runs. The analogy is imperfect, because the interaction between hormones and sexual motivation is two-way. However, the analogy correctly suggests that biology is a necessary but not sufficient explanation of human sexual behavior. The hormonal fuel is essential, but so are the psychological stimuli that turn on the engine, keep it running, and shift it into high gear.

The Psychology of Sex

11. How do internal and external stimuli contribute to sexual arousal?

Hunger and sex are different sorts of motivations. Hunger responds to a *need*. If we do not eat, we die. Sex is not in this sense a need. If we do not have sex, we may feel like dying, but we do not. Nevertheless, there are similarities between hunger and sexual motivation. Both depend on internal physiological factors. And both are influenced by external stimuli.

External Stimuli

Many studies confirm that men become aroused when they see, hear, or read erotic material. Surprising to many (because sexually explicit materials are sold mostly to men) is that most women—at least the less-inhibited women who volunteer to participate in such studies—report or exhibit nearly as much arousal to the same stimuli (Heiman, 1975; Stockton & Murnen, 1992).

People may find such arousal either pleasing or disturbing. (Those who find it disturbing often limit their exposure to such materials, just as those wishing to control hunger limit their exposure to tempting cues.) With repeated exposure, the emotional response to any erotic stimulus often "habituates" (lessens). During the 1920s, when Western women's hemlines first reached the knee, an exposed leg was a mildly erotic stimulus, as were modest (by today's standards) two-piece swimsuits and movie scenes of a mere kiss.

Can sexually explicit material have adverse effects? Research indicates that it can. Depictions of women being sexually coerced—and enjoying it—tend to increase viewers' acceptance of the false idea that women enjoy rape and tend to increase male viewers' willingness to hurt women (Malamuth & Check, 1981; Zillmann, 1989). Images of sexually attractive women and men may also lead people to devalue their own partners and relationships. After male collegians watch TV or magazine depictions of sexually attractive women, they often find an average woman, or their own girlfriends or wives, less attractive (Kenrick & Gutierres, 1980; Kenrick & others, 1989; Weaver & others, 1984). Viewing X-rated sex films similarly tends to diminish people's satisfaction with their own sexual partners (Zillmann, 1989). Erotica may create expectations that few men and women can hope to live up to.

Imagined Stimuli

Sexual motivation arises from the interplay of our physiology and our environment. But the stimuli inside our heads—our imagination—can also influence sexual arousal and desire (**FIGURE 10.13**). The brain, it has been said, is our most significant sex organ. People who, because of a spinal cord injury, have no genital sensation can still feel sexual desire (Willmuth, 1987).

"Ours is a society which stimulates interest in sex by constant titillation. . . . Cinema, television, and all the formidable array of our marketing technology project our very effective forms of titillation and our prejudices about man as a sexy animal into every corner of every hovel in the world."

Germaine Greer, 1984

Sexually explicit TV programs also divert attention from TV ads, making the ads more forgettable. Ads embedded in nonsexual and nonviolent programs more often produced memory for the products (Bushman & Bonacci, 2002).

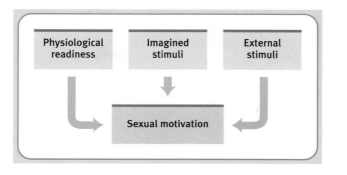

figure 10.13
Forces affecting sexual motivation
Physiology, imagination, and the environment all affect sexual motivation.

Wide-awake people become sexually aroused not only by memories of prior sexual activities but also by fantasies. Fantasies need not correspond to actual behavior. In one survey of masturbation-related fantasies (Hunt, 1974), 19 percent of women and 10 percent of men reported imagining being taken by someone overwhelmed with desire for them. Fantasy is not reality, however. To paraphrase Susan Brownmiller (1975), for women there's a big difference between fantasizing that Brad Pitt just won't take no for an answer and having a hostile stranger actually force himself on you.

About 95 percent of both men and women say they have had sexual fantasies. But men (whether gay or straight) fantasize about sex more often, more physically, and less romantically—and prefer less personal and faster-paced sex content in books and videos (Leitenberg & Henning, 1995). Fantasizing about sex does *not* indicate a sexual problem or dissatisfaction. (If anything, sexually active people have more sexual fantasies.)

"There is no difference between being raped and being run over by a truck except that afterward men ask if you enjoyed it."

Marge Piercy, "Rape Poem," 1976

Adolescent Sexuality

12. What factors influence teenagers' sexual attitudes and behaviors?

Adolescents' physical maturation fosters a sexual dimension to their emerging identity. Yet sexual expression also varies dramatically with time and culture.

Culture

We humans are one species, driven by similar motives that enhance our survival and spread our genes. Yet our attitudes toward sexual behaviors, including premarital sex and nonmarital childbearing, vary widely across the planet. In the United States, about half of ninth- to twelfth-graders report having had sexual intercourse, as do 42 percent of Canadian 16-year-olds (Boroditsky & others, 1995; Smith, 1998). Teen intercourse rates are higher in Western Europe but much lower in Arab and Asian countries and among North Americans of Asian descent (McLaughlin & others, 1997). In one survey, only 2.5 percent of 4688 unmarried Chinese students entering Hong Kong's six universities reported having had sexual intercourse (Meston & others, 1996). The variations in sexual standards from country to country help to explain the cultural differences in rates of nonmarital childbearing (**Figure 10.14**).

Sexual attitudes and behaviors also vary with time within the same culture. Among American women born before 1900, a mere 3 percent had experienced premarital sex by age 18; among today's 18-year-old women, slightly more than half have done so (Smith, 1998). (In one survey, 72 percent of 12- to 17-year-old girls who have had sex said they regretted it [Reuters, 2000].)

figure 10.14
Births to unmarried women Since 1960, the percentage of babies born to unmarried Canadian, British, and American women—one-third of whom were teens—has more than quintupled. This increase stems from two trends: a decreasing birthrate among married women and a doubling of the birthrate among unmarried women. (Data from National Center for Health Statistics; Bureau of the Census [1998], Table 1347; and British Annual Abstract of Statistics, 1999.)

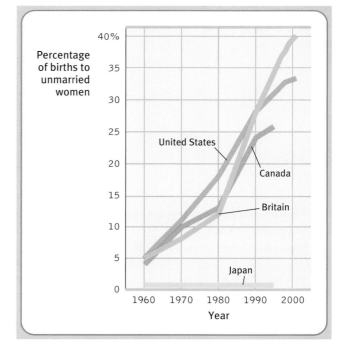

This increase in sexual activity has led to an increase in the adolescent pregnancy rate. The often impoverished futures of teen mothers and of children in father-absent homes have in turn prompted new research on teen sexuality and adolescents' use of contraceptives. "There is consensus," report Child Trends researchers, that unmarried teen childbearing "is undesirable—for the teen, for her baby, and for the larger society" (Moore & others, 2002).

Teen Pregnancy

Short of abstinence, contraceptives are the surest strategy for preventing pregnancy. Yet only one-third of sexually active male teens use condoms consistently (Sonenstein, 1992). Compared with European teens, American teens have lower rates of sex, but they also have lower rates of contraceptive use and thus higher rates of teen pregnancy and abortion (Call & others, 2002). Why? What motivates teen sexual activity, and why are sexually active teens not more motivated to use contraception? Among the contributing factors are these:

1. ***Ignorance*** Half of sexually active Canadian teen girls have mistaken ideas about which birth control methods will protect them from pregnancy and sexually transmitted diseases (Immen, 1995). Most teens also overestimate their peers' sexual activity, and that misperception may influence their own behavior (Child Trends, 2001). "Ignorant of the details of reproduction and contraception, teens often are surprised to find themselves pregnant."

2. ***Guilt related to sexual activity*** Although sexual inhibitions reduce sexual activity, they also result in lack of planned birth control for those who do engage in sex (Gerrard & Luus, 1995). Not wanting to appear deliberately sexual or promiscuous, teens may hesitate to carry and produce a condom. When, as sometimes happens, passion overwhelms intention, the result may be conception. A Columbia University study of 1990s teens who took vows pledging virginity until marriage reported that the pledgers were "much less likely" than otherwise similar adolescents to have intercourse and were "better off," with fewer health problems and better self-esteem (Bearman & Bruckner, 2001). But if they did break the vow, they were less likely than other teens to use contraception.

3. ***Minimal communication about birth control*** Many teenagers are uncomfortable discussing contraception with their parents, partners, and peers (Kotva & Schneider, 1990; Milan & Kilmann, 1987). Teens who talk freely with friends or parents and are in an exclusive relationship with a partner with whom they communicate openly are more likely to use contraceptives.

4. ***Alcohol use*** Sexually active teens are typically alcohol-using teens (National Research Council, 1987). Moreover, those who use alcohol prior to sex are less likely to use condoms (Kotchick & others, 2001). By depressing the brain centers that control judgment, inhibition, and self-awareness, alcohol tends to break down normal restraints, a phenomenon well known to sexually coercive males (page 211).

5. ***Mass media norms of unprotected promiscuity*** Planned Parenthood has complained that television and movies help define a "Go for it *now*" sexual norm. An average hour of prime-time television on the three major U.S. networks contains approximately 15 sexual acts, words, and innuendos. Nearly all of these instances involve unmarried partners, about half have no prior romantic relationship or have just met, and few communicate any concern for birth control or sexually transmitted infection (Brown & others, 2002; Kunkel, 2001; Sapolsky & Tabarlet, 1991). Portrayals of unsafe sex without consequence, contends Planned Parenthood, amounts to a campaign of sex disinformation.

Unprotected sex has led not only to an increase in teen pregnancies but also to increased rates of sexually transmitted infection (STI) (also called *STD* for *sexually transmitted disease*). Two-thirds of new infections occur in persons under 25 (ASHA, 2003). Teenage girls, because of their less mature biological development

"Will your child learn to multiply before she learns to subtract?"

Anti–teen-pregnancy poster, Children's Defense Fund

"Condoms should be used on every conceivable occasion."

Anonymous

"All of us who make motion pictures are teachers, teachers with very loud voices."

Film producer George Lucas, Academy Award ceremonies, 1992

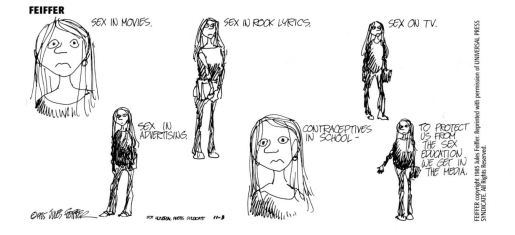

and lower levels of protective antibodies, seem especially vulnerable to STIs and associated risks of becoming infertile and developing certain cancers (Guttmacher, 1994; Morell, 1995). One response to these facts of life has been a greater emphasis on teen abstinence within some comprehensive sex education programs.

A National Longitudinal Study of Adolescent Health among 12,000 teens found that teens with high rather than average intelligence test scores more often delay sex, evidently because they appreciate possible negative consequences and are more focused on future achievement than on here-and-now pleasures (Halpern & others, 2000). Religiosity is another predictor of sexual restraint: Actively religious teens and adults more often reserve sex for marital commitment (Smith, 1998). A third major predictor of reduced teen sexuality and pregnancy is participation in service learning programs (Kirby, 2002; O'Donnell & others, 2002). In several experiments, teens who volunteer as tutors or teachers' aides or take part in community projects have lower pregnancy rates than other comparable teens randomly assigned to control conditions. Researchers are unsure why. Does service learning promote a sense of personal competence, control, and responsibility? Does it encourage more future-oriented thinking? Or does it simply reduce opportunities for unprotected sex?

To comprehend the mathematics of sexually transmitted infection, imagine an island on which all people were virgins until they first began having sex a year ago. Pat has sex with 9 people, each of whom over the same time period has sex with 9 other people, who in turn have sex with 9 others. How many "phantom" sex partners (past partners of partners) will Pat have? Ohio State researchers Laura Brannon and Timothy Brock (1994) report that the actual number—511—is more than five times the estimate given by the average student.

Given these odds, the rapid spread of STIs is not surprising. Condoms sometimes fail. But even when they don't fail, they offer no protection against certain skin-to-skin STIs—notably the human papilloma virus, which is responsible for most genital cancers (Medical Institute, 1994; NIH, 2001). Condoms do, however, reduce tenfold the risk of contracting HIV (human immunodeficiency virus—the virus that causes AIDS) from an infected partner (Pinkerton & Abramson, 1997).

In recent history, the pendulum of sexual values has swung from the European eroticism of the early 1800s to the conservative Victorian era of the late 1800s, from the libertine flapper era of the 1920s to the family values period of the 1950s. The pendulum may have begun a new swing toward commitment in the twenty-first century, as new voices decry family disintegration and call for a balance between sexual expression and restraint. In West Germany, the percentage of teens who link sex with committed love is up significantly since 1970 (Schmidt & others, 1994). And would you agree or disagree that "if two people like each other, it's all right for them to have sex even if they've known each other for a very short time"?

The percentage of first-year American college and university students who agree dropped from 52 percent in 1987 to 42 percent in 2001 (Sax & others, 2001). In 2001, virgins (54 percent) outnumbered nonvirgins (46 percent) among U.S. high school students, reversing the percentages of a decade earlier (CDC, 2002).

Sexual Orientation

13. *What does current research tell us about why some people are attracted to members of their own sex and others are attracted to members of the other sex?*

To motivate is to energize and direct behavior. So far, we have considered the energizing of sexual motivation but not its direction. We express the direction of our sexual interest in our **sexual orientation**—our enduring sexual attraction toward members of our own sex (homosexual orientation) or the other sex (heterosexual orientation). Cultures vary in their attitudes toward homosexuality. But as far as we know, all cultures in all times have been predominantly heterosexual (Bullough, 1990). Whether a culture condemns or accepts homosexuality, heterosexuality prevails and homosexuality survives.

Gay men and lesbians often recall childhood play preferences like those of the other sex (Bailey & Zucker, 1995). But most homosexual people report not becoming aware of same-sex attraction until during or shortly after puberty, and not thinking of themselves as gay or lesbian until around age 20 (Garnets & Kimmel, 1990).

Sexual Orientation Statistics

How many people are exclusively homosexual? Until recently, the popular press assumed a homosexuality rate of 10 percent. In a 2002 Gallup survey, the average American estimated that 21 percent of men are gay and 22 percent of women are lesbian (Robinson, 2002). But in both Europe and the United States, more than a dozen national surveys in the early 1990s explored sexual orientation, using methods that protected the respondent's anonymity. Their results agree in suggesting that a more accurate figure is about 3 or 4 percent of men and 1 or 2 percent of women (Laumann & others, 1994; National Center for Health Statistics, 1991; Smith, 1998). Estimates derived from the sex of unmarried partners reported in the 2000 U.S. Census suggest that 2.5 percent of the population is gay or lesbian (Tarmann, 2002). Fewer than 1 percent of survey respondents—for example, 12 people out of 7076 Dutch adults in one recent survey (Sandfort & others, 2001)— reported being actively bisexual. But a larger number of adults reported having had an isolated homosexual experience. And most people reported having had an occasional homosexual fantasy.

Health experts find it helpful to know sexual statistics, but numbers do not decide issues of human rights. Similarly, it's helpful in manufacturing school desks to know that about 10 percent of people are left-handed. But whether left-handers are 3 percent or 10 percent of the population doesn't answer the moral question of whether lefties should enjoy equal rights.

What does it feel like to be homosexual in a heterosexual culture? If you are heterosexual, one way to understand is to imagine how you would feel if you were ostracized or fired for openly admitting or displaying your feelings toward someone of the other sex; if you overheard people making crude jokes about heterosexual people; if most movies, TV shows, and advertisements portrayed (or implied) homosexuality; and if your family members were pleading with you to change your heterosexual life-style and to enter into a homosexual marriage.

Facing such reactions, homosexual people often struggle with their sexual orientation. They may at first try to ignore or deny their desires, hoping they will go away. But they don't. Then they may try to change, through psychotherapy, willpower, or

"It has been maintained for years that we each use only about 10 percent of our brain capacity; that the condom failure rate is 10 percent; and until just last year, that 10 percent of Americans are homosexual. Such statistics are partly artifacts, I suspect, of our decimal system; in a base 12 system, we'd no doubt show a similar affinity for statistics that were multiples of 8.333 percent."

John Allen Paulos, "Counting on Dyscalculia," 1993

prayer. But the feelings typically persist, as do those of heterosexual people—who are similarly incapable of becoming homosexual (Haldeman, 1994, 2001). Most of today's psychologists therefore view sexual orientation as neither willfully chosen nor willfully changed. Sexual orientation in some ways is like handedness: Most people are one way, some the other. A very few are truly ambidextrous. Regardless, the way one is endures.

Women's sexual orientation tends to be less strongly felt and potentially more fluid and changeable than men's (Diamond, 2000; Peplau & Garnets, 2000). Men's lesser sexual variability is apparent in many other ways as well, notes Roy Baumeister (2000). Across time, across cultures, across situations, and across differing levels of education, religiosity, and peer influence, adult women's sexual drive and interests are more flexible and varying than adult men's. Women, more than men, for example, prefer to alternate periods of high sexual activity with periods of almost none. Baumeister calls this phenomenon the gender difference in "erotic plasticity."

Despite elevated rates of depression and risk of suicide attempts, most gays and lesbians suffer no psychological disorder (Sandfort & others, 2001). Most people, whether straight or gay, accept their orientation—by electing celibacy; by engaging in promiscuous sex (a choice more commonly made by gay men than by lesbian women); or by entering into a committed, long-term love relationship (a choice more often made by lesbians than by gays) (Kulkin & others, 2000; Peplau, 1982; Remafedi, 1999; Weinberg & Williams, 1974). Mental health professionals are now more accepting of clients' sexual orientation. The American Psychiatric Association in 1973 dropped homosexuality from its list of "mental illnesses," as did the World Health Organization in 1993, and Japan's and China's psychiatric associations in 1995 and 2001.

Origins of Sexual Orientation

If our sexual orientation is indeed something we do not choose and seemingly cannot change, then where do these preferences come from? How do we move toward either a heterosexual or a homosexual orientation? See if you can anticipate the consensus that has emerged from hundreds of research studies by responding yes or no to the following questions:

1. Is homosexuality linked with problems in a child's relationships with parents, such as with a domineering mother and an ineffectual father, or a possessive mother and a hostile father?
2. Does homosexuality involve a fear or hatred of people of the other gender, leading individuals to direct their sexual desires toward members of their own sex?
3. Is sexual orientation linked with levels of sex hormones currently in the blood?
4. As children, were many homosexuals molested, seduced, or otherwise sexually victimized by an adult homosexual?

The answer to all these questions appears to be no (Storms, 1983). Consider the findings of lengthy Kinsey Institute interviews with nearly 1000 homosexuals and 500 heterosexuals (Bell & others, 1981; Hammersmith, 1982). The investigators assessed nearly every imaginable psychological cause of homosexuality—parental relationships, childhood sexual experiences, peer relationships, dating experiences. Their findings: Homosexuals were no more likely than heterosexuals to have been smothered by maternal love, neglected by their father, or sexually abused. And consider this: If "distant fathers" were more likely to produce homosexual sons, then shouldn't boys growing up in father-absent homes more often be gay? (They are not.) And shouldn't the rising number of such homes have led to a noticeable increase in the gay population? (It has not.)

Personal values affect sexual orientation less than they affect other forms of sexual behavior. Compared with people who rarely attend church, for example, those who attend regularly are one-third as likely to have cohabited before marriage, and they report having had many fewer sex partners. But (if male) they are just as likely to be homosexual (Smith, 1998).

Note that the scientific question is not "What causes homosexuality?" (or "What causes heterosexuality?") but "What causes differing sexual orientation?" In pursuit of answers, psychological science compares the backgrounds and physiology of people whose sexual orientations differ.

Erick has two moms Maria Christina Vlassidis (left) and Marie Tatro (center), who are lesbians, tell playmates of their son Erick, 8, that they are both his moms. Both women attend school conferences and support other aspects of his life. Studies suggest that being reared by lesbian or gay parents does not appreciably affect a child's sexual orientation.

Cynthia Johnson/ *Time* magazine

The 2000 U.S. Census found the highest percentage of same-sex unmarried partners in San Francisco, Miami, and Santa Fe (Tarmann, 2002).

Homosexual people do, however, appear more often in certain populations:

- In America's dozen largest cities, the percentage of men identifying themselves as gay jumps to 9 percent, compared with only 1 percent in rural areas (Binson & others, 1995; Laumann & others, 1994).
- One study (Ludwig, 1995) of the biographies of 1004 eminent people found homosexual and bisexual people overrepresented (11 percent of the sample), especially among poets (24 percent), fiction writers (21 percent), and artists and musicians (15 percent).
- Men who have older brothers are somewhat more likely to be gay, reports Ray Blanchard (1997, 2001). Assuming the odds of homosexuality are roughly 3 percent among first sons, they rise to about 4 percent among second sons, 5 percent for third sons, and so on for each additional older brother. The reason for this curious phenomenon—the "fraternal birth order effect"—is unclear. Blanchard suspects a defensive maternal immune response to foreign substances produced by male fetuses. The maternal antibodies may become stronger after each pregnancy with a male fetus and may prevent the fetus' brain from developing in a male-typical pattern. Women with older sisters, and women who were womb-mates of twin brothers, exhibit no such sibling effect (Rose & others, 2002).

So, what then does determine sexual orientation? One theory proposes that people develop same-sex erotic attachments if segregated by gender at the time their sex drive matures (Storms, 1981). Indeed, gay men tend to recall going through puberty somewhat earlier, when peers are more likely to be all males (Bogaert & others, 2002). But even in a tribal culture in which homosexual behavior is expected of all boys before marriage, heterosexuality prevails (Money, 1987). (As this illustrates, homosexual *behavior* does not always indicate a homosexual *orientation*.) Another theory proposes the opposite: that people develop romantic attachments to those who *differ* from, and thus are more fascinating than, the peers they associated with while growing up (Bell, 1982; Bem, 1996). The bottom line from a half-century's theory and research: If there are environmental factors that influence sexual orientation, we do not yet know what they are. If someone were to ask me, "What can I do to influence my child's sexual orientation?" my answer would have to be "I haven't a clue."

THE BRAIN AND SEXUAL ORIENTATION New research indicates that sexual orientation is at least partly biological (Hershberger, 2001). Researcher Simon LeVay (1991) discovered this while studying sections of the hypothalamus taken from deceased heterosexual and homosexual people. As a gay scientist, LeVay wanted to do "something connected with my gay identity." He knew he had to avoid biasing the results, so he did the study "blind," without knowing which donors were gay. For nine months he peered through his microscope at a cell cluster he thought might be important. Then one morning, LeVay sat down and broke the codes. His discovery: The cell cluster was reliably larger in heterosexual men than in women and homosexual men. As the brain difference became apparent, "I was almost in a state of shock. . . . I took a walk by myself on the cliffs over the ocean. I sat for half an hour just thinking what this might mean" (LeVay, 1994).

It should not surprise us that brains differ with sexual orientation. Remember our maxim: *Everything psychological is simultaneously biological.* The critical question is, when did the brain difference begin? At conception? In the womb? During childhood or adolescence? Did experience produce the difference? Or did genes or prenatal hormones (or genes via prenatal hormones)?

LeVay does not view this neural center as a sexual orientation center; rather, he sees it as an important part of the neural pathway engaged in sexual behavior. He acknowledges that it's possible that sexual behavior patterns influence the brain's anatomy. In fish, birds, rats, and humans, brain structures vary with experience—including sexual experience, reports aptly named sex researcher Marc Breedlove

"Gay men simply don't have the brain cells to be attracted to women."

Simon LeVay, The Sexual Brain, *1993*

(1997). But LeVay believes it more likely that brain anatomy influences sexual orientation. His hunch seems confirmed by the discovery of a similar hypothalamic difference between the 6 to 10 percent of male sheep that display same-sex attraction and the 90+ percent attracted to females (Larkin & others, 2002).

Laura Allen and Roger Gorski (1992) also concluded that brain anatomy influences sexual orientation after discovering that a section of the anterior commissure (fibers that, like the corpus callosum, connect right and left hemispheres) is one-third larger in homosexual men than in heterosexual men. "The emerging neuroanatomical picture," noted Brian Gladue (1994), "is that, in some brain areas, homosexual men are more likely to have female-typical neuroanatomy than are heterosexual men."

GENES AND SEXUAL ORIENTATION The evidence suggests a genetic influence on sexual orientation. "First, homosexuality does appear to run in families," note Brian Mustanski and Michael Bailey (2003). "Second, twin studies have established that genes play a substantial role in explaining individual differences in sexual orientation." Although results vary, the identical twins of homosexual individuals are somewhat more likely to also be homosexual than are the fraternal twins. However, in many identical twin pairs (especially among women) homosexual feelings are not shared, which indicates that other factors are also at work.

PRENATAL HORMONES AND SEXUAL ORIENTATION The elevated rate of homosexual orientation even in fraternal twins might also result from their sharing the same prenatal environment. In animals and some exceptional human cases, sexual orientation has been altered by abnormal prenatal hormone conditions. German researcher Gunter Dorner (1976, 1988) pioneered this research by manipulating a fetal rat's exposure to male hormones, thereby "inverting" its sexual behavior. Female sheep will likewise show homosexual behavior if their pregnant mothers are injected with testosterone during a critical gestation period (Money, 1987).

With humans, a critical period for the brain's neural-hormonal control system may exist between the middle of the second and fifth months after conception (Ellis & Ames, 1987; Gladue, 1990; Meyer-Bahlburg, 1995). Exposure to the hormone levels typically experienced by female fetuses during this time appears to predispose the person (whether female or male) to be attracted to males in later life. Some tests reveal that homosexual men have spatial abilities more like those typical of heterosexual women—a pattern consistent with the hypothesis that homosexuals were exposed to atypical prenatal hormones (Cohen, 2002; Gladue, 1994; McCormick & Witelson, 1991; Sanders & Wright, 1997).

Curiously, in some (but not all) studies, gay men have had fingerprint patterns rather like those of heterosexual women (Mustanski & others, 2002; Sanders & others, 2002). Most people have more fingerprint ridges on their right hand than on their left. Jeff Hall and Doreen Kimura (1994) first observed that this difference was greater for heterosexual males than for females and gay males. Given that fingerprint ridges are complete by the sixteenth fetal week, the researchers suspected the difference was due to prenatal hormones. Prenatal hormones also are a possible explanation for why data from 20 studies revealed that "homosexual participants had 39 percent greater odds of being non–right-handed" (Lalumière & others, 2000).

Lesbians may likewise have more male-typical anatomy. For example, the cochlea and hearing system of lesbians develop in a way that is intermediate between those of heterosexual females and heterosexual males, and which seems attributable to prenatal hormonal influence (McFadden, 2002). This phenomenon—of homosexual individuals of both sexes being intermediate between heterosexual females and males—crosses many traits (**TABLE 10.2**, page 368).

Because the physiological evidence is preliminary and controversial, some scientists remain skeptical. Rather than specifying sexual orientation, perhaps biological factors predispose a temperament that influences sexuality "in the context of individual learning and experience" (Byne & Parsons, 1993). Perhaps, theorizes Daryl Bem (1996, 1998, 2000), genes code for prenatal hormones and brain anatomy,

"Studies indicate that male homosexuality is more likely to be transmitted from the mother's side of the family."

Robert Plomin, John DeFries, Gerald McClearn, and Michael Rutter, Behavioral Genetics, 1997

"Were it not for delicately balanced combinations of genetic, neurological, hormonal, and environmental factors, largely occurring prior to birth, each and every one of us would be homosexual."

Lee Ellis and M. Ashley Ames (1987)

Gay more than straight men express interest in occupations that attract many women, such as decorator, florist, and flight attendant (Lippa, 2002). (Given that some 96 percent of men are not gay, men in such occupations may nevertheless be mostly straight.)

table 10.2 Biological Correlates of Sexual Orientation

On average (the evidence is strongest for males), various biological and behavioral traits of gays and lesbians fall between those of straight men and straight women. Tentative findings—some in need of replication—include these:

Brain differences
- One hypothalamic cell cluster is larger in straight men than in women and gay men; same difference is found in male sheep displaying other-sex versus same-sex attraction.
- Anterior commissure is larger in gay men than in women or straight men.

Genetic influences
- Shared sexual orientation is higher among identical twins than among fraternal twins.
- Sexual attraction in male fruit flies can be genetically manipulated.

Prenatal hormonal influences
- Altered prenatal hormone exposure may lead to homosexuality in humans and other animals.
- Men with several older brothers are more likely to be gay.

These brain differences and genetic and prenatal influences may contribute to observed gay-straight differences in

- spatial abilities.
- fingerprint ridge counts.
- auditory system.
- handedness.
- occupational preferences.
- relative finger lengths.
- gender nonconformity.
- age of male puberty.
- male body size.

which predispose *temperaments* that lead children to prefer gender-typical or gender-atypical activities and friends. These preferences may later lead children to feel attracted to whichever sex feels different from their own. The dissimilar-seeming sex (whether or not it conforms to one's own anatomy) becomes associated with anxiety and other forms of arousal, which eventually gets transformed into romantic arousal. The exotic becomes erotic.

Regardless of the process, the consistency of the genetic, prenatal, and brain findings has swung the pendulum toward a biological explanation (Rahman & Wilson, 2003). Nature more than nurture, most psychiatrists now believe, predisposes sexual orientation (Vreeland & others, 1995). If biological influences prove critical, such would explain why sexual orientation is so difficult to change.

Still, some people wonder: Should the cause of sexual orientation matter? Perhaps it shouldn't, but people's assumptions matter. Those who believe, as do most gays and lesbians, that sexual orientation is biologically influenced—a disposed identity, not a choice—express more accepting attitudes toward homosexual people (Allen & others, 1996; Furnham & Taylor, 1990; Kaiser, 2001; Whitley, 1990). Agreement that homosexuality is "something a person is born with" has been increasing—from 13 to 40 percent in American public opinion surveys between 1977 and 2001 (Gallup, 2002). As we might therefore expect, attitudes have become more accepting:

- Over the same years, American Gallup surveys found that support for equal job rights for gays and lesbians rose from 56 to 85 percent, and agreement that "homosexuality should be an acceptable alternative life-style" rose from 34 to 52 percent.
- In Canadian Gallup surveys between 1992 and 2001, support for same-sex marriages nearly doubled—from 24 to 46 percent (Mazzuca, 2002).
- Among entering collegians, support for laws prohibiting homosexual relationships has plummeted since 1987 (**FIGURE 10.15**).

"Evidence suggesting that biology plays an important role in the development of male and female sexual orientation is rapidly increasing."

Scott L. Hershberger (2001)

Entering collegians agreeing that "It is important to have laws prohibiting homosexual relationships."

53% in 1987

25% in 2002

figure 10.15
Changing attitudes
(Source: Annual UCLA/American Council on Education surveys of some 7 million entering collegians.)

These dramatic attitude shifts do not represent a liberalization of all sex-related attitudes. For example, in periodic national surveys, agreement that extramarital sex is "always wrong" *increased* from 69.6 percent in 1973 to 79.4 percent in 2000 (NORC, 2002).

To gay and lesbian activists, the new biological research is a double-edged sword (Diamond, 1993). If sexual orientation, like skin color and sex, is genetically influenced, that offers a further rationale for civil rights protection. Moreover, it may alleviate parents' concerns about their children having gay teachers and role models. It does, however, raise the troubling possibility that genetic markers of sexual orientation could someday be identified through fetal testing, and a fetus be aborted simply for being predisposed to an unwanted orientation.

Sex and Human Values

14. Is scientific research on sexual motivation value-free?

Recognizing that values are both personal and cultural, most sex researchers and educators strive to keep their writings on sexuality value-free.

But can the study of sexual behavior and what motivates it ever be free of values? Those who say no think that the very words we use to describe behavior often reflect our personal values. When sex researchers label sexually restrained individuals as "erotophobic" and as having "high sex guilt," they express their own values. Whether we label sexual acts we do not practice as "perversions," "deviations," or part of an "alternative sexual life-style" depends on our attitudes toward the behaviors. Labels describe, but they also evaluate.

When education about sex is separated from the context of human values, some students may get the idea that sexual intercourse is simply a recreational activity. Diana Baumrind (1982), a University of California child-rearing expert, has observed that adolescents interpret sex education that pretends to be "value-free" as meaning that adults are neutral about adolescent sexual activity. Such an implication is unfortunate, she added, because "promiscuous recreational sex poses certain psychological, social, health, and moral problems that must be faced realistically."

A sharing of love For most adults, a sexual relationship fulfills not only a biological motive, but a social need for intimacy.

Nathaniel Antman/The Image Works

Other researchers have found that teenagers who have had formal sex education are no more likely to engage in premarital sex than those who have not (Furstenberg & others, 1985; Zelnik & Kim, 1982). Moreover, we enrich our lives by knowing ourselves, by realizing that others share our feelings, by understanding what is likely to please or displease our loved one. Witness the crumbling of falsehoods about homosexuality. Witness the growing realization that some sexually explicit material can lead people to devalue and hurt others.

Perhaps we can agree that the knowledge provided by sex research is preferable to ignorance, and yet also agree that researchers' values should be stated openly, enabling us to debate them and to reflect on our own values. We should remember that scientific research on sexual motivation does not aim to define the personal meaning of sex in our own lives. You could know every available fact about sex— that the initial spasms of male and female orgasm come at 0.8-second intervals, that the female nipples expand 10 millimeters at the peak of sexual arousal, that systolic blood pressure rises some 60 points and the respiration rate to 40 breaths per minute—but fail to understand the human significance of sexual intimacy.

Surely one significance of sexual intimacy is its expression of our profoundly social nature. Sex is a socially significant act. Men and women can achieve orgasm alone, yet most people find greater satisfaction while embracing their loved one. There is a yearning for closeness in sexual motivation. Sex at its human best is life-uniting and love-renewing.

> *"The relationship between women and men should be characterized not by patronizing behavior or exploitation, but by love, partnership, and trustworthiness. . . . Sexuality should express and reinforce a loving relationship lived by equal partners."*
>
> Towards a Global Ethic, *1993 Parliament of the World's Religions*

rehearse it!

11. In the 1940s, Alfred Kinsey and his colleagues used questionnaires to investigate human sexual behavior. Their results have been criticized because
    a. their sample was not large enough.
    b. their sample was not representative of the population as a whole.
    c. they asked leading questions.
    d. both *b.* and *c.* are true.

12. In describing the sexual response cycle, Masters and Johnson noted that
    a. a plateau phase followed orgasm.
    b. men experience a refractory period during which they could not experience orgasm.
    c. the feeling that accompanies orgasm is stronger in men than in women.
    d. testosterone is released in the female as well as in the male.

13. Daily and monthly fluctuations in hormone levels do not greatly affect sexual desire in humans. Over the life span, however, hormonal changes have significant effects. A striking effect of hormonal changes on human sexual behavior is the
    a. arousing influence of erotic materials.
    b. sharp rise in sexual interest at puberty.
    c. decrease in women's sexual desire at the time of ovulation.
    d. increase in testosterone levels in castrated males.

14. Sexual behavior is motivated by internal biological factors, by external stimuli, and by imagined stimuli. An example of an external stimulus that might influence sexual behavior is
    a. blood level of testosterone.
    b. the onset of puberty.
    c. a sexually explicit film.
    d. an erotic fantasy or dream.

15. More than half of all sexually active teens either do not use contraceptives or do not use them regularly. Factors contributing to the epidemic of teen pregnancies include ignorance about reproduction and contraception, guilt about sexual behavior, mass media norms of promiscuity, insufficient communication about contraception, and
    a. the "just say no" attitude.
    b. the unavailability of abortion.
    c. the decreased rates of sexually transmitted diseases.
    d. alcohol use.

16. Sexual orientation refers to our enduring sexual attraction to members of a particular gender. Current research suggests several possible contributors to sexual orientation. Which of the following is NOT one of those contributors?
    a. Certain cell clusters in the hypothalamus
    b. A domineering mother and ineffectual father
    c. A section of fibers connecting the right and left hemispheres of the brain
    d. Exposure to hormone levels typically experienced by female fetuses

Answers can be found in Appendix C.

THE NEED TO BELONG

15. Why do some psychologists believe we have a need to belong—to affiliate with others?

If, as Barbra Streisand sings, "people who need people are the luckiest people in the world," then most people are lucky. Separated from friends or family—isolated in prison, alone at a new school, living in a foreign land—most people feel keenly their lost connections with important others. We are what Aristotle called "the social animal." We have a need to affiliate with others, even to become strongly attached to certain others in enduring, close relationships. Human beings, contended the personality theorist Alfred Adler, have an "urge to community" (Ferguson, 1989). Roy Baumeister and Mark Leary (1995) have assembled evidence for this deep *need to belong*.

Aiding Survival

Social bonds boosted our ancestors' survival rate. By keeping children close to their caregivers, attachments served as a powerful survival impulse. As adults, those who formed attachments were more likely to come together to reproduce and to stay together to nurture their offspring to maturity. To be "wretched" literally means, in its Middle English origin (*wrecche*), to be without kin nearby.

Cooperation in groups also enhanced survival. In solo combat, our ancestors were not the toughest predators. But as hunters they learned that six hands were better than two. And as foragers traveling in groups they gained protection from predators and enemies. If those who felt a need to belong were also those who survived and reproduced most successfully, their genes would in time predominate. The inevitable result: an innately social creature. People in every society on Earth belong to groups (and, as Chapter 15 explains, prefer and favor "us" over "them").

The need to connect Six days a week, women from the Philippines work as "domestic helpers" in 154,000 Hong Kong households. On Sundays, they throng to the central business district to picnic, dance, sing, talk, and laugh. "Humanity could stage no greater display of happiness," reported one observer (*Economist*, 2001).

Wanting to Belong

The need to belong colors our thoughts and emotions. We spend a great deal of time thinking about our actual and hoped-for relationships. When relationships form, we often feel joy. Falling in mutual love, people have been known to feel their cheeks ache from their irrepressible grins. Asked, "What is necessary for your happiness?" or "What is it that makes your life meaningful?" most people mention—before anything else—close, satisfying relationships with family, friends, or romantic partners (Berscheid, 1985). Happiness hits close to home.

Acting to Increase Social Acceptance

When we feel included, accepted, and loved by those important to us, our self-esteem rides high. Indeed, say Mark Leary and his colleagues (1998), our self-esteem is a gauge of how valued and accepted we feel. Much of our social behavior therefore aims to increase our belonging—our social acceptance and inclusion. To avoid rejection, we generally conform to group standards and seek to make favorable impressions (more on this in Chapter 15). To win friendship and esteem, we monitor our behavior, hoping to create the right impressions. Seeking love and belonging, we spend billions on clothes, cosmetics, and diet and fitness aids—all motivated by our quest for acceptance.

Like sexual motivation, which feeds both love and exploitation, the need to belong feeds both deep attachments and menacing threats. Out of our need to define a "we" come loving families, faithful friendships, and team spirit, but also teen gangs, ethnic rivalries, and fanatic nationalism.

Maintaining Relationships

For most of us, familiarity breeds liking, not contempt. We resist breaking social bonds. Thrown together at school, at summer camp, on a vacation cruise, people resist the group's dissolution. Hoping to maintain our relationships, we promise to

Social exclusion fosters freaking out
Most socially excluded teens do not commit violence, but some do. Charles "Andy" Williams, described by a classmate as someone his peers derided as "freak, dork, nerd, stuff like that," went on a shooting spree at his suburban California high school, killing 2 and wounding 13 (Bowles & Kasindorf, 2001).

call, to write, to come back for reunions. Parting, we feel distress. The dark side of this is that attachments can keep people in abusive relationships; the fear of being alone may seem worse than the pain of emotional or physical abuse. Even when bad relationships break, people suffer. In one 16-nation survey, separated and divorced people were only half as likely as married people to say they were "very happy" (Inglehart, 1990). After such separations, feelings of loneliness and anger—and sometimes even a strange desire to be near the former partner—are commonplace.

The fear of being alone has some basis in reality. Children who move through a series of foster homes, with repeated disruption of budding attachments, may come to have difficulty forming deep attachments. And children reared in institutions without a sense of belonging to anyone, or locked away at home under extreme neglect, become pathetic creatures—withdrawn, frightened, speechless.

When something threatens or dissolves our social ties, negative emotions—anxiety, loneliness, jealousy, guilt—overwhelm us. The bereaved often feel life is empty, pointless. When immigrants and refugees move, alone, to new places, the stress and loneliness can be depressing. After years of placing such families individually in isolated communities, today's policies encourage "chain migration" (Pipher, 2002). The second refugee Sudanese family that settles in a town generally has an easier adjustment than the first.

For children, even a brief time-out in isolation can be an effective punishment. For adults, social ostracism can be even more painful. Exile, imprisonment, and solitary confinement are progressively more severe forms of punishment. Even to be shunned—given the cold shoulder or the silent treatment, with others' eyes avoiding yours—is to have one's need to belong threatened, observe Kipling Williams and Lisa Zadro (2001). "It's the meanest thing you can do to someone, especially if you know they can't fight back. I never should have been born," said Lea, a lifelong victim of the silent treatment by her mother and grandmother. Like Lea, people often respond to social ostracism with depressed moods, initial efforts to restore their acceptance, and then withdrawal. "I came home every night and cried. I lost 25 pounds, had no self-esteem and felt that I wasn't worthy," reported Richard, after two years of silent treatment by his employer.

If rejected and unable to remedy the situation, people sometimes turn nasty. In a series of studies, Jean Twenge and her collaborators (2001, 2002; Baumeister & others, 2002) either told people (based on a personality test) that they were "the type likely to end up alone later in life" or that others whom they had met didn't want them in a group that was forming. The researchers told other participants that they would have "rewarding relationships throughout life" or that "everyone chose you as someone they'd like to work with." Those excluded became much more likely to engage in self-defeating behaviors and underperform on aptitude tests. They also exhibited more antisocial behavior, such as disparaging or aggressing (with a blast of noise) against someone who had insulted them. "If intelligent, well-adjusted, successful university students can turn aggressive in response to a small laboratory experience of social exclusion," noted the research team, "it is disturbing to imagine the aggressive tendencies that might arise from a series of important rejections or chronic exclusion from desired groups in actual social life."

Fortifying Health

Do you have close friends—people with whom you freely disclose your ups and downs? As we will see in Chapter 11, people who feel supported by close relationships live with better health and at lower risk for psychological disorder and premature death than do those who lack social support. Married people, for example, are less at risk for depression, suicide, and early death than are unattached people. All this evidence affirms Baumeister and Leary's (1995) contention that "human beings are fundamentally and pervasively motivated by a need to belong."

ACHIEVEMENT MOTIVATION

The biological perspective on motivation—the idea that physiological needs drive us to satisfy those needs—only partially explains what energizes and directs our behavior. Hunger and sex have both social and physiological components. Moreover, there are motives that, unlike hunger and sex, do not appear to satisfy any physical need. Billionaire entrepreneurs may be motivated to make ever more money, celebrities to become even more famous, dictators to achieve more power, daredevils to seek greater thrills. When fed, such motives, like our need to belong, seem not to diminish. The more we achieve, the more we may need to achieve.

Identifying Achievement Motivation

16. What characteristics are shared by people with a high need to achieve?

Think of someone you know who strives to succeed by excelling at any task where evaluation is possible. Now think of someone who is less driven. Psychologist Henry Murray (1938) defined the first person's high need for achievement, or **achievement motivation**, as a desire for significant accomplishment, for mastering skills or ideas, for control, and for rapidly attaining a high standard.

To study this motive, we first need a way to measure it. Recall from the semi-starvation studies that if driven by hunger we begin to fantasize about food. Our sexual orientation is similarly reflected in our prevalent sexual fantasies. If socially isolated, we think about those we love. Do these examples suggest a way to assess a person's need to achieve?

Murray and investigators David McClelland and John Atkinson presumed that people's fantasies would reflect their concern for achievement. So they asked research participants to invent stories about ambiguous pictures. If a person who was shown the daydreaming boy in **FIGURE 10.16** said the boy was preoccupied with pursuit of a goal, that he imagined himself performing a heroic act, or that he was feeling pride about some success, the researchers scored the response as indicating achievement concerns. If people's stories consistently included such themes, McClelland and Atkinson regarded them as having a high need for achievement.

Would you expect people whose stories express high achievement to prefer tasks that are easy, moderately challenging, or very difficult? People whose stories suggest low achievement motivation tend to choose either very easy or very difficult tasks, where failure is either unlikely or not embarrassing (Geen, 1984). Those whose stories express high achievement motivation tend to prefer moderately difficult tasks, where success is attainable yet attributable to their skill and effort. In a ring-toss game they often stand at an intermediate distance from the stake, enabling some successes while providing a suitable challenge. When things get difficult, people with a strong need to achieve do persist more (Cooper, 1983). By contrast, high school underachievers persist less in completing college degrees, holding on to jobs, and maintaining their marriages (McCall, 1994).

McClelland, D. C., et al. (1953). The achievement motive. New York: Appleton-Century Crofts. Reprinted by permission of Irvington Publishers, New York.

figure 10.16
What is this boy daydreaming about?
By analyzing responses to ambiguous photos like this, motivation researchers have sought clues to people's level of achievement motivation.

▶ **achievement motivation** a desire for significant accomplishment: for mastery of things, people, or ideas; for attaining a high standard.

Sources of Achievement Motivation

17. Why are some of us driven to excel but others are not?

What is your greatest achievement to date? What is your greatest future ambition—to attain fame? Fortune? Creative accomplishment? Security? Love? Power? Wisdom? Spiritual wholeness?

"They can because they think they can."

Virgil, Aeneid, 19 B.C.

Why, despite having similar potentials, does one person become more motivated to achieve than another? Highly motivated children (and those least likely to drop out of school) often have parents and teachers who encourage their independence from an early age and praise and reward them for their successes (Teevan & McGhee, 1972; Vallerand & others, 1997). Such parents encourage their children to dress and feed themselves and to do well in school. When their children achieve, they express delight.

Theorists speculate that the high achievement motivation displayed by such children has *emotional* roots. They learn to associate achievement with positive emotions. There may also be *cognitive* roots, as children learn to attribute their achievements to their own competence and effort, raising their expectations (Dweck & Elliott, 1983). Experiments show that even children who are bribed into an activity such as writing will sustain their interest if led to attribute their involvement internally: "You look like the kind of [girl/boy] who understands how important it is to write correctly, and who really wants to be good at it" (Cialdini & others, 1998).

So, how might organizational leaders motivate achievement in their members or employees? What might inspire workers to set high goals and work diligently to achieve them? For answers, see Appendix B: Psychology at Work.

rehearse it!

18. Achievement motivation is defined as a desire for significant accomplishment, for mastering skills or ideas, for control, and for rapidly attaining a high standard. Given a choice of tasks, high achievers would select one that is
    a. very difficult, so they have an excuse for failure.
    b. very easy, so that they can avoid failure.
    c. moderately challenging, so that their success will be attributed to their skill and effort.

    d. extremely difficult, so that when they do complete the task, they can feel superior to others performing the same task.

19. Psychologists know that achievements are not distributed in a bell curve, as intelligence scores are. Achievement therefore must be more than just raw ability. Studies of highly motivated children have found that

    a. their parents tend to encourage their independence and praise and reward their successes.
    b. their teachers and caregivers use primarily extrinsic rewards.
    c. these children are aggressive, antisocial, and self-absorbed.
    d. these children are distinguished by extraordinary natural talent.

    Answers can be found in Appendix C.

chapter review

REVIEWING

Motivation

Motivation is the energizing and directing of our behavior, as exemplified in our yearning for food, our longing for sexual intimacy, and our desire to achieve.

MOTIVATIONAL CONCEPTS

1. What underlying assumption is shared by instinct theory and evolutionary psychology?

Under Darwin's influence, early theorists viewed behavior as controlled by biological forces, such as specific instincts. When it became clear that people were naming, not explaining, various behaviors by calling them instincts, this approach fell into disfavor. The underlying idea—that genes predispose species-typical behavior—is, however, still influential in evolutionary psychology.

2. How does drive-reduction theory help us understand the forces that energize and direct some of our behavior?

Most physiological needs create aroused psychological states that drive us to reduce or satisfy those needs. The aim of drive reduction is internal stability, or homeostasis. Thus, drive reduction motivates survival behaviors, such as eating and drinking. Not only are we pushed by our internal drives, we are also pulled by external incentives. Depending on our personal experiences, some stimuli (for example, certain foods) will arouse our desires.

3. What type of motivated behavior does arousal theory attempt to explain?

Rather than reducing a physiological need or tension state, some motivated behaviors increase arousal. Curiosity-driven behaviors, for example, suggest that too little as well as too much stimulation can motivate people to seek an optimum level of arousal.

4. What is the basic idea behind Maslow's hierarchy of needs?

Maslow's hierarchy of needs expresses the idea that, until satisfied, some motives are more compelling (that is, more basic) than others. At the base of his hierarchy are physiological needs and at the top are self-actualization needs.

HUNGER

5. What physiological factors cause us to feel hungry?

Hunger's inner push primarily originates not from the stomach's contractions but from variations in body chemistry including hormones that heighten or reduce hunger. For example, we are likely to feel hungry when our blood glucose levels are low, or when the hormone ghrelin is secreted by the empty stomach. This information is integrated by the hypothalamus, which regulates the body's weight as it influences our feelings of hunger and satiety. To maintain weight, the body also adjusts its metabolic rate of energy expenditure.

6. What psychological influences affect our eating behavior and feelings of hunger?

Our preferences for certain tastes are partly genetic and universal, but also partly learned in a cultural context. The impact of psychological factors, such as challenging family settings and weight-obsessed societal pressures, on eating behavior is dramatic in people with anorexia nervosa, who keep themselves on near-starvation rations, and in those with bulimia nervosa, who binge and purge in secret. In the past half-century a dramatic increase in poor body image has coincided with a rise in eating disorders among women in Western cultures. In addition to cultural pressures, low self-esteem and negative emotions (with a possible genetic component) seem to interact with stressful life experiences to produce anorexia and bulimia.

7. What factors predispose some people to become and remain obese?

Fat is a concentrated fuel reserve stored in fat cells. Under genetic influence, the number and size of these cells determine one's body fat. Obese people find it difficult to lose weight permanently because the number of fat cells is not reduced by a diet, because fat cells require less energy expenditure than muscle cells to maintain themselves, and because the overall metabolic rate decreases when body weight drops below its set point. Those who nevertheless wish to diet should minimize exposure to food cues, boost energy expenditure through exercise, and make a lifelong change in eating patterns.

SEXUAL MOTIVATION

8. What behavior patterns must a theory of sexual motivation explain?

A theory of sexual motivation should attempt to explain the broad range of sexual behaviors that vary across time and place. Kinsey's early data-collection efforts, although criticized for their methodology, were an attempt to survey these behaviors.

9. *What are the stages of the human sexual response cycle?*

Physiologically, the human sexual response cycle normally follows a pattern of excitement, plateau, orgasm, and resolution. During the resolution phase, males enter a refractory period, a resting period in which renewed arousal and orgasm are impossible.

10. *How do sex hormones influence human sexual development and arousal?*

Sex hormones (estrogen and testosterone), in combination with the hypothalamus, help our bodies develop and function as either male or female. In many nonhuman animals, hormones also help stimulate sexual activity. In humans, they influence sexual behavior more loosely, especially once sufficient hormone levels are present.

11. *How do internal and external stimuli contribute to sexual arousal?*

External stimuli can trigger sexual arousal in both men and women. Sexually explicit materials may also lead people to perceive their partners as comparatively less appealing and to devalue their relationships. In combination with the internal hormonal push and the external pull of sexual stimuli, imagined stimuli (fantasies) help trigger sexual arousal. Some sexual disorders respond well to behavioral treatment, which assumes that people can learn to modify their sexual responses.

12. *What factors influence teenagers' sexual attitudes and behaviors?*

Adolescents' physical maturation fosters a sexual dimension to their emerging identity. But culture is a big influence, too, as is apparent from varying rates of teen intercourse and pregnancy. A near-epidemic of sexually transmitted infections has triggered new research and educational programs pertinent to adolescent sexuality.

13. *What does current research tell us about why some people are attracted to members of their own sex and others are attracted to members of the other sex?*

One's heterosexual or homosexual orientation seems neither willfully chosen nor able to be willfully changed. Preliminary new evidence links sexual orientation with genetic influences, prenatal hormones, and the size of certain brain structures. The increasing public perception that sexual orientation is biologically influenced is associated with increasing acceptance of gays and lesbians and their relationships.

14. *Is scientific research on sexual motivation value-free?*

Sex research and sex education are not value-free. Some say that sex-related values should therefore be openly acknowledged, recognizing the emotional significance of sexual expression. Human sexuality at its life-uniting and love-renewing best affirms our deep need to belong.

THE NEED TO BELONG

15. *Why do some psychologists believe we have a need to belong—to affiliate with others?*

No one is an island; we are all, as John Donne noted in 1624, part of the human continent. Our need to affiliate—to feel connected and identified with others—boosted our ancestors' chances for survival and is therefore part of our human nature. We experience our need to belong when suffering the breaking of social bonds, when feeling the gloom of loneliness or the joy of love, and when seeking social acceptance.

ACHIEVEMENT MOTIVATION

16. *What characteristics are shared by people with a high need to achieve?*

Some human behaviors are energized and directed without satisfying any apparent biological need. Achieving personal goals, for example, may be motivated by a person's social needs for competence and independence. People with a high need to achieve tend to prefer moderately challenging tasks and tend to persist in accomplishing them.

17. *Why are some of us driven to excel but others are not?*

To understand why people with similar abilities often differ widely in their achievements, psychologists have studied highly motivated children. Many achievement-motivated children have parents and teachers who encourage and affirm independent achievement. Such children may learn to associate achievement with positive emotions and to attribute their success to their own competence.

A CRITICAL THINKER'S REVIEW OF CHAPTER 10

You've now studied and reviewed **Motivation**. For even better retention, reflect on these concepts at a deeper level. If you need to refresh your memory of the six categories of critical thinking shown in parentheses below, see page 34. See if you can answer each of these questions in a short paragraph.

1. Which motivational concept explains each of these behaviors and why? (pattern recognition)
   a. On a long road trip, your stomach is growling with hunger. So, you pull off to eat at the nearest restaurant.
   b. Muriel accidentally brushes a finger against her newborn's cheek, and the baby instantly starts rooting around in an attempt to nurse.
   c. Paul and his friends have never skydived but have an opportunity to do so this weekend. So, they decide to give it a try, just for fun.

2. Louisa is a teenager who has joined the "wrong" kind of crowd at school. One night she follows the gang to an outdoor party deep in the woods. After walking a long, long way, she finally asks whether they are nearly there and mysteriously gets no response. Louisa begins to wonder about her decision to hang out with these kids. They are her only friends, but she is tired, cold, and hungry, and she's beginning to feel afraid of this group that doesn't really seem concerned about her well-being. When the group turns onto yet another dark, overgrown path, Louisa decides to make a run for it and heads for home. Using Maslow's hierarchy of needs, explain Louisa's behavior. (creative problem solving)

3. You are traveling and have not eaten anything in eight hours. As your long-awaited meal is placed in front of you, your mouth waters. Even imagining this may set your mouth to watering. What triggers this anticipatory drooling, and why do you feel so hungry? (perspective taking)

4. Imagine that you are the U.S. Surgeon General and you decide to issue a set of recommendations to every American to help reduce the alarmingly high incidence of obesity in the United States. What should your top five recommendations be to help solve this problem? (practical problem solving)

5. How might drive-reduction theory, arousal theory, and the evolutionary perspective explain our sexual motivation? (psychological reasoning)

6. We're often aware of our affiliation needs—our need for others and for the feeling that we belong. But have you ever thought about *why* we have those needs? How might a researcher in motivation explain our need to belong? (scientific problem solving)

TERMS AND CONCEPTS TO REMEMBER

motivation, p. 341
instinct, p. 342
drive-reduction theory, p. 342
homeostasis, p. 342
incentive, p. 342
hierarchy of needs, p. 343

glucose, p. 346
set point, p. 347
basal metabolic rate, p. 347
anorexia nervosa, p. 350
bulimia nervosa, p. 350
sexual response cycle, p. 358

refractory period, p. 358
sexual disorder, p. 359
estrogen, p. 359
testosterone, p. 359
sexual orientation, p. 364
achievement motivation, p. 373

To continue your study and review of Motivation, visit this book's Web site at www.worthpublishers.com/myers. You will find practice tests, review activities, and Web links for more information on topics related to Motivation.

chapter11

Emotions, Stress, and Health

No one needs to tell you that feelings add color to your life, or that in times of stress they can disrupt your life or save it. Of all the species, we seem the most emotional (Hebb, 1980). More often than any other creature, we express fear, anger, sadness, joy, and love.

We all can recall times when we have been overcome with emotion. I retain a flashbulb memory for the day I went to a huge store to drop off film and brought along Peter, my toddler first-born child. As I set Peter down and prepared to complete the paperwork, a passerby warned, "You'd better be careful or you'll lose that boy!" Not more than a few breaths later, after dropping the film in the slot, I turned and found no Peter beside me.

With mild anxiety, I peered around one end of the counter. No Peter in sight. With only slightly more anxiety, I peered around the other end. No Peter there, either. Now, with my heart accelerating, I circled the neighboring counters. Still no Peter anywhere. As anxiety turned to panic, I began racing up and down the store aisles. He was nowhere to be found. Apprised of my alarm, the store manager used the public-address system to ask customers to assist in looking for a missing child. Soon after, I passed the customer who had warned me. "I told you that you were going to lose him!" he said scornfully. With visions of kidnapping (strangers routinely adored that beautiful child), I braced for the possibility that my negligence had caused me to lose what I loved above all else, and—dread of all dreads—that I might have to return home and face my wife without our only child.

But then, as I passed the customer service counter yet again, there he was, having been found and returned by some obliging customer! In an instant, the arousal of dread spilled into the elation of ecstasy. As I clutched my son, with tears suddenly flowing, I found myself unable to speak my thanks and stumbled out of the store awash in joy.

THEORIES OF EMOTION

1. What are the components of an emotion?

Where do such emotions come from? Why do we have them? What are they made of? Emotions are our body's adaptive response. When we face challenges, emotions focus our attention and energize our action. Our heart races. We quicken our pace. All our senses go on high alert. Receiving unexpected good news, we may find our eyes tearing. We raise our hands triumphantly. We feel exuberance and a newfound confidence.

As this story illustrates, **emotions** are a mix of (1) physiological activation (heart pounding), (2) expressive behaviors (quickened pace), and (3) conscious experience, including thoughts (is this a kidnapping?) and feelings (a sense of fear, and later joy). The puzzle, as we'll see next, is how these three pieces fit together.

How do psychologists think about and study emotions? Three classic theories address two big issues about the physiology, expression, and experience of emotion.

The James-Lange and Cannon-Bard Theories

2. Does physiological arousal precede or follow an emotional experience? (Does your heart pound because you are afraid, or are you afraid because you feel your heart pounding?)

Common sense tells most of us that we cry because we are sad, lash out because we are angry, tremble because we are afraid. First comes conscious awareness, then the physiological trimmings. But to pioneering psychologist William James this commonsense view of emotion was 180 degrees out of line. According to James,

Not only emotion but most psychological phenomena (vision, sleep, memory, sex, and so forth) can be approached these three ways—physiologically, behaviorally, and cognitively.

▶ **emotion** a response of the whole organism, involving (1) physiological arousal, (2) expressive behaviors, and (3) conscious experience.

▶ **James-Lange theory** the theory that our experience of emotion is our awareness of our physiological responses to emotion-arousing stimuli.

▶ **Cannon-Bard theory** the theory that an emotion-arousing stimulus simultaneously triggers (1) physiological responses and (2) the subjective experience of emotion.

▶ **two-factor theory** Schachter's theory that to experience emotion one must (1) be physically aroused and (2) cognitively label the arousal.

"Whenever I feel afraid
I hold my head erect
And whistle a happy tune."

Richard Rodgers and Oscar Hammerstein,
The King and I, 1958

"Every moment is more intense."

Paralyzed actor Christopher Reeve (1995)

"We feel sorry because we cry, angry because we strike, afraid because we tremble" (1890, p. 1066). Perhaps you can recall a time when your car skidded on slick pavement. As it careened out of control you hit your brakes and regained control. Just after the fishtail ended, you noticed your racing heart and *then*, shaking with fright, you felt the whoosh of emotion. Your feeling of fear *followed* your body's response. James' idea, also proposed by Danish physiologist Carl Lange, is called the **James-Lange theory**.

The James-Lange theory struck U.S. physiologist Walter Cannon (1871–1943) as implausible. Cannon thought the body's responses were not distinct enough to evoke the different emotions. Does a racing heart signal fear, anger, or love? Also, changes in heart rate, perspiration, and body temperature seemed too slow to trigger sudden emotion. Cannon, and later another physiologist, Philip Bard, concluded that physiological arousal and our emotional experience occur simultaneously: The emotion-triggering stimulus is routed simultaneously to the brain's cortex, causing the subjective awareness of emotion, and to the sympathetic nervous system, causing the body's arousal. This **Cannon-Bard theory** implies that your heart begins pounding *as* you experience fear; one does not cause the other.

As long as the evidence suggested that our physiological reactions to different emotions were much the same, the James-Lange assumption that we experience our emotions through differing body states seemed improbable. But then new evidence showed subtle physiological distinctions among the emotions, and the James-Lange theory again became plausible. James struggled with his own feelings of depression and grief, and in doing so he came to believe that we can control emotions by going "through the outward motions" of whatever emotion we want to experience. "To feel cheerful," he advised, "sit up cheerfully, look around cheerfully, and act as if cheerfulness were already there." Recent findings concerning emotional effects of facial expressions are, as we will see, precisely what James might have predicted.

Let's check your understanding of the James-Lange and Cannon-Bard theories. Imagine that your brain could not sense your heart pounding or your stomach churning. According to each theory, how would this affect your experienced emotions?

Cannon and Bard would have expected you to experience emotions normally, because they believed emotions occur separately from (though simultaneously with) the body's arousal. James and Lange would have expected greatly diminished emotions because they believed that to experience emotion you must first perceive your body's arousal.

The condition you imagined actually exists in people with severed spinal cords. Psychologist George Hohmann (1966) interviewed 25 soldiers who suffered such injuries in World War II. He asked them to recall emotion-arousing incidents that occurred before and after their spinal injuries. Those with lower-spine injuries, who had lost sensation only in their legs, reported little change in their emotions. Those who could feel nothing below the neck reported a considerable decrease in emotional intensity (as James and Lange would have expected). These soldiers said that although they might act much the same as before in emotional situations, the anger, as one man confessed, "just doesn't have the heat to it that it used to. It's a mental kind of anger." But emotions expressed mostly in body areas above the neck are felt more intensely by those with high spinal-cord injury. Virtually all the men Hohmann interviewed reported increases in weeping, lumps in the throat, and getting choked up when saying good-bye, worshipping, or watching a touching movie.

Although such evidence breathed new life into the James-Lange theory, most researchers agree with Cannon and Bard that our experienced emotions also involve cognition (Averill, 1993). Whether we fear the man behind us on the dark street depends entirely on whether we interpret his actions as threatening or friendly. With James and Lange we can say that our physical reactions are an important ingredient of emotion. And with Cannon and Bard we can say that there is more to the experience of emotion than reading our physiology.

Cognition and Emotion

> *3. To experience emotions, must we consciously interpret and label them?*

Now, a second and more recent controversy: Put simply, what is the connection between what we *think* and how we *feel*? Which is the chicken and which the egg? Do our emotions always grow from our thoughts? Are our feelings always subject to our *mind's* appraisal of a situation? Or can we experience emotion apart from thinking? The answers have practical implications for self-management.

Schachter's Two-Factor Theory of Emotion

Stanley Schachter believed that our cognitions—our perceptions, memories, and interpretations—are an essential ingredient of emotion. He proposed a **two-factor theory**, in which emotions have two ingredients: physical arousal and a cognitive label (**FIGURE 11.1**). Like James and Lange, Schachter presumed that our experience of emotion grows from our awareness of our body's arousal. Yet like Cannon and Bard, Schachter also believed that emotions are physiologically similar. Thus, in his view, an emotional experience requires a conscious interpretation of the arousal.

Sometimes our arousal response to one event spills over into our response to the next event. Imagine that after an invigorating run you arrive home to find a message that you got a longed-for job. With arousal lingering from the run, would you feel more elated than if you received this news after awakening from a nap?

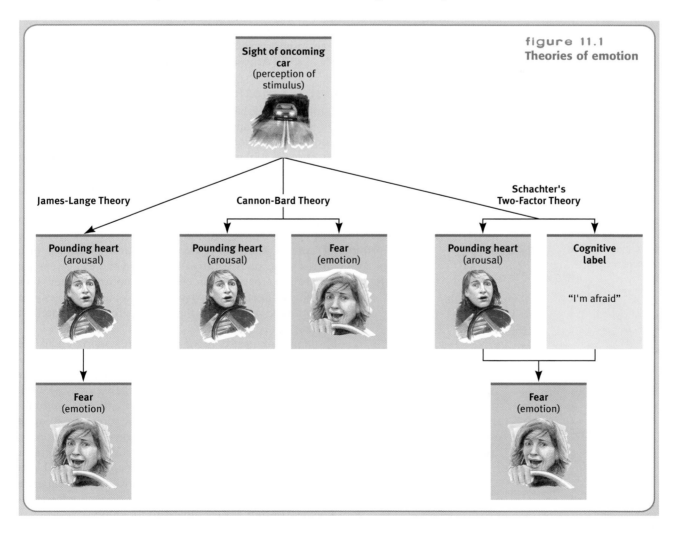

figure 11.1
Theories of emotion

Sight of oncoming car (perception of stimulus)

James-Lange Theory
Pounding heart (arousal) → **Fear** (emotion)

Cannon-Bard Theory
Pounding heart (arousal)
Fear (emotion)

Schachter's Two-Factor Theory
Pounding heart (arousal)
Cognitive label "I'm afraid"
→ **Fear** (emotion)

The spillover effect Arousal from a soccer match can fuel anger, which can descend into rioting.

To find out whether this spillover effect exists, Schachter and Jerome Singer (1962) aroused college men with injections of the hormone epinephrine. Picture yourself as one of their subjects: After receiving the injection, you go to a waiting room, where you find yourself with another person (actually an accomplice of the experimenters) who is acting either euphoric or irritated. As you observe this person, you begin to feel your heart race, your body flush, and your breathing become more rapid. If told to expect these effects from the injection, what would you feel? Schachter and Singer's subjects felt little emotion—because they attributed their arousal to the drug. But if told the injection would produce no effects, what would you feel? Perhaps you would react, as another group of subjects did, by "catching" the apparent emotion of the person you are with—becoming happy if the accomplice is acting euphoric, and testy if the accomplice is acting irritated.

This discovery—that a stirred-up state can be experienced as one emotion or another very different one, depending on how we interpret and label it—has been replicated in dozens of experiments. Although emotional arousal is not as undifferentiated as Schachter believed, arousal—from emotions as diverse as anger, fear, and sexual excitement—can spill from one emotion to another (Reisenzein, 1983; Sinclair & others, 1994; Zillmann, 1986). Insult people who have just been aroused by pedaling an exercise bike or watching rock videos and they will find it easy to misattribute their arousal to the provocation. Their feelings of anger will be greater than those of people who were similarly provoked but not previously aroused. Similarly, sexually aroused people react with more hostility in anger-provoking situations; and the arousal that lingers after an intense argument or a frightening experience may intensify sexual passion (Palace, 1995). Arousal fuels emotion; cognition channels it.

Must Cognition Precede Emotion?

So, to experience an emotion, must we first label our arousal? If Robert Zajonc (pronounced ZI-yence; 1980, 1984a) is right, the answer is no. He argues that our emotional reactions can be quicker than our interpretations of a situation; we therefore feel some emotions *before* we think. For example, a subliminally flashed smiling or angry face can prime us to feel better or worse about a follow-up stimulus (Murphy & others, 1995). Follow-up experiments confirm the lightning-quick speed of our automatic, unthinking, emotional responses (Duckworth & others, 2002; Stapel & others, 2002).

Research on neurological processes shows how we can experience emotion before cognition. Like speedy spinal reflexes that operate apart from the brain's thinking cortex, some of emotion's neural pathways also bypass the cortex. One such pathway runs from the eye or ear via the thalamus to the amygdala, an emotional control center. This eye-to-amygdala shortcut, bypassing the cortex, enables our greased-lightning emotional response before our intellect intervenes.

The amygdala sends more neural projections up to the cortex than it receives back. This makes it easier for our feelings to hijack our thinking than for our thinking to rule our feelings, note Joseph LeDoux and Jorge Armony (1999). After the cortex has further interpreted a threat, the thinking brain takes over (**FIGURE 11.2**). In the forest, we jump at the sound of rustling leaves nearby, leaving the cortex to decide later whether the sound was made by a predator or just the wind. Such an experience supports Zajonc's belief that *some* of our emotional reactions involve no deliberate thinking and that cognition is not always necessary for emotion. The heart is not always subject to the mind.

Can you recall liking something or someone immediately, without knowing why?

figure 11.2
The brain's shortcut for emotions
Sensory input may be routed both to the cortex for analysis and directly to the amygdala for a more instant emotional reaction.

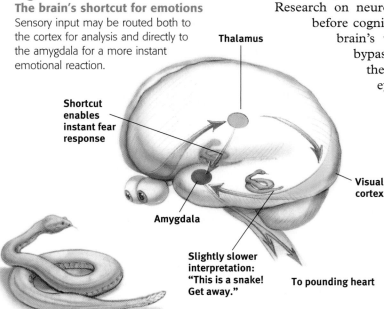

Thalamus

Shortcut enables instant fear response

Amygdala

Slightly slower interpretation: "This is a snake! Get away."

To pounding heart

Visual cortex

Emotion researcher Richard Lazarus (1991, 1998) disagreed. He conceded that our brains process and react to vast amounts of information without our conscious awareness, and he willingly granted that some emotional responses do not require *conscious* thinking. But even instantaneously felt emotions require some sort of cognitive appraisal of the situation; otherwise, he asked, how do we *know* what we are reacting to? The appraisal may be effortless and we may not be conscious of it, but it is still a mental function (**FIGURE 11.3**). Emotions arise when we *appraise* an event as beneficial or harmful to our well-being, whether we truly know it is or not. We appraise the sound of the rustling leaves as the presence of a predator. We learn after the appraisal that it was "just the wind."

To sum up, some emotional responses—especially simple likes, dislikes, and fears—involve no conscious thinking. We may fear the spider, even if we "know" it is harmless. Such responses are difficult to alter by changing our thinking.

Other emotions—including moods such as depression and complex feelings such as hatred and love—are greatly affected by our interpretations, memories, and expectations. For these emotions, as you will see in Chapter 14, learning to *think* more positively about ourselves and the world around us helps us *feel* better.

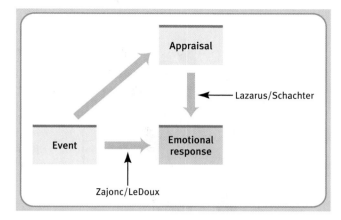

figure 11.3
Two routes to emotion
As Zajonc and LeDoux emphasize, some emotional responses are immediate, before any conscious appraisal. As Lazarus and Schachter emphasized, our appraisal and labeling of events also determines our emotional responses.

rehearse it!

1. Two important theories of emotion are the James-Lange theory and the Cannon-Bard theory. The James-Lange theory states that our experience of an emotion is a consequence of our physiological response to a stimulus; we are afraid because our heart pounds. The Cannon-Bard theory proposes that the physiological response (like heart pounding) and the subjective experience of, say, fear
   a. are unrelated.
   b. occur simultaneously.
   c. occur in the opposite order (with feelings of fear first).
   d. are regulated by the thalamus.

2. Assume that after spending an hour on a treadmill, you receive a letter saying that your scholarship to college has been approved. The two-factor theory of emotion would predict that your physical arousal will
   a. weaken your happiness.
   b. intensify your happiness.
   c. transform your happiness into relief.
   d. have no particular effect on your happiness.

3. Research suggests that we can experience an aroused state as one of several different emotions, depending on how we interpret and label the arousal. If physically aroused by swimming, then heckled by an onlooker, we may interpret our arousal as anger and

   a. become less physically aroused.
   b. feel angrier than usual.
   c. feel less angry than usual.
   d. act euphoric.

4. Robert Zajonc and Joseph LeDoux maintain that some of our emotional reactions occur before we have had the chance to label or interpret them. Richard Lazarus disagreed. These psychologists differ about whether emotional responses occur in the absence of
   a. physical arousal.
   b. the hormone epinephrine.
   c. cognitive processing.
   d. learning.

Answers can be found in Appendix C.

EMBODIED EMOTION[1]

Whether you are eagerly anticipating a long-awaited vacation, falling in love, or grieving the death of a loved one, you need little convincing that emotions involve the body. Feeling without a body is like breathing without lungs.

Emotion and Physiology

4. What physiological changes accompany emotions?

Some physical responses are easy to notice. As you hear a motorcycle rev up behind you on a dark street, your muscles tense, your stomach develops butterflies, your mouth becomes dry.

---

[1]Clinical psychophysiologist Charlotte van Oyen Witvliet contributed extensively to this sixth-edition revision of this section.

Autonomic nervous system controls physiological arousal		
Sympathetic division (arousing)		Parasympathetic division (calming)
Pupils dilate	EYES	Pupils contract
Decreases	SALIVATION	Increases
Perspires	SKIN	Dries
Increases	RESPIRATION	Decreases
Accelerates	HEART	Slows
Inhibits	DIGESTION	Activates
Secrete stress hormones	ADRENAL GLANDS	Decrease secretion of stress hormones

figure 11.4
Emotional arousal
Emotional arousal involves autonomic nervous system activation.

"Fear lends wings to his feet."

Virgil, Aeneid, 19 B.C.

One explanation of sudden death caused by a voodoo "curse" is that the terrified person's parasympathetic nervous system, which calms the body, overreacts to the extreme arousal by slowing the heart to a stop (Seligman, 1974).

figure 11.5
Arousal and performance
Performance peaks at lower levels of arousal for difficult tasks, and at higher levels for easy or well-learned tasks.

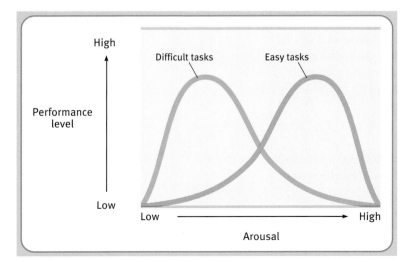

Your body also mobilizes for action in less noticeable ways. To provide energy, your liver pours extra sugar into your bloodstream. To help burn the sugar, your respiration increases to supply needed oxygen. Your digestion slows, diverting blood from your internal organs to your muscles. With blood sugar driven into the large muscles, running becomes easier. Your pupils dilate, letting in more light. To cool your stirred-up body, you perspire. If wounded, your blood would clot more quickly. After your next crisis, think of this: Without any conscious effort, your body's response to danger was wonderfully coordinated and adaptive—preparing you to fight or flee.

As we learned in Chapter 2, our *autonomic nervous system* controls our arousal (**FIGURE 11.4**). Its sympathetic division directs the adrenal glands atop the kidneys to release the stress hormones epinephrine (adrenaline) and norepinephrine (noradrenaline). The surge in epinephrine and norepinephrine increases heart rate, blood pressure, and blood sugar levels. When the crisis passes, the parasympathetic neural centers become active, calming the body. Even after the parasympathetic division inhibits further release of stress hormones, those already in the bloodstream linger awhile, so arousal diminishes gradually.

Prolonged physical arousal, produced by sustained stress, taxes the body (more on this later in this chapter). Yet in many situations arousal is adaptive. Too little arousal (say, sleepiness) can be as disruptive as extremely high levels. When you're taking an exam, it pays to be moderately aroused—alert but not trembling with nervousness.

Although we usually perform best when we feel moderately aroused, the level of arousal for optimal performance varies for different tasks. With easy or well-learned tasks, peak performance comes with relatively high arousal. With more difficult or unrehearsed tasks, optimal arousal is somewhat lower (**FIGURE 11.5**). Runners, who are performing a well-learned task, usually achieve their peak performances when highly aroused by competition. Basketball players shooting free throws—a less automatic skill—may not perform quite as well if a packed fieldhouse makes them hyper-aroused (Sokoll & Mynatt, 1984). Likewise, students who feel great anxiety during exams perform more poorly than those equally able but more confident. Teaching anxious students how to relax before an exam often enables them to perform better (Hembree, 1988).

The Physiology of Specific Emotions

5. Do different emotions activate different physiological responses?

Imagine conducting an experiment measuring the physiological responses of emotion. In each of four rooms, you have someone watching a movie: In the first, the person is viewing a horror show; in the second, a film sure to provoke anger; in the third, a sexually arousing film; in the fourth, an utterly boring movie. From the control center you monitor each person's physiological responses, measuring perspiration, breathing, and heart rates. Do you think you could tell who is frightened? Who is angry? Who is sexually aroused? Who is bored?

With training, you could probably pick out the bored viewer. But discerning physiological differences among fear, anger, and sexual arousal, with their similar arousal but differing intensities, is much more difficult (Cacioppo & others, 1997; Zillmann, 1986).

To you and me, sexual arousal, fear, and anger nevertheless *feel* different. If sexually stimulated, you will experience a genital response. If afraid, you may feel a clutching, sinking sensation in your chest and a knot in your stomach. If angry, you may feel "hot under the collar" and experience a pressing inner tension. And, despite similar arousal, fear and anger not only feel different but also *look* different. People may appear "paralyzed with fear" or "ready to explode." So, does research pinpoint any distinct physiological indicators of each emotion? Sometimes.

The finger temperatures and hormone secretions that accompany fear and anger do sometimes differ (Ax, 1953; Levenson, 1992). And, though fear and joy can prompt similar increased heart rate, they stimulate different facial muscles. During fear, brow muscles tense. During joy, muscles in the cheek and under the eye pull into a smile (Witvliet & Vrana, 1995). Emotions also differ in the brain circuits they use (Kalin, 1993; Panksepp, 1982). Observers watching (and subtly mimicking) fearful faces show more amygdala brain activity than do those watching angry faces (Whalen & others, 2001). You may recall the power of the amygdala from Chapter 2, where we saw on page 50 that stimulating one area of a cat's amygdala makes it pull back in terror at the sight of a mouse. Stimulate another area of the amygala and the cat will look enraged—pupils dilated, fur and tail erect, claws out, hissing furiously.

As people experience negative emotions such as disgust—and when they have generally negative personalities—they show more brain activity in the right prefrontal cortex than in the left. Depression-prone people also show more right frontal activity (Harmon-Jones, Abramson, & others, 2002). One man, having lost part of his right frontal lobe in brain surgery, became—his not-unhappy wife reported—less irritable and more affectionate (Goleman, 1995). My father, after a right-hemisphere stroke, lived the last two years of his life with happy gratitude and nary a complaint or negative emotion.

People with positive emotions and personalities—exuberant infants and alert, energetic, and persistently goal-directed adults—show more activity in the left frontal lobe than in the right (Davidson, Ekman, & others, 1990; Davidson, 1999, 2000). The left frontal lobe's rich supply of dopamine receptors may help explain why a peppy left hemisphere correlates with a perky disposition.

So, although emotions as varied as fear, joy, and anger involve a similar general autonomic arousal (as in similar heart rate), there are real, if subtle, physiological

"No one ever told me that grief felt so much like fear. I am not afraid, but the sensation is like being afraid. The same fluttering in the stomach, the same restlessness, the yawning. I keep on swallowing."

C. S. Lewis, A Grief Observed, *1961*

In 1966, a young man named Charles Whitman killed his wife and mother and then climbed to the top of a tower at the University of Texas and shot 38 people. An autopsy later revealed a tumor in his limbic system.

M. Greco/Stock, Boston

Emotional arousal Elated excitement and panicky fear involve similar physiological arousal. That allows us to flip rapidly between the two emotions.

Lie Detection

Given the physical indicators of emotion, might we, like Pinocchio, give some telltale sign whenever we lie? The *lie detector*, or **polygraph**, was once used mainly in law enforcement and national security work. But by the mid-1980s, 2 million Americans annually were reportedly being tested, usually by corporations screening applicants for honesty or to uncover employee theft (Holden, 1986a).

Just what do polygraphs do? First, they do not literally detect lies. Rather, they measure several physical responses that accompany emotion, such as changes in breathing, cardiovascular activity, and perspiration. While you try to relax, the examiner monitors these responses as you answer questions. Some items, called control questions, aim to make anyone a little nervous. If asked, "In the last 20 years, have you ever taken something that didn't belong to you?" many people will tell a white lie and say no, causing arousal the polygraph will detect. If your physiological reactions to critical questions ("Did you ever steal anything from your previous employer?") are weaker than to control questions, the examiner infers you are telling the truth. The assumption is that only a thief becomes agitated when denying a theft.

But there are two problems: First, our physiological arousal is much

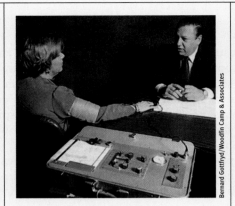

Can polygraph tests like this identify liars? To learn more, read on.

the same from one emotion to another. The polygraph cannot distinguish among anxiety, irritation, and guilt—they all prompt physiological reactivity. Second, an innocent person might also respond with heightened tension to the accusations implied by the relevant questions. Many rape victims "fail" lie detector tests when reacting emotionally while telling the truth about their assailant (Lykken, 1991). These tests err about one-third of the time. The "lie detector" could more accurately be called a fear detector. The test more often labels the innocent guilty—when the relevant question upsets an honest person—than the guilty innocent (**Figure 11.6**). Good advice, then, would be never to take a lie detector test if you are innocent.

Because the polygraph cannot discriminate the arousal of guilty lying from the arousal of fearful honesty, noted a 2002 U.S. National Academy of Sciences report, "no spy has ever been caught [by] using the polygraph." It is not for lack of trying. The FBI, CIA, and Department of Defense in the United States have spent millions of dollars testing tens of thousands of employees. Meanwhile Aldrich Ames, who enjoyed an unexplained lavish life-style as a Russian spy within the CIA, went undetected. Ames "took scores of polygraph tests and passed them all," notes Robert Park (1999). "Nobody thought to investigate the source of his sudden wealth—after all, he was passing the lie detector tests." The truth is, lie detectors can lie.

Although the polygraph is too error-prone for testing applicants and employees, police can use it to induce confessions from criminals—by scaring them into thinking that any lies will be transparent.

In a recent survey, however, more than 9 in 10 psychophysiologists and research psychologists agreed that savvy criminals and spies could beat the test by augmenting their arousal to control questions, such as by biting their tongues (Iacono & Lykken, 1997). A more effective approach to lie detection uses the *guilty knowledge test*, which assesses a suspect's physiological responses to crime-scene details known only to the police and the guilty person. If a camera and computer had been stolen, for example, the polygraph examiner could notice whether the suspect reacts strongly to the specific brand name of each. Presumably, only one guilty of the crime would have such responses. Given enough such specific probes, an innocent person will seldom be wrongly accused.

▶ **polygraph** a machine, commonly used in attempts to detect lies, that measures several of the physiological responses accompanying emotion (such as perspiration and cardiovascular, and breathing changes).

figure 11.6
How often do lie detectors lie? Benjamin Kleinmuntz and Julian Szucko (1984) had polygraph experts study the polygraph data of 50 theft suspects who later confessed to being guilty and 50 suspects whose innocence was later established by someone's confession. Had the polygraph experts been the judges, more than one-third of the innocent would have been declared guilty, and almost one-fourth of the guilty would have been declared innocent.

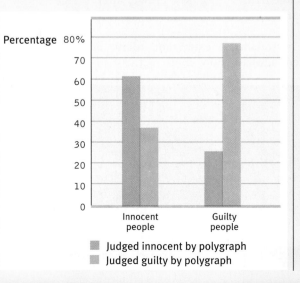

Percentage

- Judged innocent by polygraph
- Judged guilty by polygraph

differences that help explain why we experience them so differently. Moreover, most physical accompaniments of emotion appear innate and universal—the same in a village on Sumatra as in one in North America (Levenson & others, 1991).

rehearse it!

5. Emotions such as fear and anger involve a general autonomic arousal orchestrated by the sympathetic nervous system. In many situations, arousal is adaptive. For example, with a challenging task, such as taking an exam, performance is likely to be best when arousal is
   a. very high.   b. moderate.
   c. low.   d. diminishing.

6. Feelings of fear and anger involve a similar general autonomic arousal, but they activate different brain areas. For example, stimulate one area of a cat's _____ and the cat draws back in terror; stimulate another area of that structure and the cat hisses with rage.
   a. cortex
   b. hypothalamus
   c. reticular formation
   d. amygdala

Answers can be found in Appendix C.

EXPRESSED EMOTION

There is another, simpler method of deciphering people's emotions: We read their bodies, listen to their tone of voice, and study their faces.

Nonverbal Communication

6. How do we communicate nonverbally?

All of us communicate nonverbally as well as verbally. A firm handshake immediately conveys an outgoing, expressive personality (Chaplin & others, 2000). With a gaze, an averted glance, or a stare, we can communicate intimacy, submission, or dominance (Kleinke, 1986). Among those passionately in love, gazing into one another's eyes is typically prolonged and mutual (Rubin, 1970). Joan Kellerman, James Lewis, and James Laird (1989) wondered if intimate gazes would stir such feelings between strangers. To find out, they asked unacquainted male-female pairs to gaze intently for two minutes either at one another's hands or into one another's eyes. After separating, the eye-gazers reported feeling a tingle of attraction and affection. What if you do not want people to know how you feel, or if you do not even want to feel that way in the first place? Can we suppress our emotional expressions? Sometimes. But as Jane Richards and James Gross (2000) discovered, suppressing expression comes at a cost. Compared with those who simply watched a distressing film, those who diverted mental energy and attention into suppressing their emotional expressions showed impaired memory for details in the film.

Most of us are good enough at reading nonverbal cues to decipher the emotions in an old silent film. We are especially good at detecting nonverbal threats. When hearing emotions conveyed in another language, anger is the most readily detectable emotion (Scherer & others, 2001). In a crowd of faces, a single angry face will "pop out" faster than a single happy one (Fox & others, 2000; Hansen & Hansen, 1988; see **FIGURE 11.7** on page 388). By exposing different parts of emotion-laden faces, Robert Kestenbaum (1992) discovered that we read fear and anger mostly from the eyes, happiness from the mouth.

Some of us are more sensitive than others to these cues. Robert Rosenthal, Judith Hall, and their colleagues (1979) discovered this by showing hundreds of people brief film clips of portions of a person's emotionally expressive face or body, sometimes adding a garbled voice. For example, after a 2-second scene revealing only the face of an upset woman, the researchers would ask whether the woman was criticizing someone for being late or was talking about her divorce. Rosenthal and Hall reported that some people are much better than others at detecting emotion. Introverts tend to do better at reading others' emotions, although extraverts are themselves easier to read (Ambady & others, 1995).

Injected as part of the war on wrinkles, Botox paralyzes facial muscles that create wrinkles, allowing the overlying skin to relax and smooth. By erasing the subtle expressions of frown lines or twinkling eyes, might this cosmetic procedure hide subtle emotions?

"Your face, my thane, is a book where men may read strange matters."

Lady Macbeth to her husband, in William Shakespeare's Macbeth

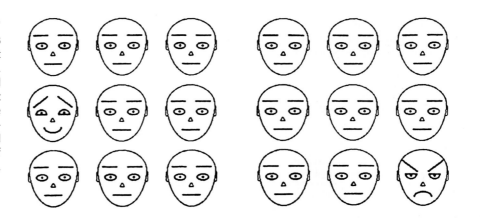

figure 11.7
Radar for threats: An angry face pops out Our emotion-detecting radar excels at detecting threats, and thus an angry face. Using stimuli such as these, Arne Öhman and his Stockholm colleagues (2001) found that people more speedily detect an angry face than a happy one. In other "Where's Waldo?"-like experiments, people more readily spotted images of threat-relevant snakes than of flowers (Öhman & others, 2001).

Experience can sensitize us to particular emotions. Shown a series of faces that morphed from sadness or fear to anger, physically abused children are much quicker than other children to see anger (**FIGURE 11.8**). Shown a face that is 60 percent fear and 40 percent anger, they are as likely to perceive anger as fear. Their perceptions become sensitively attuned to glimmers of danger that nonabused children miss.

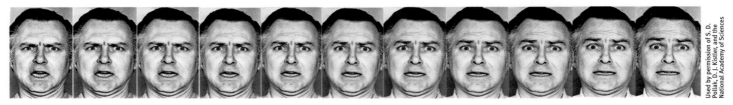

Used by permission of S. D. Pollak, D.J. Kistler, and the National Academy of Sciences

figure 11.8
Experience influences how we perceive emotions Shown the morphed middle face, evenly mixing fear or sadness with anger, physically abused children were more likely than nonabused children to perceive the face as angry (Pollak & Kistler, 2002).

Gender, Emotion, and Nonverbal Behavior

Is women's intuition, as so many believe, superior to men's? Consider: As Jackie Larsen left her Grand Marais, Minnesota, church prayer group one April 2001 morning, she encountered Christopher Bono, a clean-cut, well-mannered youth. Bono's car had broken down, and he said he was looking for a ride to meet friends in Thunder Bay. When Bono later appeared in Larsen's shop, where she had promised to help him phone his friends, she felt a pain in her stomach. Intuitively sensing that something was very wrong with this young man, she insisted that they talk outside on the sidewalk. "I said, 'I am a mother and I have to talk to you like a mother. . . . I can tell by your manners that you have a nice mother.'" At the mention of his mother, Bono's eyes fixed on her. "I don't know where my mother is," he said.

As the conversation ended, Larsen directed Bono back to the church to meet the pastor. She also called the police and suggested that they trace his license plates. The car was registered to his mother in southern Illinois. When police went to her apartment, they found blood all over and Lucia Bono dead in the bathtub. Christopher Bono, 16, was charged with first-degree murder (Biggs, 2001).

Was it a coincidence that Jackie Larsen, who saw through Bono's calm exterior, was a woman? Some psychologists would say no. In her analysis of 125 studies of sensitivity to nonverbal cues, Judith Hall (1984, 1987) discerned that women generally surpass men at reading people's emotional cues. Women's nonverbal sensitivity also gives them an edge in spotting lies (DePaulo, 1994). And women have surpassed men in discerning whether a male-female couple is a genuine romantic couple or a posed phony couple, and in discerning which of two people in a photo is the other's supervisor (Barnes & Sternberg, 1985).

Women's nonverbal sensitivity, perhaps a by-product of traditional gender roles, helps explain their greater emotional literacy. Invited by Lisa Feldman Barrett and her colleagues (2000) to describe how they would feel in certain situations, men described simpler emotional reactions. You might like to try this yourself: Ask some people how they might feel when saying good-bye to friends after graduation. Barrett's work suggests you are more likely to hear men say, simply, "I'll feel bad," and to hear women express more complex emotions: "It will be bittersweet; I'll feel both happy and sad."

Women's skill at decoding others' emotions may also contribute to their greater emotional responsiveness in positive and negative situations (Grossman & Wood, 1993; Sprecher & Sedikides, 1993; Stoppard & Gruchy, 1993). In studies of 23,000 people from 26 cultures around the world, women more than men reported themselves open to feelings (Costa & others, 2001). That helps explain the extremely strong perception that emotionality is "more true of women"—a perception expressed by nearly 100 percent of 18- to 29-year-old Americans (Newport, 2001).

When surveyed, women are also far more likely than men to describe themselves as empathic. If you have empathy, you identify with others and imagine what it must be like to walk in their shoes. You rejoice with those who rejoice and weep with those who weep. Physiological measures of empathy, such as one's heart rate while seeing another's distress, reveal a much smaller gender gap than is reported in surveys (Eisenberg & Lennon, 1983). Nevertheless, females are more likely to *express* empathy. Ann Kring and Albert Gordon (1998) observed this gender difference in videotapes of men and women students watching film clips that were sad (children with a dying parent), happy (slapstick comedy), or frightening (a man nearly falling off the ledge of a tall building). As **FIGURE 11.9** shows, the women reacted more visibly to each of the films.

In another exploration of gender and facial expression, Harold Hill and Alan Johnston (2001) animated an average head with expressions (smirks, head tosses, raised eyebrows) digitally captured from the faces of London University students as they read a joke. Despite having no anatomical clues to gender, observers could usually detect gender in the telltale expressions.

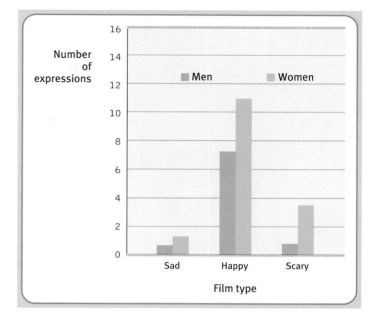

figure 11.9
Gender and expressiveness Although male and female students did not differ dramatically in self-reported emotions or physiological responses while viewing emotional films, the women's faces *showed* much more emotion. (From Kring & Gordon, 1998.)

Detecting Emotion

Hard-to-control facial muscles reveal signs of emotions you may be trying to conceal. Lifting just the inner part of your eyebrows, which few people do consciously, reveals distress or worry. Eyebrows raised and pulled together signal fear. Activated muscles under the eyes and raised cheeks suggest a natural smile. A feigned smile, such as one we make for a photographer, often continues for more than 4 or 5 seconds. Most authentic expressions have faded by that time. Feigned smiles also get switched on and off more abruptly than a genuine happy smile (Bugental, 1986).

Our brains are rather amazing detectors of these subtle expressions. Elisha Babad, Frank Bernieri, and Robert Rosenthal (1991) discovered just *how* amazing after videotaping teachers talking to unseen schoolchildren. A mere 10-second clip of either the teacher's voice or face provided enough clues for both young and old viewers to determine whether the teacher liked and admired the child he or she was addressing. Teachers may think they can conceal their feelings and stay objective, but their students can sense what their expressions and gestures reveal.

The growing awareness that we communicate through the body's silent language has led to studies of how job applicants and interviewers communicate (or miscommunicate) nonverbally. Popular guidebooks and articles offer advice on how to interpret nonverbal signals when negotiating a business deal, selling a product, or flirting. It pays to be able

Which of researcher Paul Ekman's smiles is feigned, which natural? The smile on the right engages the facial muscles of a natural smile.

Dr. Paul Ekman, University of California at San Francisco

Culver Pictures

A silent language of emotion The art of nonverbal communication reached a pinnacle early in the twentieth century as silent films became widely available. For a nickel, rapt audiences could watch performers mime a wide range of unmistakable emotions. Here Chester Conklin woos a woman on horseback while Louise Fazenda fumes. Hindu classic dance likewise uses the face and body to effectively convey 10 different emotions (Hejmadi & others, 2000).

to read feelings that leak through via subtle facial expressions, body movements, and postures. Fidgeting, for example, may reveal anxiety or boredom. More specific interpretations of postures and gestures are risky because different expressions may convey the same emotion: Either a cold stare or the avoidance of eye contact may signify hostility. And a single gesture can convey very different emotions: Folded arms, for example, can signify either irritation or relaxation.

Such gestures, facial expressions, and tones of voice are all absent in computer-based communication. E-mail communications sometimes include sideways "emoticons," such as ;-) for a knowing wink and :-(for a frown. But e-mail letters and Internet discussions otherwise lack nonverbal cues to status, personality, and age. Nobody knows what you look or sound like, or anything about your background; you are judged solely on your words. It's no wonder then that when first meeting an e-mail pen pal face to face, people are often surprised at the person they encounter.

Culture and Emotional Expression

7. Are nonverbal expressions of emotion universally understood?

The meaning of gestures varies with the culture. Some years ago, psychologist Otto Klineberg (1938) observed that in Chinese literature people clapped their hands to express worry or disappointment, laughed a great "Ho-Ho" to express anger, and stuck out their tongues to show surprise. Similarly, the North American "thumbs up" and "A-OK" signs would be insults in certain other cultures. (When former U.S. President Richard Nixon made the latter sign in Brazil, he didn't realize he was saying "Let's have sex.") Just how important cultural definitions of gestures can be was demonstrated in 1968, when North Korea publicized photos of supposedly happy officers from a captured U.S. Navy spy ship. In the photo, three of the men raised their middle fingers; they had told captors it was a "Hawaiian good luck sign" (Fleming & Scott, 1991).

Do facial expressions also have different meanings in different cultures? To find out, two investigative teams—one led by Paul Ekman, Wallace Friesen, and others (1975, 1987, 1994), the other by Carroll Izard (1977, 1994)—showed photographs of different facial expressions to people in different parts of the world and asked them to guess the emotion. You can try this yourself. Match the six emotions with the six faces of **FIGURE 11.10**.

You probably did pretty well regardless of your cultural background. A smile's a smile the world around. Ditto for anger, and to a lesser extent the other basic expressions (Elfenbein & Ambady, 1999). (There is no culture where people frown when they are happy.) Despite some differences, cultures and languages share many similarities in the ways they categorize emotions—as anger, fear, and so on. The physiological indicators of emotion also cross cultural boundaries (Levenson & others, 1992; Mesquita & Frijda, 1992).

Do people from different cultures share these similarities because they share experiences, such as American movies, the BBC, and CNN? Apparently not. Ekman and his team asked isolated people in New Guinea to display various emotions in response to such statements as, "Pretend your child has died." When the researchers showed videotapes of the New Guineans' facial reactions to North American collegians, the students read them easily. That explains why, in an experiment by Charles Bond and Adnan Atoum (2000), Americans, Jordanians, and Indians were equally adept at the difficult task of detecting videotaped lies, whether told by someone from their own country or not. Although some other research shows slightly enhanced accuracy when judging emotion from one's own culture, the telltale signs of emotion generally cross cultures (Elfenbein & Ambady, 2002).

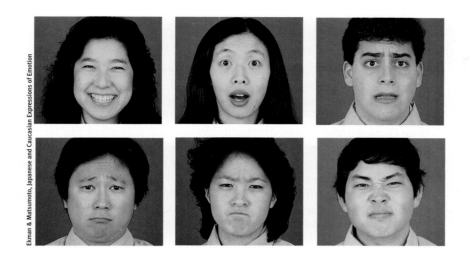

Ekman & Matsumoto, Japanese and Caucasian Expressions of Emotion

figure 11.10
Culture-specific or culturally universal expressions? As people of differing cultures and races, do our faces speak differing languages? Which face expresses disgust? Anger? Fear? Happiness? Sadness? Surprise? The answers are on page 392. (From Matsumoto and Ekman, 1989.)

Children's facial expressions—even those of blind children who have never seen a face—are also universal (Eibl-Eibesfeldt, 1971). People blind from birth spontaneously exhibit the common facial expressions associated with such emotions as joy, sadness, fear, and anger (Galati & others, 1997). The world over, children cry when distressed, shake their heads when defiant, and smile when they are happy.

The discovery that the facial muscles speak a fairly universal language would have come as no surprise to pioneering emotion researcher Charles Darwin (1809–1882). He speculated that in prehistoric times, before our ancestors communicated in words, their ability to convey threats, greetings, and submission with facial expressions helped them survive. That shared heritage, he believed, is why all humans express the basic emotions with similar facial expressions. A sneer, for example, retains elements of an animal's baring its teeth in a snarl.

Smiles, too, are social phenomena as well as emotional reflexes. Bowlers don't smile when they score a strike—they smile when they turn to face their companions (Jones & others, 1991; Kraut & Johnston, 1979). Even euphoric winners of Olympic gold medals typically don't smile when they are awaiting their ceremony but do when interacting with officials and facing the crowd and cameras (Fernández-Dols & Ruiz-Belda, 1995).

It has also been adaptive for us to *interpret* faces in particular contexts. (Recall the aggressive or frightened monster from page 181.) People judge an angry face set in a frightening situation as afraid. They judge a fearful face set in a painful situation as pained (Carroll & Russell, 1996). Movie directors harness this phenomenon by creating contexts and soundtracks that amplify our perceptions of particular emotions.

Emotional expressions may enhance our survival in other ways, too. Surprise raises the eyebrows and widens the eyes, enabling us to take in more information. Disgust wrinkles the nose, closing it from foul odors.

Although cultures share a universal facial language for basic emotions, they differ in how much emotion they express. In cultures that encourage individuality, as in Western Europe, Australia, New Zealand, and North America, emotional displays often are intense and prolonged. People focus on their own goals and attitudes and express themselves accordingly. Watching a film of someone's hand being cut, Americans grimace (whether alone or with other viewers). Japanese viewers hide their emotions when in the presence of others (Triandis, 1994). Asians rarely and briefly display negative or self-aggrandizing emotions that might disrupt communal feeling within close-knit groups (Markus & Kitayama, 1991; Matsumoto & others, 1988). Moreover, in Asian and other cultures that emphasize social connections and interdependence, displays of emotions such as sympathy, respect, and shame are more common than in the West.

"For news of the heart, ask the face."
Guinean proverb

While weightless, astronauts' fluids move toward their upper body and their faces become puffy. This makes nonverbal communication more difficult, increasing the risks of misunderstanding, especially among multinational crews (Gelman, 1989).

Answers to the questions in Figure 11.10 (page 391): From left to right, top to bottom: happiness, surprise, fear, sadness, anger, disgust.

"Refuse to express a passion and it dies. . . . If we wish to conquer undesirable emotional tendencies in ourselves, we must . . . go through the outward movements of those contrary dispositions which we prefer to cultivate."

William James, Principles of Psychology, 1890

A request from your author: Smile often as you read this book.

The Effects of Facial Expressions

8. Do our facial expressions influence our feelings?

Expressions not only communicate emotion, they also amplify and regulate it. In his 1872 book, *The Expression of the Emotions in Man and Animals*, Darwin contended that "the free expression by outward signs of an emotion intensifies it. . . . He who gives way to violent gestures will increase his rage" (p. 365).

Was Darwin right? I was driving in my car one day when the song "Put On a Happy Face" came on the radio. How phony, I thought. But I tested Darwin's hypothesis anyway, as you can, too. Fake a big grin. Now scowl. Can you feel the "smile therapy" difference?

Participants in dozens of experiments have felt a difference. For example, James Laird and his colleagues (1974, 1984, 1989) subtly induced students to make a frowning expression by asking them to "contract these muscles" and "pull your brows together" (supposedly to help the researchers attach facial electrodes). The results? The students reported feeling a little angry. Students similarly induced to smile felt happier, found cartoons more humorous, and recalled happier memories than did the frowners. People instructed to mold their faces in ways that mimicked expressions of other basic emotions also experienced those emotions. For example, they reported feeling more fear than anger, disgust, or sadness when made to construct an expression of fear: "Raise your eyebrows. And open your eyes wide. Move your whole head back, so that your chin is tucked in a little bit, and let your mouth relax and hang open a little" (Duclos & others, 1989). Going through the motions awakens the emotions.

In the absence of competing emotions, this "facial feedback" effect is subtle, yet detectable. Consider these findings:

- If subtly manipulated into furrowing their brows (**FIGURE 11.11**), people feel sadder while looking at sad photos.
- Saying the speech sounds *e* and *ah*, which activate smiling muscles, puts people—believe it or not—in a better mood than saying the German *ü* (rather like saying the English *e* and *u* together), which activates muscles associated with negative emotions (Zajonc & others, 1989).
- Just activating one of the smiling muscles by holding a pen in the teeth (rather than with the lips, which activates a frowning muscle) is enough to make cartoons seem more amusing (Strack & others, 1988). A heartier smile—made not just with the mouth but with raised cheeks that crinkle the eyes—enhances positive feelings even more while reacting to something pleasant or funny (Soussignan, 2001). Looking at oneself in a mirror further amplifies the effect (Kleinke & others, 1998). Smile warmly on the outside and you feel better on the inside. Scowl and the whole world seems to scowl back.

Sara Snodgrass and her associates (1986) observed the behavior feedback phenomenon with walking. You can duplicate her subjects' experience: Walk for a few minutes while taking short, shuffling steps, keeping your eyes downcast. Now walk around taking long strides, with your arms swinging and your eyes looking straight ahead. Can you feel your mood shift?

If assuming emotional expressions and postures triggers a feeling, then would imitating others' expressions help us feel what they are feeling? Again, the laboratory evidence is supportive. Kathleen Burns Vaughn and John Lanzetta (1981) asked some students but not others to make a pained expression whenever an electric shock was apparently delivered to

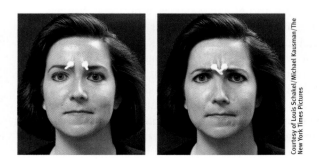

figure 11.11
How to make people frown without telling them to frown Randy Larsen, Margaret Kasimatis, and Kurt Frey's (1992) solution: Attach two golf tees above the eyebrows and ask the subjects to make the tee tips touch. Subjects felt sad while viewing scenes of war, sickness, and starvation, and even sadder with their "sad face" muscles activated.

Courtesy of Louis Schakel/Michael Kausman/The New York Times Pictures

someone they were watching. With each apparent shock, the grimacing observers perspired more and had a faster heart rate than the other observers. So one small way to become more empathic—to feel what others feel—is to let your own face mimic the other person's expression. Acting as another acts helps us feel what another feels. Indeed, natural mimicry of others' emotions helps explain why emotions are contagious (Dimberg & others, 2000; Neumann & Strack, 2000).

---

rehearse it!

7. Some nonverbal behaviors—threats and smiles, for example—are universally understood; others are not. People in different cultures are most likely to differ in their interpretations of
a. adults' facial expressions.
b. children's facial expressions.
c. frowns.
d. postures and gestures.

8. When people are induced to assume fearful expressions, they often report feeling a little fearful. This result is known as the _____ effect.

a. facial feedback
b. culture-specific
c. natural mimicry
d. emotional contagion

Answers can be found in Appendix C.

EXPERIENCED EMOTION

The ingredients of emotion include not only physiology and expressive behavior but also our conscious experience. How many distinct emotions are there? Carroll Izard (1977) isolated 10 such basic emotions (joy, interest-excitement, surprise, sadness, anger, disgust, contempt, fear, shame, and guilt), most of which are present in infancy (**FIGURE 11.12**). Izard reported that other emotions are combinations of these 10. Although Phillip Shaver and his colleagues (1996) believe that love, too, may be a basic emotion, Izard viewed it as a mixture of joy and interest-excitement.

Let's take a closer look at two of these emotions: anger and joyful happiness. What functions do they serve? What influences our experience of each?

(d) Disgust (nose wrinkled, upper lip raised, tongue pushed outward)

(e) Surprise (brows raised, eyes widened, mouth rounded in oval shape)

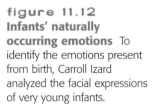

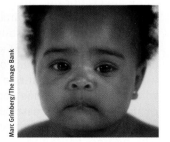

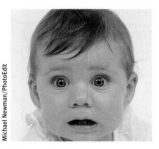

(a) Joy (mouth forming smile, cheeks lifted, twinkle in eye)

(b) Anger (brows drawn together and downward, eyes fixed, mouth squarish)

(c) Interest (brows raised or knitted, mouth softly rounded, lips may be pursed)

(f) Sadness (brow's inner corners raised, mouth corners drawn down)

(g) Fear (brows level, drawn in and up, eyelids lifted, mouth corners retracted)

figure 11.12
Infants' naturally occurring emotions To identify the emotions present from birth, Carroll Izard analyzed the facial expressions of very young infants.

"I thought it would be nice if we had a forum where we could get together and have screaming tantrums."

"Anger will never disappear so long as thoughts of resentment are cherished in the mind."

The Buddha, 500 B.C.

The cartharsis myth: Is it true?

Anger

9. What are the causes and consequences of anger?

Anger, the sages have said, is "a short madness" (Horace, 65–8 B.C.) that "carries the mind away" (Virgil, 70–19 B.C.) and that can be "many times more hurtful than the injury that caused it" (Thomas Fuller, 1654–1734). But they have also said, "noble anger" (William Shakespeare, 1564–1616) "makes any coward brave" (Cato, 234–149 B.C.) and "brings back . . . strength" (Virgil).

What makes us angry? To find out, James Averill (1983) asked people to recall or keep careful records of their experiences with anger. Most reported becoming at least mildly angry several times a week, some several times a day. The anger was often a response to friends' or loved ones' perceived misdeeds and was especially common when another person's act seemed willful, unjustified, and avoidable. But blameless annoyances—foul odors, high temperatures, a traffic jam, aches and pains—also have the power to make us angry (Berkowitz, 1990).

What do we do with our anger? And what *should* we do with it? When anger fuels physically or verbally aggressive acts we later regret, it becomes maladaptive. And it can harm us—chronic hostility is linked to heart disease (page 408). But controlled expressions of anger are more adaptive than either hostile outbursts or pent-up angry feelings. Averill's subjects recalled that when they were angry they often reacted assertively rather than hurtfully. Their anger frequently led them to talk things over with the offender, thereby lessening the aggravation.

Popular books and articles on aggression at times advise that even releasing angry feelings as hostile outbursts can be better than internalizing them. When irritated, should we go ahead and curse, tell a person off, or retaliate? Are "recovery movement" leaders right in encouraging us to rage at our dead parents, imaginatively curse the boss, or confront our childhood abuser?

Such encouragement to vent our rage is typical in individualized cultures, but it would seldom be heard in cultures where people's identity is centered more on the group. People who keenly sense their *inter*dependence see anger as a threat to group harmony (Markus & Kitayama, 1991). In Tahiti, for instance, people learn to be considerate and gentle. In Japan, from infancy on, anger expressions are less common than in Western cultures.

In Western cultures "vent your anger" advice presumes that emotional expression provides emotional release, or **catharsis**. The catharsis hypothesis maintains that we reduce anger by releasing it through aggressive action or fantasy. Experimenters report that this sometimes occurs. When people retaliate against someone who has provoked them, they may indeed calm down—*if* their counterattack is directed against the provoker, *if* their retaliation seems justifiable, and *if* their target is not intimidating (Geen & Quanty, 1977; Hokanson & Edelman, 1966). In short, expressing anger can be *temporarily* calming *if* it does not leave us feeling guilty or anxious.

However, despite the afterglow—people sometimes feel better afterward—catharsis usually fails to cleanse one's rage. More often, expressing anger breeds more anger. For one thing, it may provoke retaliation, thus escalating a minor conflict into a major confrontation. For another, expressing anger can magnify anger. (Recall Darwin's suggestion that violent gestures increase anger.) Ebbe Ebbesen and his colleagues (1975) saw this when they interviewed 100 frustrated engineers and technicians just laid off by an aerospace company. They asked some of the workers questions that released hostility, such as, "What instances can you think of where the company has not been fair with you?" When these people later filled out a questionnaire that assessed their attitudes toward the company, did this opportunity to "drain off" their hostility reduce it? Quite the contrary. Compared with those who had not vented their anger, those who had let it all out exhibited *more* hostility. Even when provoked people hit a punching bag *believing* it will be cathartic, the effect is the opposite—leading them to exhibit *more* cruelty (Bushman & others, 1999). And when they wallop a punching bag while ruminating about the person who angered them, they become even more aggressive when given a chance for revenge. "Venting to reduce anger is like using gasoline to put out a fire," concluded the researcher, Brad Bushman (2002).

Thus, although "blowing off steam" may temporarily calm us, it may also amplify the underlying hostility. And—ironically—when angry outbursts *do* calm us, they may actually be reinforcing and therefore habit forming. If stressed managers find they can drain off some of their tension by berating an employee, then the next time they feel irritated and tense they may be more likely to explode again. Think about it: The next time you are angry you are likely to do whatever has relieved your anger in the past.

What, then, is the best way to handle our anger? Experts offer two suggestions. First, wait. You can bring down the level of physiological arousal of anger by waiting. "It is true of the body as of arrows," noted Carol Tavris (1982), "what goes up must come down. Any emotional arousal will simmer down if you just wait long enough." Second, deal with anger in a way that involves neither being chronically angry over every little annoyance nor passively sulking, merely rehearsing your reasons for your anger. Ruminating inwardly about the causes of your anger serves only to increase it (Rusting & Nolen-Hoeksema, 1998). Don't join those who stifle their feelings over a series of provocations, and then suddenly overreact to a single incident (Baumeister & others, 1990). Calm yourself in other ways, such as by exercising, playing an instrument, or confiding your feelings to a friend.

Anger does communicate strength and competence (Tiedens, 2001). It can benefit a relationship when it expresses a grievance in ways that promote reconciliation rather than retaliation. Civility means not only keeping silent about trivial irritations but also communicating important ones clearly and assertively. A nonaccusing statement of feeling—perhaps letting one's housemate know that "I get irritated when you leave your dirty dishes for me to clean up"—can help resolve the conflicts that cause anger.

What if someone else's behavior really hurts you? Research suggests that the age-old response of forgiveness may be what the doctor ordered. Without letting the offender off the hook or inviting further harm, forgiveness releases anger and can calm the body. To explore the bodily effects of forgiveness, Charlotte Witvliet and her co-researchers (2001) invited college students to recall an incident where someone had hurt them. As the students mentally rehearsed forgiveness, their negative feelings—and their perspiration, blood pressure, heart rate, and facial tension—all were lower than when they rehearsed their grudges.

Wolfgang Kaehler

A cool culture Domestic violence is rare in Micronesia. This photo of community life on Pulap Island suggests one possible reason: Family life takes place in the open on this island. Relatives and neighbors who witness angry outbursts can step in before the emotion escalates into child, spouse, or elder abuse.

Happiness

10. What are the causes and consequences of happiness?

"How to gain, how to keep, how to recover happiness is in fact for most men at all times the secret motive for all they do," observed William James (1902, p. 76). Understandably so, for one's state of happiness or unhappiness colors everything. People who are happy perceive the world as safer, make decisions more easily, rate job applicants more favorably, are more cooperative, and live healthier and more energized and satisfied lives (Lyukomirsky & others, 2002; Myers, 1993). When your mood is gloomy and your thinking preoccupied, life as a whole seems depressing. Let your mood brighten and your thinking broadens and becomes more playful and creative (Fredrickson, 2002). Your relationships, your self-image, and your hopes for the future also seem more promising. Positive emotions fuel upward spirals.

Moreover—and this is one of psychology's most consistent findings—when we feel happy we are more willing to help others. In study after study, a mood-

▶ **catharsis** emotional release. In psychology, the catharsis hypothesis maintains that "releasing" aggressive energy (through action or fantasy) relieves aggressive urges.

▶ **feel-good, do-good phenomenon** people's tendency to be helpful when already in a good mood.

▶ **subjective well-being** self-perceived happiness or satisfaction with life. Used along with measures of objective well-being (for example, physical and economic indicators) to evaluate people's quality of life.

"Weeping may tarry for the night, but joy comes with the morning."

Psalms 30:5

boosting experience (finding money, succeeding on a challenging task, recalling a happy event) made people more likely to give money, pick up someone's dropped papers, volunteer time, and do other good deeds. Psychologists call it the **feel-good, do-good phenomenon** (Salovey, 1990). Happiness doesn't just feel good, it does good.

Despite the significance of happiness, psychology throughout its history has more often focused on negative emotions. Since 1887, *Psychological Abstracts* (a guide to psychology's literature) has included, as of this writing, 10,735 articles mentioning anger, 70,845 mentioning anxiety, and 86,767 mentioning depression. For every 13 articles on these topics, only one dealt with the positive emotions of joy (1161), life satisfaction (7949), or happiness (3938). There is, of course, good reason to focus on negative emotions; by making our lives miserable they drive us to seek help. But researchers are becoming increasingly interested in **subjective well-being**, assessed either as feelings of happiness (sometimes defined as a high ratio of positive to negative feelings) or as a sense of satisfaction with life. A more "positive psychology" is rapidly on the rise (see page 454).

In their research on happiness, psychologists have studied influences on both our temporary moods and our long-term life satisfaction. When studying people's hour-by-hour moods, David Watson (2000) discovered that positive emotion rises over the early part of most days and dissipates during the day's last several hours (**FIGURE 11.13**). Studying people's reports of day-to-day moods confirms that stressful events—an argument, a sick child, a car problem—trigger bad moods. No surprise there. But by the next day, the gloom nearly always lifts (Affleck & others, 1994; Bolger & others, 1989; Stone & Neale, 1984). If anything, people tend to rebound from bad days to a *better*-than-usual good mood the following day.

Apart from prolonged grief over the loss of a loved one or lingering anxiety after a trauma (such as child abuse, rape, or the terrors of war), even tragedy is not permanently depressing. Kidney dialysis patients recognize that their health is relatively poor, yet in their moment-to-moment experiences they report being just as happy as healthy nonpatients (Riis & others, 2003). Those who become blind or paralyzed usually recover near-normal levels of day-to-day happiness (Gerhart & others, 1994; Myers, 1993).

Similarly, learning that one is HIV-positive is devastating. But after five weeks of adapting to the grim news, those who tested positive felt less emotionally distraught than they had expected (Sieff & others, 1999). Likewise, faculty members up for tenure expect their lives would be deflated by a negative decision. Actually, 5 to 10 years later, those denied are not noticeably less happy than those who were awarded tenure, report Daniel Gilbert and colleagues (1998). The same is true of romantic breakups, which feel devastating. The surprising reality: *We overestimate the duration of our emotions and underestimate our capacity to adapt.*

figure 11.13
Moods across the day When psychologist David Watson (2000) sampled nearly 4500 mood reports from 150 people, he found this pattern of variation from the average level of positive and of negative emotion.

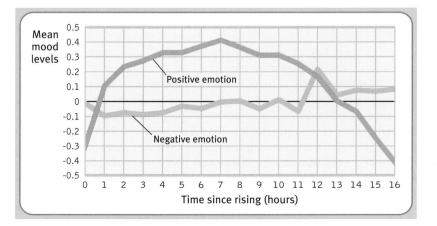

The emotional impact of dramatically positive events also dissipates sooner than we might expect. Once their rush of euphoria wears off, state lottery winners typically find their overall happiness unchanged (Brickman & others, 1978). Other research confirms that there is much more to well-being than being well-off. Many people (including most German citizens, and most new American collegians, as **FIGURE 11.14** suggests) believe they would be happier if they had more money (Csikszentmihalyi, 1999).

Mark Lemihan/AP/Wide World Photos, Inc.

Faced with adversity In 1995, an accident transformed *Superman* actor Christopher Reeve into an immobile person needing others to feed, dress, and care for him. "Maybe I should just check out," he told his wife, Dana, shortly after the accident. But within four months he reported in a Barbara Walters interview "genuine joy in being alive."

They probably would be—temporarily. Consider:

- Within most affluent countries, people with lots of money are somewhat happier than those with just enough to afford life's necessities (Di Tella & others, 2001).
- People in rich countries are also somewhat happier than those in poor countries (Steel & Ones, 2002).
- Those who have experienced a recent windfall from a lottery, an inheritance, or a surging economy often feel some elation (Diener & Oishi, 2000; Gardner & Oswald, 2001).

Yet in the long run, increased affluence hardly affects happiness. Even in Calcutta and Pakistani slums, people "are more satisfied than one might expect" (Biswas-Diener & Diener, 2001; Suhail & Chaudry, 2003). Wealth is like health: Its utter absence can breed misery, yet having it is no guarantee of happiness.

Most people agree that money can't buy happiness, but they do believe that a *little* more money would make them a *little* more happy, secure, and comfortable. So, over time, does our happiness grow, little by little, with our paychecks?

Usually not. During the last four decades, the average U.S. citizen's buying power more than doubled. The 1957 after-tax income, inflated to 1995 dollars, was $8500 per person; by 2002, thanks partly to the rich getting richer and to women's increasing employment, it was $23,000. Did this more-than-doubled wealth—enabling twice as many cars per person, and TVs, DVD players, laptops, air conditioners, and cell phones—also buy more happiness? As **FIGURE 11.15** on page 398 shows, it did not. In 1957, some 35 percent of Americans said they were "very happy," as did slightly fewer—30 percent—in 2002.

Indeed, if we can judge from statistics—a doubled divorce rate, more-than-doubled teen suicide, and mushrooming depression—contemporary Americans

"Gross national happiness is more important than gross national product."

Jigme Singye Wangchuk, King of Bhutan

"This lovely car has not brought us happiness. You agree, Morris? That is why I am now thinking in terms of having the entire house recarpeted."

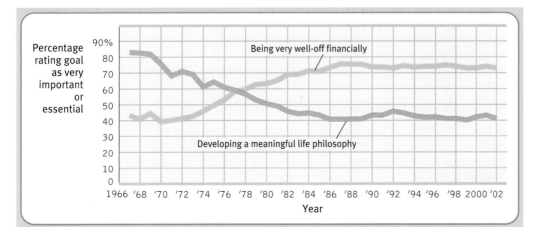

figure 11.14
The changing materialism of entering college students From 1970 through most of the 1980s, annual surveys of more than 200,000 entering U.S. college students revealed an increasing desire for wealth. (From *The American Freshman* surveys, UCLA, 1966 to 2002.)

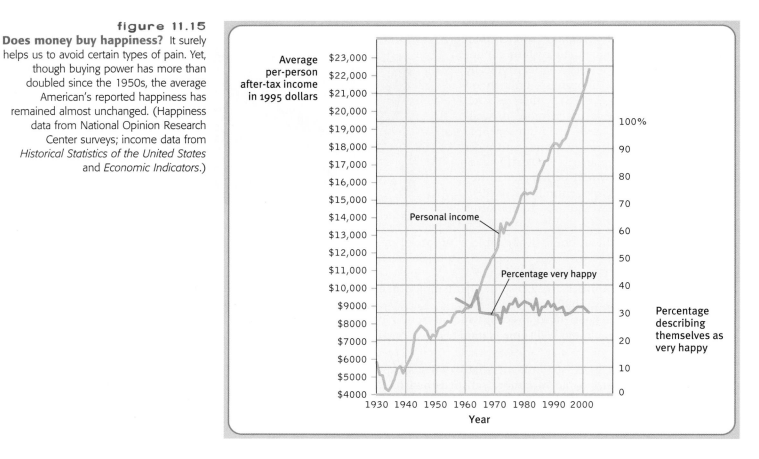

figure 11.15
Does money buy happiness? It surely helps us to avoid certain types of pain. Yet, though buying power has more than doubled since the 1950s, the average American's reported happiness has remained almost unchanged. (Happiness data from National Opinion Research Center surveys; income data from *Historical Statistics of the United States* and *Economic Indicators*.)

"But on the positive side, money can't buy happiness—so who cares?"

"No happiness lasts for long."

Seneca, *Agamemnon, 60 A.D.*

seem to be more often miserable. The same is true of the European countries, Australia, and Japan: In these countries, people enjoy better nutrition, health care, education, and science, and they are somewhat happier than those in very poor countries (Diener & Biswas-Diener, 2002; Eckersley, 2000). Yet their increasing real incomes have *not* produced increasing happiness. Such findings lob a bombshell at modern materialism: *Economic growth in affluent countries has provided no apparent boost to morale or social well-being.*

A further bombshell comes from studies showing that individuals who strive most for wealth tend to live with lower well-being, a finding that "comes through very strongly in every culture I've looked at," reports Richard Ryan (1999). This is especially so for those seeking money to prove themselves, gain power, or show off rather than support their families (Srivastava & others, 2001). Ryan's collaborator, Tim Kasser (2000, 2002), concludes from their studies that those who instead strive for "intimacy, personal growth, and contribution to the community" experience a higher quality of life. Ryan and Kasser's research echoes an earlier finding by H. W. Perkins (1991): Among 800 college alumni surveyed, those with "Yuppie values"—preferring a high income and occupational success and prestige to having very close friends and a close marriage—were twice as likely as their former classmates to describe themselves as "fairly" or "very" *un*happy. A similar correlation appears among 7167 college students surveyed in 41 countries. Those who value love more than money report much higher satisfaction with life than do their money-hungry peers (**Figure 11.16**).

Two psychological principles explain why, for all but the very poor, more money buys no more than a temporary surge of happiness and why our emotions seem attached to elastic bands that pull us back from highs or lows. In its own way, each principle suggests that happiness is relative.

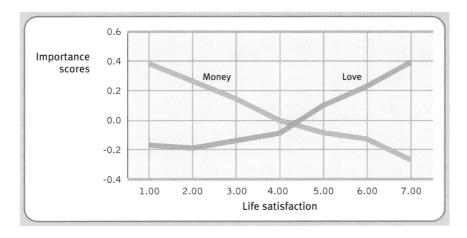

figure 11.16
Values and life satisfaction Among
college and university students worldwide,
those who report high life satisfaction give
priority to love over money. (From Diener &
Oishi, 2000.)

The Adaptation-Level Principle: Happiness Is Relative to Our Prior Experience

The **adaptation-level phenomenon** describes our tendency to judge various stimuli relative to those we have previously experienced. As psychologist Harry Helson explained, we adjust our "neutral" levels—the points at which sounds seem neither loud nor soft, temperatures neither hot nor cold, events neither pleasant nor unpleasant—based on our experience. We then notice and react to variations up or down from these levels. Adaptation researcher Allen Parducci (1995) recalls a striking example: "On the Micronesian island of Ponope, which is almost on the equator, I was told of a bitter night back in 1915 when the temperature dropped to a record-breaking 69 degrees [Fahrenheit; 21 degrees Celsius]!"

▶ **adaptation-level phenomenon** our tendency to form judgments (of sounds, of lights, of income) relative to a "neutral" level defined by our prior experience.

"Continued pleasures wear off. . . . Pleasure is always contingent upon change and disappears with continuous satisfaction."

Dutch psychologist Nico Frijda (1988)

So, could we ever create a permanent social paradise? Donald Campbell (1975) answered no: If you woke up tomorrow to your utopia—perhaps a world with no bills, no ills, all A's, someone who loves you unreservedly—you would feel euphoric, for a time. But before long, you would soon recalibrate your adaptation level. Before long you would again sometimes feel gratified (when achievements surpass expectations), sometimes feel deprived (when they fall below), and sometimes feel neutral. That helps explain why, despite the realities of triumph and tragedy, million-dollar lottery winners and people who are paralyzed report roughly similar levels of happiness. *The point to remember*: Satisfaction and dissatisfaction, success and failure—all are relative to our recent experience. Satisfaction, as Richard Ryan (1999) says, "has a short half-life."

"The mind of every man, in a longer or shorter time, returns to its natural and usual state of tranquility. In prosperity, after a certain time, it falls back to that state; in adversity, after a certain time, it rises up to it."

Adam Smith, **The Theory of Moral Sentiments**, *1759*

The Relative Deprivation Principle: Happiness Is Relative to Others' Attainments

Happiness is relative not only to our past experience but also to our comparisons with others (Lyubomirsky, 2001). We are always comparing ourselves with others. And whether we feel good or bad depends on who those others are. We are slow-witted or clumsy only when others are smart or agile.

"Shortly after I realized I had plenty, I realized there was plenty more."

▶ **relative deprivation** the perception that one is worse off relative to those with whom one compares oneself.

"I have also learned why people work so hard to succeed: It is because they envy the things their neighbors have. But it is useless. It is like chasing the wind. . . . It is better to have only a little, with peace of mind, than be busy all the time with both hands, trying to catch the wind."

Ecclesiastes 4:4

"Our poverty became a reality. Not because of our having less, but by our neighbors having more."

Will Campbell, Brother to a Dragonfly, *1977*

The effect of comparison with others helps explain why students of a given level of academic ability tend to have a higher academic self-concept if they attend a school where most other students are not exceptionally able (Marsh & Parker, 1984). If you were near the top of your class in high school, you might feel inferior upon entering a college where everyone was near the top of their class.

Two examples: To explain the frustration expressed by U.S. Air Corps soldiers during World War II, researchers formulated the concept of **relative deprivation**—the sense that we are worse off than others with whom we compare ourselves. Despite a relatively rapid promotion rate for the group, many soldiers were frustrated about their own promotion rates (Merton & Kitt, 1950). Apparently, seeing so many others being promoted inflated the soldiers' expectations. And when expectations soar above attainments, the result is disappointment. More recently, news of Alex Rodriguez's $252 million, 10-year baseball contract surely diminished other star players' satisfaction with their lesser, multimillion-dollar contracts.

Such comparisons help us understand why the middle- and upper-income people in a given country, who can compare themselves with the relatively poor, tend to be slightly more satisfied with life than their less fortunate compatriots. Nevertheless, once people reach a moderate income level, further increases do little to increase their happiness. Why? Because as people climb the ladder of success they mostly compare themselves with peers who are at or above their current level (Gruder, 1977; Suls & Tesch, 1978). "Beggars do not envy millionaires, though of course they will envy other beggars who are more successful," noted Bertrand Russell (1930, p. 90). Thus, "Napoleon envied Caesar, Caesar envied Alexander, and Alexander, I daresay, envied Hercules, who never existed. You cannot, therefore, get away from envy by means of success alone, for there will always be in history or legend some person even more successful than you are" (pp. 68–69).

Just as comparing ourselves with those who are better off creates envy, so counting our blessings as we compare ourselves with those less well off boosts our contentment. Marshall Dermer and his colleagues (1979) demonstrated this by asking University of Wisconsin-Milwaukee women to study others' deprivation and suffering. After viewing vivid depictions of how grim life was in Milwaukee in 1900, or after imagining and then writing about various personal tragedies, such as being burned and disfigured, the women expressed greater satisfaction with their own lives. Similarly, when mildly depressed people read about someone who is even more depressed, they feel somewhat better (Gibbons, 1986). "I cried because I had no shoes," states a Persian saying, "until I met a man who had no feet."

Predictors of Happiness

If, as the adaptation-level phenomenon implies, our emotions tend to balance around normal, why do some people seem so filled with joy and others so gloomy day after day? What makes one person normally happy and another less so? The answers vary somewhat by culture. Self-esteem matters more to individualistic Westerners, acceptance by others matters more to those in communal cultures (Diener & others, 2003). But across many countries, research does reveal several predictors of happiness (**TABLE 11.1**).

"Researchers say I'm not happier for being richer, but do you know how much researchers make?"

table 11.1 Happiness Is . . .

Researchers Have Found That Happy People Tend to	However, Happiness Seems Not Much Related to Other Factors, Such as
Have high self-esteem (in individualistic countries).	Age.
Be optimistic, outgoing, and agreeable.	Gender (women are more often depressed, but also more often joyful).
Have close friendships or a satisfying marriage.	Education levels.
Have work and leisure that engage their skills.	Parenthood (having children or not).
Have a meaningful religious faith.	Physical attractiveness.
Sleep well and exercise.	

Source: Summarized from DeNeve & Cooper (1998), Myers (1993, 2000), and Myers & Diener (1995, 1996).

CLOSE-UP

How to Be Happier

Happiness, like cholesterol level, is a genetically influenced trait. Yet as cholesterol is also influenced by diet and exercise, so our happiness is to some extent under our personal control. Here are some research-based suggestions for improving your mood and increasing your satisfaction with life.

1. ***Realize that enduring happiness doesn't come from financial success.*** People adapt to changing circumstances—even to wealth or a disability. Thus wealth is like health: Its utter absence breeds misery, but having it (or any circumstance we long for) doesn't guarantee happiness.

2. ***Take control of your time.*** Happy people feel in control of their lives, often aided by mastering their use of time. It helps to set goals and break them into daily aims. Although we often overestimate how much we will accomplish in any given day (leaving us frustrated), we generally *under*estimate how much we can accomplish in a year, given just a little progress every day.

3. ***Act happy.*** We can sometimes act ourselves into a frame of mind. Manipulated into a smiling expression, people feel better; when they scowl, the whole world seems to scowl back. So put on a happy face. Talk *as if* you feel positive self-esteem, are optimistic, and are outgoing. Going through the motions can trigger the emotions.

4. ***Seek work and leisure that engages your skills.*** Happy people often are in a zone called *flow*—absorbed in a task that challenges them without overwhelming them. The most expensive forms of leisure (sitting on a yacht) often provide less flow experience than gardening, socializing, or craft work.

5. ***Join the "movement" movement.*** An avalanche of research reveals that aerobic exercise not only promotes health and energy, it also is an antidote for mild depression and anxiety. Sound minds reside in sound bodies. Off your duffs, couch potatoes.

6. ***Give your body the sleep it wants.*** Happy people live active vigorous lives yet reserve time for renewing sleep and solitude. Many people suffer from sleep debt, with resulting fatigue, diminished alertness, and gloomy moods.

7. ***Give priority to close relationships.*** Intimate friendships with those who care deeply about you can help you weather difficult times. Confiding is good for soul and body. Resolve to nurture your closest relationships: to *not* take those closest to you for granted, to display to them the sort of kindness that you display to others, to affirm them, to play together and share together.

8. ***Focus beyond self.*** Reach out to those in need. Happiness increases helpfulness (those who feel good do good). But doing good also makes one feel good.

9. ***Be grateful.*** People who keep a gratitude journal—who pause each day to reflect on some positive aspect of their lives (their health, friends, family, freedom, education, senses, natural surroundings, and so on) experience heightened well-being.

10. ***Nurture your spiritual self.*** For many people, faith provides a support community, a reason to focus beyond self, and a sense of purpose and hope. That helps explain why people active in faith communities report greater than average happiness and often cope well with crisis.

Digested from David G. Myers, *The Pursuit of Happiness* (Avon Books, 1992)

Satisfying tasks and relationships affect our happiness, but always within the limits imposed by our genetic leash. From their study of 254 identical and fraternal twins, David Lykken and Auke Tellegen (1996) estimated that 50 percent of the difference among people's happiness ratings is heritable. Even identical twins raised apart are often similarly happy. Depending on our outlooks and recent experiences, our happiness fluctuates around our "happiness set point," which disposes some people to be ever upbeat and others down. But happiness, though genetically influenced, can be influenced by factors under our control. (See above Close-Up: How to Be Happier.) Given the influence of our emotions on our physical as well as emotional health, it can pay to manage one's emotions wisely.

Studies of chimpanzees in zoos reveal that happiness in chimpanzees, as rated by 200 employees, is also genetically influenced (Weiss & others, 2000, 2002).

rehearse it!

9. In some situations, venting anger—"blowing up"—seems to calm a person temporarily. In other cases, acting angry increases hostility. Experts suggest that to bring down anger, a good first step is to
   a. retaliate verbally or physically.
   b. wait or "simmer down."
   c. express anger in action or fantasy.
   d. review the grievance silently.

10. After graduating from college, you get a job and move into a large metropolitan city. At first, you find the street noise irritatingly loud, but after a while, it no longer bothers you, thus illustrating the
    a. relative deprivation principle.
    b. adaptation-level principle.

   c. feel-good, do-good phenomenon.
   d. catharsis principle.

11. A philosopher notes that one cannot escape envy by means of success alone: There will always be someone more successful, more accomplished, or richer with whom to compare oneself. In psychology this observation is embodied in the
    a. relative deprivation principle.
    b. adaptation-level principle.
    c. need to belong.
    d. feel-good, do-good phenomenon.

12. When comparing happy and unhappy people, researchers find that happy people are optimistic, outgoing, and likely to have satisfying close relation-

ships. One of the most consistent findings of psychological research is that happy people are also
   a. more likely to express anger.
   b. generally luckier than others.
   c. concentrated in the wealthier nations.
   d. more likely to help others.

13. Age, race, and gender seem not to be predictably related to subjective feelings of happiness or well-being. However, researchers have found that happy people tend to
    a. have children.
    b. score high on intelligence tests.
    c. have a meaningful religious faith.
    d. complete high school and some college education.

Answers can be found in Appendix C.

"I could cry when I think of the years I wasted accumulating money, only to learn that my cheerful disposition is genetic."

STRESS AND HEALTH

Walking along the path toward his mountain campsite, Karl hears a rustle at his feet. As he glimpses a rattlesnake, his body mobilizes for fight or flight: His muscles tense, his adrenaline flows, his heart pounds, and he flees, racing to the security of camp. Once there, Karl's muscles gradually relax and his heart rate and breathing ease.

Karen leaves her apartment one morning and, delayed by road construction, arrives at the parking lot of the commuter train station just in time to see the 8:05 pull away. Catching the next train, she arrives in the city late and elbows her way through crowds of rush-hour pedestrians. Once at her bank office, she apologizes to her first client, who wonders where Karen has been and why his quarterly investment report is not ready. Karen does her best to mollify the client. Afterward, she notices her tense muscles, clenched teeth, and churning stomach.

Karl's response to stress saved his life; Karen's, if chronic, could increase her risk of heart disease, high blood pressure, and other stress-linked health problems. Moreover, feeling under pressure, she might sleep and exercise less and smoke and drink more, further endangering her long-term health.

Stress and Stressors

11. What is stress?

Four in 10 people report frequently experiencing stress (Saad, 2001). What are they talking about? Stress is a slippery concept. It sometimes describes threats or challenges ("Karen was under a lot of stress"), other times our responses ("When Karl saw the rattler, he experienced acute stress"). Karen's missed train was a *stressor*, Karl's physical and emotional responses were a *stress reaction*, and the process by which Karen and Karl related to their environments was stress.

Thus, **stress** is not just a stimulus or a response. It is the process by which we appraise and cope with environmental threats and challenges (**FIGURE 11.17**). Stress arises less from events themselves than from how we appraise them (Lazarus, 1998). One person, alone in a house, dismisses its creaking sounds and experiences no stress; someone else suspects an intruder and becomes alarmed. One person regards a new job as a welcome challenge; someone else appraises it as risking failure.

When perceived as challenges, stressors can have positive effects, arousing and motivating us to conquer problems. Championship athletes, successful entertainers, and great teachers and leaders all thrive and excel when aroused by a challenge. Having conquered cancer or rebounded from a lost job, some people emerge with

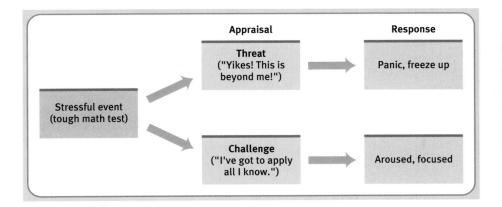

figure 11.17
Stress appraisal How we appraise an event influences how much stress we experience and how effectively we respond.

stronger self-esteem and a deepened spirituality and sense of purpose. Indeed, some stress early in life is conducive to later emotional resilience and physical growth (Landauer & Whiting, 1979). Adversity sometimes begets growth. Bad things sometimes work for good.

But stressors can also threaten us. And experiencing severe or prolonged stress may harm us. Children's physiological response to severe child abuse puts them at later risk of chronic disease (Repetti & others, 2002). Those who had post-traumatic stress reactions to heavy combat in the Vietnam War went on to suffer greatly elevated rates of circulatory, digestive, respiratory, and infectious diseases (Boscarino, 1997).

The Stress Response System

Medical interest in stress dates back to Hippocrates (460–377 B.C.). But it was not until the 1920s that Walter Cannon (1929) confirmed that the stress response is part of a unified mind-body system. He observed that extreme cold, lack of oxygen, and emotion-arousing incidents all trigger an outpouring of epinephrine (adrenaline) and norepinephrine (noradrenaline). These stress hormones enter the bloodstream from sympathetic nerve endings in the inner part of the adrenal glands. This is but one part of the sympathetic nervous system's response. When alerted by any of a number of brain pathways, the sympathetic nervous system increases heart rate and respiration, diverts blood from digestion to the skeletal muscles, dulls pain, and releases sugar and fat from the body's stores—all to prepare the body for the wonderfully adaptive response that Cannon called *fight or flight.*

Moreover, there are other alternatives to fight-or-flight. One is a common response to the stress of a loved one's death: Withdraw. Pull back. Conserve energy. Another, especially common among women, report Shelley Taylor and her colleagues (2000), is to seek and give support: "Tend and befriend."

Canadian scientist Hans Selye's (1936, 1976) 40 years of research on stress extended Cannon's findings and helped make stress a major concept in both psychology and medicine. Selye studied animals' reactions to various other stressors, such as electric shock, surgical trauma, and immobilizing restraints. He discovered that the body's adaptive response to stress was so general—like a single burglar alarm that sounds no matter what intrudes—that he called it the **general adaptation syndrome (GAS).**

Selye saw the GAS as having three phases (**FIGURE 11.18**, page 404). Let's say you suffer a physical or emotional trauma. In Phase 1, you experience an *alarm reaction* due to the sudden activation of your sympathetic nervous system. Your heart rate zooms. Blood is diverted to your skeletal muscles. You feel the faintness of shock. With your resources mobilized, you are now ready to fight the challenge during Phase 2, *resistance.* Your temperature, blood pressure, and respiration remain high, and there is a sudden outpouring of hormones. If persistent, the stress may eventually deplete your body's reserves during Phase 3, *exhaustion.* With exhaustion, you are more vulnerable to illness or even, in extreme cases, collapse and death.

▶ **stress** the process by which we perceive and respond to certain events, called *stressors,* that we appraise as threatening or challenging.

▶ **general adaptation syndrome (GAS)** Selye's concept of the body's adaptive response to stress in three stages—alarm, resistance, exhaustion.

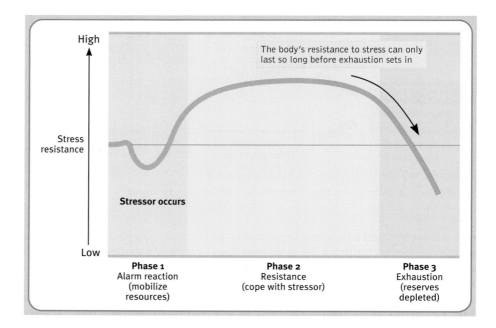

figure 11.18
Selye's general adaptation syndrome
After a trauma, the body enters an alarm phase of temporary shock. From this it rebounds, as stress resistance rises. If the stress is prolonged, wear and tear may lead to exhaustion.

Newer research reveals subtle differences in the body's reactions to different stressors. Nevertheless, few medical experts today quarrel with Selye's basic point: Although the human body comes designed to cope with temporary stress, prolonged stress can produce physical deterioration. Several recent studies have taken MRI brain scans of people who have experienced a prolonged flood of stress hormones, due to sustained child abuse, combat, or an endocrine disease (Sapolsky, 1999). Most have a shrunken hippocampus, the inner brain structure vital to laying down explicit (declarative) memories. In animals, too, various stresses—being subordinate in a group, being physically restrained, being isolated—can cause hippocampal tissue to shrink (McEwen, 1998). Such findings serve as further incentives to today's **health psychologists**, who have joined with physicians to create the interdisciplinary field of *behavioral medicine*. Health psychologists are actively exploring such questions as, What causes stress? What are the effects of stress? And how can we alleviate those effects?

Stressful Life Events

12. What events provoke stress responses?

Research has focused on our responses to three types of stressors: catastrophes, significant life changes, and daily hassles.

CATASTROPHES Catastrophes are unpredictable, large-scale events, such as war and natural disasters, that nearly everyone appraises as threatening. Although people often provide one another with aid as well as comfort after such events, the health consequences can be significant. In the three weeks after 9/11, two-thirds of Americans surveyed by University of Michigan researchers said they were having some trouble concentrating and sleeping (Wahlberg, 2001). In another national survey, New Yorkers were especially likely to report such symptoms (NSF, 2001). Sleeping pill prescriptions rose by a reported 28 percent in the New York area (HMHL, 2002).

Do other community disasters usually produce effects this great? After digesting data from 52 studies of catastrophic floods, hurricanes, and fires, Anthony Rubonis and Leonard Bickman (1991) found the typical effect more modest but nonetheless genuine. In disaster's wake, rates of psychological disorders such as depression and anxiety rose an average 17

Toxic stress On the day of its 1994 earthquake, Los Angeles experienced a fivefold increase in sudden-death heart attacks—especially in the first two hours after the quake and near its epicenter. Physical exertion (running, lifting debris) was a factor in only 13 percent of the deaths, leaving stress as the likely trigger for the others (Muller & Verrier, 1996).

percent. Refugees fleeing their homeland also suffer increased rates of psychological disorder. Their stress stems from the trauma of uprooting and family separation, and from the challenges of adjusting to a foreign culture's new language, ethnicity, climate, and social norms (Pipher, 2002; Williams & Berry, 1991). In all these cases, the health consequences often come only after prolonged stress.

▶ **health psychology** a subfield of psychology that provides psychology's contribution to behavioral medicine.

SIGNIFICANT LIFE CHANGES The second type of life event stressor is a significant personal life change—leaving home, the death of a loved one, the loss of a job, a marriage, or divorce. Life transitions and insecurities are often keenly felt during young adulthood. That helps explain why, when 15,000 Canadian adults were asked whether "you are trying to take on too many things at once," responses indicated highest stress levels among the youngest adults. The same is true of Americans: Half of adults under age 50 report "frequent" stress, as do fewer than 30 percent of those over 50 (Saad, 2001).

Some psychologists study the health effects of life changes by following people over time to see if such events precede illnesses. Others compare the life changes recalled by those who have or have not suffered a specific health problem, such as a heart attack. A review of these studies commissioned by the U.S. National Academy of Sciences revealed that people recently widowed, fired, or divorced are more vulnerable to disease (Dohrenwend & others, 1982). A Finnish study of 96,000 widowed people confirmed the phenomenon: Their risk of death doubled in the week following their partner's death (Kaprio & others, 1987). Experiencing a cluster of crises puts one even more at risk.

DAILY HASSLES As we noted earlier, our happiness stems less from enduring good fortune than from our response to daily events—an A on an exam, a gratifying letter, your team's winning the big game.

This principle works for negative events, too. Everyday annoyances—rush-hour traffic, aggravating housemates, long lines at the bank or store, too many things to do, and misplacing things—may be the most significant sources of stress (Kohn & Macdonald, 1992; Lazarus, 1990; Ruffin, 1993). Although some people can simply shrug off such hassles, others are "driven up the wall" by them.

Over time, these little stressors can add up and take a toll on our health and well-being. Hypertension (high blood pressure) rates are high among residents of urban ghettos, where the stresses that accompany poverty, unemployment, solo parenting, and overcrowding are part of daily life for some people. And these daily pressures may be compounded by racism, which—like other stressors—can have both psychological and physical consequences. Imagine thinking that some of the people you encounter each day will distrust you, dislike you, or doubt your abilities. Might you not find daily life stressful? Might such stress eventually take a toll on your health, perhaps driving up your blood pressure? Well, that describes the experiences of many African Americans as they perceive racism in their daily lives, note Rodney Clark and his colleagues (1999).

No end in sight It's not the large things that send a man to the madhouse . . . no, it's the continuing series of small tragedies . . . not the death of his love but the shoelace that snaps with no time left" (Charles Bukowski, cited by Lazarus in Wallis, 1983).

Perceived Control

Catastrophes, important life changes, and daily hassles and conflicts are especially stressful when we appraise them as both negative *and* uncontrolled. If two rats receive simultaneous shocks, but one can turn a wheel to stop the shocks, the helpless rat becomes more susceptible to ulcers and lowered immunity to disease (Laudenslager & Reite, 1984). In humans, a bacterial infection often combines with uncontrollable stress to produce the most severe ulcers (Overmier & Murison, 1997). To cure the ulcer, kill the bug with antibiotics and control the acid secretions with reduced stress.

Perceiving a loss of control, we become vulnerable to ill health. Elderly nursing home patients who have little perceived

Peter Glass

Equal incomes lead to longer lives In Kerala state, India, incomes are low, yet life expectancy is greater than in other Indian states. "Indeed," report James Lynch and his co-researchers, thanks to relative equality and to "investment in human resources, . . . [life expectancy approximates] levels seen in rich industrialized countries."

control over their activities tend to decline faster and die sooner than do those given more control over their activities (Rodin, 1986). Given control over their work environment—by being able to adjust office furnishings and control interruptions and distractions—workers, too, experience less stress (O'Neill, 1993). This helps explain why British civil service workers at the executive grades outlive those at clerical or laboring grades, and why Finnish workers with low job stress are less than half as likely to die of cardiovascular disease (strokes or heart disease) as those with a demanding job and little control. The more control workers have, the longer they live (Bosma & others, 1997, 1998; Kivimaki & others, 2002; Marmot & others, 1997).

POVERTY AND INEQUALITY Control may help explain a well-established link between economic status and longevity. In one study of 843 grave markers in an old graveyard in Glasgow, Scotland, those with the costliest, highest pillars (indicating the most affluence) tended to live the longest (Carroll & others, 1994). Likewise, Scottish regions with the least overcrowding and unemployment have the greatest longevity. Even among primates, those at the bottom of the social pecking order are more likely than their higher-status companions to become sick when exposed to a coldlike virus (Cohen & others, 1997).

People also tend to die younger in areas where there is greater income *inequality* (Kawachi & others, 1999; Lynch & others, 1998; Marmot & Wilkinson, 1999). Among developed countries, Britain and the United States, which have large income disparities between rich and poor, have life expectancies two to four years lower than those in Japan and Sweden, where income differences are less extreme. As income inequality has grown in Eastern Europe and Russia, life expectancy has decreased. A similar effect can be seen across U.S. states and Canadian provinces, where income inequality predicts lower life expectancy (**Figure 11.19**).

Some recent studies in Denmark, Japan, and the United States indicate that *income* more than inequality predicts mortality (Muller, 2002; Osler & others, 2002; Shibuya & others, 2002). Nevertheless researchers are pondering *why* in other studies inequality does predict mortality. Does the inequality–mortality correlation occur merely because extreme differences in income are flags of substantial poverty? No, the correlation remains after adjusting for average income and for the proportion of the population with low incomes. In fact, report John Lynch and his colleagues (1998, 2000), people at every income level are at greater risk of death if they live in a community with great income inequality. How, then, does inequality get under the skin? Is it because the risk of violent death is greater? Because receiving relatively low income evokes feelings of frustration and worthlessness? Because investment in public health, education, and housing is lower in such regions? Stay tuned for further research.

figure 11.19
Equality and longevity Across the American states and Canadian provinces, income equality (indexed here as proportion of income going to the poorer half of households) predicts low mortality among working-age men. (From Hertzman, 2001.)

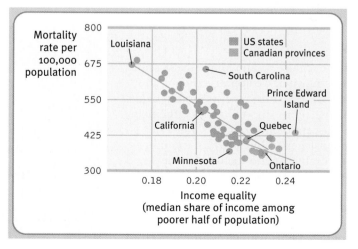

OPTIMISM–PESSIMISM One control-related factor that influences our vulnerability to stress is optimism. Psychologists Michael Scheier and Charles Carver (1992) report that optimists—people who agree with statements such as, "In uncertain times, I usually expect the best"—not only perceive more control, they cope better with stressful events and enjoy better health. During the last month of a semester, students previously identified as optimistic report less fatigue and fewer coughs, aches, and pains. During the stressful first few weeks of law school, those who are optimistic ("It's unlikely that I will fail") enjoy better moods and stronger infection-thwarting immune systems (Segerstrom & others, 1998). Optimists also respond to stress with smaller increases in blood pressure, and they recover more quickly from heart bypass surgery.

One study that followed 2428 middle-aged Finnish men for up to 10 years discovered that the number of deaths among men with a bleak, hopeless outlook was more than double that found among their optimistic counterparts (**Figure 11.20**). Another study asked 795 Americans aged 64 to 79 years if they were "hopeful about the future." When the researchers checked up on these folks about five years later, 29 percent of those answering "no" had died—more than double the 11 percent of deaths among those who said yes (Stern & others, 2001). Mayo Clinic research similarly finds that optimists tend to outlive pessimists (Maruta & others, 2002).

Those who look on the brighter side live longer. At least that was so among 180 Catholic nuns who at about 22 years of age wrote brief autobiographies. Despite living thereafter with similar life-styles and status, those expressing happiness, love, and other positive feelings lived an average seven years longer than their more dour counterparts (Danner & others, 2001). By age 80, some 54 percent of those expressing few positive emotions had died, as had only 24 percent of the most positive-spirited.

Why do perceived loss of control and pessimism predict health problems? Animal studies show—and human studies confirm—that losing control provokes an outpouring of stress hormones. When rats cannot control shock or when humans feel unable to control their environment, stress hormone levels rise and immune responses drop (Rodin, 1986). Captive animals therefore experience more stress and are more vulnerable to disease than are wild animals (Roberts, 1988). The crowding that occurs in high-density neighborhoods, prisons, and college dorms is another source of diminished feelings of control—and of elevated levels of stress hormones and blood pressure (Fleming & others, 1987; Ostfeld & others, 1987).

Long-lived winners An analysis of more than 1600 actors found that Academy Award winners lived 3.9 years longer than nonwinners, even after controlling for sex, birth year, and ethnicity (Redelmeier & Singh, 2001). That's roughly the life expectancy increase to be gained by eliminating all cancers. Multiple Oscars predicted even longer life. Katharine Hepburn, with four Oscars, lived to 96.

"A cheerful heart is a good medicine, but a downcast spirit dries up the bones."

Proverbs 17:22

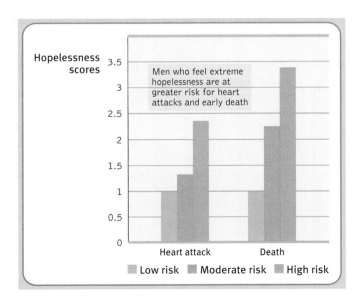

figure 11.20
Toxic hopelessness Compared with Finnish middle-aged men scoring low in hopelessness, those scoring high were two to three times more vulnerable to a heart attack over the ensuing six years, and three to four times more likely to die. (Data from Everson & others, 1996.)

▶ **coronary heart disease** the clogging of the vessels that nourish the heart muscle; the leading cause of death in many developed countries.

▶ **Type A** Friedman and Rosenman's term for competitive, hard-driving, impatient, verbally aggressive, and anger-prone people.

▶ **Type B** Friedman and Rosenman's term for easygoing, relaxed people.

▶ **psychophysiological illness** literally, "mind-body" illness; any stress-related physical illness, such as hypertension and some headaches.

▶ **lymphocytes** the two types of white blood cells that are part of the body's immune system: *B lymphocytes* form in the *b*one marrow and release antibodies that fight bacterial infections; *T lymphocytes* form in the *t*hymus and, among other duties, attack cancer cells, viruses, and foreign substances.

In both India and America, Type A bus drivers are literally hard-driving: They brake, pass, and honk their horns more often than their more easygoing Type B colleagues (Evans & others, 1987).

Stress and the Heart

13. Why are some of us more prone than others to coronary heart disease?

Although infrequent before 1900, **coronary heart disease**—the closing of the vessels that nourish the heart muscle—became by the 1950s North America's leading cause of death and remains so today. In addition to family history of the disease, many behavioral and physiological factors—smoking, obesity, a high-fat diet, physical inactivity, elevated blood pressure, and an elevated cholesterol level—increase the risk of heart disease. The psychological factors of stress and personality also play a big role.

In 1956, cardiologists Meyer Friedman, Ray Rosenman, and their colleagues stumbled upon an indication of how big that role is (Friedman & Ulmer, 1984). While studying the eating behavior of San Francisco Junior League white women and their husbands, Friedman and Rosenman discovered that the women consumed as much cholesterol and fat as their husbands did, yet they were far less susceptible to heart disease. Was it because of their female sex hormones? No, the researchers surmised, because African-American women with the same sex hormones but facing more stress than the Junior Leaguers were as prone to heart disease as their husbands.

The Junior League president thought she knew the answer: "It's the stress they have to face in their businesses, day in, day out," she said sadly. "Why, when my husband comes home at night, it takes at least one martini just to unclench his jaws."

To test the idea that stress increases vulnerability to heart disease, Friedman and Rosenman measured the blood cholesterol level and clotting speed of 40 tax accountants. From January through March, both of these coronary warning indicators were completely normal. Then, as the accountants began scrambling to finish their clients' tax returns before the April 15 filing deadline, their cholesterol and clotting measures rose to dangerous levels. In May and June, with the deadline past, the measures returned to normal. The researchers' hunch had paid off: Stress predicted heart attack risk.

The stage was set for Friedman and Rosenman's classic nine-year study of more than 3000 healthy men aged 35 to 59. At the start of the study, they interviewed each man for 15 minutes about his work and eating habits. During the interview, they noted the man's manner of talking and other behavioral patterns. Those who seemed the most reactive, competitive, hard-driving, impatient, time-conscious, supermotivated, verbally aggressive, and easily angered they called **Type A**. The roughly equal number who were more easygoing they called **Type B**. Which group do you suppose turned out to be the most coronary-prone?

By the time the study was complete, 257 of the men had suffered heart attacks; 69 percent were Type A. Moreover, not one of the "pure" Type Bs—the most mellow and laid-back of their group—had suffered a heart attack.

As often happens in science, this exciting discovery provoked enormous public interest. But after the honeymoon period, in which the finding seemed definitive and revolutionary, other researchers began asking, Is the finding reliable? If so, what is the toxic component of the Type A profile: Time-consciousness? Competitiveness? Anger? Further research found that reactive Type A individuals are more often "combat ready." When harassed or challenged, their active sympathetic nervous system redistributes bloodflow to the muscles and away from internal organs such as the liver, which removes cholesterol and fat from the blood. Thus, their blood may contain excess cholesterol and fat that later get deposited around the heart. Further stress—sometimes conflicts brought on by their own abrasiveness—may trigger the altered heart rhythms that, in those with weakened hearts, can cause sudden death (Kamarck & Jennings, 1991). In such ways, the hearts and minds of people interact.

More recent research has revealed that Type A's toxic core is negative emotions—especially the anger associated with an aggressively reactive temperament (Smith & Ruiz, 2002; Williams, 1993). The effect of an anger-prone personality appears most noticeably in studies in which interviewers assess verbal assertiveness and emotional intensity. (If you pause in the middle of a sentence, an intense, anger-prone person may jump in and finish it for you.) Among young and middle-aged adults, those who react with anger over little things are the most coronary-prone:

- One study followed 13,000 middle-aged people for five years. Among those with normal blood pressure, those who had scored high on anger were three times more likely to have had heart attacks, even after controlling for smoking and weight (Williams & others, 2000).
- Another study followed 1055 male medical students over an average of 36 years. Those who had reported being hot-tempered were five times more likely to have had a heart attack by age 55 (Chang & others, 2002).

As Charles Spielberger and Perry London (1982) put it, rage "seems to lash back and strike us in the heart muscle."

Anger is not the only toxic emotion. Depression, too, can be lethal. Consider:

- U.S. Centers for Disease Control researchers studied adults who were feeling a sense of hopelessness or at least mild depression. Compared with those without such feelings, these downhearted people were more vulnerable to heart disease in the ensuing 12 years. This was true even after controlling for differences in age, sex, smoking, and other factors linked to heart ailments (Anda & others, 1993).
- Another study (Whooley & Browner, 1998), of 7406 women age 67 or older with varying levels of depression, found significant differences in mortality, due partly to increased heart disease. Of those with no depressive symptoms, 7 percent died within six years, as did 17 percent of those with three to five depressive symptoms and 24 percent of those with six or more depressive symptoms.
- In the years following a heart attack, depressed people are four times likelier than nondepressed people to develop further heart problems (Frasure-Smith & others, 1995, 1999).

All in all, the evidence from 57 studies suggests that "depression substantially increases the risk of death, especially death by unnatural causes and cardiovascular disease" (Wulsin & others, 1999). Negative emotions have physical consequences. In addition to decreasing blood flow to parts of the heart, negative emotions may also influence a person's poor health practices and health-related decisions.

> *"The fire you kindle for your enemy often burns you more than him."*
>
> *Chinese proverb*

Stress and Susceptibility to Disease

14. How does stress make us more vulnerable to disease?

Not so long ago, the term *psychosomatic* described psychologically caused physical symptoms. To laypeople, the term implied that the symptoms were unreal—they were "merely" psychosomatic. To avoid such connotations and to describe better the genuine physiological effects of psychological states, most experts today refer instead to **psychophysiological illnesses**. These illnesses, such as hypertension and some headaches, are stress-related. A person under stress also may retain excess sodium and fluids, which, together with constriction of the arteries' muscle walls, contribute to increased blood pressure (Light & others, 1983). Let's take a closer look at some of the ways stress affects our resistance to disease.

Stress and the Immune System

Hundreds of new experiments reveal the nervous and endocrine systems' influence on the immune system (Sternberg, 2001). Your immune system is a complex surveillance system that defends your body by isolating and destroying bacteria, viruses, and other foreign substances. This system includes two types of white blood cells, called **lymphocytes**. *B lymphocytes* form in the *b*one marrow and release antibodies that fight bacterial infections. *T lymphocytes* form in the *t*hymus and other lymphatic tissue and attack cancer cells, viruses, and foreign substances—even "good" ones, such as transplanted organs. Another agent of the immune system is the *macrophage* ("big eater"), which identifies, pursues, and ingests harmful invaders. Age, nutrition, genetics, body temperature, and stress all influence the immune system's activity.

Your immune system can err in two directions. Responding too strongly, it may attack the body's own tissues, causing arthritis or an allergic reaction. Underreacting, it may allow a dormant herpes virus to erupt or cancer cells to multiply. Women are immunologically stronger than men (Morell, 1995), making them less susceptible to infections. But this very strength also makes them more susceptible to self-attacking diseases, such as lupus and multiple sclerosis.

Your immune system is not a headless horseman. Rather, it exchanges information with your brain and your hormone-secreting endocrine system. The brain regulates the secretion of stress hormones, which in turn suppress the disease-fighting lymphocytes. Thus, when animals are physically restrained, given unavoidable electric shocks, or subjected to noise, crowding, cold water, social defeat, or maternal separation, their immune systems become less active (Maier & others, 1994). One study monitored immune responses in 43 monkeys over six months (Cohen & others, 1992). Twenty-one were stressed by being housed with new roommates—three or four new monkeys—each month. (To empathize with the monkeys, recall the stress of leaving home to attend school or summer camp, and imagine having to repeat this experience monthly.) Compared with monkeys left in stable groups, the socially disrupted monkeys experienced weakened immune systems.

Stress similarly depresses the immune system of humans. Consider:

- In three separate *Skylab* missions, the immune systems of the astronauts showed reduced effectiveness immediately after the stress of reentry and splashdown (Kimzey, 1975; Kimzey & others, 1976).
- Surgical wounds heal more slowly in stressed animals and humans. In one experiment, dental students received "punch wounds" (precise small holes punched in the skin). Compared with wounds placed during summer vacation, those placed three days before a major exam healed 40 percent more slowly. In fact, report Janice Kiecolt-Glaser and her co-researchers (1998), "no student healed as rapidly during this stressful period as during vacation."
- Students' disease-fighting mechanisms are weaker during high-stress times, such as exam weeks, and on days when they are upset (Jemmott & Magloire, 1988; Stone & others, 1987). In one experiment, 47 percent of participants living stress-filled lives developed colds after a virus was dropped in their noses, but only 27 percent of those living relatively free of stress caught colds (Cohen & others, 1991).
- Managing stress may be life-sustaining. Compared with those of young adults, older adults' immune systems are more impaired by stress and depression (Kiecolt-Glaser & others, 2001, 2002). The one personality trait shared by 169 centenarians (people over 100) was their ability to manage stress well (Perls & others, 1999).

The stress effect on immunity makes physiological sense (Maier & others, 1994). It takes energy to fight infections, produce inflammations, and maintain fevers. Thus, when diseased, our bodies reduce muscular energy output by inactivity and increased sleep. But stress creates a competing energy system. Stress triggers an aroused fight-or-flight response, diverting energy from the disease-fighting system to the muscles and brain, rendering us more vulnerable to illness. The bottom line: Stress does not make us sick, but it does restrain our immune functioning, making us more vulnerable to foreign invaders.

Stress and AIDS

AIDS has become the world's fourth leading cause of death and the number one killer in Africa. AIDS, as its name tells us, is an immune disorder—an *acquired immune deficiency syndrome* caused by the human immunodeficiency virus (HIV),

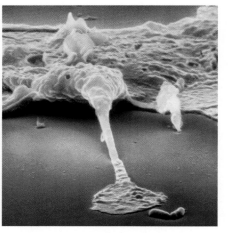

"In the eyes of God or biology or what have you, it is just very important to have women."

Immunologist Norman Talal (1995)

The immune system in action A large macrophage (at top) is about to trap and ingest a tiny bacterium (lower right). Macrophages constantly patrol our bodies in search of invaders—such as this *Escherichia coli* bacterium—and debris, such as worn-out red blood cells.

"When the heart is at ease, the body is healthy."

Chinese proverb

Lennart Nilsson/Boehringer Ingelheim International GmbH

which is spread by the exchange of bodily fluids, primarily semen and blood. If a disease spread by human contact kills slowly, as does HIV, it ironically can be lethal to more people: Those who carry the disease have time to spread it, often without realizing they are infected. When the HIV infection becomes manifest as AIDS, some years after the initial infection, the person has difficulty fighting off other diseases, such as pneumonia. Worldwide, reports the United Nations, 22 million died of AIDS in the last century. In 2002, some 42 million—half women—were infected with HIV, often without their awareness (UNAIDS, 2002). By 2020, projects the United Nations (Altman, 2002a), 65 million more will succumb to the disease. Worldwide, 15- to 24-year-olds account for half of new infections.

So if stress serves to suppress immune functioning, could it also exacerbate the course of AIDS? Researchers have found that stress and negative emotions do correlate with a progression from HIV infection to AIDS and with the speed of decline in those infected (Bower & others, 1998; Kiecolt-Glaser & Glaser, 1995; Leserman & others, 1999). HIV-infected men faced with stressful life circumstances, such as the loss of a partner, exhibit somewhat greater immune suppression and a faster disease progression.

Would efforts to reduce stress help control the disease? Although the benefits are small compared with available drug treatments, the answer appears again to be yes. Educational initiatives, bereavement support groups, cognitive therapy, and exercise programs that reduce distress have all had positive consequences for HIV-positive individuals (Baum & Posluszny, 1999; Schneiderman, 1999).

Stress and Cancer

Stress and negative emotions have also been linked to cancer's rate of progression. To explore a possible connection between stress and cancer, experimenters have implanted tumor cells into rodents or given them cancer-producing substances. Those rodents also exposed to uncontrollable stress, such as inescapable shocks, were more prone to cancer (Sklar & Anisman, 1981). With their immune systems weakened by stress, their tumors developed sooner and grew larger.

Investigators have reported that people are at increased risk for cancer within a year after experiencing depression, helplessness, or bereavement. For example, cancer occurs slightly more often than usual among those widowed, divorced, or separated. A large Swedish study revealed that people with a history of workplace stress had 5.5 times greater risk of colon cancer than those who reported no such problems, a difference not attributable to differing age, smoking, drinking, or physical characteristics (Courtney & others, 1993). Other researchers have found no link between stress and human cancer (Edelman & Kidman, 1997; Fox, 1998; Petticrew & others, 1999). Concentration camp survivors and former prisoners of war, for example, have not exhibited elevated cancer rates.

One danger in hyping reports on attitudes and cancer is that some patients may be led to blame themselves for their illness—"If only I had been more expressive, relaxed, and hopeful." A corollary danger is a "wellness macho" among the healthy, who credit their health to their healthy character and lay a guilt trip on the ill: "She has cancer? That's what you get for holding your feelings in and being so nice." Dying thus becomes the ultimate failure.

In noting the modest link between emotions and cancer prognosis, we must remember that stress does not create cancer cells. Rather, it affects their growth by weakening the body's natural defenses against a few proliferating, malignant cells. Although a relaxed, hopeful state may enhance these defenses, we should be aware of the thin line that divides science from wishful thinking. The powerful biological processes at work in advanced cancer or AIDS are not likely to be derailed by avoiding stress or maintaining a relaxed but determined spirit (Anderson, 2002; Kessler & others, 1991).

"I didn't give myself cancer."

Mayor Barbara Boggs Sigmund (1939–1990), Princeton, New Jersey

When organic causes of illness are unknown, it is tempting to invent psychological explanations. Before the germ that causes tuberculosis was discovered, personality explanations of TB were popular (Sontag, 1978).

Conditioning the Immune System

A hay fever sufferer sees the flower on the restaurant table and, not realizing it is plastic, begins to sneeze. Such experiences hint that stress is not the only psychological influence on the body's ailments. Simple classical conditioning may be an added influence. This raises an intriguing question: If conditioning affects the body's overt physiological responses, might it affect the immune system as well?

Psychologist Robert Ader and immunologist Nicholas Cohen (1985) discovered that the answer is yes. Ader came upon this discovery while researching taste aversion in rats. He paired the rats' drinking of saccharin-sweetened water with injections of a drug that happened to suppress immune functioning. After repeated pairings, sweetened water alone triggered immune suppression, as if the drug had been given (**Figure 11.21**). Such conditioned immune suppression can triple an animal's likelihood of growing a tumor when fed a carcinogen (Blom & others, 1995).

Many questions about the role of the immune system and ways to harness its healing potential remain unanswered. If it is possible to condition the immune system's suppression, should it not also be possible to condition its enhancement? Might this be one way in which placebos—treatments that have no biochemical effect—sometimes promote healing? Can a placebo sometimes elicit the same healthful state produced by an actual drug? Might negative beliefs—expecting the worst—have an opposite "nocebo" effect, as people get what they expect? Although results have been mixed, researchers are hoping to answer such questions (Hróbjartsson & Gøtzsche, 2001).

For now, we can view stress' effect on our resistance to disease (**Figure 11.22**) as a price we pay for its adaptive benefits. Stress invigorates our lives by arousing and motivating us. An unstressed life would hardly be challenging or productive. Moreover, it pays to spend our resources in fighting or fleeing an external threat. But we do so at the cost of diminished resources for fighting internal threats to health. When the stress is momentary, the cost is negligible. When uncontrollable aggravations persist, the cost may become considerable.

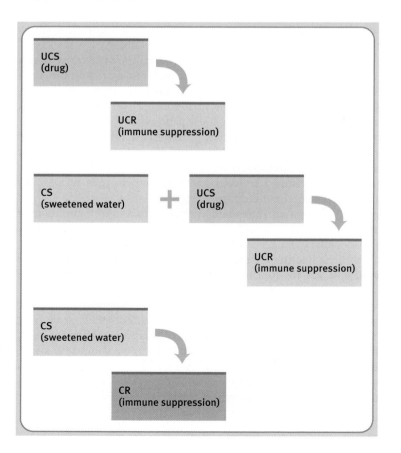

figure 11.21
The conditioning of immune suppression After Ader and Cohen (1985) associated sweetened water with a drug that causes immune suppression in rats, the inert substance alone triggered the conditioned immune response.

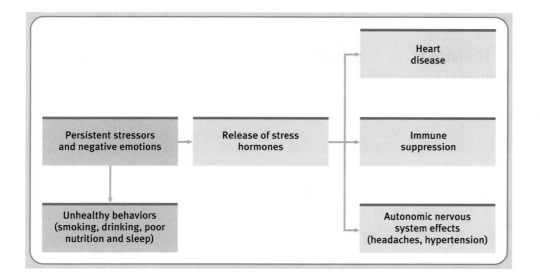

figure 11.22
Negative emotions can have a variety of health-related consequences This is especially so when experienced by "disease-prone" angry, depressed, or anxious persons.

This new behavioral medicine research provides yet another reminder of one of contemporary psychology's overriding themes. *Mind and body interact; everything psychological is simultaneously physiological.* Psychological states are physiological events that influence other parts of our physiological system. Just pausing to *think* about biting into an orange section—the sweet, tangy juice from the pulpy fruit flooding across your tongue—can trigger salivation. As the Indian sage Santi Parva recognized more than 4000 years ago, "Mental disorders arise from physical causes, and likewise physical disorders arise from mental causes." There is interplay between our heads and our health.

rehearse it!

14. The physiologist Walter Cannon described the role of the sympathetic nervous system in preparing the body for fight or flight. Hans Selye extended Cannon's findings by describing the body's adaptive response to stress in general. Selye's general adaptation syndrome (GAS) consists of an alarm reaction followed by
    a. fight or flight.
    b. resistance and exhaustion.
    c. challenge and recovery.
    d. stressful life events.

15. In the months following a catastrophe, such as an earthquake or a nuclear accident, there is a higher than usual number of short-term illnesses and stress-related psychological disorders. Following widowhood, there is an increased risk of illness and death. These findings suggest that
    a. daily hassles have adverse health consequences.
    b. experiencing a very stressful event increases one's vulnerability to illness and death.
    c. the amount of stress felt is directly related to the number of stressors involved.
    d. having a negative outlook has an adverse effect on recovery from illness.

16. Stressors are events that we appraise as threatening or challenging. Research suggests that the most significant sources of stress are
    a. catastrophes.
    b. traumatic events, such as the loss of a loved one.

    c. daily hassles.
    d. threatening events that we witness.

17. The stress we experience depends on how we perceive the events of our lives. A person (or animal) is most likely to find an event stressful and to suffer reduced immunity and other adverse health effects if the event seems
    a. painful or harmful.
    b. predictable and negative.
    c. uncontrollable and negative.
    d. both repellent and attractive.

18. Cardiologists Meyer Friedman, Ray Rosenman, and their colleagues observed that heart attacks were more frequent in Type A men—in those who appeared to be hard-driving, verbally aggressive, and anger prone. The component of Type A behavior linked most closely to coronary heart disease is
    a. living a fast-paced life-style.
    b. working in a competitive area.
    c. meeting deadlines and challenges.
    d. feeling angry and negative much of the time.

19. Stress hormones suppress the lympho-cytes, which ordinarily attack bacteria, viruses, cancer cells, and other foreign substances. The stress hormones are released mainly in response to a signal from the
    a. lymphocytes and macrophages.
    b. brain.
    c. upper respiratory tract.
    d. adrenal glands.

20. Research has shown people are at increased risk for cancer a year or so after experiencing depression, helplessness, or bereavement. In describing this link between emotions and cancer, researchers are quick to point out that
    a. accumulated stress that is not relieved by positive emotions poses the greatest threat to people who are genetically vulnerable to cancer.
    b. anger is the negative emotion most closely linked to cancer.
    c. stress does not create cancer cells, but it weakens the body's natural defenses against them.
    d. feeling optimistic about chances of survival ensures that a cancer patient will get well.

21. In testing taste aversion in rats, researchers paired the rats' drinking of saccharin-sweetened water with injections of a drug that suppressed immune functioning. After repeated pairings, sweetened water *alone* triggered immune suppression. These results suggest that
    a. the immune system is under the direct control of the hypothalamus.
    b. classical conditioning may influence the body's ailments.
    c. placebos are as effective as actual drugs in treating the body's ailments.
    d. external threats diminish our body's ability to fight internal threats.

Answers can be found in Appendix C.

PROMOTING HEALTH

Traditionally, people have sought out physicians for the diagnosis and treatment of disease. That, say health psychologists, is like ignoring a car's maintenance and going to a mechanic only when the car breaks down. Now that we realize that our attitudes and behaviors affect our health, attention is turning to health maintenance—ways of coping with stress, preventing illness, and promoting well-being.

"Is there anyone here who specializes in stress management?"

Coping With Stress

15. *What tactics can we use to manage stress and reduce stress-related ailments?*

Stressors are unavoidable. This fact, coupled with the growing awareness that recurring stress correlates with heart disease, lowered immunity, and other bodily ailments, gives us a clear message. If we cannot eliminate stress by changing or ignoring a situation, we had best manage it—by confronting or escaping the problem and taking steps to prevent its recurrence. Stress management may include aerobic exercise, biofeedback, relaxation, social support, and spirituality.

Aerobic Exercise

Aerobic exercise is sustained exercise that increases heart and lung fitness. Such exercise strengthens the body. Does it also boost the spirit?

EXERCISE AND MOOD Many studies suggest that aerobic exercise can reduce stress, depression, and anxiety. Studies indicate that the 3 in 10 Americans and 4 in 10 Canadians who exercise regularly also cope better with stressful events, exhibit more self-confidence, feel more vigor, and feel depressed and fatigued less often than those who exercise less (NCHS, 2002; Statistics Canada, 1999). In a 2002 Gallup survey, those who did not exercise were twice as likely as those who did to report being "not too happy" (Brooks, 2002). But if we state this observation the other way around—that stressed and depressed people exercise less—cause and effect become unclear.

Experiments have resolved this ambiguity by randomly assigning stressed, depressed, or anxious people either to aerobic exercise or to other treatments. In one such experiment, Lisa McCann and David Holmes (1984) assigned one third of a group of mildly depressed female college students to a program of aerobic exercise and another third to a treatment of relaxation exercises; the remaining third, a control group, received no treatment. As **FIGURE 11.23** shows, 10 weeks later the women in the aerobic exercise program reported the greatest decrease in depression. Many of them had, quite literally, run away from their troubles.

More than 150 other studies confirm that exercise reduces depression and anxiety and is therefore a useful adjunct to antidepressant drugs and

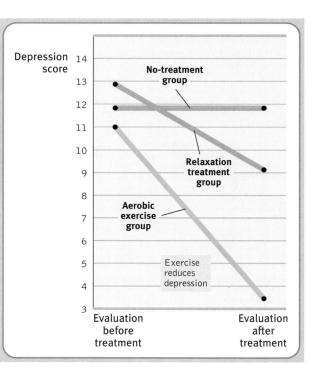

figure 11.23
Aerobic exercise and depression Mildly depressed college women who participated in an aerobic exercise program showed markedly reduced depression, compared with those who did relaxation exercises or received no treatment. (From McCann & Holmes, 1984.)

Depression score

14
13 — No-treatment group
12
11
10 — Relaxation treatment group
9
8 — Aerobic exercise group
7
6
5 — Exercise reduces depression
4
3

Evaluation before treatment — Evaluation after treatment

psychotherapy (Arent & others, 2000; Berger & Motl, 2000). Not only is exercise about as effective as drugs, some research suggests it better prevents symptom recurrence (Babyak & others, 2000; Salmon, 2001). Vigorous exercise provides a "substantial" immediate mood boost, reports David Watson (2000) from his monitoring of university students. Even a 10-minute walk stimulates two hours of increased well-being by raising energy levels and lowering tension (Thayer, 1987, 1993).

Researchers are now wondering *why* aerobic exercise alleviates stress and negative emotions. They know that exercise

- strengthens the heart, increases blood flow, keeps blood vessels open, and lowers both blood pressure and the blood pressure reaction to stress (Ford, 2002; Manson, 2002).
- orders up mood-boosting chemicals from our body's internal pharmacy—neurotransmitters such as norepinephrine, serotonin, and the endorphins (Jacobs, 1994; Salmon, 2001).
- modestly enhances cognitive abilities, such as memory (Etnier & others, 1997).
- promotes the growth of new brain cells in mice exercising daily on a running wheel regimen (Kempermann & Gage, 1999).

Perhaps the emotional benefits of exercise are also a side effect of increased body arousal and warmth, or of the muscle relaxation and sounder sleep that occur afterward. Or perhaps a sense of accomplishment and an improved physique enhance one's emotional state.

EXERCISE AND HEALTH Other research reveals that exercise not only boosts our mood, but also benefits our physical health (Dubbert, 2002). A digest of data from 43 studies revealed that, compared with inactive adults, people who exercise suffer half as many heart attacks (Powell & others, 1987). Exercise makes the muscles hungry for the "bad fats" that, if not used by the muscles, contribute to clogged arteries (Barinaga, 1997). One study following adult Finnish twins for nearly 20 years revealed that, other things being equal, occasional exercise reduced the risk of death by 29 percent, compared with no exercise. Daily conditioning exercise reduced death risk by 43 percent (Kujala & others, 1998).

By one estimate, moderate exercise adds two years to one's expected life. "Perhaps God does not subtract the time spent exercising from your allotted time on Earth," jests Martin Seligman (1994, p. 193).

The mood boost Aerobic exercise, such as running, appears to counteract depression partly by increasing arousal (replacing depression's low-arousal state) and by doing naturally what Prozac does—increasing the brain's serotonin activity.

Biofeedback and Relaxation

Knowing the damaging effects of stress, could we train people to bring their heart rate and blood pressure under conscious control? When a few psychologists started experimenting with this idea, many of their colleagues thought them foolish. After all, these functions are controlled by the autonomic ("involuntary") nervous system. Then, in the late 1960s, experiments by respected psychologists began to make the skeptics wonder. Neal Miller, for one, found that rats could modify their heartbeat if given pleasurable brain stimulation when their heartbeat increased or decreased. Later research revealed that some paralyzed humans could also learn to control their blood pressure (Miller & Brucker, 1979).

Miller was experimenting with **biofeedback**, a system of recording, amplifying, and feeding back information about subtle physiological responses. Biofeedback instruments reflect the results of a person's own efforts, thereby allowing the person to learn techniques for controlling a particular physiological response. For example, a person with chronic headaches might learn to control the tension in forehead muscles by receiving feedback about tension in those muscles. As the person relaxes the forehead muscle, the pointer on the display screen (or a tone) may go lower.

After a decade of study, however, researchers decided the initial claims for biofeedback were overblown and oversold (Miller, 1985). A 1995 National Institutes of Health panel declared that biofeedback works best on tension headaches. But other, simpler methods of relaxation, which require no expensive equipment, produce many of the same benefits.

▶ **aerobic exercise** sustained exercise that increases heart and lung fitness; may also alleviate depression and anxiety.

▶ **biofeedback** a system for electronically recording, amplifying, and feeding back information regarding a subtle physiological state, such as blood pressure or muscle tension.

Learning the "relaxation response"
Relaxation training is a component of many stress-reduction programs. At Boston's Deaconess Hospital, hypertension patients learn meditation techniques that counteract stress.

Meditation is a modern phenomenon with a long history: "Sit down alone and in silence. Lower your head, shut your eyes, breathe out gently, and imagine yourself looking into your own heart. . . . As you breathe out, say 'Lord Jesus Christ, have mercy on me.' . . . Try to put all other thoughts aside. Be calm, be patient, and repeat the process very frequently" (Gregory of Sinai, died 1346).

Might relaxation exercises alone be a natural antidote for stress? Cardiologist Herbert Benson (1996) became intrigued with this possibility when he found that experienced meditators could decrease their blood pressure, heart rate, and oxygen consumption and raise their fingertip temperature. You can experience the essence of this *relaxation response*, as Benson calls it, right now: Assume a comfortable position, breathe deeply, and relax your muscles from foot to face. Now, close your eyes and concentrate on a single word or a phrase. (About 80 percent of Benson's patients choose to focus on a favorite prayer.) When other thoughts intrude, let them drift away as you repeat your phrase continually for 10 to 20 minutes. Tibetan Buddhists deep in meditation and Franciscan nuns deep in centering prayer report a diminished sense of self, space, and time. Scans of their brains during these mystical experiences reveal the neural footprints of such spiritual feelings. A part of the parietal lobe that keeps track of where we are in space is less active than usual. A frontal lobe area involved in focused attention is more active (Newberg & D'Aquili, 2001).

Many of those who simply set aside a quiet time or two each day report enjoying the tranquility. Stress worsens pain, infertility, and insomnia, and it suppresses the immune system. Meditative relaxation counteracts all these effects, Benson reports. One astonishing study randomly assigned 73 residents of homes for the elderly either to daily meditation or to none. After three years, one-fourth of the nonmeditators had died, while all the meditators were still alive (Alexander & others, 1989). Sixty other studies find that relaxation procedures can help alleviate headaches, hypertension, anxiety, and insomnia (Stetter & Kupper, 2002).

Such findings would not surprise Meyer Friedman and his colleagues. To find out whether teaching Type A heart attack victims to relax might reduce their risk of another attack, the researchers randomly assigned hundreds of middle-aged heart attack survivors in San Francisco to one of two groups. The first group received standard advice from cardiologists concerning medications, diet, and exercise habits. The second group received similar advice plus continuing counseling on modifying their life-styles—how to slow down and relax by walking, talking, and eating more slowly; by smiling at others and laughing at themselves; by admitting mistakes; by taking time to enjoy life; and by renewing their religious faith. As **FIGURE 11.24** indicates, during the ensuing three years, the second group experienced

figure 11.24
Recurrent heart attacks and life-style modification The San Francisco Recurrent Coronary Prevention Project offered survivors of heart attacks counseling from a cardiologist. Those who were also guided in modifying their Type A life-style suffered fewer repeat heart attacks. (From Friedman & Ulmer, 1984.)

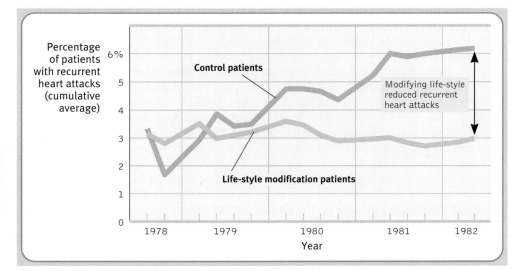

half as many repeat heart attacks as the first group. This, wrote the exuberant Friedman, is an unprecedented, spectacular reduction in heart attack recurrence. A smaller-scale British study similarly divided heart-attack–prone people into control and life-style modification groups (Eysenck & Grossarth-Maticek, 1991). During the next 13 years, it also found a 50 percent reduction in death rate among those trained to alter their thinking and life-style.

Social Support

Linda and Emily had much in common. When interviewed for a study conducted by UCLA social psychologist Shelley Taylor (1989), both Los Angeles women had married, raised three children, suffered comparable breast tumors, and recovered from surgery and six months of chemotherapy. But there was a difference. Linda, a widow in her early fifties, was living alone, her children scattered in Atlanta, Boston, and Europe. "She had become odd in ways that people sometimes do when they are isolated," reported Taylor. "Having no one with whom to share her thoughts on a daily basis, she unloaded them somewhat inappropriately with strangers, including our interviewer."

Interviewing Emily was difficult in a different way. Phone calls interrupted. Her children, all living nearby, were in and out of the house, dropping things off with a quick kiss. Her husband called from his office for a brief chat. Two dogs roamed the house, greeting visitors enthusiastically. All in all, Emily "seemed a serene and contented person, basking in the warmth of her family."

Three years later, the researchers tried to reinterview the women. Linda, they learned, had died two years before. Emily was still lovingly supported by her family and friends and was as happy and healthy as ever.

Because no two cancers are identical, we can't be certain that different social situations led to Linda's and Emily's fates. But they do illustrate a conclusion drawn from several large studies: Social support—feeling liked, affirmed, and encouraged by intimate friends and family—promotes not only happiness, but also health.

Relationships can sometimes be stressful, especially in living conditions that are crowded and lack privacy (Evans & others, 1989). "Hell is others," wrote Jean-Paul Sartre. Peter Warr and Roy Payne (1982) asked a representative sample of British adults what, if anything, had emotionally strained them the day before. Their most frequent answer? "Family."

But asked what prompted yesterday's times of pleasure, the same British sample, by an even larger margin, again answered, "Family." For most of us, family relationships provide not only our greatest heartaches (even when well-meaning, family intrusions can be stressful) but also our greatest comfort and joy. Moreover, seven massive investigations, each following thousands of people for several years, revealed that close relationships predict health. Compared with those having few social ties, people are less likely to die prematurely if supported by close relationships with friends, family, fellow workers, members of a faith community, or other support groups (Cohen, 1988; House & others, 1988; Nelson, 1988). Leukemia and heart disease patients also have enjoyed markedly increased survival rates if married or supported by family or friends (Case & others, 1992; Colon & others, 1991; Williams & others, 1992).

It has long been known that married people live longer, healthier lives than the unmarried. A seven-decades long Harvard study found that a good marriage at age 50 predicts healthy aging better than does a low cholesterol level at 50 (Vaillant, 2002). Two recent analyses conclude, after controlling for various possible explanations,

Humans aren't the only source of stress-buffering comfort. After stressful events, Medicare patients who have a dog or other companionable pet are less likely to visit their doctor (Siegel, 1990).

"Woe to one who is alone and falls and does not have another to help."

Ecclesiastes 4:10

Bob Daemmrich/Stock, Boston

Friendships are good medicine Several long-term studies of thousands of people have found that individuals with close supportive relationships are less likely than socially isolated people to die prematurely.

that marriage "improves survival prospects" (Murray, 2000) and "makes people" healthier and longer-lived (Wilson & Oswald, 2002). But marital functioning also matters. Positive, happy, supportive marriages are conducive to health; conflict-laden ones are not (Kiecolt-Glaser & Newton, 2001).

How can we explain this link between social support and health? Is it just that healthy people are more likely to marry and stay married? Or do people with supportive friends and marriage partners eat better, exercise more, sleep better, smoke less, or cope more effectively? Research indicates there are several possible reasons (Helgeson & others, 1998).

Environments that support our need to belong foster stronger immune functioning. Given ample social support, spouses of cancer patients exhibit stronger immune functioning (Baron & others, 1990). Social ties even confer resistance to cold viruses. Sheldon Cohen and his colleagues (1997) demonstrated this by putting 276 healthy volunteers in quarantine for five days after administering nasal drops laden with a cold virus. (The volunteers were paid $800 each to endure this experience.) The cold fact is that the effect of social ties is nothing to sneeze at. Age, race, sex, smoking, and other health habits being equal, those with the most social ties were least likely to catch a cold and they produced less mucus. More than 50 studies further reveal that social support calms the cardiovascular system, lowering blood pressure and stress hormones (Uchino & others, 1996, 1999).

Close relationships also provide the opportunity to *confide* painful feelings, a social support component that has now been extensively studied. In one study, health psychologists James Pennebaker and Robin O'Heeron (1984) contacted the surviving spouses of people who had committed suicide or died in car accidents. Those who bore their grief alone had more health problems than those who could express it openly. Talking about our troubles can be "open heart therapy." Older people, many of whom have lost a spouse and close friends, are somewhat less likely to enjoy such confiding (**Figure 11.25**).

Suppressed traumas sometimes eat away at us and affect our physical health. When Pennebaker surveyed more than 700 undergraduate women, he found that about 1 in 12 reported a traumatic sexual experience in childhood. Compared with women who had experienced nonsexual traumas, such as parental death or divorce, the sexually abused women—especially those who had kept their secret to themselves—reported more headaches and stomach ailments.

Actively suppressing thoughts can cause them to bubble up intrusively, preoccupying the person (Wegner, 1990). (In the next five seconds, please *don't* picture a white bear.) Disclosing suppressed thoughts may stop their intrusion. In a simulated

"I get by with a little help from my friends."

John Lennon and Paul McCartney, Sgt. Pepper's Lonely Hearts Club Band, *1967*

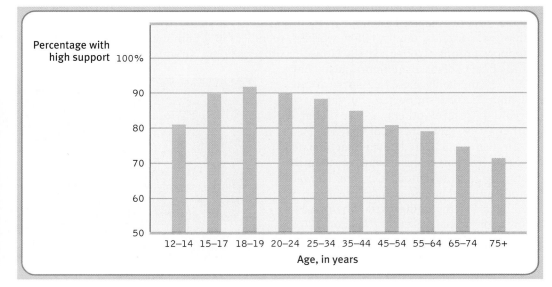

figure 11.25
Social support across the life span
Do you have someone you can confide in? Someone to count on in a crisis? Someone to count on for advice? Someone who makes you feel loved and cared for? In a national health survey, 9 in 10 young adult Canadians, but only 7 in 10 over the age of 75, indicated high social support by answering "yes" to all four questions. (Data from *Statistics Canada*, 1999, p. 133.)

confessional, Pennebaker asked volunteers to share with a hidden experimenter some upsetting events that had been preying on their minds. He asked some of the volunteers to describe a trivial event before they divulged the troubling one. Physiological measures revealed that their bodies remained tense the whole time they talked about the trivial event; they relaxed only when they later confided the cause of their turmoil.

Writing about personal traumas in a diary can also help. When volunteers in other experiments did this, they had fewer health problems during the ensuing four to six months (Pennebaker, 1990). As one subject explained, "Although I have not talked with anyone about what I wrote, I was finally able to deal with it, work through the pain instead of trying to block it out. Now it doesn't hurt to think about it."

Pennebaker and his colleagues (1989) also invited 33 Holocaust survivors to spend two hours recalling their experiences. Many did so in intimate detail never before disclosed. In the weeks following, most watched a videotape of their recollections and showed it to family and friends. Again, those who were most self-disclosing had the most improved health 14 months later. Talking about a stressful event can temporarily arouse people, but in the long run it calms them (Mendolia & Kleck, 1993). Confiding is good for the soul.

Let's summarize: Sustained emotional reactions to stressful events can be debilitating. However, the toxic impact of stressful events can be buffered by a relaxed, healthy life-style and by the comfort and aid provided by supportive friends and family (**FIGURE 11.26**).

Spirituality and Faith Communities

Throughout history, humans have suffered ills and sought healing. In response, the two healing traditions—religion and medicine—historically have joined hands in caring for the sick. These efforts were often conducted by the same person; the spiritual leader was also the healer. Maimonides was a twelfth-century rabbi and a renowned physician. Hospitals, which were first established in monasteries then spread by missionaries, often carry the names of saints or faith communities.

As medical science matured, healing and religion diverged. Rather than simply asking God to spare their children from smallpox, people began vaccinating them. Rather than seeking a spiritual healer when burning with bacterial fever, they turned to antibiotics.

The separation between religion and medicine is now shrinking. "Spirituality" has made a comeback:

- Since 1995, Harvard Medical School has annually attracted 1000 to 2000 health professionals to its Spirituality and Healing in Medicine conferences.
- Duke University has established a Center for the Study of Religion/Spirituality and Health.
- Eighty-six of America's 126 medical schools offered spirituality and health courses in 2002, up from 5 in 1992 (Koenig, 2002).
- A Yankelovich survey (1997) found 94 percent of HMO professionals and 99 percent of family physicians agreeing that "personal prayer, meditation, or other spiritual and religious practices" can enhance medical treatment.
- This renewed convergence of religion and medicine appears in such books as *The Faith Factor* (Viking, 1998), *The Healing Power of Faith* (Simon & Schuster, 1999), *Religion and Health* (Oxford University Press, 2000), and *Faith and Health* (Guilford, 2001).

figure 11.26
Coping with stress
Life events can be debilitating or not. It all depends on how we appraise them and whether the stresses are buffered by a stress-resistant disposition, healthy habits, and enduring social support.

John David Mercer/The Gamma Liaison Network/Getty Images

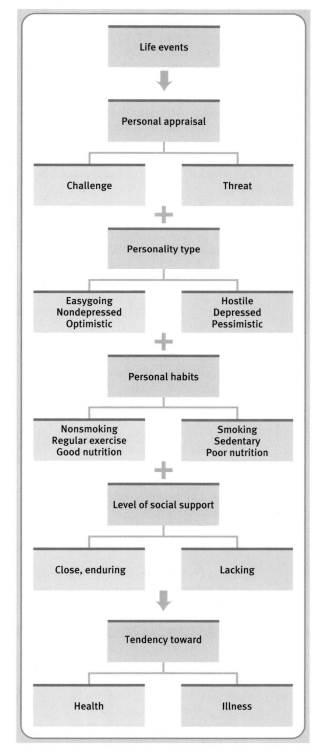

Thinking Critically About:

Alternative Medicine—New Ways to Health, or Old Snake Oil?

One health care growth market is **complementary and alternative medicine**, which encompasses acupuncture, massage therapy, homeopathy, spiritual healing, herbal remedies, chiropractic, aromatherapy, and the like. In Germany, herbal remedies and homeopathy are enormously popular. In China, herbal therapies have long flourished, as have acupuncture and acupressure therapies that claim to correct "imbalances of energy flow" (called *Qi* or *Chi*) at identifiable points close to the skin. Andrew Weil's many books on alternative medicine have sold millions of copies, putting him on the cover of *Time* magazine and gaining his Web site a reported 2.5 million monthly hits (Relman, 1998). Facing political pressure to explore such things, the U.S. National Institutes of Health established the National Center for Complementary and Alternative Medicine, which the center defines as health care treatments not taught widely in medical schools, not usually reimbursed by insurance companies, and not used in hospitals (**TABLE 11.2**). From 1998 to 2000, however, the number of U.S. hospitals offering alternative therapies doubled to 16 percent (Abelson & Brown, 2002).

So what shall we make of alternative medicine? Some aspects, such as life-style and stress management, have acknowledged validity. Do the other aspects offer, as some believe, a new medical paradigm for a new millennium? Or do they represent, as others maintain, "voodoo medicine"—a retreat from rationality and science?

Supporters of alternative medicine offer inspirational cases, such as these from Andrew Weil's books (Relman, 1998):

- A young woman diagnosed with bone cancer starts a vigorous exercise program (biking 500 miles and running 60 miles weekly), becomes vegetarian (consuming fresh fruit, juices, and whole grains), and shucks the alleged cancer.
- A woman uses "respiratory biofeedback" to end her Parkinson's-induced seizures.
- A man with scleroderma, a progressive and fatal disease of the skin and internal organs, cures himself with vinegar, lemons, aloe vera juice, and vitamin E.

But critics point out that people consult physicians for diagnosable, curable diseases and employ alternative medicine when they either are incurably ill or are basically well but feeling subpar. So an otherwise healthy person with a cold, for example, may try an herbal remedy

> *"Sickness is the manifestation of evil in the body."*
>
> **Andrew Weil,** Health and Healing, *1998*

table 11.2 Subfields of Alternative Medicine

Alternative systems of medical practice	Health care ranging from self-care according to folk principles, to care rendered in an organized health care system based on alternative traditions or practices
Bioelectromagnetic applications	The study of how living organisms interact with electromagnetic (EM) fields
Diet, nutrition, life-style changes	The knowledge of how to prevent illness, maintain health, and reverse the effects of chronic disease through dietary or nutritional intervention
Herbal medicine	Employing plant and plant products from folk medicine traditions for pharmacological use
Manual healing	Using touch and manipulation with the hands as a diagnostic and therapeutic tool
Mind-body control	Exploring the mind's capacity to affect the body, based on traditional medical systems that make use of the interconnectedness of mind and body
Pharmacological and biological treatments	Drugs and vaccines not yet accepted by mainstream medicine

Source: Offered without endorsement by the National Center for Complementary and Alternative Medicine (nccam.nih.gov)

and then credit the subsequent return to good health to alternative medicine, rather than to the body's natural regression to normal. Alternative medicine will seem especially effective with cyclical diseases, such as arthritis and allergies, as people seek therapy during the downturn and presume its effectiveness during the ensuing upturn. Add to this the healing power of belief—the placebo effect—plus the natural disappearance ("spontaneous remission") of many diseases, and voilà: Alternative medicine practices are bound to seem effective, whether they are or not. In the 1700s, even bloodletting *seemed* effective. Sometimes people improved despite the treatment; when they did not, the practitioner inferred the disease was too far advanced to be reversed.

The National Council Against Health Fraud and the editors of leading medical journals and of the *Scientific Review of Alternative Medicine* doubt the efficacy of alternative medicine therapies. They note that for most alternative medicine claims the scientific jury is not out; it hasn't yet convened. Although the U.S. government's National Center for Complementary and Alternative Medicine is funding research, the 30 research grants it awarded in 1993 had, almost six years later, produced only four studies found among the 3500 medical journals—and none of these controlled for placebo effects (Angell & Kassirer, 1998).

In November 1998, the *Journal of the American Medical Association* published seven new alternative medicine research studies. Three explored treatments that proved useless (chiropractic manipulation for tension headaches, a popular herb for weight loss, and acupuncture to control nerve pain caused by HIV). Four other treatments—an herb mixture for inflammatory bowel syndrome, an herbal remedy for bladder problems, yoga for carpal tunnel syndrome pain, and a Chinese method for inducing fetuses in the breech position to turn—showed some benefits. As always, the way to discern what works and what does not is to experiment: Randomly assign patients to receive the therapy or a placebo control. Then ask the critical question: When neither the therapist nor the patient knows who is getting the real therapy, is the real therapy effective?

"In God we trust. All others must have data."

George Lundberg, editor, Journal of the American Medical Association, *1998*

Much of today's mainstream medicine began as yesterday's alternative medicine, not all of which, like bloodletting, was refuted by controlled experiments. Natural botanical life has given us digitalis (from purple foxglove), morphine (from the opium poppy), and penicillin (from penicillium mold). In each case, the active ingredient was isolated, synthesized, and carefully verified in controlled trials. We have medical science, not alternative medicine, to thank for the antibiotics, vaccines, surgical procedures, and emergency medicine that helped lengthen our life expectancy by three decades during the last century. If you have acute chest pain, find a lump in your chest, cough up blood, or develop a high fever, you would do well to seek out someone trained in medical science—someone undergirded by research on what treatments really work best for what ailments at what doses for what lengths of time.

Indeed, said *New England Journal of Medicine* editors Marcia Angell and Jerome Kassirer (1998), "There cannot be two kinds of medicine—conventional and alternative. There is only medicine that has been adequately tested and medicine that has not, medicine that works and medicine that may or may not work. Once a treatment has been tested rigorously, it no longer matters whether it was considered alternative at the outset."

▶ **complementary and alternative medicine** unproven health care treatments not taught widely in medical schools, not used in hospitals, and not usually reimbursed by insurance companies.

Is there fire underneath all this smoke? Do religion and spirituality actually relate to health, as polls show 4 in 5 Americans have believed (Matthews & Larson, 1997)? More than a thousand studies have sought to correlate "the faith factor" with health and healing. Consider two:

- Jeremy Kark and his colleagues (1996) compared the death rates for 3900 Israelis either in one of 11 religiously orthodox or in one of 11 matched, nonreligious collective settlements (kibbutz communities). The researchers reported that over a 16-year period, "belonging to a religious collective was associated with a strong protective effect" not explained by age or economic differences. In every age group, those belonging to the religious communities were about half as likely as their nonreligious counterparts to have died. This is roughly comparable with the gender difference in mortality. (In every age group, 64 British and 60 American women die for every 100 men [*Chance News*, 1997].)
- An earlier study of 91,909 persons in one Maryland county found that those who attended religious services weekly were less likely to die during the study period than those who did not—53 percent less from coronary disease, 53 percent less from suicide, and 74 percent less from cirrhosis of the liver (Comstock & Partridge, 1972).

In response to such findings, Richard Sloan and his skeptical colleagues (1999, 2000, 2002) remind us that mere correlations can leave many factors uncontrolled. Consider one obvious possibility: Women are more religiously active than men, and women outlive men. So perhaps religious involvement is merely an expression of the gender effect on longevity.

However, several new studies find the religiosity-longevity correlation among men alone, and even more strongly among women (McCullough & others, 2000). One study that followed 5286 Californians over 28 years found that, after controlling for age, gender, ethnicity, and education, frequent religious attendees were 36 percent less likely to have died in any year (**FIGURE 11.27**).

A National Health Interview Survey (Hummer & others, 1999) followed 21,204 people over 8 years. After controlling for age, sex, race, and region, researchers found that nonattenders were 1.87 times more likely to have died than were those attending more than weekly. This translated into a life expectancy at age 20 of 83 years for frequent attenders and 75 years for infrequent attenders (**FIGURE 11.28**).

These correlational findings do not indicate that nonattenders who start attending services and change nothing else will live 8 years longer. But they do indicate that as a *predictor* of health and longevity, religious involvement rivals nonsmoking

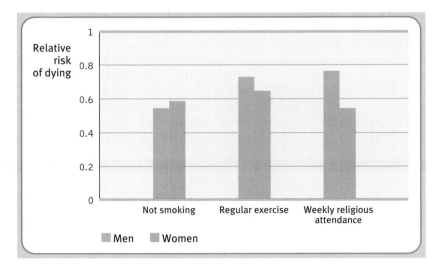

figure 11.27
Not smoking, frequent exercise, and regular religious attendance as predictors of mortality Epidemiologist William Strawbridge and his co-workers (1997, 1999; Oman & others, 2002) followed 5286 Alameda, California, adults over 28 years. After adjusting for age and education, the researchers found that not smoking, regular exercise, and religious attendance all predicted a lowered risk of death in any given year. Women attending weekly religious services, for example, were only 54 percent as likely to die in a typical study year as were nonattenders.

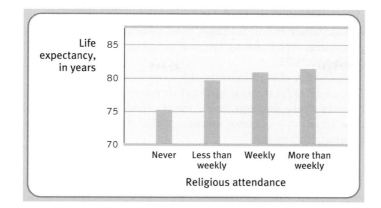

figure 11.28
Religious attendance and life expectancy In a national health survey financed by the U.S. Centers for Disease Control and Prevention, religiously active people had longer life expectancies. (Data from Hummer & others, 1999.)

and exercise effects. Such findings demand explanation. Can you imagine what "intervening variables" might account for the correlation?

First, religiously active people have healthier life-styles; for example, they smoke and drink less (Lyons, 2002; Strawbridge & others, 2001). Health-oriented, vegetarian Seventh Day Adventists have a longer-than-usual life expectancy (Berkel & de Waard, 1983). Religiously orthodox Israelis eat less fat than do their nonreligious compatriots. But such differences are not great enough to explain the dramatically reduced mortality in the religious kibbutzim, argued the Israeli researchers. In the recent American studies, too, about 75 percent of the longevity difference remains after controlling for unhealthy behaviors such as inactivity and smoking (Musick & others, 1999).

Social support is another variable that helps explain the "faith factor" (George & others, 2002). For Judaism, Christianity, and Islam, faith is not solo spirituality but a communal experience that helps satisfy the need to belong. The more than 350,000 faith communities in North America and the millions more elsewhere provide support networks for their active participants—people who are there for one another when misfortune strikes. Moreover, religion encourages another predictor of health and longevity—marriage. In the religious kibbutzim, for example, divorce is almost nonexistent.

But even after controlling for gender, unhealthy behaviors, social ties, and preexisting health problems, the mortality studies find much of the mortality reduction remaining (George & others, 2000; Powell & others, 2003). Researchers therefore speculate that a third set of intervening variables is the stress protection and enhanced well-being associated with a coherent worldview, a sense of hope for the long-term future, feelings of ultimate acceptance, and the relaxed meditation of prayer or Sabbath observance (**FIGURE 11.29**). These variables might also help to

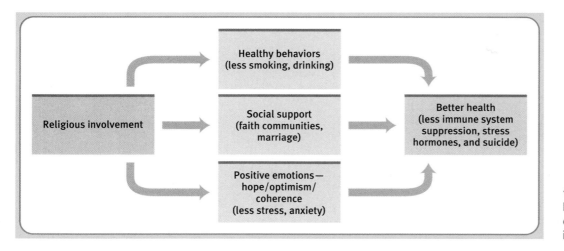

figure 11.29
Possible explanations for the correlation between religious involvement and health/longevity

explain other recent findings, such as healthier immune functioning and fewer hospital admissions among religiously active people (Koenig & Larson, 1998; Koenig & others, 1997).

Although the religion-health correlation is yet to be fully explained, Harold Pincus (1997), deputy medical director of the American Psychiatric Association, believes these findings "have made clear that anyone involved in providing health care services . . . cannot ignore . . . the important connections between spirituality, religion, and health."

rehearse it!

22. A number of studies reveal that aerobic exercise raises energy levels and helps alleviate depression and anxiety. One explanation for these emotional effects of exercise is that exercise triggers the release of mood-boosting neurotransmitters such as norepinephrine, serotonin, and the
    a. placebos.
    b. endorphins.
    c. B lymphocytes.
    d. T lymphocytes.

23. Long-term studies of thousands of people indicate that people who have close relationships—a strong social support system—are less likely to die prematurely than those who do not. These studies support the idea that
    a. social ties can be a source of stress.
    b. gender influences longevity.
    c. Type A behavior is responsible for many premature deaths.
    d. social support has a beneficial effect on health.

Answers can be found in Appendix C.

chapter review

Emotions, Stress, and Health

THEORIES OF EMOTION

1. What are the components of an emotion?

Emotions are psychological responses of the whole organism that involve an interplay among (1) physiological arousal, (2) expressive behaviors, and (3) conscious experience.

2. Does physiological arousal precede or follow an emotional experience? (Does your heart pound because you are afraid, or are you afraid because you feel your heart pounding?)

This is one of the oldest theoretical controversies regarding emotion. William James and Carl Lange proposed that we feel emotion after we notice our body responses. Walter Cannon and Philip Bard believed that we feel emotion *at the same time* that our bodies respond. Most researchers today agree with Cannon and Bard but also note that, as James and Lange pointed out, physical reactions are an important ingredient of emotion.

3. To experience emotions, must we consciously interpret and label them?

Can we experience human emotions apart from cognition? Can we feel before we think? Stanley Schachter's two-factor theory of emotion contends that the cognitive labels we put on our states of arousal are an essential ingredient of emotion. Richard Lazarus agreed that cognition is essential: Many important emotions arise from our interpretations or inferences. Robert Zajonc and Joseph LeDoux, however, believe that some simple emotional responses occur instantly, not only outside our conscious awareness but before any cognitive processing occurs. The issue has practical implications: To the degree that emotions are rooted in thinking, we can hope to change them by changing our thinking.

EMBODIED EMOTION

4. What physiological changes accompany emotions?

Emotions are both psychological and physiological. Much of the physiological activity is controlled by the autonomic nervous system's sympathetic (arousing) and parasympathetic (calming) divisions. Our performance on a task is usually best when arousal is moderate, though this varies with the difficulty of the task.

5. Do different emotions activate different physiological responses?

When two emotions are similarly arousing and negative (or positive) the physiological responses that accompany them are nearly indistinguishable to an untrained observer. However, scientists have discovered subtle differences in activity in the brain's cortical areas, in use of brain pathways, and in secretion of hormones associated with different emotions.

Polygraphs measure several physiological indicators of emotion. Although they detect lies at a rate better than chance, they are not accurate enough to justify their widespread use in business and government. The use of guilty knowledge questions may increase the accuracy of these tests.

EXPRESSED EMOTION

6. How do we communicate nonverbally?

Much of our communication is through the silent language of the body. Even very thin (seconds-long) videotaped slices of behavior can reveal feelings. Women tend to be better at reading people's emotional cues.

7. Are nonverbal expressions of emotion universally understood?

Although some gestures are culturally determined, facial expressions, such as those of happiness and fear, are common the world over. In communal cultures that value interdependence, intense displays of potentially disruptive emotions are infrequent.

8. Do our facial expressions influence our feelings?

Expressions do more than communicate emotion to others. They also amplify the felt emotion and signal the body to respond accordingly. Emotions arise from the interplay of cognition, physiology, and expressive behaviors (see **FIGURE 11.30**, page 426).

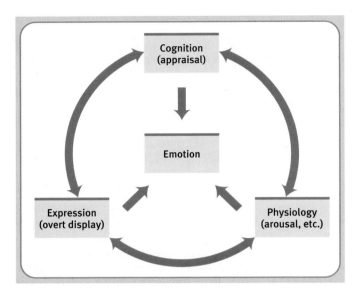

figure 11.30
The ingredients of emotion From the interplay of physiology, expression, and cognition comes emotion.

EXPERIENCED EMOTION

9. *What are the causes and consequences of anger?*

Anger is most often evoked by events that not only are frustrating or insulting but also are interpreted as willful, unjustified, and avoidable. Blowing off steam may be temporarily calming, but in the long run it does not reduce anger. Expressing anger can actually make us angrier.

10. *What are the causes and consequences of happiness?*

A good mood boosts people's perceptions of the world and their willingness to help others (the *feel-good, do-good phenomenon*). The moods triggered by the day's good or bad events seldom last beyond that day. Even significant good events, such as a substantial rise in income, seldom increase happiness for long. We can explain the relativity of happiness with the adaptation-level phenomenon and the relative deprivation principle. Nevertheless, some people are usually happier than others, and researchers have identified factors that predict such happiness.

STRESS AND HEALTH

11. *What is stress?*

Walter Cannon viewed stress, the process by which we appraise and respond to events that challenge or threaten us, as a "fight-or-flight" system. Hans Selye saw it as a three-stage (alarm-resistance-exhaustion) general adaptation syndrome (GAS).

12. *What events provoke stress responses?*

Modern research on stress assesses the health consequences of catastrophic events, significant life changes, and daily hassles. The events that tend to provoke stress responses are those that we perceive as both negative and uncontrollable. Optimists seem to cope more successfully with stress and enjoy better health.

13. *Why are some of us more prone than others to coronary heart disease?*

Coronary heart disease, North America's number one cause of death, has been linked with the competitive, hard-driving, impatient, and (especially) anger-prone Type A personality. Under stress, the body of a reactive, hostile person secretes more of the hormones that accelerate the buildup of plaque on the heart's artery walls. Type B personalities are more relaxed and easygoing.

14. *How does stress make us more vulnerable to disease?*

Stress diverts energy from the immune system, inhibiting the activities of its B and T lymphocytes and macrophages. Although stress does not cause diseases such as cancer, it may influence the disease's progression. Research indicates that conditioning also influences the immune system's responses.

PROMOTING HEALTH

15. *What tactics can we use to manage stress and reduce stress-related ailments?*

Among the components of stress-management programs are aerobic exercise, biofeedback, and relaxation. Counseling Type A heart attack survivors to slow down and relax has helped lower rates of recurring attacks. Social support also helps people cope, partly by buffering the impact of stress. Researchers are now trying to understand the active components of the religion-health correlation.

A CRITICAL THINKER'S REVIEW OF CHAPTER 11

You've now studied and reviewed **Emotions, Stress, and Health**. For even better retention, reflect on these concepts at a deeper level. If you need to refresh your memory of the six categories of critical thinking shown in parentheses below, see page 34.
See if you can answer each of these questions in a short paragraph.

1. Cindy is holding her 8-month-old baby when a fierce dog appears out of nowhere and, with teeth bared, leaps for the baby's face. Cindy immediately ducks for cover to protect the baby, screams at the dog, then notices that her heart is banging in her chest and she's broken out in a cold sweat. How would the James-Lange, Cannon-Bard, and two-factor theories explain Cindy's emotional reaction? (psychological reasoning)

2. In an alarming situation, we experience an acute physical reaction, including increased heart rate and respiration, tense muscles, and slowed digestion. If you were an evolutionary psychologist, how might you explain this reaction? (perspective taking)

3. Who tend to express more emotions—men or women? How do we know the answer to that question? (scientific problem solving)

4. Liz's roommate is a grumpy morning person. She reluctantly drags herself out of bed and then slumps her way across campus to class with a scowl—head down and feet shuffling. She typically arrives in her first class with a bad attitude. Using what you now know about the effects of our facial and bodily expressions on our experienced emotions, what could Liz suggest that might help improve her roommate's attitude? (creative problem solving)

5. Ms. Morton owns a specialty bakery. She has been reading about happiness research and was surprised to learn about the many benefits of happiness, including greater productivity on the job. She has decided to institute a happiness plan for her employees. What three or four research-based suggestions should Ms. Morton include in her plan? (practical problem solving)

6. Based on what you now know about good health, and given only the few details noted below, which of the following two college students do you think is more likely to be healthy, Terrance or Eli? Explain why. (pattern recognition)
   - *Terrance* is a bright student, yet he tends to panic before every test or class presentation. He worries that he will make a fool of himself, though he actually never has. He is too busy studying to exercise or hang out with friends. Although he is becoming overweight, he has made the college honor roll every term.
   - *Eli* is a bright student who studies hard. He likes tests and classroom discussions, because they give him a chance to demonstrate what he's been working so hard to learn, and the opportunity to learn even more. Eli runs cross country, because many of his friends are on the team, and because he thought it would be a good idea to stay in shape.

Answers can be found in Appendix C.

TERMS AND CONCEPTS TO REMEMBER

emotion, p. 379
James-Lange theory, p. 380
Cannon-Bard theory, p. 380
two-factor theory, p. 381
polygraph, p. 386
catharsis, p. 394
feel-good, do-good phenomenon, p. 396
subjective well-being, p. 396

adaptation-level phenomenon, p. 399
relative deprivation, p. 400
stress, p. 402
general adaptation syndrome (GAS), p. 403
health psychology, p. 404
coronary heart disease, p. 408
Type A, p. 408

Type B, p. 408
psychophysiological illness, p. 409
lymphocytes, p. 409
aerobic exercise, p. 414
biofeedback, p. 415
complementary and alternative medicine, p. 420

To continue your study and review of Emotions, Stress, and Health visit this book's Web site at www.worthpublishers.com/myers. You will find practice tests, review activities, and Web links for more information on topics related to Emotions, Stress, and Health.

chapter12

Personality

Lord of the Rings hobbit-hero Frodo Baggins knew that throughout his harrowing journey there was one who would never fail him—his loyal and ever-cheerful companion, Sam Gamgee. Even before they left their beloved hometown, Frodo warned Sam that the journey would not be easy:

> "It is going to be very dangerous, Sam. It is already dangerous. Most likely neither of us will come back."
>
> "If you don't come back, sir, then I shan't, that's certain," said Sam. "[The Elves told me] 'Don't you leave him!' Leave him! I said. I never mean to. I am going with him, if he climbs to the Moon; and if any of those Black Riders try to stop him, they'll have Sam Gamgee to reckon with." (Tolkien, *The Fellowship of the Ring*, p. 96)

And so they did! Later, when it became clear that Frodo had to venture into the dreaded land of Mordor without the rest of the company, it was Sam who insisted he would accompany Frodo, come what may. It was Sam who lifted Frodo's flagging spirits with songs and stories from their boyhood, and Sam upon whom Frodo leaned when he could barely take another step. When Frodo was overcome by the evil of the ring he bore, it was Sam who saved Frodo from completely succumbing to it. And in the end, it was Sam who enabled Frodo to successfully reach the end of his journey. Sam Gamgee—the cheerful, conscientious, emotionally stable optimist—never faltered in his faithfulness or his belief that they could overcome the threatening darkness.

1. What is personality?

J. R. R. Tolkien's character Sam Gamgee, as he appears and reappears throughout the trilogy, exhibits the distinctiveness and consistency that define personality. The preceding chapters have emphasized our similarity—how we all develop, perceive, learn, remember, think, and feel. This chapter emphasizes our individuality. Your individual **personality** is your characteristic pattern of thinking, feeling, and acting. If your behavior pattern is strikingly distinctive and consistent—if you are always outgoing, whether at a party or in a classroom—people are likely to say that you have a "strong" personality.

Actually, much of this book deals with personality. In earlier chapters, we considered biological influences on personality, personality development across the life span, and personality-related aspects of learning, motivation, emotion, and health. In later chapters we will study disorders of personality and social influences on personality.

In this chapter we first explore and evaluate key historic perspectives on personality. Then we consider contemporary research on our enduring traits and sense of self.

HISTORIC PERSPECTIVES ON PERSONALITY

Two historically significant perspectives established the field of personality psychology and presented some key issues for today's research:

- Sigmund Freud's *psychoanalytic* theory proposed that childhood sexuality and unconscious motivations influence personality.
- The *humanistic* approach focused on our inner capacities for growth and self-fulfillment.

The Psychoanalytic Perspective

Ask 100 people on the street to name a notable deceased psychologist, suggests Keith Stanovich (1996, p. 1), and "Sigmund Freud would be the winner hands down." In the popular mind, Freud is to psychology's history what Elvis is to rock music's history. Freud's current influence in psychological science has diminished (Robins & others, 1999). But his influence lingers in literary and film interpretation, psychiatry, and pop psychology. So, who was Freud, and what did he teach?

▶ **personality** an individual's characteristic pattern of thinking, feeling, and acting.

"There is no man who is not, at each moment, what he has been and what he will be."

Oscar Wilde, 1854–1900

Sigmund Freud, 1856–1939
"I was the only worker in a new field."

Culver Pictures

429

▶ **free association** in psychoanalysis, a method of exploring the unconscious in which the person relaxes and says whatever comes to mind, no matter how trivial or embarrassing.

▶ **psychoanalysis** Freud's theory of personality that attributes our thoughts and actions to unconscious motives and conflicts; the techniques used in treating psychological disorders by seeking to expose and interpret unconscious tensions.

▶ **unconscious** according to Freud, a reservoir of mostly unacceptable thoughts, wishes, feelings, and memories. According to contemporary psychologists, information processing of which we are unaware.

▶ **id** contains a reservoir of unconscious psychic energy that, according to Freud, strives to satisfy basic sexual and aggressive drives. The id operates on the *pleasure principle*, demanding immediate gratification.

▶ **ego** the largely conscious, "executive" part of personality that, according to Freud, mediates among the demands of the id, superego, and reality. The ego operates on the *reality principle*, satisfying the id's desires in ways that will realistically bring pleasure rather than pain.

▶ **superego** the part of personality that, according to Freud, represents internalized ideals and provides standards for judgment (the conscience) and for future aspirations.

"For seven and a half years I've worked alongside President Reagan. We've had triumphs. Made some mistakes. We've had some sex . . . uh . . . setbacks."

George H. W. Bush, 1988

After graduating from medical school in Vienna, Sigmund Freud set up a private practice, specializing in nervous disorders. Before long, however, he faced patients whose disorders made no neurological sense. For example, a patient might have lost all feeling in a hand—yet there is no sensory nerve that, if damaged, would numb the entire hand and nothing else. Freud's search for a cause for such disorders set his mind running in a direction destined to change human self-understanding.

Exploring the Unconscious

2. What was Freud's view of human personality and its development and dynamics?

Might some neurological disorders have psychological rather than physiological causes? This question led Freud to his "discovery" of the unconscious. He decided that the loss of feeling in one's hand might be caused by a fear of touching one's genitals; that blindness or deafness might be caused by not wanting to see or hear something that aroused intense anxiety. Initially, Freud thought hypnosis might unlock the door to the unconscious, but patients displayed an uneven capacity for hypnosis. He then turned to **free association**—in which he merely told the patient to relax and say whatever came to mind, no matter how embarrassing or trivial. Freud assumed that a line of mental dominoes had fallen from his patients' distant past to their troubled present. Free association, he believed, allowed him to trace that line back, producing a chain of thought leading into the patient's unconscious, thereby retrieving and releasing painful unconscious memories, often from childhood. Freud called his theory and associated techniques **psychoanalysis**.

Underlying Freud's psychoanalytic conception of personality was his belief that the mind is like an iceberg—mostly hidden. Our conscious awareness is the part of the iceberg that floats above the surface. Below the surface is the much larger, **unconscious** region containing thoughts, wishes, feelings, and memories, of which we are unaware. Some of these thoughts we store temporarily in a *preconscious* area, from which we can retrieve them into conscious awareness. Of greater interest to Freud was the mass of unacceptable passions and thoughts that he believed we *repress*, or forcibly block from our consciousness because they would be too unsettling to acknowledge. Freud believed that, although we are not consciously aware of them, these troublesome feelings and ideas powerfully influence us. In his view, our unacknowledged impulses express themselves in disguised forms—the work we choose, the beliefs we hold, our daily habits, our troubling symptoms.

For Freud the determinist, nothing was ever accidental. He believed he could glimpse the unconscious seeping not only into people's free associations, beliefs, habits, and symptoms but also into their dreams and slips of the tongue and pen. He illustrated with a financially stressed patient who, not wanting any large pills, said, "Please do not give me any bills, because I cannot swallow them." Similarly,

Freud's consulting room
Freud's office was rich with antiquities from around the world, including art work related to his ideas about unconscious motives. His famous couch, piled high with pillows, placed patients in a comfortable reclining position facing away from him to help them focus inward.

Edmund Engelman

Freud viewed jokes as expressions of repressed sexual and aggressive tendencies, and dreams as the "royal road to the unconscious." The remembered content of dreams (their *manifest content*) he believed to be a censored expression of the dreamer's unconscious wishes (the dream's *latent content*). By analyzing people's dreams, Freud believed, he could reveal the nature of their inner conflicts and release their inner tensions.

"Good morning, beheaded—uh, I mean beloved."

PERSONALITY STRUCTURE In Freud's view, human personality—including its emotions and strivings—arises from a conflict between our aggressive, pleasure-seeking biological impulses and the internalized social restraints against them. Freud believed personality is the result of our efforts to resolve this basic conflict—to express these impulses in ways that bring satisfaction without also bringing guilt or punishment.

Freud theorized that the conflict centers on three interacting systems: *id*, *ego*, and *superego* (**FIGURE 12.1**). Freud found these abstract psychological concepts "useful aids to understanding" the mind's dynamics.

The **id** has a reservoir of unconscious psychic energy constantly striving to satisfy basic drives to survive, reproduce, and aggress. The id operates on the *pleasure principle*: If not constrained by reality, it seeks immediate gratification. Think of newborn infants. Governed by the id, they cry out for satisfaction the moment they feel a need, caring nothing for the outside world's conditions and demands. Or think of people with a present rather than future time perspective—those who would sooner party now than sacrifice today's pleasure for future success and happiness. Such people ("id-dominated," Freud would have called them) more often use tobacco, alcohol, and other drugs (Keough & others, 1999).

As the **ego** develops, the young child learns to cope with the real world. The ego, operating on the *reality principle*, seeks to gratify the id's impulses in realistic ways that will bring long-term pleasure rather than pain or destruction. (Imagine what would happen if, lacking an ego, we expressed our unrestrained sexual or aggressive impulses whenever we felt them.) The ego contains our partly conscious perceptions, thoughts, judgments, and memories.

Beginning around age 4 or 5, Freud theorized, a child's ego recognizes the demands of the newly emerging **superego**, the voice of conscience that forces the ego to consider not only the real but the ideal, and that focuses solely on how one *ought* to behave. The superego strives for perfection, judging actions and producing positive feelings of pride or negative feelings of guilt. Someone with an exceptionally strong superego may be virtuous yet, ironically, guilt-ridden; another with a weak superego may be wantonly self-indulgent and remorseless.

Because the superego's demands often oppose the id's, the ego struggles to reconcile the two. It is the personality "executive," mediating the impulsive demands of the id, the restraining demands of the superego, and the real-life demands of the external world. The chaste student who is sexually attracted to someone may satisfy both id and superego by joining a volunteer organization to which the desired person belongs.

figure 12.1
Freud's idea of the mind's structure
Consciousness is like an iceberg's visible tip. Note that the id is totally unconscious, but ego and superego operate both consciously and unconsciously. (Adapted from Freud, 1933, p. 111.)

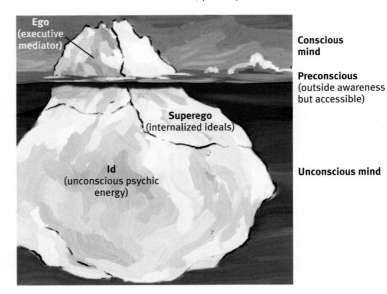

The ego struggles to reconcile the demands of superego and id, said Freud.

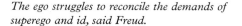

"Fifty is plenty."   "Hundred and fifty."

PERSONALITY DEVELOPMENT Analysis of his patients' histories convinced Freud that personality forms during life's first few years. Again and again his patients' symptoms seemed rooted in unresolved conflicts from early childhood. He concluded that children pass through a series of **psychosexual stages** during which the id's pleasure-seeking energies focus on distinct pleasure-sensitive areas of the body called *erogenous zones* (**TABLE 12.1**).

Freud believed that during the *phallic stage* boys seek genital stimulation, and they develop both unconscious sexual desires for their mother and jealousy and hatred for their father, whom they consider a rival. Given these feelings, boys supposedly also feel guilt and a lurking fear of punishment, perhaps by castration, from their father. Freud called this collection of feelings the **Oedipus complex** after the Greek legend of Oedipus, who unknowingly killed his father and married his mother. Some psychoanalysts believed that girls experience a parallel *Electra complex*. Freud's own thinking seemed to vary on this issue.

Children eventually cope with threatening feelings, said Freud, by repressing them and by identifying with (trying to become like) the rival parent. It's as though something inside the child decides, "If you can't beat 'em [the parent of the same sex], join 'em." Through this **identification** process, children's superegos gain strength as they incorporate many of their parents' values. Freud believed that identification with the same-sex parent provides what psychologists now call our *gender identity*—our sense of being male or female.

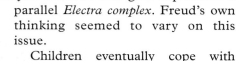

Identification
Freud believed that children cope with threatening feelings of competition with their same-sex parent by identifying with that parent.

In Freud's view, maladaptive behavior in the adult results from conflicts unresolved during earlier psychosexual stages. At any point in the oral, anal, or phallic stages, strong conflict can lock, or **fixate**, the person's pleasure-seeking energies in that stage.

For example, Freud believed that people who were either orally overindulged or deprived (perhaps by abrupt, early weaning) might fixate at the oral stage. Orally fixated adults, he thought, could exhibit either passive dependence (like that of a nursing infant) or an exaggerated denial of this dependence—perhaps by acting tough and uttering

Stage	Focus
Oral (0–18 months)	Pleasure centers on the mouth—sucking, biting, chewing
Anal (18–36 months)	Pleasure focuses on bowel and bladder elimination; coping with demands for control
Phallic (3–6 years)	Pleasure zone is the genitals; coping with incestuous sexual feelings
Latency (6 to puberty)	Dormant sexual feelings
Genital (puberty on)	Maturation of sexual interests

table 12.1 **Freud's Psychosexual Stages**

biting sarcasm. Or they might continue to seek oral gratification by excessively smoking and eating. In such ways, Freud suggested, the twig of personality is bent at an early age.

DEFENSE MECHANISMS Anxiety, said Freud, is the price we pay for civilization. As members of social groups, we must control our sexual and aggressive impulses, not act them out. But sometimes the ego fears losing control of this inner war between the demands of the id and the superego, and the result is a dark cloud of unfocused anxiety, which leaves us feeling unsettled but unsure why.

"Oh, for goodness' sake! Smoke!"

> *3. How did Freud think people defended themselves against anxiety?*

Freud proposed that the ego protects itself with **defense mechanisms**, tactics that reduce or redirect anxiety in various ways, but always by distorting reality. Here are six examples:

- **Repression** banishes anxiety-arousing thoughts and feelings from consciousness. According to Freud, *repression underlies all the other defense mechanisms*, each of which disguises threatening impulses and keeps them from reaching consciousness. Freud believed that repression explains why we do not remember our childhood lust for our parent of the other sex. However, he also believed that repression is often incomplete, that repressed urges seep out in dream symbols and slips of the tongue.
- **Regression** allows us to retreat to an earlier, more infantile stage of development. Facing the anxious first days of school, a child may regress to the oral comfort of thumb-sucking. Juvenile monkeys, when anxious, retreat to infantile clinging to their mothers or to one another (Suomi, 1987). Even homesick new college students may long for the security and comfort of home.
- In **reaction formation**, the ego unconsciously makes unacceptable impulses look like their opposites. En route to consciousness, the unacceptable proposition "I hate him" becomes "I love him." Timidity becomes daring. Feelings of inadequacy become bravado.

▶ **psychosexual stages** the childhood stages of development (oral, anal, phallic, latency, genital) during which, according to Freud, the id's pleasure-seeking energies focus on distinct erogenous zones.

▶ **Oedipus** [ED-uh-puss] **complex** according to Freud, a boy's sexual desires toward his mother and feelings of jealousy and hatred for the rival father.

▶ **identification** the process by which, according to Freud, children incorporate their parents' values into their developing superegos.

▶ **fixation** according to Freud, a lingering focus of pleasure-seeking energies at an earlier psychosexual stage, where conflicts were unresolved.

▶ **defense mechanisms** in psychoanalytic theory, the ego's protective methods of reducing anxiety by unconsciously distorting reality.

▶ **repression** in psychoanalytic theory, the basic defense mechanism that banishes anxiety-arousing thoughts, feelings, and memories from consciousness.

▶ **regression** defense mechanism in which an individual faced with anxiety retreats to a more infantile psychosexual stage, where some psychic energy remains fixated.

▶ **reaction formation** psychoanalytic defense mechanism by which the ego unconsciously switches unacceptable impulses into their opposites. Thus, people may express feelings that are the opposite of their anxiety-arousing unconscious feelings.

"The lady doth protest too much, methinks."
William Shakespeare, Hamlet, 1600

Regression Faced with a mild stressor, children and young monkeys will regress, retreating to the comfort of earlier behaviors.

● **Projection** disguises threatening impulses by attributing them to others. Thus, "He doesn't trust me" may be a projection of the actual feeling "I don't trust him" or "I don't trust myself." An El Salvadoran saying captures the idea: "The thief thinks everyone else is a thief."

● **Rationalization** occurs when we unconsciously generate self-justifying explanations to hide from ourselves the real reasons for our actions. Thus, habitual drinkers may say they drink with their friends "just to be sociable." Students who fail to study may rationalize, "All work and no play makes Jack [or Jill] a dull person."

● **Displacement** diverts sexual or aggressive impulses toward an object or person that is psychologically more acceptable than the one that aroused the feelings. Children who fear expressing anger against their parents may displace it by kicking the family pet. Students upset over an exam may snap at a roommate.

Note that all these defense mechanisms function indirectly and unconsciously, reducing anxiety by disguising our threatening impulses. Just as the body unconsciously defends itself against disease, so also, believed Freud, does the ego unconsciously defend itself against anxiety.

Assessing the Unconscious

4. What are projective tests, and what do clinicians in the Freudian tradition hope to learn from them?

Those who study personality or provide therapy need ways to evaluate personality characteristics. Methods of assessment differ because they are tailored to different personality theories. So what might be the tool of choice for analysts working in the Freudian traditions?

Such a tool would start with Freud's belief that the significant influences on our personalities arise from the unconscious, which contains residues from early childhood experiences. Evaluating personality from Freud's perspective requires a road into the unconscious mind. (Recall that Freud believed free association and dream interpretation could reveal the unconscious.) Psychoanalysts dismiss objective assessment tools, such as agree-disagree or true-false questionnaires, as merely tapping the conscious surface. Their tool of choice would be a sort of psychological x-ray—a test that sees through our surface pretensions and reveals our hidden conflicts and impulses.

Projective tests aim to provide such a view by presenting an ambiguous stimulus and then asking test-takers to describe it or tell a story about it. The stimulus has no inherent significance, so any meaning people read into it presumably is a projection of their interests and conflicts. Most widely used is the famous **Rorschach inkblot test**, introduced in 1921 by Swiss psychiatrist Hermann Rorschach [ROAR-shock]. The test assumes that what we see in its 10 inkblots reflects our inner feelings and conflicts. If we see predatory animals or weapons, the examiner may infer we have aggressive tendencies.

Is this a reasonable assumption? If so, can a psychologist use the Rorschach to understand one's personality and diagnose an emotional disorder? Recall from Chapter 9's discussion of intelligence tests that the two primary criteria of a good test are *reliability* (consistency of results) and *validity* (predicting what it's supposed to). On those criteria, how good is the Rorschach?

The Rorschach test
In this projective test, people tell what they see in a series of symmetrical inkblots. Some who use this test are confident that the interpretation of ambiguous stimuli will reveal unconscious aspects of the test-taker's personality. Others use it as an icebreaker or to supplement other information.

The "almost universal agreement among the scientific community" is that it is not very good (Sechrest & others, 1998). There is no universally accepted system for scoring and interpreting the test. If two raters were not trained in the same scoring system, their agreement on the results of any given test would be minimal. Nor has the test been very successful at predicting behavior or at discriminating between groups (for example, identifying who is suicidal and who is not). The Rorschach is not an emotional MRI.

With all the criticisms, the Rorschach remains "simultaneously, the most cherished and the most reviled of all psychological assessment tools" (Hunsley & Bailey, 1999). Clinicians—82 percent of whom report administering it at least occasionally—often cherish the Rorschach (Lilienfeld & others, 2000; Watkins & others, 1995). Judges receive Rorschach-based assessments of criminals' violence potential. Therapists use it to probe for past sexual abuse. Other clinicians view it as a diagnostic tool, a source of suggestive leads, or an icebreaker and a revealing interview technique. There is even a research-based, computer-aided coding and interpretation tool that aims to improve agreement among raters and enhance the test's validity (Erdberg, 1990; Exner, 1993).

But the evidence is insufficient to its revilers, who note that inkblot assessments would diagnose many normal adults as "strikingly pathological" (Lilienfeld & others, 2000). Other critics find "no scientific basis for justifying the use of Rorschach scales in psychological assessments" (Hunsley & Bailey, 1999) and even propose a moratorium on its clinical and forensic use (Garb, 1999). Alternative projective assessment techniques fare little better, conclude Scott Lilienfeld, James Wood, and Howard Garb (2001). "Even seasoned professionals," they warn, "can be fooled by their intuitions and their faith in tools that lack strong evidence of effectiveness. When a substantial body of research demonstrates that old intuitions are wrong, it is time to adopt new ways of thinking." Freud himself probably would have been uncomfortable with trying to diagnose patients based on tests and more interested in the therapist–patient interactions that take place during the test.

Evaluating the Psychoanalytic Perspective

5. Which of Freud's ideas did his followers accept or reject? How do Freud's ideas hold up today?

Knowing what you do about Freud's ideas, listen now to his critics.

FREUD'S EARLY DESCENDANTS AND DISSENTERS   Freud's writings were controversial, but they soon attracted followers, mostly young, ambitious physicians who formed an inner circle around their strong-minded leader. These pioneering psychoanalysts and others, whom we now call *neo-Freudians*, accepted Freud's basic ideas: the personality structures of id, ego, and superego; the importance of the unconscious; the shaping of personality in childhood; and the dynamics of anxiety and the defense mechanisms. But they did veer away from Freud in two important ways: First, they placed more emphasis on the conscious mind's role in interpreting experience and in coping with the environment. And second, they doubted that sex and aggression were all-consuming motivations. Instead, they tended to emphasize loftier motives and social interaction. The following examples illustrate.

Alfred Adler and Karen Horney [HORN-eye] agreed with Freud that childhood is important. But they believed that childhood *social*, not sexual, tensions are crucial for personality formation. Adler, who himself struggled to overcome childhood illnesses and accidents, said that much of our behavior is driven by efforts to conquer childhood feelings of inferiority, feelings that trigger our strivings for superiority and power. (Adler proposed the still-popular idea of the "inferiority complex.") Horney said childhood anxiety, caused by the dependent child's sense of helplessness, triggers our desire for love and security. Horney

"If a professional psychologist is 'evaluating' you in a situation in which you are at risk and asks you for responses to ink blots . . . walk out of that psychologist's office."

Robyn Dawes, House of Cards: Psychology and Psychotherapy Based on Myth, *1994*

"The Rorschach inkblot test has been resoundingly discredited . . . I call it the Dracula of psychological tests, because no one has been able to drive a stake through the cursed thing's heart."

Carol Tavris, "Mind Games: Psychological Warfare Between Therapists and Scientists," 2003

▶ **projection** psychoanalytic defense mechanism by which people disguise their own threatening impulses by attributing them to others.

▶ **rationalization** defense mechanism that offers self-justifying explanations in place of the real, more threatening, unconscious reasons for one's actions.

▶ **displacement** psychoanalytic defense mechanism that shifts sexual or aggressive impulses toward a more acceptable or less threatening object or person, as when redirecting anger toward a safer outlet.

▶ **projective test** a personality test, such as the Rorschach or inkblot test, that provides ambiguous stimuli designed to trigger projection of one's inner dynamics.

▶ **Rorschach inkblot test** the most widely used projective test, a set of 10 inkblots, designed by Hermann Rorschach; seeks to identify people's inner feelings by analyzing their interpretations of the blots.

Alfred Adler "The individual feels at home in life and feels his existence to be worthwhile just so far as he is useful to others and is overcoming feelings of inferiority" (*Problems of Neurosis*, 1964).

Karen Horney "The view that women are infantile and emotional creatures, and as such, incapable of responsibility and independence is the work of the masculine tendency to lower women's self-respect" (*Feminine Psychology*, 1932).

Carl Jung "We can keep from a child all knowledge of earlier myths, but we cannot take from him the need for mythology" (*Symbols of Transformation*, 1912).

"The female ... acknowledges the fact of her castration, and with it, too, the superiority of the male and her own inferiority; but she rebels against this unwelcome state of affairs."

Sigmund Freud, Female Sexuality, 1931

countered Freud's assumptions that women have weak superegos and suffer "penis envy," and she attempted to balance the bias she detected in this masculine view of psychology.

Unlike other neo-Freudians, Carl Jung—Freud's disciple-turned-dissenter—placed less emphasis on social factors and agreed with Freud that the unconscious exerts a powerful influence. But to Jung (pronounced Yoong), the unconscious contains more than our repressed thoughts and feelings. He believed we also have a **collective unconscious**, a common reservoir of images derived from our species' universal experiences. Jung said that the collective unconscious explains why, for many people, spiritual concerns are deeply rooted and why people in different cultures share certain myths and images, such as mother as a symbol of nurturance. (Today's psychologists discount the idea of inherited experiences. But many do believe that our shared evolutionary history shaped some universal dispositions.)

Freud died in 1939. Since then, some of his ideas have been incorporated into *psychodynamic theory*. "Most contemporary dynamic theorists and therapists are not wedded to the idea that sex is the basis of personality," notes Drew Westen (1996). They "do not talk about ids and egos, and do not go around classifying their patients as oral, anal, or phallic characters." What they do assume, with Freud, is that much of our mental life is unconscious, that childhood shapes our personalities and ways of becoming attached to others, and that we often struggle with inner conflicts among our wishes, fears, and values.

FREUD'S IDEAS IN THE LIGHT OF MODERN RESEARCH We critique Freud from an early twenty-first century perspective, a perspective that is itself subject to revision. Freud did not have access to all that we have since learned about human development, thinking, and emotion. He knew nothing of neurotransmitters or DNA. Thus, say Freud's admirers, to criticize his theories by comparing them with current concepts is like comparing Henry Ford's Model T with today's Mustang. To Freud's critics, however, his ideas are psychology's historical equivalent to astronomy's flat-Earth theory.

"Many aspects of Freudian theory are indeed out of date, and they should be: Freud died in 1939, and he has been slow to undertake further revisions."

Psychologist Drew Westen (1998)

Psychoanalytic theory "is on precisely the same scientific plane as the Loch Ness monster."

E. Fuller Torrey, Freudian Fraud, 1992

Both admirers and critics agree that recent research contradicts many of Freud's specific ideas. Today's developmental psychologists see our development as lifelong, not fixed in childhood. They doubt that infants' neural networks are mature enough to sustain as much emotional trauma as Freud assumed. Some think Freud overestimated parental influence and underestimated peer influence (and abuse). They also question Freud's idea that conscience and gender identity form as the child resolves the Oedipus complex at age 5 or 6. We gain our gender identity earlier and become strongly masculine or feminine even without a same-sex parent present (Frieze & others, 1978). Freud's ideas about childhood sexuality arose from his rejection of stories of childhood sexual abuse told by his female patients—stories that some scholars believe he suggested, coerced, or later misremembered and then attributed to their own childhood sexual wishes and conflicts (Esterson, 2001;

"The forward thrust of the antlers shows a determined personality, yet the small sun indicates a lack of self-confidence...."

Powell & Boer, 1994). Today, we understand how Freud's questioning might have created false memories, and we also know that childhood sexual abuse does happen.

As we saw in Chapter 6, new ideas about why we dream dispute Freud's belief that dreams disguise and fulfill wishes. And slips of the tongue can be explained as competition between similar verbal choices in our memory network. Someone who says "I don't want to do that—it's a lot of brothel" may simply be blending *bother* and *trouble* (Foss & Hakes, 1978). Researchers find little support for Freud's idea that defense mechanisms disguise sexual and aggressive impulses (though our cognitive gymnastics do indeed work to protect our self-esteem). History also has failed to support another of Freud's ideas—that sexual suppression causes psychological disorder. From Freud's time to ours, sexual suppression has diminished; psychological disorders have not.

IS REPRESSION A MYTH? Freud's entire psychoanalytic theory rests on his assumption that the human mind often *represses* painful experiences, banishing them into the unconscious. Freud and his followers thought if we could somehow uncover our past experiences, we would find them intact, like long-lost books in a dusty attic. Recover and resolve the painful repressed memories of our childhood and emotional healing would follow. Under Freud's influence, repression became a widely accepted concept, used to explain hypnotic phenomena, psychological disorders, and apparent lost and recovered memories of childhood traumas (Cheit, 1998). In one survey, 88 percent of university students believed that painful experiences commonly get pushed out of awareness and into the unconscious (Garry & others, 1994).

Actually, contend many of today's researchers, repression, if it ever occurs, is a rare mental response to terrible trauma. "Repression folklore is . . . partly refuted, partly untested, and partly untestable," says Elizabeth Loftus (1995). Consider: If the human mind indeed commonly banishes painful experiences, how do we explain these odd findings?

- Shouldn't we expect children who have witnessed a parent's murder to repress the experience? A study of sixteen 5- to 10-year-old children who had this horrific experience found that not one repressed the memory (Malmquist, 1986).
- Shouldn't survivors of Nazi death camps have banished the atrocities from consciousness? With rare exceptions, they remember all too well—although many do benefit from disclosing and talking through their experiences (Helmreich, 1992, 1994; Pennebaker, 1990).
- Shouldn't battle-scarred veterans suffer amnesia for their worst experiences? In one neurological unit in a British hospital, 35 percent of military patients arrived with amnesia after severe combat during World War II (Arrigo & Pezdek, 1997; Karon & Widener, 1997, 1998). But such cases often appear to be either concussion-related or a "false amnesia" tactic for escaping intolerable situations (Holmes, 1990, 1994). Folklore regarding recovered battlefield memories is either unconfirmed or related to therapists' use of suggestive techniques.

"I remember your name perfectly but I just can't think of your face."

Oxford professor W. A. Spooner, 1844–1930, famous for his linguistic flip-flops ("spoonerisms"). Spooner rebuked one student for "fighting a liar in the quadrangle" and another who "hissed my mystery lecture," adding "You have tasted two worms."

▶ **collective unconscious** Carl Jung's concept of a shared, inherited reservoir of memory traces from our species' history.

There are exceptions—one death camp survivor reportedly forgot for more than 30 years the snatching and shooting of her infant son (Kraft, 1996). Some researchers believe that extreme, prolonged stress, such as the stress some severely abused children experience, might disrupt memory by damaging the hippocampus (Schacter, 1996). But the far more common reality? High stress enhances memory, and negative emotional events are therefore remembered well (Christianson, 1992; Shobe & Kihlstrom, 1997).

In fact, too well: Traumatic events, such as rape and torture, haunt survivors, who experience unwanted flashbacks. They are seared onto the soul. "You see the babies," said Holocaust survivor Sally H. (1979). "You see the screaming mothers. You see hanging people. You sit and you see that face there. It's something you don't forget."

FREUD'S IDEAS AS SCIENTIFIC THEORY Psychologists also criticize Freud's theory for its scientific shortcomings. Recall from Chapter 1 that good scientific theories explain observations and offer testable hypotheses. Freud's theory rests on few objective observations and offers few hypotheses to verify or reject. (For Freud, his own recollections and interpretations of patients' free associations, dreams, and slips were evidence enough.)

What is the most serious problem with Freud's theory? It offers after-the-fact explanations of any characteristic (of one person's smoking, another's fear of horses, another's sexual orientation) yet fails to *predict* such behavior and traits. If you feel angry at your mother's death, you illustrate his theory because "your unresolved childhood dependency needs are threatened." If you do not feel angry, you again illustrate his theory because "you are repressing your anger." That, said Calvin Hall and Gardner Lindzey (1978, p. 68), "is like betting on a horse after the race has been run."

For such reasons, some of Freud's critics offer harsh words. They see a decaying Freudian edifice built on the swamplands of childhood sexuality, repression, dream analysis, and after-the-fact speculation. "When we stand on [Freud's] shoulders, we only discover that we're looking further in the wrong direction," says John Kihlstrom (1997). Freud's most searing critic, Frederick Crews (1998), likens Freud to Peter Sellers' bumbling Inspector Clouseau, albeit with a unique talent for bamboozling an entire century. What is original about Freud's ideas is not good, and what is good is not original (the unconscious mind is an idea that dates back to Plato).

So, should psychology post a "Do Not Resuscitate" order on this old theory? Freud's supporters object. To criticize Freudian theory for not making testable predictions is, they say, like criticizing baseball for not being an aerobic exercise. Is it fair to fault something for not being what it was never intended to be? Unlike many later psychoanalysts, Freud never claimed that psychoanalysis was predictive science. He merely claimed that, looking back, psychoanalysts could find meaning in our state of mind (Rieff, 1979).

Freud's supporters also note that some of his ideas *are* enduring. It was Freud who drew our attention to the unconscious and the irrational, to our defenses against anxiety, to the importance of human sexuality, and to the tension between our biological impulses and our social well-being. It was Freud who challenged our self-righteousness, punctured our pretensions, and reminded us of our potential for evil.

In science, Darwin's legacy lives, Freud's is dying (Bornstein, 2001). In the popular culture, Freud's legacy lives on. Some ideas that many people assume to be true—that childhood experiences mold personality, that dreams have meaning, that many behaviors have disguised motives—are part of that legacy. His early twentieth-century concepts penetrate our twenty-first-century language. Without realizing their source, we may speak of *ego, repression, projection, complex* (as in "inferiority complex"), *sibling rivalry, Freudian slips,* and *fixation.* "Freud's premises may have undergone a steady decline in currency within academia for many years," noted Martin Seligman (1994), "but Hollywood, the talk shows, many therapists, and the general public still love them."

"During the Holocaust, many children . . . were forced to endure the unendurable. For those who continue to suffer [the] pain is still present, many years later, as real as it was on the day it occurred."

Eric Zillmer, Molly Harrower, Barry Ritzler, and Robert Archer, **The Quest for the Nazi Personality,** 1995

"We are arguing like a man who should say, 'If there were an invisible cat in that chair, the chair would look empty; but the chair does look empty; therefore there is an invisible cat in it.'"

C. S. Lewis, **Four Loves,** 1958

"Studies have begun to converge toward a verdict . . . : there is literally nothing to be said [for] the entire Freudian system."

Frederick Crews (1996)

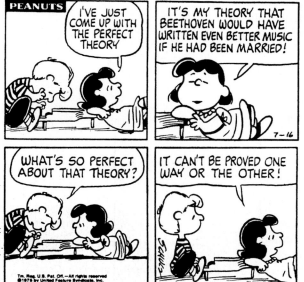

The Humanistic Perspective

6. What did humanistic psychologists view as the central feature of personality, and what was their goal in studying personality?

By 1960, some personality psychologists had become discontented with Freud's negativity. In contrast to Freud's study of the base motives of "sick" people, these *humanistic psychologists* focused on the ways "healthy" people strive for self-determination and self-realization.

Two pioneering theorists—Abraham Maslow (1908–1970) and Carl Rogers (1902–1987)—illustrate this emphasis on human potential and on seeing the world through the person's (not the researcher's) eyes.

Abraham Maslow's Self-Actualizing Person

Maslow proposed that we are motivated by a hierarchy of needs (page 343). If our physiological needs are met, we become concerned with personal safety; if we achieve a sense of security, we then seek to love, to be loved, and to love ourselves; with our love needs satisfied, we seek self-esteem. Having achieved self-esteem, we ultimately seek **self-actualization**, the process of fulfilling our potential.

Maslow (1970) developed his ideas by studying healthy, creative people rather than troubled clinical cases. He based his description of self-actualization on a study of those who seemed notable for their rich and productive lives—among them, Abraham Lincoln, Thomas Jefferson, and Eleanor Roosevelt. Maslow reported that these people shared certain characteristics: They were self-aware and self-accepting, open and spontaneous, loving and caring, and not paralyzed by others' opinions. Secure in their sense of who they were, their interests were problem-centered rather than self-centered. They focused their energies on a particular task, one they often regarded as their mission in life. Most enjoyed a few deep relationships rather than many superficial ones. Many had been moved by spiritual or personal *peak experiences* that surpassed ordinary consciousness.

▶ **self-actualization** according to Maslow, the ultimate psychological need that arises after basic physical and psychological needs are met and self-esteem is achieved; the motivation to fulfill one's potential.

Abraham Maslow "Any theory of motivation that is worthy of attention must deal with the highest capacities of the healthy and strong person as well as with the defensive maneuvers of crippled spirits" (*Motivation and Personality*, 1970).

Ted Polumbaun/TimePix/Getty Images

The picture of empathy Being open and sharing confidences is easier when the listener shows real understanding. Within such relationships people can relax and fully express their true selves.

These, said Maslow, are mature adult qualities, ones found in those who have learned enough about life to be compassionate, to have outgrown their mixed feelings toward their parents, to have found their calling, to have "acquired enough courage to be unpopular, to be unashamed about being openly virtuous, etc." Maslow's work with college students led him to speculate that those likely to become self-actualizing adults were likable, caring, "privately affectionate to those of their elders who deserve it," and "secretly uneasy about the cruelty, meanness, and mob spirit so often found in young people."

Carl Rogers' Person-Centered Perspective

Fellow humanistic psychologist Carl Rogers agreed with much of Maslow's thinking. Rogers believed that people are basically good and are endowed with self-actualizing tendencies. Unless thwarted by an environment that inhibits growth, each of us is like an acorn, primed for growth and fulfillment. Rogers (1980) believed that a growth-promoting climate required three conditions—genuineness, acceptance, and empathy.

According to Rogers, people nurture our growth by being *genuine*—by being open with their own feelings, dropping their facades, and being transparent and self-disclosing.

People also nurture growth by being *accepting*—by offering us what Rogers called **unconditional positive regard**. This is an attitude of grace, an attitude that values us even knowing our failings. It is a profound relief to drop our pretenses, confess our worst feelings, and discover that we are still accepted. In a good marriage, a close family, or an intimate friendship, we are free to be spontaneous without fearing the loss of others' esteem.

Finally, people nurture growth by being *empathic*—by sharing and mirroring our feelings and reflecting our meanings. "Rarely do we listen with real understanding, true empathy," said Rogers. "Yet listening, of this very special kind, is one of the most potent forces for change that I know."

Genuineness, acceptance, and empathy are the water, sun, and nutrients that enable people to grow like vigorous oak trees, according to Rogers. For "as persons are accepted and prized, they tend to develop a more caring attitude toward themselves" (Rogers, 1980, p. 116). As persons are empathically heard, "it becomes possible for them to listen more accurately to the flow of inner experiencings."

A father *not* offering unconditional positive regard.

"Just remember, son, it doesn't matter whether you win or lose—unless you want Daddy's love."

Rogers believed that genuineness, acceptance, and empathy nurture growth not only in the relationship between therapist and client but also between parent and child, leader and group, teacher and student, administrator and staff member—in fact, between any two human beings.

For Maslow, and even more for Rogers, a central feature of personality is one's **self-concept**—all the thoughts and feelings we have in response to the question, "Who am I?" If our self-concept is positive, we tend to act and perceive the world positively. If it is negative—if in our own eyes we fall far short of our "ideal self"—said Rogers, we feel dissatisfied and unhappy. A worthwhile goal for therapists, parents, teachers, and friends is therefore, he said, to help others know, accept, and be true to themselves.

Assessing the Self

7. How did humanistic psychologists assess a person's sense of self?

Humanistic psychologists sometimes assessed personality by asking people to fill out questionnaires that would evaluate self-concept. One questionnaire, inspired by Carl Rogers, asked people to describe themselves both as they would ideally like to be and as they actually are. When the ideal and the actual self are nearly alike, said

Rogers, the self-concept is positive. Assessing his clients' personal growth during therapy, he looked for successively closer ratings of actual and ideal self.

Some humanistic psychologists believed that any standardized assessment of personality, even a questionnaire, is depersonalizing. Rather than forcing the person to respond to narrow categories, these psychologists presumed that interviews and intimate conversation would provide a better understanding of each person's unique experiences.

Evaluating the Humanistic Perspective

8. How has the humanistic perspective on personality influenced psychology? What criticisms have been leveled against this perspective?

One thing said of Freud can also be said of the humanistic psychologists: Their impact, though waning, has been pervasive. Their ideas have influenced counseling, education, child-rearing, and management.

They have also influenced—sometimes in ways they did not intend—much of today's popular psychology. Many people have absorbed Maslow's and Rogers' ideas—that a positive self-concept is the key to happiness and success, that acceptance and empathy help nurture positive feelings about oneself, and that people are basically good and capable of self-improvement. One study found that, by a four-to-one margin, Americans believe "human nature is basically good" rather than "fundamentally perverse and corrupt" (NORC, 1985). Humanistic psychologists can also take satisfaction in the changed response to an item in a standardized personality inventory called the MMPI: Among those in the 1930s normal standardization sample, only 9 percent agreed that "I am an important person"; in the mid-1980s, more than half agreed (Holden, 1986b). Responding to a 1989 Gallup poll, 85 percent of Americans rated "having a good self-image or self-respect" as *very* important; 0 percent rated it unimportant. And 89 percent of people responding to a 1992 *Newsweek* Gallup poll rated self-esteem as very important for "motivating a person to work hard and succeed." Humanistic psychology's message has been heard.

Perhaps one reason that message has been so well received is that its emphasis on the individual self reflects and reinforces Western cultural values. Movie plots feature rugged individualists who, true to themselves, buck social convention or take the law into their own hands. Popular songs have proclaimed "I Did It My Way" and reminded us that to love yourself is "The Greatest Love of All" (Schoeneman, 1994).

The prominence of the humanistic perspective set off a backlash of criticism. First, said the critics, its concepts are vague and subjective. Consider the description of self-actualizing people as open, spontaneous, loving, self-accepting, and productive. Is this a scientific description? Isn't it merely a description of Maslow's personal values and ideals? Maslow, noted M. Brewster Smith (1978), offered impressions of his own personal heroes. Imagine another theorist who began with a different set of heroes—perhaps Napoleon, Alexander the Great, and John D. Rockefeller, Sr. This theorist would likely describe self-actualizing people as "undeterred by the needs of others," "motivated to achieve," and "obsessed with power."

Critics also objected to the idea that, as Carl Rogers put it, "The only question which matters is, 'Am I living in a way which is deeply satisfying to me, and which truly expresses me?'" (quoted by Wallach & Wallach, 1985). The individualism encouraged by humanistic psychology—trusting and acting on one's feelings, being true to oneself, fulfilling oneself—can lead to self-indulgence, selfishness, and an erosion of moral restraints (Campbell & Specht, 1985; Wallach & Wallach, 1983). Indeed, it is those who focus beyond themselves who are most likely to experience social support, to enjoy life, and to cope effectively with stress (Crandall, 1984).

▶ **unconditional positive regard** according to Rogers, an attitude of total acceptance toward another person.

▶ **self-concept** all our thoughts and feelings about ourselves, in answer to the question, "Who am I?"

"We do pretty well when you stop to think that people are basically good."

Humanistic psychologists have countered that a secure, nondefensive self-acceptance is actually the first step toward loving others. Indeed, people who feel intrinsically liked and accepted—for who they are, not just for their achievements—exhibit less-defensive attitudes (Schimel & others, 2001).

A final accusation leveled against humanistic psychology is that it fails to appreciate the reality of our human capacity for evil. Faced with global warming, overpopulation, and the spread of nuclear weapons, we may become apathetic from either of two rationalizations. One is a naive optimism that denies the threat ("People are basically good; everything will work out"). The other is a dark despair ("It's hopeless; why try?"). Action requires enough realism to fuel concern and enough optimism to provide hope. Humanistic psychology, say the critics, encourages the needed hope but not the equally necessary realism about evil.

rehearse it!

9. Abraham Maslow's hierarchy of needs proposes that we first satisfy basic physiological and psychological needs, and then we become motivated to fulfill our potential through self-actualization. Maslow based his ideas on
   a. Freudian theory.
   b. his experiences with patients.
   c. a series of laboratory experiments.
   d. his study of healthy, creative people.

10. According to Carl Rogers, a growth-promoting environment is one that

offers genuineness, acceptance, and empathy. The total acceptance Rogers advocated is called
   a. self-concept.
   b. unconditional positive regard.
   c. self-actualization.
   d. the "ideal self."

11. The humanistic perspective, which focused on the potential for human growth and self-fulfillment, has influenced counseling, education, child-rearing, and popular psychology. The

humanistic perspective has been so well received because
   a. it emphasizes the group and our social nature.
   b. it has a sound basis in scientific studies.
   c. it has predictive value as a testing instrument.
   d. its emphasis on the individual self reflects and reinforces Western cultural values.

Answers can be found in Appendix C.

CONTEMPORARY RESEARCH ON PERSONALITY

So far our tour of personality psychology has been a walk through the field's original big ideas. The psychoanalytic and humanistic theories have left a cultural legacy, and their pioneers identified issues that engage today's researchers. But in general, today's personality researchers are less interested in grand theories than in focused analyses of basic dimensions of personality and their impact on behavior, on the biological roots of these basic dimensions, on the interaction of persons and environments, and on studies of self-esteem, self-serving bias, and cultural influences on one's sense of self.

The Trait Perspective

Remember that psychoanalytic theory attempts to explain personality in terms of the dynamics that underlie behavior. It peers beneath the surface, searching for hidden motives. The trait perspective can be traced in part to a remarkable meeting in 1919, when Gordon Allport, a curious 22-year-old psychology student, interviewed Freud in Vienna. Allport soon discovered just how preoccupied the founder of psychoanalysis was with finding hidden motives.

> Soon after I had entered the famous red burlap room with pictures of dreams on the wall, he summoned me to his inner office. He did not speak to me but sat in expectant silence, for me to state my mission. I was not prepared for silence and had to think fast to find a suitable conversational gambit. I told him of an episode on the tram car on my way to his office. A small boy about 4 years of age had displayed a conspicuous dirt phobia. He kept saying to his mother, "I don't want to sit there . . . don't let that dirty man sit beside me." To him everything was *schmutzig* (filthy). His mother was a well-starched *Hausfrau*, so dominant and purposive looking that I thought the cause and effect apparent.

When I finished my story Freud fixed his kindly therapeutic eyes upon me and said, "And was that little boy you?" Flabbergasted and feeling a bit guilty, I contrived to change the subject. While Freud's misunderstanding of my motivation was amusing, it also started a deep train of thought (1967, pp. 7–8).

That train of thought ultimately led Allport to do what Freud did not do—to describe personality in terms of fundamental **traits**—people's characteristic behaviors and conscious motives (such as the professional curiosity that motivated Allport to see Freud). Meeting Freud, said Allport, "taught me that [psychoanalysis], for all its merits, may plunge too deep, and that psychologists would do well to give full recognition to manifest motives before probing the unconscious." Allport came to define personality in terms of identifiable behavior patterns. He was concerned less with *explaining* individual traits than with *describing* them.

How then do personality theorists describe and classify personalities? One way is by defining broad personality "types." An analogy may help. Imagine that you want to describe and classify apples. Someone might correctly say that every apple is unique. Still, you might find it useful to begin by classifying apples as distinct *types*—Granny Smith, MacIntosh, Red or Golden Delicious, and so forth.

One classification, especially popular in business and career counseling, attempts to sort people according to Carl Jung's personality types, based on their responses to 126 questions written by Isabel Briggs Myers (1987) and her mother, Kathleen Briggs. The *Myers-Briggs Type Indicator* is quite simple. It offers choices, such as "Do you usually value sentiment more than logic, or value logic more than sentiment?" Then it counts the test-taker's preferences, labels them as indicating, say, a "feeling" or "thinking" type, and feeds them back to the person in complimentary terms. Feeling types, for example, are told they are sensitive to values and "sympathetic, appreciative, and tactful"; thinking types are told they "prefer an objective standard of truth" and are "good at analyzing."

Most people agree with their announced type profile. It, after all, mirrors their declared preferences. They may also accept their label as a basis for being matched with work partners and tasks that supposedly suit their temperaments (although critics wonder if labeling people creates self-fulfilling prophecies). A National Research Council report, however, noted that the test's initial use outran research on its value as a predictor of job performance and that "the popularity of this instrument in the absence of proven scientific worth is troublesome" (Druckman & Bjork, 1991, p. 101; see also Pittenger, 1993). Since those cautionary words, research on the Myers-Briggs has been accumulating, thanks to periodicals such as the *Journal of Psychological Type*.

Exploring Traits

9. How do psychologists use traits to describe personality?

Classifying people as one or another distinct personality type fails to capture their full individuality. So how else could we describe their personalities? To return to our apple analogy, we might describe an apple along several trait dimensions—relatively large or small, red or yellow, sweet or sour. By placing people on several trait dimensions simultaneously, psychologists can describe countless individual personality variations. (Remember from Chapter 5 that variations on just three color dimensions—hue, saturation, and brightness—create many thousands of colors.)

What trait dimensions describe personality? If you had an upcoming blind date, what personality traits might give you an accurate sense of the person? Allport and his associate H. S. Odbert (1936) literally counted all the words in an unabridged dictionary with which one could describe people. How many were there? Almost 18,000! How, then, could psychologists condense the list to a manageable number of basic traits?

Whoopi the extravert Whoopi Goldberg seems as outgoing as her stage name implies. Trait labels such as extraversion can describe our temperaments and typical behaviors.

▶ **trait** a characteristic pattern of behavior or a disposition to feel and act, as assessed by self-report inventories and peer reports.

Joel Gordon

figure 12.2
Two personality factors
Mapmakers can tell us a lot by using two axes (north-south and east-west). Hans Eysenck and Sybil Eysenck use two primary personality factors—extraversion-introversion and stability-instability—as axes for describing personality variation. Varying combinations define other, more specific traits. (From Eysenck & Eysenck, 1963.)

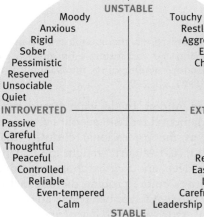

UNSTABLE

Moody	Touchy
Anxious	Restless
Rigid	Aggressive
Sober	Excitable
Pessimistic	Changeable
Reserved	Impulsive
Unsociable	Optimistic
Quiet	Active

INTROVERTED ——————— EXTRAVERTED

Passive	Sociable
Careful	Outgoing
Thoughtful	Talkative
Peaceful	Responsive
Controlled	Easygoing
Reliable	Lively
Even-tempered	Carefree
Calm	Leadership

STABLE

Bernard Wolf

FACTOR ANALYSIS One way has been to propose traits, such as anxiety, that some theory regards as basic. A newer technique is *factor analysis*, the statistical procedure described in Chapter 9 to identify clusters of test items that tap basic components of intelligence (such as spatial ability, reasoning ability, or verbal skill). Imagine that people who describe themselves as outgoing also tend to say that they like excitement and practical jokes and dislike quiet reading. Such a statistically correlated cluster of behaviors reflects a basic trait, or factor—in this case, a trait called *extraversion*.

British psychologists Hans Eysenck and Sybil Eysenck [EYE-zink] believed that we can reduce many of our normal individual variations to two or three genetically influenced dimensions, including *extraversion–introversion* and *emotional stability–instability* (**FIGURE 12.2**). Their *Eysenck Personality Questionnaire* has been given to people in 35 countries around the world, from China to Uganda to Russia. When people's answers are analyzed, the extraversion and emotionality factors inevitably emerge as basic personality dimensions (Eysenck, 1990, 1992).

There is also growing evidence that our biology influences personality factors. Extraverts seek stimulation because their normal *brain arousal* is relatively low. PET scans show that a frontal lobe area involved in behavior inhibition is less active in extraverts than in introverts (Johnson & others, 1999). Poking a hole in the frontal lobes (remember Phineas Gage in Chapter 2) pokes a hole in one's personality.

Jerome Kagan attributes differences in children's shyness and inhibition to their *autonomic nervous system* reactivity. Given a reactive autonomic nervous system, we respond to stress with greater anxiety and inhibition.

Our *genes* have much to say about the temperament and the behavioral style that help define our personality—more, it seems, than the way our parents handled us (although parents also have an influence and are very important for other aspects such as beliefs and values). The fearless, curious child may become the rock-climbing or fast-driving adult. And, as you may recall from the twin and adoption studies in Chapter 3, personality forms under the influence of genes.

Assessing Traits

10. What are personality inventories, and what are their strengths and weaknesses as trait-assessment tools?

Trait-assessment techniques profile a person's behavior patterns—often providing quick assessments of a single trait, such as extraversion, anxiety, or self-esteem. To assess several traits at once, psychologists administer **personality inventories**—longer questionnaires covering a wide range of feelings and behaviors.

The most extensively researched and widely used personality inventory is the **Minnesota Multiphasic Personality Inventory (MMPI)**. Although it assesses "abnormal" personality tendencies rather than normal personality traits, the MMPI

▶ **personality inventory** a questionnaire (often with true-false or agree-disagree items) on which people respond to items designed to gauge a wide range of feelings and behaviors; used to assess selected personality traits.

▶ **Minnesota Multiphasic Personality Inventory (MMPI)** the most widely researched and clinically used of all personality tests. Originally developed to identify emotional disorders (still considered its most appropriate use), this test is now used for many other screening purposes.

▶ **empirically derived test** a test (such as the MMPI) developed by testing a pool of items and then selecting those that discriminate between groups.

illustrates a good way of developing a personality inventory. One of its creators, Starke Hathaway (1960), compared his effort to that of Alfred Binet. Binet, as you may recall from Chapter 9, developed the first intelligence test by selecting items that discriminated children who would have trouble progressing normally in French schools. The MMPI items, too, were **empirically derived**. That is, from a large pool of items, Hathaway and his colleagues selected those on which particular diagnostic groups differed. They then grouped the questions into 10 clinical scales.

Hathaway and others initially gave hundreds of true-false statements ("No one seems to understand me"; "I get all the sympathy I should"; "I like poetry") to groups of psychologically disordered patients and to "normal" people. They retained any statement—no matter how silly it sounded—on which the patient group's answer differed from that of the normal group. "Nothing in the newspaper interests me except the comics" may seem senseless, but it just so happened that depressed people were more likely to answer "true." (Nevertheless, people have had fun spoofing the MMPI with their own mock items: "Weeping brings tears to my eyes," "Frantic screams make me nervous," and "I stay in the bathtub until I look like a raisin" [Frankel & others, 1983].)

Today's MMPI-2, renormed on a population cross-section and containing revised items, still contains 10 clinical scales (**FIGURE 12.3**). Like its predecessor, it has several validity scales, including the so-called lie scale that assesses the extent to which a person is faking in order to make a good impression (by responding "false" to statements such as "I get angry sometimes"). And it has 15 content scales assessing, for instance, work attitudes, family problems, and anger.

In contrast to the subjectivity of the projective tests favored by psychoanalysts, personality inventories are scored objectively—so objectively that a computer can administer and score them. (The computer can also provide descriptions of people who previously responded similarly.) Objectivity does not, however, guarantee validity. For example, individuals taking the MMPI for employment purposes can give socially desirable answers to create a good impression. But in so doing they may also score high on the "lie scale." Moreover, the ease of computerized testing tempts untrained administrators—including many personnel officers, educational admissions officers, and physicians—to use the test in ways for which it has not been validated (Matarazzo, 1983). Nevertheless, for better or worse, the objectivity of the MMPI contributes to its popularity and to its translation into more than 100 languages.

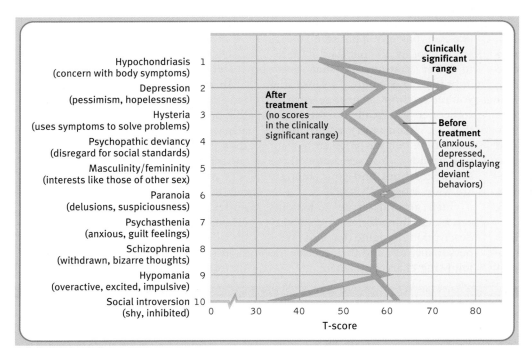

**figure 12.3
Minnesota Multiphasic Personality Inventory (MMPI) test profile** This graph plots the scores of Ed, a depressed and anxious young man, before and after psychotherapy. MMPI scores are converted to a "T-scale," such that an average score is called 50 and about two-thirds of people fall between 40 and 60. High T-scores suggest a psychological disorder. (Adapted from Butcher, 1990.)

Thinking Critically About:

How to Be a "Successful" Astrologer or Palm Reader

How should we evaluate alternative ways of assessing traits? Can we discern people's traits from the alignment of the stars and planets at the time of their birth? From their handwriting? From lines on their palms?

Astronomers scoff at the naiveté of astrology—the constellations have shifted in the millennia since astrologers formulated their predictions (Kelly, 1997, 1998). Humorists mock it: "No offense," writes Dave Barry, "but if you take the horoscope seriously your frontal lobes are the size of Raisinets." Psychologists instead ask questions: Does it work? Are birth dates correlated with character traits? Can astrologers surpass chance when given someone's birth date and asked to identify the person from a short lineup of different personality descriptions? Can people pick out their own horoscopes from a lineup of horoscopes?

The consistent answers have been: No, no, no, and no (British Psychological Society, 1993; Carlson, 1985; Kelly, 1997). Graphologists, who make predictions from handwriting samples, have similarly been found to do no better than chance when trying to discern people's occupations from examining several pages of their handwriting (Beyerstein & Beyerstein, 1992; Dean & others, 1992). Nevertheless, graphologists—and introductory psychology students—will often *perceive* correlations between personality and handwriting even where there are none (King & Koehler, 2000).

If all these perceived correlations evaporate under close scrutiny, how do astrologers and the like per-

© 2000 by Rob Pudim

suade thousands of newspapers and millions of people worldwide to buy their advice? Ray Hyman (1981), palm reader turned research psychologist, has revealed the suckering methods of astrologers, palm readers, and crystal-ball gazers. Their first technique, the "stock spiel," builds on the observation that each of us is in some ways like no one else and in other ways just like everyone else. That some things are true of us all enables the "seer" to offer statements that seem impressively accurate: "I sense that you're nursing a grudge against someone; you really ought to let that go." "You worry about things more than you let on, even to your best friends." "You are adaptable to social situations and your interests are wide-ranging."

Such generally true statements can be combined into a personality description. Imagine that you take a personality test and then receive the following character sketch:

You have a strong need for other people to like and to admire you. You have a tendency to be critical of yourself. . . . You pride yourself on being an independent thinker and do not accept other opinions without satisfactory proof. You have found it unwise to be too frank in revealing yourself to others. At times you are extraverted, affable, sociable; at other times you are introverted, wary, and reserved. Some of your aspirations tend to be pretty unrealistic (Davies, 1997; Forer, 1949).

In experiments, college students have received stock assessments like this one, drawn from statements in a newsstand astrology book. When they think the bogus feedback was prepared just for them and when it is favorable and pretty general, they nearly always rate the description as either "good" or "excellent" (Davies, 1997). Peter Glick and his co-workers (1989) found that even skeptics of astrology, when given a flattering description attributed to an astrologer, begin to think that "maybe there's something to this astrology stuff after all." An astrologer, it has been said, is someone "prepared to tell you what you think of yourself" (Jones, 2000).

French psychologist Michael Gauguelin placed an ad in a Paris newspaper offering a free personal horoscope. Ninety-four percent of those receiving the horoscope praised the description as accurate. Whose horoscope had they all actually received? That of France's Dr. Petiot, a notorious mass murderer (Kurtz, 1983).

This acceptance is called *the Barnum effect*, named in honor of master showman P. T. Barnum's dictum, "There's a sucker born every minute." So powerful is the Barnum effect that, given a choice between this stock spiel and an individualized personality description actually based on a real test, most people choose the phony generic description as being more accurate.

A second technique used by seers is to "read" our clothing, physical features, nonverbal gestures, and reactions to what they are saying. Imagine yourself as the character reader who was visited by a young woman in her late twenties or early thirties. Hyman described the woman as "wearing expensive jewelry, a wedding band, and a black dress of cheap material. The observant reader noted that she was wearing shoes which were advertised for people with foot trouble." Do these clues suggest anything?

Drawing on these observations, the character reader proceeded to amaze his client with his insights. He assumed the woman had come to see him, as did most of his female customers, because of a love or financial problem. The black dress and the wedding band led him to reason that her husband had died recently. The expensive jewelry suggested she had been financially comfortable during the marriage, but the cheap dress suggested her husband's death had left her impoverished. The therapeutic shoes signified she was now on her feet more than she had been used to, implying that she had been working to support herself since her husband's death.

If you are not as shrewd as this character reader (who correctly guessed that the woman was wondering if she should remarry in hope of ending her economic hardship), Hyman says it hardly matters. If people seek you out for a reading, start with some safe sympathy: "I sense you're having some problems lately. You seem unsure what to do. I get the feeling anoth-

er person is involved." Then tell them what they want to hear. Memorize some Barnum statements from astrology and fortune-telling manuals and use them liberally. Tell people it is their responsibility to cooperate by relating your message to their specific experiences. Later they will recall that you predicted those specific details. Phrase statements as questions, and when you detect a positive response assert the statement strongly.

Similar tactics are used by mediums who claim they can make "a really, really long-distance call"— contacting the dead. Gallup (2001) reported that 28 percent of Americans—up from 18 percent in 1990—reported believing "that people can hear from or communicate mentally with someone who has died; another 26 percent are 'not sure.'" "Validation is important!" explained the Web site of medium-to-the-masses John Edward. "Since John does not know your friends and relatives, it is very important you give feedback. A simple nod of the head, a yes or no answer goes a long way in a reading" (Waxman, 2002). Translation, say the skeptics: John will throw many things at the wall and see what sticks, then he'll run with that.

Finally, be a good listener, and later, in different words, reveal to people what they earlier revealed to you. If you dupe them, they will come.

Better yet, beware of those who, by exploiting people with these techniques, are fortune takers rather than fortune tellers.

"Madame Zelinski can provide an even more accurate reading with your date of birth and Social Security number."

table 12.2 The "Big Five" Personality Factors

Trait Dimension	Endpoints of the Dimension
Emotional stability	Calm ——— Anxious Secure ——— Insecure Self-satisfied ——— Self-pitying
Extraversion	Sociable ——— Retiring Fun-loving ——— Sober Affectionate ——— Reserved
Openness	Imaginative ——— Practical Preference for variety ——— 　　Preference for routine Independent ——— Conforming
Agreeableness	Soft-hearted ——— Ruthless Trusting ——— Suspicious Helpful ——— Uncooperative
Conscientiousness	Organized ——— Disorganized Careful ——— Careless Disciplined ——— Impulsive

Source: *Adapted from McCrae & Costa (1986, p. 1002).*

The Big Five Factors

11. Which traits seem to provide the most useful information about personality variation?

Today's trait researchers believe that earlier trait dimensions, such as the Eysencks' introverted/extraverted and unstable/stable dimensions, are important. But they do not tell the whole story. A slightly expanded set of factors—dubbed the *Big Five*—does a better job (John & Srivastava, 1999; McCrae & Costa, 1999). If a test specifies where you are on the five dimensions of **TABLE 12.2**, it has said much of what there is to say about your personality. Around the world, people describe others in terms roughly consistent with the Big Five—how agreeable they are, how extraverted they are, and so forth. The Big Five is not the last word, but for now the winning number in the personality lottery is five. The Big Five—today's "common currency for personality psychology" (Funder, 2001)—was the most active personality research topic during the 1990s and is currently our best approximation of the basic trait dimensions (Endler & Speer, 1998). If you could ask five questions about the personality of a stranger—say, that blind date you were soon to meet—querying where the person is on these five dimensions would be most revealing.

The recent wave of Big Five research explores various questions:

- *How stable are these traits?* In adulthood, the Big Five traits are quite stable, with some tendencies (emotional instability, extraversion, and openness) waning a bit in the decades after college, and others (agreeableness and conscientiousness) rising (McCrae & others, 1999; Vaidya & others, 2002).
- *How heritable are they?* Heritability of individual differences varies with the diversity of people studied, but it generally runs 50 percent or a tad more for each dimension (Loehlin & others, 1998).
- *How well do they apply to other cultures?* The Big Five dimensions describe personality in various cultures reasonably well (McCrae, 2001; Paunonen & others, 2000).

By exploring such questions, Big Five research has rejuvenated trait psychology and renewed appreciation for the importance of personality.

Evaluating the Trait Perspective

12. Does research support the consistency of personality traits over time and across situations?

Are our personality traits stable and enduring? Or does our behavior depend on where and with whom we find ourselves? J. R. R. Tolkien created characters, like the loyal Sam Gamgee, whose personality traits were consistent across various times and places. The Italian playwright Luigi Pirandello had a different view. For him, personality was ever-changing, tailored to the particular role or situation. In one of Pirandello's plays, Lamberto Laudisi describes himself: "I am really what you take me to be; though, my dear madam, that does not prevent me from also being really what your husband, my sister, my niece, and Signora Cini take me to be—because they also are absolutely right!" To which Signora Sirelli responds, "In other words you are a different person for each of us."

THE PERSON-SITUATION CONTROVERSY Who, then, typifies human personality, Tolkien's consistent Sam Gamgee or Pirandello's inconsistent Laudisi? Both. Our behavior is influenced by the interaction of our inner disposition with our environment. Still, the question lingers: Which is *more* important? Are we *more* as Tolkien or as Pirandello imagined us to be? Forced to choose, most people would probably side

"There is as much difference between us and ourselves, as between us and others."

Michel de Montaigne, Essays, 1588

Roughly speaking, the temporary, external influences on behavior are the focus of social psychology, and the enduring, inner influences are the focus of personality psychology. In actuality, behavior always depends on the interaction of persons with situations.

with Tolkien. Until the late 1960s, most psychologists would have, too. Isn't it obvious that some people are dependably conscientious and others unreliable, some cheerful and others dour, some outgoing and others shy?

When we explore this *person-situation controversy*, we look for genuine personality traits that persist over time *and* across situations. If we are to consider friendliness a trait, friendly people must act friendly at different times and places. Do they? In Chapter 4, we considered research that has followed lives through time.

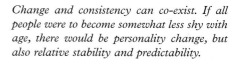

"*Mr. Coughlin over there was the founder of one of the first motorcycle gangs.*"

We noted that some scholars (especially those who study infants) are impressed with personality change; others are struck by personality stability during adulthood. As **FIGURE 12.4** illustrates, data from 152 long-term studies reveal that personality trait scores correlate with scores obtained seven years later. Interests may change—the avid collector of tropical fish may become the avid gardener. Careers may change—the determined salesperson may become a determined social worker. Relationships may change—the hostile spouse may start over with a new partner. But most people recognize their traits as their own, note Robert McCrae and Paul Costa (1994), "and it is well that they do. A person's recognition of the inevitability of his or her one and only personality is . . . the culminating wisdom of a lifetime."

The consistency of specific *behaviors* from one situation to the next is another matter. As Walter Mischel (1968, 1984) has pointed out, people do not act with predictable consistency. Mischel's studies of college students' conscientiousness revealed but a modest relationship between a student's being conscientious on one occasion (say, showing up for class on time) and being similarly conscientious on another occasion (say, turning in assignments on time). Pirandello would not have been surprised.

Mischel has also pointed out that people's scores on personality tests only mildly predict their behaviors. For example, people's scores on an extraversion test do not neatly predict how sociable they actually will be on any given occasion. If we remember such results, says Mischel, we will be more cautious about labeling and pigeonholing individuals. We will be more restrained when asked to predict whether someone is likely to violate parole, commit suicide, or be an effective employee. Years in advance, science can tell us the phase of the moon for any given date. A day in advance, meteorologists can often predict the weather. But we are much further from being able to predict how *you* will feel and act tomorrow.

In defense of traits, Seymour Epstein (1983a,b) maintained that trying to predict a specific act on the basis of a personality test result is like trying to predict your answer to a specific aptitude question on the basis of an intelligence test result. Your answer to any given question is unpredictable because it depends on so many variables (your intelligence, yes, but also your reading of the question, your momentary concentration, luck). Your *average* accuracy over many questions on several tests is more predictable. Similarly, people's *average* outgoingness, happiness, or carelessness over *many* situations is predictable, Epstein observed. When rating someone's shyness or agreeableness, this consistency enables people who know someone well to agree (Kenrick & Funder, 1988). As our best friends can verify, we *do* have personality traits—genetically influenced traits, we now know. Moreover, our traits are socially significant.

Change and consistency can co-exist. If all people were to become somewhat less shy with age, there would be personality change, but also relative stability and predictability.

figure 12.4
Personality stability With age, personality traits become more stable, as reflected in the correlation of trait scores with scores seven years later. (Data from Roberts & DelVecchio, 2000.)

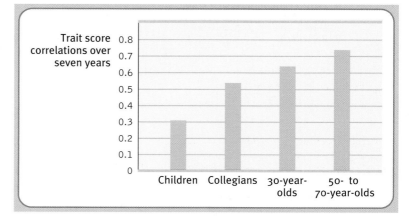

They influence our health, our thinking, and our job performance (Deary & Matthews, 1993; Hogan, 1998). The bottom line: Traits exist. We differ. And our differences matter.

CONSISTENCY OF EXPRESSIVE STYLE In unfamiliar, formal situations—perhaps as a guest in the home of a person from another culture—our traits may remain hidden as we attend carefully to social cues. In familiar, informal situations—just hanging out with friends—we feel less constrained, allowing our traits to emerge (Buss, 1989). In such situations, our expressive styles—our animation, manner of speaking, and gestures—are impressively consistent. Thus, we often form lasting impressions within a few moments of meeting someone. Nalini Ambady and Robert Rosenthal (1992, 1993) videotaped 13 Harvard University graduate students teaching undergraduate courses. Observers then viewed three thin slices of each teacher's behavior—mere 10-second clips from the beginning, middle, and end of a class—and rated each teacher's level of confidence, activeness, warmth, and so forth. These behavior ratings, based on 30 *seconds* of teaching from an entire semester, predicted amazingly well the teacher's average student ratings at the semester's end. Observing even thinner slices—three 2-second clips—yielded ratings that still correlated as high as +.72 with the student evaluations. Some people's first impressions, derived from expressive behavior, predicted other people's lasting impressions!

To sum up, we can say that at any moment the immediate situation powerfully influences a person's behavior, especially when the situation makes clear demands. We can better predict drivers' behavior at traffic lights from knowing the color of the lights than from knowing the drivers' personalities. Averaging our behavior across many occasions does, however, reveal distinct personality traits. Moreover, we can, in a flash, perceive individual differences in some traits, such as expressiveness.

rehearse it!

12. Trait theory describes personality in terms of characteristic behaviors, or traits, such as agreeableness or extraversion. A pioneering trait theorist was
a. Sigmund Freud.
b. Alfred Adler.
c. Gordon Allport.
d. Carl Rogers.

13. Trait theorists assess personality by developing a profile of a person's traits. For example, they administer personality inventories, long questionnaires that ask people to report their characteristic feelings and behaviors. The most widely used of all personality inventories is the
a. extraversion-introversion scale.
b. Person-Situation Inventory.
c. MMPI.
d. Rorschach.

14. The MMPI's items were empirically derived by testing a pool of items and selecting those that discriminate between groups. MMPI-2 contains several validity scales, which
a. can be eliminated when testing people with psychological disorders.
b. enable the test designers to judge whether the test is producing consistent results.
c. test the extent to which a person is faking in order to make a good impression.
d. appraise whether people have appropriate attitudes toward work or family problems.

15. Hans Eysenck and Sybil Eysenck defined personality in terms of two primary factors—extraversion-introversion and stability-instability. Most

researchers today believe that the Eysenck dimensions are too limiting and prefer the so-called Big Five personality factors. Which of the following is *not* one of the Big Five?
a. Conscientiousness
b. Anxiety
c. Extraversion
d. Agreeableness

16. People's scores on personality tests are only mildly predictive of their behavior. Such tests best predict
a. a person's behavior on a specific occasion.
b. a person's average behavior across many situations.
c. behavior involving a single trait, such as conscientiousness.
d. behavior that depends on situation or context.

Answers can be found in Appendix C.

The Social-Cognitive Perspective

13. In the view of social-cognitive psychologists, what mutual influences shape an individual's personality?

A modern personality perspective—the **social-cognitive perspective** proposed by Albert Bandura (1986, 2001)—emphasizes the interaction of persons and their situations. Like learning theorists, social-cognitive theorists believe we learn many of our behaviors either through conditioning or by observing others and modeling our behavior after theirs. They also emphasize the importance of mental processes: What we think about our situations affects our behavior. Instead of focusing solely on how our environment controls us (behaviorism), social-cognitive theorists focus on how we and our environment interact: How do we interpret and respond to external events? How do our schemas, our memories, and our expectations influence our behavior patterns?

Reciprocal Influences

Bandura (1986) called the process of interacting with our environment **reciprocal determinism**. "Behavior, internal personal factors, and environmental influences," he said, "all operate as interlocking determinants of each other" (**FIGURE 12.5**). For example, children's TV-viewing habits (past behavior) influence their viewing preferences (internal factor), which influence how television (environmental factor) affects their current behavior. The influences are mutual.

Consider three specific ways in which individuals and environments interact:

1. ***Different people choose different environments.*** The school you attend, the reading you do, the television programs you watch, the music you listen to, the friends you associate with—all are part of an environment you have chosen, based partly on your dispositions (Ickes & others, 1997). *You choose your environment and it then shapes you.*

2. ***Our personalities shape how we interpret and react to events.*** Anxious people, for example, are attuned to potentially threatening events (Eysenck & others, 1987). Thus, they perceive the world as threatening, and they react accordingly.

3. ***Our personalities help create situations to which we react.*** Many experiments reveal that how we view and treat people influences how they in turn treat us. If we expect someone to be angry with us, we may give the person a cold shoulder, touching off the very anger we expect. If we have an easygoing temperament we will likely enjoy close, supportive friendships (Kendler, 1997).

In such ways, we are both the products and the architects of our environments.

If all this has a familiar ring, it may be because it parallels and reinforces a pervasive theme in psychology and in this book: *Behavior emerges from the interplay of external and internal influences.* Boiling water turns an egg hard and a potato soft. A threatening environment turns one person into a hero, another into a scoundrel. *At every moment,* our behavior is influenced by our genes, our experiences, and our personalities.

Personality is seen in individual differences, as it shapes how people interpret and react to events.

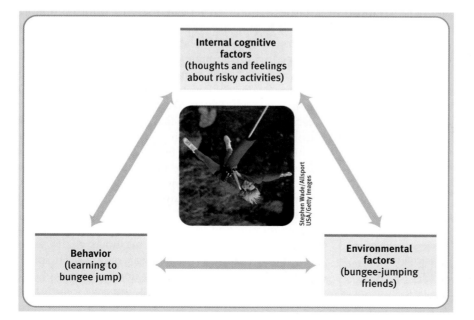

figure 12.5
Reciprocal determinism The social-cognitive perspective proposes that our personalities are shaped by the interaction of internal factors (our feelings and thoughts), our environment, and our behaviors.

▶ **personal control** our sense of controlling our environment rather than feeling helpless.

▶ **external locus of control** the perception that chance or outside forces beyond one's personal control determine one's fate.

▶ **internal locus of control** the perception that one controls one's own fate.

▶ **learned helplessness** the hopelessness and passive resignation an animal or human learns when unable to avoid repeated aversive events.

Personal Control

14. What are the causes and consequences of personal control?

In studying how we interact with our environment, social-cognitive psychologists emphasize our sense of **personal control**—whether we learn to see ourselves as controlling, or as controlled by, our environment. Psychologists have two basic ways to study the effect of personal control (or any personality factor). One: *Correlate* people's feelings of control with their behaviors and achievements. Two: *Experiment*, by raising or lowering people's sense of control and noting the effects. Let's take these one at a time.

LOCUS OF CONTROL Consider your own feelings of control. Do you believe that your life is beyond your control? That the world is run by a few powerful people? That getting a good job depends mainly on being in the right place at the right time? Or do you more strongly believe that what happens to you is your own doing? That the average person can influence government decisions? That being a success is a matter of hard work, not luck?

Hundreds of studies have compared people who differ in their perceptions of control. On the one side are those who have what psychologist Julian Rotter called an **external locus of control**—the perception that chance or outside forces determine their fate. On the other are those who perceive an **internal locus of control** and believe that to a great extent they control their own destiny. In study after study, "internals" achieve more in school, act more independently, enjoy better health, and feel less depressed than do "externals" (Lachman & Weaver, 1998; Lefcourt, 1982; Presson & Benassi, 1996). Moreover, they are better able to delay gratification and cope with various stresses, including marital problems (Miller & others, 1986).

Self-control—the ability to control impulses and delay gratification—in turn predicts good adjustment, better grades, and social success, report June Tangney and her colleagues (2004). University students who plan their day's activities and live out their day as planned are also at low risk for depression (Nezlek, 2001). None of us, however, experiences unvarying self-control. Like a muscle, self-control temporarily weakens after an exertion, replenishes with rest, and becomes stronger with exercise, report Roy Baumeister and Julia Exline (2000). Self-control requires attention and energy.

LEARNED HELPLESSNESS VERSUS PERSONAL CONTROL People who feel helpless and oppressed often perceive control as external. This perception may then deepen their feelings of resignation. In fact, this is precisely what researcher Martin Seligman (1975, 1991) and others found in experiments with both animals and people. Dogs strapped in a harness and given repeated shocks, with no opportunity to avoid them, learned a sense of helplessness. Later placed in another situation where they *could* escape the punishment by simply leaping a hurdle, the dogs cowered as if without hope. Repeatedly faced with traumatic events over which they have no control, people, too, come to feel helpless, hopeless, and depressed. Psychologists call this passive resignation **learned helplessness** (**FIGURE 12.6**). In contrast, animals able to escape the shocks in the first situation learned personal control and easily escaped the shocks in the new situation.

Part of the shock we feel in an unfamiliar culture comes from a diminished sense of control when unsure how people in the new environment will respond (Triandis, 1994). Similarly, people given little control over their world in prisons, factories, colleges, and nursing homes experience lower morale and increased stress. Measures that increase control—allowing prisoners to move chairs and control room lights and the TV, having workers participate in decision making, offering nursing home patients choices about their environment—noticeably improve health and morale

figure 12.6
Learned helplessness When animals and people experience no control over repeated bad events, they often learn helplessness.

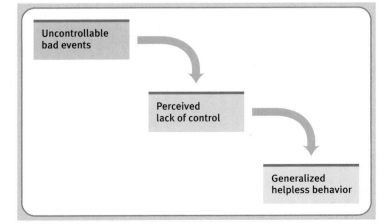

Uncontrollable bad events

→

Perceived lack of control

→

Generalized helpless behavior

(Miller & Monge, 1986; Ruback & others, 1986; Wener & others, 1987). In one famous study of nursing home patients, 93 percent of those encouraged to exert more control became more alert, active, and happy (Rodin, 1986). As researcher Ellen Langer (1983, p. 291) concluded, "Perceived control is basic to human functioning." She recommended that "for the young and old alike," it is important that we create environments that enhance our sense of control and personal efficacy.

The verdict of these studies is reassuring: Under conditions of personal freedom and empowerment, people thrive. Small wonder that the citizens of stable democracies report higher levels of happiness (Inglehart, 1990). Shortly before the democratic revolution in the former East Germany, psychologists Gabriele Oettingen and Martin Seligman (1990) studied the telltale body language of working-class men in East and West Berlin bars. Compared with their counterparts on the other side of the Wall, the empowered West Berliners much more often laughed, sat upright rather than slumped, and had upward- rather than downward-turned mouths. To paraphrase the Roman philosopher Seneca, happy are those who choose their own path.

OPTIMISM One measure of how helpless or effective you feel is where you stand on optimism-pessimism. How do you characteristically explain negative and positive events? Perhaps you have known students whose *attributional style* is negative—who attribute poor performance to their lack of ability ("I can't do this") or to situations enduringly beyond their control ("There is nothing I can do about it"). Such students are more likely to persist in getting low grades than are students who adopt the more hopeful attitude that effort, good study habits, and self-discipline can make a difference (Noel & others, 1987; Peterson & Barrett, 1987). Although mere fantasies tend not to fuel motivation and success, realistic positive expectations do (Oettingen & Mayer, 2002).

In their study of professional achievement, Seligman and Peter Schulman (1986) compared sales made by new life insurance representatives who were more or less optimistic in their outlooks. Those who put an optimistic spin on their setbacks—seeing them as flukes or as a means to learning a new approach, rather than viewing them as signs of incompetence—sold more policies during their first year and were half as likely to quit. Seligman's finding came to life for him when Bob Dell, one of the optimistic recruits who began selling for Metropolitan Life after taking Seligman's optimism test, later dialed him up and sold him a policy.

Health, too, benefits from a basic optimism. As we saw in Chapter 11, a depressed hopelessness dampens the body's disease-fighting immune system. In repeated studies, optimists have outlived pessimists or lived with fewer illnesses.

If positive thinking in the face of adversity pays dividends, so, too, can a dash of realism (Schneider, 2001). Self-disparaging explanations of past failures can depress ambition, but realistic anxiety over possible *future* failures can fuel energetic efforts to avoid the dreaded fate (Norem, 2001; Goodhart, 1986; Showers, 1992). Students who, concerned about bombing the upcoming exam, study thoroughly and get a top grade often outperform their equally able but overconfident peers. Edward Chang (2001) reports that, compared with European-American students, Asian-American students express somewhat greater pessimism—which he suspects helps explain their impressive academic achievements. Success requires enough optimism to provide hope and enough pessimism to prevent complacency.

"O God, give us grace to accept with serenity the things that cannot be changed, courage to change the things which should be changed, and the wisdom to distinguish the one from the other."

Reinhold Niebuhr, "The Serenity Prayer," 1943

Control affects well-being Nursing home residents who can arrange their own possessions, control other aspects of their daily lives, and pursue their own interests are more vigorous and happy than those who do not have these opportunities.

Toward a More Positive Psychology

During its first century, psychology understandably focused much of its attention on understanding and alleviating negative states. We have studied abuse and anxiety, depression and disease, prejudice and poverty. As Chapter 11 noted, articles on selected negative emotions since 1887 have outnumbered those on positive emotions by 13 to 1.

In ages past, notes 1998 American Psychological Association president Martin Seligman (2002), times of relative peace and prosperity have enabled cultures to turn their attention from repairing weakness and damage to promoting "the highest qualities of life." Prosperous fifth-century Athens nurtured philosophy and democracy. Flourishing fifteenth-century Florence nurtured great art. Victorian England, flush with the bounty of the British empire, nurtured honor, discipline, and duty. As we build this new millennium, Seligman believes that thriving Western cultures have a parallel opportunity to create, as a "humane, scientific monument," a more **positive psychology**—a psychology concerned not only with weakness and damage but also with strength and virtue.

Positive psychology shares with humanistic psychology an interest in advancing human fulfillment, but its origins and methodology are scientific. From these roots have grown not only the new studies of happiness and health, but also the shift in emphasis from learned helplessness and depression to optimism and thriving. Taken together, satisfaction with the past, happiness with the present, and optimism about the future define the movement's first pillar: *positive subjective well-being.*

The second pillar, *positive character*, focuses on exploring and enhancing virtues such as creativity, courage, compassion, integrity,

Martin E. P. Seligman "The main purpose of a positive psychology is to measure, understand and then build the human strengths and the civic virtues."

self-control, leadership, wisdom, and spirituality. Current research examines the roots and fruits of such virtues, sometimes by studying individuals who exemplify them in extraordinary ways.

The third pillar, *positive groups, communities, and cultures*, seeks to foster a positive social ecology, including healthy families, communal neighborhoods, effective schools, socially responsible media, and civil dialogue.

Will psychology have a more positive mission in this century? Without slighting the need to repair damage and cure disease, the supporters of positive psychology hope so. With *American Psychologist* and *British Psychologist* issues devoted to positive psychology, with new books (the *Handbook of Positive Psychology*, 2001; *A Psychology of Human Strengths*, 2003; *Flourishing: Positive Psychology and the Life Well-Lived*, 2003), and with new prizes, research awards, and summer institutes promoting positive psychology scholarship, these psychologists have reason to be positive.

▶ **positive psychology** the scientific study of optimal human functioning; aims to discover and promote strengths and virtues that enable individuals and communities to thrive.

Excessive optimism can blind us to real risks. Neil Weinstein (1980, 1982, 1996) has shown how our natural positive-thinking bias can promote "an unrealistic optimism about future life events." Most college students perceive themselves as less likely than their average classmate to develop drinking problems, drop out of school, or have a heart attack by age 40. Most late adolescents see themselves as much less vulnerable than their peers to the AIDS virus (Abrams, 1991).

Given illusory optimism, documented in some 200 research reports, people may fail to take sensible precautions. Most young Americans know that half of U.S. marriages end in divorce, but they are confident that *theirs* will not (Lehman & Nisbett, 1985). Most cigarette smokers smoke high-tar brands, but only 17 percent believe their brand has a more hazardous tar level than most others (Segerstrom & others, 1993). Compared with other women at their university, sexually active undergraduate women—especially those who do *not* consistently use effective contraception—perceive themselves as *less* vulnerable to unwanted pregnancy (Burger & Burns,

"We just haven't been flapping them hard enough."

DOONESBURY

1988). Individuals who optimistically venture into ill-fated relationships, deny the effects of smoking, or engage in unprotected sex remind us that, like pride, blind optimism may go before a fall.

Ironically, people often are most overconfident when most incompetent. That's because it often takes competence to recognize competence, note Justin Kruger and David Dunning (1999). They found that most students scoring at the low end of tests of grammar and logic believed they had scored in the top half. If you do not know what good grammar is, you may be unaware that your grammar is poor. The difficulty in recognizing one's own incompetence helps explain why so many low-scoring students are dumbfounded after doing badly on an exam.

Assessing Behavior in Situations

15. What underlying principle guides social-cognitive psychologists in their assessment of people's behavior and beliefs?

Social-cognitive researchers explore the effect of differing situations on people's behavior patterns and attitudes (Cervone & others, 2001). They study, for example, how viewing aggressive or nonaggressive models affects behavior. They assess the impact of dehumanizing situations on people's attitudes. And they examine the consistency of people's personalities in varying circumstances.

An ambitious example of such research, and one that predates social-cognitive theory, is the U.S. Army's World War II strategy for assessing candidates for spy missions. Rather than using paper-and-pencil tests, army psychologists subjected the candidates to simulated undercover conditions. They tested their ability to handle stress, solve problems, maintain leadership, and withstand intense interrogation without blowing their covers. Although it was time-consuming and expensive, this assessment of behavior in a realistic situation helped predict later success on actual spy missions (OSS Assessment Staff, 1948).

Military and educational organizations and many Fortune 500 companies are continuing this strategy in their evaluations of hundreds of thousands of people each year in assessment centers (Bray & others, 1991, 1997; Spychalski & others, 1997). AT&T has observed prospective managers doing simulated managerial work. Many colleges assess potential faculty members' teaching abilities by observing them teach, and graduate students' potentials via internships and student teaching. Armies assess their soldiers by observing them during military exercises. Most American cities with populations of 50,000 or more use assessment centers in evaluating police and fire officers (Lowry, 1997).

"I didn't think it could happen to me."
Earvin "Magic" Johnson, My Life, 1993
(after contracting HIV)

"Ignorance more freely begets confidence than does knowledge."
Charles Darwin, The Descent of Man, 1871

These procedures exploit the principle that the best means of predicting future behavior is neither a personality test nor an interviewer's intuition. Rather, it is the person's past behavior patterns in similar situations (Mischel, 1981; Ouellette & Wood, 1998; Schmidt & Hunter, 1998). As long as the situation and the person remain much the same, the best predictor of future job performance is past job performance; the best predictor of future grades is past grades; the best predictor of future aggressiveness is past aggressiveness; the best predictor of drug use in young adulthood is drug use in high school. If you can't check the person's past behavior, the next-best thing is to create an assessment situation that simulates the demands of the task so you can see how the person handles them.

A New York Times analysis of 100 rampage murders over the last half-century revealed that 55 of the killers had regularly exploded in anger and 63 had threatened violence (Goodstein & Glaberson, 2000). Most didn't, out of the blue, "just snap."

Evaluating the Social-Cognitive Perspective

16. What has the social-cognitive perspective contributed to the study of personality, and what criticisms have been leveled against it?

The social-cognitive perspective on personality sensitizes researchers to how situations affect, and are affected by, individuals. More than other perspectives, it builds from psychological research on learning and cognition. But critics charge that the social-cognitive perspective focuses so much on the situation that it fails to appreciate the person's inner traits. Where is the person in this view of personality, ask the dissenters (Carlson, 1984), and where are human emotions? True, the situation does guide our behavior. But, say the critics, in many instances our unconscious motives, our emotions, and our pervasive traits shine through. Personality traits have been shown to predict behavior at work, love, and play. Our biologically influenced traits really do matter. Consider Percy Ray Pridgen and Charles Gill. Each faced the same situation: They had jointly won a $90 million lottery jackpot (Harriston, 1993). When Pridgen learned of the winning numbers, he began trembling uncontrollably, huddled with a friend behind a bathroom door while confirming the win, then sobbed. When Gill heard the news, he told his wife and then went to sleep.

rehearse it!

17. Albert Bandura, a social-cognitive theorist, believes that interacting with our environment involves reciprocal determinism, or mutual influences among personal factors, environmental factors, and behavior. An example of an environmental factor is
  a. the presence of books in a home.
  b. a preference for outdoor play.
  c. the ability to read at a fourth-grade level.
  d. the fear of violent action on television.

18. When elderly patients take an active part in managing their own care and surroundings, their morale and health tend to improve. Such findings indicate that people do better when they perceive
  a. learned helplessness.
  b. an external locus of control.
  c. an internal locus of control.
  d. reciprocal determinism.

19. Working with animals and people, Martin Seligman studied an attitude of passive resignation, which he called *learned helplessness.* He found, for example, that a dog will respond with learned helplessness if it has received repeated shocks and has had
  a. the opportunity to escape.
  b. no control over the shocks.
  c. pain or discomfort.
  d. no food or water prior to the shocks.

20. A goal of many personality theories is to be able to predict a person's behavior in a particular situation. _____ theory is very sensitive to the way people affect, and are affected by, particular situations, but it says little about enduring traits.
  a. Psychoanalytic
  b. Humanistic
  c. Trait
  d. Social-cognitive

Answers can be found in Appendix C.

Exploring the Self

Psychology's concern with people's sense of self dates back at least to William James, who, in his 1890 *Principles of Psychology,* devoted more than 100 pages to the topic. By 1943, Gordon Allport lamented that the self had become "lost to view." Even humanistic psychology's emphasis on the self did not instigate much scientific research, but it did help renew the concept of self and keep it alive. Now, more than a century after James and outside humanistic psychology, the self is one of Western psychology's most vigorously researched topics. Every year, new studies galore appear on self-esteem, self-disclosure, self-awareness, self-schemas, self-monitoring, and so forth—more than 150,000 articles in all since 1967.

An example of more recent thinking about self is the concept of *possible selves* put forth by Hazel Markus and her colleagues (Inglehart & others, 1989; Markus & Nurius, 1986). Your possible selves include your visions of the self you dream of becoming—the rich self, the successful self, the loved and admired self. They also include the self you fear becoming—the unemployed self, the lonely self, the academically failed self. Such possible selves motivate us by laying out specific goals and calling forth the energy to work toward them. University of Michigan students in a combined undergraduate/medical school program earn higher grades if they undergo the program with a clear vision of themselves as successful doctors. Dreams do often give birth to achievements.

Underlying this research is an assumption that the self, as organizer of our thoughts, feelings, and actions, is a pivotal center of personality. From our self-focused perspective, we too readily presume that others are noticing and evaluating us. Thomas Gilovich (1996) demonstrated this **spotlight effect** by having individual Cornell University students don Barry Manilow T-shirts before entering a room with other students. Feeling self-conscious, the T-shirt wearers guessed that nearly half of their peers would take note of the shirt as they walked in. In reality, only 23 percent did. This absence of attention applies not only to our dorky clothes and bad hair but also to our nervousness, irritation, or attraction—fewer people notice than we presume (Gilovich & Savitsky, 1999). Others are also less aware than we suppose of the variability—the ups and downs—of our appearance and performance (Gilovich & others, 2002). Even after a blunder (setting off a library alarm, showing up for dinner in the wrong clothes) we "stick out like a sore thumb" less than we imagine (Savitsky & others, 2001).

"The first step to better times is to imagine them."

Chinese fortune cookie

Possible selves By giving them a chance to try out many possible selves, pretend games offer children important opportunities to grow emotionally, socially, and cognitively. This young boy may or may not grow up to be a physician, but playing adult roles will certainly bear fruit in terms of an expanded vision of what he might become.

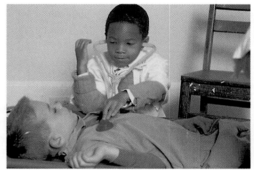

Sybil Shackman

Self-Esteem

17. Are we helped or hindered by high self-esteem?

How we *feel* about ourselves is also important. Research studies confirm the benefits of positive self-esteem and also hint at the hazards of pride.

THE BENEFITS OF SELF-ESTEEM High **self-esteem**—a feeling of self-worth—pays dividends. People who feel good about themselves (who strongly agree with self-affirming questionnaire statements) have fewer sleepless nights, succumb less easily to pressures to conform, are less likely to use drugs, are more persistent at difficult tasks, are less shy and lonely, are less likely to see rejection where none exists, and are just plain happier (Crocker & Wolfe, 1999; Leary, 1999; Murray & others, 2002; Watson & others, 2002).

Those whose self-esteem is low do not necessarily see themselves as worthless or wicked, but they seldom say good things about themselves. Such low self-esteem exacts costs. Unhappiness and despair often coexist with low self-esteem. Psychotherapy researcher Hans Strupp (1982) noted that "as soon as one listens to a patient's story, one encounters unhappiness, frustration, and despair. . . . Basic to all these difficulties are impairments in self-acceptance and self-esteem."

Low self-esteem comes in different forms. Those vulnerable to depression often feel they are falling short of their *hopes*. Those vulnerable to anxiety often feel they are falling short of what they *ought* to be (Higgins, 1987). For such people, the pain of anticipated social rejection, experienced as low self-esteem, is sometimes adaptive. As with other forms of pain, it may aid survival by motivating them to behave in ways that sustain their inclusion within a supportive group (Leary & others, 1995).

The correlational links between low self-esteem and personal problems have other possible interpretations. Psychologists Roy Baumeister and colleagues (2003), William Damon (1995), Robyn Dawes (1994), Mark Leary (1999), and Martin Seligman (1994, 2002) all doubt that self-esteem is really "the armor that protects kids" from life's problems. Could it not be the other way around? Couldn't

Dear diary, Sorry to bother you again.

LOW SELF-ESTEEM

▶ **spotlight effect** overestimating others' noticing and evaluating our appearance, performance, and blunders (as if we presume a spotlight shines on us).

▶ **self-esteem** one's feelings of high or low self-worth.

"There's a lot of talk about self-esteem these days. It seems pretty basic to me. If you want to feel proud of yourself, you've got to do things you can be proud of."

Oseola McCarty, Mississippi washerwoman, after donating $150,000 to the University of Southern Mississippi

problems and failures cause low self-esteem? Maybe self-esteem simply reflects reality. Maybe feeling good *follows* doing well. Maybe it's a side effect of meeting challenges and surmounting difficulties. Maybe self-esteem is a gauge that reads out the state of our relationships with others. If so, isn't pushing the gauge artificially higher akin to forcing a car's low fuel gauge to display "full"? And will the best boost to self-esteem therefore come not so much from our repeatedly telling children how wonderful they are as from their own effective coping and hard-won achievements?

However, an *effect* of low self-esteem does appear in experiments. Temporarily deflate people's self-image (say, by telling them they did poorly on an aptitude test or by disparaging their personality) and they will be more likely to disparage others or to express heightened racial prejudice (Ybarra, 1999). Those who are negative about themselves also tend to be thin-skinned and judgmental (Baumgardner & others, 1989; Pelham, 1993). Some "love their neighbors as themselves"; others loathe their neighbors as themselves. In experiments, those made to feel insecure often become excessively critical, as if to impress others with their own brilliance (Amabile, 1983). Such findings are consistent with Maslow's and Rogers' presumptions that a healthy self-image pays dividends. Accept yourself and you'll find it easier to accept others.

CULTURE AND SELF-ESTEEM Is it true, as so many assume, that ethnic minorities, people with disabilities, and women live lives handicapped by impoverished self-esteem? The accumulated evidence says no. For example, 261 comparisons of more than half a million people have revealed slightly *higher* self-esteem scores for black than for white children, adolescents, and young adults (Gray-Little & Hafdahl, 2000; Twenge & Crocker, 2002). The National Institute of Mental Health's 1980s study of *Psychiatric Disorders in America* similarly reveals that the rates of depression and alcoholism among African- and Hispanic-Americans are roughly comparable with those of other Americans (if anything, America's ethnic minorities suffer slightly less depression—see page 502).

Some people wonder: How can this be? Some members of "stigmatized" groups (people of color, those with disabilities, women) have faced discrimination and lower status, yet, according to Jennifer Crocker and Brenda Major (1989), they maintain their self-esteem in three ways:

- They value the things at which they excel.
- They attribute problems to prejudice.
- They do as everyone does—they compare themselves with those in their own group.

These findings help us understand why, despite the realities of prejudice, such groups report levels of happiness roughly comparable with others.

SELF-SERVING BIAS Carl Rogers (1958) once objected to the religious doctrine that humanity's problems arise from excessive self-love, or pride. He noted that most people he had known "despise themselves, regard themselves as worthless and unlovable." Mark Twain had the idea: "No man, deep down in the privacy of his heart, has any considerable respect for himself."

"To love oneself is the beginning of a life-long romance."

Oscar Wilde, An Ideal Husband, 1895

Actually, most of us have a good reputation with ourselves. In studies of self-esteem, even those who score low respond in the midrange of possible scores. (A "low" self-esteem person responds to statements such as "I have good ideas" with qualifying adjectives such as *somewhat* or *sometimes*.) Moreover, one of psychology's most provocative and firmly established recent conclusions concerns our potent **self-serving bias**—our readiness to perceive ourselves favorably (Brown, 1991; Myers, 2002). Consider these findings:

> ***People accept more responsibility for good deeds than for bad, and for successes than for failures.*** Athletes often privately credit their victories to their own prowess and their losses to bad breaks, lousy officiating, or the other team's exceptional performance. After receiving poor grades on an exam, most students in a half-dozen studies criticized the exam, not themselves. On insur-

▶ **self-serving bias** a readiness to perceive oneself favorably.

ance forms, drivers have explained accidents in such words as: "An invisible car came out of nowhere, struck my car, and vanished." "As I reached an intersection, a hedge sprang up, obscuring my vision, and I did not see the other car." "A pedestrian hit me and went under my car." The question "What have I done to deserve this?" is one we usually ask of our troubles, not our successes—those, we assume we deserve.

Most people see themselves as better than average. This is true for nearly any subjective and socially desirable dimension. In national surveys, most business executives say they are more ethical than their average counterpart. In several studies, 90 percent of business managers and more than 90 percent of college professors rated their performance as superior to that of their average peer. In Australia, 86 percent of people rate their job performance as above average, and only 1 percent as below average. The phenomenon, which reflects the overestimation of self rather than the underestimation of others (Epley & Dunning, 2000), is less striking in Asia, where people value modesty. Yet self-serving biases have been observed worldwide: among Dutch, Australian, and Chinese students; Japanese drivers; Indian Hindus; and French people of most walks of life. Ironically, people even see themselves as more immune than others to self-serving bias (Pronin & others, 2002). The world, it seems, is Garrison Keillor's Lake Wobegon writ large—a place where "all the women are strong, all the men are good-looking, and all the children are above average."

And who is at least "somewhat likely" to go to heaven? Of Americans surveyed by *U.S. News* (1997), 19 percent thought O. J. Simpson would make it. They were more optimistic about Bill Clinton (52 percent), Princess Diana (60 percent), and Michael Jordan (65 percent). The public figure closest to a perceived heavenly shoo-in was Mother Teresa (79 percent). But she was topped by the survey's respondents, 87 percent of whom believed *they* themselves were destined for eternal bliss.

Self-serving bias flies in the face of pop psychology. "All of us have inferiority complexes," wrote John Powell (1989, p. 15). "Those who seem not to have such a complex are only pretending." But additional findings remove any doubts (Myers, 2002):

- We remember and justify our past actions in self-enhancing ways.
- We exhibit an inflated confidence in our beliefs and judgments.
- We overestimate how desirably *we* would act in situations where most people behave less than admirably.
- We often seek out favorable, self-enhancing information.
- We are quicker to believe flattering descriptions of ourselves than unflattering ones, and we are impressed with psychological tests that make us look good.
- We exhibit group pride—a tendency to see our group (our school, our country, our race) as superior.

Moreover, pride does often go before a fall. Self-serving perceptions underlie conflicts ranging from blaming one's spouse for marital discord to arrogantly promoting one's own ethnic superiority. It was national self-righteousness that led both the Americans and Soviets during the arms race to say, "Your weapons threaten us, ours are for our defense." No wonder religion and literature so often warn against the perils of excessive pride.

> *"The [self-]portraits that we actually believe, when we are given freedom to voice them, are dramatically more positive than reality can sustain."*
>
> **Shelley Taylor**, Positive Illusions, *1989*

PEANUTS

Finding their self-esteem threatened, people with large egos may do more than put others down; they may react violently. Someone with a swelled head that gets deflated by insult or rejection is potentially dangerous. Brad Bushman and Roy Baumeister (1998) experimented with this "dark side of high self-esteem." They had 540 undergraduate volunteers write a paragraph, in response to which another supposed student gave them either praise ("Great essay!") or stinging criticism ("One of the worst essays I have read!"). Then the essay writers played a reaction-time game against the other student. After wins, they could assault their opponent with noise of any intensity for any duration.

Can you anticipate the result? After criticism, those with unrealistically high self-esteem were "exceptionally aggressive." They delivered three times the auditory torture of those with normal self-esteem. "Threatened egotism" more than low self-esteem, it seems, predisposes aggression. "Encouraging people to feel good about themselves when they haven't earned it" poses problems, Baumeister (2001) concludes. "Conceited, self-important individuals turn nasty toward those who puncture their bubbles of self-love."

Despite the demonstrated perils of pride, many people reject the idea of self-serving bias, insisting it overlooks those who feel worthless and unlovable and seem to despise themselves. If self-serving bias prevails, why do so many people disparage themselves? For three reasons:

- Sometimes self-directed put-downs are *subtly strategic:* They elicit reassuring strokes. Saying "No one likes me" may at least elicit "But not everyone has met you!"
- Other times, such as before a game or an exam, self-disparaging comments *prepare us for possible failure.* The coach who extols the superior strength of the upcoming opponent makes a loss understandable, a victory noteworthy.
- Self-disparagement also frequently pertains to one's *old self.* People are much more critical of their distant past selves than of their current selves—even when they have not changed (Wilson & Ross, 2001). "At 18, I was a jerk; today I'm more sensitive." In their own eyes, chumps yesterday, champs today.

Even so, it's true: All of us some of the time, and some of us much of the time, *do* feel inferior—especially when we compare ourselves with those who are a step or two higher on the ladder of status, looks, income, or ability. The deeper and more frequently we have such feelings, the more unhappy, even depressed, we are. But for most people, thinking has a naturally positive bias.

We can therefore affirm that self-affirming thinking is generally adaptive. To a point, our positive illusions are beneficial. They maintain our self-confidence, protect against anxiety and depression, and sustain our sense of well-being. "Life is the art of being well-deceived," observed the English essayist William Hazlitt.

Recognizing both the perils of self-righteousness and the dividends of positive self-esteem, psychologists Baumeister (1989), Jonathan Brown (1991), and Shelley Taylor (1989; Taylor & others, 2003) have all suggested that humans function best with modest self-enhancing illusions. Like the Japanese and European magnetic levitation trains, Brown noted, we function optimally when riding just off the rails—not so high that we gyrate and crash, yet not so in touch that we grind to a halt.

Culture and the Self

18. How does the view of self differ in individualist and collectivist cultures?

If someone were to rip away your social connections, making you a solitary refugee in a foreign land, how much of your identity would remain intact? The answer might depend in large part on whether you give greater priority to the independent self that marks **individualism** or to the interdependent self that marks **collectivism**.

"The enthusiastic claims of the self-esteem movement mostly range from fantasy to hogwash. The effects of self-esteem are small, limited, and not all good."

Roy Baumeister (1996)

"If you compare yourself with others, you may become vain and bitter; for always there will be greater and lesser persons than yourself."

Max Ehrmann, "Desiderata," 1927

▶ **individualism** giving priority to one's own goals over group goals, and defining one's identity in terms of personal attributes rather than group identifications.

▶ **collectivism** giving priority to the goals of one's group (often one's extended family or work group) and defining one's identity accordingly.

B. & C. Alexander/Photo Researchers

Collectivism By identifying with family and other groups, these yak herders in India gain a sense of "we," a set of values, a network of care.

If our solitary traveler were an individualist, a great deal of the person's identity would remain intact—the very core of his or her being, the sense of "me," the awareness of his or her personal convictions and values. Individualists give relatively greater priority to personal goals and define their identity mostly in terms of personal attributes. They strive for personal control and individual achievement. In American culture, with its relatively big "I" and small "we," 85 percent of people say it's possible "to pretty much be who you want to be" (Sampson, 2000). Being more self-contained, individualists more easily move in and out of social groups. They feel relatively free to switch churches, leave one job for another, or even to leave their extended families and migrate to a new place. Marriage is often for as long as they both shall love.

Individualism varies from person to person within any culture, of course, and cultures vary in complex ways (Oyserman & others, 2002a,b). Yet cross-cultural psychologists have discovered some variations across cultures, ranging from the individualism of the United States outside the Deep South to the collectivism of rural Asia (Hofstede, 1980; Triandis, 1994; Vandello & Cohen, 1999).

A collectivist, if set adrift in a foreign land, might experience a much greater loss of identity than would an individualist. Cut off from family, groups, and loyal friends, collectivists would lose connections that have defined who they are. In a collectivist culture, group identifications provide a sense of belonging, a set of values, a network of caring individuals, an assurance of security. In return, collectivists give priority to the goals of their groups, often their family, clan, or company, and define their identity accordingly—not as "me" but "we." In Korea, for example, people place less value on expressing a consistent, unique self-concept, and more on tradition and shared practices (Choi & Choi, 2002).

Collectivists may act shy in new groups and are more easily embarrassed than their individualist counterparts (Singelis & others, 1995, 1999). They have deeper, more stable attachments to their familiar groups and families. Compared with students in the United States, for example, students in Japan, China, and India are much less likely to complete the sentence "I am . . ." with personal traits ("I am sincere," "I am confident") and are much more likely to declare their social identities ("I am a Keio University student," "I am the third son in my family") (Cousins, 1989; Dhawan & others, 1995; Triandis, 1989a,b). Relationships are long-term. Loyalties run strong between employer and employees. No wonder, says Harry Triandis (1989b), that modern world colonization was led not by Asians, who were reluctant to cut social and family ties, but by the more individualist Europeans. And no wonder that countries colonized by Europeans willing to leave friends and family are today highly individualistic. People wanting to resettle in a new country express more concern for work and achievement, and less concern for relationships and family, than do those wanting to remain (Boneva & Frieze, 2001).

Like athletes who take more pleasure in their team's victory than in their own performance, collectivists find satisfaction in advancing their groups' interests, even at the expense of personal needs.

Valuing communal solidarity, people in collectivist cultures place a premium on maintaining harmony and making sure others never lose face. What people say reflects both what they feel (their inner attitudes) and what they presume others feel (Kashima & others, 1992). Elders and superiors are given respect. To preserve group spirit, people avoid direct confrontation, blunt honesty, and uncomfortable topics; they defer to others' wishes and display a polite, self-effacing humility (Markus & Kitayama, 1991). Thus, the individualized latté—"decaf, single shot, skinny, extra hot"—that feels so good to a North American in an espresso shop might sound more like a selfish demand in Seoul, note Heejung Kim and Hazel Markus (1999). And Korean ads are also less likely to emphasize personal choice, freedom, and uniqueness, and they more often feature people together (Markus, 2001). In collective cultures, people remember those who have done them favors, and reciprocity becomes a social art. The collectivist self is not independent but *inter*dependent (**Table 12.3**). Among collectivists—especially those influenced by the Confucian idea of self as embedded in "a web of interrelatedness"—no one is an island (Kim & Lee, 1994). Happiness is being attuned to others (Kitayama & Markus, 2000).

Both individualism and collectivism offer benefits and come at a cost. People in competitive, individualistic cultures have more personal freedom, take more pride in personal achievements, are less geographically bound to their families, and enjoy more privacy. Their less-unified cultures offer a smorgasbord of life-styles and invite individuals to construct their own identities. These cultures also celebrate innovation and creativity, and they tend to respect individual human rights. Such may help explain Ed Diener, Marissa Diener, and Carol Diener's (1995) finding that people in individualist cultures report experiencing greater happiness than do those in collectivist cultures. When individualists pursue their own ends and all goes well, life can seem rewarding.

Curiously, though, within individualist cultures, people with the strongest social ties express greatest satisfaction with their lives (Bettencourt & Door, 1997). Moreover, the seeming benefits of individualism can come at the cost of more loneliness, more divorce, more homicide, and more stress-related disease (Popenoe, 1993; Triandis & others, 1988). Individualists demand more romance and personal fulfillment in marriage, which subjects the marriage relationship to more pressure (Dion & Dion, 1993). In one survey, "keeping romance alive" was rated as important to a good marriage by 78 percent of U.S. women but only 29 percent of Japanese women (*American Enterprise*, 1992). In China, love songs often express

> *"One needs to cultivate the spirits of sacrificing the little me to achieve the benefits of the big me."*
>
> *Chinese saying*

> *Individualist proverb: "The squeaky wheel gets the grease."*

> *Collectivist proverb: "The quacking duck gets shot."*

table 12.3 Value Contrasts Between Individualism and Collectivism

Concept	Individualism	Collectivism
Self	Independent (identity from individual traits)	Interdependent (identity from belonging)
Life task	Discover and express one's uniqueness	Maintain connections, fit in
What matters	Me—personal achievement and fulfill-ment; rights and liberties; self-esteem	Us—group goals and solidarity; social responsibilities and relationships
Coping method	Change reality	Accommodate to reality
Morality	Defined by individuals (self-based)	Defined by social networks (duty-based)
Relationships	Many, often temporary or casual; confrontation acceptable	Few, close and enduring; harmony valued
Attributing behavior	Behavior reflects one's personality and attitudes	Behavior reflects social norms and roles

Sources: *Adapted from Thomas Schoeneman (1994) and Harry Triandis (1994).*

enduring commitment and friendship (Rothbaum & Tsang, 1998). As one song put it, "We will be together from now on . . . I will never change from now to forever."

In recent decades, Western individualism has increased, while the priority placed on social obligations and family ties has decreased (Yankelovich, 1993). Martin Seligman (1988) has argued that "rampant individualism carries with it two seeds of its own destruction. First, a society that exalts the individual to the extent ours now does will be ridden with depression. . . . Second, and perhaps most important, is meaninglessness [which occurs when there is no] attachment to something larger than you are."

rehearse it!

21. Psychologist Thomas Gilovich demonstrated the spotlight effect by having students wear Barry Manilow T-shirts into a room where other students were gathered. The spotlight effect is our tendency to
    a. perceive ourselves favorably and perceive others unfavorably.
    b. try out many possible selves, including the famous entertainer self.
    c. become excessively critical when made to feel insecure.
    d. overestimate others' attention to and evaluation of our appearance, performance, and blunders.

22. Researchers have found that high self-esteem is beneficial (people who feel good about themselves have fewer sleepless nights, for example, and are less likely to use drugs). Low self-esteem tends to be linked with life problems. How should this link between low self-esteem and life problems be interpreted?
    a. Life problems cause low self-esteem.
    b. The answer isn't clear because the link is correlational and does not indicate cause and effect.
    c. Low self-esteem leads to life problems.
    d. Because of the self-serving bias, we must assume that external factors cause low self-esteem.

23. Research indicates that people tend to accept responsibility for their successes or good qualities and blame circumstances or luck for their failures. This is an example of
    a. low self-esteem.
    b. self-actualization.
    c. self-serving bias.
    d. empathy.

24. Individualists and collectivists have differing identities. Compared with collectivists, individualists more often define themselves in terms of their
    a. family connections.
    b. nationality.
    c. social roles.
    d. personal achievements.

Answers can be found in Appendix C.

The Modern Unconscious Mind

19. How do contemporary psychologists view the unconscious?

We now know that Freud was right about at least one thing: We indeed have limited access to all that goes on in our minds (Erdelyi, 1985, 1988; Kihlstrom, 1990).

Although experiments point to a vast realm of out-of-sight information, the "iceberg" notion held by today's research psychologists differs from Freud's—so much so, argues Anthony Greenwald (1992), that it is time to abandon Freud's view of the unconscious. As we saw in earlier chapters, many now think of the unconscious not as seething passions and repressive censoring but as cooler information processing that occurs without our awareness. To these researchers, the unconscious involves

- the schemas that automatically control our perceptions and interpretations (Chapter 5).
- the right-hemisphere activity that enables the split-brain patient's left hand to carry out an instruction the patient cannot verbalize (Chapter 2).
- the parallel processing of different aspects of vision and thinking (Chapters 5 and 10).
- the implicit memories that operate without conscious recall, even among those with amnesia (Chapter 9).
- the emotions that activate instantly, before conscious analysis (Chapter 11).
- the self-concept and stereotypes that automatically and unconsciously influence how we process information about ourselves and others (Chapter 15).

More than we realize, we fly on autopilot. This understanding of unconscious information processing is more like the pre-Freudian view of an underground stream of thought from which spontaneous creative ideas surface.

Recent research has also provided some support for Freud's idea of defense mechanisms (even if they don't work exactly as Freud supposed). For example, Roy Baumeister and his colleagues (1998) found that people tend to see their foibles and attitudes in others, a phenomenon that Freud called projection and that today's researchers call the *false consensus effect*, the tendency to overestimate the effect to which others share our beliefs and behaviors. People who cheat on their taxes or break speed limits tend to think many others do likewise. People falsely told they are high in repressed anger or dishonesty tend more to see such in others (Schimel & others, 2003). Supportive evidence is, however, meager for other defenses, such as displacement, that are tied to instinctual energy. More evidence exists for defenses, such as reaction formation, that defend self-esteem. Defense mechanisms, Baumeister concludes, are motivated less by the seething impulses that Freud presumed than by our need to protect our self-image.

"Two passengers leaned against the ship's rail and stared at the sea. 'There sure is a lot of water in the ocean,' said one. 'Yes,' answered his friend, 'we've only seen the top of it.'"

Psychologist George A. Miller (1962)

rehearse it!

25. Sigmund Freud viewed the unconscious as a reservoir of repressed and mostly unacceptable thoughts, wishes, feelings, and memories. Which of the following is *not* part of the contemporary view of the unconscious?

a. Repressed memories of anxiety-provoking events.
b. Schemas that influence our perceptions and interpretations.

c. Parallel processing that occurs without our conscious knowledge.
d. Instantly activated emotions and implicit memories of learned skills.

Answers can be found in Appendix C.

chapter review

Personality

1. What is personality?

Like intelligence, personality is an abstract concept that cannot be seen, touched, or directly measured. To psychologists, personality is one's relatively distinctive and consistent pattern of thinking, feeling, and acting.

HISTORIC PERSPECTIVES ON PERSONALITY

2. What was Freud's view of human personality and its development and dynamics?

Sigmund Freud's treatment of emotional disorders led him to believe that they spring from unconscious dynamics, which he sought to analyze through free associations and dreams. He referred to his theory and techniques as *psychoanalysis*. He saw personality as composed of pleasure-seeking psychic impulses (the id), a reality-oriented executive (the ego), and an internalized set of ideals (the superego).

Freud believed that children develop through psychosexual stages—the oral, anal, phallic, latency, and genital stages. He suggested that our personalities are influenced by how we have resolved conflicts associated with these stages and whether we have remained fixated at any stage.

3. How did Freud think people defended themselves against anxiety?

Tensions between the demands of id and superego cause anxiety. The ego copes by using defense mechanisms, of which, repression is the most basic.

4. What are projective tests, and what do clinicians in the Freudian tradition hope to learn from them?

Projective tests attempt to assess personality by presenting ambiguous stimuli designed to reveal the unconscious. Although projective tests, such as the Rorschach inkblots, have questionable reliability and validity, many clinicians continue to use them.

5. Which of Freud's ideas did his followers accept or reject? How do Freud's ideas hold up today?

Neo-Freudians Alfred Adler and Karen Horney accepted many of Freud's ideas, as did Carl Jung. But they also argued that we have motives other than sex and aggression, and that the ego's conscious control is greater than Freud supposed.

Today's research psychologists find some of Freud's specific ideas implausible, unvalidated, or contradicted by new research, and they note that his theory offers only after-the-fact explanations. Many researchers believe that repression rarely, if ever, occurs. Nevertheless, Freud drew psychology's attention to the unconscious, to the struggle to cope with anxiety and sexuality, and to the conflict between biological impulses and social restraints. His cultural impact has been enormous.

6. What did humanistic psychologists view as the central feature of personality, and what was their goal in studying personality?

Humanistic psychologists sought to turn psychology's attention away from basic motives and environmental conditioning and toward the growth potential of healthy people, as seen through the individual's own experiences and self-concept. Abraham Maslow believed that if basic human needs are fulfilled, people will strive to actualize their highest potential. To describe self-actualization, he studied some exemplary personalities and summarized his impressions of their qualities. To nurture growth in others, Carl Rogers advised being genuine, accepting, and empathic. In such a climate, he believed, people can develop a deeper self-awareness and a more realistic and positive self-concept.

7. How did humanistic psychologists assess a person's sense of self?

Humanistic psychologists assessed personality through questionnaires on which people reported their self-concept and in therapy by seeking to understand others' subjective personal experiences.

8. How has the humanistic perspective on personality influenced psychology? What criticisms have been leveled against this perspective?

Humanistic psychology helped to renew psychology's interest in the concept of self. Nevertheless, humanistic psychology's critics complained that its concepts were vague and subjective, its values individualist and self-centered, and its assumptions naively optimistic.

CONTEMPORARY RESEARCH ON PERSONALITY

9. How do psychologists use traits to describe personality?

Rather than explain the hidden aspects of personality, trait theorists describe the predispositions that underlie our actions. For example, through factor analysis, researchers have isolated important dimensions of personality. Genetic predispositions influence many traits.

10. What are personality inventories, and what are their strengths and weaknesses as trait-assessment tools?

Personality inventories (like the MMPI) are questionnaires on which people respond to items designed to gauge a wide range of feelings and behaviors. Items on the test are empirically derived, and the tests are objectively scored. But people can fake their answers to create a good impression, and the ease of computerized testing may lead to misuse of these tests.

11. Which traits seem to provide the most useful information about personality variation?

Five personality dimensions—stability, extraversion, openness, agreeableness, and conscientiousness—offer a reasonably comprehensive picture of personality.

12. Does research support the consistency of personality traits over time and across situations?

Critics of trait theory question the consistency with which traits are expressed. Although people's traits persist over time, human behavior varies widely from situation to situation. Despite these variations, a person's *average* behavior across different situations tends to be fairly consistent. Traits matter.

13. In the view of social-cognitive psychologists, what mutual influences shape an individual's personality?

The social-cognitive perspective applies principles of learning, cognition, and social behavior to personality, with particular emphasis on the ways in which our personality influences and is influenced by our interaction with the environment. It assumes reciprocal determinism—that personal-cognitive factors interact with the environment to influence people's behavior.

14. What are the causes and consequences of personal control?

By studying how people vary in their perceived locus of control and in their experiences of learned helplessness, researchers have found that a sense of personal control helps people to cope with life. Research on learned helplessness has evolved into research on optimism and now into a broader positive psychology movement.

15. What underlying principle guides social-cognitive psychologists in their assessment of people's behavior and beliefs?

Social-cognitive researchers study how people's behaviors and beliefs both affect and are affected by their situations. The underlying principle for much of this work is that the best way to predict someone's behavior in a given situation is to observe that person's behavior in similar situations.

16. What has the social-cognitive perspective contributed to the study of personality, and what criticisms have been leveled against it?

Though faulted for underemphasizing the importance of unconscious dynamics, emotions, and inner traits, the social-cognitive perspective builds on psychology's well-established concepts of learning and cognition and reminds us of the power of social situations.

17. Are we helped or hindered by high self-esteem?

Research confirms the importance of high self-esteem. But it also warns of the dangers of unrealistically high self-esteem. The self-serving bias, for example, leads us to perceive ourselves favorably, often causing us to overestimate our abilities and underestimate our faults.

18. How does the view of self differ in individualist and collectivist cultures?

Individuals and cultures vary in giving priority to "me" or "we"—to personal control and individual achievement or to social connections and solidarity. Self-reliant *individualism* defines identity in terms of personal goals and attributes; socially connected *collectivism* gives priority to group goals and to one's social identity and commitments.

19. How do contemporary psychologists view the unconscious?

Freud's view of the unconscious—a reservoir of repressed and mostly unacceptable thoughts, wishes, feelings, and memories—has not survived empirical scrutiny. But current information-processing research confirms that our access to all that goes on in our mind is very limited. The current view of the unconscious is that it consists of schemas that control our perceptions; parallel processing (as in vision) that occurs without our conscious knowledge; implicit memories of learned skills; instantly activated emotions; and self-concepts and stereotypes that filter information about ourselves and others.

Psychology's false consensus effect (the tendency to overestimate the effect to which others share our beliefs and behaviors) bears a resemblance to Freud's projection defense mechanism. Reaction formation also seems to happen. But current theorists believe that the motivation triggering defense mechanisms is a need to protect our self-image, not a well of instinctual energy or impulses.

A CRITICAL THINKER'S REVIEW OF CHAPTER 12

You've now studied and reviewed **Personality**. For even better retention, reflect on these concepts at a deeper level. If you need to refresh your memory of the six categories of critical thinking shown in parentheses below, see page 34. See if you can answer each of these questions in a short paragraph.

1. While your roommate is out, you take the opportunity to line up her shoes and boots, because it has been bothering you to have them scattered all over the floor. Upon her return, she notices and comments, "Oh, you are so anal retentive!" Who is responsible for this term, and how did it become a part of our everyday language? (creative problem solving)

2. After feeling a lot of stress, Genevieve consulted a therapist, Dr. Weaver, who told her, "You are a wonderful person. You should be true to your own needs above all else." Genevieve, worried that Dr. Weaver was simply flattering her, decided to try another therapist. When Genevieve told her second therapist, Dr. Carter, about this incident, he said, "That kind of blind support can lead to selfishness and problems in coping with stress. I believe in a more behavioral approach to helping." Dr. Weaver incorporates methods from which perspective? How might she reply to Dr. Carter's critique? (perspective taking)

3. Your friend Franklin claims he knows all his instructors so well that he could predict how any of them would behave in any number of situations. However, when the two of you are out one night, Franklin is shocked to find his reticent physics teacher out on the dance floor having a wild and crazy time. What personality controversy does this story illustrate? Explain. (practical problem solving)

4. Research suggests that optimism is a powerfully positive trait—helping us to feel better both psychologically and physically. However, most research in this area is *correlational*. How should this affect how we interpret this finding? (scientific problem solving)

5. English essayist William Hazlitt said, "Life is the art of being well-deceived." What psychological principles might this comment illustrate? (pattern recognition)

6. Participants in an experiment were told that they were high in either repressed anger or dishonesty, and they then tended to see more of those qualities in *others*. What psychological concept helps us to understand this reaction? (psychological reasoning)

TERMS AND CONCEPTS TO REMEMBER

personality, p. 429

free association, p. 430

psychoanalysis, p. 430

unconscious, p. 430

id, p. 431

ego, p. 431

superego, p. 431

psychosexual stages, p. 432

Oedipus [ED-uh-puss] complex, p. 432

identification, p. 432

fixation, p. 432

defense mechanisms, p. 433

repression, p. 433

regression, p. 433

reaction formation, p. 433

projection, p. 434

rationalization, p. 434

displacement, p. 434

projective test, p. 434

Rorschach inkblot test, p. 434

collective unconscious, p. 436

self-actualization, p. 439

unconditional positive regard, p. 440

self-concept, p. 440

trait, p. 443

personality inventory, p. 444

Minnesota Multiphasic Personality Inventory (MMPI), p. 444

empirically derived test, p. 445

social-cognitive perspective, p. 450

reciprocal determinism, p. 451

personal control, p. 452

external locus of control, p. 452

internal locus of control, p. 452

learned helplessness, p. 452

positive psychology, p. 454

spotlight effect, p. 457

self-esteem, p. 457

self-serving bias, p. 458

individualism, p. 460

collectivism, p. 460

To continue your study and review of Personality visit this book's Web site at www.worthpublishers.com/myers. You will find practice tests, review activities, and Web links for more information on topics related to Personality.

chapter13

Psychological Disorders

I felt the need to clean my room at home in Indianapolis every Sunday and would spend four to five hours at it. I would take every book out of the bookcase, dust and put it back. At the time I loved doing it. Then I didn't want to do it anymore, but I couldn't stop. The clothes in my closet hung exactly two fingers apart. . . . I made a ritual of touching the wall in my bedroom before I went out because something bad would happen if I didn't do it the right way. I had a constant anxiety about it as a kid, and it made me think for the first time that I might be nuts.

Marc, diagnosed with obsessive-compulsive disorder (from Summers, 1996)

Whenever I get depressed it's because I've lost a sense of self. I can't find reasons to like myself. I think I'm ugly. I think no one likes me. . . . I become grumpy and short-tempered. Nobody wants to be around me. I'm left alone. Being alone confirms that I am ugly and not worth being with. I think I'm responsible for everything that goes wrong.

Greta, diagnosed with depression (from Thorne, 1993, p. 21)

Voices, like the roar of a crowd, came. I felt like Jesus; I was being crucified. It was dark. I just continued to huddle under the blanket, feeling weak, laid bare and defenseless in a cruel world I could no longer understand.

Stuart, diagnosed with schizophrenia (from Emmons & others, 1997)

People are fascinated by the exceptional, the unusual, the abnormal. "The sun shines and warms and lights us and we have no curiosity to know why this is so," observed Ralph Waldo Emerson, "but we ask the reason of all evil, of pain, and hunger, and [unusual] people." But why such fascination with disturbed people? Do we see in them something of ourselves? At various moments, all of us feel, think, or act the way disturbed people do much of the time. We, too, get anxious, depressed, withdrawn, suspicious, deluded, or antisocial, just less intensely and more briefly. It's no wonder then that studying psychological disorders may at times evoke an eerie sense of self-recognition, one that illuminates the dynamics of our own personality. "To study the abnormal is the best way of understanding the normal," proposed William James (1842–1910).

Another reason for our curiosity is that so many of us have felt, either personally or through friends or family members, the bewilderment and pain of a psychological disorder, which can bring unexplained physical symptoms, irrational fears, or even the feeling that life is not worth living.

No known culture is free of the two terrible maladies this chapter examines in depth—depression and schizophrenia (Castillo, 1997; Draguns, 1990a,b, 1997). Some 450 million people worldwide suffer psychological disorders, according to the World Health Organization (WHO, 2001). The WHO also reports that, worldwide, mental disorders have accounted for 15.4 percent of the years of life lost due to death or disability—scoring slightly below cardiovascular conditions and slightly above cancer (Murray & Lopez, 1996). As members of the human family, few of us go through life unacquainted with the reality of psychological disturbance.

"We are all mad at some time or another."
Battista Mantuanus, Eclogues, 1500

Tony Ray Jones/Magnum Photos

A benign obsession British street cleaner Snowy Farr's eccentric behavior may indeed be atypical, but clinicians would not label it disordered because it is neither particularly disturbing nor maladaptive.

"Who in the rainbow can draw the line where the violet tint ends and the orange tint begins? Distinctly we see the difference of the colors, but where exactly does the one first blendingly enter into the other? So with sanity and insanity?"

Herman Melville, Billy Budd, Sailor, 1924

"If a man is in a minority of one, we lock him up."

Oliver Wendell Holmes, 1841–1935

PERSPECTIVES ON PSYCHOLOGICAL DISORDERS

1. Where should we draw the line between normality and disorder?

Most people would agree that someone who is too depressed to get out of bed for weeks at a time has a psychological disorder. But what about those who, having experienced a loss, are unable to resume their usual social activities? Where should we draw the line between sadness and depression? Between zany creativity and bizarre irrationality? Between normality and abnormality? How should we *define* psychological disorders? Equally important, how should we *understand* disorders—as sicknesses that need to be diagnosed and cured, or as natural responses to a troubling environment? How should we *classify* psychological disorders? Can we do so in a way that allows us to help disturbed people without stigmatizing them with labels?

Defining Psychological Disorders

Many mental health workers view **psychological disorders** as *harmful dysfunctions* (Spitzer, 1997; Wakefield, 1997). They label behavior as harmful and dysfunctional when they judge it to be *atypical, disturbing, maladaptive,* and *unjustifiable.*

The emotions and perceptions of Marc, Greta, and Stuart are indeed "*abnormal*" (atypical). Being different from most other people in one's culture is *part* of what it takes to define a psychological disorder.

But there is more to a disorder than being atypical. Olympic gold medalists are abnormal in their physical abilities, and they are heroes. To be considered disordered, an atypical behavior must also be one that other people find *disturbing*.

Standards of acceptability for behaviors vary from place to place. In some cultures, people routinely behave in ways (such as going about naked) that in other cultures would be grounds for arrest. In at least one cultural context—wartime—even mass killing may be viewed as heroic.

Standards of acceptability also vary over time. On December 9, 1973, homosexuality was an illness. By day's end on December 10, it was not. The American Psychiatric Association had dropped homosexuality as a disorder (because more and more of its members no longer equated being gay with having psychological problems). Later it *added* nicotine dependence (because it deemed smoking both addictive and self-destructive).

Atypical and disturbing behaviors are more likely to be considered disordered when judged harmful. Indeed, many clinicians define disorders as behaviors that are *maladaptive*—as when a smoker's nicotine dependence causes physical damage. By this yardstick, even typical behaviors, such as the occasional despondency that many college students feel, may signal a psychological disorder—if they become disabling.

Finally, abnormal behavior is most likely to be considered disordered when others find it rationally *unjustifiable*. Stuart claimed to hear voices and people presumed he was deranged. But actress Shirley MacLaine could wear a crystal on her neck and say, "See the outer bubble of white light watching you. It is part of you," and not be seen as disordered because enough people found her rational (Friedrich, 1987).

Understanding Psychological Disorders

2. What theoretical models or perspectives can help us understand psychological disorders?

To explain puzzling behavior, people in earlier times often presumed that strange forces—the movements of the stars, godlike powers, or evil spirits—were at work. "The devil made him do it," you might have said had you lived during the Middle Ages. The cure might have been to get rid of the evil force—by placating the great powers or exorcising the demon. Until the last two centuries, "mad" people were sometimes caged in zoolike conditions or given "therapies" appropriate to a demon: beatings, burning, or castration. In other times, therapy might have included pulling teeth, removing lengths of intestines, cauterizing the clitoris, or receiving transfusions of animal blood (Farina, 1982).

The Medical Perspective

In opposition to such brutal treatment, reformers such as Philippe Pinel (1745–1826) in France insisted madness was not demon possession but a sickness of the mind caused by severe stresses and inhumane conditions. For Pinel and other reformers, "moral treatment" included boosting patients' morale by unchaining them, talking with them, and replacing brutality with gentleness, isolation with activity, and filth with clean air and sun.

When physicians later discovered that syphilis infects the brain and distorts the mind, health reformers and medical workers refocused on physical causes for disorders and treatments that would cure them. Today, the medical perspective is familiar and recognizable to us in the terminology of the mental *health* movement: A mental *illness* (also called a psycho*pathology*) needs to be *diagnosed* on the basis of its *symptoms* and *cured* through *therapy*, which may include *treatment* in a psychiatric *hospital*. In the 1800s, the assumption of this **medical model**—that psychological disorders are sicknesses—provided the impetus for further reform as hospitals replaced asylums.

The medical perspective has gained credibility from recent discoveries. As we will see, genetically influenced abnormalities in brain structure and biochemistry contribute to a number of disorders (Andreasen, 2001). "Mental illnesses are diagnosable disorders of the brain," declares a White House fact sheet on mental illness (1999). Two of the most troubling, depression and schizophrenia, are often treated medically. As we will also see, psychological factors, such as traumatic stress, also play an important role.

The Bio-Psycho-Social Perspective

Today's psychologists contend that *all* behavior, whether called normal or disordered, arises from the interaction of nature (genetic and physiological factors) and nurture (past and present experiences). To presume that a person is "mentally ill" attributes the condition solely to an internal problem—to a "sickness" that must be found and cured. Maybe there *is* no deep, internal problem. Maybe instead there is a growth-blocking difficulty in the person's environment, in the person's current interpretations of events, or in the person's bad habits and poor social skills.

Evidence of environmental effects comes from links between disorder and culture. As noted earlier, some major disorders, such as depression and schizophrenia, occur worldwide. From Asia to Africa and across the Americas, the core symptoms of schizophrenia include irrationality and incoherent speech (Brislin, 1993; Draguns, 1990b). But other disorders are culture-bound (Beardsley, 1994; Castillo, 1997). Different cultures have different sources of stress, and they produce different ways of coping. Anorexia nervosa and bulimia, for example, are disorders that occur mostly in Western cultures. *Susto*, marked by severe anxiety, restlessness, and a fear of black magic, is found in Latin America. *Taijin-kyofusho*, which combines social anxiety about one's appearance with a readiness to blush and a fear of eye contact, appears in Japan. Such disorders may share an underlying dynamic (such as anxiety) while differing in the symptoms (an eating problem or a type of fear) manifested in a particular culture.

Today, most mental health workers assume that disorders are influenced by genetic predispositions and physiological states. And by inner psychological dynamics. And by social and cultural circumstances. To get the whole picture, we

▶ **psychological disorder** a "harmful dysfunction" in which behavior is judged to be atypical, disturbing, maladaptive, and unjustifiable.

▶ **medical model** the concept that diseases have physical causes that can be diagnosed, treated, and, in most cases, cured. When applied to psychological disorders, the medical model assumes that these "mental" illnesses can be diagnosed on the basis of their symptoms and cured through therapy, which may include treatment in a psychiatric hospital.

"It's no measure of health to be well adjusted to a profoundly sick society."

Krishnamurti, 1895–1986

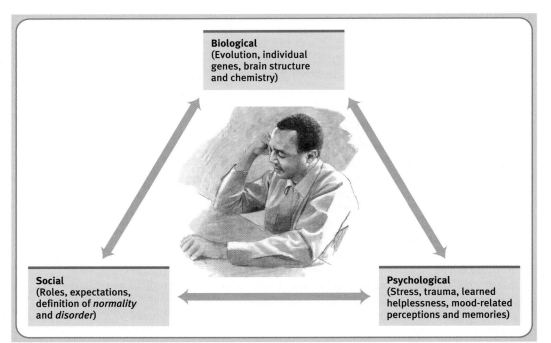

figure 13.1
The bio-psycho-social perspective
Today's psychology studies how biological, psychological, and social factors interact to produce specific psychological disorders.

need an interdisciplinary **bio-psycho-social perspective** (**Figure 13.1**). The bio-psycho-social perspective recognizes that mind and body are inseparable. Thus stress and negative emotions contribute to physical illness, and physical abnormalities contribute experiences of pain or malaise. We are mind embodied.

Classifying Psychological Disorders

3. How and why do clinicians classify psychological disorders?

In biology and the other sciences, classification creates order. To classify an animal as a mammal says a great deal—that it is warm-blooded, has hair or fur, and nourishes its young with milk. In psychiatry and psychology, too, classification orders and describes symptoms. To classify a person's disorder as "schizophrenia" suggests that the person talks incoherently, hallucinates or has delusions (bizarre beliefs), shows either little emotion or inappropriate emotion, or is socially withdrawn. Thus, "schizophrenia" provides a handy shorthand for describing a complex disorder.

In psychiatry and psychology, diagnostic classification aims not only to describe a disorder, but also to predict its future course, imply appropriate treatment, and stimulate research into its causes. Indeed, to study a disorder we must first name and describe it. The current authoritative scheme for classifying psychological disorders is the American Psychiatric Association's *Diagnostic and Statistical Manual of Mental Disorders* (Fourth Edition), nicknamed **DSM-IV**. This 1994 volume, now updated as a 2000 "text revision" (DSM-IV-TR), will be more substantially revised as DSM-V, to appear about 2010. (A book of case illustrations accompanying DSM-IV provides the basis for much of this chapter.) DSM-IV was developed in coordination with the tenth edition of the World Health Organization's *International Classification of Diseases* (ICD-10).

The very idea of "diagnosing" people's problems in terms of their "symptoms" presumes a mental "illness." As a result, some practitioners are not enthralled with this medical terminology, but most find DSM-IV a helpful and practical tool. It is also financially necessary: Most North American health insurance companies require a DSM-IV diagnosis.

To be helpful and useful, DSM-IV categories must be reliable. If one psychiatrist or psychologist diagnoses someone as having, say, "catatonic schizophrenia," what are the chances that another mental health worker will independently give the same diagnosis? With the DSM-IV's diagnostic guidelines, the chances are good.

"I'm always like this, and my family was wondering if you could prescribe a mild depressant."

CLOSE-UP

The "unDSM"—A Diagnostic Manual of Human Strengths

One facet of the fast-expanding positive psychology movement (see page 454) is an effort, led by psychologists Christopher Peterson and Martin Seligman (2004), to create a classification system for human strengths and virtues. A manual that orders and defines harmful dysfunctions has been helpful, these researchers note. Why not also have a companion manual that similarly orders and defines human strengths—thinking-feeling-action tendencies that contribute to the *good* life, for self and others?

Like the DSM-IV, *The Values in Action Classification of Strengths* (nicknamed "VIA") draws insights from many researchers in proposing a common vocabulary that lends itself to cross-cultural under-

standing and to the budding science of strengths. Like the DSM, the VIA manual will offer assessment strategies, and also questionnaires, that help researchers assess six clusters of 24 strengths:

Wisdom and Knowledge
- curiosity
- love of learning
- critical judgment and openmindedness
- creativity
- perspective (wisdom)

Courage (overcoming opposition)
- bravery/valor
- industry and perseverance
- integrity and honesty
- vitality (zest and enthusiasm)

Love
- kindness
- intimate attachment
- social intelligence

Justice
- citizenship and teamwork
- fairness and equity
- leadership

Temperance
- humility
- self-control
- prudence and caution
- forgiveness and mercy

Transcendence
- appreciation of beauty, awe/wonder
- gratitude
- hope and optimism
- playfulness and humor
- spirituality and purpose

Following these guidelines, clinicians answer a series of objective questions about observable behaviors, such as, "Is the person afraid to leave home?" In one study, 16 psychologists used this structured-interview procedure to diagnose 75 psychiatric patients as suffering from (1) depression, (2) generalized anxiety, or (3) some other disorder (Riskind & others, 1987). Without knowing the first psychologist's diagnosis, another psychologist viewed a videotape of each interview and offered a second opinion. For 83 percent of the patients, the two opinions agreed.

Some critics fault the manual for casting too wide a net and bringing "almost any kind of behavior within the compass of psychiatry" (Eysenck & others, 1983). These critics point to behaviors ranging from irrational fear of humiliation and embarrassment (social phobia) to persistently breaking rules at home or school (conduct disorder). As the number of disorder categories has swelled, from 60 in the 1950s' DSM to 400 in today's, so has the number of adults who meet the criteria for at least one psychiatric ailment—nearly 30 percent in one recent year, according to one national survey (Regier & others, 1998).

Labeling Psychological Disorders

4. Why do some psychologists criticize the use of diagnostic labels?

The DSM has other critics who register a more fundamental complaint—that these labels are at best arbitrary and at worst value judgments masquerading as science. Once we label a person, we view that person differently (Farina, 1982). Labels create preconceptions that guide our perceptions and our interpretations. It is better, some clinicians say, to study the roots of specific symptoms, such as distorted thoughts or perceptions, than to study catchall categories, such as schizophrenia (Persons, 1986).

▶ **bio-psycho-social perspective** a contemporary perspective which assumes that biological, psychological, and sociocultural factors combine and interact to produce psychological disorders.

▶ **DSM-IV** the American Psychiatric Association's *Diagnostic and Statistical Manual of Mental Disorders* (Fourth Edition), a widely used system for classifying psychological disorders. Presently distributed in an updated "text revision" (DSM-IV-TR).

Thinking Critically About:

Insanity and Responsibility

My brain . . . my genes . . . my bad upbringing made me do it. Such defenses were anticipated by Shakespeare's *Hamlet*. If I wrong someone when not myself, he explained, "then Hamlet does it not, Hamlet denies it. Who does it then? His madness." Such is the essence of a legal insanity defense, created in 1843 after a deluded Scotsman tried to shoot the prime minister (who he thought was persecuting him) but killed an assistant by mistake. Like President Reagan's near assassin, John Hinckley, the Scotsman, Daniel M'Naughten, was sent to a mental hospital rather than to prison.

In both cases, the public was outraged. "Hinckley Insane, Public Mad," declared one headline. And they were mad again when a deranged Jeffrey Dahmer in 1991 admitted murdering 15 young men and eating parts of their bodies. They were mad in 1998 when 15-year-old Kip Kinkel, driven by "those voices in my head," killed his parents and 2 fellow Springfield, Oregon, students and wounded 25 others. And they were mad in 2002 when Andrea Yates, after being taken off her anti-psychotic medication, was tried in Texas for drowning her five children. The public was mad enough that all of these people were sent to jails, not hospitals, following their arrests.

These cases are not uncommon. A 1999 U.S. Justice Department study found that 283,000 jail and prison inmates had severe mental disorders. This is about 16 percent of the U.S. inmate population and considerably more than the 209,000 psychiatric inpatients in all types of hospitals (Bureau of the Census, 2002; Butterfield, 1999). Many people who have been executed or are on death row have been limited by mental retardation or motivated by delusional voices. Larry Robison (1999) was twice hospitalized for paranoid schizophrenia, as were his brother, sister, uncle, and grandfa-

Elaine Thompson/AP Photo

Jail or hospital? Theodore Kaczynski lived in a shack for some 20 years, rarely bathed, sent bombs to strangers (killing 3 and injuring 23 more), and was diagnosed by his state-appointed psychiatrist with paranoid schizophrenia. Should Kaczynski be jailed as a criminal or hospitalized as mentally ill?

ther. When denied further treatment after insurance coverage ran out, Robison was discharged and killed five people. On January 21, 2000, he was executed by the state of Texas.

Questions to consider: Who should we hold responsible for such crimes? The people who commit them, or the "madness" that clouds their vision? Should we treat or should we punish executives who sexually harass their employees and then plead guilty to alcoholism or "sex addiction" (not to being jerks)? Should we fire the nasty co-worker who behaves with "disregard for, and violation of, the rights of others" (the definition of antisocial personality disorder) or protect him because he suffers from a disability?

Many sick crimes are the products of sick minds—and the malfunctioning brains and abusive nurturing that often produced them. But if the heinousness of a crime becomes synonymous with mental incompetence, does this create a social basis for evading responsibility (like the person who, having just killed his parents, then demands mercy because he is an orphan)? If some superpsychologist were to understand the biological and environmental basis for everything—for generosity and for vandalism—society would probably still wish to hold people responsible for both.

In the most controversial demonstration of the biasing power of diagnostic labels, David Rosenhan (1973) and seven others went to mental hospital admissions offices, complaining of "hearing voices" that were saying "empty," "hollow," and "thud." Apart from this complaint and giving false names and occupations, they answered all questions truthfully. All eight were diagnosed as mentally ill.

That these normal people were misdiagnosed is unsurprising. As one psychiatrist noted, if someone swallowed blood, went to an emergency room, and spat it up, would we fault the doctor for diagnosing a bleeding ulcer? What followed the diagnosis *was* startling. Until being released (an average of 19 days later), the "patients" exhibited no further symptoms. Yet the clinicians were able to "discover" the causes of their disorders after analyzing their (quite normal) life histories. They said one person was reacting to mixed emotions about his parents. Even the normal behaviors of the "patients," such as taking notes, were often misinterpreted as symptoms.

Other studies also confirm that labels affect how we perceive people. Ellen Langer and her colleagues (1974, 1980) had people rate an interviewee they thought was either normal (a job applicant) or out of the ordinary (a psychiatric or cancer patient). All raters saw the identical videotape. Those who watched unlabeled interviewees perceived them as normal; those who watched supposed patients perceived them as "different from most people." Therapists (who thought they were evaluating a psychiatric patient) perceived the interviewee as "frightened of his own aggressive impulses," a "passive, dependent type," and so forth. A label can serve a useful purpose. But as Rosenhan discovered, it can also have "a life and an influence of its own."

Tipper Gore "I had clinical depression, recognized it, and went to a social worker. I got diagnosed and then successfully treated. I hope that will encourage people to seek treatment if they think they are suffering from depression."

The stigmatizing power of labels was illustrated when a female associate of psychologist Stewart Page (1977) called 180 people in Toronto who were advertising furnished rooms for rent. When she merely asked if the room was still available, the answer was nearly always yes. When she instead said she was about to be released from a mental hospital, the answer three times out of four was no (as it was when she said she was calling for her brother who was about to be released from jail). Some who answered no were later called by a second person who simply asked if the room was still available. Nearly always it was. Surveys in Western Europe have uncovered similar attitudes toward those labeled mentally ill. But as we better understand many psychological disorders as diseases of the brain, not failures of character, the stigma seems to be lifting (Solomon, 1996). Public figures are feeling freer to "come out" and speak with candor about their struggles with disorders such as depression. And the more often people have contact with mental health patients, the more accepting their attitudes are (Kolodziej & Johnson, 1996).

"One of the unpardonable sins, in the eyes of most people, is for a man to go about unlabeled. The world regards such a person as the police do an unmuzzled dog, not under proper control."

T. H. Huxley, Evolution and Ethics, 1893

Given media images of psychological disorders, it is hardly surprising that stereotypes linger. Movies, for example, sometimes offer reasonably accurate and sympathetic portrayals of disorder, as in the portrayal of mathematician John Nash's schizophrenia in *A Beautiful Mind*. But movies often stereotype mental health patients as homicidal (Hannibal Lecter in *Silence of the Lambs*) or as freaks (Woody Allen as *Zelig*) (Hyler & others, 1991; Wahl, 1992). People with schizophrenia are more likely than others to commit violent crime, especially if they also abuse alcohol (Citrome & Volavka, 1999; Tiihonen & others, 1997). However, at least 9 in 10 people with disorders are *not* dangerous; instead, they are anxious, depressed, or withdrawn. And *if* they steer clear of alcohol and drugs, those released from mental hospitals are no more prone to violence than are their neighbors (Steadman & others, 1998). Indeed, reports the U.S. Surgeon General's Office (1999, p. 7), "There is very little risk of violence or harm to a stranger from casual contact with an individual who has a mental disorder."

Labels not only can bias perceptions, they can also change reality. When teachers are told certain students are "gifted," when students expect someone to be "hostile," or when interviewers check to see whether someone is "extraverted," they may act in ways that elicit the very behavior expected (Snyder, 1984). Someone who was led to think you are nasty may treat you coldly, leading you to respond as a mean-spirited person would. Labels can serve as self-fulfilling prophecies.

But let us also remember the benefits of diagnostic labels. Mental health professionals use labels to communicate about their cases, to comprehend the underlying causes, and to control the outcomes.

r e h e a r s e   i t !

1. Although some psychological disorders are culture-bound, others are universal. For example, in every known culture there are people who suffer from
   a. bulimia nervosa.
   b. anorexia nervosa.
   c. schizophrenia.
   d. susto.

2. To be labeled "disordered," a behavior must usually be atypical, disturbing, unjustifiable, and maladaptive. For example, we all wash our hands; physicians may well wash their hands 100 times a day. But if a person washes his hands 100 times a day for no apparent reason and is unable to do much else, the behavior will be labeled disordered because it is, among other things,
   a. unjustifiable and maladaptive.
   b. not explained by the medical model.
   c. harmful to others.
   d. untreatable.

3. In the past, people considered to be mad or insane were beaten, punished, or caged. A more modern approach is to equate psychological disorders with sickness and to refer the "mentally ill" to hospitals, where they can be treated as patients. This more modern approach is called the
   a. social-cultural perspective.
   b. psychological model.
   c. medical model.
   d. diagnostic model.

4. Many psychologists adhere to the idea that psychological disorders are sicknesses arising from an internal problem. Others contend that other factors may be involved—for example, a growth-blocking difficulty in the person's environment or the person's bad habits and poor social skills. Psychologists who take the second approach to psycholog-

ical disorders are said to be advocates of the _____ perspective.
   a. medical
   b. biomedical
   c. bio-psycho-social
   d. social-cultural

5. The American Psychiatric Association's system of classifying psychological disorders is found in the *Diagnostic and Statistical Manual of Mental Disorders (Fourth Edition)*, or DSM-IV. One study found that psychologists using DSM-IV agreed on a diagnosis for more than 80 percent of patients. The DSM-IV's reliability stems in part from its reliance on
   a. structured-interview procedure.
   b. in-depth histories of the patients.
   c. input from patients' family and friends.
   d. the theories of Pinel, Freud, and others.

Answers can be found in Appendix C.

▶ **anxiety disorders** psychological disorders characterized by distressing, persistent anxiety or maladaptive behaviors that reduce anxiety.

▶ **generalized anxiety disorder** an anxiety disorder in which a person is continually tense, apprehensive, and in a state of autonomic nervous system arousal.

▶ **panic disorder** an anxiety disorder marked by a minutes-long episode of intense dread in which a person experiences terror and accompanying chest pain, choking, or other frightening sensations.

▶ **phobia** an anxiety disorder marked by a persistent, irrational fear and avoidance of a specific object or situation.

ANXIETY DISORDERS

5. What are anxiety disorders, and how do they differ from the ordinary worries and fears we all experience?

Anxiety is part of life. Speaking in front of a class, peering down from a ledge, or waiting to play in a big game, any one of us might feel anxious. At one time or another, most of us feel enough anxiety that we fail to make eye contact or we avoid talking to someone—"shyness," we call it. Fortunately for most of us, our uneasiness is not intense and persistent. If it becomes so, we may have one of the **anxiety disorders**, marked by distressing, persistent anxiety or maladaptive behaviors that reduce anxiety. In this section we focus on four of these disorders:

- *Generalized anxiety disorder*, in which a person is unexplainably and continually tense and uneasy
- *Panic disorder*, in which a person experiences sudden episodes of intense dread
- *Phobias*, in which a person feels irrationally afraid of a specific object or situation
- *Obsessive-compulsive disorder*, in which a person is troubled by repetitive thoughts or actions

Taken together, these are the most common mental disorders.

Generalized Anxiety Disorder and Panic Disorder

Tom, a 27-year-old electrician, complains of dizziness, sweating palms, heart palpitations, and ringing in his ears. He feels edgy and sometimes finds himself shaking. With reasonable success he hides his symptoms from his family and co-workers. Nevertheless, he has had few social contacts since the symptoms began two years ago. He occasionally has to leave work. His family doctor and a neurologist can find no physical problem.

Tom's unfocused, out-of-control, negative feelings suggest **generalized anxiety disorder**. The symptoms of this disorder are commonplace; their persistence is not. Sufferers, two-thirds of whom are women, are continually tense and jittery, worried about bad things that might happen, and plagued by muscular tension, agitation, and sleeplessness. The tension and apprehension may leak out through furrowed

Gender and anxiety: Eight months after 9/11, more U.S. women (34 percent) than men (19 percent) told Gallup (2002) they were still less willing than before 9/11 to go into skyscrapers or fly on planes. In early 2003, more women (57 percent) than men (36 percent) were "somewhat worried" about becoming a terrorist victim (Jones, 2003).

brows, twitching eyelids, trembling, perspiration, or fidgeting. Concentration is difficult, as attention switches from worry to worry. One of the worst characteristics of generalized anxiety disorder is that the person cannot identify, and therefore cannot deal with or avoid, its cause. To use Freud's term, the anxiety is "free-floating."

Panic disorder is to anxiety what a tornado is to a windy day. It strikes suddenly, wreaks havoc, and disappears. For the 1 person in 75 who suffers the disorder, anxiety suddenly escalates into a terrifying *panic attack*—a minutes-long episode of intense fear that something horrible is about to happen. Heart palpitations, shortness of breath, choking sensations, trembling, or dizziness typically accompany the panic, which may be misperceived as a heart attack. The false alarm experience is unpredictable and so frightening that after several attacks, the sufferers develop a *panic disorder*. They come to fear the fear itself and to avoid situations where the panic has struck before. Smokers have a two- to fourfold risk of a first-time panic attack (Breslau & Klein, 1999; Goodwin & Hamilton, 2002).

One woman recalled suddenly feeling "hot and as though I couldn't breathe. My heart was racing and I started to sweat and tremble and I was sure I was going to faint. Then my fingers started to feel numb and tingly and things seemed unreal. It was so bad I wondered if I was dying and asked my husband to take me to the emergency room. By the time we got there (about 10 minutes) the worst of the attack was over and I just felt washed out" (Greist & others, 1986).

Agoraphobia is fear or avoidance of situations in which escape might be difficult or help unavailable when panic strikes. Given such fear, people may avoid being outside the home, being in a crowd, being on a bus or even on an elevator. After spending five years sailing the world, Charles Darwin began suffering panic disorder at age 28. Because of the attacks, he moved to the country, avoided social gatherings, and traveled only in his wife's company. But the relative seclusion did free him to focus on developing his evolutionary theory. "Even ill health," he reflected, "has saved me from the distraction of society and its amusements" (quoted in Ma, 1997).

Lighting up doesn't lighten up Daily smokers are two to four times more likely than others to have a first-time panic attack. Their risk may be higher because nicotine is a stimulant.

Phobias

Phobias *focus* anxiety on a specific object, activity, or situation. (See **Figure 13.2** for one ranking of some common and less common fears.) Phobias are irrational fears that disrupt behavior. They are a common psychological disorder many people accept and live with. Some *specific phobias*, however, are incapacitating. Marilyn, a 28-year-old homemaker, so fears thunderstorms that she feels anxious

figure 13.2
Some common and uncommon fears
This national survey ranked the relative fear levels of Americans to some sources of anxiety. A fear becomes a phobia if it provokes a compelling but irrational desire to avoid the dreaded object or situation. (From *Public Opinion*, 1984.)

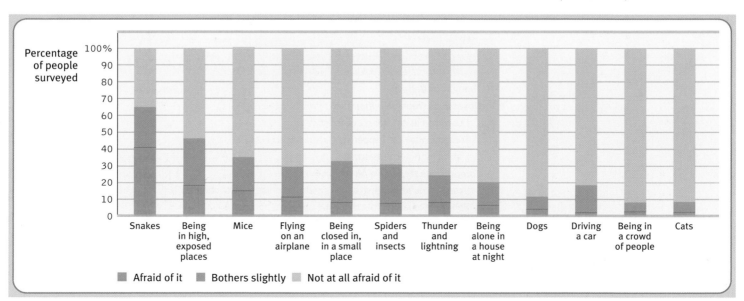

▶ **obsessive-compulsive disorder** an anxiety disorder characterized by unwanted repetitive thoughts (obsessions) and/or actions (compulsions).

as soon as a weather forecaster mentions possible storms later in the week. If her husband is away and a storm is forecast, she sometimes stays with a close relative. During a storm, she hides from windows and buries her head to avoid seeing the lightning. She is otherwise healthy and happy.

Some people suffer from irrational fears of specific animals or insects, or of heights, or blood, or tunnels. Sometimes it is possible to avoid the stimulus that arouses the fear: One can hide during thunderstorms or avoid high places. With a *social phobia*, an intense fear of being scrutinized by others, the anxious person will avoid potentially embarrassing social situations. The person may avoid speaking up, eating out, or going to parties—or will sweat, tremble, or have diarrhea when doing so. Social phobia is shyness taken to an extreme.

Obsessive-Compulsive Disorder

As with generalized anxiety and phobias, we can see aspects of our own behavior in **obsessive-compulsive disorder**. We may at times be obsessed with senseless or offensive thoughts that will not go away. Or we may engage in compulsive, rigid behavior-checking, ordering, cleaning, hoarding. We recheck a locked door, step over cracks in the sidewalk, or line up our books and pencils "just so" before studying.

Obsessive thoughts and compulsive behaviors cross the fine line between normality and disorder when they become so persistent that they interfere with the way we live or when they cause distress. Checking to see that the door is locked is normal; checking 10 times is not. Washing your hands is normal; washing so often that your skin becomes raw is not. (**TABLE 13.1** offers more examples.) At some time during their lives, often during their late teens or twenties, 2 to 3 percent of people cross that line from normal preoccupations and fussiness to debilitating disorder (Karno & others, 1988). The obsessive thoughts become so haunting, the compulsive rituals so senselessly time-consuming, that effective functioning becomes impossible.

Older people are less often plagued by obsessive-compulsive disorder than are teens and young adults (Samuels & Nestadt, 1997). A 40-year follow-up study of 144 Swedish people diagnosed around 1950 found that, for most, the obsessions and compulsions had gradually lessened, though only 1 in 5 had completely recovered (Skoog & Skoog, 1999). Anxiety disorders all engage our anticipation of future events, about which older adults, it seems, are less apprehensive.

table 13.1 Common Obsessions and Compulsions Among Children and Adolescents With Obsessive-Compulsive Disorder	
Thought or Behavior	**Percentage Reporting Symptom**
Obsessions (repetitive thoughts)	
Concern with dirt, germs, or toxins	40
Something terrible happening (fire, death, illness)	24
Symmetry, order, or exactness	17
Compulsions (repetitive behaviors)	
Excessive hand washing, bathing, tooth brushing, or grooming	85
Repeating rituals (in/out of a door, up/down from a chair)	51
Checking doors, locks, appliances, car brake, homework	46

Source: *Adapted from Rapoport, 1989.*

Explaining Anxiety Disorders

6. What are the sources of the anxious feelings and thoughts that characterize anxiety disorders?

Anxiety is both a feeling and a cognition—a doubt-laden appraisal of one's safety or social skill. How do these anxious feelings and cognitions arise? Freud's psychoanalytic perspective assumed that, beginning in childhood, people repress intolerable impulses, ideas, and feelings and that this submerged mental energy sometimes produces mystifying symptoms such as anxiety. However, many of today's psychologists have turned away from Freud to two contemporary perspectives—learning and biological.

The Learning Perspective

FEAR CONDITIONING When bad events happen unpredictably and uncontrollably, anxiety often develops (Chorpita & Barlow, 1998). Researchers have linked general anxiety with classical conditioning of fear. In the laboratory, they have created chronically anxious, ulcer-prone rats by giving them unpredictable electric shocks (Schwartz, 1984). Like assault victims who report feeling anxious when entering the neighborhood of the attack, the rats become apprehensive in their lab environment. For many victims of post-traumatic stress disorder, anxiety swells with any reminder of their trauma (see Close-Up: The Wounds of War, page 480). Such experiences might help explain why anxious people are hyperattentive to possible threats, and how panic-prone people come to associate anxiety with certain cues (Bouton & others, 2001; Mineka & Zinbarg, 1996). In one survey, 58 percent of those with social phobia experienced their disorder after a traumatic event (Ost & Hugdahl, 1981).

Recall from Chapter 7 that dogs learn to fear neutral stimuli associated with shock, that infants come to fear furry objects associated with frightening noises, and that adults can become terrified of incidental stimuli linked with traumatic experiences. As infants become mobile they experience falls and near-falls—and become increasingly afraid of heights (Campos & others, 1992).

Through such conditioning, the short list of naturally painful and frightening events can multiply into a long list of human fears. My car was once struck by another whose driver missed a stop sign. For months afterward, I felt a twinge of unease when any car approached from a side street. Marilyn's phobia may have been similarly conditioned during a terrifying or painful experience associated with a thunderstorm. Some specific learning processes might also have contributed to her anxiety:

STIMULUS GENERALIZATION Conditioned fears may remain long after we have forgotten the experiences that produced them (Jacobs & Nadel, 1985). Moreover, some fears arise from *stimulus generalization*. A person who fears heights after a fall may be afraid of airplanes without ever having flown.

REINFORCEMENT Once phobias and compulsions arise, reinforcement helps maintain them. Avoiding or escaping the feared situation reduces anxiety, thus reinforcing the phobic behavior. Feeling anxious or fearing a panic attack, a person may go or stay inside (Antony & others, 1992). Compulsive behaviors similarly reduce anxiety. If washing your hands relieves your feelings of unease, you will likely wash your hands again when the feelings return.

OBSERVATIONAL LEARNING We might also learn fear through observational learning—by observing others' fears. As we saw in Chapter 11, wild monkeys transmit their fear of snakes to their offspring. Human parents similarly transmit their fears to their children.

An emotional high Although we humans seem biologically predisposed to fear heights—certainly an adaptive response—this construction worker seems fearless. The biological perspective helps us understand why most people would be terrified in this situation.

John Coletti/Stock, Boston

CLOSE-UP

The Wounds of War: Post-Traumatic Stress Disorder

During the fighting in Vietnam, Jack's platoon was repeatedly under fire. In one ambush, his closest friend was killed while Jack was standing a few feet away. Jack himself killed one of his enemies in a brutal assault. Years later, images of these events intrude on him as flashbacks and nightmares. He still jumps at the sound of a cap gun or the backfire of a car. When annoyed by his family or friends, he lashes out in ways he seldom did before Vietnam. To calm his continuing anxiety, he drinks more than he should.

Such has been the experience of many combat veterans, accident and disaster survivors, and sexual assault victims, including an estimated two-thirds of prostitutes (Brewin & others, 1999; Farley & others, 1998; Taylor & others, 1998). Stretch a metal spring and it will snap back—unless stretched too far. Traumatic stress—experiencing or witnessing severely threatening, uncontrollable events with a sense of fear, helplessness, or horror—can produce *post-traumatic stress disorder* (PTSD), symptoms of which include haunting memories and nightmares, a numbed social withdrawal, jumpy anxiety, and insomnia (Goodman & others, 1993; Kessler, 2000; Wilson & others, 1988). The more frequent and severe the assault experiences, the more adverse the outcomes (Golding, 1999).

After witnessing atrocities or living in life-threatening circumstances, children of the world's war zones and violent neighborhoods show similar symptoms (Garbarino, 1991, 1992). Their sense of basic trust erodes; many experience fearful wariness, troubled sleep, nightmares, and a sense of hopelessness about their future. This "learned helplessness" on the part of children who have repeatedly suffered abuse appears to make them more vulnerable to post-traumatic stress if assaulted as adults (Mineka & Zinbarg, 1996).

To pin down the frequency of PTSD, the U.S. Centers for Disease Control (1988) compared 7000 Vietnam combat veterans with 7000 noncombat veterans who served during the same years. Combat stress more than doubled a veteran's risk of alcohol abuse, depression, or anxiety. Studies of U.S. and Israeli soldiers reveal that the more terrifying and prolonged the battle experience, the greater the psychological casualties (King & King, 1991; Solomon, 1990). Roughly 15 percent of all Vietnam veterans, for example, reported post-traumatic stress symptoms. This rate was halved among those who never saw combat and tripled among those who experienced heavy combat. And among soldiers held captive in Vietnam, the more torture they suffered, the greater its psychological toll (Mollica & others, 1998).

Civilians, too, exhibit a stress "dose-response" relationship. PTSD rates vary from 4 percent among those who have experienced a natural disaster to up to 50 percent among those who have been kidnapped, held captive, tortured, or

The Biological Perspective

There is more to anxiety than simple conditioning, as evident from how few people develop lasting phobias after suffering traumas. The biological perspective can broaden our understanding, though it, too, is limited. It cannot, for example, explain the sharp increase in the anxiety levels of both children and college students over the last half-century, which appears related to such things as fraying social support accompanying family breakup (Twenge, 2000). But the biological perspective does help explain why we learn some fears more readily and why some individuals are more vulnerable.

NATURAL SELECTION We humans seem biologically prepared to fear threats faced by our ancestors. Most of our phobias focus on such objects: spiders, snakes, and other animals; closed spaces and heights; storms and darkness. (Those fearless about these occasional threats were less likely to survive and leave descendants.) It is easy to condition but hard to extinguish fears of such stimuli (Davey, 1995; Öhman, 1986). Many of our modern fears may also have an evolutionary

raped (Brewin & others, 2000; Brody, 2000; Kessler, 2000). The greater one's emotional distress during a trauma, the higher the risk for posttraumatic symptoms (Ozer & others, 2003).

A month after 9/11, a survey of Manhattan residents indicated that 8.5 percent were suffering PTSD, most as a result of the terrorist acts (Galea & others, 2002). Among those living near the World Trade Center, 20 percent reported such telltale signs as nightmares, severe anxiety, and fear of public places. In all, some 400,000 people in the greater New York area met the diagnosis, said Columbia University researchers (Susser & others, 2002).

Some psychologists, however, believe that PTSD is overdiagnosed, due partly to a broadening definition of *trauma* (which originally meant direct exposure to serious threat, such as combat or rape [McNally, 2003]). PTSD is actually infrequent, say the critics, and no good purpose is served by patholo-gizing normal stress reactions (Wakefield & Spitzer, 2002). More than 9 in 10 New Yorkers, although understandably stunned and grief-stricken by 9/11, did *not* respond pathologically, and by the following January the stress symptoms of the rest had mostly subsided (Galea & others, 2002). Similarly, most combat-stressed veterans live productive lives. Most political dissidents who survive dozens of episodes of torture do *not* later exhibit post-traumatic stress disorder (Mineka & Zinbarg, 1996).

Although suffering some lingering stress symptoms, most American Jews who survived the Holocaust trauma—experiencing starvation, beatings, lost freedom, the murders of loved ones—went on to live productive lives. In fact, compared with other American Jews of the same age, these survivors have been *less* likely to have seen a psychotherapist (18 percent versus 31 percent) and *more* likely to have had stable marriages (83 percent versus 62 percent).

Moreover, virtually none has committed a criminal act. Researcher William Helmreich (1992, p. 276) reflects on their successes:

The story of the survivors is one of courage and strength, of people who are living proof of the indomitable will of human beings to survive and of their tremendous capacity for hope. It is not a story of remarkable people. It is a story of just how remarkable people can be.

Psychologist Peter Suedfeld (1998, 2000), who as a boy survived the Holocaust under conditions of privation while his mother died in Auschwitz, has also documented the resilience of Holocaust survivors. The successes of Southeast Asian "boat people" who escaped war and immigrated to America further testify to the "hardiness and resilience of the survivors," notes Suedfeld. "It is not always true that 'What doesn't kill you makes you stronger,' but it is often true; and, in addition, what doesn't kill you may reveal to you just how strong you really are."

explanation. For example, a fear of flying may also come from our biological past, which predisposes us to fear confinement and heights.

Moreover, consider what people tend *not* to learn to fear. World War II air raids produced remarkably few lasting phobias. As the air blitz continued, the British, Japanese, and German populations became not more panicked, but rather more indifferent to planes not in their immediate neighborhood (Mineka & Zinbarg, 1996). Evolution has not prepared us to fear bombs dropping from the sky.

Just as our phobias focus on dangers faced by our ancestors, our compulsive acts typically exaggerate behaviors that contributed to our species' survival. Grooming gone wild becomes hair pulling. Washing up becomes ritual hand washing. Checking territorial boundaries becomes checking and rechecking an already locked door (Rapoport, 1989).

GENES Some people more than others seem genetically predisposed to particular fears and high anxiety. Pair a traumatic event with a sensitive, high-strung temperament and the result may be a new phobia. Identical twins often develop similar

figure 13.3
A PET scan of the brain of a person with obsessive-compulsive disorder
The scan reveals an abnormally high metabolic activity (red areas) in the frontal lobes, seen at the top of the photo. This is visible in a region of the left hemisphere's frontal lobe involved in directing attention.

phobias, in some cases even when raised separately (Carey, 1990; Eckert & others, 1981). One pair of 35-year-old female identical twins independently developed claustrophobia. They also became so afraid of water that each would gingerly wade backward into the ocean, and then only up to the knees. Among monkeys, fearfulness runs in families. Individual monkeys react more strongly to stress if their close biological relatives are anxiously reactive (Suomi, 1986). Among humans, vulnerability to anxiety disorder rises when the afflicted relative is an identical twin (Barlow, 1988; Hettema & others, 2001; Kendler & others, 1992, 1999, 2002a,b).

PHYSIOLOGY Generalized anxiety, panic attacks, and even obsessions and compulsions are biologically measurable as an overarousal of brain areas involved in impulse control and habitual behaviors. PET scans of persons with obsessive-compulsive disorder (**FIGURE 13.3**) reveal unusually high activity in an area of the frontal lobes just above the eyes (Rauch & Jenike, 1993; Resnick, 1992). When the disordered brain detects that something is amiss, it generates a mental hiccup of repeating thoughts or actions (Gehring & others, 2000).

Fear-learning experiences can traumatize the brain, by creating fear circuits within the amygdala (Armony & others, 1998). Some antidepressant drugs dampen this fear-circuit activity and its associated obsessive-compulsive behavior.

rehearse it!

6. When anxiety is so distressing, uncontrollable, or persistent that it results in maladaptive behavior, the person is said to have an anxiety disorder. If a person's anxiety takes the form of an irrational fear of a specific object or situation—for example, an irrational fear of thunderstorms or closed spaces—the disorder is called
   a. a phobia.
   b. a panic attack.
   c. generalized anxiety.
   d. an obsessive-compulsive disorder.

7. The experience of anxiety often involves physical symptoms, such as trembling, dizziness, chest pains, or choking sensations. An episode of intense dread, typically accompanied by such symptoms and by feelings of terror, is called

   a. generalized or chronic anxiety.
   b. a social phobia.
   c. a panic attack.
   d. an obsessive fear.

8. Marina has always been concerned with cleanliness and neatness. Her mother never had to remind her to clean her room. When Marina became consumed with the need to clean the entire house and refused to participate in any other activities, her family consulted a therapist, who diagnosed her as having
   a. obsessive-compulsive disorder.
   b. generalized anxiety disorder.
   c. a phobia.
   d. a panic attack.

9. Rats subjected to unpredictable shocks in the laboratory become chronically anxious. To the learning researcher this suggests that anxiety is a response to

   a. a phobia.
   b. biological factors.
   c. a genetic predisposition.
   d. fear conditioning.

10. Psychologists have different ideas about the causes of phobias. For example, some psychologists stress the importance of biological predispositions, noting that we seem predisposed to fear certain stimuli. Psychologists of the learning perspective, on the other hand, maintain that phobias are
    a. the result of individual genetic makeup.
    b. a way of repressing unacceptable impulses.
    c. conditioned fears.
    d. a symptom of having been abused as a child.

Answers can be found in Appendix C.

DISSOCIATIVE AND PERSONALITY DISORDERS

Among the most bewildering disorders are the rare *dissociative disorders*, in which a person appears to experience a sudden loss of memory or change in identity, and the socially dysfunctional *personality disorders*.

Dissociative Disorders

7. What are dissociative disorders, and why are they controversial?

▶ **dissociative disorders** disorders in which conscious awareness becomes separated (dissociated) from previous memories, thoughts, and feelings.

▶ **dissociative identity disorder** a rare dissociative disorder in which a person exhibits two or more distinct and alternating personalities. Also called *multiple personality disorder*.

When a situation becomes overwhelmingly stressful, those diagnosed with a **dissociative disorder** are said to dissociate themselves from it. Their conscious awareness becomes separated from painful memories, thoughts, and feelings. (Note that this explanation presumes the existence of repressed memories, which have recently been questioned, as discussed in Chapters 8 and 12.)

Certain symptoms of dissociation are not so rare. Now and then, many people may have a sense of being unreal, of being separated from their body, of watching themselves as if in a movie. Perhaps you can recall getting in your car and driving to some unintended location while your mind was preoccupied elsewhere. Facing trauma, such detachment may actually protect a person from being overwhelmed by emotion. Only when such experiences are severe and prolonged do they suggest a dissociative disorder.

The king of dissociative disorders is the presumed massive dissociation of self from ordinary consciousness in those with **dissociative identity disorder**. These people are said to have two or more distinct identities that alternately control the person's behavior. The person with this disorder may be prim and proper one moment and loud and flirtatious the next. Each personality has its own voice and mannerisms, and the original one typically denies any awareness of the other(s).

The "Hillside Strangler" Kenneth Bianchi is shown here at his trial.

Although people diagnosed as having multiple personalities are usually not violent, there have been cases in which the person reportedly became dissociated into a "good" and a "bad" (or aggressive) personality—a modest version of the Dr. Jekyll/Mr. Hyde split immortalized in Robert Louis Stevenson's story. One unusual case involved Kenneth Bianchi, who was on trial for the "Hillside Strangler" rapes and murders of 10 California women. During a hypnosis session with Bianchi, psychologist John Watkins (1984) "called forth" a hidden personality: "I've talked a bit to Ken, but I think that perhaps there might be another part of Ken that I haven't talked to, another part that maybe feels somewhat differently from the part that I've talked to. . . . Would you talk with me, Part, by saying, 'I'm here'?" Bianchi answered "Yes" and then claimed to be "Steve."

When speaking as Steve, Bianchi stated that he hated Ken because Ken was nice and that he (Steve), aided by a cousin, had murdered women. He also claimed that Ken knew nothing about his existence and that Ken was innocent of the murders. Was Bianchi's second personality a ruse, simply a way of disavowing responsibility for his actions? Yes. Bianchi—a practiced liar who had read about multiple personality in psychology books—was later convicted.

Exploring our capacity for personality shifts, Nicholas Spanos (1986, 1994, 1996) asked college students to pretend they were accused murderers being examined by a psychiatrist. When given the same hypnotic treatment Bianchi received, most spontaneously expressed a second personality. This discovery made Spanos wonder: Are dissociative identities simply a more extreme version of our normal human capacity to vary the "selves" we present—as when we might display a goofy, loud self while hanging out with friends, and a subdued, respectful self around grandparents. Are clinicians who discover multiple personalities merely triggering fantasy-prone people's enactment of a role? If so, can such people then convince themselves of the authenticity of their own role enactments? Are they like actors, who commonly report "losing themselves" in their roles? (Recall from Chapter 6 that Spanos also raised these questions about the hypnotic state. Given that most multiple personality patients are highly hypnotizable, whatever explains one condition—dissociation or role playing—may help explain the other.)

"Pretense may become reality."

Chinese Proverb

Those who accept dissociative identity as a genuine disorder find support in the distinct brain and body states associated with differing personalities (Putnam, 1991). Handedness, too, sometimes switches with personality (Henninger, 1992). Subtle memories of one personality's experience sometimes fail to transfer to another personality (Eich & others, 1997). In one study, ophthalmologists detected shifting visual acuity and eye-muscle balance as patients switched personalities. These changes did not occur among control subjects trying to simulate multiple personality (Miller & others, 1991).

Skeptics nevertheless find it suspicious that the disorder became so popular in the late twentieth century. In North America, the number of diagnoses exploded from only 2 reported cases per decade from 1930 to 1960, to more than 20,000 in the 1980s (McHugh, 1995a). The average number of displayed personalities also

"Would it be possible to speak with the personality that pays the bills?"

"Though this be madness, yet there is method in 't."

William Shakespeare, Hamlet, 1600

mushroomed—from 3 to 12 per patient (Goff & Simms, 1993). How could such a dramatic disorder have gone unnoticed for so long? Isn't the sudden increase just what one would expect after the role of multiple personality was well publicized in books and films of that time, including *The Three Faces of Eve* and *Sybil*? Many clinicians have never encountered a case of dissociative identity and the disorder is almost nonexistent outside North America, although in other cultures some people are said to be "possessed" by an alien spirit (Aldridge-Morris, 1989; Kluft, 1991). In Britain, the diagnosis—which some consider "a wacky American fad" (Cohen, 1995)—is rare. In India and Japan, it is essentially nonexistent.

To skeptics, these findings point to a cultural phenomenon—a disorder created by therapists in a particular social context (Merskey, 1992). Patients do not enter therapy saying "Allow me to introduce myselves." Rather, note skeptics, therapists go fishing for multiple personalities: "Have you ever felt like another part of you does things you can't control? Does this part of you have a name? Can I talk to the angry part of you?" Once patients permit a therapist to talk, by name, "to the part of you that says those angry things" they have begun acting out the fantasy. The result may be a real phenomenon, which patients may experience as another self. Yet, say skeptics, "It is no coincidence" that multiple personality studies began among practitioners of hypnosis and that symptoms are most dramatic *after* beginning therapy (Goff, 1993; Piper, 1998).

With the dissociative disorders, as with the anxiety disorders, both psychoanalytic and learning perspectives see the symptoms as ways of dealing with anxiety. Psychoanalysts see them as defenses against the anxiety caused by the eruption of unacceptable impulses. Learning theorists see them as behaviors reinforced by anxiety reduction.

Others view dissociative disorders as post-traumatic disorders—a natural, protective response to "histories of childhood trauma" (Putnam, 1995). Researchers debate whether most dissociative identity disorder patients suffered physical, sexual, or emotional abuse as children (Gleaves, 1996; Lilienfeld & others, 1999). One study of 12 murderers diagnosed with dissociative identity disorder did find that 11 of them had suffered severe, torturous child abuse (Lewis & others, 1997). One was set afire by his parents. Another was used in child pornography and was scarred from being made to sit on a stove burner. Perhaps, then, multiple personalities are the desperate efforts of the traumatized to flee inward.

But then why, wonder the skeptics, did the children of the Holocaust, after enduring boxcars, concentration camps, and their parents' murders, not develop dissociative identity disorders? Is it because the condition is either contrived by fantasy-prone, emotionally vulnerable people, or constructed out of the therapist-patient interaction? If so, history's verdict will not be sympathetic. "This epidemic will end in the way that the witch craze ended in Salem," predicts psychiatrist Paul McHugh (1995b). "The [multiple personality phenomenon] will be seen as manufactured, the 'repressed memory' explanation will be recognized as misguided, and psychiatrists will become immunized against the practices that generated these artifacts."

Personality Disorders

8. What characteristics are typical of personality disorders?

▶ **personality disorders** psychological disorders characterized by inflexible and enduring behavior patterns that impair social functioning.

▶ **antisocial personality disorder** a personality disorder in which the person (usually a man) exhibits a lack of conscience for wrongdoing, even toward friends and family members. May be aggressive and ruthless or a clever con artist.

Personality disorders are inflexible and enduring patterns of behavior that impair one's social functioning. One cluster of disorders expresses anxiety, such as a fearful sensitivity to rejection that predisposes the withdrawn *avoidant personality disorder*. A second cluster expresses eccentric behaviors, such as the social disengagement of the *schizoid personality disorder*.

A third cluster exhibits dramatic or impulsive behaviors. A person with a *histrionic personality disorder* displays shallow, attention-getting emotions and goes to great lengths to gain others' praise and reassurance. Those with *narcissistic personality disorder* exaggerate their own importance, aided by success fantasies. They find criticism hard to accept, often reacting with rage or shame. Those with *borderline personality disorder* have an unstable identity, unstable relationships, and unstable emotions. If personality is one's enduring pattern of thinking, feeling, and acting, then a markedly unstable sense of self defines a "borderline personality."

The most troubling of these impulsive personality disorders is the **antisocial personality disorder**. The person (formerly called a *sociopath* or a *psychopath*) is typically a male whose lack of conscience becomes plain before age 15, as he begins to lie, steal, fight, or display unrestrained sexual behavior. About half of such children become antisocial adults—unable to keep a job, irresponsible as a spouse and parent, and assaultive or otherwise criminal (Farrington, 1991). When the antisocial personality combines a keen intelligence with amorality, the result may be a charming and clever con artist—or worse.

Despite their antisocial behavior, most criminals do not fit the description of antisocial personality disorder. Why? Because most criminals actually show responsible concern for their friends and family members. Antisocial personalities feel little and fear little, and in extreme cases, the results can be horrifyingly tragic. Henry Lee Lucas reported that at age 13 he strangled a woman who refused to have sex with him. He at one time confessed to having bludgeoned, suffocated, stabbed, shot, or mutilated some 360 women, men, and children during his 32 years of crime. During the last 6 years of his reign of terror, Lucas teamed with Elwood Toole, who reportedly slaughtered about 50 people whom he "didn't think was worth living anyhow." It ended when Lucas confessed to stabbing and dismembering his 15-year-old common-law wife, who was Toole's niece.

The antisocial personality expresses little regret over violating others' rights. "Once I've done a crime, I just forget it," said Lucas. Toole was equally matter-of-fact: "I think of killing like smoking a cigarette, like another habit" (Darrach & Norris, 1984).

As with mood disorders and schizophrenia, the antisocial personality disorder is woven of both biological and psychological strands. No single gene codes for a complex behavior such as crime, but twin and adoption studies reveal that biological relatives of certain individuals are at increased risk for antisocial behavior (Rhee & Waldman, 2002). Their genetic vulnerability appears as a fearless approach to life. When they await aversive events, such as electric shocks or loud noises, they show little autonomic nervous system arousal (Hare, 1975). Even as youngsters, before committing any crime, they react with lower levels of stress hormones than do others their age (**Figure 13.4**).

Some studies have detected the early signs of antisocial behavior in children as young as ages 3 to 6 (Caspi & others, 1996; Tremblay & others, 1994). Boys who later became aggressive or antisocial as adolescents tended, as young children, to have been impulsive, uninhibited, unconcerned with social rewards, and low in anxiety. If channeled in more productive directions, such fearlessness may lead to courageous heroism, adventurism, or star-level athleticism (Poulton & Milne, 2002). Lacking a sense of social responsibility, the same disposition produces a cool con artist or killer (Lykken, 1995).

Genetic influences help wire the brain. Adrian Raine (1999) compared PET scans of 41 murderers' brains with those from people of similar age and sex. Raine found reduced activity in the murderers' frontal lobe, which helps control impulses (**Figure 13.5**, page 486). This was especially true for those who murdered impulsively. In a follow-up study, Raine and his team (2000) found that repeat violent criminal offenders had 11 percent less frontal lobe neural tissue than normal. This helps explain why people with antisocial personality disorder exhibit marked deficits in frontal lobe cognitive functions, such as planning, organization, and inhibition (Morgan & Lilienfeld, 2000).

figure 13.4
Cold-blooded arousability and risk of crime Levels of the stress hormone adrenaline were measured in two groups of 13-year-old Swedish boys. In both stressful and nonstressful situations, those who were later convicted of a crime (as 18- to 26-year-olds) showed relatively low arousal. (From Magnusson, 1990.)

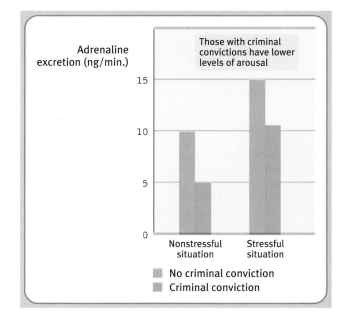

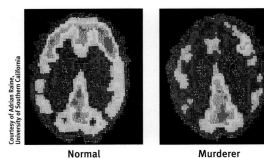

Normal   Murderer

figure 13.5
Murderous minds PET scans illustrate reduced activation in a murderer's frontal cortex—a brain area that helps brake impulsive, aggressive behavior. (From Raine, 1999.)

Courtesy of Adrian Raine, University of Southern California

Genetics alone is hardly the whole story of antisocial crime, however. Relative to 1960, the average American in 1995 (before the late 1990s crime decline) was twice as likely to be murdered, four times as likely to report being raped, four times as likely to report being robbed, and five times as likely to report being assaulted (FBI, *Uniform Crime Reports*). Violent crime was also surging in other Western nations. Yet the human gene pool had hardly changed. Or consider the British social experiment begun in 1787, exiling 160,000 criminals to Australia. The descendants of these exiles, carrying their ancestors' supposed "criminal genes," have helped create a civilized democracy whose crime rate is similar to Britain's. Genetic predispositions do put some individuals more at risk for antisocial conduct than others; biological as well as environmental influences explain why 5 to 6 percent of offenders commit 50 to 60 percent of crimes (Lyman, 1996). But we must look to sociocultural factors to explain the modern epidemic of violence.

rehearse it!

11. Dissociative identity disorder is relatively rare. This disorder is controversial because
    a. criminals have used it as a defense.
    b. it was reported frequently in the 1920s but rarely today.
    c. it is almost never reported outside North America.

    d. its symptoms are nearly identical to those of obsessive-compulsive disorder.

12. Unlike other psychological disorders, personality disorders need not involve any apparent anxiety, depression, or loss of contact with reality. A personali-

ty disorder, such as antisocial personality, is characterized by
    a. the presence of multiple personalities.
    b. disorganized thinking.
    c. enduring and maladaptive personality traits.
    d. elevated level of autonomic nervous system arousal.

Answers can be found in Appendix C.

© The New Yorker Collection, 1988, Gahan Wilson from cartoonbank.com. All Rights Reserved.

"Listen, everybody feels a little depressed around this time of year!"

For some people, recurring depression during winter's dark months constitutes a seasonal affective disorder. For others, winter darkness means more blue moods. When asked "Have you cried today?" Americans answered "yes" more often in the winter:

	Percent answering yes	
	Men	*Women*
August	4%	7%
December	8%	21%

Source: Time/CNN survey, 1994

MOOD DISORDERS

9. What are mood disorders, and what forms do they take?

The emotional extremes of **mood disorders** come in two principal forms: (1) *major depressive disorder*, in which the person experiences prolonged hopelessness and lethargy until usually rebounding to normality, and (2) *bipolar disorder* (formerly called *manic depressive disorder*), in which the person alternates between depression and *mania*, an overexcited, hyperactive state.

Major Depressive Disorder

Perhaps you know what depression feels like. If you are like most college students, at some time during this year—more likely the dark months of winter than the bright days of summer—you will probably experience a few of the symptoms of depression (Beck & Young, 1978). You may feel deeply discouraged about the future, dissatisfied with your life, or isolated from others. You may lack the energy to get things done or even to force yourself out of bed; be unable to concentrate, eat, or sleep normally; or even wonder if you would be better off dead. Perhaps academic success came easily to you in high school, and now you find that disappointing grades jeopardize your goals. Maybe social stresses, such as feeling you don't belong or the breakup of a romance, have plunged you into despair. And maybe brooding has at times only worsened your self-torment.

You are not alone. Depression is the "common cold" of psychological disorders—an expression that effectively describes its pervasiveness but certainly not its seriousness. Although phobias are more common, depression is the number one reason people seek mental health services. Moreover, it is the leading cause of disability worldwide (WHO, 2002).

As anxiety is a response to threat of future loss, depression is often a response to past and current loss. To feel bad in reaction to profoundly sad events (such as a significant loss) is to be in touch with reality. In such times, depression is like a car's low-oil-pressure light—a signal that warns us to stop and take protective measures. Recall that, biologically speaking, life's purpose is not happiness but survival and reproduction. To this end, coughing, vomiting, and various forms of pain protect the body from dangerous toxins. Similarly, depression is a sort of psychic hibernation: It slows us down, avoids attracting predators, restrains futile effort, and evokes support. To grind temporarily to a halt and ruminate, as depressed people do, is to reassess one's life when feeling threatened, and to redirect energy in more promising ways. From this perspective, there is sense to suffering.

But when does this response become seriously maladaptive? The line separating life's normal "downs" from major depression is difficult to draw. Joy, contentment, sadness, and despair are different points on a continuum, points at which any of us may be found at any given moment.

Major depressive disorder occurs when signs of depression (including lethargy, feelings of worthlessness, or loss of interest in family, friends, and activities) last two weeks or more without any notable cause. The difference between a blue mood after bad news and a mood disorder is like the difference between gasping for breath after a hard run and being chronically short of breath. To sense what depression feels like, suggest some clinicians, imagine combining the anguish of grief with the sluggishness of jet lag.

Bipolar Disorder

With or without therapy, episodes of major depression usually end, and people temporarily or permanently return to their previous behavior patterns. However, some people rebound to the opposite emotional extreme—a euphoric, hyperactive, wildly optimistic **manic episode**. If depression is living in slow motion, mania is fast forward. Alternation between depression and mania signals **bipolar disorder**. During the manic phase of bipolar disorder, the person is typically overtalkative, overactive, elated (though easily irritated if crossed); has little need for sleep; and shows fewer sexual inhibitions. Speech is loud, flighty, and hard to interrupt.

One of mania's maladaptive symptoms is grandiose optimism and self-esteem, which may lead to reckless investments, spending sprees, and unsafe sex. Although people in a manic state find advice irritating, they need protection from their own poor judgment. In milder forms, however, the energy and free-flowing thinking of

▶ **mood disorders** psychological disorders characterized by emotional extremes. See *major depressive disorder*, *manic episode*, and *bipolar disorder*.

▶ **major depressive disorder** a mood disorder in which a person, for no apparent reason, experiences two or more weeks of depressed moods, feelings of worthlessness, and diminished interest or pleasure in most activities.

▶ **manic episode** a mood disorder marked by a hyperactive, wildly optimistic state.

▶ **bipolar disorder** a mood disorder in which the person alternates between the hopelessness and lethargy of depression and the overexcited state of mania. (Formerly called manic-depressive disorder.)

"Depression . . . is well adapted to make a creature guard itself against any great or sudden evil."

Charles Darwin, The Life and Letters of Charles Darwin, 1887

Creativity and bipolar disorders
History has given us many creative artists, composers, and writers with bipolar disorder, including (top, left to right) Walt Whitman, Virginia Woolf, Edgar Allan Poe, (bottom, left to right) Samuel Clemens (Mark Twain), Ernest Hemingway, and Margot Kidder.

mania can fuel creativity. History offers many examples of creative bipolar people, from Walt Whitman and Ernest Hemingway to actress Margot Kidder. Bipolar disorder is especially common among creative artists (Jamison, 1993, 1995). George Frideric Handel (1685–1759), who many believe suffered a mild form of bipolar disorder, composed his nearly four-hour-long *Messiah* during three weeks of intense, creative energy (Keynes, 1980). Robert Schumann composed 51 musical works during two years of mania (1840 and 1849) and none during 1844, when he was severely depressed (Slater & Meyer, 1959). Creative professionals who rely on precision and logic (architects, designers, journalists) less often suffer bipolar disorder than those who rely on emotional expression and vivid imagery (poets, novelists, entertainers), reports Arnold Ludwig (1995).

It is as true of emotions as of everything else: What goes up comes down. Before long, the elated mood either returns to normal or plunges into a depression. Though as maladaptive as major depression, bipolar disorder is much less common, occurring in about 1 percent of the population. Unlike major depression, it afflicts as many men as women. It often strikes after a steady routine of daily activities, and it disrupts sleep (Malkoff-Schwartz & others, 1998; Reilly-Harrington & others, 1999).

Explaining Mood Disorders

10. What causes mood disorders, and what might explain the Western world's rising incidence of depression among youth and young adults?

Because depression profoundly affects so many people, it understandably has been the subject of thousands of studies. Psychologists are working to develop a theory of mood disorders that will suggest ways to treat and prevent them. Researcher Peter Lewinsohn and his colleagues (1985, 1998) summarized the facts that any theory of depression must explain. Among them are the following:

● ***Many behavioral and cognitive changes accompany depression.*** Depressed people are inactive and feel unmotivated. They are sensitive to negative happenings, expect negative outcomes, and more often recall negative information. In a depressed mood, we expect our team to lose, our grades to fall, our love to fail. When the depression lifts, these behavioral and cognitive accompaniments disappear. Nearly half the time depressed people exhibit symptoms of another disorder, such as anxiety or drug or alcohol abuse.

● ***Depression is widespread.*** Its commonality suggests that its causes, too, must be common.

● ***Compared with men, women are twice as vulnerable to major depression*** (**FIGURE 13.6**). In general, women are most vulnerable to passive disorders—internalized states, such as depression, anxiety, and inhibited sexual desire. Men's disorders are more active—alcohol abuse, antisocial conduct, lack of impulse control (see Table 13.3 on page 502). When women get sad they often get sadder than men do. When men get mad, they often get madder than women do.

figure 13.6
Gender and depression Interviews with 38,000 adults in 10 countries confirm what many smaller studies have found: Women's risk of major depression is double that of men's. Lifetime risk of depression also varies by culture—from 1.5 percent in Taiwan to 19 percent in Beirut. (Data from Weissman & others, 1996.)

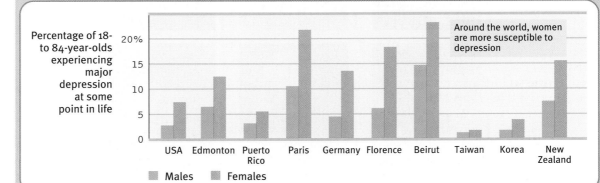

Percentage of 18- to 84-year-olds experiencing major depression at some point in life

Around the world, women are more susceptible to depression

USA Edmonton Puerto Rico Paris Germany Florence Beirut Taiwan Korea New Zealand

■ Males ■ Females

- *Most major depressive episodes self-terminate.* Therapy can speed recovery, yet most people suffering major depression return to normal without professional help. The plague of depression comes and, a few weeks or months later, it usually goes. It sometimes recurs later.
- *Stressful events related to work, marriage, and close relationships often precede depression.* A family member's death, a job loss, a marital crisis, or a physical assault increase one's risk of depression. One study followed 2000 people over time. It found that the risk of the onset of depression in the ensuing month ranged from less than 1 percent among those who had experienced no stressful life event to 24 percent among those with three such stresses (Kendler, 1998). The early loss of a parent due to death or separation also increases later vulnerability to depression (Agid & others, 1999).

To these facts we can add one more: The dramatic increase in anxiety levels noted earlier is also true of depression. *With each new generation, the rate of depression is increasing.* What is more, the disorder is striking earlier (now often in the late teens). This is true not only in Canada and the United States but also in Germany, Italy, France, Lebanon, New Zealand, Taiwan, and Puerto Rico (Cross-National Collaborative Group, 1992). In Australia, 12 percent of adolescents interviewed reported symptoms of depression. Most hid it from their parents; almost 90 percent of their parents perceived their depressed teen as *not* suffering depression (Sawyer & others, 2000).

In North America, today's young adults are three times as likely as their grandparents to report having recently—or ever—suffered depression (despite the grandparents' many more years of being at risk). In one National Institute of Mental Health study of 18,244 Americans, only 1 percent of those born before 1905 had suffered major depression by age 75. Of those born since 1955, 6 percent had experienced depression by age 25. Asked "Have you ever felt that you were going to have a nervous breakdown?" 17 percent of Americans said "yes" in 1957, as did 24 percent in 1996 (Swindle & others, 2000). The increase appears authentic, *not* simply the result of people being more willing to disclose depression. Young adult Canadians are similarly most vulnerable to depression (*Statistics Canada*, 1999).

As you might expect, researchers understand and interpret these facts in ways that reflect their different perspectives. Psychoanalytic theory, applying Freud's ideas about the importance of early childhood experiences and unconscious impulses, suggested that depression occurs when significant losses evoke feelings associated with losses experienced in childhood. Loss of a romantic relationship or a job might evoke feelings associated with the loss of the intimate relationship with one's mother. Alternatively, unresolved anger toward one's parents might be turned inward against the self. Today's bio-psycho-social perspective is replacing these Freudian explanations with biological and cognitive explanations.

The Biological Perspective

Most mental health research dollars of late have funded explorations of biological influences on mood disorders. Depression is a whole-body disorder. It involves genetic predispositions, biochemical imbalances, negative thoughts, and melancholy mood.

GENETIC INFLUENCES We have long known that mood disorders run in families. The risk of major depression and bipolar disorder increases if you have a depressed parent or sibling (Sullivan & others, 2000). If one identical twin is diagnosed as suffering major depressive disorder, the chances are about 1 in 2 that at some time the other twin will be, too. If one identical twin has bipolar disorder, the chances are 7 in 10 that the other twin will at some point be diagnosed similarly. Among fraternal twins, the corresponding odds are just under 1 in 5 (Tsuang & Faraone, 1990). The greater similarity of identical twins' depressive tendencies even occurs among twins reared apart (DiLalla & others, 1996). Moreover, adopted people who suffer a mood disorder often have close biological relatives who suffer mood disorders, become dependent on alcohol, or commit suicide (Wender & others, 1986).

About 50 percent of those who recover from depression will suffer another episode within two years. Recovery is more likely to be enduring the later the first episode strikes, the longer patients stay well, the fewer their previous episodes, the less stress they experience, and the more social support they have (Belsher & Costello, 1988; Fergusson & Woodward, 2002; Kendler & others, 2001).

"I see depression as the plague of the modern era."

Lewis Judd, former chief, National Institute of Mental Health, 2000

CLOSE-UP

Suicide

"But life, being weary of these worldly bars, / Never lacks power to dismiss itself."

William Shakespeare,
Julius Caesar, *1599*

Each year some 1 million despairing people worldwide will say no to life by electing a permanent solution to what may be a temporary problem (WHO, 2000).

To find out who commits suicide, researchers have compared the suicide rates of different groups.

- *National differences* The suicide rates of England, Italy, and Spain are little more than half those of Canada, Australia, and the United States; Austria and Finnish suicide rates are about double (WHO, 2002a). Within Europe, the most suicide-prone people (Lithuanians) have been 15 times more likely to kill themselves than the least (Portuguese).
- *Racial differences* White Americans are nearly twice as likely as black Americans to kill themselves (NIMH, 2002).

- *Gender differences* Women are much more likely than men to attempt suicide. But men are two to four times more likely (depending on the country) to succeed (**FIGURE 13.7**). (An exception is suicide-prone China, where women account for most suicides [WHO, 2002c]). Men are more likely to use lethal methods, such as firing a bullet into the head, the method of choice in 6 of 10 U.S. suicides.
- *Age differences and trends* The suicide rate surges among older men (Figure 13.7). Across the Western world, suicide rates have also surged since 1960 among older teens, especially males (Eckersley & Dear, 2002). American, Australian, British, Canadian, and New Zealand suicide rates of 15- to 25-year-olds all doubled or more than doubled in the 30 years after 1960, paralleling the increasing late teen and early twenties rates of anxiety and depression.

- *Other group differences* Suicide rates are much higher among the rich, the nonreligious, and those who are single, widowed, or divorced (Hoyer & Lund, 1993; Stack, 1992; Stengel, 1981). In both the United States and Australia, the teen suicide surge was almost entirely among males (Hassan & Carr, 1989). Gay and lesbian youth much more often suffer distress and attempt suicide than do their heterosexual peers (Goldfried, 2001).

People seldom commit suicide while in the depths of depression, when energy and initiative are lacking. It is when they begin to rebound and become capable of following through that the risk increases. Teenage suicides may follow a traumatic event, such as a romantic breakup or a guilt-provoking antisocial act; they are often linked with drug and alcohol abuse (Fowler & others, 1986; Kolata, 1986). Compared with people who suffer no disorder, those addicted to alcohol are

Gene-hunters' pursuit of bipolar-DNA links Linkage studies seek to identify aberrant genes in family members suffering the disorder. These Pennsylvania Amish family members—an isolated population sharing a common life-style and some vulnerability to the disorder—have been among the volunteer subjects.

Jerry Irwin Photography

A search for the genes that put people at risk for depression is now under way. At least 15 groups worldwide are sleuthing the genes that make one vulnerable to bipolar disorder (Veggeberg, 1996). To tease out which genes are implicated, researchers use *linkage analysis*. First, they find families that have had the disorder across several generations. Then they draw blood from both affected and unaffected family members and examine their DNA, looking for differences. The anticipated

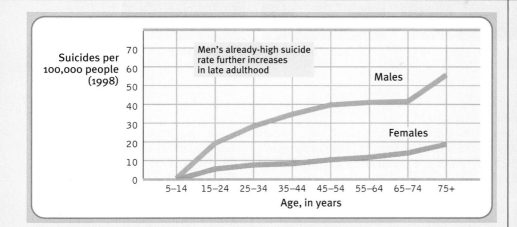

figure 13.7
Suicide rates by gender and age
Worldwide suicide rates are higher among males than among females. The highest rates of all are found among older men. (From WHO, 2002a.)

roughly 100 times more likely to commit suicide; some 3 percent of them do (Murphy & Wetzel, 1990). Even among those who have attempted suicide, those who abuse alcohol are five times more likely than others to kill themselves eventually (Beck & Steer, 1989).

Social suggestion may trigger the final act. Following highly publicized suicides and TV programs featuring suicide, known suicides increase. So do fatal auto "accidents" and private airplane crashes (pages 545–546).

Among the elderly, suicide is sometimes chosen as an alternative to current or future suffering. In people of all ages, suicide is not necessarily an act of hostility or revenge, but may instead be a way of switching off unendurable pain (Shneidman, 1987).

In retrospect, families and friends may recall signs that they believe should have forewarned them—verbal hints, giving possessions away, or withdrawal and preoccupation with death. Those who have been depressed have at least five times the general population's risk of suicide (Bostwick & Pankratz, 2000). One-third of those who kill themselves have tried to kill themselves previously.

Few who talk of suicide or think suicidal thoughts (a number that includes one-third of all adolescents and college students) actually attempt suicide, and few of those who attempt it complete the act (Yip, 1998). The United States, for example, records about 30,000 suicides annually, but a half-million emergency room visits for attempted suicide (Surgeon General, 1999). Still, most who do commit suicide had talked of it. And anyone who does threaten suicide is at least sending a signal of being desperate or feeling despondent. So, if a friend talks of suicide, it's important to listen and to direct the friend to professional help.

outcome of linkage research is a complex picture—many genes have small effects that can combine to put some people at greater risk for depression.

THE DEPRESSED BRAIN Genes act by directing biochemical events that, down the line, influence behavior. The biochemical key is the neurotransmitters, those messenger molecules that shuttle signals between nerve cells. Norepinephrine, a neurotransmitter that increases arousal and boosts mood, is scarce during depression and overabundant during mania. Most people with a history of depression are also habitual smokers. Although their smoking typically precedes their depression, depressed people may also self-medicate by smoking, which can temporarily increase norepinephrine and boost mood (HMHL, 2002).

A second neurotransmitter, serotonin, is also scarce during depression. Drugs that alleviate mania reduce norepinephrine; drugs that relieve depression tend to increase norepinephrine or serotonin supplies by blocking either their reuptake (as Prozac, Zoloft, and Paxil do with serotonin) or their chemical breakdown.

figure 13.8
The ups and downs of bipolar disorder PET scans show that brain energy consumption rises and falls with the patient's emotional switches. Red areas are where the brain rapidly consumes glucose.

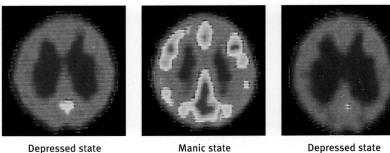

Depressed state
(May 17)

Manic state
(May 18)

Depressed state
(May 27)

Repetitive physical exercise, such as jogging, reduces depression as it increases serotonin (Jacobs, 1994).

Using modern scanning machines, researchers are also spotting neurological signs of depression. Many recent studies have found the brains of depressed people to be less active, indicating a slowed-down state (**FIGURE 13.8**). The left frontal lobe, which is active during positive emotions, is likely to be inactive in depressed states (Davidson & others, 2002). MRI scans have even shown the frontal lobes to be 7 percent smaller in severely depressed patients (Coffey & others, 1993). The hippocampus, a memory processing center linked with the brain's emotional circuitry, is vulnerable to stress-related damage. By boosting serotonin, which stimulates hippocampus neuron growth, antidepressant drugs may promote recovery from depression (Jacobs & others, 2000).

The Social-Cognitive Perspective

Some people slide into depression for no obvious reason, even when life has been going well. Often, however, biological factors accompany psychological reactions to experience (**FIGURE 13.9**). The mind's negative thoughts somehow influence biochemical events that in a vicious cycle amplify depressing thoughts.

Recent research reveals how *self-defeating beliefs* feed the vicious cycle. Depressed people view life through dark glasses. Their intensely negative assumptions about themselves, their situation, and their future lead them to magnify bad experiences and minimize good ones. Listen to Norman, a Canadian college professor, recalling his depression:

> I [despaired] of ever being human again. I honestly felt subhuman, lower than the lowest vermin. Furthermore, I was self-deprecatory and could not understand why anyone would want to associate with me, let alone love me. . . . I was positive that I was a fraud and a phony and that I didn't deserve my Ph.D. I didn't deserve to have tenure; I didn't deserve to be a Full Professor. . . . I didn't deserve the research grants I had been awarded; I couldn't understand how I had written books and journal articles. . . . I must have conned a lot of people. (Endler, 1982, pp. 45–49)

figure 13.9
Depression—an ailing mind in an ailing body Altering any one component of the chemistry-cognition-mood circuit can alter the others.

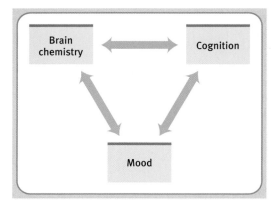

Self-defeating beliefs may arise from *learned helplessness*. As we saw in Chapter 12, both dogs and humans act depressed, passive, and withdrawn after experiencing uncontrollable painful events. Gender differences in uncontrollable stress help explain why women have been twice as vulnerable to depression. Women more often than men have been abused or made to feel helpless, and they may respond more strongly to stress (Hankin & Abramson 2001; Mazure & others, 2002; Nolen-Hoeksema, 2001). Thirty-five percent of women and 16 percent of men entering American colleges feel "frequently overwhelmed by all I have to do" (Sax & others, 2002). (Men report spending more of their time in "light anxiety" activities such as sports, TV watching, and partying, possibly avoiding activities that might make them feel overwhelmed.)

PEANUTS

Drawing by Charles Schulz;
© 1956 Reprinted by permission of
United Feature Syndicate, Inc.

NEGATIVE THOUGHTS FEED NEGATIVE MOODS Why do life's unavoidable failures lead some people, but not others, to become depressed? The difference lies partly with people's *attributions* of blame. We have some choice of whom or what to blame for our failures. If you fail a test and blame yourself, you may feel stupid and depressed. If you externalize the blame—perhaps attributing your failure to an unfair test—you are more likely to feel angry.

Depressed people tend to explain bad events in terms that are *stable* ("It's going to last forever"), *global* ("It's going to affect everything I do"), and *internal* ("It's all my fault"). Lyn Abramson, Gerald Metalsky, and Lauren Alloy (1989) theorized that the result of these pessimistic, overgeneralized, self-blaming attributions is a depressing sense of hopelessness. If you tend to see bad grades, social rejection, and work problems as inevitable and your own fault, and if you ruminate about such things, then when bad things happen you will probably experience the blues.

Martin Seligman (1991, 1995) argues that depression is common among young Westerners because of epidemic hopelessness stemming from the rise of individualism and the decline of commitment to religion and family. When facing failure or rejection, contends Seligman, the self-focused individual takes on personal responsibility for problems and has nothing to fall back on for hope. In non-Western cultures, where close-knit relationships and cooperation are the norm, major depression is less common and less tied to self-blame over personal failure. In Japan, for example, depressed people instead tend to report feeling shame over letting others down (Draguns, 1990a).

NEGATIVE MOODS FEED NEGATIVE THOUGHTS There is, however, a chicken-and-egg problem with the social-cognitive explanation of depression. Self-defeating beliefs, self-blame, and negative attributions surely do support depression. Peter Barnett and Ian Gotlib (1988) note that such cognitions are *indicators* of depression. Depressing thoughts *coincide* with a depressed mood. But do they *cause* depression, any more than a speedometer's reading 70 mph causes a car's speed? Before or after being depressed, people's thoughts are less negative. Perhaps this is because, as we noted in our discussion of state-dependent memory (page 274), a depressed mood triggers negative thoughts. If you temporarily put people in a bad or sad mood, their memories, judgments, and expectations suddenly become more pessimistic.

DEPRESSION'S VICIOUS CYCLE "A recipe for severe depression is preexisting pessimism encountering failure," noted Martin Seligman (1991, p. 78). Depression, as we have seen, is often brought on by stressful experiences—losing a job, getting divorced or rejected, suffering physical trauma—anything that disrupts your sense of who you are and why you are a worthy human being. Such brooding after failure can be adaptive; one may gain insights during times of depressed inactivity that can later lead to more effective strategies for interacting with the world. But depression-prone people respond to bad events in an especially self-focused, self-blaming way (Mor & Winquist, 2002; Pyszczynski & others, 1991; Wood & others, 1990a,b). Their self-esteem fluctuates more rapidly up with boosts and down with threats (Butler & others, 1994). When down, their brooding amplifies their negative feelings, which in turn trigger depression's other cognitive and behavioral symptoms.

"I have learned to accept my mistakes by referring them to a personal history which was not of my making."

B. F. Skinner (1983)

Greg Gibson/AP Photo

Surviving depression CBS correspondent Mike Wallace became debilitated by severe depression during a tough libel trial. "Depression is palpable," he says. "You begin to feel like a fake and a fraud. You second-guess everything about everything."

"Man never reasons so much and becomes so introspective as when he suffers, since he is anxious to get at the cause of his sufferings."

Luigi Pirandello, Six Characters in Search of an Author, 1922

CLOSE-UP

Loneliness

Loneliness—the painful awareness that one's social relationships are deficient—is both a contributor to depression and its own problem. The deficiency stems from a mismatch between one's actual and desired social contacts. One person may feel lonely when isolated, another when in a crowd. "In America, there is loneliness but no solitude," writes Mary Pipher (2002); "there are crowds but no community." In Los Angeles, observed her daughter, "There are 10 million people around me but nobody knows my name."

Aloneness often breeds loneliness. People who are alone—unmarried, unattached, and often young—are more likely to feel lonely. Dutch psychologist Jenny de Jong-Gierveld (1987) has speculated that the emphasis on individual fulfillment and the downgrading of stable relationships and commitment to others are "loneliness-provoking factors." Work-related moves also make for fewer long-term family and social ties and increased loneliness (Dill & Anderson, 1999).

People commonly experience one or more of four types of loneliness (Beck & Young, 1978). To be lonely is to feel *excluded* from a group you would like to belong to; to feel *unloved* and uncared about by those around you; to feel *constricted* and unable to share your private concerns with anyone; or to feel *alienated*, or different, from those in your community.

Like people suffering from depression, lonely people tend to blame themselves, attributing their deficient social relationships to their own inadequacies (Snodgrass, 1987). There may be a basis for this self-blame: Chronically lonely people tend to be shy, self-conscious, and lacking in self-esteem, and to be perceived as less socially competent and attractive (Cheek & Melchior, 1990; Lau & Gruen, 1992; Vaux, 1988). They often find it hard to introduce themselves, make phone calls, and participate in groups (Rook, 1984; Spitzberg & Hurt, 1987). In addition, believing in their own social unworthiness restricts them from noticing and remembering positive feedback and from taking steps that would reduce their loneliness (Frankel & Prentice-Dunn, 1990). Thus, the very factors that work to create and maintain the cycle of depression can also produce a cycle of loneliness.

"*This epidemic of morbid meditation is a disease that women suffer much more than men. Women can ruminate about anything and everything—our appearance, our families, our career, our health.*"

Susan Nolen-Hoeksema, Women Who Think Too Much: How to Break Free of Overthinking and Reclaim Your Life, 2003

This cycle also helps explain women's doubled risk of depression. When trouble strikes, women tend to think, men tend to act. Women often have vivid recall for both wonderful and horrid experiences; men more vaguely recall such experiences (Seidletz & Diener, 1998). This gender difference in emotional memory may feed women's greater rumination over negative events and explain why fewer entering American college men than women reported being "frequently overwhelmed" (Sax & others, 2002). In contrast, being withdrawn, self-focused, and complaining elicits rejection (Furr & Funder, 1998; Gotlib & Hammen, 1992). In one study, researchers Stephen Strack and James Coyne (1983) noted that "depressed persons induced hostility, depression, and anxiety in others and got rejected. Their guesses that they were not accepted were not a matter of cognitive distortion." Weary of the person's fatigue, hopeless attitude, and lethargy, a spouse may threaten to leave or a boss may begin to question the person's competence. Indeed, people in the throes of depression are at high risk for divorce, job loss, and other stressful life events. Misery may love another's company, but company does not love another's misery.

Susan Nolen-Hoeksema and Jannay Morrow (1991) illustrated the link between brooding and depression. They happened to assess Stanford University students' moods and ruminations 2 weeks before the 1989 earthquake devastated much of their area. Those identified as prone to brood over negative events showed more symptoms of depression both 10 days and 7 weeks after the earthquake. If you have an optimistic way of interpreting events, a failure or stress is unlikely to provoke depression (Seligman, 1991). And even if you do fall prey to depression, you are more likely to recover quickly (Metalsky & others, 1993; Needles & Abramson, 1990).

Might Charlie Brown be helped by an optimism-training program?

What might you expect of new college students who are not depressed but do exhibit a pessimistic cognitive style (some of whom are about to satisfy Seligman's depression recipe: pessimism encountering failure)? Lauren Alloy and her collaborators (1999) monitored Temple University and University of Wisconsin students every 6 weeks for 2.5 years. Among those identified as having pessimistic thinking styles, 17 percent had a first episode of major depression, as did only 1 percent of those who began college with optimistic thinking styles. Follow-up research has found that students who exhibit optimism as they begin college develop more social support, which contributes to a lowered risk of depression (Brissette & others, 2002).

Knowing that there is two-way traffic between depressed mood and negative thinking, might we train depression-prone people to think more positively? That, as the next chapter explains, is an aim of cognitive therapy. It's also the aim of the Penn Optimism Program for 9- to 13-year-old children targeted as at risk for depression. The program puts children through 12 small-group sessions, each lasting two hours, in which they learn to tune into their thoughts when facing tough situations and to imagine alternatives to negative thoughts. The leader might, for example, present a cartoon depicting a child being called a name and invite the children to brainstorm positive ways to cope. In early experiments, the training halved the proportion of children suffering depression for up to two ensuing years (Gillham & others, 1995).

We can now assemble the pieces of the depression puzzle (**Figure 13.10**): (1) Negative, stressful events interpreted through (2) a ruminating, pessimistic explanatory style create (3) a hopeless, depressed state that (4) hampers the way the person thinks and acts. This, in turn, fuels (1) negative experiences such as rejection. It's a cycle we can all recognize. Bad moods feed on themselves: When we *feel* down, we *think* negatively and remember bad experiences. On the brighter side, we can break the cycle of depression at any of these points—by moving to a different environment, by reversing our self-blame and negative attributions, by turning our attention outward, or by engaging in more pleasant activities and more competent behavior.

Winston Churchill called depression a "black dog" that periodically hounded him. Poet Emily Dickinson was so afraid of bursting into tears in public that she spent much of her adult life in seclusion (Patterson, 1951). Abraham Lincoln was so withdrawn and brooding as a young man that his friends feared he might take his own life (Kline, 1974). As each of these lives reminds us, people can and do struggle through depression. Most regain their capacity to love, to work, and even to succeed at the highest levels.

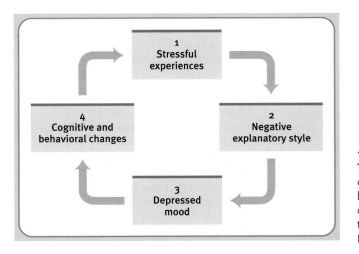

figure 13.10
The vicious cycle of depression This cycle can be broken at any point. Chapter 14 describes some therapeutic techniques. (Adapted from Lewinsohn & others, 1985.)

SCHIZOPHRENIA

If depression is the common cold of psychological disorders, chronic schizophrenia is the cancer. Nearly 1 in 100 people will develop schizophrenia, joining the estimated 24 million across the world who suffer one of humanity's most dreaded disorders (WHO, 2002d). It typically strikes as young people are maturing into adulthood, it knows no national boundaries, and it affects males and females about equally often (though men tend to be struck earlier and more severely).

Symptoms of Schizophrenia

11. What patterns of thinking, perceiving, feeling, and behaving characterize schizophrenia?

Literally translated, **schizophrenia** means "split mind." It refers not to a multiple-personality split but rather to a split from reality that shows itself in disorganized thinking, disturbed perceptions, and inappropriate emotions and actions.

Disorganized Thinking

Imagine trying to communicate with Maxine, a young woman whose thoughts spill out in no logical order. Her biographer, Susan Sheehan (1982, p. 25), observed her saying aloud to no one in particular,

> This morning, when I was at Hillside [Hospital], I was making a movie. I was surrounded by movie stars. The X-ray technician was Peter Lawford. The security guard was Don Knotts. That Indian doctor in Building 40 was Lou Costello. I'm Mary Poppins. Is this room painted blue to get me upset? My grandmother died four weeks after my eighteenth birthday.

As this strange monologue illustrates, the thinking of a person with schizophrenia is fragmented, bizarre, and distorted by false beliefs, called **delusions** ("I'm Mary Poppins"). Jumping from one idea to another may occur even within sentences, creating a sort of "word salad." One young man begged for "a little more allegro in the treatment," and suggested that "liberationary movement with a view to the widening of the horizon" will "ergo extort some wit in lectures." Those with *paranoid* tendencies are particularly prone to delusions of persecution.

Many psychologists believe disorganized thoughts result from a breakdown in selective attention. Recall from Chapter 6 that we normally have a remarkable capacity for selective attention—for, say, giving our undivided attention to one voice at a

▶ **schizophrenia** a group of severe disorders characterized by disorganized and delusional thinking, disturbed perceptions, and inappropriate emotions and actions.

▶ **delusions** false beliefs, often of persecution or grandeur, that may accompany psychotic disorders.

party while filtering out competing sensory stimuli. Schizophrenia sufferers cannot do this. They also have difficulty clearing their working memory of distracting information and inhibiting irrelevant material (Schooler & others, 1997; Holden, 2003). Thus, an irrelevant stimulus or an extraneous part of the preceding thought easily distracts them. Minute stimuli, such as the grooves on a brick or the inflections of a voice, may distract their attention from the whole scene or from the speaker's meaning. As one former patient recalled, "What had happened to me . . . was a breakdown in the filter, and a hodge-podge of unrelated stimuli were distracting me from things which should have had my undivided attention" (MacDonald, 1960, p. 218).

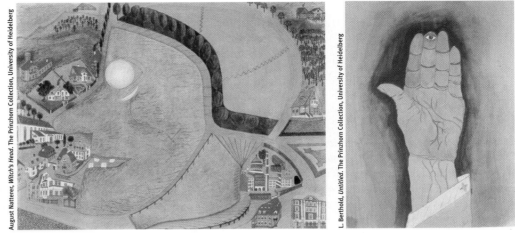

August Natterer, *Witch's Head*. The Prinzhorn Collection, University of Heidelberg

L. Berthold, *Untitled*. The Prinzhorn Collection, University of Heidelberg

Photos of paintings by Krannert Museum, University of Illinois at Urbana-Champaign

Art by people diagnosed with schizophrenia Commenting on the kind of art work shown here, poet and art critic John Ashbery wrote: "The lure of the work is strong, but so is the terror of the unanswerable riddles it proposes."

Disturbed Perceptions

A person with schizophrenia may perceive things that are not there. Such *hallucinations* (sensory experiences without sensory stimulation) are usually auditory. The person may hear voices that make insulting statements or give orders. The voices may tell the patient that she is bad or that he must burn himself with a cigarette lighter. Less commonly, people see, feel, taste, or smell things that are not there. Hallucinations have been compared to dreams breaking into waking consciousness. When the unreal seems real, the resulting perceptions are at best bizarre, at worst terrifying.

Inappropriate Emotions and Actions

The emotions of schizophrenia are often utterly inappropriate. Maxine's emotions seemed split off from reality. She laughed after recalling her grandmother's death. On occasion, she became angry for no apparent reason or cried when others laughed. Other victims of schizophrenia sometimes lapse into *flat affect*, a zombielike state of apparent apathy.

Motor behavior may also be inappropriate. The person may perform senseless, compulsive acts, such as continually rocking or rubbing an arm. Those who exhibit *catatonia* may remain motionless for hours on end and then become agitated.

As you can imagine, such disorganized thinking, disturbed perceptions, and inappropriate emotions and actions profoundly disrupt social relationships. During their most severe periods, people with schizophrenia live in a private inner world, preoccupied with illogical ideas and unreal images. Given a supportive environment, some eventually recover to enjoy a normal life or experience bouts of schizophrenia only intermittently. Others remain socially withdrawn and isolated throughout much of their lives.

Subtypes of Schizophrenia

12. What forms does schizophrenia take?

We have thus far described schizophrenia as if it were a single disorder. Actually, it is a cluster of disorders. The subtypes share some common features, but they also have some distinguishing symptoms (**TABLE 13.2**). Schizophrenia patients with *positive symptoms* may experience hallucinations, are often disorganized and deluded in their talk, and may exhibit inappropriate laughter, tears, or rage. Those with *negative symptoms* have toneless voices, expressionless faces, or mute and rigid bodies.

table 13.2 Subtypes of Schizophrenia	
Paranoid:	Preoccupation with delusions or hallucinations
Disorganized:	Disorganized speech or behavior, or flat or inappropriate emotion
Catatonic:	Immobility (or excessive, purposeless movement), extreme negativism, and/or parrotlike repeating of another's speech or movements
Undifferentiated:	Many and varied symptoms
Residual:	Withdrawal, after hallucinations and delusions have disappeared

Thus positive symptoms are the *presence* of inappropriate behaviors, and negative symptoms are the *absence* of appropriate behaviors. Because schizophrenia is more than one disorder, these varied symptoms could have more than one cause.

Sometimes, as in the case of Maxine, schizophrenia develops gradually, emerging from a long history of social inadequacy (which helps explain why those predisposed to schizophrenia often end up in the lower socioeconomic levels, or even homeless). Other times it appears suddenly, seemingly as a reaction to stress. One rule holds true around the world (World Health Organization, 1979): When schizophrenia is a slow-developing process (called *chronic*, or *process*, schizophrenia), recovery is doubtful. When, in reaction to particular life stresses, a previously well-adjusted person develops schizophrenia rapidly (called *acute*, or *reactive*, schizophrenia), recovery is much more likely. Those with chronic schizophrenia often exhibit the negative symptom of withdrawal. Men, whose schizophrenia develops on average four years earlier than women's, more often exhibit negative symptoms and chronic schizophrenia (Räsänen & others, 2000). The outlook is better for those exhibiting positive symptoms—they more often have a reactive condition that responds to drug therapy (Fenton & McGlashan, 1991, 1994; Fowles, 1992).

Understanding Schizophrenia

13. What causes schizophrenia?

Schizophrenia is not only the most dreaded psychological disorder but also one of the most heavily researched. Most of the new research studies link it with brain abnormalities and genetic predispositions. Schizophrenia is a disease of the brain exhibited in symptoms of the mind.

Brain Abnormalities

Might imbalances in brain chemistry underlie schizophrenia? Scientists have long known that strange behaviors could have strange chemical causes. The saying "mad as a hatter" refers to the psychological deterioration of British hatmakers whose brains, it was later discovered, were slowly poisoned as they moistened the brims of mercury-laden felt hats with their lips (Smith, 1983). As we saw on page 215, scientists are clarifying the mechanism by which chemicals such as LSD produce hallucinations. These discoveries hint that schizophrenia symptoms might have a biochemical key.

DOPAMINE OVERACTIVITY One such key to schizophrenia involves the neurotransmitter dopamine. When researchers examined schizophrenia patients' brains after death, they found an excess of receptors for dopamine—in fact, a sixfold excess for the so-called D4 dopamine receptor (Seeman & others, 1993; Wong & others, 1986). The researchers speculate that such a high level may intensify brain signals in schizophrenia, creating positive symptoms such as hallucinations and paranoia. As we might therefore expect, drugs that block dopamine receptors often lessen the symptoms; drugs that increase dopamine levels, such as amphetamines and cocaine, sometimes intensify them (Swerdlow & Koob, 1987). Dopamine overactivity may underlie patients' overreacting to irrelevant external and internal stimuli.

BRAIN ANATOMY Modern brain-scanning techniques reveal that many people with chronic schizophrenia have abnormal brain activity. Some have abnormally low brain activity in the frontal lobes (Pettegrew & others, 1993; Resnick, 1992). One study took PET scans of brain activity while people were hallucinating (Silbersweig & others, 1995). When participants heard a voice or saw something, their brains became vigorously active in several core regions, including the thalamus, a structure deep in the brain that filters incoming sensory signals and transmits them to the cortex.

Many studies have found enlarged, fluid-filled areas and a corresponding shrinkage of cerebral tissue in schizophrenia patients (Wright & others, 2000). One study even found abnormalities in the brains of people who would *later* develop schizophrenia (Pantelis & others, 2002). The greater the shrinkage, the worse the thought

"When someone asks me to explain schizophrenia I tell them, you know how sometimes in your dreams you are in them yourself and some of them feel like real nightmares? My schizophrenia was like I was walking through a dream. But everything around me was real. At times, today's world seems so boring and I wonder if I would like to step back into the schizophrenic dream, but then I remember all the scary and horrifying experiences."

Stuart Emmons, Craig Geisler,
Kalman J. Kaplan, and Martin Harrow,
Living With Schizophrenia, 1997

Studying the neurophysiology of schizophrenia Psychiatrist E. Fuller Torrey is collecting the brains of hundreds of those who died as young adults and suffered disorders such as schizophrenia and bipolar disorder. Torrey is making tissue samples available to researchers worldwide.

Chris Usher

disorder tends to be (Nelson & others, 1998; Shenton, 1992). The thalamus is one smaller-than-normal area, which may explain why people with schizophrenia have difficulty filtering sensory input and focusing attention (Andreasen & others, 1994). The bottom line of various brain studies, reports Nancy Andreasen (1997, 2001), is that schizophrenia involves not a single brain abnormality but problems with several brain regions and their interconnections.

Naturally, scientists wonder what causes these brain abnormalities. One possibility is a prenatal problem. Low birth weight and birth complications such as oxygen deprivation are known risk factors for schizophrenia (Buka & others, 1999; Zornberg & others, 2000). People conceived during the peak of the Dutch wartime famine also later displayed a doubled rate of schizophrenia (Susser & others, 1996).

MATERNAL VIRUS DURING MIDPREGNANCY Another possible culprit is a midpregnancy viral infection that impairs fetal brain development. Can you imagine some ways to test this fetal-virus idea? Scientists exploring this possibility have asked the following questions:

- Are people at increased risk of schizophrenia if, during the middle of their fetal development, their country experienced a flu epidemic?
- Are people born in densely populated areas, where viral diseases spread more readily, at greater risk for schizophrenia?
- Are those born during the winter and spring months—after the fall-winter flu season—also at increased risk?
- In the Southern Hemisphere, where the seasons are the reverse of the Northern Hemisphere, are the months of above-average schizophrenia births similarly reversed?
- Are mothers who report being sick with influenza during pregnancy more likely to bear children who develop schizophrenia?
- Does blood drawn from pregnant women whose offspring develop schizophrenia show higher-than-normal levels of antibodies that suggest a viral infection?

The answer to all these questions appears to be yes, suggesting that prenatal viral infections do play a contributing role (Myers, 2004).

Schizophrenia has other causes (as genetics research makes plain). Moreover, the children of some 98 percent of women who catch the flu during their second trimester of pregnancy do *not* develop schizophrenia. Nevertheless, these converging lines of evidence suggest that prenatal viral infections play a contributing role. They also strengthen the Centers for Disease Control (2003) recommendation that "women who will be more than three months pregnant during the flu season" have a flu shot.

Why might a second-trimester maternal flu bout put fetuses at risk? Is it the virus itself? The mother's immune response to it? Medications taken? (Wyatt & others, 2001). Does the infection weaken the brain's supportive glial cells, leading to reduced synaptic connections (Moises & others, 2002)? At this point, the answer is not clear.

Genetic Factors

Might people also inherit a predisposition to certain brain abnormalities? The evidence strongly suggests that, yes, some do. The nearly 1 in 100 odds of any person's being diagnosed with schizophrenia become about 1 in 10 among those who have an afflicted sibling or parent, and close to 1 in 2 among those who have an afflicted identical twin (**FIGURE 13.11**). Although there are barely more than a dozen such known cases, it appears that an identical twin of a person with schizophrenia retains that 1-in-2 chance, whether the twins are reared together or apart (Plomin & others, 1997).

figure 13.11
Risk of developing schizophrenia
The lifetime risk of developing schizophrenia varies with one's genetic relatedness to someone having this disorder. Across countries, barely more than 1 in 10 fraternal twins, but some 5 in 10 identical twins, share a schizophrenia diagnosis. (Adapted from Gottesman, 2001.)

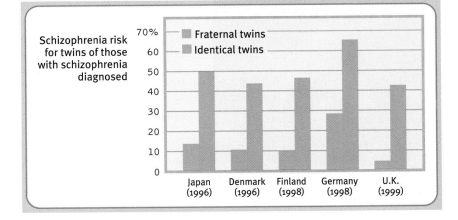

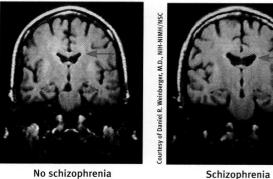

No schizophrenia   Schizophrenia

Schizophrenia in identical twins
When twins differ, only the one afflicted with schizophrenia typically has enlarged, fluid-filled cranial cavities (Suddath & others, 1990). The difference between the twins implies some nongenetic factor, such as a virus, is also at work.

The Genain quadruplets The odds that any four people picked at random would all be diagnosed with schizophrenia are 1 in 100 million. But genetically identical sisters Nora, Iris, Myra, and Hester Genain all have the disease. Two of the sisters have more severe forms of the disorder than the others, suggesting the influence of environmental as well as biological factors.

Even with identical twins there may be a prenatal environmental component. About two-thirds of identical twins share the same placenta and blood. (They usually also have opposite handedness to their co-twin.) If an identical twin has schizophrenia, the co-twin's chances of being similarly afflicted are 6 in 10 if they shared a single placenta, but only 1 in 10 if the twins had separate placentas (Davis & others, 1995a,b; Phelps & others, 1997). Twins who share a placenta are more likely to experience the same prenatal viruses. So it's possible that shared germs as well as shared genes produce identical twin similarities.

Adoption studies, however, confirm that the genetic link is real (Gottesman, 1991). Children adopted by someone who develops schizophrenia seldom "catch" the disorder. Rather, adopted children have an elevated risk if a biological parent is diagnosed with schizophrenia. One intriguing study of 87,907 Israelis also found that the older the biological father—and thus the more opportunities for the DNA in his sperm cells to have mutated—the greater the risk of offspring with schizophrenia (Malaspina & others, 2001).

With the genetic factor established, researchers are now sleuthing specific genes that, in some combination, might predispose schizophrenia-inducing brain abnormalities. Despite tantalizing findings, the culprit genes have proven elusive. The genetic contribution to schizophrenia is beyond question. But the genetic role is not as straightforward as the inheritance of eye color. A complex disorder such as schizophrenia is surely influenced by "multiple genes of small effects."

Also remember that half the twins who share identical genes with a schizophrenia victim do *not* develop the disorder. Thus, behavior geneticists Susan Nicol and Irving Gottesman (1983) concluded that some people "have a genetic predisposition to the disorder but that this predisposition by itself is not sufficient for the development of schizophrenia." Other factors—including the prenatal viral infections mentioned above, but also nutritional deprivation and oxygen deprivation at birth—may be ingredients for the disease.

Our knowledge of human genetics and of genetic influences upon maladies such as schizophrenia and bipolar disorder is exploding. So, can scientists develop genetic tests that reveal who is at risk? If so, will people in the future subject their embryos to genetic testing (and gene repair or abortion) if they are at risk for a psychological or physical malady? Might they take their egg and sperm to the genetics lab for screening before combining them to produce an embryo? Or will children be tested for genetic risks and given appropriate preventive treatments? In this brave new twenty-first-century world, such questions await answers.

Psychological Factors

If genetically predisposed physiological abnormalities do not, by themselves, cause schizophrenia, neither do prenatal and psychological factors alone. It remains true, as Nicol and Gottesman (1983) noted more than two decades ago, that "no environmental causes have been discovered that will invariably, or even with moderate probability, produce schizophrenia in persons who are not related to" a person with schizophrenia. Psychologists long ago ceased blaming parents; no longer do they attribute schizophrenia to cold and capricious "refrigerator mothers."

Nevertheless, if genes predispose some people to *react* to particular experiences by developing schizophrenia, then there must be identifiable triggering experiences. Researchers have asked: Can difficulties in family communications be a contributing factor? Can stress trigger schizophrenia?

The answer to each question is maybe. The psychological triggers of schizophrenia have proved elusive, and they may vary with the type of schizophrenia and its speed of onset—whether it is a slow-developing chronic schizophrenia or a sudden and acute reaction to stress. Young people with schizophrenia do have disturbed communications with their parents. But is this a cause or a result of their disorder?

And stressful experiences, brain abnormalities, and schizophrenia's symptoms do often occur together. But as the bio-psycho-social perspective emphasizes, the traffic between brain biochemistry and psychological experiences runs both ways. Social withdrawal does often occur in adolescence or early adulthood, coinciding with the stresses of having to become independent, assert oneself, and achieve social success and intimacy. So, is schizophrenia the maladaptive coping reaction of biologically vulnerable people? Do abnormalities in the dopamine system and in brain anatomy render a person hypersensitive to stress (Walker & Diforio, 1997)?

Most of us can relate more easily to the ups and downs of mood disorders than to the strange thoughts, perceptions, and behaviors of schizophrenia. Sometimes our thoughts do jump around, but we do not talk nonsensically. Occasionally we feel unjustly suspicious of someone, but we do not fear that the world is plotting against us. Often our perceptions err, but rarely do we see or hear things that are not there. We have felt regret after laughing at someone's misfortune, but we rarely giggle in response to bad news. At times we just want to be alone, but we do not live in social isolation. However, millions of people around the world do talk strangely, suffer delusions, hear nonexistent voices, see things that are not there, laugh or cry at inappropriate times, or withdraw into private imaginary worlds. The quest to solve the cruel puzzle of schizophrenia therefore continues.

rehearse it!

18. Schizophrenia patients often show disorganized thinking and disturbed perceptions. They may speak illogically and may hear voices urging self-destruction. Hearing voices in the absence of any auditory stimulation is an example of a(n)
    a. delusion or false belief.
    b. inappropriate emotion.
    c. word salad.
    d. hallucination.

19. Schizophrenia is actually a cluster of disorders characterized by positive or negative symptoms. A person with positive symptoms is most likely to experience
    a. catatonia.
    b. delusions.
    c. withdrawal.
    d. flat emotion.

20. Stressful events, faulty family communications, and, especially, inherited abnormalities in brain chemistry and structure are all possible factors in the development of schizophrenia. Chances for recovery are best when
    a. onset is sudden, in response to stress.
    b. deterioration occurs gradually, during childhood.
    c. no environmental causes can be identified.
    d. there is a detectable brain abnormality.

Answers can be found in Appendix C.

RATES OF PSYCHOLOGICAL DISORDERS

14. How many people suffer, or have suffered, from a psychological disorder? Does the risk vary with ethnicity or gender?

How prevalent are the various disorders? Who is most vulnerable to them? At what times of life? To answer such questions, the U.S. National Institute of Mental Health (NIMH) undertook a short census of psychological disorders during the 1980s. Researchers conducted lengthy, structured interviews with a representative sample of nearly 20,000 people in five different regions of the country, then projected their findings to the entire U.S. population. After asking hundreds of questions that probed for symptoms—"Has there ever been a period of two weeks or more when you felt like you wanted to die?"—the researchers estimated both the current and the lifetime prevalence of various disorders.

How many people suffer, or have suffered, a psychological disorder? More than most of us suppose:

● Summarizing the NIMH study, and a later government survey, William Narrow and his colleagues (2002) estimate that 1 in 6 Americans suffers clinically significant mental disorders.

● Britain's Office of National Statistics (2002) recently reported a similar 1 in 6 rate of active disorders.

Does a full moon trigger "madness" in some people? James Rotton and I. W. Kelly (1985) examined data from 37 studies that related lunar phase to crime, homicides, crisis calls, and mental hospital admissions. Their conclusion: There is virtually no evidence of "moon madness." Nor does lunar phase correlate with suicides, assaults, emergency room visits, or traffic disasters (Martin & others, 1992; Raison & others, 1999).

● An Australian government survey of 10,600 adults found that in any 12 months, slightly less than 1 in 6 "have a mental disorder" (Andrews & others, 1999). Another Australian government study of 4500 children and adolescents concluded that 1 in 7 had "mental health problems" (Sawyer & others, 2000).

These surprisingly high rates reflect the inclusion of institutionalized as well as community samples, and they surely also reflect how well many people manage to hide disorders such as a phobia, alcohol abuse, or depression. **TABLE 13.3** shows the relative prevalence in the United States of most of the disorders we have considered among three ethnic groups, among men and women, and in the whole population.

The incidence of serious psychological disorders is doubly high among those below the poverty line (Centers for Disease Control, 1992). Like so many other correlations, the poverty–disorder association raises a chicken-and-egg question: Does poverty cause disorders? Or do disorders cause poverty? It's both, though the answer varies with the disorder. Schizophrenia understandably leads to poverty. Yet the stresses and demoralization of poverty can also precipitate disorders, especially depression in women and substance abuse in men (Dohrenwend & others, 1992).

Those who experience a psychological disorder usually do so by early adulthood. "Over 75 percent of our sample with any disorder had experienced its first symptoms by age 24," reported Lee Robins and Darrel Regier (1991, p. 331). The symptoms of antisocial personality disorder and of phobias appear earliest, by a median age of 8 and 10, respectively. Symptoms of alcohol abuse, obsessive-compulsive disorder, bipolar disorder, and schizophrenia appear at a median age near 20. Major depression often hits somewhat later, at a median age of 25. Such findings make clear the need for research and treatment to help the growing number of people, especially teenagers and young adults, who suffer the bewilderment and pain of a psychological disorder.

Although mindful of the pain, we can also be encouraged by the many successful people—including Leonardo da Vinci, Isaac Newton, and Leo Tolstoy—who pursued brilliant careers while enduring psychological difficulties. The bewilderment, fear, and sorrow caused by psychological disorders are real. But, as Chapter 14 shows, hope, too, is real.

table 13.3 Percentage of Americans Who Have Ever Experienced Psychological Disorders

Disorder	White	Ethnicity Black	Hispanic	Gender Men	Women	Total
Alcohol abuse or dependence	13.6%	13.8%	16.7%	23.8%	4.6%	13.8%
Generalized anxiety	3.4	6.1	3.7	2.4	5.0	3.8
Phobias	9.7	23.4	12.2	10.4	17.7	14.3
Obsessive-compulsive disorder	2.6	2.3	1.8	2.0	3.0	2.6
Mood disorder	8.0	6.3	7.8	5.2	10.2	7.8
Schizophrenia	1.4	2.1	0.8	1.2	1.7	1.5
Antisocial personality	2.6	2.3	3.4	4.5	0.8	2.6

Source: *Data from Robins & Regier, 1991. Similar gender differences, though with somewhat higher rates of disorder, come from the U.S. National Comorbidity Survey (Kessler & others, 1994).*

rehearse it!

21. On the basis of an NIMH report and a later government survey, researchers note that 1 in 6 American adults are currently experiencing a psychiatric disorder. Despite differences in the prevalence of disorders among ethnic groups and between men and women, all groups are vulnerable. One factor that crosses ethnic and gender lines and is closely correlated with serious psychological disorder is
a. age.
b. education.
c. poverty.
d. religious faith.

Answers can be found in Appendix C.

chapter review

REVIEWING

Psychological Disorders

PERSPECTIVES ON PSYCHOLOGICAL DISORDERS

1. Where should we draw the line between normality and disorder?

Between normality and abnormality lies not a gulf but a somewhat arbitrary line. Where we draw that line depends on how atypical, disturbing, maladaptive, and unjustifiable a person's behavior is.

2. What theoretical models or perspectives can help us understand psychological disorders?

The medical model's assumption that psychological disorders are mental "illnesses" displaced earlier views that demons and evil spirits were to blame. However, critics question the medical model's labeling of psychological disorders as sicknesses. Most mental health workers today adopt a bio-psycho-social perspective. They assume that disorders are influenced by genetic predisposition, physiological states, psychological dynamics, and social circumstances.

3. How and why do clinicians classify psychological disorders?

Many psychiatrists and psychologists use the *Diagnostic and Statistical Manual of Mental Disorders* (DSM-IV) for naming and describing psychological disorders in treatment and research. Diagnostic labels facilitate mental health professionals' communications and research, and most health insurance policies in North America require DSM-IV diagnoses before they will pay for therapy.

4. Why do some psychologists criticize the use of diagnostic labels?

Critics point out the price we pay for the benefits of classifying disorders: Labels can create preconceptions that unfairly stigmatize people and bias our perceptions of their past and present behavior.

ANXIETY DISORDERS

5. What are anxiety disorders, and how do they differ from the ordinary worries and fears we all experience?

Anxiety is classified as a psychological disorder only when it becomes distressing or persistent, or is characterized by maladaptive behaviors intended to reduce it.

Those who suffer a *generalized anxiety disorder* may for no clear reason feel persistently and uncontrollably tense and uneasy. Anxiety escalates into periodic episodes of intense dread for those suffering *panic disorder*. Those with a *phobic disorder* may be irrationally afraid of a specific object or situation. Persistent and repetitive thoughts and actions characterize *obsessive-compulsive disorder*.

6. What are the sources of the anxious feelings and thoughts that characterize anxiety disorders?

The psychoanalytic perspective viewed anxiety disorders as the discharging of repressed impulses. Psychologists now tend to consider these disorders from the learning and biological perspectives. The learning perspective sees anxiety disorders as a product of fear conditioning, stimulus generalization, reinforcement, and observational learning. The biological perspective considers possible evolutionary, genetic, and physiological influences.

DISSOCIATIVE AND PERSONALITY DISORDERS

7. What are dissociative disorders, and why are they controversial?

Dissociative disorders occur when, under stress, a person's conscious awareness becomes dissociated (separated) from previous memories, thoughts, and feelings. Most mysterious of all dissociative disorders are cases of dissociative identity (multiple personality). The afflicted person is said to have two or more distinct personalities, with the original typically unaware of the other(s). Skeptics question whether this disorder may be a cultural phenomenon, finding it suspicious that the disorder has just recently become popular and is virtually nonexistent outside North America.

8. What characteristics are typical of personality disorders?

Personality disorders are enduring, maladaptive patterns of behavior that impair social functioning. For society, the most troubling of these is the remorseless and fearless antisocial personality.

MOOD DISORDERS

9. What are mood disorders, and what forms do they take?

Mood disorders are characterized by emotional extremes. The two principal forms are *major depressive disorder* and *bipolar disorder*. In major depressive disorder, the person—without apparent reason—descends for weeks or months into deep unhappiness, lethargy, and feelings of worthlessness before rebounding to normality. In the less common bipolar disorder, the person alternates between the hopelessness and lethargy of depression and the hyperactive, wildly optimistic, impulsive phase of mania.

10. *What causes mood disorders, and what might explain the Western world's rising incidence of depression among youth and young adults?*

Current research on depression is vigorously exploring two sets of influences. The first focuses on genetic predispositions and neurotransmitter abnormalities. The second views the cycle of depression from a social-cognitive perspective, in the light of cyclic self-defeating beliefs, learned helplessness, negative attributions, and stressful experiences.

SCHIZOPHRENIA

Schizophrenia typically strikes during late adolescence. It affects men and women about equally, and it seems to occur in all cultures.

11. *What patterns of thinking, perceiving, feeling, and behaving characterize schizophrenia?*

Schizophrenia shows itself in disorganized thinking (nonsensical talk and delusions, which may stem from a breakdown of selective attention); disturbed perceptions (including hallucinations); and inappropriate emotions and actions. It is rarely a one-time episode.

12. *What forms does schizophrenia take?*

Schizophrenia is a set of disorders that emerge either gradually from a chronic history of social inadequacy (in which case the outlook is dim) or suddenly in reaction to stress (in which case the prospects for recovery are brighter). Positive symptoms are defined as the presence of inappropriate behaviors; negative symptoms, as the absence of appropriate behaviors. The subtypes vary in their cause and onset.

13. *What causes schizophrenia?*

Multiple causes converge to create schizophrenia. Researchers have linked certain forms of schizophrenia with brain abnormalities, such as enlarged, fluid-filled cerebral cavities, or increased receptors for the neurotransmitter dopamine, known to be a major player in this disorder. Prenatal viral infections are one possible cause. Twin and adoption studies also point to a genetic predisposition that, in conjunction with environmental factors, may bring about schizophrenia.

RATES OF PSYCHOLOGICAL DISORDERS

14. *How many people suffer, or have suffered, from a psychological disorder? Does the risk vary with ethnicity or gender?*

A 1980s National Institute of Mental Health survey of nearly 20,000 institutionalized and community residents, and a later government survey, revealed that 1 in 6 U.S. adults was currently experiencing a psychological disorder. Risk does vary with ethnicity and gender, and the incidence of serious disorders is doubly high below the poverty line. Among Americans who have ever experienced a psychological disorder, the three most common were phobic disorder, alcohol abuse or dependence (with men outnumbering women 5 to 1), and mood disorder (with women outnumbering men 2 to 1).

A CRITICAL THINKER'S REVIEW OF CHAPTER 13

You've now studied and reviewed **Psychological Disorders**. For even better retention, reflect on these concepts at a deeper level. If you need to refresh your memory of the six categories of critical thinking shown in parentheses below, see page 34. See if you can answer each of these questions in a short paragraph.

1. Raphael's therapist has taken pains to learn all about his medical history and has asked him many questions about how he interacts with others and how he handles day-to-day stress and problematic situations. What perspective does this therapist seem to be operating from, and why is this beneficial for Raphael? (perspective taking)

2. Kirsten has a phobia for heights. She cannot climb a spiral staircase without going pale and gripping the handrail desperately. In an attempt to help, her therapist starts by introducing the concepts of natural selection and learning. Kirsten is bewildered. Where do you think her therapist is going with this discussion? (creative problem solving)

3. When you show your depressed friend Figure 13.10 on page 495, he responds, "You see? Depression is a vicious cycle and there's no way out!" What hope could you offer? (practical problem solving)

4. Phineas Gage was made famous by a tragic and dramatic 1848 accident. He suffered serious brain damage when a tamping rod shot through the frontal lobe of his brain. Gage changed from an even-tempered, likeable young man to an irreverent and irritable character. Which explanation of personality disorders does this famous story support? Why? (pattern recognition)

5. Does a full moon trigger "madness" in some people? How might you test that question? (scientific problem solving)

6. Paniotis' mother suffers from schizophrenia, and Paniotis believes it is because she has lived in poverty for so many years. Could he be right? What is the relationship between poverty and psychological disorders such as schizophrenia? (psychological reasoning)

Answers can be found in Appendix C.

TERMS AND CONCEPTS TO REMEMBER

To continue your study and review of Psychological Disorders, visit this book's Web site at www.worthpublishers.com/myers. You will find practice tests, review activities, and Web links for more information on topics related to Psychological Disorders.

chapter14

Therapy

We have treated psychological disorders with a bewildering variety of harsh and gentle methods: by cutting holes in the head and by giving warm baths and massages; by restraining, bleeding, or "beating the devil" out of people; by placing them in sunny, serene environments; by administering drugs and electric shocks; and by talking—talking about childhood experiences, about current feelings, about maladaptive thoughts and behaviors.

The transition from brutal to gentler treatments occurred thanks to the efforts of reformers such as Philippe Pinel in France and Dorothea Dix in the United States, Canada, and Scotland. Both advocated constructing mental hospitals to offer more humane methods of treatment. As we shall see, however, the introduction of therapeutic drugs and community-based treatment programs has largely emptied mental health hospitals since the mid-1950s.

Today's favored treatment depends on the therapist's viewpoint. Those who believe that psychological disorders are learned will tend to favor psychological therapies. Those who view disorders as biologically rooted are likely to advocate medication as well. Those who believe that disorders are responses to social conditions will, in addition, want to reform the "sick" environment. Many therapists seek to integrate insights from each of these views.

We can classify therapies into two main categories: The *psychological therapies* employ structured interactions (usually verbal) between a trained professional and a client with a problem. The *biomedical therapies* act directly on the patient's nervous system.

Dorothea Dix (1802–1887) "I . . . call your attention to the state of the Insane Persons confined within this Commonwealth, in cages."

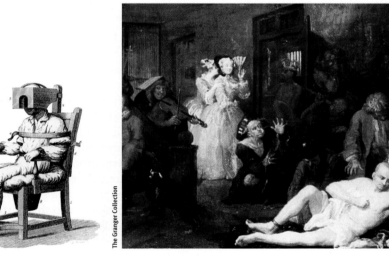

The history of treatment The chair on the far left was designed by Benjamin Rush (1746–1813) "for the benefit of maniacal patients." Rush, a founder of the movement for more humane treatment of the mentally ill, believed they required restraint to regain their sensibilities. At left, William Hogarth's (1697–1764) engraving of St. Mary of Bethlehem hospital in London (commonly called Bedlam) depicts the treatment of mental disorders in the eighteenth century. Visitors paid to gawk at the patients as if they were viewing zoo animals.

THE PSYCHOLOGICAL THERAPIES

Psychological therapy, or **psychotherapy**, is "a planned, emotionally charged, confiding interaction between a trained, socially sanctioned healer and a sufferer" (Frank, 1982). Some 250 types of psychotherapy have been identified (Parloff, 1987). We will look at only the most influential. Each is built on one or more of psychology's major theories: psychoanalytic, humanistic, behavioral, and cognitive.

Although each technique is distinctive, there are common threads. Therapists who view disorders as an interplay of bio-psycho-social influences may welcome a combination of treatments. Indeed, half of psychotherapists describe themselves as taking an **eclectic approach**, by using a blend of therapies (Beitman & others, 1989; Castonguay & Goldfried, 1994). Depending on the client and the problem, an eclectic therapist will draw from a variety of techniques. Closely related to eclecticism is *psychotherapy integration*. Rather than picking and choosing methods, integration advocates aim to combine them into a single, coherent system.

▶ **psychotherapy** an emotionally charged, confiding interaction between a trained therapist and someone who suffers from psychological difficulties.

▶ **eclectic approach** an approach to psychotherapy that, depending on the client's problems, uses techniques from various forms of therapy.

▶ **psychoanalysis** Sigmund Freud's therapeutic technique. Freud believed the patient's free associations, resistances, dreams, and transferences—and the therapist's interpretations of them—released previously repressed feelings, allowing the patient to gain self-insight.

▶ **resistance** in psychoanalysis, the blocking from consciousness of anxiety-laden material.

▶ **interpretation** in psychoanalysis, the analyst's noting supposed dream meanings, resistances, and other significant behaviors in order to promote insight.

▶ **transference** in psychoanalysis, the patient's transfer to the analyst of emotions linked with other relationships (such as love or hatred for a parent).

Psychoanalysis

1. What are the aims and methods of psychoanalysis, and how have they been adapted in psychodynamic therapy?

Although few clinicians today practice therapy as Sigmund Freud did, many of his techniques and assumptions survive, especially in the *psychodynamic* therapies (see page 509). Freudian terminology has also crept into our modern vocabulary. Let's look, then, at classical **psychoanalysis** as practiced by Freud himself.

Aims

As we noted in Chapter 12, Freud assumed that many psychological problems are fueled by childhood's residue of repressed impulses and conflicts. It is therefore the analyst's job to bring these repressed feelings into conscious awareness where the patient can deal with them. By gaining insight into the origins of the disorder—by fulfilling the ancient imperative to "know thyself" in a deep way—the patient "works through" the buried feelings. The theory presumes that healthier, less anxious living becomes possible when patients release the energy they had previously devoted to id-ego-superego conflicts.

Methods

Psychoanalysis is historical reconstruction. It aims to unearth the past in hope of unmasking the present. But how?

When Freud discarded hypnosis as unreliable, he turned to *free association*. Imagine yourself as a patient using the free association technique. The analyst invites you to relax, perhaps by lying on a couch. He or she will probably help you focus attention on your own thoughts and feelings by sitting out of your line of vision. Beginning with a childhood memory, a dream, or a recent experience, you say aloud whatever comes to your mind from moment to moment. It sounds easy, but soon you notice how often you edit your thoughts as you speak, omitting what seems trivial, irrelevant, or shameful. Even in the safe presence of the analyst, you may pause momentarily before uttering an embarrassing thought. You may make a joking remark or change the subject to something less threatening. Sometimes your mind may go blank or you may find yourself unable to remember important details.

To the psychoanalyst, these blocks in the flow of your free associations indicate **resistance**. They hint that anxiety lurks and that you are repressing sensitive material. The analyst will want to make you aware of your resistances and then **interpret** their meaning, providing *insight* into underlying wishes, feelings, and conflicts. If offered at the right moment, the analyst's interpretation—of, say, your not wanting to talk about your mother—may illuminate what you are avoiding and demonstrate how this resistance fits with other pieces of your psychological puzzle.

Classical psychoanalysis The placement of the analyst's chair out of view is thought to minimize distraction and make it easier for the patient—relaxed on a couch—to verbalize whatever comes to mind.

Freud believed that another clue to repressed impulses is your dream's *latent content*—its underlying but censored meaning. Thus, after inviting you to report a dream, the analyst may offer a dream analysis, suggesting its meaning.

During many such sessions you will probably disclose to your analyst more of yourself than you have ever revealed to anyone else. Because psychoanalytic theory emphasizes the formative power of childhood experiences, much of what you reveal will pertain to your earliest memories. You may find yourself experiencing strong positive or negative feelings for your analyst. When this happens, Freud would say you are actually *transferring* your strongest feelings from earlier relationships (with family members or other important people) to the analyst. Analysts and other therapists believe that this **transference** exposes long-repressed feelings, such as dependency or mingled love and anger, giving you a belated chance to work through them with your analyst's help. But psychoanalysis is not just about excavating your childhood past. By examining your feelings toward the analyst you may also gain insight into your current relationships.

Note how much of psychoanalysis is built on the assumption that repressed memories exist. As we noted in Chapter 8, that assumption is now questioned. This challenge—to an assumption so basic to much of professional and popular psychology—is provoking intense debate.

Critics also say psychoanalysts' interpretations are hard to refute. If, in response to the analyst's suggested interpretation, you say, "Yes! I see now," your acceptance confirms the analyst's interpretation. If you emphatically say, "No! Not so!" some analysts may take your denial as more resistance, also confirming the interpretation. Psychoanalysts acknowledge it's hard to prove or disprove their interpretations. But they insist that interpretations often are a great help to patients. Psychoanalysis is therapy, not science.

Traditional psychoanalysis takes time, up to several years of several sessions a week, and it is expensive. (Three times a week for just two years at more than $100 per hour comes to at least $30,000.) This helps explain why, outside of New York City, Quebec, France, and Germany, relatively few therapists offer it (Goode, 2003).

"In the mental-health profession, we try to avoid negative labels, like 'a hundred and fifty bucks an hour—that's crazy!' or 'three fifty-minute sessions a week—that's insane!'"

Woody Allen, after awakening from suspended animation in the movie Sleeper: *"I haven't seen my analyst in 200 years. He was a strict Freudian. If I'd been going all this time, I'd probably almost be cured by now."*

Psychodynamic Therapy

Influenced by Freud, *psychodynamic* therapists try to understand a patient's current symptoms by exploring childhood experiences. They also probe for supposed repressed, emotion-laden information, seeking to help the person gain insight into the unconscious roots of problems and work through newly resurrected feelings. But these therapists may talk to the patient face to face (rather than out of the line of vision), once a week (rather than several times weekly), and for only a few weeks or months (rather than several years).

No brief excerpt can exemplify psychodynamic therapy's probing of the past, but we can illustrate these therapists' goal of enabling insight via their interpretations. In the following interaction, therapist David Malan responds to all that he has heard from a depressed patient by suggesting insights into her problems. Note how Malan interprets the woman's earlier remarks (when he listened as she did most of the talking) and suggests that her relationship with him reveals a characteristic pattern of behavior (1978, pp. 133–134).

> ***Malan:*** *I get the feeling that you're the sort of person who needs to keep active. If you don't keep active, then something goes wrong. Is that true?*
>
> ***Patient:*** *Yes.*
>
> ***Malan:*** *I get a second feeling about you and that is that you must, underneath all this, have an awful lot of very strong and upsetting feelings. Somehow they're there but you aren't really quite in touch with them. Isn't this right? I feel you've been like that as long as you can remember.*
>
> ***Patient:*** *For quite a few years, whenever I really sat down and thought about it I got depressed, so I tried not to think about it.*
>
> ***Malan:*** *You see, you've established a pattern, haven't you? You're even like that here with me, because in spite of the fact that you're in some trouble and you feel that the bottom is falling out of your world, the way you're telling me this is just as if there wasn't anything wrong.*

Interpersonal psychotherapy, a brief (12- to 16-session) alternative to psychodynamic therapy has been found effective with depressed patients (Weissman, 1999). Like psychodynamic therapies, interpersonal psychotherapy aims to help people gain insight into the roots of their difficulties. But rather than focusing on undoing past hurts and offering interpretations, interpersonal therapy focuses on current relationships and assists people in improving their relationship skills. Its goal is not personality change but symptom relief in the here and now.

Face-to-face therapy In this type of therapy session, the couch has disappeared. But the influence of psychoanalytic theory may not have, especially if the therapist probes for the origin of the patient's symptoms by seeking information from the patient's childhood.

▶ **client-centered therapy** a humanistic therapy, developed by Carl Rogers, in which the therapist uses techniques such as active listening within a genuine, accepting, empathic environment to facilitate clients' growth. (Also called *person-centered therapy*.)

▶ **active listening** empathic listening in which the listener echoes, restates, and clarifies. A feature of Rogers' client-centered therapy.

Interpersonal psychotherapy goals can be illustrated with the case of Anna (not her real name), a 34-year-old married businesswoman. Five months after receiving a promotion, with accompanying responsibilities and longer hours, Anna experienced increased tensions with her husband over his wanting a second child. She began feeling depressed, had trouble sleeping, became irritable, and was gaining weight. A psychodynamic therapist would likely help Anna gain insight into her angry impulses and her defenses against anger. An interpersonal therapist would similarly want the patient to gain insight but would also engage Anna's thinking on immediate issues—how to balance work and home, how to resolve the dispute with her husband, and how to express emotion more effectively (Markowitz & others, 1998).

Humanistic Therapies

2. What are the basic themes of humanistic therapy, such as Rogers' client-centered approach?

As we noted in Chapter 12, the humanistic perspective has emphasized people's inherent potential for self-fulfillment. Not surprisingly, then, humanistic therapists aim to boost self-fulfillment by helping people grow in self-awareness and self-acceptance. Unlike psychoanalytic therapists, humanistic therapists tend to focus on

- the *present* and *future* more than the past. They explore feelings as they occur, rather than achieving insights into the childhood origins of the feelings.
- *conscious* rather than unconscious thoughts.
- taking immediate *responsibility* for one's feelings and actions, rather than uncovering hidden determinants.
- promoting *growth* instead of curing illness. Thus, those in therapy are "clients" rather than "patients."

One widely used humanistic technique is Carl Rogers' (1961, 1980) **client-centered therapy**. A client-centered therapist focuses on the person's conscious self-perceptions rather than on the therapist's own interpretations. The therapist listens, without judging or interpreting, and refrains from directing the client toward certain insights, a strategy labeled *nondirective* therapy.

Believing that most people already possess the resources for growth, Rogers encouraged therapists to exhibit *genuineness, acceptance*, and *empathy*. When therapists drop their facades and genuinely express their true feelings, when they enable their clients to feel unconditionally accepted, and when they empathically sense and reflect their clients' feelings, the clients may deepen their self-understanding and self-acceptance (Hill & Nakayama, 2000). As Rogers (1980, p. 10) explained,

> Hearing has consequences. When I truly hear a person and the meanings that are important to him at that moment, hearing not simply his words, but him, and when I let him know that I have heard his own private personal meanings, many things happen. There is first of all a grateful look. He feels released. He wants to tell me more about his world. He surges forth in a new sense of freedom. He becomes more open to the process of change.
>
> I have often noticed that the more deeply I hear the meanings of the person, the more there is that happens. Almost always, when a person realizes he has been deeply heard, his eyes moisten. I think in some real sense he is weeping for joy. It is as though he were saying, "Thank God, somebody heard me. Someone knows what it's like to be me."

"Hearing" refers to Rogers' technique of **active listening**—echoing, restating, and seeking clarification of what the person expresses (verbally or nonverbally) and acknowledging the expressed feelings. Active listening is now an accepted part of therapeutic counseling practices in many schools, colleges, and clinics. The counselor listens attentively and interrupts only to restate and confirm the client's feelings, to accept what the client is expressing, or to seek clarification. The following excerpt between Rogers and a male client illustrates how a therapist using this approach

"We have two ears and one mouth that we may listen the more and talk the less."

Zeno, 335–263 B.C., Diogenes Laertius

seeks to provide a psychological mirror that helps clients see themselves more clearly.

Client: *I just ain't no good to nobody, never was, and never will be.*

Rogers: *Feeling that now, hm? That you're just no good to yourself, no good to anybody. Never will be any good to anybody. Just that you're completely worthless, huh?— Those really are lousy feelings. Just feel that you're no good at all, hm?*

Client: *Yeah.* (Muttering in low, discouraged voice) *That's what this guy I went to town with just the other day told me.*

Rogers: *This guy that you went to town with really told you that you were no good? Is that what you're saying? Did I get that right?*

Client: *M-hm.*

Rogers: *I guess the meaning of that if I get it right is that here's somebody that—meant something to you and what does he think of you? Why, he's told you that he thinks you're no good at all. And that just really knocks the props out from under you.* (Client weeps quietly.) *It just brings the tears.* (Silence of 20 seconds)

Client: (Rather defiantly) *I don't care though.*

Rogers: *You tell yourself you don't care at all, but somehow I guess some part of you cares because some part of you weeps over it. (Meador & Rogers, 1984, p. 167)*

Active listening Carl Rogers (right) empathized with a client during this group therapy session.

Can a therapist be a perfect mirror, without selecting and interpreting what is reflected? Rogers conceded that one cannot be *totally* nondirective. Nevertheless, he believed that the therapist's most important contribution is to accept and understand the client. Given a nonjudgmental, grace-filled environment that provides *unconditional positive regard*, people internalize unconditional positive self-regard; they may accept even their worst traits and feel valued and whole.

If you want to listen more actively in your own relationships, three hints may help (keep in mind that practicing these is not easy):

1. **Paraphrase.** Check your understandings by summarizing the speaker's words in your own words.
2. **Invite clarification.** "What might be an example of that?" may encourage the speaker to say more.
3. **Reflect feelings.** "It sounds frustrating" might mirror what you're sensing from the speaker's body language and intensity.

rehearse it!

1. All of the psychological therapies involve verbal interactions between a trained professional and a person with a problem. A therapist who encourages people to relate their dreams and searches for the unconscious roots of their problems is drawing from
   a. psychoanalysis.
   b. humanistic therapies.
   c. person-centered therapy.
   d. nondirective therapy.

2. According to psychoanalytic theory, a patient's emotional relationship with the therapist mirrors other important relationships in the patient's life—for example, an early relationship with a parent. Developing strong feelings for the analyst is an important part of the psychoanalytic process and is called
   a. transference.
   b. resistance.
   c. interpretation.
   d. empathy.

3. Humanistic therapists focus on present experience—on becoming aware of feelings as they arise and taking responsibility for them. Compared with psychoanalysts, humanistic therapists are more likely to emphasize
   a. hidden or repressed feelings.
   b. childhood experiences.
   c. psychological disorders.
   d. self-fulfillment and growth.

4. Especially important to Carl Rogers' person-centered therapy is the technique of active listening. The therapist who practices active listening
   a. engages in free association.
   b. exposes the patient's resistances.
   c. restates and clarifies the client's statements.
   d. directly challenges the client's self-perceptions.

Answers can be found in Appendix C.

Behavior Therapies

3. What are the assumptions and techniques of the behavior therapies?

The therapies we have considered so far assume that, for rational people at least, psychological problems diminish as self-awareness grows. The psychoanalyst expects problems to subside as people gain insight into their unresolved and unconscious tensions. The humanistic therapist expects problems to abate as people "get in touch with their feelings." Behavior therapists, however, doubt the healing power of self-awareness. They assume that problem behaviors *are* the problems. For example, you can become aware of why you are highly anxious during exams and still be anxious. So, instead of trying to resolve a presumed underlying problem, **behavior therapy** applies learning principles to eliminate the unwanted behavior. To treat phobias or sexual disorders, behavior therapists do not delve deep below the surface looking for inner causes. They view maladaptive symptoms as learned behaviors, which they try to replace with constructive behaviors.

Classical Conditioning Techniques

One cluster of behavior therapies derives from principles developed in Pavlov's conditioning experiments (pages 228–230). As Pavlov and others showed, we learn various behaviors and emotions through classical conditioning. So, are maladaptive symptoms examples of conditioned responses? If so, might reconditioning be a solution? One such conditioning therapy was developed by learning theorist O. H. Mowrer for chronic bed-wetters. The child sleeps on a liquid-sensitive pad connected to an alarm. Moisture on the pad triggers the alarm, waking the child. With sufficient repetition, this association of urinary relaxation with waking up stops the bed-wetting. In three out of four cases the treatment is effective, and the success provides a boost to the child's self-image (Christophersen & Edwards, 1992; Houts & others, 1994).

Another example: If a claustrophobic fear of elevators is a learned aversion to the stimulus of being in a confined space, then might one unlearn the fear by counterconditioning the fear response? **Counterconditioning** pairs the trigger stimulus with a new response that is incompatible with fear. For example, repeatedly pairing the enclosed space of the elevator with a relaxed response may displace the fear response.

Two specific counterconditioning techniques are *systematic desensitization* and *aversive conditioning*.

SYSTEMATIC DESENSITIZATION Picture this scene reported in 1924 by Mary Cover Jones, an associate of the behaviorist John B. Watson: Three-year-old Peter is petrified of rabbits and other furry objects. (Unlike Little Albert's laboratory-conditioned fear of white rats, described in Chapter 7, Peter's fear arose during the course of his life at home and is more intense.) Jones aims to replace Peter's fear of rabbits with a conditioned response that is incompatible with fear. Her strategy is to associate the fear-evoking rabbit with the pleasurable, relaxed response associated with eating.

As Peter begins his midafternoon snack, Jones introduces a caged rabbit on the other side of the huge room. Peter, eagerly munching away on his crackers and drinking his milk, hardly notices. On succeeding days, she gradually moves the rabbit closer and closer. Within two months, Peter is tolerating the rabbit in his lap, even stroking it while he eats. Moreover, his fear of other furry objects subsides as well, having been "countered," or replaced, by a relaxed state that cannot coexist with fear (Fisher, 1984; Jones, 1924).

Unfortunately for those who might have been helped by her counterconditioning procedures, Jones' story of Peter and the rabbit did not immediately become part of psychology's lore. It was more than 30 years later that psychiatrist Joseph Wolpe (1958; Wolpe & Plaud, 1997) refined Jones' technique into what has become the most widely used method of behavior therapy: the **exposure therapies**. Exposure

What might a psychoanalyst say about this therapy for bed-wetting? How might a behavior therapist reply?

▶ **behavior therapy** therapy that applies learning principles to the elimination of unwanted behaviors.

▶ **counterconditioning** a behavior therapy procedure that conditions new responses to stimuli that trigger unwanted behaviors; based on classical conditioning. Includes *systematic desensitization* and *aversive conditioning*.

▶ **exposure therapies** behavioral techniques, such as systematic desensitization, that treat anxieties by exposing people (in imagination or actuality) to the things they fear and avoid.

▶ **systematic desensitization** a type of counterconditioning that associates a pleasant relaxed state with gradually increasing anxiety-triggering stimuli. Commonly used to treat phobias.

therapies expose people to what they normally avoid. As people can habituate to the sound of a train passing their new apartment, so, with repeated exposure, can they become less responsive to things that once petrified them.

One widely used exposure therapy is **systematic desensitization**. Wolpe assumed, as did Jones, that you cannot simultaneously be anxious and relaxed. Therefore, if you can repeatedly relax when facing anxiety-provoking stimuli, you can gradually eliminate your anxiety. The trick is to proceed gradually.

Let's see how this might work with a common phobia. Imagine yourself afraid of public speaking. A behavior therapist might first ask for your help in constructing a hierarchy of anxiety-triggering speaking situations. Your anxiety hierarchy could range from mildly anxiety-provoking situations, such as speaking up in a small group of friends, to panic-provoking situations, such as having to address a large audience.

Using *progressive relaxation*, the therapist trains you to relax one muscle group after another, until you achieve a drowsy state of complete relaxation and comfort. Then the therapist asks you to imagine, with your eyes closed, a mildly anxiety-arousing situation: You are having coffee with a group of friends and are trying to decide whether to speak up. If imagining the scene causes you to feel any anxiety, you signal your tension by raising your finger, and the therapist instructs you to switch off the mental image and go back to deep relaxation. This imagined scene is repeatedly paired with relaxation until you feel no trace of anxiety.

The therapist progresses up the constructed anxiety hierarchy, using the relaxed state to desensitize you to each imagined situation. After several therapy sessions, you practice what you had imagined in actual situations, beginning with relatively easy tasks and gradually moving to more anxiety-filled ones. Conquering your anxiety in an actual situation, not just in your imagination, raises your self-confidence (Foa & Kozak, 1986; Williams, 1987). Eventually, you may even become a confident public speaker.

For those unable to vividly imagine an anxiety-arousing situation and too terrified or embarrassed to experience the situation in reality, *virtual reality exposure therapy* offers an efficient middle ground. Wearing a head-mounted display unit that projects a three-dimensional virtual world, the fearful person is immersed into a lifelike series of scenes. Experiments led by several research teams in Atlanta and elsewhere have treated people with fear of flying, fear of heights, fear of particular animals, and fear of public speaking (Gershon & others, 2002; Rothbaum & others, 1995, 1997). People with a fear of flying, for example, can peer out a virtual window of a simulated plane, feel vibrations, and hear the engine roar as the plane taxis down the runway and takes off. In initial experiments, those experiencing virtual reality exposure therapy have experienced greater relief from their fears—in real life—than have those in control groups.

THE FAR SIDE® BY GARY LARSON

© 1986 FarWorks, Inc. All Rights Reserved/Dist. by Creators Syndicate

The Far Side® by Gary Larson © 1986 FarWorks, Inc. All Rights Reserved. Used with permission.

Professor Gallagher and his controversial technique of simultaneously confronting the fear of heights, snakes and the dark.

Bob Mahoney/The Image Works

Bob Mahoney/The Image Works

Virtual reality exposure therapy
Within the confines of a room, virtual reality technology exposes people to vivid simulations of feared stimuli, such as a plane's takeoff.

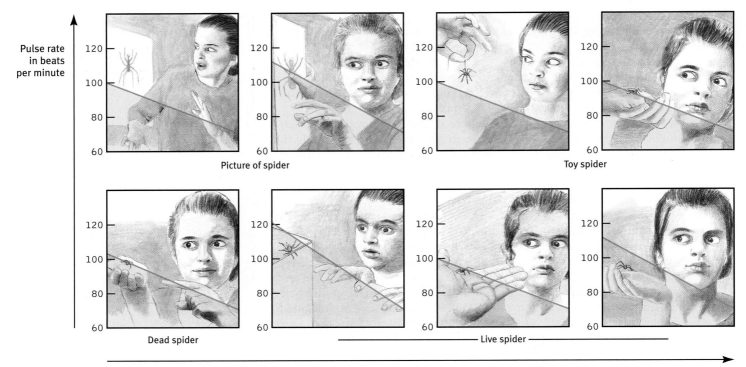

Pulse rate in beats per minute

Picture of spider

Toy spider

Dead spider

Live spider

Time

figure 14.1
Systematic desensitization of a phobia Beverly, who is terribly afraid of spiders, is exposed to progressively more threatening stimuli, but she adapts to each one in turn, as shown by her pulse rate's return to near-normal. She tolerates first a picture of a spider, then a toy spider, then a dead spider, and finally a live one. Notice that the therapist is modeling appropriate behavior for Beverly. (Adapted from Gilling & Brightwell, 1982.)

Therapists sometimes combine systematic desensitization with observational learning and other techniques. Using this combined approach, they have helped people overcome disruptive fears of snakes, spiders, and dogs (**Figure 14.1**). Notice that the systematic desensitization and modeling procedures make no attempt to help the person achieve insight into the fear's underlying cause. Simply changing maladaptive behaviors can help people feel better about themselves.

AVERSIVE CONDITIONING In systematic desensitization, the therapist helps the client substitute a positive (relaxed) response for a negative (fearful) response to a harmless stimulus. In **aversive conditioning**, the therapist tries to replace a positive response to a harmful stimulus (such as alcohol) with a negative (aversive) response. Thus, aversive conditioning is the reverse of systematic desensitization—it seeks to condition an aversion to something the client *should* avoid.

The procedure is simple: It associates the unwanted behavior with unpleasant feelings. To treat nail biting, one can paint the fingernails with a yucky-tasting nail polish (Baskind, 1997). To treat alcoholism, an aversion therapist offers the client appealing drinks laced with a drug that produces severe nausea. By linking the drinking of alcohol with violent nausea, the therapist seeks to transform the person's reaction to alcohol from positive to negative (see **Figure 14.2**; also recall the taste-aversion experiments with rats and coyotes in Chapter 7). Arthur Wiens and Carol Menustik (1983) studied 685 alcoholic patients who completed an aversion therapy program at a Portland, Oregon, hospital. One year later, after returning for several booster treatments of alcohol-sickness pairings, 63 percent were still successfully abstaining. But after three years, only 33 percent had remained abstinent.

Does aversive conditioning work? In the short run it may. But, as we saw in Chapter 7, the problem is that cognition influences conditioning. People know that outside the therapist's office they can drink without fear of nausea. Their ability to discriminate between the aversive conditioning situation and all other situations can limit the treatment's effectiveness. Thus, it is often used in combination with another treatment.

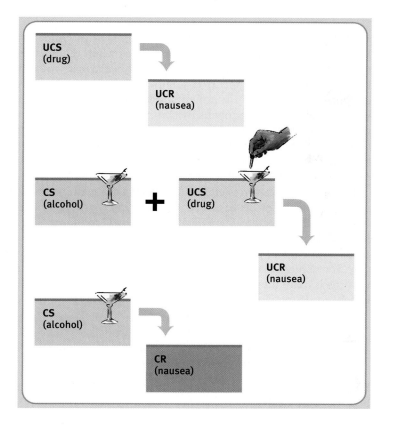

figure 14.2
Aversion therapy for alcoholism After repeatedly imbibing an alcoholic drink mixed with a drug that produces severe nausea, some people with a history of alcohol abuse develop at least a temporary conditioned aversion to alcohol.

Operant Conditioning

Recall from Chapter 7 that voluntary behaviors are strongly influenced by their consequences. This simple fact enables behavior therapists to reinforce desired behaviors and to withhold reinforcement for, or to punish, undesired behaviors. Using operant conditioning to solve specific behavior problems has raised hopes for some cases thought to be hopeless. Children with mental retardation have been taught to care for themselves. Socially withdrawn children with autism have learned to interact. People with schizophrenia have been helped to behave more rationally in their hospital ward. In such cases, therapists use positive reinforcers to shape behavior in the step-by-step manner described on pages 238–239.

In extreme cases, treatment must be intensive. In one study, 19 withdrawn, uncommunicative 3-year-olds with autism participated in a 2-year, 40-hour-a-week program in which their parents attempted to shape their behavior (Lovaas, 1987). The combination of positively reinforcing desired behaviors and ignoring or punishing aggressive and self-abusive behaviors worked wonders. By first grade, 9 of the 19 children were functioning successfully in school and exhibiting normal intelligence. Only 1 of 40 comparable children who did not undergo this treatment showed similar improvement.

Rewards used to modify behavior vary. For some people, the reinforcing power of attention or praise is sufficient. Others require concrete rewards, such as food. In institutional settings, therapists may create a **token economy**. When patients display appropriate behavior, such as getting out of bed, washing, dressing, eating, talking coherently, cleaning up their rooms, or playing cooperatively, they receive a token or plastic coin as a positive reinforcer. Later, they can exchange their accumulated tokens for various rewards, such as candy, watching television, trips to town, or better living quarters. Token economies have been successfully applied in various settings (homes, classrooms, hospitals, institutions for the delinquent) and among members of various populations (including disturbed children and people with schizophrenia and other mental disabilities).

▶ **aversive conditioning** a type of counter-conditioning that associates an unpleasant state (such as nausea) with an unwanted behavior (such as drinking alcohol).

▶ **token economy** an operant conditioning procedure that rewards desired behavior. A patient exchanges a token of some sort, earned for exhibiting the desired behavior, for various privileges or treats.

Critics of such *behavior modification* express two concerns. The first is practical: What happens when the reinforcers stop, as when the person leaves the institution? Could the person become so dependent on extrinsic rewards that the appropriate behaviors quickly disappear? If so, how can behavior therapists make the appropriate behaviors durable? Proponents of behavior modification respond that they may wean patients from the tokens by shifting them toward other rewards, such as social approval, more typical of life outside the institution. They may also train people to behave in ways that are intrinsically rewarding. For example, as a withdrawn person becomes more socially competent, the intrinsic satisfactions of social interaction may help the person maintain the behavior.

The second concern is ethical: Is it right for one human to control another's behavior? Those who set up token economies typically deprive people of something they desire and then decide which behaviors they will reinforce. To critics, the whole behavior modification process has an authoritarian taint. Advocates reply that control already exists; rewards and punishers are already maintaining destructive behavior patterns. So why not reinforce adaptive behavior instead? They argue that treatment with positive rewards is more humane than being institutionalized or punished, and that the right to effective treatment and to an improved life justifies temporary deprivation.

Cognitive Therapies

4. What are the goals and techniques of the cognitive therapies?

We have seen how behavior therapists treat specific fears and problem behaviors. But how do they deal with major depression or general anxiety? When anxiety has no focus, developing a hierarchy of anxiety-triggering situations is difficult. The cognitive revolution that has profoundly changed psychology during the last four decades has also influenced how therapists treat these less clearly defined psychological problems.

The **cognitive therapies** assume that our thinking colors our feelings (**FIGURE 14.3**), that between the event and our response lies the mind. As we noted in Chapter 13, self-blaming and overgeneralized explanations of bad events are an integral part of the vicious cycle of depression. The person experiencing depression interprets a suggestion as criticism, disagreement as dislike, praise as flattery, friendliness as

"Life does not consist mainly, or even largely, of facts and happenings. It consists mainly of the storm of thoughts that are forever blowing through one's mind."

Mark Twain, 1835–1910

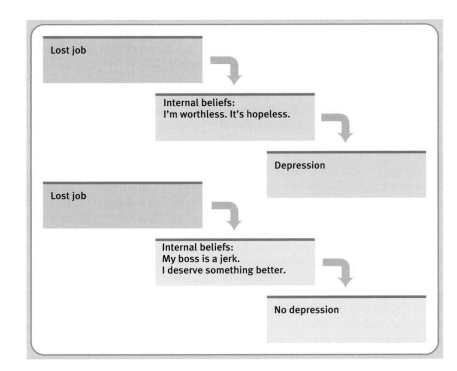

figure 14.3
A cognitive perspective on psychological disorders The person's emotional reactions are produced not directly by the event but by the person's thoughts in response to the event.

pity. Ruminating on such thoughts sustains the bad mood. If depressing thinking patterns are learned, then surely they can be replaced. Cognitive therapists therefore try in various ways to teach people new, more constructive ways of thinking. If people are miserable, they can be helped to change their minds.

Cognitive therapist Aaron Beck was originally trained in Freudian techniques. As Beck analyzed the dreams of patients with depression, he found recurring negative themes of loss, rejection, and abandonment that extended into their waking thoughts. Such negativity even extends into therapy, as clients recall and rehearse their failings and worst impulses (Kelly, 2000). So in their form of cognitive therapy, Beck and his colleagues (1979) instead seek to reverse clients' catastrophizing beliefs about themselves, their situations, and their futures. They attempt to convince depressed people to take off the dark glasses through which they view life, and their technique is a gentle questioning that aims to help people discover their irrationalities (Beck & others, 1979, pp. 145–146):

> **Patient:** *I agree with the descriptions of me but I guess I don't agree that the way I think makes me depressed.*
> **Beck:** *How do you understand it?*
> **Patient:** *I get depressed when things go wrong. Like when I fail a test.*
> **Beck:** *How can failing a test make you depressed?*
> **Patient:** *Well, if I fail I'll never get into law school.*
> **Beck:** *So failing the test means a lot to you. But if failing a test could drive people into clinical depression, wouldn't you expect everyone who failed the test to have a depression? . . . Did everyone who failed get depressed enough to require treatment?*
> **Patient:** *No, but it depends on how important the test was to the person.*
> **Beck:** *Right, and who decides the importance?*
> **Patient:** *I do.*
> **Beck:** *And so, what we have to examine is your way of viewing the test (or the way that you think about the test) and how it affects your chances of getting into law school. Do you agree?*
> **Patient:** *Right.*
> **Beck:** *Do you agree that the way you interpret the results of the test will affect you? You might feel depressed, you might have trouble sleeping, not feel like eating, and you might even wonder if you should drop out of the course.*
> **Patient:** *I have been thinking that I wasn't going to make it. Yes, I agree.*
> **Beck:** *Now what did failing mean?*
> **Patient:** *(tearful) That I couldn't get into law school.*
> **Beck:** *And what does that mean to you?*
> **Patient:** *That I'm just not smart enough.*
> **Beck:** *Anything else?*
> **Patient:** *That I can never be happy.*
> **Beck:** *And how do these thoughts make you feel?*
> **Patient:** *Very unhappy.*
> **Beck:** *So it is the meaning of failing a test that makes you very unhappy. In fact, believing that you can never be happy is a powerful factor in producing unhappiness. So, you get yourself into a trap—by definition, failure to get into law school equals "I can never be happy."*

Cognitive therapists often combine the reversal of self-defeating thinking with efforts to modify behavior. This integrated therapy, called **cognitive-behavior therapy**, aims to alter the way people act (behavior therapy) and to alter the way they think (cognitive therapy). It seeks to make people aware of their irrational negative thinking, to replace it with new ways of thinking, *and* to practice the more positive approach in everyday settings.

An example: We often think in words. Therefore, getting people to change what they say to themselves is an effective way to change their thinking. Perhaps you can identify with the anxious students who before an exam make matters worse with

▶ **cognitive therapy** therapy that teaches people new, more adaptive ways of thinking and acting; based on the assumption that thoughts intervene between events and our emotional reactions.

▶ **cognitive-behavior therapy** a popular integrated therapy that combines cognitive therapy (changing self-defeating thinking) with behavior therapy (changing behavior).

self-defeating thoughts: "This exam's probably going to be impossible. All these other students seem so relaxed and confident. I wish I were better prepared. Anyhow, I'm so nervous I'll forget everything." To change such negative self-talk, Donald Meichenbaum (1977, 1985) offers *stress inoculation training*. He trains people to restructure their thinking in stressful situations. Sometimes it may be enough simply to say more positive things to oneself: "Relax. The exam may be hard, but it will be hard for everyone else, too. I studied harder than most people. Besides, I don't need a perfect score to get a good grade." In experiments, depression-prone children and college students exhibit a halved rate of future depression after being trained to dispute their negative thoughts (Seligman, 2002).

GROUP AND FAMILY THERAPIES

5. In what group contexts do people receive therapy?

Except for traditional psychoanalysis, the therapies we have considered may also occur in therapist-led small groups. Group therapy does not provide the same degree of therapist involvement with each client; however, it saves therapists' time and clients' money—and it often is no less effective than individual therapy (Fuhriman & Burlingame, 1994). Therapists frequently suggest group therapy for people experiencing family conflicts or those whose behavior is distressing to others. For up to 90 minutes a week, the therapist guides the interactions of 6 to 10 people as they engage issues and react to one another.

Group sessions also offer a unique benefit: The social context allows people both to discover that others have problems similar to their own and to try out new ways of behaving. It can help to receive feedback—perhaps being reassured that you look poised even though you feel anxious and self-conscious. And it can be a relief to find that you are not alone—to learn that others, despite their apparent composure, share your problems and your troublesome feelings.

This has been the experience of a wide range of participants in self-help and support groups (Yalom, 1985). In an individualistic age, with more and more people living alone or feeling isolated, the popularity of support groups—for the bereaved, the divorced, the addicted, and those simply seeking fellowship and growth—reflects a longing for community and connectedness. More than 100 million Americans belong to small religious, interest, or self-help groups that meet regularly—and 9 in 10 report that group members "support each other emotionally" (Gallup, 1994). One analysis (Davison & others, 2000) of online support groups and more than 14,000 self-help groups reports that most support groups focus on stigmatized, embarrassing, hard-to-discuss illnesses. AIDS patients are 250 times more likely than hypertension patients to be in support groups. Breast cancer patients have formed 40 times as many support groups as have heart disease patients. Those who struggle with anorexia and alcoholism often join groups; those with migraines and ulcers do not.

The grandparent of support groups, Alcoholics Anonymous (AA), reportedly has 60,000 chapters in 112 countries. Its famous 12-step strategy, emulated by many other self-help groups, asks members to admit their powerlessness, to seek help from a higher power and from one another, and (the twelfth step) to take the message to others in need of it. In one eight-year, $27 million investigation, people seeking treatment for alcoholism reduced their drinking sharply and to roughly the same degree whether randomly assigned to a therapy based on AA principles and AA participation or to cognitive-behavior therapy or to a "motivational therapy" (Project Match, 1997).

One special type of group interaction, **family therapy**, assumes that no person is an island, that we live and grow in relation to others, especially our families. We do struggle to differentiate ourselves from our families, but we also need to connect with them emotionally. Some of our problem behaviors arise from the tension between

With an estimated 1.8 million members worldwide, AA is said to be "the largest organization on Earth that nobody wanted to join" (Finlay, 2000).

▶ **family therapy** therapy that treats the family as a system. Views an individual's unwanted behaviors as influenced by or directed at other family members; attempts to guide family members toward positive relationships and improved communication.

these two tendencies, which can create family stress. Patients often come to therapists seeking help in their relationships with family members.

Unlike most psychotherapy, which focuses on what happens inside the person's own skin, family therapists work with family groups to heal relationships and to mobilize family resources. Their aim is to help family members discover the role they play within their family's social system. A child's rebellion, for example, affects and is affected by other family tensions. Family therapists also attempt—usually with some success, research suggests (Hazelrigg & others, 1987; Shadish & others, 1993)—to open up communication within the family or to help family members discover new ways of preventing or resolving conflicts.

Stacy Pick/Stock, Boston

Family therapy This type of therapy often acts as a preventive mental health strategy. The therapist helps family members understand how their ways of relating to one another create problems. The treatment's emphasis is not on changing the individuals but on changing their relationships and interactions.

rehearse it!

5. Behavior therapies apply learning principles to the treatment of problems such as phobias and alcoholism. In such treatment, the behavior therapist's goal is to
   a. identify and treat the underlying causes of the problem.
   b. improve learning and insight.
   c. eliminate the unwanted behavior.
   d. improve communication and social sensitivity.

6. Behavior therapists assume that phobias and other maladaptive behaviors are conditioned responses. They attempt to extinguish these responses or to use counterconditioning to produce new responses to old stimuli. Two counterconditioning techniques are systematic desensitization and
   a. resistance.
   b. aversive conditioning.
   c. transference.
   d. active listening.

7. The technique of systematic desensitization, developed by Joseph Wolpe, teaches people to relax in the presence of progressively more anxiety-provoking stimuli. Systematic desensitization has been found to be especially effective in the treatment of
   a. phobias.
   b. depression.
   c. alcoholism.
   d. bed-wetting.

8. Some institutions have used token economies to shape behavior. They hand out tokens. People who display a desired behavior or take a step in the right direction earn tokens, which may later be exchanged for other rewards. Token economics are an application of
   a. classical conditioning.
   b. counterconditioning.
   c. cognitive therapy.
   d. operant conditioning.

9. Aaron Beck's form of cognitive therapy teaches people to stop attributing failures to personal inadequacy, and success to external circumstances. This form of cognitive therapy has been shown to be especially effective in treating
   a. mental retardation.
   b. phobias.
   c. alcoholism.
   d. depression.

10. Psychotherapy is in large part an individual process, although most therapies may occur in therapist-led small groups. The social context of this group therapy tells people that others have problems similar to theirs and allows them to act out alternative behaviors. One type of group therapy, family therapy, serves as a
    a. source of psychoanalysis.
    b. preventive mental health strategy.
    c. self-help group.
    d. type of behavior therapy.

Answers can be found in Appendix C.

EVALUATING PSYCHOTHERAPIES

Advice columnist Ann Landers frequently advised her troubled letter writers to get professional help. One response urged the writer "not to give up. Hang in there until you find [a psychotherapist] who fills the bill. It's worth the effort." On the same day, she advised a second letter writer, "There are many excellent mental health facilities in your city. I urge you to make an appointment at once" (Farina & Fisher, 1982). Many share Ann Landers' confidence in psychotherapy's effectiveness. The National Institute of Mental Health estimates that 15 percent of Americans seek help for psychological and addictive disorders each year (**FIGURE 14.4**, page 520). In 1997 alone, 9.7 million Americans—up from 7.9 million in 1987—visited mental health professionals for psychotherapy (Olfson & others, 2002).

figure 14.4
Where do people turn for help? The National Institute of Mental Health reports that 19 million Americans a year seek help for psychological difficulties. About two in five seek out a mental health worker, such as a psychologist or psychiatrist. (Data from Regier & others, 1993.)

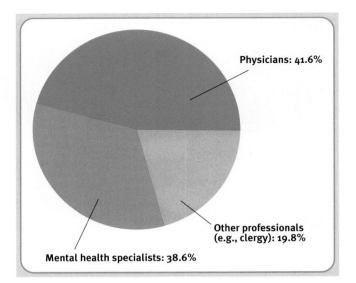

Physicians: 41.6%

Other professionals (e.g., clergy): 19.8%

Mental health specialists: 38.6%

Before 1950, the primary mental health providers were psychiatrists. Since then, demand has outgrown the psychiatric profession, and now most psychotherapy is done by clinical and counseling psychologists; clinical social workers; pastoral, marital, abuse, and school counselors; and psychiatric nurses. Much of it is done through community mental health programs, which provide outpatient therapy, crisis phone lines, and halfway houses for those making the transition from hospitalization to independent living. With such an enormous outlay of time, money, effort, and hope, it is important to ask: Is the faith that Ann Landers and millions of others worldwide place in these therapists justified? And is the *Wall Street Journal* (1999) therefore wrong to suppose that including psychotherapy in health insurance plans would lead to "endless payments for dubious benefits of apparently marginal problems"?

Is Psychotherapy Effective?

6. Does psychotherapy work? Who decides?

The question, though simply put, is not simply answered. For one thing, measuring therapy's effectiveness is not like taking your body's temperature to see if your fever has gone away. If you and I were to undergo psychotherapy, how would we gauge its effectiveness? By how we feel about our progress? How our therapist feels about it? How our friends and family feel about it? How our behavior has changed?

Clients' Perceptions

If clients' testimonials were the only yardstick, we could strongly affirm the effectiveness of psychotherapy. Three out of four clients describe themselves as satisfied, and one in two reports being "very satisfied" (Lebow, 1982). When 2900 *Consumer Reports* readers (1995; Kotkin & others, 1996; Seligman, 1995) related their experiences with mental health professionals, 89 percent said they were at least "fairly well satisfied." Among those who recalled feeling *fair* or *very poor* when beginning therapy, 9 in 10 now were feeling *very good, good,* or at least *so-so.* We have their word for it—and who should know better?

We should not dismiss these testimonials lightly. People enter therapy because they are suffering, and most leave feeling better about themselves. But there are several reasons why client testimonials do not persuade psychotherapy's skeptics:

- **People often enter therapy in crisis.** When, with the normal ebb and flow of events, the crisis passes, people may attribute their improvement to the therapy.
- **Positive expectations can enhance healing.** Thanks to the *placebo effect* (Chapter 1), patients' beliefs sometimes make ineffective therapies seem effective.
- **Unusual events and emotions tend, with time, to "regress" (return) toward their average state.** When things hit bottom, we may try anything, and whatever we try—going to a psychotherapist, starting yoga, doing aerobic exercise—is more likely to be followed by improvement than by further descent.

"The real purpose of [the] scientific method is to make sure Nature hasn't misled you into thinking you know something that you actually don't."

Robert Pirsig, Zen and the Art of Motorcycle Maintenance, *1974*

● *Clients may need to believe the therapy was worth the effort.* To admit investing time and money in something ineffective is like admitting to having one's car serviced repeatedly by a mechanic who never fixes it. Self-justification is a powerful human motive.

● *Clients generally like their therapists and speak kindly of them.* Even if the clients' problems remain, say the critics, "they work hard to find something positive to say. The therapist had been very understanding, the client had gained a new perspective, he learned to communicate better, his mind was eased, anything at all so as not to have to say treatment was a failure" (Zilbergeld, 1983, p. 117).

Clinicians' Perceptions

If clinicians' perceptions accurately reflected therapeutic effectiveness, we would have even more reason to celebrate. Case studies of successful treatment abound. Furthermore, every therapist treasures compliments from clients as they say good-bye or later express their gratitude. The problem is that clients justify entering psychotherapy by emphasizing their woes, justify leaving therapy by emphasizing their well-being, and stay in touch only if satisfied. Therapists are aware of failures, but they are mostly the failures of *other* therapists—those whose clients, having experienced only temporary relief, are now seeking a new therapist for their recurring problems. Thus, the same person with the same recurring difficulty—the same old weight problem, depression, or marital difficulty—may be a "success" story in several therapists' files.

Because people enter therapy when they are extremely unhappy, and usually leave when they are less extremely unhappy, most therapists, like most clients, testify to therapy's success—regardless of the treatment. Although "treatments" have varied widely, from chains to counseling, every generation views its own approach as more enlightened.

Outcome Research

How, then, can we objectively measure the effectiveness of psychotherapy? What types of people and problems are best helped, and by what type of psychotherapy? The questions have both academic and personal relevance. If you or someone you care about feels anxious or depressed, or suffers some psychological disorder, it is crucial for you to understand the likelihood of psychotherapy's being of help.

In hopes of better assessing psychotherapy's effectiveness, psychologists have turned to controlled research studies. Similar research in the 1800s transformed medicine from concocted treatments (bleeding, purging, infusions of plant and metal substances) into a science. The transformation occurred when skeptical physicians began to realize that many patients got better on their own, that most of the fashionable treatments were doing no good, and that sorting fact from superstition required following illnesses closely—with and without a particular treatment. Typhoid fever patients, for example, often improved after being bled, convincing most physicians that the treatment worked. Not until a control group was given mere bed rest—and 70 percent were observed to improve after five weeks of fever—did physicians learn, to their shock, that their treatments were, at best, worthless (Thomas, 1992).

In psychology, the opening challenge in what became a spirited debate over such research was issued by British psychologist Hans Eysenck (1952). He summarized studies showing that two-thirds of those suffering nonpsychotic disorders improve markedly after undergoing psychotherapy. To this day, no one disputes that optimistic estimate.

So why then are we still debating psychotherapy's effectiveness? Because Eysenck also reported similar improvement among *untreated* persons, such as those who were on waiting lists. With or without psychotherapy, he said, roughly two-thirds improved noticeably. Time was a great healer.

"Fortunately, [psycho]analysis is not the only way to resolve inner conflicts. Life itself still remains a very effective therapist."

Karen Horney, Our Inner Conflicts, 1945

The avalanche of criticism prompted by Eysenck's conclusions did reveal short-comings in his analyses. Also, in 1952 Eysenck could find only 24 studies of psychotherapy outcomes to analyze. Today, there are hundreds. The best of these "randomized clinical trials" randomly assign people on a waiting list to therapy or to no therapy. Afterward, researchers evaluate.

In the first statistical digest of these studies, Mary Lee Smith and her colleagues (1980) combined the results of 475 investigations. For psychotherapists, the welcome result was that "the evidence overwhelmingly supports the efficacy of psychotherapy" (p. 183). **FIGURE 14.5** depicts their finding—that the average therapy client ends up better off than 80 percent of the untreated individuals on waiting lists. The claim is more modest than it first appears—by definition, about 50 percent of untreated people also are better off than the average untreated person. Nevertheless, Smith and her collaborators exulted that "psychotherapy benefits people of all ages as reliably as schooling educates them, medicine cures them, or business turns a profit" (p. 183).

Newer research summaries confirm that psychotherapy works (Kopta & others, 1999; Shadish & others, 2000). In one ambitious study, the National Institute of Mental Health compared three depression treatments: cognitive therapy, interpersonal therapy, and a standard drug therapy. Twenty-eight experienced therapists at research sites in Norman, Oklahoma; Washington, DC; and Pittsburgh, Pennsylvania, were trained in one of the three methods and randomly assigned their share of the 239 participants suffering from depression. Patients in all three groups improved more than did those in a control group who received merely an inert medication and supportive attention, encouragement, and advice. Among patients who completed a full 16-week treatment program, the depression had lifted for slightly more than half of those in each treatment group—but for only 29 percent of those in the control group (Elkin & others, 1989). This verdict echoes the results of the earlier outcome studies: *Those not undergoing therapy often improve, but those undergoing therapy are more likely to improve.*

Often, however, the improvement was not permanent. Only one in four patients undergoing psychotherapy and one in six undergoing drug therapy both recovered and experienced no relapse within 18 months (Shea & others, 1992). So, extravagant expectations that psychotherapy will transform your life and personality seem unwarranted. Still, Eysenck's pessimism also seems unwarranted. *On average*, psychotherapy is somewhat effective—and is also cost-effective when compared with the greater costs of medical care for psychologically related ailments. When people seek psychological treatment, their search for medical treatment drops—by 16 percent in one digest of 91 studies (Chiles & others, 1999).

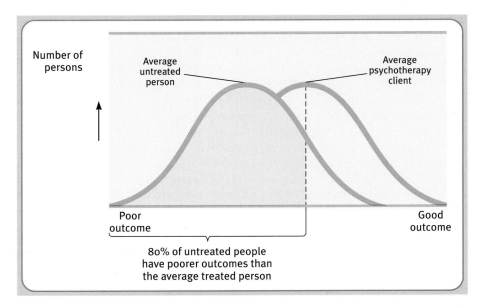

figure 14.5
Treatment versus no treatment These two normal distribution curves based on data from 475 studies show the improvement of untreated people and psychotherapy clients. The outcome for the average therapy client surpassed that for 80 percent of the untreated people. (Adapted from Smith & others, 1980.)

The annual cost of psychological disorders and substance abuse—including crime, accidents, lost work, and treatment—is staggering. Thus, just as an investment in prenatal and well-baby care *reduces* long-term costs, so will an investment in almost any effective treatment for psychological problems. Anything that boosts employees' psychological well-being will reduce medical costs, improve work efficiency, and diminish absenteeism. Studies by health insurers show that mental health treatment can more than pay for itself with reduced medical costs (American Psychological Association, 1991).

But note that *on average* refers to no one therapy in particular. It is like saying, "Surgery is somewhat effective," or reassuring lung-cancer patients that "on average," medical treatment of health problems is effective. What people want to know is not the effectiveness of therapy in general but the effectiveness of particular treatments for their particular problems.

The Relative Effectiveness of Different Therapies

7. Are some therapies more effective than others?

So what can we tell people considering therapy, and those paying for it, about *which* psychotherapy will be most effective for their problem?

Despite claims of superiority by advocates of different types of therapy, the statistical summary conducted by Mary Lee Smith and her colleagues (1977, 1980) revealed no one type of therapy as generally superior. Newer evidence also indicates little if any connection between clinicians' experience, training, supervision, and licensing and their clients' outcomes (Bickman, 1999; Luborsky & others, 2002; Seligman, 1995). Was the dodo bird in *Alice in Wonderland* right: "Everyone has won and all must have prizes"?

A recent Society of Clinical Psychology task force is working to answer that question by identifying treatments shown to be beneficial in controlled treatment studies (Chambless & others, 1997; Norcross, 2002). The task force has pinpointed some elements of effective therapy, such as empathy. And it offers lists of "empirically supported therapies," including, for example, cognitive-behavior therapy for bulimia, and behavioral conditioning therapies for specific behavior problems such as bed-wetting, phobias, compulsions, or sexual disorders (Bowers & Clum, 1988; Giles, 1983; Hunsley & DiGiulio, 2002). Just as physicians offer particular treatments for specific medical problems, so psychotherapists are aiming toward particular treatments for specific psychological problems.

Indeed, therapy is most effective when the problem is clear-cut (Singer, 1981; Westen & Morrison, 2001). Those who experience phobias or panic, who are unassertive, or who are frustrated by sexual performance problems can hope for improvement. Those who suffer depression and anxiety will usually benefit in the short term but often relapse later. Those who have chronic schizophrenia or who wish to change their whole personality are unlikely to benefit from psychotherapy alone (Zilbergeld, 1983). The more specific the problem, the greater the hope.

"Different sores have different salves."

English proverb

Evaluating Alternative Therapies

8. How do alternative therapies stand up to psychology's critical thinking methods?

The tendency of abnormal states of mind to "regress" to normal, combined with the placebo effect, creates fertile soil for pseudotherapies. Bolstered by anecdotes, heralded by the media, praised on the Internet, alternative therapies can spread like wildfire. Princess Diana typified the modern fascination with alternative healers by seeking out spiritualists, a hypnotherapist, an "anger-release" therapist, reflexologists,

table 14.1 Comparison of Psychology Citations and Web Sites			
Topic	Psychology journal citations*	Web sites**	Ratio
Systematic desensitization	2,277	8,930	1 to 4
Thought field therapy	126	19,100	1 to 152
Therapeutic touch	300	53,900	1 to 180
St. John's wort (herbal remedy)	155	352,000	1 to 2,271
Enneagram (personality typing)	24	179,000	1 to 7,458

*Using PsychInfo, September 2003
**Using Google, September 2003

aromatherapists, colonic irrigationists, and a "mind-body" therapist (Smith, 1999). She had much company. In one national survey, 57 percent of those with a history of anxiety attacks and 54 percent of those with a history of depression had used alternative treatments such as relaxation techniques, herbal medicine, massage, and spiritual healing (Kessler & others, 2001).

What can we say of such alternative therapies? Testimonials aside—every therapy, whether effective or not, will *seem* effective to some—what does the evidence say? Which are empirically validated?

About most, there is no evidence, because their proponents and devotees feel no need for controlled research. For them, personal experience is evidence enough. So which therapies do get systematically evaluated? To gauge scientific versus popular interest in various treatments and assessment techniques, clinical researcher Scott Lilienfeld (1998) suggests comparing the number of times each is mentioned in electronic searches of psychology's literature and on the World Wide Web. As **TABLE 14.1** shows, some topics exist almost exclusively on the Web.

In earlier chapters, we critically evaluated alternative therapies such as subliminal self-help tapes, recovery of supposedly repressed memories, and hypnotherapy. Let's now consider three more. As we do, remember that sifting sense from nonsense requires the scientific attitude: being skeptical but not cynical, open to surprises but not gullible.

Therapeutic Touch

Among the most popular recent alternative therapies is *therapeutic touch*. Its tens of thousands of practitioners worldwide (many of whom are nurses) move their hands a few inches from a patient's body, purportedly "pushing energy fields into balance." Advocates say these manipulations help heal everything from headaches to burns to cancer (Krieger, 1993). Skeptics say the evidence shows no healing power beyond the placebo effect (Scheiber & Selby, 1997).

To put therapeutic touch to the test, fourth-grader Emily Rosa and her mother, a nurse, schemed a simple experiment (Rosa & others, 1998). Why not test healers' ability to detect the supposed energy field by inviting them to rest their hands, palms up, on a flat surface? (Thanks to a screen, the healers wouldn't see their own or Emily's hands.) After the toss of a coin, Emily would hover her hand over one of the practitioner's hands to see if the practitioner could detect that this hand rather than the other was receiving the energy field. Shortly before, skeptic James Randi had offered $742,000 to anyone who could detect a human energy field under similar conditions. Only one person agreed to be tested by Randi, and that volunteer had left the experiment in a huff after achieving only chance results.

Apparently less threatened by a 9-year-old girl doing a science fair project, and not fully realizing that this was a serious research project, 21 practitioners agreed to be tested by Emily for 10 trials each. Could they beat chance—50 percent? They could not, averaging but 47 percent correct. A year later when the trials were repeated—this time allowing each practitioner to "feel" Emily's energy field in each hand and then choose which hand Emily would use—the practitioners got 41 percent correct. The results, published in the prestigious *Journal of the American Medical Association*, caused its editor to conclude that the supposed human energy field "does not exist" and that, barring new evidence, patients should "save their money." Perhaps, say critics of this experiment, Emily's hands were held too far from the practitioner's hands. But when body heat is shielded by a thin sheet of glass, people cannot detect the presence of unseen hands (Long & others, 1999). Thus, the tentative scientific verdict is that therapeutic touch (actually nontouch) does not work, nor is there any credible theory that predicts why it might.

Eye Movement Desensitization and Reprocessing (EMDR)

Walking in a park one day, Francine Shapiro (1989) observed that anxious thoughts vanished as her eyes spontaneously darted about. From this experience she developed a novel anxiety treatment: *eye movement desensitization and reprocessing* (EMDR). While people imagined traumatic scenes, Shapiro triggered eye movements by waving her finger in front of their eyes. She tried this on 22 people haunted by old traumatic memories, and all reported marked reductions in their distress after just one therapeutic session. This extraordinary result triggered an enormous response from mental health professionals, 40,000 of whom from 52 countries have undergone training (EMDR, 2002). Not since the similarly charismatic Franz Anton Mesmer introduced "animal magnetism" (hypnosis) more than two centuries ago (also after feeling inspired by an outdoor experience) has a new therapy attracted so many devotees so quickly.

Does it work? For 84 to 100 percent of single-trauma victims participating in four recent studies, the answer is yes, reports Shapiro (1999, 2002). (When EMDR did not fare well in other trials, Shapiro argued that the therapists were not properly trained.) Moreover, the treatment need take no more than three 90-minute sessions. A Society of Clinical Psychology task force on empirically validated treatments acknowledges that the treatment is "probably efficacious" for the treatment of nonmilitary post-traumatic stress disorder (Chambless & others, 1997). Encouraged by their seeming successes, EMDR therapists are now applying the technique to other anxiety disorders, such as panic disorder, and, with Shapiro's (1995, 2002) encouragement, to a wide range of complaints, including pain, grief, paranoid schizophrenia, rage, and guilt.

EMDR is a therapy that thousands adore, and thousands more dismiss as a sham—"an excellent vehicle for illustrating the differences between scientific and pseudoscientific therapy techniques," suggest James Herbert and seven others (2000). Why should rapidly moving one's eyes while recalling traumas be therapeutic, wondered skeptics. Indeed, eye movements, it seems, are not the therapeutic ingredient. When they tested the therapy without the eye movements—with finger tapping, for example, or with eyes fixed straight ahead while the therapist's finger wagged—the therapeutic results were the same (Cahill & others, 1999; Davidson & Parker, 2001; Lohr & others, 1999). What is therapeutic, the skeptics suspect, is the combination of desensitization—repeatedly reliving traumatic memories in a safe and reassuring context—and a robust placebo effect. Had Mesmer's pseudotherapy been compared with no treatment at all, notes Richard McNally (1999), it, too, (thanks to the healing power of positive belief) could have been found "probably efficacious."

Light Exposure Therapy

Have you ever found yourself oversleeping, gaining weight, and feeling lethargic during the dark mornings and overcast days of winter? For some people, especially women and those living far from the equator, the wintertime blahs constitute a form of depression known as *seasonal affective disorder*, for which the appropriate acronym

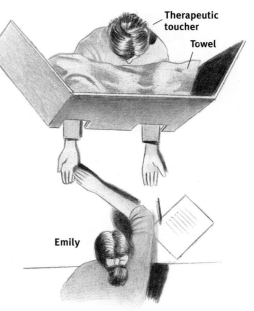

Testing the energy field Could therapeutic touch practitioners detect a nearby hand? To find out, Emily Rosa tossed a coin and, unobserved by the healer, held her hand over the practitioner's right or left hand.

Studies indicate that EMDR is "just as effective with fixed eyes. If that conclusion is right, what's useful in the therapy (chiefly behavioral desensitization) is not new, and what's new is superfluous."

Harvard Mental Health Letter, *2002*

Light therapy To counteract winter depression, some people spend time each morning in front of a box that emits intense light that mimics natural outdoor light.

is SAD. To counteract these dark spirits, National Institute of Mental Health researchers in the early 1980s had a bright idea: Give SAD people a timed daily dose of intense light. Light exposure, as we noted in Chapter 6, can tweak the circadian clock. When clinical experience indicated that light exposure could also relieve symptoms associated with wintertime depression, manufacturers produced "light boxes" that can now be rented or purchased from health supply and lighting stores.

Is this another placebo effect, attributable to people's expectations? Recent studies shed light on this therapy. In one, Charmane Eastman and her colleagues (1998) exposed some SAD patients to 90 minutes of bright light and others to a sham placebo treatment—a hissing "negative ion generator" about which the staff expressed similar enthusiasm (but which unknown to the patients was not turned on). After four weeks of exposure, 61 percent of those exposed to morning light had greatly improved, as had 50 percent of those exposed to evening light and 32 percent of those exposed to the placebo treatment. Two other studies, led by Michael Terman and Jiuan Su Terman (1998, 2001), found that 30 minutes of light exposure produced relief for more than half the people receiving morning light therapy and for one-third receiving evening light therapy. Another study, led by Alfred Lewy (1998), replicated the morning light effect and identified a possible biological mechanism. With SAD patients, morning light exposure shifted secretion of the hormone melatonin to an earlier time. The verdict: For many people, morning bright light does indeed dim SAD symptoms.

Commonalities Among Psychotherapies

9. What three elements are shared by all forms of psychotherapy?

Good therapists may have differing perspectives, yet share much in common, including compassion, sensitivity, and empathy. Jerome Frank (1982), Marvin Goldfried (Goldfried & Padawer, 1982), Hans Strupp (1986), and Bruce Wampold (2001) studied the common ingredients of various therapies and suggested that they all offer at least three benefits: hope for demoralized people; a new perspective on oneself and the world; and an empathic, trusting, caring relationship. These "nonspecific" factors aren't all that therapy offers, but they are important (Barker & others, 1988; Jones & others, 1988; Roberts & others, 1993). They are part of what the growing numbers of self-help and support groups offer their members. And they have been part of what traditional healers offer (Jackson, 1992). Healers—special people to whom others disclose their suffering—have for centuries listened in order to understand and to empathize, reassure, advise, console, interpret, or explain.

"I utilize the best from Freud, the best from Jung, and the best from my Uncle Marty, a very smart fellow."

"Therapy that reviews childhood endlessly has a century-long history of being ineffective. All therapy that works for depression, anxiety, and sexual problems focuses on exactly what is going wrong now and on how to correct it."

Martin E. P. Seligman, **What You Can Change and What You Can't**, *1994*

Hope for Demoralized People

People who seek therapy typically feel anxious, depressed, devoid of self-esteem, and incapable of turning things around. What any therapy offers is the expectation that, with commitment from the therapy seeker, things can and will get better. Apart from the particular therapeutic technique, this belief may itself function as a placebo, promoting improved morale, new feelings of self-efficacy, and diminished symptoms (Prioleau & others, 1983). In psychotherapy experiments, the placebo treatment may be listening to inspirational tapes, attending group discussions, or taking a fake pill.

The finding that improvement is greater for placebo-treated people than for untreated people (although not as great as for those receiving actual psychotherapy) suggests that one reason therapies help is that they offer hope. Said another way, therapy outcomes vary with the attitude of the person seeking help—the person's motivation, confidence, and commitment. Each therapy, in its individual way, may harness the person's own healing powers. And that, says psychiatrist Jerome Frank, helps us understand why all sorts of treatments—including some folk healing rites known to be powerless apart from the participants' beliefs—may in their own time and place produce cures.

A New Perspective

Every therapy offers people a plausible explanation of their symptoms and an alternative way of looking at themselves or responding to their worlds. Therapy can offer new experiences as well, ones that help people change their behaviors and their views of themselves. Armed with a believable fresh perspective, they may approach life with a new attitude.

An Empathic, Trusting, Caring Relationship

Regardless of their therapeutic technique, effective therapists are empathic people who seek to understand another's experience; whose care and concern the client feels; and whose respectful listening, reassurance, and advice earn the client's trust and respect. In a National Institute of Mental Health depression-treatment study, the most effective therapists were those who were perceived as most empathic and caring and who established the closest therapeutic bonds with their clients (Blatt & others, 1996). In another study, Marvin Goldfried and his associates (1998) analyzed taped therapy sessions from 36 recognized master therapists. Some were cognitive-behavior therapists, others were psychodynamic-interpersonal therapists. Regardless, the striking finding was how *similar* the therapists were during the parts of their sessions they considered most significant. At key moments, the empathic therapists of both persuasions would help clients evaluate themselves, link one aspect of their lives with another, and gain insight into their interactions with others. Indeed, some believe warmth and empathy are hallmarks of healers everywhere, whether psychiatrists, witch doctors, or shamans (Torrey, 1986).

That all therapies offer *hope* through a *fresh perspective* offered by a *caring person* is supported by an analysis of 39 studies. Each study compared treatment offered by professional therapists with treatment offered by laypeople: friendly professors, people who had had a few hours' training in empathic listening skills, and college students supervised by a professional clinician. The result? The "paraprofessionals," as these briefly trained people are called, typically proved as effective as the professionals (Christensen & Jacobson, 1994). Although most of the problems they treated were mild, the trained paraprofessionals were—believe it or not—as effective as professionals even when dealing with more disturbed adults, such as those diagnosed with serious depression.

To recap, people who seek help usually improve. So do many of those who do not undergo psychotherapy. Our resilience is a tribute to our human resourcefulness and to our capacity to care for one another. Although the therapist's orientation and experience appear not to matter much, people who receive some psychotherapy usually improve more than those who do not. People with clearcut, specific problems often improve the most.

Part of what all therapies offer is hope, a fresh way of looking at life, and an empathic, caring relationship. That may explain why the empathy and friendly counsel of paraprofessionals are often as helpful as professional psychotherapy. And that may also explain why people who feel supported by close relationships—who enjoy the fellowship and friendship of caring people—are less likely to need or seek therapy (Frank, 1982; O'Connor & Brown, 1984).

Mark Antman/The Image Works

A caring relationship Effective therapists form a bond of trust with their patients.

CLOSE-UP

A Consumer's Guide to Psychotherapists

When should a person seek the help of a mental health professional? Life for everyone is marked by a mix of serenity and stress, blessing and bereavement, good moods and bad. When troubling thoughts and emotions interfere with your normal living, you might consider talking to a professional. The American Psychological Association offers these common trouble signals:

- Feelings of hopelessness
- Deep and lasting depression
- Self-destructive behavior, such as alcohol and drug abuse
- Disruptive fears
- Sudden mood shifts
- Thoughts of suicide
- Compulsive rituals, such as hand washing
- Sexual difficulties

If you are looking for a therapist, it may be wise to first have a pre-

table 14.2 Therapists and Their Training

Type	Description
Clinical psychologists	Most are psychologists with a Ph.D. and expertise in research, assessment, and therapy, supplemented by a supervised internship. About half work in agencies and institutions, half in private practice.
Clinical or psychiatric social workers	A two-year Master of Social Work graduate program plus postgraduate supervision prepares some social workers to offer psychotherapy, mostly to people with everyday personal and family problems. About half have earned the National Association of Social Workers' designation of clinical social worker.
Counselors	Marriage and family counselors specialize in problems arising from family relations. Pastoral counselors provide counseling to countless people. Abuse counselors work with substance abusers and with spouse, child, and sexual abusers and their victims.
Psychiatrists	These physicians specialize in the treatment of psychological disorders. Not all psychiatrists have had extensive training in psychotherapy, but as M.D.s they can prescribe medications. Thus, they tend to see those with the most serious problems. Many have a private practice.

liminary consultation with two or three. You can describe your problem and learn each therapist's treatment approach. You can ask questions about the therapist's values, credentials (**TABLE 14.2**), and fees. And you can assess your own feelings about each one.

Culture and Values in Psychotherapy

10. How do differences in culture and values influence the relationship between a therapist and a client?

All therapies offer hope, and nearly all therapists attempt to enhance their clients' sensitivity, openness, personal responsibility, and sense of purpose (Jensen & Bergin, 1988). But on certain matters of moral and cultural diversity, therapists may differ from one another and from their clients (Kelly, 1990). In Canada and the United States, for example, about 1 person in 25 is a self-proclaimed atheist or agnostic, as are (depending on the survey) one-fifth to one-half of psychiatrists and clinical psychologists (Gallup, 1993; Lukoff & others, 1992). In Britain, two-thirds of psychiatrists say they are atheists (Neeleman & Persaud, 1995). That raises an intriguing issue: What values prevail in psychotherapy? What values *should* prevail? Should it matter that highly religious people prefer religiously similar therapists (Worthington & others, 1996)?

Albert Ellis, a well-known therapist, and Allen Bergin, co-editor of the *Handbook of Psychotherapy and Behavior Change*, illustrate how sharply values can differ. Ellis (1980) assumes that "no one and nothing is supreme," that "self-gratification" should be encouraged, and that "unequivocal love, commitment, service, and . . . fidelity to any interpersonal commitment, especially marriage, leads to harmful consequences." Bergin (1980) assumes the opposite—that "because God is supreme, humility and the acceptance of divine authority are virtues," that "self-control and committed love and self-sacrifice are to be encouraged," and that "infidelity to any interpersonal commitment, especially marriage, leads to harmful consequences." Bergin and Ellis disagree more radically than most therapists regarding what values are healthiest. In so doing, however, they illustrate what they agree on: that psychotherapists' personal beliefs and values influence their practice. Knowing that clients tend to adopt their therapists' values (Worthington & others, 1996), Bergin and Ellis also agree that therapists should divulge their values more openly.

Value differences also can become significant when a therapist from one culture meets a client from another. In North America, Europe, and Australia, for example, most therapists reflect their culture's individualism (often giving priority to personal desires and identity). Clients who are immigrants from Asian countries, which expect people to be mindful of others' expectations, may therefore have problems with therapies that require them to think only of their own well-being. Such differences help explain the reluctance of some minority populations to use mental health services (Sue, 1990). Recognizing that therapists and clients may differ in values, communication styles, and language, many therapy training programs now provide training in cultural sensitivity and recruit members of underrepresented culture groups.

rehearse it!

11. The question "Is psychotherapy effective?" has been the subject of hundreds of scientific studies and innumerable personal accounts. The most enthusiastic or optimistic view of psychotherapy comes from
    a. outcome research.
    b. psychologist Hans Eysenck.
    c. reports of clinicians and clients.
    d. a government study of treatment for depression.

12. On average, troubled people who undergo therapy are more likely to improve than those who do not, and therapy tends to be most effective

when the problem is clear-cut and specific. Studies show that _____ therapy is most effective overall.
    a. behavior
    b. humanistic
    c. psychodynamic
    d. no one type of

13. People's belief that a treatment will help them is often sufficient to cause some improvement. A neutral treatment, such as an inert pill, that improves morale and diminishes symptoms is an example of
    a. a placebo effect.
    b. preventive mental health.

    c. an empathic perspective.
    d. EMDR therapy.

14. Those who offer or receive alternative therapies usually feel that testimonials are enough evidence of the success of the therapy. One alternative therapy that has passed the test of critical evaluation is
    a. hypnotherapy.
    b. light exposure therapy.
    c. eye movement desensitization and reprocessing.
    d. therapeutic touch.

Answers can be found in Appendix C.

THE BIOMEDICAL THERAPIES

Psychotherapy is one way to treat psychological disorders. The other is physically changing the brain's functioning—by altering its chemistry with drugs, by overloading its circuits with electroconvulsive shock, or by disconnecting its circuits through psychosurgery. Although psychologists can provide "talking" therapies, psychiatrists (as medical doctors) offer most of the biomedical therapies.

Drug Therapies

11. What are the most common forms of biomedical therapies? What criticisms have been leveled against drug therapies?

By far the most widely used biomedical treatments today are the drug therapies. When introduced in the 1950s, modern drug therapy greatly reduced the need for psychosurgery or hospitalization. The discoveries in **psychopharmacology** (the study of drug effects on mind and behavior) revolutionized the treatment of people with severe disorders, liberating hundreds of thousands from hospital confinement. Thanks to drug therapy—and to efforts to minimize involuntary hospitalization and to support people with community mental health programs—the resident population of state and county mental hospitals in the United States today is a fraction of what it was a half-century ago (**FIGURE 14.6**, page 530).

"The mentally ill were out of the hospital, but in many cases they were simply out on the streets, less agitated but lost, still disabled but now uncared for."

Lewis Thomas, Late Night Thoughts on Listening to Mahler's Ninth Symphony, *1983*

▶ **psychopharmacology** the study of the effects of drugs on mind and behavior.

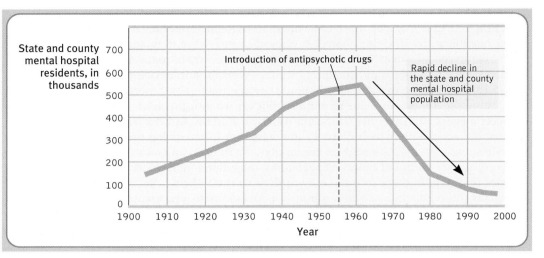

figure 14.6
The emptying of U.S. mental hospitals After the widespread introduction of antipsychotic drugs, starting in about 1955, the number of residents in state and county mental hospitals declined sharply. But in the rush to deinstitutionalize the mentally ill, many people who were ill-equipped to care for themselves were left homeless on city streets. (Data from the National Institute of Mental Health and Bureau of the Census, 2002.)

"If this doesn't help you don't worry, it's a placebo."

"No twisted thought without a twisted molecule."

Attributed to psychologist Ralph Gerard

Herself renewed Thanks to clozapine, Daphne Moss went "from hating the sunshine in the morning to loving it." No longer suffering from the paranoid delusion that her parents were witches, Moss began teaching school and living independently.

Almost any new treatment, including drug therapy, is greeted by an initial wave of enthusiasm as many people apparently improve. But that enthusiasm often diminishes after researchers subtract the rate of (1) normal recovery among untreated persons and (2) recovery due to the placebo effect, which arises from the positive expectations of patients and mental health workers alike. So, to evaluate the effectiveness of any new drug, researchers use the *double-blind technique*. Half the patients receive the drug, the other half a similar-appearing placebo. Neither the staff nor the patients know who gets which. The good news: In double-blind studies, several types of drugs have proven useful in treating psychological disorders.

Antipsychotic Drugs

The revolution in drug therapy for psychological disorders began with the accidental discovery that certain drugs, used for other medical purposes, calmed psychotic patients. These *antipsychotic* drugs, such as chlorpromazine (sold as Thorazine), dampen responsiveness to irrelevant stimuli. Thus they provide the most help to schizophrenia patients experiencing positive symptoms, such as auditory hallucinations and paranoia (Lehman & others, 1998; Lenzenweger & others, 1989). Patients exhibiting negative symptoms, such as apathy and withdrawal, often do not respond well to these antipsychotic drugs. A newer drug, clozapine (marketed as Clozaril), does sometimes enable "awakenings" in such people. It also sometimes helps those who have positive symptoms but have not responded to other drugs. In 1 or 2 percent of cases, clozapine has a toxic effect on white blood cells, necessitating regular blood tests.

The molecules of antipsychotic drugs are similar enough to molecules of the neurotransmitter dopamine to occupy its receptor sites and block its activity (Pickar & others, 1984; Taubes, 1994). (Clozapine also blocks serotonin activity.) This finding—that most antipsychotic drugs block dopamine receptors—reinforces the idea that an overactive dopamine system contributes to schizophrenia.

Antipsychotics such as Thorazine are powerful drugs. They can produce sluggishness, tremors, and twitches similar to those of Parkinson's disease, which is marked by too little dopamine (Kaplan & Saddock, 1989). (Clozapine has few such side effects.) Another complication is that one person's effective dose may be another person's overdose. Only by carefully monitoring the dosage and its effects can psychiatrist and patient tread the fine line between relieving symptoms and causing extremely unpleasant side effects. But with the appropriate dosage, combined with life-skills programs and family support, hundreds of thousands of people with schizophrenia who had been consigned to the back wards of mental hospitals have returned to work and to near-normal lives.

Antianxiety Drugs

Like alcohol, *antianxiety* agents, such as Xanax or Valium, depress central nervous system activity (and so should not be used in combination with alcohol). Used in combination with other therapy, an antianxiety drug can help a person learn to cope with frightening situations and fear-triggering stimuli.

The criticism sometimes made of the behavior therapies—that they reduce symptoms without resolving underlying problems—is also made of antianxiety drugs. Unlike the behavior therapies, they may be used as an ongoing treatment. However, "popping a Xanax" at the first sign of tension can produce psychological dependence on the drug. (The immediate relief reinforces a person's tendency to take drugs when anxious.) When heavy users stop taking the drug, they may experience both increased anxiety and insomnia, driving them back to the drug for relief.

Antidepressant Drugs

As the antianxiety drugs can calm people down from a state of anxiety, the *antidepressants* sometimes lift people up from a state of depression. Most antidepressants work by increasing the availability of the neurotransmitters norepinephrine or serotonin, which elevate arousal and mood and appear scarce during depression. Consider fluoxetine, which 38 million users worldwide have known as Prozac (Goode, 2000). Prozac and other serotonin-enhancing drugs have been prescribed not only to patients with depression but also to those with obsessive-compulsive disorder, two-thirds of whom respond with "partial symptom reduction" (Pigott & Seay, 1997).

Prozac partially blocks the reabsorption and removal of serotonin from synapses (**FIGURE 14.7**). Because they slow the synaptic vacuuming up of serotonin, Prozac, and its cousins Zoloft and Paxil, are therefore called "selective-serotonin-reuptake-inhibitor" drugs (SSRIs). Other antidepressants work by blocking the reabsorption of both norepinephrine and serotonin or by inhibiting an enzyme that breaks down neurotransmitters such as serotonin. These drugs, though no less effective, have

Perhaps you can guess an occasional side effect of L-dopa, a drug that raises dopamine levels for Parkinson's patients: hallucinations.

"I think the dosage needs adjusting. I'm not nearly as happy as the people in the ads."

figure 14.7
Biology of antidepressants Shown here is the action of Prozac, which partially blocks the reuptake of serotonin.

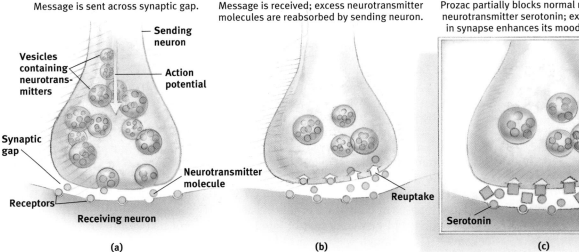

Message is sent across synaptic gap.

Vesicles containing neurotrans-mitters

Sending neuron

Action potential

Synaptic gap

Neurotransmitter molecule

Receptors

Receiving neuron

(a)

Message is received; excess neurotransmitter molecules are reabsorbed by sending neuron.

Reuptake

(b)

Prozac partially blocks normal reuptake of the neurotransmitter serotonin; excess serotonin in synapse enhances its mood-lifting effect.

Prozac

Serotonin

(c)

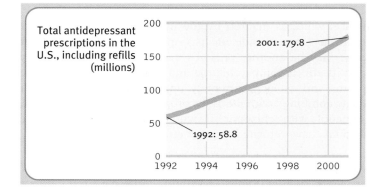

figure 14.8
Modifying mood Antidepressant prescriptions have soared. (Data from Goode, 2002.)

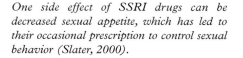

One side effect of SSRI drugs can be decreased sexual appetite, which has led to their occasional prescription to control sexual behavior (Slater, 2000).

more potential side effects, such as dry mouth, weight gain, hypertension, or dizzy spells (Anderson, 2000; Mulrow, 1999). (Administering such drugs by a patch, bypassing the intestines and liver, helps reduce such side effects [Bodkin & Amsterdam, 2002].)

The greater popularity of SSRI drugs helps explain why 89 percent of patients diagnosed with depression in 2001 received medication from their physicians, up from 70 percent in 1987, the year before SSRIs were introduced (Stafford & others, 2000). That, plus increasing numbers seeking help for depression, helps explain a reported tripling in the total number of antidepressant prescriptions since 1992 (**Figure 14.8**). The drugs are especially popular in North America, which accounted for 75 percent of the $13.4 billion in worldwide sales of antidepressant drugs in 2000 (IMS, 2002).

Be advised: Patients who begin taking antidepressants do not wake up the next day singing "Oh, what a beautiful morning!" Although the influence of antidepressants on neurotransmission does occur within hours, their full psychological effect often requires four weeks. One possible reason for the delayed effect is that increased serotonin seems to promote neurogenesis—the birth of new brain cells, perhaps reversing stress-induced loss of brain cells (Duman & others, 2001; Jacobs & others, 2000). Antidepressant drugs are not the only way to give the body a lift. Aerobic exercise, which helps calm people who feel anxious and energize those who feel depressed, does about as much good, and with positive side effects (see pages 414–415). And cognitive therapy, by helping the patient reverse a now-habitual negative thinking style, can boost the drug-aided relief from depression and reduce the post-treatment risk of relapse (Hollon & others, 2002; Keller & others, 2000).

Everyone agrees that people with depression often improve after a month on antidepressants. But after allowing for natural recovery (the regression to normal called "spontaneous recovery") and the placebo effect, how big is the drug effect? Not big, report Irving Kirsch and his colleagues (1998, 2002) from their analyses of double-blind clinical trials: Placebos produced improvement that was 75 percent or so of the active drug's effect. Another research team analyzed data from 45 studies. Given antidepressants, 41 percent of participants improved; given placebos, 31 percent improved (Khan & others, 2000).

Another chemical—the simple salt **lithium**—can be an effective mood stabilizer for those suffering the manic-depressive swings of bipolar disorder. Australian physician John Cade discovered this in the 1940s when he administered lithium to a severely manic patient. Although his reason for doing so was misguided—he thought lithium had calmed excitable guinea pigs when actually it had made them sick— Cade found that in less than a week the patient became perfectly well (Snyder, 1986). With continued lithium use, emotional highs and lows typically stabilize. After suffering mood swings for years, about 7 in 10 people with bipolar disorder benefit from a long-term daily dose of this cheap salt (Solomon & others, 1995). Their risk of suicide is but one-sixth that of bipolar patients not taking lithium (Tondo & others, 1997). Although we do not fully understand why, lithium works.

"First of all I think you should know that last quarter's sales figures are interfering with my mood-stabilizing drugs."

Electroconvulsive Therapy

12. What is electroconvulsive therapy? When is it used?

A more controversial brain manipulation occurs through shock treatment, or **electroconvulsive therapy (ECT)**. When ECT was first introduced in 1938, the wide-awake patient was strapped to a table and jolted with roughly 100 volts of electricity to the brain, producing racking convulsions and brief unconsciousness. ECT therefore gained a barbaric image, one that lingers still. Today, however, patients first receive a general anesthetic so they are not conscious, and a muscle relaxant to prevent injury from convulsions. Then a psychiatrist momentarily electrically shocks the unconscious patient's brain. Within 30 minutes, the patient awakens and remembers nothing of the treatment or of the hours preceding it (**Figure 14.9**).

Psychiatrists usually limit ECT to treatment of severe depression. (It tends to be ineffective in treating other psychological disorders.) After three such sessions each week for two to four weeks, 80 percent or more of people receiving ECT improve markedly, showing some memory loss for the treatment period but no discernible brain damage (Bergsholm & others, 1989; Coffey, 1993). "A miracle had happened in two weeks," reported noted research psychologist Norman Endler (1982) after ECT alleviated his deep depression. A 1985 panel of the National Institutes of Health, as well as newer research reviews, confirm that ECT is an effective treatment for severe depression in patients who have not responded to drug therapy (Consensus Conference, 1985; Parker & others, 1992). By 2001, confidence in ECT had further increased, with a *Journal of the American Medical Association* editorial concluding that "the results of ECT in treating severe depression are among the most positive treatment effects in all of medicine" (Glass, 2001).

How does ECT work? After more than 50 years, no one knows for sure. One recipient likened ECT to smallpox vaccine, which was saving lives before we knew how it worked. Perhaps electrical shock increases the release of norepinephrine, a neurotransmitter that elevates arousal and mood and seems in short supply during depression. Or perhaps the shock-induced seizures cause the brain to react by calming neural centers where overactivity produces depression.

ECT is credited with saving many from suicide and is now administered with briefer pulses that disrupt memory less (Fink, 1998). Yet its Frankensteinlike image continues. No matter how impressive the results, the idea of electrically shocking people into convulsions still strikes many as barbaric, especially given our ignorance about why ECT works. Moreover, ECT-treated patients, like other patients with a history of depression, are vulnerable to relapse. Nevertheless, electroconvulsive therapy is, in the minds of many psychiatrists and patients, a lesser evil than severe depression's misery, anguish, and risk of suicide.

Hopes are now rising for gentler alternatives for jump-starting the depressed brain. Some patients with chronic depression have found relief through a chest implant that intermittently stimulates the vagus nerve, which sends signals to the brain's mood-related limbic system (Marangell & others,

▶ **lithium** a chemical that provides an effective drug therapy for the mood swings of bipolar (manic-depressive) disorders.

▶ **electroconvulsive therapy (ECT)** a biomedical therapy for severely depressed patients in which a brief electric current is sent through the brain of an anesthetized patient.

The medical use of electricity is an ancient practice. Physicians treated the Roman Emperor Claudius (10 B.C.–A.D. 54) for headaches by pressing electric eels to his temples.

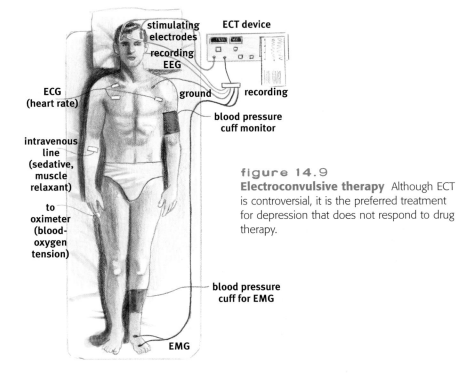

figure 14.9
Electroconvulsive therapy Although ECT is controversial, it is the preferred treatment for depression that does not respond to drug therapy.

Steve Liss/Time Life/Getty Images

Kitty Dukakis, who disclosed her struggle with depression after her husband's 1988 U.S. presidential campaign, has reported a "wonderful" response to ECT treatments (Smith, 2003).

2002). Depressed moods also seem to improve when repeated pulses surge through a magnetic coil held close to a person's skull above the right eyebrow. The painless procedure—called *repetitive transcranial magnetic stimulation* (rTMS)—is performed on wide-awake patients for 20 to 30 minutes for 2 to 4 weeks. Some studies have confirmed the therapeutic effect (Janicak & others, 2002; Klein & others, 1999; Schiffer & others, 2002; Wasserman & Lisanby, 2001). One idea is that the stimulation energizes depressed patients' relatively inactive left frontal lobe (Helmuth, 2001).

Psychosurgery

13. Under what conditions might psychosurgery be considered for changing behavior or moods?

Because its effects are irreversible, **psychosurgery**—surgery that removes or destroys brain tissue—is the most drastic and the least-used biomedical intervention for changing behavior. In the 1930s, Portuguese physician Egas Moniz developed what became the best-known psychosurgical operation: the **lobotomy**. Moniz found that cutting the nerves connecting the frontal lobes with the emotion-controlling centers of the inner brain calmed uncontrollably emotional and violent patients. After shocking the patient into a coma, a neurosurgeon would hammer an icepicklike instrument through each eye socket into the brain, then wiggle it to sever connections running up to the frontal lobes. The whole procedure was crude but easy and inexpensive, and it took only about 10 minutes. During the 1940s and 1950s, tens of thousands of severely disturbed people were "lobotomized," and Moniz was honored with a Nobel prize (Valenstein, 1986).

Although the intention was simply to disconnect emotion from thought, the effect was often more drastic: The lobotomy produced a permanently lethargic, immature, impulsive personality. During the 1950s, after some 35,000 people had been lobotomized in the United States alone, calming drugs became available and psychosurgery was largely abandoned. Today, lobotomies are almost never performed, and other psychosurgery is used only in extreme cases. For example, if a patient suffers uncontrollable seizures, surgeons can deactivate the specific nerve clusters that cause or transmit the convulsions. MRI-guided precision surgery is also occasionally done to cut the circuits involved in severe obsessive-compulsive disorder (Sachdev & Sachdev, 1997). Because such beneficial operations are irreversible, however, neurosurgeons perform them only as a last resort.

Mind-body interaction The biomedical therapies assume that mind and body are a unit: Affect one and you will affect the other.

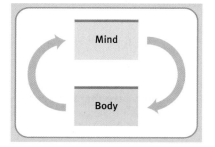

Mind

Body

The effectiveness of the biomedical therapies reminds us of a fundamental lesson: We find it convenient to talk of separate psychological and biological influences, but everything psychological is also biological. Every thought and feeling depends on the functioning brain. Every creative idea, every moment of joy or anger, every period of depression emerges from the electrochemical activity of the living brain. The influence is two-way: When therapy relieves obsessive-compulsive behavior, PET scans reveal a calmer brain (Schwartz & others, 1996).

PREVENTING PSYCHOLOGICAL DISORDERS

14. What is the rationale for preventive mental health programs?

Psychotherapies and biomedical therapies tend to locate the cause of psychological disorders within the person with the disorder. We infer that people who act cruelly must be cruel and that people who act "crazy" must be "sick." We attach labels to such people, thereby distinguishing them from "normal" folks. It follows, then, that we try to treat "abnormal" people by giving them insight into their problems, by changing their thinking, and/or by controlling them with drugs.

There is an alternative viewpoint: We could interpret many psychological disorders as understandable responses to a disturbing and stressful society. According to this view, it is not just the person who needs treatment, but also the person's social context. Better to prevent a problem by reforming a sick situation and by developing people's coping competencies than to wait for a problem to arise and then treat it.

A story about the rescue of a drowning person from a rushing river illustrates this viewpoint: Having successfully administered first aid to the first victim, the rescuer spots another struggling person and pulls her out, too. After a half-dozen repetitions, the rescuer suddenly turns and starts running away while the river sweeps yet another floundering person into view. "Aren't you going to rescue that fellow?" asks a bystander. "Heck, no," the rescuer replies. "I'm going upstream to find out what's pushing all these people in."

Preventive mental health is upstream work. It seeks to prevent psychological casualties by identifying and alleviating the conditions that cause them. George Albee (1986) believes there is abundant evidence that poverty, meaningless work, constant criticism, unemployment, racism, and sexism undermine people's sense of competence, personal control, and self-esteem. Such stresses increase their risk of depression, alcoholism, and suicide.

Albee contends that we who care about preventing psychological casualties should therefore support programs that alleviate poverty, discrimination, and other demoralizing situations. We eliminated smallpox not by treating the afflicted but by inoculating the unafflicted. We conquered yellow fever by controlling mosquitos. Prevention of psychological problems means empowering those who have learned an attitude of helplessness, changing environments that breed loneliness, renewing the disintegrating family, and bolstering parents' and teachers' skills at nurturing children's achievements and resulting self-esteem. Indeed, "Everything aimed at improving the human condition, at making life more fulfilling and meaningful, may be considered part of primary prevention of mental or emotional disturbance" (Kessler & Albee, 1975, p. 557).

There is, however, more to the story of psychological disorders than toxic environments and pessimism. Anxiety disorders, major depression, bipolar disorder, and schizophrenia are known biological events. Yet Albee reminds us again of one of this book's themes: *A human being is an integrated bio-psycho-social system.* For years we have trusted our bodies to physicians and our minds to psychiatrists and psychologists. That neat separation no longer seems valid. Stress affects body chemistry and health. And chemical imbalances, whatever their cause, can produce schizophrenia and depression. "*Mens sana in corpore sano,*" says an ancient Latin adage: A healthy mind in a healthy body.

▶ **psychosurgery** surgery that removes or destroys brain tissue in an effort to change behavior.

▶ **lobotomy** a now-rare psychosurgical procedure once used to calm uncontrollably emotional or violent patients. The procedure cut the nerves that connect the frontal lobes to the emotion-controlling centers of the inner brain.

"It is better to prevent than to cure."
Peruvian folk wisdom

"Mental disorders arise from physical ones, and likewise physical disorders arise from mental ones."
The Mahabharata, c. A.D. 200

---

rehearse it!

15. Antipsychotic drugs are used to calm schizophrenia patients so that they can live outside the hospital. The drugs often bring relief from auditory hallucinations and other troubling symptoms. However, some of them can have unpleasant side effects, most notably
    a. hyperactivity.
    b. convulsions and momentary memory loss.
    c. sluggishness, tremors, and twitches.
    d. paranoia.

16. Valium and Xanax, which depress central nervous system activity, are among the most heavily prescribed and abused drugs. These drugs are referred to as _____ drugs.

    a. antipsychotic.   c. antidepressant.
    b. antianxiety.   d. antineurotic.

17. One substance that often brings relief to patients suffering the manic-depressive mood swings of bipolar disorder is
    a. dopamine.   c. lithium.
    b. Xanax.   d. Valium.

18. Two controversial biomedical therapies are electroconvulsive therapy (shock treatment) and lobotomy (a type of psychosurgery). Lobotomy, once used to treat uncontrollably violent patients, is no longer an accepted treatment. Electroconvulsive therapy, however, remains in use as a treatment for

    a. severe obsessive-compulsive disorder.
    b. severe depression.
    c. schizophrenia.
    d. anxiety disorders.

19. Being poor or unemployed undermines a person's self-esteem and sense of competence. An approach that seeks to alleviate poverty and other demoralizing situations that put people at high risk for developing psychological disorders is
    a. biomedical therapy.
    b. the humanistic approach.
    c. empathy and active listening.
    d. preventive mental health.

Answers can be found in Appendix C.

chapter review

REVIEWING

Therapy

THE PSYCHOLOGICAL THERAPIES

The psychological therapies treat psychological disorders by means of structured interactions. The major psychotherapies derive from the familiar psychoanalytic, humanistic, behavioral, and cognitive perspectives on psychology. Today, many therapists employ either an eclectic approach, using a variety of therapies, or psychotherapy integration, which attempts to combine the various approaches into one coherent system.

1. What are the aims and methods of psychoanalysis, and how have they been adapted in psychodynamic therapy?

Those influenced by the psychoanalytic perspective try to help people gain insight into the unconscious origins of their disorders and to work through the accompanying feelings. To do so, an analyst may draw on techniques such as free association and dream analysis, and interpret resistances and transference to the therapist of long-repressed feelings. Traditional psychoanalysis, which is no longer practiced widely, is criticized for assuming repression, for after-the-fact interpretations, and for being time-consuming and costly. The more common psychodynamic therapy is influenced by the psychoanalytic perspective's concern for providing insight by exploring childhood experiences, but it offers a briefer treatment form.

2. What are the basic themes of humanistic therapy, such as Rogers' client-centered approach?

Unlike psychoanalysts, humanistic therapists focus on clients' current conscious feelings and on their taking responsibility for their own growth. Carl Rogers, in his person-centered therapy, used active listening to express genuineness, acceptance, and empathy.

3. What are the assumptions and techniques of the behavior therapies?

Behavior therapists do not attempt to explain the origin of problems or to promote self-awareness. Instead, they attempt to modify the problem behaviors themselves. Thus, they may countercondition behaviors through systematic desensitization or aversive conditioning. Or they may apply operant conditioning principles with behavior modification techniques, such as token economies.

4. What are the goals and techniques of the cognitive therapies?

The cognitive therapies, such as Aaron Beck's cognitive therapy for depression, aim to change self-defeating thinking by training people to look at themselves in new, more positive ways. Cognitive behavior therapy also helps clients to regularly practice new ways of thinking and talking.

GROUP AND FAMILY THERAPIES

5. In what group contexts do people receive therapy?

Many therapeutic techniques can also be applied in a group context. Self-help and support groups, such as AA, engage many millions of people. Family therapy treats the family as an interactive system from which problems may arise.

EVALUATING PSYCHOTHERAPIES

6. Does psychotherapy work? Who decides?

Because the positive testimonials of clients and therapists cannot prove that therapy is actually effective, psychologists have conducted hundreds of outcome studies of psychotherapy. These studies indicate that (1) people who remain untreated often improve; (2) those who receive psychotherapy are more likely to improve, regardless of what kind of therapy they receive and for how long; (3) those with clear-cut, specific problems often receive the greatest benefits from therapy; but (4) placebo treatments or the sympathy and friendly counsel of paraprofessionals also tend to produce more improvement than occurs when people receive no treatment.

7. Are some therapies more effective than others?

Statistical analyses of different types of therapies indicate that no one type of therapy is superior to all others. Some therapies do, however, seem to be well-suited to specific psychological examples. Behavioral conditioning, for example, is effective in treating phobias and compulsions.

8. How do alternative therapies stand up to psychology's critical thinking methods?

Of the three alternative therapies considered—therapeutic touch, EMDR, and light exposure therapy—only light exposure therapy held up under scientific testing. It does seem to relieve the symptoms of seasonal affective disorder (SAD).

9. What three elements are shared by all forms of psychotherapy?

Despite their differences, all psychotherapies offer three benefits to demoralized people: hope, a fresh perspective, and (if the therapist is effective) an empathic, trusting, and caring relationship.

10. How do differences in culture and values influence the relationship between a therapist and a client?

Therapists differ in the values that influence their aims. Value differences may also create problems when a therapist from one culture works with a client from another culture. Before seeking therapy, one might ask about the therapist's treatment approach and values, as well as the person's credentials and fees.

THE BIOMEDICAL THERAPIES

The biomedical therapies treat psychological disorders by altering neural functions.

11. *What are the most common forms of biomedical therapies? What criticisms have been leveled against drug therapies?*

The most widely used biomedical therapies are the antipsychotic drugs, used in treating schizophrenia, which block dopamine activity; antianxiety drugs, which depress central nervous system activity; and antidepressant drugs, which increase the availability of serotonin and norepinephrine. Lithium is a mood stabilizer prescribed for those with bipolar disorder.

12. *What is electroconvulsive therapy? When is it used?*

ECT is a biomedical therapy in which a brief electric current is sent through the brain of an anesthetized patient. Although controversial, ECT remains an effective, last-resort treatment for many people with severe depression who have not responded to drug therapy. Researchers are also exploring newer alternatives, such as magnetic brain stimulation.

13. *Under what conditions might psychosurgery be considered for changing behavior or moods?*

Although radical psychosurgical procedures such as lobotomy were once popular, neurosurgeons now rarely perform brain surgery to alleviate specific problems. Even when MRI-guided precision surgery is considered, it is a treatment of last resort because its effects are irreversible.

PREVENTING PSYCHOLOGICAL DISORDERS

14. *What is the rationale for preventive mental health programs?*

Advocates of preventive mental health programs argue that many psychological disorders could be prevented. Their aim is to change oppressive, esteem-destroying environments into more benevolent, nurturing environments that foster individual growth and self-confidence.

A CRITICAL THINKER'S REVIEW OF CHAPTER 14

You've now studied and reviewed **Therapy**. For even better retention, reflect on these concepts at a deeper level. If you need to refresh your memory of the six categories of critical thinking shown in parentheses below, see page 34. See if you can answer each of these questions in a short paragraph.

1. Keesha's therapist is attempting to resolve her extreme anxiety about being around other people by counterconditioning that anxiety. Which technique is her therapist using: psychoanalytic or behavior therapy? Explain. (perspective taking)

2. Dr. Keller is trying to help mildly depressed Alana develop more adaptive ways of thinking and acting. He believes that if Alana learns healthier ways of interpreting everyday events, she will be able to think her way out of her negative feelings. Which psychological therapy is Dr. Keller employing: cognitive or psychoanalytic? Explain. (pattern recognition)

3. Carlos, who suffers from depression, is participating in a scientific study of the effectiveness of different therapeutic approaches. Carlos visits the campus clinic daily, where he picks up a pill from a drop box but does not meet with anyone. Others in the same study receive a pill along with some counseling. A third group receives counseling but no pill. After taking his daily pill for several weeks, Carlos reports that he feels better and says he thinks the pills are working. However, the "pills" he has been taking contain only inert substances—they are "sugar pills." What effect has occurred here? (scientific problem solving)

4. Luca is in therapy to work through his debilitating anxiety. After several weeks, he is functioning fairly normally and decides to end his therapy session. His therapist asks Luca to complete a survey rating how effective his therapy has been, and Luca gives his therapist a glowing report. With Luca's permission, the therapist shares his responses with a prospective client as evidence of his effectiveness as a therapist. Do surveys like this speak to a therapist's effectiveness? What else do we need to consider when determining psychotherapy's effectiveness? (creative problem solving)

5. Your co-worker swears that St. John's wort is the cure for all ills. He says there is scientific support for his claim, pointing out the huge number of Web sites that mention this herbal remedy. Based on what you've learned in this chapter, how might you challenge his claim? (practical problem solving)

6. Your childhood friend is suffering severe, relentless depression. She has tried many different types of therapy, but nothing is working. Her doctors are now recommending electroconvulsive therapy (ECT), but her father is adamantly opposed. He saw the movie *One Flew Over the Cuckoo's Nest* and says that ECT is just another radical biomedical approach like the lobotomy. What could you tell him about today's ECT that might help him feel more comfortable with this approach? (psychological reasoning)

TERMS AND CONCEPTS TO REMEMBER

psychotherapy, p. 507
eclectic approach, p. 507
psychoanalysis, p. 508
resistance, p. 508
interpretation, p. 508
transference, p. 508
client-centered therapy, p. 510
active listening, p. 510

behavior therapy, p. 512
counterconditioning, p. 512
exposure therapies, p. 512
systematic desensitization, p. 513
aversive conditioning, p. 514
token economy, p. 515
cognitive therapy, p. 516
cognitive-behavior therapy, p. 517

family therapy, p. 518
psychopharmacology, p. 529
lithium, p. 532
electroconvulsive therapy (ECT), p. 533
psychosurgery, p. 534
lobotomy, p. 534

chapter15

Social Psychology

Each of us recalls our whereabouts on 9/11. I was talking by phone with my daughter, Laura, who was on the street in her Manhattan neighborhood, describing the tumultuous scene, when suddenly she yelled, "Oh my gosh! Oh my gosh!" as the second World Trade Center tower fell before her eyes. By almost anyone's definition, this catastrophic violence—accomplished by a mere 19 men with box cutters—was an evil act, to which the communal response was fear mixed with anger. A bully's single kick that collapses a nearly finished sandcastle triggers both fright and outrage. So, too, after 9/11, as millions responded both with anxiety about what might come next and with a desire for revenge.

But the cataclysm also triggered an outpouring of love and compassion. From around the country and the world, money and countless truckloads of food, clothing, and teddy bears—more than New Yorkers could possibly use—poured in. People in Toledo, Fargo, and Stockholm wept for those who wept. There on 6th Avenue and 24th Street, strangers hugged and talked, trying to make sense of senseless destruction. Although few transfusions would be needed, willing donors formed long lines at blood banks. "Everywhere I go I see concern," Laura wrote that evening.

> I see compassion. I see people with many differences united. I don't see violence. I don't see impatience. I don't see cruelty. Except when I look at that cloud of smoke, a constant backdrop all day. People are helping each other. People are desperate to do whatever they can.
>
> In the midst of this nightmare, I am utterly filled with love for the people of this city. It is incredible to witness their response. I am covered in goose bumps. My faith in humanity rises over that cloud and I see goodness and respect.

We watch and we wonder: What drives people to feel such hatred and to destroy so many innocent lives? Where do such prejudices—and the counterprejudices that arose after 9/11—come from? And what motivates the heroic altruism of those who died trying to save others and of the many more who reached out to those coping with loss?

As the 9/11 horror so compellingly demonstrates, we are social animals. Depending on who or what influences our thinking, we may assume the best or the worst in others. And depending on our attitudes, we may approach them with closed fists or open arms.

"We cannot live for ourselves alone," remarked the novelist Herman Melville. "Our lives are connected by a thousand invisible threads." **Social psychologists** explore these connections by scientifically studying how we *think about, influence,* and *relate to* one another.

SOCIAL THINKING

Especially when the unexpected occurs, we analyze why people act as they do. Does her warmth reflect romantic interest, or is that how she relates to everyone? Does his absenteeism signify illness, laziness, or a stressful work atmosphere? Was the horror of 9/11 the work of crazed evil people, or of unremarkable people socialized by and responding to life events?

Attributing Behavior to Persons or to Situations

1. How do we tend to explain others' behavior? How do we explain our own behavior?

After studying how people explain others' behavior, Fritz Heider (1958) proposed an **attribution theory**. Heider noted that people usually attribute others' behavior either to their internal dispositions or to their external situations. A teacher, for example, may wonder whether a child's hostility reflects an aggressive personality (*a dispositional attribution*) or whether the child is reacting to stress or abuse (*a situational attribution*).

▶ **social psychology** the scientific study of how we think about, influence, and relate to one another.

▶ **attribution theory** the theory that we tend to give a causal explanation for someone's behavior, often by crediting either the situation or the person's disposition.

539

The fundamental attribution error
If our new colleague at work acts grouchy, we may infer that he's a grouchy person, discounting his having lost sleep over a family worry, having a flat tire on the way to work, and being unable to find a parking place.

B. Busco/The Image Bank/Getty Images

Recall from Chapter 12 that personality psychologists study the enduring, inner determinants of behavior that help to explain why different people *act differently in a given situation. Social psychologists study the social influences that help explain why the same person will act differently in* different situations.

"Calling [9/11] senseless, mindless, insane, or the work of madmen is wrong . . . [it] fails to adopt the perspective of the perpetrators, as an act with a clearly defined purpose that we must understand in order to challenge it most effectively."

Psychologist Philip G. Zimbardo, "Fighting Terrorism by Understanding Man's Capacity for Evil," September 16, 2001

In class, we notice that Julie seldom talks; over coffee, Jack talks nonstop. Attributing their behaviors to their personal dispositions, we decide Julie is shy and Jack is outgoing. Because people do have enduring personality traits, such attributions are sometimes valid. However, we often fall prey to the **fundamental attribution error**, overestimating the influence of personality and underestimating the influence of situations. In class, Jack may be as quiet as Julie. Catch Julie at a party and you may hardly recognize your quiet classmate.

An experiment by David Napolitan and George Goethals (1979) illustrates the phenomenon. They had Williams College students talk, one at a time, with a young woman who acted either aloof and critical or warm and friendly. Beforehand, they told half the students the woman's behavior would be spontaneous. They told the other half the truth—that she had been instructed to *act* friendly (or unfriendly). What effect do you suppose this information had?

None. The students disregarded the information. If the woman acted friendly, they inferred she really was a warm person. If she acted unfriendly, they inferred she really was a cold person. In other words, they attributed her behavior to her personal disposition *even when told that her behavior was situational*—that she was merely acting that way for purposes of the experiment.

You, too, have surely committed the fundamental attribution error. In judging whether your psychology instructor is shy or outgoing, you have perhaps by now inferred that he or she has an outgoing personality. But you know your instructor only from the classroom, a situation that demands outgoing behavior. Catch the instructor in a different situation and you might be surprised (as some of my students have been when confronting me in a pick-up basketball game). Outside their assigned roles, professors seem less professorial, presidents less presidential, servants less servile.

The instructor, on the other hand, observes his or her own behavior in many different situations—in the classroom, in meetings, at home—and so might say, "Me, outgoing? It all depends on the situation. In class or with good friends, yes, I'm outgoing. But at conventions I'm really rather shy."

So, when explaining *our own* behavior, we are sensitive to how our behavior changes with the situations we encounter. When explaining *others'* behavior, particularly after observing them in only one type of situation, we often commit the fundamental attribution error: We disregard the situation and leap to unwarranted conclusions about their personality traits. We initially assumed that Nazi death camp commanders had notably vile personalities, when in reality many were unremarkable men who went home after the day's brutality and relaxed over a good book and the strains of classical music. We initially assumed that the 9/11 terrorists were obviously crazy, when actually they went unnoticed in their neighborhoods, health clubs, and favorite restaurants.

Those whom we know well we observe in varied situations, which restrains our attributing their behavior solely to their dispositions (Idson & Mischel, 2001). But with strangers, we make dispositional attributions because we focus our attention more on the person than on the situational context. Meanwhile, the person's own attention focuses more on the situation to which he or she is reacting. Reversing the perspectives of actor and observer—by having each view a videotape replay of the situation from the other's perspective—also reverses the attributions (Lassiter & Irvine, 1986; Storms, 1973). Seeing the world from the actor's perspective, the observers better appreciate the situation. Taking the observer's point of view, the actors better appreciate their own personal style.

The Effects of Attribution

In everyday life we often struggle to explain others' actions. A jury must decide whether a shooting was malicious or in self-defense. An unhappy wife and husband each ponder why the other behaves so selfishly. An interviewer must judge whether the applicant's geniality is genuine. When we make such judgments, our attributions—either to the person or to the situation—have important consequences (Fincham & Bradbury, 1993; Fletcher & others, 1990). Happily married couples attribute a spouse's tart-tongued remark to a temporary situation ("She must have had a bad day at work"). Unhappily married persons attribute the same remark to a mean disposition ("Why did I marry such a hostile person?").

Or consider the political effects of attribution: How do you explain poverty or unemployment? Researchers in Britain, India, Australia, and the United States (Furnham, 1982; Pandey & others, 1982; Wagstaff, 1982; Zucker & Weiner, 1993) report that political conservatives tend to attribute such social problems to the personal dispositions of the poor and unemployed themselves: "People generally get what they deserve. Those who don't work are often freeloaders. Anybody who takes the initiative can still get ahead." "Society is not to blame for crime, criminals are," said one U.S. presidential candidate (Dole, 1996). Political liberals (and social scientists) are more likely to blame past and present situations: "If you or I had to live with the same poor education, lack of opportunity, and discrimination, would we be any better off?" To understand 9/11 and prevent such terrorism in the future, they say, consider the perceived grievances and the situations that breed terrorists.

Managers also have to make attributions. In evaluating employees, they are likely to attribute poor performance to personal factors, such as low ability or lack of motivation. But remember the actor's viewpoint: Workers doing poorly on a job recognize situational influences, such as inadequate supplies, poor working conditions, difficult co-workers, or impossible demands (Rice, 1985).

The point to remember: Our attributions—to individuals' dispositions or to their situations—have real consequences.

"Otis, shout at that man to pull himself together."

▶ **fundamental attribution error** the tendency for observers, when analyzing another's behavior, to underestimate the impact of the situation and to overestimate the impact of personal disposition.

▶ **attitude** a belief and feeling that predisposes one to respond in a particular way to objects, people, and events.

Attitudes and Actions

2. Does what we think predict what we will do, or does what we do shape what we will think?

Attitudes are beliefs and feelings that predispose our reactions to objects, people, and events. If we *believe* someone is mean, we may *feel* dislike for the person and *act* unfriendly. "Change the way people think," said South African civil rights martyr Steve Biko, "and things will never be the same." Such is the power of persuasion.

Our attitudes predict our behavior imperfectly. As **Figure 15.1** illustrates, the external situation also influences behavior. The American public's overwhelming support for President George W. Bush's preparation to attack Iraq motivated Democratic leaders to vote to

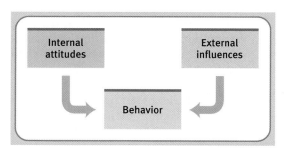

figure 15.1
Attitudes, external influences, and behavior Our behavior is affected by our inner attitudes as well as by external social influences.

Attitudes follow behavior Cooperative actions, such as those performed by people on sports teams, feed mutual liking. Such attitudes, in turn, promote positive behavior.

Actions

Attitudes

support Bush despite their private reservations (Nagourney, 2002). Nevertheless, our attitudes *will* guide our actions when other influences are minimal, when the attitude is specific to the behavior, and when we are keenly aware of our attitudes.

Now consider a more surprising principle: People also come to believe in what they have stood up for. Many streams of evidence confirm that *attitudes follow behavior*. Here are two.

The Foot-in-the-Door Phenomenon

During the Korean War, many captured U.S. soldiers were imprisoned in war camps run by Chinese communists. Without using brutality, the captors secured the collaboration of hundreds of their prisoners in various activities. Some merely ran errands or accepted favors. Others made radio appeals and false confessions. Still others informed on fellow prisoners and divulged military information. When the war ended, 21 prisoners chose to stay with the communists. More returned home "brainwashed"—convinced that communism was a good thing for Asia.

A key ingredient of the Chinese "thought-control" program was its effective use of the **foot-in-the-door phenomenon**—a tendency for people who agree to a small action to comply later with a larger one. The Chinese gradually escalated their demands on the prisoners, beginning with harmless requests (Schein, 1956). Having "trained" the prisoners to speak or write trivial statements, the communists then asked them to copy or create something more important, noting, perhaps, the flaws of capitalism. The prisoners then participated in group discussions, wrote self-criticisms, or uttered public confessions. After doing so, perhaps to gain privileges, they often adjusted their beliefs toward consistency with their public acts.

The point is simple, says Robert Cialdini (1993): To get people to agree to something big, "start small and build." Be wary of those who would exploit you with the tactic. This chicken-and-egg spiral of actions feeding attitudes feeding actions enables behavior to escalate. A trivial act makes the next act easier. Succumb to a temptation and you will find the next temptation harder to resist. In experiments, doing became believing when people induced to harm an innocent victim—by making nasty comments or delivering electric shocks—began to disparage their victim. Others induced to speak or write on behalf of a position they had qualms about began to believe their own words. Teens who publicly pledge virginity until marriage have sex less often than similar teens not induced to pledge (Bearman & Brückner, 2001). Saying becomes believing.

The action-attitude spiral

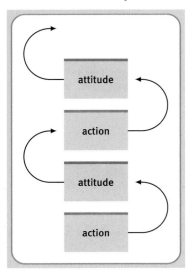

attitude

action

attitude

action

Fortunately, the attitudes-follow-behavior principle works as well for good deeds as for bad. The foot-in-the-door tactic can help boost charitable contributions, blood donations, and product sales. In one experiment, researchers posing as safe-driving volunteers asked Californians to permit the installation of a large, poorly lettered "Drive Carefully" sign in their front yards. Only 17 percent consented. They approached other home owners with a small request first: Would they display a 3-inch high "Be a Safe Driver" sign? Nearly all readily agreed. When reapproached two weeks later to allow the large, ugly sign in their front yards, 76 percent consented (Freedman & Fraser, 1966).

Racial attitudes likewise follow behavior. In the years immediately following the introduction of school desegregation and the passage of the Civil Rights Act of 1964, white Americans expressed diminishing racial prejudice. And as Americans in different regions came to act more alike—thanks to more uniform national standards against discrimination—they began to think more alike. Experiments confirm the observation: Moral action strengthens moral convictions.

The bottom line: Evil acts shape the self. But so do acts of good will. Act as though you like someone, and you soon will. We love people for the good we do them as well as for the good they do us.

Role Playing Affects Attitudes

When you adopt a new **role**—when you become a college student, marry, or begin a new job—you strive to follow the social prescriptions. At first, your behaviors may feel phony, because you are *acting* the role. The first weeks in the military feel artificial—as if one is pretending to be a soldier. The first weeks of a marriage may feel like "playing house." Before long, however, what began as play-acting in the theater of life becomes *you*. This helps explain why women who do administrative or professional work develop, over time, more confident and assertive personalities (Roberts, 1997).

Researchers have confirmed this effect by assessing people's attitudes before and after they adopt a new role, sometimes in laboratory situations, sometimes in everyday situations, such as before and after taking a job. In one laboratory study, college students volunteered to spend time in a simulated prison devised by psychologist Philip Zimbardo (1972). Some he randomly designated as guards; he gave them uniforms, billy clubs, and whistles and instructed them to enforce certain rules. The remainder became prisoners; they were locked in barren cells and forced to wear humiliating outfits. After a day or two in which the volunteers self-consciously "played" their roles, the simulation became real—too real. Most of the guards developed disparaging attitudes, and some devised cruel and degrading routines. One by one, the prisoners broke down, rebelled, or became passively resigned, causing Zimbardo to call off the study after only six days.

In real life, Greece's military junta during the early 1970s was training another group of men to become torturers (Staub, 1989). The men's indoctrination into their roles occurred in small steps. First, the trainee stood guard outside the interrogation cells—the "foot in the door." Next, he stood guard inside. Only then was he ready to become actively involved in the questioning and torture. As the nineteenth-century writer Nathaniel Hawthorne noted, "No man, for any considerable period, can wear one face to himself and another to the multitude without finally getting bewildered as to which may be true." What we do, we gradually become.

Why Do Our Actions Affect Our Attitudes?

Without doubt, then, actions can affect attitudes, sometimes turning prisoners into collaborators, doubters into believers, or mere acquaintances into friends. But why? One explanation is that we feel motivated to justify our actions. When we are aware that our attitudes and actions don't coincide, we experience tension, called *cognitive dissonance*. To relieve this tension, according to the **cognitive dissonance theory** proposed by Leon Festinger, we often bring our attitudes into line with our actions.

"If the King destroys a man, that's proof to the King it must have been a bad man."

Thomas Cromwell, in Robert Bolt's
A Man for All Seasons, 1960

Social roles are powerful Initially both the obedient recruit and the abusive sergeant may have consciously adopted the behavior expected of them. In time, they may become the characters they are playing.

"Fake it until you make it."

Alcoholics Anonymous saying

▶ **foot-in-the-door phenomenon** the tendency for people who have first agreed to a small request to comply later with a larger request.

▶ **role** a set of expectations (norms) about a social position, defining how those in the position ought to behave.

▶ **cognitive dissonance theory** the theory that we act to reduce the discomfort (dissonance) we feel when two of our thoughts (cognitions) are inconsistent. For example, when our awareness of our attitudes and of our actions clash, we can reduce the resulting dissonance by changing our attitudes.

figure 15.2
When attitudes follow behavior, cognitive dissonance lessens.

Fiona's attitude:

The tuition here is too high

Fiona's behavior:

THE SCHOOL NEEDS THE MONEY!

Cognitive dissonance
(awareness that attitude and behavior are inconsistent)

Dissonance resolved

Maybe the school has a point

It is as if we rationalize, "If I chose to do it (or say it), I must believe in it." The less coerced and more responsible we feel for a troubling act, the more dissonance we feel. The more dissonance we feel, the more motivated we are to find consistency, such as changing our attitudes to help justify the act.

Dozens of experiments have confirmed cognitive dissonance by making people feel responsible for behavior that is inconsistent with their attitudes and that has foreseeable consequences. As a subject in one of these experiments, you might agree for a measly $2 to help a researcher by writing an essay that supports something you don't believe in (perhaps a tuition increase). Feeling responsible for the statements (which are not consistent with your attitudes), you would probably feel dissonance, especially if you thought an administrator would be reading your essay. How would you reduce the uncomfortable dissonance? One way would be to start believing your phony words. Your pretense becomes your reality (**FIGURE 15.2**).

The attitudes-follow-behavior principle has some heartening implications. Although we cannot directly control all our feelings, we can influence them by altering our behavior. If we are down in the dumps, we can do as cognitive therapists advise and talk in more positive, self-accepting ways with fewer self–put-downs. If we are unloving, we can become more loving by behaving as if we were so—by doing thoughtful things, expressing affection, giving affirmation. "Assume a virtue, if you have it not," says Hamlet to his mother. "For use can almost change the stamp of nature." *The point to remember:* Changing our behavior can change how we think and how we feel. Just do it.

"Sit all day in a moping posture, sigh, and reply to everything with a dismal voice, and your melancholy lingers. . . . If we wish to conquer undesirable emotional tendencies in ourselves, we must . . . go through the outward movements of those contrary dispositions which we prefer to cultivate."

William James, Principles of Psychology, 1890

rehearse it!

1. In explaining a person's behavior we tend to make the fundamental attribution error—we overestimate the impact of internal factors (such as disposition, or personality) and underestimate the impact of the situation in which the behavior occurs. Thus, if we encounter a person seemingly high on drugs, we might attribute the person's behavior to
   a. moral weakness or an addictive personality.
   b. peer pressure.
   c. the easy availability of the drug on city streets.
   d. society's acceptance of drug use.

2. During the Korean War, the Chinese "brainwashed" captured American soldiers to think that communism was a good thing for Asia. A key ingredient in this process was their use of people's tendency to more readily agree to a larger request if they have already agreed to a small request. This tendency is called
   a. the fundamental attribution error.
   b. the foot-in-the-door phenomenon.
   c. the behavior-follows-attitudes principle.
   d. role playing.

3. When we are aware of a discrepancy between our attitudes and our behavior, cognitive dissonance theory predicts that we will act to reduce the discomfort or dissonance we feel. The theory explains why
   a. people who act against their attitudes tend to change their attitudes.
   b. attitudes predict actions when social pressures are minimized.
   c. changing an attitude—through persuasion—often fails to result in behavioral changes.
   d. people are hypocritical, talking one way and acting another.

Answers can be found in Appendix C.

SOCIAL INFLUENCE

Social psychology's great lesson is the enormous power of social influence. This influence can be seen in our conformity, compliance, and group behavior. Suicides, bomb threats, airplane hijackings, and UFO sightings all have a curious tendency to come in clusters. Armed with principles of social influence, advertisers, salespeople, and campaign workers aim to sway our decisions to buy, to donate, to vote. Isolated with others who share their grievances, dissenters may gradually become rebels, and rebels may become terrorists. During a lengthy stay in another part of the world, we may struggle with the new cultural norms. On campus, we wear blue jeans; on New York's Wall Street or London's Bond Street, we wear suits and ties. Let's examine the pull of these social strings. How strong are they? How do they operate?

Niche conformity Are these students asserting their individuality or identifying themselves with others of the same microculture?

Conformity and Obedience

3. What do experiments on conformity and compliance reveal about the power of social influence?

Behavior is contagious.

- One person giggles, coughs, or yawns, and others in the group soon do the same. A cluster of people stand gazing upward, and passersby pause to do likewise.
- Laughter, even canned laughter, can be infectious. Bartenders and street musicians know to "seed" their tip containers with money to suggest that others have given.
- Sickness can also be contagious. In the anxious 9/11 aftermath, more than two dozen elementary and middle schools had outbreaks of children reporting red rashes, sometimes causing parents to wonder whether biological terrorism was at work (Talbot, 2002). Some cases may have been stress-related, but mostly, said health experts, people were just noticing normal early acne, insect bites, eczema, and dry skin from overheated classrooms.

We are natural mimics—an effect Tanya Chartrand and John Bargh (1999) call "the chameleon effect." Unconsciously mimicking others' expressions, postures, and voice tones helps us feel what they are feeling. This helps explain why we feel happier around happy people than around depressed ones, and why studies of groups of British nurses and accountants reveal "mood linkage"—sharing up and down moods (Totterdell & others, 1998). Just hearing someone reading a neutral text with either a happy- or sad-sounding voice creates "mood contagion" in listeners (Neumann & Strack, 2000).

Chartrand and Bargh demonstrated the chameleon effect when they had students work in a room alongside someone—a confederate working for the experimenter—who rubbed his or her face and, on another occasion, alongside a confederate who shook his or her foot. Participants tended to rub their own face when with the face-rubbing person and shake their own foot with the foot-shaking person. Such automatic mimicry is part of empathy, and the most empathic people mimic—and are liked—the most.

Sometimes the effects of suggestibility are more serious. In the eight days following the 1999 shooting rampage at Colorado's Columbine High School, every U.S. state except Vermont experienced threats of copycat violence. Pennsylvania alone recorded 60 such threats (Cooper, 1999). Sociologist David Phillips and his colleagues (1985, 1989) found that suicides, too, sometimes increase following a highly publicized suicide. In the wake of Marilyn Monroe's suicide on August 6, 1962, the number of August suicides in the United States exceeded the usual count by 200. Although not all studies have confirmed the copycat suicide phenomenon, suicides have sometimes occurred in local clusters. Within an 18-day span, one 1500-student high school recorded 2 completed suicides, 7 attempted suicides, and 23 students with suicidal thoughts.

▶ **conformity** adjusting one's behavior or thinking to coincide with a group standard.

▶ **normative social influence** influence resulting from a person's desire to gain approval or avoid disapproval.

▶ **informational social influence** influence resulting from one's willingness to accept others' opinions about reality.

NON SEQUITUR   by WILEY

What caused these suicide clusters? Do people act similarly because of their influence on one another? Or because they are simultaneously exposed to the same events and conditions? Seeking answers, social psychologists have conducted experiments on group pressure and conformity.

Group Pressure and Conformity

Suggestibility is a subtle type of **conformity**. To study conformity (adjusting our behavior or thinking toward some group standard), Solomon Asch (1955) devised a simple test. As a participant in the study, you arrive at the experiment location in time to take a seat at a table where five people are already seated. The experimenter asks which of three comparison lines is identical to a standard line (**FIGURE 15.3**). You see clearly that the answer is Line 2 and await your turn to say so after the others. Your boredom with this experiment begins to show when the next set of lines proves equally easy.

Now comes the third trial, and the correct answer seems just as clear-cut, but the first person gives what strikes you as a wrong answer: "Line 3." When the second person and then the third and fourth give the same wrong answer, you sit up straight and squint. When the fifth person agrees with the first three, you feel your heart begin to pound. The experimenter then looks to you for your answer. Torn between the unanimity of your five fellow respondents and the evidence of your own eyes, you feel tense and much less sure of yourself than you were moments ago. You hesitate before answering, wondering whether you should suffer the discomfort of being the oddball. What answer do you give?

In the experiments conducted by Asch and others after him, thousands of college students have experienced this conflict. Answering such questions alone, they erred less than 1 percent of the time. But the odds were quite different when several others—confederates working for the experimenter—answered incorrectly. Asch reports that more than one-third of the time, these "intelligent and well-meaning" college students were then "willing to call white black" by going along with the group.

figure 15.3
Asch's conformity experiments Which of the three comparison lines is equal to the standard line? What do you suppose most people would say after hearing five others say, "Line 3"? In this photo from one of Asch's experiments, the subject (center) shows the severe discomfort that comes from disagreeing with the responses of other group members.

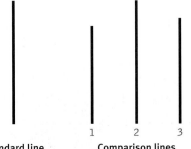

Standard line   Comparison lines

CONDITIONS THAT STRENGTHEN CONFORMITY Asch's procedure became the model for later investigations. Although experiments have not always found so much conformity, they do reveal that conformity increases when

- one is made to feel incompetent or insecure.
- the group has at least three people.
- the group is unanimous. (The support of a single fellow dissident greatly increases social courage.)
- one admires the group's status and attractiveness.
- one has made no prior commitment to any response.
- others in the group observe one's behavior.
- one's culture strongly encourages respect for social standards.

Thus, we might predict the behavior of Joe, an enthusiastic but insecure new fraternity member: Noting that the 40 other members appear unanimous in their plans for a fund-raiser, Joe is unlikely to voice his dissent.

REASONS FOR CONFORMING Why do we clap when others clap, eat as others eat, believe what others believe, even see what others see? Frequently, it is to avoid rejection or to gain social approval. In such cases, we are responding to what social psychologists call **normative social influence**. We are sensitive to social norms—understood rules for accepted and expected behavior—because the price we pay for being different may be severe.

Marco Lokar knows. During the 1991 Persian Gulf War, Lokar, an Italian, was the only Seton Hall University basketball player who chose not to display an American flag on his uniform. As the team traveled, the fans' abusive responses to his nonconforming behavior became unbearable, so he left the team and returned to Italy. Toni Smith also knows. In 2003, when the Manhattanville College basketball player likewise dissented from the impending war with Iraq—by turning sideways and not looking at the flag during the pregame national anthem—similar outrage resulted. In one game at another college, students stood and chanted "Leave the country!"

Respecting norms is not the only reason we conform: Groups may provide valuable information, and only an uncommonly stubborn person will *never* listen to others. When we accept others' opinions about reality, we are responding to **informational social influence**. "Those who never retract their opinions love themselves more than they love truth," observed the eighteenth-century French essayist, Joseph Joubert.

Our view of social influence as bad or good depends on our values. When influence supports what we approve, we applaud those who are "open-minded" and "sensitive" enough to be "responsive." When influence supports what we disapprove, we scorn the "submissive conformity" of those who comply with others' wishes. As we saw in Chapter 12, cultures vary in the value they place on individualism or collectivism. Western Europeans and people in most English-speaking countries tend to prize individualism more than conformity and obedience. These values are reflected in social influence experiments that have been conducted in 17 countries: In individualist cultures, conformity rates are lower (Bond & Smith, 1996).

Obedience

Social psychologist Stanley Milgram (1963, 1974) knew that people often comply with social pressures. But how would they respond to outright commands? To find out, he undertook what have become social psychology's most famous and controversial experiments. Imagine yourself as one of the nearly 1000 participants in Milgram's 20 experiments.

Responding to an advertisement, you come to Yale University's psychology department to participate in an experiment. Professor Milgram's assistant explains that the study concerns the effect of punishment on learning. You and another person draw slips from a hat to see who will be the "teacher" (which your slip says) and who will be the "learner." The learner is then led to an adjoining room and strapped

"Have you ever noticed how one example—good or bad—can prompt others to follow? How one illegally parked car can give permission for others to do likewise? How one racial joke can fuel another?"

Marian Wright Edelman,
The Measure of Our Success, *1992*

Stanley Milgram (1933–1984) The late social psychologist's obedience experiments now "belong to the self-understanding of literate people in our age" (Sabini, 1986).

into a chair that is wired through the wall to an electric shock machine. You sit in front of the machine, which has switches labeled with voltages. Your task: to teach and then test the learner on a list of word pairs. You are to punish the learner for wrong answers by delivering brief electric shocks, beginning with a switch labeled "15 Volts—Slight Shock." After each of the learner's errors, you are to move up to the next higher voltage. With each flick of a switch, lights flash, relay switches click on, and an electric buzzing fills the air.

If you comply with the experimenter's instructions, you hear the learner grunt when you flick the third, fourth, and fifth switches. After you activate the eighth switch (labeled "120 Volts—Moderate Shock"), the learner shouts that the shocks are painful. After the tenth switch ("150 Volts—Strong Shock"), he cries, "Get me out of here! I won't be in the experiment anymore! I refuse to go on!" When you hear these pleas, you draw back. But the experimenter prods you: "Please continue—the experiment requires that you continue." If you still resist, he insists, "It is absolutely essential that you continue," or "You have no other choice, you *must* go on."

If you obey, you hear the learner's protests escalate to shrieks of agony as you continue to raise the shock level with each succeeding error. After the 330-volt level, the learner refuses to answer and soon falls silent. Still, the experimenter pushes you toward the final, 450-volt switch, ordering you to ask the questions and, if no correct answer is given, to administer the next shock level.

How far do you think you would follow the experimenter's commands? When Milgram surveyed people before conducting the experiment, most declared they would stop playing such a sadistic role soon after the learner first indicated pain and certainly before he shrieked in agony. This also was the prediction made by each of 40 psychiatrists whom Milgram asked to guess the outcome. When Milgram actually conducted the experiment with men aged 20 to 50, he was astonished to find that 63 percent complied fully—right up to the last switch. Ten later studies that included women found women's compliance rates were similar to men's (Blass, 1999).

Did the "teachers" figure out the hoax—that no shock was being delivered? Did they guess the learner was a confederate who only pretended to feel the shocks? Did they realize the experiment was really testing their willingness to comply with commands to inflict punishment? No, the teachers typically displayed genuine agony: They sweated, trembled, laughed nervously, and bit their lips.

Milgram's use of deception and stress triggered a debate over his research ethics. In his own defense, Milgram pointed out that, after the participants learned of the deception and actual research purposes, virtually none regretted taking part. When 40 of the "teachers" who had agonized most were later interviewed by a psychiatrist, none appeared to be suffering emotional aftereffects. All in all, said Milgram, the experiments provoked less stress than university students experience when facing and failing big exams (Blass, 1996).

Wondering whether the participants obeyed because the learners' protests were not convincing, Milgram repeated the experiment, with 40 new teachers. This time his confederate mentioned a "slight heart condition" while being strapped into the chair, and then he complained and screamed more intensely as the shocks became more punishing. Still, 65 percent of the new teachers complied fully (**FIGURE 15.4**).

In later experiments, Milgram discovered that subtle details of a situation powerfully influence people. When he varied the social conditions, the proportion of fully compliant participants varied from 0 to 93 percent. Obedience was highest when

- the person giving the orders was close at hand and was perceived to be a legitimate authority figure.
- the authority figure was supported by a prestigious institution. Compliance was somewhat lower when Milgram dissociated his experiments from Yale University. (The 9/11 terrorists apparently obeyed orders to kill which they believed expressed the will of their ultimate authority—Allah, who would reward them in the afterlife.)

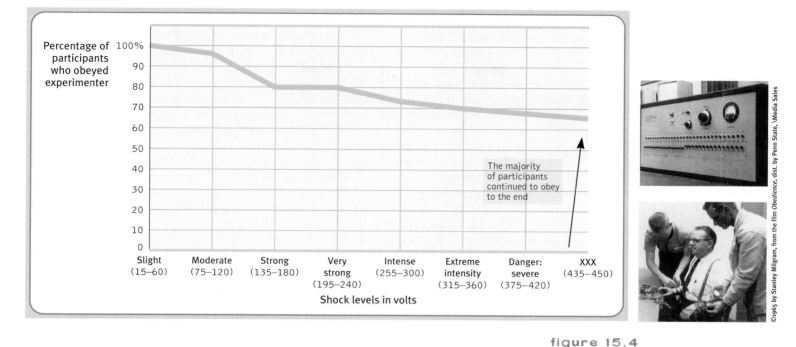

The majority of participants continued to obey to the end

Percentage of participants who obeyed experimenter

Shock levels in volts:
Slight (15–60), Moderate (75–120), Strong (135–180), Very strong (195–240), Intense (255–300), Extreme intensity (315–360), Danger: severe (375–420), XXX (435–450)

figure 15.4
Milgram's follow-up obedience experiment In a repeat of the earlier experiment, 65 percent of the adult male "teachers" fully obeyed the experimenter's commands to continue. They did so despite the "learner's" earlier mention of a heart condition and despite hearing cries of protest after 150 volts and agonized protests after 330 volts. (Data from Milgram, 1974.)

- the victim was depersonalized or at a distance, even in another room. (Similarly, in combat with an enemy they can see, many soldiers either do not fire their rifles or do not aim them properly. Such refusals to kill are rare among those who operate the more distant weapons of artillery or aircraft [Padgett, 1989].)

- there were no role models for defiance; that is, no other subjects were seen disobeying the experimenter.

The power of legitimate, close-at-hand authorities is dramatically apparent in stories of those who complied with orders to carry out the atrocities of the Holocaust, and those who didn't. Obedience, alone, hardly explains the Holocaust; anti-Semitic ideology engaged eager killers as well (Mastroianni, 2002). But obedience was a factor. In the summer of 1942 nearly 500 middle-aged German reserve police officers were dispatched to Jozefow, Poland, in German-occupied territory. On July 13, the group's visibly upset commander informed his recruits, mostly family men, that they had been ordered to round up the village's Jews, who were said to be aiding the enemy. Able-bodied men were to be sent to work camps, and all the rest were to be shot on the spot. Given a chance to refuse participation in the executions, only about a dozen immediately did so. Within 17 hours, the remaining 485 officers killed 1500 helpless women, children, and elderly by shooting them in the back of the head as they lay face down. Hearing the pleadings of the victims, and seeing the gruesome results, some 20 percent of the officers did eventually dissent, managing either to miss their victims or to wander away and hide until the slaughter was over (Browning, 1992). But in real life, as in Milgram's experiments, the disobedient were the minority.

Another story was being played out in the French village of Le Chambon, where French Jews destined for deportation to Germany were being sheltered by villagers who openly defied orders to cooperate with the "New Order." The villagers' ancestors had themselves been persecuted and their pastors had been teaching them to "resist whenever our adversaries will demand of us obedience contrary to the orders of the Gospel" (Rochat, 1993). Ordered by police to give a list of sheltered Jews, the head pastor modeled defiance: "I don't know of Jews, I only know of human beings." Without realizing how long and terrible the war would be, or how much punishment and poverty they would suffer, the resisters made an initial commitment to resist. Supported by their beliefs, their role models, their interaction with one another, and their own initial acts, they remained defiant to the war's end.

Standing up for democracy Some individuals—roughly one in three in Milgram's experiments—resist social coercion, as did this unarmed man in Beijing, by single-handedly challenging an advancing line of tanks the day after the 1989 Tiananmen Square student uprising was suppressed.

"Drive off the cliff, James, I want to commit suicide."

Lessons From the Conformity and Obedience Studies

What do the Asch and Milgram experiments teach us about ourselves? How does judging the length of a line or flicking a shock switch relate to everyday social behavior? Recall from Chapter 1 that psychological experiments aim not to re-create the literal behaviors of everyday life but to capture and explore the underlying processes that shape those behaviors. Asch and Milgram devised experiments in which the subjects had to choose between adhering to their own standards and being responsive to others, a dilemma we all face frequently.

In Milgram's experiments, the participants were also torn between what they should respond to—the pleas of the victim or the orders of the experimenter. Their moral sense warned them not to harm another, yet it also prompted them to obey the experimenter and to be a good research participant. With kindness and obedience on a collision course, obedience usually won.

Such experiments demonstrate that strong social influences can make people conform to falsehoods or capitulate to cruelty. "The most fundamental lesson of our study," Milgram noted, is that "ordinary people, simply doing their jobs, and without any particular hostility on their part, can become agents in a terrible destructive process" (1974, p. 6). Milgram did not entrap his "teachers" by asking them first to zap "learners" with enough electricity to make their hair stand on end. Rather, he exploited the foot-in-the-door effect, beginning with a little tickle of electricity and escalating step by step. In the minds of those throwing the switches, the small action became justified, making the next act tolerable. In Jozefow, in Le Chambon, and in Milgram's experiments, those who resisted usually did so early. After the first acts of compliance or resistance, attitudes began to follow and justify behavior.

So it happens when people succumb, gradually, to evil. In any society, great evils sometimes grow out of people's compliance with lesser evils. The Nazi leaders suspected that most German civil servants would resist shooting or gassing Jews directly, but they found them surprisingly willing to handle the paperwork of the Holocaust (Silver & Geller, 1978). Likewise, when Milgram asked 40 men to administer the learning test while someone else did the shocking, 93 percent complied. Contrary to images of devilish villains, evil does not require monstrous characters; all it takes is ordinary people corrupted by an evil situation—ordinary soldiers who follow orders to shoot, ordinary students who follow orders to haze initiates into their group, ordinary employees who follow orders to produce and market harmful products. Before leading the 9/11 attacks, Mohamed Atta reportedly was a sane, rational person who had been a "good boy" and an excellent student from a close-knit family—not someone who fits our image of evil monster.

"I was only following orders."

Adolf Eichmann, Director of Nazi deportation of Jews to concentration camps

"The normal reaction to an abnormal situation is abnormal behavior."

James Waller, Becoming Evil: How Ordinary People Commit Genocide and Mass Killing, 2002

Group Influence

4. How does the mere presence of others influence our actions? How does our behavior change when we act as part of a group?

How do groups affect our behavior? To find out, social psychologists study the various influences that operate in the simplest of groups—one person in the presence of another—and those that operate in more complex groups, such as families, teams, and committees.

Individual Behavior in the Presence of Others

Appropriately, social psychology's first experiments focused on the simplest of all questions about social behavior: How are we influenced by the mere presence of others—by people watching us or joining us in various activities?

SOCIAL FACILITATION Having noticed that cyclists' racing times were faster when they competed against each other than when they competed with a clock, Norman Triplett (1898) hypothesized that the presence of others boosts performance. To test his hypothesis, Triplett had adolescents wind a fishing reel as rapidly

▶ **social facilitation** improved performance of tasks in the presence of others; occurs with simple or well-learned tasks but not with tasks that are difficult or not yet mastered.

▶ **social loafing** the tendency for people in a group to exert less effort when pooling their efforts toward attaining a common goal than when individually accountable.

as possible. He discovered that they wound the reel faster in the presence of some-one doing the same thing. This phenomenon of stronger performance in others' presence is called **social facilitation**. For example, after a light turns green, driv-ers take about 15 percent less time to travel the first 100 yards when another car is beside them at the intersection than when they are alone (Towler, 1986).

But now things get tricky. On tougher tasks (learning nonsense syllables or solv-ing complex multiplication problems), people perform *less* well when observers or others working on the same task are present. Further studies revealed why the pres-ence of others sometimes helps and sometimes hinders performance (Guerin, 1986; Zajonc, 1965). When others observe us, we become aroused. This arousal strength-ens the most *likely* response—the correct one on an easy task, an incorrect one on a difficult task. Thus, when we are being observed, we perform well-learned tasks more quickly and accurately and unmastered tasks less quickly and accurately. James Michaels and his associates (1982) found that expert pool players who made 71 per-cent of their shots when alone made 80 percent when four people came to watch them. Poor shooters, who made 36 percent of their shots when alone, made only 25 percent when watched. The energizing effect of an enthusiastic audience probably contributes to the home advantage enjoyed by various sports teams. Studies of more than 80,000 college and professional athletic events in Canada, the United States, and England reveal that home teams win about 6 in 10 games (somewhat fewer for baseball and football, somewhat more for basketball and soccer—see **TABLE 15.1**).

The point to remember: What you do well, you are likely to do even better in front of an audience, especially a friendly audience; what you normally find difficult may seem all but impossible when you are being watched.

Social facilitation also helps explain a funny effect of crowding: Comedy records that are mildly amusing to people in an uncrowded room seem funnier in a dense-ly packed room (Aiello & others, 1983; Freedman & Perlick, 1979). As comedians and actors know, a "good house" is a full one. The arousal triggered by crowding amplifies other reactions, too. If sitting close to one another, participants in exper-iments like a friendly person even more, an unfriendly person even less (Schiffenbauer & Schiavo, 1976; Storms & Thomas, 1977).

SOCIAL LOAFING Social facilitation experiments test the effect of others' presence on performance on an individual task, such as shooting pool. But what happens to performance when people perform the task as a group? In a team tug-of-war, for example, do you suppose the effort that a person puts forth would be more than, less than, or the same as the effort he or she would exert in a one-on-one tug-of-war? To find out, Alan Ingham and his fellow researchers (1974) asked blindfolded University of Massachusetts students to "pull as hard as you can" on a rope. When Ingham fooled the students into believing three others were also pulling behind them, they exerted only 82 percent as much effort as when they knew they were pulling alone.

To describe this diminished effort, Bibb Latané (1981; Jackson & Williams, 1988) coined the term **social loafing**. In 78 experiments conducted in the United States, India, Thailand, Japan, China, and Taiwan, social loafing occurred on vari-ous tasks, though it was especially common among men in individualistic cultures (Karau & Williams, 1993). In one of Latané's experiments, blindfolded people seat-ed in a group clapped or shouted as loud as they could while listening through headphones to the sound of loud clapping or shouting. When told they were doing it with the others, these people produced about one-third less noise than when they thought their individual efforts were identifiable.

Why? First, people acting as part of a group feel less accountable and therefore worry less about what others think. Second, they may view their contribution as dis-pensable (Harkins & Szymanski, 1989; Kerr & Bruun, 1983). As many leaders of organizations know—and as you have perhaps observed on student group assign-ments—if group members share equally in the group's benefits regardless of how much they contribute, some may slack off. Unless highly motivated and identified with their group, they may *free-ride* on the other group members' efforts.

table 15.1 Home Advantage in Major Team Sports

Sport	Home Team Games Studied	Home Team Winning Percentage
Baseball	23,034	53.5%
Football	2,592	57.3
Ice hockey	4,322	61.1
Basketball	13,596	64.4
Soccer	37,202	69.0

From Courneya & Carron, 1992

Social facilitation Skilled athletes often find they are "on" before an audience. What they do well, they do even better when people are watching.

Michelle Agins/NYT Pictures

▶ **deindividuation** the loss of self-awareness and self-restraint occurring in group situations that foster arousal and anonymity.

▶ **group polarization** the enhancement of a group's prevailing attitudes through discussion within the group.

▶ **groupthink** the mode of thinking that occurs when the desire for harmony in a decision-making group overrides a realistic appraisal of alternatives.

DEINDIVIDUATION So, the presence of others can arouse people (as in the social facilitation experiments) or can diminish their feelings of responsibility (as in the social loafing experiments). But sometimes the presence of others both arouses people *and* diminishes their sense of responsibility. The result can be uninhibited behavior ranging from a food fight in the dining hall or screaming at a basketball referee to vandalism or rioting. Abandoning normal restraints to the power of the group is termed **deindividuation**. To be deindividuated is to be less self-conscious and less restrained when in a group situation.

Deindividuation often occurs when group participation makes people feel aroused and anonymous. In one experiment, New York University women dressed in depersonalizing Ku Klux Klan–style hoods delivered twice as much electric shock to a victim as did identifiable women (Zimbardo, 1970). (As in all such experiments, the "victim" did not actually receive the shocks.) Similarly, tribal warriors who depersonalize themselves with face paints or masks are more likely than those with exposed faces to kill, torture, or mutilate captured enemies (Watson, 1973). Whether in a mob, at a rock concert, at a ballgame, or at worship, to lose self-consciousness (to become deindividuated) is to become more responsive to the group experience.

Effects of Group Interaction

5. What are group polarization and groupthink?

We have examined the conditions under which being in the presence of others can

● make easy tasks easier and difficult tasks harder.
● tempt people to free-ride on the efforts of others or motivate them to exert themselves.
● enhance humor or fuel mob violence.

Research shows that interacting with others can also have both bad and good effects.

GROUP POLARIZATION Educational researchers have noted that, over time, initial differences between groups of college students tend to grow. If the first-year students at College X tend to be more intellectually oriented than those at College Y, that difference will probably be amplified by the time they are seniors. Similarly, if the political conservatism of students who join fraternities and sororities is greater than that of students who do not, the gap in the political attitudes of the two groups will probably widen as they progress through college (Wilson & others, 1975). Likewise, notes Eleanor Maccoby (2002) from her decades of observing gender development, girls talk more intimately than boys do and play and fantasize less aggressively—and these gender differences widen over time as they interact mostly with their own gender.

This enhancement of a group's prevailing tendencies—called **group polarization**—occurs when people within a group discuss attitudes that most of them either favor or oppose. Group polarization can have beneficial results, as when it amplifies a sought-after spiritual awareness or strengthens the resolve of those in a self-help group. But it can also have dire consequences. For example, George Bishop and I discovered that when a low-prejudice group of high school students discussed racial issues, their attitudes became more accepting. When high-prejudice students discussed the same issues, they became more prejudiced (**Figure 15.5**). Discussion among like-minded people may backfire. This happened when adolescents at risk for delinquency emerged from such discussions with *increased* negative behaviors (Dishion & others, 1999).

The 9/11 terrorists were not born terrorists; their actions were the fruit of a long process that engaged the polarizing effect of interaction among the like-minded. Ditto for other suicide terrorists. After analyzing terrorist organizations around the world, psychologists Clark McCauley and Mary Segal (1987; McCauley, 2002) noted that the terrorist mentality does not erupt suddenly. Rather, it arises among people who get together because of a grievance and then become more and more extreme as they interact in isolation from any moderating influences. "To the best of my knowledge," reports terrorism researcher Ariel Merari (2002), "there has not been a single case of suicide terrorism which was done on a personal whim."

The Internet provides a new medium for group polarization. Its tens of thousands of virtual groups enable bereaved parents, peacemakers, and teachers to find solace and support from kindred spirits. But the Internet also enables people who share interests in government cover-ups, extraterrestrial visitors, white supremacy, Y2K collapse, or citizen militias to find one another and to find support for their shared suspicions (McKenna & Bargh, 1998). Future experiments will reveal whether electronic discussions mirror the polarizing effects of face-to-face discussions. With their views echoing one another's, will nerds become nerdier, goths gothier, conspiracy wackos wackier?

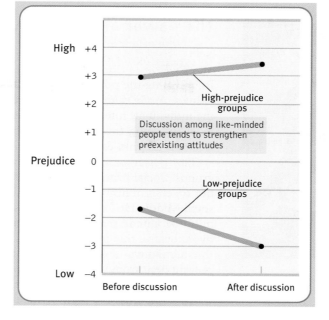

figure 15.5
Group polarization
If a group is like-minded, discussion strengthens its prevailing opinions. Talking over racial issues increased prejudice in a high-prejudice group of high school students and decreased it in a low-prejudice group. (Data from Myers & Bishop, 1970.)

GROUPTHINK Does group interaction ever distort important decisions? Social psychologist Irving Janis began to think so as he read historian Arthur M. Schlesinger, Jr.'s account of how President John F. Kennedy and his advisers blundered into an ill-fated plan to invade Cuba with 1400 CIA-trained Cuban exiles. When the invaders were easily captured and soon linked to the U.S. government, Kennedy wondered in hindsight, "How could we have been so stupid?"

To find out, Janis (1982) studied the decision-making procedures that led to the fiasco. He discovered that the soaring morale of the recently elected president and his advisers fostered undue confidence in the plan. To preserve the good group feeling, any dissenting views were suppressed or self-censored, especially after the President voiced his enthusiasm for the scheme. Since no one spoke strongly against the idea, everyone assumed consensus support. To describe this harmonious but unrealistic group thinking, Janis coined the term **groupthink**.

Janis and others then examined other historical fiascos—the failure to anticipate the 1941 Japanese attack on Pearl Harbor, the escalation of the Vietnam War, the U.S. Watergate cover-up, the Chernobyl nuclear reactor accident (Reason, 1987), and the U.S. space shuttle *Challenger* explosion (Esser & Lindoerfer, 1989). They discovered that in these cases, too, groupthink was fed by overconfidence, conformity, self-justification, and group polarization. Overconfidence appears also to have contributed to the FBI and CIA's failure to take seriously their agents' warnings that Arabs in flight-training schools might be plotting to fly planes into buildings such as the World Trade Center.

Despite such fiascos and tragedies, Janis also knew that, with some types of problems, two heads are better than one. So he also studied instances in which U.S. presidents and their advisers collectively made good decisions, such as when the Truman administration formulated the Marshall Plan, which offered assistance to Europe after World War II, and when the Kennedy administration worked to keep the Soviets from installing missiles in Cuba. In such instances—and in the business world, too, Janis believed—groupthink is prevented when a leader welcomes various opinions, invites experts' critiques of developing plans, and assigns people to identify possible problems. Just as the suppression of dissent bends a group toward bad decisions, so open debate often shapes good ones. None of us is as smart as all of us.

"One's impulse to blow the whistle on this nonsense was simply undone by the circumstances of the discussion."
Arthur M. Schlesinger, Jr., A Thousand Days, *1965*

"Truth springs from argument among friends."
Philosopher David Hume, 1711–1776

Gandhi As the life of Mahatma Gandhi powerfully testifies, a consistent and persistent minority voice can sometimes sway the majority. The nonviolent appeals and fasts of the Hindu nationalist and spiritual leader were instrumental in winning India's independence from Britain in 1947.

The Power of Individuals

6. How much power do we have as individuals? Can a minority sway a majority?

In affirming the power of social influence, we must not overlook our power as individuals. *Social control* (the power of the situation) and *personal control* (the power of the individual) interact. People aren't billiard balls. When feeling pressured, we may react by doing the opposite of what is expected, thereby reasserting our sense of freedom (Brehm & Brehm, 1981).

The power of committed individuals also appears in their influence on their groups. Social history is often made by a minority that sways the majority. Were this not so, communism would have remained an obscure theory, Christianity would be a small Middle Eastern sect, and Rosa Parks' refusal to sit at the back of the bus would not have ignited the civil rights movement. Technological history, too, is often made by innovative minorities who overcome the majority's resistance to change. To many, the railroad was a nonsensical idea; some farmers even feared that train noise would prevent hens from laying eggs. People derided Robert Fulton's steamboat as "Fulton's Folly." As Fulton later said, "Never did a single encouraging remark, a bright hope, a warm wish, cross my path." Much the same reaction greeted the printing press, the telegraph, the incandescent lamp, and the typewriter (Cantril & Bumstead, 1960).

European social psychologists have sought to better understand *minority influence—* the power of one or two individuals to sway majorities (Moscovici, 1985). They investigated groups in which one or two individuals consistently expressed a controversial attitude or an unusual perceptual judgment. They repeatedly found that a minority that unswervingly holds to its position is far more successful in swaying the majority than is a minority that waffles. Holding consistently to a minority opinion will not make you popular, but it may make you influential. This is especially so if your self-confidence stimulates others to consider why you react as you do. Although people often follow the majority view publicly, they may privately develop sympathy for the minority view. Even when a minority's influence is not yet visible, it may be persuading some members of the majority to rethink their views (Wood & others, 1994). The powers of social influence are enormous, but so are the powers of the committed individual.

---

rehearse it!

4. Conformity involves adjusting our thinking and behavior toward others in the group. Researchers have found that a person is most likely to conform to a group if
   a. the group members have diverse opinions.
   b. the person feels competent and secure.
   c. the group consists of at least three people.
   d. other group members will not observe the person's behavior.

5. In a classic experiment on obedience, Stanley Milgram tested research participants' (the "teachers") willingness to comply with a command to deliver what they believed to be painful high-voltage shocks to another person. More than 60 percent complied with the commands to deliver stronger and stronger shocks. Milgram's later experiments showed that the rate of compliance was highest when
   a. the victim was at a distance from the "teacher."
   b. the victim was close at hand.

   c. other "teachers" refused to go along with the experimenter.
   d. the "teachers" believed the victim had a heart condition.

6. In the presence of others we become aroused: Professional sports teams play better before a crowd. Social facilitation—improved performance in the presence of others—occurs with
   a. any physical task.
   b. new learning.
   c. a well-learned task.
   d. competitive sports or activities only.

7. When people are part of a group working toward a common goal, their individual efforts are diminished. Latané and his colleagues called this
   a. minority influence.
   b. social facilitation.
   c. social loafing.
   d. group polarization.

8. In a group situation that fosters arousal and anonymity, a person sometimes loses self-consciousness and self-control. This phenomenon, called *deindividuation*, is best illustrated by

   a. improved performance in front of an audience.
   b. unrestrained behavior at a mass rally.
   c. evasion of responsibility in a group clean-up effort.
   d. denial of one's own perceptions in the face of an opposing consensus.

9. If a group is like-minded, discussion strengthens its prevailing opinion. This effect is called
   a. groupthink.
   b. minority influence.
   c. group polarization.
   d. social facilitation.

10. Group interaction has the potential of distorting important group decisions. For example, when a group's desire for harmony overrides its realistic appraisal of alternatives, _____ has occurred.
    a. group polarization
    b. groupthink
    c. social facilitation
    d. deindividuation

Answers can be found in Appendix C.

SOCIAL RELATIONS

We have sampled how we *think* about and *influence* one another. Now we come to social psychology's third focus—how we *relate* to one another. We will ponder the bad and the good: from prejudice, aggression, and conflict, to attraction, altruism, and peacemaking.

Prejudice

Prejudice means "prejudgment." It is an unjustifiable and usually negative attitude toward a group—often a different cultural, ethnic, or gender group. Like all attitudes, **prejudice** is a mixture of *beliefs* (often overgeneralized and called **stereotypes**), *emotions* (hostility, envy, or fear), and predispositions to *action* (to discriminate). To *believe* that overweight people are gluttonous, to *feel* disgust for an overweight person, and to be hesitant to hire or date an overweight person is to be prejudiced. Prejudice is a negative *attitude;* **discrimination** is a negative *behavior.*

Like other forms of prejudgment, prejudices are schemas that influence how we notice and interpret events. In one study, most white participants perceived a white man shoving a black man as "horsing around." When they saw a black man shove a white man, they interpreted the act as "violent" (Duncan, 1976). Our preconceived ideas about people bias our impressions of their behavior. Prejudgments color perceptions.

How Prejudiced Are People?

To find out, we can assess what they say and what they do. To judge by what Americans say, racial and gender attitudes have changed dramatically in the last half-century (**FIGURE 15.6**). Nearly everyone agrees that children of all races should attend the same schools and that women and men should receive the same pay for the same job. In Western Europe, where many "guest workers" and refugees have settled in recent years, "modern prejudice" (rejecting immigrant minorities for supposedly nonracial reasons) is replacing blatant prejudice (Jackson & others, 2001; Pettigrew, 1998).

As blatant prejudice wanes, subtle prejudice lingers. In socially intimate settings (dating, dancing, marrying), many people admit they would feel uncomfortable with someone of another race. This fact helps explain why, in a survey of students at 390 colleges and universities, 53 percent of African-American students felt excluded from school activities (Hurtado & others, 1994). (Similar feelings were

Does perception change with race? Skin color and facial features are the visible frosting on the physiological cake. On average, any two randomly chosen humans are 99.8 percent alike in the alphabetic sequence in their genetic code. Only 6 percent of their 0.2 percent difference—.012 percent in all—is racial (Hoffman, 1994; Vines, 1995).

Courtesy of Colors magazine

▶ **prejudice** an unjustifiable (and usually negative) attitude toward a group and its members. Prejudice generally involves stereotyped beliefs, negative feelings, and a predisposition to discriminatory action.

▶ **stereotype** a generalized (sometimes accurate but often overgeneralized) belief about a group of people.

▶ **discrimination** unjustifiable negative behavior toward a group or its members.

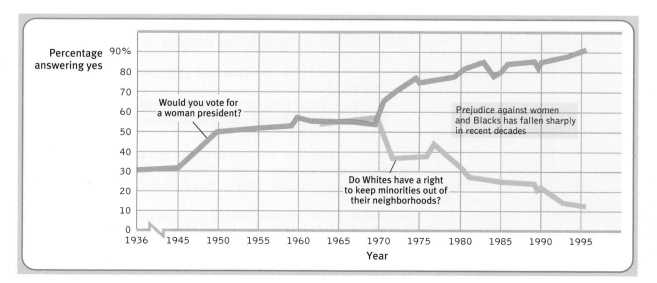

figure 15.6 Prejudice over time Late twentieth-century Americans expressed much less racial and gender prejudice than they did three decades previous (Niemi & others, 1989; T. Smith, personal communication).

reported by 24 percent of Asian-Americans, 16 percent of Mexican-Americans, and 6 percent of European-Americans.) On NBA basketball teams, where most of the players and all the top scorers have been African-American in recent years, a similar majority–minority dynamic can lead some white minority players to feel lonely or disrespected (Waller, 1998).

Three recent experiments illustrate that prejudice can be not only subtle but also apparently unconscious:

- Anthony Greenwald and his colleagues (1998) showed that even people who deny harboring racial or gender prejudice may carry negative associations. For example, 9 in 10 white respondents took longer to identify pleasant words (such as *peace* and *paradise*) as "good" when good was presented with black rather than white faces.
- Kent Harber (1998) asked white university women to evaluate a flawed essay said to be written by a black or a white fellow student. When the writer was said to be black, the ratings were markedly *higher*. Harsh criticisms—"When I read college work this bad I just want to lay my head down on the table and cry"—were never given the supposedly black-authored essays. Did the evaluators calibrate their evaluations to their racial stereotypes, Harber wondered, leading them to patronize the black writers with less exacting standards? If so, such low expectations and the resulting "inflated praise and insufficient criticism" may hinder minority student achievement.
- Two research teams were curious about the shooting of an unarmed man in the doorway of his Bronx apartment building by officers who mistook his wallet for a gun. Each research team reenacted the situation, by asking people to press buttons quickly to "shoot" or not shoot men who suddenly appeared on screen holding either a gun or a harmless object such as a flashlight or bottle (Correll & others, 2002; Greenwald & others, 2003). People (both Blacks and Whites, in one of the studies) more often mistakenly shot targets who were Black.

Around the world, ethnic hatreds persist openly, and gender prejudice and discrimination persist, too. Worldwide, women are more likely to live in poverty (Lipps, 1999). Worldwide, two-thirds of children without basic schooling are girls. Thus, there are an estimated 313 million illiterate men and 549 million illiterate women (UNESCO, 2002). In Saudi Arabia, women are not allowed to drive. In Western countries, we pay more to those (usually men) who take care of our streets than to those (usually women) who take care of our children. And despite gender equality in intelligence scores, people tend to perceive their fathers as more intelligent than their mothers (Furnham & Rawles, 1995).

Nowhere are female infants left out on a hillside to die of exposure, as was the practice in ancient Greece. Yet even today boys are often valued more than their sisters. And with testing that enables sex-selective abortions,

- South Korean male births have exceeded female births by 14 percent (instead of the normal 5 percent).
- China now has almost 120 boy babies for every 100 girls (Fathalla, 1999; *Nando Times*, 1999; Walfish, 2001).
- in Punjab, India's most prosperous farming state, 126 boys are born for every 100 girls—despite India's having outlawed sex-determination tests since 1994 (Dugger, 2001).

Sex-selective neglect and abortions have resulted in China and India together having 76 million fewer females than they should have (Klasen, 1994). Globally, up to 100 million women are missing (Fathalla, 1999). (You read that right: 100 *million* "missing women.")

Suppose that you could only have one child. Would you prefer that it be a boy or a girl? When Gallup asked that question of Americans, two-thirds expressed a gender preference, and for two-thirds of those—in 2003 as in 1941—it was for a boy (Lyons, 2003). But the news isn't all bad for girls and women. Most people *feel* more positively

"Unhappily the world has yet to learn how to live with diversity."

Pope John Paul II,
Address to the United Nations, 1995

▶ **ingroup** "Us"—people with whom one shares a common identity.

▶ **outgroup** "Them"—those perceived as different or apart from one's ingroup.

about "women" in general than they do about "men" (Eagly, 1994; Haddock & Zanna, 1994). People see women as having some traits, such as nurturance, sensitivity, and less aggressiveness, that most people prefer (Swim, 1994). Perhaps that's why people prefer slightly feminized computer-generated men's and women's faces to slightly masculinized faces. Researcher David Perrett and his colleagues (1998) speculate that a slightly feminized male face connotes kindness, cooperativeness, and other traits of a good father. When the British Broadcasting Company invited 18,000 women to guess which of the men in **FIGURE 15.7** was most likely to place a personal ad seeking a "special lady to love and cherish forever," 66 percent guessed the slightly feminized face B.

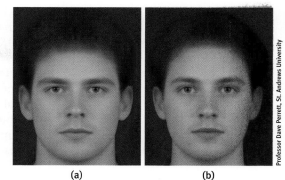

(a)　　　　　　(b)

figure 15.7
Who do you like best? Which one placed an ad seeking a long-term relationship? (See page 562.)

Social Roots of Prejudice

7. What are the social and emotional roots of prejudice?

Why does prejudice arise? Inequalities, social divisions, and emotional scapegoating are partly responsible.

SOCIAL INEQUALITIES When some people have money, power, and prestige and others do not, the "haves" usually develop attitudes that justify things as they are. In the extreme case, slave owners perceived slaves as innately lazy, ignorant, and irresponsible—the very traits that "justified" enslaving them. More commonly, women have been perceived as unassertive but sensitive and therefore suited for the caretaking tasks they have traditionally performed (Hoffman & Hurst, 1990). In short, prejudice rationalizes inequalities.

Discrimination also increases prejudice through the reactions it provokes in its victims, another example of a self-fulfilling prophecy. In his classic 1954 book, *The Nature of Prejudice*, Gordon Allport noted that being a victim of discrimination can produce either self-blame or anger. Both reactions may create new grounds for prejudice through the classic *blame-the-victim* dynamic. If the circumstances of ghetto life breed a higher crime rate, someone can then use the higher crime rate to justify continuing the discrimination that helped to create the ghetto.

"You cannot oppress people for over three centuries and then say it is all over and expect them to put on suits and ties and [be] attaché-carrying citizens and go to work on Wall Street."

Shelby Steele, "The New Segregation," 1992

US AND THEM: INGROUP AND OUTGROUP Thanks to our ancestral need to belong, we are a group-bound species. We cheer for our groups, kill for them, die for them. Indeed, we define who we are—our identities—partly in terms of our groups. Australian psychologists John Turner (1987) and Michael Hogg (1996) note that through our *social identities* we associate ourselves with certain groups and contrast ourselves with others. When Ian identifies himself as a man, an Aussie, a Labourite, a University of Sydney student, a Catholic, and a MacGregor, he knows who he is.

The social definition of who you are also implies who you are not. Mentally drawing a circle that defines "us" (the **ingroup**) excludes "them" (the **outgroup**).

The ingroup Scotland's famed "Tartan Army" football fans, shown here during a match against archrival England, share a social identity that defines "us" (the Scottish ingroup) and "them" (the English outgroup).

*"All good people agree,
And all good people say
All nice people, like us, are We
And everyone else is They.
But if you cross over the sea
Instead of over the way
You may end by (think of it)
looking on We
As only a sort of They."*

Rudyard Kipling, "We and They," 1926

"If the Tiber reaches the walls, if the Nile does not rise to the fields, if the sky doesn't move or the Earth does, if there is famine, if there is plague, the cry is at once: 'The Christians to the lion!'"

Tertullian, Apologeticus, A.D. 197

Such group identifications typically promote an **ingroup bias**—a favoring of one's own group. Even arbitrarily creating an us–them distinction—by grouping people with the toss of a coin—leads people to show favoritism to their own group when dividing any rewards (Tajfel, 1982; Wilder, 1981).

The urge to distinguish enemies from friends and to have one's group be dominant predisposes prejudice against strangers (Whitley, 1999). To Greeks of the classical era, all non-Greeks were "barbarians." Most children believe their own school is better than the other schools in town. In high schools, students often form cliques—jocks, preppies, stoners, skaters, gangsters, freaks, geeks—and disparage those outside their group. Even chimpanzees have been seen to wipe clean the spot where they were touched by a chimp from another group (Goodall, 1986).

SCAPEGOATING Prejudice springs not only from the divisions of society but also from the passions of the heart. Prejudice may express anger: When things go wrong, finding someone to blame can provide a target, a scapegoat, for one's anger. Following 9/11, some outraged people lashed out at innocent Arab-Americans, about whom negative stereotypes blossomed. Calls to eliminate Saddam Hussein, whom Americans had been grudgingly tolerating, also increased. "Fear and anger create aggression, and aggression against citizens of different ethnicity or race creates racism and, in turn, new forms of terrorism," noted Philip Zimbardo (2001).

Evidence for this **scapegoat theory** of prejudice comes from high prejudice levels among economically frustrated people and from experiments in which a temporary frustration intensifies prejudice. Nazi leader Hermann Rausching once explained the Nazis' need to scapegoat: "If the Jew did not exist, we should have to invent him" (quoted by Koltz, 1983). Passions produce prejudice.

In addition to providing a convenient emotional outlet for anger, despised outgroups can also boost ingroup members' self-esteem. In experiments, students who experience failure or are made to feel insecure will often restore their self-esteem by disparaging a rival school or another person (Cialdini & Richardson, 1980; Crocker & others, 1987). To boost our own sense of status, it helps to have others to denigrate. That is why a rival's misfortune sometimes provides a twinge of pleasure. By contrast, those made to feel loved and supported become more open to and accepting of others who differ (Mikulincer & Shaver, 2001).

Cognitive Roots of Prejudice

8. What are the cognitive roots of prejudice?

Prejudice springs from the divisions of society, the passions of the heart, and also from the mind's natural workings. Stereotyped beliefs are a by-product of how we cognitively simplify the world.

CATEGORIZATION One way we simplify our world is to categorize. A chemist categorizes molecules as organic and inorganic. A mental health professional categorizes psychological disorders by types. In categorizing people into groups, however, we often stereotype them. Stereotypes may contain a germ of truth, but they bias our perceptions. Jeff Stone and his colleagues (1997) demonstrated this by having Princeton University students listen to a radio broadcast of a university basketball game while evaluating the performance of one player. Influenced by their expectations, those introduced to him with a photo of a black player gave him a better performance evaluation than did those who had been shown a photo of a white player.

Categorization also biases our perceptions of diversity. We view ourselves as individuals, but we overestimate the similarity of people within groups other than our own. "They"—the members of some other group—seem to look and act alike, but

Do racial stereotypes influence perceptions? Augustana College's black students' and white students' reactions to the O. J. Simpson "not guilty" criminal trial verdict mirrored racial differences in perceptions of his guilt or innocence. In part, people's reactions reflected their stereotypes of white police officers as either honest or oppressive.

Larry Fischer/AP/Wide World Photos

"we" are diverse (Bothwell & others, 1989). If we could see ourselves from a penguin's perspective, we would all look alike—much as penguins all look alike to us (though not to their fellow penguins). We are keenly sensitive to differences within our group, less so to differences within other groups. To those in one ethnic group, members of another often seem more alike in appearance, personality, and attitudes than they are. With experience, however, people get better at recognizing individual faces from another group. For example, people of European descent more accurately identify individual African faces if they have watched a great deal of basketball on television, exposing them to many African-heritage faces (Li & others, 1996).

VIVID CASES As noted in Chapter 9's discussion of the availability heuristic, we often judge the frequency of events by instances that readily come to mind. In a classic experiment, Myron Rothbart and his colleagues (1978) showed how we can overgeneralize from vivid, memorable cases. They divided University of Oregon student volunteers into two groups, then showed them information about 50 men. The first group's list included 10 men arrested for nonviolent crimes, such as forgery. The second group's list included 10 men arrested for violent crimes, such as assault. Later when both groups recalled how many men on their list had committed any sort of crime, the second group overestimated the number. Vivid (violent) cases are readily available to our memory and therefore influence our judgments of a group (**FIGURE 15.8**).

THE JUST-WORLD PHENOMENON As we noted earlier, people often justify their prejudice by blaming its victims. Bystanders, too, may blame victims by assuming the world is just and therefore "people get what they deserve." In experiments, merely observing someone receive painful shocks has led many people to think less of the victim (Lerner, 1980). This **just-world phenomenon** reflects an idea we commonly teach our children—that good is rewarded and evil is punished. From this it is but a short leap to assume that those who succeed must be good and those who suffer must be bad. Such reasoning enables the rich to see both their own wealth and the poor's misfortune as justly deserved. As one German civilian is said to have remarked when visiting the Bergen-Belsen concentration camp shortly after World War II, "What terrible criminals these prisoners must have been to receive such treatment."

Hindsight bias is also at work here (Carli & Leonard, 1989). Have you ever heard people say that rape victims, abused spouses, or people with AIDS got what they deserved? In some countries, women who have been raped have been sentenced to severe punishment for having violated a law against adultery (Mydans, 2002). An experiment by Ronnie Janoff-Bulman and her collaborators (1985) illustrates this phenomenon of blaming the victim. When given a detailed account of a date that ended with the woman's being raped, people perceived the woman's behavior as at least partly to blame. In hindsight, they thought, "She should have known better." (Blaming the victim also serves to reassure people that it couldn't happen to them.) Others who were given the same account, with the rape ending deleted, did not perceive the woman's behavior as inviting rape. Only when victimized was she faulted for her behavior.

Aggression

The most destructive force in our social relations is aggression. In psychology, *aggression* has a more precise meaning than it does in everyday usage. The assertive, persistent salesperson is not aggressive. Nor is the dentist who makes you wince with pain. But the person who passes along a vicious rumor about you, the person who verbally assaults you, and the attacker who mugs you are aggressive. In psychology, **aggression** is any physical or verbal behavior intended to hurt or destroy,

figure 15.8
Vivid cases feed stereotypes The 9/11 Muslim terrorists created, in many minds, an exaggerated stereotype of Muslims as terror-prone. Actually, reported a National Research Council panel on terrorism, when offering this inexact illustration, most terrorists are not Muslim and "the vast majority of Islamic people have no connection with and do not sympathize with terrorism" (Smelser & Mitchell, 2002).

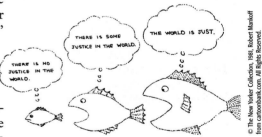

▶ **ingroup bias** The tendency to favor one's own group.

▶ **scapegoat theory** The theory that prejudice offers an outlet for anger by providing someone to blame.

▶ **just-world phenomenon** the tendency of people to believe that the world is just and people therefore get what they deserve and deserve what they get.

▶ **aggression** any physical or verbal behavior intended to hurt or destroy.

In the last 25 years in the United States, guns caused some 800,000 suicidal, homicidal, and accidental deaths. Compared with people of the same sex, race, age, and neighborhood, those who keep a gun in the home (ironically, often for protection) are nearly three times more likely to be murdered in the home— nearly always by a family member or close acquaintance. For every self-defense use of a gun in the home, there are 4 unintentional shootings, 7 criminal assaults or homicides, and 11 attempted or completed suicides (Kellermann & others, 1993, 1997, 1998).

whether done reactively out of hostility or proactively as a calculated means to an end. Thus, murders and assaults that occurred as hostile outbursts are aggression. So were the 110 million war-related deaths that took place during the last century, many of which were cool and calculated.

Aggression research affirms that behavior emerges from the interaction of biology and experience. For a gun to fire, the trigger must be pulled; with some people, as with hair-trigger guns, it doesn't take much to trip an explosion. Let us look first at biological factors that influence our thresholds for aggressive behavior, then at the psychological factors that pull the trigger.

The Biology of Aggression

9. What biological factors make us more prone to hurt one another?

According to one view, argued by Sigmund Freud and others, our species has a volcanic potential to erupt in aggression. Freud thought that we harbor not only positive survival instincts but also a self-destructive "death instinct," which we usually displace toward others as aggression or release in socially approved activities such as the arts or sports.

Aggression varies too widely from culture to culture and person to person to be considered an unlearned instinct, as Freud supposed. But biology does influence aggression. Stimuli that trigger aggressive behavior operate through our biological system. We can look for biological influences at three levels—genetic, neural, and biochemical. Our genes engineer our individual nervous systems, which operate electrochemically.

GENETIC INFLUENCES Animals have been bred for aggressiveness—sometimes for sport, sometimes for research. Twin studies suggest that genes influence human aggression as well (Miles & Carey, 1997; Rowe & others, 1999). If one identical twin admits to "having a violent temper," the other twin will often independently admit the same. Fraternal twins are much less likely to respond similarly. Researchers are now searching for genetic markers found in those who commit the most violence. (One is already well-known, and is carried by half the human race: the Y chromosome.)

NEURAL INFLUENCES Animal and human brains have neural systems that, when stimulated, inhibit or produce aggressive behavior (Moyer, 1983). Consider:

- The domineering leader of a caged monkey colony had a radio-controlled electrode implanted in a brain area that, when stimulated, inhibits aggression. When researchers placed the button that activated the electrode in the colony's cage, one small monkey learned to push it every time the boss became threatening.
- A mild-mannered woman had an electrode implanted in her brain's limbic system (in the amygdala) by neurosurgeons seeking to diagnose a disorder.

"It's a guy thing."

A lean, mean fighting machine—the testosterone-laden female hyena The hyena's unusual embryology pumps testosterone into female fetuses. The result is revved-up young female hyenas who seem born to fight.

Because the brain has no sensory receptors, she was unable to feel the stimulation. But at the flick of a switch she snarled, "Take my blood pressure. Take it now," then stood up and began to strike the doctor.

● Intensive evaluation of 15 death-row inmates revealed that all 15 had suffered a severe head injury. Although most neurologically impaired people are not violent, researcher Dorothy Lewis and her colleagues (1986) inferred that unrecognized neurological disorders may be part of the violence recipe. Other studies of violent criminals have revealed diminished activity in the frontal lobes, which play an important role in controlling impulses (Amen & others 1996; Davidson & others, 2000; Raine, 1999).

So, does the brain have a "violence center" that produces aggression when stimulated? Actually, no one spot in the brain controls aggression, because aggression is a complex behavior that occurs in particular contexts. Rather, the brain has neural systems that facilitate aggression, making it more likely, given the presence of provocation and the absence of deterrents. And it has a frontal lobe system for inhibiting aggression, making aggression more likely if this system is damaged, inactive, or disconnected.

BIOCHEMICAL INFLUENCES Hormones, alcohol, and other substances in the blood influence the neural systems that control aggression. A raging bull will become a gentle Ferdinand when its testosterone level is reduced by castration. The same is true of castrated mice. When injected with testosterone, the castrated mice once again become aggressive.

Although humans are less sensitive to hormonal changes, violent criminals tend to be muscular young males with lower-than-average intelligence scores, low levels of the neurotransmitter serotonin, and higher-than-average testosterone levels (Dabbs & others, 2001a; Pendick, 1994). Drugs that sharply reduce their testosterone levels also subdue their aggressive tendencies. High testosterone correlates with irritability, low tolerance for frustration, assertiveness, and impulsiveness— qualities that predispose somewhat more aggressive responses to provocation (Dabbs & others, 2001b; Harris, 1999). Among both teenage boys and adult men, high testosterone levels correlate with delinquency, hard drug use, and aggressive-bullying responses to frustration (Berman & others, 1993; Dabbs & Morris, 1990; Olweus & others, 1988). With age, testosterone levels—and aggressiveness—diminish.

Alcohol, for biological and psychological reasons, unleashes aggressive responses to frustration (Bushman, 1993; Ito & others, 1996; Taylor & Chermack, 1993). (Just *thinking* you've imbibed alcohol has some effect; but so, too, does unknowingly ingesting alcohol slipped into a drink.) Police data and prison surveys reinforce conclusions drawn from experiments on alcohol and aggression. Aggression-prone people are more likely to drink and to become violent when intoxicated (White & others, 1993). People who have been drinking commit 4 in 10 violent crimes and 3 in 4 acts of spousal abuse (Greenfeld, 1998).

The Psychology of Aggression

10. What psychological factors may trigger aggressive behavior?

Biological factors influence the ease with which aggression is triggered. But what psychological factors pull the trigger?

AVERSIVE EVENTS Although suffering sometimes builds character, it may also bring out the worst in us. Studies in which animals or humans experience unpleasant events reveal that those made miserable often make others miserable (Berkowitz, 1983, 1989).

Being blocked short of a goal also increases people's readiness to aggress. This phenomenon is called the **frustration-aggression principle**: Frustration creates anger, which may in some people generate aggression, especially in the presence of an aggressive cue, such as a gun. Recall that organisms often respond to stress with a "fight-or-flight" reaction. After the frustration and stress of 9/11, Americans responded with a readiness to fight.

Deindividuation + competition + alcohol = aggression A 1985 riot at a soccer game in Brussels left 38 dead and 437 injured. Aroused by the competition and loaded with alcohol, English fans lost all restraint when provoked by Italian fans. They attacked the Italians, who retreated and were then crushed against a wall.

"We could avoid two-thirds of all crime simply by putting all able-bodied young men in cryogenic sleep from the age of 12 through 28."

David T. Lykken, *The Antisocial Personalities, 1995*

▶ **frustration-aggression principle** the principle that frustration—the blocking of an attempt to achieve some goal—creates anger, which can generate aggression.

figure 15.9
Uncomfortably hot weather and aggressive reactions Between 1980 and 1982 in Houston, murders and rapes were more common on days over 91 degrees Fahrenheit (33 degrees centigrade), as shown in the graph at right. This finding is consistent with those from laboratory experiments in which people working in a hot room react to provocations with greater hostility. (From Anderson & Anderson, 1984.)

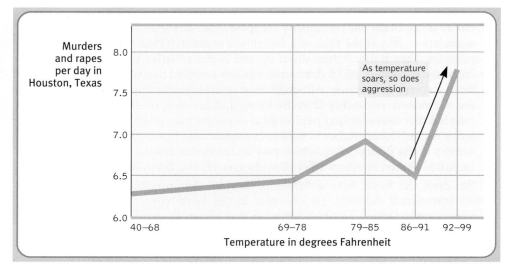

Answers to questions in Figure 15.7 (page 557): Research suggests that subtly feminized features convey a likeable image, which people tend to associate more with committed dads than with promiscuous cads. Thus, most women picked computer-generated face B in response to both questions.

Like frustration, other aversive stimuli—physical pain, personal insults, foul odors, hot temperatures, cigarette smoke, and a host of others—can also evoke hostility. For example, violent crime and spousal abuse rates are higher during hotter years, seasons, months, and days (**FIGURE 15.9**). When people are hot, they think, feel, and act more aggressively. From the available data, Craig Anderson and his colleagues (2000) project that, other things being equal, global warming of 4 degrees Fahrenheit (about 2 degrees centigrade) would induce more than 50,000 additional assaults and murders in the United States alone.

LEARNING TO EXPRESS AND INHIBIT AGGRESSION Aggression may be a natural response to aversive events, but learning can alter natural reactions. Animals naturally eat when they are hungry. But if appropriately rewarded or punished, they can be taught either to overeat or to starve.

Our reactions are more likely to be aggressive in situations where experience has taught us that aggression pays. Children whose aggression successfully intimidates other children may become more aggressive. Animals that have successfully fought to get food or mates become increasingly ferocious.

Different cultures model, reinforce, and evoke different tendencies toward violence. For example, crime rates are higher in countries marked by a great disparity between rich and poor (Triandis, 1994). Richard Nisbett and Dov Cohen (1996) show how violence can vary by culture within a country. They analyzed violence among white Americans in southern U.S. towns settled by Scots-Irish herders whose tradition emphasized "manly honor," the use of arms to protect one's flock, and a history of coercive slavery. To this day, their cultural descendants have triple the homicide rates and are more supportive of physically punishing children, of warfare initiatives, and of uncontrolled gun ownership than are their white counterparts in New England towns settled by Puritan, Quaker, and Dutch farmer-artisans.

Social influence also appears in high violence rates among cultures and families that experience minimal father care (Triandis, 1994). For example, the U.S. Bureau of Justice Statistics reports that 70 percent of imprisoned juveniles did not grow up with two parents (Beck & others, 1988). (An absent parent is usually a father.) The correlation between father absence and violence in the United States holds for all races, income levels, and locations (Myers, 2000).

It is important, however, to note how many individuals are leading gentle, even heroic lives amid social stresses, reminding us again that individuals differ. The person matters. That people differ over time and place reminds us that environments differ. Situations matter. Like all behavior, aggressive behavior arises from the interaction of persons and situations.

Once established, however, aggressive behavior patterns are difficult to change. To foster a kinder, gentler world we had best model and reward sensitivity and cooperation from an early age, perhaps by training parents to discipline without modeling violence. Modeling violence—screaming and hitting—is precisely what exasperated parents often do. Parents of delinquent youngsters typically discipline with beatings, thus modeling aggression as a method of dealing with problems (Patterson & others, 1982, 1992). They also frequently cave into (reward) their children's tears and temper tantrums.

Parent-training programs advise a more positive approach. They encourage parents to reinforce desirable behaviors and to frame statements positively ("When you finish loading the dishwasher you can go play," rather than "If you don't load the dishwasher, there'll be no playing"). One "aggression-replacement program" that brought down re-arrest rates of juvenile offenders and gang members taught the youths and their parents communication skills, trained them in how to control anger, and encouraged more thoughtful moral reasoning (Goldstein & others, 1998).

SEXUAL AGGRESSION AND THE MEDIA   Parents are hardly the only aggression models. As we noted in Chapter 7, observing TV violence tends to desensitize people to cruelty and prime them to respond aggressively when provoked. Does the media effect extend to sexual violence?

A woman's risk of rape has varied across cultures and times but is generally greater today than half a century ago (Koss & others, 1994). In surveys, about one-fifth of women report that a man has forced them to do something sexually, about one-half report some form of unwanted sexual coercion, and most report experiencing verbal sexual harassment (Craig & others, 1989; Laumann & others, 1994; Sandberg & others, 1985). Similar levels of sexual coercion were found in Canadian, Australian, and New Zealand surveys (Koss & others, 1994; Patton & Mannison, 1995).

What factors might explain this increase in sexual aggression? Alcohol consumption—often linked with aggression—has not increased. We do know that sexually coercive men typically are sexually unrestrained and hostile in their relationships with women (**Figure 15.10**). Might changes in the media have contributed to such tendencies?

Coinciding with the increase in sexual aggression was the rise of the home video business, giving easier access to R-rated "slasher films" and X-rated films. Content analyses reveal that most X-rated films depict quick, casual sex between strangers, but that scenes of rape and sexual exploitation of women by men are also common (Cowan & others, 1988; NCTV, 1987; Yang & Linz, 1990). Added to this, reports the National Research Council (2002), are 400,000 for-profit pornography Internet sites. In one survey of collegians, 10 percent of women and 28.4 percent of men acknowledged accessing sexually explicit material on the Internet more often than "rarely" (Goodson & others, 2001). Although the explosion in Internet pornography has not been accompanied by a further increase in reported rapes, researchers nevertheless wonder whether images of sexual exploitation influence sexual aggression.

Rape scenes often portray the victim at first fleeing and resisting her attacker, but then becoming aroused and finally driven to ecstasy. In less graphic form, the same unrealistic script—she resists, he persists, she melts—is commonplace on TV and in romance novels. In *Gone With the Wind*, Scarlett O'Hara is carried to bed screaming and wakes up singing. Most rapists accept this "rape myth"—the idea that some women invite or enjoy rape and get "swept away" while being "taken" (Brinson, 1992). (In actuality, rape is very traumatic, and it frequently harms women's reproductive and sexual health [Golding, 1996].)

Laboratory experiments reveal that repeatedly watching X-rated films (even if nonviolent) makes one's own partner seem less attractive (page 360), makes a woman's friendliness seem more sexual, and makes sexual aggression seem less serious (Harris, 1994). In one such experiment, Dolf Zillmann and Jennings Bryant

"Why do we kill people who kill people to show that killing people is wrong?"

National Coalition to Abolish the Death Penalty, 1992

figure 15.10
Men who sexually coerce women   The recipe for coercion against women combines an impersonal approach to sex with a hostile masculinity. (Adapted from Malamuth, 1996.)

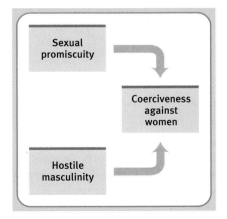

In follow-up studies, Zillmann (1989) found that after massive exposure to X-rated sexual films, men and women became more accepting of extramarital sex, of women's sexual submission to men, and of a man's seducing a 12-year-old girl. As people heavily exposed to televised crime perceive the world as more dangerous, so people heavily exposed to pornography see the world as more sexual.

Pornography *means different things to different people. Following Webster's dictionary, some define pornography as erotic depictions intended to excite sexual arousal. Others define it as sexual materials that exploit, degrade, or subordinate women.*

"What we're trying to do is raise the level of awareness of violence against women and pornography to at least the level of awareness of racist and Ku Klux Klan literature."

Gloria Steinem (1988)

(1984) showed undergraduates six brief, sexually explicit films each week for six weeks. A control group viewed nonerotic films during the same six-week period. Three weeks later, both groups read a newspaper report about a man convicted but not yet sentenced for raping a hitchhiker. When asked to suggest an appropriate prison term, those who had viewed sexually explicit films recommended sentences half as long as those recommended by the control group.

Experiments cannot elicit actual sexual violence, but they can assess a man's willingness to hurt a woman. Often the research gauges the effect of violent versus nonviolent erotic films on men's willingness to deliver supposed electric shocks to women who had earlier provoked them. These experiments suggest that it's not the eroticism but rather the depictions of sexual *violence* (whether in R-rated slasher films or X-rated films) that most directly affect men's acceptance and performance of aggression against women. A conference of 21 social scientists, including many of the researchers who conducted these experiments, produced a consensus (Surgeon General, 1986): "Pornography that portrays sexual aggression as pleasurable for the victim increases the acceptance of the use of coercion in sexual relations." Contrary to much popular opinion, viewing such depictions does not provide an outlet for bottled-up impulses. Rather, "in laboratory studies measuring short-term effects, exposure to violent pornography increases punitive behavior toward women."

TV VIOLENCE, PORNOGRAPHY, AND SOCIETY Significant behaviors, such as violence, usually have many determinants, making any single explanation an oversimplification. Asking what causes violence is therefore like asking what causes cancer. Those who study, say, the effects of asbestos exposure on cancer rates may remind us that asbestos is indeed a cancer cause, but only one among many. Likewise, report Neil Malamuth and his colleagues (1991, 1995), several factors can create a predisposition to sexual violence; they include not only the media but also dominance motives, disinhibition by alcohol, and a history of child abuse. Still, if media depictions of violence can disinhibit and desensitize; if viewing sexual violence fosters hostile, domineering attitudes and behaviors; and if viewing pornography leads viewers to trivialize rape, devalue their partners, and engage in uncommitted sex, then media influence is not a minor issue.

Social psychologists attribute the media's influence partly to the *social scripts* they provide. When we find ourselves in new situations, uncertain how to act, we rely on social scripts—mental tapes for how to act— provided by our culture. After so many episodes of "Power Rangers," followed by Bruce Willis and Arnold Schwarzenegger action films, youngsters may acquire a script that gets played when they face real-life conflicts. Challenged, they may "act like a man" by intimidating or eliminating the threat (see Thinking Critically About on page 565). Likewise, after viewing multiple sexual innuendoes and acts in most prime-time TV hours—often involving impulsive or short-term relationships—youths may acquire sexual scripts they later enact in real-life relationships (Kunkel & others, 2001; Sapolsky & Tabarlet, 1991).

Might public consciousness be raised by making people aware of the information you have just been reading? In the 1940s, movies often depicted African-Americans as childlike superstitious buffoons. Today, we would not tolerate such images. In the 1960s and 1970s, some rock music and movies glamorized drug use. Responding to a tidal change in cultural attitudes, the entertainment industry now more often portrays the dark side of drug use. Even cigarette smoking in movies largely disappeared until the 1990s, when its reappearance was accompanied by a new surge in teen smoking rates. In response to growing public concern about violence in the media, television violence levels declined in the early 1990s (Gerbner & others, 1993). The growing sensitivity to violence has raised hopes that entertainers, producers, and audiences might someday look back with embarrassment on the days when movies "entertained" people with scenes of torture, mutilation, and sexual coercion.

Thinking Critically About:

Do Video Games Teach or Release Violence?

Violent video games became an issue for public debate in 1999 after teen assassins in Paducah, Kentucky, and Littleton, Colorado, seemed to mimic the carnage in the splatter games they had so often played. In 2002, two Grand Rapids, Michigan, teens and a man in his early twenties spent part of a night drinking beer and playing Grand Theft Auto III, using cars to run down simulated pedestrians, then beating them with fists, leaving a bloody body behind (Kolker, 2002). Then they went driving on a real drive, spotted a 38-year-old man on a bicycle, ran him down with their car, got out, stomped and punched him, and returned home to play the game some more. (The man, a father of three, died six days later.) When youths play such games, do they learn social scripts? Interactive games transport the player into their own vivid reality. When someone assumes the video game identity of Clare Redfield in Resident Evil 2 and sprays bullets into Zombie cops, whose bodies slump, twitch, and hemorrhage, is anything being learned?

"It'll be like the LA riots, the Oklahoma bombing, WWI, Vietnam, Duke, and Doom all mixed together."

Journal entry by
Columbine killer Eric Harris, 1998

Most pack-a-day smokers don't die of lung cancer. Most abused children don't become abusive adults. And most young people who spend hundreds of hours in these mass murder simulators won't

Mark C. Burnett/Stock, Boston

Desensitizing violence

become teen assassins. Still, mindful that smoking and child abuse are risk factors, we wonder: If passively viewing violence elevates aggressive responses to provocation and lowers sensitivity to cruelty, what will be the effect of actively role-playing aggression? Although very few will commit slaughter, will many become desensitized to violence and more violence-prone?

Thirty-five recent studies of more than 4000 people offer some answers (Anderson & Bushman, 2001). Mary Ballard and Rose Wiest (1998) observed a rising level of arousal and feelings of hostility in college men as they played Mortal Kombat. Other studies have found that video games can prime aggressive thoughts and increase aggression. Consider this report from Craig Anderson and Karen Dill (2000): University men who have spent the most hours playing violent

video games tend to be the most physically aggressive (for example, to acknowledge having hit or attacked someone else). In an experiment, those randomly assigned to play a game involving bloody murders with groaning victims (rather than to play nonviolent Myst) became more hostile. On a follow-up task, they also were more likely to blast intense noise at a fellow student. Anderson (2001) believes that, due partly to the more repetitive and active participation of game play, violent video games have even greater effects "than the well-documented effects of exposure to violent television and movies."

Although much remains to be learned, these studies again disconfirm the *catharsis hypothesis*—the idea that we feel better if we "blow off steam" by venting our emotions (Chapter 11). Playing violent video games *increases* aggressive thoughts, emotions, and behaviors. The behavior effect is not huge, notes Anderson (2003), but it is larger than the effect of homework on academic achievement. The studies also challenge the rationalization of one video game company's CEO—that we are "violent by nature [and] need release valves." Expressing anger breeds more anger, and practicing violence breeds more violence.

"Absent the combination of extremely violent video games and these boys' incredibly deep involvement . . . this massacre would not have occurred."

Lawsuit against video game makers by
Columbine victims' families, 2001

▶ **conflict** a perceived incompatibility of actions, goals, or ideas.

▶ **social trap** a situation in which the conflicting parties, by rationally pursuing their self-interests, become caught in mutually destructive behavior.

Conflict

11. What social processes fuel conflict?

We live in surprising times. With astonishing speed, democratic movements have swept away totalitarian rule in Eastern European countries, and hopes for a new world order have displaced the Cold War chill. And yet, the world spends $2 billion every day for arms and armies, money that could be used for housing, nutrition, education, and health. Knowing that wars begin in human minds, psychologists have wondered: What in the human mind causes destructive conflict? How might the perceived threats of social diversity be replaced by a spirit of cooperation?

To a social psychologist, a **conflict** is a seeming incompatibility of actions, goals, or ideas. The elements of conflict are much the same at all levels, from nations at war, to cultural disputes within a society, to individuals in a marital dispute. In each situation, people become enmeshed in a potentially destructive social process that can produce results no one wants. Among the destructive processes are social traps and distorted perceptions.

Social Traps

In some situations, we can enhance our collective well-being by pursuing our personal interests. As capitalist Adam Smith wrote in *The Wealth of Nations* (1776), "It is not from the benevolence of the butcher, the brewer, or the baker that we expect our dinner, but from their regard to their own interest." In other situations, the parties involved may become caught up in mutually harmful behavior as they pursue their own ends. Such situations are **social traps**.

Consider the simple game matrix in **Figure 15.11**, which is similar to those used in experiments with countless thousands of people. In this game, both sides can win or both can lose, depending on the players' individual choices. Pretend you are Person 1, and that you and Person 2 will each receive the amount shown after you separately choose either A or B. (You might invite someone to look at the matrix with you and take the role of Person 2.) Which do you choose—A or B?

As you ponder the game, you will discover that you and Person 2 are caught in a dilemma. If you both choose A, you both benefit, making $5 each. Neither of you benefits if you both choose B, for neither of you makes anything. Nevertheless, on any single trial you serve your own interests if you choose B: You can't lose, and you might make $10. But the same is true for the other person. Hence, the social trap: As long as you both pursue your own immediate best interest and choose B, you will both end up with nothing—the typical result—when you could have made $5.

Many real-life situations similarly pit our individual interests against our communal well-being. Individual whalers reasoned that the few whales they took would not threaten the species and that if they didn't take them other whalers would anyway. The result: Some species of whales became endangered. The individual car owner and home owner reasons, "It would cost me comfort or money to buy a more fuel-efficient car and furnace. Besides, the fossil fuels I burn don't noticeably add to the greenhouse gases." When enough others reason similarly, the collective result threatens disaster—global warming.

Social traps challenge us to find ways of reconciling our right to

figure 15.11
Social trap game matrix By pursuing our self-interest and not trusting others, we can end up losers. To illustrate this, imagine playing the game to the right. The pink triangles show the outcomes for Person 1, which depend on the choices made by both players. If you were Person 1, would you choose A or B? (This game is called a "non–zero-sum game" because the outcomes need not add up to zero; both sides can win or both can lose.)

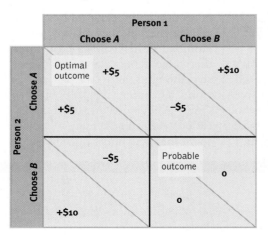

pursue our personal well-being with our responsibility for the well-being of all. Psychologists are therefore exploring ways to convince people to cooperate for their mutual betterment—through agreed-upon *regulations*, through better *communication*, and through promoting *awareness* of our responsibilities toward community, nation, and the whole of humanity (Dawes, 1980; Linder, 1982; Sato, 1987). Under such conditions, people more often cooperate, whether it be in playing a laboratory game or the real game of life.

Enemy Perceptions

Psychologists have noted that those in conflict have a curious tendency to form diabolical images of one another. These distorted images are ironically similar, so similar in fact that we call them *mirror-image perceptions*: As we see "them"—as untrustworthy and evil intentioned—so "they" see us. Each demonizes the other.

In the early twenty-first century, many Americans came to loathe Saddam Hussein. Like the "evil" Saddam Hussein, declared George W. Bush (2001), "some of today's tyrants are gripped by an implacable hatred of the United States of America. They hate our friends, they hate our values, they hate democracy and freedom and individual liberty. Many care little for the lives of their own people." Hussein (2002) reciprocated the perception, seeing the United States as "an evil tyrant" that, with Satan as its protector, lusts for oil and aggressively attacks those who "defend what is right." To Hussein's foreign minister, George W. Bush was today's wicked "Pharaoh" (Klinkenborg, 2002).

The point is not that truth must lie midway between two such views (one may be more accurate). The point is that enemy perceptions often form mirror images. Moreover, as enemies change, so do perceptions. In American minds and media, the "bloodthirsty, cruel, treacherous" Japanese of World War II later became our "intelligent, hardworking, self-disciplined, resourceful allies" (Gallup, 1972).

Biased perceptions—whether of individuals or of groups or nations—have deep psychological roots. The *self-serving bias* leads each party to accept credit for good deeds and to shuck the blame for bad deeds (Chapter 12). Although two nations admit to a buildup of military forces, the *fundamental attribution error* leads each to see the other's actions as arising from an aggressive disposition, and to view its own buildup as necessary self-defense. Information about each other's actions is then filtered, interpreted, and remembered through preconceived *stereotypes*. Group interaction among like-minded policymakers may *polarize* these tendencies, leading to *groupthink*, whereby each sees its own group as more moral, thereby justifying retaliation. In Soviet–U.S. relations, such biases resulted in the social perceptions that fueled the Cold War arms race: Each side (1) wished for mutual arms reduction, but (2) wanted above all to avoid disarming while the other armed, and (3) perceived the other side as wanting above all to gain an arms advantage (Plous, 1993).

Another result of such perceptions is a vicious cycle of hostility. If Victor believes Samantha is annoyed with him, he may snub her, causing her to act in ways that justify his perception. As with individuals, so with countries. Perceptions confirm themselves by influencing the other country to react in ways that seem to justify them. This is an example of what's called the *self-fulfilling prophecy*.

We have pondered the bad side of our social relations—prejudice, aggression, and conflict. Is there a good side? There is—attraction, altruism, and peacemaking.

A social trap In the Atlantic waters off Newfoundland, those who fished knew that their individual catch was their livelihood and, by itself, hardly depleted the whole fish population. Such reasoning by everyone, including outsiders with mega-trawlers, depleted fish stocks. The result: Newfoundland's fishing fleet sat idle and an economy was in ruins during a 1990s fishing moratorium. This unemployed fisherman was forced to use his boat for firewood.

Keith Gosse/The Evening Telegram

"Why do you see the speck that is in your brother's eye, but do not notice the log that is in your own eye?"

Jesus, Luke 6:41–42

Attraction

12. Why do we befriend or fall in love with some people but not with others?

Pause a moment and think about your relationships with two people—a close friend, and someone who stirred in you feelings of romantic love. What is the psychological chemistry that binds us together in these special sorts of friendship that help us cope with all other relationships? Social psychology suggests some answers.

The Psychology of Attraction

We endlessly wonder how we can win others' affection and what makes our own affections flourish or fade. Does familiarity breed contempt, or does it intensify our affection? Do birds of a feather flock together? Or do opposites attract? Is beauty only skin deep or does attractiveness matter greatly?

PROXIMITY Before friendships become close, they must begin. *Proximity*—geographic nearness—is perhaps the most powerful predictor of friendship. Proximity provides opportunities for aggression, but much more often it breeds liking. Study after study reveals that people are most likely to like, and even to marry, those who live in the same neighborhood, who sit nearby in class, who work in the same office, who share the same parking lot. Look around.

Why is proximity so conducive to liking? Obviously, part of the answer is the greater availability of those we often meet. But there is more to it than that. For one thing, repeated exposure to novel stimuli—be they nonsense syllables, musical selections, geometric figures, Chinese characters, human faces, or the letters of our own name—increases our liking for them (Moreland & Zajonc, 1982; Zajonc, 2001; Nuttin, 1987). This phenomenon, exploited by advertisers, we call the **mere exposure effect**. Within certain limits (Bornstein, 1989, 1999), familiarity breeds fondness. Richard Moreland and Scott Beach (1992) demonstrated this by having

Familiarity breeds acceptance When this rare white penguin was born in the Sydney, Australia, zoo, his tuxedoed peers ostracized him. Zookeepers thought they would need to dye him black to gain acceptance. But after three weeks of contact, the other penguins came to accept him.

Rex USA

four equally attractive women silently attend a 200-student class for zero, 5, 10, or 15 class sessions. At the end of the course, students were shown slides of each woman and asked to rate each one's attractiveness. The most attractive? The ones they'd seen most often. The phenomenon will come as no surprise to the young Taiwanese man who wrote more than 700 letters to his girlfriend, urging her to marry him. She did marry—the mail carrier (Steinberg, 1993).

No face is more familiar than one's own. And that explains why, when Lisa DeBruine (2002) had McMaster University students play a social trap-type game with a supposed other player, they were more trusting and cooperative when the other person's picture face had some features of their own face morphed into it. In me I trust. For our ancestors, the mere exposure phenomenon was adaptive. What was familiar was generally safe and approachable. What was unfamiliar was more often dangerous and threatening. Robert Zajonc (1998) concludes that evolution has hard-wired into us the tendency to bond with those who are familiar and to be wary of those who are unfamiliar. Gut-level prejudice against those culturally different may thus be a primitive, automatic emotional response (Devine, 1995).

PHYSICAL ATTRACTIVENESS Once proximity affords you contact, what most affects your first impressions: The person's sincerity? Intelligence? Personality? Hundreds of experiments reveal that it is something far more superficial: Appearance.

For people taught that "beauty is only skin deep" and that "appearances can be deceiving," the power of physical attractiveness is unnerving. In one early study, Elaine Hatfield and her co-workers (Walster & others, 1966) randomly matched new University of Minnesota students for a Welcome Week dance. Before the dance, each took a battery of personality and aptitude tests. On the night of the blind date, the couples danced and talked for more than two hours and then took a brief intermission to rate their dates. What determined whether they liked each other? So far as the researchers could determine, only one thing mattered: Physical attractiveness (which had been rated by the researchers beforehand). Both the men and the women liked good-looking dates best. Although women are more likely than men to *say* that another's looks don't affect them, a man's looks do affect women's behavior (Feingold, 1990; Sprecher, 1989; Woll, 1986).

People's physical attractiveness has wide-ranging effects. It predicts their frequency of dating, their feelings of popularity, and others' initial impressions of their personalities. We perceive attractive people to be healthier, happier, more sensitive, more successful, and more socially skilled, though not more honest or compassionate (Eagly & others, 1991; Feingold, 1992; Hatfield & Sprecher, 1986). Attractive, well-dressed people are more likely to make a favorable impression on potential employers and to enjoy occupational success (Cash & Janda, 1984; Langlois & others, 2000; Solomon, 1987).

An analysis of 100 top-grossing films since 1940 found that attractive characters were portrayed as morally superior to unattractive characters (Smith & others, 1999). But Hollywood modeling doesn't explain why, to judge from their gazing times, even babies prefer attractive over unattractive faces (Langlois & others, 1987). So do some blind people, discovered University of Birmingham professor John Hull (1990, p. 23) after going blind. A colleague's remarking on a woman's beauty would strangely affect his feelings. He finds this "deplorable . . . but I still feel it. . . . What can it matter to me what sighted men think of women . . . yet I do care what sighted men think, and I do not seem able to throw off this prejudice."

That looks are important may seem unfair and unenlightened. Two thousand years ago the Roman statesman Cicero felt the same way: "The final good and the supreme duty of the wise person is to resist appearance." Cicero might be reassured by two other findings about attractiveness.

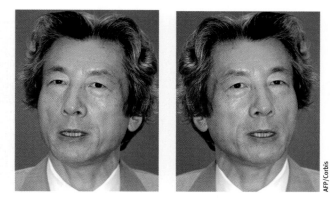

The mere exposure effect The mere exposure effect applies even to ourselves. Because the human face is not perfectly symmetrical, the face we see in the mirror is not the same as the one our friends see. Most of us prefer the familiar mirror image, while our friends like the reverse (Mita & others, 1977). The Prime Minister Junichiro Koizumi known to the Japanese people is shown at left. The person Koizumi sees in the mirror each morning is shown at right, and that's the photo he would probably prefer.

"Personal beauty is a greater recommendation than any letter of introduction."

Aristotle, Apothegems, 330 B.C.

Percentage of Men and Women Who "Constantly Think About Their Looks"

	Men	Women
Canada	18%	20%
United States	17	27
Mexico	40	45
Venezuela	47	65

From Roper Starch survey, reported by McCool (1999).

▶ **mere exposure effect** the phenomenon that repeated exposure to novel stimuli increases liking of them.

When Neanderthals fall in love.

First, people's attractiveness is surprisingly unrelated to their self-esteem and happiness (Diener & others, 1995; Major & others, 1984). One reason may be that, except after comparing themselves with superattractive people, few people (thanks, perhaps, to the mere exposure effect) view themselves as unattractive (Thornton & Moore, 1993). Another reason is that strikingly attractive people are sometimes suspicious that praise for their work may simply be a reaction to their looks. When less attractive people are praised, they are more likely to accept it as sincere (Berscheid, 1981).

Cicero might also find comfort in knowing that attractiveness judgments are relative. The standards by which judges crown Miss Universe hardly apply to the whole planet. Rather, beauty is in the eye of the culture—most accepted standards of beauty are influenced by one's place and time. Hoping to look attractive, people in different cultures have pierced their noses, lengthened their necks, bound their feet, and dyed or painted their skin and hair. They have gorged themselves to achieve a full figure or liposuctioned fat to achieve a slim one, applied chemicals hoping to rid themselves of unwanted hair or regrow wanted hair, strapped on leather garments to make their breasts seem smaller or surgically filled their breasts with silicone and put on Wonder Bras to make them look bigger. In North America, the ultra-thin ideal of the Roaring Twenties gave way to the soft, voluptuous Marilyn Monroe ideal of the 1950s, only to be replaced by the lean yet busty ideal of the 1990s. Americans now spend more on beauty supplies than on education and social services combined and, when still not satisfied, underwent 8.5 million cosmetic medical treatments in 2001, including plastic surgeries, Botox injections to smooth wrinkles, and laser hair removal (Wall, 2002). Yet since 1970 the number of women unhappy with their appearance has substantially increased (Feingold & Mazella, 1998).

Some aspects of attractiveness, however, do cross place and time (Langlois & others, 2000). As we noted in Chapter 3, men in 37 cultures, from Australia to Zambia, judge women as more attractive if they have a youthful appearance. Women feel attracted to healthy-looking men, but especially to those who seem mature, dominant, and affluent.

Cultural standards aside, attractiveness also depends on our feelings about the person. In a Rodgers and Hammerstein musical, Prince Charming asks Cinderella, "Do I love you because you're beautiful, or are you beautiful because I love you?"

New York Times *columnist Maureen Dowd on liposuction (January 19, 2000): "Women in the 50's vacuumed. Women in the 00's are vacuumed. Our Hoovers have turned on us!"*

"Love is a dirty trick played on us to achieve the continuation of the species."

Novelist W. Somerset Maugham, 1874–1965

Extreme makeover In affluent, beauty-conscious cultures, increasing numbers of people—including former President Clinton's sexual harassment accuser, Paula Jones—have turned to cosmetic surgery to improve their looks. If money were no concern, might you ever do the same?

In the eye of the beholder Conceptions of attractiveness vary by culture. Moreover, the current concept of attractiveness in Kenya, Morocco, and Scandinavia may well change in the future.

Chances are it's both. As we see our loved ones again and again, their physical imperfections grow less noticeable and their attractiveness grows more apparent (Beaman & Klentz, 1983; Gross & Crofton, 1977). Shakespeare said it in *A Midsummer Night's Dream*: "Love looks not with the eyes, but with the mind." Until you got to know him, E.T. was uglier than Darth Vader. Come to love someone and watch beauty grow.

"Love has ever in view the absolute loveliness of that which it beholds."

George MacDonald, Unspoken Sermons, *1867*

SIMILARITY Let's say that proximity has brought you into contact with someone and that your appearance has made a favorable first impression. What now influences whether acquaintances develop into friends? For example, as you get to know someone better, is the chemistry better if you are opposites or if you are alike?

It makes a good story—extremely different types living in harmonious union: Rat, Mole, and Badger in *The Wind in the Willows*, Frog and Toad in Arnold Lobel's books. The stories delight us by expressing what we seldom experience, for we tend *not* to like dissimilar people (Rosenbaum, 1986). In real life, opposites retract. Birds that flock together usually *are* of a feather. Friends and couples are far more likely to share common attitudes, beliefs, and interests (and, for that matter, age, religion, race, education, intelligence, smoking behavior, and economic status) than are randomly paired people. Much as you and I may dismiss such differences, seeing ourselves as one human family in a global village, we can't hang out with 6 billion people. Moreover, the more alike people are, the more their liking endures (Byrne, 1971). Journalist Walter Lippmann was right to suppose that love is best sustained "when the lovers love many things together, and not merely each other." Similarity breeds content.

Proximity, attractiveness, and similarity are not the only determinants of attraction. We also like those who like us, especially when our self-image is low. When we believe someone likes us, we respond to them more warmly, which leads them to like us even more (Curtis & Miller, 1986). To be liked is powerfully rewarding.

Indeed, a simple reward theory of attraction—that we will like those whose behavior is rewarding to us and that we will continue relationships that offer more rewards than costs—can explain all the findings we have considered so far. When a person lives or works in close proximity with someone else, it costs less time and effort to develop the friendship and enjoy its benefits. Attractive people are aesthetically pleasing, and associating with them can be socially rewarding. Those with similar views reward us by validating our own.

Romantic Love

13. Does our love for a partner remain the same as time passes?

Occasionally, people move quickly from initial impressions, to friendship, to the more intense, complex, and mysterious state of romantic love. Elaine Hatfield (1988) distinguishes two types of love: temporary passionate love and a more enduring companionate love.

A popular (but generally unsupported) idea: Opposites attract.

▶ **passionate love** An aroused state of intense positive absorption in another, usually present at the beginning of a love relationship.

▶ **companionate love** the deep affectionate attachment we feel for those with whom our lives are intertwined.

▶ **equity** a condition in which people receive from a relationship in proportion to what they give to it.

▶ **self-disclosure** revealing intimate aspects of oneself to others.

▶ **altruism** unselfish regard for the welfare of others.

"When two people are under the influence of the most violent, most insane, most delusive, and most transient of passions, they are required to swear that they will remain in that excited, abnormal, and exhausting condition continuously until death do them part."

George Bernard Shaw, Man and Superman, *1903*

Passionate love to companionate love
The quality of love changes as a relationship matures from passionate absorption to affectionate attachment.

HI & LOIS

PASSIONATE LOVE Noting that arousal is a key ingredient of **passionate love**, Hatfield suggests that the two-factor theory of emotion (page 381) can help us understand this intense positive absorption in another. The theory assumes that (1) emotions have two ingredients—physical arousal plus cognitive appraisal—and that (2) arousal from any source can enhance one emotion or another, depending on how we interpret and label the arousal.

In tests of this theory, college men have been aroused by fright, by running in place, by viewing erotic materials, or by listening to humorous or repulsive monologues. They were then introduced to an attractive woman and asked to rate her (or their girlfriend). Unlike unaroused men, those who were stirred up attributed some of their arousal to the woman or girlfriend and felt more attracted to her (Carducci & others, 1978; Dermer & Pyszczynski, 1978; White & Kight, 1984).

Outside the laboratory, Donald Dutton and Arthur Aron (1974, 1989) went to two bridges across British Columbia's rocky Capilano River. One, a swaying footbridge, was 230 feet above the rocks; the other was low and solid. An attractive young female accomplice intercepted men coming off each bridge, sought their help in filling out a short questionnaire, and then offered her phone number in case they wanted to hear more about her project. Far more of those who had just crossed the high bridge—which left their hearts pounding—accepted the number and later called the woman. To be revved up and to associate some of that arousal with a desirable person is to feel the pull of passion. Adrenaline makes the heart grow fonder.

COMPANIONATE LOVE Although the spark of romantic love often endures, the intense absorption in the other, the thrill of the romance, the giddy "floating on a cloud" feeling always fades. Does this mean the French are correct in saying that "love makes the time pass and time makes love pass"? Or can friendship and commitment keep a relationship going after the passion cools?

Hatfield notes that as love matures it becomes a steadier **companionate love**—a deep, affectionate attachment. There may be adaptive wisdom to this change from passion to affection. Passionate love often produces children, whose survival is aided by the parents' waning obsession with one another. Social psychologist Ellen Berscheid and her colleagues (1984) note that the failure to appreciate passionate love's limited half-life can doom a relationship: "If the inevitable odds against eternal passionate love in a relationship were better understood, more people might choose to be satisfied with the quieter feelings of satisfaction and contentment." Indeed, recognizing the short duration of passionate love, some societies have deemed such feelings an irrational reason for marrying. Better, such cultures say, to choose (or have someone choose for you) a partner with a compatible background and interests. Non-Western cultures, where people rate love less important for marriage, do have lower divorce rates (Levine & others, 1995).

One key to a gratifying and enduring relationship is **equity**: Both partners receive in proportion to what they give. When equity exists—when both partners freely give and receive, when they share decision making—their chances for sustained and satisfying companionate love are good (Gray-Little & Burks, 1983; Van Yperen & Buunk, 1990). Mutually sharing self and possessions, giving and getting emotional support, promoting and caring about one another's welfare are at the core of every type of loving relationship (Sternberg & Grajek, 1984). It's true for lovers, for parent and child, and for intimate friends.

Another vital ingredient of loving relationships is intimacy. A strong friendship or marriage offers **self-disclosure**, the revealing of intimate details about ourselves—our likes and dislikes, our dreams and worries, our proud and shameful moments. "When I am with my friend," noted the Roman statesman Seneca, "me thinks I am alone, and as much at liberty to speak anything as to think it." Self-disclosure breeds liking, and liking breeds self-disclosure (Collins & Miller, 1994). As one person reveals a little, the other reciprocates, the first then reveals more, and on and on, as friends or lovers move to deeper intimacy. Each increase in intimacy rekindles passion (Baumeister & Bratslavsky, 1999).

One experiment marched pairs of volunteer students through 45 minutes of increasingly self-disclosing conversation—from "When did you last sing to yourself" to "When did you last cry in front of another person? By yourself?" By the experiment's end, those experiencing the escalating intimacy felt remarkably close to their conversation partner, much closer than others who had spent the time with small-talk questions such as "What was your high school like?" (Aron & others, 1997). Given self-disclosing intimacy plus mutually supportive equality, the odds favor enduring companionate love.

Altruism

14. Why do we help others? When are we most—and least—likely to help?

"In what I like to call the Great Asymmetry," noted Stephen Jay Gould (2001) shortly after 9/11, "every spectacular incident of evil will be balanced by 10,000 acts of kindness, too often unnoted and invisible as the 'ordinary' efforts of a vast majority." The spectacular evils of that day indeed elicited a greater number of spectacular kindnesses:

- As they bucked the stream of humanity heading down the staircases, hundreds of New York firefighters, each laden with 70 pounds and more of lifesaving gear, were charging up in what was to become their last act of helping.
- As the last of four hijacked planes advanced toward its own horrific destiny, several heroic passengers huddled together, plotted resistance, declared "Let's roll!" and somehow deflected the plane and themselves into the soil of an empty field.
- Seeing the tragedy unfold, people across the country felt compelled to help. They begged to give blood, overwhelmed the city with donated items, and contributed over $500 million to assist victims, their families, and the devastated community.

Such goodness in response to badness exemplifies **altruism**—the unselfish regard for the welfare of others. Altruism became a major concern of social psychologists after an especially vile act of sexual violence. On March 13, 1964, a stalker repeatedly stabbed Kitty Genovese, then raped her as she lay dying outside her Queens, New York, apartment at 3:30 A.M. "Oh, my God, he stabbed me!" Genovese screamed into the early morning stillness. "Please help me!" Windows opened and lights went on as 38 of her neighbors heard her screams. Her attacker fled and then returned to stab her eight more times and rape her again. Not until he had fled for good did anyone so much as call the police, at 3:50 A.M.

"When a match has equal partners then I fear not."

Aeschylus, Prometheus Bound, *478 B.C.*

"Probably no single incident has caused social psychologists to pay as much attention to an aspect of social behavior as Kitty Genovese's murder."

R. Lance Shotland (1984)

▶ **bystander effect** the tendency for any given bystander to be less likely to give aid if other bystanders are present.

▶ **social exchange theory** the theory that our social behavior is an exchange process, the aim of which is to maximize benefits and minimize costs.

Bystander Intervention

Reflecting on the Genovese murder and other such tragedies, most commentators were outraged by the bystanders' "apathy" and "indifference." Rather than blaming the onlookers, social psychologists John Darley and Bibb Latané (1968b) attributed their inaction to an important situational factor—the presence of others. Given certain circumstances, they suspected, most of us might behave similarly.

After staging emergencies under various conditions, Darley and Latané assembled their findings into a decision scheme: We will help only if the situation enables us first to *notice* the incident, then to *interpret* it as an emergency, and finally to *assume responsibility* for helping (**FIGURE 15.12**). For the New York City firefighters near the World Trade Center on 9/11, both the emergency and their responsibility for helping were crystal clear.

At each step, the presence of other bystanders turns people away from the path that leads to helping. In the laboratory and on the street, people in a group of strangers are more likely than solitary individuals to keep their eyes focused on what they themselves are doing or where they are going. If they notice an unusual situation, they may infer from the blasé reactions of the other passersby that the situation is not an emergency. "The person lying on the sidewalk must be drunk," they think, and move on.

But sometimes, as with the Genovese murder, the emergency is unambiguous and people still fail to help. The witnesses looking out through their windows noticed the incident, correctly interpreted the emergency, and yet failed to assume responsibility. Why? To find out, Darley and Latané (1968a) simulated a physical emergency in their laboratory. University students participated in a discussion over an intercom. Each student was in a separate cubicle, and only the person whose microphone was switched on could be heard. One of the students was an accomplice of the experimenters. When his turn came, he made sounds as though he were having an epileptic seizure and called for help.

How did the other students react? As **FIGURE 15.13** shows, those who believed only they could hear the victim—and therefore thought they bore total responsibility for helping him—usually went to his aid. Those who thought others also could hear were more likely to react as did Kitty Genovese's neighbors. When more people shared responsibility for helping—when there was "diffusion of responsibility"—any single listener was less likely to help.

In hundreds of additional experiments, psychologists have studied the factors that influence bystanders' willingness to relay an emergency phone call, aid a stranded motorist, donate blood, pick up dropped books, contribute money, and give time. For example, Latané, James Dabbs (1975), and 145 collaborators took 1497 elevator rides in three cities and "accidentally" dropped eight to ten coins or pencils in front of 4813 fellow passengers. The women coin droppers were more likely to receive help than were the men—a gender difference often reported by other researchers (Eagly & Crowley, 1986). But the major finding was the

figure 15.12
The decision-making process for bystander intervention Before helping, one must first notice an emergency, then correctly interpret it, and then feel responsible. (From Darley & Latané, 1968b.)

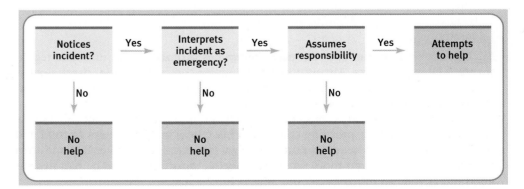

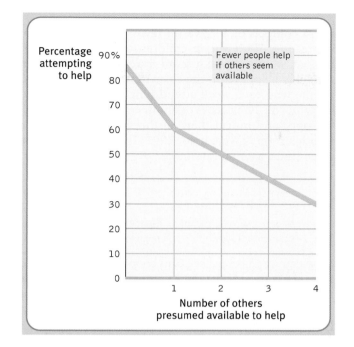

Percentage attempting to help

Fewer people help if others seem available

Number of others presumed available to help

figure 15.13
Responses to a simulated physical emergency When people thought they alone heard the calls for help from a person they believed to be having an epileptic seizure, they usually helped. But when they thought four others were also hearing the calls, fewer than a third responded. (From Darley & Latané, 1968a.)

bystander effect—any particular bystander was less likely to give aid with other bystanders present. When alone with the person in need, 40 percent helped; when there were five other bystanders, only 20 percent helped.

From their observations of behavior in tens of thousands of such "emergencies," altruism researchers have discerned some additional patterns. The *best* odds of our helping someone occur when

- we have just observed someone else being helpful.
- we are not in a hurry.
- the victim appears to need and deserve help.
- the victim is in some way similar to us.
- we are in a small town or rural area.
- we are feeling guilty.
- we are focused on others and not preoccupied.
- we are in a good mood.

This last result, that happy people are helpful people, is one of the most consistent findings in all of psychology. No matter how people are cheered—whether by being made to feel successful and intelligent, by thinking happy thoughts, by finding money, or even by receiving a posthypnotic suggestion—they become more generous and more eager to help (Carlson & others, 1988).

"Oh, make us happy and you make us good!"
Robert Browning, The Ring and the Book, *1868*

The Psychology of Helping

Why do we help? One widely held view is that self-interest underlies all human interactions: Our constant goal is to maximize rewards and minimize costs. Accountants call it cost–benefit analysis. Philosophers call it utilitarianism. Social psychologists call it **social exchange theory**. If you are pondering whether to donate blood, you may weigh the costs of doing so (time, discomfort, and anxiety) against the benefits (reduced guilt, social approval, good feelings). If you anticipate rewards from helping that exceed the costs, you help.

But why do we leave tips for people we will never see again and give directions to strangers? Social expectations also influence helping. They prescribe how we ought to behave, often to our mutual benefit. Through socialization, we learn the *reciprocity norm*, the expectation that we should return help, not harm, to those who have helped us. In our relations with others of similar status, the reciprocity

▶ **superordinate goals** shared goals that override differences among people and require their cooperation.

norm compels us to give (in favors, gifts, or social invitations) about as much as we receive. With young children and others who cannot give as much as they receive, we also learn a *social responsibility norm*—that we should help those who need our help, even if the costs outweigh the benefits. In repeated Gallup surveys, people who each week attend religious services often exhibit the social responsibility norm: They report volunteering more than twice as many hours in helping the poor and infirm than do those who rarely or never attend religious services (Hodgkinson & Weitzman, 1992; Independent Sector, 2002). They also give away three times as much money.

Peacemaking

15. How can we transform feelings of prejudice, aggression, and conflict into attitudes that promote peace?

"You cannot shake hands with a clenched fist."

Indira Gandhi, 1971

How can we make peace? Can cooperation, communication, and conciliation transform the antagonisms fed by prejudice, aggression, and various conflicts into attitudes that promote peace? Research indicates that in some cases they can.

Cooperation

Does it help to put two conflicting parties into close contact? It depends. When such contact is noncompetitive and between parties with equal status, such as fellow store clerks, it may help. Initially prejudiced co-workers of different races have, in such circumstances, usually come to accept one another. Among Europeans, friendly contact with ethnic minorities has led to less prejudice (Pettigrew, 1969, 1997). However, mere contact is not always enough. In most desegregated middle and junior high schools in the United States, white and black students resegregate themselves in the lunchrooms and on the school grounds (Schofield, 1986).

Contact alone was not enough to defuse intense conflicts instigated by researcher Muzafer Sherif (1966). He placed 22 Oklahoma City boys in two separate areas of a Boy Scout camp. He then put the two groups through a series of competitive activities, with prizes going to the victors. Before long, each group became intensely proud of itself and hostile to the other group's "sneaky," "smart-alecky stinkers." Food wars broke out during meals. Cabins were ransacked. Fistfights had to be broken up by members of the camp staff. When Sherif brought the two groups together, they avoided one another, except to taunt and threaten.

Nevertheless, within a few days Sherif transformed these young enemies into jovial comrades. He gave them **superordinate goals**—shared goals that overrode their differences and that could be achieved only through cooperation. A planned disruption of the camp water supply necessitated that all 22 boys work together to restore water. Renting a movie in those pre-VCR days required their pooled

Superordinate goals override differences Cooperative efforts to achieve shared goals are an effective way to break down social barriers.

resources. A stalled truck needed the combined force of all the boys pulling and pushing together to get it moving. Having used isolation and competition to make strangers into enemies, Sherif used shared predicaments and goals to reconcile the enemies and make them friends. What reduced conflict was not mere contact, but *cooperative* contact.

A shared predicament—a fearsome external threat and a superordinate desire to overcome it—likewise had a powerfully unifying effect in the weeks after 9/11. Nothing breeds solidarity quite like a common enemy. As suicide attacks in Israel can unify partisan Jews, and as Israeli military attacks on Palestinians can unify diverse Muslims, so Americans immediately felt that "we" were under attack. Gallup-surveyed approval of "our President" shot up from 51 percent the week before the attack to a highest-ever level of 90 percent 10 days after, just surpassing the previous approval rating record of 89 percent enjoyed by his father, George Bush, at the climax of the 1991 Persian Gulf War (Newport, 2002). In chat groups and everyday speech, even the word *we* (relative to *I*) surged in the immediate aftermath (Pennebaker, 2002).

John Dovidio and Samuel Gaertner (1999) report that cooperation has especially positive effects when it leads people to define a new, inclusive group that dissolves their former subgroups. Seat the members of two groups not on opposite sides, but alternately around the table. Give them a new, shared name. Have them work together. Such experiences change "us and them" into "we." Those once perceived as being in another group now are seen as part of one's own group. One 18-year-old New Jersey man would not be surprised. After 9/11, he explained a shift in his social identity: "I just thought of myself as black. But now I feel like I'm an American, more than ever" (Sengupta, 2001).

During the 1970s, several teams of educational researchers simultaneously wondered: If cooperative contacts between members of rival groups encourage positive attitudes, could we apply this principle in multicultural schools? Could we promote interracial friendships by replacing competitive classroom situations with cooperative ones? And could cooperative learning maintain or even enhance student achievement? Many experiments confirm that in all three cases, the answer is yes (Johnson & Johnson, 1989, 1994; Slavin, 1989). Members of interracial groups who work together on projects and play together on athletic teams typically come to feel friendly toward those of the other race. So do those who engage in cooperative classroom learning. So encouraging are these results that more than 25,000 teachers have introduced interracial cooperative learning into their classrooms (Kohn, 1987). Working with fellow students in all their diversity sets the stage, declared the Carnegie Council on Adolescent Development (1989), for "adult work life and for citizenship in a multicultural society."

The power of cooperative activity to make friends of former enemies has led psychologists to urge increased international exchange and cooperation (Klineberg, 1984). As we engage in mutually beneficial trade, as we work to protect our common destiny on this fragile planet, and as we become more aware that our hopes and fears are shared, we can change misperceptions that lead to fragmentation and conflict into a solidarity based on common interests. Although we will never love all our differences or be friends with everyone, we can, as we work toward shared goals, grow to accept and value human diversity.

Communication

In the social trap game we considered earlier, people are usually distrustful and pursue their individual interests as a defense against exploitation. But when they are allowed to discuss the dilemma and negotiate, cooperation increases (Jorgenson & Papciak, 1981).

When real-life conflicts do become intense, a third-party mediator—a marriage counselor, labor mediator, diplomat, community volunteer—may facilitate much-needed communication (Rubin & others, 1994). Mediators help each party to voice its viewpoint and to understand the other's. By leading each side to think about the other's underlying needs and goals, the mediator aims to replace a competitive *win-lose* orientation with a cooperative *win-win* orientation that aims at a mutually beneficial resolution. A classic example: Two friends, after quarreling over an orange, agreed to split it. One squeezed his half for juice. The other used the peel from her half to make a cake. If only the two had understood each other's motives, they could have hit on the win-win solution of one having all the juice, the other all the peel.

Such understanding and cooperative resolution is most needed, yet least likely, in times of anger or crisis (Bodenhausen & others, 1994; Tetlock, 1988). When conflicts intensify, images become more stereotyped, communication more difficult, and judgments more rigid.

"Most of us have overlapping identities which unite us with very different groups. We can love what we are, without hating what—and who—we are not. We can thrive in our own tradition, even as we learn from others."

*U.N. Secretary General Kofi Annan
Nobel Prize Lecture, 2001*

"I am prepared this day to declare myself a citizen of the world, and to invite everyone everywhere to embrace this broader vision of our interdependent world, our common quest for justice, and ultimately for Peace on Earth."

Father Theodore Hesburgh, The Human Imperative, *1974*

"To begin with, I would like to express my sincere thanks and deep appreciation for the opportunity to meet with you. While there are still profound differences between us, I think the very fact of my presence here today is a major breakthrough."

▶ **GRIT** **Graduated and Reciprocated Initiatives in Tension-Reduction—a strategy designed to decrease international tensions.**

Conciliation

When tension and suspicion peak, cooperation and communication may become impossible. Each party is likely to threaten, coerce, or retaliate. In the weeks before the Persian Gulf War, President George Bush threatened, in the full glare of publicity, to "kick Saddam's ass." Saddam Hussein communicated in kind, threatening to make Americans "swim in their own blood."

Under such conditions, is there an alternative to war or surrender? Social psychologist Charles Osgood (1962, 1980) has advocated a strategy of "Graduated and Reciprocated Initiatives in Tension-Reduction," nicknamed **GRIT**. In applying GRIT, one side first announces its recognition of mutual interests and its intent to reduce tensions. It then initiates one or more small, conciliatory acts. Without weakening one's retaliatory capability, this modest beginning opens the door for reciprocation by the other party. Should the enemy respond with hostility, one reciprocates in kind. But so, too, with any conciliatory response. Thus, President Kennedy's gesture of stopping atmospheric nuclear tests began a series of reciprocated conciliatory acts that culminated in the 1993 atmospheric test-ban treaty.

In laboratory experiments, GRIT has been the most effective strategy known for increasing trust and cooperation (Lindskold & others, 1978–1988). Even during intense personal conflict, when communication has been nonexistent, a small conciliatory gesture—a smile, a touch, a word of apology—may work wonders. Conciliations allow both parties to begin edging down the tension ladder to a safer rung where communication and mutual understanding can begin.

And how good that such can happen, for civilization advances not by cultural isolation—maintaining walls around ethnic enclaves—but by tapping the knowledge, the skills, and the arts that are each culture's legacy to the whole human race. Thomas Sowell (1991) notes that, thanks to cultural sharing, every modern society is enriched by a cultural mix. We have China to thank for paper and printing, and for the magnetic compass that opened the great explorations. We have Egypt to thank for trigonometry. We have the Islamic world and India's Hindus to thank for our Arabic numerals. While celebrating and claiming these cultural legacies, we can also welcome the enrichment of today's social diversity. We can view ourselves as individual instruments in a human orchestra. And we can therefore affirm our own culture's heritage while building bridges of communication, understanding, and cooperation across cultural traditions.

---

rehearse it!

18. Repeated exposure to a stimulus—including a new human face—increases our liking of the stimulus. This *mere exposure effect* helps explain why proximity is a powerful predictor of friendship and marriage, and why, for example, people tend to marry someone
    a. about as attractive as themselves.
    b. who lives or works nearby.
    c. of similar religious or ethnic background.
    d. who has similar attitudes and habits.

19. Male subjects who are aroused by various stimuli and then introduced to an attractive woman tend to attribute their arousal to the woman, and to report positive feelings toward her. This supports the two-factor theory of emotion, which assumes that emotions such as passionate love consist of physical arousal plus
    a. a reward.
    b. proximity.

c. companionate love.
    d. our interpretation of that arousal.

20. Companionate love is described as a deep, affectionate attachment. _____ is (are) vital to the maintenance of such loving relationships.
    a. Equity and self-disclosure
    b. Physical attraction
    c. Intense positive absorption
    d. Passionate love

21. Many factors determine whether a bystander will come to the aid of a stranger in an emergency. One is the bystander effect, which states that a particular bystander is *less* likely to give aid if
    a. the victim is similar to the bystander in appearance.
    b. no one else is present.
    c. other people are present.
    d. the incident occurs in a deserted or rural area.

22. Social expectations influence helping. For example, through socialization, we are taught that we should help those who need our help. This is called
    a. the reciprocity norm.
    b. social exchange theory.
    c. the social responsibility norm.
    d. a GRIT strategy.

23. Social psychologists have attempted to define the circumstances that facilitate conflict resolution. One way of fostering cooperation is by providing contentious groups with superordinate goals, which are
    a. the goals of friendly competition.
    b. shared goals that override differences.
    c. goals for winning at negotiations.
    d. goals for reducing conflict through increased contact.

Answers can be found in Appendix C.

chapter review

REVIEWING

Social Psychology

Social psychologists study how people think about, influence, and relate to one another.

SOCIAL THINKING

1. How do we tend to explain others' behavior? How do we explain our own behavior?

We generally explain people's behavior by attributing it either to internal dispositions or to external situations. In accounting for others' actions, we often underestimate the influence of the situation, thus committing the fundamental attribution error. When we explain our own behavior, however, we more often point to the situation and not to ourselves.

2. Does what we think predict what we will do, or does what we do shape what we will think?

Attitudes predict behavior only under certain conditions, as when other influences are minimized, when the attitude is specific to the behavior, and when people are aware of their attitudes.

Studies of the foot-in-the-door phenomenon and of role playing reveal that our actions can also modify our attitudes, especially when we feel responsible for those actions. Cognitive dissonance theorists explain that behavior shapes attitudes because people feel discomfort when their actions go against their feelings and beliefs; they reduce the discomfort by bringing their attitudes more into line with what they have done.

SOCIAL INFLUENCE

3. What do experiments on conformity and compliance reveal about the power of social influence?

As suggestibility studies demonstrate, when we are unsure about our judgments, we are likely to adjust them toward the group standard. Solomon Asch found that under certain conditions people will conform to a group's judgment even when it is clearly incorrect. We may conform either to gain social approval (normative social influence) or because we welcome the information that others provide (informational social influence). In Stanley Milgram's famous experiments, people torn between obeying an experimenter and responding to another's pleas to stop the shocks usually chose to obey orders, even though obedience appeared to mean harming another person. Social influence is potent.

4. How does the mere presence of others influence our actions? How does our behavior change when we act as part of a group?

Experiments on social facilitation reveal that the presence of either observers or co-actors can arouse individuals, boosting their performance on easy tasks but hindering it on difficult ones. When people pool their efforts toward a group goal, social loafing may occur as individuals free-ride on others' efforts. When a group experience arouses people and makes them anonymous, they may become less self-aware and self-restrained, a psychological state known as deindividuation.

5. What are group polarization and groupthink?

Within groups, discussions among like-minded members often produce group polarization, an enhancement of the group's prevailing attitudes. This is one cause of groupthink, the tendency for harmony-seeking groups to make unrealistic decisions after suppressing unwelcome information.

6. How much power do we have as individuals? Can a minority sway a majority?

The power of the group is great, but so is the power of the individual. Even a small minority sometimes sways a group, especially when the minority expresses its views consistently.

SOCIAL RELATIONS

7. What are the social and emotional roots of prejudice?

Prejudice is a mixture of beliefs (often stereotypes), emotions, and predispositions to action. It often arises as those who enjoy social and economic superiority attempt to justify the status quo. Even the temporary assignment of people to groups can cause an ingroup bias. Prejudice may also boost self-esteem and focus on a scapegoat the anger caused by frustration.

8. What are the cognitive roots of prejudice?

Research reveals how our ways of processing information—for example, by overestimating similarities when we categorize people or by noticing and remembering vivid cases—work to create stereotypes. In addition, favored social groups often rationalize their higher status with the just-world phenomenon.

9. What biological factors make us more prone to hurt one another?

Aggressive behavior, like all behavior, is a product of nature and nurture. Although psychologists dismiss the idea that aggression is instinctual, aggressiveness is genetically influenced. Moreover, certain areas of the brain, when stimulated, activate or inhibit aggression, and these neural areas are biochemically influenced.

10. What psychological factors may trigger aggressive behavior?

A variety of psychological factors also fuel aggression's fire. Aversive events heighten people's hostility. Such stimuli are especially likely to trigger aggression in those rewarded for their own aggression, those who have learned aggression from role models, and those who have been influenced by media violence. Enacting violence in video games also heightens aggressive behavior. Such factors desensitize people to cruelty and prime them to behave aggressively when provoked. Media influences may also cultivate the rape myth (the idea that some women invite or enjoy rape) and make sexual aggression seem less terrible.

11. What social processes fuel conflict?

Conflicts between individuals and cultures often arise from destructive social processes. These include social traps, in which each party, by protecting and pursuing its self-interest, creates an outcome no one wants. The spiral of conflict also feeds and is fed by distorted mirror-image perceptions, in which each party views itself as moral and the other as untrustworthy and evil-intentioned.

12. Why do we befriend or fall in love with some people but not with others?

Three factors are known to affect our liking for one another. *Proximity*—geographical nearness—is conducive to attraction, partly because mere exposure to novel stimuli enhances liking. *Physical attractiveness* influences social opportunities and the way one is perceived. As acquaintanceship moves toward friendship, *similarity* of attitudes and interests greatly increases liking.

13. Does our love for a partner remain the same as time passes?

We can view passionate love as an aroused state that we cognitively label as love. The strong affection of companionate love, which often emerges as a relationship matures, is enhanced by an equitable relationship and by intimate self-disclosure.

14. Why do we help others? When are we most—and least—likely to help?

In response to incidents where bystanders did not intervene in emergencies, social psychologists undertook experiments that revealed a bystander effect: Any given bystander is less likely to help if others are present. The bystander effect is especially apparent in situations where the presence of others inhibits one's noticing the event, interpreting it as an emergency, or assuming responsibility for offering help. Many factors, including mood, also influence willingness to help someone in distress.

Social exchange theory proposes that our social behaviors—even our helpful acts—maximize our benefits (which may include our own good feelings) and minimize our costs. Our desire to help is also affected by social norms, which prescribe reciprocating the help we have received and being socially responsible toward those in need.

15. How can we transform feelings of prejudice, aggression, and conflict into attitudes that promote peace?

Enemies sometimes become friends, especially when the circumstances favor cooperation to achieve superordinate goals, understanding through communication, and reciprocated conciliatory gestures.

A CRITICAL THINKER'S REVIEW OF CHAPTER 15

You've now studied and reviewed **Social Psychology.** For even better retention, reflect on these concepts at a deeper level. If you need to refresh your memory of the six categories of critical thinking shown in parentheses below, see page 34. See if you can answer each of these questions in a short paragraph.

1. Driving to school one wintry day, Marco narrowly misses a car that slides through a red light. "Slow down! What a terrible driver," he thinks to himself. Moments later, Marco himself slips through an intersection and yelps, "Wow! These roads are awful. The city snow plows need to get out here." What social psychology principle has Marco just demonstrated? Explain. (perspective taking)

2. You are organizing a Town Hall-style meeting of fiercely competitive political candidates. To add to the fun, friends have suggested handing out masks of the candidates' faces for supporters to wear. Is this a good idea? What phenomenon might these masks engage? (pattern recognition)

3. Your brother is not comfortable visiting nursing homes or being around older people. He regrets this, because it means he hardly ever spends time with your elderly grandmother who lives in a nursing home and dearly loves family visits. How might your brother change his behavior in a way that would also change his thinking about the elderly? What theory would explain the change? (psychological reasoning)

4. Mrs. Lewis wants to collect unique pieces of art from her third-grade class for a farewell project the school is doing for a beloved, retiring principal. She knows from past experience that when the students work side by side, they often conform to what their classmates are doing, and the result is a lot of similarity. What have we learned from social science research about the conditions that strengthen conformity? How might these findings help Mrs. Lewis? (scientific problem solving)

5. Why didn't anybody help Kitty Genovese? What social relations principle did this incident illustrate? (creative problem solving)

6. Two of your best friends have had a few run-ins and have decided they are "enemies." What could you suggest they do that might help them make peace? (practical problem solving)

Answers can be found in Appendix C.

TERMS AND CONCEPTS TO REMEMBER

social psychology, p. 539

attribution theory, p. 539

fundamental attribution error, p. 540

attitude, p. 541

foot-in-the-door phenomenon, p. 542

role, p. 543

cognitive dissonance theory, p. 543

conformity, p. 546

normative social influence, p. 547

informational social influence, p. 547

social facilitation, p. 551

social loafing, p. 551

deindividuation, p. 552

group polarization, p. 552

groupthink, p. 553

prejudice, p. 555

stereotype, p. 555

discrimination, p. 555

ingroup, p. 557

outgroup, p. 557

ingroup bias, p. 558

scapegoat theory, p. 558

just-world phenomenon, p. 559

aggression, p. 559

frustration-aggression principle, p. 561

conflict, p. 566

social trap, p. 566

mere exposure effect, p. 568

passionate love, p. 572

companionate love, p. 572

equity, p. 573

self-disclosure, p. 573

altruism, p. 573

bystander effect, p. 575

social exchange theory, p. 575

superordinate goals, p. 576

GRIT, p. 578

To continue your study and review of Social Psychology, visit this book's Web site at www.worthpublishers.com/myers. You will find practice tests, review activities, and Web links for more information on topics related to Social Psychology.

appendix A

Statistical Reasoning in Everyday Life

Statistics are tools that help us see and interpret what the unaided eye might miss. To be an educated person today is to be able to apply simple statistical principles to everyday reasoning. One needn't remember complicated formulas to think more clearly and critically about data.

1. What is the first important point to remember when assessing studies that use statistical reasoning?

Unaided by statistics, top-of-the-head estimates often misread reality and mislead the public. Someone throws out a big round number. Others echo it, and before long the big round number becomes a public myth. A few examples:

- *One percent of Americans (2.7 million) are homeless.* Or is it 300,000, an earlier estimate by the federal government? Or 600,000, the estimate by the Urban Institute (Crossen, 1994)?
- *Ten percent of people are lesbians or gay men.* Or is it 2 to 3 percent, as suggested by various national surveys (Chapter 10)?
- *We ordinarily use but 10 percent of our brain.* Or is it closer to 100 percent? (Which 90 percent, or even 10 percent, would you be willing to sacrifice?)

The point to remember: Doubt big, round, undocumented numbers. Rather than swallow top-of-the-head estimates, focus on thinking smarter by applying simple statistical principles to everyday reasoning.

DESCRIBING DATA

Once researchers have gathered their raw data, their first task is to *organize* it. One way is to use a simple *bar graph*, as in **FIGURE A.1** (page A-2), which displays a distribution of trucks of different brands still on the road after a decade. When reading statistical graphs such as this, take care. Depending on what people want to emphasize, they can design the graph to make a difference look small or big. So think smart: When viewing figures in magazines and on television, read the scale labels and note their range.

Measures of Central Tendencies

2. What are the three measures of central tendency, and which is most affected by extreme scores?

The next step is to summarize the data using three measures of "central tendency," a single score that represents a whole set of scores. The simplest measure is the **mode**, the most frequently occurring score. The most commonly reported measure is the **mean**, or arithmetic average—the total sum of all the scores divided by the number of scores. On a divided highway, the median is the middle. So, too, with data: The **median** is the middle score. If you arrange all the scores in order from the highest to the lowest, half will be above the median and half will be below it.

Describing Data
Measures of Central Tendencies
Measures of Variation
Correlation: A Measure of Relationships

Making Inferences
When Is a Difference Reliable?
When Is a Difference Significant?

▶ **mode** the most frequently occurring score in a distribution.

▶ **mean** the arithmetic average of a distribution, obtained by adding the scores and then dividing by the number of scores.

▶ **median** the middle score in a distribution; half the scores are above it and half are below it.

figure A.1
Read the scale labels An American truck manufacturer offered a graph (a)—with actual brand names included—to suggest the much greater durability of its trucks. Note, however, how the apparent difference shrinks as the vertical scale changes (graph b).

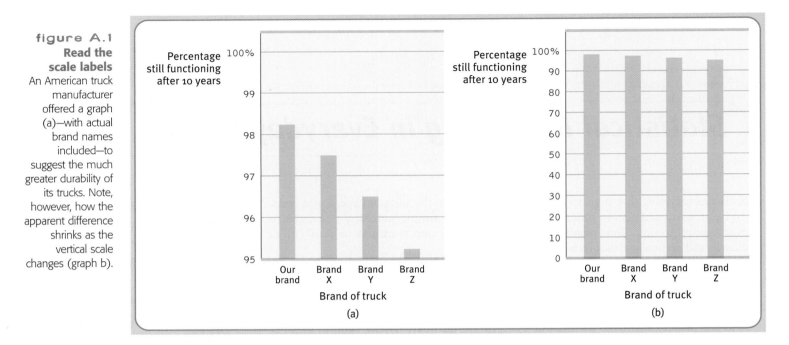

Measures of central tendency neatly summarize data. But consider what happens to the mean when a distribution is lopsided or *skewed*. With income data, for example, the mode, median, and mean often tell very different stories (**FIGURE A.2**). This happens because the mean is biased by a few extreme scores. When Microsoft founder Bill Gates sits down in an intimate cafe, its average (mean) patron instantly becomes a billionaire. Understanding this, you can see how a British newspaper could accurately run the headline "Income for 62% Is Below Average" (Waterhouse, 1993).

"The poor are getting poorer, but with the rich getting richer it all averages out in the long run."

figure A.2
A skewed distribution This graphic representation of the distribution of incomes illustrates the three measures of central tendency—mode, median, and mean. Note how just a few high incomes make the mean—the fulcrum point that balances the incomes above and below—deceptively high.

Because the bottom *half* of British income earners receive only a *quarter* of the national income pie, most British people, like most people everywhere, make less than the mean. Professional athletes' incomes also form skewed distributions. In 1998, 66 percent of the National Basketball Association's 411 players made less than the average (mean) player salary (DuPree, 1998). The average ($2.24 million) was, of course, inflated by a few superstar salaries, led by Michael Jordan's $33.14 million.

The point to remember: Always note which measure of central tendency is reported. Then, if it is a mean, consider whether a few atypical scores could be distorting it.

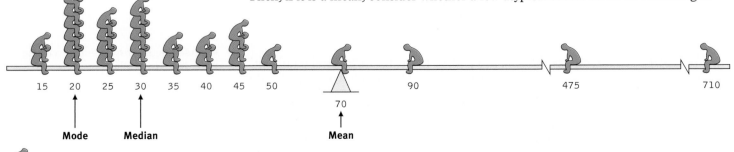

Mode   Median   Mean

One family   Income per family in thousands of dollars

Measures of Variation

3. What is the most useful measure of variation in a set of data?

Knowing the value of an appropriate measure of central tendency can tell us a great deal. But it also helps to know something about the amount of *variation* in the data— how similar or diverse the scores are. Averages derived from scores with low variability are more reliable than averages based on scores with high variability. Consider a basketball player who scored between 13 and 17 points in each of her first 10 games in a season. Knowing this, we would be more confident that she would score near 15 points in her next game than if her scores had varied from 5 to 25 points.

The **range** of scores—the gap between the lowest and highest scores—provides only a crude estimate of variation because a couple of extreme scores in an otherwise uniform group, such as the $475,000 and $710,000 in Figure A.2, will create a deceptively large range.

The more useful measure of how much scores deviate from one another is the **standard deviation**. Because it uses information from each score, it better gauges whether scores are packed together or dispersed. (The computation assembles information about how much individual scores differ from the mean.)

You can grasp the meaning of the standard deviation more easily if you consider how scores tend to be distributed in nature. Large numbers of data—heights, weights, intelligence scores, grades (though not incomes)—often form a roughly symmetrical, bell-shaped distribution. Most cases fall near the mean, and fewer cases fall near either extreme. This bell-shaped distribution is so typical that we call the curve it forms the **normal curve**.

As **FIGURE A.3** shows, a useful property of the normal curve is that roughly 68 percent of the cases fall within one standard deviation on either side of the mean. About 95 percent of cases fall within two standard deviations. Thus, Chapter 9 notes that about 68 percent of people taking an intelligence test will score within ±15 points of 100. About 95 percent will score within ±30 points.

▶ **range** the difference between the highest and lowest scores in a distribution.

▶ **standard deviation** a measure of score variability based on how much individual scores differ from the mean. (Technical note: A standard deviation is computed by [1] calculating the deviation of each score from the mean, [2] squaring those deviations, [3] finding their average, and [4] finding the square root of this average.)

▶ **normal curve** (normal distribution) a symmetrical, bell-shaped curve that describes the distribution of many types of data; most scores fall near the mean (68 percent fall within one standard deviation of it) and fewer and fewer near the extremes.

▶ **correlation coefficient** a statistical measure of the extent to which two factors vary together, and thus of how well either factor predicts the other. Scores with a *positive correlation coefficient* go up and down together (as with high school and college GPAs). A *negative correlation coefficient* indicates that one score falls as the other rises (as in the relationship between self-esteem and depression).

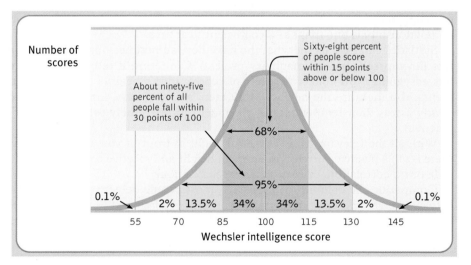

figure A.3
The normal curve Scores on aptitude tests tend to form a normal, or bell-shaped, curve. For example, the Wechsler scale calls the average score 100.

Correlation: A Measure of Relationships

4. What does it mean when we say that two things are correlated?

Throughout this book we often ask how much two things relate: How closely related are the personality scores of identical twins? How well do intelligence test scores predict achievement? How often does stress lead to disease? Describing behavior is a first step toward predicting it. When surveys and naturalistic observations reveal that one trait or behavior accompanies another, we say the two *correlate*. As we noted in Chapter 1, a **correlation coefficient** is a statistical measure of

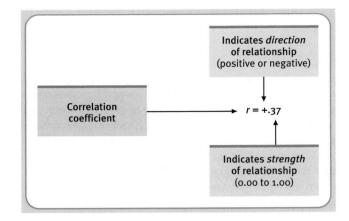

relationship (**FIGURE A.4**). It reveals how closely two things vary together and thus how well either one *predicts* the other. Knowing how much the number of one's close friends *correlates* with happiness tells us how well friendships *predict* happiness. But they do not tell you which causes which. (Can you speculate possible explanations for a positive correlation?)

To get a feel for whether one set of scores relates to a second set, we can plot, or display, the data, as in **FIGURE A.5**, which shows perfect positive and negative correlations. A correlation's possible range is as follows:

- **+1.00**, which means that one set of scores increases in direct proportion to the other's increase.
- **0.00**, meaning that the scores are unrelated.
- **−1.00**, which means that one set of scores goes up precisely as the other goes down.

Note that a correlation's being negative has nothing to do with its strength or weakness; a negative correlation means two things relate inversely. (As tooth brushing goes up from zero, tooth decay goes down.) A weak correlation, indicating little or no relationship, is one that has a coefficient near zero.

Statistics can help us see what the naked eye sometimes misses. To demonstrate this for yourself, try an imaginary project. Wondering if tall people are more or less easygoing, you collect two sets of scores: men's heights and men's temperaments. You measure the heights of 20 men, and you have someone else independently assess their temperaments (from zero for extremely calm to 100 for highly reactive).

With all the relevant data (**TABLE A.1**) right in front of you, can you tell whether there is (1) a positive correlation between height and reactive temperament, (2) very little or no correlation, or (3) a negative correlation?

Comparing the columns in Table A.1, most people detect very little relationship between height and temperament. In fact, the correlation in this imaginary example is moderately positive, +0.63, as you could see if you plotted the data on a graph, as

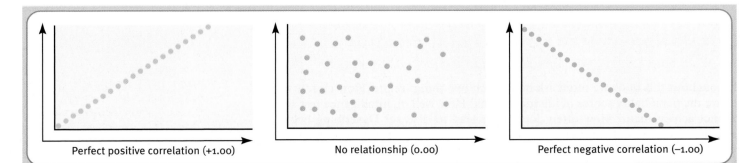

Perfect positive correlation (+1.00)   No relationship (0.00)   Perfect negative correlation (−1.00)

in **FIGURE A.6**. The upward slope of the cluster of points as one moves to the right shows that the two sets of scores (height and reactivity) tend to rise together.

If we fail to see a relationship when data are presented as systematically as in Table A.1, how much less likely are we to notice them in everyday life? To see what is right in front of us, we sometimes need statistical illumination. We can easily see evidence of gender discrimination when given statistically summarized information about job level, seniority, performance, gender, and salary. But we often see no discrimination when the same information dribbles in, case by case (Twiss & others, 1989).

The point to remember: Although the correlation coefficient tells us nothing about cause and effect, it *can* help us see the world more clearly by revealing the actual extent to which two things relate.

5. What is regression toward the mean?

Correlations not only make visible the relationships that we might otherwise miss, they also restrain our "seeing" nonexistent relationships. As Chapter 1 explained, a perceived correlation that does not really exist is an *illusory correlation*. When we *believe* there is a relationship between two things, we are likely to *notice* and *recall* instances that confirm our belief. If we believe that dreams are forecasts of actual events, we may notice and recall confirming instances more than disconfirming instances. The result is an illusory correlation.

Illusory correlations feed an *illusion of control*—that chance events are subject to our personal control. Gamblers, remembering their lucky rolls, may come to believe they can influence the roll of the dice by again throwing gently for low numbers and hard for high numbers. The illusion that uncontrollable events correlate with our actions is also fed by a statistical phenomenon called **regression toward the mean**. Average results are more typical than extreme results. Thus, after an unusual event, things tend to return toward their average level; extraordinary happenings tend to be followed by more ordinary ones.

The point may seem obvious, yet we regularly miss it. Thus, we sometimes attribute what may be a normal statistical regression (the expected falling back to normal) to something we have done. Examples are abundant:

- Students who score much lower or higher on an exam than they usually do are likely, when retested, to return to their average.
- Unusual ESP subjects who defy chance when first tested nearly always lose their "psychic powers" when retested (a phenomenon parapsychologists have called the "decline effect").

table A.1 **Height and Temperament of 20 Men**		
Subject	Height in inches	Temperament
1	80	75
2	63	66
3	61	60
4	79	90
5	74	60
6	69	42
7	62	42
8	75	60
9	77	81
10	60	39
11	64	48
12	76	69
13	71	72
14	66	57
15	73	63
16	70	75
17	63	30
18	71	30
19	68	84
20	70	39

▶ **regression toward the mean** the tendency for extremes of unusual scores or events to fall back (regress) toward the average.

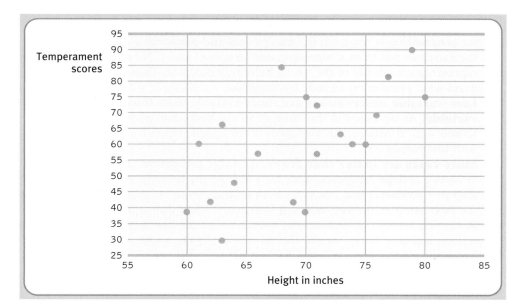

figure A.6
Height and temperament This graph displays data from 20 imagined people. Each point represents the data for one person. The upward slope indicates a positive correlation. The wide spread of the dots indicates the correlation is much lower than the perfect 1.0 correlation shown in Figure A.5.

● Scientists who win a Nobel prize—an extraordinary accomplishment—almost always experience diminished accomplishments thereafter, leading some to believe that winning a Nobel hinders creativity.

● People have also noticed a seeming "*Sports Illustrated* jinx"—that athletes whose peak performances get them on the cover of the magazine will then suffer a decline in their performance. Edward Schall and Gary Smith (2002) illustrated regression from exceptional performance in the year-to-year performance of all major league baseball players since 1900. Eighty percent of those with a high batting average (.300 or higher) had lower averages the next year. And 80 percent of pitchers who allowed few earned runs (average 3.00 or less) allowed more runs the next year.

Failure to recognize regression is the source of many superstitions and of some ineffective practices as well. When day-to-day behavior has a large element of chance fluctuation, we may notice that others' behavior improves (regresses toward average) after we criticize them for very bad performance, and that it worsens (regresses toward average) after we warmly praise them for an exceptionally fine performance. Ironically, then, regression toward the average can mislead us into feeling rewarded for having criticized others and into feeling punished for having praised them (Tversky & Kahneman, 1974).

The point to remember: When a fluctuating behavior returns to normal, there is no need to invent fancy explanations for why it does so. Regression toward the mean is probably at work.

MAKING INFERENCES

Data are "noisy." One group's average score (women's salaries) could conceivably differ from another's (men's salaries) not because of any real difference but merely due to chance fluctuation in the people sampled. How confidently, then, can we infer that an observed difference accurately estimates the true difference?

When Is a Difference Reliable?

6. When can we safely generalize from a sample?

In deciding when it is safe to generalize from a sample, we should keep three principles in mind. Let's look at each in turn.

1. **Representative samples are better than biased samples.** The best basis for generalizing is not from the exceptional and memorable cases one finds at the extremes but from a representative sample of cases. No research involves a representative sample of the whole human population. Thus, it pays to keep in mind what population a study has sampled.

2. **Less-variable observations are more reliable than those that are more variable.** As we noted in the example of the basketball player whose points scored were consistent, an average is more reliable when it comes from scores with low variability.

3. **More cases are better than fewer.** An eager prospective university student visits two college campuses, each for a day. At the first, the student randomly attends two classes and discovers both instructors to be witty and engaging. At the next campus, the two sampled instructors seem dull and uninspiring. Returning home, the student tells friends about the "great teachers" at the first school, and the "bores" at the second school. Again, we know it but we ignore it: Small samples provide less reliable estimates of the average than do large samples. The proportion of heads in samples of 10 coin tosses varies more than in samples of 100 tosses.

Said differently, *averages based on more cases are more reliable* (less variable) than averages based on only a few cases. Knowing this, answer a question posed by Christopher Jepson, David Krantz, and Richard Nisbett (1983) to University of Michigan introductory psychology students:

> The registrar's office at the University of Michigan has found that usually about 100 students in Arts and Sciences have a 4.00 GPA at the end of their first term at the University. However, only about 10 to 15 students graduate with a 4.00 GPA. What do you think is the most likely explanation for the fact that there are more 4.00 GPAs after one term than at graduation?

How did you answer? Most students in the study came up with plausible causes for the drop in GPA, such as, "Students tend to work harder at the beginning of their college careers than toward the end." Fewer than a third recognized the statistical phenomenon clearly at work: Averages based on fewer courses are more variable, which guarantees a greater number of extremely low and high GPAs at the end of the first term.

The point to remember: Don't be overly impressed by a few anecdotes. Generalizations based on a few unrepresentative cases are unreliable.

When Is a Difference Significant?

7. What do we mean when we say that an observed difference is significant?

We can justifiably have the most confidence when we generalize from samples that (1) are representative of the population we wish to study, (2) give us consistent rather than highly variable data, and (3) are large rather than small. These principles extend to the inferences we make about differences between groups.

Statistical tests help us determine significance by indicating the reliability of differences. Here is the logic behind them: When *averages* from two samples are each *reliable* measures of their respective populations (as when each is based on many observations that have small variability), then their difference (sometimes even a very small difference) is likely to be reliable as well. (The less the variability in women's and men's aggression scores, the more confidence we would have that any observed difference is reliable.) But when the *difference* between the sample averages is *large*, we have even more confidence that the difference between them reflects a real difference in their populations.

In short, *when the sample averages are reliable and the difference between them is large*, we say the difference has **statistical significance**. This simply means that the difference we observed is probably not due to chance variation between the samples. In judging statistical significance, psychologists are conservative. They are like juries who must presume innocence until guilt is proven. For most psychologists, proof beyond a reasonable doubt means not making much of a finding unless the odds of its occurring by chance are less than 5 percent (an arbitrary criterion).

▶ **statistical significance** a statistical statement of how likely it is that an obtained result occurred by chance.

PEANUTS

When reading about research, you should remember that, given large enough or homogeneous enough samples, a difference between them may be "statistically significant" yet have little practical significance. For example, comparisons of intelligence test scores among several hundred-thousand first-born and later-born individuals indicate that there is a highly significant tendency for first-born individuals within a family to have higher average scores than their later-born siblings (Zajonc & Markus, 1975). But because the scores differ by only one or two points, the difference has little practical importance. Such findings have caused some psychologists to advocate alternatives to significance testing (Hunter, 1997). Better, they say, to use other ways to express a finding's magnitude and reliability.

The point to remember: Statistical significance indicates the *likelihood* that a result will happen by chance. It does not indicate the *importance* of the result.

rehearse it!

A.1 The three measures of central tendency are the mode, the mean, and the median. Which of these three measures is most easily distorted by a few very large or very small scores?
a. The mode
b. The mean
c. The median
d. They are equally vulnerable to distortion from atypical scores.

A.2 The standard deviation is the most useful measure of variation in a set of data. The standard deviation tells us
a. the difference between the highest and lowest scores in a distribution.
b. the extent to which the sample being used deviates from the bigger population it represents.

c. how much individual scores differ from the mode.
d. how much individual scores differ from the mean.

A.3 A correlation coefficient is a statistical measure of the extent to which two factors, such as two sets of scores, vary together. In a _____ correlation, the scores would travel up and down together; in a (an) _____ correlation, one score would fall as the other rises.
a. positive; negative
b. positive; illusory
c. negative; inverse
d. strong; weak

A.4 Statistical significance is a measure of how likely it is that an observed difference is real and not due to chance alone. When sample averages are _____ and the difference between them is _____, we can say the difference has statistical significance.
a. reliable; large
b. reliable; small
c. due to chance; large
d. due to chance; small

Answers found in Appendix C.

appendix a review

REVIEWING

Statistical Reasoning in Everyday Life

Having gathered this raw data, researchers must organize and summarize it. They then draw inferences from the data and assess the significance of the findings.

DESCRIBING DATA

1. *What is the first important point to remember when assessing studies that use statistical reasoning?*

   Doubt big, round, undocumented numbers. Think smarter by applying simple statistical reasoning.

2. *What are the three measures of central tendency, and which is most affected by extreme scores?*

   Always note which measure of central tendency—the mean (the arithmetic average), the median (the middle score), or the mode (the most frequently occurring score) is reported. Then, if it is a mean, consider whether a few atypical scores could be distorting it.

3. *What is the most useful measure of variation in a set of data?*

   Standard deviations provide the most reliable measure of variation. Many types of data form a normal curve. When looking at statistical graphs in books and magazines and on television ads and news broadcasts, think critically: Always read the scale labels and note their range.

4. *What does it mean when we say that two things are correlated?*

   A correlation coefficient tells us the extent to which two things relate, and thus how well one predicts the other. Correlation coefficients cannot tell cause and effect, but they do make visible relationships we might miss, and they restrain us from seeing nonexistent relationships.

5. *What is regression toward the mean?*

   Fluctuating behaviors tend to return to normal. There is no need to invent fancy explanations for why they do so. Regression toward the mean is probably at work.

MAKING INFERENCES

6. *When can we safely generalize from a sample?*

   To safely generalize from a sample, we would want it to be representative of the population we wish to study, to provide consistent (not highly variable) data, and to be large rather than small. Don't be overly impressed by a few anecdotes; generalizations based on only a few cases are unreliable.

7. *What do we mean when we say that an observed difference is significant?*

   Statistical significance indicates the *likelihood* that a result will occur by chance. It does not indicate the importance of the result.

TERMS AND CONCEPTS TO REMEMBER

mode, p. A-1
mean, p. A-1
median, p. A-1

range, p. A-3
standard deviation, p. A-3
normal curve, p. A-3

correlation coefficient, p. A-3
regression toward the mean, p. A-5
statistical significance, p. A-7

To continue your study and review of Statistical Reasoning in Everyday Life, visit this book's Web site at www.worthpublishers.com/myers. You will find practice tests, review activities, and Web links for more information on topics related to Statistical Reasoning in Everyday Life.

appendix B

Psychology at Work

The healthy life, said Freud, is filled by love and by work. For most of us, work is life's biggest single waking activity. To live is to work. Work helps satisfy several levels of human needs. Work supports us. Work connects us. Work defines us. Meeting someone for the first time, and wondering "Who are you?" we may ask, "So, what do you do?"

If we feel dissatisfied with our work-related pay, relationships, or identity, we may change where or for whom we work, as 16 percent of Australians did in just the year 2000 (Trewin, 2001). Most people therefore have neither a single vocation nor a predictable career path. Two decades from now, most of you reading this book will be doing work you cannot now imagine. To prepare you and others for this unknown future, many colleges and universities focus less on training your job skills and more on enlarging your capacities for understanding, thinking, and communicating in any work environment.

Sometimes work is drudgery, toil, the daily grind. It is clenched jaws, tension headaches, and accidents. Insecurity, struggle, and weariness. Yet, as Studs Terkel (1972, p. xi) has written, work is also a search "for daily meaning as well as daily bread, for recognition as well as cash."

Work is indeed both a bane and a blessing—but it's more a blessing. Or so it seems to those without work. In almost every industrialized nation surveyed, people report markedly lower well-being if unemployed (**FIGURE B.1**). Idleness may sound like bliss. Oh, to be able to escape the rat race and spend time sunbathing on a Bahamian beach, or curled up on the couch watching *Law and Order* or *Coronation Street* reruns, or just vegetating. Yet when we get excess leisure time, we may feel purposeless.

Amy Wrzensniewski and her colleagues (1997, 2001) have identified person-to-person variations in people's attitudes toward their work. Across various occupations, some people view their work as a *job*, a necessary way to make money, but not a positive and fulfilling activity. Others view their work as a *career*, an opportunity to advance from one position to a better position. The rest view their work as a *calling*, a fulfilling and socially useful activity. Those who view work as a calling report the highest satisfaction with their work and their lives.

- **Personnel Psychology**
  Close-Up: I/O Psychology at Work
  Harnessing Strengths
  Close-Up: Discovering Your Strengths
  Do Interviews Predict Performance?
  Appraising Performance

- **Organizational Psychology**
  Satisfaction and Engagement
  Managing Well

- **Human Factors Psychology**

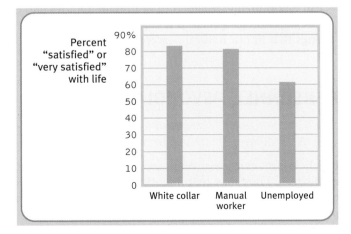

figure B.1
The bane of unemployment To want work but not have work is to feel less satisfied with life. Data from 169,776 adults in 16 nations (Ingelhart, 1990).

This finding would not surprise Mihaly Csikszentmihalyi (1990, 1999), who has observed that people's quality of life increases when they are purposefully engaged. Between the anxiety of being overwhelmed and stressed, and the apathy of being underwhelmed and bored, lies a zone in which people experience **flow**. Csikszentmihalyi (chick-SENT-me-hi) formulated the flow concept after studying artists who would spend hour after hour painting or sculpting with enormous concentration. Immersed in a project, they worked as if nothing else mattered, and then promptly forgot about it once they finished. The artists seemed driven less by the external rewards of producing art—money, praise, promotion—than by the intrinsic rewards of creating the work. His later observations of dancers, chess players, surgeons, writers, parents, mountain climbers, Australian sailors, elderly Koreans, Alpine farmers, and Japanese, Italian, and American teenagers confirmed an overriding principle: It's exhilarating to flow with an activity that fully engages our skills. Flow experiences boost our sense of self-esteem, competence, and well-being. When people are beeped at random intervals and asked to report what they are doing and how much they are enjoying themselves, those who are vegetating usually report little sense of flow and little satisfaction. People report more positive feelings when interrupted while doing something active, something that engages their skills, be it play or work. Purposeful work enriches our lives.

Work is changing, from farming to manufacturing to "knowledge work." More and more work is "outsourced" to temporary employees and consultants who communicate electronically from virtual workplaces in remote locations. (This book and its teaching package are developed and produced by a team of people in a dozen cities, from Alaska to Florida.) As work changes, will our attitudes toward our work also change? Will our satisfaction with work increase or decrease? Will the "psychological contract"—the subjective sense of mutual obligations between workers and employers—become more or less trusting and secure? These are among the questions that fascinate psychologists who study work-related behavior.

Industrial-organizational (I/O) psychology is a fast-growing profession that applies psychology's principles to the workplace (see Close-Up: I/O Psychology at Work). Here we consider three main subfields:

- **Personnel psychology**, which applies psychology's methods and principles to selecting and evaluating workers. Personnel psychologists match people with jobs, by identifying and placing well-suited candidates.
- **Organizational psychology**, which considers how work environments and management styles influence worker motivation, satisfaction, and productivity. Organizational psychologists modify jobs and supervision in ways that boost morale and productivity.
- **Human factors psychology**, which explores how machines and environments can be optimally designed to fit human abilities and expectations. Human factors psychologists help to design appliances, machines, Web sites, and work settings that fit our natural perception.

▶ **flow** a completely involved, focused state of consciousness, with diminished awareness of self and time, resulting from optimal engagement of one's skills.

▶ **industrial-organizational (I/O) psychology** the application of psychological concepts and methods to optimizing human behavior in workplaces.

▶ **personnel psychology** a subfield of I/O psychology that focuses on employee recruitment, selection, placement, training, appraisal, and development.

▶ **organizational psychology** a subfield of I/O psychology that examines organizational influences on worker satisfaction and productivity and facilitates organizational change.

▶ **human factors psychology** a subfield of I/O psychology that explores how people and machines interact and how machines and physical environments can be adapted to human behaviors.

PERSONNEL PSYCHOLOGY

1. What tools and techniques do personnel psychologists use to marry the individual's strengths with the organization's needs?

Psychologists can assist organizations at various stages of selecting and assessing employees. They may help identify needed job skills, decide upon selection methods, recruit and evaluate applicants, introduce and train new employees, and appraise their performance.

I/O Psychology at Work

As scientists, consultants, and management professionals, industrial-organizational psychologists are found working in varied areas:

Personnel Psychology

Selecting and placing employees
- Developing and validating assessment tools for selecting, placing, and promoting workers
- Analyzing job content
- Optimizing worker placements

Training and developing employees
- Identifying needs
- Designing training programs
- Evaluating training programs

Appraising performance
- Developing criteria
- Measuring individual performance
- Measuring organizational performance

Organizational Psychology

Developing organizations
- Analyzing organizational structures
- Maximizing worker satisfaction and productivity
- Facilitating organizational change

Enhancing quality of worklife
- Expanding individual productivity
- Identifying elements of satisfaction
- Redesigning jobs

Human Factors (Engineering) Psychology
- Designing optimum work environments
- Optimizing person–machine interactions
- Developing systems technologies

Adapted from the Society of Industrial and Organizational Psychology (siop.org)

Harnessing Strengths

As a new AT&T human resource executive, psychologist Mary Tenopyr's (1997) first assignment was a problem: Customer service representatives were failing at a high rate. After concluding that many of the hires were ill-matched to the demands of their new job, Tenopyr developed a new selection instrument:

1. She asked new applicants to respond to various questions (without as yet making any use of their responses).
2. She followed up later to assess which of the applicants excelled on the job.
3. She identified the individual items on the earlier test that best predicted who would succeed.

The happy result of her data-driven work was a new test that enabled AT&T to identify likely-to-succeed customer representatives.

As this illustrates, personnel selection aims to match people's strengths with work that enables them and their organizations to flourish. Marry the strengths of people with the tasks of organizations and the result is often prosperity and profit.

Your strengths are any enduring qualities that can be productively applied. Are you naturally curious? Persuasive? Charming? Persistent? Competitive? Analytical? Empathic? Organized? Articulate? Neat? Mechanical? Any such trait, if matched with suitable work, can function as a strength. (See Close-Up: Discovering Your Strengths, page B-4.)

Unfortunately, reports Marcus Buckingham (2001), "The corporate world is appallingly bad at capitalizing on the strengths of its people." Buckingham based this conclusion on Gallup surveys of nearly 2 million employees in 63 countries. Today, only 20 percent of employees surveyed globally strongly agree that every day they have the "opportunity to do what I do best" (Buckingham & Clifton,

Artistic strengths At age 21, Henri Matisse was a sickly and often depressed lawyer's clerk. When his mother gave him a box of paints to cheer him up one day, he felt the darkness lift and his energy surge. He began to fill his days with painting and drawing and went on to art school and a life as one of the world's great painters. For Matisse, doing art felt like "a comfortable armchair." That is how exercising our strengths often feels.

CLOSE-UP

Discovering Your Strengths

You can use some of the techniques personnel psychologists have developed to identify your own strengths and pinpoint types of work that will likely prove satisfying and successful. Marcus Buckingham and Donald Clifton (2001) suggest asking yourself:

- What activities give me pleasure? (Bringing order out of chaos? Playing host? Helping others? Challenging sloppy thinking?)
- What activities leave me wondering, "When can I do this again?" (rather than "When will this be over?")?
- What sort of challenges do I relish (and which do I dread)?

- What sort of tasks do I learn easily (and which do I struggle with)?

Some people find themselves in flow—their skills engaged and time flying—when teaching, or selling, or writing, or cleaning, or consoling, or creating, or repairing. If an activity feels good, if it comes easily, if you look forward to it, then look deeper and see your strengths at work.

Satisfied and successful people, Buckingham and Clifton report, devote far less time to correcting their deficiencies than to accentuating their strengths. Top performers are "rarely well rounded," the researchers found (p. 26). Instead, they have sharpened their existing

"To be what we are, and to become what we are capable of becoming, is the only end of life."

Robert Louis Stevenson,
Of Men and Books, 1882

skills. Given the persistence of our traits and temperaments, most of us are better advised to identify and employ our talents than to focus on our deficiencies, they argue. Better to recognize activities that we quickly learn and become absorbed in—and to further develop those strengths—than to sign up for assertiveness training if shy, public speaking courses if nervous and soft-spoken, or drawing classes if stick figures express our artistic talent.

2001). Ironically, the longer employees are with an organization and the higher they climb, the *less* likely they are to strongly agree that their strengths are daily in play. The organization's goal may be productive efficiency, rather than engaging workers' strengths, but the two often go hand in hand.

Buckingham and his colleague Donald Clifton say that the first step to a stronger organization is instituting a strengths-based selection system. Thus, as a manager, you would first identify a group of the most effective people in any role—the ones you'd want to hire more of—and compare their strengths to a group of the least effective people in that role. In defining these groups, you would try to measure performance as objectively as possible. In one Gallup study of more than 5000 telecommunications customer service representatives, those evaluated most favorably by their managers were strong in "harmony" and "responsibility," while those actually rated most effective by customers were strong in energy, assertiveness, and eagerness to learn. So if you discovered that your best software developers are analytical, disciplined, and eager to learn, you would want to focus employment ads less on experience than on the strengths that mark your successful software developers: "Do you take a logical and systematic approach to problem solving [analytical]? Are you a perfectionist who strives for timely completion of your projects [disciplined]? Do you want to learn to use SQL, Java, and Perl [learner]? If you can say yes to these questions, then please call. . . ."

Identifying people's strengths and matching strengths to work is a first step toward workplace effectiveness. Personnel managers use various tools to assess applicants' strengths and decide who is best-suited to the job. In Chapter 9, we discuss how psychologists assess candidates using ability tests. And in Chapter 12, we explore personality tests and "assessment centers" that enable observations of behaviors on simulated job tasks. For now, let's consider the job interview.

Do Interviews Predict Performance?

It takes only a few seconds for an employment interviewer to sense an applicant's animation, extraversion, warmth, and speaking voice. The speed with which we form impressions of others was shown after psychologist Frank Bernieri and his colleagues spent six weeks training two people in job-interviewing skills. The two interviewers then spent 15 to 20 minutes interviewing 98 volunteers of varied ages and evaluating each on a six-page form. Later, one of Bernieri's undergraduate students, Tricia Prickett, decided to see just how quickly impressions form (Prickett & others, 2000). She showed people 15-second clips of each applicant knocking on the door, coming in, shaking hands, and sitting down. Amazingly, after just 15 seconds the strangers were able to predict the interviewers' ratings of traits related to likability, self-assuredness, and competence. "The strength of the correlation was extraordinary," reflected Bernieri (2000). But do these first impressions lead to reliable assessments?

The Interviewer Illusion

Given how quickly they form impressions, interviewers understandably feel confident in their ability to predict long-term job performance from an unstructured, get-acquainted interview. What's shocking is how error-prone those predictions are. Whether predicting job or graduate school success, interviewers' judgments are weak predictors. From their review of 85 years of personnel selection research, I/O psychologists Frank Schmidt and John Hunter (1998; Schmidt, 2002) determined that for all but less-skilled jobs, general mental ability best predicts on-the-job performance. Subjective overall evaluations from informal interviews are better than handwriting analysis (which is worthless). But informal interviews are less informative than aptitude tests, work samples, job knowledge tests, and past job performance. If there's a contest between what our gut tells us about someone and what test scores, work samples, and past performance tell us, we should distrust our gut.

Interviewers often overrate their discernment, a phenomenon psychologist Richard Nisbett (1987) has labeled the *interviewer illusion*. "I have excellent interviewing skills, and so don't need reference checking as much as someone who doesn't have my ability to read people," is a comment sometimes heard by I/O consultants. Four interesting effects help create this gap between interviewers' intuition and the resulting reality:

- *Interviews disclose the interviewee's good intentions, which are less revealing than habitual behaviors* (Ouellette & Wood, 1998). Intentions matter. People can change. But the best predictor of the person we will be is the person we have been. Wherever we go, we take ourselves along.
- *Interviewers more often follow the successful careers of those they have hired than the successful careers of those they have rejected and lost track of.* This missing feedback enables interviewers to persuade themselves of their hiring ability.
- *Interviewers presume that people are what they seem to be in the interview situation.* As Chapter 15 explains, we discount the enormous influence of varying situations and mistakenly presume, when meeting others, that what we see is what we will get. But mountains of research on everything from chattiness to conscientiousness reveals that how we behave reflects not only our enduring traits, but the details of the particular situation (wanting to impress in a job interview).
- *Interviewers' preconceptions and moods color how they perceive interviewees' responses* (Cable & Gilovich, 1998; Macan & Dipboye, 1994). If we instantly like a person who perhaps is similar to ourselves, we may interpret the person's assertiveness as indicating "confidence" rather than "arrogance." When told randomly selected applicants have been prescreened, interviewers are disposed to judge them more favorably.

"Between the idea and reality . . . falls the shadow."

T. S. Eliot, "The Hollow Men"

▶ **structured interviews** interview process that asks the same job-relevant questions of all applicants, each of whom is rated on established scales.

So, gut feelings gleaned from unstructured interviews are only modestly predictive. An interview does provide a sense of someone's personality—their expressiveness, warmth, and verbal ability, for example. But this information reveals less about the person's behavior toward others in different situations than we tend to suppose. Hoping to improve prediction and selection, personnel psychologists have put people in simulated work situations (see page 455), scoured for information on past performance, aggregated evaluations from multiple interviews, administered tests, and developed job-specific interviews.

Structured Interviews

Unlike casual conversation aimed at getting a feel for someone, **structured interviews** offer a disciplined method of collecting information. A personnel psychologist may analyze a job, script questions, and train interviewers. The interviewers then put the same questions, in the same order, to all applicants, and rate each applicant on established scales.

In an *unstructured* interview, someone might ask, "How organized are you?" "How well do you get along with people?" or "How do you handle stress?" Street-smart applicants know how to score high: "Although I sometimes drive myself too hard, I handle stress by prioritizing and delegating, and by making sure I leave time for sleep and exercise."

By contrast, structured interviews pinpoint strengths (attitudes, behaviors, knowledge, and skills) that distinguish high performers in a particular line of work. The process then derives job-specific situations and asks candidates to explain how they would handle them, and how they handled similar situations in their prior employment. "Tell me about a time when you were caught between conflicting demands, without time to accomplish both. How did you handle that?"

To reduce memory distortions and bias, the interviewer takes notes and makes ratings as the interview proceeds and avoids irrelevant and follow-up questions. The structured interview therefore feels less warm, but that can be explained to the applicant: "This conversation won't typify how we relate to each other in this organization."

Michael Campion and his colleagues (1998) conclude that "one of the most strongly supported conclusions" from employment interview research is that "structuring the interview enhances its reliability and validity and, hence, its usefulness for prediction and decision making." Another review of 150 findings revealed that structured interviews had double the predictive accuracy of unstructured seat-of-the-pants interviews (Schmidt & Hunter, 1998; Wiesner & Cronshaw, 1988).

If, instead, we let our intuitions bias the hiring process, notes Malcolm Gladwell (2000), then "all we will have done is replace the old-boy network, where you hired your nephew, with the new-boy network, where you hire whoever impressed you most when you shook his hand. Social progress, unless we're careful, can merely be the means by which we replace the obviously arbitrary with the not so obviously arbitrary."

To recap, personnel psychologists assist organizations in analyzing jobs, recruiting well-suited applicants, selecting and placing employees, and, appraising their performance (**FIGURE B.2**)—the topic we turn to next.

figure B.2
Personnel psychologists' tasks
Personnel psychologists consult in human resource activities, from job definition to employee appraisal.

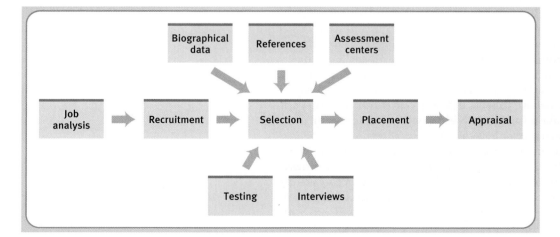

Appraising Performance

Performance appraisal serves organizational purposes: It helps decide who to retain, how to appropriately reward and pay people, and how to better harness their strengths, sometimes with job shifts or promotions. Performance appraisal also serves individual purposes: Its feedback affirms workers' strengths and helps motivate needed improvements.

Performance appraisal methods include

- *checklists* on which supervisors simply check behaviors that describe the worker ("always attends to customers' needs," "takes long breaks").
- *graphic rating scales* on which a supervisor checks the extent to which a worker is dependable, productive, and so forth.
- *behavior rating scales* on which a supervisor checks behaviors that best describe a worker's performance. If rating the extent to which a worker "follows procedures," the supervisor might mark the employee somewhere between "often takes shortcuts" and "always follows established procedures" (Levy, 2003).

In some organizations, performance feedback comes not only from supervisors but also from all organizational levels. If you join an organization that practices *360-degree feedback* you will rate yourself, your manager will rate you, you will rate your manager, and your peers and customers will rate you both (Green, 2002; **FIGURE B.3**). The net result is often more open communication and more complete appraisal.

Performance appraisal, like other social judgments, is vulnerable to bias (Murphy & Cleveland, 1995). *Halo errors* occur when one's overall evaluation of an employee, or of a trait such as their friendliness, biases ratings of their specific work-related behaviors, such as their reliability. *Leniency* and *severity errors* reflect evaluators' tendencies to be either too easy or too harsh on everyone. *Recency errors* occur when raters focus only on easily remembered recent behavior. By encouraging multiple raters and developing objective, job-relevant performance measures, personnel psychologists seek to support their organizations while also helping employees perceive the appraisal process as fair.

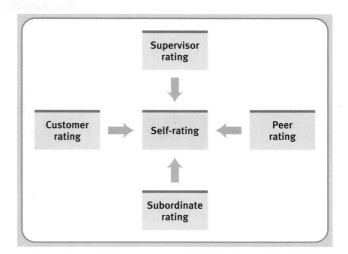

figure B.3
360-degree feedback With multisource 360-degree feedback, one's knowledge, skills, and behaviors are rated by self and surrounding others. Professors, for example, may be rated by their department chairs, their students, and their colleagues. After receiving all these ratings, professors discuss the 360-degree feedback with their department chair.

ORGANIZATIONAL PSYCHOLOGY

2. How do organizational psychologists help organizations to energize and direct people's behavior in the workplace?

The matching of talents to work, and the appraisal of work, matter. So does motivation. Organizational psychologists seek ways to engage and motivate ordinary people doing ordinary jobs.

Satisfaction and Engagement

Employee satisfaction is a priority concern for I/O psychologists because work is such a big part of life. Satisfaction with work feeds satisfaction with life. Moreover, decreased job stress feeds improved health (Chapter 11).

Does employee satisfaction also contribute to successful organizations? Positive moods at work do contribute to creativity, persistence, and helpfulness (Brief & Weiss, 2002). But are engaged, happy workers also less often absent? Less likely to quit? Less prone to theft? More punctual? More productive? Conclusive evidence of satisfaction's benefits is, some have said, the holy grail of I/O psychology. One statistical digest of prior research found a significant .30 correlation between

table B.1 The Gallup Workplace Audit

Overall Satisfaction—On a 5-point scale, where 5 is extremely satisfied and 1 is extremely dissatisfied, how satisfied are you with (Name of Company) as a place to work?

On a scale of 1 to 5, where 1 is strongly disagree and 5 is strongly agree, please indicate your agreement with the following items.

1. I know what is expected from me at work.
2. I have the materials and equipment I need to do my work right.
3. At work, I have the opportunity to do what I do best every day.
4. In the last seven days, I have received recognition or praise for doing good work.
5. My supervisor, or someone at work, seems to care about me as a person.
6. There is someone at work who encourages my development.
7. At work, my opinions seem to count.
8. The mission/purpose of my company makes me feel my job is important.
9. My associates (fellow employees) are committed to doing quality work.
10. I have a best friend at work.
11. In the last six months, someone at work has talked to me about my progress.
12. This last year, I have had opportunities at work to learn and grow.

Note: These statements are proprietary and copyrighted by The Gallup Organization. They may not be printed or reproduced in any manner without the written consent of The Gallup Organization. Reprinted here by permission.

individual job satisfaction and performance (Judge & others, 2001). Other studies find satisfaction associated with lower rates of lateness, absenteeism, and turnover (Blau, 1994; Horn & Griffeth, 1991; Sagie, 1998).

Positive data also come from the biggest-ever study, a recent analysis of Gallup data from more than 198,000 employees in nearly 8000 business units of 36 large companies (including some 1100 bank branches, 1200 stores, and 4200 teams or departments). James Harter, Frank Schmidt, and Theodore Hayes (2002) explored correlations between various measures of organizational success and *employee engagement*—the extent of workers' involvement, satisfaction, and enthusiasm. Engaged workers, as **TABLE B.1** indicates, say they know what's expected of them, have what they need to do their work, feel fulfilled in their work, have regular opportunities to do what they do best, perceive that they are part of something significant, and have opportunities to learn and develop.

The overall result: Business units with engaged employees have more loyal customers, less turnover, higher productivity, and greater profits. "Business units above the median on employee engagement had a 70 percent higher success rate than those below the median," reported the research team. Business units in the top quarter on employee engagement averaged about $100,000 more in monthly revenue. A separate analysis for a company with 275 retail stores found that annual turnover was 55 percent among stores whose employee engagement was in the top quarter, and 75 percent among stores with employees in the bottom quarter (Harter, 2000).

Engaged employees facilitate organizational success Best Buy's 400 electronic goods stores have nearly identical product layout and operations manuals. Yet some stores have much more engaged employees—and more profitable performance. The store with the highest engagement scores is in the top tenth of stores in having profits beyond budget. And the store with the least engaged employees is in the bottom tenth (Buckingham, 2001).

Capital-Journal/David Eulitt/AP/Wide World Photos

Managing Well

Every leader dreams of managing in ways that enhance people's satisfaction, engagement, and productivity and their organization's success. Effective leaders harness job-relevant strengths, set goals, and choose an appropriate leadership style.

Harnessing Job-Relevant Strengths

"The major challenge for CEOs over the next 20 years will be the effective deployment of human assets," observes Marcus Buckingham (2001). That challenge is "about psychology. It's about getting [individuals] to be more productive, more focused, more fulfilled than [they were] yesterday." To do so, he and others maintain, effective leaders want first to select the right people. Then, they aim to discern their employees' natural talents, adjust their work roles to suit their talents, and develop those talents into great strengths (**FIGURE B.4**). For example, should every college professor at a given school be expected to teach the same load, advise the same number of students, serve on the same number of committees, and engage in the same amount of research? Or should each person's job description be tailored to harness their unique strengths?

Managers who excel spend less time trying to instill talents that aren't there and more time developing and drawing out what is there. Rather than focus on people's weaknesses, and pack them off to training seminars to fix those problems, good managers revel in their employees' strengths. They focus training time on educating people about their strengths and building upon them (which means not promoting people into roles ill-suited to their strengths). They celebrate engaged and productive employees in every organizational role.

This positive psychology builds upon a basic principle of operant conditioning (Chapter 7): To teach a behavior, catch an organism doing something right and reinforce it. The best animal trainers for theme park performances and television attempt to find something the animal does naturally, catch the animal doing it, and give positive reinforcement. Whale trainers pay scant attention to mistakes, but give attention and rewards when the whale performs a desired behavior. These principles also apply to reinforcing employees. It sounds simple, but many managers are like parents who, when a child returns home with A grades, except for a D in Biology, focus on the D and ignore the A's.

Great managers build upon their employees' talents, concludes Kenneth Tucker (2002). Great managers

- start by helping people identify and measure their talents.
- match tasks to talents and then give people freedom to do what they do best.
- care how their people feel about their work.
- reinforce positive behaviors through recognition and reward.

Setting Specific, Challenging Goals

In study after study, people merely asked to do their best do not do so. But specific, challenging goals do motivate higher achievement, especially when combined with progress reports (Locke & Latham, 2002). Specific, measurable objectives, such as those you might set in planning your course work, serve to direct attention, promote effort, motivate persistence, and stimulate creative strategies. When people share in setting a goal and find the goal challenging yet attainable, reaching it boosts their self-evaluation (White & others, 1995). Moreover, when people state not only goals but also "implementation intentions"—action plans that specify when, where, and how they will march toward achieving those goals—they become more focused in their work and on-time completion becomes more likely (Koestner & others, 2002;

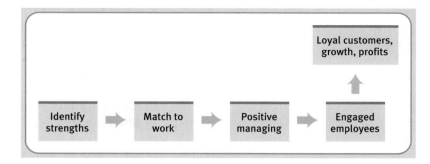

figure B.4
On the right path The Gallup Organization path to organizational success (adapted from Fleming, 2001).

Harnessing unique strengths
Great managers spend less time trying to train what got left out of someone than drawing out what got put in.

Chuck Savage/Corbis

Koole & Spijker, 2000). (Before beginning each new edition of this book, my editor and I "manage by objectives"—we agree on target dates for the completion of each chapter draft.) So, to motivate high productivity, effective leaders work with people to define explicit goals, elicit commitments to implementation plans, and provide feedback on progress.

Choosing an Appropriate Leadership Style

Leadership varies from a boss-focused directive style to a democratic style that empowers workers in setting goals and strategies. Which works best may depend on the situation and the leader. The best leadership style for leading a discussion may not be the best style for leading troops on a charge (Fiedler, 1981). Moreover, different leaders are suited to different styles. Some excel at **task leadership**—setting standards, organizing work, and focusing attention on goals. Being goal-oriented, task leaders are good at keeping a group centered on its mission. Typically, they have a directive style, which can work well if the leader is bright enough to give good orders (Fiedler, 1987).

Other managers excel at **social leadership**—mediating conflicts and building high-achieving teams (Evans & Dion, 1991). Social leaders often have a democratic style: They delegate authority and welcome the participation of team members. Many experiments show that social leadership is good for morale. Subordinates usually feel more satisfied and motivated when they can participate in decision making (Burger, 1987; Spector, 1986).

Because effective leadership styles vary with the situation and the person, the once-popular "great person" theory of leadership—that all great leaders share certain traits—now seems overstated. But a leader's personality does matter. Effective leaders of laboratory groups, work teams, and large corporations tend to exude a self-confident "charisma" (House & Singh, 1987; Shamir & others, 1993). Their charisma is a mix of a *vision* of some goal, an ability to *communicate* it clearly and simply, and enough optimism and faith in their group to *inspire* others to follow. Leadership of this kind—"transformational leadership"—motivates others to identify with and commit themselves to the group's mission.

Peter Smith and Monir Tayeb (1989) have compiled data from studies in India, Taiwan, and Iran indicating that effective managers—whether in coal mines, banks, or government offices—often exhibit a high degree of *both* task and social leadership. As achievement-minded people, effective managers certainly care about how well work is done, yet at the same time they are sensitive to their subordinates' needs.

Whether managers favor a directive approach or a participative-democratic approach depends, according to one classic leadership theory, on their assumptions about human motivation. Douglas McGregor (1960) identified two contrasting

> "Good leaders don't ask more than their constituents can give, but they often ask—and get—more than their constituents intended to give or thought it was possible to give."
>
> John W. Gardner, Excellence, 1984

views. **Theory X** managers assume that workers are basically lazy, error-prone, and extrinsically motivated by money. Thus, they need simple tasks, close monitoring, and incentives to work harder. **Theory Y** managers make very different assumptions—that people are intrinsically motivated to work for reasons beyond money—for example, to promote self-esteem, enjoy satisfying relations with others, and fulfill their potential. Thus, given enough freedom and challenge, employees will strive to demonstrate their competence and creativity. Theory Y managers are more likely to give employees control over work procedures, to welcome employee participation in decision making, and to have creative and satisfied subordinates (Deci & others, 1989). In one national survey of American workers, those in family-friendly organizations offering flexible-time hours reported feeling greater loyalty to their employers (Roehling & others, 2001).

Theory Y is one guiding force behind the contemporary move by many businesses to increase employee participation in making decisions, a management style common in Sweden and Japan and increasingly elsewhere (Naylor, 1990; Sundstrom & others, 1990). Although managers often think better of work they have directly supervised, studies reveal a "voice effect": If given a chance to voice their opinion during a decision-making process, people will respond more positively to the decision (van den Bos & Spruijt, 2002). And as we noted earlier, positive engaged employees are a mark of thriving organizations.

The rags-to-riches Harley-Davidson story illustrates the potential of inviting workers to participate in decision making (Teerlink & Ozley, 2000). In 1987, the struggling company began transforming its "command-and-control" management process to a "joint vision process." The aim: "To push decision-making, planning, and strategizing from a handful of people at the top, down throughout the organization. We wanted all the employees to think every day about how to improve the company," reports CEO Jeffrey Bleustein (2002). In the mid-1990s, Harley signed a cooperative agreement with its unions that included them "in decision-making in virtually every aspect of the business." Consensus decision-making can take longer, but "when the decision is made, it gets implemented quickly and the commitment is by the group," says Bleustein. The result is more engaged workers and also more satisfied stockholders. Every $1 of Harley-Davidson stock purchased in 1987 was, 15 years later, worth $150. In recognition of its soaring earnings and devoted customers, *Forbes* named Harley its 2002 Company of the Year.

We have considered *personnel* psychology (the I/O subfield that focuses on employee selection, placement, appraisal, and development). And we have considered *organizational* psychology (the I/O subfield that focuses on worker satisfaction and productivity and on organizational change). Finally, we turn to *human factors* psychology, which explores the human-machine interface.

Harley-Davidson's CEO, Jeffrey Bleustein

HUMAN FACTORS PSYCHOLOGY

3. How do human factors psychologists help create user-friendly technology?

I love our VCR, though I still haven't figured out how to make it "express record." Our stove is wonderful, except for the moments I spend puzzling over which control works which burner. The push-bar doors on our campus buildings are sturdy, though occasionally frustrating when I push the wrong end. The extra buttons on my phone are handy, though when transferring a call I still must look up which buttons to press.

Human factors psychologists study such technological puzzles to understand how people and machines interact. Psychologist Donald Norman (1988) suggests how simple design changes could reduce some of our frustrations. For example, by exploiting "natural mapping" we could design stove controls that require no labels

▶ **task leadership** goal-oriented leadership that sets standards, organizes work, and focuses attention on goals.

▶ **social leadership** group-oriented leadership that builds teamwork, mediates conflict, and offers support.

▶ **Theory X** assumes that workers are basically lazy, error-prone, and extrinsically motivated by money and, thus, should be directed from above.

▶ **Theory Y** assumes that, given challenge and freedom, workers are intrinsically motivated to achieve self-esteem and to demonstrate their competence and creativity.

figure B.5
Natural mapping (a) With traditionally positioned stove controls, a person must read the labels to figure out which knob works which burner. (b) By positioning the controls in a natural map, which the brain understands at a glance, we can eliminate the need to ponder written instructions just to boil water.

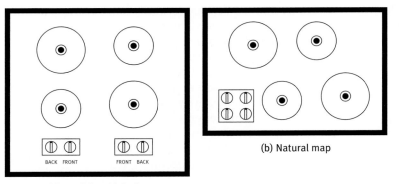

(a) Traditional labeling

(b) Natural map

(**FIGURE B.5**). ATM machines are internally more complex than VCRs, yet, thanks to human factor psychologists working with engineers, ATMs are easier to operate. TiVo has solved the TV recording problem with a simple point-and-click menu system ("record that one").

Norman (2001), who hosts a Web site (jnd.org) on designing equipment to fit people, bemoans the complexity of assembling his new high-definition TV, receiver, speakers, digital recorder, DVD player, VCR, and seven remotes into a usable home theater system. An MIT alumnus with a PhD, he notes, "I was VP of Advanced Technology at Apple. I can program dozens of computers in dozens of languages. I understand television, really, I do. . . . It doesn't matter: I am overwhelmed." If only the makers of home entertainment equipment would minimize cords and cables by bundling audio, visual, control, and power lines into a single cable. If only a single control could operate a point-and-click menu. If only engineers would routinely work with human factors psychologists to test their designs and instructions on average people.

Technology developers often suffer the "curse of knowledge," which leads them to assume that others share their knowledge (Camerer & others, 1989; Nickerson, 1999). The developers often mistakenly assume that what's clear to them will similarly be clear to others. (Recall from Chapter 1 that once we know an anagram's solution—WREAT → WATER—it seems that it should be obvious to others, too.) They realize others lack their expertise, yet they underestimate how confusing their explanations and instructions can be. When you know a thing, it's hard to mentally simulate what it's like not to know.

Understanding human factors can do more than enable us to design for reduced frustration; it can help avoid disaster. After beginning commercial flights in the late 1960s, the Boeing 727 was involved in several landing accidents caused by pilot error. Psychologist Conrad Kraft (1978) noted a common setting for these accidents: All took place at night, and all involved landing short of the runway after crossing a dark stretch of water or unilluminated ground. Kraft reasoned that, beyond the runway, city lights would project a larger retinal image if on a rising terrain. This would make the ground seem farther away than it was. By recreating these conditions in flight simulations, Kraft discovered that pilots were deceived into thinking they were flying safely, higher than their actual altitudes (**FIGURE B.6**). Aided by Kraft's finding, the airlines began requiring the co-pilot to monitor the altimeter—calling out altitudes during the descent—and the accidents diminished.

Today's Boeing psychologists are at work on other human factors problems (Murray, 1998): How should airlines best train and manage mechanics to reduce the maintenance errors that underlie about 50 percent of flight delays and 15 percent of accidents? What illumination and typeface would make on-screen flight data easiest to read? How would warning messages be most effectively worded—as an

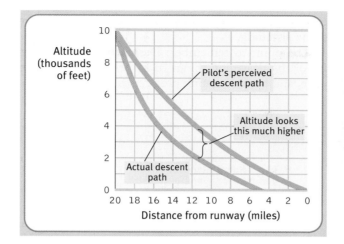

figure B.6
The human factor in misperception
Lacking distance cues when approaching a runway from over a dark surface, pilots simulating a night landing tended to fly too low. (From Kraft, 1978.)

action statement ("pull up") rather than a problem statement ("ground proximity")? In studying these and other issues, human factors psychologists strive to increase both safety and productivity.

As psychologists, their most powerful tool is research. If an organization wonders what sort of Web design (emphasizing content? speed? graphical features?) will most effectively draw in visitors and entice them to return, a human factors psychologist will want to test responses to several alternatives. If NASA wonders what sort of spacecraft design will best facilitate sleeping, work, and morale, their human factors psychologists will want to test the alternatives. If the designers of Palm Beach, Florida's "butterfly ballot" had not suffered the curse of knowledge in the 2000 presidential election—by assuming all voters would understand which hole to punch if they wished to vote for Al Gore—and had instead user-tested their ballot design, the United States might have elected a different president.

Consider, finally, the available "assistive listening" technologies in various auditoriums, churches, and theaters. One technology, commonly available in the United States, requires people with hearing loss to use a special device: a headset attached to a pocket-sized portable receiver that detects infrared or FM signals from the room's sound system. The well-meaning people who design, purchase, and install these systems correctly understand that the technology puts clear sound directly into the user's ears. But, alas, few people with hearing loss elect the hassle of checking out the system and the embarrassment of wearing a conspicuous headset. Most such units therefore sit unused in closets. Britain and the Scandinavian countries have instead installed "loop systems" that broadcast customized sound directly through a person's own hearing aids. A discrete touch of a switch can transform a suitably equipped hearing aid into an in-the-ear-loudspeaker. A loop system (a special amplifier attached to a wire encircling an audience) can also work in homes, enabling TV sound or phone conversation to broadcast directly through hearing aids (see www.hearingloop.org). When offered

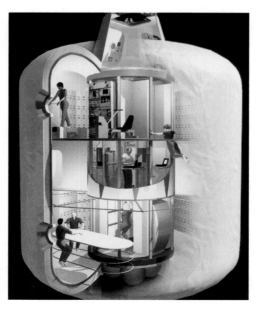

How not to go mad while going to Mars
Future astronauts headed to Mars will be confined in conditions of monotony, stress, and weightlessness for months on end. To help design and evaluate a workable human environment, such as this Transit Habitation (Transhab) Module, NASA engages human factors psychologists (Weed, 2001; Wichman, 1992).

convenient, inconspicuous, personalized sound, many more people elect to use assistive listening.

The point to remember: Designers and engineers should consider the human factor, by designing things to fit people, by being mindful of the curse of knowledge, and by user-testing products before production and distribution.

rehearse it!

B.1. Industrial/organizational psychologists apply psychology's concepts and methods to optimizing human behavior in the workplace. The three main divisions within I/O psychology are _____, _____, and _____ psychology.
  a. motivational; management; small group
  b. personnel; organizational; human factors
  c. motivational; personnel; human factors
  d. personnel; management; small group

B.2. People who view their work as a calling report the highest satisfaction with their work and with their lives. When engaged in their work, these people often experience _____, a focused state of consciousness, with diminished awareness of themselves and of time.
  a. stress   b apathy
  c. flow   d. facilitation

B.3. A personnel psychologist analyzed the tasks and responsibilities attached to the job of creative director in a Web design firm. The psychologist then scripted a set of questions that would be asked of all applicants. Then the firm's interviewers were trained to ask these questions, take notes, rate applicants' responses and avoid irrelevant follow-up questions. This personnel selection technique is known as a (an)

  a. structured interview.
  b. unstructured interview.
  c. performance appraisal checklist.
  d. behavior rating scale.

B.4. Performance appraisal helps organizations retain and reward workers and make the best use of their talents. It also gives feedback to employees on their individual performance. If you rate your own performance and your manager's, and your manager, your peers, and your customers rate your performance and your manager's, your organization is using
  a. flow procedure.
  b. graphic feedback.
  c. structured interviews.
  d. 360-degree feedback.

B.5. Task leadership is goal-oriented, whereas social leadership is group-oriented. Research indicates that effective managers exhibit
  a. only task leadership.
  b. only social leadership.
  c. both task and social leadership, depending on the situation and the person.
  d. task leadership for building teams and social leadership for setting standards.

B.6. Managers' assumptions about human motivation influence their management style and the extent to which they encourage employees to partici-

pate in decision making. _____ _____ managers assume that workers are basically lazy, error-prone, and extrinsically motivated by money. _____ managers assume that workers who are given challenges and freedom will be intrinsically motivated to achieve self-esteem and to demonstrate competence and creativity.
  a. Task leadership; social leadership
  b. Social leadership; task leadership
  c. Theory X; Theory Y
  d. Theory Y; Theory X

B.7. Human factors psychologists explore ways that machines and physical environments can be adapted to human behaviors to reduce users' frustration and to avoid accidents. One tendency these psychologists watch carefully is the "curse of knowledge," which is
  a. the idea that a little bit of knowledge is dangerous for the user.
  b. users' tendencies to override machines and resort to familiar habits.
  c. engineers' and designers' tendencies to assume that users are idiots and need overly detailed instructions.
  d. engineers' and designers' tendencies to assume that others share their knowledge.

Answers can be found in Appendix C.

appendix review

REVIEWING

Psychology at Work

For most people, work is a huge part of life. At its best, when work puts us in "flow," work can be satisfying and enriching. What, then, enables worker motivation, productivity, and satisfaction? I/O psychology studies behavior in the workplace through its primary subfields: personnel psychology, organizational psychology, and human factors psychology.

PERSONNEL PSYCHOLOGY

1. What tools and techniques do personnel psychologists use to marry the individual's strengths with the organization's needs?

Personnel psychologists aim to identify people's strengths and to match them with organizational tasks. Subjective interviews lead to quickly formed impressions, but they also frequently foster an illusory overconfidence in one's ability to predict employee success. Structured interviews, pinpointing job-relevant strengths, enhance interview reliability and validity. Personnel psychologists also assist organizations in appraisal that boosts organization, motivates individuals, and is welcomed as fair.

ORGANIZATIONAL PSYCHOLOGY

2. How do organizational psychologists help organizations to energize and direct people's behavior in the workplace?

To motivate employees to achieve, smart managers aim to create an engaged, committed, satisfied workforce. Effective leaders build on people's strengths, work with them to set specific and challenging goals, and adapt their leadership style to their situation.

HUMAN FACTORS PSYCHOLOGY

3. How do human factors psychologists help create user-friendly technology?

Human factors psychologists study how people perceive and use machines, and how machines and physical environments can be better suited to that use. Such studies have improved aircraft safety and have made many machines and technological devices less frustrating and easier to use.

TERMS AND CONCEPTS TO REMEMBER

flow, p. B-2

industrial-organizational (I/O) psychology, p. B-2

personnel psychology, p. B-2

organizational psychology, p. B-2

human factors psychology, p. B-2

structured interviews, p. B-6

task leadership, p. B-10

social leadership, p. B-10

Theory X, p. B-11

Theory Y, p. B-11

To continue your study and review of Psychology at Work, visit this book's Web site at www.worthpublishers.com/myers. You will find practice tests, review activities, and Web links for more information on topics related to Psychology at Work.

appendix C

Answers to Rehearse It and Critical Thinking Questions

Rehearse It Answer Key

1. d, 2. d, 3. a, 4. c, 5. b, 6. a, 7. d, 8. c, 9. a, 10. d, 11. c, 12. c, 13. c, 14. d, 15. b, 16. a, 17. c, 18. c, 19. c, 20. c, 21. c, 22. b, 23. b, 24. d.

Critical Thinker's Review Answer Key

1. Why do many psychologists try to consider questions or issues from more than one perspective? (psychological reasoning)

ANSWER: Narrowing one's focus to just one perspective can lead to incomplete answers to important questions. The various perspectives—neuroscience, evolutionary, behavior genetics, psychodynamic, behavioral, cognitive, and social-cultural—*complement* rather than contradict one another. Considering several perspectives on a question or an issue helps psychologists come up with more complete answers.

2. Matthew's friend asks, "Are you ready for the history test?" Matthew scans his notes and everything looks familiar, so he says, confidently, "Yes." However, Matthew's performance on the test is not impressive. What human tendency is Matthew displaying, and why is it important to study more than we think is needed? (practical problem solving)

ANSWER: Matthew has a classic and common case of overconfidence. Psychological research teaches us that we have a strong tendency to be more confident than correct. Keeping this in mind and overpreparing will help students do their best on tests.

3. Outside the community library, you are approached by a woman with what she claims is a survey on whether the city should hire an additional librarian. She says, "Do you agree that our city dollars should not be wasted on extraneous municipal staff positions?" What does the wording of this question tell you about what this woman hopes to accomplish? (perspective taking)

ANSWER: The wording of her question clearly indicates this woman is biased against the new hire. Asking immediately if you "agree," and using words such as "wasted" and "extraneous" are clear indicators that she has an agenda. She is not conducting a scientific survey in an effort to collect data on public opinion. Rather, she is attempting to sway public opinion toward her own perspective.

4. Here are three recently reported correlations, with interpretations drawn by journalists. Knowing just these correlations, can you come up with other possible explanations? (creative problem solving)

    a. Alcohol use is associated with violence.
      Journalists' interpretation: Drinking lowers inhibitions, unleashing aggressive behavior.

    b. Educated people live longer, on average, than less-educated people.
      Journalists' interpretation: Education lengthens life and enhances health.

c. Teens engaged in team sports use drugs, smoke, have sex, carry weapons, and eat junk food less often than teens who do not engage in team sports. *Journalists' interpretation:* Team sports encourage healthy living.

ANSWER:

a. Perhaps anger triggers drinking, or perhaps the same genes or environment predisposes both drinking and aggression. (In this case, researchers have found that drinking can indeed unleash aggressive behavior.)

b. Perhaps some third factor is responsible; perhaps richer people can afford more education *and* better health care. (Research supports *this* conclusion as well.)

c. Perhaps some third factor explains this correlation—teens who use drugs, smoke, have sex, carry weapons, and eat junk food may be "loners" who do not enjoy playing on any team or who have been rejected by their peers.

5. Why, when testing a new drug for blood pressure, would we learn more about its effectiveness from giving it to half of the participants in a group of 1000 than to all 1000 participants? (scientific problem solving)

ANSWER: To determine whether this drug is medically effective—not just serving as a placebo—we must compare its effect on those randomly assigned to receive it (the experimental condition) with those who receive a placebo (the control condition). The only difference between the groups is whether they received the actual drug. So, if blood pressure is lower in the experimental group, then we know that the drug itself has produced this effect, not just the participants' knowledge that they are being treated. (placebo effect)

6. In what ways does the field of psychology *fit* your preconceptions (what you expected when you signed up for the class) and in what ways has it surprised you so far? (pattern recognition)

ANSWER: Answers will vary.

CHAPTER 2   *Neuroscience and Behavior*

Rehearse It Answer Key

1. b, 2. b, 3. c, 4. d, 5. b, 6. c, 7. a, 8. b, 9. b, 10. c, 11. d, 12. a, 13. b, 14. d, 15. b, 16. c, 17. d, 18. d, 19. c, 20. c, 21. b, 22. c, 23. d, 24. b, 25. a, 26. b, 27. a, 28. a.

Critical Thinker's Review Answer Key

1. Knowing what you now know about the endorphin response, explain why the immediate pain you experience from a paper cut could possibly be greater than the pain from a terrible accident that severed your arm. (pattern recognition)

ANSWER: Endorphins are our naturally occurring painkillers. They are released in response to severe pain. Your body would not release endorphins in response to a minor injury such as a paper cut, so you would feel that pain, but endorphins would most likely be released in response to a severed arm. Endorphin response can make some severely injured people indifferent to pain.

2. One way researchers have learned about normal neurotransmitter functioning is by introducing a non-natural substance, such as the drug morphine, and watching where it goes in our body. What might researchers learn from watching this process? (scientific problem solving)

ANSWER: If an introduced drug, such as morphine, is taken up by receptor sites in our bodies and has an effect (in this case, elevating mood and easing pain), then researchers can assume we have naturally occurring feel-good neurotransmitters that normally occupy those receptor sites. Otherwise, the sites would not be there.

3. **Imagine that you are a neuroscientist, and you are trying to help a right-handed man whose neural deficiency seems to be preventing him from successfully using a fork. Describe for your patient and his family how the information would normally flow through the various parts of his nervous system. (practical problem solving)**

   ANSWER: The left hemisphere of your patient's brain would normally activate and guide the muscles of his right arm and hand via his peripheral nervous system's motor neurons. As he picked up the fork, his brain would also process the information from his sensory nervous system, enabling it to continue to guide the fork to his mouth.

4. **What information could a neuroscientist working with the patient in Question 3 acquire from a single MRI scan of the patient's brain? Why might a functional MRI be a more useful technique in this case? (psychological reasoning)**

   ANSWER: A single MRI scan would produce a detailed picture of the brain's soft tissues at one moment in time, which might disclose structural defects but would not reveal how the brain is functioning. A functional MRI would be more useful because it would provide a series of photos taken less than a second apart, offering more specific information about what is happening, or not happening, in the patient's brain when he attempts to use a fork.

5. **Imagine that you lost a thumb. What would happen in your sensory cortex in response to this change? How would you experience the sensory cortex change? (perspective taking)**

   ANSWER: If your sensory cortex was no longer receiving input from your missing thumb, the adjacent regions of the sensory cortex would become more sensitive in response. You might have increased sensitivity in the tissue (for example, a finger) that transmits to those adjacent regions.

6. **Geniene is having trouble speaking. We know her problem is not an inability to speak, because when someone tells her what to say, she can repeat it with reasonable accuracy. However, she is unable to read aloud. Besides the inability to read aloud, Geniene appears to have normal vision. What two areas in Geniene's brain may be causing her problem? (creative problem solving)**

   ANSWER: Geniene cannot translate words on a printed page to spoken words, so she appears to be having trouble in her angular gyrus and/or her Wernicke's area, where written words are processed. Since she is able to speak normally, she seems not to have problems in her Broca's area or motor cortex.

CHAPTER 3 *The Nature and Nurture of Behavior*

Rehearse It Answer Key

1. c, 2. b, 3. c, 4. c, 5. b, 6. b, 7. b, 8. a, 9. c, 10. b, 11. b, 12. d, 13. b, 14. c.

Critical Thinker's Review Answer Key

1. **Whose explanation of gender differences in sexuality do you find most persuasive—that of evolutionary psychologists or their critics? Now switch gears completely and write a few persuasive lines about the explanation with which you are least likely to align yourself. Do you still feel as strongly opposed to that perspective? (perspective taking)**

   ANSWER: Evolutionary psychologists explain that our sexuality is driven by our ancestors' drive for reproductive success, and that over time natural selection would have favored people whose traits helped them to reproduce and care for their offspring. They believe this helps explain why men tend to mate more widely, and to be more attracted to youthful features in women that suggest reproductive capacity, and why women tend to mate more selectively and to prefer mature, dominant, bold, and affluent men—all of whom could presumably provide protection and resources for children. The critics of the evolutionary perspective take issue with such hindsight explanations and point out exceptions to these tendencies, such as other members of the primate family in which females mate with numerous males. They also emphasize the effects of cultural expectations on our behaviors, noting that we are not "hard-wired."

2. How might behavior geneticists investigate the heritability of intelligence with sets of identical twins raised together and sets of fraternal twins raised together? (scientific problem solving)

ANSWER: Behavior geneticists studying the heritability of intelligence would be interested in determining the extent to which variation in intelligence levels among individuals can be attributed to their differing genes. First, they would collect and compare data on the intelligence levels of the identical twins raised together. Second, they would collect and compare data on the intelligence levels of the fraternal twins raised together. Finally, they would compare the similarity in intelligence levels of the identical twins with the similarity in intelligence levels of the fraternal twins. If the intelligence levels of the identical twins are significantly more similar than the intelligence levels of the fraternal twins (which is what researchers have, indeed, found), then we can infer that there is significant heritability of this trait.

3. Steven is a third-grader who for his age is very large, strong, and "tough" looking. However, Steven has a sweet, sensitive personality. Use the concept of genetic and environmental interaction to explain how Steven could be drawn into a group of bullies in his school. (psychological reasoning)

ANSWER: The outward appearance dictated by Steven's genes—a big, tough-looking kid—is going to affect how his classmates perceive him. They will expect him to be tough, and the school bullies may expect him to be "one of them." Steven's own tendencies toward sweetness may very well win over, but he may struggle with how people react to him.

4. Many researchers have recently concluded that the shared home environment has less effect on children's development than is often supposed, and that peer influences matter more than we realized. What evidence supports that conclusion? (practical problem solving)

ANSWER: Despite sharing the same home, adopted siblings vary nearly as widely in personalities and abilities as do children paired at random. Although children may pick up manners and values from their home environments, peer influences definitely matter. Here are two possible examples from research results: (1) When parents speak with one accent and peers with another, children will inevitably adopt the accent of their peers. (2) Teens tend to pick up the smoking habit from friends and not from parents.

5. Why are so few women worldwide in top leadership positions? Use what you have learned about the nature and nurture of gender to try to explain this phenomenon. (creative problem solving)

ANSWER: Men's physiology does make them somewhat more likely to be dominant and aggressive. This could partly explain their greater presence in top leadership roles. However, cultural effects and gender role expectations probably play a larger role. We know gender roles are *not* biologically predetermined, because in some societies boys and girls receive essentially the same upbringing and later experience little division of labor by gender.

6. James states that our evolutionary heritage has fixed our gender-specific behaviors. He claims "guys can't help being jerks who run around in search of one-night stands." His friend Charlie retorts that humans have exhibited dramatic behavior variations across cultures and over time. Explain why Charlie's argument counters James' statement. (pattern recognition)

ANSWER: Humans have indeed exhibited wildly different behaviors *across cultures* and *over time*. Across cultures, Europeans expect eye contact, Asians find it offensive. In some nomadic food-gathering cultures, women and men share work roles; in industrialized cultures, work is divided along gender lines. Over time, U.S. women in Victorian times would not bare an ankle; young women today select undergarments knowing that they will be partly revealed by fashionable clothing. If our behavior can change according to our environment, then it is not solely dictated by our genetic or evolutionary history.

CHAPTER 4 *The Developing Person*

Rehearse It Answer Key

1. b, 2. c, 3. a, 4. a, 5. b, 6. c, 7. b, 8. d, 9. d, 10. a, 11. b, 12. b, 13. c, 14. b, 15. d, 16. c, 17. d, 18. b, 19. b, 20. a, 21. d, 22. d, 23. c, 24. b, 25. b.

Critical Thinker's Review Answer Key

1. Your friend—a heavy smoker—hopes to become pregnant soon. She says she will stop smoking as soon as she learns she is pregnant. What can you tell her to convince her that the time to stop smoking is before she is pregnant? (psychological reasoning)

> *ANSWER:* Cigarette smoke is a *teratogen*—an agent that can reach the embryo or fetus during prenatal development and cause harm. The most harmful effects of teratogens occur during the first trimester of pregnancy, often before a woman even knows she is pregnant. So, the time to quit smoking is before there is a chance that the pregnancy has begun.

2. Ugandan babies tend to begin walking at an earlier age than babies of European descent. Researchers have presumed that this difference is a product of the infants' nurture. Others might wonder if credit should instead go to their genetically predisposed nature. How might we test these alternatives? (scientific problem solving)

> *ANSWER:* As Chapter 3 suggested, we can evaluate nature's and nurture's relative contributions by allowing one to vary while the other remains constant. In the absence of twin studies one might, for example, compare the age of walking of Ugandan babies raised in Uganda with that of Ugandan babies raised in Europe. Or, within Uganda, one might compare the walking age of similarly reared infants of European and Ugandan ancestry.

3. How do Piaget's first three stages of cognitive development explain why young children are *not* just miniature adults in the way they think? (creative problem solving)

> *ANSWER:* Infants in the *sensorimotor stage* tend to be focused only on their own perceptions of the world and may, for example, be unaware that objects continue to exist when unseen. A *preoperational* child is still egocentric (unable to take another's point of view) and incapable of appreciating simple logic, such as the reversibility of operations. A preteen in the *concrete operational stage* is beginning to think logically about concrete events but not about abstract concepts.

4. To predict whether a teenager smokes marijuana, you can ask how many of the teen's friends smoke it. One explanation for this correlation is peer influence. What's another? (perspective taking)

> *ANSWER:* There may also be a *selection effect*. Adolescents tend to sort themselves into like-minded groups—the jocks, the geeks, the druggies, and so forth. Those who smoke pot may similarly seek out other teenagers who also smoke it.

5. Jacintha would like to study adult memory in university professors. She is considering a longitudinal study, in which the same people are restudied and retested over a long period of time. She would need to test the professors repeatedly over the next 30 years. However, she is not sure she wants to spend 30 years completing this study! What approach could Jacintha use instead that would allow her to complete this study much more quickly? (pattern recognition)

> *ANSWER:* Jacintha could use the cross-sectional approach, in which people of different ages are compared with one another. So, she would instead study university professors of many different ages and compare their results.

6. **Mr. Johnson, a counselor at a nearby high school, is trying hard to help students deal with the recent, tragic death of a classmate. Mr. Johnson is convinced that the students must all express their grief openly, and go through several specific stages of grieving, before they will be "healed." Some of the students he's trying to help seem to be feeling worse than ever. What can you tell Mr. Johnson that might help him deal with the students more effectively? (practical problem solving)**

> *ANSWER:* Research has shown that the normal range of grieving responses is much wider than Mr. Johnson supposes. For example, those who express their grief openly do not overcome their sadness more quickly than those who grieve privately, and there are no predictable stages through which grieving people can be expected to pass on the path to healing. Mr. Johnson would therefore be wise to address each student's needs individually.

CHAPTER 5 *Sensation and Perception*

Rehearse It Answer Key

1. d, 2. b, 3. b, 4. d, 5. b, 6. d, 7. b, 8. c, 9. c, 10. b, 11. a, 12. d, 13. b, 14. a, 15. b, 16. c, 17. a, 18. c, 19. d, 20. c, 21. d, 22. b, 23. c, 24. c, 25. a, 26. c, 27. b, 28. d, 29. a.

Critical Thinker's Review Answer Key

1. **For the purposes of this book, we discuss sensation and perception separately, but in reality the distinction is hazy. What is the rough distinction between sensation and perception, and why is it considered hazy? (psychological reasoning)**

> *ANSWER:* Sensation refers to the bottom-up process by which the physical sensory system receives and represents stimuli. Perception refers to the top-down mental process of organizing and interpreting the sensory input. In everyday life, these two processes blend imperceptibly, as, for example, when we instantaneously interpret the pitch and tone of a voice on the phone saying the one syllable "Hi!" and recognize that it is Mom.

2. **Olivia is the director of a children's choir that is barely scraping by financially. She really needs to raise the yearly tuition from $500 to $750, but she doesn't want to lose families in the process. Keeping in mind Weber's law, how would you suggest she accomplish her goals? (creative problem solving)**

> *ANSWER:* We have learned from Weber's law that a difference will not be perceived unless it varies by a certain proportion. If she can manage it, Olivia would be wise to raise the yearly tuition gradually over several years—perhaps adding $35 per year—until she reaches her target amount. That way the difference will not be perceived as too dramatic.

3. **Deirdre is intensely interested in the sense of smell. She often talks about how many of her memories are connected to smells, and she claims that smell is more complex than our senses of vision, touch, or taste. How might she support this claim—how is smell different from these other senses? (scientific problem solving)**

> *ANSWER:* We have three types of color receptors (red, green, and blue), four basic touch senses (pressure, warmth, cold, and pain), and four basic taste sensations (sweet, sour, salty, bitter). But we have no basic smell receptors. Instead, 1000 odor receptors, individually and in combination, recognize some 10,000 discernible odors.

4. **John has completely color-deficient vision. What sorts of dangers and challenges does this present in his daily life? (perspective taking)**

> *ANSWER:* People with normal color vision sometimes do not realize how many color cues they use each day. John has to be careful when selecting food in buffet lines or at the grocery store—especially when it is wrapped in plastic and he cannot rely on his sense of smell. Without color vision, he will not see discolored meat or spots of green mold on cheese. Interpreting traffic lights

can also be problematic, especially if they are more elaborate than the traditional three vertical circles (for example, with left-turn green/red arrows) and if he is first in line at the light (and cannot take his cue from other drivers). Other daily challenges include selecting matching clothes.

5. How does the study of illusions inform our understanding of normal perceptions? (pattern recognition)

ANSWER: Perceptual illusions reveal the ways we organize and interpret sensory information. Our occasional misperceptions demonstrate the workings of our normally effective perceptual processes. For example, the perceived relationship between distance and size is generally valid, but under special circumstances it can lead us astray—as when it helps create the moon illusion.

6. Tatiana and Ariana watch a television show with lions hunting zebras. Tatiana is upset at the carnage, while Ariana is matter-of-fact about the life-feeds-on-life principle. How could context and perceptual set have affected their very different points of view? (practical problem solving)

ANSWER: The *context* in which the two women are watching the show would definitely affect the way they perceive its content. If Tatiana had a day full of sad news, she may be more likely to be upset by the program. Tatiana and Ariana will also be affected by *perceptual set*—our mental disposition to perceive one thing and not another. Perhaps Ariana was raised in a family that viewed the world through a more scientific lens than Tatiana's family, for example.

CHAPTER 6 *States of Consciousness*

Rehearse It Answer Key

1. c, 2. a, 3. a, 4. b, 5. b, 6. d, 7. c, 8. d, 9. d, 10. a, 11. c, 12. a, 13. c, 14. c, 15. c, 16. a, 17. d, 18. c, 19. d, 20. c, 21. a, 22. b.

Critical Thinker's Review Answer Key

1. Your friend Jake is intently watching TV in the next room. You call out "Mind if I eat the last cookie?" There is no response, so you eat it. Jake is later angry, because he insists that you never asked. How can you show Jake that "selective attention" really exists? (scientific problem solving)

ANSWER: You might tell Jake about the incredible "change blindness" experiments that had subjects so intently focused on responding to a request for directions that they did not even notice a new person standing in the place of the original questioner! (See Figure 6.2.) You could point out that Jake must have been so focused on the TV show that he did not hear your voice, and that we are capable of focusing our attention on only a few of the myriad of visual, auditory, and other stimuli bombarding us.

2. Eliza shows classic signs of sleep deprivation. She has a hard time concentrating, and she often falls asleep during even the most interesting lectures. She claims she gets plenty of sleep, yet she always has to set her alarm and often hits the "snooze" button several times before getting out of bed in the morning. She drinks a lot of cola at night while studying, because she says it quenches her thirst. She also regularly works out at night before going to bed. And her bedtimes and wake-up times fluctuate wildly throughout the week. Based on what you've learned from reading about sleep research, what changes would you recommend to Eliza so that she can feel more alert during the day? (practical problem solving)

ANSWER: Eliza should try to get to bed and wake up at the same time every day. Research shows that a regular sleep schedule can help people feel more energetic during the day. Eliza should also avoid drinking caffeinated beverages such as cola at night, because caffeine is a stimulant that can interfere with sleep. Exercising regularly helps us sleep better, but exercising too late in the day can interfere with sleep. She would do better to exercise in the morning or afternoon. If she has to wake to an alarm every day, Eliza may also not be getting *enough* sleep. She should try going to bed earlier each night.

3. Karena is convinced she is suffering from narcolepsy. She has a tendency to fall asleep at what she considers inopportune times, such as late at night while watching TV with friends, or when she's in the library trying to study. When she falls asleep—leaning back on the couch or with her head on her desk—she is hard to awaken. She says she often begins dreaming during these "naps." What questions do we need to ask of Karena to help her determine whether she is truly suffering from narcolepsy? What else could be causing her to nod off? (pattern recognition)

ANSWER: We need to ask Karena how much sleep she is getting, and what quality of sleep she is getting. For example, is her home in a rowdy dormitory, where noise levels wake her up intermittently throughout the night? If she is extremely sleep-deprived, or is experiencing disrupted sleep, she would be more likely to fall asleep during quiet times, and she could experience REM rebound—the tendency for REM sleep to increase following REM sleep deprivation. Karena's symptoms do not seem to indicate narcolepsy, which would be marked by brief sleep periods (usually less than 5 minutes each) rather than long naps, and sleep onset at emotionally intense times rather than quiet, sleepy times.

4. Byron was not doing well in his university courses, and he had a hard time mustering the energy to get out of bed each day. A friend suggested he see a hypnotist to help uncover and resolve the inner conflicts she is sure are disrupting his functioning. After several sessions, Byron became convinced he had been abducted by aliens, who landed on his rooftop in their spaceship and performed painful medical procedures on him. He is understandably upset and, because he worries the aliens will come back, he cannot sleep at night. What can you tell Byron about hypnosis and recall of forgotten events that will help dispel his fears? (perspective taking)

ANSWER: You could tell Byron that although you can only imagine how terrified he must feel, hypnosis is really not a magic window into our past, but is simply a state of heightened suggestibility—a condition in which we are more likely to take someone's suggestions. This can be beneficial, as when hypnosis is used for pain control, or highly damaging, as when a hypnotist's beliefs work their way into a subject's recollections and create false memories. You could reassure Byron that, although he is in the company of thousands of others who have supposedly recovered such memories of abduction, there is no scientific evidence that such abductions have ever occurred.

5. A U.S. government survey of 27,616 current or former alcohol drinkers found that 40 percent of those who began drinking before age 15 grew dependent on alcohol. The same was true of only 10 percent of those who first imbibed at ages 21 or 22 (Grant & Dawson, 1998). What possible explanations can you think of for this correlation between early use and later abuse? (creative problem solving)

ANSWER: Possible explanations include (1) a biological predisposition to both early use and later abuse, (2) brain changes and taste preferences induced by early use, and (3) enduring habits, attitudes, activities, and/or peer relationships that are conducive to alcohol use.

6. Your parents lecture you about not drinking and driving, but then they often drive themselves home after having several drinks with friends. When you point out this inconsistency, they tell you that they are older and can "handle it" better than a young adult. Using what you now know about the physiological effects of alcohol, explain why this is not true. (psychological reasoning)

ANSWER: It is true that most older adults have been driving longer than younger adults, and so may have to focus less energy and attention on the task. Yet alcohol has the same physiological effects regardless of age. Alcohol slows the sympathetic nervous system, which lowers inhibitions, slows reaction time, causes deterioration of skilled performance, reduces the ability to make good judgments, and focuses attention on immediate rather than long-term consequences. Even those who have developed a "tolerance" for alcohol will experience these same physiological effects, all of which will make for a much more dangerous driver.

CHAPTER 7 *Learning*

Rehearse It Answer Key

1. c, 2. c, 3. a, 4. b, 5. d, 6. b, 7. b, 8. d, 9. c, 10. a, 11. b, 12. b, 13. c, 14. b, 15. d, 16. a, 17. a, 18. c, 19. c.

Critical Thinker's Review Answer Key

1. Holden is feeling somewhat lonely during his first week away at college. While unpacking his things, he finds his dog's old toy at the bottom of his duffle bag. The smell of the toy brings to mind many happy times playing with his dog at home and makes him feel better. Why does Holden feel better? Would Holden's roommate also feel better if he smelled the toy? Use the terminology you've learned in this chapter to explain. (pattern recognition)

ANSWER: Holden has associated the smell of playing with his dog to the feeling of being happy and loved. This is classical conditioning. The unconditioned stimulus (UCS) is playing with the dog. The unconditioned response (UCR) is feeling accepted and loved. The conditioned stimulus (CS) is the smell of the dog's toy, which, after being present many, many times with actual playing with the dog, has come to trigger the conditioned response (CR) of feeling accepted and loved. The smell of the toy would most likely *not* make Holden's roommate feel better, unless he also has learned to associate dog smells with happy times.

2. Two-year-old Antonia received a painful hornet sting in the ear. Now she is terribly afraid of all flying bugs, including flies and mosquitoes. Use principles of conditioning to explain Antonia's fears and to suggest what her parents might do to help her overcome them. (practical problem solving)

ANSWER: Antonia was classically conditioned—through just one painful incident—to associate pain with hornets. The UCS is the sting, the UCR is pain, the CS is flying hornets, and the CR is fear. That fear has been *generalized* to include all flying bugs. Her parents could help her learn to *discriminate* between hornets and the more harmless varieties of flying insects to lessen her fears. Time will also help, as long as she does not receive another sting, because her fears will eventually extinguish if the CS (flying insects) is repeatedly presented without the UCS (painful sting).

3. Ian has learned about positive reinforcement in his psychology course, and he would like to use this technique to help his two school-aged sons develop good study habits. Ian decides that after each son finishes his homework, he will be allowed to watch television. This seems to be working for his older son, who works hard for this privilege, but not for his younger son, who doesn't seem to care about the television but does seem to enjoy his father's frequent visits to his room to check on his homework progress. Why aren't the younger son's study habits being improved by Ian's efforts? Use principles of operant conditioning to explain. (perspective taking)

ANSWER: A reinforcer is any event that increases the frequency of a preceding response. Our interests, experiences, and personalities all affect what we find reinforcing, and sometimes the same event is reinforcing to one person and not to another. Ian's efforts to condition more focused homework completion—using TV watching as a reinforcer—will be successful *only* if his sons consider TV watching desirable. Watching television is something the older son wants to be able to do, and his homework efforts seem to have improved accordingly. However, Ian may actually be reinforcing his younger son for NOT finishing his homework! The younger son seems to find Dad's visits to the room where he is working much more reinforcing than TV!

4. Five-year-old Thomas has already gotten into trouble several times at his new school for hitting his classmates. Whenever things don't go his way, he

lashes out physically. When the teacher discusses the problem with Thomas' parents, she learns that the parents often use physical punishment at home but feel it's "not working." They are eager to help change Thomas' disruptive behaviors. What research results might the teacher offer to help Thomas' parents modify his behavior? (creative problem solving)

> *ANSWER:* The teacher might explain to Thomas' parents that physical punishment often increases aggressiveness in children by demonstrating that aggression is a way to cope with problems. She could also explain that although punishment of any kind may suppress unwanted behavior, the effects are often only temporary—the child learns to avoid that behavior only while in the presence of the one doling out the punishment. The teacher could tell Thomas' parents that it may be more effective to try to guide Thomas toward more desirable behavior by reinforcing appropriate behaviors. Catching him doing something right and rewarding him for it may help increase the desirable behaviors.

5. Lily has an idea for her thesis paper in psychology. She has noticed wildly varying scores on the vocabulary portion of her city's schools' standardized testing of 12-year-olds. She wonders whether teaching styles—specifically views on *latent learning* of vocabulary, the idea that children expand their vocabulary naturally while reading many different types of literature and seeing new words in context—may be related in any way to those scores. She knows that some city schools believe in latent learning of vocabulary. Other schools believe children will broaden their vocabulary only by doing specific exercises that drill them on the meaning of lists of vocabulary words. How might Lily test whether these two different ways of learning are related to the standardized test scores? (scientific problem solving)

> *ANSWER:* Lily might create a list of the schools that rely on latent learning, and a second list of the schools that do not. Then she could examine the test scores from the students at those schools to see if either method leads to higher vocabulary scores (higher than expected, relative to smaller score differences in other academic abilities).

6. Jason's parents and older friends all smoke, but they advise him not to. Juan's parents and friends don't smoke, but they say nothing to deter him from doing so. Who will be more likely to start smoking, Jason or Juan? (psychological reasoning)

> *ANSWER:* Although both saying and doing can influence people, experiments suggest that children more often do as others do and say as they say. Generalizing this finding to smoking, we can expect that Jason will be more likely to start smoking.

CHAPTER 8 *Memory*

Rehearse It Answer Key

> 1. b, 2. a, 3. b, 4. a, 5. d, 6. c, 7. b, 8. c, 9. c, 10. b, 11. a, 12. a, 13. d, 14. a, 15. d, 16. d, 17. d, 18. c, 19. a, 20. b, 21. c.

Critical Thinker's Review Answer Key

1. In a week, you will be expected to participate in a graded discussion of key historical figures in your World History class. What strategy could you employ to learn and retain information about these people so that you are ready by next week? What might you do to make sure you retain this information beyond next week? (practical problem solving)

> *ANSWER:* You could, for example, make the names and life details personally meaningful—relating what you are learning to your own life. This will make it all much more memorable. To ensure long-term retention, you should overlearn this information by going over your notes repeatedly, and spacing your rehearsals over the course of several weeks rather than cramming them too close together.

2. Your friend tells you that her brother, Brad, was in a car accident six months ago, and his neurologist told the family that Brad's hippocampus was severely damaged and he would no longer be able to form new memories of events, images,

or names. Your friend has noticed that Brad has learned to do a new jigsaw puzzle, and that his skill at using an exercise bike in his physical therapy class is steadily improving. She wonders if this is evidence that the neurologist's diagnosis was wrong. What can you tell your friend? (pattern recognition)

> *ANSWER:* Unfortunately, Brad's memory of skills is not evidence that his hippocampus is still functioning. The hippocampus is a limbic system structure essential to the formation of *explicit* memories—those in which we recall facts and personally experienced events. The cerebellum and other ancient brain areas process *implicit* memories of skills and procedures, such as doing jigsaw puzzles and riding a bike.

3. **Your biology instructor favors fill-in-the-blank tests; your psychology instructor uses nothing but multiple-choice questions. In which class might it be easier to do well on the tests? Explain. (psychological reasoning)**

> *ANSWER:* It may be easier to do well on the psychology tests, because multiple-choice questions are based on recognition, which requires only that you identify things you have previously learned. The biology tests may be harder, because they require recall—retrieving from your memory bank information you hopefully learned earlier in your studying.

4. **After Shonte's store is robbed at gunpoint, she is asked to go to the police department to identify possible suspects. When she sees the lineup of men who supposedly fit the description she gave after the robbery, she really isn't sure which one of them did it. She points to a man on the far left and says, "I think it might have been him." The attending officer responds, "He *does* look like a criminal, doesn't he?! That's great, you got him. Nice work." Later in court, Shonte *confidently* testifies that she's sure the man she identified in the lineup was the culprit. However, DNA evidence contradicts Shonte's eyewitness testimony. Using what you know about memory construction, explain how Shonte's confidence level about identifying the suspect could have changed so dramatically. (perspective taking)**

> *ANSWER:* The police officer fueled the *misinformation effect* by making supportive comments about Shonte's initial, tentative identification. Shonte incorporated this misleading information into her own memory of the event, remembering that she had been much more confident about identifying the suspect than she actually was.

5. **What would happen if we had perfect memories? What might life be like if we remembered *all* our waking experiences and *all* our dreams? (creative problem solving)**

> *ANSWER:* Given the commonality of source amnesia, we would confuse real experiences with dreams. When meeting someone, we might therefore be unsure whether we were reacting to something they previously did or to something we dreamed they did. William Dement (1999, p. 298) thinks this "would put a great burden on your sanity. . . . I truly believe that the wall of memory is a blessed protection." We also would remember much useless information, such as old phone numbers and previous checkbook balances.

6. **Your friend Casey tells you she is sure she is ready for the big chemistry test. She says she doesn't need to take the self-test at the end of the chapter, because she has looked through her notes many times, and everything looks very familiar. Why might Casey not be ready for the test? Explain. (scientific problem solving)**

> *ANSWER:* Casey needs to work through the self-test, or have a friend test her, as well as read through her notes to be sure she is ready for the test. We are easily lulled into thinking we are prepared because we *recognize* material we have learned (reading our notes). Taking the self-test will test Casey's *recall* of information and will also help determine the gaps in her knowledge so she can focus her study time appropriately.

CHAPTER 9 *Thinking, Language, and Intelligence*

Rehearse It Answer Key

1. a, 2. b, 3. c, 4. d, 5. b, 6. d, 7. c, 8. d, 9. b, 10. a, 11. b, 12. a, 13. d, 14. c, 15. c, 16. b, 17. d, 18. c, 19. b, 20. a, 21. c, 22. c.

Critical Thinker's Review Answer Key

1. **Your cousin Sam is a 22-year-old smoker who has refused to fly since the U.S. terrorist attacks of 9/11. Instead he drives himself on long road trips. What could you say to Sam to explain why his risk assessment doesn't make sense? (perspective taking)**

> *ANSWER:* We all have to work to think smart about risks. We fear what our ancestral history has prepared us to fear, including heights and confinement (and therefore flying). Our ancestors did not have the opportunity to develop a fear of cars or cigarettes, both of which are far more dangerous to us today. We also fear what we cannot control, including being flown by someone else rather than being behind the wheel ourselves, though statistically we are far more likely to die in a car accident than in a plane crash. We fear what is immediate—what may happen right now if we fly (probably nothing)—rather than what is more likely to happen to us in the long-term—death or illness in 20 years if we keep smoking. Finally, we fear what is readily available in our memories, such as a crashing plane, rather than some distant image of a winded smoker struggling up a flight of stairs.

2. **If children are not yet even speaking, would they nevertheless benefit from having parents and other caregivers read to them? (creative problem solving)**

> *ANSWER:* Indeed they would, because well before age 1 children are learning to detect words among the stream of spoken sounds and to discern grammatical rules. Before age 1 they also are babbling with the phonemes of their own language. More than many parents realize, their infants are soaking up language. As researcher Peter Jusczyk reminds us, "Little ears are listening."

3. **If your dog barks at a stranger at the front door, does this qualify as *language?* What if the dog yips in a telltale way to let you know she needs to go out? (pattern recognition)**

> *ANSWER:* These are definitely communications. But if language is words and how we combine them grammatically to communicate meaning, few scientists would label a dog's barking and yipping as language.

4. **Joseph is a student at Harvard Law School. He carries a straight-A average, writes a small column for the *Harvard Law Review,* and will be working for a Supreme Court Justice the year after he graduates. Joseph's grandmother, Judith, is very proud of her grandson and says he is way more intelligent than she ever was. But Joseph is also very proud of Judith. As a young woman, Judith was imprisoned by the Nazis. When the war ended, she walked out of Germany, contacted an agency helping refugees travel to the United States, and began a new life as an assistant chef in her cousin's restaurant. According to the definition of intelligence in this chapter, why is Joseph not the only intelligent person in this story? (psychological reasoning)**

> *ANSWER:* Intelligence is the ability to learn, solve problems, and adapt to new situations, which Joseph has demonstrated in his school and career work. Judith also clearly fits this description, given all that she accomplished after her release.

5. **Fiona wants to find out if leg strength predicts running speed. She correlates the muscular strength of the 10 fastest runners in her school with their 100-meter times—and finds only a weak correlation. But even if strong muscles do enable speed, we could have expected this result. Why? Is Fiona's study *valid?* (scientific problem solving)**

> *ANSWER:* Fiona's study is not valid, because it does not measure what it is supposed to measure. Fiona tested only those within a narrow range of speeds, so her sample will tell us only about those within this narrow range of speed and will not tell us anything about leg strength and running speed in the general population. Perhaps if her tests had included a wider range, from the slowest runners to the fastest, the correlation would have been stronger.

6. **The Romanos have enrolled their 2-year-old son, who they believe is gifted, in a special program that claims to "give your child a superior mind." Why is this endeavor of questionable value? (practical problem solving)**

ANSWER: First, two years is generally too young an age for reliably predicting future intelligence. More important, there is no proven way to create a "superbaby." Extreme conditions, such as malnutrition, abuse, sensory deprivation, and social isolation can indeed retard normal development. But research has shown that as long as young children have attentive caregivers and are experiencing a normal environment with everyday sights, sounds, and speech, programs for raising their intelligence seem to have no substantial long-term effects.

CHAPTER 10 *Motivation*

Rehearse It Answer Key

1. b, 2. d, 3. c, 4. c, 5. a, 6. b, 7. a, 8. c, 9. b, 10. d, 11. d, 12. b, 13. b, 14. c, 15. d, 16. b, 17. c, 18. c, 19. a.

Critical Thinker's Review Answer Key

1. Which motivational concept explains each of these behaviors and why? (pattern recognition)

> A. On a long road trip, your stomach is growling with hunger. So, you pull off to eat at the nearest restaurant.
> B. Muriel accidentally brushes a finger against her newborn's cheek, and the baby instantly starts rooting around in an attempt to nurse.
> C. Paul and his friends have never skydived but have the opportunity to do so this weekend. So, they decide to give it a try, just for fun.

ANSWER: Drive-reduction theory—the idea that physical needs create an aroused state that drives us to reduce the need—explains the road stop. *Instincts* explain the infant's rooting reflex. We are born pre-wired to seek nourishment. Paul and his friends' sky-diving can only be explained by a need they feel to seek *optimum arousal*. In this case, they are clearly motivated to increase arousal!

2. Louisa is a teenager who has joined the "wrong" kind of crowd at school. One night she follows the gang to an outdoor party deep in the woods. After walking a long, long way, she finally asks whether they are nearly there and mysteriously gets no response. Louisa begins to wonder about her decision to hang out with these kids. They are her only friends, but she is tired, cold, and hungry, and she's beginning to feel afraid of this group that doesn't really seem concerned about her well-being. When the group turns onto yet another dark, overgrown path, Louisa decides to make a run for it and heads for home. Using Maslow's hierarchy of needs, explain Louisa's behavior. (creative problem solving)

ANSWER: Maslow used a pyramid to illustrate that we give some needs higher priority than others. Our belonging and love needs are halfway up the pyramid—less important than safety needs and physiological needs. Maslow might say that Louisa is willing to follow the gang of kids in hopes of meeting her need to belong and be accepted and to avoid alienation as long as her physiological needs have been met, and as long as she feels safe. When those two, more important needs are not being met, she wisely abandons the effort to meet her social needs.

3. You are traveling and have not eaten anything in eight hours. As your long-awaited meal is placed in front of you, your mouth waters. Even imagining this may set your mouth to watering. What triggers this anticipatory drooling, and why do you feel so hungry? (perspective taking)

ANSWER: You, like Pavlov's dogs, have learned through *classical conditioning* to respond to the cues—the sight and aroma—that signal the food about to enter your mouth. Both *physiological cues* (eight hours of deprivation have left you with low-blood sugar) and *psychological cues* (the anticipation of the tasty meal) have heightened your experienced hunger.

4. Imagine that you are the U.S. Surgeon General, and you decide to issue a set of recommendations to every American to help reduce the alarmingly high incidence of obesity in the United States. What should your top five recommendations be to help solve this problem? (practical problem solving)

ANSWER: There are many possible answers here, but the following should probably be included in any set of recommendations:

A. First, use the Body Mass Index (BMI) formula (on p. 349 of this chapter) to calculate your BMI and determine whether you need to lose weight, and if so how much.

B. If you are in the "overweight," category, and especially if you are in the "obese" or "morbidly obese" categories, set up a reasonable timeframe to lose enough weight to be back in the "healthy" category. The National Institute of Health suggests shooting for a 10 percent weight reduction over the course of six months (1998).

C. Try to boost your metabolism by exercising. Dieting failures often result from lack of activity.

D. Avoid temptation! It is much easier to maintain self-control in your eating habits if you simply avoid buffet tables full of fatty foods and take alternate routes so that you are not walking past bakeries and sweet shops. Never grocery shop on an empty stomach. If you binge, do not despair and give up entirely. Just work back into your established eating plan as soon as possible.

E. Eat healthy foods (unprocessed and naturally colorful foods are generally best), and never miss breakfast. Time your consumption patterns so that you eat less as the day goes by rather than more. Do not, for example, eat a big meal at night.

5. How might drive-reduction theory, arousal theory, and the evolutionary perspective explain our sexual motivation? (psychological reasoning)

ANSWER: Drive-reduction theory could imply that hormonal influences create a driven (physiologically aroused) state that compels us to reduce the drive. Arousal theory could add that people sometimes *seek* the pleasure and stimulation of arousal. Evolutionary psychologists would remind us that those motivated to have sex were more likely to leave descendants—us—than others who lacked sexual motivation.

6. We're often aware of our affiliation needs—our need for others and for the feeling that we belong. But have you ever thought about *why* you have those needs? How might a researcher in motivation explain our need to belong? (scientific problem solving)

ANSWER: Researchers might call upon drive-reduction theory to explain that being threatened and afraid drive us to find safety in the company of others (thus reducing our aroused state). Researchers could also mention arousal theory, which suggests that we welcome optimal levels of arousal, and that the presence of others is arousing. Researchers might also consider the findings of evolutionary psychologists, who have noted that our ancestors hunted and survived threats as group-dwelling creatures. In numbers there were food and safety. As their descendants, we therefore are disposed to live in groups, connected to supportive others.

CHAPTER 11   *Emotions, Stress, and Health*

Rehearse It Answer Key

1. b, 2. b, 3. b, 4. c, 5. b, 6. d, 7. d, 8. a, 9. b, 10. b, 11. a, 12. d, 13. c, 14. b, 15. b, 16. c, 17. c, 18. d, 19. b, 20. c, 21. b, 22. b, 23. d.

Critical Thinker's Review Answer Key

1. Cindy is holding her 8-month-old baby when a fierce dog appears out of nowhere and, with teeth bared, leaps for the baby's face. Cindy immediately ducks for cover to protect the baby, screams at the dog, then notices that her heart is banging in her chest and she's broken out in a cold sweat. How would the James-Lange, Cannon-Bard, and two-factor theories explain Cindy's emotional reaction? (psychological reasoning)

ANSWER: The James-Lange theory would say that Cindy's emotional reaction consists of her awareness of her physiological responses to the dog attack. The

Cannon-Bard theory would say that her fear experience happened simultaneously with her physiological arousal. Schacter's two-factor theory would presume that Cindy's emotional reaction stemmed from her interpreting and labeling the arousal.

2. **In an alarming situation, we experience an acute physical reaction, including increased heart rate and respiration, tense muscles, and slowed digestion. If you were an evolutionary psychologist, how might you explain this reaction? (perspective taking)**

ANSWER: Evolutionary psychologists would presume that all such reactions prepare the organism to cope and survive. They would consider the adaptive value of each response. For example, slowed digestion allows the body to direct all its resources to a fight-or-flight response. Those among our ancestors who did not respond adaptively would have been less likely to produce descendants than those who did.

3. **Who tend to express more emotion—men or women? How do we know the answer to that question? (scientific problem solving)**

ANSWER: Women tend to surpass men not only at detecting emotion but also at expressing certain emotions (though men have slightly surpassed women in conveying anger). Researchers discovered this male-female difference by showing people brief, silent clips of men's and women's faces expressing various emotions and by observing who is most skilled at reading and sending emotions.

4. **Liz's roommate is a grumpy morning person. She reluctantly drags herself out of bed and then slumps her way across campus to class with a scowl—head down and feet shuffling. She typically arrives in her first class with a bad attitude. Using what you now know about the effects of our facial and bodily expressions on our experienced emotions, what could Liz suggest that might help improve her roommate's attitude? (creative problem solving)**

ANSWER: Liz might tell her roommate about ways our expressions can affect the way we feel. For example, if we scowl, we tend to feel more irritable. Liz might suggest that her roommate try walking to class briskly with her head held high and a pleasant expression on her face. This cannot hurt, and it might help her build a more positive attitude!

5. **Ms. Morton owns a specialty bakery. She has been reading about happiness research and was surprised to learn about the many benefits of happiness, including greater productivity on the job. She has decided to institute a happiness plan for her employees. What three or four research-based suggestions should Ms. Morton include in her plan? (practical problem solving)**

ANSWER: Although happiness is genetically influenced, a number of factors under our control can also influence happiness levels. They include giving up the idea that money can buy happiness; *acting* happy (smiling instead of scowling); seeking "flow" in work and leisure activity by building focus and a sense of purpose; exercising; getting enough sleep; maintaining close relationships; reaching out to help others; expressing gratitude rather than taking credit for everything yourself; and nurturing spirituality.

6. **Based on what you now know about good health, and given only the few details noted below, which of the following two college students do you think is more likely to be healthy, Terrance or Eli? Explain why. (pattern recognition)**

- *Terrance* is a bright student, yet he tends to panic before every test or class presentation. He worries that he will make a fool of himself, though he actually never has. He is too busy studying to exercise or hang out with friends. Although he is becoming overweight, he has made the college honor roll every term.

- *Eli* is a bright student who studies hard. He likes tests and classroom discussions, because they give him a chance to demonstrate what he's been working so hard to learn, and the opportunity to learn more. Eli runs cross-country, because many of his friends are on the team, and he thought it would be a good idea to stay in shape.

ANSWER: Based on this information, Eli will tend to be healthier than Terrance. Eli appraises difficult life events as challenges rather than threats, and Eli seems to have a more optimistic outlook than Terrance. Eli exercises regularly and seems to enjoy a higher level of social support. All these factors contribute to general levels of good health.

CHAPTER 12 *Personality*

Rehearse It Answer Key

1. b, 2. c, 3. b, 4. b, 5. b, 6. d, 7. d, 8. a, 9. d, 10. b, 11. d, 12. c, 13. c, 14. c, 15. b, 16. b, 17. a, 18. c, 19. b, 20. d, 21. d, 22. b, 23. c, 24. d, 25. a.

Critical Thinker's Review Answer Key

1. While your roommate is out, you take the opportunity to line up her shoes and boots, because it has been bothering you to have them scattered all over the floor. Upon her return, she notices and comments, "Oh, you are so anal retentive!" Who is responsible for this term, and how did it become a part of our everyday language? (creative problem solving)

ANSWER: Although Freud's current influence in psychological science has diminished, his influence on popular culture has not. Many terms that are common in our language stem from Freud's theories, including the term "anal retentive." Freud believed that children progress through a series of psychosexual stages, including the anal stage. Freud referred to those fixated at the anal stage as "anal retentive" and suggested that they struggle with control issues.

2. After feeling a lot of stress, Genevieve consulted a therapist, Dr. Weaver, who told her, "You are a wonderful person. You should be true to yourself and fulfill your own needs above all else." Genevieve, worried that Dr. Weaver was simply flattering her, decided to try another therapist. When Genevieve told her second therapist, Dr. Carter, about this incident, he said, "That kind of blind support can lead to selfishness and problems in coping with stress. I believe in a more behavioral approach to helping." Dr. Weaver incorporates methods from which perspective? How might Dr. Weaver reply to Dr. Carter's critique? (perspective taking)

ANSWER: Dr. Weaver seems to be incorporating methods from the humanistic perspective in her approach. If she were a strict humanist, she might tell Dr. Carter that when her clients feel truly accepted they are then able to love others. Dr. Weaver might also argue that behavioral treatments for problems can be depersonalizing, and that only face-to-face interviews provide an adequate understanding of each person's unique situation.

3. Your friend Franklin claims he knows all his instructors so well that he could predict how any of them would behave in any number of situations. However, when the two of you are out one night, Franklin is shocked to find his reticent physics teacher out on the dance floor having a wild and crazy time. What personality controversy does this story illustrate? Explain. (practical problem solving)

ANSWER: This story nicely illustrates the person-situation controversy. Although certain personality *traits* do persist over time and across situations, an individual's *behavior* is much harder to predict. Our behaviors do tend to shift depending upon the situation. A physics teacher may seem quiet in the classroom, where such behavior is expected, yet she may be much more outgoing in a party atmosphere.

4. Research suggests that optimism is a powerfully positive trait—helping us to feel better both psychologically and physically. However, most research in this area is *correlational*. How should this affect how we interpret this finding? (scientific problem solving)

ANSWER: Research on optimism has shown a *correlation* between an optimistic outlook and better physical and emotional health. It is important to keep in mind that correlational research does not identify cause and effect, so it does not tell us whether optimism leads to better health, or whether better health leads to a more optimistic outlook. (Other research does give us a clue, by studying how today's optimism predicts future health and by experiments that train more optimistic thinking.)

5. English essayist William Hazlitt said, "Life is the art of being well-deceived." What psychological principles might this comment illustrate? (pattern recognition)

ANSWER: Hazlitt's comment could be taken to illustrate Freud's defense mechanisms, all of which are said to protect the self from painful self-knowledge. It also illustrates the pervasive self-serving bias. Hazlitt's words seem to suggest that living well means having an exaggerated, positive perception of one's traits. Indeed, most people in individualistic cultures today do enjoy a strong self-serving bias, but current research suggests that a dose of reality is essential to truly artful living.

6. Participants in an experiment were told that they were high in either repressed anger or dishonesty, and they then tended to see more of those qualities in *others*. What psychological concept helps us to understand this reaction? (psychological reasoning)

ANSWER: This reaction (drawn from a research study [Schimel & others, 2003]) is a nearly perfect illustration of the false consensus effect—the tendency to overestimate the extent to which others share our beliefs and behaviors. The false consensus effect is similar to Freud's projection—a defense mechanism in which one unconsciously disguises threatening impulses by attributing them to others.

CHAPTER 13 *Psychological Disorders*

Rehearse It Answer Key

1. c, 2. a, 3. c, 4. c, 5. a, 6. a, 7. c, 8. a, 9. d, 10. c, 11. c, 12. c, 13. b, 14. c, 15. a, 16. d, 17. d, 18. d, 19. b, 20. a, 21. c.

Critical Thinker's Review Answer Key

1. Raphael's therapist has taken pains to learn all about his medical history and has asked him many questions about how he interacts with others and how he handles day-to-day stress and problematic situations. What perspective does this therapist seem to be operating from, and why is this beneficial for Raphael? (perspective taking)

ANSWER: Raphael's therapist seems to be taking the bio-psycho-social perspective. This means he is exploring the biological, psychological, and social factors that could be affecting the way Raphael is functioning. Raphael will probably benefit because this perspective is more complete than any one of the three alone.

2. Kirsten has a phobia for heights. She cannot climb a spiral staircase without going pale and gripping the handrail desperately. In an attempt to help, her therapist starts by introducing the concepts of natural selection and learning. Kirsten is bewildered. Where do you think her therapist is going with this discussion? (creative problem solving)

ANSWER: Natural selection and learning represent two popular explanations for anxiety disorders of all kinds, including phobias. We are biologically predisposed to fear the threats faced by our ancestors. If our ancestors had not feared heights, for example, they probably would not have survived to leave descendents. Thus, the therapist might explain that although her fear has become debilitating, and that is problematic, it is not unnatural for Kirsten to have *some* fear of heights. We also often *learn* fears by being conditioned with powerfully negative experiences, (perhaps Kirsten had a particularly fearful height-related experience in her childhood, such as falling from a playground ladder); by generalizing from specific learned fears (of playground ladders) to other related fears (open staircases); by having our fears reinforced (avoiding stairs reduces Kirsten's anxiety and thus reinforces her avoidance behavior); or by observing others (perhaps Kirsten's mother had a phobia for heights and Kirsten imitated her behavior).

3. When you show your depressed friend Figure 13.10 on page 495, he responds, "You see? Depression is a vicious cycle and there's no way out!" What hope could you offer? (practical problem solving)

ANSWER: There are actually several points at which the vicious cycle may be broken: (1) seeking a less stressful environment, (2) reversing self-blaming explanations, (3) turning self-focused attention to other tasks, and (4) engaging in more positive, helpful behavior.

4. Phineas Gage was made famous by a tragic and dramatic 1848 accident. He suffered serious brain damage when a tamping rod shot through the frontal lobe of his brain. Gage changed from an even-tempered, likable young man to an irreverent and irritable character. Which explanation of personality disorders does this famous story support? Why? (pattern recognition)

ANSWER: The story of Phineas Gage provides solid support for the biological explanation of personality disorders. Gage's brain damage was so dramatic that people were surprised he survived it. He survived physically, but the accident changed his personality—and the rest of his life—completely.

5. Does a full moon trigger "madness" in some people? How might you test that question? (scientific problem solving)

ANSWER: Here is how James Rotton and I. W. Kelly (1985) did it. They examined data from 37 studies that related lunar phase to crime, homicides, crisis calls, and mental hospital admissions. Their conclusion: There is virtually no evidence of "moon madness." Nor does lunar phase correlate with suicides, assaults, emergency room visits, or traffic disasters (Byrnes & Kelly, 1992; Kelly & others, 1990; Martin & others, 1992).

6. Paniotis' mother suffers from schizophrenia, and Paniotis believes it is because she has lived in poverty for so many years. Could he be right? What is the relationship between poverty and psychological disorders such as schizophrenia? (psychological reasoning)

ANSWER: Paniotis could be right. Poverty-related stresses can indeed help trigger disorders. But he may also have the explanation backwards, because disabling disorders can also contribute to poverty. Thus, poverty and psychological disorders are often a chicken-and-egg situation, and it is hard to know which came first.

CHAPTER 14　*Therapy*

Rehearse It Answer Key

1. a, 2. a, 3. d, 4. c, 5. c, 6. b, 7. a, 8. d, 9. d, 10. b, 11. c, 12. d, 13. a, 14. b, 15. c, 16. b, 17. c, 18. b, 19. d.

Critical Thinker's Review Answer Key

1. Keesha's therapist is attempting to resolve her extreme anxiety about being around other people by counterconditioning that anxiety. Which technique is her therapist using: psychoanalytic or behavior therapy? Explain. (perspective taking)

ANSWER: Keesha's therapist is employing behavior therapy techniques. Behaviorists believe that by using learning principles, including conditioning, we can learn healthier behaviors, and "un-learn" problem behaviors. In counterconditioning, a person learns new responses to stimuli (such as social settings) that had been triggering unwanted behaviors (such as avoidance).

2. Dr. Keller is trying to help mildly depressed Alana develop more adaptive ways of thinking and acting. He believes that if Alana learns healthier ways of interpreting everyday events, she will be able to think her way out of her negative feelings. Which psychological therapy is Dr. Keller employing: cognitive or psychoanalytic? Explain. (pattern recognition)

ANSWER: Dr. Keller is taking a cognitive approach to helping Alana resolve her difficulties. He is assuming that thoughts intervene between events and our emotional reactions to those events.

3. Carlos, who suffers from depression, is participating in a scientific study of the effectiveness of different therapeutic approaches. Carlos visits the campus clinic daily, where he picks up a pill from a drop box but does not meet with anyone. Others in the same study receive a pill along with some counseling. A third group receives counseling but no pill. After taking his daily pill for several weeks, Carlos reports that he feels better and that the pills are working. However, the "pills" he has been taking contain only inert substances—they are "sugar pills." What effect has occurred here? (scientific problem solving)

ANSWER: Carlos has experienced the powerful placebo effect, in which expectations alone bring about a change in thoughts or behaviors. Carlos believed he was being treated with medication, because he was taking a pill. This belief alone changed the way he behaved and the way he felt.

4. Luca is in therapy to work through his debilitating anxiety. After several weeks, he is functioning fairly normally and decides to end his therapy session. His therapist asks Luca to complete a survey rating how effective his therapy has been, and Luca gives his therapist a glowing report. With Luca's permission, the therapist shares his survey with another prospective client as evidence of his effectiveness as a therapist. Do surveys like this speak to a therapist's effectiveness? What else do we need to consider when determining psychotherapy's effectiveness? (creative problem solving)

ANSWER: Clients' perceptions, such as Luca's, are important, but we need to keep in mind that clients often enter therapy in crisis—with nowhere to go but up. So, most people will improve rather than get worse whether they are in or out of therapy. Clients also tend to want to believe their therapy was worth the time and money, so are more likely to give positive reports and say nice things about their therapists. In considering psychotherapy's effectiveness, we also need to consider outcome research, which compares the results of different therapies (and of no therapy).

5. Your co-worker swears that St. John's wort is the cure for all ills. He says there is scientific support for his claim, pointing out the huge number of Web sites that mention this herbal remedy. Based on what you've learned in this chapter, how might you challenge his claim? (practical problem solving)

ANSWER: You might suggest that your co-worker compare the number of times St. John's wort is mentioned on the World Wide Web with the number of times it is mentioned in an electronic search of psychology's literature (peer-reviewed psychology journals). He will find that this herbal remedy has very few journal citations, but a huge number of related Web sites. These are indications of high popular interest and low scientific support.

6. Your childhood friend is suffering severe, relentless depression. She has tried many different types of therapy, but nothing is working. Her doctors are now recommending electroconvulsive therapy (ECT), but your friend's father is adamantly opposed. He saw the movie *One Flew Over the Cuckoo's Nest* and says that ECT is just another radical biomedical approach like the lobotomy. What could you tell your friend's father about today's ECT that might help him feel more comfortable with this approach? (psychological reasoning)

ANSWER: You might tell him that ECT as performed today is quite different from the harsh early version introduced in 1938 and portrayed in *One Flew Over the Cuckoo's Nest*. Patients now receive a general anesthetic, so they are not conscious, and a muscle relaxant to prevent injuries from convulsions. The electricity transmitted to the brain is also now administered in briefer pulses that disrupt memory less. Although we do not completely understand how ECT works, this therapy has been credited with preventing many from committing suicide and is widely recognized as an effective, last-resort treatment for severe depression. This is quite a contrast to the huge decline in the use of the lobotomy, which is almost never performed today.

CHAPTER 15 *Social Psychology*

Rehearse It Answer Key

1. a, 2. b, 3. a, 4. c, 5. a, 6. c, 7. c, 8. b, 9. c, 10. b, 11. b, 12. b, 13. d, 14. c, 15. c, 16. c, 17. c, 18. b, 19. d, 20. a, 21. c, 22. c, 23. b.

Critical Thinker's Review Answer Key

1. Driving to school one wintry day, Marco narrowly misses a car that slides through a red light. "Slow down! What a terrible driver," he thinks to himself. Moments later, Marco himself slips through an intersection and yelps, "Wow! These roads are awful. The city snow plows need to get out here." What social psychology principle has Marco just demonstrated? Explain. (perspective taking)

> *ANSWER:* By attributing the other person's behavior to the person ("what a terrible driver") and his own to the situation ("these roads are awful"), Marco exhibits the *fundamental attribution error.*

2. You are organizing a Town Hall–style meeting of fiercely competitive political candidates. To add to the fun, friends have suggested handing out masks of the candidates' faces for supporters to wear. Is this a good idea? What phenomenon might these masks engage? (pattern recognition)

> *ANSWER:* The anonymity provided by the masks, combined with the arousal of the contentious setting, might create *deindividuation* (lessened self-awareness and self-restraint). This may not be such a great idea, because it could lead to aggressive outbursts.

3. Your brother is not comfortable visiting nursing homes or being around older people. He regrets this, because it means he hardly ever spends time with your elderly grandmother who lives in a nursing home and dearly loves family visits. How might your brother change his behavior in a way that would also change his thinking about the elderly? What theory would explain the change? (psychological reasoning)

> *ANSWER:* If your brother decides to visit your grandmother regularly, despite his discomfort, this would be inconsistent with his negative attitudes about the elderly. *Cognitive dissonance theory* suggests that he would then bring his attitudes into line with his actions and change the way he thinks about this group.

4. Mrs. Lewis wants to collect unique pieces of art from her third grade class for a farewell project the school is doing for a beloved, retiring principal. She knows from past experience that when the students work side by side, they often conform to what their classmates are doing, and the result is a lot of similarity. What have we learned from social science research about the conditions that strengthen conformity? How might these findings help Mrs. Lewis? (scientific problem solving)

> *ANSWER:* We have learned that those most likely to conform are those who feel incompetent or insecure, are in a group of at least three people, are experiencing unanimous agreement among the others in the group, admire the group's status and attractiveness, have not made a prior commitment to any response, are being observed, and are in a culture that encourages respect for social standards. Mrs. Lewis could employ these findings to her advantage. She should first do her best to help each student feel comfortable with the project and confident in his or her abilities to complete it. She could have students work alone and not present their work to the class later (so they will not feel "observed"). She might also ask the students in advance to commit to doing their very best and to expressing themselves and not worrying about what others think of what they are doing.

5. Why didn't anybody help Kitty Genovese? What social relations principle did this incident illustrate? (creative problem solving)

> *ANSWER:* The Kitty Genovese tragedy illustrated the *bystander effect.* This occurs because, in the presence of others, an individual is less likely to notice a situation, correctly interpret it as an emergency, and then take

responsibility for offering help. When Kitty Genovese was attacked, many people—too many people—heard her cries for help. Each assumed the other would help, and no one did.

6. Two of your best friends have had a few run-ins and have decided they are "enemies." What could you suggest they do that might help them make peace? (practical problem solving)

ANSWER: Cooperation, communication, and conciliation should be your main goals. Your friends need to have contact with each other in a situation that requires cooperation but is not in any way competitive. Perhaps they could go on a camping outing, where all members of the party need to depend on one another. And, because conflict often results from misunderstanding, you might point this out and help your friends reestablish their lines of communication. Finally, you could urge each friend to give a little. A small conciliatory act from one friend, such as agreeing to plan a camping outing, will hopefully lead to a responding, small conciliatory act from the other friend.

APPENDIX A   *Statistical Reasoning in Everyday Life*

Rehearse It Answer Key

A1. b, **A2.** d, **A3.** a, **A4.** a.

APPENDIX B   *Psychology at Work*

Rehearse It Answer Key

B1. b, **B2.** c, **B3.** a, **B4.** d, **B5.** c, **B6.** c, **B7.** d.

A

absolute threshold   the minimum stimulation needed to detect a particular stimulus 50 percent of the time.

accommodation (1)   adapting one's current understandings (schemas) to incorporate new information.

accommodation (2)   the process by which the eye's lens changes shape to focus near or far objects on the retina.

achievement motivation   a desire for significant accomplishment: for mastery of things, people, or ideas; for attaining a high standard.

achievement test   a test designed to assess what a person has learned.

acquisition   the initial stage in classical conditioning; the phase associating a neutral stimulus with an unconditioned stimulus so that the neutral stimulus comes to elicit a conditioned response. In operant conditioning, the strengthening of a reinforced response.

action potential   a neural impulse; a brief electrical charge that travels down an axon. The action potential is generated by the movement of positively charged atoms in and out of channels in the axon's membrane.

active listening   empathic listening in which the listener echoes, restates, and clarifies. A feature of Rogers' client-centered therapy.

adaptation-level phenomenon   our tendency to form judgments (of sounds, of lights, of income) relative to a "neutral" level defined by our prior experience.

adolescence   the transition period from childhood to adulthood, extending from puberty to independence.

adrenal [ah-DREEN-el] **glands**   a pair of endocrine glands just above the kidneys. The adrenals secrete the hormones epinephrine (adrenaline) and norepinephrine (noradrenaline), which help to arouse the body in times of stress.

aerobic exercise   sustained exercise that increases heart and lung fitness; may also alleviate depression and anxiety.

aggression   any physical or verbal behavior intended to hurt or destroy.

algorithm   a methodical, logical rule or procedure that guarantees solving a particular problem. Contrasts with the usually speedier—but also more error-prone—use of *heuristics*.

alpha waves   the relatively slow brain waves of a relaxed, awake state.

altruism   unselfish regard for the welfare of others.

amnesia   the loss of memory.

amphetamines   drugs that stimulate neural activity, causing speeded-up body functions and associated energy and mood changes.

amygdala [uh-MIG-duh-la]   two almond-shaped neural clusters that are components of the limbic system and are linked to emotion.

anorexia nervosa   an eating disorder in which a normal-weight person (usually an adolescent female) diets and becomes significantly (15 percent or more) underweight, yet, still feeling fat, continues to starve.

antisocial personality disorder   a personality disorder in which the person (usually a man) exhibits a lack of conscience for wrongdoing, even toward friends and family members. May be aggressive and ruthless or a clever con artist.

anxiety disorders   psychological disorders characterized by distressing, persistent anxiety or maladaptive behaviors that reduce anxiety.

aphasia   impairment of language, usually caused by left hemisphere damage either to Broca's area (impairing speaking) or to Wernicke's area (impairing understanding).

applied research   scientific study that aims to solve practical problems.

aptitude test   a test designed to predict a person's future performance; *aptitude* is the capacity to learn.

assimilation   interpreting one's new experience in terms of one's existing schemas.

association areas   areas of the cerebral cortex that are not involved in primary motor or sensory functions; rather, they are involved in higher mental functions such as learning, remembering, thinking, and speaking.

associative learning   learning that certain events occur together. The events may be two stimuli (as in classical conditioning) or a response and its consequences (as in operant conditioning).

attachment   an emotional tie with another person; shown in young children by their seeking closeness to the caregiver and showing distress on separation.

attitude   a belief and feeling that predisposes one to respond in a particular way to objects, people, and events.

attribution theory   the theory that we tend to give a causal explanation for someone's behavior, often by crediting either the situation or the person's disposition.

audition   the sense of hearing.

automatic processing   unconscious encoding of incidental information, such as space, time, and frequency, and of well-learned information, such as word meanings.

autonomic [aw-tuh-NAHM-ik] **nervous system**   the part of the peripheral nervous system that controls the glands and the muscles of the internal organs (such as the heart). Its sympathetic division arouses; its parasympathetic division calms.

availability heuristic   estimating the likelihood of events based on their availability in memory; if instances come readily to mind (perhaps because of their vividness), we presume such events are common.

aversive conditioning   a type of counterconditioning that associates an unpleasant state (such as nausea) with an unwanted behavior (such as drinking alcohol).

axon   the extension of a neuron, ending in branching terminal fibers, through which messages pass to other neurons or to muscles or glands.

B

babbling stage   beginning by about 4 months, the stage of speech development in which the infant spontaneously utters various sounds at first unrelated to the household language.

barbiturates   drugs that depress the activity of the central nervous system, reducing anxiety but impairing memory and judgment.

basal metabolic rate   the body's resting rate of energy expenditure.

basic research   pure science that aims to increase the scientific knowledge base.

basic trust   according to Erik Erikson, a sense that the world is predictable and trustworthy; said to be formed during infancy by appropriate experiences with responsive caregivers.

behavior genetics   the study of the relative power and limits of genetic and environmental influences on behavior.

behavior therapy   therapy that applies learning principles to the elimination of unwanted behaviors.

behaviorism   the view that psychology (1) should be an objective science that (2) studies behavior without reference to mental processes. Most research psychologists today agree with (1) but not with (2).

belief perseverance   clinging to one's initial conceptions after the basis on which they were formed has been discredited. (*Confirmation bias*—searching for belief-support information—contributes to belief perseverance.)

binocular cues   depth cues, such as retinal disparity and convergence, that depend on the use of two eyes.

bio-psycho-social perspective   a contemporary perspective which assumes that biological, psychological, and sociocultural factors combine and interact to produce psychological disorders.

biofeedback   a system for electronically recording, amplifying, and feeding back information regarding a subtle physiological state, such as blood pressure or muscle tension.

biological psychology   a branch of psychology concerned with the links between biology and behavior. (Some biological psychologists call themselves *behavioral neuroscientists, neuropsychologists, behavior geneticists, physiological psychologists,* or *biopsychologists.*)

bipolar disorder   a mood disorder in which the person alternates between the hopelessness and lethargy of depression and the overexcited state of mania. (Formerly called manic-depressive disorder.)

blind spot   the point at which the optic nerve leaves the eye, creating a "blind" spot because no receptor cells are located there.

bottom-up processing   analysis that begins with the sense receptors and works up to the brain's integration of sensory information.

brainstem   the oldest part and central core of the brain, beginning where the spinal cord swells as it enters the skull; the brainstem is responsible for automatic survival functions.

Broca's area   controls language expression—an area of the frontal lobe, usually in the left hemisphere, that directs the muscle movements involved in speech.

bulimia nervosa   an eating disorder characterized by episodes of overeating, usually of high-calorie foods, followed by vomiting, laxative use, fasting, or excessive exercise.

bystander effect   the tendency for any given bystander to be less likely to give aid if other bystanders are present.

C

Cannon-Bard theory   the theory that an emotion-arousing stimulus simultaneously triggers (1) physiological responses and (2) the subjective experience of emotion.

case study   an observation technique in which one person is studied in depth in the hope of revealing universal principles.

catharsis   emotional release. In psychology, the catharsis hypothesis maintains that "releasing" aggressive energy (through action or fantasy) relieves aggressive urges.

central nervous system (CNS)   the brain and spinal cord.

cerebellum [sehr-uh-BELL-um]   the "little brain" attached to the rear of the brainstem; it helps coordinate voluntary movement and balance.

cerebral [seh-REE-bruhl] **cortex**   the intricate fabric of interconnected neural cells that covers the cerebral hemispheres; the body's ultimate control and information-processing center.

chromosomes   threadlike structures made of DNA molecules that contain the genes.

chunking   organizing items into familiar, manageable units; often occurs automatically.

circadian [ser-KAY-dee-an] **rhythm**   the biological clock; regular bodily rhythms (for example, of temperature and wakefulness) that occur on a 24-hour cycle.

classical conditioning   a type of learning in which an organism comes to associate stimuli. A neutral stimulus that signals an unconditioned stimulus (UCS) begins to produce a response that anticipates and prepares for the unconditioned stimulus. Also called *Pavlovian conditioning.*

client-centered therapy   a humanistic therapy, developed by Carl Rogers, in which the therapist uses techniques such as active listening within a genuine, accepting, empathic environment to facilitate clients' growth. (Also called *person-centered therapy.*)

clinical psychology   a branch of psychology that studies, assesses, and treats people with psychological disorders.

cochlea [KOHK-lee-uh]   a coiled, bony, fluid-filled tube in the inner ear through which sound waves trigger nerve impulses.

cognition   all the mental activities associated with thinking, knowing, remembering, and communicating.

cognitive dissonance theory   the theory that we act to reduce the discomfort (dissonance) we feel when two of our thoughts (cognitions) are inconsistent. For example, when our awareness of our attitudes and of our actions clash, we can reduce the resulting dissonance by changing our attitudes.

cognitive map   a mental representation of the layout of one's environment. For example, after exploring a maze, rats act as if they have learned a cognitive map of it.

cognitive therapy   therapy that teaches people new, more adaptive ways of thinking and acting; based on the assumption that thoughts intervene between events and our emotional reactions.

cognitive-behavior therapy   a popular integrated therapy that combines cognitive therapy (changing self-defeating thinking) with behavior therapy (changing behavior).

collective unconscious   Carl Jung's concept of a shared, inherited reservoir of memory traces from our species' history.

collectivism   giving priority to the goals of one's group (often one's extended family or work group) and defining one's identity accordingly.

color constancy   perceiving familiar objects as having consistent color, even if changing illumination alters the wavelengths reflected by the object.

companionate love   the deep affectionate attachment we feel for those with whom our lives are intertwined.

complementary and alternative medicine   unproven health care treatments not taught widely in medical schools, not used in hospitals, and not usually reimbursed by insurance companies.

concept   a mental grouping of similar objects, events, ideas, or people.

concrete operational stage   in Piaget's theory, the stage of cognitive development (from about 6 or 7 to 11 years of age) during which children gain the mental operations that enable them to think logically about concrete events.

conditioned reinforcer   a stimulus that gains its reinforcing power through its association with a primary reinforcer; also known as *secondary reinforcer.*

conditioned response (CR)   in classical conditioning, the learned response to a previously neutral conditioned stimulus (CS).

conditioned stimulus (CS)   in classical conditioning, an originally irrelevant stimulus that, after association with an unconditioned stimulus (UCS), comes to trigger a conditioned response.

cones   receptor cells that are concentrated near the center of the retina and that function in daylight or in well-lit conditions. The cones detect fine detail and give rise to color sensations.

confirmation bias   a tendency to search for information that confirms one's preconceptions.

conflict   a perceived incompatibility of actions, goals, or ideas.

conformity   adjusting one's behavior or thinking to coincide with a group standard.

consciousness   our awareness of ourselves and our environment.

conservation   the principle (which Piaget believed to be a part of concrete operational reasoning) that properties such as mass, volume, and number remain the same despite changes in the forms of objects.

content validity   the extent to which a test samples the behavior that is of interest (such as a driving test that samples driving tasks).

continuous reinforcement   reinforcing the desired response every time it occurs.

control condition   the condition of an experiment that contrasts with the experimental condition and serves as a comparison for evaluating the effect of the treatment.

convergence   a binocular cue for perceiving depth; the extent to which the eyes converge inward when looking at an object.

coronary heart disease   the clogging of the vessels that nourish the heart muscle; the leading cause of death in many developed countries.

corpus callosum [KOR-pus kah-LOW-sum]   the large band of neural fibers connecting the two brain hemispheres and carrying messages between them.

correlation coefficient   a statistical measure of the extent to which two factors vary together, and thus of how well either factor predicts the other.

counterconditioning   a behavior therapy procedure that conditions new responses to stimuli that trigger unwanted behaviors; based on classical conditioning. Includes *systematic desensitization* and *aversive conditioning*.

creativity   the ability to produce novel and valuable ideas.

criterion   the behavior (such as future college grades) that a test (such as the SAT) is designed to assess; thus, the measure used in defining whether the test has predictive validity.

critical period   an optimal period shortly after birth when an organism's exposure to certain stimuli or experiences produces proper development.

critical thinking   thinking that does not blindly accept arguments and conclusions. Rather, it examines assumptions, discerns hidden values, evaluates evidence, and assesses conclusions.

cross-sectional study   a study in which people of different ages are compared with one another.

crystallized intelligence   one's accumulated knowledge and verbal skills; tends to increase with age.

culture   the enduring behaviors, ideas, attitudes, and traditions shared by a large group of people and transmitted from one generation to the next.

D

defense mechanisms   in psychoanalytic theory, the ego's protective methods of reducing anxiety by unconsciously distorting reality.

deindividuation   the loss of self-awareness and self-restraint occurring in group situations that foster arousal and anonymity.

déjà vu   that eerie sense that "I've experienced this before." Cues from the current situation may subconsciously trigger retrieval of an earlier experience.

delta waves   the large, slow brain waves associated with deep sleep.

delusions   false beliefs, often of persecution or grandeur, that may accompany psychotic disorders.

dendrite   the bushy, branching extensions of a neuron that receive messages and conduct impulses toward the cell body.

dependent variable   the experimental factor—in psychology, the behavior or mental process—that is being measured; the variable that may change in response to manipulations of the independent variable.

depressants   drugs (such as alcohol, barbiturates, and opiates) that reduce neural activity and slow body functions.

depth perception   the ability to see objects in three dimensions although the images that strike the retina are two-dimensional; allows us to judge distance.

developmental psychology   a branch of psychology that studies physical, cognitive, and social change throughout the life span.

difference threshold   the minimum difference between two stimuli required for detection 50 percent of the time. We experience the difference threshold as a just noticeable difference. (Also called *just noticeable difference* or *jnd.*)

discrimination (1)   in classical conditioning, the learned ability to distinguish between a conditioned stimulus and stimuli that do not signal an unconditioned stimulus.

discrimination (2)   unjustifiable negative behavior toward a group or its members.

displacement   psychoanalytic defense mechanism that shifts sexual or aggressive impulses toward a more acceptable or less threatening object or person, as when redirecting anger toward a safer outlet.

dissociation   a split in consciousness, which allows some thoughts and behaviors to occur simultaneously with others.

dissociative disorders   disorders in which conscious awareness becomes separated (dissociated) from previous memories, thoughts, and feelings.

dissociative identity disorder   a rare dissociative disorder in which a person exhibits two or more distinct and alternating personalities. Also called *multiple personality disorder.*

DNA (deoxyribonucleic acid)   a complex molecule containing the genetic information that makes up the chromosomes.

double-blind procedure   an experimental procedure in which both the research participants and the research staff are ignorant (blind) about whether the research participants have received the treatment or a placebo. Commonly used in drug-evaluation studies.

Down syndrome   a condition of retardation and associated physical disorders caused by an extra chromosome in one's genetic makeup.

dream   a sequence of images, emotions, and thoughts passing through a sleeping person's mind. Dreams are notable for their hallucinatory imagery, discontinuities, and incongruities, and for the dreamer's delusional acceptance of the content and later difficulties remembering it.

drive-reduction theory   the idea that a physiological need creates an aroused tension state (a drive) that motivates an organism to satisfy the need.

DSM-IV   the American Psychiatric Association's *Diagnostic and Statistical Manual of Mental Disorders* (Fourth Edition), a widely used system for classifying psychological disorders. Presently distributed in an updated "text revision" (DSM-IV-TR).

E

echoic memory   a momentary sensory memory of auditory stimuli; if attention is elsewhere, sounds and words can still be recalled within 3 or 4 seconds.

eclectic approach   an approach to psychotherapy that, depending on the client's problems, uses techniques from various forms of therapy.

Ecstasy (MDMA)   a synthetic stimulant and mild hallucinogen. Produces euphoria and social intimacy, but with short-term health risks and longer-term harm to serotonin-producing neurons and to mood and cognition.

effortful processing   encoding that requires attention and conscious effort.

ego   the largely conscious, "executive" part of personality that, according to Freud, mediates among the demands of the id, superego, and reality. The ego operates on the *reality principle*, satisfying the id's desires in ways that will realistically bring pleasure rather than pain.

egocentrism   in Piaget's theory, the preoperational child's inability to take another's point of view.

electroconvulsive therapy (ECT)   a biomedical therapy for severely depressed patients in which a brief electric current is sent through the brain of an anesthetized patient.

electroencephalogram (EEG)   an amplified recording of the waves of electrical activity that sweep across the brain's surface. These waves are measured by electrodes placed on the scalp.

embryo   the developing human organism from about 2 weeks after fertilization through the second month.

emotion   a response of the whole organism, involving (1) physiological arousal, (2) expressive behaviors, and (3) conscious experience.

emotional intelligence   the ability to perceive, express, understand, and regulate emotions.

empirically derived test   a test (such as the MMPI) developed by testing a pool of items and then selecting those that discriminate between groups.

empiricism   the view that (a) knowledge comes from experience via the senses, and (b) science flourishes through observation and experiment.

encoding   the processing of information into the memory system—for example, by extracting meaning.

endocrine [EN-duh-krin] **system**   the body's "slow" chemical communication system; a set of glands that secrete hormones into the bloodstream.

endorphins [en-DOR-fins]   "morphine within"—natural, opiatelike neurotransmitters linked to pain control and to pleasure.

environment   every nongenetic influence, from prenatal nutrition to the people and things around us.

equity   a condition in which people receive from a relationship in proportion to what they give to it.

estrogen   a sex hormone, secreted in greater amounts by females than by males. In nonhuman female mammals, estrogen levels peak during ovulation, promoting sexual receptivity.

evolutionary psychology   the study of the evolution of behavior and the mind, using principles of natural selection.

experiment   a research method in which an investigator manipulates one or more factors (independent variables) to observe the effect on some behavior or mental process (the dependent variable). By random assignment of participants, the experiment controls other relevant factors.

experimental condition   the condition of an experiment that exposes participants to the treatment, that is, to one version of the independent variable.

explicit memory   memory of facts and experiences that one can consciously know and "declare." (Also called *declarative memory*.)

exposure therapies   behavioral techniques, such as systematic desensitization, that treat anxieties by exposing people (in imagination or actuality) to the things they fear and avoid.

external locus of control   the perception that chance or outside forces beyond one's personal control determine one's fate.

extinction   the diminishing of a conditioned response; occurs in classical conditioning when an unconditioned stimulus (UCS) does not follow a conditioned stimulus (CS); occurs in operant conditioning when a response is no longer reinforced.

extrasensory perception (ESP)   the controversial claim that perception can occur apart from sensory input. Said to include *telepathy, clairvoyance,* and *precognition.*

extrinsic motivation   a desire to perform a behavior due to promised rewards or threats of punishment.

F

factor analysis   a statistical procedure that identifies clusters of related items (called *factors*) on a test; used to identify different dimensions of performance that underlie one's total score.

family therapy   therapy that treats the family as a system. Views an individual's unwanted behaviors as influenced by or directed at other family members; attempts to guide family members toward positive relationships and improved communication.

feature detectors   nerve cells in the brain that respond to specific features of the stimulus, such as shape, angle, or movement.

feel-good, do-good phenomenon   people's tendency to be helpful when already in a good mood.

fetal alcohol syndrome (FAS)   physical and cognitive abnormalities in children caused by a pregnant woman's heavy drinking. In severe cases, symptoms include noticeable facial misproportions.

fetus   the developing human organism from 9 weeks after conception to birth.

figure-ground   the organization of the visual field into objects (the *figures*) that stand out from their surroundings (the *ground*).

fixation (1)   the inability to see a problem from a new perspective; an impediment to problem solving.

fixation (2)   according to Freud, a lingering focus of pleasure-seeking energies at an earlier psychosexual stage, where conflicts were unresolved.

fixed-interval schedule   in operant conditioning, a schedule of reinforcement that reinforces a response only after a specified time has elapsed.

fixed-ratio schedule   in operant conditioning, a schedule of reinforcement that reinforces a response only after a specified number of responses.

flashbulb memory   a clear memory of an emotionally significant moment or event.

fluid intelligence   one's ability to reason speedily and abstractly; tends to decrease during late adulthood.

foot-in-the-door phenomenon   the tendency for people who have first agreed to a small request to comply later with a larger request.

formal operational stage   in Piaget's theory, the stage of cognitive development (normally beginning about age 12) during which people begin to think logically about abstract concepts.

framing   the way an issue is posed; how an issue is framed can significantly affect decisions and judgments.

fraternal twins   twins who develop from separate eggs. They are genetically no closer than non-twin brothers and sisters, but they share a fetal environment.

free association   in psychoanalysis, a method of exploring the unconscious in which the person relaxes and says whatever comes to mind, no matter how trivial or embarrassing.

frequency   the number of complete wavelengths that pass a point in a given time (for example, per second).

frontal lobes   the portion of the cerebral cortex lying just behind the forehead; involved in speaking and muscle movements and in making plans and judgments.

frustration-aggression principle   the principle that frustration—the blocking of an attempt to achieve some goal—creates anger, which can generate aggression.

functional fixedness   the tendency to think of things only in terms of their usual functions; an impediment to problem solving.

functionalism   a school of psychology that focused on how mental and behavioral processes function—how they enable the organism to adapt, survive, and flourish.

fundamental attribution error the tendency for observers, when analyzing another's behavior, to underestimate the impact of the situation and to overestimate the impact of personal disposition.

G

gate-control theory the theory that the spinal cord contains a neurological "gate" that blocks pain signals or allows them to pass on to the brain. The "gate" is opened by the activity of pain signals traveling up small nerve fibers and is closed by activity in larger fibers or by information coming from the brain.

gender in psychology, the characteristics, whether biologically or socially influenced, by which people define *male* and *female*.

gender identity one's sense of being male or female.

gender role a set of expected behaviors for males and for females.

gender schema theory the theory that children learn from their cultures a concept of what it means to be male and female and that they adjust their behavior accordingly.

gender-typing the acquisition of a traditional masculine or feminine role.

general adaptation syndrome (GAS) Selye's concept of the body's adaptive response to stress in three stages—alarm, resistance, exhaustion.

general intelligence (*g*) a factor that Spearman and others believed underlies specific mental abilities and is therefore measured by every task on an intelligence test.

generalization the tendency, once a response has been conditioned, for stimuli similar to the conditioned stimulus to elicit similar responses.

generalized anxiety disorder an anxiety disorder in which a person is continually tense, apprehensive, and in a state of autonomic nervous system arousal.

genes the biochemical units of heredity that make up the chromosomes; a segment of DNA capable of synthesizing a protein.

gestalt an organized whole. Gestalt psychologists emphasized our tendency to integrate pieces of information into meaningful wholes.

glucose the form of sugar that circulates in the blood and provides the major source of energy for body tissues. When its level is low, we feel hunger.

GRIT Graduated and Reciprocated Initiatives in Tension-Reduction—a strategy designed to decrease international tensions.

group polarization the enhancement of a group's prevailing attitudes through discussion within the group.

grouping the perceptual tendency to organize stimuli into coherent groups.

groupthink the mode of thinking that occurs when the desire for harmony in a decision-making group overrides a realistic appraisal of alternatives.

H

habituation decreasing responsiveness with repeated stimulation. As infants gain familiarity with repeated exposure to a visual stimulus, their interest wanes and they look away sooner.

hallucinations false sensory experiences, such as seeing something in the absence of an external visual stimulus.

hallucinogens psychedelic ("mind-manifesting") drugs, such as LSD, that distort perceptions and evoke sensory images in the absence of sensory input.

health psychology a subfield of psychology that provides psychology's contribution to behavioral medicine.

heritability the proportion of variation among individuals that we can attribute to genes. The heritability of a trait may vary, depending on the range of populations and environments studied.

heuristic a simple thinking strategy that often allows us to make judgments and solve problems efficiently; usually speedier but also more error-prone than *algorithms*.

hidden observer Hilgard's term describing a hypnotized subject's awareness of experiences, such as pain, that go unreported during hypnosis.

hierarchy of needs Maslow's pyramid of human needs, beginning at the base with physiological needs that must first be satisfied before higher-level safety needs and then psychological needs become active.

hindsight bias the tendency to believe, after learning an outcome, that one would have foreseen it. (Also known as the *I-knew-it-all-along phenomenon*.)

hippocampus a neural center located in the limbic system that helps process explicit memories for storage.

homeostasis a tendency to maintain a balanced or constant internal state; the regulation of any aspect of body chemistry, such as blood glucose, around a particular level.

hormones chemical messengers, mostly those manufactured by the endocrine glands, that are produced in one tissue and affect another.

hue the dimension of color that is determined by the wavelength of light; what we know as the color names *blue, green*, and so forth.

hypnosis a social interaction in which one person (the hypnotist) suggests to another (the subject) that certain perceptions, feelings, thoughts, or behaviors will spontaneously occur.

hypothalamus [hi-po-THAL-uh-muss] a neural structure lying below (*hypo*) the thalamus; it directs several maintenance activities (eating, drinking, body temperature), helps govern the endocrine system via the pituitary gland, and is linked to emotion.

hypothesis a testable prediction, often implied by a theory.

I

iconic memory a momentary sensory memory of visual stimuli; a photographic or picture-image memory lasting no more than a few tenths of a second.

id contains a reservoir of unconscious psychic energy that, according to Freud, strives to satisfy basic sexual and aggressive drives. The id operates on the *pleasure principle*, demanding immediate gratification.

identical twins twins who develop from a single fertilized egg that splits in two, creating two genetically identical organisms.

identification the process by which, according to Freud, children incorporate their parents' values into their developing superegos.

identity one's sense of self; according to Erikson, the adolescent's task is to solidify a sense of self by testing and integrating various roles.

illusory correlation the perception of a relationship where none exists.

imagery mental pictures; a powerful aid to effortful processing, especially when combined with semantic encoding.

implicit memory retention independent of conscious recollection. Also called *procedural memory*.

imprinting the process by which certain animals form attachments during a critical period very early in life.

incentive a positive or negative environmental stimulus that motivates behavior.

independent variable the experimental factor that is manipulated; the variable whose effect is being studied.

individualism giving priority to one's own goals over group goals, and defining one's identity in terms of personal attributes rather than group identifications.

informational social influence influence resulting from one's willingness to accept others' opinions about reality.

ingroup "Us"—people with whom one shares a common identity.

ingroup bias The tendency to favor one's own group.

inner ear the innermost part of the ear, containing the cochlea, semicircular canals, and vestibular sacs.

insight   a sudden and often novel realization of the solution to a problem; it contrasts with strategy-based solutions.

insomnia   recurring problems in falling or staying asleep.

instinct   a complex behavior that is rigidly patterned throughout a species and is unlearned.

intelligence   the mental abilities needed to select, adapt to, and shape environments. It involves the abilities to profit from experience, solve problems, reason, and successfully meet challenges and achieve goals.

intelligence quotient (IQ)   defined originally as the ratio of mental age (*ma*) to chronological age (*ca*) multiplied by 100 (thus, IQ = *ma/ca* × 100). On contemporary intelligence tests, the average performance for a given age is assigned a score of 100.

intensity   the amount of energy in a light or sound wave, which we perceive as brightness or loudness, as determined by the wave's amplitude.

interaction   the idea that one factor (such as environment) depends on another factor (such as heredity).

internal locus of control   the perception that one controls one's own fate.

interneurons   central nervous system neurons that internally communicate and intervene between the sensory inputs and motor outputs.

interpretation   in psychoanalysis, the analyst's noting supposed dream meanings, resistances, and other significant behaviors in order to promote insight.

intimacy   in Erikson's theory, the ability to form close, loving relationships; a primary developmental task in late adolescence and early adulthood.

intrinsic motivation   a desire to perform a behavior for its own sake and to be effective.

J

James-Lange theory   the theory that our experience of emotion is our awareness of our physiological responses to emotion-arousing stimuli.

just-world phenomenon   the tendency of people to believe that the world is just and people therefore get what they deserve and deserve what they get.

K

kinesthesis [kin-ehs-THEE-sehs]   the system for sensing the position and movement of individual body parts.

L

language   our spoken, written, or signed words and the ways we combine them to communicate meaning.

latent content   according to Freud, the underlying meaning of a dream (as distinct from its manifest content). Freud believed that a dream's latent content functions as a safety valve.

latent learning   the idea that animals, like people, can learn from experience, with or without reinforcement. For example, after exploring a maze for 10 days, rats received a food reward at the end of the maze. They quickly demonstrated their prior learning of the maze—by immediately doing as well as (and even better than) rats that had been reinforced for running the maze.

law of effect   Thorndike's principle that behaviors followed by favorable consequences become more likely.

learned helplessness   the hopelessness and passive resignation an animal or human learns when unable to avoid repeated aversive events.

learning   a relatively permanent change in an organism's behavior due to experience.

lesion [LEE-zhuhn]   tissue destruction. A brain lesion is a naturally or experimentally caused destruction of brain tissue.

limbic system   a doughnut-shaped system of neural structures at the border of the brainstem and cerebral hemispheres; associated with emotions such as fear and aggression and drives such as those for food and sex. Includes the hippocampus, amygdala, and hypothalamus.

linguistic determinism   Whorf's hypothesis that language determines the way we think.

lithium   a chemical that provides an effective drug therapy for the mood swings of bipolar (manic-depressive) disorders.

lobotomy   a now-rare psychosurgical procedure once used to calm uncontrollably emotional or violent patients. The procedure cut the nerves that connect the frontal lobes to the emotion-controlling centers of the inner brain.

long-term memory   the relatively permanent and limitless storehouse of the memory system.

long-term potentiation (LTP)   an increase in a synapse's firing potential after brief, rapid stimulation. Believed to be a neural basis for learning and memory.

longitudinal study   research in which the same people are restudied and retested over a long period.

LSD   a powerful hallucinogenic drug; also known as *acid* (*lysergic acid diethylamide*).

lymphocytes   the two types of white blood cells that are part of the body's immune system: *B lymphocytes* form in the *b*one marrow and release antibodies that fight bacterial infections; *T lymphocytes* form in the *t*hymus and, among other duties, attack cancer cells, viruses, and foreign substances.

M

major depressive disorder   a mood disorder in which a person, for no apparent reason, experiences two or more weeks of depressed moods, feelings of worthlessness, and diminished interest or pleasure in most activities.

manic episode   a mood disorder marked by a hyperactive, wildly optimistic state.

manifest content   according to Freud, the remembered story line of a dream (as distinct from its latent content).

maturation   biological growth processes that enable orderly changes in behavior, relatively uninfluenced by experience.

medical model   the concept that diseases have physical causes that can be diagnosed, treated, and, in most cases, cured. When applied to psychological disorders, the medical model assumes that these "mental" illnesses can be diagnosed on the basis of their symptoms and cured through therapy, which may include treatment in a psychiatric hospital.

medulla [muh-DUL-uh]   the base of the brainstem; controls heartbeat and breathing.

memory   the persistence of learning over time through the storage and retrieval of information.

menarche [meh-NAR-key]   the first menstrual period.

menopause   the time of natural cessation of menstruation; also refers to the biological changes a woman experiences as her ability to reproduce declines.

mental age   a measure of intelligence test performance devised by Binet; the chronological age that most typically corresponds to a given level of performance. Thus, a child who does as well as the average 8-year-old is said to have a mental age of 8.

mental retardation   a condition of limited mental ability, indicated by an intelligence score below 70 and difficulty in adapting to the demands of life; varies from mild to profound.

mere exposure effect   the phenomenon that repeated exposure to novel stimuli increases liking of them.

middle ear   the chamber between the eardrum and cochlea containing three tiny bones (hammer, anvil, and stirrup) that concentrate the vibrations of the eardrum on the cochlea's oval window.

Minnesota Multiphasic Personality Inventory (MMPI) the most widely researched and clinically used of all personality tests. Originally developed to identify emotional disorders (still considered its most appropriate use), this test is now used for many other screening purposes.

mirror neurons frontal lobe neurons that fire when performing certain actions or when observing another doing so. The brain's mirroring of another's action may enable imitation, language learning, and empathy.

misinformation effect incorporating misleading information into one's memory of an event.

mnemonics [nih-MON-iks] memory aids, especially those techniques that use vivid imagery and organizational devices.

modeling the process of observing and imitating a specific behavior.

monocular cues distance cues, such as linear perspective and overlap, available to either eye alone.

mood disorders psychological disorders characterized by emotional extremes. See *major depressive disorder*, *manic episode*, and *bipolar disorder*.

mood-congruent memory the tendency to recall experiences that are consistent with one's current good or bad mood.

motivation a need or desire that energizes and directs behavior.

motor cortex an area at the rear of the frontal lobes that controls voluntary movements.

motor neurons neurons that carry outgoing information from the central nervous system to the muscles and glands.

MRI (magnetic resonance imaging) a technique that uses magnetic fields and radio waves to produce computer-generated images that distinguish among different types of soft tissue; allows us to see structures within the brain.

mutation a random error in gene replication that leads to a genetic change.

myelin [MY-uh-lin] **sheath** a layer of fatty tissue segmentally encasing the fibers of many neurons; enables vastly greater transmission speed of neural impulses as the impulse hops from one node to the next.

N

narcolepsy a sleep disorder characterized by uncontrollable sleep attacks. The sufferer may lapse directly into REM sleep, often at inopportune times.

natural selection the principle that, among the range of inherited trait variations, those that lead to increased reproduction and survival will most likely be passed on to succeeding generations.

naturalistic observation observing and recording behavior in naturally occurring situations without trying to manipulate and control the situation.

nature-nurture issue the longstanding controversy over the relative contributions that genes and experience make to the development of psychological traits and behaviors.

near-death experience an altered state of consciousness reported after a close brush with death (such as through cardiac arrest); often similar to drug-induced hallucinations.

nerves neural "cables" containing many axons. These bundled axons, which are part of the peripheral nervous system, connect the central nervous system with muscles, glands, and sense organs.

nervous system the body's speedy, electrochemical communication system, consisting of all the nerve cells of the peripheral and central nervous systems.

neuron a nerve cell; the basic building block of the nervous system.

neurotransmitters chemical messengers that traverse the synaptic gaps between neurons. When released by the sending neuron, neurotransmitters travel across the synapse and bind to receptor sites on the receiving neuron, thereby influencing whether that neuron will generate a neural impulse.

night terrors a sleep disorder characterized by high arousal and an appearance of being terrified; unlike nightmares, night terrors occur during Stage 4 sleep, within 2 or 3 hours of falling asleep, and are seldom remembered.

norm an understood rule for accepted and expected behavior. Norms prescribe "proper" behavior.

normal curve the symmetrical bell-shaped curve that describes the distribution of many physical and psychological attributes. Most scores fall near the average, and fewer and fewer scores lie near the extremes.

normative social influence influence resulting from a person's desire to gain approval or avoid disapproval.

O

object permanence the awareness that things continue to exist even when not perceived.

observational learning learning by observing others.

obsessive-compulsive disorder an anxiety disorder characterized by unwanted repetitive thoughts (obsessions) and/or actions (compulsions).

occipital [ahk-SIP-uh-tuhl] **lobes** the portion of the cerebral cortex lying at the back of the head; includes the visual areas, which receive visual information from the opposite visual field.

Oedipus [ED-uh-puss] **complex** according to Freud, a boy's sexual desires toward his mother and feelings of jealousy and hatred for the rival father.

one-word stage the stage in speech development, from about age 1 to 2, during which a child speaks mostly in single words.

operant behavior behavior that operates on the environment, producing consequences.

operant chamber a chamber, also known as a *Skinner box*, containing a bar or key that an animal can manipulate to obtain a food or water reinforcer, with attached devices to record the animal's rate of bar pressing or key pecking. Used in operant conditioning research.

operant conditioning a type of learning in which behavior is strengthened if followed by a reinforcer or diminished if followed by a punisher.

operational definition a statement of the procedures (operations) used to define research variables. For example, *intelligence* may be operationally defined as what an intelligence test measures.

opiates opium and its derivatives, such as morphine and heroin; they depress neural activity, temporarily lessening pain and anxiety.

opponent-process theory the theory that opposing retinal processes (red-green, yellow-blue, white-black) enable color vision. For example, some cells are stimulated by green and inhibited by red; others are stimulated by red and inhibited by green.

optic nerve the nerve that carries neural impulses from the eye to the brain.

outgroup "Them"—those perceived as different or apart from one's ingroup.

overconfidence the tendency to be more confident than correct—to overestimate the accuracy of one's beliefs and judgments.

P

panic disorder an anxiety disorder marked by a minutes-long episode of intense dread in which a person experiences terror and accompanying chest pain, choking, or other frightening sensations.

parallel processing the processing of several aspects of a problem simultaneously; the brain's natural mode of information processing for many functions, including vision. Contrasts with the step-by-step (serial) processing of most computers and of conscious problem solving.

parapsychology the study of paranormal phenomena, including ESP and psychokinesis.

parasympathetic nervous system the division of the autonomic nervous system that calms the body, conserving its energy.

parietal [puh-RYE-uh-tuhl] **lobes**   the portion of the cerebral cortex lying at the top of the head and toward the rear; includes the sensory cortex.

partial (intermittent) reinforcement   reinforcing a response only part of the time; results in slower acquisition of a response but much greater resistance to extinction than does continuous reinforcement.

passionate love   an aroused state of intense positive absorption in another, usually present at the beginning of a love relationship.

perception   the process of organizing and interpreting sensory information, enabling us to recognize meaningful objects and events.

perceptual adaptation   in vision, the ability to adjust to an artificially displaced or even inverted visual field.

perceptual constancy   perceiving objects as unchanging (having consistent lightness, color, shape, and size) even as illumination and retinal images change.

perceptual set   a mental predisposition to perceive one thing and not another.

peripheral nervous system (PNS)   the sensory and motor neurons that connect the central nervous system (CNS) to the rest of the body.

personal control   our sense of controlling our environment rather than feeling helpless.

personal space   the buffer zone we like to maintain around our bodies.

personality   an individual's characteristic pattern of thinking, feeling, and acting.

personality disorders   psychological disorders characterized by inflexible and enduring behavior patterns that impair social functioning.

personality inventory   a questionnaire (often with true-false or agree-disagree items) on which people respond to items designed to gauge a wide range of feelings and behaviors; used to assess selected personality traits.

PET (positron emission tomography) scan   a visual display of brain activity that detects where a radioactive form of glucose goes while the brain performs a given task.

phobia   an anxiety disorder marked by a persistent, irrational fear and avoidance of a specific object or situation.

physical dependence   a physiological need for a drug, marked by unpleasant withdrawal symptoms when the drug is discontinued.

pitch   a tone's highness or lowness; depends on frequency.

pituitary gland   the endocrine system's most influential gland. Under the influence of the hypothalamus, the pituitary regulates growth and controls other endocrine glands.

placebo effect   any effect on behavior caused by a placebo.

placebo [pluh-SEE-bo; Latin for "I shall please"]   an inert substance or condition that may be administered instead of a presumed active agent, such as a drug, to see if it triggers the effects believed to characterize the active agent.

plasticity   the brain's capacity for modification, as evident in brain reorganization following damage (especially in children) and in experiments on the effects of experience on brain development.

polygraph   a machine, commonly used in attempts to detect lies, that measures several of the physiological responses accompanying emotion (such as perspiration and cardiovascular and breathing changes).

population   all the cases in a group, from which samples may be drawn for a study. (Note: Except for national studies, this does *not* refer to a country's whole population.)

positive psychology   the scientific study of optimal human functioning; aims to discover and promote strengths and virtues that enable individuals and communities to thrive.

posthypnotic amnesia   supposed inability to recall what one experienced during hypnosis; induced by the hypnotist's suggestion.

posthypnotic suggestion   a suggestion, made during a hypnosis session, to be carried out after the subject is no longer hypnotized; used by some clinicians to help control undesired symptoms and behaviors.

predictive validity   the success with which a test predicts the behavior it is designed to predict; it is assessed by computing the correlation between test scores and the criterion behavior. (Also called *criterion-related validity*.)

prejudice   an unjustifiable (and usually negative) attitude toward a group and its members. Prejudice generally involves stereotyped beliefs, negative feelings, and a predisposition to discriminatory action.

preoperational stage   in Piaget's theory, the stage (from about 2 to 6 or 7 years of age) during which a child learns to use language but does not yet comprehend the mental operations of concrete logic.

primary reinforcer   an innately reinforcing stimulus, such as one that satisfies a biological need.

primary sex characteristics   the body structures (ovaries, testes, and external genitalia) that make sexual reproduction possible.

priming   the activation, often unconsciously, of particular associations in memory.

proactive interference   the disruptive effect of prior learning on the recall of new information.

projection   psychoanalytic defense mechanism by which people disguise their own threatening impulses by attributing them to others.

projective test   a personality test, such as the Rorschach or inkblot test, that provides ambiguous stimuli designed to trigger projection of one's inner dynamics.

prosocial behavior   positive, constructive, helpful behavior. The opposite of antisocial behavior.

prototype   a mental image or best example of a category. Matching new items to the prototype provides a quick and easy method for including items in a category (as when comparing feathered creatures to a prototypical bird, such as a robin).

psychiatry   a branch of medicine dealing with psychological disorders; practiced by physicians who sometimes provide medical (for example, drug) treatments as well as psychological therapy.

psychoactive drug   a chemical substance that alters perceptions and mood.

psychoanalysis   Freud's theory of personality and therapeutic technique that attributes our thoughts and actions to unconscious motives and conflicts. Freud believed the patient's free associations, resistances, dreams, and transferences—and the therapist's interpretations of them—released previously repressed feelings, allowing the patient to gain self-insight.

psychological dependence   a psychological need to use a drug, such as to relieve negative emotions.

psychological disorder   a "harmful dysfunction" in which behavior is judged to be atypical, disturbing, maladaptive, and unjustifiable.

psychology   the science of behavior and mental processes.

psychopharmacology   the study of the effects of drugs on mind and behavior.

psychophysics   the study of relationships between the physical characteristics of stimuli, such as their intensity, and our psychological experience of them.

psychophysiological illness   literally, "mind-body" illness; any stress-related physical illness, such as hypertension and some headaches.

psychosexual stages   the childhood stages of development (oral, anal, phallic, latency, genital) during which, according to Freud, the id's pleasure-seeking energies focus on distinct erogenous zones.

psychosurgery   surgery that removes or destroys brain tissue in an effort to change behavior.

psychotherapy   an emotionally charged, confiding interaction between a trained therapist and someone who suffers from psychological difficulties.

puberty   the period of sexual maturation, during which a person becomes capable of reproducing.

punishment   an event that *decreases* the behavior that it follows.

R

random assignment   assigning participants to experimental and control conditions by chance, thus minimizing preexisting differences between those assigned to the different groups.

random sample   a sample that fairly represents a population because each member has an equal chance of inclusion.

rationalization   defense mechanism that offers self-justifying explanations in place of the real, more threatening, unconscious reasons for one's actions.

reaction formation   psychoanalytic defense mechanism by which the ego unconsciously switches unacceptable impulses into their opposites. Thus, people may express feelings that are the opposite of their anxiety-arousing unconscious feelings.

recall   a measure of memory in which the person must retrieve information learned earlier, as on a fill-in-the-blank test.

reciprocal determinism   the interacting influences between personality and environmental factors.

recognition   a measure of memory in which the person need only identify items previously learned, as on a multiple-choice test.

reflex   a simple, automatic, inborn response to a sensory stimulus, such as the knee-jerk response.

refractory period   a resting period after orgasm, during which a man cannot achieve another orgasm.

regression   defense mechanism in which an individual faced with anxiety retreats to a more infantile psychosexual stage, where some psychic energy remains fixated.

rehearsal   the conscious repetition of information, either to maintain it in consciousness or to encode it for storage.

reinforcer   in operant conditioning, any event that *strengthens* the behavior it follows.

relative deprivation   the perception that one is worse off relative to those with whom one compares oneself.

relearning   a memory measure that assesses the amount of time saved when learning material for a second time.

reliability   the extent to which a test yields consistent results, as assessed by the consistency of scores on two halves of the test, on alternate forms of the test, or on retesting.

REM rebound   the tendency for REM sleep to increase following REM sleep deprivation (created by repeated awakenings during REM sleep).

REM sleep   rapid eye movement sleep, a recurring sleep stage during which vivid dreams commonly occur. Also known as *paradoxical sleep,* because the muscles are relaxed (except for minor twitches) but other body systems are active.

replication   repeating the essence of a research study, usually with different participants in different situations, to see whether the basic finding extends to other participants and circumstances.

representativeness heuristic   judging the likelihood of things in terms of how well they seem to represent, or match, particular prototypes; may lead one to ignore other relevant information.

repression   in psychoanalytic theory, the basic defense mechanism that banishes anxiety-arousing thoughts, feelings, and memories from consciousness.

resistance   in psychoanalysis, the blocking from consciousness of anxiety-laden material.

respondent behavior   behavior that occurs as an automatic response to some stimulus.

reticular formation   a nerve network in the brainstem that plays an important role in controlling arousal.

retina   the light-sensitive inner surface of the eye, containing the receptor rods and cones plus layers of neurons that begin the processing of visual information.

retinal disparity   a binocular cue for perceiving depth: By comparing images from the two eyeballs, the brain computes distance—the greater the disparity (difference) between the two images, the closer the object.

retrieval   the process of getting information out of memory storage.

retroactive interference   the disruptive effect of new learning on the recall of old information.

rods   retinal receptors that detect black, white, and gray; necessary for peripheral and twilight vision, when cones don't respond.

role   a set of expectations (norms) about a social position, defining how those in the position ought to behave.

rooting reflex   a baby's tendency, when touched on the cheek, to open the mouth and search for the nipple.

Rorschach inkblot test   the most widely used projective test, a set of 10 inkblots, designed by Hermann Rorschach; seeks to identify people's inner feelings by analyzing their interpretations of the blots.

S

savant syndrome   a condition in which a person otherwise limited in mental ability has an exceptional specific skill, such as in computation or drawing.

scapegoat theory   The theory that prejudice offers an outlet for anger by providing someone to blame.

schema   a concept or framework that organizes and interprets information.

schizophrenia   a group of severe disorders characterized by disorganized and delusional thinking, disturbed perceptions, and inappropriate emotions and actions.

secondary sex characteristics   nonreproductive sexual characteristics, such as female breasts and hips, male voice quality and body hair.

selective attention   the focusing of conscious awareness on a particular stimulus, as in the cocktail party effect.

self-actualization   according to Maslow, the ultimate psychological need that arises after basic physical and psychological needs are met and self-esteem is achieved; the motivation to fulfill one's potential.

self-concept   all our thoughts and feelings about ourselves, in answer to the question, "Who am I?"

self-disclosure   revealing intimate aspects of oneself to others.

self-esteem   one's feelings of high or low self-worth.

self-serving bias   a readiness to perceive oneself favorably.

sensation   the process by which our sensory receptors and nervous system receive and represent stimulus energies from our environment.

sensorimotor stage   in Piaget's theory, the stage (from birth to about 2 years of age) during which infants know the world mostly in terms of their sensory impressions and motor activities.

sensory adaptation   diminished sensitivity as a consequence of constant stimulation.

sensory cortex   the area at the front of the parietal lobes that registers and processes body sensations.

sensory interaction   the principle that one sense may influence another, as when the smell of food influences its taste.

sensory memory   the immediate, initial recording of sensory information in the memory system.

sensory neurons   neurons that carry incoming information from the sense receptors to the central nervous system.

serial position effect   our tendency to recall best the last and first items in a list.

set point   the point at which an individual's "weight thermostat" is supposedly set. When the body falls below this weight, an increase in hunger and a lowered metabolic rate may act to restore the lost weight.

sexual disorder   a problem that consistently impairs sexual arousal or functioning.

sexual orientation   an enduring sexual attraction toward members of either one's own sex (homosexual orientation) or the other sex (heterosexual orientation).

sexual response cycle   the four stages of sexual responding described by Masters and Johnson—excitement, plateau, orgasm, and resolution.

shaping   an operant conditioning procedure in which reinforcers guide behavior toward closer and closer approximations of a desired goal.

short-term memory   activated memory that holds a few items briefly, such as the seven digits of a phone number while dialing, before the information is stored or forgotten. *Working memory* is a similar concept that focuses more on the processing of briefly stored information.

sleep   periodic, natural, reversible loss of consciousness—as distinct from unconsciousness resulting from a coma, general anesthesia, or hibernation. (Adapted from Dement, 1999.)

sleep apnea   a sleep disorder characterized by temporary cessations of breathing during sleep and consequent momentary reawakenings.

social clock   the culturally preferred timing of social events such as marriage, parenthood, and retirement.

social exchange theory   the theory that our social behavior is an exchange process, the aim of which is to maximize benefits and minimize costs.

social facilitation   improved performance of tasks in the presence of others; occurs with simple or well-learned tasks but not with tasks that are difficult or not yet mastered.

social learning theory   the theory that we learn social behavior by observing and imitating and by being rewarded or punished.

social loafing   the tendency for people in a group to exert less effort when pooling their efforts toward attaining a common goal than when individually accountable.

social psychology   the scientific study of how we think about, influence, and relate to one another.

social trap   a situation in which the conflicting parties, by rationally pursuing their self-interests, become caught in mutually destructive behavior.

social-cognitive perspective   views behavior as influenced by the interaction between persons (and their thinking) and their social context.

somatic nervous system   the division of the peripheral nervous system that controls the body's skeletal muscles. Also called the *skeletal nervous system*.

source amnesia   attributing to the wrong source an event that we have experienced, heard about, read about, or imagined. (Also called *source misattribution*.) Source amnesia, along with the misinformation effect, is at the heart of many false memories.

spacing effect   the tendency for distributed study or practice to yield better long-term retention than is achieved through massed study or practice.

split brain   a condition in which the two hemispheres of the brain are isolated by cutting the connecting fibers (mainly those of the corpus callosum) between them.

spontaneous recovery   the reappearance, after a rest period, of an extinguished conditioned response.

spotlight effect   overestimating others' noticing and evaluating our appearance, performance, and blunders (as if we presume a spotlight shines on us).

SQ3R   a study method incorporating five steps: *S*urvey, *Q*uestion, *R*ead, *R*ehearse, *R*eview.

standardization   defining meaningful scores by comparison with the performance of a pretested "standardization group."

Stanford-Binet   the widely used American revision (by Terman at Stanford University) of Binet's original intelligence test.

stereotype   a generalized (sometimes accurate but often overgeneralized) belief about a group of people.

stereotype threat   a self-confirming concern that one will be evaluated based on a negative stereotype.

stimulants   drugs (such as caffeine, nicotine, and the more powerful amphetamines and cocaine) that excite neural activity and speed up body functions.

storage   the retention of encoded information over time.

stranger anxiety   the fear of strangers that infants commonly display, beginning by about 8 months of age.

stress   the process by which we perceive and respond to certain events, called *stressors*, that we appraise as threatening or challenging.

structuralism   an early school of psychology that used introspection to explore the elemental structure of the human mind.

subjective well-being   self-perceived happiness or satisfaction with life. Used along with measures of objective well-being (for example, physical and economic indicators) to evaluate people's quality of life.

subliminal   below one's absolute threshold for conscious awareness.

superego   the part of personality that, according to Freud, represents internalized ideals and provides standards for judgment (the conscience) and for future aspirations.

superordinate goals   shared goals that override differences among people and require their cooperation.

survey   a technique for ascertaining the self-reported attitudes or behaviors of people, usually by questioning a representative, random sample of them.

sympathetic nervous system   the division of the autonomic nervous system that arouses the body, mobilizing its energy in stressful situations.

synapse [SIN-aps]   the junction between the axon tip of the sending neuron and the dendrite or cell body of the receiving neuron. The tiny gap at this junction is called the *synaptic gap* or *cleft*.

systematic desensitization   a type of counterconditioning that associates a pleasant relaxed state with gradually increasing anxiety-triggering stimuli. Commonly used to treat phobias.

T

telegraphic speech   early speech stage in which a child speaks like a telegram—"go car"—using mostly nouns and verbs and omitting "auxiliary" words.

temperament   a person's characteristic emotional reactivity and intensity.

temporal lobes   the portion of the cerebral cortex lying roughly above the ears; includes the auditory areas, each of which receives auditory information primarily from the opposite ear.

teratogens   agents, such as chemicals and viruses, that can reach the embryo or fetus during prenatal development and cause harm.

testosterone   the most important of the male sex hormones. Both males and females have it, but the additional testosterone in males stimulates the growth of the male sex organs in the fetus and the development of the male sex characteristics during puberty.

thalamus [THAL-uh-muss]   the brain's sensory switchboard, located on top of the brainstem; it directs messages to the sensory receiving areas in the cortex and transmits replies to the cerebellum and medulla.

THC   the major active ingredient in marijuana; triggers a variety of effects, including mild hallucinations.

theory   an explanation using an integrated set of principles that organizes and predicts observations.

theory of mind   people's ideas about their own and others' mental states—about their feelings, perceptions, and thoughts and the behaviors these might predict.

threshold   the level of stimulation required to trigger a neural impulse.

token economy   an operant conditioning procedure that rewards desired behavior. A patient exchanges a token of some sort, earned for exhibiting the desired behavior, for various privileges or treats.

tolerance   the diminishing effect with regular use of the same dose of a drug, requiring the user to take larger and larger doses before experiencing the drug's effect.

top-down processing   information processing guided by higher-level mental processes, as when we construct perceptions drawing on our experience and expectations.

trait   a characteristic pattern of behavior or a disposition to feel and act, as assessed by self-report inventories and peer reports.

transference   in psychoanalysis, the patient's transfer to the analyst of emotions linked with other relationships (such as love or hatred for a parent).

two-factor theory   Schachter's theory that to experience emotion one must (1) be physically aroused and (2) cognitively label the arousal.

two-word stage   beginning about age 2, the stage in speech development during which a child speaks mostly two-word statements.

Type A   Friedman and Rosenman's term for competitive, hard-driving, impatient, verbally aggressive, and anger-prone people.

Type B   Friedman and Rosenman's term for easygoing, relaxed people.

U

unconditional positive regard   according to Rogers, an attitude of total acceptance toward another person.

unconditioned response (UCR)   in classical conditioning, the unlearned, naturally occurring response to the unconditioned stimulus (UCS), such as salivation when food is in the mouth.

unconditioned stimulus (UCS)   in classical conditioning, a stimulus that unconditionally— naturally and automatically— triggers a response.

unconscious   according to Freud, a reservoir of mostly unacceptable thoughts, wishes, feelings, and memories. According to contemporary psychologists, information processing of which we are unaware.

V

validity   the extent to which a test measures or predicts what it is supposed to. (See also *content validity* and *predictive validity*.)

variable-interval schedule   in operant conditioning, a schedule of reinforcement that reinforces a response at unpredictable time intervals.

variable-ratio schedule   in operant conditioning, a schedule of reinforcement that reinforces a response after an unpredictable number of responses.

vestibular sense   the sense of body movement and position, including the sense of balance.

visual capture   the tendency for vision to dominate the other senses, as when we perceive voices in films as coming from the screen we see rather than from the projector behind us.

visual cliff   a laboratory device for testing depth perception in infants and young animals.

W

wavelength   the distance from the peak of one light or sound wave to the peak of the next. Electromagnetic wavelengths vary from the short blips of cosmic rays to the long pulses of radio transmission.

Weber's law   the principle that, to be perceived as different, two stimuli must differ by a constant minimum percentage (rather than a constant amount).

Wechsler Adult Intelligence Scale (WAIS)   the WAIS is the most widely used intelligence test; contains verbal and performance (nonverbal) subtests.

Wernicke's area   controls language reception—a brain area involved in language comprehension and expression; usually in the left temporal lobe.

withdrawal   the discomfort and distress that follow discontinuing the use of an addictive drug.

X

X chromosome   the sex chromosome found in both men and women. Females have two X chromosomes; males have one. An X chromosome from each parent produces a female child.

Y

Y chromosome   the sex chromosome found only in males. When paired with an X sex chromosome from the mother, it produces a male child.

Young-Helmholtz trichromatic (three-color) theory   the theory that the retina contains three different color receptors—one most sensitive to red, one to green, one to blue—which when stimulated in combination can produce the perception of any color.

Z

zygote   the fertilized egg; it enters a 2-week period of rapid cell division and develops into an embryo.

Aas, H., & Klepp, K-I. (1992). Adolescents' alcohol use related to perceived norms. *Scandinavian Journal of Psychology, 33,* 315–325. (p. 219)

Abbey, A. (1991). Acquaintance rape and alcohol consumption on college campuses: How are they linked? *Journal of American College Health, 39,* 165–169. (p. 210)

Abelson, R., & Brown, P. L. (2002, April 13). Alternative medicine is finding its niche in nation's hospitals. *New York Times* (www.nytimes.com). (p. 420)

Abrams, D. (1991). AIDS: What young people believe and what they do. Paper presented at the British Association for the Advancement of Science conference. (p. 454)

Abrams, D. B., & Wilson, G. T. (1983). Alcohol, sexual arousal, and self-control. *Journal of Personality and Social Psychology, 45,* 188–198. (p. 211)

Abrams, M. (2002, June). Sight unseen—Restoring a blind man's vision is now a real possibility through stem-cell surgery. But even perfect eyes cannot see unless the brain has been taught to use them. *Discover, 23,* 54–60. (p. 176)

Abramson, L. Y., Metalsky, G. I., & Alloy, L. B. (1989). Hopelessness depression: A theory-based subtype. *Psychological Review, 96,* 358–372. (p. 493)

Acock, A. C., & Demo, D. H. (1994). *Family diversity and well-being.* Thousand Oaks, CA: Sage. (p. 90)

Adelmann, P. K., Antonucci, T. C., Crohan, S. F., & Coleman, L. M. (1989). Empty nest, cohort, and employment in the well-being of midlife women. *Sex Roles, 20,* 173–189. (p. 131)

Ader, R., & Cohen, N. (1985). CNS-immune system interactions: Conditioning phenomena. *Behavioral and Brain Sciences, 8,* 379–394. (p. 412)

Advertising Age (1958, February 10). "Phone now," said CBC subliminally—but nobody did. P. 8. (p. 144)

Affleck, G., Tennen, H., Urrows, S., & Higgins, P. (1994). Person and contextual features of daily stress reactivity: Individual differences in relations of undesirable daily events with mood disturbance and chronic pain intensity. *Journal of Personality and Social Psychology, 66,* 329–340. (p. 396)

Agid, O., Shapira, B., Zislin, J., Ritsner, M., Hanin, B., Murad, H., Troudart, T., Bloch, M., Heresco-Levy, U., & Lerer, B. (1999). Environment and vulnerability to major psychiatric illness: A case control study of early parental loss in major depression, bipolar disorder and schizophrenia. *Molecular Psychiatry, 4,* 163–172. (p. 489)

Aiello, J. R., Thompson, D. D., & Brodzinsky, D. M. (1983). How funny is crowding anyway? Effects of room size, group size, and the introduction of humor. *Basic and Applied Social Psychology, 4,* 193–207. (p. 551)

Ainsworth, M. D. S. (1973). The development of infant-mother attachment. In B. Caldwell & H. Ricciuti (Eds.), *Review of child development research* (Vol. 3). Chicago: University of Chicago Press. (p. 111)

Ainsworth, M. D. S. (1979). Infant-mother attachment. *American Psychologist, 34,* 932–937. (p. 111)

Albee, G. W. (1986). Toward a just society: Lessons from observations on the primary prevention of psychopathology. *American Psychologist, 41,* 891–898. (p. 535)

Alcock, J. E. (1981). *Parapsychology: Science or magic?* Oxford: Pergamon. (p. 274)

Aldrich, M. S. (1989). Automobile accidents in patients with sleep disorders. *Sleep, 12,* 487–494. (p. 199)

Aldridge-Morris, R. (1989). *Multiple personality: An exercise in deception.* Hillsdale, NJ: Erlbaum. (p. 484)

Alexander, C. N., Langer, E. J., Newman, R. I., Chandler, H. M., & Davies, J. L. (1989). Transcendental meditation, mindfulness, and longevity: An experimental study with the elderly. *Journal of Personality and Social Psychology, 57,* 950–964. (p. 416)

Allard, F., & Burnett, N. (1985). Skill in sport. *Canadian Journal of Psychology, 39,* 294–312. (p. 264)

Allen, J. B., Repinski, D. J., Ballard, J. C., & Griffin, B. W. (1996). Beliefs about the etiology of homosexuality may influence attitudes toward homosexuals. Paper presented to the American Psychological Society convention. (p. 368)

Allen, L. S., & Gorski, R. A. (1992). Sexual orientation and the size of the anterior commisure in the human brain. *Proceedings of the National Academy of Sciences, 89,* 7199–7202. (p. 367)

Alloy, L. B., Abramson, L. Y., Whitehouse, W. G., Hogan, M. E., Tashman, N. A., Steinberg, D. L., Rose, D. T., & Donovan, P. (1999). Depressogenic cognitive styles: Predictive validity, information processing and personality characteristics, and developmental origins. *Behaviour Research and Therapy, 37,* 503–531. (p. 495)

Allport, G. W. (1967). Gordon W. Allport. In E. G. Boring & G. Lindzey (Eds.), *A history of psychology in autobiography* (Vol. V). New York: Appleton-Century-Crofts. (pp. 442–443)

Allport, G. W., & Odbert, H. S. (1936). Trait-names: A psycho-lexical study. *Psychological Monographs, 47*(1). (p. 443)

Altman, L. K. (1999, June 28). Study says gay men reducing levels of risky sexual behavior. *New York Times* (www.nytimes.com). (p. 73)

Altman, L. K. (2002b, July 5). Modest anti-AIDS efforts offer huge payoff, studies say. *New York Times* (www.nytimes.com). (p. 299)

Alwin, D. F. (1990). Historical changes in parental orientations to children. In N. Mandell (Ed.), *Sociological studies of child development* (Vol. 3). Greenwich, CT: JAI Press. (p. 88)

Amabile, T. M. (1983). *The social psychology of creativity.* New York: Springer-Verlag. (p. 458)

Amabile, T. M., & Hennessey, B. A. (1992). The motivation for creativity in children. In A. K. Boggiano & T. S. Pittman (Eds.), *Achievement and motivation: A social-developmental perspective.* New York: Cambridge University Press. (p. 322)

Ambady, N., Hallahan, M., & Rosenthal, R. (1995). On judging and being judged accurately in zero-acquaintance situations. *Journal of Personality and Social Psychology, 69,* 518–529. (p. 387)

Ambady, N., & Rosenthal, R. (1992). Thin slices of expressive behavior as predictors of interpersonal consequences: A meta-analysis. *Psychological Bulletin, 111,* 256–274. (p. 450)

Ambady, N., & Rosenthal, R. (1993). Half a minute: Predicting teacher evaluations from thin slices of nonverbal behavior and physical attractiveness. *Journal of Personality and Social Psychology, 64,* 431–441. (p. 450)

Amen, D. G., Stubblefield, M., Carmichael, B., & Thisted, R. (1996). Brain SPECT findings and aggressiveness. *Annals of Clinical Psychiatry, 8,* 129–137. (p. 561)

American Enterprise (1992, January/February). Women, men, marriages & ministers. P. 106. (p. 462)

American Psychiatric Association. (1994). *Diagnostic and statistical manual of mental disorders (Fourth Edition).* Washington, DC: American Psychiatric Press. (p. 325)

American Psychological Association. (1991). Medical cost offset. Washington, DC: American Psychological Association Practice Directorate. (p. 523)

American Psychological Association. (1992). Ethical principles of psychologists and code of conduct. *American Psychologist, 47,* 1597–1611. (p. 30)

Anda, R., Williamson, D., Jones, D., Macera, C., Eaker, E., Glassman, A., & Marks, J. (1993). Depressed affect, hopelessness, and the risk of ischemic heart disease in a cohort of U.S. adults. *Epidemiology, 4,* 285–294. (p. 409)

Andersen, R. E., Crespo, C. J., Bartlett, S. J., Cheskin, L. J., & Pratt, M. (1998). Relationship of physical activity and television watching with body weight and level of fatness among children. *Journal of the American Medical Association, 279,* 938–942. (p. 356)

Andersen, S. M. (1998). Service Learning: A National Strategy for Youth Development. A position paper issued by the Task Force on Education Policy. Washington, DC: Institute for Communitarian Policy Studies, George Washington University. (p. 119)

Anderson, A. K., & Phelps, E. A. (2000). Expression without recognition: Contributions of the human amygdala to emotional communication. *Psychological Science, 11,* 106–111. (p. 50)

Anderson, B. L. (2002). Biobehavioral outcomes following psychological interventions for cancer patients. *Journal of Consulting and Clinical Psychology, 70,* 590–610. (p. 411)

Anderson, C. A. (2000). Violent video games increase aggression and violence. Testimony to the U.S. Senate Commerce, Science, and Transportation Committee hearing on "The impact of interactive violence on children," March 21, 2000. (p. 565)

Anderson, C. A. (2003). Video games and aggressive behavior. In D. Ravitch & J. P. Viteritti (Eds.), *Kids stuff: Marketing sex and violence to America's children.* Baltimore, MD: Johns Hopkins University Press. (p. 565)

Anderson, C. A., & Anderson, D. C. (1984). Ambient temperature and violent crime: Tests of the linear and curvilinear hypotheses. *Journal of Personality and Social Psychology, 46,* 91–97. (p. 562)

Anderson, C. A., Anderson, K. B., Dorr, N., DeNeve, K. M., & Flanagan, M. (2000). Temperature and aggression. *Advances in Experimental Social Psychology, 32,* 63–133. (p. 562)

Anderson, C. A., & Bushman, B. J. (2001). Effects of violent video games on aggressive behavior, aggressive cognition, aggressive affect physiological arousal, and prosocial behavior: A meta-analytic review of the scientific literature. *Psychological Science, 12,* 353–359. (p. 565)

Anderson, C. A., & Dill, K. E. (2000). Video games and aggressive thoughts, feelings, and behavior in the laboratory and in life. *Journal of Personality and Social Psychology, 78,* 772–790. (p. 565)

Anderson, C. A., Lindsay, J. J., & Bushman, B. J. (1999). Research in the psychological laboratory: Truth or triviality? *Current Directions in Psychological Science, 8,* 3–9. (p. 28)

Anderson, I. M. (2000). Selective serotonin reuptake inhibitors versus tricyclic antidepressants: A meta-analysis of efficacy and tolerability. *Journal of Affective Disorders, 58,* 19–36. (pp. 531–532)

Anderson, R. C., Pichert, J. W., Goetz, E. T., Schallert, D. L., Stevens, K. V., & Trollip, S. R. (1976). Instantiation of general terms. *Journal of Verbal Learning and Verbal Behavior, 15,* 667–679. (p. 273)

Andreasen, N. C. (1997). Linking mind and brain in the study of mental illnesses: A project for a scientific psychopathology. *Science, 275,* 1586–1593. (p. 499)

Andreasen, N. C. (2001). *Brave new brain: Conquering mental illness in the era of the genome.* New York: Oxford University Press. (pp. 471, 499)

Andreasen, N. C., Arndt, S., Swayze, V., II, Cizadlo, T., & Flaum, M. (1994). Thalamic abnormalities in schizophrenia visualized through magnetic resonance image averaging. *Science, 266,* 294–298. (p. 499)

Andrews, G., Hall, W., Teesson, M., & Henderson, S. (1999, April). *The mental health of Australians.* Canberra: Mental Health Branch, Commonwealth Department of Health and Aged Care. (p. 502)

Angell, M., & Kassirer, J. P. (1998). Alternative medicine: The risks of untested and unregulated remedies. *New England Journal of Medicine, 17,* 839–841. (p. 421)

Angelsen, N. K., Vik, T., Jacobsen, G., & Bakketeig, L. S. (2001). Breast feeding and cognitive development at age 1 and 5 years. *Archives of Disease in Childhood,* 85, 183–188. (p. 24)

Angoff, W. H. (1987). The nature-nurture debate, aptitudes, and group differences. Presidential address to American Psychological Association Division 5. (p. 331)

Annan, K. A. (2001). We can love what we are, without hating who—and what—we are not. Nobel Peace Prize lecture. (pp. 89, 577)

Anstis, S. (2000, November 4). Anecdote reported by A. Onion, Kaleidoscope vision. ABCNews.com. Originally reported in S. Anstis, "Visual adaptation to a negative, brightness-reversed world: Some preliminary observations. In G. A. Carpenter & S. Grossberg, *Neural networks for vision and image processing.* Cambridge, MA: MIT Press. (p. 177)

Antony, M. M., Brown, T. A., & Barlow, D. H. (1992). Current perspectives on panic and panic disorder. *Current Directions in Psychological Science, 1,* 79–82. (p. 479)

Antrobus, J. (1991). Dreaming: Cognitive processes during cortical activation and high afferent thresholds. *Psychological Review, 98,* 96–121. (p. 203)

Archer, J. (1996). Sex differences in social behavior: Are the social role and evolutionary explanations compatible? *American Psychologist, 51,* 909–917. (p. 91)

Arenson, K. W. (1997, May 4). Romanian woman breaks male grip on top math prize. *New York Times* News Service (in *Grand Rapids Press,* p. A7). (p. 333)

Arent, S. M., Landers, D. M., & Etnier, J. L. (2000). The effects of exercise on mood in older adults: A meta-analytic review. *Journal of Aging and Physical Activity, 8,* 407–430. (pp. 414–415)

Armony, J. L., Quirk, G. J., & Le Doux, J. E. (1998). Differential effects of amygdala lesions on early and late plastic components of auditory cortex spike trains during fear conditioning. *Journal of Neuroscience, 18,* 2592–2601. (p. 482)

Arnett, J. J. (1999). Adolescent storm and stress, reconsidered. *American Psychologist, 54,* 317–326. (p. 115)

Aron, A., Melinat, E., Aron, E. N., Vallone, R. D., & Bator, R. J. (1997). The experimental generation of interpersonal closeness: A procedure and some preliminary findings. *Personality and Social Psychology Bulletin, 23,* 363–377. (p. 573)

Aronson, E. (2001, April 13). Newsworthy violence. E-mail to SPSP discussion list, drawing from *Nobody Left to Hate.* New York: Freeman, 2000. (p. 122)

Arrigo, J. M., & Pezdek, K. (1997). Lessons from the study of psychogenic amnesia. *Current Directions in Psychology, 6,* 148–152. (p. 437)

Asch, S. E. (1955). Opinions and social pressure. *Scientific American, 193,* 31–35. (pp. 546–547)

Aserinsky, E. (1988, January 17). Personal communication. (p. 191)

ASHA (2003). STD statistics. American Social Health Association (www.ashastd.org/stdfaqs/statistics.html). (p. 362)

Assanand, S., Pinel, J. P. J., & Lehman, D. R. (1998). Personal theories of hunger and eating. *Journal of Applied Social Psychology, 28,* 998–1015. (p. 347)

Astin, A. W., Parrott, S. A., Korn, W. S., & Sax, L. J. (1997). *The American freshman: Thirty year trends, 1966–1996.* Los Angeles, CA: Higher Education Research Institute, UCLA. (p. 217)

Atkinson, R. (1988). *The teenage world: Adolescent self-image in ten countries.* New York: Plenum Press. (p. 88)

Atkinson, R. C., & Schiffrin, R. M. (1968). Human memory: A control system and its control processes. In K. Spence (Ed.), *The psychology of learning and motivation* (Vol. 2). New York: Academic Press. (p. 259)

Atwell, R. H. (1986, July 28). Drugs on campus: A perspective. *Higher Education & National Affairs,* p. 5. (p. 211)

Au, T. K., Knightly, L. M., Jun, S-A., & Oh, J. S. (2002). Overhearing a language during childhood. *Psychological Science, 13,* 238–242. (p. 305)

August, D., & Hakuta, K. (1998). *Educating language–minority children.* Washington, DC: National Academy of Sciences. (p. 309)

Austin, E. J., Deary, I. J., Whiteman, M. C., Fowkes, F. G. R., Pedersen, N. L., Rabbitt, P., Bent, N., & McInnes, L. (2002). Relationships between ability and personality: Does intelligence contribute positively to personal and social adjustment? *Personality and Individual Differences, 32,* 1391–1411. (p. 324)

Australian Bureau of Statistics. (1999). *Australia now—A statistical profile: Health—overweight and obesity* (www.abs.gov.au). (p. 354)

Averill, J. R. (1983). Studies on anger and aggression: Implications for theories of emotion. *American Psychologist, 38,* 1145–1160. (p. 394)

Averill, J. R. (1993). William James's other theory of emotion. In M. E. Donnelly (Ed.), *Reinterpreting the legacy of William James.* Washington, DC: American Psychological Association. (p. 380)

Avery, R. D., et al. (1994, December 13). Mainstream science on intelligence. *Wall Street Journal,* p. A-18. (p. 331)

Ax, A. F. (1953). The physiological differentiation of fear and anger in humans. *Psychosomatic Medicine, 15,* 433–442. (p. 385)

Axel, R. (1995, October). The molecular logic of smell. *Scientific American,* pp. 154–159. (p. 163)

Azar, B. (1998, June). Why can't this man feel whether or not he's standing up? *APA Monitor* (www.apa.org/monitor/jun98/touch.html). (p. 164)

Babad, E., Bernieri, F., & Rosenthal, R. (1991). Students as judges of teachers' verbal and nonverbal behavior. *American Educational Research Journal, 28,* 211–234. (p. 389)

Babyak, M., Blumenthal, J. A., Herman, S., Khatri, P., Doraiswamy, M., Moore, K., Craighead, W. W., Baldewics, T. T., & Krishnan, K. R. (2000). Exercise treatment for major depression: Maintenance of therapeutic benefit at ten months. *Psychosomatic Medicine, 62,* 633–638. (p. 415)

Bachman, J., Wadsworth, K., O'Malley, P., Johnston, L., & Schulenberg, J. (1997). *Smoking, drinking, and drug use in young adulthood: The impact of new freedoms and new responsibilities.* Mahwah, NJ: Erlbaum. (p. 219)

Baddeley, A. D. (1982). *Your memory: A user's guide.* New York: Macmillan. (p. 261)

Bahrick, H. P. (1984). Semantic memory content in permastore: 50 years of memory for Spanish learned in school. *Journal of Experimental Psychology: General, 111,* 1–29. (p. 277)

Bahrick, H. P., Bahrick, L. E., Bahrick, A. S., & Bahrick, P. E. (1993). Maintenance of foreign language vocabulary and the spacing effect. *Psychological Science, 4,* 316–321. (p. 261)

Bahrick, H. P., Bahrick, P. O., & Wittlinger, R. P. (1975). Fifty years of memory for names and faces: A cross-sectional approach. *Journal of Experimental Psychology: General, 104,* 54–75. (p. 272)

Bailey, J. M., Gaulin, S., Agyei, Y., & Gladue, B. A. (1994). Effects of gender and sexual orientation on evolutionary relevant aspects of human mating psychology. *Journal of Personality and Social Psychology, 66,* 1081–1093. (p. 73)

Bailey, J. M., Kirk, K. M., Zhu, G., Dunne, M. P., & Martin, N. G. (2000). Do individual differences in sociosexuality represent genetic or environmentally contingent strategies? Evidence from the Australian twin registry. *Journal of Personality and Social Psychology, 78,* 537–545. (p. 72)

Bailey, J. M., & Zucker, K. J. (1995). Childhood sex-typed behavior and sexual orientation: A conceptual analysis and quantitative review. *Developmental Psychology, 31,* 43–55. (p. 364)

Baillargeon, R. (1995). A model of physical reasoning in infancy. In C. Rovee-Collier & L. P. Lipsitt (Eds.), *Advances in infancy research* (Vol. 9). Stamford, CT: Ablex. (p. 106)

Baillargeon, R. (1998). Infants' understanding of the physical world. In M. Sabourin, F. I. M. Craik, & M. Roberts (Eds.), *Advances in psychological science, Vol. 2: Biological and cognitive aspects.* Hove, England: Psychology Press. (p. 106)

Baker, E. L. (1987). The state of the art of clinical hypnosis. *International Journal of Clinical and Experimental Hypnosis, 35,* 203–214. (p. 205)

Baker, M. C. (2001). *The atoms of language: The mind's hidden rules of grammar.* New York: Basic Books. (p. 305)

Ballard, M. E., & Wiest, J. R. (1998). Mortal Kombat: The effects of violent videogame play on males' hostility and cardiovascular responding. *Journal of Applied Social Psychology, 26,* 717–730. (p. 565)

Bandura, A. (1986). *Social foundations of thought and action: A social-cognitive theory.* Englewood Cliffs, NJ: Prentice-Hall. (pp. 450–451)

Bandura, A. (2001). Social cognitive theory: An agentic perspective. *Annual Review of Psychology, 52,* 1–26. (pp. 450–451)

Bandura, A., Ross, D., & Ross, S. A. (1961). Transmission of aggression through imitation of aggressive models. *Journal of Abnormal and Social Psychology, 63,* 575–582. (p. 249)

Barber, T. X. (2000). A deeper understanding of hypnosis: Its secrets, its nature, its essence. *American Journal of Clinical Hypnosis, 42,* 208–272. (p. 206)

Barinaga, M. (1992). The brain remaps its own contours. *Science, 258,* 216–218. (p. 58)

Barinaga, M. B. (1997). How exercise works its magic. *Science, 276,* 1325. (p. 415)

Barker, S. L., Funk, S. C., & Houston, B. K. (1988). Psychological treatment versus nonspecific factors: A meta-analysis of conditions that engender comparable expectations for improvement. *Clinical Psychology Review, 8,* 579–594. (p. 526)

Barlow, D. H. (1988). *Anxiety and its disorders: The nature and treatment of anxiety and panic.* New York: Guilford. (p. 482)

Barnes, M. L., & Sternberg, R. J. (1989). Social intelligence and decoding of nonverbal cues. *Intelligence, 13,* 263–287. (p. 388)

Barnett, P. A., & Gotlib, I. H. (1988). Psychosocial functioning and depression: Distinguishing among antecedents, concomitants, and consequences. *Psychological Bulletin, 104,* 97–126. (p. 493)

Baron, R. A. (1988). Negative effects of destructive criticism: Impact on conflict, self-efficacy, and task performance. *Journal of Applied Psychology, 73,* 199–207. (p. 246)

Baron, R. S., Cutrona, C. E., Hicklin, D., Russell, D. W., & Lubaroff, D. M. (1990). Social support and immune function among spouses of cancer patients. *Journal of Personality and Social Psychology, 59,* 344–352. (p. 418)

Barr, R. (1991, October). In *The Evening Standard,* 9. (p. 285)

Barrett, L. F., Lane, R. D., Sechrest, L., & Schwartz, G. E. (2000). Sex differences in emotional awareness. *Personality and Social Psychology Bulletin, 26,* 1027–1035. (pp. 388–389)

Barry, D. (1995, September 17). Teen smokers, too, get cool, toxic, waste-blackened lungs. *Asbury Park Press,* p. D3. (p. 219)

Barry, D. (1998, January 30). Beauty and the beast. *Miami Herald.* (p. 351)

Barry, D. (1998). *Dave Barry turns 50*. New York: Crown Publishers. (p. 125)

Barry, D. (2002, April 26). *The Dave Barry 2002 Calendar*. Kansas City: Andrews McMeel. (p. 354)

Baruch, G. K., & Barnett, R. (1986). Role quality, multiple role involvement, and psychological well-being in midlife women. *Journal of Personality and Social Psychology, 51*, 578–585. (p. 132)

Bashore, T. R., Ridderinkhof, K. R., & van der Molen, M. W. (1997). The decline of cognitive processing speed in old age. *Current Directions in Psychological Science, 6*, 163–169. (p. 126)

Baskind, D. E. (1997, December 14). Personal communication, from Delta College. (p. 514)

Bass, L. E., & Kane-Williams, E. (1993). Stereotype or reality: Another look at alcohol and drug use among African American children. U.S. Department of Health and Human Services, *Public Health Reports, 108* (Supplement 1), 78–84. (p. 219)

Bauer, P. J. (2002). Long-term recall memory: Behavioral and neuro-developmental changes in the first 2 years of life. *Current Directions in Psychology, 11*, 137–141. (p. 103)

Baum, A., & Posluszny, D. M. (1999). Health psychology: Mapping biobehavioral contributions to health and illness. *Annual Review of Psychology, 50*, 137–163. (p. 411)

Baumeister, R. F. (1989). The optimal margin of illusion. *Journal of Social and Clinical Psychology, 8*, 176–189. (pp. 300, 460)

Baumeister, R. F. (1996). Should schools try to boost self-esteem? Beware the dark side. *American Educator, 20*, 14019, 43. (p. 460)

Baumeister, R. F. (2000). Gender differences in erotic plasticity: The female sex drive as socially flexible and responsive. *Psychological Bulletin, 126*, 347–374. (p. 365)

Baumeister, R. F. (2001, April). Violent pride: Do people turn violent because of self-hate, or self-love? *Scientific American*, pp. 96–101. (p. 460)

Baumeister, R. F., & Bratslavsky, E. (1999). Passion, intimacy, and time: Passionate love as a function of change in intimacy. *Personality and Social Psychology Review, 3*, 49–67. (p. 573)

Baumeister, R. F., Campbell, J., Krueger, J. I., & Vohs, K. D. (2003). Does high self-esteem cause better performance, interpersonal success, happiness or healthier lifestyles? *Psychological Science in the Public Interest, 4*, 1–44. (p. 457)

Baumeister, R. F., Catanese, K. R., & Vohs, K. D. (2001). Is there a gender difference in strength of sex drive? Theoretical views, conceptual distinctions, and a review of relevant evidence. *Personality and Social Psychology Review, 5*, 242–273. (p. 72)

Baumeister, R. F., Dale, K., & Sommer, K. L. (1998). Freudian defense mechanisms and empirical findings in modern personality and social psychology: Reaction formation, projection, displacement, undoing, isolation, sublimation, and denial. *Journal of Personality, 66*, 1081–1125. (p. 464)

Baumeister, R. F., & Exline, J. J. (2000). Self-control, morality, and human strength. *Journal of Social and Clinical Psychology, 19*, 29–42. (p. 452)

Baumeister, R. F., & Leary, M. R. (1995). The need to belong: Desire for interpersonal attachments as a fundamental human motivation. *Psychological Bulletin, 117*, 497–529. (pp. 371, 372–373)

Baumeister, R. F., Stillwell, A., & Wotman, S. R. (1990). Victim and perpetrator accounts of interpersonal conflict: Autobiographical narratives about anger. *Journal of Personality and Social Psychology, 59*, 994–1005. (p. 395)

Baumeister, R. F., Twenge, J. M., & Nuss, C. K. (2002). Effects of social exclusion on cognitive processes: Anticipated aloneness reduces intelligent thought. *Journal of Personality and Social Psychology, 83*, 817–827. (p. 372)

Baumgardner, A. H., Kaufman, C. M., & Levy, P. E. (1989). Regulating affect interpersonally: When low esteem leads to greater enhancement. *Journal of Personality and Social Psychology, 56*, 907–921. (p. 458)

Baumrind, D. (1982). Adolescent sexuality: Comment on Williams' and Silka's comments on Baumrind. *American Psychologist, 37*, 1402–1403. (p. 369)

Baumrind, D. (1996). The discipline controversy revisited. *Family Relations, 45*, 405–414. (p. 114)

Bavelier, D., Tomann, A., Hutton, C., Mitchell, T., Corina, D., Liu, G., & Neville, H. (2000). Visual attention to the periphery is enhanced in congenitally deaf individuals. *Journal of Neuroscience, 20*, 1–6. (p. 58)

Beaman, A. L., & Klentz, B. (1983). The supposed physical attractiveness bias against supporters of the women's movement: A meta-analysis. *Personality and Social Psychology Bulletin, 9*, 544–550. (p. 571)

Beardsley, L. M. (1994). Medical diagnosis and treatment across cultures. In W. J. Lonner & R. Malpass (Eds.), *Psychology and culture*. Boston: Allyn & Bacon. (p. 471)

Beardsley, T. (1996, July). Waking up. *Scientific American*, pp. 14, 18. (p. 196)

Bearman, P. S., & Brückner, H. (2001). Promising the future: Virginity pledges and first intercourse. *American Journal of Sociology, 106*, 859–912. (pp. 362, 542)

Beauchamp, G. K. (1987). The human preference for excess salt. *American Scientist, 75*, 27–33. (p. 348)

Beck, A. J., Kline, S. A., & Greenfeld, L. A. (1988). Survey of youth in custody, 1987. U.S. Department of Justice, Bureau of Justice Statistics Special Report. (p. 562)

Beck, A. T., Rush, A. J., Shaw, B. F., & Emery, G. (1979). *Cognitive therapy of depression*. New York: Guilford Press. (p. 517)

Beck, A. T., & Steer, R. A. (1989). Clinical predictors of eventual suicide: A 5- to 10-year prospective study of suicide attempters. *Journal of Affective Disorders, 17*, 203–209. (p. 491)

Beck, A. T., & Young, J. E. (1978, September). College blues. *Psychology Today*, pp. 80–92. (pp. 486, 494)

Beeman, M., Friedman, R. B., Grafman, J., Perez, E., Diamond, S., & Lindsay, M. B. (1994). Summation priming and coarse semantic coding in the right hemisphere. *Journal of Cognitive Neuroscience, 6*, 26–45. (p. 62)

Beeman, M. J., & Chiarello, C. (1998). Complementary right- and left-hemisphere language comprehension. *Current Directions in Psychological Science, 7*, 2–8. (p. 62)

Beitman, B. D., Goldfried, M. R., & Norcross, J. C. (1989). The movement toward integrating the psychotherapies: An overview. *American Journal of Psychiatry, 146*, 138–147. (p. 507)

Bell, A. P. (1982, November/December). Sexual preference: A postscript. (SIECUS Report, 11, No. 2) *Church and Society*, pp. 34–37. (p. 366)

Bell, A. P., Weinberg, M. S., & Hammersmith, S. K. (1981). *Sexual preference: Its development in men and women*. Bloomington: Indiana University Press. (p. 365)

Belsher, G., & Costello, C. G. (1988). Relapse after recovery from unipolar depression: A critical review. *Psychological Bulletin, 104*, 84–96. (p. 489)

Belsky, J., Lang, M., & Huston, T. L. (1986). Sex typing and division of labor as determinants of marital change across the transition to parenthood. *Journal of Personality and Social Psychology, 50*, 517–522. (p. 131)

Bem, D. J. (1984). Quoted in *The Skeptical Inquirer, 8*, 194. (p. 180)

Bem, D. J. (1996). Exotic becomes erotic: A developmental theory of sexual orientation. *Psychological Review, 103*, 320–335. (pp. 366, 367–368)

Bem, D. J. (1998). Is EBE theory supported by the evidence? Is it androcentric? A reply to Peplau et al. (1998). *Psychological Review, 105*, 395–398. (pp. 367–368)

Bem, D. J. (2000). Exotic becomes erotic: Interpreting the biological correlates of sexual orientation. *Archives of Sexual Behavior, 29,* 531–548. (pp. 367–368)

Bem, D. J., & Honorton, C. (1994). Does psi exist? Replicable evidence for an anomalous process of information transfer. *Psychological Bulletin, 115,* 4–18. (p. 180)

Bem, D. J., Palmer, J., & Broughton, R. S. (2001). Updating the Ganzfeld database: A victim of its own success? *Journal of Parapsychology, 65,* 207–218. (p. 181)

Benbow, C. P., Lubinski, D., Shea, D. L., & Eftekhari-Sanjani, H. (2000). Sex differences in mathematical reasoning ability at age 13: Their status 20 years later. *Psychological Science, 11,* 474–2000. (p. 333)

Bennett, W. I. (1995). Beyond overeating. *New England Journal of Medicine, 332,* 673–674. (p. 356)

Benson, H. (1996). *Timeless healing: The power and biology of belief.* New York: Scribner. (p. 416)

Benson, P. L., Sharma, A. R., & Roehlkepartain, E. C. (1994). *Growing up adopted: A portrait of adolescents and their families.* Minneapolis: Search Institute. (p. 79)

Berenbaum, S. A., Korman, K., & Leveroni, C. (1995). Early hormones and sex differences in cognitive abilities. *Learning and Individual Differences, 7,* 303–321. (p. 334)

Berger, B. G., & Motl, R. W. (2000). Exercise and mood: A selective review and synthesis of research employing the profile of mood states. *Journal of Applied Sports Psychology, 12,* 69–92. (pp. 414–415)

Bergin, A. E. (1980). Psychotherapy and religious values. *Journal of Consulting and Clinical Psychology, 48,* 95–105. (pp. 528–529)

Bergsholm, P., Larsen, J. L., Rosendahl, K., & Holsten, F. (1989). Electroconvulsive therapy and cerebral computed tomography. *Acta Psychiatrica Scandinavia, 80,* 566–572. (p. 533)

Berkel, J., & de Waard, F. (1983). Mortality pattern and life expectancy of Seventh Day Adventists in the Netherlands. *International Journal of Epidemiology, 12,* 455–459. (p. 423)

Berkowitz, L. (1983). Aversively stimulated aggression: Some parallels and differences in research with animals and humans. *American Psychologist, 38,* 1135–1144. (p. 561)

Berkowitz, L. (1989). Frustration-aggression hypothesis: Examination and reformulation. *Psychological Bulletin, 106,* 59–73. (p. 561)

Berkowitz, L. (1990). On the formation and regulation of anger and aggression: A cognitive-neoassociationistic analysis. *American Psychologist, 45,* 494–503. (p. 394)

Berman, M., Gladue, B., & Taylor, S. (1993). The effects of hormones, Type A behavior pattern, and provocation on aggression in men. *Motivation and Emotion, 17,* 125–138. (p. 561)

Berndt, T. J. (1992). Friendship and friends' influence in adolescence. *Current Directions in Psychological Science, 1,* 156–159. (p. 121)

Bernieri, F. (2000, May 29). Quoted by M. Gladwell, "The new-boy network: What do job interviews really tell us?" *New Yorker,* pp. 68–86. (p. B–5)

Berry, D. S., & McArthur, L. Z. (1986). Perceiving character in faces: The impact of age-related craniofacial changes on social perception. *Psychological Bulletin, 100,* 3–18. (p. 232)

Berscheid, E. (1981). An overview of the psychological effects of physical attractiveness and some comments upon the psychological effects of knowledge of the effects of physical attractiveness. In G. W. Lucker, K. Ribbens, & J. A. McNamara (Eds.), *Psychological aspects of facial form* (Craniofacial growth series). Ann Arbor: Center for Human Growth and Development, University of Michigan. (p. 570)

Berscheid, E. (1985). Interpersonal attraction. In G. Lindzey & E. Aronson (Eds.), *The handbook of social psychology.* New York: Random House. (p. 371)

Berscheid, E., Gangestad, S. W., & Kulakowski, D. (1984). Emotion in close relationships: Implications for relationship counseling. In S. D. Brown & R. W. Lent (Eds.), *Handbook of counseling psychology.* New York: Wiley. (p. 572)

Bettencourt, R. A., & Dorr, N. (1997). Collective self-esteem as a mediator of the relationship between allocentrism and subjective well-being. *Personality and Social Psychology Bulletin, 23,* 955–964. (p. 462)

Beyerstein, B., & Beyerstein, D. (Eds.) (1992). *The write stuff: Evaluations of graphology.* Buffalo, NY: Prometheus Books. (p. 446)

Bhatt, R. S., Wasserman, E. A., Reynolds, W. F., Jr., & Knauss, K. S. (1988). Conceptual behavior in pigeons: Categorization of both familiar and novel examples from four classes of natural and artificial stimuli. *Journal of Experimental Psychology: Animal Behavior Processes, 14,* 219–234. (p. 238)

Bialystok, E. (2001). *Bilingualism in development, language, literacy, and cognition.* New York: Cambridge University Press. (p. 309)

Bickman, L. (1999). Practice makes perfect and other myths about mental health services. *American Psychologist, 54,* 965–978. (p. 523)

Biello, S. M., & Dafters, R. I. (2001). MDMA and fenfluramine alter the response of the circadian clock to a serotonin agonist in vitro. *Brain Research, 920,* 202–209. (p. 215)

Biggs, V. (2001, April 13). Murder suspect captured in Grand Marais. *Cook County News-Herald.* (p. 388)

Binet, A., & Simon, T. (1905; reprinted 1916). New methods for the diagnosis of the intellectual level of subnormals. In A. Binet & T. Simon, *The development of intelligence in children.* Baltimore: Williams & Wilkins. (p. 316)

Binson, D., Michaels, S., Stall, R., Coates, T. J., Gagnon, J. H., & Catania, J. A. (1995). Prevalence and social distribution of men who have sex with men: United States and its urban centers. *Journal of Sex Research, 32,* 245–254. (p. 366)

Bishop, G. D. (1991). Understanding the understanding of illness: Lay disease representations. In J. A. Skelton & R. T. Croyle (Eds.), *Mental representation in health and illness.* New York: Springer-Verlag. (p. 294)

Biswas-Diener, R., & Diener, E. (2001). Making the best of a bad situation: Satisfaction in the slums of Calcutta. *Social Indicators Research, 55,* 329–352. (p. 397)

Bjork, R. A. (1978). The updating of human memory. In G. H. Bower (Ed.), *The psychology of learning and motivation* (Vol. 12). New York: Academic Press. (p. 275)

Bjork, R. A. (1999). Assessing our own competence: Heuristics and illusions. In D. Gopher & A. Koriat (Eds.), *Attention and performance XVII. Cognitive regulation of performance: Interaction of theory and application.* Cambridge, MA: MIT Press. (p. 261)

Bjork, R. A. (2000, July/August). Toward one world of psychological science. *APS Observer,* p. 3. (p. 7)

Bjorklund, D. F., & Green, B. L. (1992). The adaptive nature of cognitive immaturity. *American Psychologist, 47,* 46–54. (p. 109)

Blackmore, S. (1999). *The meme machine.* Oxford: Oxford University Press. (p. 248)

Blackmore, S. (2000, October). The power of memes. *Scientific American,* pp. 63–73. (p. 248)

Blakemore, S-J., Wolpert, D. M., & Frith, C. D. (1998). Central cancellation of self-produced tickle sensation. *Nature Neuroscience, 1,* 635–640. (p. 159)

Blanchard, R. (1997). Birth order and sibling sex ratio in homosexual versus heterosexual males and females. *Annual Review of Sex Research, 8,* 27–67. (p. 366)

Blanchard, R. (2001). Fraternal birth order and the maternal immunie hypothesis of male homosexuality. *Hormones and Behavior, 40,* 105–114. (p. 366)

Blass, T. (1996). Stanley Milgram: A life of inventiveness and controversy. In G. A. Kimble, C. A. Boneau, & M. Wertheimer (Eds.), *Portraits of pioneers in psychology* (Vol. II). Washington, DC and Mahwah, NJ: American Psychological Association and Lawrence Erlbaum Publishers. (p. 548)

Blass, T. (1999). The Milgram paradigm after 35 years: Some things we now know about obedience to authority. *Journal of Applied Social Psychology, 29,* 955–978. (p. 548)

Blatt, S. J., Sanislow, C. A., III, Zuroff, D. C., & Pilkonis, P. (1996). Characteristics of effective therapists: Further analyses of data from the National Institute of Mental Health Treatment of Depression Collaborative Research Program. *Journal of Consulting and Clinical Psychology, 64,* 1276–1284. (p. 527)

Blau, G. (1994). Developing and testing a taxonomy of lateness behavior. *Journal of Applied Psychology, 76,* 959–970. (p. B–8)

Bleustein, J. (2002, June 15). Quoted in "Harley retooled," by S. S. Smith, *American Way Magazine.* (p. B–11)

Blom, J. M. C., Tamarkin, L., Shiber, J. R., & Nelson, R. J. (1995). Learned immunosuppression is associated with an increased risk of chemically-induced tumors. *Neuroimmunomodulation, 2,* 92–99. (p. 412)

Bloom, F. E. (1993, January/February). What's new in neurotransmitters. *BrainWork,* pp. 7–9. (p. 40)

Bloom, S. R. (2002, September/October). Quoted in Researchers identify natural appetite suppressant. *BrainWork.* (p. 347)

Blum, K., Cull, J. G., Braverman, E. R., & Comings, D. E. (1996). Reward deficiency syndrome. *American Scientist, 84,* 132–145. (p. 52)

Bodenhausen, G. V., Sheppard, L. A., & Kramer, G. P. (1994). Negative affect and social judgment: The differential impact of anger and sadness. *European Journal of Social Psychology, 24,* 45–62. (p. 577)

Bodkin, J. A., & Amsterdam, J. D. (2002). Transdermal selegiline in major depression: A double-blind, placebo-controlled, parallel-group study in outpatients. *American Journal of Psychiatry, 159,* 1869–1875. (p. 532)

Boehm, K. E., Schondel, C. K., Marlowe, A. L., & Manke-Mitchell, L. (1999). Teens' concerns: A national evaluation. *Adolescence, 34,* 523–528. (p. 122)

Boesch-Achermann, H., & Boesch, C. (1993). Tool use in wild chimpanzees: New light from dark forests. *Current Directions in Psychological Science, 2,* 18–21. (p. 312)

Bogaert, A. F., Friesen, C., & Klentrou, P. (2002). Age of puberty and sexual orientation in a national probability sample. *Archives of Sexual Behavior, 31,* 73–81. (p. 366)

Boggiano, A. K., Barrett, M., Weiher, A. W., McClelland, G. H., & Lusk, C. M. (1987). Use of the maximal-operant principle to motivate children's intrinsic interest. *Journal of Personality and Social Psychology, 53,* 866–879. (p. 244)

Boggiano, A. K., Harackiewicz, J. M., Bessette, M. M., & Main, D. S. (1985). Increasing children's interest through performance-contingent reward. *Social Cognition, 3,* 400–411. (p. 244)

Bogin, B. (1998, February). The tall and the short of it (range of height in humans demonstrates plasticity of human species). *Discover.* (p. 331)

Bohman, M., & Sigvardsson, S. (1990). Outcome in adoption: Lessons from longitudinal studies. In D. Brodzinsky & M. Schechter (Eds.), *The psychology of adoption.* New York: Oxford University Press. (p. 79)

Bolger, N., DeLongis, A., Kessler, R. C., & Schilling, E. A. (1989). Effects of daily stress on negative mood. *Journal of Personality and Social Psychology, 57,* 808–818. (p. 396)

Bonanno, G. A. (2001). Grief and emotion: Experience, expression, and dissociation. In M. Stroebe, W. Stroebe, R. O. Hansson, & H. Schut (Eds.), *New handbook of bereavement: Consciousness, coping, and care.* Cambridge: Cambridge University Press. (p. 133)

Bonanno, G. A., & Kaltman, S. (1999). Toward an integrative perspective on bereavement. *Psychological Bulletin, 125,* 760–777. (p. 133)

Bond, C. F., Jr., & Atoum, A. O. (2000). International deception. *Personality and Social Psychology Bulletin, 26,* 385–395. (p. 390)

Bond, C. F., Jr., Pitre, U., & Van Leeuwen, M. D. (1991). Encoding operations and the next-in-line effect. *Personality and Social Psychology Bulletin, 17,* 435–441. (p. 261)

Bond, M. H. (1988). Finding universal dimensions of individual variation in multi-cultural studies of values: The Rokeach and Chinese values surveys. *Journal of Personality and Social Psychology, 55,* 1009–1015. (p. 88)

Bond, R., & Smith, P. B. (1996). Culture and conformity: A meta-analysis of studies using Asch's (1952b, 1956) line judgment task. *Psychological Bulletin, 119,* 111–137. (p. 547)

Boneva, B. S., & Frieze, I. H. (2001). Toward a concept of a migrant personality. *Journal of Social Issues, 57,* 477–491. (p. 461)

Boring, E. G. (1930). A new ambiguous figure. *American Journal of Psychology, 42,* 444–445. (p. 177)

Bornstein, M. H. (1989). Stability in early mental development: From attention and information processing in infancy to language and cognition in childhood. In M. G. Bornstein & N. A. Krasnegor (Eds.), *Stability and continuity in mental development: Behavioral and biological perspectives.* Hillsdale, NJ: Erlbaum. (p. 111)

Bornstein, M. H., Tal, J., Rahn, C., Galperin, C. Z., Pecheux, M-G., Lamour, M., Toda, S., Azuma, H., Ogino, M., & Tamis-LeMonda, C. S. (1992a). Functional analysis of the contents of maternal speech to infants of 5 and 13 months in four cultures: Argentina, France, Japan, and the United States. *Developmental Psychology, 28,* 593–603. (p. 89)

Bornstein, M. H., Tamis-LeMonda, C. S., Tal, J., Ludemann, P., Toda, S., Rahn, C. W., Pecheux, M-G., Azuma, H., Vardi, D. (1992b). Maternal responsiveness to infants in three societies: The United States, France, and Japan. *Child Development, 63,* 808–821. (p. 89)

Bornstein, R. F. (1989). Exposure and affect: Overview and meta-analysis of research, 1968–1987. *Psychological Bulletin, 106,* 265–289. (p. 568)

Bornstein, R. F. (1999). Source amnesia, misattribution, and the power of unconscious perceptions and memories. *Psychoanalytic Psychology, 16,* 155–178. (p. 568)

Bornstein, R. F. (2001). The impending death of psychoanalysis. *Psychoanalytic Psychology, 18,* 3–20. (p. 438)

Bornstein, R. F., Galley, D. J., Leone, D. R., & Kale, A. R. (1991). The temporal stability of ratings of parents: Test-retest reliability and influence of parental contact. *Journal of Social Behavior and Personality, 6,* 641–649. (p. 275)

Boroditsky, R., Fisher, W., & Sand, M. (1995, July). Teenagers and contraception. Section of the Canadian contraception study. *Journal of the Society of Obstetricians and Gynaecologists of Canada,* Special Supplement, pp. 22–25. (p. 361)

Boscarino, J. A. (1997). Diseases among men 20 years after exposure to severe stress: Implications for clinical research and medical care. *Psychosomatic Medicine, 59,* 605–614. (p. 403)

Bosma, H., Marmot, M. G., Hemingway, H., Nicolson, A. C., Brunner, E., & Stansfeld, S. A. (1997). Low job control and risk of coronary heart disease in Whitehall II (prospective cohort) study. *British Medical Journal, 314,* 558–565. (p. 406)

Bosma, H., Peter, R., Siegrist, J., & Marmot, M. (1998). Two alternative job stress models and the risk of coronary heart disease. *American Journal of Public Health, 88,* 68–74. (p. 406)

Bostwick, J. M., & Pankratz, V. S. (2000). Affective disorders and suicide risk: A re-examination. *American Journal of Psychiatry, 157,* 1925–1932. (p. 491)

Bothwell, R. K., Brigham, J. C., & Malpass, R. S. (1989). Cross-racial identification. *Personality and Social Psychology Bulletin, 15,* 19–25. (pp. 558–559)

Bouchard, T. J., Jr. (1981, December 6). Interview on *Nova: Twins* [program broadcast by the Public Broadcasting Service]. (p. 77)

Bouchard, T. J., Jr. (1995). Longitudinal studies of personality and intelligence: A behavior genetic and evolutionary psychology perspective. In D. H. Saklofske & M. Zeidner (Eds.), *International handbook of personality and intelligence.* New York: Plenum. (p. 328)

Bouchard, T. J., Jr. (1996a). IQ similarity in twins reared apart: Finding and responses to critics. In R. Sternberg & C. Grigorenko (Eds.), *Intelligence: Heredity and environment.* New York: Cambridge University Press. (pp. 326, 328)

Bouchard, T. J., Jr., & McGue, M. (1990). Genetic and rearing environmental influences on adult personality: An analysis of adopted twins reared apart. *Journal of Personality, 58*, 263. (pp. 19, 77)

Bouton, M. E., Mineka, S., & Barlow, D. H. (2001). A modern learning theory perspective on the etiology of panic disorder. *Psychological Review, 108*, 4–32. (p. 479)

Bowden, E. M., & Beeman, M. J. (1998). Getting the right idea: Semantic activation in the right hemisphere may help solve insight problems. *Psychological Science, 9*, 435–440. (p. 62)

Bower, G. H. (1983). Affect and cognition. *Philosophical Transaction: Royal Society of London, Series B, 302*, 387–402. (p. 274)

Bower, G. H. (1986). Prime time in cognitive psychology. In P. Eelen (Ed.), *Cognitive research and behavior therapy: Beyond the conditioning paradigm.* Amsterdam: North Holland Publishers. (p. 273)

Bower, G. H., Clark, M. C., Lesgold, A. M., & Winzenz, D. (1969). Hierarchical retrieval schemes in recall of categorized word lists. *Journal of Verbal Learning and Verbal Behavior, 8*, 323–343. (p. 264)

Bower, G. H., & Morrow, D. G. (1990). Mental models in narrative comprehension. *Science, 247*, 44–48. (p. 262)

Bower, J. E., Kemeny, M. E., Taylor, S. E., & Fahey, J. L. (1998). Cognitive processing, discovery of meaning, CD4 decline, and AIDS-related mortality among bereaved HIV-seropositive men. *Journal of Consulting and Clinical Psychology, 66*, 979–986. (p. 411)

Bowers, K. S. (1984). Hypnosis. In N. Endler & J. M. Hunt (Eds.), *Personality and behavioral disorders* (2nd ed.). New York: Wiley. (pp. 204, 205)

Bowers, K. S. (1987, July). Personal communication. (p. 205)

Bowers, T. G., & Clum, G. A. (1988). Relative contribution of specific and nonspecific treatment effects: Meta-analysis of placebo-controlled behavior therapy research. *Psychological Bulletin, 103*, 315–323. (p. 523)

Bowles, S., & Kasindorf, M. (2001, March 6). Friends tell of picked-on but 'normal' kid. *USA Today*, p. 4A. (p. 372)

Boyatzis, C. J., Matillo, G. M., & Nesbitt, K. M. (1995). Effects of the 'Mighty Morphin Power Rangers' on children's aggression with peers. *Child Study Journal, 25*, 45–55. (p. 252)

Boynton, R. M. (1979). *Human color vision.* New York: Holt, Rinehart & Winston. (p. 154)

Braden, J. P. (1994). *Deafness, deprivation, and IQ.* New York: Plenum. (p. 331)

Bradshaw, J. (1990). *Homecoming: Reclaiming and championing your inner child.* New York: Bantam Books. (p. 82)

Brainerd, C. J. (1996). Piaget: A centennial celebration. *Psychological Science, 7*, 191–195. (p. 104)

Brandon, S., Boakes, J., Glaser, & Green, R. (1998). Recovered memories of childhood sexual abuse: Implications for clinical practice. *British Journal of Psychiatry, 172*, 294–307. (p. 286)

Brannon, L. A., & Brock, T. C. (1994). Perilous underestimation of sex partners' sexual histories in calculating personal AIDS risk. Paper presented to the American Psychological Society convention. (p. 363)

Bransford, J. D., & Johnson, M. K. (1972). Contextual prerequisites for understanding: Some investigations of comprehension and recall. *Journal of Verbal Learning and Verbal Behavior, 11*, 717–726. (pp. 262, 263)

Braun, S. (1996). New experiments underscore warnings on maternal drinking. *Science, 273*, 738–739. (p. 100)

Braun, S. (2001, Spring). Seeking insight by prescription. *Cerebrum*, pp. 10–21. (p. 214)

Bray, D. W., & Byham, W. C. (1991, Winter). Assessment centers and their derivatives. *Journal of Continuing Higher Education*, pp. 8–11. (p. 455)

Bray, D. W., Byham, W., interviewed by Mayes, B. T. (1997). Insights into the history and future of assessment centers: An interview with Dr. Douglas W. Bray and Dr. William Byham. *Journal of Social Behavior and Personality, 12*, 3–12. (p. 455)

Bray, G. A. (1969). Effect of caloric restriction on energy expenditure in obese patients. *Lancet, 2*, 397–398. (p. 353)

Brayne, C., Spiegelhalter, D. J., Dufouil, C., Chi, L-Y., Dening, T. R., Paykel, E. S., O'Connor, D. W., Ahmed, A., McGee, M. A., & Huppert, F. A. (1999). Estimating the true extent of cognitive decline in the old old. *Journal of the American Geriatrics Society, 47*, 1283–1288. (p. 128)

Bread for the World. (2002). The feasibility of ending hunger. Washington, DC: Alliance to End Hunger, Bread for the World Institute. (pp. 299, 344)

Breedlove, S. M. (1997). Sex on the brain. *Nature, 389*, 801. (pp. 366–367)

Brehm, S., & Brehm, J. W. (1981). *Psychological reactance: A theory of freedom and control.* New York: Academic Press. (p. 554)

Breland, K., & Breland, M. (1961). The misbehavior of organisms. *American Psychologist, 16*, 661–664. (p. 245)

Brenner, M. (1973). The next-in-line effect. *Journal of Verbal Learning and Verbal Behavior, 12*, 320–323. (p. 261)

Breslau, N., & Klein, D. F. (1999). Smoking and panic attacks: An epidemiologic investigation. *Archives of General Psychiatry, 56*, 1141–1147. (p. 477)

Bressan, P., & Dal Martello, M. F. (2002). Talis pater, talis filius: Perceived resemblance and the belief in genetic relatedness. *Psychological Science, 13*, 213–218. (p. 177)

Brewer, C. L. (1990). Personal correspondence. (p. 80)

Brewer, C. L. (1996). Personal communication. (p. 8)

Brewer, W. F. (1977). Memory for the pragmatic implications of sentences. *Memory & Cognition, 5*, 673–678. (p. 262)

Brewin, C. R., Andrews, B., Rose, S., & Kirk, M. (1999). Acute stress disorder and posttraumatic stress disorder in victims of violent crime. *American Journal of Psychiatry, 156*, 360–366. (p. 480)

Brewin, C. R., Andrews, B., & Valentine, J. D. (2000). Meta-analysis of risk factors for posttraumatic stress disorder in trauma-exposed adults. *Journal of Consulting and Clinical Psychology, 68*, 748–766. (pp. 480–481)

Brickman, P., Coates, D., & Janoff-Bulman, R. J. (1978). Lottery winners and accident victims: Is happiness relative? *Journal of Personality and Social Psychology, 36*, 917–927. (p. 397)

Brief, A. P., & Weiss, H. M. (2002). Organizational behavior: Affect in the workplace. *Annual Review of Psychology, 53*, 279–307. (p. B–7)

Brinson, S. L. (1992). The use and opposition of rape myths in prime-time television dramas. *Sex Roles, 27*, 359–375. (p. 563)

Briscoe, D. (1997, February 16). Women lawmakers still not in charge. Associated Press (in *Grand Rapids Press*, p. A23). (p. 91)

Brislin, R. W. (1988). Increasing awareness of class, ethnicity, culture, and race by expanding on students' own experiences. In I. Cohen (Ed.), *The G. Stanley Hall Lecture Series.* Washington, DC: American Psychological Association. (p. 86)

Brislin, R. W. (1993). *Understanding culture's influence on behavior.* Fort Worth, TX: Harcourt Brace. (p. 471)

Brissette, I., & Cohen, S. (2002). The contribution of individual differences in hostility to the associations between daily interpersonal conflict, affect, and sleep. *Personality and Social Psychology Bulletin, 28*, 1265–1274. (p. 198)

Brissette, I., Scheier, M. F., & Carver, C. S. (2002). The role of optimism in social network development, coping, and psychological adjustment during a life transition. *Journal of Personality and Social Psychology, 82,* 102–111. (p. 495)

British Psychological Society. (1993). Ethical principles for conducting research with human participants. *The Psychologist: Bulletin of the British Psychological Society, 6,* 33–36. (pp. 30, 446)

Brody, J. E. (1999, November 30). Yesterday's precocious puberty is norm today. *New York Times* (www.nytimes.com). (p. 117)

Brody, J. E. (2000, March 21). When post-traumatic stress grips youth. *New York Times* (www.nytimes.com). (pp. 480–481)

Brody, J. E. (2002, November 26). When the eyelids snap shut at 65 miles an hour. *New York Times* (www.nytimes.com). (p. 196)

Brody, N. (1997). Dispositional paradigms: Comment on Eysenck (1997) and the biosocial science of individual differences. *Journal of Personality and Social Psychology, 73*(6), 1242–1245. (p. 320)

Brodzinsky, D. M., & Schechter, M. D. (Eds.) (1990). *The psychology of adoption.* New York: Oxford University Press. (p. 79)

Bronner, E. (1998, February 25). U.S. high school seniors among worst in math and science. *New York Times* (www.nytimes.com). (pp. 332–333)

Brooks, D. J. (2001, April). "Creationism" has strong following in U.S. Gallup News Service article reprinted in *Emerging Trends* from Princeton Religion Research Center, pp. 4–5. (p. 72)

Brooks, D. J. (2002, October 8). Running down the road to happiness. *Gallup Tuesday Briefing* (www.gallup.com). (p. 414)

Brown, E. L., & Deffenbacher, K. (1979). *Perception and the senses.* New York: Oxford University Press. (p. 158)

Brown, J. D. (1991). Accuracy and bias in self-knowledge. In C. R. Snyder & D. F. Forsyth (Eds.), *Handbook of social and clinical psychology: The health perspective.* New York: Pergamon Press. (pp. 458, 460)

Brown, J. D., Steele, J. R., & Walsh-Childers, K. (2002). Sexual teens, sexual media: Investigating media's influence on adolescent sexuality. Mahwah, NJ: Erlbaum. (p. 362)

Brown, J. L., & Pollitt, E. (1996, February). Malnutrition, poverty and intellectual development. *Scientific American,* pp. 38–43. (p. 329)

Brown, P. J. (1993). Cultural perspectives on the etiology and treatment of obesity. In A. J. Stunkard & T. A. Wadden (Eds.), *Obesity: Theory and therapy,* 2nd ed. New York: Raven Press. (p. 354)

Brown, R. (1986). Linguistic relativity. In S. H. Hulse & B. F. Green, Jr. (Eds.), *One hundred years of psychological research in America.* Baltimore: Johns Hopkins University Press. (p. 308)

Brown, R., & Kulik, J. (1982). Flashbulb memories. In U. Neisser (Ed.), *Memory observed.* San Francisco: Freeman. (p. 258)

Brown, S. W., Garry, M., Loftus, E., Silver, B., DuBois, K., & DuBreuil, S. (1996). People's beliefs about memory: Why don't we have better memories? Paper presented at the American Psychological Society convention. (pp. 267, 281)

Brownell, K. D., & Jeffery, R. W. (1987). Improving long-term weight loss: Pushing the limits of treatment. *Behavior Therapy, 18,* 353–374. (p. 355)

Brownell, K. D., & Wadden, T. A. (1992). Etiology and treatment of obesity: Understanding a serious, prevalent, and refractory disorder. *Journal of Consulting and Clinical Psychology, 60,* 505–517. (p. 354)

Browning, C. (1992). *Ordinary men: Reserve police battalion 101 and the final solution in Poland.* New York: HarperCollins. (p. 549)

Brownmiller, S. (1975). *Against our will: Men, women, and rape.* New York: Simon and Schuster. (p. 361)

Bruce, D., Dolan, A., & Phillips-Grant, K. (2000). On the transition from childhood amnesia to the recall of personal memories. *Psychological Science, 11,* 360–364. (p. 103)

Bruck, M., & Ceci, S. J. (1999). The suggestibility of children's memory. *Annual Review of Psychology, 50,* 419–439. (p. 284)

Bruck, M., Ceci, S. J., & Hembrooke, H. (1998, February). Reliability and credibility of young children's reports: From research to policy and practice. *American Psychologist, 53*(2), 136–151. (p. 284)

Bruer, J. T. (1999). *The myth of the first three years: A new understanding of early brain development and lifelong learning.* New York: Free Press. (p. 329)

Brumberg, J. J. (2000). *Fasting girls: The history of anorexia nervosa.* New York: Vintage. (p. 350)

Buckingham, M. (2001, August). Quoted by P. LaBarre, "Marcus Buckingham thinks your boss has an attitude problem." *The Magazine* (fastcompany.com/online/49/buckingham.html). (pp. B–3, B–8, B–9)

Buckingham, M., & Clifton, D. O. (2001). *Now, discover your strengths.* New York: Free Press. (pp. B–3 to B–4)

Buehler, R., Griffin, D., & Ross, M. (1994). Exploring the "planning fallacy": Why people underestimate their task completion times. *Journal of Personality and Social Psychology, 67,* 366–381. (p. 299)

Bugelski, B. R., Kidd, E., & Segmen, J. (1968). Image as a mediator in one-trial paired-associate learning. *Journal of Experimental Psychology, 76,* 69–73. (p. 263)

Bugental, D. B. (1986). Unmasking the "polite smile": Situational and personal determinants of managed affect in adult-child interaction. *Personality and Social Psychology Bulletin, 12,* 7–16. (p. 389)

Buka, S. L., Goldstein, J. M., Seidman, L. J., Zornberg, G., Donatelli, J-A. A., Denny, L. R., & Tsuang, M. T. (1999). Prenatal complications, genetic vulnerability, and schizophrenia: The New England longitudinal studies of schizophrenia. *Psychiatric Annals, 29,* 151–156. (p. 499)

Bullough, V. (1990). The Kinsey scale in historical perspective. In D. P. McWhirter, S. A. Sanders, & J. M. Reinisch (Eds.), *Homosexuality/heterosexuality: Concepts of sexual orientation.* New York: Oxford University Press. (p. 364)

Buquet, R. (1988). Le reve et les deficients visuels (Dreams and the visually-impaired). *Psychanalyse-a-l'Universite, 13,* 319–327. (p. 200)

Bureau of the Census. (1998). *Statistical abstract of the United States 1998.* Washington, DC: U.S. Government Printing Office. (p. 361)

Bureau of the Census. (2002). *Statistical abstract of the United States 2002.* Washington, DC: U.S. Government Printing Office. (pp. 131, 474)

Burger, J. M. (1987). Increased performance with increased personal control: A self-presentation interpretation. *Journal of Experimental Social Psychology, 23,* 350–360. (p. B–10)

Burger, J. M., & Burns, L. (1988). The illusion of unique invulnerability and the use of effective contraception. *Personality and Social Psychology Bulletin, 14,* 264–270. (pp. 454–455)

Buri, J. R., Louiselle, P. A., Misukanis, T. M., & Mueller, R. A. (1988). Effects of parental authoritarianism and authoritativeness on self-esteem. *Personality and Social Psychology Bulletin, 14,* 271–282. (p. 114)

Burish, T. G., & Carey, M. P. (1986). Conditioned aversive responses in cancer chemotherapy patients: Theoretical and developmental analysis. *Journal of Counseling and Clinical Psychology, 54,* 593–600. (p. 234)

Busch, C. M., Zonderman, A. B., & Costa, P. T. (1994). Menopausal transition and psychological distress in a nationally representative sample: Is menopause associated with psychological distress? *Journal of Aging and Health, 6,* 209–228. (p. 125)

Bush, G. W. (2001, May 1). Speech to the National Defense University, Washington, DC. (p. 567)

Bushman, B. J. (1993). Human aggression while under the influence of alcohol and other drugs: An integrative research review. *Current Directions in Psychological Science, 2,* 148–152. (p. 561)

Bushman, B. J. (2002). Does venting anger feed or extinguish the flame? Catharsis, rumination, distraction, anger, and aggressive responding. *Personality and Social Psychology Bulletin, 28,* 724–731. (p. 395)

Bushman, B. J., & Anderson, C. A. (2001). Media violence and the American public: Scientific facts versus media misinformation. *American Psychologist, 56,* 477–489. (pp. 250, 252)

Bushman, B. J., & Baumeister, R. F. (1998). Threatened egotism, narcissism, self-esteem, and direct and displaced aggression: Does self-love or self-hate lead to violence? *Journal of Personality and Social Psychology, 75,* 219–229. (p. 460)

Bushman, B. J., Baumeister, R. F., & Stack, A. D. (1999). Catharsis, aggression, and persuasive influence: Self-fulfilling or self-defeating prophecies? *Journal of Personality and Social Psychology, 76,* 367–376. (pp. 394–395)

Bushman, B. J., & Bonaci, A. M. (2002). Violence and sex impair memory for television ads. *Journal of Applied Psychology, 87,* 557–564. (pp. 279, 360)

Buss, A. H. (1989). Personality as traits. *American Psychologist, 44,* 1378–1388. (p. 450)

Buss, D. M. (1991). Evolutionary personality psychology. *Annual Review of Psychology, 42,* 459–491. (p. 80)

Buss, D. M. (1994). The strategies of human mating: People worldwide are attracted to the same qualities in the opposite sex. *American Scientist, 82,* 238–249. (p. 74)

Buss, D. M. (1995). Evolutionary psychology: A new paradigm for psychological science. *Psychological Inquiry, 6,* 1–30. (p. 73)

Buss, D. M. (1996). Sexual conflict: Evolutionary insights into feminism and the "battle of the sexes." In D. M. Buss & N. M. Malamuth (Eds.), *Sex, power, conflict: Evolutionary and feminist perspectives.* New York: Oxford University Press. (p. 73)

Buss, D. M. (2000). *The dangerous passion: Why jealousy is as necessary as love and sex.* New York: The Free Press. (p. 73)

Bussey, K., & Bandura, A. (1999). Social cognitive theory of gender development and differentiation. *Psychological Review, 106,* 676–713. (p. 92)

Butcher, J. N. (1990). *The MMPI-2 in psychological treatment.* New York: Oxford University Press. (p. 445)

Butler, A. C., Hokanson, J. E., & Flynn, H. A. (1994). A comparison of self-esteem lability and low trait self-esteem as vulnerability factors for depression. *Journal of Personality and Social Psychology, 66,* 166–177. (p. 493)

Butler, R. A. (1954, February). Curiosity in monkeys. *Scientific American,* pp. 70–75. (p. 343)

Butterfield, F. (1999, July 12). Experts say study confirms prison's new role as mental hospital. *New York Times* (www.nytimes.com). (p. 474)

Byne, W., & Parsons, B. (1993). Human sexual orientation: The biologic theories reappraised. *Archives of General Psychiatry, 50,* 228–239. (p. 367)

Byrne, D. (1971). *The attraction paradigm.* New York: Academic Press. (p. 571)

Byrne, D. (1982). Predicting human sexual behavior. In A. G. Kraut (Ed.), *The G. Stanley Hall Lecture Series* (Vol. 2). Washington, DC: American Psychological Association. (p. 359)

Byrne, R. W. (1991, May/June). Brute intellect. *The Sciences,* pp. 42–47. (p. 312)

Byrne, R. W., & Russon, A. E. (1998). Learning by imitation: A hierarchical approach. *Behavioral and Brain Sciences, 21,* 667–721. (p. 248)

Byrnes, G., & Kelly, I. W. (1992). Crisis calls and lunar cycles: a twenty-year review. *Psychological Reports, 71,* 779–785. (p. C–18)

Cable, D. M., & Gilovich, T. (1998). Looked over or overlooked? Prescreening decisions and postinterview evaluations. *Journal of Personality and Social Psychology, 83,* 501–508. (p. B–5)

Cacioppo, J. T., Berntson, G. G., Klein, D. J., & Poehlmann, K. M. (1997). The psychophysiology of emotion across the lifespan. *Annual Review of Gerontology and Geriatrics, 17,* 27. (p. 385)

Cahill, L., Prins, B., Weber, M., & McGaugh, J. L. (1994). (Beta)-adrenergic activation and memory for emotional events. *Nature, 371,* 702–704. (p. 269)

Cahill, S. P., Carrigan, M. H., & Frueh, B. C. (1999). Does EMDR work? And if so, why? A critical review of controlled outcome and dismantling research. *Journal of Anxiety Disorders, 13,* 5–33. (p. 525)

Call, K. T., Riedel, A. A., Hein, K., McLoyd, V., Petersen, A., & Kipke, M. (2002). Adolescent health and well-being in the twenty-first century: A global perspective. *Journal of Research on Adolescence, 12,* 69–98. (p. 362)

Calle, E. E., Thun, M. J., Petrelli, J. M., Rodriguez, C., & Health, C. W., Jr. (1999). Body-mass index and mortality in a prospective cohort of U.S. adults. *New England Journal of Medicine, 341,* 1097–1105. (p. 352)

Calvin, W. H. (1996). *The cerebral code: Thinking a thought in the mosaics of the mind.* Cambridge, MA: MIT Press. (p. 53)

Camerer, C. F., Loewenstein, G., & Weber, M. (1989). The curse of knowledge in economic settings: An experimental analysis. *Journal of Political Economy, 97,* 1232–1254. (p. B–12)

Campbell, D. T. (1975). On the conflicts between biological and social evolution and between psychology and moral tradition. *American Psychologist, 30,* 1103–1126. (p. 399)

Campbell, D. T., & Specht, J. C. (1985). Altruism: Biology, culture, and religion. *Journal of Social and Clinical Psychology, 3*(1), 33–42. (p. 441)

Campbell, S. (1986). *The Loch Ness Monster: The evidence.* Willingborough, Northamptonshire, U.K.: Acquarian Press. (p. 180)

Camper, J. (1990, February 7). Drop pompom squad, U. of I. rape study says. *Chicago Tribune,* p. 1. (p. 210)

Campion, M., Palmer, D. K., & Campion, J. E. (1998). Structured employment interviews to improve reliability, validity, and users' reactions. *Current Directions in Psychological Science, 7,* 77–82. (p. B–6)

Campos, J. J., Bertenthal, B. I., & Kermoian, R. (1992). Early experience and emotional development: The emergence of wariness and heights. *Psychological Science, 3,* 61–64. (pp. 168, 479)

Cannon, W. B. (1929). *Bodily changes in pain, hunger, fear, and rage.* New York: Branford. (pp. 346, 403)

Cannon, W. B., & Washburn, A. (1912). An explanation of hunger. *American Journal of Physiology, 29,* 441–454. (p. 345)

Cantor, N., & Kihlstrom, J. F. (1987). *Personality and social intelligence.* Englewood Cliffs, NJ: Prentice-Hall. (p. 319)

Cantril, H., & Bumstead, C. H. (1960). *Reflections on the human venture.* New York: New York University Press. (p. 554)

Caplan, N., Choy, M. H., & Whitmore, J. K. (1992, February). Indochinese refugee families and academic achievement. *Scientific American,* pp. 36–42. (pp. 85, 332)

Carducci, B. J., Cosby, P. C., & Ward, D. D. (1978). Sexual arousal and interpersonal evaluations. *Journal of Experimental Social Psychology, 14,* 449–457. (p. 572)

Carey, G. (1990). Genes, fears, phobias, and phobic disorders. *Journal of Counseling and Development, 68,* 628–632. (pp. 481–482)

Carli, L. L., & Leonard, J. B. (1989). The effect of hindsight on victim derogation. *Journal of Social and Clinical Psychology, 8,* 331–343. (p. 559)

Carlson, M. (1995, August 29). Quoted by S. Blakeslee, In brain's early growth, timetable may be crucial. *New York Times,* pp. C1, C3. (p. 113)

Carlson, M., Charlin, V., & Miller, N. (1988). Positive mood and helping behavior: A test of six hypotheses. *Journal of Personality and Social Psychology, 55,* 211–229. (p. 575)

Carlson, R. (1984). What's social about social psychology? Where's the person in personality research? *Journal of Personality and Social Psychology, 47*, 1304–1309. (p. 456)

Carlson, S. (1985). A double-blind test of astrology. *Nature, 318*, 419–425. (p. 446)

Carnegie Council on Adolescent Development. (1989, June). *Turning points: Preparing American youth for the 21st century.* (The report of the Task Force on Education of Young Adolescents.) New York: Carnegie Corporation. (p. 577)

Carroll, D., Davey Smith, G., & Bennett, P. (1994, March). Health and socio-economic status. *The Psychologist*, pp. 122–125. (p. 406)

Carroll, J. M., & Russell, J. A. (1996). Do facial expressions signal specific emotions? Judging emotion from the face in context. *Journal of Personality and Social Psychology, 70*, 205–218. (p. 391)

Carskadon, M. (2002). *Adolescent sleep patterns: Biological, social, and psychological influences.* New York: Cambridge University Press. (p. 195)

Carter, R. (1998). *Mapping the mind.* Berkeley, CA: University of California Press. (p. 40)

Cartwright, R. D. (1978). *A primer on sleep and dreaming.* Reading, MA: Addison-Wesley. (p. 193)

Case, R. B., Moss, A. J., Case, N., McDermott, M., & Eberly, S. (1992). Living alone after myocardial infarction: Impact on prognosis. *Journal of the American Medical Association, 267*, 515–519. (p. 417)

Casey, B. J., Giedd, J. N., & Thomas, K. M. (2000). Structural and functional brain development and its relation to cognitive development. *Biological Psychology, 54*, 241–257. (p. 117)

Cash, T. F., & Henry, P. E. (1995). Women's body images: The results of a national survey in the U.S.A. *Sex Roles, 33*, 19–28. (pp. 350–351)

Cash, T., & Janda, L. H. (1984, December). The eye of the beholder. *Psychology Today*, pp. 46–52. (p. 569)

Caspi, A. (2000). The child is father of the man: Personality continuities from childhood to adulthood. *Journal of Personality and Social Psychology, 78*, 158–172. (p. 79)

Caspi, A., Moffitt, T. E., Newman, D. L., & Silva, P. A. (1996). Behavioral observations at age 3 years predict adult psychiatric disorders: Longitudinal evidence from a birth cohort. *Archives of General Psychiatry, 53*, 1033–1039. (p. 485)

Cassandro, V. J., & Simonton, D. K. (2003). Creativity and genius. In C. L. M. Keyes & J. Haidt (Eds.), *Flourishing: Positive psychology and the life well-lived.* Washington, DC: American Psychological Association. (p. 324)

Cassidy, J., & Shaver, P. R. (1999). *Handbook of attachment.* New York: Guilford. (p. 111)

Castillo, R. J. (1997). *Culture and mental illness: A client-centered approach.* Pacific Grove, CA: Brooks/Cole. (pp. 469, 471)

Castonguay, L. G., & Goldfried, M. R. (1994). Psychotherapy integration: An idea whose time has come. *Applied & Preventive Psychology, 3*, 159–172. (p. 507)

Cattell, R. B. (1963). Theory of fluid and crystallized intelligence: A critical experiment. *Journal of Educational Psychology, 54*, 1–22. (p. 128)

Cavalli-Sforza, L., Menozzi, P., & Piazza, A. (1994). *The history and geography of human genes.* Princeton, NJ: Princeton University Press. (p. 332)

CDC (Centers for Disease Control). (2002, September 27). Trends in sexual risk behaviors among high school students—United States, 1991–2002. *MMWR, 51*(38): 856–859 (www.cdc.gov/mmwr). (p. 364)

Ceci, S. J. (1993). Cognitive and social factors in children's testimony. Master Lecture, American Psychological Association convention. (pp. 284, 285)

Ceci, S. J., & Bruck, M. (1993). Child witnesses: Translating research into policy. *Social Policy Report* (Society for Research in Child Development), *7(3)*, 1–30. (p. 284)

Ceci, S. J., & Bruck, M. (1995). *Jeopardy in the courtroom: A scientific analysis of children's testimony.* Washington, DC: American Psychological Association. (p. 284)

Ceci, S. J., Huffman, M. L. C., Smith, E., & Loftus, E. F. (1994). Repeatedly thinking about a non-event: Source misattributions among preschoolers. *Consciousness and Cognition, 3*, 388–407. (p. 284)

Ceci, S. J., & Liker, J. K. (1986). A day at the races: A study of IQ, expertise, and cognitive complexity. *Journal of Experimental Psychology: General, 115*, 255–266. (p. 319)

Ceci, S. J., & Williams, W. M. (1997). Schooling, intelligence, and income. *American Psychologist, 52*, 1051–1058. (p. 330)

Centers for Disease Control. (1991). Body-weight perceptions and selected weight-management goals and practices of high school students—United States, 1990. *Morbidity and Mortality Weekly Report, 40*, 741, 747–750. (p. 355)

Centers for Disease Control. (1992, September 16). Serious mental illness and disability in the adult household population: United States, 1989. *Advance Data* No. 218 from *Vital and Health Statistics*, National Center for Health Statistics. (p. 502)

Centers for Disease Control. (2003). Who should get a flu shot (influenza vaccine). National Center for Infectious Diseases (http://www.cdc.gov/ncidod/diseases/flu/who.htm). (p. 499)

Centers for Disease Control Vietnam Experience Study. (1988). Health status of Vietnam veterans. *Journal of the American Medical Association, 259*, 2701–2709. (p. 480)

Centerwall, B. S. (1989). Exposure to television as a risk factor for violence. *American Journal of Epidemiology, 129*, 643–652. (p. 251)

Cerella, J. (1985). Information processing rates in the elderly. *Psychological Bulletin, 98*, 67–83. (p. 126)

Cervone, D., Shadel, W. G., & Jencius, S. (2001). Social-cognitive theory of personality assessment. *Personality and Social Psychology Review, 5*, 33–51. (p. 455)

Chalmers, R. (1995, September 19). Sizing sizzle of mutuals. *Edmonton Journal*, p. E1. (p. 23)

Chambless, D. L., Baker, M. J., Baucom, D. H., Beutler, L. E., Calhoun, K. S., Crits-Christoph, P., Daiuto, A., DeRubeis, R., Detweiler, J., Haaga, D. A. F., Johnson, S. B., McCurry, S., Mueser, K. T., Pope, K. S., Sanderson, W. C., Shoham, V., Stickle, T., Williams, D. A., & Woody, S. R. (1997). Update on empirically validated therapies, II. *The Clinical Psychologist, 51*(1), 3–16. (pp. 523, 525)

Chamove, A. S. (1980). Nongenetic induction of acquired levels of aggression. *Journal of Abnormal Psychology, 89*, 469–488. (p. 250)

Chance News (1997, 25 November). More on the frequency of letters in texts. Dart.Chance@Dartmouth.edu (p. 18)

Chance News (1997, 30 December). Gender and mortality statistics. Dart.Chance@Dartmouth.edu. (p. 422)

Chang, E. C. (2001). Cultural influences on optimism and pessimism: Differences in Western and Eastern construals of the self. In E. C. Chang (Ed.), *Optimism and pessimism.* Washington, DC: APA Books. (p. 453)

Chang, P. P., Ford, D. E., Meoni, L. A., Wang, N-Y., & Klag, M. J. (2002). Anger in young men and subsequent premature cardiovascular disease: The precursors study. *Archives of Internal Medicine, 162*, 901–906. (p. 409)

Chaplin, W. F., Phillips, J. B., Brown, J. D., Clanton, N. R., & Stein, J. L. (2000). Handshaking, gender, personality, and first impressions. *Journal of Personality and Social Psychology, 79*, 110–117. (p. 387)

Charles, S. T., Reynolds, C. A., & Gatz, M. (2001). Age-related differences and change in positive and negative affect over 23 years. *Journal of Personality and Social Psychology, 80*, 136–151. (p. 132)

Chartrand, T. L., & Bargh, J. A. (1999). The chameleon effect: The perception-behavior link and social interaction. *Journal of Personality and Social Psychology, 76*, 893–910. (p. 545)

Chase, W. G., & Simon, H. A. (1973). Perception in chess. *Cognitive Psychology, 4,* 55–81. (p. 264)

Chassin, L., Presson, C. C., Sherman, S. J., & McGrew, J. (1987). The changing smoking environment for middle and high school students: 1980–1983. *Journal of Behavioral Medicine, 10,* 581–593. (p. 213)

Chaudhari, N., Landin, A. M., & Roper, S. D. (2000). A metabotropic glutamate receptor variant functions as a taste receptor. *Nature Neuroscience, 3,* 113–119. (p. 162)

Chaves, J. F. (1989). Hypnotic control of clinical pain. In N. P. Spanos & J. F. Chaves (Eds.), *Hypnosis: The cognitive-behavioral perspective.* Buffalo, NY: Prometheus Books. (p. 206)

Cheek, J. M., & Melchior, L. A. (1990). Shyness, self-esteem, and self-consciousness. In H. Leitenberg (Ed.), *Handbook of social and evaluation anxiety.* New York: Plenum. (pp. 88, 494)

Cheit, R. E. (1998). Consider this, skeptics of recovered memory. *Ethics & Behavior, 8,* 141–160. (p. 437)

Chess, S., & Thomas, A. (1987). *Know your child: An authoritative guide for today's parents.* New York: Basic Books. (pp. 79, 112)

Child Trends. (2001, August). Facts at a glance. (www.childtrends.org). (p. 362)

Chiles, J. A., Lambert, M. J., & Hatch, A. L. (1999). The impact of psychological interventions on medical cost offset: A meta-analytic review. *Clinical Psychology: Science and Practice, 6,* 204–220. (p. 522)

Chisholm, K. (1998). A three-year follow-up of attachment and indiscriminate friendliness in children adopted from Romanian orphanages. *Child Development, 69,* 1092–1106. (p. 113)

Choi, I., & Choi, Y. (2002). Culture and self-concept flexibility. *Personality and Social Psychology Bulletin, 28,* 1508–1517. (p. 461)

Chomsky, N. (1959). Review of B. F. Skinner's *Verbal behavior. Language, 35,* 26–58. (p. 305)

Chomsky, N. (1972). *Language and mind.* New York: Harcourt Brace Jovanovich. (p. 302)

Chomsky, N. (1987). Language in a psychological setting. Sophia Linguistic Working Papers in Linguistics, No. 22, Sophia University, Tokyo. (p. 305)

Chorney, M. J., Chorney, K., Seese, N., Owen, M. J., Daniels, J., McGuffin, P., Thompson, L. A., Detterman, D. K., Benbow, C., Lubinski, D., Eley, T., & Plomin, R. (1998). A quantitative trait locus associated with cognitive ability in children. *Psychological Science, 9,* 159–166. (p. 327)

Chorpita, B. F., & Barlow, D. H. (1998). The development of anxiety: The role of control in the early environment. *Psychological Bulletin, 124,* 3–21. (p. 479)

Christensen, A., & Jacobson, N. S. (1994). Who (or what) can do psychotherapy: The status and challenge of nonprofessional therapies. *Psychological Science, 5,* 8–14. (p. 527)

Christianson, S. A. (1992). Emotional stress and eyewitness memory: A critical review. *Psychological Bulletin, 112,* 284–309. (p. 438)

Christophersen, E. R., & Edwards, K. J. (1992). Treatment of elimination disorders: State of the art 1991. *Applied & Preventive Psychology, 1,* 15–22. (p. 512)

Chugani, H. T., & Phelps, M. E. (1986). Maturational changes in cerebral function in infants determined by [18]FDG Positron Emission Tomography. *Science, 231,* 840–843. (p. 103)

CIA (2002, February). *Chiefs of state and cabinet members of foreign governments* (www.msad.state.mn.us/onlinecareerfair/human/Bethlockard.htm). (p. 91)

Cialdini, R. B. (1993). *Influence: Science and practice* (3rd ed.). New York: HarperCollins. (p. 542)

Cialdini, R. B., Eisenberg, N., Green, B. L., Rhoads, K., & Bator, R. (1998). Undermining the undermining effect of reward on sustained interest. *Journal of Applied Social Psychology, 28,* 249–263. (p. 374)

Cialdini, R. B., & Richardson, K. D. (1980). Two indirect tactics of image management: Basking and blasting. *Journal of Personality and Social Psychology, 39,* 406–415. (p. 558)

Citrome, L., & Volavka, J. (1999). Schizophrenia: Violence and comorbidity. *Current Opinion in Psychiatry, 12,* 47–51. (p. 475)

Clancy, S. A., McNally, R. J., Schachter, D. L., Lenzenweger, M. F., & Pitman, R. K. (2002). Memory distortion in people reporting abduction by aliens. *Journal of Abnormal Psychology, 111,* 455–461. (p. 282)

Clancy, S. A., Schacter, D. L., McNally, R. J., & Pitman, R. K. (2000). False recognition in women reporting recovered memories of sexual abuse. *Psychological Science, 11,* 26–31. (p. 282)

Clark, R., Anderson, N. B., Clark, V. R., & Williams, D. R. (1999). Racism as a stressor for African Americans: A biopsychosocial model. *American Psychologist, 54,* 805–816. (p. 405)

Coffey, C. E. (Ed.) (1993). *Clinical science of electroconvulsive therapy.* Washington, DC: American Psychiatric Press. (p. 533)

Coffey, C. E., Lucke, J. F., Saxton, J. A., Ratcliff, G., Unitas, L. J., Billig, B., & Bryan, R. N. (1998). Sex differences in brain aging: A quantitative magnetic resonance imagine study. *Archives of Neurology, 55,* 169–179. (p. 126)

Coffey, C. E., Wilkinson, W. E., Weiner, R. D., Parashos, I. A., Djang, W. T., Webb, M. C., Figiel, G. S., & Spritzer, C. E. (1993). Quantitative cerebral anatomy in depression: A controlled magnetic resonance imaging study. *Archives of General Psychiatry, 50,* 7–16. (p. 492)

Cogan, J. C., Bhalla, S. K., Sefa-Dedeh, A., & Rothblum, E. D. (1996). A comparison study of United States and African students on perceptions of obesity and thinness. *Journal of Cross-Cultural Psychology, 27,* 98–113. (p. 349)

Cohen, D. (1995, June 17). Now we are one, or two, or three. *New Scientist,* pp. 14–15. (p. 484)

Cohen, G., Conway, M. A., & Maylor, E. A. (1994, September). Flashbulb memories in older adults. *Psychology & Aging, 9(3),* 454–463. (p. 127)

Cohen, K. M. (2002). Relationships among childhood sex-atypical behavior, spatial ability, handedness, and sexual orientation in men. *Archives of Sexual Behavior, 31,* 129–143. (p. 367)

Cohen, S. (1988). Psychosocial models of the role of social support in the etiology of physical disease. *Health Psychology, 7,* 269–297. (p. 417)

Cohen, S., Doyle, W. J., Skoner, D. P., Rabin, B. S., & Gwaltney, J. M., Jr. (1997). Social ties and susceptibility to the common cold. *Journal of the American Medical Association, 277,* 1940–1944. (p. 418)

Cohen, S., Line, S., Manuck, S. B., Rabin, B. S., Heise, E. R., & Kaplan, J. R. (1997). Chronic social stress, social status, and susceptibility to upper respiratory infections in nonhuman primates. *Psychosomatic Medicine, 59,* 213–221. (p. 406)

Cohen, S., Tyrrell, D. A. J., & Smith, A. P. (1991). Psychological stress and susceptibility to the common cold. *New England Journal of Medicine, 325,* 606–612. (p. 410)

Coile, D. C., & Miller, N. E. (1984). How radical animal activists try to mislead humane people. *American Psychologist, 39,* 700–701. (p. 29)

Cole, K. C. (1998). *The universe and the teacup: The mathematics of truth and beauty.* New York: Harcourt Brace. (p. 212)

Coleman, J. C. (1980). *The nature of adolescence.* London: Methuen. (p. 115)

Coleman, P. D., & Flood, D. G. (1986). Dendritic proliferation in the aging brain as a compensatory repair mechanism. In D. F. Swaab, E. Fliers, M. Mirmiram, W. A. Van Gool, & F. Van Haaren (Eds.), *Progress in brain research* (Vol. 20). New York: Elsevier. (p. 126)

Collins, D. W., & Kimura, D. (1997). A large sex difference on a two-dimensional mental rotation task. *Behavioral Neuroscience, 111*, 845–849. (p. 333)

Collins, N. L., & Miller, L. C. (1994). Self-disclosure and liking: A meta-analytic review. *Psychological Bulletin, 116*, 457–475. (p. 573)

Collins, W. A., Maccoby, E. E., Steinberg, L., Hetherington, E. M., & Bornstein, M. H. (2000). Contemporary research on parenting: The case for nature and nurture. *American Psychologist, 55*, 218–232. (p. 85)

Colon, E. A., Callies, A. L., Popkin, M. K., & McGlave, P. B. (1991). Depressed mood and other variables related to bone marrow transplantation survival in acute leukemia. *Psychosomatics, 32*, 420–425. (p. 417)

Commission on Violence and Youth. (1993). Violence and youth: Psychology's response. Washington, DC: American Psychological Association. (p. 251)

Commissioner of Official Languages. (1999). *Annual Report 1998.* Minister of Public Works and Government Services Canada, Cat. No. SF1–1998. (p. 309)

Comstock, G. W., & Partridge, K. B. (1972). Church attendance and health. *Journal of Chronic Disease, 25*, 665–672. (p. 422)

Conner, M., & McMillan, B. (1999). Interaction effects in the theory of planned behaviour: Studying cannabis use. *British Journal of Social Psychology, 38*, 195–222. (p. 217)

Consensus Conference. (1985). Electroconvulsive therapy. *Journal of the American Medical Association, 254*, 2103–2108. (p. 533)

Consumer Reports. (1995, November). Does therapy help? pp. 734–739. (p. 520)

Conway, M., & Ross, M. (1984). Getting what you want by revising what you had. *Journal of Personality and Social Psychology, 47*, 738–748. (p. 280)

Cook, E. W., III, Hodes, R. L., & Lang, P. J. (1986). Preparedness and phobia: Effects of stimulus content on human visceral conditioning. *Journal of Abnormal Psychology, 95*, 195–207. (p. 234)

Cooper, K. J. (1999, May 1). This time, copycat wave is broader. *Washington Post* (www.washingtonpost.com). (pp. 249, 545)

Cooper, W. H. (1983). An achievement motivation nomological network. *Journal of Personality and Social Psychology, 44*, 841–861. (p. 373)

Coopersmith, S. (1967). *The antecedents of self-esteem.* San Francisco: Freeman. (p. 114)

Corballis, M. C. (1999, March-April). The gestural origins of language. *American Scientist*, pp. 138–145. (p. 313)

Corballis, M. C. (2002). *From hand to mouth: The origins of language.* Princeton: Princeton University Press. (p. 313)

Coren, S. (1996). *Sleep thieves: An eye-opening exploration into the science and mysteries of sleep.* New York: Free Press. (pp. 195–196, 198)

Corina, D. P. (1998). The processing of sign language: Evidence from aphasia. In B. Stemmer & H. A. Whittaker (Eds.), *Handbook of neurolinguistics.* San Diego: Academic Press. (p. 62)

Corina, D. P., Vaid, J., & Bellugi, U. (1992). The linguistic basis of left hemisphere specialization. *Science, 255*, 1258–1260. (p. 62)

Correll, J., Park, B., Judd, C. M., & Wittenbrink, B. (2002). The police officer's dilemma: Using ethnicity to disambiguate potentially threatening individuals. *Journal of Personality and Social Psychology, 83*, 1314–1329. (p. 556)

Costa, P. T., Jr., & McCrae, R. R. (1989). Personality continuity and the changes of adult life. In M. Storandt & G. R. VandenBos (Eds.), *The adult years: Continuity and change.* Washington, DC: American Psychological Association. (p. 135)

Costa, P. T., Jr., Terracciano, A., & McCrae, R. R. (2001). Gender differences in personality traits across cultures: Robust and surprising findings. *Journal of Personality and Social Psychology, 81*, 322–331. (p. 389)

Courneya, K. S., & Carron, A. V. (1992). The home advantage in sports competitions: A literature review. *Journal of Sport and Exercise Psychology, 14*, 13–27. (p. 551)

Courtney, J. G., Longnecker, M. P., Theorell, T., & de Verdier, M. G. (1993). Stressful life events and the risk of colorectal cancer. *Epidemiology, 4*, 407–414. (p. 411)

Cousins, N. (1989). *Head first: The biology of hope.* New York: Dutton. (p. 461)

Cowan, G., Lee, C., Levy, D., & Snyder, D. (1988). Dominance and inequality in X-rated videocassettes. *Psychology of Women Quarterly, 12*, 299–311. (p. 563)

Cowan, N. (1988). Evolving conceptions of memory storage, selective attention, and their mutual constraints within the human information-processing system. *Psychological Bulletin, 104*, 163–191. (p. 266)

Cowan, N. (1994). Mechanisms of verbal short-term memory. *Current Directions in Psychological Science, 3*, 185–189. (p. 266)

Cowan, N. (2001). The magical number 4 in short-term memory: A reconsideration of mental storage capacity. *Behavioral and Brain Sciences, 24*, 87–185. (p. 266)

Cowart, B. J. (1981). Development of taste perception in humans: Sensitivity and preference throughout the life span. *Psychological Bulletin, 90*, 43–73. (p. 162)

Crabbe, J. C. (2002). Genetic contributions to addiction. *Annual Review of Psychology, 53*, 435–462. (p. 218)

Crabtree, S. (2002, January 22). Gender roles reflected in teen tech use. *Gallup Tuesday Briefing* (www.gallup.com). (p. 121)

Craig, M. E., Kalichman, S. C., & Follingstad, D. R. (1989). Verbal coercive sexual behavior among college students. *Archives of Sexual Behavior, 18*, 421–434. (p. 563)

Craik, F. I. M., & Watkins, M. J. (1973). The role of rehearsal in short-term memory. *Journal of Verbal Learning and Verbal Behavior, 12*, 599–607. (p. 262)

Crandall, C. S. (1988). Social contagion of binge eating. *Journal of Personality and Social Psychology, 55*, 588–598. (p. 350)

Crandall, C. S. (1994). Prejudice against fat people: Ideology and self-interest. *Journal of Personality and Social Psychology, 66*, 882–894. (p. 352)

Crandall, C. S. (1995). Do parents discriminate against their heavyweight daughters? *Personality and Social Psychology Bulletin, 21*, 724–735. (p. 352)

Crandall, J. E. (1984). Social interest as a moderator of life stress. *Journal of Personality and Social Psychology, 47*, 164–174. (p. 441)

Crawford, M., Chaffin, R., & Fitton, L. (1995). Cognition in social context. *Learning and Individual Differences, 7*, 341–362. (p. 334)

Crews, F. (1996). The verdict on Freud. *Psychological Science, 7*, 63–68. (p. 438)

Crews, F. (Ed.) (1998). *Unauthorized Freud: Doubters confront a legend.* New York: Viking. (p. 438)

Crocker, J., & Major, B. (1989). Social stigma and self-esteem: The self-protective properties of stigma. *Psychological Review, 89*, 608–630. (p. 458)

Crocker, J., Thompson, L. L., McGraw, K. M., & Ingerman, C. (1987). Downward comparison, prejudice, and evaluation of others: Effects of self-esteem and threat. *Journal of Personality and Social Psychology, 52*, 907–916. (p. 558)

Crocker, J., & Wolfe, C. (1999). Rescuing self-esteem: A contingencies of worth perspective. Unpublished manuscript, University of Michigan. (p. 457)

Croft, R. J., Klugman, A., Baldeweg, T., & Gruzelier, J. H. (2001). Electrophysiological evidence of serotonergic impairment in long-term MDMA ("Ecstasy") users. *American Journal of Psychiatry, 158*, 1687–1692. (p. 215)

Crook, T. H., & West, R. L. (1990). Name recall performance across the adult life-span. *British Journal of Psychology, 81*, 335–340. (p. 127)

Cross-National Collaborative Group. (1992). The changing rate of major depression. *Journal of the American Medical Association, 268,* 3098–3105. (p. 489)

Crossen, C. (1994). *Tainted truth: The manipulation of fact in America.* New York: Simon & Schuster. (p. A–1)

Crowell, J. A., & Waters, E. (1994). Bowlby's theory grown up: The role of attachment in adult love relationships. *Psychological Inquiry, 5,* 1–22. (p. 111)

Csikszentmihalyi, M. (1990). *Flow: The psychology of optimal experience.* New York: Harper & Row. (p. B–2)

Csikszentmihalyi, M. (1999). If we are so rich, why aren't we happy? *American Psychologist, 54,* 821–827. (pp. 397, B–2)

Curtis, R. C., & Miller, K. (1986). Believing another likes or dislikes you: Behaviors making the beliefs come true. *Journal of Personality and Social Psychology, 51,* 284–290. (p. 571)

Czeisler, C. A., Allan, J. S., Strogatz, S. H., Ronda, J. M., Sanchez, R., Rios, C. D., Freitag, W. O., Richardson, G. S., & Kronauer, R. E. (1986). Bright light resets the human circadian pacemaker independent of the timing of the sleep-wake cycle. *Science, 233,* 667–671. (p. 190)

Czeisler, C. A., Duffy, J. F., Shanahan, T. L., Brown, E. N., Mitchell, J. F., Rimmer, D. W., Ronda, J. M., Silva, E. J., Allan, J. S., Emens, J. S., Dijk, D-J., & Kronauer, R. E. (1999). Stability, precision, and near-24-hour period of the human circadian pacemaker. *Science, 284,* 2177–2181. (p. 191)

Czeisler, C. A., Kronauer, R. E., Allan, J. S., & Duffy, J. F. (1989). Bright light induction of strong (type O) resetting of the human circadian pacemaker. *Science, 244,* 1328–1333. (p. 190)

Dabbs, J. M., Jr. (2000). Heroes, rogues, and lovers: Testosterone and behavior. New York: McGraw-Hill. (pp. 359, 360)

Dabbs, J. M., Jr., Bernieri, F. J., Strong, R. K., Campo, R., & Milun, R. (2001b). Going on stage: Testosterone in greetings and meetings. *Journal of Research in Personality, 35,* 27–40. (p. 561)

Dabbs, J. M., Jr., & Morris, R. (1990). Testosterone, social class, and antisocial behavior in a sample of 4,462 men. *Psychological Science, 1,* 209–211. (p. 561)

Dabbs, J. M., Jr., Riad, J. K., & Chance, S. E. (2001a). Testosterone and ruthless homicide. *Personality and Individual Differences, 31,* 599–603. (p. 561)

Dabbs, J. M., Jr., Ruback, R. B., & Besch, N. F. (1987). Male saliva testosterone following conversations with male and female partners. Paper presented at the American Psychological Association convention. (p. 359)

Damasio, A. R. (1994). *Descartes error: Emotion, reason, and the human brain.* New York: Grossett/Putnam & Sons. (p. 319)

Damasio, H., Grabowski, T., Frank, R., Galaburda, A. M., & Damasio, A. R. (1994). The return of Phineas Gage: Clues about the brain from the skull of a famous patient. *Science, 264,* 1102–1105. (p. 56)

Damon, W. (1995). *Greater expectations: Overcoming the culture of indulgence in America's homes and schools.* New York: Free Press. (pp. 104, 457)

Danner, D. D., Snowdon, D. A., & Friesen, W. V. (2001). Positive emotions in early life and longevity: Findings from the Nun Study. *Journal of Personality and Social Psychology, 80,* 804–813. (p. 407)

Danso, H., & Esses, V. (2001). Black experimenters and the intellectual test performance of white participants: The tables are turned. *Journal of Experimental Social Psychology, 37,* 158–165. (p. 335)

Darley, J. M., & Latané, B. (1968a). Bystander intervention in emergencies: Diffusion of responsibility. *Journal of Personality and Social Psychology, 8,* 377–383. (pp. 574–575)

Darley, J. M., & Latané, B. (1968b, December). When will people help in a crisis? *Psychology Today,* pp. 54–57, 70–71. (p. 574)

Darrach, B., & Norris, J. (1984, August). An American tragedy. *Life,* pp. 58–74. (p. 485)

Daum, I., & Schugens, M. M. (1996). On the cerebellum and classical conditioning. *Psychological Science, 5,* 58–61. (p. 271)

Davey, G. C. L. (1992). Classical conditioning and the acquisition of human fears and phobias: A review and synthesis of the literature. *Advances in Behavior Research and Therapy, 14,* 29–66. (p. 234)

Davey, G. C. L. (1995). Preparedness and phobias: Specific evolved associations or a generalized expectancy bias? *Behavioral and Brain Sciences, 18,* 289–297. (p. 480)

Davidoff, J., Davies, I., & Roberson, D. (1999). Colour categories in a stone-age tribe. *Nature, 398,* 203–204. (pp. 308–309)

Davidson, P. R., & Parker, K. C. H. (2001). Eye movement desensitization and reprocessing (EMDR): A meta-analysis. *Journal of Consulting and Clinical Psychology, 69,* 305–317. (p. 525)

Davidson, R. (2000). Affective style, psychopathology, and resilience: Brain mechanisms and plasticity. *American Psychologist, 55,* 1196–1209. (p. 385)

Davidson, R. J. (1999). Biological bases of personality. In V. J. Darlega, B. A. Winstead, & W. H. Jones. (Eds.) *Personality: Contemporary theory and research.* Chicago: Nelson-Hall. (p. 385)

Davidson, R. J., Ekman, P., Saron, C. D., Senulis, J. A., & Friesen, W. V. (1990). Approach/withdrawal and cerebral asymmetry: Emotional expression and brain physiology: I. *Journal of Personality and Social Psychology, 58,* 330–341. (p. 385)

Davidson, R. J., Pizzagalli, D., Nitschke, J. B., & Putnam, K. (2002). Depression: Perspectives from affective neuroscience. *Annual Review of Psychology, 53,* 545–574. (p. 492)

Davidson, R. J., Putnam, K. M., & Larson, C. L. (2000). Dysfunction in the neural circuitry of emotion regulation—a possible prelude to violence. *Science, 289,* 591–594. (p. 561)

Davies, D. R., Matthews, G., & Wong, C. S. K. (1991). Aging and work. *International Review of Industrial and Organizational Psychology, 6,* 149–211. (p. 130)

Davies, M. F. (1997). Positive test strategies and confirmatory retrieval processes in the evaluation of personality feedback. *Journal of Personality and Social Psychology, 73,* 574–583. (p. 446)

Davies, P. (1992). *The mind of God: The scientific basis for a rational world.* New York: Simon & Schuster. (p. 95)

Davies, P. (1999). *The fifth miracle: The search for the origin and meaning of life.* New York: Simon & Schuster. (p. 95)

Davis, J. O., & Phelps, J. A. (1995a). Twins with schizophrenia: Genes or germs? *Schizophrenia Bulletin, 21,* 13–18. (pp. 83, 500)

Davis, J. O., Phelps, J. A., & Bracha, H. S. (1995b). Prenatal development of monozygotic twins and concordance for schizophrenia. *Schizophrenia Bulletin, 21,* 357–366. (p. 500)

Davison, K. P., Pennebaker, J. W., & Dickerson, S. S. (2000). Who talks? The social psychology of illness support groups. *American Psychologist, 55,* 205–217. (p. 518)

Dawes, R. M. (1980). Social dilemmas. *Annual Review of Psychology, 31,* 169–193. (p. 567)

Dawes, R. M. (1994). *House of cards: Psychology and psychotherapy built on myth.* New York: Free Press. (pp. 435, 457)

Dawkins, R. (1998). *Unweaving the rainbow.* Boston: Houghton Mifflin. (p. 94)

Dawkins, R. (1999, April 8). Is science killing the soul (a discussion with Richard Dawkins and Steven Pinker). www.edge.org (p. 187)

Day, N. L., Leech, S. L., Richardson, G. A., Cornelius, M. D., Robles, N., & Larkby, C. (2002). Prenatal alcohol exposure predicts continued deficits in offspring size at 14 years of age. *Alcoholism: Clinical & Experimental Research, 26,* 1584–1591. (p. 100)

Dean, G. A., Kelly, I. W., Saklofske, D. H., & Furnham, A. (1992). Graphology and human judgment. In B. Beyerstein & D. Beyerstein (Eds.), *The write stuff: Evaluations of graphology*. Buffalo, NY: Prometheus Books. (p. 446)

Deary, I. J., & Matthews, G. (1993). Personality traits are alive and well. *The Psychologist: Bulletin of the British Psychological Society, 6*, 299–311. (p. 450)

de Boysson-Bardies, B., Halle, P., Sagart, L., & Durand, C. (1989). A cross linguistic investigation of vowel formats in babbling. *Journal of Child Language, 16*, 1–17. (p. 303)

DeBruine, L. M. (2002). Facial resemblance enhances trust. *Proceedings of the Royal Society of London, 269*, 1307–1312. (p. 569)

Deci, E. L., Connell, J. P., & Ryan, R. M. (1989). Self-determination in a work organization. *Journal of Applied Psychology, 74*, 580–590. (p. B–11)

Deci, E. L., Koestner, R., & Ryan, R. M. (1999, November). A meta-analytic review of experiments examining the effects of extrinsic rewards on intrinsic motivation. *Psychological Bulletin, 125(6)*, 627–668. (p. 244)

Deci, E. L., & Ryan, R. M. (1985). *Intrinsic motivation and self-determination in human behavior.* New York: Plenum Press. (p. 244)

Deci, E. L., & Ryan, R. M. (1992). The initiation and regulation of intrinsically motivated learning and achievement. In A. K. Boggiano & T. S. Pittman (Eds.), *Achievement and motivation: A social-developmental perspective.* New York: Cambridge University Press. (p. 244)

Deci, E. L., & Ryan, R. M. (2000). The "what" and "why" of goal pursuits: Human needs and the self-determination of behavior. *Psychological Inquiry, 11*, 227–268. (p. 244)

de Courten-Myers, G. M. (2002, May 9). Personal correspondence. (p. 53)

de Cuevas, J. (1990, September-October). "No, she held them loosely." *Harvard Magazine*, pp. 60–67. (p. 305)

de Jong-Gierveld, J. (1987). Developing and testing a model of loneliness. *Journal of Personality and Social Psychology, 53*, 119–128. (p. 494)

De Koninck, J. (2000). Waking experiences and dreaming. In M. Kryger, T. Roth, & W. Dement (Eds.), *Principles and practice of sleep medicine, 3rd ed.* Philadelphia: Saunders. (p. 201)

Delaney, P. F., Ericsson, K. A., Weaver, G. E., & Mahadevan, S. (1999). Accounts of the memorist Rajan's exceptional performance: Comparing three theoretical proposals. Paper presented to the American Psychological Society convention. (p. 267)

Delgado, J. M. R. (1969). *Physical control of the mind: Toward a psychocivilized society.* New York: Harper & Row. (p. 53)

DeLoache, J. S. (1995). Early understanding and use of symbols: The model model. *Current Directions in Psychological Science, 4*, 109–113. (p. 107)

DeLoache, J. S., & Brown, A. L. (1987, October-December). Differences in the memory-based searching of delayed and normally developing young children. *Intelligence, 11*(4), 277–289. (p. 107)

Dement, W. (1997, September). What all undergraduates should know about how their sleeping lives affect their waking lives. Stanford University: www-leland.stanford.edu/~dement/sleepless.html (pp. 195, 199)

Dement, W. C. (1978). *Some must watch while some must sleep.* New York: Norton. (pp. 192, 199)

Dement, W. C. (1999). *The promise of sleep.* New York: Delacorte Press. (pp. 191–193, 195–196, 199, C–11)

Dement, W. C., & Wolpert, E. A. (1958). The relation of eye movements, body mobility, and external stimuli to dream content. *Journal of Experimental Psychology, 55*, 543–553. (p. 201)

Dempster, F. N. (1988). The spacing effect: A case study in the failure to apply the results of psychological research. *American Psychologist, 43*, 627–634. (p. 261)

Denes-Raj, V., Epstein, S., & Cole, J. (1995). The generality of the ratio-bias phenomenon. *Personality and Social Psychology Bulletin, 21*, 1083–1092. (p. 300)

DeNeve, K. M., & Cooper, H. (1998). The happy personality: A meta-analysis of 137 personality traits and subjective well-being. *Psychological Bulletin, 124*, 197–229. (p. 400)

Dennerstein, L., Dudley, E., Guthrie, J., & Barrett-Connor, E. (2000). Life satisfaction, symptoms, and the menopausal transition. *Medscape Women's Health, 5(4)* (www.medscape.com). (p. 125)

Denton, K., & Krebs, D. (1990). From the scene to the crime: The effect of alcohol and social context on moral judgment. *Journal of Personality and Social Psychology, 59*, 242–248. (p. 210)

D'Eon, J. L. (1989). Hypnosis in the control of labor pain. In N. P. Spanos & J. F. Chaves (Eds.), *Hypnosis: The cognitive-behavioral perspective.* Buffalo, NY: Prometheus Books. (p. 206)

DePaulo, B. M. (1994). Spotting lies: Can humans learn to do better?" *Current Directions in Psychological Science 3*, 83–86. (p. 388)

Dermer, M., Cohen, S. J., Jacobsen, E., & Anderson, E. A. (1979). Evaluative judgments of aspects of life as a function of vicarious exposure to hedonic extremes. *Journal of Personality and Social Psychology, 37*, 247–260. (p. 400)

Dermer, M., & Pyszczynski, T. A. (1978). Effects of erotica upon men's loving and liking responses for women they love. *Journal of Personality and Social Psychology, 36*, 1302–1309. (p. 572)

DeSteno, D., Petty, R. E., Wegener, D. T., & Rucker, D. D. (2000). Beyond valence in the perception of likelihood: The role of emotion specificity. *Journal of Personality and Social Psychology, 78*, 397–416. (p. 275)

Deutsch, J. A. (1972, July). Brain reward: ESP and ecstasy. *Psychology Today*, pp. 46–48. (p. 52)

Deutsch, M. (1991). Egalitarianism in the laboratory and at work. In R. Vermunt & H. Steensma (Eds.), *Social justice in human relations.* New York: Plenum. (p. 246)

DeValois, R. L., & DeValois, K. K. (1975). Neural coding of color. In E. C. Carterette & M. P. Friedman (Eds.), *Handbook of perception: Vol. V. Seeing.* New York: Academic Press. (p. 155)

Devine, P. G. (1995). Prejudice and outgroup perception. In A. Tesser (Ed.), *Advanced social psychology.* New York: McGraw-Hill. (p. 569)

Devlin, B., Daniels, M., & Roeder, K. (1997). The heritability of IQ. *Nature, 388*, 468–471. (p. 327)

de Waal, F. B. M. (1999, December). The end of nature versus nurture. *Scientific American*, pp. 94–99. (p. 94)

de Waal, F. B. M., & Johanowicz, D. L. (1993). Modification of reconciliation behavior through social experience: An experiment with two macaque species. *Child Development, 64*, 897–908. (p. 248)

Dey, E. L., Astin, A. W., & Korn, W. S. (1991). *The American freshman: Twenty-five year trends.* Los Angeles: Higher Education Research Institute, UCLA. (p. 91)

Dhawan, N., Roseman, I. J., Naidu, R. K., Thapa, K., & Rettek, S. I. (1995). Self-concepts across two cultures: India and the United States. *Journal of Cross-Cultural Psychology, 26*, 606–621. (p. 461)

Diaconis, P. (2002, August 11). Quoted by L. Belkin, The odds of that. *New York Times* (www.nytimes.com). (p. 22)

Diaconis, P., & Mosteller, F. (1989). Methods for studying coincidences. *Journal of the American Statistical Association, 84*, 853–861. (p. 22)

Diamond, J. (1989, May). The great leap forward. *Discover*, pp. 50–60. (p. 302)

Diamond, J. (2001, February). A tale of two reputations: Why we revere Darwin and give Freud a hard time. *Natural History*, pp. 20–24. (p. 72)

Diamond, L. M. (2000). Sexual identity, attractions, and behavior among young sexual-minority women over a 2-year period. *Developmental Psychology, 36*, 241–250. (p. 365)

Diamond, R. (1993). Genetics and male sexual orientation (letter). *Science, 261,* p. 1258. (p. 369)

Dickens, W. T., & Flynn, J. R. (2001). Heritability estimates versus large environmental effects: The IQ paradox resolved. *Psychological Review, 108,* 346–349. (p. 328)

Diener, E., & Biswas-Diener, R. (2002). Will money increase subjective well-being? A literature review and guide to needed research. *Social Indicators Research, 57,* 119–169. (p. 398)

Diener, E., Diener, M., & Diener, C. (1995). Factors predicting the subjective well-being of nations. *Journal of Personality and Social Psychology, 69,* 851–864. (p. 462)

Diener, E., & Oishi, S. (2000). Money and happiness: Income and subjective well-being across nations. In E. Diener & E. M. Suh (Eds.), *Subjective well-being across cultures.* Cambridge, MA: MIT Press. (pp. 397, 398)

Diener, E., Oishi, S., & Lucas, R. E. (2003). Personality, culture, and subjective well-being: Emotional and cognitive evaluations of life. *Annual Review of Psychology, 54,* 403–425. (p. 400)

Diener, E., Wirtz, D., & Oishi, S. (2001). End effects of rated life quality: The James Dean effect. *Psychological Science, 12,* 124–128. (p. 161)

Diener, E., Wolsic, B., & Fujita, F. (1995). Physical attractiveness and subjective well-being. *Journal of Personality and Social Psychology, 69,* 120–129. (p. 570)

Dietz, W. H., Jr., & Gortmaker, S. L. (1985). Do we fatten our children at the television set? Obesity and television viewing in children and adolescents. *Pediatrics, 75,* 807–812. (p. 356)

DiLalla, D. L., Carey, G., Gottesman, I. I., & Bouchard, T. J., Jr. (1996). Heritability of MMPI personality indicators of psychopathology in twins reared apart. *Journal of Abnormal Psychology, 105,* 491–499. (pp. 77, 489)

Dill, J. C., & Anderson, C.A. (1999). Loneliness, shyness, and depression: The etiology and interrelationships of everyday problems in living. In T. Joiner and J.C. Coyne (Eds.) *The interactional nature of depression: Advances in interpersonal approaches.* Washington, D.C.: American Psychological Association. (p. 494)

Dimberg, U., Thunberg, M., & Elmehed, K. (2000). Unconscious facial reactions to emotional facial expressions. *Psychological Science, 11,* 86–89. (pp. 249, 393)

Dimberg, U., Thunberg, M., & Grunedal, S. (2002). Facial reactions to emotional stimuli: Automatically controlled emotional responses. *Cognition and Emotion, 16,* 449–472. (p. 249)

Dindia, K., & Allen, M. (1992). Sex differences in self-disclosure: A meta-analysis. *Psychological Bulletin, 112,* 106–124. (p. 121)

Dinges, N. G., & Hull, P. (1992). Personality, culture, and international studies. In D. Lieberman (Ed.), *Revealing the world: An interdisciplinary reader for international studies.* Dubuque, IA: Kendall-Hunt. (p. 308)

Dion, K. K., & Dion, K. L. (1993). Individualistic and collectivistic perspectives on gender and the cultural context of love and intimacy. *Journal of Social Issues, 49,* 53–69. (p. 462)

Dion, K. K., & Dion, K. L. (2001). Gender and cultural adaptation in immigrant families. *Journal of Social Issues, 57,* 511–521. (p. 91)

Discover (1996, May). A fistful of risks. Pp. 82–83. (p. 212)

Dishion, T. J., McCord, J., & Poulin, F. (1999). When interventions harm: Peer groups and problem behavior. *American Psychologist, 54,* 755–764. (p. 552)

Di Tella, R., MacCulloch, R. J., & Oswald, A. J. (2001). The macroeconomics of happiness. Warwick Economic Research Paper No. 615, Department of Economics, University of Warwick. (p. 397)

Doherty, E. W., & Doherty, W. J. (1998). Smoke gets in your eyes: Cigarette smoking and divorce in a national sample of American adults. *Families, Systems, and Health, 16,* 393–400. (p. 212)

Dohrenwend, B., Pearlin, L., Clayton, P., Hamburg, B., Dohrenwend, B. P., Riley, M., & Rose, R. (1982). Report on stress and life events. In G. R. Elliott & C. Eisdorfer (Eds.), *Stress and human health: Analysis and implications of research* (A study by the Institute of Medicine/National Academy of Sciences). New York: Springer. (p. 405)

Dohrenwend, B. P., Levav, I., Shrout, P. E., Schwartz, S., Naveh, G., Link, B. G., Skodol, A. E., & Stueve, A. (1992). Socioeconomic status and psychiatric disorders: The causation-selection issue. *Science, 255,* 946–952. (p. 502)

Dolan, R. J. (2002). Emotion, cognition, and behavior. *Science, 298,* 1191–1194. (p. 272)

Dole, R. (1996, April 20). Quoted by M. Duffy, Look who's talking. *Time,* p. 48. (p. 541)

Dolezal, H. (1982). *Living in a world transformed.* New York: Academic Press. (p. 177)

Domhoff, G. W. (1996). *Finding meaning in dreams: A quantitative approach.* New York: Plenum. (p. 200)

Domhoff, G. W. (1999). New directions in the study of dream content using the Hall and Van de Castle coding system. *Dreaming, 9,* 115–137. (p. 200)

Domhoff, W. G. (2003). *The scientific study of dreams: Neural networks, cognitive development, and content analysis.* Washington, DC: APA Books. (p. 203)

Domjan, M. (1992). Adult learning and mate choice: Possibilities and experimental evidence. *American Zoologist, 32,* 48–61. (p. 230)

Domjan, M. (1994). Formulation of a behavior system for sexual conditioning. *Psychonomic Bulletin & Review, 1,* 421–428. (p. 230)

Domjan, M. (1997). Behavior systems and the demise of equipotentiality: Historical antecedents and evidence from sexual conditioning. In M. E. Bouton & M. S. Fanselow (Eds.), *Learning, motivation, and cognition: The functional behaviorism of Robert C. Bolles.* Washington, DC: American Psychological Association. (p. 230)

Domjan, M., Blesbois, E., & Williams, J. (1998). The adaptive significance of sexual conditioning: Pavlovian control of sperm release. *Psychological Science, 9,* 411–415. (p. 230)

Donnerstein, E. (1998). Why do we have those new ratings on television. Invited address to the National Institute on the Teaching of Psychology. (pp. 250, 251, 252)

Donnerstein, E., Linz, D., & Penrod, S. (1987). *The question of pornography.* New York: Free Press. (p. 252)

Dorner, G. (1976). *Hormones and brain differentiation.* Amsterdam: Elsevier Scientific. (p. 367)

Dorner, G. (1988). Neuroendocrine response to estrogen and brain differentiation in heterosexuals, homosexuals, and transsexuals. *Archives of Sexual Behavior, 17,* 57–75. (p. 367)

Doty, R. L., Shaman, P., Applebaum, S. L., Giberson, R., Siksorski, L., & Rosenberg, L. (1984). Smell identification ability: Changes with age. *Science, 226,* 1441–1443. (p. 125)

Doty, R. W. (1998). The five mysteries of the mind, and their consequences. *Neuropsychologia, 36,* 1069–1076. (p. 268)

Dovidio, J. F., & Gaertner, S. L. (1999). Reducing prejudice: Combating intergroup biases. *Current Directions in Psychological Science, 8,* 101–105. (p. 577)

Downing, P. E., Jiang, Y., & Shuman, M. (2001). A cortical area selective for visual processing of the human body. *Science, 293,* 2470–2473. (p. 151)

Draguns, J. G. (1990a). Normal and abnormal behavior in cross-cultural perspective: Specifying the nature of their relationship. *Nebraska Symposium on Motivation 1989, 37,* 235–277. (pp. 469, 493)

Draguns, J. G. (1990b). Applications of cross-cultural psychology in the field of mental health. In R. W. Brislin (Ed.), *Applied cross-cultural psychology.* Newbury Park, CA: Sage. (pp. 469, 471)

Druckman, D., & Bjork, R. A. (1991). *In the mind's eye: Enhancing human performance.* National Academy Press: Washington, DC. (p. 443)

Druckman, D., & Bjork, R. A. (Eds.) (1994). *Learning, remembering, believing: Enhancing human performance.* Washington, DC: National Academy Press. (pp. 205, 206)

Druckman, D., & Swets, J. A. (Eds.). (1988). *Enhancing human performance: Issues, theories, and techniques.* Washington, DC: National Academy Press. (p. 181)

Dubbert, P. M. (2002). Physical activity and exercise: Recent advances and current challenges. *Journal of Consulting and Clinical Psychology, 70,* 526–537. (p. 415)

Duckworth, K. L., Bargh, J. A., Garcia, M., & Chaiken, S. (2002). The automatic evaluation of novel stimuli. *Psychological Science, 13,* 513–519. (p. 382)

Duclos, S. E., Laird, J. D., Sexter, M., Stern, L., & Van Lighten, O. (1989). Emotion-specific effects of facial expressions and postures on emotional experience. *Journal of Personality and Social Psychology, 57,* 100–108. (p. 392)

Dugatkin, L. A. (2002, Winter). Watching culture shape even guppy love. *Cerebrum,* pp. 51–66. (p. 248)

Duggan, J. P., & Booth, D. A. (1986). Obesity, overeating, and rapid gastric emptying in rats with ventromedial hypothalamic lesions. *Science, 231,* 609–611. (p. 346)

Dugger, C. W. (2001, April 22). Abortion in India is tipping scales sharply against girls. *New York Times* (www.nytimes.com). (p. 556)

Duman, R. S., Nakagawa, S., & Malberg, J. (2001). Regulation of adult neurogenesis by antidepressant treatment. *Neuropsychopharmacology, 25,* 836–844. (p. 532)

Duncan, B. L. (1976). Differential social perception and attribution of intergroup violence: Testing the lower limits of stereotyping of blacks. *Journal of Personality and Social Psychology, 34,* 590–598. (p. 555)

Duncan, G. J., Hill, M. S., & Hoffman, S. D. (1988). Welfare dependence within and across generations. *Science, 239,* 467–471. (p. 297)

Duncker, K. (1945). On problem solving. *Psychological Monographs, 58* (Whole no. 270). (pp. 296, 299)

Dunson, D. B., Colombo, B., & Baird, D. D. (2002). Changes with age in the level and duration of fertility in the menstrual cycle. *Human Reproduction, 17,* 1399–1403. (p. 124)

DuPree, D. (1998, 26 February). Jordan's $33.14M tops NBA. *USA Today,* p. C1. (p. A–2)

Durston, S., Hulshoff, P., Hilleke, E., Casey, B. J., Giedd, J. N., Buitelaar, J. K., & van Engeland, H. (2001). Anatomical MRI of the developing human brain: What have we learned? *Journal of the American Academy of Child and Adolescent Psychiatry, 40,* 1012–1020. (p. 117)

Dutton, D. G., & Aron, A. (1989). Romantic attraction and generalized liking for others who are sources of conflict-based arousal. *Canadian Journal of Behavioural Sciences, 21,* 246–257. (p. 572)

Dutton, D. G., & Aron, A. P. (1974). Some evidence for heightened sexual attraction under conditions of high anxiety. *Journal of Personality and Social Psychology, 30,* 510–517. (p. 572)

Dweck, C. S., & Elliott, E. S. (1983). Achievement motivation. In P. Mussen & E. M. Hetherington (Eds.), *Handbook of child psychology* (Vol. IV). New York: Wiley. (p. 374)

Eagly, A. (1994). Are people prejudiced against women? Donald Campbell Award invited address, American Psychological Association convention. (pp. 556–557)

Eagly, A. H., Ashmore, R. D., Makhijani, M. G., & Kennedy, L. C. (1991). What is beautiful is good, but . . .: A meta-analytic review of research on the physical attractiveness stereotype. *Psychological Bulletin, 110,* 109–128. (p. 569)

Eagly, A. H., & Crowley, M. (1986). Gender and helping behavior: A meta-analytic review of the social psychological literature. *Psychological Bulletin, 100,* 283–308. (p. 574)

Eagly, A. H., & Wood, W. (1999). The origins of sex differences in human behavior: Evolved dispositions versus social roles. *American Psychologist, 54,* 408–423. (p. 74)

Eastman, C. L., Boulos, Z., Terman, M., Campbell, S. S., Dijk, D-J., & Lewy, A. J. (1995). Light treatment for sleep disorders: Consensus report. VI. Shift work. *Journal of Biological Rhythms, 10,* 157–164. (p. 190)

Eastman, C. L., Young, M. A., Fogg, L. F., Liu, L., & Meaden, P. M. (1998). Bright light treatment of winter depression: A placebo-controlled trial. *Archives of General Psychiatry, 55,* 883–889. (p. 526)

Ebbesen, E. B., Duncan, B., & Konecni, V. J. (1975). Effects of content of verbal aggression on future verbal aggression: A field experiment. *Journal of Experimental Social Psychology, 11,* 192–204. (p. 394)

Ebbinghaus, H. (1885). *Über das Gedachtnis.* Leipzig: Duncker & Humblot. Cited in R. Klatzky (1980), *Human memory: Structures and processes.* San Francisco: Freeman. (p. 261)

Ebbinghaus, H. (1885/1964). *Memory: A contribution to experimental psychology* (tr. by H. A. Ruger & C. E. Bussenius). New York: Dover. (p. 277)

Eccles, J. S., Jacobs, J. E., & Harold, R. D. (1990). Gender role stereotypes, expectancy effects, and parents' socialization of gender differences. *Journal of Social Issues, 46,* 183–201. (p. 334)

Eckensberger, L. H. (1994). Moral development and its measurement across cultures. In W. J. Lonner & R. Malpass (Eds.), *Psychology and culture.* Boston: Allyn and Bacon. (p. 119)

Eckersley, R. (2000). The mixed blessings of material progress: Diminishing returns in the pursuit of happiness. *Journal of Happiness Studies, 1,* 267–292. (p. 398)

Eckersley, R., & Dear, K. (2002). Correlates of youth suicide. *Social Science and Medicine, 55,* 1891–1935. (p. 490)

Eckert, E. D., Heston, L. L., & Bouchard, T. J., Jr. (1981). MZ twins reared apart: Preliminary findings of psychiatric disturbances and traits. In L. Gedda, P. Paris, & W. D. Nance (Eds.), *Twin research: Vol. 3. Pt. B. Intelligence, personality, and development.* New York: Alan Liss. (pp. 480–481)

Economist. (2001, December 20). An anthropology of happiness. *The Economist* (www.economist.com/world/asia). (p. 371)

Edelman, S., & Kidman, A. D. (1997). Mind and cancer: Is there a relationship? A review of the evidence. *Australian Psychologist, 32,* 1–7. (p. 411)

Edwards, C. P. (1981). The comparative study of the development of moral judgment and reasoning. In R. H. Munroe, R. L. Munroe, & B. B. Whiting (Eds.), *Handbook of cross-cultural human development.* New York: Garland Press. (p. 119)

Edwards, C. P. (1982). Moral development in comparative cultural perspective. In D. A. Wagner & H. W. Stevenson (Eds.), *Cultural perspectives on child development.* San Francisco: Freeman. (p. 119)

Ehrlichman, H., & Halpern, J. N. (1988). Affect and memory: Effects of pleasant and unpleasant odors on retrieval of happy and unhappy memories. *Journal of Personality and Social Psychology, 55,* 769–779. (p. 164)

Eibl-Eibesfeldt, I. (1971). *Love and hate: The natural history of behavior patterns.* New York: Holt, Rinehart & Winston. (p. 391)

Eich, E. (1990). Learning during sleep. In R. B. Bootzin, J. F. Kihlstrom, & D. L. Schacter (Eds.), *Sleep and cognition.* Washington, DC: American Psychological Association. (p. 201)

Eich, E., Macaulay, D., Loewenstein, R. J., & Dihle, P. H. (1997). Memory, amnesia, and dissociative identity disorder. *Psychological Science, 8,* 417–422. (p. 483)

Eich, J. E. (1980). The cue-dependent nature of state-dependent retrieval. *Memory and Cognition, 8,* 157–173. (p. 210)

Eisenberg, N., Cumberland A., & Spinrad, T. L. (1998a). Parental socialization of emotion. *Psychological Inquiry, 9,* 241–271. (p. 85)

Eisenberg, N., & Lennon, R. (1983). Sex differences in empathy and related capacities. *Psychological Bulletin, 94,* 100–131. (p. 389)

Eisenberg, N., Spinrad, T. L., & Cumberland, A. (1998b). The socialization of emotion: Reply to commentaries. *Psychological Inquiry, 9,* 317–333. (p. 85)

Eisenberger, R., & Rhoades, L. (2001). Incremental effects of reward on creativity. *Journal of Personality and Social Psychology, 81,* 728–741. (p. 244)

Ekman, P. (1994). Strong evidence for universals in facial expressions: A reply to Russell's mistaken critique. *Psychological Bulletin, 115,* 268–287. (p. 390)

Ekman, P., & Friesen, W. V. (1975). *Unmasking the face.* Englewood Cliffs, NJ: Prentice-Hall. (p. 390)

Ekman, P., Friesen, W. V., O'Sullivan, M., Chan, A., Diacoyanni-Tarlatzis, I., Heider, K., Krause, R., LeCompte, W. A., Pitcairn, T., Ricci-Bitti, P. E., Scherer, K., Tomita, M., & Tzavaras, A. (1987). Universals and cultural differences in the judgments of facial expressions of emotion. *Journal of Personality and Social Psychology, 53,* 712–717. (p. 390)

Elbert, T., Pantev, C., Wienbruch, C., Rockstroh, B., & Taub, E. (1995). Increased cortical representation of the fingers of the left hand in string players. *Science, 270,* 305–307. (p. 84)

Elfenbein, H. A., & Ambady, N. (1999). Does it take one to know one? A meta-analysis of the universality and cultural specificity of emotion recognition. Unpublished manuscript, Harvard University. (p. 390)

Elfenbein, H. A., & Ambady, N. (2002). On the universality and cultural specificity of emotion recognition: A meta-analysis. *Psychological Bulletin, 128,* 203–235. (p. 390)

Elkin, I., Shea, T., Watkins, J. T., Imber, S. D., Sotsky, S. M., Collins, J. F., Glass, D. R., Pilkonis, P. A., Leber, W. R., Docherty, J. P., Fiester, S. J., & Parloff, M. B. (1989). National Institute of Mental Health treatment of depression collaborative research program. *Archives of General Psychiatry, 46,* 971–983. (p. 522)

Elkind, D. (1970). The origins of religion in the child. *Review of Religious Research, 12,* 35–42. (p. 118)

Elkind, D. (1978). *The child's reality: Three developmental themes.* Hillsdale, NJ: Erlbaum. (p. 118)

Ellis, A., & Becker, I. M. (1982). *A guide to personal happiness.* North Hollywood, CA: Wilshire Book Co. (p. 236)

Ellis, B. J., & Garber, J. (2000). Psychosocial antecedents of variation in girls' pubertal timing: Maternal depression, stepfather presence, and marital and family stress. *Child Development, 71,* 485–501. (p. 116)

Ellis, B. J., McFadyen-Ketchum, S., Dodge, K. A., Pettit, G. S., & Bates, J. E. (1999). Quality of early family relationships and individual differences in the timing of pubertal maturation in girls: A longitudinal test of an evolutionary model. *Journal of Personality and Social Psychology, 77,* 387–401. (p. 116)

Ellis, L., & Ames, M. A. (1987). Neurohormonal functioning and sexual orientation: A theory of homosexuality-heterosexuality. *Psychological Bulletin, 101,* 233–258. (p. 367)

Emde, R. N., Plomin, R., Robinson, J., Corley, R., DeFries, J., Fulker, D. W., Reznick, J. S., Campos, J., Kagan, J., & Zahn-Waxler, C. (1992). Temperament, emotion, and cognition at fourteen months: The MacArthur Longitudinal Twin Study. *Child Development, 63,* 1437–1455. (p. 80)

Emerging Trends (1997, September). Teens turn more to parents than friends on whether to attend church. Princeton, NJ: Princeton Religion Research Center, p. 5. (p. 123)

Emmons, S., Geisler, C., Kaplan, K. J., & Harrow, M. (1997). *Living with schizophrenia.* Muncie, IN: Taylor and Francis (Accelerated Development). (p. 469)

Empson, J. A. C., & Clarke, P. R. F. (1970). Rapid eye movements and remembering. *Nature, 227,* 287–288. (p. 202)

Emslie, C., Hunt, K., & Macintyre, S. (2001). Perceptions of body image among working men and women. *Journal of Epidemiology and Community Health, 55,* 406–407. (p. 351)

Endler, N. S. (1982). *Holiday of darkness: A psychologist's personal journey out of his depression.* New York: Wiley. (pp. 482, 533)

Endler, N. S., & Speer, R. L. (1998). Personality psychology: Research trends for 1993–1995. *Journal of Personality, 66,* 621–669. (p. 448)

Engen, T. (1987). Remembering odors and their names. *American Scientist, 75,* 497–503. (p. 164)

Engle, R. W. (2002). Working memory capacity as executive attention. *Current Directions in Psychological Science, 11,* 19–23. (p. 260)

Epley, N., & Dunning, D. (2000). Feeling "holier than thou": Are self-serving assessments produced by errors in self- or social prediction? *Journal of Personality and Social Psychology, 79,* 861–875. (p. 459)

EPOCH (2000). *Legal reforms: Corporal punishment of children in the family* (www.stophitting.com/laws/legalReform.php). (p. 243)

Epstein, S. (1983a). Aggregation and beyond: Some basic issues on the prediction of behavior. *Journal of Personality, 51,* 360–392. (p. 449)

Epstein, S. (1983b). The stability of behavior across time and situations. In R. Zucker, J. Aronoff, & A. I. Rabin (Eds.), *Personality and the prediction of behavior.* San Diego: Academic Press. (p. 449)

Erdberg, P. (1990). Rorschach assessment. In G. Goldstein & M. Hersen (Eds.), *Handbook of psychological assessment,* 2nd ed. New York: Pergamon. (p. 435)

Erdelyi, M. H. (1985). *Psychoanalysis: Freud's cognitive psychology.* New York: Freeman. (p. 463)

Erdelyi, M. H. (1988). Repression, reconstruction, and defense: History and integration of the psychoanalytic and experimental frameworks. In J. Singer (Ed.), *Repression: Defense mechanism and cognitive style.* Chicago: University of Chicago Press. (p. 463)

Erel, O., & Burman, B. (1995). Interrelatedness of marital relations and parent-child relations: A meta-analytic review. *Psychological Bulletin, 118,* 108–132. (p. 131)

Erikson, E. H. (1963). *Childhood and society.* New York: Norton. (p. 119)

Erikson, E. H. (1983, June). A conversation with Erikson (by E. Hall). *Psychology Today,* pp. 22–30. (p. 112)

Ernsberger, P., & Koletsky, R. J. (1999). Biomedical rationale for a wellness approach to obesity: An alternative to a focus on weight loss. *Journal of Social Issues, 55,* 221–260. (pp. 349, 356)

Eron, L. D. (1987). The development of aggressive behavior from the perspective of a developing behaviorism. *American Psychologist, 42,* 435–442. (p. 251)

Esser, J. K., & Lindoerfer, J. S. (1989). Groupthink and the space shuttle *Challenger* accident: Toward a quantitative case analysis. *Journal of Behavioral Decision Making, 2,* 167–177. (p. 553)

Esterson, A. (2001). The mythologizing of psychoanalytic history: Deception and self-deception in Freud's accounts of the seduction theory episode. *History of Psychiatry, 12,* 329–352. (p. 437)

Etnier, J. L., Salazar, W., Landers, D. M., Petruzzello, S. J., Han, M., & Nowell, P. (1997). The influence of physical fitness and exercise upon cognitive functioning: A meta-analysis. *Journal of Sport & Exercise Psychology, 19,* 249–277. (p. 415)

ETS. (1992). Three reports shed new light on gender differences in testing. *ETS Developments, 37*(3), 4–7. (p. 332)

Evans, C. R., & Dion, K. L. (1991). Group cohesion and performance: A meta-analysis. *Small Group Research, 22,* 175–186. (p. B–10)

Evans, G. W., Palsane, M. N., & Carrere, S. (1987). Type A behavior and occupational stress: A cross-cultural study of blue-collar workers. *Journal of Personality and Social Psychology, 52,* 1002–1007. (p. 408)

Evans, G. W., Palsane, M. N., Lepore, S. J., & Martin, J. (1989). Residential density and psychological health: The mediating effects of social support. *Journal of Personality and Social Psychology, 57,* 994–999. (p. 417)

Everson, S. A., Goldberg, D. E., Kaplan, G. A., Cohen, R. D., Pukkala, E., Tuomilehto, J., & Salonen, J. T. (1996). Hopelessness and risk of mortality and incidence of myocardial infarction and cancer. *Psychosomatic Medicine, 58,* 113–121. (p. 407)

Exner, J. E. (1993). *The Rorschach: A comprehensive system, Vol. 1. Basic foundations* (3rd ed.). New York: Wiley. (p. 435)

Eysenck, H. J. (1952). The effects of psychotherapy: An evaluation. *Journal of Consulting Psychology, 16,* 319–324. (pp. 521–522)

Eysenck, H. J. (1990, April 30). An improvement on personality inventory. *Current Contents: Social and Behavioral Sciences, 22(18),* 20. (p. 444)

Eysenck, H. J. (1992). Four ways five factors are *not* basic. *Personality and Individual Differences, 13,* 667–673. (p. 444)

Eysenck, H. J., & Grossarth-Maticek, R. (1991). Creative novation behaviour therapy as a prophylactic treatment for cancer and coronary heart disease: Part II—Effects of treatment. *Behaviour Research and Therapy, 29,* 17–31. (p. 417)

Eysenck, H. J., Wakefield, J. A., Jr., & Friedman, A. F. (1983). Diagnosis and clinical assessment: The DSM-III. *Annual Review of Psychology, 34,* 167–193. (p. 473)

Eysenck, M. W., MacLeod, C., & Mathews, A. (1987). Cognitive functioning and anxiety. *Psychological Research, 49,* 189–195. (p. 451)

Eysenck, S. B. G., & Eysenck, H. J. (1963). The validity of questionnaire and rating assessments of extraversion and neuroticism, and their factorial stability. *British Journal of Psychology, 54,* 51–62. (p. 444)

Faber, N. (1987, July). Personal glimpse. *Reader's Digest,* p. 34. (p. 321)

Fagan, J. F., III (1992). Intelligence: A theoretical viewpoint. *Current Directions in Psychological Science, 1,* 82–86. (p. 332)

Fairburn, C. G., Cowen, P. J., & Harrison, P. J. (1999). Twin studies and the etiology of eating disorders. *International Journal of Eating Disorders, 26,* 349–358. (p. 350)

Fantz, R. L. (1961, May). The origin of form perception. *Scientific American,* pp. 66–72. (p. 101)

Farina, A. (1982). The stigma of mental disorders. In A. G. Miller (Ed.), *In the eye of the beholder.* New York: Praeger. (pp. 471, 473)

Farina, A., & Fisher, J. D. (1982). Beliefs about mental disorders: Findings and implications. In G. Weary & H. L. Mirels (Eds.), *Integrations of clinical and social psychology.* New York: Oxford University Press. (p. 519)

Farley, M, Baral, I., Kiremire, M., & Sezgin, U. (1998). Prostitution in five countries: Violence and post-traumatic stress disorder. *Feminism and Psychology, 8,* 405–426. (p. 480)

Farley, T., & Cohen, D. (2001, December). Fixing a fat nation. *Washington Monthly* (www.washingtonmonthly.com/features/2001/0112.farley.cohen.html). (p. 354)

Farrington, D. P. (1991). Antisocial personality from childhood to adulthood. *The Psychologist: Bulletin of the British Psychological Society, 4,* 389–394. (p. 485)

Fathalla, M. (1999). The missing millions. *People & the Planet.* www.oneworld.org/patp (p. 556)

Feder, H. H. (1984). Hormones and sexual behavior. *Annual Review of Psychology, 35,* 165–200. (p. 359)

Feeney, J. A., & Noller, P. (1990). Attachment style as a predictor of adult romantic relationships. *Journal of Personality and Social Psychology, 58,* 281–291. (p. 112)

Feingold, A. (1990). Gender differences in effects of physical attractiveness on romantic attraction: A comparison across five research paradigms. *Journal of Personality and Social Psychology, 59,* 981–993. (p. 569)

Feingold, A. (1992). Good-looking people are not what we think. *Psychological Bulletin, 111,* 304–341. (p. 569)

Feingold, A., & Mazzella, R. (1998). Gender differences in body image are increasing. *Psychological Science, 9,* 190–195. (pp. 350, 570)

Feminist Psychologist. (2002, Winter). Justice for Mary Whiton Calkins. P. 11. (p. 4)

Fenton, W. S., & McGlashan, T. H. (1991). Natural history of schizophrenia subtypes: II. Positive and negative symptoms and long-term course. *Archives of General Psychiatry, 48,* 978–986. (p. 498)

Fenton, W. S., & McGlashan, T. H. (1994). Antecedents, symptom progression, and long-term outcome of the deficit syndrome in schizophrenia. *American Journal of Psychiatry, 151,* 351–356. (p. 498)

Ferguson, E. D. (1989). Adler's motivational theory: An historical perspective on belonging and the fundamental human striving. *Individual Psychology, 45,* 354–361. (p. 371)

Fergusson, D. M., & Woodward, L. G. (2002). Mental health, educational, and social role outcomes of adolescents with depression. *Archives of General Psychiatry, 59,* 225–231. (p. 489)

Fernandez, E., & Turk, D. C. (1989). The utility of cognitive coping strategies for altering pain perception: A meta-analysis. *Pain, 38,* 123–135. (p. 161)

Fernandez-Dols, J-M., & Ruiz-Belda, M-A. (1995). Are smiles a sign of happiness? Gold medal winners at the Olympic Games. *Journal of Personality and Social Psychology, 69,* 1113–1119. (p. 391)

Ferris, C. F. (1996, March). The rage of innocents. *The Sciences,* pp. 22–26. (p. 113)

Fiedler, F. E. (1981). Leadership effectiveness. *American Behavioral Scientist, 24,* 619–632. (p. B–10)

Fiedler, F. E. (1987, September). When to lead, when to stand back. *Psychology Today,* pp. 26–27. (p. B–10)

Fiedler, K., Nickel, S., Muehlfriedel, T., & Unkelbach, C. (2001). Is mood congruency an effect of genuine memory or response bias? *Journal of Experimental Social Psychology, 37,* 201–214. (p. 274)

Field, T. (2001). Massage therapy facilitates weight gain in preterm infants. *Current Directions in Psychological Science, 10,* 51–54. (p. 84)

Fincham, F. D., & Bradbury, T. N. (1993). Marital satisfaction, depression, and attributions: A longitudinal analysis. *Journal of Personality and Social Psychology, 64,* 442–452. (p. 541)

Fink, G. R., Markowitsch, H. J., Reinkemeier, M., Bruckbauer, T., Kessler, J., & Heiss, W-D. (1996). Cerebral representation of one's own past: Neural networks involved in autobiographical memory. *Journal of Neuroscience, 16,* 4275–4282. (p. 271)

Fink, M. (1998). ECT and managed care. *Journal Watch Psychiatry, 4,* pp. 76, 73. (p. 533)

Finlay, S. W. (2000). Influence of Carl Jung and William James on the origin of alcoholics anonymous. *Review of General Psychology, 4,* 3–12. (p. 518)

Finucci, J. M., & Childs, B. (1981). Are there really more dyslexic boys than girls? In A. Ansara, N. Geschwind, A. Galaburda, M. Albert, & N. Gartrell (Eds.), *Sex differences in dyslexia.* Towson, MD: The Orton Dyslexia Society. (p. 332)

Fischhoff, B. (1982). Debiasing. In D. Kahneman, P. Slovic, & A. Tversky (Eds.), *Judgment under uncertainty: Heuristics and biases.* New York: Cambridge University Press. (p. 300)

Fischhoff, B., Slovic, P., & Lichtenstein, S. (1977). Knowing with certainty: The appropriateness of extreme confidence. *Journal of Experimental Psychology: Human Perception and Performance, 3,* 552–564. (p. 298)

Fisher, H. E. (1993, March/April). After all, maybe it's biology. *Psychology Today,* pp. 40–45. (p. 130)

Fisher, H. T. (1984). Little Albert and Little Peter. *Bulletin of the British Psychological Society, 37,* 269. (p. 512)

Fitch, R. H., & Denenberg, V. H. (1998). A role for ovarian hormones in sexual differentiation of the brain. *Behavioral and Brain Sciences, 21,* 311–352. (p. 90)

Fleming, I., Baum, A., & Weiss, L. (1987). Social density and perceived control as mediator of crowding stress in high-density residential neighborhoods. *Journal of Personality and Social Psychology, 52,* 899–906. (p. 407)

Fleming, J. H. (2001, Winter/Spring). Introduction to the special issue on linkage analysis. *The Gallup Research Journal,* pp. i–vi. (p. B–9)

Fleming, J. H., & Scott, B. A. (1991). The costs of confession: The Persian Gulf War POW tapes in historical and theoretical perspective. *Contemporary Social Psychology, 15,* 127–138. (p. 390)

Fletcher, G. J. O., Fitness, J., & Blampied, N. M. (1990). The link between attributions and happiness in close relationships: The roles of depression and explanatory style. *Journal of Social and Clinical Psychology, 9,* 243–255. (p. 541)

Flynn, J. R. (1987). Massive IQ gains in 14 nations: What IQ tests really measure. *Psychological Bulletin, 101,* 171–191. (p. 332)

Flynn, J. R. (1999). Searching for justice: The discovery of IQ gains over time. *American Psychologist, 54,* 5–20. (p. 332)

Foa, E. B., & Kozak, M. J. (1986). Emotional processing of fear: Exposure to corrective information. *Psychological Bulletin, 99,* 20–35. (p. 513)

Ford, E. S. (2002). Does exercise reduce inflammation? Physical activity and C-reactive protein among U. S. adults. *Epidemiology, 13,* 561–569. (p. 415)

Foree, D. D., & LoLordo, V. M. (1973). Attention in the pigeon: Differential effects of food-getting versus shock-avoidance procedures. *Journal of Comparative and Physiological Psychology, 85,* 551–558. (p. 245)

Forer, B. R. (1949). The fallacy of personal validation: A classroom demonstration of gullibility. *Journal of Abnormal and Social Psychology, 44,* 118–123. (p. 446)

Forgas, J. P., Bower, G. H., & Krantz, S. E. (1984). The influence of mood on perceptions of social interactions. *Journal of Experimental Social Psychology, 20,* 497–513. (p. 275)

Foss, D. J., & Hakes, D. T. (1978). *Psycholinguistics: An introduction to the psychology of language.* Englewood Cliffs, NJ: Prentice-Hall. (p. 437)

Fouts, R. (1997). *Next of kin: What chimpanzees have taught me about who we are.* New York: Morrow. (p. 314)

Fouts, R. S. (1992). Transmission of a human gestural language in a chimpanzee mother-infant relationship. *Friends of Washoe, 12/13,* pp. 2–8. (p. 314)

Fouts, R. S., & Bodamer, M. (1987). Preliminary report to the National Geographic Society on: "Chimpanzee intrapersonal signing." *Friends of Washoe, 7(1),* 4–12. (p. 314)

Fowler, M. J., Sullivan, M. J., & Ekstrand, B. R. (1973). Sleep and memory. *Science, 179,* 302–304. (p. 278)

Fowler, R. C., Rich, C. L., & Young, D. (1986). San Diego suicide study: II. Substance abuse in young cases. *Archives of General Psychiatry, 43,* 962–965. (p. 490)

Fowles, D. C. (1992). Schizophrenia: Diathesis-stress revisited. *Annual Review of Psychology, 43,* 303–336. (p. 498)

Fox, B. H. (1998). Psychosocial factors in cancer incidence and prognosis. In P. M. Cinciripini & others (Eds.), *Psychological and behavioral factors in cancer risk.* New York: Oxford University Press. (p. 411)

Fox, E., Lester, V., Russo, R., Bowles, R. J., Pichler, A., & Dutton, K. (2000). Facial expression of emotion: Are angry faces detected more efficiently? *Cognition and Emotion, 14,* 61–92. (p. 387)

Fracassini, C. (2000, August 27). Holidaymakers led by the nose in sales quest. *Scotland on Sunday.* (p. 164)

Fraley, R. C. (2002). Attachment stability from infancy to adulthood: Meta-analysis and dynamic modeling of developmental mechanisms. *Personality and Social Psychology Review, 6,* 123–151. (p. 112)

Frank, J. D. (1982). Therapeutic components shared by all psychotherapies. In J. H. Harvey & M. M. Parks (Eds.), *The Master Lecture Series: Vol. 1. Psychotherapy research and behavior change.* Washington, DC: American Psychological Association. (pp. 507, 526, 527)

Frank, R. (1999). *Luxury fever: Why money fails to satisfy in an era of excess.* New York: Free Press. (p. 88)

Frank, S. J. (1988). Young adults' perceptions of their relationships with their parents: Individual differences in connectedness, competence, and emotional autonomy. *Developmental Psychology, 24,* 729–737. (p. 123)

Frankel, A., & Prentice-Dunn, S. (1990). Loneliness and the processing of self-relevant information. *Journal of Social and Clinical Psychology, 9,* 303–315. (p. 494)

Frankel, A., Strange, D. R., & Schoonover, R. (1983). CRAP: Consumer rated assessment procedure. In G. H. Scherr & R. Liebmann-Smith (Eds.), *The best of The Journal of Irreproducible Results.* New York: Workman Publishing. (p. 445)

Frankenburg, W., Dodds, J., Archer, P., Shapiro, H., & Bresnick, B. (1992). The Denver II: A major revision and restandardization of the Denver Developmental Screening Test. *Pediatrics, 89,* 91–97. (p. 104)

Franz, E. A., Waldie, K. E., & Smith, M. J. (2000). The effect of callosotomy on novel versus familiar bimanual actions: A neural dissociation between controlled and automatic processes? *Psychological Science, 11,* 82–85. (p. 61)

Frasure-Smith, N., Lesperance, F., Juneau, M., Talajic, M., & Bourassa, M. G. (1999). Gender, depression, and one-year prognosis after myocardial infarction. *Psychosomatic Medicine, 61,* 26–37. (p. 409)

Frasure-Smith, N., Lesperance, F., & Talajic, M. (1995). The impact of negative emotions on prognosis following myocardial infarction: Is it more than depression? *Health Psychology, 14,* 388–398. (p. 409)

Fredrickson, B. L. (2002). Positive emotions. In C. R. Snyder & S. J. Lopez (Eds.), *Handbook of positive psychology.* New York: Oxford. (p. 395)

Fredrickson, B. L., & Kahneman, D. (1993). Duration neglect in retrospective evaluations of affective episodes. *Journal of Personality and Social Psychology, 65,* 45–55. (p. 263)

Fredrickson, B. L., Roberts, T-A., Noll, S. M., Quinn, D. M., & Twenge, J. M. (1998). That swimsuit becomes you: Sex differences in self-objectification, restrained eating, and math performance. *Journal of Personality and Social Psychology, 75,* 269–284. (p. 351)

Freedman, D. J., Riesenhuber, M., Poggio, T., & Miller, E. K. (2001). Categorical representation of visual stimuli in the primate prefrontal cortex. *Science, 291,* 312–316. (p. 311)

Freedman, J. L. (1978). *Happy people.* San Diego: Harcourt Brace Jovanovich. (p. 132)

Freedman, J. L. (1988). Television violence and aggression: What the evidence shows. In S. Oskamp (Ed.), *Television as a social issue.* Newbury Park, CA: Sage. (p. 251)

Freedman, J. L., & Fraser, S. C. (1966). Compliance without pressure: The foot-in-the-door technique. *Journal of Personality and Social Psychology, 4,* 195–202. (p. 543)

Freedman, J. L., & Perlick, D. (1979). Crowding, contagion, and laughter. *Journal of Experimental Social Psychology, 15,* 295–303. (p. 551)

Freeman, W. J. (1991, February). The physiology of perception. *Scientific American,* 78–85. (p. 152)

French, C. C., O'Donnell, H., & Williams, L. (2001, March 28). Hypnotic susceptibility, paranormal belief and reports of 'crystal power.' Paper presented to the British Psychological Society Centenary Annual Conference, Glasgow. (p. 206)

Freud, S. (1933). *New introductory lectures on psychoanalysis.* New York: Carlton House. (p. 431)

Freud, S. (1935; reprinted 1960). *A general introduction to psychoanalysis.* New York: Washington Square Press. (p. 130)

Friedman, M., & Ulmer, D. (1984). *Treating Type A behavior—and your heart.* New York: Knopf. (pp. 408, 416)

Friedrich, O. (1987, December 7). New age harmonies. *Time,* pp. 62–72. (p. 470)

Frieze, I. H., Parsons, J. E., Johnson, P. B., Ruble, D. N., & Zellman, G. L. (1978). *Women and sex roles: A social psychological perspective.* New York: Norton. (p. 437)

Frijda, N. H. (1988). The laws of emotion. *American Psychologist, 43,* 349–358. (p. 399)

Frith, U., & Frith, C. (2001). The biological basis of social interaction. *Current Directions in Psychological Science, 10,* 151–155. (p. 108)

Fritsch, G., & Hitzig, E. (1870; reprinted 1960). On the electrical excitability of the cerebrum. In G. Von Bonin (Trans.), *Some papers on the cerebral cortex.* Springfield, IL: Charles C. Thomas. (p. 53)

Fromkin, V., & Rodman, R. (1983). *An introduction to language* (3rd ed.). New York: Holt, Rinehart & Winston. (p. 304)

Fry, A. F., & Hale, S. (1996). Processing speed, working memory, and fluid intelligence: Evidence for a developmental cascade. *Psychological Science, 7,* 237–241. (p. 126)

Fuhriman, A., & Burlingame, G. M. (1994). Group psychotherapy: Research and practice. In A. Fuhriman & G. M. Burlingame (Eds.), *Handbook of group psychotherapy.* New York: Wiley. (p. 518)

Fuller, M. J., & Downs, A. C. (1990). Spermarche is a salient biological marker in men's development. Poster presented at the American Psychological Society convention. (p. 117)

Funder, D. C. (2001). Personality. *Annual Review of Psychology, 52,* 197–221. (p. 448)

Funder, D. C., & Block, J. (1989). The role of ego-control, ego-resiliency, and IQ in delay of gratification in adolescence. *Journal of Personality and Social Psychology, 57,* 1041–1050. (p. 119)

Furlow, F. B., & Thornhill, R. (1996, January/February). The orgasm wars. *Psychology Today,* pp. 42–46. (p. 358)

Furnham, A. (1982). Explanations for unemployment in Britain. *European Journal of Social Psychology, 12,* 335–352. (p. 541)

Furnham, A. (2001). Self-estimates of intelligence: Culture and gender difference in self and other estimates of both general (g) and multiple intelligences. *Personality and Individual Differences, 31,* 1381–1405. (p. 332)

Furnham, A., & Baguma, P. (1994). Cross-cultural differences in the evaluation of male and female body shapes. *International Journal of Eating Disorders, 15,* 81–89. (p. 349)

Furnham, A., Hosoe, T., & Tang, T. L-P. (2002a). Male hubris and female humility? A cross-cultural study of ratings of self, parental, and sibling multiple intelligence in American, Britain, and Japan. *Intelligence, 30,* 101–115. (p. 332)

Furnham, A., & Rawles, R. (1995). Sex differences in the estimation of intelligence. *Journal of Social Behavior and Personality, 10,* 741–748. (p. 556)

Furnham, A., Reeves, E., & Bughani, S. (2002b). Parents think their sons are brighter than their daughters: Sex differences in parental self-estimations and estimations of their children's multiple intelligences. *Journal of Genetic Psychology, 163,* 24–39. (p. 332)

Furnham, A., & Taylor, L. (1990). Lay theories of homosexuality: Aetiology, behaviours, and 'cures.' *British Journal of Social Psychology, 29,* 135–147. (p. 368)

Furr, R. M., & Funder, D. C. (1998). A multimodal analysis of personal negativity. *Journal of Personality and Social Psychology, 74,* 1580–1591. (p. 494)

Furstenberg, F. F., Jr., Moore, K. A., & Peterson, J. L. (1985). Sex education and sexual experience among adolescents. *American Journal of Public Health, 75,* 1331–1332. (p. 370)

Gabbay, F. H. (1992). Behavior-genetic strategies in the study of emotion. *Psychological Science, 3,* 50–55. (p. 80)

Gabrieli, J. D. E., Desmond, J. E., Demb, J. E., Wagner, A. D., Stone, M. V., Vaidya, C. J., & Glover, G. H. (1996). Functional magnetic resonance imaging of semantic memory processes in the frontal lobes. *Psychological Science, 7,* 278–283. (p. 271)

Galambos, N. L. (1992). Parent-adolescent relations. *Current Directions in Psychological Science, 1,* 146–149. (p. 122)

Galanter, E. (1962). Contemporary psychophysics. In R. Brown, E. Galanter, E. H. Hess, & G. Mandler (Eds.), *New directions in psychology.* New York: Holt Rinehart, & Winston. (p. 142)

Galati, D., Scherer, K. R., & Ricci-Bitti, P. E. (1997). Voluntary facial expression of emotion: Comparing congenitally blind with normally sighted encoders. *Journal of Personality and Social Psychology, 73,* 1363–1379. (p. 391)

Gale, C. R., & Martyn, C. N. (1996). Breastfeeding, dummy use and adult intelligence. *Lancet, 347,* 1072–1075. (p. 24)

Galea, S., Boscarino, J., Resnick, H., & Vlahov, D. (2002). Mental health in New York City after the September 11 terrorist attacks: Results from two population surveys. Chapter 7. In R. W. Manderscheid & M. J. Henderson (Eds.), *Mental-Health, United States, 2001.* Washington, DC: Superintendent of Documents, U.S. Government Printing Office. (p. 481)

Gallup. (2001, June 8). Americans' belief in psychic and paranormal phenomena is up over last decade. Gallup Organization poll report by F. Newport & M. Strausberg (www.gallup.com/poll/releases/pr01608.asp). (p. 447)

Gallup. (2002, February 21). Homosexual relations. The Gallup Organization (www.gallup.com/poll/topics/homosexual.asp). (p. 368)

Gallup. (2002, June 11). Poll insights: The gender gap—post Sept. 11th fear. The Gallup Organization (www.gallup.com/poll/pollInsights). (p. 476)

Gallup. (2002). Alcohol and drinking (results of November 8–11, 2001 survey) (www.gallup.com/poll/topics/alcohol.asp). (p. 218)

Gallup, G. G., Jr., & Suarez, S. D. (1985). Alternatives to the use of animals in psychological research. *American Psychologist, 40,* 1104–1111. (p. 29)

Gallup, G. H. (1972). *The Gallup poll: Public opinion 1935–1971* (Vol. 3). New York: Random House. (p. 567)

Gallup, G. H., Jr. (1994, October). Millions finding care and support in small groups. *Emerging Trends,* pp. 2–5. (p. 518)

Gallup, G., Jr. (2002, April 30). Education and youth. *Gallup Tuesday Briefing* (www.gallup.com/poll/tb/educaYouth/20020430.asp). (p. 250)

Gallup Organization. (1993). Other hemispheres may think our religion is alien and exotic. *PRRC Emerging Trends, 15,* 1–3. (p. 528)

Gangestad, S. W., & Simpson, J. A. (2000). The evolution of human mating: Trade-offs and strategic pluralism. *Behavioral and Brain Sciences, 23.* (p. 74)

Garb, H. N. (1999). Call for a moratorium on the use of the Rorschach inkblot test in clinical and forensic settings. *Assessment, 6,* 313–315. (p. 435)

Garbarino, J., Dubrow, N., & Kostelny, K. (1992). *Children in danger: Coping with the consequences of community violence.* San Francisco: Jossey-Bass Inc. (p. 480)

Garbarino, J., Kostelny, K., & Dubrow, N. (1991). What children can tell us about living in danger. *American Psychologist, 46,* 376–383. (p. 480)

Garcia, J., & Gustavson, A. R. (1997, January). Carl R. Gustavson (1946–1996): Pioneering wildlife psychologist. *APS Observer,* pp. 34–35. (p. 234)

Garcia, J., & Koelling, R. A. (1966). Relation of cue to consequence in avoidance learning. *Psychonomic Science, 4*, 123–124. (p. 233)

Gardner, H. (1983). *Frames of mind: The theory of multiple intelligences.* New York: Basic Books. (p. 317)

Gardner, H. (1998, March 19). An intelligent way to progress. *The Independent* (London), p. E4. (p. 318)

Gardner, H. (1998, November 5). Do parents count? *New York Review of Books* (www.nybooks.com). (pp. 85, 319)

Gardner, H. (1999, February). Who owns intelligence? *Atlantic Monthly,* pp. 67–76. (p. 317)

Gardner, H. (1999). *Multiple views of multiple intelligence.* New York: Basic Books. (p. 320)

Gardner, J., & Oswald, A. (2001). Does money buy happiness? A longitudinal study using data on windfalls. Working paper, Department of Economics, Cambridge University. (p. 397)

Gardner, R. A., & Gardner, B. I. (1969). Teaching sign language to a chimpanzee. *Science, 165,* 664–672. (p. 312)

Gardner, R. M., & Tockerman, Y. R. (1994). A computer-TV video methodology for investigating the influence of somatotype on perceived personality traits. *Journal of Social Behavior and Personality, 9,* 555–563. (p. 352)

Garfield, C. (1986). *Peak performers: The new heroes of American business.* New York: Morrow. (p. 310)

Garner, D. M., & Wooley, S. C. (1991). Confronting the failure of behavioral and dietary treatments for obesity. *Clinical Psychology Review, 11,* 729–780. (p. 355)

Garnets, L., & Kimmel, D. (1990). Lesbian and gay dimensions in the psychological study of human diversity. Master lecture, American Psychological Association convention. (p. 364)

Garry, M., & Loftus, E. F., & Brown, S. W. (1994). Memory: A river runs through it. *Consciousness and Cognition, 3,* 438–451. (p. 437)

Garry, M., Manning, C. G., Loftus, E. F., & Sherman, S. J. (1996). Imagination inflation: Imagining a childhood event inflates confidence that it occurred. *Psychonomic Bulletin & Review, 3,* 208–214. (p. 282)

Garza, D. L., & Feltz, D. L. (1998). Effects of selected mental practice on performance, self-efficacy, and competition confidence of figure skaters. *The Sports Psychologist, 12,* 1–15. (p. 310)

Gates, W. (1998, July 20). Charity begins when I'm ready (interview). *Fortune* (www.pathfinder.com/fortune/1998/980720/bil7.html). (p. 319)

Gawin, F. H. (1991). Cocaine addiction: Psychology and neurophysiology. *Science, 251,* 1580–1586. (p. 214)

Gazzaniga, M. S. (1967, August). The split brain in man. *Scientific American,* pp. 24–29. (p. 60)

Gazzaniga, M. S. (1983). Right hemisphere language following brain bisection: A 20–year perspective. *American Psychologist, 38,* 525–537. (p. 60)

Gazzaniga, M. S. (1988). *Mind matters: How mind and brain interact to create our conscious lives.* Boston: Houghton Mifflin. (p. 61)

Gazzaniga, M. S. (1988). Organization of the human brain. *Science, 245,* 947–952. (p. 209)

Gazzaniga, M. S. (1992). *Nature's mind: The biological roots of thinking, emotions, sexuality, language, and intelligence.* New York: Basic Books. (p. 58)

Gazzaniga, M. S. (1997). Brain, drugs, and society. *Science, 275,* 459. (p. 209)

Geary, D. C. (1995). Sexual selection and sex differences in spatial cognition. *Learning and Individual Differences, 7,* 289–301. (p. 333)

Geary, D. C. (1996). Sexual selection and sex differences in mathematical abilities. *Behavioral and Brain Sciences, 19,* 229–247. (p. 333)

Geary, D. C. (1998). *Male, female: The evolution of human sex differences.* Washington, DC: American Psychological Association. (p. 73)

Geary, D. C., Salthouse, T. A., Chen, G-P., & Fan, L. (1996). Are East Asian versus American differences in arithmetical ability a recent phenomenon? *Developmental Psychology, 32,* 254–262. (p. 332)

Geen, R. G. (1984). Human motivation: New perspectives on old problems. In A. M. Rogers & C. J. Scheirer (Eds.), *The G. Stanley Hall Lecture Series* (Vol. 4). Washington, DC: American Psychological Association. (p. 373)

Geen, R. G., & Quanty, M. B. (1977). The catharsis of aggression: An evaluation of a hypothesis. In L. Berkowitz (Ed.), *Advances in experimental social psychology* (Vol. 10). New York: Academic Press. (p. 394)

Geen, R. G., & Thomas, S. L. (1986). The immediate effects of media violence on behavior. *Journal of Social Issues, 42(3),* 7–28. (p. 252)

Gehring, W. J., Wimle, J., & Nisenson, L. G. (2000). Action-monitoring dysfunction in obsessive-compulsive disorder. *Psychological Science, 11(1),* 1–6. (p. 482)

Geldard, F. A. (1972). *The human senses* (2nd ed.). New York: Wiley. (p. 153)

Gelman, D. (1989, May 15). Voyages to the unknown. *Newsweek,* pp. 66–69. (p. 391)

Genesee, F., & Gándara, P. (1999). Bilingual education programs: A cross-national perspective. *Journal of Social Issues, 55,* 665–685. (p. 309)

George, L. K., Ellison, C. G., & Larson, D. B. (2002). Explaining the relationships between religious involvement and health. *Psychological Inquiry, 13,* 190–200. (p. 423)

George, L. K., Larson, D. B., Koenig, H. G., & McCullough, M. E. (2000). Spirituality and health: What we know, what we need to know. *Journal of Social and Clinical Psychology, 19,* 102–116. (p. 423)

Gerard, R. W. (1953, September). What is memory? *Scientific American,* pp. 118–126. (p. 268)

Gerbner, G. (1990). Stories that hurt: Tobacco, alcohol, and other drugs in the mass media. In H. Resnik (Ed.), *Youth and drugs: Society's mixed messages.* Rockville, MD: Office for Substance Abuse Prevention, U.S. Department of Health and Human Services. (p. 217)

Gerbner, G. (1993, June). Women and minorities on television: A study in casting and fate. A report to the Screen Actors Guild and the American Federation of Radio and Television Artists. (p. 250)

Gerbner, G., Gross, L., Morgan, M., & Signorielli, N. (1994). Growing up with television: The cultivation perspective. In J. Bryant, & D. Zillman (Eds.), *Media Effects: Advances in theory and research.* Hillsdale, NJ: Lawrence Erlbaum Associates, Inc., 17–41. (p. 250)

Gerbner, G., Morgan, M., & Signorielli, N. (1993). Television violence profile No. 16: The turning point from research to action. Annenberg School for Communication, University of Pennsylvania. (p. 564)

Gerhart, K. A., Koziol-McLain, J., Lowenstein, S. R., & Whiteneck, G. G. (1994). Quality of life following spinal cord injury: Knowledge and attitudes of emergency care providers. *Annals of Emergency Medicine, 23,* 807–812. (p. 396)

Gerrard, M., & Luus, C. A. E. (1995). Judgments of vulnerability to pregnancy: The role of risk factors and individual differences. *Personality and Social Psychology Bulletin, 21,* 160–171. (p. 362)

Gershon, J., Anderson, P., Graap, K., Zimand, E., Hodges, L., & Rothbaum, B. O. (2002). Virtual reality exposure therapy in the treatment of anxiety disorders, *Scientific Review of Mental Health Practice, 1,* 76–81. (p. 513)

Gerstein, E. R. (2002). Manatees, bioacoustics and boats. *American Scientist, 90,* 154–163. (p. 142)

Geschwind, N. (1979, September). Specializations of the human brain. *Scientific American,* pp. 180–199. (p. 56)

Gfeller, J. D., Lynn, S. J., & Pribble, W. E. (1987). Enhancing hypnotic susceptibility: Interpersonal and rapport factors. *Journal of Personality and Social Psychology, 52,* 586–595. (p. 206)

Gibbons, F. X. (1986). Social comparison and depression: Company's effect on misery. *Journal of Personality and Social Psychology, 51,* 140–148. (p. 400)

Gibbs, W. W. (1996, June). Mind readings. *Scientific American,* pp. 34–36. (p. 54)

Gibbs, W. W. (2002, August). Saving dying languages. *Scientific American,* pp. 79–85. (p. 305)

Gibson, E. J., & Walk, R. D. (1960, April). The "visual cliff." *Scientific American,* pp. 64–71. (p. 167)

Gibson, H. B. (1995, April). Recovered memories. *The Psychologist,* pp. 153–154. (p. 205)

Gilbert, D. T., Pinel, E. C., Wilson, T. D., Blumberg, S. J., & Wheatley, T. P. (1998). Immune neglect: A source of durability bias in affective forecasting. *Journal of Personality and Social Psychology, 75,* 617–638. (p. 396)

Giles, D. E., Dahl, R. E., & Coble, P. A. (1994). Childbearing, developmental, and familial aspects of sleep. In J. M. Oldham & M. B. Riba (Eds.), *Review of Psychiatry,* (Vol. 13). Washington, DC: American Psychiatric Press. (p. 193)

Giles, T. R. (1983). Probable superiority of behavioral interventions—II: Empirical status of the equivalence of therapies hypothesis. *Journal of Behavior Therapy and Experimental Psychiatry, 14,* 189–196. (p. 523)

Gillham, J. E., Reivich, K. J., Jaycox, L. H., & Seligman, M. E. P. (1995). Preventing depressive symptoms in schoolchildren: Two year follow-up. *Psychological Science, 6,* 343–351. (p. 495)

Gilligan, C. (1982). *In a different voice: Psychological theory and women's development.* Cambridge, MA: Harvard University Press. (p. 121)

Gilligan, C., Lyons, N. P., & Hanmer, T. J. (Eds.). (1990). *Making connections: The relational worlds of adolescent girls at Emma Willard School.* Cambridge, MA: Harvard University Press. (p. 121)

Gilling, D., & Brightwell, R. (1982). *The human brain.* New York: Facts on File. (p. 514)

Gilovich, T. (1991). *How we know what isn't so: The fallibility of human reason in everyday life.* New York: Free Press. (p. 21)

Gilovich, T. D. (1996). The spotlight effect: Exaggerated impressions of the self as a social stimulus. Unpublished manuscript, Cornell University. (p. 457)

Gilovich, T., Kruger, J., & Medvec, V. H. (2002). The spotlight effect revisted: Overestimating the manifest variability of our actions and appearance. *Journal of Experimental Social Psychology, 38,* 93–99. (p. 457)

Gilovich, T., & Medvec, V. H. (1995). The experience of regret: What, when, and why. *Psychological Review, 102,* 379–395. (p. 132)

Gilovich, T., & Savitsky, K. (1999). The spotlight effect and the illusion of transparency: Egocentric assessments of how we are seen by others. *Current Directions in Psychological Science, 8,* 165–168. (p. 457)

Gilovich, T., Vallone, R., & Tversky, A. (1985). The hot hand in basketball: On the misperception of random sequences. *Cognitive Psychology, 17,* 295–314. (p. 23)

Gingerich, O. (1999, February 6). Is there a role for natural theology today? *The Real Issue* (www.origins.org/real/n9501/natural.html). (p. 95)

Gladue, B. A. (1990). Hormones and neuroendocrine factors in atypical human sexual behavior. In J. R. Feierman (Ed.), *Pedophilia: Biosocial dimensions.* New York: Springer-Verlag. (p. 367)

Gladue, B. A. (1994). The biopsychology of sexual orientation. *Current Directions in Psychological Science, 3,* 150–154. (p. 367)

Gladwell, M. (2000, May 9). The new-boy network: What do job interviews really tell us? *New Yorker,* pp. 68–86. (p. B–6)

Glass, R. M. (2001). Electroconvulsive therapy: Time to bring it out of the shadows. *Journal of the American Medical Association, 285,* 1346–1348. (p. 533)

Glater, J. D. (2001, March 26). Women are close to being majority of law students. *New York Times* (www.nytimes.com). (p. 91)

Gleaves, D. H. (1996). The sociocognitive model of dissociative identity disorder: A reexamination of the evidence. *Psychological Bulletin, 120,* 42–59. (p. 484)

Glenn, N. D. (1975). Psychological well-being in the postparental stage: Some evidence from national surveys. *Journal of Marriage and the Family, 37,* 105–110. (p. 131)

Glick, P., Gottesman, D., & Jolton, J. (1989). The fault is not in the stars: Susceptibility of skeptics and believers in astrology to the Barnum effect. *Personality and Social Psychology Bulletin, 15,* 572–583. (pp. 446–447)

Godden, D. R., & Baddeley, A. D. (1975). Context-dependent memory in two natural environments: On land and underwater. *British Journal of Psychology, 66,* 325–331. (pp. 273, 274)

Goel, V., & Dolan, R. J. (2001). The functional anatomy of humor: Segregating cognitive and affective components. *Nature Neuroscience, 4,* 237–238. (p. 56)

Goff, D. C. (1993). Reply to Dr. Armstrong. *Journal of Nervous and Mental Disease, 181,* 604–605. (p. 484)

Goff, D. C., & Simms, C. A. (1993). Has multiple personality disorder remained consistent over time? *Journal of Nervous and Mental Disease, 181,* 595–600. (pp. 483–484)

Goff, L. M., & Roediger, III, H. L. (1998). Imagination inflation for action events: Repeated imaginings lead to illusory recollections. *Memory and Cognition, 26,* 20–33. (p. 282)

Gold, M., & Yanof, D. S. (1985). Mothers, daughters, and girlfriends. *Journal of Personality and Social Psychology, 49,* 654–659. (p. 122)

Goldfried, M. R. (2001). Integrating gay, lesbian, and bisexual issues into mainstream psychology. *American Psychologist, 56,* 977–988. (p. 490)

Goldfried, M. R., & Padawer, W. (1982). Current status and future directions in psychotherapy. In M. R. Goldfried (Ed.), *Converging themes in psychotherapy: Trends in psychodynamic, humanistic, and behavioral practice.* New York: Springer. (p. 526)

Goldfried, M. R., Raue, P. J., & Castonguay, L. G. (1998). The therapeutic focus in significant sessions of master therapists: A comparison of cognitive-behavioral and psychodynamic-interpersonal interventions. *Journal of Consulting and Clinical Psychology, 66,* 803–810. (p. 527)

Goldin-Meadow, S., Nusbaum, H., Kelly, S. D., & Wagner, S. (2001). Explaining math: Gesturing lightens the load. *Psychological Science, 12,* 516–522. (p. 313)

Golding, J. M. (1996). Sexual assault history and women's reproductive and sexual health. *Psychology of Women Quarterly, 20,* 101–121. (p. 563)

Golding, J. M. (1999). Sexual-assault history and the long-term physical health problems: Evidence from clinical and population epidemiology. *Current Directions in Psychological Science, 8,* 191–194. (p. 480)

Goldstein, A. P., Glick, B., & Gibbs, J. C. (1998). *Aggression replacement training: A comprehensive intervention for aggressive youth* (rev. ed.). Champaign, IL: Research Press. (p. 563)

Goldstein, I. (2000, August). Male sexual circuitry. *Scientific American,* pp. 70–75. (p. 46)

Goldstein, I., Lue, T. F., Padma-Nathan, H., Rosen, R. C., Steers, W. D., & Wicker, P. A. (1998). Oral sildenafil in the treatment of erectile dysfunction. *New England Journal of Medicine, 338,* 1397–1404. (p. 25)

Goleman, D. (1995). *Emotional intelligence.* New York: Bantam. (p. 385)

Goodall, J. (1968). The behaviour of free-living chimpanzees in the Gombe Stream Reserve. *Animal Behaviour Monographs, 1,* 161–311. (p. 82)

Goodall, J. (1986). *The chimpanzees of Gombe: Patterns of behavior.* Cambridge, MA: Harvard University Press. (p. 558)

Goodall, J. (1998). Learning from the chimpanzees: A message humans can understand. *Science, 282,* 2184–2185. (p. 18)

Goode, E. (1999, April 13). If things taste bad, 'phantoms' may be at work. *New York Times* (www.nytimes.com). (p. 160)

Goode, E. (2000, July 18). Once again, Prozac take center stage, in furor. *New York Times* (www.nytimes.com). (p. 531)

Goode, E. (2002, June 30). Antidepressants life clouds, but lose 'miracle drug' label. *New York Times* (www.nytimes.com). (p. 532)

Goode, E. (2003, January 28). Even in the age of Prozac, some still prefer the couch. *New York Times* (www.nytimes.com). (p. 509)

Goodhart, D. E. (1986). The effects of positive and negative thinking on performance in an achievement situation. *Journal of Personality and Social Psychology, 51,* 117–124. (p. 453)

Goodman, E. (2000). Depressive symptoms and cigarette smoking among teens. *Pediatrics, 106,* 4, 748–756. (p. 212)

Goodman, G. S., Rudy, L., Bottoms, B. L., & Aman, B. (1990). Children's concerns and memory: Issues of ecological validity in the study of children's eyewitness testimony. In R. Fivush & J. A. Hudson (Eds.), *Knowing and remembering in young children.* New York: Cambridge University Press. (p. 284)

Goodman, L. A., Koss, M. P., & Russo, N. F. (1993). Violence against women: Mental health effects. Part II. Conceptualizations of posttraumatic stress. *Applied & Preventive Psychology, 2,* 123–130. (p. 480)

Goodson, P., McCormick, D., & Evans, A. (2001). Searching for sexually explicit materials on the Internet: An exploratory study of college students' behavior and attitudes. *Archives of Sexual Behavior, 30,* 101–118. (p. 563)

Goodstein, L., & Glaberson, W. (2000, April 9). The well-marked roads to homicidal rage. *New York Times* (www.nytimes.com). (p. 456)

Goodwin, C. J. (1991). Misportraying Pavlov's apparatus. *American Journal of Psychology, 104,* 135–141. (p. 229)

Goodwin, F. K., & Morrison, A. R. (1999). Scientists in bunkers: How appeasement of animal rights activism has failed. *Cerebrum, 1(2),* 50–62. (p. 29)

Goodwin, R., & Hamilton, S. P. (2002). Cigarette smoking and panic: The role of neuroticism. *American Journal of Psychiatry, 159,* 1208–1213. (p. 477)

Gopnik, A., & Meltzoff, A. N. (1986). Relations between semantic and cognitive development in the one-word stage: The specificity hypothesis. *Child Development, 57,* 1040–1053. (p. 309)

Goranson, R. E. (1978). *The hindsight effect in problem solving.* Unpublished manuscript, cited by G. Wood (1984), Research methodology: A decision-making perspective. In A. M. Rogers & C. J. Scheirer (Eds.), *The G. Stanley Hall Lecture Series* (Vol. 4). Washington, DC: American Psychological Association. (p. 12)

Gore, A., Jr. (1992). *Earth in the balance: Ecology and the human spirit.* Boston: Houghton-Mifflin. (p. 297)

Gore-Felton, C., Koopman, C., Thoresen, C., Arnow, B., Bridges, E., & Spiegel, D. (2000). Psychologists' beliefs and clinical characteristics: Judging the veracity of childhood sexual abuse memories. *Professional Psychology: Research and Practice, 31,* 372–377. (p. 286)

Gortmaker, S. L., Must, A., Perrin, J. M., Sobol, A. M., & Dietz, W. H. (1993). Social and economic consequences of overweight in adolescence and young adulthood. *New England Journal of Medicine, 329,* 1008–1012. (p. 352)

Gotlib, I. H., & Hammen, C. L. (1992). *Psychological aspects of depression: Toward a cognitive-interpersonal integration.* New York: Wiley. (p. 494)

Gottesman, I. I. (1991). *Schizophrenia genesis: The origins of madness.* New York: Freeman. (p. 500)

Gottesman, I. I. (2001). Psychopathology through a life span—genetic prism. *American Psychologist, 56,* 867–881. (p. 499)

Gottfredson, L. S. (2002a). Where and why *g* matters: Not a mystery. *Human Performance, 15,* 25–46. (p. 318)

Gottfredson, L. S. (2002b). *g:* Highly general and highly practical. In R. J. Sternberg & E. L. Grigorenko (Eds.), *The general factor of intelligence: How general is it?* Mahwah, NJ: Erlbaum. (p. 318)

Gould, S. J. (1981). *The mismeasure of man.* New York: Norton. (p. 316)

Gould, S. J. (1997, June 12). Darwinian fundamentalism. *The New York Review of Books, XLIV*(10), 34–37. (p. 74)

Gould, S. J. (2001, September 26). A time of gifts. *New York Times* (www.nytimes.com). (p. 573)

Grady, C. L., & McIntosh, A. R., Horwitz, B., Maisog, J. M., Ungeleider, L. G., Mentis, M. J., Pietrini, P., Schapiro, M. B., & Haxby, J. V. (1995). Age-related reductions in human recognition memory due to impaired encoding. *Science, 269,* 218–221. (p. 276)

Graf, P. (1990). Life-span changes in implicit and explicit memory. *Bulletin of the Psychonomic Society, 28,* 353–358. (p. 128)

Graham, J. W., Marks, G., & Hansen, W. B. (1991). Social influence processes affecting adolescent substance use. *Journal of Applied Psychology, 76,* 291–298. (p. 219)

Grant, B. F., & Dawson, D. A. (1998). Age of onset of drug use and its association with DSM-IV drug abuse and dependence: Results from the national Longitudinal Alcohol Epidemiologic Survey. *Journal of Substance Abuse, 10,* 163–173. (p. C–8)

Gray-Little, B., & Burks, N. (1983). Power and satisfaction in marriage: A review and critique. *Psychological Bulletin, 93,* 513–538. (p. 573)

Gray-Little, B., & Hafdahl, A. R. (2000). Factors influencing racial comparisons of self-esteem: A quantitative review. *Psychological Bulletin, 126,* 26–54. (p. 458)

Greeley, A. (1994). Marital infidelity. *Society, 31,* 9. (p. 18)

Greeley, A. M. (1991). *Faithful attraction.* New York: Tor Books. (p. 18)

Green, B. (2002). Listening to leaders: Feedback on 360-degree feedback one year later. *Organizational Development Journal, 20,* 8–16. (p. B–7)

Green, J. T., & Woodruff-Pak, D. S. (2000). Eyeblink classical conditioning: Hippocampal formation is for neutral stimulus associations as cerebellum is for association-response. *Psychological Bulletin, 126,* 138–158. (p. 271)

Greene, R. L. (1987). Effects of maintenance rehearsal on human memory. *Psychological Bulletin, 102,* 403–413. (p. 262)

Greenfeld, L. A. (1998). *Alcohol and crime: An analysis of national data on the prevalence of alcohol involvement in crime.* Washington, DC: Document NCJ–168632, Bureau of Justice Statistics (www.ojp.usdoj.gov/bjs). (p. 561)

Greenough, W. T., Black, J. E., & Wallace, C. S. (1987). Experience and brain development. *Child Development, 58,* 539–559. (p. 84)

Greenwald, A. G. (1992). New look 3: Unconscious cognition reclaimed. *American Psychologist, 47,* 766–779. (p. 463)

Greenwald, A. G. (1992). Subliminal semantic activation and subliminal snake oil. Paper presented to the American Psychological Association Convention, Washington, DC. (p. 26)

Greenwald, A. G., McGhee, D. E., & Schwartz, J. L. K. (1998). Measuring individual differences in implicit cognition: The implicit association test. *Journal of Personality and Social Psychology, 74,* 1464–1480. (p. 556)

Greenwald, A. G., Oakes, M. A., & Hoffman, H. (2003). Targets of discrimination: Effects of race on responses to weapons holders. *Journal of Experimental Social Psychology, 39,* 399–405. (p. 556)

Greenwald, A. G., Spangenberg, E. R., Pratkanis, A. R., & Eskenazi, J. (1991). Double-blind tests of subliminal self-help audiotapes. *Psychological Science, 2,* 119–122. (p. 26)

Greenwood, M. R. C. (1989). Sexual dimorphism and obesity. In A. J. Stunkard & A. Baum (Eds.). *Perspectives in behavioral medicine: Eating, sleeping, and sex.* Hillsdale, NJ: Erlbaum. (p. 349)

Greer, G. (1984, April). The uses of chastity and other paths to sexual pleasures. *MS,* pp. 53–60, 96. (p. 360)

Gregory, R. L. (1978). *Eye and brain: The psychology of seeing* (3rd ed.). New York: McGraw-Hill. (p. 176)

Gregory, R. L., & Gombrich, E. H. (Eds.). (1973). *Illusion in nature and art.* New York: Charles Scribner's Sons. (p. 182)

Greif, E. B., & Ulman, K. J. (1982). The psychological impact of menarche on early adolescent females: A review of the literature. *Child Development, 53*, 1413–1430. (p. 117)

Greist, J. H., Jefferson, J. W., & Marks, I. M. (1986). *Anxiety and its treatment: Help is available.* Washington, DC: American Psychiatric Press. (p. 477)

Grilo, C. M., & Pogue-Geile, M. F. (1991). The nature of environmental influences on weight and obesity: A behavior genetic analysis. *Psychological Bulletin, 110*, 520–537. (p. 354)

Grobstein, C. (1979, June). External human fertilization. *Scientific American*, pp. 57–67. (p. 100)

Gross, A. E., & Crofton, C. (1977). What is good is beautiful. *Sociometry, 40*, 85–90. (p. 571)

Grossberg, S. (1995). The attentive brain. *American Scientist, 83*, 438–449. (p. 181)

Grossman, M., & Wood, W. (1993). Sex differences in intensity of emotional experience: A social role interpretation. *Journal of Personality and Social Psychology, 65*, 1010–1022. (p. 389)

Gruder, C. L. (1977). Choice of comparison persons in evaluating oneself. In J. M. Suls & R. L. Miller (Eds.), *Social comparison processes.* New York: Hemisphere. (p. 400)

Guerin, B. (1986). Mere presence effects in humans: A review. *Journal of Personality and Social Psychology, 22*, 38–77. (p. 551)

Gundersen, E. (2001, August 1). MTV is a many splintered thing. *USA Today*, pp. D1, D2. (p. 250)

Gustavson, C. R., Garcia, J., Hankins, W. G., & Rusiniak, K. W. (1974). Coyote predation control by aversive conditioning. *Science, 184*, 581–583. (p. 234)

Gustavson, C. R., Kelly, D. J., & Sweeney, M. (1976). Prey-lithium aversions I: Coyotes and wolves. *Behavioral Biology, 17*, 61–72. (p. 234)

Gutmann, D. (1977). The cross-cultural perspective: Notes toward a comparative psychology of aging. In J. E. Birren & K. Warner Schaie (Eds.), *Handbook of the psychology of aging.* New York: Van Nostrand Reinhold. (p. 121)

Guttmacher Institute. (1994). *Sex and America's teenagers.* New York: Alan Guttmacher Institute. (p. 363)

Guttmacher Institute. (2000). *Fulfilling the promise: Public policy and U.S. family planning clinics.* New York: Alan Guttmacher Institute. (p. 123)

H., Sally (1979, August). Videotape recording number T–3, Fortunoff Video Archive of Holocaust Testimonies. New Haven, CT: Yale University Library. (p. 438)

Haber, R. N. (1970, May). How we remember what we see. *Scientific American*, pp. 104–112. (p. 258)

Hackel, L. S., & Ruble, D. N. (1992). Changes in the marital relationship after the first baby is born: Predicting the impact of expectancy disconfirmation. *Journal of Personality and Social Psychology, 62*, 944–957. (p. 131)

Haddock, G., & Zanna, M. P. (1994). Preferring "housewives" to "feminists." *Psychology of Women Quarterly, 18*, 25–52. (pp. 556–557)

Halberstadt, J. B., & Niedenthal, P. M., & Kushner, J. (1995). Resolution of lexical ambiguity by emotional state. *Psychological Science, 6*, 278–281. (p. 182)

Haldeman, D. C. (1994). The practice and ethics of sexual orientation conversion therapy. *Journal of Consulting and Clinical Psychology, 62*, 221–227. (pp. 364–365)

Haldeman, D. C. (2002). Gay rights, patient rights: The implications of sexual orientation conversion therapy. *Professional Psychology: Research and Practice, 33*, 260–264. (pp. 364–365)

Hall, C. S., Dornhoff, W., Blick, K. A., & Weesner, K. E. (1982). The dreams of college men and women in 1950 and 1980: A comparison of dream contents and sex differences. *Sleep, 5*, 188–194. (p. 200)

Hall, C. S., & Lindzey, G. (1978). *Theories of personality* (2nd ed.). New York: Wiley. (p. 438)

Hall, G. (1997). Context aversion, Pavlovian conditioning, and the psychological side effects of chemotherapy. *European Psychologist, 2*, 118–124. (p. 234)

Hall, G. S. (1904). *Adolescence: Its psychology and its relations to physiology, anthropology, sex, crime, religion and education* (Vol. I). New York: Appleton-Century-Crofts. (p. 115)

Hall, J. A. (1984). *Nonverbal sex differences: Communication accuracy and expressive style.* Baltimore: Johns Hopkins University Press. (p. 388)

Hall, J. A. (1987). On explaining gender differences: The case of nonverbal communication. In P. Shaver & C. Hendrick (Eds.), *Review of Personality and Social Psychology, 7*, 177–200. (p. 388)

Hall, J. A. Y., & Kimura, D. (1994). Dermatoglyphic asymmetry and sexual orientation in men. *Behavioral Neuroscience, 108*, 1203–1206. (p. 367)

Halpern, C. T., Joyner, K., Udry, J. R., & Suchindran, C. (2000). Smart teens don't have sex (or kiss much either). *Journal of Adolescent Health, 26*, 213–225. (p. 363)

Halpern, D. F. (1991). Cognitive sex differences: Why diversity is a critical research issue. Paper presented to the American Psychological Association convention. (p. 333)

Halpern, D. F. (2000). Sex-related ability differences: Changing perspectives, changing minds. Mahwah, NJ: Erlbaum. (pp. 332, 333)

Halsey, A. H., & Webb, J. (2000). *Twentieth-century British social trends.* Basingstoke: Macmillan. (p. 354)

Hamann, S., Monarch, E. S., & Goldstein, F. C. (2002). Impaired fear conditioning in Alzheimer's disease. *Neuropsychologica, 40*, 1187–1195. (p. 269)

Hamill, R., Wilson, T. D., & Nisbett, R. E. (1980). Insensitivity to sample bias: Generalizing from atypical cases. *Journal of Personality and Social Psychology, 39*, 578–589. (p. 297)

Hammersmith, S. K. (1982, August). *Sexual preference: An empirical study from the Alfred C. Kinsey Institute for Sex Research.* Paper presented at the meeting of the American Psychological Association, Washington, DC. (p. 365)

Hampson, R. (2000, April 10). In the end, people just need more room. *USA Today*, p. 19A. (p. 354)

Hankin, B. L., & Abramson, L. Y. (2001). Development of gender differences in depression: An elaborated cognitive vulnerability-transactional stress theory. *Psychological Bulletin, 127*, 773–796. (p. 492)

Hansen, C. H., & Hansen, R. D. (1988). Finding the face-in-the-crowd: An anger superiority effect. *Journal of Personality and Social Psychology, 54*, 917–924. (p. 387)

Harber, K. D. (1998), Feedback to minorities: Evidence of a positive bias. *Journal of Personality and Social Psychology, 74*, 622–628. (p. 556)

Hardin, C., & Banaji, M. R. (1993). The influence of language on thought. *Social Cognition, 11*, 277–308. (p. 308)

Hare, R. D. (1975). Psychophysiological studies of psychopathy. In D. C. Fowles (Ed.), *Clinical applications of psychophysiology.* New York: Columbia University Press. (p. 485)

Harkins, S. G., & Szymanski, K. (1989). Social loafing and group evaluation. *Journal of Personality and Social Psychology, 56*, 934–941. (p. 551)

Harlow, H. F., Harlow, M. K., & Suomi, S. J. (1971). From thought to therapy: Lessons from a primate laboratory. *American Scientist, 59*, 538–549. (p. 110)

Harmon-Jones, E., Abramson, L. Y., Sigelman, J., Bohlig, A., Hogan, M. E., & Harmon-Jones, C. (2002). Proneness to hypomania/mania symptoms or depression symptoms and asymmetrical frontal cortical responses to an anger-evoking event. *Journal of Personality and Social Psychology, 82,* 610–618. (p. 385)

Harris, B. (1979). Whatever happened to Little Albert? *American Psychologist, 34,* 151–160. (p. 235)

Harris, J. A. (1999). Review and methodological considerations in research on testosterone and aggression. *Aggression and Violent Behavior, 4,* 273–291. (p. 561)

Harris, J. R. (1998). *The nurture assumption.* New York: Free Press. (pp. 78, 85, 112)

Harris, J. R. (2000a). Beyond the nurture assumption: Testing hypotheses about the child's environment. In J. G. Borkowski & S. L. Ramey (Eds.), *Parenting and the child's world: Influences on academic, intellectual, and social-emotional development.* Washington, DC: APA Books. (p. 85)

Harris, R. J. (1994). The impact of sexually explicit media. In J. Brant & D. Zillmann (Eds.), *Media effects: Advances in theory and research.* Hillsdale, NJ: Erlbaum. (p. 563)

Harrison, Y., & Horne, J. A. (2000). The impact of sleep deprivation on decision making: A review. *Journal of Experimental Psychology: Applied, 6,* 236–249. (p. 196)

Harriston, K. A. (1993, December 24). 1 shakes, 1 snoozes; both win $45 million. *Washington Post* release (in *Tacoma News Tribune,* pp. A1, A2). (p. 456)

Harter, J. K. (2000, Winter/Spring). The linkage of employee perceptions to outcomes in a retail environment—cause and effect? *Gallup Research Journal,* pp. 25–38. (p. B–8)

Harter, J. K., Schmidt, F. L., & Hayes, T. L. (2002). Business-unit-level relationship between employee satisfaction, employee engagement, and business outcomes: A meta-analysis. *Journal of Applied Psychology, 87,* 268–279. (p. B–8)

Hartmann, E. (1981, April). The strangest sleep disorder. *Psychology Today,* pp. 14, 16, 18. (p. 199)

Hartmann, E. (1984). *The nightmare: The psychology and biology of terrifying dreams.* New York: Basic Books. (p. 199)

Harvey, S. M. (1987). Female sexual behavior: Fluctuations during the menstrual cycle. *Journal of Psychosomatic Research, 31,* 101–110. (p. 359)

Hassan, R., & Carr, J. (1989). Changing patterns of suicide in Australia. *Australian and New Zealand Journal of Psychiatry, 23,* 226–234. (p. 490)

Hatfield, E. (1988). Passionate and companionate love. In R. J. Sternberg & M. L. Barnes (Eds.), *The psychology of love.* New Haven: Yale University Press. (p. 571)

Hatfield, E., & Sprecher, S. (1986). *Mirror, mirror . . . The importance of looks in everyday life.* Albany: State University of New York Press. (p. 569)

Hathaway, S. R. (1960). *An MMPI Handbook* (Vol. 1, Foreword). Minneapolis: University of Minnesota Press. (Revised edition, 1972). (p. 445)

Hawkes, N. (2002, September 10). Fat children may die before their parents (report on presentation to the British Association for the Advancement of Science). *Times of London,* p. 3. (p. 354)

Haxby, J. V. (2001, July 7). Quoted by B. Bower, Faces of perception. *Science News,* pp. 10–12. See also J. V. Haxby, M. I. Gobbini, M. L. Furey, A. Ishai, J. L. Schouten & P. Pietrini, Distributed and overlapping representations of faces and objects in ventral temporal cortex. *Science, 293,* 2425–2430. (p. 151)

Hazelrigg, M. D., Cooper, H. M., & Borduin, C. M. (1987). Evaluating the effectiveness of family therapies: An integrative review and analysis. *Psychological Bulletin, 101,* 428–442. (p. 519)

Hearold, S. (1986). A synthesis of 1043 effects of television on social behavior. In G. Comstock (Ed.), *Public communication and behavior.* New York: Academic Press. (p. 251)

Hebb, D. O. (1980). *Essay on mind.* Hillsdale, NJ: Erlbaum. 9–16. (pp. 235, 379)

Hebert, R. (2001, September). Doing a number on memory. *APS Observer,* pp. 1, 7–11. (p. 264)

Hedges, L. V., & Nowell, A. (1995). Sex differences in mental test scores, variability, and numbers of high-scoring individuals. *Science, 269,* 41–45. (pp. 332–333)

Heider, F. (1958). *The psychology of interpersonal relations.* New York: Wiley. (p. 539)

Heiman, J. R. (1975, April). The physiology of erotica: Women's sexual arousal. *Psychology Today,* 90–94. (p. 360)

Heishman, S. J., Kozlowski, L. T., & Henningfield, J. E. (1997). Nicotine addiction: Implications for public health policy. *Journal of Social Issues, 53,* 13–33. (p. 213)

Hejmadi, A., Davidson, R. J., & Rozin, P. (2000). Exploring Hindu Indian emotion expressions: Evidence for accurate recognition by Americans and Indians. *Psychological Science, 11,* 183–187. (p. 390)

Helgeson, V. S., Cohen, S., & Fritz, H. L. (1998). Social ties and cancer. In P. M. Cinciripini & others (Eds.), *Psychological and behavioral factors in cancer risk.* New York: Oxford University Press. (p. 418)

Helmreich, W. B. (1992). *Against all odds: Holocaust survivors and the successful lives they made in America.* New York: Simon & Schuster. (pp. 113, 437, 481)

Helmreich, W. B. (1994). Personal correspondence. Department of Sociology, City University of New York. (p. 437)

Helmuth, L. (2001). Boosting brain activity from the outside in. *Science, 292,* 1284–1286. (p. 534)

Hembree, R. (1988). Correlates, causes, effects, and treatment of test anxiety. *Review of Educational Research, 58,* 47–77. (p. 384)

Henderlong, J., & Lepper, M. R. (2002). The effects of praise on children's intrinsic motivation: A review and synthesis. *Psychological Bulletin, 128,* 774–795. (p. 244)

Henkel, L. A., Franklin, N., & Johnson, M. K. (2000, Mar.). Cross-modal source monitoring confusions between perceived and imagined events. *Journal of Experimental Psychology: Learning, Memory, & Cognition, 26,* 321–335. (p. 283)

Henninger, P. (1992). Conditional handedness: Handedness changes in multiple personality disordered subject reflect shift in hemispheric dominance. *Consciousness and Cognition, 1,* 265–287. (p. 483)

Herbert, B. (2001, July 23). Economics 202 at Big Tobacco U. *New York Times* (www.nytimes.com). (p. 212)

Herbert, J. D., Lilienfeld, S. O., Lohr, J. M., Montgomery, R. W., O'Donohue, W. T., Rosen, G. M., & Tolin, D. F. (2000). Science and pseudoscience in the development of eye movement desensitization and reprocessing: Implications for clinical psychology. *Clinical Psychology Review, 20,* 945–971. (p. 525)

Herman, C. P., & Polivy, J. (1980). Restrained eating. In A. J. Stunkard (Ed.), *Obesity.* Philadelphia: Saunders. (p. 356)

Herman-Giddens, M. E., Wang, L., & Koch, G. (2001). Secondary sexual characteristics in boys: Estimates from the National Health and Nutrition Examination Survey III, 1988–1994. *Archives of Pediatrics and Adolescent Medicine, 155,* 1022–1028. (p. 116)

Herrmann, D. (1982). Know thy memory: The use of questionnaires to assess and study memory. *Psychological Bulletin, 92,* 434–452. (p. 288)

Herrnstein, R. J., & Loveland, D. H. (1964). Complex visual concept in the pigeon. *Science, 146,* 549–551. (p. 238)

Hershberger, S. L. (2001). Biological factors in the development of sexual orientation. In C. J. Patterson & A. R. D'Augelli (Eds.), *Lesbian, gay, and bisexual identities and youth: Psychological perspectives.* New York: Oxford. (pp. 366, 368)

Hershenson, M. (1989). *The moon illusion.* Hillsdale, NJ: Erlbaum. (p. 173)

Hertzman, C. (2001, November-December). Health and human society. *American Scientist, 89,* 538–545. (p. 406)

Herz, R. S. (2001). Ah sweet skunk! Why we like or dislike what we smell. *Cerebrum, 3*(4), 31–47. (p. 163)

Hess, E. H. (1956, July). Space perception in the chick. *Scientific American,* pp. 71–80. (p. 176)

Hettema, J. M., Neale, M. C., & Kendler, K. S. (2001). A review and meta-analysis of the genetic epidemiology of anxiety disorders. *American Journal of Psychiatry, 158,* 1568–1578. (p. 482)

Hickok, G., Bellugi, U., & Klima, E. S. (2001, June). Sign language in the brain. *Scientific American,* pp. 58–65. (p. 62)

Higgins, E. T. (1987). Self-discrepancy: A theory relating self and affect. *Psychological Review, 94,* 319–340. (p. 457)

Hilgard, E. R. (1986). *Divided consciousness: Multiple controls in human thought and action.* New York: Wiley. (p. 207)

Hilgard, E. R. (1987). *Psychology in America: A historical survey.* New York: Oxford University Press. (p. 4)

Hilgard, E. R. (1992). Dissociation and theories of hypnosis. In E. Fromm & M. R. Nash (Eds.), *Contemporary hypnosis research.* New York: Guilford. (p. 207)

Hill, C. E., & Nakayama, E. Y. (2000). Client-centered therapy: Where has it been and where is it going? A comment on Hathaway. *Journal of Clinical Psychology, 56,* 961–875. (p. 510)

Hill, H., & Johnston, A. (2001). Categorizing sex and identity from the biological motion of faces. *Current Biology, 11,* 880–885. (p. 389)

Hingson, R. W., Heeren, T., Zakocs, R. C., Kopstein, A., & Wechsler, H. (2002). Magnitude of alcohol-related mortality and morbidity among U.S. college students ages 18–24. *Journal of Studies on Alcohol, 63,* 136–144. (p. 211)

Hintzman, D. L. (1978). *The psychology of learning and memory.* San Francisco: Freeman. (p. 264)

Hinz, L. D., & Williamson, D. A. (1987). Bulimia and depression: A review of the affective variant hypothesis. *Psychological Bulletin, 102,* 150–158. (p. 350)

Hirst, W., Neisser, U., & Spelke, E. (1978, June). Divided attention. *Human Nature,* pp. 54–61. (p. 207)

HMHL (2002, January). Disaster and trauma. *Harvard Mental Health Letter,* pp. 1–5. (p. 404)

HMHL (2002, August). Smoking and depression. *Harvard Mental Health Letter,* pp. 6–7. (p. 491)

Hobson, J. A. (1988). *The dreaming brain.* New York: Basic Books. (p. 203)

Hobson, J. A. (1995, September). Quoted by C. H. Colt, The power of dreams. *Life,* pp. 36–49. (p. 202)

Hodgkinson, V. A., & Weitzman, M. S. (1992). *Giving and volunteering in the United States.* Washington, DC: Independent Sector. (p. 576)

Hoebel, B. G., & Teitelbaum, P. (1966). Effects of forcefeeding and starvation on food intake and body weight in a rat with ventromedial hypothalamic lesions. *Journal of Comparative and Physiological Psychology, 61,* 189–193. (p. 346)

Hoffman, C., & Hurst, N. (1990). Gender stereotypes: Perception or rationalization? *Journal of Personality and Social Psychology, 58,* 197–208. (p. 557)

Hoffman, D. D. (1998). *Visual intelligence: How we create what we see.* New York: Norton. (p. 151)

Hoffman, H. G., Patterson, D. R., Carrougher G. J., & Sharar, S. (2001). The effectiveness of virtual reality based pain control with multiple treatments. *Clinical Journal of Pain, 17,* 229–235. (p. 161)

Hoffman, P. (1994, November). The science of race. *Discover,* p. 4. (p. 555)

Hofstede, G. (1980). *Culture's consequences: International differences in work-related values.* Beverly Hills: Sage. (p. 461)

Hogan, R. (1998). Reinventing personality. *Journal of Social and Clinical Psychology, 17,* 1–10. (p. 450)

Hogg, M. A. (1996). Intragroup processes, group structure and social identity. In W. P. Robinson (Ed.), *Social groups and identies: Developing the legacy of Henri Tajfel.* Oxford: Butterworth Heinemann. (p. 557)

Hohmann, G. W. (1966). Some effects of spinal cord lesions on experienced emotional feelings. *Psychophysiology, 3,* 143–156. (p. 380)

Hokanson, J. E., & Edelman, R. (1966). Effects of three social responses on vascular processes. *Journal of Personality and Social Psychology, 3,* 442–447. (p. 394)

Holahan, C. K., & Sears, R. R. (1995). *The gifted group in later maturity.* Stanford, CA: Stanford University Press. (p. 324)

Holden, C. (1980a). Identical twins reared apart. *Science, 207,* 1323–1325. (p. 77)

Holden, C. (1980b, November). Twins reunited. *Science, 80,* 55–59. (p. 77)

Holden, C. (1986a). Days may be numbered for polygraphs in the private sector. *Science, 232,* 705. (p. 386)

Holden, C. (1986b). Researchers grapple with problems of updating classic psychological test. *Science, 233,* 1249–1251. (p. 441)

Holden, C. (1993). Wake-up call for sleep research. *Science, 259,* 305. (p. 195)

Holden, C. (2003). Deconstructing schizophrenia. *Science, 299,* 333–335. (p. 497)

Holden, G. W., & Miller, P. C. (1999). Enduring and different: A meta-analysis of the similarity in parents' child rearing. *Psychological Bulletin, 125,* 223–254. (p. 114)

Hollis, K. L. (1997). Contemporary research on Pavlovian conditioning: A "new" functional analysis. *American Psychologist, 52,* 956–965. (p. 230)

Hollon, S. D., Thase, M. E., & Markowitz, J. C. (2002). Treatment and prevention of depression. *Psychological Science in the Public Interest, 3,* 39–77. (p. 532)

Holmes, A., & Conway, M. A. (1999). Generation identity and the reminiscence bump: Memory for public and private events. *Journal of Adult Development, 6,* 21–34. (p. 127)

Holmes, D. S. (1990). The evidence for repression: An examination of sixty years of research. In J. Singer (Ed.), *Repression and dissociation: Implications for personality theory, psychopathology, and health.* Chicago: University of Chicago Press. (p. 437)

Holmes, D. S. (1994). Is there evidence for repression? No. (Unexpurgated version on an article which was rewritten by the *Harvard Mental Health Letter* and published as "Is there evidence for repression? Doubtful," June, 1994, pp. 4–6.) (p. 437)

Holzman, P. S., & Matthysse, S. (1990). The genetics of schizophrenia: A review. *Psychological Science, 1,* 279–286. (p. 145)

Hom, P. W., & Griffeth, R. W. (1991). Structural equations modeling test of a turnover theroy: Cross sectional and longitudinal analyses. *Journal of Applied Psychology, 76,* 350–366. (p. B–8)

Hooper, J., & Teresi, D. (1986). *The three-pound universe.* New York: Macmillan. (p. 52)

Hooykaas, R. (1972). *Religion and the rise of modern science.* Grand Rapids, MI: Eerdmans. (p. 14)

Horn, J. L. (1982). The aging of human abilities. In J. Wolman (Ed.), *Handbook of developmental psychology.* Englewood Cliffs, NJ: Prentice-Hall. (p. 128)

House, J. S., Landis, K. R., & Umberson, D. (1988). Social relationships and health. *Science, 241,* 540–545. (p. 417)

House, R. J., & Singh, J. V. (1987). Organizational behavior: Some new directions for I/O psychology. *Annual Review of Psychology, 38,* 669–718. (p. B–10)

Houts, A. C., Berman, J. S., & Abramson, H. (1994). Effectiveness of psychological and pharmacological treatments for nocturnal enuresis. *Journal of Consulting and Clinical Psychology, 62,* 737–745. (p. 512)

Howard Hughes Medical Institute (1997). *Seeing, hearing, and smelling the world.* Chevy Chase, MD: Howard Hughes Medical Institute. Also available at: www.hhmi.org/senses/ (p. 158)

Howe, M. L. (1997). Children's memory for traumatic experiences. *Learning and Individual Differences, 9,* 153–174. (p. 284)

Howe, M. L., & Courage, M. L. (1993). On resolving the enigma of infantile amnesia. *Psychological Bulletin, 113,* 305–326. (p. 103)

Hoyer, G., & Lund, E. (1993). Suicide among women related to number of children in marriage. *Archives of General Psychiatry, 50,* 134–137. (p. 490)

Hróbjartsson, A., & Gøtzsche, P. C. (2001). Is the placebo powerless? An analysis of clinical trials comparing placebo with no treatment. *New England Journal of Medicine, 344,* 1594–602. (p. 412)

Hubel, D. H. (1979, September). The brain. *Scientific American,* pp. 45–53. (p. 145)

Hubel, D. H., & Wiesel, T. N. (1979, September). Brian mechanisms of vision. *Scientific American,* pp. 150–162. (p. 150)

Hublin, C., Kaprio, J., Partinen, M., Heikkila, K., & Koskenvuo, M. (1997). Prevalence and genetics of sleepwalking—A population-based twin study. *Neurology, 48,* 177–181. (p. 199)

Hublin, C., Kaprio, J., Partinen, M., & Koskenvuo, M. (1998). Sleeptalking in twins: Epidemiology and psychiatric comorbidity. *Behavior Genetics, 28,* 289–298. (p. 199)

Hucker, S. J., & Bain, J. (1990). Androgenic hormones and sexual assault. In W. Marshall, R. Law, & H. Barbaree (Eds.), *The handbook on sexual assault.* New York: Plenum. (p. 359)

Hughes, H. C. (1999). *Sensory exotica: A world beyond human experience.* Cambridge, MA: MIT Press. (p. 142)

Hugick, L. (1989, July). Women play the leading role in keeping modern families close. *Gallup Report,* No. 286, pp. 27–34. (p. 121)

Hull, J. G., Young, R. D., & Jouriles, E. (1986). Applications of the self-awareness model of alcohol consumption: Predicting patterns of use and abuse. *Journal of Personality and Social Psychology, 51,* 790–796. (p. 211)

Hull, J. M. (1990). *Touching the rock: An experience of blindness.* New York: Vintage Books. (pp. 273, 569)

Hulme, C., & Tordoff, V. (1989). Working memory development: The effects of speech rate, word length, and acoustic similarity on serial recall. *Journal of Experimental Child Psychology, 47,* 72–87. (p. 266)

Hummer, R. A., Rogers, R. G., Nam, C. B., & Ellison, C. G. (1999). Religious involvement and U.S. adult mortality. *Demography, 36,* 273–285. (pp. 422–423)

Hunsley, J., & Bailey, J. M. (1999). The clinical utility of the Rorschach: Unfulfilled promises and an uncertain future. *Psychological Assessment, 11*(3), 266–277. (p. 435)

Hunsley, J., & Di Giulio, G. (2002). Dodo bird, phoenix, or urban legend? The question of psychotherapy equivalence. *Scientific Review of Mental Health Practice, 1,* 11–22. (p. 523)

Hunt, M. (1974). *Sexual behavior in the 1970s.* Chicago: Playboy Press. (p. 361)

Hunt, M. (1982). *The universe within.* New York: Simon and Schuster. (p. 329)

Hunt, M. (1990). *The compassionate beast: What science is discovering about the humane side of humankind.* New York: William Morrow. (p. 10)

Hunt, M. (1993). *The story of psychology.* New York: Doubleday. (pp. 3, 4, 5, 236, 324)

Hunter, J. E. (1997). Needed: A ban on the significance test. *Psychological Science, 8,* 3–7. (p. A–8)

Hunter, S., & Sundel, M. (Eds.). (1989). *Midlife myths: Issues, findings, and practice implications.* Newbury Park, CA: Sage. (p. 129)

Hurtado, S., Dey, E. L., & Trevino, J. G. (1994). Exclusion or self-segregation? Interaction across racial/ethnic groups on college campuses. Paper presented at the American Educational Research Association annual meeting. (p. 555)

Hussein, S. (2002, July 17 and August 28). Speeches to the Iraqi people as reported by various media. (p. 567)

Huston, A. C., Donnerstein, E., Fairchild, H., Feshbach, N. D., Katz, P. A., & Murray, J. P. (1992). *Big world, small screen: The role of television in American society.* Lincoln, NE: University of Nebraska Press. (p. 250)

Hyde, J. S. (1983, November). *Bem's gender schema theory.* Paper presented at GLCA Women's Studies Conference, Rochester, IN. (p. 281)

Hyde, J. S., Fennema, E., & Lamon, S. J. (1990). Gender differences in mathematics performance: A meta-analysis. *Psychological Bulletin, 107,* 139–155. (p. 332)

Hyler, S., Gabbard, G. O., & Schneider, I. (1991). Homicidal maniacs and narcissistic parasites: Stigmatization of mentally ill persons in the movies. *Hospital and Community Psychiatry, 42,* 1044–1048. (p. 475)

Hyman, R. (1981). Cold reading: How to convince strangers that you know all about them. In K. Frazier (Ed.), *Paranormal borderlands of science.* Buffalo, NY: Prometheus. (p. 446)

Hyman, R. (1994). Anomaly or artifact? Comments on Bem and Honorton. *Psychological Bulletin, 115,* 19–24. (pp. 180–181)

Hyman, R. (1996, March/April). Evaluation of the military's twenty-year program on psychic spying. *The Skeptical Inquirer,* pp. 21–23, 27. (pp. 180–181)

Hyman, R. (1996, March/April). The evidence for psychic functioning: Claims vs. reality. *The Skeptical Inquirer,* pp. 24–26. (pp. 180–181)

Iacono, W. G., & Lykken, D. T. (1997). The validity of the lie detector: Two surveys of scientific opinion. *Journal of Applied Psychology, 82,* 426–433. (p. 386)

Ickes, W., Snyder, M., & Garcia, S. (1997). Personality influences on the choice of situations. In R. Hogan, J. Johnson, & S. Briggs (Eds.). *Handbook of Personality Psychology.* San Diego, CA: Academic Press. (p. 451)

Idson, L. C., & Mischel, W. (2001). The personality of familiar and significant people: The lay perceiver as a social-cognitive theorist. *Journal of Personality and Social Psychology, 80,* 585–596. (p. 540)

Ikonomidou, C., Bittigau, P., Ishimaru, M. J., Wozniak, D. F., Koch, C., Genz, K., Price, M. T., Stefovska, V., Hoerster, F., Tenkova, T., Dikranian, K., & Olney, J. W. (2000). Ethanol-induced apoptotic neurodegeneration and fetal alcohol syndrome. *Science, 287,* 1056–1060. (p. 101)

Immen, W. (1995, July 16). Canadians ignore 'safe sex' warning. *Toronto Globe and Mail* (in *Grand Rapids Press,* p. A22). (p. 362)

IMS (2002, September 21). Antidepressants. IMS Health (www.imshealth.com). (p. 532)

Independent Sector. (2002). *Faith and philanthropy: The connection between charitable giving behavior and giving to religion.* Washington, DC: Independent Sector. (p. 576)

Ingham, A. G., Levinger, G., Graves, J., & Peckham, V. (1974). The Ringelmann effect: Studies of group size and group performance. *Journal of Experimental Social Psychology, 10,* 371–384. (p. 551)

Inglehart, M. R., Markus, H., & Brown, D. R. (1989). The effects of possible selves on academic achievement—A panel study. In J. P. Forgas & J. M. Innes (Eds.), *Recent advances in social psychology: An international perspective.* New York: Elsevier Science Publishers. (p. 457)

Inglehart, R. (1990). *Culture shift in advanced industrial society.* Princeton, NJ: Princeton University Press. (pp. 132, 133, 372, 453, B–1)

Inzlicht, M., & Ben-Zeev, T. (2000). A threatening intellectual environment: Why females are susceptible to experiencing problem-solving deficits in the presence of males. *Psychological Science, 11,* 365–371. (p. 335)

IPU (2002, April 10). Women in national parliaments. Inter-Parliamentary Union (www.ipu.org/wmn-e/world.htm). (p. 91)

Irwin, M., Mascovich, A., Gillin, J. C., Willoughby, R., Pike, J., & Smith, T. L. (1994). Partial sleep deprivation reduces natural killer cell activity in humans. *Psychosomatic Medicine, 56,* 493–498. (p. 196)

Isham, W. P., & Kamin, L. J. (1993). Blackness, deafness, IQ, and *g. Intelligence, 17,* 37–46. (p. 309)

Iversen, L. L. (2000). *The science of marijuana.* New York: Oxford. (p. 216)

Iverson, J. M., & Goldin-Meadow, S. (1998). Why people gesture when they speak. *Nature, 396,* 228. (p. 313)

Iyer, P. (1993, April). The soul of an intercontinental wanderer. *Harper's, 286,* 13–17. (p. 86)

Izard, C. E. (1977). *Human emotions.* New York: Plenum Press. (pp. 390, 393)

Izard, C. E. (1994). Innate and universal facial expressions: Evidence from developmental and cross-cultural research. *Psychological Bulletin, 115,* 288–299. (p. 390)

Izard, C., Fine, S., Schultz, D., Mostow, A., Ackerman, B., & Younstrom, E. (2001). Emotion knowledge as a predictor of social behavior and academic competence in children at risk. *Psychological Science, 12,* 18–23. (p. 319)

Jackson, J. M., & Williams, K. D. (1988). Social loafing: A review and theoretical analysis. Unpublished manuscript, Fordham University. (p. 551)

Jackson, J. S., Brown, K. T., Brown, T. N., & Marks, B. (2001). Contemporary immigration policy orientations among dominant-group members in western Europe. *Journal of Social Issues, 57,* 431–456. (p. 555)

Jackson, S. W. (1992). The listening healer in the history of psychological healing. *American Journal Psychiatry, 149,* 1623–1632. (p. 526)

Jacobs, B. L. (1987). How hallucinogenic drugs work. *American Scientist, 75,* 386–392. (p. 215)

Jacobs, B. L. (1994). Serotonin, motor activity, and depression-related disorders. *American Scientist, 82,* 456–463. (pp. 415, 492)

Jacobs, B. L., van Praag, H., & Gage, F. H. (2000). Adult brain neurogenesis and psychiatry: A novel theory of depression. *Molecular Psychiatry, 5,* 262–269. (p. 492)

Jacobs, B. L., van Praag, H., & Gage, F. H. (2000). Depression and the birth and death of brain cells. *American Scientist, 88,* 340–345. (p. 532)

Jacobs, W. J., & Nadel, L. (1985). Stress-induced recovery of fears and phobias. *Psychological Bulletin, 92,* 512–531. (p. 479)

Jaffee, S., & Hyde, J. S. (2000). Gender differences in moral orientation: A meta-analysis. *Psychological Bulletin, 126,* 703–726. (p. 119)

Jakicic, J. M., Winters, C., Lang, W., & Wing R. R. (1999). Effects of intermittent exercise and use of home exercise equipment on adherence, weight loss, and fitness in overweight women. *Journal of the American Medical Association, 282,* 1554–1560. (p. 356)

James, K. (1986). Priming and social categorizational factors: Impact on awareness of emergency situations. *Personality and Social Psychology Bulletin, 12,* 462–467. (p. 273)

James, W. (1890). *The principles of psychology* (Vol. 2). New York: Holt. (pp. 275, 288, 380, 392)

James, W. (1902; reprinted 1958). *Varieties of religious experience.* New York: Mentor Books. (p. 395)

Jameson, D. (1985). Opponent-colors theory in light of physiological findings. In D. Ottoson & S. Zeki (Eds.), *Central and peripheral mechanisms of color vision.* New York: Macmillan. (p. 155)

Jamison, K. R. (1993). *Touched with fire: Manic-depressive illness and the artistic temperament.* New York: Free Press. (p. 488)

Jamison, K. R. (1995, February). Manic-depressive illness and creativity. *Scientific American,* pp. 62–67. (p. 488)

Janicak, P. G., Dowd, S. M., Martis, B., Alam, D., Beedle, D., Krasuski, J., Strong, M. J., Sharma, R., Rosen, C., & Viana, M. (2002). Repetitive transcranial magnetic stimulation versus electroconvulsive therapy for major depression: Preliminary results of randomized trial. *Biological Psychiatry, 51,* 659–667. (p. 534)

Janis, I. L. (1982). *Groupthink: Psychological studies of policy decisions and fiascoes.* Boston: Houghton Mifflin. (p. 553)

Janis, I. L. (1986). Problems of international crisis management in the nuclear age. *Journal of Social Issues, 42(2),* 201–220. (p. 296)

Janoff-Bulman, R., Timko, C., & Carli, L. L. (1985). Cognitive biases in blaming the victim. *Journal of Experimental Social Psychology, 21,* 161–177. (p. 559)

Jeffery, R. W., Drewnowski, A., Epstein, L. H., Stunkard, A. J., Wilson, G. T., Wing, R. R., & Hill, D. R. (2000). Long-term maintenance of weight loss: Current status. *Health Psychology, 19,* No. 1 (Supplement), 5–16. (pp. 355, 356)

Jemmott, J. B., III, & Magloire, K. (1988). Academic stress, social support, and secretory immunoglobulin A. *Journal of Personality and Social Psychology, 55,* 803–810. (p. 410)

Jenkins, J. G., & Dallenbach, K. M. (1924). Obliviscence during sleep and waking. *American Journal of Psychology, 35,* 605–612. (pp. 278, 279)

Jenkins, J. M., & Astington, J. W. (1996). Cognitive factors and family structure associated with theory of mind development in young children. *Developmental Psychology, 32,* 70–78. (p. 108)

Jensen, J. P., & Bergin, A. E. (1988). Mental health values of professional therapists: A national interdisciplinary survey. *Professional Psychology: Research and Practice, 19,* 290–297. (p. 528)

Jepson, C., Krantz, D. H., & Nisbett, R. E. (1983). Inductive reasoning: Competence or skill. *The Behavioral and Brain Sciences, 3,* 494–501. (p. A–7)

Jervis, R. (1985, April 2). Quoted in D. Goleman, Political forces come under new scrutiny of psychology. *The New York Times,* pp. C1, C4. (p. 301)

Jing, H. (1999, Summer). China faces myriad psychological challenges of modernization. *Psychology International* (APA newsletter), p. 7. (p. 7)

John, O. P., & Srivastava, S. (1999). The Big Five trait taxonomy: History, measurement, and theoretical perspectives. In L. A. Pervin & O. P. John (Eds.), *Handbook of personality: Theory and research.* New York: Guilford. (p. 448)

Johnson, D. F. (1997, Winter). Margaret Floy Washburn. *Psychology of Women Newsletter,* pp. 17, 22. (p. 5)

Johnson, D. L., Swank, P. R., Howie, V. M., Baldwin, C. D., & Owen, M. (1996). Breast feeding and children's intelligence. *Psychological Reports, 79,* 1179–1185. (p. 24)

Johnson, D. L., Wiebe, J. S., Gold, S. M., Andreasen, N. C., Hichwa, R. D., Watkins, G. L., & Ponto, L. L. B. (1999). Cerebral blood flow and personality: A positron emission tomography study. *American Journal of Psychiatry, 156,* 252–257. (p. 444)

Johnson, D. W., & Johnson, R. T. (1989). *Cooperation and competition: Theory and research.* Edina, MN: Interaction Book. (p. 577)

Johnson, D. W., & Johnson, R. T. (1994). Constructive conflict in the schools. *Journal of Social Issues, 50(1),* 117–137. (p. 577)

Johnson, J. G., Cohen, P., Kotler, L., Kasen, S., & Brook, J. S. (2002). Psychiatric disorders associated with risk for the development of eating disorders during adolescence and early adulthood. *Journal of Consulting and Clinical Psychology, 70,* 1119–1128. (p. 350)

Johnson, J. G., Cohen, P., Smailes, E. M., Kasen, S., & Brook, J. S. (2002). Television viewing and aggressive behavior during adolescence and adulthood. *Science, 295,* 2468–2471. (p. 251)

Johnson, J. S., & Newport, E. L. (1991). Critical period effects on universal properties of language: The status of subjacency in the acquisition of a second language. *Cognition, 39,* 215–258. (p. 307)

Johnson, L. C. (2001, July 10). The declining terrorist threat. *New York Times* (www.nytimes.com). (p. 298)

Johnson, M. E., & Hauck, C. (1999). Beliefs and opinions about hypnosis held by the general public: A systematic evaluation. *American Journal of Clinical Hypnosis, 42,* 10–20. (p. 205)

Johnson, M. H., & Morton, J. (1991). *Biology and cognitive development: The case of face recognition.* Oxford: Blackwell Publishing. (p. 101)

Johnston, L. D., O'Malley, P. M., Bachman, J. G., & Schulenberg, J. E. (2004). *Monitoring the future national results on adolescent drug use: Overview of key findings, 2003.* Bethesda, MD: National Institute on Drug Abuse. (pp. 213, 217, 218, 219)

Jones, E. E., Cumming, J. D., & Horowitz, M. J. (1988). Another look at the nonspecific hypothesis of therapeutic effectiveness. *Journal of Consulting and Clinical Psychology, 56,* 48–55. (p. 526)

Jones, J. M. (2003, February 12). Fear of terrorism increases amidst latest warning. *Gallup News Service* (www.gallup.com/releases/pr030212.asp). (p. 476)

Jones, L. (2000, December). Skeptics New Year quiz. *Skeptical Briefs,* p. 11. (p. 447)

Jones, M. C. (1924). A laboratory study of fear: The case of Peter. *Journal of Genetic Psychology, 31,* 308–315. (pp. 512–513)

Jones, S. S., Collins, K., & Hong, H-W. (1991). An audience effect on smile production in 10–month-old infants. *Psychological Science, 2,* 45–49. (p. 391)

Jones, W. H., Carpenter, B. N., & Quintana, D. (1985). Personality and interpersonal predictors of loneliness in two cultures. *Journal of Personality and Social Psychology, 48,* 1503–1511. (p. 28)

Jorgenson, D. O., & Papciak, A. S. (1981). The effects of communication, resource feedback, and identifiability on behavior in a simulated commons. *Journal of Experimental Social Psychology, 17,* 373–385. (p. 577)

Joseph, J. (2001). Separated twins and the genetics of personality differences: A critique. *American Journal of Psychology, 114,* 1–30. (p. 78)

Judge, T. A., Thoresen, C. J., Bono, J. E., & Patton, G. K. (2001). The job satisfaction/job performance relationship: A qualitative and quantitative review. *Psychological Bulletin, 127,* 376–407. (pp. B–7 to B–8)

Kagan, J. (1976). Emergent themes in human development. *American Scientist, 64,* 186–196. (p. 113)

Kagan, J. (1984). *The nature of the child.* New York: Basic Books. (p. 110)

Kagan, J. (1990). Interview with M. V. Ellis & E. S. Robbins, In Celebration of nature: A dialogue with Jerome Kagan. *Journal of Counseling and Development, 68,* 623–627. (p. 79)

Kagan, J. (1995). On attachment. *Harvard Review of Psychiatry, 3,* 104–106. (p. 111)

Kagan, J. (1998). *Three seductive ideas.* Cambridge, MA: Harvard University Press. (p. 135)

Kagan, J., Arcus, D., Snidman, N., Feng, W. Y., Hendler, J., & Greene, S. (1994). Reactivity in infants: A cross-national comparison. *Developmental Psychology, 30,* 342–345. (p. 79)

Kagan, J., Lapidus, D. R., & Moore, M. (December, 1978). Infant antecedents of cognitive functioning: A longitudinal study. *Child Development, 49*(4), 1005–1023. (p. 135)

Kagan, J., Snidman, N., & Arcus, D. M. (1992). Initial reactions to unfamiliarity. *Current Directions in Psychological Science, 1,* 171–174. (pp. 79, 80)

Kahneman, D. (1999). Assessments of objective happiness: A bottom-up approach. In D. Kahneman, E. Diener, & N. Schwartz (Eds.), *Understanding well-being: Scientific perspectives on enjoyment and suffering.* New York: Russell Sage Foundation. (p. 161)

Kahneman, D., Fredrickson, B. L., Schreiber, C. A., & Redelmeier, D. A. (1993). When more pain is preferred to less: Adding a better end. *Psychological Science, 4,* 401–405. (p. 161)

Kahneman, D., Knetsch, J. L., & Thaler, R. (1986). Fairness as a constraint on profit seeking: Entitlements in the market. *American Economic Review, 76,* 728–741. (p. 300)

Kahneman, D., & Tversky, A. (1972). Subjective probability: A judgment of representativeness. *Cognitive Psychology, 3,* 430–454. (p. 21)

Kail, R. (1991). Developmental change in speed of processing during childhood and adolescence. *Psychological Bulletin, 109,* 490–501. (p. 126)

Kaiser (2001). Inside-out: A report on the experiences of lesbians, gays and bisexuals in America and the public's views on issues and policies related to sexual orientation. The Henry J. Kaiser Foundation (www.kff.org). (p. 368)

Kalin, N. H. (1993, May). The neurobiology of fear. *Scientific American,* pp. 94–101. (p. 385)

Kamarck, T., & Jennings, J. R. (1991). Biobehavioral factors in sudden cardiac death. *Psychological Bulletin, 109,* 42–75. (p. 408)

Kamena, M. (1998). Repressed/false childhood sexual abuse memories: A survey of therapists. Paper presented to the Sexual Abuse memories Symposium at the American Psychological Association convention. (p. 285)

Kandel, D. B., & Raveis, V. H. (1989). Cessation of illicit drug use in young adulthood. *Archives of General Psychiatry, 46,* 109–116. (p. 220)

Kandel, E. R., & Schwartz, J. H. (1982). Molecular biology of learning: Modulation of transmitter release. *Science, 218,* 433–443. (p. 268)

Kann, L., Warren, W., Collins, J. L., Ross, J., Collins, B., Kolbe, L. J. (1993). Results from the national school-based 1991 Youth Risk Behavior Survey and progress toward achieving related health objectives for the nation. U.S. Department of Health and Human Services, *Public Health Reports, 108* (Supplement 1), 47–55. (p. 219)

Kaplan, H. I., & Saddock, B. J. (Eds.). (1989). *Comprehensive textbook of psychiatry, V.* Baltimore, MD: Williams and Wilkins. (pp. 530–531)

Kaplowitz, P. B. (2001). Earlier onset of puberty in girls: Relation to increased body mass index and race. *Pediatrics, 108,* 347–353. (p. 116)

Kaprio, J., Koskenvuo, M., & Rita, H. (1987). Mortality after bereavement: A prospective study of 95,647 widowed persons. *American Journal of Public Health, 77,* 283–287. (p. 405)

Karacan, I., Aslan, C., & Hirshkowitz, M. (1983). Erectile mechanisms in man. *Science, 220,* 1080–1082. (p. 194)

Karacan, I., Goodenough, D. R., Shapiro, A., & Starker, S. (1966). Erection cycle during sleep in relation to dream anxiety. *Archives of General Psychiatry, 15,* 183–189. (pp. 193–194)

Karau, S. J., & Williams, K. D. (1993). Social loafing: A meta-analytic review and theoretical integration. *Journal of Personality and Social Psychology, 65,* 681–706. (p. 551)

Kark, J. D., Shemi, G., Friedlander, Y., Martin, O., Manor, O., & Blondheim, S. H. (1996). Does religious observance promote health? Mortality in secular vs. religious kibbutzim in Israel. *American Journal of Public Health, 86,* 341–346. (p. 422)

Karni, A., Meyer, G., Rey-Hipolito, C., Jezzard, P., Adams, M. M., Turner, R., & Ungerleider, L. G. (1998). The acquisition of skilled motor performance: Fast and slow experience-driven changes in primary motor cortex. *Proceedings of the National Academy of Sciences, 95,* 861–868. (p. 84)

Karni, A., & Sagi, D. (1994). Dependence on REM sleep for overnight improvement of perceptual skills. *Science, 265,* 679–682. (p. 202)

Karno, M., Golding, J. M., Sorenson, S. B., & Burnam, A. (1988). The epidemiology of obsessive-compulsive disorder in five US communities. *Archives of General Psychiatry, 45,* 1094–1099. (p. 478)

Karon, P. B., & Widener, A. (1998). Repressed memories: The real story. *Professional Psychology: Research and Practice, 29,* 482–487. (p. 437)

Karon, P. B., & Widener, A. J. (1997). Repressed memories and World War II: Lest we forget. *Professional Psychology: Research and Practice, 28,* 338–340. (p. 437)

Kashima, Y., Siegal, M., Tanaka, K., & Kashima, E. S. (1992). Do people believe behaviours are consistent with attitudes? Towards a cultural psychology of attribution processes. *British Journal of Social Psychology, 31,* 111–124. (p. 462)

Kasser, T. (2002). *The high price of materialism.* Cambridge, MA: MIT Press. (p. 398)

Kasser, T. (2000). Two versions of the American dream: Which goals and values make for a high quality of life? In E. Diener (Ed.), *Advances in quality of life theory and research.* Dordrecht, Netherlands: Kluwer. (p. 398)

Kaufman, A. S., Reynolds, C. R., & McLean, J. E. (1989). Age and WAIS-R intelligence in a national sample of adults in the 20– to 74–year age range: A cross-sectional analysis with educational level controlled. *Intelligence, 13,* 235–253. (p. 129)

Kaufman, J., & Zigler, E. (1987). Do abused children become abusive parents? *American Journal of Orthopsychiatry, 57,* 186–192. (p. 113)

Kaufman, L., & Kaufman, J. H. (2000). Explaining the moon illusion. *Proceedings of the National Academy of Sciences, 97,* 500–505. (p. 174)

Kawachi, I., Kennedy, B. P., Wilkinson, R. G., & Kawachi, K. W. (Eds.) (1999). *Society and population health reader: Income inequality and health.* New York: New Press. (p. 406)

Keesey, R. E., & Corbett, S. W. (1983). Metabolic defense of the body weight set-point. In A. J. Stunkard & E. Stellar (Eds.), *Eating and its disorders.* New York: Raven Press. (p. 347)

Keller, M. B., McCullough, J. P., Klein, D. N., Arnow, B., Dunner, D. L., Gelenberg, A. J., Markowitz, J. C., Nemeroff, C. B., Russell, J. M., Thase, M. E., Trivedi, M. H., & Zajecka J. (2000), A comparison of nefazodone, the cognitive behavioral-analysis system of psychothrapy, and their combination for the treatment of chronic depression. *New England Journal of Medicine, 342,* 1462–1470. (p. 532)

Kellerman, J., Lewis, J., & Laird, J. D. (1989). Looking and loving: The effects of mutual gaze on feelings of romantic love. *Journal of Research in Personality, 23,* 145–161. (p. 387)

Kellermann, A. L. (1997). Comment: Gunsmoke—changing public attitudes toward smoking and firearms. *American Journal of Public Health, 87,* 910–913. (p. 560)

Kellermann, A. L., Rivara, F. P., Rushforth, N. B., Banton, H. G., Feay, D. T., Francisco, J. T., Locci, A. B., Prodzinski, J., Hackman, B. B., & Somes, G. (1993). Gun ownership as a risk factor for homicide in the home. *New England Journal of Medicine, 329,* 1084–1091. (p. 560)

Kellermann, A. L., Somes, G. Rivara, F. P., Lee, R. K., & Banton, J. G. (1998). Injuries and deaths due to firearms in the home. *Journal of Trauma, 45,* 263-267. (p. 560)

Kelley, J., & De Graaf, N. D. (1997). National context, parental socialization, and religious belief: Results from 15 nations, *American Sociological Review, 62,* 639–659. (p. 79)

Kelling, S. T., & Halpern, B. P. (1983). Taste flashes: Reaction times, intensity, and quality. *Science, 219,* 412–414. (p. 162)

Kelly, A. E. (2000). Helping construct desirable identities: A self-presentational view of psychotherapy. *Psychological Bulletin, 126,* 475–494. (p. 517)

Kelly, I. W. (1997). Modern astrology: A critique. *Psychological Reports, 81,* 1035–1066. (p. 446)

Kelly, I. W. (1998). Why astrology doesn't work. *Psychological Reports, 82,* 527–546. (p. 446)

Kelly, I. W., Laverty, W. H., & Saklofske, D. (1990). Geophysical variables and behavior: LXIV. An empirical investigation of the relationship between worldwide automobile traffic disasters and lunar cycles: No relationship. *Psychological Reports, 67,* 987–994. (p. C–18)

Kelly, T. A. (1990). The role of values in psychotherapy: A critical review of process and outcome effects. *Clinical Psychology Review, 10,* 171–186. (p. 528)

Kempe, R. S., & Kempe, C. C. (1978). *Child abuse.* Cambridge, MA: Harvard University Press. (p. 113)

Kempermann, G., & Gage, F. H. (1999, May). New nerve cells for the adult brain. *Scientific American,* pp. 48–53. (p. 415)

Kempermann, G., Kuhn, H. G., & Gage, F. H. (May, 1998). *Journal of Neuroscience, 18*(9), 3206–3212. (p. 126)

Kendall-Tackett, K. A., Williams, L. M., & Finkelhor, D. (1993). Impact of sexual abuse on children: A review and synthesis of recent empirical studies. *Psychological Bulletin, 113,* 164–180. (pp. 113, 285)

Kendler, K. S. (1996). Parenting: A genetic-epidemiologic perspective. *The American Journal of Psychiatry, 153,* 11–20. (p. 114)

Kendler, K. S. (1997). Social support: A genetic-epidemiologic analysis. *American Journal of Psychiatry, 154,* 1398–1404. (p. 451)

Kendler, K. S. (January, 1998). Major depression and the environment: A psychiatric genetic perspective. *Pharmacopsychiatry, 31(1),* 5–9. (p. 489)

Kendler, K. S., Jacobson, K. C., Myers, J., & Prescott, C. A. (2002a). Sex differences in genetic and environmental risk factors for irrational fears and phobias. *Psychological Medicine, 32,* 209–217. (p. 482)

Kendler, K. S., Karkowski, L. M., & Prescott, C. A. (1999). Fears and phobias: Reliability and heritability. *Psychological Medicine, 29,* 539–553. (p. 482)

Kendler, K. S., Myers, J., & Prescott, C. A. (2002b). The etiology of phobias: An evaluation of the stress-diathesis model. *Archives of General Psychiatry, 59,* 242–248. (p. 482)

Kendler, K. S., Neale, M. C., Kessler, R. C., Heath, A. C., & Eaves, L. J. (1992). Generalized anxiety disorder in women: A population-based twin study. *Archives of General Psychiatry, 49,* 267–272. (p. 482)

Kendler, K. S., Thornton, L. M., & Gardner, C. O. (2001). Genetic risk, number of previous depressive episodes, and stressful life events in predicting onset of major depression. *American Journal of Psychiatry, 158,* 582–586. (p. 489)

Kennedy, S., & Over, R. (1990). Psychophysiological assessment of male sexual arousal following spinal cord injury. *Archives of Sexual Behavior, 19,* 15–27. (p. 46)

Kenrick, D. T., & Funder, D. C. (1988). Profiting from controversy: Lessons from the person-situation debate. *American Psychologist, 43,* 23–34. (p. 449)

Kenrick, D. T., & Gutierres, S. E. (1980). Contrast effects and judgments of physical attractiveness: When beauty becomes a social problem. *Journal of Personality and Social Psychology, 38,* 131–140. (p. 360)

Kenrick, D. T., Gutierres, S. E., & Goldberg, L. L. (1989). Influence of popular erotica on judgments of strangers and mates. *Journal of Experimental Social Psychology, 25,* 159–167. (p. 360)

Keough, K. A., Zimbardo, P. G., & Boyd, J. N. (1999). Who's smoking, drinking, and using drugs? Time perspective as a predictor of substance use. *Basic and Applied Social Psychology, 2,* 149–164. (p. 431)

Kerr, N. L., & Bruun, S. E. (1983). Dispensability of member effort and group motivation losses: Free-rider effects. *Journal of Personality and Social Psychology, 44,* 78–94. (p. 551)

Kessler, M., & Albee, G. (1975). Primary prevention. *Annual Review of Psychology, 26,* 557–591. (p. 535)

Kessler, R. C. (2000). Posttraumatic stress disorder: The burden to the individual and to society. *Journal of Clinical Psychiatry, 61*(suppl. 5), 4–12. (pp. 480, 481)

Kessler, R. C., Foster, C., Joseph, J., Ostrow, D., Wortman, C., Phair, J., & Chmiel, J. (1991). Stressful life events and symptom onset in HIV infection. *American Journal of Psychiatry, 148,* 733–738. (p. 411)

Kessler, R. C., McGonagle, K. A., Zhao, S., Nelson, C. B., Hughes, M., Eshleman, S., Wittchen, H-U., & Kendler, K. S. (1994). Lifetime and 12-month prevalence of DSM-III-R psychiatric disorders in the United States. *Archives of General Psychiatry, 51,* 8–19. (p. 502)

Kessler, R. C., Soukup, J., Davis, R. B., Foster, D. F., Wilkey, S. A., Van Rompay, M. I., & Eisenberg, D. M. (2001). The use of complementary and alternative therapies to treat anxiety and depression in the United States. *American Journal of Psychiatry, 158,* 289–294. (p. 524)

Kestenbaum, R. (1992). Feeling happy versus feeling good: The processing of discrete and global categories of emotional expressions by children and adults. *Developmental Psychology, 28,* 1132–1142. (p. 387)

Keynes, M. (1980, December 20/27). Handel's illnesses. *The Lancet,* pp. 1354–1355. (p. 488)

Keys, A., Brozek, J., Henschel, A., Mickelsen, O., & Taylor, H. L. (1950). *The biology of human starvation.* Minneapolis: University of Minnesota Press. (p. 345)

Keys, L. (2001, May 27). Once isolated nation falls for TV. Associated Press (*Grand Rapids Press,* p. A14). (p. 250)

Khan, A., Warner, H. A., & Brown, W. A. (2000). Symptom reduction and suicide risk inpatients treated with placebo in antidepressant clinical trials. *Archives of General Psychiatry, 57,* 311–317. (p. 532)

Kiecolt-Glaser, J. K., & Glaser, R. (1995). Psychoneuorimmunology and health consequences: Data and shared mechanisms. *Psychosomatic Medicine, 57,* 269–274. (p. 411)

Kiecolt-Glaser, J. K., & Glaser, R. (2001, February). Stress and immunity: Age enhances the risks. *Current Directions in Psychological Science, 10,* 18–21. (p. 410)

Kiecolt-Glaser, J. K., McGuire, L., Robles, T. F., & Glaser, R. (2002). Emotions, morbidity, and mortality. *Annual Review of Psychology, 53,* 83–107. (p. 410)

Kiecolt-Glaser, J. K., & Newton, T. L. (2001). Marriage and health: His and hers. *Psychological Bulletin, 127,* 472–503. (p. 418)

Kiecolt-Glaser, J. K., Page, G. G., Marucha, P. T., MacCallum, R. C., & Glaser, R. (1998). Psychological influences on surgical recovery: Perspectives from psychoneuroimmunology. *American Psychologist, 53,* 1209–1218. (p. 410)

Kihlstrom, J. F. (1985). Hypnosis. *Annual Review of Psychology, 36,* 385–418. (p. 204)

Kihlstrom, J. F. (1990). Awareness, the psychological unconscious, and the self. Address to the American Psychological Association convention. (p. 281)

Kihlstrom, J. F. (1990). The psychological unconscious. In L. A. Pervin (Ed.), *Handbook of personality: Theory and research.* New York: Guilford Press. (p. 463)

Kihlstrom, J. F. (1994). The social construction of memory. Paper presented at the American Psychological Society convention. (p. 283)

Kihlstrom, J. F. (1997, November 11). Freud as giant pioneer on whose shoulders we should stand. Social Psychology listserv posting (spsp@stolaf.edu). (p. 438)

Kihlstrom, J. F., & McConkey, K. M. (1990). William James and hypnosis: A centennial reflection. *Psychological Science, 1,* 174–177. (p. 208)

Kim, H., & Markus, H. R. (1999). Deviance or uniqueness, harmony or conformity? A cultural analysis. *Journal of Personality and Social Psychology, 77,* 785–800. (p. 462)

Kim, K. H. S., Relkin, N. R., Lee, K-M., & Hirsch, J. (1997). Distinct cortical areas associated with native and second languages. *Nature, 388,* 171–174. (p. 307)

Kim, Y., & Lee, S-H. (1994). The Confucian model of morality, justice, selfhood and society: Implications for modern society. In *The universal and particular natures of Confucianism.* The Academy of Korean Studies. (p. 462)

Kimball, M. M. (1989). A new perspective on women's math achievement. *Psychological Bulletin, 105,* 198–214. (p. 332)

Kimble, G. A. (1956). *Principles of general psychology.* New York: Ronald. (p. 233)

Kimble, G. A. (1981). *Biological and cognitive constraints on learning.* Washington, DC: American Psychological Association. (p. 233)

Kimzey, S. L. (1975). The effects of extended spaceflight on hematologic and immunologic systems. *Journal of the American Medical Women's Association, 30(5),* 218–232. (p. 410)

Kimzey, S. L., Johnson, P. C., Ritzman, S. E., & Mengel, C. E. (1976, April). Hematology and immunology studies: The second manned Skylab mission. *Aviation, Space, and Environmental Medicine,* pp. 383–390. (p. 410)

King, D. W., & King, L. A. (1991). Validity issues in research on Vietnam veteran adjustment. *Psychological Bulletin, 109,* 107–124. (p. 480)

King, R. N., & Koehler, D. J. (2000). Illusory correlations in graphological interference. *Journal of Experimental Psychology: Applied, 6,* 336–348. (p. 446)

Kinnier, R. T., & Metha, A. T. (1989). Regrets and priorities at three stages of life. *Counseling and Values, 33,* 182–193. (p. 132)

Kinsey, A. C., Pomeroy, W., & Martin, C. (1948). *Sexual behavior in the human male.* Philadelphia: Saunders. (p. 357)

Kinsey, A. C., Pomeroy, W., Martin, C., & Gebhard, P. (1953). *Sexual behavior in the human female.* Philadelphia: Saunders. (p. 357)

Kirby, D. (2002). Effective approaches to reducing adolescent unprotected sex, pregnancy, and childbearing. *Journal of Sex Research, 39,* 51–57. (p. 363)

Kirkpatrick, L. (1999). Attachment and religious representations and behavior. In J. Cassidy & P. R. Shaver (1999), *Handbook of attachment.* New York: Guilford. (p. 111)

Kirsch, I. (1996). Hypnotic enhancement of cognitive-behavioral weight loss treatments: Another meta-reanalysis. *Journal of Consulting and Clinical Psychology, 64,* 517–519. (p. 205)

Kirsch, I., & Braffman, W. (2001). Imaginative suggestibility and hypnotizability. *Current Directions in Psychological Science, 10,* 57–61. (p. 204)

Kirsch, I., & Lynn, S. J. (1995). The altered state of hypnosis. *American Psychologist, 50,* 846–858. (p. 208)

Kirsch, I., & Lynn, S. J. (1998a). Dissociation theories of hypnosis. *Psychological Bulletin, 123,* 100–115. (p. 208)

Kirsch, I., & Lynn, S. J. (1998b). Social-cognitive alternatives to dissociation theories of hypnotic induction. *Review of General Psychology, 2,* 66–80. (p. 208)

Kirsch, I., Montgomery, G., & Sapirstein, G. (1995). Hypnosis as an adjunct to cognitive-behavioral psychotherapy: A meta-analysis. *Journal of Consulting and Clinical Psychology, 63,* 214–220. (p. 205)

Kirsch, I., Moore, T. J., Scoboria, A., & Nicholls, S. S. (2002, July 15). New study finds little difference between effects of antidepressants and placebo. *Prevention and Treatment* (journals.apa.org/prevention). (p. 532)

Kirsch, I., & Sapirstein, G. (1998). Listening to Prozac but hearing placebo: A meta-analysis of antidepressant medication. *Prevention and Treatment, 1,* posted June 26 at (journals.apa.org/prevention/volume1). (pp. 25, 532)

Kitayama, S., & Markus, H. R. (2000). The pursuit of happiness and the realization of sympathy: Cultural patterns of self, social relations, and well-being. In E. Diener & E. M. Suh (Eds.), *Subjective well-being across cultures.* Cambridge, MA: MIT Press. (p. 462)

Kivimaki, M., Leino-Arjas, P., Luukkonen, R., Rihimaki, H., & Kirjonen, J. (2002). Work stress and risk of cardiovascular mortality: Prospective cohort study of industrial employees. *British Medical Journal, 325*, 857. (p. 406)

Klasen, S. (1994). "Missing women" reconsidered. *World Development, 22.* (p. 556)

Klayman, J., & Ha, Y-W. (1987). Confirmation, disconfirmation, and information in hypothesis testing. *Psychological Review, 94*, 211–228. (p. 295)

Klein, E., Kreinin, I., Chistyakov, A., Koren, D., Mecz, L., Marmur, S., Ben-Shachar, D., & Feinsod, M. (1999). Therapeutic efficacy of right prefrontal slow repetitive transcranial magnetic stimulation in major depression. *Archives of General Psychiatry, 56*, 315–320. (p. 534)

Klein, S. B., & Kihlstrom, J. F. (1998). On bridging the gap between social-personality psychology and neuropsychology. *Personality and Social Psychology Review, 2* , 228–242. (p. 108)

Kleinfeld, J. (1998). The myth that schools shortchange girls: Social science in the service of deception. Washington, DC: Women's Freedom Network. Available from ERIC, Document ED423210, and via www.uaf.edu/northern/schools/myth.html (p. 332)

Kleinke, C. L. (1986). Gaze and eye contact: A research review. *Psychological Bulletin, 100*, 78–100. (p. 387)

Kleinke, C. L., Peterson, T. R., & Rutledge, T. R. (1998). Effects of self-generated facial expressions on mood. *Journal of Personality and Social Psychology, 74*, 272–279. (p. 392)

Kleinmuntz, B., & Szucko, J. J. (1984). A field study of the fallibility of polygraph lie detection. *Nature, 308*, 449–450. (p. 386)

Kleitman, N. (1960, November). Patterns of dreaming. *Scientific American*, pp. 82–88. (p. 191)

Klemm, W. R. (1990). Historical and introductory perspectives on brainstem-mediated behaviors. In W. R. Klemm & R. P. Vertes (Eds.), *Brainstem mechanisms of behavior.* New York: Wiley. (p. 47)

Kline, D., & Schieber, F. (1985). Vision and aging. In J. E. Birren & K. W. Schaie (Eds.), *Handbook of the psychology of aging.* New York: Van Nostrand Reinhold. (p. 125)

Kline, N. S. (1974). *From sad to glad.* New York: Ballantine Books. (p. 495)

Klineberg, O. (1938). Emotional expression in Chinese literature. *Journal of Abnormal and Social Psychology, 33*, 517–520. (p. 390)

Klineberg, O. (1984). Public opinion and nuclear war. *American Psychologist, 39*, 1245–1253. (p. 577)

Klinke, R., Kral, A., Heid, S., Tillein, J., & Hartmann, R. (1999). Recruitment of the auditory cortex in congenitally deaf cats by long-term cochlear electrostimulation. *Science, 285*, 1729–1733. (p. 176)

Klinkenborg, V. (2002, December 16). Living under the virtual volcano of video games this holiday season. *New York Times* (www.nytimes.com). (p. 567)

Klohnen, E. C., & Bera, S. (1998). Behavioral and experiential patterns of avoidantly and securely attached women across adulthood: A 31-year longitudinal perspective. *Journal of Personality and Social Psychology, 74*, 211–223. (p. 135)

Kluft, R. P. (1991). Multiple personality disorder. In A. Tasman & S. M. Goldfinger (Eds.), *Review of Psychiatry*, (Vol. 10). Washington, DC: American Psychiatric Press. (p. 484)

Klüver, H., & Bucy, P. C. (1939). Preliminary analysis of functions of the temporal lobes in monkeys. *Archives of Neurology and Psychiatry, 42*, 979–1000. (p. 50)

Knapp, S., & VandeCreek, L. (2000, August). Recovered memories of childhood abuse: Is there an underlying professional consensus? *Professional Psychology: Research and Practice, 31*, 365–371. (p. 286)

Knickmeyer, E. (2001, August 7). In Africa, big is definitely better. Associated Press (*Seattle Times*, p. A7). (p. 350)

Koenig, H. (2002, October 9). Personal communication, from Director of Center for the Study of Religion/Spirituality and Health, Duke University. (p. 419)

Koenig, H. G., Cohen, H. J., George, L, K., Hays, J. C., Larson, D. B., & Blazer, D. G. (1997). Attendance at religious services, interleukin-6, and other biological indicators of immune function in older adults. *International Journal of Psychiatry in Medicine, 23*, 233–250. (pp. 423–424)

Koenig, H. G., & Larson, D. B. (1998). Use of hospital services, religious attendance, and religious affiliation. *Southern Medical Journal, 91*, 925–932. (pp. 423–424)

Koestner, R., Lekes, N., Powers, T. A., & Chicoine, E. (2002). Attaining personal goals: Self-concordance plus implementation intentions equals success. *Journal of Personality and Social Psychology, 83*, 231–244. (pp. B–9 to B–10)

Kohlberg, L. (1981). *The philosophy of moral development: Essays on moral development* (Vol. I). San Francisco: Harper & Row. (p. 118)

Kohlberg, L. (1984). *The psychology of moral development: Essays on moral development* (Vol. II). San Francisco: Harper & Row. (p. 118)

Kohler, I. (1962, May). Experiments with goggles. *Scientific American*, pp. 62–72. (p. 177)

Köhler, W. (1925; reprinted 1957). *The mentality of apes.* London: Pelican. (p. 312)

Kohn, A. (1987, October). It's hard to get left out of a pair. *Psychology Today*, pp. 53–57. (p. 577)

Kohn, P. M., & Macdonald, J. E. (1992). The survey of recent life experiences: A decontaminated hassles scale for adults. *Journal of Behavioral Medicine, 15*, 221–236. (p. 405)

Kolata, G. (1986). Youth suicide: New research focuses on a growing social problem. *Science, 233*, 839–841. (p. 490)

Kolata, G. (1987). Metabolic catch-22 of exercise regimens. *Science, 236*, 146–147. (p. 356)

Kolb, B. (1989). Brain development, plasticity, and behavior. *American Psychologist, 44*, 1203–1212. (p. 58)

Kolb, B., & Whishaw, I. Q. (1998). Brain plasticity and behavior. *Annual Review of Psychology, 49*, 43–64. (pp. 58, 83)

Kolers, P. A. (1975). Specificity of operations in sentence recognition. *Cognitive Psychology, 7*, 289–306. (p. 260)

Kolker, K. (2002, December 8). Video violence disturbs some; others scoff at influence. *Grand Rapids Press*, pp. A1, A12. (p. 565)

Kolodziej, M. E., & Johnson, B. T. (1996). Interpersonal contact and acceptance of persons with psychiatric disorders: A research synthesis. *Journal of Consulting and Clinical Psychology, 64*, 1387–1396. (p. 475)

Koltz, C. (1983, December). Scapegoating. *Psychology Today*, pp. 68–69. (p. 558)

Koole, S., & Spijker, M. (2000). Overcoming the planning fallacy through willpower: Effects of implementation intentions on actual and predicted task-completion times. *European Journal of Social Psychology, 30*, 873–888. (pp. B–9 to B–10)

Kopta, S. M., Lueger, R. J., Saunders, S. M., & Howard, K. I. (1999). Individual psychotherapy outcome and process research: Challenges leading to greater turmoil or a positive transition? *Annual Review of Psychology, 30*, 441–469. (p. 522)

Koss, M. P., Heise, L., & Russo, N. P. (1994). The global health burden of rape. *Psychology of Women Quarterly, 18*, 509–537. (p. 563)

Kosslyn, S. M., & Koenig, O. (1992). *Wet mind: The new cognitive neuroscience.* New York: Free Press. (p. 45)

Kosslyn, S. M., Thompson, W. L., Costantini-Ferrando, M. F., Alpert, N. M., & Spiegel, D. (2000). Hypnotic visual illusion alters color processing in the brain. *American Journal of Psychiatry, 157,* 1279–1284. (p. 207)

Kotchick, B. A., Shaffer, A., & Forehand, R. (2001). Adolescent sexual risk behavior: A multi-system perspective. *Clinical Psychology Review, 21,* 493–519. (p. 362)

Kotkin, M., Daviet, C., & Gurin, J. (1996). The *Consumer Reports* mental health survey. *American Psychologist, 51,* 1080–1082. (p. 520)

Kotva, H. J., & Schneider, H. G. (1990). Those "talks"—general and sexual communication between mothers and daughters. *Journal of Social Behavior and Personality, 5,* 603–613. (p. 362)

Kraft, C. (1978). A psychophysical approach to air safety: Simulator studies of visual illusions in night approaches. In H. L. Pick, H. W. Leibowitz, J. E. Singer, A. Steinschneider, & H. W. Stevenson (Eds.), *Psychology: From research to practice.* New York: Plenum Press. (pp. B–12 to B–13)

Kraft, R. (1996, December 2, and 1994, July 20). Personal correspondence (from Otterbein College) regarding Holocaust memories. (p. 438)

Kramer, A. F., Hahn, S., Cohen, N. J., Banich, M. T., McAuley, E., Harrison, C. R., Chason, J., Vakil, E., Bardell, L., Boileau, R. A., & Colcombe, A. (1999). Ageing, fitness and neurocognitive function. *Nature, 400,* 418–419. (p. 126)

Kraus, N., Malmfors, T., & Slovic, P. (1992). Intuitive toxicology: Expert and lay judgments of chemical risks. *Risk Analysis, 12,* 215–232. (p. 300)

Krauss, R. M. (1998). Why do we gesture when we speak? *Current Directions in Psychology, 7,* 54–60. (p. 313)

Kraut, R. E., & Johnston, R. E. (1979). Social and emotional messages of smiling: An ethological approach. *Journal of Personality and Social Psychology, 37,* 1539–1553. (p. 391)

KRC Research & Consulting. (2001, August 7). Memory isn't quite what it used to be (survey for General Nutrition Centers). *USA Today,* p. D1. (p. 127)

Krebs, D. L., & Van Hesteren, F. (1994). The development of altruism: Toward an integrative model. *Developmental Review, 14,* 103–158. (p. 119)

Kreiger, D. (1993). *Accepting your power to heal: The personal practice of therapeutic touch.* Santa Fe, NM: Bear. (p. 524)

Kring, A. M., & Gordon, A. H. (1998). Sex differences in emotion: Expression, experience, and physiology. *Journal of Personality and Social Psychology, 74,* 686–703. (p. 389)

Krosnick, J. A., & Alwin, D. F. (1989). Aging and susceptibility to attitude change. *Journal of Personality and Social Psychology, 57,* 416–425. (p. 135)

Krosnick, J. A., Betz, A. L., Jussim, L. J., & Lynn, A. R. (1992). Subliminal conditioning of attitudes. *Personality and Social Psychology Bulletin, 18,* 152–162. (p. 143)

Kruger, J., & Dunning, D. (1999). Unskilled and unaware of it: How difficulties in recognizing one's own incompetence lead to inflated self-assessments. *Journal of Personality and Social Psychology, 77,* 1121–1134. (p. 455)

Krupa, D. J., Thompson, J. K., & Thompson, R. F. (1993). Localization of a memory trace in the mammalian brain. *Science, 260,* 989–991. (p. 271)

Kubey, R., & Csikszentmihalyi, M. (2002, February). Television addiction is no mere metaphor. *Scientific American,* pp. 74–80. (p. 250)

Kuhl, P. K., & Meltzoff, A. N. (1982). The bimodal perception of speech in infancy. *Science, 218,* 1138–1141. (p. 303)

Kujala, U. M., Kaprio, J., Sarna, S., & Koskenvuo, M. (1998). Relationship of leisure-time physical activity and mortality: The Finnish twin cohort. *Journal of the American Medical Association, 279,* 440–444. (p. 415)

Kulkin, H. S., Chauvin, E. A., & Percle, G. A. (2000). Suicide among gay and lesbian adolescents and young adults: A review of the literature. *Journal of Homosexuality, 40,* 1–29. (p. 365)

Kunkel, D. (2001, February 4). Sex on TV. Menlo Park, CA: Henry J. Kaiser Family Foundation (www.kff.org). (p. 362)

Kunkel, D., Cope-Farrar, K., Biely, E., Farinola, W. J. M., & Donnerstein, E. (2001). *Sex on TV (2): A biennial report to the Kaiser Family Foundation.* Menlo Park, CA: Kaiser Family Foundation. (p. 564)

Kurtz, P. (1983, Spring). Stars, planets, and people. *The Skeptical Inquirer,* pp. 65–68. (p. 447)

Kutas, M. (1990). Event-related brain potential (ERP) studies of cognition during sleep: Is it more than a dream? In R. R. Bootzin, J. F. Kihlstrom, & D. Schacter (Eds.), *Sleep and cognition.* Washington, DC: American Psychological Association. (p. 193)

Labouvie-Vief, G., & Schell, D. A. (1982). Learning and memory in later life. In B. B. Wolman (Ed.), *Handbook of developmental psychology.* Englewood Cliffs, NJ: Prentice-Hall. (p. 128)

Lacayo, R. (1995, June 12). Violent reaction. *Time,* pp. 25–39. (p. 17)

Lachman, M. E., & Weaver, S. L. (1998). The sense of control as a moderator of social class differences in health and well-being. *Journal of Personality and Social Psychology, 74,* 763–773. (p. 452)

Ladd, E. C. (1998, August/September). The tobacco bill and American public opinion. *The Public Perspective,* pp. 5–19. (p. 220)

Ladd, G. T. (1887). *Elements of physiological psychology.* New York: Scribner's. (p. 187)

Laird, J. D. (1974). Self-attribution of emotion: The effects of expressive behavior on the quality of emotional experience. *Journal of Personality and Social Psychology, 29,* 475–486. (p. 392)

Laird, J. D. (1984). The real role of facial response in the experience of emotion: A reply to Tourangeau and Ellsworth, and others. *Journal of Personality and Social Psychology, 47,* 909–917. (p. 392)

Laird, J. D., Cuniff, M., Sheehan, K., Shulman, D., & Strum, G. (1989). Emotion specific effects of facial expressions on memory for life events. *Journal of Social Behavior and Personality, 4,* 87–98. (p. 392)

Lalumière, M. L., Blanchard, R., & Zucker, K. J. (2000). Sexual orientation and handedness in men and women: A meta-analysis. *Psychological Bulletin, 126,* 575–592. (p. 367)

Lambert, W. E. (1992). Challenging established views on social issues: The power and limitations of research. *American Psychologist, 47,* 533–542. (p. 309)

Lambert, W. E., Genesee, F., Holobow, N., & Chartrand, L. (1993). Bilingual education for majority English-speaking children. *European Journal of Psychology of Education, 8,* 3–22. (p. 309)

Lampinen, J. M. (2002). What exactly is déjà vu? *Scientific American* (scieam.com/askexpert/biology/biology63). (p. 274)

Landauer, T. K. (1986). How much do people remember? Some estimates of the quantity of learned information in long-term memory. *Cognitive Science, 10,* 477–493. (p. 267)

Landauer, T. K. (2001, September). Quoted by R. Herbert, You must remember this. *APS Observer,* p. 11. (p. 261)

Landauer, T. K., & Whiting, J. W. M. (1979). Correlates and consequences of stress in infancy. In R. Munroe, B. Munroe & B. Whiting (Eds.), *Handbook of Cross-Cultural Human Development.* New York: Garland. (p. 403)

Landry, M. J. (2002). MDMA: A review of epidemiologic data. *Journal of Psychoactive Drugs, 34,* 163–169. (p. 214)

Langer, E. J. (1983). *The psychology of control.* Beverly Hills, CA: Sage. (p. 453)

Langer, E. J., & Abelson, R. P. (1974). A patient by any other name . . . : Clinician group differences in labeling bias. *Journal of Consulting and Clinical Psychology, 42,* 4–9. (p. 475)

Langer, E. J., & Imber, L. (1980). The role of mindlessness in the perception of deviance. *Journal of Personality and Social Psychology, 39,* 360–367. (p. 475)

Langlois, J. H., Kalakanis, L., Rubenstein, A. J., Larson, A., Hallam, M., & Smoot, M. (2000). Maxims or myths of beauty? A meta-analytic and theoretical review. *Psychological Bulletin, 126,* 390–423. (pp. 569, 570)

Langlois, J. H., Roggman, L. A., Casey, R. J., Ritter, J. M., Rieser-Danner, L. A., & Jenkins, V. Y. (1987). Infant preferences for attractive faces: Rudiments of a stereotype? *Developmental Psychology, 23,* 363–369. (p. 569)

Larkin, K., Resko, J. A., Stormshak, F., Stellflug, J. N., & Roselli, C. E. (2002). Neuroanatomical correlates of sex and sexual partner preference in sheep. Society for Neuroscience convention. (p. 367)

Larsen, R. J., & Diener, E. (1987). Affect intensity as an individual difference characteristic: A review. *Journal of Research in Personality, 21,* 1–39. (p. 79)

Larsen, R. J., Kasimatis, M., & Frey, K. (1992). Facilitating the furrowed brow: An unobtrusive test of the facial feedback hypothesis applied to unpleasant affect. *Cognition and Emotion, 6,* 321–338. (p. 392)

Larson, R. W. (2001). How U.S. children and adolescents spend time: What it does (and doesn't) tell us about their development. *Current Directions in Psychological Science, 10,* 160–164. (p. 122)

Larson, R. W., & Verma, S. (1999). How children and adolescents spend time across the world: Work, play, and developmental opportunities. *Psychological Bulletin, 125,* 701–736. (p. 332)

Larzelere, R. E. (1996). A review of the outcomes of parental use of nonabusive or customary physical punishment. *Pediatrics, 78,* 824–828. (p. 242)

Larzelere, R. E. (1999). The intervention selection bias. Unpublished manuscript. Boys Town, NE: Boys Town. (p. 242)

Larzelere, R. E. (2000). Child outcomes of non-abusive and customary physical punishment by parents: An updated literature review. *Clinical Child and Family Psychology Review, 3,* 199–221. (p. 242)

Lashley, K. S. (1950). In search of the engram. In *Symposium of the Society for Experimental Biology* (Vol. 4). New York: Cambridge University Press. (p. 268)

Lassiter, G. D., & Irvine, A. A. (1986). Video-taped confessions: The impact of camera point of view on judgments of coercion. *Journal of Personality and Social Psychology, 16,* 268–276. (p. 540)

Latané, B. (1981). The psychology of social impact. *American Psychologist, 36,* 343–356. (p. 551)

Latané, B., & Dabbs, J. M., Jr. (1975). Sex, group size and helping in three cities. *Sociometry, 38,* 180–194. (p. 574)

Lau, S., & Gruen, G. E. (1992). The social stigma of loneliness: Effect of target person's and perceiver's sex. *Personality and Social Psychology Bulletin, 18,* 182–189. (p. 494)

Laudenslager, M. L., & Reite, M. L. (1984). Losses and separations: Immunological consequences and health implications. *Review of Personality and Social Psychology, 5,* 285–312. (p. 405)

Laumann, E. O., Gagnon, J. H., Michael, R. T., & Michaels, S. (1994). *The social organization of sexuality: Sexual practices in the United States.* Chicago: University of Chicago Press. (pp. 73, 364, 366, 563)

Lazarus, R. S. (1990). Theory-based stress measurement. *Psychological Inquiry, 1,* 3–13. (p. 405)

Lazarus, R. S. (1991). Progress on a cognitive-motivational-relational theory of emotion. *American Psychologist, 46,* 352–367. (p. 383)

Lazarus. R. S. (1998). *Fifty years of the research and theory of R. S. Lazarus: An analysis of historical and perennial issues.* Mahwah, NJ: Erlbaum. (pp. 383, 402)

Lea, S. E. G. (2000). Towards an ethical use of animals. *The Psychologist, 13,* 556–557. (p. 29)

Leach, P. (1993). Should parents hit their children? *The Psychologist: Bulletin of the British Psychological Society, 6,* 216–220. (p. 243)

Leach, P. (1994). *Children first.* New York: Knopf. (p. 243)

Leary, M. R. (1999). The social and psychological importance of self-esteem. In R. M. Kowalski & M. R. Leary (Eds.), *The social psychology of emotional and behavioral problems.* Washington, DC: APA Books. (p. 457)

Leary, M. R., Haupt, A. L., Strausser, K. S., & Chokel, J. T. (1998). Calibrating the sociometer: The relationship between interpersonal appraisals and state self-esteem. *Journal of Personality and Social Psychology, 74,* 1290–1299. (p. 371)

Leary, M. R., Schreindorfer, L. S., & Haupt, A. L. (1995). The role of low self-esteem in emotional and behavioral problems: Why is low self-esteem dysfunctional? *Journal of Social and Clinical Psychology, 14,* 297–314. (p. 457)

Leary, W. E. (1998, September 28). Older people enjoy sex, survey says. *New York Times* (www.nytimes.com). (p. 125)

Lebow, J. (1982). Consumer satisfaction with mental health treatment. *Psychological Bulletin, 91,* 244–259. (p. 520)

Lederer, R. (1987). *Anguished English.* Charleston, SC: Wyrick & Co. (p. 87)

Le Doux, J. (1996). *The emotional brain: The mysterious underpinnings of emotional life.* New York: Simon & Schuster. (p. 271)

Le Doux, J. E. (2002). *The synaptic self.* London: Macmillan. (p. 84)

Le Doux, J. E. (2002, October 8). Quoted by C. Dreifus, Taking a clinical look at human emotions. *New York Times* (www.nytimes.com). (p. 94)

Le Doux, J. E., & Armony, J. (1999). Can neurobiology tell us anything about human feelings? In D. Dahneman, E. Diener, & N. Schwartz (Eds.), *Well-being: The foundations of hedonic psychology.* New York: Sage. (p. 382)

Lefcourt, H. M. (1982). *Locus of control: Current trends in theory and research.* Hillsdale, NJ: Erlbaum. (p. 452)

Lehman, A. F., Steinwachs, D. M., Dixon, L. B., Goldman, H. H., Osher, F., Postrado, L., Scott, J. E., Thompson, J. W., Fahey, M., Fischer, P., Kasper, J. A., Lyles, A., Skinner, E. A., Buchanan, R., Carpenter, W. T., Jr., Levine, J., McGlynn, E. A., Rosenheck, R., & Zito, J. (1998). Translating research into practice: The schizophrenia patient outcomes research team (PORT) treatment recommendations. *Schizophrenia Bulletin, 24,* 1–10. (p. 530)

Lehman, D. R., & Nisbett, R. E. (1985). Effects of higher education on inductive reasoning. Unpublished manuscript, University of Michigan. (p. 454)

Lehman, D. R., Wortman, C. B., & Williams, A. F. (1987). Long-term effects of losing a spouse or child in a motor vehicle crash. *Journal of Personality and Social Psychology, 52,* 218–231. (p. 133)

Leibowitz, H. W. (1985). Grade crossing accidents and human factors engineering. *American Scientist, 73,* 558–562. (p. 171)

Leigh, B. C. (1989). In search of the seven dwarves: Issues of measurement and meaning in alcohol expectancy research. *Psychological Bulletin, 105,* 361–373. (p. 211)

Leitenberg, H., & Henning, K. (1995). Sexual fantasy. *Psychological Bulletin, 117,* 469–496. (pp. 360, 361)

Lemonick, M. D. (2002, June 3). Lean and hungrier. *Time,* p. 54. (p. 346)

Lennox, B. R., Bert, S., Park, G., Jones, P. B., & Morris, P. G. (1999). Spatial and temporal mapping of neural activity associated with auditory hallucinations. *Lancet, 353,* 644. (p. 55)

Lenzenweger, M. F., Dworkin, R. H., & Wethington, E. (1989). Models of positive and negative symptoms in schizophrenia: An empirical evaluation of latent structures. *Journal of Abnormal Psychology, 98,* 62–70. (p. 530)

Lepper, M. R., Anderson, C. A., & Ross, L. (December, 1980). Perseverance of social theories: The role of explanation in the persistence of discredited information. *Journal of Personality & Social Psychology, 39,* 1037–1049. (p. 301)

Lerner, M. J. (1980). *The belief in a just world: A fundamental delusion.* New York: Plenum Press. (p. 559)

Leserman, J., Jackson, E. D., Petitto, J. M., Golden, R. N., Silva, S. G., Perkins, D. O., Cai, J., Folds, J. D., & Evans, D. L. (1999). Progression to AIDS: The effects of stress, depressive symptoms, and social support. *Psychosomatic Medicine, 61,* 397–406. (p. 411)

LeVay, S. (1991). A difference in hypothalamic structure between heterosexual and homosexual men. *Science, 253,* 1034–1037. (pp. 366–367)

Levenson, R. W. (1992). Autonomic nervous system differences among emotions. *Psychological Science, 3,* 23–27. (p. 385)

Levenson, R. W., Ekman, P., Heider, K., & Friesen, W. V. (1991). Emotion and autonomic nervous system activity in an Indonesian culture. Unpublished manuscript, University of California, Berkeley. (p. 387)

Levenson, R. W., Ekman, P., Heider, K., & Friesen, W. V. (1992). Emotion and autonomic nervous system activity in the Minangkabau of West Sumatra. *Journal of Personality and Social Psychology, 62,* 972–988. (p. 390)

Levin, I. P., & Gaeth, G. J. (1988). How consumers are affected by the framing of attribute information before and after consuming the product. *Journal of Consumer Research, 15,* 374–378. (p. 300)

Levine, J. A., Eberhardt, N. L., & Jensen, M. D. (1999). Role of nonexercise activity thermogenesis in resistance to fat gain in humans. *Science, 283,* 212–214. (p. 347)

Levine, R. V., & Norenzayan, A. (1999). The pace of life in 31 countries. *Journal of Cross-Cultural Psychology, 30,* 178–205. (pp. 19, 87)

Levine, R. V., Sato, S., Hashimoto, T., & Verma, J. (1995). Love and marriage in eleven cultures. *Journal of Cross-Cultural Psychology, 26,* 554–571. (p. 572)

Levy, P. E. (2003). *Industrial/organizational psychology: Understanding the workplace.* Boston: Houghton Mifflin. (p. B–7)

Lewinsohn, P. M., Hoberman, H., Teri, L., & Hautziner, M. (1985). An integrative theory of depression. In S. Reiss & R. Bootzin (Eds.), *Theoretical issues in behavior therapy.* Orlando, FL: Academic Press. (pp. 488, 495)

Lewinsohn, P. M., Rohde, P., & Seeley, J. R. (1998). Major depressive disorder in older adolescents: Prevalence, risk factors, and clinical implications. *Clinical Psychology Review, 18,* 765–794. (p. 488)

Lewinsohn, P. M., & Rosenbaum, M. (1987). Recall of parental behavior by acute depressives, remitted depressives, and nondepressives. *Journal of Personality and Social Psychology, 52,* 611–619. (p. 275)

Lewis, C. S. (1960). *Mere Christianity.* New York: Macmillan. (p. 3)

Lewis, C. S. (1967). *Christian reflections.* Grand Rapids, MI: Eerdmans. (p. 276)

Lewis, D. O., Pincus, J. H., Bard, B., Richardson, E., Prichep, L. S., Feldman, M., & Yeager, C. (1988). Neuropsychiatric, psychoeducational, and family characteristics of 14 juveniles condemned to death in the United States. *American Journal of Psychiatry, 145,* 584–589. (p. 113)

Lewis, D. O., Pincus, J. H., Feldman, M., Jackson, L., & Bard, B. (1986). Psychiatric, neurological, and psychoeducational characteristics of 15 death row inmates in the United States. *American Journal of Psychiatry, 143,* 838–845. (p. 561)

Lewis, D. O., Yeager, C. A., Swica, Y., Pincus, J. H., & Lewis, M. (1997). Objective documentation of child abuse and dissociation in 12 murderers with dissociative identity disorder. *American Journal of Psychiatry, 154,* 1703–1710. (p. 484)

Lewis, M. (1992). Commentary. *Human Development, 35,* 44–51. (p. 275)

Lewontin, R. (1982). *Human diversity.* New York: Scientific American Library. (pp. 71, 332)

Lewy, A. J., Bauer, V. K., Cutler, N, L., Sack, R. L., Ahmed, S., Thomas, K. H., Blood, M. L., & Jackson, J. M. L. (1998). Morning vs evening light treatment of patients with winter depression. *Archives of General Psychiatry, 55,* 890–896. (p. 526)

Li, J. C., Dunning, D., & Malpass, R. L. (1996). Cross-racial identification among European-Americans Basketball fandom and the contact hypothesis. Unpublished manuscript, Cornell University. (p. 559)

Licata, A., Taylor, S., Berman, M., & Cranston, J. (1993). Effects of cocaine on human aggression. *Pharmacology Biochemistry and Behavior, 45,* 549–552. (p. 214)

Lichtman, S. W., Pisarska, K., Berman, E. R., Pestone, M., Dowling, H., Offenbacher, E., Weisel, H., Heshka, S., Matthews, D. E., & Heymsfield, S. B. (1992). Discrepancy between self-reported and actual caloric intake and exercise in obese subjects. *New England Journal of Medicine, 327,* 1893–1898. (p. 354)

Light, K. C., Koepke, J. P., Obrist, P. A., & Willis, P. W., Jr. (1983). Psychological stress induces sodium and fluid retention in men at high risk for hypertension. *Science, 220,* 429–431. (p. 409)

Lilienfeld, S. O. (1998). Pseudoscience in contemporary clinical psychology: What it is and what we can do about it. *The Clinical Psychologist, 51(4),* 3–5. (p. 524)

Lilienfeld, S. O., Lynn, S. J., Kirsch, I., Chaves, J. F., Sarbin, T. R., Ganaway, G. K., & Powell, R. A. (1999). Dissociative identity disorder and the sociocognitive model: Recalling the lessons of the past. *Psychological Bulletin, 125,* 507–523. (p. 484)

Lilienfeld, S. O., Wood, J. M., & Garb, H. N. (2000). The scientific status of projective techniques. *Psychological Science in the Public Interest, 1,* 27–66. (p. 435)

Lilienfeld, S. O., Wood, J. M., & Garb, H. N. (2001, May). What's wrong with this picture? *Scientific American,* pp. 81–87. (p. 435)

Lin, L., Faraco, J., Li, R., Kadotani, H., Rogers, W., Lin, X., Qiu, X., de Jong, P. J., Nishino, S., & Mignot E. (1999). The sleep disorder canine narcolepsy is caused by a mutation in the hypocretin (orexin) receptor 2 gene. *Cell, 98,* 365–376. (p. 199)

Linder, D. (1982). Social trap analogs: The tragedy of the commons in the laboratory. In V. J. Derlega & J. Grzelak (Eds.), *Cooperative and helping behavior: Theories and research.* New York: Academic Press. (p. 567)

Lindskold, S. (1978). Trust development, the GRIT proposal, and the effects of conciliatory acts on conflict and cooperation. *Psychological Bulletin, 85,* 772–793. (p. 578)

Lindskold, S. (1986). GRIT: Reducing distrust through carefully introduced conciliation. In S. Worchel & W. G. Austin (Eds.), *Psychology of intergroup relations* (2nd ed.). Chicago: Nelson-Hall. (p. 578)

Lindskold, S., & Han, G. (1988). GRIT as a foundation for integrative bargaining. *Personality and Social Psychology Bulletin, 14,* 335–345. (p. 578)

Lindskold, S., Han, G., & Betz, B. (1986). Repeated persuasion in interpersonal conflict. *Journal of Personality and Social Psychology, 51,* 1183–1188. (p. 578)

Lindskold, S., Walters, P. S., & Koutsourais, H. (1983). Cooperators, competitors, and response to GRIT. *Journal of Conflict Resolution, 27,* 521–532. (p. 578)

Linville, P. W., Fischer, G. W., & Fischhoff, B. (1992). AIDS risk perceptions and decision biases. In J. B. Pryor & G. D. Reeder (Eds.), *The social psychology of HIV infection.* Hillsdale, NJ: Erlbaum. (p. 300)

Lippa, R. A. (2002). Gender-related traits of heterosexual and homosexual men and women. *Archives of Sexual Behavior, 31,* 83–98. (p. 367)

Lippman, J. (1992, October 25). Global village is characterized by a television in every home. *Los Angeles Times* Syndicate (in *Grand Rapids Press,* p. F9. (p. 250)

Lipps, H. M. (1999). *A new psychology of women: Gender, culture, and ethnicity.* Mountain View, CA: Mayfield Publishing. (p. 556)

Livingstone, M., & Hubel, D. (1988). Segregation of form, color, movement, and depth: Anatomy, physiology, and perception. *Science, 240,* 740–749. (p. 152)

Locke, E. A., & Latham, G. P. (2002). Building a practically useful theory of goal setting and task motivation. *American Psychologist, 57,* 705–717. (p. B–9)

Loehlin, J. C., McCrae, R. R., & Costa, P. T., Jr. (1998). Heritabilities of common and measure-specific components of the Big Five personality factors. *Journal of Research in Personality, 32,* 431–453. (p. 448)

Loehlin, J. C., & Nichols, R. C. (1976). *Heredity, environment, and personality.* Austin: University of Texas Press. (p. 76)

Loewenstein, G., & Furstenberg, F. (1991). Is teenage sexual behavior rational? *Journal of Applied Social Psychology, 21,* 957–986. (p. 240)

Loftus, E. F. (1979). The malleability of human memory. *American Scientist, 67,* 313–320. (p. 282)

Loftus, E. F. (1980). *Memory: Surprising new insights into how we remember and why we forget.* Reading, MA: Addison-Wesley. (pp. 204–205)

Loftus, E. F. (1993). The reality of repressed memories. *American Psychologist, 48,* 518–537. (p. 287)

Loftus, E. (1995, March/April). Remembering dangerously. *Skeptical Inquirer,* pp. 20–29. (p. 437)

Loftus, E. F. (2001, November). Imagining the past. *The Psychologist, 14,* 584–587. (p. 282)

Loftus, E. F., Coan, J., & Pickrell, J. E. (1996). Manufacturing false memories using bits of reality. In L. Reder (Ed.), *Implicit memory and metacognition.* Mahway, NJ: Erlbaum. (p. 286)

Loftus, E. F., & Ketcham, K. (1994). *The myth of repressed memory.* New York: St. Martin's Press. (pp. 267, 268, 286)

Loftus, E. F., Levidow, B., & Duensing, S. (1992). Who remembers best? Individual differences in memory for events that occurred in a science museum. *Applied Cognitive Psychology, 6,* 93–107. (p. 282)

Loftus, E. F., & Loftus, G. R. (1980). On the permanence of stored information in the human brain. *American Psychologist, 35,* 409–420. (p. 267)

Loftus, E. F., Milo, E. M., & Paddock, J. R. (1995). The accidental executioner: Why psychotherapy must be informed by science. *The Counseling Psychologist, 23,* 300–309. (p. 285)

Loftus, E. F., & Palmer, J. C. (October, 1974). Reconstruction of automobile destruction: An example of the interaction between language and memory. *Journal of Verbal Learning & Verbal Behavior, 13(5),* 585–589. (pp. 281–282)

Loftus, G. R. (1992). When a lie becomes memory's truth: Memory distortion after exposure to misinformation. *Current Directions in Psychological Science, 1,* 121–123. (p. 282)

Logue, A. W. (1998a). Laboratory research on self-control: Applications to administration. *Review of General Psychology, 2,* 221–238. (p. 240)

Logue, A. W. (1998b). Self-control. In W. T. O'Donohue, (Eds.), *Learning and behavior therapy.* Boston, MA: Allyn & Bacon. (p. 240)

Lohr, J. M., Lilienfeld, S. O., Tolin, D. F., & Herbert, J. D. (1999). Eye movement desensitization and reprocessing: An analysis of specific versus nonspecific treatment factors. *Journal of Anxiety Disorders, 13,* 185–207. (p. 525)

London, P. (1970). The rescuers: Motivational hypotheses about Christians who saved Jews from the Nazis. In J. Macaulay & L. Berkowitz (Eds.), *Altruism and helping behavior.* New York: Academic Press. (p. 250)

Long, R., Bernhardt, P., & Evans, W. (1999). Perception of conventional sensory cues as an alternative to the postulated 'human energy field' of therapeutic touch. *Scientific Review of Alternative Medicine, 3(2),* (http://www.hcrc.org/contrib/long/sram-tt.html). (p. 525)

Looy, H. (2001). Sex differences: Evolved, constructed, and designed. *Journal of Psychology and Theology, 29,* 301–313. (p. 75)

Lopez, A. D. (1999). Measuring the health hazards of tobacco: Commentary. *Bulletin of the World Health Organization, 77(1),* 82–83. (p. 212)

Lord, C. G., Lepper, M. R., & Preston, E. (1984). Considering the opposite: A corrective strategy for social judgment. *Journal of Personality and Social Psychology, 47,* 1231–1247. (p. 301)

Lord, C. G., Ross, L., & Lepper, M. (1979). Biased assimilation and attitude polarization: The effects of prior theories on subsequently considered evidence. *Journal of Personality and Social Psychology, 37,* 2098–2109. (p. 301)

Lorenz, K. (1937). The companion in the bird's world. *Auk, 54,* 245–273. (p. 111)

Los Angeles Times (1998, 14 March). Daughters give birth on same day. P. A15. (p. 22)

Louie, K., & Wilson, M. A. (2001). Temporally structured replay of awake hippocampal ensemble activity during rapid eye movement sleep. *Neuron, 29,* 145–156. (p. 202)

Lourenco, O., & Machado, A. (1996). In defense of Piaget's theory: A reply to 10 common criticisms. *Psychological Review, 103,* 143–164. (p. 109)

Lovaas, O. I. (1987). Behavioral treatment and normal educational and intellectual functioning in young autistic children. *Journal of Consulting and Clinical Psychology, 55,* 3–9. (p. 515)

Love, S. M. (2002, July 16). Preventive medicine, properly practiced. *New York Times* (www.nytimes.com). (p. 25)

Lowry, P. E. (1997). The assessment center process: New directions. *Journal of Social Behavior and Personality, 12,* 53–62. (p. 455)

Lu, Z.-L., Williamson, S. J., & Kaufman, L. (1992). Behavioral lifetime of human auditory sensory memory predicted by physiological measures. *Science, 258,* 1668–1670. (p. 266)

Lubinski, D., & Benbow, C. P. (1992). Gender differences in abilities and preferences among the gifted: Implications for the math-science pipeline. *Current Directions in Psychological Science, 1,* 61–66. (p. 332)

Lubinski, D., & Benbow, C. P. (2000). States of excellence. *American Psychologist,* 137–150. (p. 324)

Lubinski, D., Webb, R. M., Morelock, M. J., & Benbow, C. P. (2001). Top 1 in 10,000: A 10-year follow-up of the profoundly gifted. *Journal of Applied Psychology, 86,* 718–729. (p. 324)

Luborsky, L., Rosenthal, R., Diguer, L., Andrusyna, T. P., Berman, J. S., Levitt, J. T., Seligman, D. A., & Krause, E. D. (2002). The dodo bird verdict is alive and well—mostly. *Clinical Psychology: Science and Practice, 9,* 2–34. (p. 523)

Lucas, A., Morley, R., & Cole, T. J. (1998). Randomised trial of early diet in preterm babies and later intelligence quotient. *British Medical Journal, 317,* 1481–1487. (p. 24)

Lucas, A., Morley, R., Cole, T. J., Lister, G., & Leeson-Payne, C. (1992). Breast milk and subsequent intelligence quotient in children born preterm. *Lancet, 339,* 261–264. (p. 24)

Ludwig, A. M. (1995). *The price of greatness: Resolving the creativity and madness controversy.* New York: Guilford Press. (pp. 366, 488)

Lukoff, D., Lu, F., & Turner, R. (1992). Toward a more culturally sensitive DSM-IV: Psychoreligious and psychospiritual problems. *Journal of Nervous and Mental Disease, 180,* 673–682. (p. 528)

Luria, A. M. (1968). In L. Solotaroff (Trans.), *The mind of a mnemonist.* New York: Basic Books. (p. 258)

Lykken, D. T. (1991). Science, lies, and controversy: An epitaph for the polygraph. Invited address upon receipt of the Senior Career Award for Distinguished Contribution to Psychology in the Public Interest, American Psychological Association convention. (p. 386)

Lykken, D. T. (1995). *The antisocial personalities.* Hillsdale, NJ: Erlbaum. (p. 485)

Lykken, D. T. (1999). *Happiness.* New York: Golden Books. (p. 326)

Lykken, D. T. (2001). Happiness—stuck with what you've got? *The Psychologist, 14,* 470–473. (p. 78)

Lykken, D. T., & Tellegen, A. (1996). Happiness is a stochastic phenomenon. *Psychological Science, 7*, 186–189. (p. 401)

Lyman, D. R. (1996). Early identification of chronic offenders: Who is the fledgling psychopath? *Psychological Bulletin, 120*, 209–234. (p. 486)

Lynch, G., & Staubli, U. (1991). Possible contributions of long-term potentiation to the encoding and organization of memory. *Brain Research Reviews, 16*, 204–206. (p. 269)

Lynch, J. W., Kaplan, G. A., Pamuk, E. R., Cohen, R. D., Heck, K. E., Balfour, J. L., & Yen, I. H. (1998). Income inequality and mortality in metropolitan areas of the United States. *American Journal of Public Health, 88*, 1074–1080. (p. 406)

Lynch, J. W., Smith, G. D., Kaplan, G. A., & House, J. S. (2000). Income inequality and health: A neo-material interpretation. *British Medical Journal, 320*, 1200–1204. (p. 406)

Lynn, M. (1988). The effects of alcohol consumption on restaurant tipping. *Personality and Social Psychology Bulletin, 14*, 87–91. (p. 210)

Lynn, R. (1987). Japan: Land of the rising IQ. A reply to Flynn. *Bulletin of the British Psychological Society, 40*, 464–468. (p. 331)

Lynn, R. (1991, Fall/Winter). The evolution of racial differences in intelligence. *The Mankind Quarterly, 32*, 99–145. (p. 331)

Lynn, S. J., & Rhue, J. W. (1986). The fantasy-prone person: Hypnosis, imagination, and creativity. *Journal of Personality and Social Psychology, 51*, 404–408. (p. 204)

Lynn, S. J., Rhue, J. W., & Weekes, J. R. (1990). Hypnotic involuntariness: A social cognitive analysis. *Psychological Review, 97*, 169–184. (p. 206)

Lyons, L. (2002, June 25). Are spiritual teens healthier? *Gallup Tuesday Briefing*, Gallup Organization (www.gallup.com/poll/tb/religValue/20020625b.asp). (p. 423)

Lytton, H., & Romney, D. M. (1991). Parents' differential socialization of boys and girls: A meta-analysis. *Psychological Bulletin, 109*, 267–296. (p. 92)

Lyubomirsky, S. (2001). Why are some people happier than others? The role of cognitive and motivational processes in well-being. *American Psychologist, 56*, 239–249. (p. 399)

Lyubomirsky, S., King, L. A., & Diener, E. (2002). Is happiness a good thing? The benefits of long-term positive affect. Unpublished manuscript, Department of Psychology, University of California, Riverside. (p. 395)

Ma, L. (1997, September). On the origin of Darwin's ills. *Discover*, p. 27. (p. 477)

Maas, J. B. (1999). *Power sleep. The revolutionary program that prepares your mind for peak performance.* New York: HarperCollins. (pp. 195, 196, 198)

Macaluso, E., Frith, C. D., & Driver, J. (2000). Modulation of human visual cortex by crossmodal spatial attention. *Science, 289*, 1206–1208. (p. 162)

Macan, T. H., & Dipboye, R. L. (1994). The effects of the application on processing of information from the employment interview. *Journal of Applied Social Psychology, 24*, 1291. (p. B–5)

Maccoby, E. E. (1990). Gender and relationships: A developmental account. *American Psychologist, 45*, 513–520. (p. 121)

Maccoby, E. E. (1995). Divorce and custody: The rights, needs, and obligations of mothers, fathers, and children. *Nebraska Symposium on Motivation, 42*, 135–172. (p. 91)

Maccoby, E. E. (1998). *The paradox of gender.* Cambridge, MA: Harvard University Press. (p. 121)

Maccoby, E. E. (2002). Gender and group process: A developmental perspective. *Current Directions in Psychological Science, 11*, 54–58. (p. 552)

MacDonald, N. (1960). Living with schizophrenia. *Canadian Medical Association Journal, 82*, 218–221. (p. 497)

MacDonald, T. K., Fong, G. T., Zanna, M. P., & Martineau, A. M. (2000). Alcohol myopia and condom use: Can alcohol intoxication be asso-

ciated with more prudent behavior? *Journal of Personality and Social Psychology, 78*, 605–619. (p. 211)

MacDonald, T. K., Zanna, M. P., & Fong, G. T. (1995). Decision making in altered states: Effects of alcohol on attitudes toward drinking and driving. *Journal of Personality and Social Psychology, 68*, 973–985. (p. 210)

MacDonald, T. K., Zanna, M. P., & Fong, G. T. (1996). Why common sense goes out the window: The effects of alcohol on intentions to use condoms. *Personality and Social Psychology Bulletin, 22*, 763–775. (p. 211)

MacFarlane, A. (1978, February). What a baby knows. *Human Nature*, pp. 74–81. (p. 102)

Macfarlane, J. W. (1964). Perspectives on personality consistency and change from the guidance study. *Vita Humana, 7*, 115–126. (p. 115)

MacKay, D. G. (1983). Prescriptive grammar and the pronoun problem. In B. Thorne, C. Kramarae, & N. Henley (Eds.), *Language, gender and society.* Rowley, MA: Newbury House. (p. 309)

MacKinnon, D. W., & Hall, W. B. (1972). Intelligence and creativity. In *Proceedings, XVIIth International Congress of Applied Psychology* (Vol. 2). Brussels: Editest. (p. 321)

MacLeod, C., & Campbell, L. (1992). Memory accessibility and probability judgments: An experimental evaluation of the availability heuristic. *Journal of Personality and Social Psychology, 63*, 890–902. (p. 297)

MacNeilage, P. F., & Davis, B. L. (2000). On the origin of internal structure of word forms. *Science, 288*, 527–531. (p. 303)

Maes, H. H. M., Neale, M. C., & Eaves, L. J. (1997). Genetic and environmental factors in relative body weight and human adiposity. *Behavior Genetics, 27*, 325–351. (p. 354)

Magnusson, D. (1990). Personality research—challenges for the future. *European Journal of Personality, 4*, 1–17. (p. 485)

Mahowald, M. W., & Ettinger, M. G. (1990). Things that go bump in the night: The parsomias revisted. *Journal of Clinical Neurophysiology, 7*, 119–143. (p. 192)

Maier, S. F., Watkins, L. R., & Fleshner, M. (1994). Psychoneuroimmunology: The interface between behavior, brain, and immunity. *American Psychologist, 49*, 1004–1017. (p. 410)

Major, B., Carrington, P. I., & Carnevale, P. J. D. (1984). Physical attractiveness and self-esteem: Attribution for praise from an other-sex evaluator. *Personality and Social Psychology Bulletin, 10*, 43–50. (p. 570)

Malamuth, N. M. (1996). Sexually explicit media, gender differences, and evolutionary theory. *Journal of Communication, 46*, 8–31. (p. 563)

Malamuth, N. M., & Check, J. V. P. (1981). The effects of media exposure on acceptance of violence against women: A field experiment. *Journal of Research in Personality, 15*, 436–446. (p. 360)

Malamuth, N. M., Linz, D., Heavey, C. L., Barnes, G., & Acker, M. (1995). Using the confluence model of sexual aggression to predict men's conflict with women: A 10-year follow-up study. *Journal of Personality and Social Psychology, 69*, 353–369. (p. 564)

Malamuth, N. M., Sockloskie, R. J., Koss, M. P., & Tanaka, J. S. (1991). Characteristics of aggressors against women: Testing a model using a national sample of college students. *Journal of Consulting and Clinical Psychology, 59*, 670–681. (p. 564)

Malan, D. H. (1978). "The case of the secretary with the violent father." In H. Davanloo (Ed.), *Basic principles and techniques in short-term dynamic psychotherapy.* New York: Spectrum. (p. 509)

Malaspina, D., Harlap, S., Fennig, S., Heiman, D., Nahon, D., Feldman, D., & Susser, E. S. (2001). Advancing paternal age and the risk of schizophrenia. *Archives of General Psychiatry, 58*, 361–367. (p. 500)

Malinosky-Rummell, R., & Hansen, D. J. (1993). Long-term consequences of childhood physical abuse. *Psychological Bulletin, 114*, 68–79. (p. 113)

Malkiel, B. (1985). *A random walk down Wall Street* (4th ed.). New York: Norton. (p. 298)

Malkiel, B. G. (1989). Is the stock market efficient? *Science, 243,* 1313–1318. (p. 23)

Malkiel, B. G. (1995, June). Returns from investing in equity mutual funds 1971 to 1991. *Journal of Finance,* pp. 549–572. (pp. 23, 298)

Malkoff-Schwartz, S., Frank, E., Anderson, B., Sherrill, J. T., Siegel, L., Patterson, D., & Kupfer, D. J. (1998). Stressful life events and social rhythm disruption in the onset of manic and depressive bipolar episodes. *Archives of General Psychiatry, 55,* 702–707. (p. 488)

Malloy, E. A. (1994, June 7). Report of the Commission on Substance Abuse at Colleges and Universities, reported by *Associated Press.* (p. 211)

Malmquist, C. P. (1986). Children who witness parental murder: Post-traumatic aspects. *Journal of the American Academy of Child Psychiatry, 25,* 320–325. (p. 437)

Malnic, B., Hirono, J., Sato, T., & Buck, L. B. (1999). Combinatorial receptor codes for odors. *Cell, 96,* 713–723. (p. 163)

Manber, R., Bootzin, R. R., Acebo, C., & Carskadon, M. A. (1996). The effects of regularizing sleep-wake schedules on daytime sleepiness. *Sleep, 19,* 432–441. (p. 198)

Mandel, D. (1983, March 13). One man's holocaust: Part II. The story of David Mandel's journey through hell as told to David Kagan. *Wonderland Magazine (Grand Rapids Press),* pp. 2–7. (p. 341)

Manson, J. E. (2002). Walking compared with vigorous exercise for the prevention of cardiovascular events in women. *New England Journal of Medicine, 347,* 716–725. (p. 415)

Maquet, P. (2001). The role of sleep in learning and memory. *Science, 294,* 1048–1052. (p. 202)

Maquet, P., Peters, J-M., Aerts, J., Delfiore, G., Degueldre, C., Luxen, A., & Franck, G. (1996). Functional neuroanatomy of human rapid-eye-movement sleep and dreaming. *Nature, 383,* 163–166. (p. 203)

Marangell, L. B., Rush, A. J., George, M. S., Sackeim, H. A., Johnson, C. R., Husain, M. M., Nahas, Z., & Lisanby, S. H. (2002). Vagus nerve stimulation (VNS) for major depressive episodes: One year outcomes. *Biological Psychiatry, 51,* 280–287. (pp. 533–534)

Marcus, G. F., Vijayan, S., Rao, S. B., & Vishton, P. M. (1999). Rule learning by seven-month-old infants. *Science, 283,* 77–80. (p. 306)

Margolis, M. L. (2000). Brahms' lullaby revisited: Did the composer have obstructive sleep apnea? *Chest, 118,* 210–213. (p. 199)

Markowitsch, H. J. (1995). Which brain regions are critically involved in the retrieval of old episodic memory? *Brain Research Reviews, 21,* 117–127. (p. 271)

Markowitz, J. C., Svartberg, M., & Swartz, H. A. (1998). Is IPT time-limited psychodynamic psychotherapy? *Journal of Psychotherapy Practice and Research, 7,* 185–195. (p. 510)

Markus, G. B. (1986). Stability and change in political attitudes: Observe, recall, and "explain." *Political Behavior, 8,* 21–44. (p. 283)

Markus, H. (2001, October 7). Culture and the good life. Address to the Positive Psychology Summit conference, Washington, DC. (p. 462)

Markus, H., & Kitayama, S. (1991). Culture and the self: Implications for cognition, emotion, and motivation. *Psychological Review, 98,* 224–253. (pp. 308, 391, 394, 462)

Markus, H., & Nurius, P. (1986). Possible selves. *American Psychologist, 41,* 954–969. (p. 457)

Marlatt, G. A. (1991). Substance abuse: Etiology, prevention, and treatment issues. Master lecture, American Psychological Association convention. (pp. 211, 240)

Marmot, M. G., Bosma, H., Hemingway, H., Brunner, E., & Stansfeld, S. (1997). Contribution fo job control and other risk factors to social variations in coronary heart disease incidents. *Lancet, 350,* 235–239. (p. 406)

Marmot, M. G., & Wilkinson, R. G. (Eds.) (1999). *Social determinants of health.* Oxford: Oxford University Press. (p. 406)

Marschark, M., Richman, C. L., Yuille, J. C., & Hunt, R. R. (1987). The role of imagery in memory: On shared and distinctive information. *Psychological Bulletin, 102,* 28–41. (p. 263)

Marsh, H. W., & Parker, J. W. (1984). Determinants of student self-concept: Is it better to be a relatively large fish in a small pond even if you don't learn to swim as well? *Journal of Personality and Social Psychology, 47,* 213–231. (p. 400)

Marshall, M. J. (2002). *Why spanking doesn't work.* Springville, UT: Bonneville Books. (p. 242)

Marteau, T. M. (1989). Framing of information: Its influences upon decisions of doctors and patients. *British Journal of Social Psychology, 28,* 89–94. (p. 300)

Martin, C. L., Ruble, D. N., & Szkrybalo, J. (2002). Cognitive theories of early gender development. *Psychological Bulletin, 128,* 903–933. (p. 92)

Martin, R. J., White, B. D., & Hulsey, M. G. (1991). The regulation of body weight. *American Scientist, 79,* 528–541. (p. 347)

Martin, S. J., Kelly, I. W., & Saklofske, D. H. (1992). Suicide and lunar cycles: A critical review over 28 years. *Psychological Reports, 71,* 787–795. (pp. 501, C–18)

Maruta, T., Colligan, R. C., Malinchoc, M., & Offord, K. P. (2002). Optimism-pessimism assessed in the 1960s and self-reported health status 30 years later. *Mayo Clinic Proceedings, 77,* 748–753. (p. 407)

Maslow, A. H. (1970). *Motivation and personality* (2nd ed.). New York: Harper & Row. (pp. 343–344, 439)

Maslow, A. H. (1971). *The farther reaches of human nature.* New York: Viking Press. (p. 343)

Mason, C., & Kandel, E. R. (1991). Central visual pathways. In E. R. Kandel, J. H. Schwartz, & T. M. Jessell, *Principles of neural science* (3rd ed.). New York: Elsevier. (p. 43)

Masse, L. C., & Tremblay, R. E. (1997). Behavior of boys in kindergarten and the onset of substance use during adolescence. *Archives of General Psychiatry, 54,* 62–68. (p. 218)

Masten, A. S. (2001). Ordinary magic: Resilience processes in development. *American Psychologist, 56,* 227–238. (p. 113)

Masters, W. H., & Johnson, V. E. (1966). *Human sexual response.* Boston: Little, Brown. (p. 358)

Mastroianni, G. R. (2002). Milgram and the Holocaust: A reexamination. *Journal of Theoretical and Philosophical Psychology, 22,* 158–173. (p. 549)

Matarazzo, J. D. (1983). Computerized psychological testing. *Science, 221,* 323. (p. 445)

Matsumoto, D. (1994). *People: Psychology from a cultural perspective.* Pacific Grove, CA: Brooks/Cole. (p. 308)

Matsumoto, D., & Ekman, P. (1989). American-Japanese cultural differences in intensity ratings of facial expressions of emotion. *Motivation and Emotion, 13,* 143–157. (p. 391)

Matsumoto, D., Kudoh, T., Scherer, K., & Wallbott, H. (1988). Antecedents of and reactions to emotions in the United States and Japan. *Journal of Cross-Cultural Psychology, 19,* 267–286. (p. 391)

Matthews, D. A., & Larson, D. B. (1997). *The faith factor: An annotated bibliography of clinical research on spiritual subjects,* Vol. I-IV. Rockville, MD: National Institute for Healthcare Research and Georgetown University Press. (p. 422)

Matthews, K. A. (1992). Myths and realities of the menopause. *Psychosomatic Medicine, 54,* 1–9. (p. 125)

Maurer, D., Lewis, T. L., Brent, H. P., & Levin, A. V. (1999). Rapid improvement in the acuity of infants after visual input. *Science, 286,* 108–110. (p. 176)

Maurer, D., & Maurer, C. (1988). *The world of the newborn.* New York: Basic Books. (p. 101)

May, C., & Hasher, L. (1998). Synchrony effects in inhibitory control over thought and action. *Journal of Experimental Psychology: Human Perception and Performance, 24,* 363–380. (p. 190)

May, C. P., Hasher, L., & Stoltzfus, E. R. (1993). Optimal time of day and the magnitude of age differences in memory. *Psychological Science, 4,* 326–330. (p. 128)

Mazure, C., Keita, G., & Blehar, M. (2002). *Summit on women and depression: Proceedings and recommendations.* Washington, DC: American Psychological Association (www.apa.org/pi/wpo/women&depression.pdf). (p. 492)

Mazzuca, J. (2002, July 2). Same-sex parenting: Does public back Rosie? The Gallup Organization (www.gallup.com/poll/tb/religValue/20020702.asp). (p. 368)

Mazzuca, J. (2002, August 20). Teens shrug off movie sex and violence. *Gallup Tuesday Briefing* (www.gallup.com/poll/tb/educayouth/20020820b.asp). (p. 252)

McAneny, L. (1996, September). Large majority think government conceals information about UFO's. *Gallup Poll Monthly,* pp. 23–26. (p. 274)

McBurney, D. H. (1996). *How to think like a psychologist: Critical thinking in psychology.* Upper Saddle River, NJ: Prentice-Hall. (p. 55)

McBurney, D. H., & Collings, V. B. (1984). *Introduction to sensation and perception* (2nd ed.). Englewood Cliffs, NJ: Prentice-Hall. (pp. 174–175)

McBurney, D. H., & Gent, J. F. (1979). On the nature of taste qualities. *Psychological Bulletin, 86,* 151–167. (p. 162)

McCall, R. B. (1994). Academic underachievers. *Current Directions in Psychological Science, 3,* 15–19. (p. 373)

McCall, R. B., Evahn, C., & Kratzer, L. (1992). High school underachievers. Newbury Park, CA: Sage. (p. 332)

McCann, I. L., & Holmes, D. S. (1984). Influence of aerobic exercise on depression. *Journal of Personality and Social Psychology, 46,* 1142–1147. (p. 414)

McCann, U. D., Eligulashvili, V., & Ricaurte, G. A. (2001). (+-)3,4-Methylenedioxymethamphetamine ('Ecstasy')-induced serotonin neurotoxicity: Clinical studies. *Neuropsychobiology, 42,* 11–16. (p. 215)

McCarthy, P. (1986, July). Scent: The tie that binds? *Psychology Today,* pp. 6, 10. (p. 163)

McCaul, K. D., & Malott, J. M. (1984). Distraction and coping with pain. *Psychological Bulletin, 95,* 516–533. (p. 161)

McCauley, C. R. (2002). Psychological issues in understanding terrorism and the response to terrorism. In C. E. Stout (Ed.), *The psychology of terrorism, Vol. 3.* Westport, CT: Praeger/Greenwood. (pp. 552–553)

McCauley, C. R., & Segal, M. E. (1987). Social psychology of terrorist groups. In C. Hendrick (Ed.), *Group processes and intergroup relations.* Beverly Hills, CA: Sage. (pp. 552–553)

McClearn, G. E., Johansson, B., Berg, S., Pedersen, N. L., Ahern, F., Petrill, S. A., & Plomin, R. (1997). Substantial genetic influence on cognitive abilities in twins 80 or more years old. *Science, 276,* 1560–1563. (p. 328)

McClintock, M. K., & Herdt, G. (December, 1996). Rethinking puberty: The development of sexual attraction. *Current Directions in Psychological Science, 5(6),* 178–183. (p. 116)

McCloskey, M., Wible, C. G., & Cohen, N. J. (1988). Is there a special flashbulb-memory mechanism? *Journal of Experimental Psychology: General, 117,* 171–181. (p. 258)

McClure, E. B. (2000). A meta-analytic review of sex differences in facial expression processing and their development in infants, children, and adolescents. *Psychological Bulletin, 126,* 424–453. (p. 334)

McConkey, K. M. (1995). Hypnosis, memory, and the ethics of uncertainty. *Australian Psychologist, 30,* 1–10. (p. 205)

McConnell, R. A. (1991). National Academy of Sciences opinion on parapsychology. *Journal of the American Society for Psychical Research, 85,* 333–365. (p. 178)

McCool, G. (1999, October 26). Mirror-gazing Venezuelans top of vanity stakes. *Toronto Star* (via web.lexis-nexis.com). (p. 569)

McCormick, C. M., & Witelson, S. F. (1991). A cognitive profile of homosexual men compared to heterosexual men and women. *Psychoneuroendocrinology, 16,* 459–473. (p. 367)

McCrae, R. R. (2001). Trait psychology and culture. *Journal of Personality, 69,* 819–846. (p. 448)

McCrae, R. R., & Costa, P. T., Jr. (1986). Clinical assessment can benefit from recent advances in personality psychology. *American Psychologist, 41,* 1001–1003. (p. 448)

McCrae, R. R., & Costa, P. T., Jr. (1990). *Personality in adulthood.* New York: Guilford. (p. 130)

McCrae, R. R., & Costa, P. T., Jr. (1994). The stability of personality: Observations and evaluations. *Current Directions in Psychological Science, 3,* 173–175. (pp. 135, 449)

McCrae, R. R., & Costa, P. T., Jr. (1999). A five-factor theory of personality. In L. A. Pervin & O. P. John (Eds.), *Handbook of personality: Theory and research.* New York: Guilford. (p. 448)

McCrae, R. R., Costa, P. T., Jr., de Lirna, M. P., Simoes, A., Ostendorf, F., Angleitner, A., Marusic, I., Bratko, D., Caprara, G. V., Barbaranelli, C., Chae, J-H., & Piedmont, R. L. (1999). Age differences in personality across the adult life span: Parallels in five cultures. *Developmental Psychology, 35,* 466–477. (p. 448)

McCrae, R. R., Costa, P. T., Jr., Ostendorf, F., Angleitner, A., Hrebickova, M., Avia, M. D., Sanz, J., Sanchez-Bernardos, M. L., Kusdil, M. E., Woodfield, R., Saunders, P. R., & Smith, P. B. (2000). Nature over nurture: Temperament, personality, and life span development. *Journal of Personality and Social Psychology, 78,* 173–186. (p. 80)

McCullough, M. E., Hoyt, W. T., Larson, D. B., Koenig, H. G., & Thoresen, C. (2000). Religious involvement and mortality: A meta-analytic review. *Health Psychology, 19,* 211–222. (p. 422)

McDaniel, M. A., Maier, S. F., & Einstein, G. O. (2002). "Brain-specific" nutrients: A memory cure? *Psychological Science in the Public Interest, 3,* 12–38. (p. 269)

McEwen, B. S. (1998). Protective and damaging effects of stress mediators. *Seminars in Medicine of the Beth Israel Deaconess Medical Center, 338,* 171–179. (p. 404)

McFadden, D. (2002). Masculinization effects in the auditory system. *Archives of Sexual Behavior, 31,* 99–111. (p. 367)

McFarland, C., & Ross, M. (1987). The relation between current impressions and memories of self and dating partners. *Psychological Bulletin, 13,* 228–238. (p. 283)

McGaugh, J. L. (1994). Quoted by B. Bower, Stress hormones hike emotional memories. *Science News, 146,* p. 262. (p. 269)

McGaugh, J. L. (2000). Memory—a century of consolidation. *Science, 287,* 248–251. (pp. 269, 271)

McGhee, P. E. (June, 1976). Children's appreciation of humor: A test of the cognitive congruency principle. *Child Development, 47(2),* 420–426. (p. 108)

McGrath, M. J., & Cohen, D. B. (1978). REM sleep facilitation of adaptive waking behavior: A review of the literature. *Psychological Bulletin, 85,* 24–57. (p. 202)

McGregor, D. (1960). *The human side of enterprise.* New York: McGraw-Hill. (pp. B–10 to B–11)

McGue, M., & Bouchard, T. J., Jr. (1998). Genetic and environmental influences on human behavioral differences. *Annual Review of Neuroscience, 21,* 1–24. (p. 78)

McGue, M., Bouchard, T. J., Jr., Iacono, W. G., & Lykken, D. T. (1993). Behavioral genetics of cognitive ability: A life-span perspective. In R. Plomin & G. E. McClearn (Eds.), *Nature, nurture and psychology.* Washington, DC: American Psychological Association. (pp. 327–328)

McGuire, M. T., Wing, R. R., Klem, M. L., Lang, W., & Hill, J. O. (1999). What predicts weight regain in a group of successful weight losers? *Journal of Consulting and Clinical Psychology, 67,* 177–185. (p. 356)

McGuire, W. J. (1986). The myth of massive media impact: Savings and salvagings. In G. Comstock (Ed.), *Public communication and behavior.* Orlando, FL: Academic Press. (p. 251)

McGurk, H., & MacDonald, J. (1976). Hearing lips and seeing voices. *Nature, 264,* 746–748. (p. 162)

McHugh, P. R. (1995a). Witches, multiple personalities, and other psychiatric artifacts. *Nature Medicine, 1(2),* 110–114. (p. 483)

McHugh, P. R. (1995b). Resolved: Multiple personality disorder is an individually and socially created artifact. *Journal of the American Academy of Child and Adolescent Psychiatry, 34,* 957–959. (p. 484)

McHugh, P. R., & Moran, T. H. (1978). Accuracy of the regulation of caloric ingestion in the rhesus monkey. *American Journal of Physiology, 235,* R29–34. (p. 345)

McKenna, K. Y. A., & Bargh, J. A. (1998). Coming out in the age of the Internet: Identity "demarginalization" through virtual group participation. *Journal of Personality and Social Psychology, 75,* 681–694. (p. 553)

McKinlay, J. B., McKinlay, S. M., & Brambilla, D. J. (1987a). Health status and utilization behavior associated with menopause. *American Journal of Epidemiology, 125,* 110–121. (p. 125)

McKinlay, J. B., McKinlay, S. M., & Brambilla, D. J. (1987b). The relative contributions of endocrine changes and social circumstances to depression in mid-aged women. *Journal of Health and Social Behavior, 28,* 345–363. (p. 125)

McLaughlin, C. S., Chen, C., Greenberger, E., & Biermeier, C. (1997). Family, peer, and individual correlates of sexual experience among Caucasian and Asian American late adolescents. Journal of Personality and Social Psychology, *Journal of Research on Adolescence, 7,* 33–53. (p. 361)

McNally, R. J. (1999). EMDR and Mesmerism: A comparative historical analysis. *Journal of Anxiety Disorders, 13,* 225–236. (p. 525)

McNally, R. J. (2003). Progress and controversy in the study of posttraumatic stress disorder. *Annual Review of Psychology, 54,* 229–252. (p. 481)

McNally, R. J., Clancy, S. A., & Schacter, D. L. (2001). Directed forgetting of trauma cues in adults reporting repressed or recovered memories of childhood sexual abuse. *Journal of Abnormal Psychology, 110,* 151–156. (p. 282)

McNally, R. J., Clancy, S. A., Schacter, D. L., & Pitman, R. K. (2000). Personality profiles, dissociation, and absorption in women reporting repressed, recovered, or continuous memories of childhood sexual abuse. *Journal of Consulting and Clinical Psychology, 68,* 1033–1037. (p. 282)

McNeil, B. J., Pauker, S. G., & Tversky, A. (1988). On the framing of medical decisions. In D. E. Bell, H. Raiffa, & A. Tversky (Eds.), *Decision making: Descriptive, normative, and prescriptive interactions.* New York: Cambridge, 1988. (p. 300)

Meador, B. D., & Rogers, C. R. (1984). Person-centered therapy. In R. J. Corsini (Ed.), *Current psychotherapies* (3rd ed.). Itasca, IL: Peacock. (p. 511)

Meaney, M. J., Aitken, D. H., Van Berkel, C., Bhatnagar, S., & Sapolsky, R. M. (1988). Effect of neonatal handling on age-related impairments associated with the hippocampus. *Science, 239,* 766–768. (p. 84)

Medical Institute for Sexual Health. (1994, April). Condoms ineffective against human papilloma virus. *Sexual Health Update, 2.* (p. 363)

Meichenbaum, D. (1977). *Cognitive-behavior modification: An integrative approach.* New York: Plenum Press. (p. 518)

Meichenbaum, D. (1985). *Stress inoculation training.* New York: Pergamon. (p. 518)

Meier, R. P. (1991). Language acquisition by deaf children. *American Scientist, 79,* 60–70. (p. 307)

Meltzoff, A. N. (1988). Infant imitation after a 1-week delay: Long-term memory for novel acts and multiple stimuli. *Developmental Psychology, 24,* 470–476. (p. 249)

Meltzoff, A. N., & Moore, M. K. (1989). Imitation in newborn infants: Exploring the range of gestures imitated and the underlying mechanisms. *Developmental Psychology, 25,* 954–962. (p. 249)

Meltzoff, A. N., & Moore, M. K. (1997). Explaining facial imitation: A theoretical model. *Early Development and Parenting, 6,* 179–192. (p. 249)

Melzack, R. (1984). The myth of painless childbirth. *Pain, 19,* 321–337. (p. 161)

Melzack, R. (1990, February). The tragedy of needless pain. *Scientific American,* pp. 27–33. (p. 209)

Melzack, R. (1992, April). Phantom limbs. *Scientific American,* pp. 120–126. (p. 160)

Melzack, R. (1993). Distinguished contribution series. *Canadian Journal of Experimental Psychology, 47,* 615–629. (p. 160)

Melzack, R. (1998, February). Quoted in Phantom limbs. *Discover,* p. 20. (p. 160)

Melzack, R., & Wall, P. D. (1965). Pain mechanisms: A new theory. *Science, 150,* 971–979. (p. 160)

Melzack, R., & Wall, P. D. (1983). *The challenge of pain.* New York: Basic Books. (p. 160)

Mendolia, M., & Kleck, R. E. (1993). Effects of talking about a stressful event on arousal: Does what we talk about make a difference? *Journal of Personality and Social Psychology, 64,* 283–292. (p. 419)

Merari, A. (2002). Explaining suicidal terrorism: theories versus empirical evidence. Invited address to the American Psychological Association. (p. 553)

Merriman, J. (1999, May 13). These pounds aren't sterling. *Reuters* (www.abcnews.go.com). (p. 354)

Merskey, H. (1992). The manufacture of personalities: The production of multiple personality disorder. *British Journal of Psychiatry, 160,* 327–340. (p. 484)

Merton, R. K. (1938; reprinted 1970). *Science, technology and society in seventeenth-century England.* New York: Fertig. (p. 14)

Merton, R. K., & Kitt, A. S. (1950). Contributions to the theory of reference group behavior. In R. K. Merton & P. F. Lazarsfeld (Eds.), *Continuities in social research: Studies in the scope and method of the American soldier.* Glencoe, IL: Free Press. (p. 400)

Mesquita, B., & Frijda, N. H. (1992). Cultural variations in emotions: A review. *Psychological Bulletin, 112,* 179–204. (p. 390)

Messer, D. (2000). Language acquisition. *The Psychologist, 13,* 138–143. (p. 305)

Messer, W. S., & Griggs, R. A. (1989). Student belief and involvement in the paranormal and performance in introductory psychology. *Teaching of Psychology, 16,* 187–191. (p. 179)

Mestel, R. (1997, April 26). Get real, Siggi. *New Scientist* (www.newscientist.com/ns/970426/siggi.html). (p. 201)

Meston, C. M., & Frohlich, P. F. (2000). The neurobiology of sexual function. *Archives of General Psychiatry, 57,* 1012–1030. (p. 359)

Meston, C. M., Trapnell, P. D., & Gorzalka, B. B. (1996). Ethnic and gender differences in sexuality: Variations in sexual behavior between Asian and non-Asian university students. *Archives of Sexual Behavior, 25,* 33–72. (p. 361)

Metalsky, G. I., Joiner, T. E., Jr., Hardin, T. S., & Abramson, L. Y. (1993). Depressive reactions to failure in a naturalistic setting: A test of the hopelessness and self-esteem theories of depression. *Journal of Abnormal Psychology, 102*, 101–109. (p. 494)

Metcalfe, J. (1998). Cognitive optimism: Self-deception or memory-based processing heuristics. *Personality and Social Psychology Review, 2*, 100–110. (p. 298)

Meuwissen, I., & Over, R. (1992). Sexual arousal across phases of the human menstrual cycle. *Archives of Sexual Behavior, 21*, 101–119. (p. 359)

Meyer-Bahlburg, H. F. L. (1995). Psychoneuroendocrinology and sexual pleasure: The aspect of sexual orientation. In P. R. Abramson & S. D. Pinkerton (Eds.), *Sexual nature/sexual culture.* Chicago: University of Chicago Press. (p. 367)

Michaels, J. W., Bloomel, J. M., Brocato, R. M., Linkous, R. A., & Rowe, J. S. (1982). Social facilitation and inhibition in a natural setting. *Replications in Social Psychology, 2*, 21–24. (p. 551)

Middlebrooks, J. C., & Green, D. M. (1991). Sound localization by human listeners. *Annual Review of Psychology, 42*, 135–159. (p. 158)

Mikulincer, M., Babkoff, H., Caspy, T., & Sing, H. (1989). The effects of 72 hours of sleep loss on psychological variables. *British Journal of Psychology, 80*, 145–162. (p. 195)

Mikulincer, M., & Shaver, P. R. (2001). Attachment theory and intergroup bias: Evidence that priming the secure base schema attenuates negative reactions to our-groups. *Journal of Personality and Social Psychology, 81*, 97–115. (p. 558)

Milan, R. J., Jr., & Kilmann, P. R. (1987). Interpersonal factors in premarital contraception. *Journal of Sex Research, 23*, 289–321. (p. 362)

Miles, D. R., & Carey, G. (1997). Genetic and environmental architecture of human aggression. *Journal of Personality and Social Psychology, 72*, 207–217. (p. 560)

Milgram, S. (1963). Behavioral study of obedience. *Journal of Abnormal & Social Psychology, 67(4)*, 371–378. (p. 547)

Milgram, S. (1974). *Obedience to authority.* New York: Harper & Row. (pp. 547, 549)

Miller, E. J., Smith, J. E., & Trembath, D. L. (2000). The "skinny" on body size requests in personal ads. *Sex Roles, 43*, 129–141. (p. 352)

Miller, G. A. (1956). The magical number seven, plus or minus two: Some limits on our capacity for processing information. *Psychological Review, 63*, 81–97. (p. 266)

Miller, G. A. (1962). *Psychology: The science of mental life.* New York: Harper & Row. (p. 464)

Miller, G. A., & Gildea, P. M. (1987, September). How children learn words. *Scientific American*, pp. 94–99. (p. 302)

Miller, J. G., & Bersoff, D. M. (1995). Development in the context of everyday family relationships: Culture, interpersonal morality and adaptation. In M. Killen and D. Hart (Eds.), *Morality in everyday life: A developmental perspective.* New York: Cambridge University Press. (p. 119)

Miller, K. I., & Monge, P. R. (1986). Participation, satisfaction, and productivity: A meta-analytic review. *Academy of Management Journal, 29*, 727–753. (pp. 452–453)

Miller, L. C., Putcha-Bhagavatula, A., & Pedersen, W. C. (2002). Men's and women's mating preferences: distinct evolutionary mechanisms? *Current Directions in Psychological Science, 11*, 88–93. (p. 74)

Miller, L. K. (1999). The Savant Syndrome: Intellectual impairment and exceptional skill. *Psychological Bulletin, 125*, 31–46. (p. 318)

Miller, N. E. (1983). Understanding the use of animals in behavioral research: Some critical issues. *Annals of the New York Academy of Sciences, 406*, 113–118. (p. 29)

Miller, N. E. (1985, February). Rx: biofeedback. *Psychology Today*, pp. 54–59. (p. 415)

Miller, N. E. (1995). Clinical-experimental interactions in the development of neuroscience: A primer for nonspecialists and lessons for young scientists. *American Psychologist, 50*, 901–911. (p. 346)

Miller, N. E., & Brucker, B. S. (1979). A learned visceral response apparently independent of skeletal ones in patients paralyzed by spinal lesions. In N. Birbaumer & H. D. Kimmel (Eds.), *Biofeedback and self-regulation.* Hillsdale, NJ: Erlbaum. (p. 415)

Miller, P. A., Eisenberg, N., Fabes, R. A., & Shell, R. (1996). Relations of moral reasoning and vicarious emotion to young children's prosocial behavior toward peers and adults. *Developmental Psychology, 32*, 210–219. (p. 119)

Miller, P. C., Lefcourt, H. M., Holmes, J. G., Ware, E. E., & Saleh, W. E. (1986). Marital locus of control and marital problem solving. *Journal of Personality and Social Psychology, 51*, 161–169. (p. 452)

Miller, S. D., Blackburn, T., Scholes, G., White, G. L., & Mamalis, N. (1991). Optical differences in multiple personality disorder: A second look. *Journal of Nervous and Mental Disease, 179*, 132–135. (p. 483)

Mills, M., & Melhuish, E. (1974). Recognition of mother's voice in early infancy. *Nature, 252*, 123–124. (p. 102)

Milner, D. A. (2003). Visual awareness and the primate brain. In M. A. Jeeves (Ed.), *Human nature.* London: Routledge. (p. 152)

Milton, J., & Wiseman, R. (1999). Does psi exist? Lack of replication of an anomalous process of information transfer. *Psychological Bulletin, 125*, 387–391. (p. 181)

Milton, J., & Wiseman, R. (2001). Does psi exist? Reply to Storm and Ertel (2001). *Psychological Bulletin, 127*, 434–438. (p. 181)

Mineka, S., & Zinbarg, R. (1996). Conditioning and ethological models of anxiety disorders: Stress-in-dynamic-context anxiety models. In D. Hope (Ed.), *Perspectives on anxiety, panic, and fear. Nebraska symposium on motivation.* Lincoln, NE: University of Nebraska Press. (pp. 479, 480, 481)

Mischel, W. (1968). *Personality and assessment.* New York: Wiley. (p. 449)

Mischel, W. (1981). Current issues and challenges in personality. In L. T. Benjamin, Jr. (Ed.), *The G. Stanley Hall Lecture Series* (Vol. 1). Washington, DC: American Psychological Association. (p. 456)

Mischel, W. (1984). Convergences and challenges in the search for consistency. *American Psychologist, 39*, 351–364. (p. 449)

Mischel, W., Shoda, Y., & Peake, P. K. (1988). The nature of adolescent competencies predicted by preschool delay of gratification. *Journal of Personality and Social Psychology, 54*, 687–696. (p. 119)

Mischel, W., Shoda, Y., & Rodriguez, M. L. (1989). Delay of gratification in children. *Science, 244*, 933–938. (pp. 119, 240)

Mita, T. H., Dermer, M., & Knight, J. (1977). Reversed facial images and the mere-exposure hypothesis. *Journal of Personality and Social Psychology, 35*, 597–601. (p. 569)

Mitchell, T. R., Thompson, L., Peterson, E., & Cronk, R. (1997). Temporal adjustments in the evaluation of events: The "rosy view." *Journal of Experimental Social Psychology, 33*, 421–448. (p. 263)

Moffitt, T. E., Caspi, A., Harrington, H., & Milne, B. J. (2002). Males on the life-course-persistent and adolescence-limited antisocial pathways: Follow-up at age 26 years. *Development and Psychopathology, 14*, 179–207. (p. 135)

Moises, H. W., Zoega, T., & Gottesman, I. I. (2002, 3 July). The glial growth factors deficiency and synaptic destabilization hypothesis of schizophrenia. *BMC Psychiatry, 2:8* (www.biomedcentral.com/1471–244X/2/8). (p. 499)

Mollica, R. F., McInnes, K., Pham, T., Fawzi, M. C. S., Murphy, E., & Lin, L. (1998). The dose-effect relationships between torture and psychiatric symptoms in Vietnamese ex-political detainees and a comparison group. *Journal of Nervous and Mental Diseases, 186*, 543–553. (p. 480)

Monaghan, P. (1992, September 23). Professor of psychology stokes a controversy on the reliability and repression of memory. *Chronicle of Higher Education*, pp. A9–A10. (p. 286)

Mondloch, C. J., Lewis, T. L., Budreau, D. R., Maurer, D., Dannemiller, J. L., Stephens, B. R., & Kleiner-Gathercoal, K. A. (1999). Face perception during early infancy. *Psychological Science, 10,* 419–422. (p. 101)

Money, J. (1987). Sin, sickness, or status? Homosexual gender identity and psychoneuroendocrinology. *American Psychologist, 42,* 384–399. (pp. 366, 367)

Money, J., Berlin, F. S., Falck, A., & Stein, M. (1983). *Antiandrogenic and counseling treatment of sex offenders.* Baltimore: Department of Psychiatry and Behavioral Sciences, The Johns Hopkins University School of Medicine. (pp. 359–360)

Montgomery, G. H., DuHamel, K. H., & Redd, W. H. (2000). A meta-analysis of hypnotically induced analgesia: How effective is hypnosis? *International Journal of Clinical and Experimental Hypnosis, 48,* 138–153. (p. 206)

Moody, R. (1976). *Life after life.* Harrisburg, PA: Stackpole Books. (p. 215)

Mook, D. G. (1983). In defense of external invalidity. *American Psychologist, 38,* 379–387. (p. 27)

Moorcroft, W. (1993). *Sleep, dreaming, and sleep disorders: An introduction* (2nd ed.). Landam, MD: University Press of America. (p. 196)

Moorcroft, W. H. (2003). *Understanding sleep and dreaming.* New York: Kluwer/Plenum. (pp. 192, 194, 197)

Moore, D. W. (2002, February 12). Eyes wide open: Americans, sleep and stress. *Gallup Tuesday Briefing* (www.gallup.com/poll/tb/healthcare/20020212.asp). (p. 198)

Moore, K. A., Jekielek, S. M., & Emig, C. (2002, June). Marriage from a child's perspective: how does family structure affect children, and what can we do about it? Washington, DC: Child Trends Research Brief (www.childtrends.org). (p. 362)

Moore, T. E. (1988). The case against subliminal manipulation. *Psychology and Marketing, 5,* 297–316. (p. 144)

Mor, N., & Winquist, J. (2002). Self-focused attention and negative affect: A meta-analysis. *Psychological Bulletin, 128,* 638–662. (p. 493)

Moreland, R. L., & Beach, S. R. (1992). Exposure effects in the classroom: The development of affinity among students. *Journal of Experimental Social Psychology, 28,* 255–276. (pp. 568–569)

Moreland, R. L., & Zajonc, R. B. (1982). Exposure effects in person perception: Familiarity, similarity, and attraction. *Journal of Experimental Social Psychology, 18,* 395–415. (p. 568)

Morell, V. (1995). Attacking the causes of "silent" infertility. *Science, 269,* 775–776. (pp. 362–363)

Morell, V. (1995). Zeroing in on how hormones affect the immune system. *Science, 269,* 773–775. (p. 410)

Morelli, G. A., Rogoff, B., Oppenheim, D., & Goldsmith, D. (1992). Cultural variation in infants' sleeping arrangements: Questions of independence. *Developmental Psychology, 26,* 604–613. (p. 88)

Morgan, A. B., & Lilienfeld, S. O. (2000). A meta-analytic review of the relation between antisocial behavior and neuropsychological measures of executive function. *Clinical Psychology Review, 20,* 113–136. (p. 485)

Morin, R., & Brossard, M. A. (1997, March 4). Communication breakdown on drugs. *Washington Post,* pp. A1, A6. (p. 122)

Morris, R. L. (2000). Parapsychology in the 21st century. *Journal of Parapsychology, 64,* pp. 123–137. (p. 178)

Mortensen, E. L., Michaelsen, K. F., Sanders, S. A., & Reinisch, J. M. (2002). The association between duration of breastfeeding and adult intelligence. *Journal of the American Medical Association, 287,* 2365–2371. (p. 24)

Moruzzi, G., & Magoun, H. W. (1949). Brain stem reticular formation and activation of the EEG. *Electroencephalography and Clinical Neurophysiology, 1,* 455–473. (p. 47)

Moscovici, S. (1985). Social influence and conformity. In G. Lindzey & E. Aronson (Eds.), *The handbook of social psychology* (3rd ed). Hillsdale, N.J.: Erlbaum. (p. 554)

Moser, P. W. (1987, May). Are cats smart? Yes, at being cats. *Discover,* pp. 77–88. (p. 152)

Mosher, D. L., & Anderson, R. D. (1986). Macho personality, sexual aggression, and reactions to guided imagery of realistic rape. *Journal of Research in Personality, 20,* 77–94. (p. 210)

Moss, H. A., & Susman, E. J. (1980). Longitudinal study of personality development. In O. G. Brim, Jr., & J. Kagan (Eds.), *Constancy and change in human development.* Cambridge, MA: Harvard University Press. (p. 135)

Moyer, K. E. (1983). The physiology of motivation: Aggression as a model. In C. J. Scheier & A. M. Rogers (Eds.), *G. Stanley Hall Lecture Series* (Vol. 3). Washington, DC: American Psychological Association. (p. 560)

Mroczek, D. K. (2001). Age and emotion in adulthood. *Current Directions in Psychological Science, 10,* 87–90. (p. 132)

Mroczek, D. K., & Kolarz, D. M. (1998). The effect of age on positive and negative affect: A developmental perspective on happiness. *Journal of Personality and Social Psychology, 75,* 1333–1349. (p. 129)

Muhlnickel, W., Elbert, T., Taub, E., & Flor, H. (1998). Reorganization of auditory cortex in tinnitus. *Proceedings of the National Academy of Sciences, 95,* 10340–10343. (p. 55)

Muller, A. (2002). Education, income inequality, and morality: A multiple regression analysis. *British Medical Journal, 324,* 23–26. (p. 406)

Muller, J. E., Mittleman, M. A., Maclure, M., Sherwood, J. B., & Tofler, G. H. (1996). Triggering myocardial infarction by sexual activity. *Journal of the American Medical Association, 275,* 1405–1409. (p. 358)

Muller, J. E., & Verrier, R. L. (1996). Triggering of sudden death—Lessons from an earthquake. *New England Journal of Medicine, 334,* 461–461. (p. 404)

Mullin, C. R., & Linz, D. (1995). Desensitization and resensitization to violence against women: Effects of exposure to sexually violent films on judgments of domestic violence victims. *Journal of Personality and Social Psychology, 69,* 449–459. (p. 252)

Mulrow, C. D. (1999, March). Treatment of depression—newer pharmacotherapies, summary. *Evidence Report/Technology Assessment, 7.* Agency for Health Care Policy and Research, Rockville, MD. (http://www.ahrq.gov/clinic/deprsumm.htm). (pp. 531–532)

Murphy, G. E., & Wetzel, R. D. (1990). The lifetime risk of suicide in alcoholism. *Archives of General Psychiatry, 47,* 383–392. (pp. 490–491)

Murphy, K. R., & Cleveland, J. N. (1995). *Understanding performance appraisal: Social, organizational, and goal-based perspectives.* Thousand Oaks, CA: Sage. (p. B–7)

Murphy, S. T., Monahan, J. L., & Miller, L. C. (1998). Inference under the influence: The impact of alcohol and inhibition conflict on women's sexual decision making. *Personality and Social Psychology Bulletin, 24,* 517–528. (p. 211)

Murphy, S. T., Monahan, J. L., & Zajonc, R. B. (1995). Additivity of nonconscious affect: Combined effects of priming and exposure. *Journal of Personality and Social Psychology, 69,* 589–602. (p. 382)

Murphy, S. T., & Zajonc, R. B. (1993). Affect, cognition, and awareness: Affective priming with optimal and suboptimal stimulus exposures. *Journal of Personality and Social Psychology, 64,* 723–739. (p. 143)

Murphy, T. N. (1982). Pain: Its assessment and management. In R. J. Gatchel, A. Baum, & J. E. Singer (Eds.), *Handbook of psychology and health: Vol. I. Clinical psychology and behavioral medicine: Overlapping disciplines.* Hillsdale, NJ: Erlbaum. (p. 161)

Murray, B. (1998, May). Psychology is key to airline safety at Boeing. *The APA Monitor,* p. 36. (p. B–12)

Murray, C., & Herrnstein, R. J. (1994, October 31). Race, genes and I.Q.—An apologia. *New Republic,* pp. 27–37. (p. 331)

Murray, C. J., & Lopez, A. D. (Eds.) (1996). *The global burden of disease: A comprehensive assessment of mortality and disability from diseases, injuries, and risk factors in 1990 and projected to 2020.* Cambridge, MA: Harvard University Press. (p. 469)

Murray, H. (1938). *Explorations in personality.* New York: Oxford University Press. (p. 373)

Murray, H. A., & Wheeler, D. R. (1937). A note on the possible clairvoyance of dreams. *Journal of Psychology, 3,* 309–313. (p. 179)

Murray, J. E. (2000). Marital protection and marital selection: Evidence from a historical-prospective sample of American men. *Demography, 37,* 511–521. (pp. 417–418)

Murray, S. L., Rose, P., Bellavia, G. M., Holmes, J. G., & Kusche, A. G. (2002). When rejection stings: How self-esteem constrains relationship-enhancement processes. *Journal of Personality and Social Psychology, 83,* 556–573. (p. 457)

Musick, M. A., Herzog, A. R., & House, J. S. (1999). Volunteering and mortality among older adults: Findings from a national sample. *Journals of Gerontology, 54B,* 173–180. (p. 423)

Mustanski, B. S., Bailey, J. M., & Kaspar, S. (2002). Dermatoglyphics, handedness, sex, and sexual orientation. *Archives of Sexual Behavior, 31,* 113–122. (p. 367)

Mydans, S. (2002, May 17). In Pakistan, rape victims are the 'criminals.' *New York Times* (www.nytimes.com). (p. 559)

Myers, D. G. (1993). *The pursuit of happiness.* New York: Avon Books. (pp. 395, 396, 400, 401)

Myers, D. G. (2000). *The American paradox: Spiritual hunger in an age of plenty.* New Haven: Yale University Press. (pp. 88, 131, 400, 562)

Myers, D. G. (2002). *Intuition: Its powers and perils.* New Haven: Yale University Press. (pp. 4, 23)

Myers, D. G. (2002). *Social psychology.* New York: McGraw-Hill. (pp. 458, 459)

Myers, D. G. (2004). *Psychology.* New York: Worth Publishers. (p. 499)

Myers, D. G., & Bishop, G. D. (1970). Discussion effects on racial attitudes. *Science, 169,* 78–779. (pp. 552, 553)

Myers, D. G., & Diener, E. (1995). Who is happy? *Psychological Science, 6,* 10–19. (p. 400)

Myers, D. G., & Diener, E. (1996, May). The pursuit of happiness. *Scientific American,* pp. 54–56. (p. 400)

Myers, I. B. (1987). *Introduction to type: A description of the theory and applications of the Myers-Briggs Type Indicator.* Palo Alto, CA: Consulting Psychologists Press. (p. 443)

Nagourney, A. (2002, September 25). For remarks on Iraq, Gore gets praise and scorn. *New York Times* (www.nytimes.com). (pp. 541–542)

Nando Times. (1999, January 7). China reportedly has 20 percent more males than females. www.nandotimes.com (p. 556)

Napolitan, D. A., & Goethals, G. R. (1979). The attribution of friendliness. *Journal of Experimental Social Psychology, 15,* 105–113. (p. 540)

Narrow, W. E., Rae, D. S., Robins, L. N., & Regier, D. A. (2002). Revised prevalence estimates of mental disorders in the United States. *Archives of General Psychiatry, 59,* 115–123. (p. 501)

Nash, M. R. (2001, July). The truth and the hype of hypnosis. *Scientific American,* pp. 47–55. (p. 205)

National Academy of Sciences. (1999). *Marijuana and medicine: Assessing the science base* (by J. A. Benson, Jr. & S. J. Watson, Jr.). Washington, DC: National Academy Press. (p. 216)

National Academy of Sciences, Institute of Medicine. (1982). *Marijuana and health.* Washington, DC: National Academic Press. (p. 216)

National Center for Health Statistics. (1990). *Health, United States, 1989.* Washington, DC: U.S. Department of Health and Human Services. (p. 126)

National Center for Health Statistics. (1991). Family structure and children's health: United States, 1988, *Vital and Health Statistics, Series 10, No. 178,* CHHS Publication No. PHS 91–1506 by Deborah A. Dawson. (p. 364)

National Center for Health Statistics. (1994). National Health Interview Survey. (p. 158)

National Center for Health Statistics. (2002, April). Leisure-time physical activity among adults: United States 1997–1998. *Advance Data from Vital and Health Statistics, No. 325.* Washington, DC: U. S. Department of Health and Human Services. (p. 414)

National Institute of Mental Health. (1982). *Television and behavior: Ten years of scientific progress and implications for the eighties.* Washington, DC: U. S. Government Printing Office. (p. 252)

National Institutes of Health. (1998). Clinical guidelines on the identification evaluation and treatment of overweight and obesity in adults. Executive summary, Obesity Education Initiative, National heart, Lung, and Blood Institute. (p. 356)

National Research Council. (1987). *Risking the future: Adolescent sexuality, pregnancy, and childbearing.* Washington, DC: National Academy Press. (p. 362)

National Research Council. (1990). *Human factors research needs for an aging population.* Washington, DC: National Academy Press. (p. 126)

National Research Council. (2002, May 2). No single solution for protecting kids from Internet pornography. Synopsis of *Youth, pornography, and the Internet.* Washington, DC: National Academy Press. (p. 563)

National Safety Council. (2001). Data from 1995 to 1999 summarized in personal correspondence from Kevin T. Fearn, NSC Research and Statistics Department. (p. 298)

National Sleep Foundation. (2000). Sleep in America survey. www.sleep-foundation.com. (p. 195)

Naylor, T. H. (1990). Redefining corporate motivation, Swedish style. *Christian Century, 107,* 566–570. (p. B–11)

NCTV News. (1987, July-August). More research links harmful effects to non-violent porn. P. 12. (p. 563)

Needles, D. J., & Abramson, L. Y. (1990). Positive life events, attributional style, and hopefulness: Testing a model of recovery from depression. *Journal of Abnormal Psychology, 99,* 156–165. (p. 494)

Neeleman, J., & Persaud, R. (1995). Why do psychiatrists neglect religion? *British Journal of Medical Psychology, 68,* 169–178. (p. 528)

Neese, R. M. (1991, November/December). What good is feeling bad? The evolutionary benefits of psychic pain. *The Sciences,* pp. 30–37. (pp. 159, 234)

Neisser, U. (1997). The ecological study of memory. *Philosophical Transactions of the Royal Society of London, 352,* 1697–1701. (p. 258)

Neisser, U. (1997b). Rising scores on intelligence tests. *American Scientist, 85,* 440–447. (p. 330)

Neisser, U., Boodoo, G., Bouchard, T. J., Jr., Boykin, A. W., Brody, N., Ceci, S. J., Halpern, D. F., Loehlin, J. C., Perloff, R., Sternberg, R. J., & Urbina, S. (1996). Intelligence: Knowns and unknowns. *American Psychologist, 51,* 77–101. (pp. 327, 331, 335)

Neisser, U., & Harsch, N. (1992). Phantom flashbulbs: False recollections of hearing the news about *Challenger.* In E. Winograd & U. Neisser (Eds.), *Affect and accuracy in recall: Studies of "flashbulb" memories.* New York: Cambridge University Press. (p. 282)

Neisser, U., Winograd, E., & Weldon, M. S. (1991). Remembering the earthquake: "What I experienced" vs. "How I heard the news." Paper presented to the Psychonomic Society convention. (p. 269)

Neitz, J., Geist, T., & Jacobs, G. H. (1989). Color vision in the dog. *Visual Neuroscience, 3,* 119–125. (p. 154)

Nelson, G., Hoon, M. A., Chandrashekar, J., Zhang, Y., Ryba, N. J., Nicholas, J. P., & Zuker, C. S. (2001). Mammalian sweet taste receptors. *Cell, 106,* 381–390. (p. 162)

Nelson, K. (1993). The psychological and social origins of autobiographical memory. *Psychological Science, 4,* 7–13. (p. 103)

Nelson, M. D., Saykin, A. J., Flashman, L. A., & Riordan, H. J. (1998). Hippocampal volume reduction in schizophrenia as assessed by magnetic resonance imaging. *Archives of General Psychiatry, 55,* 433–440. (pp. 498–499)

Nelson, N. (1988). *A meta-analysis of the life-event/health paradigm: The influence of social support.* Philadelphia: Temple University Ph.D. dissertation. (p. 417)

Nephew, T. M., Williams, G. D., Stinson, F. S., Nguyen, K., & Dufour, M. C. (1999). Surveillance report #51: Apparent per capita alcohol consumption: National, state, and regional trends, 1977–1997. Bethesda, MD: National Institute on Alcohol Abuse and Alcoholism. (p. 218)

Neubauer, P. B., & Neubauer, A. (1990). *Nature's thumbprint: The new genetics of personality.* Reading, MA: Addison-Wesley. (p. 82)

Neumann, R., & Strack, F. (2000). "Mood contagion": The automatic transfer of mood between persons. *Journal of Personality and Social Psychology, 79,* 211–223. (pp. 393, 545)

Nevin, J. A. (1988). Behavioral momentum and the partial reinforcement effect. *Psychological Bulletin, 103,* 44–56. (p. 241)

Newberg, A., & D'Aquili, E. (2001). *Why God won't go away: Brain science and the biology of belief.* New York: Simon and Schuster. (p. 416)

Newcomb, M. D., & Bentler, P. M. (1988). Impact of adolescent drug use and social support on problems of young adults: A longitudinal study. *Journal of Abnormal Psychology, 97,* 64–75. (p. 216)

Newcomb, M. D., & Harlow, L. L. (1986). Life events and substance use among adolescents: Mediating effects of perceived loss of control and meaninglessness in life. *Journal of Personality and Social Psychology, 51,* 564–577. (p. 219)

Newman, A. J., Bavelier, D., Corina, D., Jezzard, P., & Neville, H. J. (2002). A critical period for right hemisphere recruitment in American Sign Language processing. *Nature Neuroscience, 5,* 76–80. (p. 307)

Newman, L. S., & Baumeister, R. F. (1996). Toward an explanation of the UFO abduction phenomenon: Hypnotic, elaboration, extraterrestrial sado-masochism, and spurious memories. *Psychological Inquiry, 7,* 99–126. (p. 205)

Newport, E. L. (1990). Maturational constraints on language learning. *Cognitive Science, 14,* 11–28. (p. 307)

Newport, F. (2001, February). Americans see women as emotional and affectionate, men as more aggressive. *The Gallup Poll Monthly,* pp. 34–38. (p. 389)

Newport, F. (2002, July 29). Bush job approval update. Gallup News Service (www.gallup.com/poll/releases/pr020729.asp). (pp. 576–577)

Neylan, T. C., Metzler, T. J., Best, S. R., Weiss, D. S., Fagan, J. A., Liberman, A., Rogers, C., Vedantham, K., Brunet, A., Lipsey, T. L., & Marmar, C. R. (2002). Critical incident exposure and sleep quality in police officers. *Psychosomatic Medicine, 64,* 345–352. (p. 198)

Nezlek, J. B. (2001). Daily psychological adjustment and the planfulness of day-to-day behavior. *Journal of Social and Clinical Psychology, 20,* 452–475. (p. 452)

Nickell, J. (1996, May/June). A study of fantasy proneness in the thirteen cases of alleged encounters in John Mack's *Abduction. Skeptical Inquirer,* pp. 18–20, 54. (p. 205)

Nickerson, R. S. (1999). How we know—and sometimes misjudge—what others know: Imputing one's own knowledge to others. *Psychological Bulletin, 125,* 737–759. (p. B–12)

Nicol, S. E., & Gottesman, I. I. (1983). Clues to the genetics and neurobiology of schizophrenia. *American Scientist, 71,* 398–404. (p. 500)

Nicolaus, L. K., Cassel, J. F., Carlson, R. B., & Gustavson, C. R. (1983). Taste-aversion conditioning of crows to control predation on eggs. *Science, 220,* 212–214. (p. 234)

Niemi, R. G., Mueller, J., & Smith, T. W. (1989). *Trends in public opinion: A compendium of survey data.* New York: Greenwood Press. (pp. 213, 555)

Nigro, G. (1984). Cited by U. Neisser, The role of invariant structures in the control of movement. In M. Frese & J. Sabini (Eds.), *Goal directed behavior: The concept of action in psychology.* Hillsdale, NJ: Erlbaum. (p. 310)

NIH (2001, July 20). Workshop summary: Scientific evidence on condom effectiveness for sexually transmitted disease (STD) prevention. Bethesda: National Institute of Allergy and Infectious Diseases, National Institutes of Health. (p. 363)

NIMH (2002, April 26). U.S. suicide rates by age, gender, and racial group. National Institute of Mental Health (www.nimh.nih.gov/research/suichart.cfm). (p. 490)

Nisbett, R. E. (1987). Lay personality theory: Its nature, origin, and utility. In N. E. Grunberg, R. E. Nisbett, & others, *A distinctive approach to psychological research: The influence of Stanley Schachter* (Hillsdale, NJ: 1987). (p. B–5)

Nisbett, R. E., & Borgida, E. (1975). Attribution and the psychology of prediction. *Journal of Personality and Social Psychology, 32,* 932–943. (p. 302)

Nisbett, R. E., & Cohen, D. (1996). *Culture of honor: The psychology of violence in the South.* Boulder, CO: Westview Press. (p. 562)

Nisbett, R. E., & Ross, L. (1980). *Human inference: Strategies and shortcomings of social judgment.* Englewood Cliffs, NJ: Prentice-Hall. (p. 296)

Noel, J. G., Forsyth, D. R., & Kelley, K. N. (1987). Improving the performance of failing students by overcoming their self-serving attributional biases. *Basic and Applied Social Psychology, 8,* 151–162. (p. 453)

Nolen-Hoeksema, S. (2001). Gender differences in depression. *Current Directions in Psychological Science, 10,* 173–176. (p. 492)

Nolen-Hoeksema, S., & Larson, J. (1999). *Coping with loss.* Mahwah, NJ: Erlbaum. (p. 133)

Nolen-Hoeksema, S., & Morrow, J. (1991). A prospective study of depression and post-traumatic stress symptoms following a natural disaster: The 1989 Loma Prieta earthquake. *Journal of Personality and Social Psychology, 61,* 115–121. (p. 494)

NORC (National Opinion Research Center) (1985, October/November). Images of the world. *Public Opinion,* p. 38. (p. 441)

NORC (National Opinion Research Center). (2002). Percent saying sex with person other than spouse is always or almost always wrong. National Opinion Research Center General Social Survey of 2000 (www.csa.berkeley.edu:7502). (p. 369)

Norcross, J. C. (Ed.). (2002). *Psychotherapy relationships that work: Therapist contributions and responsiveness to patient needs.* New York: Oxford University Press. (p. 523)

Norem, J. K. (2001). *The Positive Power of Negative Thinking: Using Defensive Pessimism to Harness Anxiety and Perform at Your Peak.* Basic Books. (p. 453)

Norman, D. A. (1988). *The psychology of everyday things.* New York: Basic Books. (pp. B–11 to B–12)

Norman, D. A. (2001). The perils of home theater (www.jnd.org/dn.mss/ProblemsOfHomeTheater.html). (p. B–12)

Norton, K. L., Olds, T. S., Olive, S., & Dank, S. (1996). Ken and Barbie at life size. *Sex Roles, 34,* 287–294. (p. 351)

Nowak, R. (1994). Nicotine scrutinized as FDA seeks to regulate cigarettes. *Science, 263,* 1555–1556. (p. 213)

NSF (2001, October 24). Public bounces back after Sept. 11 attacks, national study shows. *NSF News,* National Science Foundation (www.nsf.gov/od/lpa/news/press/ol/pr0185.htm). (p. 404)

Nuttin, J. M., Jr. (1987). Affective consequences of mere ownership: The name letter effect in twelve European languages. *European Journal of Social Psychology, 17,* 381–402. (p. 568)

O'Connor, P., & Brown, G. W. (1984). Supportive relationships: Fact or fancy? *Journal of Social and Personal Relationships, 1,* 159–175. (p. 527)

O'Donnell, L., Stueve, A., O'Donnell, C., Duran, R., San Doval, A., Wilson, R. F., Haber, D., Perry, E., & Pleck, J. H. (2002). Long-term reduction in sexual initiation and sexual activity among urban middle schoolers in the reach for health service learning program. *Journal of Adolescent Health, 31,* 93–100. (p. 363)

Oetting, E. R., & Beauvais, F. (1987). Peer cluster theory, socialization characteristics, and adolescent drug use: A path analysis. *Journal of Counseling Psychology, 34,* 205–213. (p. 220)

Oetting, E. R., & Beauvais, F. (1990). Adolescent drug use: Findings of national and local surveys. *Journal of Social and Personal Relationships, 1,* 159–175. (p. 220)

Oettingen, G., & Mayer, D. (2002). The motivating function of thinking about the future: Expectations versus fantasies. *Journal of Personality and Social Psychology, 83,* 1198–1212. (p. 453)

Oettingen, G., & Seligman, M. E. P. (1990). Pessimism and behavioural signs of depression in East versus West Berlin. *European Journal of Social Psychology, 20,* 207–220. (p. 453)

Offer, D., Ostrov, E., Howard, K. I., & Atkinson, R. (1988). *The teenage world: Adolescents' self-image in ten countries.* New York: Plenum. (p. 122)

Office of National Statistics. (2002). *The social and economic circumstances of adults with mental disorders* (report based on the analysis of the ONS Survey of Psychiatric Morbidity Among Adults in Great Britain carried out in 2000). Norwich: HMSO. (p. 501)

Ohman, A. (1986). Face the beast and fear the face: Animal and social fears as prototypes for evolutionary analyses of emotion. *Psychophysiology, 23,* 123–145. (p. 480)

Öhman, A., Lundqvist, D., & Esteves, F. (2001). The face in the crowd revisited: A threat advantage with schematic stimuli. *Journal of Personality and Social Psychology, 80,* 381–396. (p. 388)

Oishi, S., Diener, E. F., Lucas, R. E., & Suh, E. M. (1999). Cross-cultural variations in predictors of life satisfaction: Perspectives from needs and values. *Personality and Social Psychology Bulletin, 25,* 980–990. (p. 344)

Olds, J. (1975). Mapping the mind onto the brain. In F. G. Worden, J. P. Swazey, & G. Adelman (Eds.), *The neurosciences: Paths of discovery.* Cambridge, MA: MIT Press. (p. 51)

Olds, J., & Milner, P. (1954). Positive reinforcement produced by electrical stimulation of the septal area and other regions of rat brain. *Journal of Comparative and Physiological Psychology, 47,* 419–427. (p. 51)

Olfson, M., Marcus, S. C., Druss, B., & Pincus, H. A. (2002). New research—National trends in the use of outpatient psychotherapy. *The American Journal of Psychiatry, 159,* 1914–1921. (p. 519)

Oliner, S. P., & Oliner, P. M. (1988). *The altruistic personality: Rescuers of Jews in Nazi Europe.* New York: Free Press. (p. 250)

Olney, B. (1998, July 9). As baseball's second-half begins, Mark McGwire leads the Maris chase. *New York Times* (www.nytimes.com). (p. 310)

Olweus, D., Mattsson, A., Schalling, D., & Low, H. (1988). Circulating testosterone levels and aggression in adolescent males: A causal analysis. *Psychosomatic Medicine, 50,* 261–272. (p. 561)

Oman, D., Kurata, J. H., Strawbridge, W. J., & Cohen, R. D. (2002). Religious attendance and cause of death over 31 years. *International Journal of Psychiatry in Medicine, 32,* 69–89. (p. 422)

O'Neil, J. (2002, September 3). Vital Signs: Behavior: Parent smoking and teenage sex. *New York Times.* (p. 20)

O'Neill, M. J. (1993). The relationship between privacy, control, and stress responses in office workers. Paper presented to the Human Factors and Ergonomics Society convention. (p. 406)

Oren, D. A., & Terman, M. (1998). Tweaking the human circadian clock with light. *Science, 279,* 333–334. (p. 190)

Orne, M. T., & Evans, F. J. (1965). Social control in the psychological experiment: Antisocial behavior and hypnosis. *Journal of Personality and Social Psychology, 1,* 189–200. (p. 205)

Osborne, L. (1999, October 27). A linguistic big bang. *New York Times Magazine* (www.nytimes.com). (p. 305)

Osgood, C. E. (1962). *An alternative to war or surrender.* Urbana: University of Illinois Press. (p. 578)

Osgood, C. E. (1980). *GRIT: A strategy for survival in mankind's nuclear age?* Paper presented at the Pugwash Conference on New Directions in Disarmament. (p. 578)

Osler, M., Prescott, E., Grønbæk, M., Christensen, U., Due, P., & Engholm G. (2002). Income inequality, individual income, and mortality in Danish adults. *British Medical Journal, 324,* 13–16. (p. 406)

OSS Assessment Staff. (1948). *The assessment of men.* New York: Rinehart. (p. 455)

Ost, L. G., & Hugdahl, K. (1981). Acquisition of phobias and anxiety response patterns in clinical patients. *Behaviour Research and Therapy, 16,* 439–447. (p. 479)

Ostfeld, A. M., Kasl, S. V., D'Atri, D. A., & Fitzgerald, E. F. (1987). *Stress, crowding, and blood pressure in prison.* Hillsdale, NJ: Erlbaum. (p. 407)

Ouellette, J. A., & Wood, W. (1998). Habit and intention in everyday life: The multiple processes by which past behavior predicts future behavior. *Psychological Bulletin, 124,* 54–74. (pp. 456, B–5)

Overmier, J. B., & Murison, R. (1997). Animal models reveal the "psych" in the psychosomatics of peptic ulcers. *Current Directions in Psychological Science, 6,* 180–184. (p. 405)

Oyserman, D., Coon, H. M., & Kemmelmeier, M. (2002a). Rethinking individualism and collectivism: Evaluation of theoretical assumptions and meta-analyses. *Psychological Bulletin, 128,* 3–72. (p. 461)

Oyserman, D., Kemmelmeier, M., & Coon, H. M. (2002b). Cultural psychology, a new look: Reply to Bond (2002), Fiske (2002), Kitayama (2002), and Miller (2002). *Psychological Bulletin, 128,* 110–117. (p. 461)

Ozer, E. J., Best, S. R., Lipsey, T. L., & Weiss, D. S. (2003). Predictors of posttraumatic stress disorder and symptoms in adults: A meta-analysis. *Psychological Bulletin, 129,* 52–73. (p. 481)

Özgen, E., & Davies, I. R. L. (2002). Acquisition of categorical color perception: A perceptual learning approach to linguistic relativity hypothesis. *Journal of Experimental Psychology: General, 131,* 477–493. (p. 308)

Pacifici, R., Zuccaro, P., Farre, M., Pichini, S., Di Carlo, S., Roset, P. N., Ortuno, J., Pujadus, M., Bacosi, A., Menoyo, E., Segura, J., & de la Torre, R. (2001). Effects of repeated doses of MDMA ("Ecstasy") on cell-mediated immune response in humans. *Life Sciences, 69,* 2931–2941. (p. 215)

Padgett, V. R. (1989). Predicting organizational violence: An application of 11 powerful principles of obedience. Paper presented to the American Psychological Association convention. (p. 549)

Padilla, R. V., & Benavides, A. H. (Eds.) (1992). *Critical perspectives on bilingual education research.* Tempe, AZ: Bilingual Press. (p. 309)

Page, S. (1977). Effects of the mental illness label in attempts to obtain accommodation. *Canadian Journal of Behavioral Science, 9,* 84–90. (p. 475)

Paikoff, R. L., & Brooks-Gunn, J. (1991). Do parent-child relationships change during puberty? *Psychological Bulletin, 110,* 47–66. (p. 122)

Paivio, A. (1986). *Mental representations: A dual coding approach.* New York: Oxford University Press. (p. 263)

Palace, E. M. (1995). Modification of dysfunctional patterns of sexual response through autonomic arousal and false physiological feedback. *Journal of Consulting and Clinical Psychology, 63,* 604–615. (p. 382)

Pallier, C., Colomé, A., & Sebastián-Gallés, N. (2001). The influence of native-language phonology on lexical access: Exemplar-based versus abstract lexical entries. *Psychological Science, 12,* 445–448. (pp. 303–304)

Palmer, S., Schreiber, C., & Box, C. (1991). Remembering the earthquake: "Flashbulb" memory for experienced vs. reported events. Paper presented to the Psychonomic Society convention. (p. 269)

Pandey, J., Sinha, Y., Prakash, A., & Tripathi, R. C. (1982). Right-left political ideologies and attribution of the causes of poverty. *European Journal of Social Psychology, 12,* 327–331. (p. 541)

Panksepp, J. (1982). Toward a general psychobiological theory of emotions. *Behavioral and Brain Sciences, 5,* 407–467. (p. 385)

Pantelis, C., Velakoulis, D., McGorry, P. D., Wood, S. J., Suckling, J., Phillips, L. J., Yung, A. R., Bullmore, E. T., Brewer, W., Soulsby, B., Desmond, P., & McGuire, P. K. (2002). Neuroanatomical abnormalities before and after onset of psychosis: A cross-sectional and longitudinal MRI comparison. *The Lancet,* published online at image.thelancet.com/extras/01art9092web.pdf. (p. 498)

Parducci, A. (1995). *Happiness, pleasure, and judgment: The contextual theory and its applications.* Hillsdale, NJ: Erlbaum. (p. 399)

Park, R. L. (1999). Liars never break a sweat. *New York Times,* July 12, 1999 (www.nytimes.com). (p. 386)

Parker, G., Roy, K., Hadzi, P. D., Pedic, F. (1992). Psychotic (delusional) depression: A meta-analyis of physical treatments. *Journal of Affective Disorders, 24,* 17–24. (p. 533)

Parker, S., Nichter, M., Nichter, M., & Vuckovic, N. (1995). Body image and weight concerns among African American and white adolescent females: Differences that make a difference. *Human Organization, 54,* 103–114. (p. 349)

Parloff, M. B. (1987, February). Psychotherapy: An import from Japan. *Psychology Today,* pp. 74–75. (p. 507)

Passell, P. (1993, March 9). Like a new drug, social programs are put to the test. *New York Times,* pp. C1, C10. (p. 27)

Pate, J. E., Pumariega, A. J., Hester, C., & Garner, D. M. (1992). Cross-cultural patterns in eating disorders: A review. *Journal of the American Academy of Child and Adolescent Psychiatry, 31,* 802–809. (p. 350)

Patterson, F. (1978, October). Conversations with a gorilla. *National Geographic,* pp. 438–465. (p. 313)

Patterson, G. R., Chamberlain, P., & Reid, J. B. (1982). A comparative evaluation of parent training procedures. *Behavior Therapy, 13,* 638–650. (pp. 243, 563)

Patterson, G. R., Reid, J. B., & Dishion, T. J. (1992). *Antisocial boys.* Eugene, OR: Castalia. (p. 563)

Patterson, R. (1951). *The riddle of Emily Dickinson.* Boston: Houghton Mifflin. (p. 495)

Patton, W., & Mannison, M. (1995). Sexual coercion in dating situations among university students: Preliminary Australian data. *Australian Journal of Psychology, 47,* 66–72. (p. 563)

Paulesu, E., Demonet, J-F., Fazio, F., McCrory, E., Chanoine, V., Brunswick, N., Cappa, S. F., Cossu, G., Habib, M., Frith, C. D., & Frith, U. (2001). Dyslexia: Cultural diversity and biological unity. *Science, 291,* 2165–2167. (p. 28)

Paunonen, S. V., Zeidner, M., Engvik, H. A., Oosterveld, P., & Maliphant, R. (2000). The nonverbal assessment of personality in five cultures. *Journal of Cross-Cultural Psychology, 31,* 220–239. (p. 448)

Paus, T., Zijdenbos, A., Worsley, K., Collins, D. L., Blumenthal, J., Giedd, J. N., Rapoport, J. L., & Evans, A. C. (1999) Structural maturation of neural pathways in children and adolescents: In vivo study. *Science, 283,* 1908–1911. (p. 103)

Pavlov, I. (1927). *Conditioned reflexes: An investigation of the physiological activity of the cerebral cortex.* Oxford: Oxford University Press. (pp. 228, 232)

Pedersen, N. L., Plomin, R., McClearn, G. E., & Friberg, L. (1988). Neuroticism, extraversion, and related traits in adult twins reared apart and reared together. *Journal of Personality and Social Psychology, 55,* 950–957. (p. 77)

Pedersen, W. C., Miller, L. C., Putcha-Bhagavatula, A. D., & Yang, Y. (2002). Evolved sex differences in the number of partners desired? The long and the short of it. *Psychological Science, 13,* 147–161. (p. 74)

Pekkanen, J. (1982, June). Why do we sleep? *Science, 82,* p. 86. (p. 197)

Pelham, B. W. (1993). On the highly positive thoughts of the highly depressed. In R. F. Baumeister (Ed.), *Self-esteem: The puzzle of low self-regard.* New York: Plenum. (p. 458)

Pendick, D. (1994, January/February). The mind of violence. *BrainWork: The Neuroscience Newsletter,* pp. 1–3, 5. (p. 561)

Penfield, W. (1969). Consciousness, memory, and man's conditioned reflexes. In K. Pigram (Ed.), *On the biology of learning.* New York: Harcourt, Brace & World. (p. 267)

Pennebaker, J. (1990). *Opening up: The healing power of confiding in others.* New York: William Morrow. (pp. 419, 437)

Pennebaker, J. W. (2002, January 28). Personal communication. (p. 577)

Pennebaker, J. W., Barger, S. D., & Tiebout, J. (1989). Disclosure of traumas and health among Holocaust survivors. *Psychosomatic Medicine, 51,* 577–589. (p. 419)

Pennebaker, J. W., & O'Heeron, R. C. (1984). Confiding in others and illness rate among spouses of suicide and accidental death victims. *Journal of Abnormal Psychology, 93,* 473–476. (p. 418)

Peplau, L. A. (1982). Research on homosexual couples: An overview. *Journal of Homosexuality, 8(2),* 3–8. (p. 365)

Peplau, L. A., & Garnets, L. D. (2000). A new paradigm for understanding women's sexuality and sexual orientation. *Journal of Social Issues, 56,* 329–350. (p. 365)

Pepperberg, I. M. (2002). Cognitive and communicative abilities of grey parrots. *Current Directions in Psychological Science, 11,* 83–87. (p. 312)

Perkins, H. W. (1991). Religious commitment, Yuppie values, and well-being in post-collegiate life. *Review of Religious Research, 32,* 244–251. (p. 398)

Perlmutter, M. (1983). Learning and memory through adulthood. In M. W. Riley, B. B. Hess, & K. Bond (Eds.), *Aging in society: Selected reviews of recent research.* Hillsdale, NJ: Erlbaum. (p. 128)

Perls, T., Silver, M. H., & Lauerman, J. F. (1999). *Living to 100: Lessons in living to your maximum potential at any age.* Thorndike Press: ME.

Perrett, D. I., Harries, M., Misflin, A. J., & Chitty, A. J. (1988). Three stages in the classification of body movements by visual neurons. In H. B. Barlow, C. Blakemore, & M. Weston Smith (Eds.), *Images and understanding.* Cambridge: Cambridge University Press. (p. 151)

Perrett, D. I., Hietanen, J. K., Oram, M. W., & Benson, P. J. (1992). Organization and functions of cells responsive to faces in the temporal cortex. *Philosophical Transactions of the Royal Society of London: Series B, 335,* 23–30. (p. 151)

Perrett, D. I., Lee, K. J., Penton-Voak, I., Rowland, D., Yoshikawa, S., Burt, D. M., Henzi, S. P., Castles, D. L., Akamatsu, S. (1998, August). Effects of sexual dimorphism on facial attractiveness. *Nature, 394,* 884–887. (p. 557)

Perrett, D. I., May, K. A., & Yoshikawa, S. (1994). Facial shape and judgments of female attractiveness. *Nature, 368,* 239–242. (p. 151)

Persons, J. B. (1986). The advantages of studying psychological phenomena rather than psychiatric diagnoses. *American Psychologist, 41,* 1252–1260. (p. 473)

Pert, C. (1986). Quoted in J. Hooper & D. Teresi, *The three-pound universe.* New York: Macmillan. (p. 51)

Pert, C. B., & Snyder, S. H. (1973). Opiate receptor: Demonstration in nervous tissue. *Science, 179,* 1011–1014. (p. 41)

Perugini, E. M., Kirsch, I., Allen, S. T., Coldwell, E., Meredith, J., Montgomery, G. H., & Sheehan, J. (1998). Surreptitious observation of responses to hypnotically suggested hallucinations: A test of the compliance hypothesis. *International Journal of Clinical and Experimental Hypnosis, 46,* 191–203. (p. 207)

Peschel, E. R., & Peschel, R. E. (1987). Medical insights into the castrati in opera. *American Scientist, 75,* 578–583. (p. 359)

Peters, T. J., & Waterman, R. H., Jr. (1982). *In search of excellence: Lessons from America's best-run companies.* New York: Harper & Row. (p. 246)

Peterson, C., & Barrett, L. C. (1987). Explanatory style and academic performance among university freshmen. *Journal of Personality and Social Psychology, 53,* 603–607. (p. 453)

Peterson, C., Peterson, J., & Skevington, S. (1986). Heated argument and adolescent development. *Journal of Social and Personal Relationships, 3,* 229–240. (p. 118)

Peterson, C., & Seligman, M. E. P. (Eds.). (2004). *Character strengths and virtues: A handbook and classification.* Washington, DC: American Psychological Association. (p. 473)

Peterson, L. R., & Peterson, M. J. (1959). Short-term retention of individual verbal items. *Journal of Experimental Psychology, 58,* 193–198. (p. 266)

Petitto, L. A., & Marentette, P. F. (1991). Babbling in the manual mode: Evidence for the ontogeny of language. *Science, 251,* 1493–1496. (pp. 303, 307)

Pettegrew, J. W., Keshavan, M. S., & Minshew, N. J. (1993). 31P nuclear magnetic resonance spectroscopy: Neurodevelopment and schizophrenia. *Schizophrenia Bulletin, 19,* 35–53. (p. 498)

Petticrew, M., Fraser, J. M., & Regan, M. F. (1999). Adverse life events and risk of breast cancer: A meta-analysis. *British Journal of Health Psychology, 4,* 1–17. (p. 411)

Pettigrew, T. F. (1969). Racially separate or together? *Journal of Social Issues, 25,* 43–69. (p. 576)

Pettigrew, T. F. (1997). Generalized intergroup contact effects on prejudice. *Personality and Social Psychology Bulletin, 23,* 173–185. (p. 576)

Pettigrew, T. F. (1998). Reactions toward the new minorities of western Europe. *Annual Review of Sociology, 24,* 77–103. (p. 555)

Phelps, J. A., Davis J. O., & Schartz, K. M. (1997). Nature, nurture, and twin research strategies. *Current Directions in Psychological Science, 6,* 117–120. (pp. 83, 500)

Phillips, D. P. (1985). Natural experiments on the effects of mass media violence on fatal aggression: Strengths and weaknesses of a new approach. In L. Berkowitz (Ed.), *Advances in experimental social psychology* (Vol. 19). Orlando, FL: Academic Press. (p. 545)

Phillips, D. P., Carstensen, L. L., & Paight, D. J. (1989). Effects of mass media news stories on suicide, with new evidence on the role of story content. In D. R. Pfeffer (Ed.), *Suicide among youth: Perspectives on risk and prevention.* Washington, DC: American Psychiatric Press. (p. 545)

Phillips, J. L. (1969). *Origins of intellect: Piaget's theory.* San Francisco: Freeman. (p. 107)

Piaget, J. (1930). *The child's conception of physical causality.* London: Routledge & Kegan Paul. (p. 105)

Piaget, J. (1932). *The moral judgment of the child.* New York: Harcourt, Brace & World. (p. 118)

Pickar, D., Labarca, R., Linnoila, M., Roy, A., Hommer, D., Everett, D., & Payl, S. M. (1984). Neuroleptic-induced decrease in plasma homovanillic acid and antipsychotic activity in schizophrenic patients. *Science, 225,* 954–957. (p. 530)

Pigott, T. A., & Seay, S. (1997). Pharmacotherapy of obsessive-compulsive disorder. *International Review of Psychiatry, 9,* 133–147. (p. 531)

Pike, K. M., & Rodin, J. (1991). Mothers, daughters, and disordered eating. *Journal of Abnormal Psychology, 100,* 198–204. (p. 350)

Pillemer, D. (1998). *Momentous events, vivid memories.* Cambridge: Harvard University Press, 1998. (p. 103)

Pillemer, D. G. (1995). What is remembered about early childhood events? Invited paper presentation to the American Psychological Society convention. (p. 127)

Pincus, H. A. (1997) Commentary: Spirituality, religion, and health: Expanding, and using the knowledge base. *Mind/Body Medicine, 2,* 49. (p. 424)

Pinel, J. P. J. (1993). *Biopsychology* (2nd ed). Boston: Allyn & Bacon. (pp. 346–347)

Pingitore, R., Dugoni, B. L., Tindale, R. S., & Spring, B. (1994). Bias against overweight job applicants in a simulated employment interview. *Journal of Applied Psychology, 79,* 909–917. (p. 352)

Pinker, S. (1990, September-October). Quoted by J. de Cuevas, "No, she holded them loosely." *Harvard Magazine,* pp. 60–67. (p. 302)

Pinker, S. (1995). The language instinct. *The General Psychologist, 31,* 63–65. (p. 314)

Pinker, S. (1998). Words and rules. *Lingua, 106,* 219–242. (p. 302)

Pinker, S. (2002, September 9). A biological understanding of human nature: A talk with Steven Pinker. The Edge Third Culture Mail List (www.edge.org). (p. 78)

Pinkerton, S. D., & Abramson, P. R. (1997). Condoms and the prevention of AIDS. *American Scientist, 85,* 364–373. (p. 363)

Pipe, M-E. (1996). Children's eyewitness memory. *New Zealand Journal of Psychology, 25,* 36–43. (p. 284)

Piper, A., Jr. (1998, Winter). Multiple personality disorder: Witchcraft survives in the twentieth century. *Skeptical Inquirer,* pp. 44–50. (p. 484)

Pipher, M. (2002). *The middle of everywhere: The world's refugees come to our town.* New York: Harcourt Brace. (pp. 87, 372, 405, 494)

Pittenger, D. J. (1993). The utility of the Myers-Briggs Type Indicator. *Review of Eduational Research, 63,* 467–488. (p. 443)

Pliner, P. (1982). The effects of mere exposure on liking for edible substances. *Appetite: Journal for Intake Research, 3,* 283–290. (p. 348)

Pliner, P., Pelchat, M., & Grabski, M. (1993). Reduction of neophobia in humans by exposure to novel foods. *Appetite, 20,* 111–123. (p. 348)

Pliner, P., & Pelchat, M. L. (1991). Neophobia in humans and the special status of foods of animal origin. *Appetite, 16,* 205–218. (p. 348)

Plomin, R. (1999). Genetics and general cognitive ability. *Nature, 402* (Suppl), C25–C29. (pp. 317, 326)

Plomin, R. (2001). Genetics and behaviour. *The Psychologist, 14,* 134–139. (p. 326)

Plomin, R. (2003). General cognitive ability. In R. Plomin, J. C. DeFries, I. W. Craig, & P. McGuffin (Eds.), *Behavioral genetics in a postgenomic world.* Washington, DC: APA Books. (p. 327)

Plomin, R., & Bergeman, C. S. (1991). The nature of nurture: Genetic influence on "environmental" measures. *Behavioral and Brain Sciences, 14,* 373–427. (p. 81)

Plomin, R., Corley, R., Caspi, A., Fulker, D. W., & DeFries, J. (1998). Adoption results for self-reported personality: Evidence for nonadditive genetic effects? *Journal of Personality and Social Psychology, 75,* 211–219. (p. 78)

Plomin, R., & Crabbe, J. (2000). DNA. *Psychological Bulletin, 126,* 806–828. (p. 70)

Plomin, R., & Daniels, D. (1987). Why are children in the same family so different from one another? *Behavioral and Brain Sciences, 10,* 1–60. (p. 82)

Plomin, R., & DeFries, J. C. (1998, May). The genetics of cognitive abilities and disabilities. *Scientific American,* pp. 62–69. (p. 328)

Plomin, R., DeFries, J. C., McClearn, G. E., & Rutter, M. (1997). *Behavioral genetics.* New York: Freeman. (pp. 71, 328, 354, 367, 499)

Plomin, R., Fulker, D. W., Corley, R., & DeFries, J. C. (1997). Nature, nurture and cognitive development from 1 to 16 years: A parent-offspring adoption study. *Psychological Science, 8,* 442–447. (p. 76)

Plomin, R., McClearn, G. E., Pedersen, N. L., Nesselroade, J. R., & Bergeman, C. S. (1988). Genetic influence on childhood family environment perceived retrospectively from the last half of the life span. *Developmental Psychology, 24,* 37–45. (p. 81)

Plomin, R., Reiss, D., Hetherington, E. M., & Howe, G. W. (January, 1994). Nature and nurture: Genetic contributions to measures of the family environment. *Developmental Psychology, 30*(1), 32–43. (p. 81)

Plous, S. (1993). The nuclear arms race: Prisoner's dilemma or perceptual dilemma? *Journal of Peace Research, 30,* 163–179. (p. 567)

Plous, S., & Herzog, H. A. (2000). Poll shows researchers favor lab animal protection. *Science, 290,* 711. (p. 29)

Polivy, J., & Herman, C. P. (1985). Dieting and binging: A causal analysis. *American Psychologist, 40,* 193–201. (p. 356)

Polivy, J., & Herman, C. P. (1987). Diagnosis and treatment of normal eating. *Journal of Personality and Social Psychology, 55,* 635–644. (p. 356)

Polivy, J., & Herman, C. P. (2002). Causes of eating disorders. *Annual Review of Psychology, 53,* 187–213. (p. 350)

Pollak, S., Cicchetti, D., & Klorman, R. (1998). Stress, memory, and emotion: Developmental considerations from the study of child maltreatment. *Developmental Psychopathology, 10,* 811–828. (p. 232)

Pollak, S. D., & Kistler, D. J. (2002). Early experience is associated with the development of categorical representations for facial expressions of emotion. *Proceedings of the National Academy of Sciences, 99,* 9072–9076. (p. 388)

Pollard, R. (1992). 100 years in psychology and deafness: A centennial retrospective. Invited address to the American Psychological Association convention, Washington, DC. (p. 309)

Polusny, M. A., & Follette, V. M. (1995). Long-term correlates of child sexual abuse: Theory and review of the empirical literature. *Applied & Preventive Psychology, 4,* 143–166. (p. 113)

Poole, D. A., & Lindsay, D. S. (1995). Interviewing preschoolers: Effects of nonsuggestive techniques, parental coaching and leading questions on reports of nonexperienced events. *Journal of Experimental Child Psychology, 60,* 129–154. (p. 284)

Poole, D. A., & Lindsay, D. S. (2001). Children's eyewitness reports after exposure to misinformation from parents. *Journal of Experimental Psychology: Applied, 7,* 27–50. (p. 284)

Poole, D. A., & Lindsay, D. S. (2002). Reducing child witnesses' false reports of misinformation from parents. *Journal of Experimental Child Psychology, 81,* 117–140. (p. 284)

Poole, D. A., Lindsay, D. S., Memon, A., & Bull, R. (1995). Psychotherapy and the recovery of memories of childhood sexual abuse: U.S. and British practitioners' opinions, practices, and experiences. *Journal of Consulting and Clinical Psychology, 63,* 426–437. (p. 285)

Poon, L. W. (1987). Myths and truisms: Beyond extant analyses of speed of behavior and age. Address to the Eastern Psychological Association convention. (p. 126)

Pope, H. G., & Yurgelun-Todd, D. (1996). The residual cognitive effects of heavy marijuana use in college students. *Journal of the American Medical Association, 275,* 521–527. (p. 216)

Popenoe, D. (1993). The evolution of marriage and the problem of step-families: A biosocial perspective. Paper presented at the National Symposium on Stepfamilies, Pennsylvania State University. (p. 462)

Poremba, A., & Gabriel, M. (2001). Amygdalar efferents initiate auditory thalamic discriminative training-induced neuronal activity. *Journal of Neuroscience, 21,* 270–278. (p. 50)

Porkka-Heiskanen, T., Strecker, R. E., Thakkar, M., Bjorkum, A. A., Greene, R. W., & McCarley, R. W. (1997). Adenosine: A mediator of the sleep-inducing effects of prolonged wakefulness. *Science, 276,* 1265–1268. (p. 197)

Porter, D., & Neuringer, A. (1984). Music discriminations by pigeons. *Journal of Experimental Psychology: Animal Behavior Processes, 10,* 138–148. (p. 238)

Porter, R. P. (1998). Twisted tongues: The failure of bilingual education. Washington, DC: The Communitarian Network (www.gwu.edu/~ccps/pop_biling.html). (p. 309)

Porter, S., Birt, A. R., Yuille, J. C., & Lehman, D. R. (2000, Nov.). Negotiating false memories: Interviewer and rememberer characteristics relate to memory distortion. *Psychological Science, 11,* 507–510. (p. 282)

Posavac, H. D., Posavac, S. S., & Posavac, E. J. (1998). Exposure to media images of female attractiveness and concern with body weight among young women. *Sex Roles, 38,* 187–201. (p. 351)

Posner, M. I., & Carr, T. H. (1992). Lexical access and the brain: Anatomical constraints on cognitive models of word recognition. *American Journal of Psychology, 105,* 1–26. (p. 56)

Poulton, R., & Milne, B. J. (2002). Low fear in childhood is associated with sporting prowess in adolescence and young adulthood. *Behaviour Research and Therapy, 40,* 1191–1197. (p. 485)

Powell, J. (1989). *Happiness is an inside job.* Valencia, CA: Tabor. (p. 459)

Powell, K. E., Thompson, P. D., Caspersen, C. J., & Kendrick, J. S. (1987). Physical activity and the incidence of coronary heart disease. *Annual Review of Public Health, 8,* 253–287. (p. 415)

Powell, L. H., Schahabi, L., & Thoresen, C. E. (2003). Religion and spirituality: Linkages to physical health. *American Psychologist, 58,* 36–52. (p. 423)

Powell, R. A., & Boer, D. P. (1994). Did Freud mislead patients to confabulate memories of abuse? *Psychological Reports, 74,* 1283–1298. (p. 437)

Pratkanis, A. R. (1992). The cargo-cult science of subliminal persuasion. *Skeptical Inquirer, 16,* 260–272. (p. 143)

Pratkanis, A. R., Eskenazi, J., & Greenwald, A. G. (1994). What you expect is what you believe (but not necessarily what you get): A test of the effectiveness of subliminal self-help audiotapes. *Basic and Applied Social Psychology, 15,* 251–276. (p. 144)

Pratto, F. (1996). Sexual politics: The gender gap in the bedroom, the cupboard, and the cabinet. In D. M. Buss & N. M. Malamuth (Eds.), *Sex, power, conflict: Evolutionary and feminist perspectives.* New York: Oxford University Press. (p. 91)

Prentice, D. A., & Miller, D. T. (1993). Pluralistic ignorance and alcohol use on campus: Some consequences of misperceiving the social norm. *Journal of Personality and Social Psychology, 64,* 243–256. (p. 220)

Presley, C. A., Meilman, P. W., & Lyerla, R. (1997). *Alcohol and drugs on American college campuses: Issues of violence and harrassment.* Carbondale, IL: Core Institute, Southern Illinois University. (p. 210)

Presson, P. K., & Benassi, V. A. (1996). Locus of control orientation and depressive symptomatology: A meta-analysis. *Journal of Social Behavior and Personality, 11,* 201–212. (p. 452)

Prickett, J. T., Gada-Jain, N., & Bernieri, F. J. (2000, May). The importance of first impressions in a job interview. Presented at the annual meeting of the Midwestern Psychological Association, Chicago, IL. (p. B–5)

Prioleau, L., Murdock, M., & Brody, N. (1983). An analysis of psychotherapy versus placebo studies. *The Behavioral and Brain Sciences, 6,* 275–310. (p. 526)

Project Match Research Group. (1997). Matching alcoholism treatments to client heterogeneity: Project MATCH posttreatment drinking outcomes. *Journal of Studies on Alcohol, 58,* 7–29. (p. 518)

Pronin, E., Lin, D. Y., & Ross, L. (2002). The bias blind spot: Perceptions of bias in self versus others. *Personality and Social Psychology Bulletin, 28,* 369–381. (p. 459)

Provine, R. R. (2001). *Laughter: A scientific investigation.* New York: Penguin. (p. 19)

Public Opinion. (1984, August/September). Phears and Phobias, p. 32. (p. 477)

Putnam, F. W. (1991). Recent research on multiple personality disorder. *Psychiatric Clinics of North America, 14,* 489–502. (p. 483)

Putnam, F. W. (1995). Rebuttal of Paul McHugh. *Journal of the American Academy of Child and Adolescent Psychiatry, 34,* 963. (p. 484)

Putnam, R. (2000). *Bowling alone.* New York: Simon and Schuster. (p. 88)

Pyszczynski, T., Hamilton, J. C., Greenberg, J., & Becker, S. E. (1991). Self-awareness and psychological dysfunction. In C. R. Snyder & D. O. Forsyth (Eds.), *Handbook of social and clinical psychology: The health perspective.* New York: Pergamon. (p. 493)

Quinn, P. C. (2002). Category representation in young infants. *Current Directions in Psychological Science, 11,* 66–70. (p. 102)

Quinn, P. C., Bhatt, R. S., Brush, D., Grimes, A., & Sharpnack, H. (2002). Development of form similarity as a Gestalt grouping principle in infancy. *Psychological Science, 13,* 320–328. (pp. 166, 168)

Quinn, P. J., Williams, G. M., Najman, J. M., Andersen, M. J., & Bor, W. (2001). The effect of breastfeeding on child development at 5 years: A cohort study. *Journal of Paediatrics & Child Health, 3,* 465–469. (p. 24)

Radford, B. (2002, November/December). Psychics wrong about Chandra Levy. *Skeptical Inquirer,* p. 9. (p. 179)

Raine, A. (1999). Murderous minds: Can we see the mark of Cain? *Cerebrum: The Dana Forum on Brain Science 1(1),* 15–29. (pp. 485–486, 561)

Raine, A., Lencz, T., Bihrle, S., LaCasse, L., & Colletti, P. (2000). Reduced prefrontal gray matter volume and reduced autonomic activity in antisocial personality disorder. *Archives of General Psychiatry, 57,* 119–127. (p. 485)

Rainville, P., Duncan, G. H., Price, D. D., Carrier, B., & Bushnell, M. C. (1997). Pain affect encoded in human anterior cingulate but not somatosensory cortex. *Science, 277,* 968–971. (p. 206)

Raison, C. L., Klein, H. M., & Steckler, M. (1999). The mood and madness reconsidered. *Journal of Affective Disorders, 53,* 99–106. (p. 501)

Rajecki, D. W., Bledsoe, S. B., & Rasmussen, J. L. (1991). Successful personal ads: Gender differences and similarities in offers, stipulations, and outcomes. *Basic and Applied Social Psychology, 12,* 457–469. (p. 73)

Ramachandran, V. S., & Blakeslee, S. (1998). *Phantoms in the brain: Probing the mysteries of the human mind.* New York: Morrow. (pp. 45, 58, 61, 160)

Ramey, S. L., & Ramey, C. T. (1992). Early educational intervention with disadvantaged children—To what effect? *Applied and Preventive Psychology, 1,* 131–140. (p. 329)

Rand, C. S. W., & Macgregor, A. M. C. (1990). Morbidly obese patients' perceptions of social discrimination before and after surgery for obesity. *Southern Medical Journal, 83,* 1390–1395. (p. 353)

Rand, C. S. W., & Macgregor, A. M. C. (1991). Successful weight loss following obesity surgery and perceived liability or morbid obesity. *Internal Journal of Obesity, 15,* 577–579. (p. 353)

Randi, J. (1999, February 4). 2000 Club mailing list e-mail letter. (p. 179)

Rapoport, J. L. (1989, March). The biology of obsessions and compulsions. *Scientific American,* pp. 83–89. (pp. 478, 481)

Räsänen, S., Pakaslahti, A., Syvalahti, E., Jones, P. B., & Isohanni, M. (2000). Sex differences in schizophrenia: A review. *Nordic Journal of Psychiatry, 54,* 37–45. (p. 498)

Rauch, S. L., & Jenike, M. A. (1993). Neurobiological models of obsessive-compulsive disorder. *Psychomatics, 34,* 20–32. (p. 482)

Ray, O., & Ksir, C. (1990). *Drugs, society, and human behavior* (5th ed.). St. Louis: Times Mirror/Mosby. (p. 214)

Raynor, H. A., & Epstein, L. H. (2001). Dietary variety, energy regulation, and obesity. *Psychological Bulletin, 127,* 325–341. (p. 356)

Reason, J. (1987). The Chernobyl errors. *Bulletin of the British Psychological Society, 40,* 201–206. (p. 553)

Reason, J., & Mycielska, K. (1982). *Absent-minded? The psychology of mental lapses and everyday errors.* Englewood Cliffs, NJ: Prentice-Hall. (p. 181)

Redelmeier, D. A., & Singh, S. M. (2001). Survival in Academy Award–winning actors and actresses. *Annals of Internal Medicine, 134,* 955–962. (p. 407)

Reed, P. (2000). Serial position effects in recognition memory for odors. *Journal of Experimental Psychology: Learning, Memory, and Cognition, 26,* 411–422. (p. 261)

Reeve, C. (1995). ABC 20/20, October 6, 1995, and Associated Press report, October 17, 1995 (in *Holland Sentinel,* p. A12). (p. 380)

Reeve, C. L., & Hakel, M. D. (2002). Asking the right questions about *g. Human Performance, 15,* 47–74. (p. 318)

Regier, D. A., Kaelber, C. T., Rae, D. S., Farmer, M. E., Knauper, B., Kessler, R. C., & Norquist, G. S. (1998). Limitations of diagnostic criteria and assessment instruments for mental disorders: Implications for research and policy. *Archives of General Psychiatry, 55,* 109–115. (p. 473)

Regier, D. A., Narrow, W. E., Rae, D. S., Manderscheid, R. W., Locke, B. Z., & Goodwin, F. K. (1993). The de facto U.S. mental and addictive disorders service system: Epidemiologic catchment area prospective 1-year prevalence rates of disorders and services. *Archives of General Psychiatry, 50,* 85–94. (p. 520)

Reichman, J. (1998). *I'm not in the mood: What every woman should know about improving her libido.* New York: Morrow. (p. 359)

Reilly-Harrington, N. A., Alloy, L. B., Fresco, D. M., & Whitehouse, W. G. (1999). Cognitive styles and life events interact to predict bipolar and unipolar symptomatology. *Journal of Abnormal Psychology, 108,* 567–578. (p. 488)

Reisenzein, R. (1983). The Schachter theory of emotion: Two decades later. *Psychological Bulletin, 94,* 239–264. (p. 382)

Reiser, M. (1982). *Police psychology.* Los Angeles: LEHI. (p. 178)

Relman, A. S. (1998, December 14). A trip to stonesville. *New Republic* (www.thenewrepublic.com). (p. 420)

Remafedi, G. (1999). Suicide and sexual orientation: Nearing the end of controversy? *Archives of General Psychiatry, 56,* 885–886. (p. 365)

Remley, A. (1988, October). From obedience to independence. *Psychology Today,* pp. 56–59. (p. 88)

Reneman, L., Lavalaye, J., Schmand, B., De Wolff, F. A., Van Den Brink, W., Den Heeten, G., & Booij, J. (2001). Cortical serotonin transporter density and verbal memory in individuals who stopped using 3, 4-methylenedioxy-methampetamine. *Archives of General Psychiatry, 58,* 901–908. (p. 215)

Renner, M. J. (1992). Curiosity and exploration. In L. R. Squire (Ed.), *Encyclopedia of Learning and Memory.* New York: Macmillan. (p. 343)

Renner, M. J., & Renner, C. H. (1993). Expert and novice intuitive judgments about animal behavior. *Bulletin of the Psychonomic Society, 31,* 551–552. (p. 83)

Renner, M. J., & Rosenzweig, M. R. (1987). Enriched and impoverished environments: Effects on brain and behavior. New York: Springer-Verlag. (p. 83)

Repetti, R. L., Taylor, S. E., & Seeman, T. E. (2002). Risky families: Family social environments and the mental and physical health of offspring. *Psychological Bulletin, 128,* 330–366. (p. 403)

Rescorla, R. A., & Wagner, A. R. (1972). A theory of Pavlovian conditioning: Variations in the effectiveness of reinforcement and nonreinforcement. In A. H. Black & W. F. Perokasy (Eds.), *Classical conditioning II: Current theory.* New York: Appleton-Century-Crofts. (p. 233)

Resnick, M. D., Bearman, P. S., Blum, R. W., Bauman, K. E., Harris, K. M., Jones, J., Tabor, J., Beuhring, T., Sieving, R., Shew, M., Bearinger, L. H., & Udry, J. R. (1997). Protecting adolescents from harm: Findings from the National Longitudinal Study on Adolescent Health. *Journal of the American Medical Association, 278,* 823–832. (pp. 20, 122)

Resnick, R. A., O'Regan, J. K., & Clark, J. J. (1997). To see or not to see: The need for attention to perceive changes in scenes. *Psychological Science, 8,* 368–373. (p. 188)

Resnick, S. M. (1992). Positron emission tomography in psychiatric illness. *Current Directions in Psychological Science, 1,* 92–98. (pp. 482, 498)

Responsive Community. (1996, Fall). Age vs. weight. Page 83 (reported from a *Wall Street Journal* survey). (p. 355)

Reuters. (2000, July 5). Many teens regret decision to have sex (National Campaign to Prevent Teen Pregnancy survey). www.washingtonpost.com (p. 361)

Reynolds, A. J., Temple, J. A., Robertson, D. L., & Manri, E. A. (2001). Long-term effects of an early childhood intervention on educational achievement and juvenile arrest. *Journal of the American Medical Association, 285,* 2339–2346. (p. 330)

Rhee, S. H., & Waldman, I. D. (2002). Genetic and environmental influences on antisocial behavior: A meta-analysis of twin and adoption studies. *Psychological Bulletin, 128,* 490–529. (p. 485)

Rhodes, S. R. (1983). Age-related differences in work attitudes and behavior: A review and conceptual analysis. *Psychological Bulletin, 93,* 328–367. (p. 126)

Rice, B. (1985, September). Performance review: The job nobody likes. *Psychology Today,* pp. 30–36. (p. 541)

Rice, M. E., & Grusec, J. E. (1975). Saying and doing: Effects on observer performance. *Journal of Personality and Social Psychology, 32,* 584–593. (p. 250)

Richards, J. M., & Gross, J. J. (2000). Emotion regulation and memory: The cognitive costs of keeping one's cool. *Journal of Personality and Social Psychology, 79,* 410–424. (p. 387)

Rieff, P. (1979). *Freud: The mind of a moralist* (3rd ed.). Chicago: University of Chicago Press. (p. 438)

Riis, J., Loewenstein, G., Baron, J., Jepson, C., Fagerlin, A., & Ubel, P. A. (2003). Ignorance of hedonic adaptation to hemo-dialysis: A study using ecological momentary assessment. Unpublished manuscript, University of Michigan. (p. 396)

Ring, K. (1980). *Life at death: A scientific investigation of the near-death experience.* New York: Coward, McCann & Geoghegan. (p. 215)

Riskind, J. H., Beck, A. T., Berchick, R. J., Brown, G., & Steer, R. A. (1987). Reliability of DSM-III diagnoses for major depression and generalized anxiety disorder using the structured clinical interview for DSM-III. *Archives of General Psychiatry, 44,* 817–820. (p. 473)

Rizzolatti, G., Fadiga, L., Fogassi, L., & Gallese, V. (2002). From mirror neurons to imitation: Facts and speculations. In A. N. Meltzoff & W. Prinz (Eds.), *The imitative mind: Development, evolution, and brain bases.* Cambridge: Cambridge University Press, 2002. (p. 249)

Roberts, A. H., Kewman, D. G., Mercier, L., & Hovell, M. (1993). The power of nonspecific effects in healing: Implications for psychosocial and biological treatments. *Clinical Psychology Review, 13,* 375–391. (p. 526)

Roberts, B. W. (1997). Plaster or plasticity: Are adult work experiences associated with personality change in women? *Journal of Personality, 65,* 205–232. (p. 543)

Roberts, B. W., Caspi, A., & Moffitt, T. E. (2001). The kids are alright: Growth and stability in personality development from adolescence to adulthood. *Journal of Personality and Social Psychology, 81,* 670–683. (p. 135)

Roberts, B. W., & DelVecchio, W. F. (2000). The rank-order consistency of personality traits from childhood to old age: A quantitative review of longitudinal studies. *Psychological Bulletin, 126,* 3–25. (p. 449)

Roberts, B. W., Robins, R. W., Caspi, A., & Trzesniewski, K. H. (2003). Personality trait development in adulthood. In J. L. Mortimer & M. Shanahan (Eds.), *Handbook of the life course* (New York: Plenum Press). (p. 135)

Roberts, L. (1988). Beyond Noah's ark: What do we need to know? *Science, 242,* 1247. (p. 407)

Roberts, T-A. (1991). Determinants of gender differences in responsiveness to others' evaluations. *Dissertation Abstracts International, 51*(8–B). (p. 121)

Robins, L., & Regier, D. (Eds.). (1991). *Psychiatric disorders in America.* New York: Free Press. (p. 502)

Robins, R. W., Gosling, S. D., & Craik, K. H. (1999). An empirical analysis of trends in psychology. *American Psychologist, 54,* 117–128. (p. 429)

Robins, R. W., Trzesniewski, K. H., Tracy, J. L., Gosling, S. D., & Potter, J. (2002). Global self-esteem across the lifespan. *Psychology and Aging, 17,* 423–434. (p. 121)

Robinson, J. (2002, October 8). What percentage of the population is gay? *Gallup Tuesday Briefing* (www.gallup.com/poll/tb/religValue/20021008b.asp). (p. 364)

Robinson, J. L., Kagan, J., Reznick, J. S., & Corley, R. (1992). The heritability of inhibited and uninhibited behavior: A twin study. *Developmental Psychology, 28,* 1030–1037. (p. 80)

Robinson, T. E., & Berridge, K. C. (2003). Addiction. *Annual Review of Psychology, 54,* 25–53. (p. 209)

Robinson, T. N. (1999). Reducing children's television viewing to prevent obesity. *Journal of the American Medical Association, 282,* 1561–1567. (p. 356)

Robison, L. (1999). Why our MENTALLY ILL son is on DEATH ROW. www.swuuc.org/fjuuc/Courier/robison.htm. See also www.larryrobison.org (p. 474)

Rochat, F. (1993). How did they resist authority? Protecting refugees in Le Chambon during World War II. Paper presented at the American Psychological Association convention. (p. 549)

Rock, I., & Palmer, S. (1990, December). The legacy of Gestalt psychology. *Scientific American,* pp. 84–90. (pp. 165, 166)

Rodin, J. (1986). Aging and health: Effects of the sense of control. *Science, 233,* 1271–1276. (pp. 405–406, 407, 453)

Roediger, H. L., III, Wheeler, M. A., & Rajaram, S. (1993). Remembering, knowing, and reconstructing the past. In D. L. Medin (Ed.), *The psychology of learning and motivation: Advances in research and theory* (Vol. 30). Orlando, FL: Academic Press. (p. 282)

Roehling, M. V. (2000). Weight-based discrimination in employment: psychological and legal aspects. *Personnel Psychology, 52(4),* 969–1016. (p. 352)

Roehling, P. V., Roehling, M. V., & Moen, P. (2001). The relationship between work-life policies and practices and employee loyalty: A life course perspective. *Journal of Family and Economic Issues, 22,* 141–170. (p. B–11)

Roesser, R. (1998). What you should know about hearing conservation. Better Hearing Institute (www.betterhearing.org). (p. 158)

Rogers, C. R. (1961). *On becoming a person: A therapist's view of psychotherapy.* Boston: Houghton Mifflin. (p. 510)

Rogers, C. R. (1980). *A way of being.* Boston: Houghton Mifflin. (pp. 440, 510)

Rogers, S. (1992–1993, Winter). How a publicity blitz created the myth of subliminal advertising. *Public Relations Quarterly,* pp. 12–17. (p. 143)

Rogers, S. (1994). Subliminal advertising: Grand scam of the 20th century. Paper presented to the American Academy of Advertising convention. (p. 143)

Rohan, M. J., & Zanna, M. P. (1996). Value transmission in families. In C. Seligman, J. M. Olson, & M. P. Zanna (Eds.), *The psychology of values: The Ontario Symposium* (Vol. 8). Malwah, NJ: Erlbaum. (p. 79)

Rohner, R. P. (1986). *The warmth dimension: Foundations of parental accept-ance-rejection theory.* Newbury Park, CA: Sage. (p. 89)

Rohner, R. P., & Veneziano, R. A. (2001). The importance of father love: History and contemporary evidence. *Review of General Psychology, 5,* 382–405. (pp. 112, 114)

Rokach, A., Orzeck, T., Moya, M., & Exposito, F. (2002). Causes of loneliness in North America and Spain. *European Psychologist, 7,* 70–79. (p. 28)

Rook, K. S. (1984). Promoting social bonding: Strategies for helping the lonely and socially isolated. *American Psychologist, 39,* 1389–1407. (p. 494)

Rosa, L., Rosa, E., Sarner, L., & Barrett, S. (1998). A close look at therapeutic touch. *Journal of the American Medical Association, 279,* 1005–1010. (pp. 524–525)

Rosch, E. (1974). Linguistic relativity. In A. Silverstein (Ed.), *Human communication: Theoretical perspectives.* New York: Halsted Press. (p. 308)

Rosch, E. (1978). Principles of categorization. In E. Rosch & B. L. Lloyd (Eds.), *Cognition and categorization.* Hillsdale, NJ: Erlbaum. (p. 294)

Rose, J. S., Chassin, L., Presson, C. C., & Sherman, S. J. (1999). Peer influences on adolescent cigarette smoking: A prospective sibling analysis. *Merrill-Palmer Quarterly, 45,* 62–84. (p. 85)

Rose, R. J., Kaprio, J., Winter, T., Dick, D. M., Viken, R. J., Pulkkinen, L., & Koskenvuo, M. (2002). Femininity and fertility in sis-ters with twin brothers: Prenatal androgenization? Cross-sex socialization? *Psychological Science, 13,* 263–266. (p. 366)

Rose, S. (1999). Precis of *Lifelines: Biology, freedom, determinism. Behavioral and Brain Sciences, 22,* 871–921. (p. 75)

Rosenbaum, M. (1986). The repulsion hypothesis: On the nondevelop-ment of relationships. *Journal of Personality and Social Psychology, 51,* 1156–1166. (p. 571)

Rosenhan, D. L. (1973). On being sane in insane places. *Science, 179,* 250–258. (p. 474)

Rosenthal, R., Hall, J. A., Archer, D., DiMatteo, M. R., & Rogers, P. L. (1979). The PONS test: Measuring sensitivity to nonverbal cues. In S. Weitz (Ed.), *Nonverbal communication* (2nd ed.). New York: Oxford University Press. (pp. 334, 387)

Rosenzweig, M. R. (1984). Experience, memory, and the brain. *American Psychologist, 39,* 365–376. (p. 83)

Ross, M., McFarland, C., & Fletcher, G. J. O. (1981). The effect of attitude on the recall of personal histories. *Journal of Personality and Social Psychology, 40,* 627–634. (p. 280)

Ross, M., Xun, W. Q. E., & Wilson, A. E. (2002). Language and the bicultural self. *Personality and Social Psychology Bulletin, 28,* 1040–1050. (p. 308)

Rossi, P. J. (1968). Adaptation and negative aftereffect to lateral optical displacement in newly hatched chicks. *Science, 160,* 430–432. (p. 176)

Roth, T., Roehrs, T., Zwyghuizen-Doorenbos, A., Stpeanski, E., & Witting, R. (1988). Sleep and memory. In I. Hindmarch & H. Ott (Eds.), *Benzodiazepine receptor ligans, memory and information processing.* New York: Springer-Verlag. (p. 201)

Rothbart, M., Fulero, S., Jensen, C., Howard, J., & Birrell, P. (1978). From individual to group impressions: Availability heuristics in stereotype formation. *Journal of Experimental Social Psychology, 14,* 237–255. (p. 559)

Rothbart, M. K., Ahadi, S. A., & Evans, D. E. (2000). Temperament and personality: Origins and outcomes. *Journal of Personality and Social Psychology, 78,* 122–135. (p. 80)

Rothbaum, B. O., Hodges, L. F., Kooper, R., Opdyke, D., Williford, J., & North, M. M. (1995). Effectiveness of computer-generated (virtual reality) graded exposure in the treatment of acrophobia. *American Journal of Psychiatry, 152,* 626–628. (p. 513)

Rothbaum, B. O., Hodges, L., & Kooper, R. (1997). Virtual reality exposure therapy. *Journal of Psychotherapy Practice and Research, 6,* 219–226. (p. 513)

Rothbaum, F., & Tsang, B. Y-P. (1998). Lovesongs in the United States and China: On the nature of romantic love. *Journal of Cross-Cultural Psychology, 29,* 306–319. (pp. 462–463)

Rothman, A. J., & Salovey, P. (1997). Shaping perceptions to motivate healthy behavior: The role of message framing. *Psychological Bulletin, 121,* 3–19. (p. 300)

Rothstein, W. G. (1980). The significance of occupations in work careers: An empirical and theoretical review. *Journal of Vocational Behavior, 17,* 328–343. (p. 132)

Rotton, J., & Kelly, I. W. (1985). Much ado about the full moon: A meta-analysis of lunar-lunacy research. *Psychological Bulletin, 97,* 286–306. (pp. 501, C–18)

Rovee-Collier, C. (1989). The joy of kicking: Memories, motives, and mobiles. In P. R. Solomon, G. R. Goethals, C. M. Kelley, & B. R. Stephens (Eds.), *Memory: Interdisciplinary approaches.* New York: Springer-Verlag. (p. 103)

Rovee-Collier, C. (1993). The capacity for long-term memory in infancy. *Current Directions in Psychological Science, 2,* 130–135. (p. 273)

Rovee-Collier, C. (1997). Dissociations in infant memory: Rethinking the development of implicit and explicit memory. *Psychological Review, 104,* 467–498. (p. 103)

Rowe, D. C. (1990). As the twig is bent? The myth of child-rearing influ-ences on personality development. *Journal of Counseling and Development, 68,* 606–611. (p. 78)

Rowe, D. C. (1997). A place at the policy table? Behavior genetics and estimates of family environmental effects on IQ. *Intelligence, 24,* 133–158. (p. 331)

Rowe, D. C., Almeida, D. M., & Jacobson, K. C. (1999). School con-text and genetic influences on aggression in adolescence. *Psychological Science, 10,* 277–280. (p. 560)

Rowe, D. C., Jacobson, K. C., & Van den Oord, E. J. C. G. (1999). Genetic and environmental influences on vocabulary IQ: Parental educa-tion level as moderator. *Child Development, 70(5),* 1151–1162. (p. 328)

Rowe, D. C., Vazsonyi, A. T., & Flannery, D. J. (1994). No more than skin deep: Ethnic and racial similarity in developmental process. *Psychological Review, 101(3),* 396. (p. 89)

Rowe, D. C., Vazsonyi, A. T., & Flannery, D. J. (1995). Ethnic and racial similarity in developmental process: A study of academic achieve-ment. *Psychological Science, 6,* 33–38. (p. 89)

Rozin, P. (1976). The selection of food by rats, humans and other animals. In J. Rosenblatt, R. A. Hinde, C. Beer, & E. Shaw (Eds.), *Advances in the study of behavior* (Vol. 6). New York: Academic Press. (p. 348)

Rozin, P., Dow, S., Mosovitch, M., & Rajaram, S. (1998). What causes humans to begin and end a meal? A role for memory for what has been eaten, as evidenced by a study of multiple meal eating in amnesic patients. *Psychological Science, 9,* 392–396. (p. 348)

Rozin, P., Millman, L., & Nemeroff, C. (1986). Operation of the laws of sympathetic magic in disgust and other domains. *Journal of Personality and Social Psychology, 50,* 703–712. (p. 232)

Ruback, R. B., Carr, T. S., & Hopper, C. H. (1986). Perceived control in prison: Its relation to reported crowding, stress, and symptoms. *Journal of Applied Social Psychology, 16,* 375–386. (pp. 452–453)

Rubin, D. C., Rahhal, T. A., & Poon, L. W. (1998). Things learned in early adulthood are remembered best. *Memory and Cognition, 26,* 3–19. (p. 127)

Rubin, J. Z., Pruitt, D. G., & Kim, S. H. (1994). *Social conflict: Escalation, stalemate, and settlement.* New York: McGraw-Hill. (p. 577)

Rubin, L. B. (1985). *Just friends: The role of friendship in our lives.* New York: Harper & Row. (p. 121)

Rubin, Z. (1970). Measurement of romantic love. *Journal of Personality and Social Psychology, 16,* 265–273. (p. 387)

Rubonis, A. V., & Bickman, L. (1991). Psychological impairment in the wake of disaster: The disaster-psychopathology relationship. *Psychological Bulletin, 109,* 384–399. (p. 404)

Ruchlis, H. (1990). *Clear thinking: A practical introduction.* Buffalo, NY: Prometheus Books. (p. 294)

Ruffin, C. L. (1993). Stress and health—little hassles vs. major life events. *Australian Psychologist, 28,* 201–208. (p. 405)

Rule, B. G., & Ferguson, T. J. (1986). The effects of media violence on attitudes, emotions, and cognitions. *Journal of Social Issues, 42(3),* 29–50. (p. 252)

Rumbaugh, D. M. (1977). *Language learning by a chimpanzee: The Lana project.* New York: Academic Press. (p. 313)

Rumbaugh, D. M. (1994, February 15). Remarks on *Nova: Can chimps talk?* PBS Television. (pp. 314–315)

Rumbaugh, D. M., & Savage-Rumbaugh, S. (1978). Chimpanzee language research: Status and potential. *Behavior Research Methods & Instrumentation, 10,* 119–131. (p. 314)

Rumbaugh, D. M., & Savage-Rumbaugh, S. (1994, January/February). Language and apes. *Psychology Teacher Network,* pp. 2–5, 9. (p. 314)

Rupp, R. (1998). *How we remember and why we forget.* New York: Three Rivers Press. (p. 257)

Rushton, J. P. (1975). Generosity in children: Immediate and long-term effects of modeling, preaching, and moral judgment. *Journal of Personality and Social Psychology, 31,* 459–466. (p. 250)

Rushton, J. P. (1990). Race differences, r/K theory, and a reply to Flynn. *The Psychologist: Bulletin of the British Psychological Society, 5,* 195–198. (p. 331)

Rushton, J. P. (1998). The "Jensen effect" and the "Spearman-Jensen hypothesis" of black-white IQ differences. *Intelligence, 26,* 217–225. (p. 331)

Russell, B. (1930/1985). *The conquest of happiness.* London: Unwin Paperbacks. (p. 400)

Rusting, C. L., & Nolen-Hoeksema, S. (1998). Regulating responses to anger: Effects of rumination and distraction on angry mood. *Journal of Personality and Social Psychology, 74,* 790–803. (p. 395)

Rutter, M., and the English and Romanian Adoptees (ERA) study team. (1998). Developmental catch-up, and deficit, following adoption after severe global early privation. *Journal of Child Psychology and Psychiatry, 39,* 465–476. (p. 113)

Ryan, L., Hatfield, C., & Hofstetter, M. (2002). Caffeine reduces time-of-day effects on memory performance in older adults. *Psychological Science, 13,* 68–71. (p. 128)

Ryan, R. (1999, February 2). Quoted by Alfie Kohn, In pursuit of affluence, at a high price. *New York Times* (www.nytimes.com). (pp. 398, 399)

Ryckman, R. M., Robbins, M. A., Kaczor, L. M., & Gold J. A. (1989). Male and female raters' stereotyping of male and female physiques. *Personality and Social Psychology Bulletin, 15,* 244–251. (p. 352)

Saad, L. (2001, December 17). Americans' mood: Has Sept. 11 made a difference? Gallup Poll News Service (www.gallup.com/poll/releases/pr011217.asp). (pp. 402, 405)

Saad, L. (2002, July 30). Dieter's dilemma: Bagel or bacon? *Gallup Tuesday Briefing,* Gallup Organization (www.gallup.com/poll/tb/healthcare/20020730.asp). (p. 354)

Sabini, J. (1986). Stanley Milgram (1933–1984). *American Psychologist, 41,* 1378–1379. (p. 547)

Sachdev, P., & Sachdev, J. (1997). Sixty years of psychosurgery: Its present status and its future. *Australian and New Zealand Journal of Psychiatry, 31,* 457–464. (p. 534)

Sacks, O. (1985). *The man who mistook his wife for a hat.* New York: Summit Books. (pp. 164, 269–270)

Sacks, O. (1990). *Seeing voices: A journey into the world of the deaf.* New York: HarperCollins. (p. 309)

Sadato, N., Pascual-Leone, A., Grafman, J., Ibanez, V., Deiber, M-P., Dold, G., & Hallett, M. (1996). Activation of the primary visual cortex by Braille reading in blind subjects. *Nature, 380,* 526–528. (p. 58)

Saffran, J. R., Aslin, R. N., & Newport, E. L. (1996). Statistical learning by 8-month-old infants. *Science, 274,* 1926–1928. (p. 306)

Sagan, C. (1987, February 1). The fine art of baloney detection. *Parade.* (p. 179)

Sagan, C., & Druyan, A. (1992). *Shadows of forgotten ancestors: A search for who we are.* New York: Random House. (p. 312)

Sagie, A. (1998). Employee absenteeism, organizational commitment, and job satisfaction: Another look. *Journal of Vocational Behavior, 52,* 156–171. (p. B–8)

Sakurai, T., Amemiya, A., Ishii, M., Matsuzaki, I., Chemelli, R. M., Tanaka, H., Williams, S. C., Richardson, J. A., Kozlowski, G. P., Wilson, S., Arch, J. R. S., Buckingham, R. E., Haynes, A. C., Carr, S. A., Annan, R. S., McNulty, D. E., Liu, W-S., Terrett, J. A., Elshourbagy, N. A., Bergsma, D. J., Yanagisawa, M. (1998). Orexins and orexin receptors: A family of hypothalamic neuropeptides and G protein-coupled receptors that regulate feeding behavior. *Cell, 92,* 573–585. (p. 346)

Salmon, P. (2001). Effects of physical exercise on anxiety, depression, and sensitivity to stress: A unifying theory. *Clinical Psychology Review, 21,* 33–61. (p. 415)

Salovey, P. (1990, January/February). Interview. *American Scientist,* pp. 25–29. (p. 396)

Salovey, P., & Mayer, J. D. (1990). Emotional intelligence. *Imagination, Cognition, and Personality, 9,* 185–211. (p. 319)

Salovey, P., Mayer, J. D., & Caruso, D. (2002). The positive psychology of emotional intelligence. In C. R. Snyder & S. J. Lopez (Eds.), *Handbook of positive psychology.* New York: Oxford. (p. 319)

Sampson, E. E. (2000). Reinterpreting individualism and collectivism: Their religious roots and monologic versus dialogic person–other relationship. *American Psychologist, 55,* 1425–1432. (p. 461)

Samuels, J., & Nestadt, G. (1997). Epidemiology and genetics of obsessive-compulsive disorder. *International Review of Psychiatry, 9,* 61–71. (p. 478)

Samuels, S., & McCabe, G. (1989). Quoted by P. Diaconis & F. Mosteller, Methods for studying coincidences. *Journal of the American Statistical Association, 84,* 853–861. (p. 22)

Sandberg, G. G., Jackson, T. L., & Petretic-Jackson, P. (1985). *Sexual aggression and courtship violence in dating relationships.* Paper presented at the meeting of the Midwestern Psychological Association. (p. 563)

Sanders, G., Sjodin, M., & de Chastelaine, M. (2002). On the elusive nature of sex differences in cognition hormonal influences contributing to within-sex variation. *Archives of Sexual Behavior, 31,* 145–152. (p. 367)

Sanders, G., & Wright, M. (1997). Sexual orientation differences in cerebral asymmetry and in the performance of sexually dimorphic cognitive and motor tasks. *Archives of Sexual Behavior, 26,* 463–479. (p. 367)

Sandfort, T. G. M., de Graaf, R., Bijl, R., & Schnabel, P. (2001). Same-sex sexual behavior and psychiatric disorders. *Archives of General Psychiatry, 58,* 85–91. (pp. 364, 365)

Sanford, A. J., Fray, N., Stewart, A., & Moxey, L. (2002). Perspective in statements of quantity, with implications for consumer psychology. *Psychological Science, 13,* 130–134. (p. 300)

Sanz, C., Blicher, A., Dalke, K., Gratton-Fabri, L., McClure-Richards, T., & Fouts, R. (1998, Winter-Spring). Enrichment object use: Five chimpanzees' use of temporary and semi-permanent enrichment objects. *Friends of Washoe, 19(1,2),* 9–14. (p. 312)

Sapadin, L. A. (1988). Friendship and gender: Perspectives of professional men and women. *Journal of Social and Personal Relationships, 5,* 387–403. (p. 121)

Sapolsky, B. S., & Tabarlet, J. O. (1991). Sex in primetime television: 1979 versus 1989. *Journal of Broadcasting and Electronic Media, 35,* 505–516. (pp. 362, 564)

Sapolsky, R. (1999, March). Stress and your shrinking brain. *Discover,* pp. 116–120. (p. 404)

Sato, K. (1987). Distribution of the cost of maintaining common resources. *Journal of Experimental Social Psychology, 23,* 19–31. (p. 567)

Savage-Rumbaugh, E. S., Murphy, J., Sevcik, R. A., Brakke, K. E., Williams, S. L., & Rumbaugh, D. M., with commentary by Bates, E. (1993). Language comprehension in ape and child. *Monographs of the Society for Research in Child Development, 58(233),* 1–254. (p. 314)

Savoy, C., & Beitel, P. (1996). Mental imagery for basketball. *International Journal of Sport Psychology, 27,* 454–462. (p. 310)

Sawyer, M. G., Arney, F. M., Baghurst, P. A., Clark, J. J., Graetz, B. W., Kosky, R. J., Nurcombe, B., Patton, G. C., Prior, M. R., Raphael, B., Rey, J., Whaites, L. C., & Zubrick, S. R. (2000). *The mental health of young people in Australia.* Canberra: Mental Health and Special Programs Branch, Commonwealth Department of Health and Aged Care. (pp. 489, 502)

Sax, L. J., Lindholm, J. A., Astin, A. W., Korn, W. S., & Mahoney, K. M. (2001). *The American freshman: National norms for Fall 2001.* Los Angeles, CA: Higher Education Research Institute, UCLA. (pp. 72, 364)

Sax, L. J., Lindholm, J. A., Astin, A. W., Korn, W. S., & Mahoney, K. M. (2002). *The American freshman: National norms for Fall 2002.* Los Angeles, CA: Higher Education Research Institute, UCLA. (pp. 91, 217, 492, 494)

Scarborough, E., & Furumoto, L. (1987). *Untold lives: The first generation of American women psychologists.* New York: Columbia University Press. (p. 4)

Scarr, S. (1984, May). What's a parent to do? A conversation with E. Hall. *Psychology Today,* pp. 58–63. (p. 329)

Scarr, S. (1989). Protecting general intelligence: Constructs and consequences for interventions. In R. J. Linn (Ed.), *Intelligence: Measurement, theory, and public policy.* Champaign: University of Illinois Press. (p. 318)

Scarr, S. (1990). Back cover comments on J. Dunn & R. Plomin (1990). *Separate lives: Why siblings are so different.* New York: Basic Books. (p. 81)

Scarr, S. (1993, May/June). Quoted by *Psychology Today,* Nature's thumbprint: So long, superparents, p. 16. (p. 82)

Schab, F. R. (1991). Odor memory: Taking stock. *Psychological Bulletin, 109,* 242–251. (p. 164)

Schachter, S., & Singer, J. E. (1962). Cognitive, social and physiological determinants of emotional state. *Psychological Review, 69,* 379–399. (p. 382)

Schacter, D. L. (1992). Understanding implicit memory: A cognitive neuroscience approach. *American Psychologist, 47,* 559–569. (p. 270)

Schacter, D. L. (1996). *Searching for memory: The brain, the mind, and the past.* New York: Basic Books. (pp. 126, 270, 271, 283, 438)

Schacter, D. L. (1999). The seven sins of memory: Insights from psychology and cognitive neuroscience. *American Psychologist, 54,* 182–201. (p. 276)

Schaie, K. W., & Geiwitz, J. (1982). *Adult development and aging.* Boston: Little, Brown. (p. 128)

Schall, E. M., & Smith, G. (2002). Do baseball players regress toward the mean? Unpublished manuscript, Claremont College (www.economics.pomona.edu/GarySmith). (p. A–6)

Schall, T., & Smith, G. (2000, Fall). Career trajectories in baseball. *Chance,* pp. 35–38. (p. 124)

Scheiber, B., & Selby, C. (1997, May-June). UAB final report of therapeutic touch—An appraisal. *Skeptical Inquirer, 21,* 53–54. (p. 524)

Scheier, M. F., & Carver, C. S. (1992). Effects of optimism on psychological and physical well-being: Theoretical overview and empirical update. *Cognitive Therapy and Research, 16,* 201–228. (p. 407)

Schein, E. H. (1956). The Chinese indoctrination program for prisoners of war: A study of attempted brainwashing. *Psychiatry, 19,* 149–172. (p. 542)

Scherer, K. R., Banse, R., & Wallbott, H. G. (2001). Emotion inferences from vocal expression correlate across languages and cultures. *Journal of Cross-Cultural Psychology, 32,* 76–92. (p. 387)

Schiavi, R. C., & Schreiner-Engel, P. (1988). Nocturnal penile tumescence in healthy aging men. *Journal of Gerontology: Medical Sciences, 43,* M146–150. (p. 194)

Schiffenbauer, A., & Schiavo, R. S. (1976). Physical distance and attraction: An intensification effect. *Journal of Experimental Social Psychology, 12,* 274–282. (p. 551)

Schiffer, F., Stinchfield, Z., & Pascual-Leone, A. (2002). Prediction of clinical response to transcranial magnetic stimulation for depression by baseline lateral visual-field stimulation. *Neuropsychiatry, Neuropsychology and Behavioral Neurology, 15,* 18–27. (p. 534)

Schimel, J., Arndt, J., Pyszczynski, T., & Greenberg, J. (2001). Being accepted for who we are: Evidence that social validation of the intrinsic self reduces general defensiveness. *Journal of Personality and Social Psychology, 80,* 35–52. (p. 442)

Schimel, J., Greenberg, J., & Martens, A. (2003). Evidence that projection of a feared trait can serve a defensive function. *Personality and Social Psychology Bulletin, 29,* 969–979. (p. 464)

Schmidt, F. L. (2002). The role of general cognitive ability and job performance: Why there cannot be a debate. *Human Performance, 15,* 187–210. (p. B–5)

Schmidt, F. L., & Hunter, J. E. (1998). The validity and utility of selection methods in personnel psychology: Practical and theoretical implications of 85 years of research findings. *Psychological Bulletin, 124,* 262–274. (pp. 320, 456, B–5, B–6)

Schmidt, G., Klusmann, D., Zeitzschel, U., & Lange, C. (1994). Changes in adolescents' sexuality between 1970 and 1990 in West-Germany. *Archives of Sexual Behavior, 23,* 489–513. (p. 363)

Schnaper, N. (1980). Comments germane to the paper entitled "The reality of death experiences" by Ernst Rodin. *Journal of Nervous and Mental Disease, 168,* 268–270. (p. 215)

Schneider, S. L. (2001). In search of realistic optimism: Meaning, knowledge, and warm fuzziness. *American Psychologist, 56,* 250–263. (p. 453)

Schneiderman, N. (1999). Behavioral medicine and the management of HIV/AIDS. *International Journal of Behavioral Medicine, 6,* 3–12. (p. 411)

Schoeneman, T. J. (1994). *Individualism.* In V. S. Ramachandran (Ed.), *Encyclopedia of Human Behavior.* San Diego: Academic Press. (pp. 441, 462)

Schofield, J. W. (1986). Black-White contact in desegregated schools. In M. Hewstone & R. Brown (Eds.), *Contact and conflict in intergroup encounters.* Oxford: Basil Blackwell. (p. 576)

Schonfield, D., & Robertson, B. A. (1966). Memory storage and aging. *Canadian Journal of Psychology, 20,* 228–236. (p. 127)

Schooler, C., Neumann, E., Caplan, L. J., & Roberts, B. R. (1997). A time course analysis of Stroop interference and facilitation: Comparing normal individuals and individuals with schizophrenia. *Journal of Experimental Psychology: General, 126,* 19–36. (p. 497)

Schooler, J. W., Gerhard, D., & Loftus, E. F. (1986). Qualities of the unreal. *Journal of Experimental Psychology: Learning, Memory, and Cognition, 12,* 171–181. (p. 282)

Schulenberg, J., Bachman, J. G., O'Malley, P. M., & Johnston, L. D. (March, 1994). High school educational success and subsequent substance use: A panel analysis following adolescents into young adulthood. *Journal of Health & Social Behavior, 35(1),* 45–62. (p. 213)

Schuman, H., & Scott, J. (June, 1989). Generations and collective memories. *American Sociological Review, 54(3),* 359–381. (p. 127)

Schwartz, B. (1984). *Psychology of learning and behavior* (2nd ed.). New York: Norton. (pp. 235, 479)

Schwartz, J. M., Stoessel, P. W., Baxter, L. R., Jr., Martin, K. M., & Phelps, M. E. (1996). Systematic changes in cerebral glucose metabolic rate after successful behavior modification treatment of obsessive-compulsive disorder. *Archives of General Psychiatry, 53,* 109–113. (p. 534)

Schwarz, N., Strack, F., Kommer, D., & Wagner, D. (1987). Soccer, rooms, and the quality of your life: Mood effects on judgments of satisfaction with life in general and with specific domains. *European Journal of Social Psychology, 17,* 69–79. (p. 275)

Scott, W. A., Scott, R., & McCabe, M. (1991). Family relationships and children's personality: A cross-cultural, cross-source comparison. *British Journal of Social Psychology, 30,* 1–20. (p. 89)

Sechrest, L., Stickle, T. R., & Stewart, M. (1998). The role of assessment in clinical psychology. In A. Bellack, M. Hersen (Series eds.) & C. R. Reynolds (Vol. ed.), *Comprehensive clinical psychology: Vol 4: Assessment.* New York: Pergamon. (p. 435)

Seeman, P., Guan, H-C., & Van Tol, H. H. M. (1993). Dopamine D4 receptors elevated in schizophrenia. *Nature, 365,* 441–445. (p. 498)

Segal, N. L. (1999). *Entwined lives: Twins and what they tell us about human behavior.* New York: Dutton. (p. 77)

Segall, M. H., Dasen, P. R., Berry, J. W., & Poortinga, Y. H. (1990). *Human behavior in global perspective: An introduction to cross-cultural psychology.* New York: Pergamon. (pp. 72, 91, 109)

Segerstrom, S. C., McCarthy, W. J., Caskey, N. H., Gross, T. D., & Jarvik, M. E. (1993). Optimistic bias among cigarette smokers. *Journal of Applied Social Psychology, 23,* 1606–1618. (p. 454)

Segerstrom, S. C., Taylor, S. E., Kemeny, M. E., & Fahey, J. L. (1998). Optimism is associated with mood, coping, and immune change in response to stress. *Journal of Personality and Social Psychology, 74,* 1646–1655. (p. 407)

Seidlitz, L., & Diener, E. (1998). Sex differences in the recall of affective experiences. *Journal of Personality and Social Psychology, 74,* 262–271. (p. 494)

Sekiyama, K., Miyauchi, S., Imaruoka, T., Egusa, H., & Tashiro, T. (2000). Body image as a visuomotor transformation device revealed in adaptation to reversed vision. *Nature, 407,* 374–377. (p. 177)

Self, C. E. (1994). *Moral culture and victimization in residence halls.* Dissertation: Thesis (M.A.). Bowling Green University. (p. 220)

Seligman, M. E. P. (1974, May). Submissive death: Giving up on life. *Psychology Today,* pp. 80–85. (p. 384)

Seligman, M. E. P. (1975). *Helplessness: On depression, development and death.* San Francisco: Freeman. (p. 452)

Seligman, M. E. P. (1988, October). Boomer blues. *Psychology Today,* pp. 50–55. (p. 463)

Seligman, M. E. P. (1991). *Learned optimism.* New York: Knopf. (pp. 452, 493, 494)

Seligman, M. E. P. (1994). *What you can change and what you can't.* New York: Knopf. (pp. 82, 415, 438, 457)

Seligman, M. E. P. (1995). The effectiveness of psychotherapy: The *Consumer Reports* study. *American Psychologist, 50,* 965–974. (p. 493, 520, 523)

Seligman, M. E. P. (2002). *Authentic happiness: Using the new positive psychology to realize your potential for lasting fulfillment.* New York: Free Press. (pp. 454, 457, 518)

Seligman, M. E. P., & Schulman, P. (1986). Explanatory style as a predictor of productivity and quitting among life insurance sales agents. *Journal of Personality and Social Psychology, 50,* 832–838. (p. 453)

Seligman, M. E. P., & Yellen, A. (1987). What is a dream? *Behavior Research and Therapy, 25,* 1–24. (p. 191)

Selye, H. (1936). A syndrome produced by diverse nocuous agents. *Nature, 138,* 32. (p. 403)

Selye, H. (1976). *The stress of life.* New York: McGraw-Hill. (p. 403)

Senghas, A., & Coppola, M. (2001). Children creating language: How Nicaraguan Sign Language acquired a spatial grammar. *Psychological Science, 12,* 323–328. (p. 305)

Sengupta, S. (2001, October 10). Sept. 11 attack narrows the racial divide. *New York Times* (www.nytimes.com). (p. 577)

Serdula, M. K., Mokdad, A., Williamson, D. F., Galuska, D. A., Mendlein, J. M., & Heath, G. W. (1999). Prevalence of attempting weight loss and strategies for controlling weight. *Journal of the American Medical Association, 282,* 1353–1358. (pp. 355, 356)

Service, R. F. (1994). Will a new type of drug make memory-making easier? *Science, 266,* 218–219. (p. 269)

Seto, M. C., & Barbaree, H. E. (1995). The role of alcohol in sexual aggression. *Clinical Psychology Review, 15,* 545–566. (p. 211)

Shadish, W. R., Matt, G. E., Navarro, A. M., & Phillips, G. (2000). The effects of psychological therapies under clinically representative conditions: A meta-analysis. *Psychological Bulletin, 126,* 512–529. (p. 522)

Shadish, W. R., Montgomery, L. M., Wilson, P., Wilson, M. R., Bright, I., & Okwumabua, T. (1993). Effects of family and marital psychotherapies: A meta-analysis. *Journal of Consulting and Clinical Psychology, 61,* 992–1002. (p. 519)

Shafir, E., & LeBoeuf, R. A. (2002). Rationality. *Annual Review of Psychology, 53,* 491–517. (pp. 301–302)

Shamir, B., House, R. J., & Arthur, M. B. (1993). The motivational effects of charismatic leadership: A self-concept based theory. *Organizational Science, 4(4),* 577–594. (p. B–10)

Shapiro, F. (1989). Efficacy of the eye movement desensitization procedure in the treatment of traumatic memories. *Journal of Traumatic Stress, 2,* 199–223. (p. 525)

Shapiro, F. (1995). *Eye movement desensitization and reprocessing: Basic principles, protocols, and procedures.* New York: Guilford. (p. 525)

Shapiro, F. (1999). Eye movement desensitization and reprocessing (EMDR) and the anxiety disorders: Clinical and research implications of an integrated psychotherapy treatment. *Journal of Anxiety Disorders, 13,* 35–67. (p. 525)

Shapiro, F. (Ed.) (2002). *EMDR as an integrative psychotherapy approach: Experts of diverse orientations explore the paradigm prism.* Washington, DC: APA Books. (p. 525)

Sharma, A. R., McGue, M. K., & Benson, P. L. (1998). The psychological adjustment of United States adopted adolescents and their non-adopted siblings. *Child Development, 69,* 791–802. (p. 79)

Shaver, P. R., & Hazan, C. (1993). Adult romantic attachment: Theory and evidence. In D. Perlman & W. Jones (Eds.), *Advances in personal relationships* (Vol. 4). Greenwich, CT: JAI. (p. 112)

Shaver, P. R., Morgan, H. J., & Wu, S. (1996). Is love a basic emotion? *Personal Relationships, 3,* 81–96. (p. 393)

Shaw, H. L. (1989–90). Comprehension of the spoken word and ASL translation by chimpanzees (Pan troglodytes). *Friends of Washoe, 9(1/2),* 8–19. (p. 314)

Shea, M. T., Elkin, I., Imber, S. D., Sotsky, S. M., Watkins, J. T., Collins, J. F., Pilkonis, P. A., Beckham, E., Glass, D. R., Dolan, R. T., & Parloff, M. B. (1992). Course of depressive symptoms over follow-up: Findings from the National Institute of Mental Health Treatment of Depression Collaborative Research Program. *Archives of General Psychiatry, 49,* 782–787. (p. 522)

Sheehan, S. (1982). *Is there no place on earth for me?* Boston: Houghton Mifflin. (p. 496)

Shenton, M. E. (1992). Abnormalities of the left temporal lobe and thought disorder in schizophrenia: A quantitative magnetic resonance imaging study. *New England Journal of Medicine, 327,* 604–612. (pp. 498–499)

Shepard, R. N. (1990). *Mind sights.* New York: Freeman. (pp. 30, 173, 182)

Shepherd, C. (1997, April). News of the weird. *Funny Times*, p. 15. (p. 77)

Shepherd, C. (1999, June). News of the weird. *Funny Times*, p. 21. (p. 354)

Sherif, M. (1966). *In common predicament: Social psychology of intergroup conflict and cooperation.* Boston: Houghton Mifflin. (p. 576)

Sherman, P. W., & Flaxman, S. M. (2001). Protecting ourselves from food. *American Scientist, 89,* 142–151. (p. 348)

Sherry, D., & Vaccarino, A. L. (1989). Hippocampus and memory for food caches in black-capped chickadees. *Behavioral Neuroscience, 103,* 308–318. (p. 271)

Shettleworth, S. J. (1973). Food reinforcement and the organization of behavior in golden hamsters. In R. A. Hinde & J. Stevenson-Hinde (Eds.), *Constraints on learning.* London: Academic Press. (p. 245)

Shettleworth, S. J. (1993). Where is the comparison in comparative cognition? Alternative research programs. *Psychological Science, 4,* 179–184. (p. 267)

Shibuya, K., Hashimoto, H., & Yano, E. (2002). Individual income, income distribution, and self-rated health in Japan. *British Medical Journal, 324,* 16–20. (p. 406)

Shneidman, E. (1987, March). At the point of no return. *Psychology Today,* pp. 54–58. (p. 491)

Shobe, K. K., & Kihlstrom, J. F. (June, 1997). Is traumatic memory special? *Current Directions in Psychological Science, 6(3),* 70–74. (p. 438)

Shotland, R. L. (1984, March 12). Quoted in Maureen Dowd, 20 years after the murder of Kitty Genovese, the question remains: Why? *The New York Times,* p. B1. (p. 573)

Showers, C. (1992). The motivational and emotional consequences of considering positive or negative possibilities for an upcoming event. *Journal of Personality and Social Psychology, 63,* 474–484. (p. 453)

Shulman, P. (2000, June). The girl who loved math. *Discover,* pp. 67–70. (p. 333)

Sieff, E. M., Dawes, R. M., & Loewenstein, G. (1999). Anticipated versus actual reaction to HIV test results. *The American Journal of Psychology, 112,* 297–313. (p. 396)

Siegel, J. (2000, Winter). Recent developments in narcolepsy research: An explanation for patients and the general public. *Narcolepsy Network Newsletter,* pp. 1–2. (p. 199)

Siegel, J. M. (1990). Stressful life events and use of physician services among the elderly: The moderating role of pet ownership. *Journal of Personality and Social Psychology, 58,* 1081–1086. (p. 417)

Siegel, R. K. (1977, October). Hallucinations. *Scientific American,* pp. 132–140. (p. 215)

Siegel, R. K. (1980). The psychology of life after death. *American Psychologist, 35,* 911–931. (p. 215)

Siegel, R. K. (1982, October). Quoted by J. Hooper, Mind tripping. *Omni,* pp. 72–82, 159–160. (p. 215)

Siegel, R. K. (1984, March 15). Personal communication. (p. 215)

Siegel, R. K. (1990). *Intoxication.* New York: Pocket Books. (pp. 209, 211, 213, 214, 216)

Siegler, R. S., & Ellis, S. (1996). Piaget on childhood. *Psychological Science, 7,* 211–215. (p. 105)

Silbersweig, D. A., Stern, E., Frith, C., Cahill, C., Holmes, A., Grootoonk, S., Seaward, J., McKenna, P., Chua, S. E., Schnorr, L., Jones, T., & Frackowiak, R. S. J.. (1995). A functional neuroanatomy of hallucinations in schizophrenia. *Nature, 378,* 176–179. (p. 498)

Silva, A. J., Stevens, C. F., Tonegawa, S., & Wang, Y. (1992). Deficient hippocampal long-term potentiation in alpha-calcium-calmodulin kinase II mutant mice. *Science, 257,* 201–206. (p. 269)

Silva, C. E., & Kirsch, I. (1992). Interpretive sets, expectancy, fantasy proneness, and dissociation as predictors of hypnotic response. *Journal of Personality and Social Psychology, 63,* 847–856. (p. 204)

Silver, M., & Geller, D. (1978). On the irrelevance of evil: The organization and individual action. *Journal of Social Issues, 34,* 125–136. (p. 550)

Silverman, I., & Eals, M. (1992). Sex differences in spatial abilities: Evolutionary theory and data. In J. H. Barkow, L. Cosmides, & J. Tooby (Eds.), *The adapted mind: Evolutionary psychology and the generation of culture.* New York: Oxford University Press. (p. 333)

Silverman, I., & Phillips, K. (1998). The evolutionary psychology of spatial sex differences. In C. Crawford & D. L. Krebs (Eds.), *Handbook of Evolutionary Psychology: Ideas, Issues, and Applications.* Mahwah, NJ: Erlbaum. (p. 333)

Silverman, K., Evans, S. M., Strain, E. C., & Griffiths, R. R. (1992). Withdrawal syndrome after the double-blind cessation of caffeine consumption. *New England Journal of Medicine, 327,* 1109–1114. (p. 212)

Silverman, P. S., & Retzlaff, P. D. (1986). Cognitive stage regression through hypnosis: Are earlier cognitive stages retrievable? *International Journal of Clinical and Experimental Hypnosis, 34,* 192–204. (p. 205)

Simons, D. J. (1996). In sight, out of mind: When object representations fail. *Psychological Science, 7,* 301–305. (p. 188)

Simons, D. J., & Levin, D. T. (1998). Failure to detect changes to people during a real-world interaction. *Psychonomic Bulletin and Review, 5,* 644–649. (p. 188)

Simonton, D. K. (1988). Age and outstanding achievement: What do we know after a century of research? *Psychological Bulletin, 104,* 251–267. (p. 129)

Simonton, D. K. (1990). Creativity in the later years: Optimistic prospects for achievement. *The Gerontologist, 30,* 626–631. (p. 129)

Simonton, D. K. (1992). The social context of career success and course for 2,026 scientists and inventors. *Personality and Social Psychology Bulletin, 18,* 452–463. (p. 322)

Simonton, D. K. (2000). Creativity: Cognitive, personal, developmental, and social aspects. *American Psychologist, 55,* 151–158. (p. 321)

Simonton, D. K. (2000). Methodological and theoretical orientation and the long-term disciplinary impact of 54 eminent psychologists. *Review of General Psychology, 4,* 13–24. (p. 252)

Simpson, J. A., Rholes, W. S., & Nelligan, J. S. (1992). Support seeking and support giving within couples in an anxiety-provoking situation: The role of attachment styles. *Journal of Personality and Social Psychology, 62,* 434–446. (p. 112)

Sinclair, R. C., Hoffman, C., Mark, M. M., Martin, L. L., & Pickering, T. L. (1994). Construct accessibility and the misattribution of arousal: Schachter and Singer revisited. *Psychological Science, 5,* 15–18. (p. 382)

Singelis, T. M., Bond, M. H., Sharkey, W. F., & Lai, C. S. Y. (1999). Unpackaging culture's influence on self-esteem and embarrassability: The role of self-construals. *Journal of Cross-Cultural Psychology, 30,* 315–341. (p. 461)

Singelis, T. M., & Sharkey, W. F. (1995). Culture, self-construal, and embarrassability. *Journal of Cross-Cultural Psychology, 26,* 622–644. (p. 461)

Singer, J. L. (1981). Clinical intervention: New developments in methods and evaluation. In L. T. Benjamin, Jr. (Ed.), *The G. Stanley Hall Lecture Series* (Vol. 1). Washington, DC: American Psychological Association. (p. 523)

Singh, D. (1993). Adaptive significance of female physical attractiveness: Role of waist-to-hip ratio. *Journal of Personality and Social Psychology, 65,* 293–307. (p. 73)

Singh, D. (1995b). Female health, attractiveness, and desirability for relationships: Role of breast asymmetry and waist-to-hip ratio. *Ethology and Sociobiology, 16,* 465–481. (p. 73)

Singh, S. (1997). *Fermat's enigma: The epic quest to solve the world's greatest mathematical problem.* New York: Bantam Books. (p. 321)

Singh, S., & Riber, K. A. (November, 1997). Fermat's last stand. *Scientific American,* pp. 68–73. (pp. 320, 322)

Sipski, M. L., Alexander, C. J., & Rosen, R. C. (1999). Sexual response in women with spinal cord injuries: Implications for our understanding of the able bodied. *Journal of Sex & Marital Therapy, 25,* 11–22. (p. 46)

Sirenteanu, R. (1999). Switching on the infant brain. *Science, 286,* 59, 61. (p. 176)

Sjöstrum, L. (1980). Fat cells and body weight. In A. J. Stunkard (Ed.), *Obesity.* Philadelphia: Saunders. (p. 353)

Skinner, B. F. (1953). *Science and human behavior.* New York: Macmillan. (p. 241)

Skinner, B. F. (1956). A case history in scientific method. *American Psychologist, 11,* 221–233. (p. 242)

Skinner, B. F. (1957). *Verbal behavior.* Englewood Cliffs, NJ: Prentice-Hall. (p. 304)

Skinner, B. F. (1961, November). Teaching machines. *Scientific American,* pp. 91–102. (p. 241)

Skinner, B. F. (1983, September). Origins of a behaviorist. *Psychology Today,* pp. 22–33. (pp. 245, 493)

Skinner, B. F. (1985). *Cognitive science and behaviorism.* Unpublished manuscript, Harvard University. (pp. 304–305)

Skinner, B. F. (1986). What is wrong with daily life in the western world? *American Psychologist, 41,* 568–574. (p. 246)

Skinner, B. F. (1988). The school of the future. Address to the American Psychological Association convention. (p. 246)

Skinner, B. F. (1989). Teaching machines. *Science, 243,* 1535. (p. 246)

Skinner, B. F. (1990). Address to the American Psychological Association convention. (p. 243)

Sklar, L. S., & Anisman, H. (1981). Stress and cancer. *Psychological Bulletin, 89,* 369–406. (p. 411)

Skoog, G., & Skoog, I. (1999). A 40-year follow-up of patients with obsessive-compulsive disorder. *Archives of General Psychiatry, 56,* 121–127. (p. 478)

Skov, R. B., & Sherman, S. J. (1986). Information-gathering processes: Diagnosticity, hypothesis-confirmatory strategies, and perceived hypothesis confirmation. *Journal of Experimental Social Psychology, 22,* 93–121. (p. 295)

Slater, A. (1994, February 15). Personal correspondence. (p. 102)

Slater, E., & Meyer, A. (1959). *Confinia Psychiatra.* Basel: S. Karger AG. (p. 488)

Slater, L. (2000, November 19). How do you cure a sex addict? *New York Times Magazine* (www.nytimes.com). (p. 532)

Slavin, R. E. (1989). Cooperative learning and student achievement. In R. E. Slavin (Ed.), *School and classroom organization.* Hillsdale, NJ: Erlbaum. (p. 577)

Sloan, R. P., & Bagiela E. (2002). Claims about religious involvement and health outcomes. *Annals of Behavioral Medicine, 24,* 14–21. (p. 422)

Sloan, R. P., Bagiella, E., & Powell, T. (1999). Religion, spirituality, and medicine. *Lancet, 353,* 664–667. (p. 422)

Sloan, R. P., Bagiella, E., VandeCreek, L., & Poulos, P. (2000). Should physicians prescribe religious activities? *New England Journal of Medicine, 342,* 1913–1917. (p. 422)

Slovic, P. (1987). Perception of risk. *Science, 236,* 280–285. (p. 298)

Slovic, P., Finucane, M., Peters, E., & MacGregor, D. G. (2002). The affect heuristic. In T. Gilovich, D. Griffin, & D. Kahneman (Eds.), *Intuitive judgment: Heuristics and biases.* New York: Cambridge University Press. (p. 213)

Slovic, P., & Fischhoff, B. (1977). On the psychology of experimental surprises. *Journal of Experimental Psychology: Human Perception and Performance, 3,* 544–551. (p. 11)

Small, M. F. (1997). Making connections. *American Scientist, 85,* 502–504. (p. 89)

Small, M. F. (2002, July). What you can learn from drunk monkeys. *Discover,* pp. 40–45. (p. 219)

Smart, R. G., Adlaf, E. M., & Walsh, G. W. (1991). The Ontario student drug use survey: Trends between 1977 and 1991. Toronto: Addiction Research Foundation. (p. 217)

Smelser, N. J., & Mitchell, F. (Eds.) (2002). *Terrorism: Perspectives from the behavioral and social sciences.* Washington, DC: National Research Council, National Academies Press. (p. 559)

Smith, A. (1983). Personal correspondence. (p. 498)

Smith, D. V., & Margolskee, R. F. (2001, March). Making sense of taste. *Scientific American,* pp. 32–39. (p. 162)

Smith, J. E., Waldorf, V. A., & Trembath, D. L. (1990). "Single white male looking for thin, very attractive . . ." *Sex Roles, 23,* 675–685. (p. 352)

Smith, K. H., & Rogers, M. (1994). Effectiveness of subliminal messages in television commercials: Two experiments. *Journal of Applied Psychology, 79,* 866–874. (p. 144)

Smith, M. B. (1978). Psychology and values. *Journal of Social Issues, 34,* 181–199. (p. 441)

Smith, M. L., & Glass, G. V. (1977). Meta-analysis of psychotherapy outcome studies. *American Psychologist, 32,* 752–760. (p. 523)

Smith, M. L., Glass, G. V., & Miller, R. L. (1980). *The benefits of psychotherapy.* Baltimore: Johns Hopkins Press. (p. 522)

Smith, P. B., & Tayeb, M. (1989). Organizational structure and processes. In M. Bond (Ed.), *The cross-cultural challenge to social psychology.* Newbury Park, CA: Sage. (p. B–10)

Smith, P. F. (1995). Cannabis and the brain. *New Zealand Journal of Psychology, 24,* 5–12. (p. 216)

Smith, S. B. (1999). Diana in search of herself : Portrait of a troubled princess. New York: Times Books. (pp. 523–524)

Smith, S. M., McIntosh, W. D., & Bazzini, D. G. (1999). Are the beautiful good in Hollywood? An investigation of the beauty-and-goodness stereotype on film. *Basic and Applied Social Psychology, 21,* 69–80. (p. 569)

Smith, T. W. (1997). Personal correspondence. Data from the General Social Survey, National Opinion Research Center, University of Chicago. (p. 555)

Smith, T. W. (1998, December). American sexual behavior: Trends, sociodemographic differences, and risk behavior. National Opinion Research Center GSS Topical Report No. 25. (pp. 361, 363, 364–365)

Smith, T. W., & Ruiz, J. M. (2002). Psychosocial influences on the development and course of coronary heart disease: Current status and implications for research and practice. *Journal of Consulting and Clinical Psychology, 70,* 548–568. (p. 408)

Smolak, L., & Murnen, S. K. (2002). A meta-analytic examination of the relationship between child sexual abuse and eating disorders. *International Journal of Eating Disorders, 31,* 136–150. (p. 350)

Smoreda, Z., & Licoppe, C. (2000). Gender-specific use of the domestic telephone. *Social Psychology Quarterly, 63,* 238–252. (p. 121)

Snarey, J. R. (1985). Cross-cultural universality of social-moral development: A critical review of Kohlbergian research. *Psychological Bulletin, 97,* 202–233. (p. 119)

Snarey, J. R. (1987, June). A question of morality. *Psychology Today,* pp. 6–7. (p. 119)

Snodgrass, M. A. (1987). The relationships of differential loneliness, intimacy and characterological attributional style to duration of loneliness. *Journal of Social Behavior and Personality, 2,* 173–186. (p. 494)

Snodgrass, S. E., Higgins, J. G., & Todisco, L. (1986). The effects of walking behavior on mood. Paper presented at the American Psychological Association convention. (p. 392)

Snyder, F., & Scott, J. (1972). The psychophysiology of sleep. In N. S. Greenfield & R. A. Sterbach (Eds.), *Handbook of psychophysiology.* New York: Holt, Rinehart & Winston. (p. 202)

Snyder, M. (1984). When belief creates reality. In L. Berkowitz (Ed.), *Advances in experimental social psychology* (Vol. 18). New York: Academic Press. (p. 475)

Snyder, S. H. (1984). Neurosciences: An integrative discipline. *Science, 225,* 1255–1257. (p. 39)

Snyder, S. H. (1986). *Drugs and the brain.* New York: Scientific American Library. (p. 532)

Sokoll, G. R., & Mynatt, C. R. (1984). *Arousal and free throw shooting.* Paper presented at the meeting of the Midwestern Psychological Association. (p. 384)

Solomon, D. A., Keitner, G. I., Miller, I. W., Shea, M. T., & Keller, M. B. (1995). Course of illness and maintenance treatments for patients with bipolar disorder. *Journal of Clinical Psychiatry, 56,* 5–13. (p. 532)

Solomon, J. (1996, May 20). Breaking the silence. *Newsweek,* pp. 20–22. (p. 475)

Solomon, M. (1987, December). Standard issue. *Psychology Today,* pp. 30–31. (p. 569)

Solomon, Z. (1990). Does the war end when the shooting stops? The psychological toll of war. *Journal of Applied Social Psychology, 20,* 1733–1745. (p. 480)

Sommer, R. (1969). *Personal space.* Englewood Cliffs, NJ: Prentice-Hall. (p. 87)

Sonenstein, F. L. (1992). Condom use. *Science, 257,* 861. (p. 362)

Sontag, S. (1978). *Illness as metaphor.* New York: Farrar, Straus, & Giroux. (p. 411)

Soussignan, R. (2001). Duchenne smile, emotional experience, and autonomic reactivity: A test of the facial feedback hypothesis. *Emotion, 2,* 52–74. (p. 392)

Sowell, T. (1991, May/June). Cultural diversity: A world view. *American Enterprise,* pp. 44–55. (p. 578)

Spanos, N. P. (1982). A social psychological approach to hypnotic behavior. In G. Weary & H. L. Mirels (Eds.), *Integrations of clinical and social psychology.* New York: Oxford. (p. 205)

Spanos, N. P. (1986). Hypnosis, nonvolitional responding, and multiple personality: A social psychological perspective. *Progress in Experimental Personality Research, 14,* 1–62. (p. 483)

Spanos, N. P. (1991). Hypnosis, hypnotizability, and hypnotherapy. In C. R. Snyder & D. R. Forsyth (Eds.), *Handbook of social and clinical psychology: The health perspective.* New York: Pergamon Press. (p. 205)

Spanos, N. P. (1994). Multiple identity enactments and multiple personality disorder: A sociocognitive perspective. *Psychological Bulletin, 116,* 143–165. (pp. 207, 483)

Spanos, N. P. (1996). *Multiple identities and false memories: A sociocognitive perspective.* Washington, DC: American Psychological Association Books. (pp. 205, 207, 483)

Spanos, N. P., & Coe, W. C. (1992). A Social-psychological approach to hypnosis. In E. Fromm & M. R. Nash (Eds.), *Contemporary hypnosis research.* New York: Guilford. (p. 206)

Spanos, N. P., Radtke, L., & Bertrand, L. D. (1985). Hypnotic amnesia as a strategic enactment: Breaching amnesia in highly susceptible subjects. *Journal of Personality and Social Psychology, 47,* 1155–1169. (p. 204)

Spector, P. E. (1986). Perceived control by employees: A meta-analysis of studies concerning autonomy and participation at work. *Human Relations, 39,* 1005–1016. (p. B-10)

Spelke, E. S. (2000). Core knowledge. *American Psychologist, 55,* 1233–1243. (p. 106)

Spencer, J., Quinn, P. C., Johnson, M. H., & Karmiloff-Smith, A. (1997). Heads you win, tails you lose: Evidence for young infants categorizing mammals by head and facial attributes. *Early Development & Parenting, 6,* 113–126. (p. 102)

Spencer, S. J., Steele, C. M., & Quinn, D. M. (1997). Stereotype threat and women's math performance. Unpublished manuscript, Hope College. (p. 335)

Sperling, G. (1960). The information available in brief visual presentations. *Psychological Monographs, 74* (Whole No. 498). (pp. 265–266)

Sperry, R. W. (1964). *Problems outstanding in the evolution of brain function.* James Arthur Lecture, American Museum of Natural History, New York. Cited by R. Ornstein (1977), *The psychology of consciousness* (2nd ed.). New York: Harcourt Brace Jovanovich. (p. 61)

Sperry, R. W. (1985). Changed concepts of brain and consciousness: Some value implications. *Zygon, 20,* 41–57. (p. 152)

Spiegel, K., Leproult, R., & Van Cauter, E. (1999). Impact of sleep debt on metabolic and endrocrine function. *Lancet, 354,* 1435–1439. (p. 196)

Spielberger, C., & London, P. (1982). Rage boomerangs. *American Health, 1,* 52–56. (p. 409)

Spitzberg, B. H., & Hurt, H. T. (1987). The relationship of interpersonal competence and skill to reported loneliness across time. *Journal of Social Behavior and Personality, 2,* 157–172. (p. 494)

Spitzer, R. L. (1997). Brief comments from a psychiatric nosologist weary from his own attempts to define mental disorder: Why Ossorio's definition muddles and Wakefield's "harmful dysfunction" illuminates the issues. *Clinical Psychology Science and Practice, 4,* 259–266. (p. 470)

Spradley, J. P., & Phillips, M. (1972). Culture and stress: A quantitative analysis. *American Anthropologist, 74,* 518–529. (p. 87)

Sprecher, S. (1989). The importance to males and females of physical attractiveness, earning potential, and expressiveness in initial attraction. *Sex Roles, 21,* 591–607. (p. 569)

Sprecher, S., & Sedikides, C. (1993). Gender differences in perceptions of emotionality: The case of close heterosexual relationships. *Sex Roles, 28,* 511–530. (p. 389)

Springer, S. P., & Deutsch, G. (1985). *Left brain, right brain.* San Francisco: Freeman. (p. 62)

Spychalski, A., Quinones, M. A., & Gaugler, B. B. (1997). A survey of assessment center practices in the United States. *Personnel Psychology, 50,* 71–90. (p. 455)

Squire, L. R. (1992). Memory and the hippocampus: A synthesis from findings with rats, monkeys, and humans. *Psychological Review, 99,* 195–231. (p. 271)

Squire, L., & Zola-Morgan, S. (1991). The medial temporal lobe memory system. *Science, 253,* 1380–1386. (p. 271)

Srivastava, A., Locke, E. A., & Bartol, K. M. (2001). Money and subject well-being: It's not the money, it's the motives. *Journal of Personality and Social Psychology, 80,* 959–971. (p. 398)

Stack, S. (1992). Marriage, family, religion, and suicide. In R. Maris, A. Berman, J. Maltsberger, & R. Yufit (Eds.), *Assessment and prediction of suicide.* New York: Guilford Press. (p. 490)

Stafford, R. S., MacDonald, E. A., & Finkelstein, S. N. (2001). National patterns of medication treatment for depression, 1987 to 2001. *Primary Care Companion Journal of Clinical Psychiatry, 3,* 232–235. (p. 532)

Stanford University Center for Narcolepsy. (2002). Narcolepsy is a serious medical disorder and a key to understanding other sleep disorders (www.med.stanford.edu/school/Psychiatry/narcolepsy). (p. 199)

Stanley, J. C. (1997). Varieties of intellectual talent. *Journal of Creative Behavior, 31,* 93–119. (p. 324)

Stanovich, K. (1996). *How to think straight about psychology.* New York: HarperCollins. (p. 429)

Stapel, D. A., Koomen, W., & Ruys, K. I. (2002). The effects of diffuse and distinct affect. *Journal of Personality and Social Psychology, 83,* 60–74. (p. 382)

Statistics Canada. (1999). *Statistical report on the health of Canadians.* Prepared by the Federal, Provincial and Territorial Advisory Committee on Population Health for the Meeting of Ministers of Health, Charlottetown, PEI, September 16–17, 1999. (pp. 122, 354, 414, 418, 489)

Statistics Canada. (2002). CANSIM II, table 105–0027 (www.statcan.ca/english/Pgdb/health07a.htm). (p. 86)

Staub, E. (1989). *The roots of evil: The psychological and cultural sources of genocide.* New York: Cambridge University Press. (p. 543)

Steadman, H. J., Mulvey, E. P., Monahan, J., Robbins, P. C., Appelbaum, P. S., Grisso, T., Roth, L. H., & Silver, E. (1998). Violence by people discharged from acute psychiatric inpatient facilities and by other in the same neighborhoods. *Archives of General Psychiatry, 55,* 393–401. (p. 475)

Steel, P., & Ones, D. S. (2002). Personality and happiness: A national-level analysis. *Journal of Personality and Social Psychology, 83,* 767–781. (p. 397)

Steele, C. (1990, May). A conversation with Claude Steele. *APS Observer,* pp. 11–17. (p. 331)

Steele, C. M. (1997). A threat in the air: How stereotypes shape intellectual identity and performance. *American Psychologist, 52,* 613–629. (p. 335)

Steele, C. M., & Josephs, R. A. (1990). Alcohol myopia: Its prized and dangerous effects. *American Psychologist, 45,* 921–933. (p. 211)

Steele, C. M., Spencer, S. J., & Aronson, J. (2002). Contending with group image: The psychology of stereotype and social identity threat. *Advances in Experimental Social Psychology, 34,* 379–440. (p. 335)

Stein, J. A., Newcomb, M. D., & Bentler, P. M. (1986). Stability and change in personality: A longitudinal study from early adolescence to young adulthood. *Journal of Research In Personality, 20,* 276–291. (p. 135)

Steinberg, L. (1987, September). Bound to bicker. *Psychology Today,* pp. 36–39. (p. 122)

Steinberg, L., & Morris, A. S. (2001). Adolescent development. *Annual Review of Psychology, 52,* 83–110. (pp. 114, 117, 122)

Steinberg, N. (1993, February). Astonishing love stories (from an earlier United Press International report). *Games,* p. 47. (p. 569)

Steinem, G. (1988). Six great ideas that television is missing. In G. Comstock (Ed.), *Public communication and behavior.* New York: Academic Press. (p. 564)

Steinmetz, J. E. (1999). The localization of a simple type of learning and memory: The cerebellum and classical eyeblink conditioning. *Contemporary Psychology, 7,* 72–77. (p. 271)

Stellar, E. (1985). Hunger in animals and humans. Distinguished lecture to the Eastern Psychological Association convention. (p. 348)

Stengel, E. (1981). Suicide. In *The new encyclopaedia britannica, macropaedia* (Vol. 17, pp. 777–782). Chicago: Encyclopaedia Britannica. (p. 490)

Stern, M., & Karraker, K. H. (1989). Sex stereotyping of infants: A review of gender labeling studies. *Sex Roles, 20,* 501–522. (p. 182)

Stern, S. L., Dhanda, R., & Hazuda, H. P. (2001). Hopelessness predicts mortality in older Mexican and European Americans. *Psychosomatic Medicine, 63,* 344–351. (p. 407)

Sternberg, E. M. (2001). *The balance within: The science connecting health and emotions.* New York: Freeman. (p. 409)

Sternberg, R. J. (1985). *Beyond IQ: A triarchic theory of human intelligence.* New York: Cambridge University Press. (p. 318)

Sternberg, R. J. (1988). Applying cognitive theory to the testing and teaching of intelligence. *Applied Cognitive Psychology, 2,* 231–255. (p. 321)

Sternberg, R. J. (1997). *Successful intelligence.* New York: Plume. (p. 315)

Sternberg, R. J. (1998). Principles of teaching for successful intelligence. *Educational Psychologist, 33,* 65–72. (p. 319)

Sternberg, R. J. (1999). The theory of successful intelligence. *Review of General Psychology, 3,* 292–316. (pp. 318, 319)

Sternberg, R. J. (2000). Presidential aptitude in Science. (p. 319)

Sternberg, R. J., & Grajek, S. (1984). The nature of love. *Journal of Personality and Social Psychology, 47,* 312–329. (p. 573)

Sternberg, R. J., & Lubart, T. I. (1991). An investment theory of creativity and its development. *Human Development,* 1–31. (p. 321)

Sternberg, R. J., & Lubart, T. I. (1992). Buy low and sell high: An investment approach to creativity. *Psychological Science, 1,* 1–5. (p. 321)

Sternberg, R. J., & Wagner, R. K. (1993). The *g*-ocentric view of intelligence and job performance is wrong. *Current Directions in Psychological Science, 2,* 1–5. (p. 319)

Sternberg, R. J., Wagner, R. K., Williams, W. M., & Horvath, J. A. (1995). Testing common sense. *American Psychologist, 50,* 912–927. (p. 319)

Stetter, F., & Kupper, S. (2002). Autogenic training: A meta-analysis of clinical outcome studies. *Applied Psychophysiology and Biofeedback, 27,* 45–98. (p. 416)

Stevenson, H. W. (1992, December). Learning from Asian schools. *Scientific American,* pp. 70–76. (p. 332)

Stewart, B. (2002, April 6). Recall of the wild. *New York Times* (www.nytimes.com). (p. 30)

Stewart, D. (2000, February). Driving the wrong way. *The Psychologist,* pp. 64–65. (p. 169)

Stice, E. (2002). Risk and maintenance factors for eating pathology: A meta-analytic review. *Psychological Bulletin, 128,* 825–848. (p. 350)

Stice, E., & Shaw, H. E. (1994). Adverse effects of the media portrayed thin-ideal on women and linkages to bulimic symptomatology. *Journal of Social and Clinical Psychology, 13,* 288–308. (p. 351)

Stice, E., Spangler, D., & Agras, W. S. (2001). Exposure to media-portrayed thin-ideal images adversely affects vulnerable girls: A longitudinal experiment. *Journal of Social and Clinical Psychology, 20,* 270–288. (p. 351)

Stickgold, R. (2000, March 7). Quoted by S. Blakeslee, For better learning, researchers endorse "sleep on it" adage. *New York Times,* p. F2. (p. 202)

Stickgold, R., Hobson, J. A., Fosse, R., & Fosse, M. (2001). Sleep, learning, and dreams: Off-line memory processing. *Science, 294,* 1052–1057. (p. 202)

Stickgold, R., James, L., & Hobson, J. A. (2000). Visual discrimination learning requires sleep after training. *Nature Neuroscience, 3,* 1237–1238. (p. 202)

Stickgold, R., Malia, A., Maquire, D., Roddenberry, D., & O'Connor, M. (2000, October 13). Replaying the game: Hypnagogic images in normals and amnesics. *Science, 290,* 350–353. (p. 270)

Stickgold, R., Whidbee, D., Schirmer, B., Patel, V., & Hobson, J. A. (2000). Visual discrimination task improvement: A multi-step process occurring during sleep. *Journal of Cognitive Neuroscience, 12,* 246–254. (p. 201)

Stith, S. M., Rosen, K. H., Middleton, K. A., Busch, A. L., Lunderberg, K., & Carlton, R. P. (2000). The intergenerational transmission of spouse abuse: A meta-analysis. *Journal of Marriage and the Family, 62,* 640–654. (p. 249)

Stock, R. W. (1995, July 13). Reducing the risk for older drivers. *New York Times,* p. C1. (p. 126)

Stockton, M. C., & Murnen, S. K. (1992). Gender and sexual arousal in response to sexual stimuli: A meta-analytic review. Presented at the American Psychological Society convention. (p. 360)

Stone, A. A., Cox, D. S., Valdimarsdottir, H., Jandor, L., & Neale, J. M. (1987). Evidence that secretory IgA antibody is associated with daily mood. *Journal of Personality and Social Psychology, 52,* 988–993. (p. 410)

Stone, A. A., & Neale, J. M. (1984). Effects of severe daily events on mood. *Journal of Personality and Social Psychology, 46,* 137–144. (p. 396)

Stone, J., Perry, Z. W., & Darley, J. M. (1997). "White men can't jump": Evidence for the perceptual confirmation of racial stereotypes following a basketball game. *Basic and Applied Social Psychology, 19*(3), 291–306. (p. 558)

Stoolmiller, M. (1999). Implications of the restricted range of family environments for estimates of heritability and nonshared environment in behavior-genetic adoption studies. *Psychological Bulletin, 125,* 392–409. (p. 79)

Stoppard, J. M., & Gruchy, C. D. G. (1993). Gender, context, and expression of positive emotion. *Personality and Social Psychology Bulletin, 19,* 143–150. (p. 389)

Storm, L., & Ertel, S. (2001). Does psi exist? Comments on Milton and Wiseman's (1999) meta-analysis of Ganzfeld research. *Psychological Bulletin, 127,* 424–433. (p. 181)

Storm, L., & Ertel, S. (2002). The Ganzfeld debate continued: A response to Milton and Wiseman (2001). *The Journal of Parapsychology, 66,* 73–82. (p. 181)

Storms, M. D. (1973). Videotape and the attribution process: Reversing actors' and observers' points of view. *Journal of Personality and Social Psychology, 27,* 165–175. (p. 540)

Storms, M. D. (1981). A theory of erotic orientation development. *Psychological Review, 88,* 340–353. (p. 366)

Storms, M. D. (1983). *Development of sexual orientation.* Washington, DC: Office of Social and Ethical Responsibility, American Psychological Association. (p. 365)

Storms, M. D., & Thomas, G. C. (1977). Reactions to physical closeness. *Journal of Personality and Social Psychology, 35,* 412–418. (p. 551)

Strack, F., Martin, L., & Stepper, S. (1988). Inhibiting and facilitating conditions of the human smile: A nonobtrusive test of the facial feedback hypothesis. *Journal of Personality and Social Psychology, 54,* 768–777. (p. 392)

Strack, S., & Coyne, J. C. (1983). Social confirmation of dysphoria: Shared and private reactions to depression. *Journal of Personality and Social Behavior, 44,* 798–806. (p. 494)

Strahan, E. J., Spencer, S. J., & Zanna, M. P. (2002). Subliminal priming and persuasion: Striking while the iron is hot. *Journal of Experimental Social Psychology, 38,* 556–568. (p. 143)

Stratton, G. M. (1986). Some preliminary experiments on vision without inversion of the retinal image. *Psychological Review, 3,* 611–617. (p. 177)

Straub, R. O., Seidenberg, M. S., Bever, T. G., & Terrace, H. S. (1979). Serial learning in the pigeon. *Journal of the Experimental Analysis of Behavior, 32,* 137–148. (p. 313)

Straus, M. A., & Gelles, R. J. (1980). *Behind closed doors: Violence in the American family.* New York: Anchor/Doubleday. (p. 243)

Straus, M. A., Sugarman, D. B., & Giles-Sims, J. (1997). Spanking by parents and subsequent antisocial behavior of children. *Archives of Pediatric Adolescent Medicine, 151,* 761–767. (p. 243)

Strawbridge, W. J. (1999). Mortality and religious involvement: A review and critique of the results, the methods, and the measures. Paper presented at a Harvard University conference on religion and health, sponsored by the National Institiue for Healthcare Research and the John Templeton Foundation. (p. 422)

Strawbridge, W. J., Cohen, R. D., & Shema, S. J. (1997). Frequent attendance at religious services and mortality over 28 years. *American Journal of Public Health, 87,* 957–961. (p. 422)

Strawbridge, W. J., Shema, S. J., Cohen, R. D., & Kaplan, G. A. (2001). Religious attendance increases survival by improving and maintaining good health behaviors, mental health, and social relationships. *Annals of Behavioral Medicine, 23,* 68–74. (p. 423)

Strayer, D. L., & Johnston, W. A. (2001). Driven to distraction: Dual-task studies of simulated driving and conversing on a cellular telephone. *Psychological Science, 12,* 462–466. (p. 188)

Strentz, H. (1986, January 1). Become a psychic and amaze your friends! *Atlanta Journal,* p. 15A. (p. 178)

Striegel-Moore, R. H., Silberstein, L. R., & Rodin, J. (1993). The social self in bulimia nervosa: Public self-consciousness, social anxiety, and perceived fraudulence. *Journal of Abnormal Psychology, 102,* 297–303. (p. 350)

Stroebe, M., Stroebe, W., & Schut, H. (2001). Gender differences in adjustment to bereavement: An empirical and theoretical review. *Review of General Psychology, 5,* 62–83. (p. 133)

Stroebe, M., Stroebe, W., Schut, H., Zech, E., & van den Bout, J. (2002). Does disclosure of emotions facilitate recovery from bereavement? Evidence from two prospective studies. *Journal of Consulting and Clinical Psychology, 70,* 169–178. (p. 133)

Strupp, H. H. (1982). The outcome problem in psychotherapy: Contemporary perspectives. In J. H. Harvey & M. M. Parks (Eds.), *The master lecture series: Vol. 1. Psychotherapy research and behavior change.* Washington, DC: American Psychological Association. (p. 457)

Strupp, H. H. (1986). Psychotherapy: Research, practice, and public policy (How to avoid dead ends). *American Psychologist, 41,* 120–130. (p. 526)

Stumpf, H., & Jackson, D. N. (1994). Gender-related differences in cognitive abilities: Evidence from a medical school admissions testing program. *Personality and Individual Differences, 17,* 335–344. (p. 333)

Stunkard, A. J., Harris, J. R., Pedersen, N. L., & McClearn, G. E. (1990). A separated twin study of the body mass index. *New England Journal of Medicine, 322,* 1483–1487. (p. 354)

Suddath, R. L., Christison, G. W., Torrey, E. F., Casanova, M. F., & Weinberger, D. R. (1990). Anatomical abnormalities in the brains of monozygotic twins discordant for schizophrenia. *New England Journal of Medicine, 322,* 789–794. (p. 500)

Sue, D. W. (1990). Culture-specific strategies in counseling: A conceptual framework. *Professional Psychology: Research and Practice, 21,* 424–433. (p. 529)

Suedfeld, P. (1998). Homo invictus: The indomitable species. *Canadian Psychology, 38,* 164–173. (p. 481)

Suedfeld, P. (2000). Reverberations of the Holocaust fifty years later: Psychology's contributions to understanding persecution and genocide. *Canadian Psychology, 41,* 1–9. (p. 481)

Suedfeld, P., & Mocellin, J. S. P. (1987). The "sensed presence" in unusual environments. *Environment and Behavior, 19,* 33–52. (p. 215)

Suinn, R. M. (1997). Mental practice in sports psychology: Where have we been, Where do we go? *Clinical Psychology: Science and Practice.* (p. 310)

Sullivan, P. F., Neale, M. C., & Kendler, K. S. (2000). Genetic epidemiology of major depression: Review and meta-analysis. *American Journal of Psychiatry, 157,* 1552–1562. (p. 489)

Suls, J. M., & Tesch, F. (1978). Students' preferences for information about their test performance: A social comparison study. *Journal of Experimental Social Psychology, 8,* 189–197. (p. 400)

Summers, M. (1996, December 9). Mister clean. *People Weekly,* pp. 139–142. (p. 469)

Sundstrom, E., De Meuse, K. P., & Futrell, D. (1990). Work teams: Applications and effectiveness. *American Psychologist, 45,* 120–133. (p. B–11)

Suomi, S. J. (1986). Anxiety-like disorders in young nonhuman primates. In R. Gettleman (Ed.), *Anxiety disorders of childhood.* New York: Guilford Press. (p. 482)

Suomi, S. J. (1987). Genetic and maternal contributions to individual differences in rhesus monkey biobehavioral development. In N. A. Krasnegor & others (Eds.), *Perinatal development: A psychobiological perspective.* Orlando, FL: Academic Press. (p. 433)

Suppes, P. Quoted by R. H. Ennis (1982). Children's ability to handle Piaget's propositional logic: A conceptual critique. In S. Modgil & C. Modgil (Eds.), *Jean Piaget: Consensus and controversy.* New York: Praeger. (p. 108)

Surgeon General. (1986). *The Surgeon General's workshop on pornography and public health*, June 22–24. Report prepared by E. P. Mulvey & J. L. Haugaard and released by Office of the Surgeon General on August 4, 1986. (p. 564)

Surgeon General. (1999). *Mental health: A report of the Surgeon General.* Rockville, MD: U.S. Department of Health and Human Services. (pp. 475, 491)

Susser, E., Neugenbauer, R., Hoek, H. W., Brown, A. S., Lin, S., Labovitz, D., & Gorman, J. M. (1996). Schizophrenia after prenatal famine. *Archives of General Psychiatry, 53(1)*, 25–31 (p. 499)

Susser, E. S., Herman, D. B., & Aaron, B. (2002, August). Combating the terror of terrorism. *Scientific American*, pp. 70–77. (p. 481)

Sweat, J. A., & Durm, M. W. (1993). Psychics: Do police departments really use them? *Skeptical Inquirer, 17*, 148–158. (pp. 178–179)

Swerdlow, N. R., & Koob, G. F. (1987). Dopamine, schizophrenia, mania, and depression: Toward a unified hypothesis of cortico-stiato-pallido-thalamic function (with commentary). *Behavioral and Brain Sciences, 10*, 197–246. (p. 498)

Swim, J. K. (1994). Perceived versus meta-analytic effect sizes: An assessment of the accuracy of gender stereotypes. *Journal of Personality and Social Psychology, 66*, 21–36. (p. 557)

Swindle, R., Jr., Heller, K., Bescosolido, B., & Kikuzawa, S. (2000). Responses to nervous breakdowns in America over a 40-year period: Mental health policy implications. *American Psychologist, 55*, 740–749. (p. 489)

Taha, F. A. (1972). A comparative study of how sighted and blind perceive the manifest content of dreams. *National Review of Social Sciences, 9(3)*, 28. (p. 200)

Taheri, S., Zeitzer, J. M., & Mignot, E. (2002). The role of hypocretins (orexins) in sleep regulation and narcolepsy. *Annual Review of Neuroscience, 25*, 283–313. (p. 199)

Tajfel, H. (Ed.). (1982). *Social identity and intergroup relations.* New York: Cambridge University Press. (p. 558)

Talal, N. (1995). Quoted by V. Morell, Zeroing in on how hormones affect the immune system. *Science, 269*, 773–775. (p. 410)

Talbot, M. (2001, February 14). A desire to duplicate. *New York Times* (www.nytimes.com). (p. 76)

Talwar, S. K., Xu, S., Hawley, E. S., Weiss, S. A., Moxon, K. A., & Chapin, J. K. (2002). Rat navigation guided by remote control. *Nature, 417*, 37–38. (p. 51)

Tamres, L. K., Janicki, D., & Helgeson, V. S. (2002). Sex differences in coping behavior: A meta-analytic review and an examination of relative coping. *Personality and Social Psychology Review, 6*, 2–30. (p. 121)

Tanda, G., Pontieri, F. E., & Di Chiara, G. (1997). Cannabinoid and heroin activation of mesolimbic dopamine transmission by a common mu-1 opioid receptor mechanism. *Science, 276*, 2048–2050. (p. 216)

Tang, S-H., & Hall, V. C. (1995). The overjustification effect: A meta-analysis. *Applied Cognitive Psychology, 9*, 365–404. (p. 244)

Tangney, J. P., Baumeister, R. F., & Boone, A. L. (2004). High self-control predicts good adjustment, less pathology, better grades, and interpersonal success. *Journal of Personality*, in press. (p. 452)

Tannen, D. (1990). *You just don't understand: Women and men in conversation.* New York: Morrow. (pp. 28, 121)

Tannenbaum, P. (2002, February). Quoted by R. Kubey & M. Csikszentmihalyi, Television addiction is no mere metaphor. *Scientific American*, pp. 74–80. (p. 145)

Tanner, J. M. (1978). *Fetus into man: Physical growth from conception to maturity.* Cambridge, MA: Harvard University Press. (p. 116)

Tarmann, A. (2002, May/June). Out of the closet and onto the Census long form. *Population Today, 30*, pp. 1, 6. (pp. 364–366)

Taubes, G. (1994). Will new dopamine receptors offer a key to schizophrenia? *Science, 265*, 1034–1035. (p. 530)

Taubes, G. (2001). The soft science of dietary fat. *Science, 291*, 2536–2545. (p. 356)

Taubes, G. (2002, July 7). What if it's all been a big fat lie? *New York Times* (www.nytimes.com). (p. 356)

Tavris, C. (1982, November). Anger defused. *Psychology Today*, pp. 25–35. (p. 395)

Taylor, S., Kuch, K., Koch, W. J., Crockett, D. J., & Passey, G. (1998). The structure of posttraumatic stress symptoms. *Journal of Abnormal Psychology, 107*, 154–160. (p. 480)

Taylor, S. E. (1989). *Positive illusions.* New York: Basic Books. (pp. 300, 417, 459, 460)

Taylor, S. E., Cousino, L. K., Lewis, B. P., Gruenewald, T. L., Gurung, R. A. R., & Updegraff, J. A. (2000). Biobehavioral responses to stress in females: Tend-and-befriend, not fight-or-flight. *Psychological Review, 107*, 411–430. (p. 403)

Taylor, S. E., Lerner, J. S., Sherman, D. K., Sage, R. M., & McDowell, N. K. (2003). Portrait of the self-enhancer: Well adjusted and well liked or maladjusted and friendless? *Journal of Personality and Social Psychology, 84*, 165–176. (p. 460)

Taylor, S. E., Pham, L. B., Rivkin, I. D., & Armor, D. A. (1998). Harnessing the imagination: Mental simulation, self-regulation, and coping. *American Psychologist, 53*, 429–439. (p. 310)

Taylor, S. P., & Chermack, S. T. (1993). Alcohol, drugs and human physical aggression. *Journal of Studies on Alcohol*, Supplement No. 11, 78–88. (p. 561)

Teerlink, R., & Ozley, L. (2000). More than a motorcycle: The leadership journey at Harley-Davidson. Cambridge, MA: Harvard Business School Press. (p. B–11)

Teevan, R. C., & McGhee, P. E. (1972). Childhood development of fear of failure motivation. *Journal of Personality and Social Psychology, 21*, 345–348. (p. 374)

Teghtsoonian, R. (1971). On the exponents in Stevens' law and the constant in Ekinan's law. *Psychological Review, 78*, 71–80. (p. 144)

Teicher, M. H. (2002, March). The neurobiology of child abuse. *Scientific American*, pp. 68–75. (p. 114)

Tenopyr, M. L. (1997). Improving the workplace: Industrial/organizational psychology as a career. In R. J. Sternberg (Ed.), *Career paths in psychology: Where your degree can take you.* Washington, DC: American Psychological Association. (p. B–3)

Teran-Santos, J., Jimenez-Gomez, A., & Cordero-Guevara, J. (1999). The association between sleep apnea and the risk of traffic accidents. *New England Journal of Medicine, 340*, 847–851. (p. 199)

Terkel, S. (1972). *Working: People talk about what they do all day and how they feel about what they do.* New York: Pantheon Books, 1972. (p. B–1)

Terman, J. S., Terman, M., Lo, E-S., & Cooper, T. B. (2001). Circadian time of morning light administration and therapeutic response in winter depression. *Archives of General Psychiatry, 58*, 69–73. (p. 526)

Terman, M., Terman, J. S., & Ross, D. C. (1998). A controlled trial of timed bright light and negative air ionization for treatment of winter depression. *Archives of General Psychiatry, 55*, 875–882. (p. 526)

Terrace, H. S. (1979, November). How Nim Chimpsky changed my mind. *Psychology Today*, pp. 65–76. (p. 314)

Tesser, A., Forehand, R., Brody, G., & Long, N. (1989). Conflict: The role of calm and angry parent-child discussion in adolescent development. *Journal of Social and Clinical Psychology, 8*, 317–330. (p. 122)

Tetlock, P. E. (1988). Monitoring the integrative complexity of American and Soviet policy rhetoric: What can be learned? *Journal of Social Issues, 44*, 101–131. (p. 577)

Thannickal, T. C., Moore, R. Y., Nienhuis, R., Ramanathan, L., Gulyani, S., Aldrich, M., Cornford, M., & Siegel, J. M. (2000). Reduced number of hypocretin neurons in human narcolepsy. *Neuron, 27,* 469–474. (p. 199)

Thatcher, R. W., Walker, R. A., & Giudice, S. (1987). Human cerebral hemispheres develop at different rates and ages. *Science, 236,* 1110–1113. (pp. 103, 135)

Thayer, R. E. (1987). Energy, tiredness, and tension effects of a sugar snack versus moderate exercise. *Journal of Personality and Social Psychology, 52,* 119–125. (p. 415)

Thayer, R. E. (1993). Mood and behavior (smoking and sugar snacking) following moderate exercise: A partial test of self-regulation theory. *Personality and Individual Differences, 14,* 97–104. (p. 415)

Thomas, A., & Chess, S. (1986). The New York Longitudinal Study: From infancy to early adult life. In R. Plomin & J. Dunn (Eds.), *The study of temperament: Changes, continuities, and challenges.* Hillsdale, NJ: Erlbaum. (p. 135)

Thomas, G. V., & Blackman, D. (1991). Are animal experiments on the way out? *The Psychologist, 14,* 208–212. (p. 29)

Thomas, L. (1983). *The youngest science: Notes of a medicine watcher.* New York: Viking Press. (p. 41)

Thomas, L. (1992). *The fragile species.* New York : Scribner's. (pp. 95, 521)

Thomas, W. P., & Collier, V. P. (1998). Two languages are better than one. *Educational Leadership, 55,* 23–36. (p. 309)

Thompson, C. P., Frieman, J., & Cowan, T. (1993). Rajan's memory. Paper presented to the American Psychological Society convention. (p. 267)

Thompson, G. (1998, December 14). As obesity in children increases, so do cases of adult-onset diabetes. *New York Times* (www.nytimes.com). (p. 354)

Thompson, J. K., Jarvie, G. J., Lahey, B. B., & Cureton, K. J. (1982). Exercise and obesity: Etiology, physiology, and intervention. *Psychological Bulletin, 91,* 55–79. (p. 356)

Thompson, J. K., & Stice, E. (2001). Thin-ideal internalization: Mounting evidence for a new risk factor for body-image disturbance and eating pathology. *Current Directions in Psychological Science, 10,* 181–183. (p. 350)

Thompson, P. M., Cannon, T. D., Narr, K. L., van Erp, T., Poutanen, V-P., Huttunen, M., Lönnqvist, J., Standerskjöld-Nordenstam, C-G., Kaprio, J., Khaledy, M., Dail, R., Zoumalan, C. I., & Toga, A. W. (2001). Genetic influences on brain structure. *Nature Neuroscience, 4,* 1253–1258. (p. 327)

Thompson, P. M., Giedd, J. N., Woods, R. P., MacDonald, D., Evans, A. C., & Toga, A. W. (2000). Growth patterns in the developing brain detected by using continuum mechanical tensor maps. *Nature, 404,* 190–193. (p. 103)

Thomson, R., & Murachver, T. (2001). Predicting gender from electronic discourse. *British Journal of Social Psychology, 40,* 193–208 (and personal correspondence from T. Murachver, May 23, 2002). (p. 121)

Thorndike, A. L., & Hagen, E. P. (1977). Measurement and evaluation in psychology and education. New York: Macmillan. (p. 323)

Thorne, J., with Larry Rothstein (1993). *You are not alone: Words of experience and hope for the journey through depression.* New York: HarperPerennial. (p. 469)

Thornton, B., & Moore, S. (1993). Physical attractiveness contrast effect: Implications for self-esteem and evaluations of the social self. *Personality and Social Psychology Bulletin, 19,* 474–480. (p. 570)

Thorpe, W. H. (1974). *Animal nature and human nature.* London: Metheun. (p. 315)

Tiedens, L. Z. (2001). Anger and advancement versus sadness and subjugation: The effect of negative emotion expressions on social status conferral. *Journal of Personality and Social Psychology, 80,* 86–94. (p. 395)

Tiihonen, J., Isohanni, M., Rasanen, P., Koiranen, M., & Moring, J. (1997). Specific major mental disorders and criminality: A 26-year prospective study of the 1966 northern Finland birth cohort. *American Journal of Psychiatry, 154,* 840–845. (p. 475)

Tikkanen, T. (2001). Psychology in Europe: A growing profession with high standards and a bright future. *European Psychologist, 6,* 144–146. (p. 7)

Tinbergen, N. (1951). *The study of instinct.* Oxford: Clarendon. (p. 342)

Tirrell, M. E. (1990). Personal communication. (pp. 230–231)

Todes, D. P. (1997). From the machine to the ghost within: Pavlov's transition from digestive physiology to conditional reflexes. *American Psychologist, 52,* 947–955. (p. 229)

Tolchin, M. (1994, April 17). Major airlines go two years without a fatality. *New York Times* report (in *Grand Rapids Press,* p. A10). (p. 299)

Tolkien, J. R. R. (1965). *The fellowship of the ring.* Boston: Houghton Mifflin Co. (p. 429)

Tolstoy, L. (1904). *My confessions.* Boston: Dana Estes. (p. 8)

Tondo, L., Jamison, K. R., & Baldessarini, R. J. (1997). Effect of lithium maintenance on suicidal behavior in major mood disorders. In D. M. Stoff & J. J. Mann (Eds.), *The neurobiology of suicide: From the bench to the clinic.* New York: New York Academy of Sciences. (p. 532)

Toni, N., Buchs, P.-A., Nikonenko, I., Bron, C. R., & Muller, D. (1999). LTP promotes formation of multiple spine synapses between a single axon terminal and a dendrite. *Nature, 402,* 421–42. (p. 268)

Torrey, E. F. (1986). *Witchdoctors and psychiatrists.* New York: Harper & Row. (p. 527)

Totterdell, P., Kellett, S., Briner, R. B., & Teuchmann, K. (1998). Evidence of mood linkage in work groups. *Journal of Personality and Social Psychology, 74,* 1504–1515. (p. 545)

Tovee, M. J., Mason, S. M., Emery, J. L., McCluskey, S. E., & Cohen-Tovee, E. M. (1997). Supermodels: Stick insects or hourglasses? *The Lancet, 350,* 1474–1475. (p. 351)

Towler, G. (1986). From zero to one hundred: Coaction in a natural setting. *Perceptual and Motor Skills, 62,* 377–378. (p. 551)

Treffert, D. A., & Wallace, G. L. (2002). Island of genius—The artistic brilliance and dazzling memory that sometimes accompany autism and other disorders hint at how all brains work. *Scientific American, 286,* 76–86. (p. 317)

Treisman, A. (1987). Properties, parts, and objects. In K. R. Boff, L. Kaufman, & J. P. Thomas (Eds.), *Handbook of perception and human performance.* New York: Wiley. (p. 166)

Tremblay, R. E., Pihl, R. O., Vitaro, F., & Dobkin, P. L. (1994). Predicting early onset of male antisocial behavior from preschool behavior. *Archives of General Psychiatry, 51,* 732–739. (p. 485)

Trewin, D. (2001). *Australian social trends 2001.* Canberra: Australian Bureau of Statistics. (pp. 86, 90, 250, B–1)

Triandis, H. C. (1981). Some dimensions of intercultural variation and their implications for interpersonal behavior. Paper presented at the American Psychological Association convention. (p. 87)

Triandis, H. C. (1989a). The self and social behavior in differing cultural contexts. *Psychological Review, 96,* 506–520. (p. 461)

Triandis, H. C. (1989b). Cross-cultural studies of individualism and collectivism. In J. J. Berman (Ed.), *Nebraska symposium on motivation 1989* (Vol. 37). Lincoln, NE: University of Nebraska Press. (p. 461)

Triandis, H. C. (1994). *Culture and social behavior.* New York: McGraw-Hill. (pp. 87–88, 391, 452, 461, 462, 562)

Triandis, H. C., Bontempo, R., Villareal, M. J., Asai, M., & Lucca, N. (1988). Individualism and collectivism: Cross-cultural perspectives on self-ingroup relationships. *Journal of Personality and Social Psychology, 54,* 323–338. (p. 462)

Trickett, P. K., & McBride-Chang, C. (1995). The developmental impact of different forms of child abuse and neglect. *Developmental Review, 15*, 311–337. (p. 113)

Trimble, J. E. (1994). Cultural variations in the use of alcohol and drugs. In W. J. Lonner & R. Malpass (Eds.), *Psychology and culture.* Boston: Allyn & Bacon. (p. 219)

Triplett, N. (1898). The dynamogenic factors in pacemaking and competition. *American Journal of Psychology, 9*, 507–533. (pp. 550–551)

Trolier, T. K., & Hamilton, D. L. (1986). Variables influencing judgments of correlational relations. *Journal of Personality and Social Psychology, 50*, 879–888. (p. 21)

Trut, L. N. (1999). Early canid domestication: The farm-fox experiment. *American Scientist, 87*, 160–169. (p. 70)

Tsang, Y. C. (1938). Hunger motivation in gastrectomized rats. *Journal of Comparative Psychology, 26*, 1–17. (p. 345)

Tsien, J. Z. (April, 2000). Building a brainier mouse. *Scientific American,* 62–68. (p. 327)

Tsuang, M. T., & Faraone, S. V. (1990). *The genetics of mood disorders.* Baltimore, MD: Johns Hopkins University Press. (p. 489)

Tuber, D. S., Miller, D. D., Caris, K. A., Halter, R., Linden, F., & Hennessy, M. B. (1999). Dogs in animal shelters: Problems, suggestions, and needed expertise. *Psychological Science, 10*, 379–386. (p. 30)

Tucker, K. A. (2002). I believe you can fly. *Gallup Management Journal* (www.gallupjournal.com/CA/st/20020520.asp). (p. B–9)

Tulving, E. (1996, August 18). Quoted in J. Gatehouse, Technology revealing brain's secrets. *Montreal Gazette,* p. A3. (p. 271)

Turner, C. W., Hesse, B. W., & Peterson-Lewis, S. (1986). Naturalistic studies of the long-term effects of television violence. *Journal of Social Issues, 42*(3), 7–28. (p. 251)

Turner, J. C. (1987). *Rediscovering the social group: A self-categorization theory.* New York: Basil Blackwell. (p. 557)

Tversky, A. (1985, June). Quoted in K. McKean, Decisions, decisions. *Discover,* pp. 22–31. (p. 296)

Tversky, A., & Kahneman, D. (1974). Judgment under uncertainty: Heuristics and biases. *Science, 185*, 1124–1131. (pp. 296, A–6)

Twenge, J. M. (2000). The age of anxiety? Birth cohort change in anxiety and neuroticism, 1952–1993. *Journal of Personality and Social Psychology, 79*, 1007–1021. (p. 480)

Twenge, J. M. (2001). Changes in women's assertiveness in response to status and roles: A cross-temporal meta-analysis, 1931–1993. *Journal of Personality and Social Psychology, 8*, 133–145. (p. 91)

Twenge, J. M., Baumeister, R. F., Tice, D. M., & Stucke, T. S. (2001). If you can't join them, beat them: Effects of social exclusion on aggressive behavior. *Journal of Personality and Social Psychology, 81*, 1058–1069. (p. 372)

Twenge, J. M., & Campbell, W. K. (2001). Age and birth cohort differences in self-esteem: A cross-temporal meta-analysis. *Personality and Social Psychology Review, 5*, 321–344. (p. 121)

Twenge, J. M., Catanese, K. R., & Baumeister, R. F. (2002). Social exclusion causes self-defeating behavior. *Journal of Personality and Social Psychology, 83*, 606–615. (p. 372)

Twenge, J. M., & Crocker, J. (2002). Race and self-esteem: Meta-analyses comparing Whites, Blacks, Hispanics, Asians, and American Indians and comment on Gray-Little and Hafdahl (2000). *Psychological Bulletin, 128*, 371–408. (p. 458)

Twiss, C., Tabb, S., & Crosby, F. (1989). Affirmative action and aggregate data: The importance of patterns in the perception of discrimination. In F. Blanchard & F. Crosby (Eds.), *Affirmative action: Social psychological perspectives.* New York: Springer-Verlag. (p. A–5)

Uchino, B. N., Cacioppo, J. T., & Kiecolt-Glaser, J. K. (1996). The relationship between social support and physiological processes: A review with emphasis on underlying mechanisms and implications for health. *Psychological Bulletin, 119*, 488–531. (p. 418)

Uchino, B. N., Uno, D., & Holt-Lunstad, J. (1999). Social support, physiological processes, and health. *Current Directions in Psychological Science, 8*, 145–148. (p. 418)

Udry, J. R. (2000). Biological limits of gender construction. *American Sociological Review, 65*, 443–457. (p. 90)

Ulrich, R. E. (1991). Animal rights, animal wrongs and the question of balance. *Psychological Science, 2*, 197–201. (p. 29)

UNAIDS. (2002, December). AIDS epidemic update (www.unaids.org). (p. 411)

Underwood, B. J. (1957). Interference and forgetting. *Psychological Review, 64*, 49–60. (p. 278)

UNESCO (2002, July). Regional adult illiteracy rate and population by gender (www.uis.unesco.org). (p. 556)

United Nations. (1992). *1991 demographic yearbook.* New York: United Nations. (p. 130)

Urbany, J. E., Bearden, W. O., & Weilbaker, D. C. (1988). The effect of plausible and exaggerated reference prices on consumer perceptions and price search. *Journal of Consumer Research, 15*, 95–110. (p. 300)

U.S. News & World Report. (1997, March 31). Oprah: A heavenly body? Survey finds talk-show host a celestial shoo-in. P. 18. (p. 459)

Vaidya, J. G., Gray, E. K., Haig, J., & Watson, D. (2002). On the temporal stability of personality: Evidence for differential stability and the role of life experiences. *Journal of Personality and Social Psychology, 83*, 1469–1484. (p. 448)

Vaillant, G. E. (2002). *Aging well: Surprising guideposts to a happier life from the landmark Harvard study of adult development.* Boston: Little, Brown. (p. 417)

Valenstein, E. S. (1986). *Great and desperate cures: The rise and decline of psychosurgery.* New York: Basic Books. (p. 534)

Vallerand, R. J., Fortier, M. S., & Guay, F. (1997). Self-determination and persistence in a real-life setting: Toward a motivational model of high school dropout. *Journal of Personality and Social Psychology, 72*, 1161–1176. (p. 374)

Vance, E. B., & Wagner, N. N. (1976). Written descriptions of orgasm: A study of sex differences. *Archives of Sexual Behavior, 5*, 87–98. (p. 358)

Vandell, D. L. (2000). Parents, peer groups, and other socializing influences. *Developmental Psychology, 36*, 699–710. (p. 85)

Vandello, J. A., & Cohen, D. (1999). Patterns of individualism and collectivism across the United States. *Journal of Personality and Social Psychology, 77*, 279–292. (p. 461)

Vandenberg, S. G., & Kuse, A. R. (1978). Mental rotations: A group test of three-dimensional spatial visualization. *Perceptual and Motor Skills, 47*, 599–604. (p. 333)

van den Boom, D. (1990). Preventive intervention and the quality of mother-infant interaction and infant exploration in irritable infants. In W. Koops, H. J. G. Soppe, J. L. van der Linden, P. C. M. Molenaar, & J. J. F. Schroots (Eds.), *Developmental psychology behind the dikes: An outline of developmental psychology research in The Netherlands.* The Netherlands: Uitgeverij Eburon. Cited by C. Hazan & P. R. Shaver (1994). Deeper into attachment theory. *Psychological Inquiry, 5*, 68–79. (p. 112)

van den Bos, K., & Spruijt, N. (2002). Appropriateness of decisions as a moderator of the psychology of voice. *European Journal of Social Psychology, 32*, 57–72. (p. B–11)

Van Dyke, C., & Byck, R. (1982, March). Cocaine. *Scientific American,* pp. 128–141. (p. 214) van IJzendoorn, M. H., & Kroonenberg, P. M. (1988). Cross-cultural patterns of attachment: A meta-analysis of the strange situation. *Child Development, 59,* 147–156. (p. 111)

Van Leeuwen, M. S. (1978). A cross-cultural examination of psychological differentiation in males and females. *International Journal of Psychology, 13,* 87–122. (p. 91)

Van Leeuwen, M. S. (1982). IQism and the just society: Historical background. *Journal of the American Scientific Affiliation, 34,* 193–201. (p. 322)

van Schaik, C. P., Ancrenaz, M., Borgen, G., Galdikas, B., Knott, C. D., Singleton, I., Suzuki, A., Utami, S. S., & Merrill, M. (2003). Orangutan cultures and the evolution of material culture. *Science, 299,* 102–105. (p. 312)

Van Yperen, N. W., & Buunk, B. P. (1990). A longitudinal study of equity and satisfaction in intimate relationships. *European Journal of Social Psychology, 20,* 287–309. (p. 573)

Vaughn, K. B., & Lanzetta, J. T. (1981). The effect of modification of expressive displays on vicarious emotional arousal. *Journal of Experimental Social Psychology, 17,* 16–30. (p. 392)

Vaux, A. (1988). Social and personal factors in loneliness. *Journal of Social and Clinical Psychology, 6,* 462–471. (p. 494)

Vecera, S. P., Vogel, E. K., & Woodman, G. F. (2002). Lower region: A new cue for figure-ground assignment. *Journal of Experimental Psychology: General, 13,* 194–205. (p. 170)

Veggeberg, S. K. (1996, March-April). Manic depression: Gene-Hunters' hopes rise. *BrainWork,* pp. 1–2. (p. 490)

Vekassy, L. (1977). Dreams of the blind. *Magyar Pszichologiai Szemle, 34,* 478–491. (p. 200)

Vemer, E., Coleman, M., Ganong, L. H., & Cooper, H. (1989). Marital satisfaction in remarriage: A meta-analysis. *Journal of Marriage and the Family, 51,* 713–725. (p. 131)

Venn, J. (1986). Hypnosis and the Lamaze method: A reply to Wideman and Singer. *American Psychologist, 41,* 475–476. (p. 206)

Verhaeghen, P., & Salthouse, T. A. (1997). Meta-analyses of age-cognition relations in adulthood: Estimates of linear and nonlinear age effects and structural models. *Psychological Bulletin, 122,* 231–249. (p. 126)

Vigliocco, G., & Hartsuiker, R. J. (2002). The interplay of meaning, sound, and syntax in sentence production. *Psychological Bulletin, 128,* 442–472. (p. 303)

Vines, G. (1995, July 8). Genes in black and white. *New Scientist,* pp. 34–37. (p. 555)

Vining, E. P. G., Freeman, J. M., Pillas, D. J., Uematsu, S., Carson, B. S., Brandt, J., Boatman, D., Pulsifer, M. B., & Zukerberg, A. (1997). Why would you remove half a brain? The outcome of 58 children after hemispherectomy—The Johns Hopkins Experience: 1968 to 1996. *Pediatrics, 100,* 163–171. (p. 59)

Vita, A. J., Terry, R. B., Hubert, H. B., & Fries, J. F. (1998). Aging, health risks, and cumulative disability. *New England Journal of Medicine, 338,* 1035–1041. (p. 212)

Vohs, K., Voelz, Z., Pettit, J., Bardone, A., Katz, J., Abramson, L., Heatherton, T., & Joiner, T. (2001). Perfectionism, body dissatisfaction, and self-esteem: An interactive model of bulimic symptom development. *Journal of Social and Clinical Psychology, 20,* 476–497. (p. 350)

von Senden, M. (1932; reprinted 1960). In P. Heath (Trans.), *Space and sight: The perception of space and shape in the congenitally blind before and after operation.* Glencoe, IL: Free Press. (p. 176)

Vreeland, C. N., Gallagher, B. J., III, & McFalls, J. A., Jr. (1995). The beliefs of members of the American Psychiatric Association on the etiology of male homosexuality: A national survey. *Journal of Psychology, 129,* 507–517. (p. 368)

Wadden, T. A., Vogt, R. A., Foster, G. D., & Anderson, D. A. (1998). Exercise and the maintenance of weight loss: 1-year follow-up of a con-trolled clinical trial. *Journal of Consulting and Clinical Psychology, 66,* 429–433. (p. 356)

Wagstaff, G. (1982). Attitudes to rape: The "just world" strikes again? *Bulletin of the British Psychological Society, 13,* 275–283. (p. 541)

Wahl, O. F. (1992). Mass media images of mental illness: A review of the literature. *Journal of Community Psychology, 20,* 343–352. (p. 475)

Wahlberg, D. (2001, October 11). We're more depressed, patriotic, poll finds. *Grand Rapids Press,* p. A15. (p. 404)

Wakefield, J. C. (1997). Normal inability versus pathological disability: Why Ossorio's definition of mental disorder is not sufficient. *Clinical Psychology Science and Practice, 4,* 249–258. (p. 470)

Wakefield, J. C., & Spitzer, R. L. (2002). Lowered estimates—but of what? *Archives of General Psychiatry, 59,* 129–130. (p. 481)

Walfish, D. (2001). National count reveals major societal changes. *Science, 292,* 1823. (p. 556)

Walker, E. F., & Diforio, D. (1997). Schizophrenia: A neural diathesis-stress model. *Psychological Bulletin, 104,* 667–685. (p. 501)

Wall, B. (2002, August 24–25). Profit matures along with baby boomers. *International Herald Tribune,* p. 13. (p. 570)

Wall, P. (2000). *Pain: The science of suffering.* New York: Columbia University Press. (p. 160)

Wall Street Journal. (1999, December 17). Money and misery. Editorial, p. A14. (p. 520)

Wallach, M. A., & Wallach, L. (1983). *Psychology's sanction for selfishness: The error of egoism in theory and therapy.* New York: Freeman. (p. 441)

Wallach, M. A., & Wallach, L. (1985, February). How psychology sanctions the cult of the self. *Washington Monthly,* pp. 46–56. (p. 441)

Waller, D. (1995, December 11). The vision thing. *Time,* p. 48. (p. 181)

Waller, J. (1998). *Face to face: The changing state of racism across America.* New York: Plenum. (p. 556)

Wallis, C. (1983, June 6). Stress: Can we cope? *Time,* pp. 48–54. (p. 405)

Wallis, C. (1987, October 12). Back off, buddy: A new Hite report stirs up a furor over sex and love in the '80s. *Time,* pp. 68–73. (p. 18)

Walster (Hatfield), E., Aronson, V., Abrahams, D., & Rottman, L. (1966). Importance of physical attractiveness in dating behavior. *Journal of Personality and Social Psychology, 4,* 508–516. (p. 569)

Wampold, B. E. (2001). *The great psychotherapy debate: Models, methods, and findings.* Mahwah, NJ: Erlbaum. (p. 526)

Ward, A., & Mann, T. (2000). Don't mind if I do: Disinhibited eating under cognitive load. *Journal of Personality and Social Psychology, 78,* 753–763. (p. 356)

Ward, C. (1994). Culture and altered states of consciousness. In W. J. Lonner & R. Malpass (Eds.), *Psychology and culture.* Boston: Allyn & Bacon. (p. 211)

Ward, K. D., Klesges, R. C., & Halpern, M. T. (1997). Predictors of smoking cessation and state-of-the-art smoking interventions. *Journal of Socies Issues, 53,* 129–145. (p. 213)

Warr, P., & Payne, R. (1982). Experiences of strain and pleasure among British adults. *Social Science and Medicine, 16,* 1691–1697. (p. 417)

Wason, P. C. (1960). On the failure to eliminate hypotheses in a conceptual task. *Quarterly Journal of Experimental Psychology, 12,* 129–140. (p. 295)

Wasserman, E. A. (1993). Comparative cognition: Toward a general understanding of cognition in behavior. *Psychological Science, 4,* 156–161. (p. 238)

Wasserman, E. A. (1995). The conceptual abilities of pigeons. *American Scientist, 83,* 246–255. (p. 311)

Wasserman, E. M., & Lisanby, S. H. (2001). Therapeutic application of repetitive transcranial magnetic stimulation: A review. *Clinical Neurophysiology, 112,* 1367–1377. (p. 534)

Waterhouse, R. (1993, July 19). Income for 62 percent is below average pay. *The Independent*, p. 4. (p. A–2)

Waterman, A. S. (1988). Identity status theory and Erikson's theory: Commonalities and differences. *Developmental Review, 8,* 185–208. (p. 120)

Watkins, C. E., Campbell, V. L., Nieberding, R., & Hallmark, R. (1995). Contemporary practice of psychological assessment by clinical psychologists. *Professional Psychology: Research and Practice, 26,* 54–60. (p. 435)

Watkins, J. G. (1984). The Bianchi (L. A. Hillside Strangler) case: Sociopath or multiple personality? *International Journal of Clinical and Experimental Hypnosis, 32,* 67–101. (p. 483)

Watson, D. (2000). *Mood and temperament.* New York: Guilford Press. (pp. 396, 415)

Watson, D., Suls, J., & Haig, J. (2002). Global self-esteem in relation to structural models of personality and affectivity. *Journal of Personality and Social Psychology, 83,* 185–197. (p. 457)

Watson, J. B. (1913). Psychology as the behaviorist views it. *Psychological Review, 20,* 158–177. (pp. 187, 228, 235)

Watson, J. B. (1924). *Behaviorism.* New York: Norton. (p. 53)

Watson, J. B., & Rayner, R. (1920). Conditioned emotional reactions. *Journal of Experimental Psychology, 3,* 1–14. (p. 235)

Watson, R. I., Jr. (1973). Investigation into deindividuation using a cross-cultural survey technique. *Journal of Personality and Social Psychology, 25,* 342–345. (p. 552)

Watson, S. J., Benson, J. A., Jr., & Joy, J. E. (2000). NEWS AND VIEWS—Marijuana and medicine: Assessing the science base: A summary of the 1999 Institute of Medicine report. *Archives of General Psychiatry, 57,* 547–553. (p. 216)

Waxman, S. (2002, June 13). Shooting crap: Alleged psychic John Edward actually gambles on hope and basic laws of statistics. *Salon* (www.salon.com/people/feature/2002/06/13/probability/index.html). (p. 447)

Wayment, H. A., & Peplau, L. A. (1995). Social support and well-being among lesbian and heterosexual women: A structural modeling approach. *Personality and Social Psychology Bulletin, 21,* 1189–1199. (p. 131)

Weaver, J. B., Masland, J. L., & Zillmann, D. (1984). Effect of erotica on young men's aesthetic perception of their female sexual partners. *Perceptual and Motor Skills, 58,* 929–930. (p. 360)

Webb, W. B. (1992). *Sleep: The gentle tyrant.* Bolton, MA: Anker Publishing. (pp. 193, 198)

Webb, W. B., & Campbell, S. S. (1983). Relationships in sleep characteristics of identical and fraternal twins. *Archives of General Psychiatry, 40,* 1093–1095. (p. 195)

Wechsler, D. (1972). "Hold" and "Don't Hold" tests. In S. M. Chown (Ed.), *Human aging.* New York: Penguin. (p. 128)

Wechsler, H., Davenport, A., Dowdall, G., Moeykens, B., & Castillo, S. (1994). Health and behavioral consequences of binge drinking in college. *Journal of the American Medical Association, 272,* 1672–1677. (p. 211)

Wechsler, H., Lee, J. E., Kuo, M., Seibring, M., Nelson, T. F., & Lee, H. (2002). Trends in college binge drinking during a period of increased prevention efforts. *Journal of American College Health, 50,* 203–217. (p. 211)

Weed, W. S. (2001, May). Can we go to Mars without going crazy? *Discover*, pp. 31–43. (p. B–13)

Wegner, D. M. (1990). *White bears and other unwanted thoughts: Suppression, obsession, and the psychology of mental control.* New York: Penguin Books. (p. 418)

Weinberg, M. S., & Williams, C. (1974). *Male homosexuals: Their problems and adaptations.* New York: Oxford University Press. (p. 365)

Weinstein, N. D. (1980). Unrealistic optimism about future life events. *Journal of Personality and Social Psychology, 39,* 806–820. (p. 454)

Weinstein, N. D. (1982). Unrealistic optimism about susceptibility to health problems. *Journal of Behavioral Medicine, 5,* 441–460. (p. 454)

Weinstein, N. D. (1996, October 4). 1996 optimistic bias bibliography. Distributed via internet (weinstein_c@aesop.rutgers.edu). (p. 454)

Weiss, A., King, J. E., & Enns, R. M. (2002). Subjective well-being is heritable and genetically correlated with dominance in chimpanzees (*Pan troglodytes*). *Journal of Personality and Social Psychology, 83,* 1141–1149. (p. 401)

Weiss, A., King, J. E., & Figueredo, A. J. (2000). The heritability of personality factors in chimpanzees (*Pan troglodytes*). *Behavior Genetics, 30,* 213–221. (pp. 78, 401)

Weissman, M. M. (1999). Interpersonal psychotherapy and the health care scene. In D. S. Janowsky (Ed.), *Psychotherapy indications and outcomes.* Washington, DC: American Psychiatric Press. (p. 509)

Weissman, M. M., Bland, R. C., Canino, G. J., Faravelli, C., Greenwald, S., Hwu, H-G., Joyce, P. R., Karam, E. G., Lee, C-K., Lellouch, J., Lepine, J-P., Newman, S. C., Rubio-Stepic, M., Wells, J. E., Wickramaratne, P. J., Wittchen, H-U., & Yeh, E-K. (1996). Cross-national epidemiology of major depression and bipolar disorder. *Journal of the American Medical Association, 276,* 293–299. (p. 488)

Weisz, J. R., Rothbaum, F. M., & Blackburn, T. C. (1984). Standing out and standing in: The psychology of control in America and Japan. *American Psychologist, 39,* 955–969. (p. 86)

Wellman, H. M., Cross, D., & Watson, J. (2001). Meta-analysis of theory-of-mind development: The truth about false belief. *Child Development, 72,* 655–684. (p. 108)

Wellman, H. M., & Gelman, S. A. (1992). Cognitive development: Foundational theories of core domains. *Annual Review of Psychology, 43,* 337–375. (p. 106)

Wells, G. L. (1981). Lay analyses of causal forces on behavior. In J. Harvey (Ed.), *Cognition, social behavior and the environment.* Hillsdale, NJ: Erlbaum. (p. 225)

Wender, P. H., Kety, S. S., Rosenthal, D., Schulsinger, F., Ortmann, J., & Lunde, I. (1986). Psychiatric disorders in the biological and adoptive families of adopted individuals with affective disorders. *Archives of General Psychiatry, 43,* 923–929. (p. 489)

Wener, R., Frazier, W., & Farbstein, J. (1987, June). Building better jails. *Psychology Today*, pp. 40–49. (pp. 452–453)

Werker, J. F. (1989). Becoming a native listener. *American Scientist, 77,* 54–59. (p. 303)

Westen, D. (1996). Is Freud really dead? Teaching psychodynamic theory to introductory psychology. Presentation to the Annual Institute on the Teaching of Psychology, St. Petersburg Beach, Florida. (p. 436)

Westen, D. (1998). The scientific legacy of Sigmund Freud: Toward a psychodynamically informed psychological science. *Psychological Bulletin, 124,* 333–371. (p. 436)

Westen, D., & Morrison, K. (2001). A multidimensional meta-analysis of treatments for depression, panic, and generalized anxiety disorder: An empirical examination of the status of empirically supported therapies. *Journal of Consulting and Clinical Psychology, 69,* 875–899. (p. 523)

Whalen, P. J., Shin, L. M., McInerney, S. C., Fisher, H., Wright, C. I., & Rauch, S. L. (2001). A functional MRI study of human amygdala responses to facial expressions of fear versus anger. *Emotion, 1,* 70–83. (p. 385)

White, G. L., & Kight, T. D. (1984). Misattribution of arousal and attraction: Effects of salience of explanations for arousal. *Journal of Experimental Social Psychology, 20,* 55–64. (p. 572)

White, H. R., Brick, J., & Hansell, S. (1993). A longitudinal investigation of alcohol use and aggression in adolescence. *Journal of Studies on Alcohol*, Supplement No. 11, 62–77. (p. 561)

White House. (1999, June 7). White House fact sheet on myths and facts about mental illness. Washington, DC: White House Press Office. (p. 471)

White, K. M. (1983). Young adults and their parents: Individuation to mutuality. *New Directions for Child Development, 22,* 61–76. (p. 123)

White, L., & Edwards, J. (1990). Emptying the nest and parental well-being: An analysis of national panel data. *American Sociological Review, 55*, 235–242. (p. 131)

White, P. H., Kjelgaard, M. M., & Harkins, S. G. (1995). Testing the contribution of self-evaluation to goal-setting effects. *Journal of Personality and Social Psychology, 69*, 69–79. (p. B–9)

Whitehead, B. D., & Popenoe, D. (2001). *The state of our unions 2001: The social health of marriage in America.* Rutgers University: The National Marriage Project. (p. 131)

Whiten, A., & Boesch, C. (2001, January). Cultures of chimpanzees. *Scientific American*, pp. 60–67. (p. 312)

Whiten, A., & Byrne, R. W. (1988). Tactical deception in primates. *Behavioral and Brain Sciences, 11*, 233–244, 267–273. (p. 19)

Whiting, B. B., & Edwards, C. P. (1988). *Children of different worlds: The formation of social behavior.* Cambridge, MA: Harvard University Press. (p. 88)

Whitley, B. E., Jr. (1990). The relationships of heterosexuals' attributions for the causes of homosexuality to attitudes toward lesbians and gay men. *Personality and Social Psychology Bulletin, 16*, 369–377. (p. 368)

Whitley, B. E., Jr. (1999). Right-wing authoritarianism, social dominance orientation, and prejudice. *Journal of Personality and Social Psychology, 77*, 126–134. (p. 558)

WHO (2000). Mental health and brain disorders. Geneva: World Health Organization (www.who.int/mental_health). (p. 490)

WHO (2001). The World Health Report 2001. Mental Health: New Understanding, New Hope. (p. 469)

WHO (2002). The global burden of disease. Geneva: World Health Organization (www.who.int/msa/mnh/ems/dalys/intro.htm). (pp. 212, 486)

WHO (2002a, September 4). Suicide rates. World Health Organization (www5.who.int/mental_health). (pp. 490, 491)

WHO (2002c, December 9). China: WHO lauds launch of nation's first suicide prevent center: Xinhua news. World Health Organization (www5.who.int/mental_health). (p. 490)

WHO (2002d). Schizophrenia. World Health Organization (www5.who.int/mental_health). (p. 496)

Whooley, M. A., & Browner, W. S. (1998). Association between depressive symptoms and mortality in older women. *Archives of Internal Medicine, 158*, 2129–2135. (p. 409)

Whorf, B. L. (1956). Science and linguistics. In J. B. Carroll (Ed.), *Language, thought, and reality: Selected writings of Benjamin Lee Whorf.* Cambridge, MA: MIT Press. (p. 308)

Wichman, H. (1992). *Human factors in the design of spacecraft.* Stony Brook, NY: State University of New York. (p. B–13)

Wickelgren, W. A. (1977). *Learning and memory.* Englewood Cliffs, NJ: Prentice-Hall. (p. 263)

Widom, C. S. (1989a). Does violence beget violence? A critical examination of the literature. *Psychological Bulletin, 106*, 3–28. (p. 113)

Widom, C. S. (1989b). The cycle of violence. *Science, 244*, 160–166. (p. 113)

Wiens, A. N., & Menustik, C. E. (1983). Treatment outcome and patient characteristics in an aversion therapy program for alcoholism. *American Psychologist, 38*, 1089–1096. (p. 514)

Wierson, M., & Forehand, R. (1994). Parent behavioral training for child noncompliance: Rationale, concepts, and effectiveness. *Current Directions in Psychological Science, 3*, 146–149. (pp. 246–247)

Wierzbicki, M. (1993). Psychological adjustment of adoptees: A meta-analysis. *Journal of Clinical Child Psychology, 22*, 447–454. (p. 79)

Wiesel, T. N. (1982). Postnatal development of the visual cortex and the influence of environment. *Nature, 299*, 583–591. (p. 176)

Wiesner, W. H., & Cronshow, S. P. (1988). A meta-analytic investigation of the impact of interview format and degree of structure on the validity of the employment interview. *Journal of Occupational Psychology, 61*, 275–290. (p. B–6)

Wigdor, A. K., & Garner, W. R. (1982). *Ability testing: Uses, consequences, and controversies.* Washington, DC: National Academy Press. (p. 335)

Wilder, D. A. (1981). Perceiving persons as a group: Categorization and intergroup relations. In D. L. Hamilton (Ed.), *Cognitive processes in stereotyping and intergroup behavior.* Hillsdale, NJ: Erlbaum. (p. 558)

Wilford, J. N. (1999, February 9). New findings help balance the cosmological books. *New York Times* (www.nytimes.com). (p. 95)

Williams, C. L., & Berry, J. W. (1991). Primary prevention of acculturative stress among refugees. *American Psychologist, 46*, 632–641. (p. 405)

Williams, J. E., Paton, C. C., Siegler, I. C., Eigenbrodt, M. L., Nieto, F. J., & Tyroler, H. A. (2000). Anger proneness predicts coronary heart disease risk: Prospective analysis from the artherosclerosis risk in communities (ARIC) study. *Circulation, 101,* 17, 2034–2040. (p. 409)

Williams, K. D., & Zadro, L. (2001). Ostracism: On being ignored, excluded and rejected. In M. Leary (Ed.), *Rejection.* New York: Oxford University Press. (p. 372)

Williams, R. (1993). *Anger kills.* New York: Times Books. (p. 408)

Williams, R. B., Barefoot, J. C., Califf, R. M., Haney, T. L., Saunders, W. B., Pryor, D. B., Hlatky, M. A., Siegler, I. C., & Mark, D. B. (1992). Prognostic importance of social and economic resources among medically treated patients with angiographically documented coronary artery disease. *Journal of the American Medical Association, 267*, 520–524. (p. 417)

Williams, S. L. (1987). Self-efficacy and mastery-oriented treatment for severe phobias. Paper presented to the American Psychological Association convention. (p. 513)

Willmuth, M. E. (1987). Sexuality after spinal cord injury: A critical review. *Clinical Psychology Review, 7*, 389–412. (p. 360)

Wilson, A. E., & Ross, M. (2001). From chump to champ: People's appraisals of their earlier and present selves. *Journal of Personality and Social Psychology, 80*, 572–584. (p. 460)

Wilson, C. M., & Oswald, A. J. (2002). How does marriage affect physical and psychological health? A survey of the longitudinal evidence. Working paper, University of York and Warwick University. (pp. 417–418)

Wilson, J. P., Harel, Z., & Kahana, B. (1988). *Human adaptation to extreme stress: From the Holocaust to Vietnam.* New York: Plenum Press. (p. 480)

Wilson, R. C., Gaft, J. G., Dienst, E. R., Wood, L., & Bavry, J. L. (1975). *College professors and their impact on students.* New York: Wiley. (p. 552)

Wilson, R. S. (1979). Analysis of longitudinal twin data: Basic model and applications to physical growth measures. *Acta Geneticae medicae et Gemellologiae, 28*, 93–105. (p. 104)

Wilson, R. S., & Matheny, A. P., Jr. (1986). Behavior-genetics research in infant temperament: The Louisville twin study. In R. Plomin & J. Dunn (Eds.), *The study of temperament: Changes, continuities, and challenges.* Hillsdale, NJ: Erlbaum. (p. 79)

Wilson, T. D. (2002). *Strangers to ourselves: Discovering the adaptive unconscious.* Cambridge: Harvard University Press. (p. 188)

Wilson, W. R. (1979). Feeling more than we can know: Exposure effects without learning. *Journal of Personality and Social Psychology, 37*, 811–821. (p. 188)

Windholz, G. (1989, April-June). The discovery of the principles of reinforcement, extinction, generalization, and differentiation of conditional reflexes in Pavlov's laboratories. *Pavlovian Journal of Biological Science, 26*, 64–74. (p. 232)

Windholz, G. (1997). Ivan P. Pavlov: An overview of his life and psychological work. *American Psychologist, 52*, 941–946. (p. 230)

Winn, P. (1995). The lateral hypothalamus and motivated behavior: An old syndrome reassessed and a new perspective gained. *Current Directions in Psychological Science, 4,* 182–187. (p. 347)

Winner, E. (2000). The origins and ends of giftedness. *American Psychologist, 55,* 159–169. (p. 324)

Wiseman, R. (2002). Laugh Lab—final results. University of Hertfordshire (www.laughlab.co.uk). (p. 295)

Wiseman, R., Jeffreys, C., Smith, M., & Nyman, A. (1999). The psychology of the seance. *The Skeptical Inquirer, 23(2),* 30–33. (p. 283)

Witelson, S. F., Kigar, D. L., & Harvey, T. (1999). The exceptional brain of Albert Einstein. *The Lancet, 353,* 2149–2153. (p. 56)

Witvliet, C. V. O., Ludwig, T., & Vander Laan, K. (2001). Granting forgiveness or harboring grudges: Implications for emotions, physiology, and health. *Psychological Science, 12,* 117–123. (p. 395)

Witvliet, C. V. O., & Vrana, S. R. (1995). Psychophysiological responses as indices of affective dimensions. *Psychophysiology, 32,* 436–443. (p. 385)

Wixted, J. T., & Ebbesen, E. B. (1991). On the form of forgetting. *Psychological Science, 2,* 409–415. (p. 277)

Wolfson, A. R., & Carskadon, M. A. (1998). Sleep schedules and daytime functioning in adolescents. *Child Development, 69,* 875–887. (p. 202)

Woll, S. (1986). So many to choose from: Decision strategies in videodating. *Journal of Social and Personal Relationships, 3,* 43–52. (p. 569)

Wolpe, J. (1958). *Psychotherapy by reciprocal inhibition.* Stanford, CA: Stanford University Press. (p. 512)

Wolpe, J., & Plaud, J. J. (1997). Pavlov's contributions to behavior therapy: The obvious and the not so obvious. *American Psychologist, 52,* 966–972. (pp. 512–513)

Wong, D. F., Wagner, H. N., Tune, L. E., Dannals, R. F., et al. (1986). Positron emission tomography reveals elevated D_2 dopamine receptors in drug-naive schizophrenics. *Science, 234,* 1588–1593. (p. 498)

Wong, M. M., & Csikszentmihalyi, M. (1991). Affiliation motivation and daily experience: Some issues on gender differences. *Journal of Personality and Social Psychology, 60,* 154–164. (p. 121)

Wood, G. (1979). The knew-it-all-along effect. *Journal of Experimental Psychology: Human Perception and Performance, 4,* 345–353. (p. 11)

Wood, J. M., Bootzin, R. R., Kihlstrom, J. F., & Schacter, D. L. (1992). Implicit and explicit memory for verbal information presented during sleep. *Psychological Science, 3,* 236–239. (p. 261)

Wood, J. V., Saltzberg, J. A., & Goldsamt, L. A. (1990a). Does affect induce self-focused attention? *Journal of Personality and Social Psychology, 58,* 899–908. (p. 493)

Wood, J. V., Saltzberg, J. A., Neale, J. M., Stone, A. A., & Rachmiel, T. B. (1990b). Self-focused attention, coping responses, and distressed mood in everyday life. *Journal of Personality and Social Psychology, 58,* 1027–1036. (p. 493)

Wood, W., & Eagly, A. (2002). A cross-cultural analysis of the behavior of women and men: Implications for the origins of sex differences. *Psychological Bulletin, 128,* 699–727. (p. 75)

Wood, W., Lundgren, S., Ouellette, J. A., Busceme, S., & Blackstone, T. (1994). Minority influence: A meta-analytic review of social influence processes. *Psychological Bulletin, 115,* 323–345. (p. 554)

Wood, W., Wong, F. Y., & Chachere, J. G. (1991). Effects of media violence on viewers' aggression in unconstrained social interaction. *Psychological Bulletin, 109,* 371–383. (p. 251)

Woods, N. F., Dery, G. K., & Most, A. (1983). Recollections of menarche, current menstrual attitudes, and premenstrual symptoms. In S. Golub (Ed.), *Menarche: The transition from girl to woman.* Lexington, MA: Lexington Books. (p. 117)

World Health Organization. (1979). *Schizophrenia: An international follow-up study.* Chicester, England: Wiley. (p. 498)

Worobey, J., & Blajda, V. M. (1989). Temperament ratings at 2 weeks, 2 months, and 1 year: Differential stability of activity and emotionality. *Developmental Psychology, 25,* 257–263. (p. 79)

Worthington, E. L., Jr. (1989). Religious faith across the life span: Implications for counseling and research. *The Counseling Psychologist, 17,* 555–612. (p. 118)

Worthington, E. L., Jr., Kurusu, T. A., McCullogh, M. E., & Sandage, S. J. (1996). Empirical research on religionand psychotherapeutic processes and outcomes: A 10-year review and research prospectus. *Psychological Bulletin, 119,* 448–487. (pp. 528, 529)

Wortman, C. B., & Silver, R. C. (1989). The myths of coping with loss. *Journal of Consulting and Clinical Psychology, 57,* 349–357. (p. 133)

Wren, C. S. (1999, April 8). Drug survey of children finds middle school a pivotal time. *New York Times* (www.nytimes.com). (pp. 219–220)

Wright, I. C., Rabe-Hesketh, S., Woodruff, P. W. R., David, A. S., Murray, R. M., & Bullmore, E. T. (2000). Meta-analysis of regional brain volumes in schizophrenia. *American Journal of Psychiatry, 157,* 16–25. (p. 498)

Wright, P. H. (1989). Gender differences in adults' same- and cross-gender friendships. In R. G. Adams & R. Blieszner (Eds.), *Older adult friendships: Structure and process.* Newbury Park, CA: Sage. (p. 121)

Wright, W. (1998). *Born that way: Genes, behavior, personality.* New York: Knopf. (p. 77)

Wrzesniewski, A., McCauley, C. R., Rozin, P., & Schwartz, B. (1997). Jobs, careers, and callings: People's relations to their work. *Journal of Research in Personality, 31,* 21–33. (p. B–1)

Wuethrich, B. (2001, March). Features—GETTING STUPID—Surprising new neurological behavioral research reveals that teenagers who drink too much may permanently damage their brains and seriously compromise their ability to learn. *Discover, 56,* 56–64. (p. 210)

Wulsin, L. R., Vaillant, G. E., & Wells, V. E. (1999). A systematic review of the mortality of depression. *Psychosomatic Medicine, 61,* 6–17. (p. 409)

Wyatt, J. K., & Bootzin, R. R. (1994). Cognitive processing and sleep: Implications for enhancing job performance. *Human Performance, 7,* 119–139. (pp. 201, 261)

Wyatt, R. J., Henter, I., & Sherman-Elvy, E. (2001). Tantalizing clues to preventing schizophrenia. *Cerebrum: The Dana Forum on Brain Science, 3,* pp. 15–30. (p. 499)

Wynn, K. (1992). Addition and subtraction by human infants. *Nature, 358,* 749–759. (pp. 106–107)

Wynn, K. (2000). Findings of addition and subtraction in infants are robust and consistent: reply to Wakeley, Rivera, and Langer. *Child Development, 71,* 1535–1536. (p. 106)

Wynn, K., Bloom, P., & Chiang, W-C. (2002). Enumeration of collective entities by 5-month-old infants. *Cognition, 83,* B55-B62. (p. 106)

Wynn, V., & Gilhooly, K. (1999). The veracity of memories for what you were doing and who you were with when you heard of the death of Diana. *British Psychological Society 1999 Proceedings, 71,* 47. (p. 258)

Xu, Y., & Corkin, S. (2001). H.M. revisits the Tower of Hanoi puzzle. *Neuropsychology, 15,* 69–79. (p. 270)

Yalom, I. D. (1985). *The theory and practice of group psychotherapy* (3rd ed.). New York: Basic Books. (p. 518)

Yang, N., & Linz, D. (1990). Movie ratings and the content of adult videos: The sex-violence ratio. *Journal of Communication, 40(2),* 28–42. (p. 563)

Yankelovich Partners. (1993). *Inside affluent America.* Westport, CT: Yankelovich Partners. (p. 463)

Yankelovich Partners. (1995, May/June). Growing old. *American Enterprise,* p. 108. (p. 124)

Yankelovich Partners. (1997, December 15). Ability of spirituality to help people who are sick. (Press release.) (p. 419)

Yarnell, P. R., & Lynch, S. (1970, April 25). Retrograde memory immediately after concussion. *Lancet*, pp. 863–865. (p. 269)

Yates, A. (1989). Current perspectives on the eating disorders: I. History, psychological and biological aspects. *Journal of the American Academy of Child and Adolescent Psychiatry, 28*, 813–828. (p. 350)

Yates, A. (1990). Current perspectives on the eating disorders: II. Treatment, outcome, and research directions. *Journal of the American Academy of Child and Adolescent Psychiatry, 29*, 1–9. (p. 350)

Yates, W. R. (2000). Testosterone in psychiatry. *Archives of General Psychiatry, 57*, 155–156. (p. 360)

Ybarra, O. (1999). Misanthropic person memory when the need to self-enhance is absent. *Personality and Social Psychology Bulletin, 25*, 261–269. (p. 458)

Yip, P. S. F. (1998). Age, sex, marital status and suicide: An empirical study of east and west. *Psychological Reports, 82*, 311–322. (p. 491)

Yirmiya, N., Erel, O., Shaken, M., & Solomonica-Levi, D. (1998). Meta-analyses comparing theory of mind abilities of individuals with autism, individuals with mental retardation, and normally developing individuals. *Psychological Bulletin, 124*, 283–307. (p. 108)

Zajonc, R. B. (1965). Social facilitation. *Science, 149*, 269–274. (p. 551)

Zajonc, R. B. (1980). Feeling and thinking: Preferences need no inferences. *American Psychologist, 35*, 151–175. (p. 382)

Zajonc, R. B. (1984a). On the primacy of affect. *American Psychologist, 39*, 117–123. (p. 382)

Zajonc, R. B. (1984b, July 22). Quoted by D. Goleman, Rethinking IQ tests and their value. *The New York Times*, p. D22. (p. 316)

Zajonc, R. B. (1998). Emotions. In D. Gilbert, S. T. Fiske, & G. Lindzey (Eds.), *Handbook of social psychology*, 4th ed. New York: McGraw-Hill. (p. 569)

Zajonc, R. B. (2001). Mere exposure: A gateway to the subliminal. *Current Directions in Psychological Science, 10*, 224–228. (p. 568)

Zajonc, R. B., & Markus, G. B. (1975). Birth order and intellectual development. *Psychological Review, 82*, 74–88. (p. A–8)

Zajonc, R. B., Murphy, S. T., & Inglehart, M. (1989). Feeling and facial efference: Implications of the vascular theory of emotions. *Psychological Review, 96*, 395–416. (p. 392)

Zeidner, M. (1990). Perceptions of ethnic group modal intelligence: Reflections of cultural stereotypes or intelligence test scores? *Journal of Cross-Cultural Psychology, 21*, 214–231. (p. 331)

Zelnick, M., & Kim, Y. J. (1982). Sex education and its association with teenage sexual activity, pregnancy, and contraceptive use. *Family Planning Perspectives, 14(3)*, 117–126. (p. 370)

Zigler, E. F. (1987). Formal schooling for four-year-olds? No. *American Psychologist, 42*, 254–260. (p. 329)

Zigler, E., & Styfco, S. J. (2001). Extended childhood intervention prepared children for school and beyond. *Journal of the American Medical Association, 285*, 2378–2380. (p. 330)

Zilbergeld, B. (1983). *The shrinking of America: Myths of psychological change.* Boston: Little, Brown. (pp. 521, 523)

Zillmann, D. (1986). Effects of prolonged consumption of pornography. Background paper for *The Surgeon General's workshop on pornography and public health*, June 22–24. Report prepared by E. P. Mulvey & J. L. Haugaard and released by Office of the Surgeon General on August 4, 1986. (pp. 382, 385)

Zillmann, D. (1989). Effects of prolonged consumption of pornography. In D. Zillmann & J. Bryant (Eds.), *Pornography: Research advances and policy considerations.* Hillsdale, NJ: Erlbaum. (pp. 360, 564)

Zillmann, D., & Bryant, J. (1984). Effects of massive exposure to pornography. In N. Malamuth & E. Donnerstein (Eds.), *Pornography and sexual aggression.* Orlando, FL: Academic Press. (pp. 563–564)

Zimbardo, P. G. (1970). The human choice: Individuation, reason, and order versus deindividuation, impulse, and chaos. In W. J. Arnold & D. Levine (Eds.), *Nebraska Symposium on Motivation, 1969.* Lincoln, NE: University of Nebraska Press. (p. 552)

Zimbardo, P. G. (1972, April). Pathology of imprisonment. *Transaction/Society*, pp. 4–8. (p. 543)

Zimbardo, P. G. (2001, September 16). Fighting terrorism by understanding man's capacity for evil. Op Ed Essay distributed by spsp-discuss@stolaf.edu. (p. 558)

Zornberg, G. L., Buka, S. L., & Tsuang, M. T. (2000). At issue: The problem of obstetrical complications and schizophrenia. *Schizophrenia Bulletin, 26*, 249–256. (p. 499)

Zucker, G. S., & Weiner, B. (1993). Conservatism and perceptions of poverty: An attributional analysis. *Journal of Applied Social Psychology, 23*, 925–943. (p. 541)

Zuckerman, M. (1979). *Sensation seeking: Beyond the optimal level of arousal.* Hillsdale, NJ: Erlbaum. (p. 343)

1948
- Alfred Kinsey and his colleagues publish *Sexual Behavior in the Human Male.*
- B. F. Skinner publishes *Walden Two,* a novel that describes a Utopian community based on positive reinforcement, which becomes a clarion call for applying psychological principles in everyday living, especially communal living.
- Ernest R. Hilgard publishes *Theories of Learning,* which was required reading for several generations of psychology students in North America.

1949
- Raymond B. Cattell publishes the Sixteen Personality Factor Questionnaire (16PF).
- Canadian psychologist Donald O. Hebb publishes *The Organization of Behavior: A Neuropsychological Theory,* in which he outlines a new and influential conceptualization of how the nervous system functions.

1950
- Solomon Asch publishes studies of effects of conformity on judgments of line length.
- Erik Erikson publishes *Childhood and Society,* outlining stages of psychosocial development.

1951
- Carl Rogers publishes *Client-Centered Therapy.*

1953
- Eugene Aserinski and Nathaniel Kleitman describe rapid eye movements (REM) that occur during sleep.
- Janet Taylor publishes the Manifest Anxiety Scale in the *Journal of Abnormal Psychology.*

1954
- Abraham Maslow publishes *Motivation and Personality,* in which he proposes a hierarchy of motives ranging from physiological needs to self-actualization.
- James Olds and Peter Milner, McGill University neuropsychologists, describe rewarding effects of electrical stimulation of the hypothalamus in rats.
- Gordon Allport publishes *The Nature of Prejudice.*

1956
- George Miller publishes a *Psychological Review* article titled "The Magical Number Seven, Plus or Minus Two: Some Limits on Our Capacity for Processing Information," in which he coins the term *chunk* for memory researchers.

1957
- Robert Sears, Eleanor Maccoby, and Harry Levin publish *Patterns of Child Rearing.*
- Charles Ferster and B. F. Skinner publish *Schedules of Reinforcement.*
- Noam Chomsky publishes a critical review of B. F. Skinner's *Verbal Behavior* in the journal titled *Language.*

1959
- Eleanor Gibson and Richard Walk publish, "The Visual Cliff," in which they report their research on infants' depth perception.
- Harry Harlow publishes an article titled "The Nature of Love," outlining his work on attachment in monkeys.

1968
- Richard Atkinson and Richard Schiffrin publish their influential three-stage memory model involving sensory memory (SM), short-term memory (STM), and long-term memory (LTM).
- Neal E. Miller publishes an article in *Science* describing instrumental conditioning of autonomic responses, which stimulates research on biofeedback.

1969
- Albert Bandura publishes *Principles of Behavior Modification.*
- George Miller publishes his APA presidential address, "Psychology as a Means of Promoting Human Welfare," in which he emphasizes the importance of "giving psychology away."

1971
- Kenneth B. Clark is the first African-American president of the American Psychological Association.
- Albert Bandura publishes *Social Learning Theory.*
- Allan Paivio publishes *Imagery and Verbal Processes.*
- B. F. Skinner publishes *Beyond Freedom and Dignity.*

1972
- Elliot Aronson publishes *The Social Animal.*
- Fergus Craik and Robert Lockhart publish "Levels of Processing: A Framework for Memory Research" in *Journal of Verbal Learning and Verbal Behavior.*
- Robert Rescorla and Allan Wagner publish their associative model of Pavlovian conditioning.
- Asian-American Psychological Association is founded.

1973
- Ethologists Karl von Frisch, Konrad Lorenz, and Nikolaas Tinbergen receive the Nobel Prize for their research on animal behavior.

1974
- The American Psychological Association's Division 2 (Teaching of Psychology) first publishes its journal, *Teaching of Psychology,* with Robert S. Daniel as editor.
- Eleanor Maccoby and Carol Jacklin publish *The Psychology of Sex Differences.*

1976
- Ralph Nader presents an invited address, "Bringing Psychology into the Consumer Movement," at the annual meeting of the American Psychological Association in Washington, DC.

1978
- Sandra Wood Scarr and Richard A. Weinberg publish "IQ Test Performance of Black Children Adopted by White Families" in *American Psychologist.*
- Psychologist Herbert A. Simon, Carnegie-Mellon University, wins a Nobel Prize for pioneering research on computer simulations of human thinking and problem solving.

1979
- James J. Gibson publishes *The Ecological Approach to Visual Perception.*
- Elizabeth Loftus publishes *Eyewitness Testimony.*

1981
- Ellen Langer is the first woman to be granted tenure in the Department of Psychology at Harvard University.